"I strongly recommend this book to any individual or [illegible] *their IP Service Routing knowledge and hands-on implementation skills and know-how. This comprehensive self-study guide not only leads to a valuable certification at the NRS II level, it covers a wide range of critical IP subject areas in a thorough and practical manner to help you better support your mission, business, and customers."*

—Gary Horn
Vice President, Technology Services and CTO, Advocate Health Care

"This book is a comprehensive source of information necessary for NRS II certification as well as a working tool for the beginning to intermediate level engineer. The topics are inclusive from routing protocols to Layer 2 and Layer 3 VPNs, and lead the student through the information required to pass the challenging certification exams. It also doubles as an invaluable reference for the working network engineer configuring the 7750 SR platform in a service provider environment."

—Douglas Bruyer
Alcatel-Lucent 3RP No. 52

"This in-depth guide to the NRS II certification provides extensive coverage of current IP/MPLS technologies and their implementation in modern service provider networks. It is an invaluable tool for helping you obtain your NRS II certification, while developing the important skills needed to support your network and customers. I highly recommend this book to anyone who wants to acquire a deeper knowledge of IP/MPLS routing."

—Geir Jensen
Alcatel-Lucent SRA No. 97, Senior Network Architect
NextGenTel, part of TeliaSonera

"Use this book to learn the skills for building and supporting modern IP networks. It is one of the best I have seen for explaining some of the more complicated areas of MPLS. I would recommend this to someone who is going after the NRS II certification or who is looking for a good technical reference."

—Dan Snyder
CCIE No. 12405, Alcatel-Lucent SRA No. 42
Senior Network Architect, UPMC

Alcatel-Lucent Network Routing Specialist II (NRS II) Self-Study Guide

Preparing for the NRS II Certification Exams

Glenn Warnock, Alcatel-Lucent SRA No. 2
Amin Nathoo, Alcatel-Lucent SRA No. 37

WILEY
John Wiley & Sons, Inc.

Alcatel-Lucent Network Routing Specialist II (NRS II) Self-Study Guide: Preparing for the NRS II Certification Exams

Published by
John Wiley & Sons, Inc.
10475 Crosspoint Boulevard
Indianapolis, IN 46256
www.wiley.com

Published by John Wiley & Sons, Inc., Indianapolis, Indiana

Published simultaneously in Canada

ISBN: 978-0-470-94772-2

ISBN: 978-1-118-17811-9 (ebk)

ISBN: 978-1-118-17812-6 (ebk)

ISBN: 978-1-118-17813-3 (ebk)

Manufactured in the United States of America

C10005111_101018

Library of Congress Control Number: 2011935814

Dedicated to my father, Richard G. Warnock—you quietly inspired my sense of curiosity and passion for teaching and the value of hard work. This book would never have been started without the bedrock of my family—my wife, Maggie, and my daughter and son, Jana and Kim. And Fred—I know you would be proud.

—Glenn

To my parents, for their support over the years.

—Amin

Credits

Executive Editor
Carol Long

Project Editor
Tom Dinse

Production Editor
Kathleen Wisor

Copy Editor
Cate Caffrey

Editorial Manager
Mary Beth Wakefield

Freelancer Editorial Manager
Rosemarie Graham

Associate Director of Marketing
David Mayhew

Marketing Manager
Ashley Zurcher

Business Manager
Amy Knies

Production Manager
Tim Tate

Vice President and
Executive Group Publisher
Richard Swadley

Vice President and Executive Publisher
Neil Edde

Associate Publisher
Jim Minatel

Project Coordinator, Cover
Katie Crocker

Compositor
Craig Woods,
Happenstance Type-O-Rama

Proofreaders
James Saturnio, Word One
Louise Watson, Word One

Indexer
Johnna VanHoose Dinse

Vertical Websites Project Manager 1
Laura Moss-Hollister

Vertical Websites Assistant Project Manager
Jenny Swisher

Vertical Websites Associate Producers
Josh Frank
Marilyn Hummel

About the Authors

Glenn Warnock earned a B.Sc. in Computer Science from the University of Ottawa in 1977—in the early prehistory of Ethernet, the Internet, and fiber optics. He became fascinated with the possibilities of networking technologies while working for AT&T Canada and Apple Canada. Since he delivered his first course, "Programming in Pascal," in 1979, teaching has also been an important and rewarding part of Glenn's career. He was attracted to Alcatel-Lucent in 2006 by the potential of the 7750 SR and the opportunity to participate in the development of the Service Routing Certification program. The success of both has exceeded his optimistic expectations. He can be reached on Twitter at @Glenn_Warnock.

Amin Nathoo is a telecom professional with 11 years of experience working for Alcatel-Lucent. He has worked as a SW engineer in the research and development of various Alcatel-Lucent networking products in the Multiservice WAN and Access Networking divisions, and as a customer support engineer for IPD products in the Technical Expertise Center of Alcatel-Lucent. Amin has a Service Routing Architect certification and is currently a Subject Matter Expert in IP/MPLS networking on the Service Routing Certification team. Amin is an accredited Professional Engineer and holds a bachelor's degree in Engineering Science from the University of Western Ontario.

Acknowledgments

There would be no reason for the existence of this book without the Alcatel-Lucent Service Router products. To Basil Alwan and everyone in product development and support who are responsible for the 7750 SR, the 7450 ESS, the 7705 SAR, and the 7210 SAS, thank you for making these great products. We are honoured to be part of such an outstanding group.

The content of this book is entirely based on the three SRC courses—Interior Routing Protocols, Multiprotocol Label Switching, and Services Architecture. That means that this book is a joint effort of the SRC Subject Matter Experts group, past and present, who have all contributed to this content. Current members are Bo Li, Connie Kwan, Dave Watts, Ghassan Shaheen, Latif Ahmed, Michael Weir, Mira Ghafary, and Ray Belleville. We are also greatly indebted to the Alcatel-Lucent University SRC instructors who teach and contribute to the development of these courses. We are proud to be members of this skilled and committed team.

We are very dependent on the engineering and support groups within Alcatel-Lucent who work with the products daily and write much of the reference material on which we base our courses. Especially important to us are the SR TEC (Technical Excellence Center) and NDE (Network Design Engineering) groups. They are always ready to share their knowledge and help answer any questions we have.

There are many in Alcatel-Lucent who contributed to the existence of this book through their constant support, particularly Barry Denroche and Don Joyce. Stephanie Chasse has followed our every step and made sure we got every single one accomplished. Bernie May has been relentless in his pursuit of opportunities to promote this book (and he's only just getting started!). And, of course, Karyn Lennon has been critical to the completion of this project. Karyn's experience, commitment, and great track record with previous SRC publications practically guaranteed our success.

We would not have the confidence to publish such a book without the critical eyes of our technical reviewers. Special thanks to Ghassan Shaheen, who reviewed every chapter and all the practical exercises. Lieven Levrau and Alastair Johnson made invaluable contributions. Thanks also to the teams of Mustapha Aissaoui and Alfred Nothaft for their review, including Palak Mehta, Santosh Ramamurthy, and Pradeep Jain. Others who made technical contributions include Gilles Geerts and Ziggy Droogmans. Thanks to Rod Hoekman for his input on the SR Product group.

We greatly appreciate the support of some of our key customers who reviewed early proofs and provided valuable feedback and encouragement. Special thanks to Jaco Boshoff, Doug Bruyer, Geir Jensen, Dan Snyder, and Gary Horn.

The job of producing the illustrations is a large and important one. Our thanks to Bryan Charbonneau, Alex Cedzynski, and Pat Desjardins for their efforts and to Meta Murphy for assembling this talented and efficient team. The team at Wiley that makes this such a professional publication is mostly invisible to us, but our thanks to Tom Dinse for providing a calm and effective interface to this skilled group.

—*The authors*

I express my appreciation for the opportunity to work on this book and to everyone within IPD who gave us the time to do our best possible effort. I'm also greatly indebted to the many folks within IPD Customer Support and beyond who have given their time to help me in learning these technologies. Finally, my greatest appreciation and admiration to all of you who are committed to your own learning and self-development by working toward the NRS II certification.

—*Glenn Warnock*

I especially thank Glenn Warnock for welcoming me to work on this publication after much of the planning and work were already under way, and for coordinating efforts with many of the other parties involved in the development of this book, allowing me the luxury of focus. I express my gratitude to Karyn Lennon for giving me the opportunity to work on this book and balancing my schedule with my other deliverables. I could not imagine performing my day-to-day job without the help and support from members of the IPD SRC development team who have contributed directly and indirectly to this publication.

—*Amin Nathoo*

Contents

Foreword

IP networks are supporting phenomenal change worldwide. Smartphones and tablets have untethered the Internet and communications, information, entertainment and commerce are available anytime, anywhere. Advances in networking, computing and storage technologies are also changing how we interact and conduct business. And at the heart of this change are advanced Service Routing platforms under the management and control of networking engineers like you.

Your investment in this Service Routing Certification self-study program from Alcatel-Lucent will help you and your organization acquire the technical skills, knowledge, and competency needed to succeed in this dynamic and fast-paced environment. The challenges are great. Customers are demanding a more diverse set of applications and services, across many more devices. This greatly impacts how service providers, mobile operators, and enterprise and vertical customers build, operate and maintain their IP networks.

The continuous scaling of networks at the lowest per-bit delivery cost is critical to meeting these new challenges—equaled only by the need to extract greater value from the network to support new business models and revenues. This is the foundation of the Alcatel-Lucent High Leverage Network™ vision—carefully architected changes to basic router and network design in order to scale routing performance while also scaling service sophistication. This is what we call *Service Routing*—a concept we introduced with the world's first Service Router, and which is now deployed by more than 400 service provider customers around the world.

The business, organizational, and customer value of having highly trained personnel with professional certifications in the areas of IP/MPLS and Ethernet-based networks and services has never been greater. Congratulations on taking this important step forward to attain your Network Routing Specialist II certification. With this certification you will be well positioned to help your company or customer succeed in this exciting new world of advanced IP communications and collaboration.

—*Basil Alwan*
President, IP Division and Head of Portfolio Strategy,
Alcatel-Lucent Networks Group

Introduction

This book is based on the following courses from the SRC program: Alcatel-Lucent's "Interior Routing Protocols," "Multiprotocol Label Switching (MPLS)," and "Services Architecture." It will help you prepare to take and pass the exams required to achieve the Alcatel-Lucent Network Routing Specialist II (NRS II) certification. Like the SRC courses, this book explains the details of IP routing and MPLS label distribution and introduces Layer 2 and Layer 3 Virtual Private Network (VPN) services. It is intended for network professionals who have experience with IP and Ethernet networking technologies.

Although the primary focus of the book is to prepare you for the Alcatel-Lucent NRS II lab exam, NRSII4A0, the protocols and technologies described are at the core of today's IP/MPLS Virtual Private Networks and thus are useful as reference even for those not intending to take the exam.

Upon completing this book, you should be able to:

- Describe the strengths and limitations of traditional IP routing.
- Describe the common Layer 2 technologies supported by the Alcatel-Lucent 7750 Service Router (SR).
- Configure and verify IP interfaces and static routes on the 7750 SR.
- Describe the addressing and basic operation of IPv6.
- Explain how the shortest path first (SPF) algorithm is used by link-state routing protocols to construct the route table.
- Describe the Open Shortest Path First (OSPF) link-state database and different link-state advertisements (LSAs).
- Describe the differences between OSPFv3 and OSPFv2.
- Describe the Intermediate System to Intermediate System (IS-IS) link-state database and link-state protocol data units (PDUs).
- Explain how IS-IS is enhanced for routing IPv6.
- Explain why hierarchy is necessary for a link-state routing protocol and how it is implemented in OSPF and IS-IS.
- Configure and verify OSPF and IS-IS on the 7750 SR.
- Describe the basic terminology and concepts of Multiprotocol Label Switching (MPLS).

- Describe the purpose and operation of Label Distribution Protocol (LDP).
- Describe the purpose and operation of Resource Reservation Protocol–Traffic Engineering (RSVP-TE).
- Explain how MPLS is used for BGP and IPv6 shortcuts.
- Explain the Constrained Shortest Path First (CSPF) algorithm and how it is used for traffic-engineered label switched paths (LSPs).
- Configure and verify CSPF-enabled LSPs.
- Explain how RSVP-TE signals bandwidth reservations for LSPs.
- Configure resource reservations and DiffServ traffic engineering for LSPs on the 7750 SR.
- Explain the operation of fast reroute and secondary LSPs.
- Configure and verify redundancy using fast reroute and secondary LSPs on the 7750 SR.
- Describe the service infrastructure used on the 7750 SR for implementing VPN services.
- Describe the operation of the different types of Virtual Private Wire Services (VPWS) on the 7750 SR.
- Describe the purpose and operation of a Virtual Private Local Area Network Service (VPLS).
- Configure and verify an epipe and VPLS on the 7750 SR.
- Describe the components and operation of a Virtual Private Routed Network (VPRN).
- Configure and verify a VPRN and Internet Enhanced Service (IES) on the 7750 SR.
- Troubleshoot and manage VPN service networks using operation, administration, and management (OAM) tools on the 7750 SR.

Achieving the NRS II certification requires a solid understanding of these technologies and the ability to configure them on the Alcatel-Lucent 7750 SR. Besides describing these technologies in detail, the book provides many examples of how they are configured and verified on the 7750 SR. In addition, most chapters contain practical exercises that will help solidify your understanding of the material and how to apply that knowledge. The CD included with the book contains solutions to the exercises with a detailed explanation of the configuration. Even if you do not have easy access to a network of 7750 SRs for practice, you can still follow the examples of how to perform the configuration. The SRC Exam Preparation Service provides you with remote access to a SR lab environment and practice scenarios that will help you practice for the NRS II lab exam. Learn more about this service at `www.alcatel-lucent.com/src/examprep`.

How This Book Is Organized

The book is divided into three sections, corresponding to the three courses that lead to the NRS II (Network Routing Specialist II) certification. Although we provide a brief overview of Layer 2 and IP networking, we assume that you have already completed the NRS I (Network Routing Specialist I) certification. The three sections of the book are the following:

- **IP Networking**—This section corresponds to the Alcatel-Lucent "Interior Routing Protocols" course and will help you prepare for the written exam, 4A0-101.
- **Multiprotocol Label Switching**—This section corresponds to the Alcatel-Lucent "Multiprotocol Label Switching" course and will help you prepare for the written exam, 4A0-103.
- **VPN Services**—This section corresponds to the Alcatel-Lucent "Service Architecture" course and will help you prepare for the written exam, 4A0-104.

The first section comprises Chapters 1 through 10. Chapter 1 introduces the concept of an IP/MPLS service network and provides a brief overview of the Alcatel-Lucent Service Router Product group. Chapter 2 provides an overview of the technologies that perform the actual physical transmission of data across the Internet. These are described in more detail in the NRS I Self-Study Guide (*Alcatel-Lucent Scalable IP Networks Self-Study Guide: Preparing for the Network Routing Specialist I (NRS I) Certification Exam (4A0-100).*Wiley Publishing, Inc. ISBN: 978-0470429068) and the Alcatel-Lucent "Scalable IP Networks" course.

Chapter 3 reviews the nature of the IP address and how IP data is forwarded across the network. This is also described in more detail in the NRS I Self-Study Guide, Chapter 3 also introduces IPv6, including IPv6 addressing and the basic operation of an IPv6 network.

Chapter 4 introduces dynamic IP routing and the two routing protocols most often used within a service provider's network: Open Shortest Path First (OSPF) and Intermediate System to Intermediate System (IS-IS). The focus is on the general operational behavior of these protocols and how they calculate the best route to destinations in the network. An overview of Border Gateway Protocol (BGP) is also provided in this chapter. BGP was originally designed to support routing of IP data between service providers. BGP is also used for the exchange of routing information in some Virtual Private Networks (VPNs).

BGP routing is a complex subject and is only lightly covered here because our focus is on routing within a service provider network. At the time of writing (2011), MPLS services are mainly deployed only within a single service provider's network.

Chapters 5 through 7 provide a detailed examination of the OSPF routing protocol. Chapter 5 focuses on single-area networks and the methods used to exchange topology information between routers. In Chapter 6, we look at the additional capabilities that allow us to build multi-area networks. Chapter 7 covers OSPFv3, which is the version of OSPF enhanced to carry IPv6 routing information.

Chapters 8 through 10 provide a detailed examination of the IS-IS routing protocol. Chapter 8 describes the operation of single-area networks, and Chapter 9 describes the configuration and operation of IS-IS in a multi-area network. Chapter 10 describes the enhancements to IS-IS that allow it to be used for IPv6 networks.

OSPF and IS-IS perform a similar function—the exchange of routing information inside a single administrative routing domain. Both protocols use the shortest path first (SPF) algorithm, provide very similar results, and have very similar capabilities. However, their operation is quite different, and both protocols are found in service provider and enterprise networks.

MPLS is a technology that adds to the capabilities of an IP network. However, MPLS depends very much on the underlying foundation of the IP network, which is why an understanding of IP routing protocols is important to understanding the operation of an MPLS network. MPLS is not a routing protocol, and although it enables the creation of tunnels across an IP network, it is still very much dependent on IP routing for determining the paths of these tunnels. In addition, MPLS routers use IP to exchange the messages needed to establish and maintain these tunnels.

Chapters 11 through 16 describe MPLS. Chapter 11 introduces basic MPLS concepts and terminology. We show how data is transported over an MPLS network on label switched paths (LSPs) and how these LSPs are created through the distribution of label information.

Chapter 12 introduces Label Distribution Protocol (LDP), a simple protocol used for the distribution of MPLS labels. LSPs established using LDP always follow the path determined by the routing protocol. This means that LDP does not provide the traffic engineering or enhanced resiliency described above, but its LSPs can support VPN services.

Chapter 13 introduces Resource Reservation Protocol–Traffic Engineering (RSVP-TE), which supports the enhancements to IP of traffic engineering and faster resiliency. This chapter focuses on the operation of RSVP-TE, including the protocol messages and the basics of path selection. The chapter also describes how LDP and RSVP-TE can be used to create shortcuts across the service provider MPLS network. These shortcuts could be used to carry external transit IP traffic or to carry IPv6 packets across an IPv4 core network.

Chapter 14 introduces the concept of constraint-based routing and its application to building traffic-engineered LSPs (TE-LSPs). We examine the extensions to OSPF and IS-IS that support traffic engineering and how they are used by RSVP-TE to select the path for the LSP. Traffic-engineering calculations are performed across a single area only. This chapter also describes how LDP-over-RSVP can be used to create an LSP joining TE-LSPs across different areas.

Chapter 15 describes how bandwidth resources can be reserved with RSVP-TE LSPs to support dynamic allocation of resources for specific traffic types. The operational aspects of bandwidth reservations are described, including preemption by higher-priority LSPs. DiffServ-aware traffic engineering is also described.

Chapter 16 explains how RSVP-TE can be used to define redundant paths through the network to be used in the event of a failure. This allows the service provider to build a highly resilient network that has much better availability than a simple IP network and can achieve failover times on the order of 50 milliseconds.

Chapters 17 through 21 describe how Virtual Private Network (VPN) services are built on the foundation of an IP/MPLS network. Chapter 17 introduces the concept of a pseudowire and the signaling used to establish a VPN service. It also describes the terminology and infrastructure used to support VPN services on the 7750 SR.

Chapter 18 describes the different types of Virtual Private Wire Services (VPWS) that can be built on a 7750 SR. These simple point-to-point Layer 2 services are epipes, apipes, fpipes, cpipes, and ipipes. The different encapsulation types supported for customer traffic and MTU considerations are also described.

Chapter 19 introduces the Virtual Private LAN Service (VPLS), which is a point-to-multipoint Ethernet service similar to a virtual Ethernet switch. We describe the virtual switch behavior, including Media Access Control (MAC) address learning and the flooding behavior of the VPLS. We also introduce several VPLS topologies, including the hierarchical VPLS.

Chapter 20 introduces Layer 3 services. These are the Internet Enhanced Service (IES) and the Virtual Private Routed Network (VPRN). The IES can be used to provide a Layer 3 interface to a customer in the context of a service network. The VPRN service is used by a customer who wants to connect multiple sites as if they were all connected to a virtual IP router. We also show how the VPRN can be used to interconnect customer IPv6 networks using an IPv4/MPLS core network.

Chapter 21 introduces some of the basic operations, administration, and maintenance (OAM) tools that can be used to manage and troubleshoot an IP/MPLS service network. It also describes how the 7750 SR can mirror traffic on a port or other service component to a local port or to a remote location across the service network.

Conventions Used in the Book

The command-line interface (CLI) commands used in the examples in this book are included in a separate text box, as shown in Listing 1. In the code listings, user input is indicated by bold font (also shown in Listing 1). When a CLI command is used inline along with the main text, it is indicated by the use of monofont text, like this: `show router route-table`.

Listing 1 Viewing the route table with locally connected networks

```
*A:R1# show router route-table

===============================================================================
Route Table (Router: Base)
===============================================================================
Dest Prefix                                     Type    Proto     Age        Pref
      Next Hop[Interface Name]                                        Metric
-------------------------------------------------------------------------------
10.1.2.0/27                                     Local   Local     00h03m40s   0
      toR2                                                            0
10.1.3.0/27                                     Local   Local     00h03m13s   0
      toR3                                                            0
10.10.10.1/32                                   Local   Local     00h04m10s   0
      system                                                          0
-------------------------------------------------------------------------------
No. of Routes: 3
===============================================================================
```

A standard set of icons is used throughout the book. A representation of these icons and their meanings is listed under the section, "Standard Icons."

Audience

This book is targeted to network professionals who have experience with IP and Ethernet networks and are preparing for the Alcatel-Lucent NRS II lab exam (NRSII4A0). Although the topics covered are helpful to any networking professional, the level of detail and the particular aspects of the technologies covered match explicitly what is needed to prepare for the exam.

This book provides a brief overview of Layer 2 technologies and IPv4 basics, but assumes that you have had some experience with these technologies. It assumes no prior knowledge of MPLS, IPv6, or VPN services. It is expected that you will have had some exposure to the CLI and the basic operation of one or more of the routers in the Alcatel-Lucent Service Router product group, because this is required to achieve the Alcatel-Lucent NRS I certification. A solid understanding of and experience with configuring the 7750 SR or one of the other Alcatel-Lucent Service Routers is necessary to pass the NRS II lab exam.

Feedback Is Welcome

It would be our great pleasure to hear from you. Please forward any comments or suggestions for improvements to the following e-mail address: `sr.publications@alcatel-lucent.com`.

Welcome to your preparation guide for the Alcatel-Lucent NRS II certification. Good luck with your studies, your exams, and your career with the Alcatel-Lucent Service Router products!

—*Glenn Warnock*
Alcatel-Lucent SRA No. 2

—*Amin Nathoo*
Alcatel-Lucent SRA No. 37

The Alcatel-Lucent Service Routing Certification Program Overview

The Alcatel-Lucent Service Routing Certification (SRC) program is designed to arm individuals with the knowledge and skills needed for building and supporting today's advanced IP/MPLS networks and services. The comprehensive SRC program curriculum is based on Alcatel-Lucent's unique and innovative *Service Routing* technology and our Service Router product portfolio, which has been deployed by hundreds of the world's most progressive service providers for delivering next-generation residential, business, and mobile services.

The SRC program currently consists of 11 courses and 4 certifications. Courses and certifications are designed to meet the varying roles, objectives, abilities, and experience levels of the students. Each course focuses on a specific IP subject area and set of learning objectives to create the learning foundation for each of the following certifications:

- **Alcatel-Lucent Network Routing Specialist I (NRS I) certification**—Designed to teach the fundamentals of IP/MPLS for beginners
- **Alcatel-Lucent Network Routing Specialist II (NRS II) certification**—Designed for the beginning to intermediate-level engineer or support person
- **Alcatel-Lucent Triple Play Routing Professional (3RP) certification**—Designed for more advanced personnel with specialization in residential IP services delivery
- **Alcatel-Lucent Service Routing Architect (SRA) certification**—Our most advanced certification, designed for engineers who need to be experts in all aspects of designing, building, and supporting IP/MPLS networks

Alcatel-Lucent is also introducing a mobility-focused certification into the SRC program. It is designed for the network professional at the NRS II level who is specializing in mobile transport for the LTE Evolved Packet Core.

To achieve a certification, you must complete all of the written exams required for the certification. In addition to written exams, you must pass a practical lab exam for the NRS II and SRA certifications. Courses and required exams for each certification are summarized on our website at `www.alcatel-lucent.com/src`. There is no need to plan for a certification in order to enroll in a course—the program curriculum is ideal for anyone needing to advance his or her knowledge and skill set in any of the course subject areas.

Alcatel-Lucent provides credit for some Cisco and Juniper IP certifications. Visit `www.alcatel-lucent.com/src/exemptions` for a detailed overview of certification exemptions.

All SRC courses are delivered by highly trained IP/MPLS subject matter experts. In addition to lectures, each course includes a significant amount of hands-on lab training and exercises to ensure that you gain proficiency in configuration, provisioning, and troubleshooting. SRC courses are delivered at select Alcatel-Lucent locations globally. Private classes can also be delivered on-site at a customer-designated location or other third-party site through advance arrangement.

SRC program participants will greatly benefit from Alcatel-Lucent's extensive research and development knowledge and the applied knowledge that comes from building advanced networks around the world. A recognized industry leader, Alcatel-Lucent has long been a pioneer in IP/MPLS networks and products. We introduced our innovative Service Routing platform in 2003 and have continued to remain at the leading edge of service routing product technology and innovation. We continue to partner with hundreds of the world's most progressive service providers as they roll out next-generation consumer, business, and mobile services.

The *Alcatel-Lucent Network Routing Specialist II Self-Study Guide* is published by the Alcatel-Lucent Service Routing Certification (SRC) program team.

For further information on the SRC program, including details on course and exam registration, please visit `http://www.alcatel-lucent.com/src`.

Alcatel-Lucent Network Routing Specialist II Exams

To achieve the Alcatel-Lucent Network Routing Specialist II certification, you need to complete four written exams and one practical lab exam.

Written exams are delivered by Prometric, a leading global provider of testing and assessment services. Prometric offers exam registration online, by telephone or by walk-in (in selected locations). The exams are delivered in English in a secure and supervised environment at Prometric's global test sites.

Each written exam consists of 60 randomly generated questions. You have 90 minutes to complete each of the NRS II written exams, with the exception of the Alcatel-Lucent Scalable IP Networks exam (4A0-100), for which you have 75 minutes to complete all questions. There are no written exam prerequisites; written exams can be completed in any order. You will be sent a notification once Alcatel-Lucent has received the exam result (typically within five business days).

Written exams that apply to the Alcatel-Lucent NRS II certification include the following:

- **Alcatel-Lucent Scalable IP Networks (4A0-100)**
- **Alcatel-Lucent Interior Routing Protocols (4A0-101)**
- **Alcatel-Lucent Multiprotocol Label Switching (4A0-103)**
- **Alcatel-Lucent Services Architecture (4A0-104)**

Upon successful completion of the written exams, you are eligible to complete the NRS II Lab Exam (NRSII4A0). This exam is a 3 1/2-hour practical exam that tests your ability to configure basic services and the supporting technologies on the Alcatel-Lucent 7750 Service Router (SR). The NRS II Lab Exam (NRSII4A0) is delivered at select Alcatel-Lucent sites. You can register for the exam at `www.alcatel-lucent.com/src/examreg`.

Once you have passed all four written exams and the practical lab exam, you will receive the Alcatel-Lucent Network Routing Specialist II certification.

For assistance in preparing for exams, you can use the Alcatel-Lucent SRC Exam Preparation Service available at `www.alcatel-lucent.com/src/examprep`.

Visit `www.alcatel-lucent.com/src` for more information on the SRC program.

Visit the Prometric site at `www.prometric.com/alcatel-lucent` to register for the written exams.

Accessing a Service Router Lab: The SRC Exam Preparation Service

The SRC Exam Preparation service (SRC ExamPrep) is an ideal companion to the NRS II Self-Study Guide. The service provides private, remote access to a Service Router lab environment so that you can work on the NRS II lab exercises included in the self-study guide or prepare for the NRS II lab exam (NRSII4A0) required for certification.

The SRC ExamPrep service is an Alcatel-Lucent–managed offering. The service includes the following main components:

- Dedicated, remote access to an Alcatel-Lucent Service Router lab consisting of six fully-meshed Alcatel-Lucent Service Routers

- Access to a suite of more than 30 detailed lab "practice" scenarios along with the optimal solutions for each. The NRS II lab scenarios are designed specifically to help you prepare for the NRS II lab exam.
- Access to a set of traffic simulation and analysis tools

Scheduling SRC lab access time is flexible and easy. Equipment is conveniently available 24 hours a day, 7 days a week. Starting point configurations for each of the lab scenarios can be auto-configured, and router and network configurations can be saved and automatically restored between lab sessions.

Get started today by visiting the SRC ExamPrep website at `http://www.alcatel-lucent.com/src/examprep`.

Standard Icons

PE Router

P Router

MDU

Router

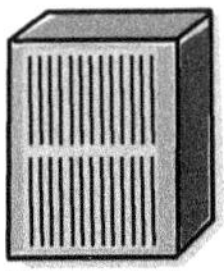

Switch

Hub

PC
(Host)

File Server

Network

Failure

Enterprise

Internet

Residential
Home Services

Cell Site

Video

Voice

I

IP Networking

1 IP/MPLS Service Networks

The Alcatel-Lucent NRS II exam topics covered in this chapter include the following:

- Characteristics of IP
- Internet overview
- Alcatel-Lucent 7750 Service Router product group
- 7750 Service Router
- 7705 Service Aggregation Router
- 7450 Ethernet Service Switch
- 7210 Service Access Switch

In this chapter, we describe the development of the Internet and the characteristics of the Internet protocol (IP). We see how IP networks have evolved and the requirements of networking technology today. Multiprotocol Label Switching (MPLS) addresses some of the limitations of IP networking and provides a foundation for building service networks. The chapter concludes with an overview of the Alcatel-Lucent Service Router product group.

1.1 Internet Protocol

Development of the Internet protocol (IP) started in 1974 and was formally defined in RFC 791 ("Request for Comments for Internet Protocol") published in 1981. TCP/IP (Transmission Control Protocol/Internet Protocol) became the standard protocol of the ARPANET (Advanced Research Projects Agency Network) on January 1, 1983—many consider this the birth of the Internet. The NSFNET (National Science Foundation Network) was created in 1986 with backbone links of 56 kb/s; these were soon upgraded to 1.5 Mb/s. Incredibly, today we're deploying links that support 100,000 Mb/s, and we're still using the same version of IP!

Characteristics of IP

The phenomenal growth of the Internet to date is to some extent a result of the characteristics of IP. Some of the characteristics that lead to IP's global dominance are the following:

- **Simplicity**—This is the most important characteristic contributing to the success of IP. It means that new hardware and software supporting IP are easily developed, more easily deployed, and more easily managed. Simplicity also leads to lower cost, another characteristic of IP networks.
- **Accessibility**—This is also a very important contributing factor to the success of IP. Development of the first Internet standards was an open and collaborative process, an approach that has continued to this day. All standards documents are freely available and usually easy to understand. In an age when the only question is whether to use IPv4 or IPv6, it's easy to forget that 20 years ago there were many different communications protocols in use, and most were proprietary. The OSI (Open System Interconnect) protocols were open, but the standards documents were expensive, complex, and difficult to follow, making them much less accessible than IP.

- **Resiliency**—This was one of the original design goals for IP and was achieved through the connectionless nature and simplicity of the protocol. IP routing protocols react quickly to changes in the network topology and simply change the next-hop to which they forward packets for a particular destination. It is understood that IP provides an unreliable, connectionless service, thus the higher-layer protocols provide connection-oriented features as required.

The simplicity of IP results in some serious limitations as the Internet reaches a size, complexity, and diversity of applications that was unimaginable to the early developers of the protocol. Some of the major shortcomings of IP include the following:

- **Traffic engineering**—This is the ability to use a more sophisticated approach to routing traffic across the network. IP uses a simple hop-by-hop approach to forward traffic across the most direct path, but for today's networks and applications, this is often not the most suitable route. *Traffic engineering* allows for the use of other criteria and knowledge of the complete topology of the network to find an optimal path for a varied mix of traffic types.
- **Quality of service (QoS)**—This is the ability to prioritize different traffic types and provide a different service level to each. Usually these service levels relate to delivery and delay guarantees. For example, a voice-over-IP application used for a real-time conversation requires a small delay and relatively low packet loss, whereas an e-mail application can tolerate much greater delay and can easily retransmit lost packets. A simple IP network provides the same level of service to all applications (*best effort*).
- **High resiliency**—High resiliency, or high availability, goes beyond the resiliency of IP to provide connectivity that is nearly always on. We can build redundancy into a network with IP routing protocols so that most equipment failures result in an outage lasting only a few seconds. We hardly notice such an outage when surfing the Web or sending e-mails, but we are not nearly as tolerant when using IP-TV (broadcast television over IP) to watch our favorite sporting event. More demanding applications typically strive for failover in less than 50 milliseconds—1/20 of a second.
- **IPv4 address space**—The IPv4 address space is effectively exhausted. The number of devices connected to the Internet continues to grow exponentially, and every one needs a unique address. There are measures that have been developed to extend the IPv4 address space, but ultimately the increased address space of IPv6 is required.

QoS is a topic for another book, but this book addresses the other three issues listed above. A key technology in adding these capabilities to an IP network is Multiprotocol Label Switching (MPLS). We will see that MPLS is effectively a tunneling technology that allows us to build a variety of different networks using the base technology of an IP network.

Although the global, public Internet is the network that interconnects us all, in reality there is an even larger demand for *private* networks. These private networks may interconnect corporate enterprises to their different geographical locations or to their partners and customers. Or they may be used to deliver specific services in a controlled manner, such as mobile services or IP-TV delivery.

Service providers are increasingly adopting IP/MPLS networks to provide these private network services. IP/MPLS provides a cost-effective, flexible foundation for deploying a wide variety of private network services.

The Internet

The 1980s were really the experimental years of the Internet as it grew throughout universities and American research institutions. TCP/IP was included in the free UNIX distributions of the time, which definitely helped spread the understanding and use of TCP/IP. The fact that the RFC documents that define all Internet protocols are freely available and generally easy to understand also helped spread its acceptance. Key characteristics of the Internet in the 1980s were the following:

- Experimental nature of the Internet
- Development of IP routing software (IS-IS, OSPF, BGP)
- Routing typically handled by general-purpose mini-computers running routing software

During the 1990s, the Internet spread into the commercial world and a much broader public awareness. Major characteristics of this decade included the following:

- Development of the Hypertext Transfer Protocol (HTTP) and the World Wide Web
- Availability of high-speed Internet access using ADSL (Asymmetric Digital Subscriber Line) and cable networks
- Purpose-built routers including specialized hardware designed specifically for IP forwarding

- Exponential growth in size and bandwidth of the Internet
- Maturation of BGP (Border Gateway Protocol)

In the first decade of the new millennium, the Internet spread beyond the relatively simple domain of e-mail and web traffic into new domains with more demanding requirements. Characteristics of the first decade of 2000 included the following:

- Continued massive bandwidth increases
- The YouTube phenomena—ubiquitous video and massive amounts of user-generated content
- Support of data services in the mobile network
- The introduction of MPLS to create a more sophisticated service layer over IP
- Routers capable of providing quality of service differentiation in an IP network

What can we expect in the second decade of the new millennium? More of the same—and then some:

- Continued massive bandwidth increases
- The cloud—our data and applications moving to the network
- Video everywhere
- Greatly enhanced control plane for network components to improve and simplify management of the network
- Everything anywhere—by the end of the decade, everything we manufacture will connect to the Internet, and we'll have access to it from anywhere.

1.2 Alcatel-Lucent 7750 Service Router Product Group

The original Alcatel-Lucent Service Router was the Alcatel-Lucent 7750 SR, introduced in 2003. Since that time, other products have been added to the Service Router product family, all built around the SR-OS (SR Operating System) and all managed by the 5620 SAM (Service Aware Manager). Two of the products, the Alcatel-Lucent 7750 SR and the Alcatel-Lucent 7450 ESS, use FP network processors developed in-house to ensure leading-edge performance, density, and advanced services, with no compromise between speed and advanced service delivery.

The 7750 SR was conceived and developed specifically for IP/MPLS Virtual Private Network (VPN) services such as Virtual Private Wire Services (VPWS),

Virtual Private LAN Service (VPLS), and Virtual Private Routed Network (VPRN). The system architecture, hardware, and software fully support the provisioning and configuration of IP/MPLS networks with Layer 2 and Layer 3 VPN services. The SR product group supports a wide range of access interfaces. Broadly, these include the following:

- Ethernet interfaces from 100 Mb/s to 100 Gb/s
- Packet over SONET/SDH (POS) from OC-3c/STM-1c to OC-192c/STM-64c
- Circuit Emulation Service (CES) at OC-3/STM-1 and OC-12/STM-4
- Asynchronous Transfer Mode (ATM) at OC-3c/STM-1c and OC-12c/STM-4c

The primary focus of the Service Router product group is the IP services market. This covers a broad range of IP routers and switches from small hardened devices in a remote cell site to very large routers in a central office (CO) routing thousands of connections and terabits of data into the service provider core network. Although many edge routers today are simple IP routers, service providers are increasingly recognizing the benefits of deploying IP/MPLS service routers to support the diverse connectivity requirements and applications in today's network. Three key areas where IP/MPLS service routing is finding application today are the following:

- **Residential service delivery**—This requires the reliable delivery of video, voice, and high-speed Internet services over an IP network. The network must provide differentiated quality of service to different traffic types and efficiently manage the service parameters for thousands of subscribers.
- **Mobile Packet Core and backhaul**—This is evolving to a fully IP-based packet network. The mobile backhaul must support the increasing demand for data in existing mobile networks in a cost-effective manner while providing a path to support the deployment of fourth-generation LTE (Long Term Evolution) networks.
- **Business service delivery**—This must provide cost-effective connectivity and bandwidth options while supporting legacy technologies. A reliable and secure service is required with defined and measured service level guarantees.

Not all of the routers in the SR product group support all the features and capabilities of the 7750 SR, but all use the same core operating system and the same command-line interface (CLI) commands for configuring and managing the network. All the examples and exercises in this book were created on the 7750 SR but will function the same way on any other router in the product group, except in the circumstances in which it does not support the specific feature.

In the sections below, we provide a brief introduction and overview of the members of the SR product family at the time of writing (June 2011). The four major product families in the Service Router product group are the following:

- 7750 Service Router
- 7705 Service Aggregation Router
- 7450 Ethernet Service Switch
- 7210 Service Access Switch

7750 Service Router

The Alcatel-Lucent 7750 Service Router (SR) portfolio is a suite of multiservice routers that deliver high-performance, high-availability routing with service-aware operations, administration, management, and provisioning. The 7750 SR integrates the scalability, resiliency, and predictability of MPLS along with the bandwidth and economics of Ethernet and a broad selection of legacy interfaces, to enable a converged network infrastructure for the delivery of next-generation services.

The 7750 SR's advanced and comprehensive feature set enables it to be deployed as a Broadband Network Gateway (BNG) for residential services, as a Multiservice Edge (MSE) for Carrier Ethernet and IP VPN business services, as the aggregation router in mobile backhaul applications, or as a mobile packet core for 2G, 3G, and LTE wireless networks. With support for service-enabled, high-density 10GigE, 40 GigE, and 100GigE interfaces, the 7750 SR is well suited for edge and core routing applications.

The 7750 SR is available in four chassis variants, as shown in Figure 1.1, and scales gracefully from 90 Gb/s to 2 Tb/s of capacity. From left to right with the 7750 SR-7c in the foreground, the routers are as follows:

- 7750 SR-12
- 7750 SR-7
- 7750 SR-12c
- 7750 SR-7c

Figure 1.1 7750 Service Router product family.

7705 Service Aggregation Router

The Alcatel-Lucent 7705 SAR portfolio is optimized for multiservice adaptation, aggregation, and routing, especially onto a modern Ethernet and IP/MPLS infrastructure. It is available in compact, low-power consumption platforms delivering highly available services over resilient and flexible network topologies.

The 7705 SAR is well suited to the aggregation and backhaul of 2G, 3G, and LTE mobile traffic—providing cost-effective scaling and the transformation to IP/MPLS networking. Business services modernization is supported in the transition from legacy to consolidated, packet-based operation. Hugely reduced equipment footprints are achievable with reduced energy costs. Industries, enterprises, and government organizations can achieve reliable and resilient support of legacy and advanced services.

The 7705 SAR is available in three chassis variants:

- 7705 SAR-18
- 7705 SAR-8
- 7705 SAR-F

The 7705 SAR family in Figure 1.2 shows the SAR-F, the SAR-8, and the SAR-18, front to back.

Figure 1.2 7705 SAR family.

7450 Ethernet Service Switch

The 7450 ESS is a highly scalable platform designed to support residential service delivery, business VPN services, and mobile backhaul applications at the Carrier Ethernet service edge. The 7450 ESS integrates the scalability, resiliency, and predictability of MPLS, along with the bandwidth and economics of Ethernet, to enable a metro-wide, converged packet aggregation infrastructure using Carrier Ethernet to deliver next-generation services.

Designed as a service delivery platform, the 7450 ESS enables a broadly scalable service offering based on MPLS-enabled Carrier Ethernet. Comprehensive Carrier Ethernet and IP/MPLS feature and protocol support allows a full complement of residential, business, and mobile service applications across a range of topologies, from point-to-point to any-to-any, from fully meshed to ring-based. The 7450 ESS enables providers to flexibly offer any combination of Ethernet or IP-based services in a highly scalable (up to 2 Tb/s) platform that can support hundreds of thousands of end users in a metro area with ease.

The 7450 ESS is available in four chassis variants:

- 7450 ESS-12
- 7450 ESS-7
- 7450 ESS-6
- 7450 ESS-6v

The ESS family in Figure 1.3 shows the ESS-7 on the left and the ESS-6 on the right with the ESS-12 behind.

Figure 1.3 7450 ESS family.

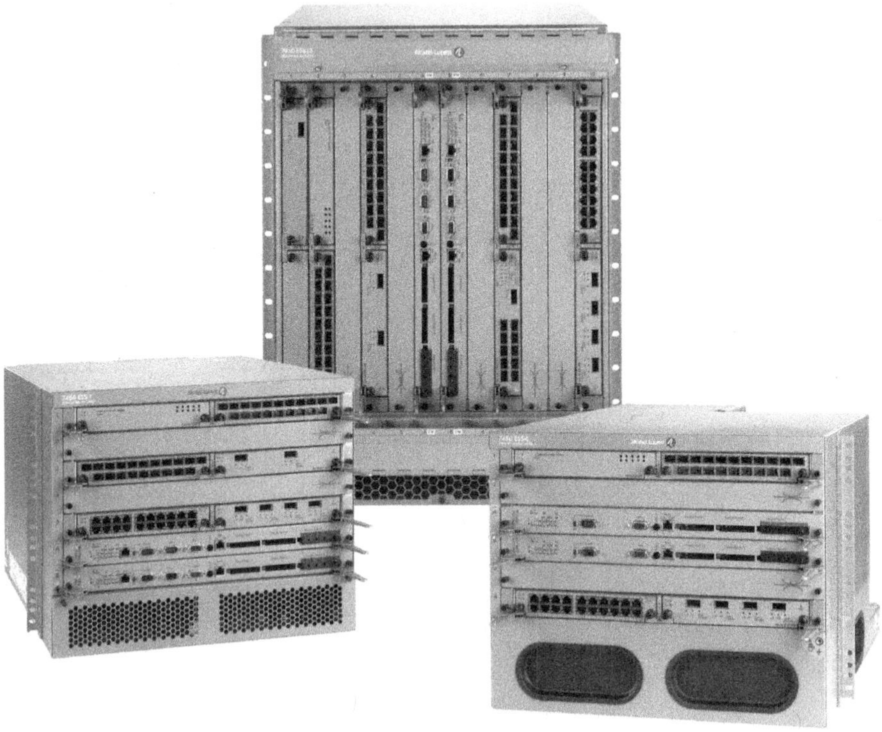

7210 Service Access Switch

The Alcatel-Lucent 7210 SAS (Service Access Switch) family of compact, Ethernet-edge, and aggregation devices enables the delivery of advanced Carrier Ethernet services to the customer edge and extends the reach of MPLS-enabled Carrier Ethernet aggregation networks into smaller network locations. Available in a wide range of compact form factors, the 7210 SAS enables fixed and wireless service providers, multiservice operators (MSOs), as well as industry and enterprise customers to build out cost-optimized Carrier Ethernet infrastructure for business, residential, and mobile services delivery.

The 7210 SAS family is available in a range of platform variants, including two that support extended temperature ranges (ETRs). The current variants are the following:

- 7210 SAS-X
- 7210 SAS-M (10GigE and 10GigE–ETR)
- 7210 SAS-M
- 7210 SAS-E
- 7210 SAS-D (SAS-D and SAS-D–ETR)

Figure 1.4 shows the 7210 SAS-E (on top) and the 7210 SAS-M.

Figure 1.4 7210 SAS-E and SAS-M.

5620 Service Aware Manager (SAM)

The Alcatel-Lucent 5620 SAM (Service Aware Manager) provides end-to-end service-aware management of all-IP networks and the services they deliver, going well beyond the traditional boundaries of element- and network-management systems. The 5620 SAM manages all network domains end-to-end as well as the multiple interdependent layers on which service delivery depends. With unified element, network, and service-aware management, service providers can more effectively manage mobile, business, and residential services.

The 5620 SAM consists of four integrated modules:

- **5620 SAM Element Manager (SAM-E)**—The 5620 SAM Element Manager (SAM-E) module provides traditional Fault, Configuration, Accounting, Performance, and Security (FCAPS) management functionality for element management and is the base platform for all 5620 SAM modules.
- **5620 SAM Provisioning (SAM-P)**—The 5620 SAM Provisioning (SAM-P) module provides network configuration and service provisioning.
- **5620 SAM Assurance (SAM-A)**—The 5620 SAM Assurance (SAM-A) module provides physical, network, and service topology views; and operations, administration, and maintenance (OAM) service-diagnostics tools.
- **5620 SAM OSS Integration (SAM-O)**—The 5620 SAM OSS Integration (SAM-O) module provides an open interface for integration with external applications and operations support systems (OSSs).

The 5620 SAM provides extensive management for all the products in the 7750 Service Router product group as well as many others in the Alcatel-Lucent High Leverage Network.

Chapter Review

Now that you have completed this chapter, you should be able to:

- List the key strengths and weaknesses of IP.
- Describe the overall evolution of the Internet.
- List the product families making up the Alcatel-Lucent Service Router product group.

2

Layer 2: The Physical Components of the Internet

The Alcatel-Lucent NRS II exam topics covered in this chapter include the following:

- Overview of Layer 2 technologies
- Format and transmission of Ethernet frames
- Ethernet switching
- VLANs
- SONET/SDH and POS
- ATM

This chapter provides a quick overview of common Layer 2 technologies—the physical components that make up the Internet. The most attention is given to Ethernet, the most widely used Layer 2 technology today. We look at how Ethernet frames are transmitted and examine the fields of the Ethernet header. We also take a brief look at the operation of an Ethernet switch. Support for VLANs (virtual LANs, Local Area Networks) is an important attribute of modern Ethernet switches, and we describe the purpose and operation of VLANs. The chapter concludes with a quick survey of some other important Layer 2 technologies. SONET/SDH (Synchronous Optical Network/Synchronous Digital Hierarchy) is the most widely used technology for long-distance optical transmission and provides a foundation for both the POS (Packet over SONET/SDH) and ATM (Asynchronous Transfer Mode) protocols.

Pre-Assessment

The following assessment questions will help you understand what areas of the chapter you should review in more detail to prepare for the NRS II exam. You can also use the CD that accompanies this book to take all the assessment tests and review the answers.

1. Which of the following is a circuit switched protocol?

A. POS

B. ATM

C. IP

D. Ethernet

2. What does a switch do when it receives a frame with an unknown destination MAC address?

A. It sends an ICMP destination unreachable to the source.

B. It sends an ICMP redirect to the source.

C. It silently discards the frame.

D. It floods the frame to all ports except the one the frame was received on.

E. It holds the packet for the configured time-out value and discards it if the source is still not known.

3. How is communication accomplished between two users on separate VLANs?

A. The users must be relocated to the same VLAN.

B. A third VLAN must be created, and both users must be given membership.

C. A router must be used to route the packets at the IP layer.

D. The users on separate VLANs must use an IP address on the same subnet to trigger a direct VLAN transfer on the switch.

E. No special mechanism is required.

4. For what reason was TDM initially developed?

A. To support high-bandwidth video applications

B. As a technology to offer improvements over ATM with respect to QoS

C. To meet the demands of the emerging Internet

D. For the PSTN

E. To support the cellular network

5. Which ATM adaptation layer is used for connectionless non-real time data such as IP?

A. AAL1

B. AAL2

C. AAL3

D. AAL4

E. AAL5

2.1 Purpose and Functions of a Layer 2 Protocol

An Internet application such as a web browser gives its data to the transport layer for delivery to a remote system. The transport layer packages the application data into transport layer segments that are delivered by the network or IP (Internet Protocol) layer (Layer 3). The IP layer constructs a packet with an IP address that uniquely identifies the source and destination network device in the internetwork. The packet may then be transmitted over several different physical networks (Layer 2) before it reaches its destination.

The network hardware and protocols that transmit data in the Internet are most often called *Layer 2*. This is because they perform the functions of Layer 1 and Layer 2 of the OSI (Open Systems Interconnection) model. IP provides a common structure and address plan for all devices of the Internet, but in order to transmit data, IP uses a widely diverse range of technologies that are collectively known as Layer 2 (see Figure 2.1).

Figure 2.1 The physical network technologies used to transmit data in the Internet comprise Layers 1 and 2 of the OSI model.

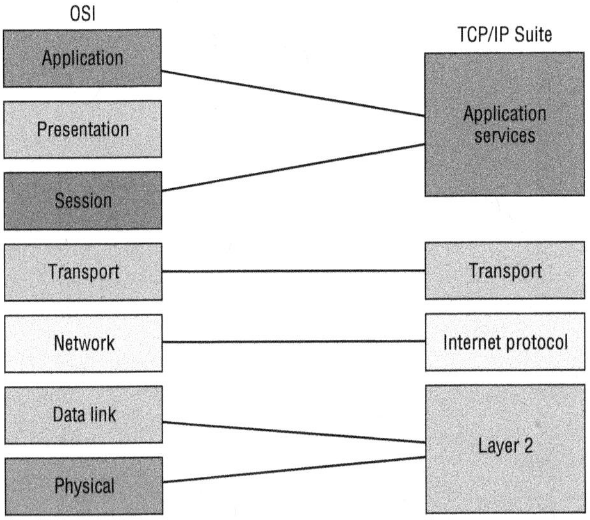

In any specific physical network, the data link layer (or Layer 2) is responsible for encapsulating the packet into a frame for transmission. The frame header usually contains source and destination addresses and other fields relating to the transmission of the data. The format and meaning of these fields vary depending on the particular Layer 2 protocol. Besides addresses, the Layer 2 header typically contains a checksum field to verify that the frame has not been corrupted in transmission. The frame also contains framing information that identifies the start and end of the frame on the physical transmission media. Once the frame is constructed, it is physically transmitted to the other Layer 2 device.

Layer 2 networks can be classified broadly into point-to-point networks, circuit-based networks, and broadcast networks (Figure 2.2). Point-to-point networks support direct connections between two endpoints. Circuit-based networks contain a collection of devices with point-to-point connections, each of which may contain many circuits. Data is transmitted on individual circuits and may include a circuit identifier. In a broadcast network, data is transmitted on a shared medium and therefore may be received by a number of devices. Frames in a broadcast network contain an address to identify the sender and intended recipient.

Figure 2.2 Layer 2 networks can be classified as point-to-point, circuit-based, or broadcast networks.

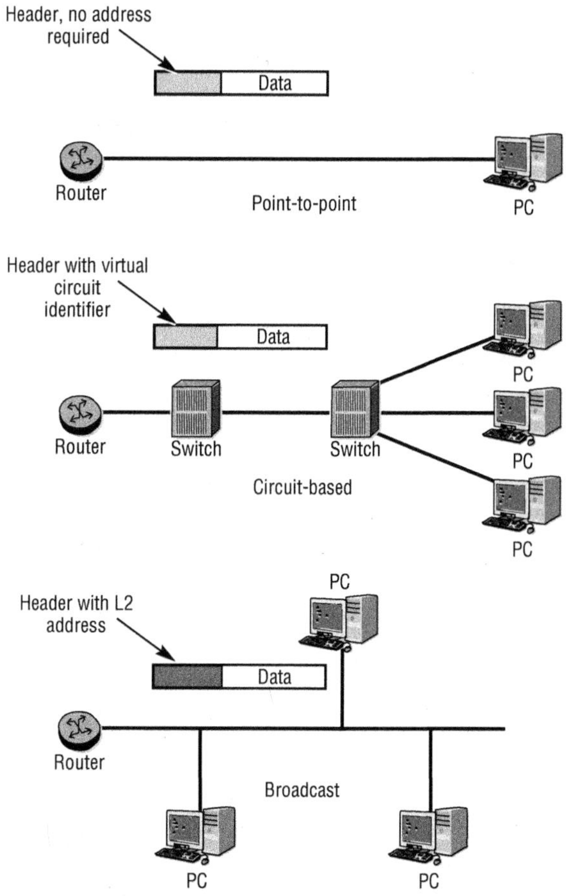

The Layer 2 network is used to deliver data between two Layer 3 devices (routers or end systems). The scope of the Layer 2 frame is the local Layer 2 network. In an IP network, data is transmitted from an end system to an IP router and then between routers across the network. Each router creates a Layer 2 frame to transmit the IP packet to another router across the network. The frame remains intact until it reaches the other router. This router receives the frame and extracts the IP packet. The connection to the next router may use a different Layer 2 technology, and a new frame is created for transmission to the next router.

Figure 2.3 shows IP routers connected by a variety of Layer 2 networks and the transmission of an IP packet across the network. The IP packet is constructed by the sending end system and remains (essentially) unchanged as it is transmitted across the different Layer 2 networks that make up the Internet.

Today, the most widely used Layer 2 protocol is Ethernet, which was originally used only as a local area network (LAN) technology. It is now being used frequently in metropolitan area networks (MANs) and wide area networks (WANs).

Figure 2.3 IP provides a common, global format for the transmission of data over a variety of Layer 2 networks.

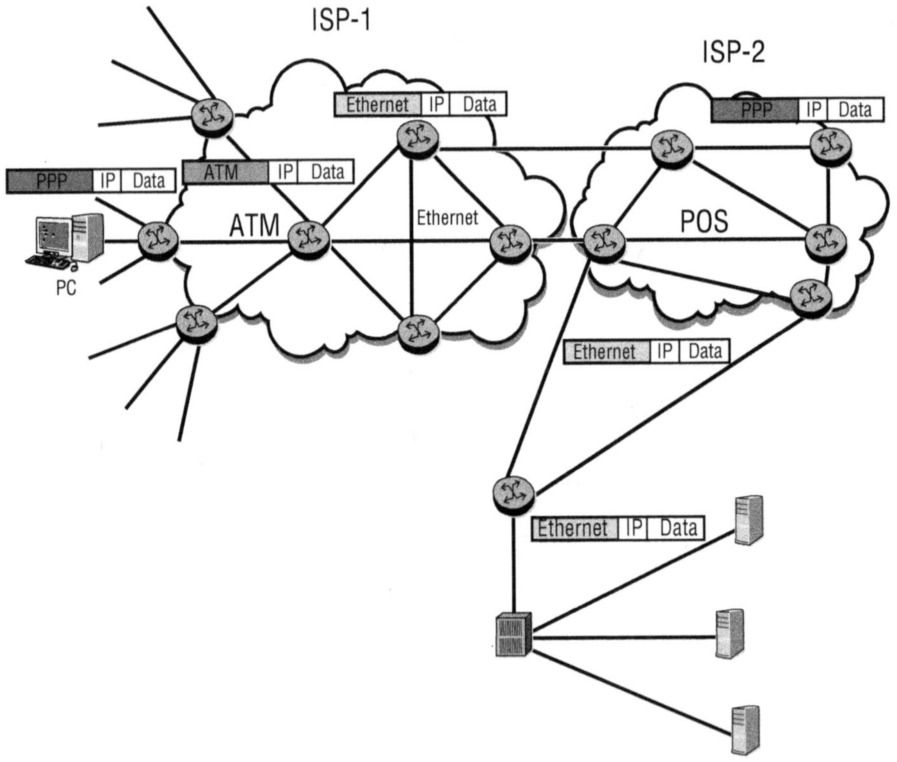

Technologies traditionally used in MANs and WANs include TDM (time division multiplexing), ATM (Asynchronous Transfer Mode), and POS (Packet over SONET/SDH). The remainder of this chapter provides an overview of the common Layer 2 technologies of the Internet.

2.2 Ethernet

Ethernet is the most widely used Layer 2 technology of the Internet. It is gradually replacing other Layer 2 technologies such as ATM and POS because of its simplicity and low cost.

Understanding Ethernet Transmissions

Ethernet is a broadcast technology. In early Ethernet networks, end systems were all attached to a shared cable. Later, end systems were attached to hubs that simply replicated a transmission received on one port to all the other ports. Since the transmission media is shared by many systems, a method is needed to control access to the media—Ethernet uses Carrier Sense Multiple Access with Collision Detection (CSMA/CD). The algorithm used by CSMA/CD is the following:

1. All systems are connected to a common, shared media (Multiple Access). A system wishing to transmit listens to the media to determine if it is free for transmission (Carrier Sense).
2. If the media is available, the end system transmits its frame.
3. If another system transmits at the same time, there is a collision (Collision Detection). In this case, both systems wait a random period of time before attempting another transmission.

We say the media is *half-duplex* because it is shared and when two end systems are communicating, only one system can transmit at a time. As shown by Figure 2.4, when Host A is transmitting, Hosts B, C, and D are unable to transmit.

The systems attached to an Ethernet cable or a hub as shown in Figure 2.4 are said to be in a *common collision domain* since the transmission by one system is seen, or sensed, by all the others and has the potential to collide with their transmissions.

In modern Ethernet networks, systems are usually attached to an Ethernet switch. A switch is a more intelligent device than a hub. Instead of simply replicating the signal seen on one port on all other ports, the switch examines the Ethernet frame it receives and only transmits on the port connected to the destination system. We need to understand the structure of the Ethernet frame to understand the operation of an Ethernet switch, so we will return to the switch after a brief study of the Ethernet frame.

Figure 2.4 On shared media, other devices are unable to transmit when one device is transmitting.

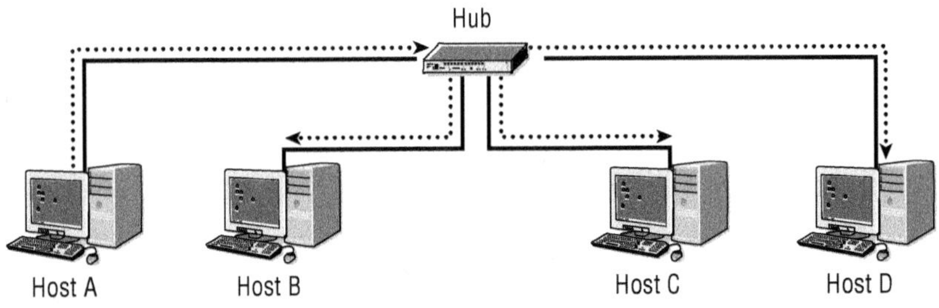

The Ethernet Frame

The original Ethernet standard defined the minimum frame size as 64 bytes and the maximum as 1,518 bytes. These numbers include all bytes from the destination MAC (Media Access Control) address field to the frame check sequence field. The preamble and Start Frame Delimiter (SFD) fields are not included when calculating the size of a frame. Later, standards increased the size of Ethernet frames, and modern switches often support jumbo frames, which can be more than 9,000 bytes. Figure 2.5 shows the structure of an Ethernet frame.

Figure 2.5 The standard Ethernet frame is a minimum of 64 bytes and a maximum of 1,518 bytes.

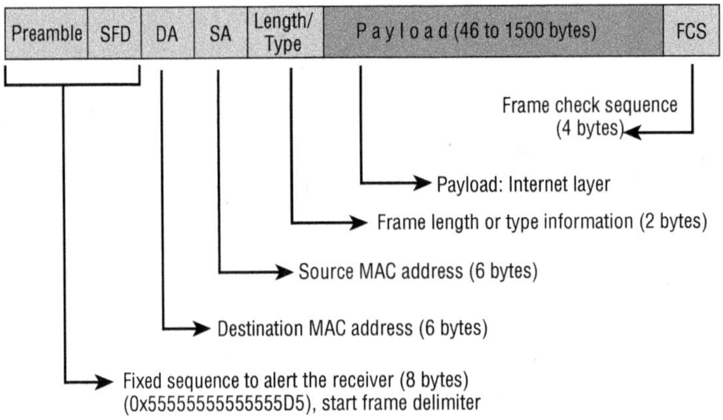

The different fields of the Ethernet frame are described below:

- **Preamble**—Ethernet is an asynchronous communications protocol because the transmission of a frame can occur at any time. The preamble is required to identify the beginning of the Ethernet frame. The preamble is a 56-bit pattern of alternating ones and zeroes. It is immediately followed by the Start Frame Delimiter.
- **Start Frame Delimiter (SFD)**—The SFD is always 10101011 and indicates the beginning of the actual Ethernet frame. Note that it continues the pattern of the preamble with the last bit changed to 1.
- **Destination address (DA)**—The address of the system meant to receive the frame.
- **Source address (SA)**—The address of the machine transmitting the frame.
- **Length/Type**—The payload length or type field (also known as *Ethertype*). There are actually two types of Ethernet frames—the original version sometimes known as DIX (Digital-Intel-Xerox) or more commonly as Ethernet II, and the IEEE version known as 802.3. If the value in this field is less than 1,536, the Ethernet frame is an 802.3 frame and this field is interpreted as length. If the value is 1,536 or greater, the Ethernet frame is an Ethernet II frame and the field is interpreted as type, or Ethertype. Today, nearly all Ethernet traffic is Ethernet II.
- **Data/Padding (also known as payload)**—The payload contains the actual data for transmission in the Ethernet frame. In the service networks supported by the Alcatel-Lucent 7750 SR, this would usually be either an IP packet or an MPLS (Multiprotocol Label Switching) frame. These protocols are transported in Ethernet II frames.

  An Ethernet frame must be a minimum of 64 bytes long. Therefore, if the data field is less than 46 bytes in length, padding is included to bring the total frame length to 64 bytes.
- **Frame Check Sequence (FCS)**—The FCS is the final part of the frame and is used to verify that the frame was not corrupted during transmission. The FCS is a value calculated by the sender based on the entire contents of the frame. The recipient uses the same formula to calculate the FCS value as it receives the frame. If the frame FCS does not match the calculated value, the frame is discarded.

Ethernet Addressing

An Ethernet frame contains a destination and a source address to identify the sender and the intended recipient. As shown in Figure 2.6, an Ethernet address (or MAC address) contains 6 bytes. The first 3 bytes are the OUI (Organizationally Unique Identifier), which is assigned to the manufacturer by the IEEE. The last 3 bytes are assigned by the organization owning the OUI. It is their responsibility to ensure that the remaining 3 bytes are unique for every MAC address they use.

Figure 2.6 In a MAC address, the three high-order bytes are assigned by the IEEE to an organization. The organization assigns the three low-order bytes to ensure a unique address.

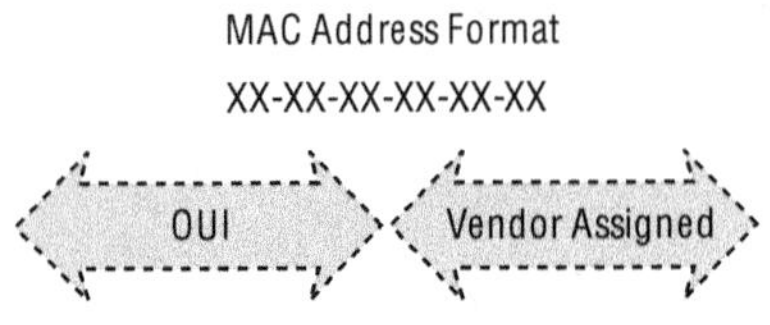

The addresses discussed so far are called *unicast* addresses because they uniquely identify a single node on any Ethernet network. Ethernet also supports broadcast and multicast addresses. A frame sent to the broadcast address has a destination address that is all ones and is intended for all systems on the network. A frame sent to a multicast address represents a group of systems on the network. Systems that wish to receive the traffic for a group must join the group. An Ethernet multicast address has the eighth bit from the left set to one (lowest bit of the highest-order byte).

When a switch receives traffic sent to the broadcast or multicast address, it is flooded out all ports. Some switches have additional functionality that enables them to discover the interested multicast receivers so that the switch does not have to flood multicast traffic.

Ethernet Switching

In an older Ethernet network, with the end systems attached to a single cable or to a hub, any transmission by one system is received by everyone. Although all systems receive the frame, the Ethernet hardware ignores frames unless the destination is its own MAC address, the broadcast address, or a multicast address they wish to receive. Since all systems receive the frame and have the possibility that their transmissions will collide, this is known as a collision domain.

When systems are connected to an Ethernet switch, the switch transmits only on the port attached to the destination system, and therefore each port is a separate collision domain. Modern Ethernet technologies use separate wires or optical fibers for transmit and receive; thus a system connected to a switch can transmit and receive simultaneously.

Many switches have the capacity to switch traffic between all ports simultaneously; thus the throughput of a switched Ethernet network is many times greater than a traditional network on a coaxial cable or connected to a hub (see Figure 2.7).

Figure 2.7 On an Ethernet switch, devices can transmit and receive simultaneously on all ports.

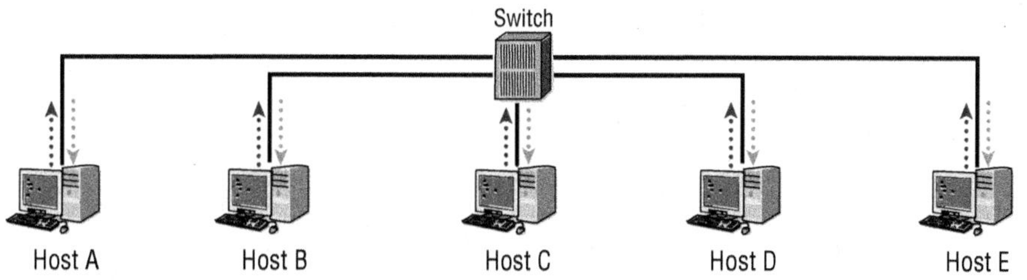

In order to determine the destination for a specific frame, an Ethernet switch maintains a table called the *forwarding database* (FDB). The FDB maps Ethernet destination MAC addresses to specific ports on the switch. When the switch receives a frame on any of its ports, the source address and port number are added to the FDB. When the switch receives a frame with a destination MAC address that has an entry in the FDB, the frame is transmitted only on the port associated with the destination address. When the switch receives a frame for a destination address that is not in the FDB, the frame is flooded (transmitted out all ports).

Each port on an Ethernet switch is a separate collision domain since transmissions on one port do not collide with transmissions on other ports. However, broadcast transmissions are flooded on all ports; thus an Ethernet switch is said to form a single broadcast domain. Ethernet broadcast traffic is not transmitted through an IP router, so an IP router separates Ethernet broadcast domains. Figure 2.8 shows a network with multiple hubs, switches, and routers. There is a collision domain for each switch or router port, for a total of eight in this network, and a broadcast domain for each router port, for a total of three.

Ethernet Standards

The original Ethernet operated on a thick coaxial cable that operated at 10 Mbps (megabits per second) with a maximum length of 500 meters. Today Ethernet standards are defined at rates of 10 Mbps, 100 Mbps, 1 Gbps, and 10 Gbps for operation on unshielded twisted pair and fiber optic cable. Figure 2.9 lists some of the commonly used variants of Ethernet.

Figure 2.8 Each port on a switch is a separate collision domain; each port on a router is a separate broadcast domain.

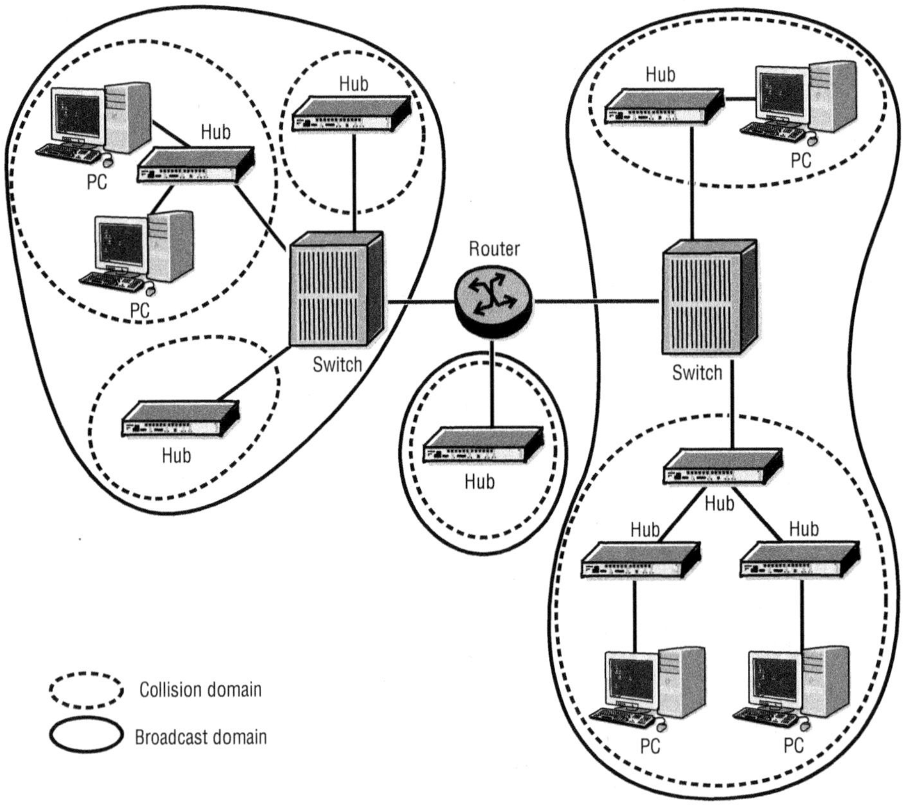

2.3 Ethernet VLANs

Most Ethernet switches also support the creation of virtual LANs, or VLANs. VLANs separate the Ethernet switch into multiple virtual switches. Each VLAN is a separate broadcast domain and corresponds to a distinct virtual switch. Systems connected to different VLANs cannot exchange data directly—data must be routed to move between VLANs. There are several methods of defining VLANs, but usually the ports on an Ethernet switch are configured to belong to a specific VLAN.

In Figure 2.10, VLANs subdivide the Ethernet switch into multiple, logical switches. Note that there are no logical interconnections between these logical switches. Therefore, broadcast traffic that is generated by a host in one VLAN stays within that

VLAN, making each VLAN a separate broadcast domain. In the diagram, Ports 1 and 5 are members of VLAN 102, Ports 2 and 7 are members of VLAN 103, and Ports 3 and 6 are members of VLAN 101. Traffic between systems connected to Ports 1 and 2 cannot be exchanged directly through the switch but must be routed.

Figure 2.9 There are many different versions of the Ethernet standard to support transmission over different media at different speeds.

Ethernet	Designation	Type	Wavelength	Distance	Fiber Type
10/100Base	TX	Copper	—	100 m	—
100Base	FX	Optical SFP	1310 nm	2 km	Multimode
	FX-SM	Optical SFP	1310 nm	25 km	Single-mode
Gigabit Ethernet	TX	Copper	—	100 m	—
	SX	Optical SFP	850 nm	550 m	Multimode
	LX	Optical SFP	1310 nm	10 km	Single-mode
	ZX	Optical SFP	1550 nm	70 km	Single-mode
	CWDM	Optical SFP	1470 nm to 1610 nm	70 km	Single-mode
10 Gigabit Ethernet	LW/LR	Optical SFP	1310 nm	10 km	Single-mode
	EW/ER	Optical SFP	1550 nm	40 km	Single-mode
	SR	Optical SFP	850 nm	300 m	Multimode
	LR	Optical SFP	850 nm	10 km	Single-mode
	ZR	Optical SFP	1550 nm	80 km	Single-mode
	T	Copper	—	30-100 m	—
	CX4	Copper	—	15 m	—

Usually, hosts are not VLAN-aware, and therefore no special configuration is required on the hosts. VLAN configuration is done on the switch, and ports are assigned on a VLAN-by-VLAN basis.

VLAN Tags

In a network with multiple Ethernet switches, the sharing of VLANs between switches is achieved by the insertion of a header with a 32-bit VLAN field inserted into the Ethernet header. The format and use of this field are defined by the IEEE 802.1Q standard. The VLAN identifier (VID) uses 12 bits of this 32-bit VLAN field and provides 4,094 possible VLAN destinations for each Ethernet frame (VIDs 0 and 4095 are usually not used). A VID is assigned to each VLAN, and by using the same VID on different, connected switches, the VLAN can be extended across multiple switches. This is known as *VLAN trunking* and allows the use of one high-bandwidth port, such as a gigabit Ethernet port, to carry the VLAN traffic between switches instead of using one port for each VLAN (see Figure 2.11).

Figure 2.10 VLANs segregate an Ethernet switch into multiple, separate virtual switches.

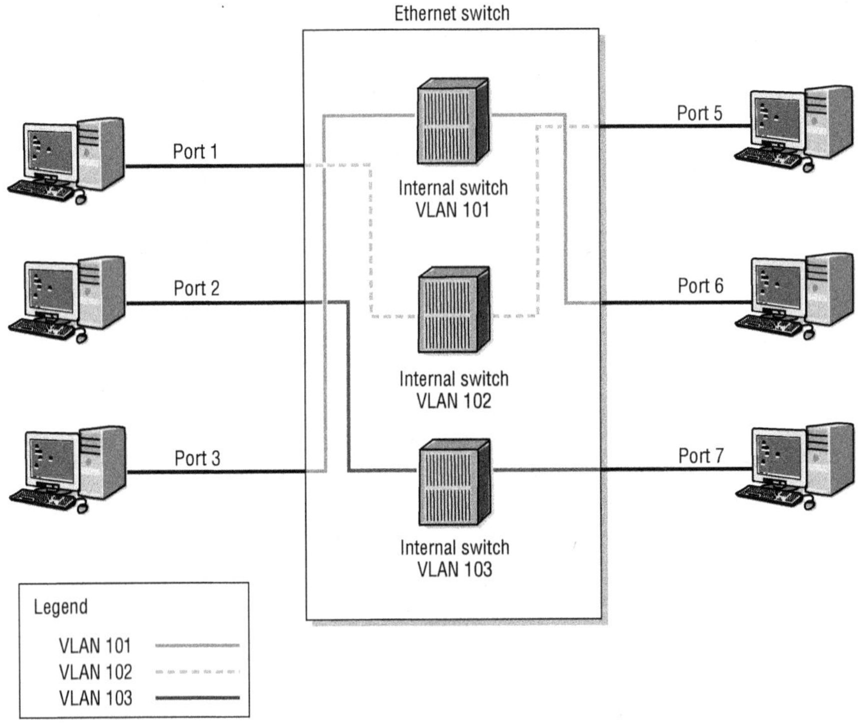

The VLAN field is inserted after the source MAC address, before the Ethertype/Length field, and can be divided into two parts—the VLAN tag type and the VLAN tag field (see Figure 2.12). The VLAN tag type is an additional Ethertype field with a fixed value (hex value 0x8100) that indicates an 802.1Q VLAN tag. The VLAN tag field is 2 bytes, of which 12 bits are used for the VID. The VLAN tag field is followed by the original Ethertype field describing the payload.

The tag control information has three parts:

- **Priority value (user priority)**—A 3-bit value that specifies a frame's priority or class of service.
- **CFI (Canonical Format Indicator)**—Always set to 0 for Ethernet switches.
- **VID**—A 12-bit value that identifies the VLAN that the frame belongs to. If the VID is 0, the tag header contains only priority information.

An Ethernet switch maintains a separate FDB for each VID and uses the VID to determine which FDB it will use to find the destination. When a tagged frame reaches the destination switch port, the VLAN header is typically removed.

Figure 2.11 The VLAN tag allows the transmission of data for multiple distinct VLANs over the same physical connection.

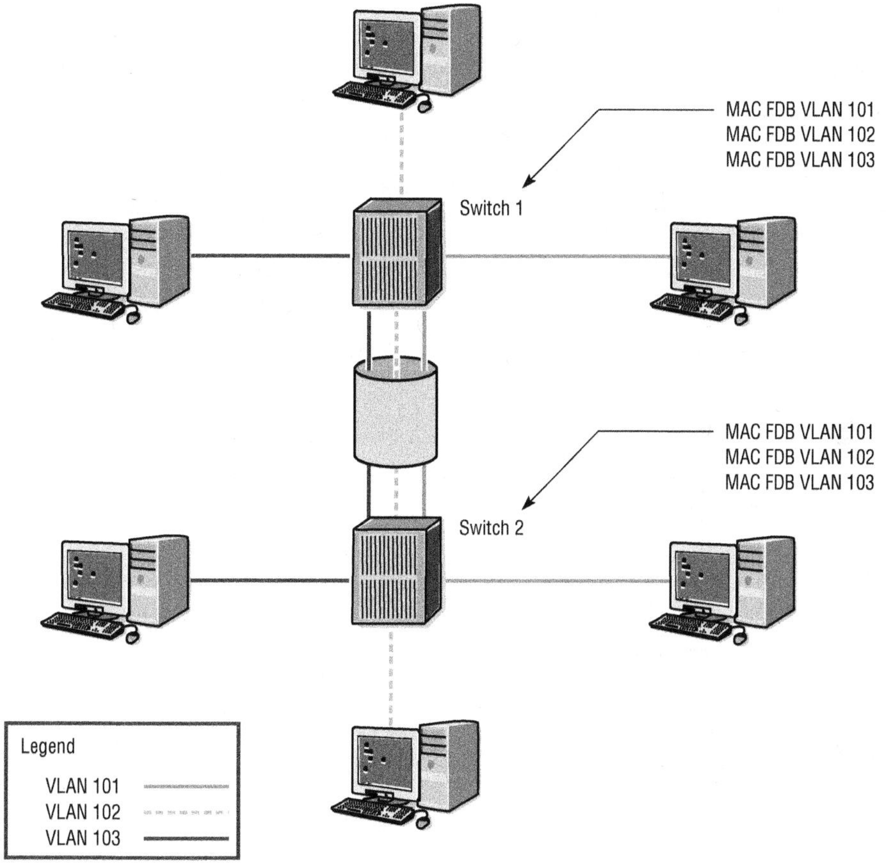

VLAN Stacking (Q-in-Q)

A restriction of Ethernet VLANs is the limited number of VIDs. With 12 bits used for the VID, there are only 4,096 possibilities. Because VLAN 0 and 4095 are reserved, the switch is really only capable of supporting 4,094 VLANs—not a significant number if it is compared with the expanding growth of networks. One of the solutions to this restriction is VLAN stacking, also known as Q-in-Q. With VLAN stacking, a service provider's customers can use their own VLAN tags to identify VLANs on their networks, and the service provider can add an outer VLAN tag to identify and connect their customers' sites. A standardized approach to Q-in-Q is defined as an extension to 802.1Q in IEEE 802.1ad ("Provider Bridges") (see Figure 2.13).

Figure 2.12 The VLAN field is a 32-bit field inserted directly after the source address in the Ethernet header.

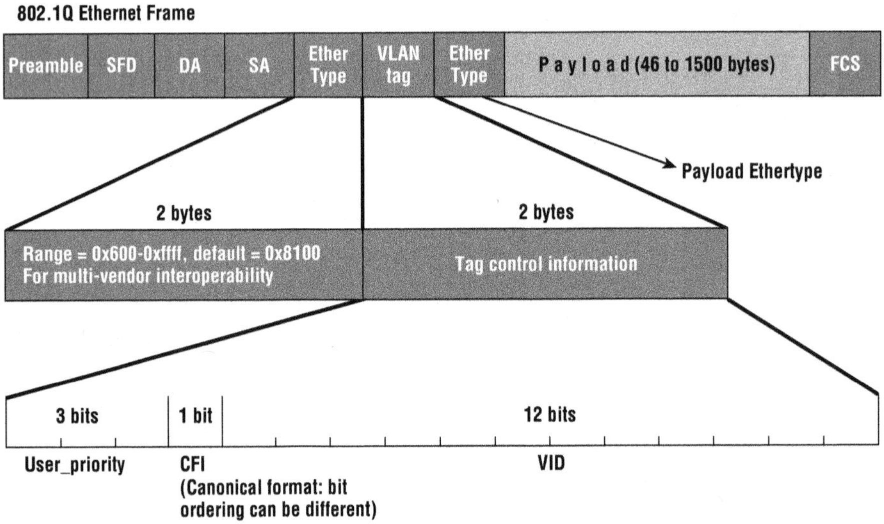

Figure 2.13 Q-in-Q adds an additional VLAN field to the header. Often the outer tag is used by the service provider, while the inner tag is used by the customer.

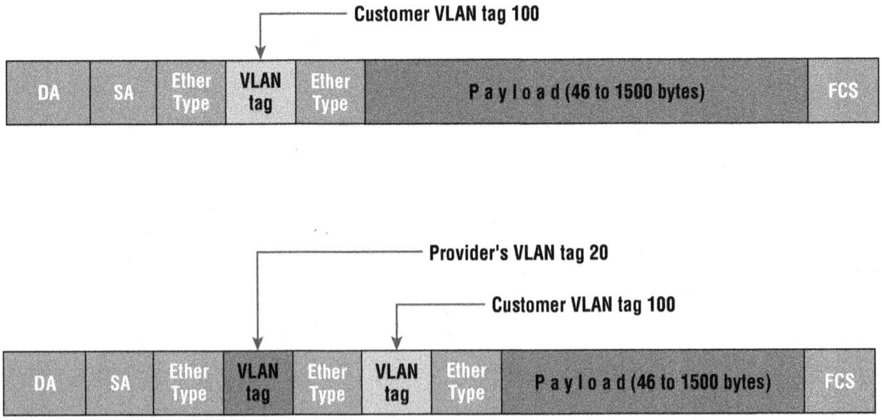

2.4 SONET/SDH, POS, and ATM

TDM was developed to support digital data transmission in the public switched telephone network (PSTN). It supports the multiplexing of multiple, lower-bandwidth circuits into one higher-bandwidth circuit. In the 1980s, SONET/SDH (Synchronous Optical Network/Synchronous Digital Hierarchy) was developed to define standardized formats for multiplexing voice circuits over optical networks. Since the 1990s, the volume of data traffic has been increasing much more than voice traffic, and additional technologies have been developed for carrying data traffic over SONET/SDH networks. These include ATM and POS.

Time Division Multiplexing

When digital technologies were introduced into the PSTN in the 1960s, the analog voice signal was sampled 8,000 times per second using an 8-bit sample. This meant a constant 64 Kbps was required for a simple voice circuit. Therefore, in a TDM network, frames are defined using a fixed unit of time—125 microseconds, or 8,000 frames per second. Although TDM was designed and developed for voice communications equipment, it is now widely used for data communications as well. TDM is a synchronous technology since accurate timing between the end systems is necessary to define the frame.

In the T-carrier system used in North America and Japan, 24 voice circuits are bundled to create the DS1 (Digital Signal 1), commonly known as the T1. Each frame of 24×8 bits has an additional bit added for framing to make 193 bits per frame. Since 8,000 frames are transmitted per second, this necessitates a signaling rate of 1.544 Mbps (see Figure 2.14).

The E-carrier system was developed later and is used in the rest of the world outside North America and Japan. The principle is similar since the E-carrier rates are defined to carry multiple voice circuits of 64 Kbps. The E1 basic rate uses a 2.048-Mbps signaling rate to carry 32 circuits. Thirty circuits are available for voice or data with 64 Kbps used for framing and 64 Kbps reserved for signaling (see Figure 2.15).

The basic T1 or E1 signal can be multiplexed again to higher data rates, such as the T3 or E3.

Figure 2.14 A T1 frame carries 8 bits for each of 24 channels plus one framing bit. A single T1 frame is transmitted in 125 microseconds.

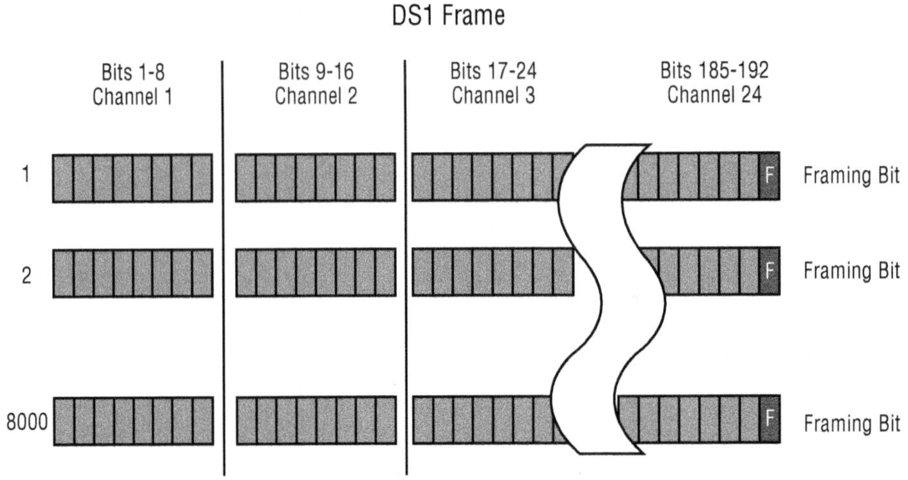

Figure 2.15 An E1 frame carries 8 bits for each of 30 channels plus 8 bits of framing and 8 bits of signaling. A single E1 frame is transmitted in 125 microseconds.

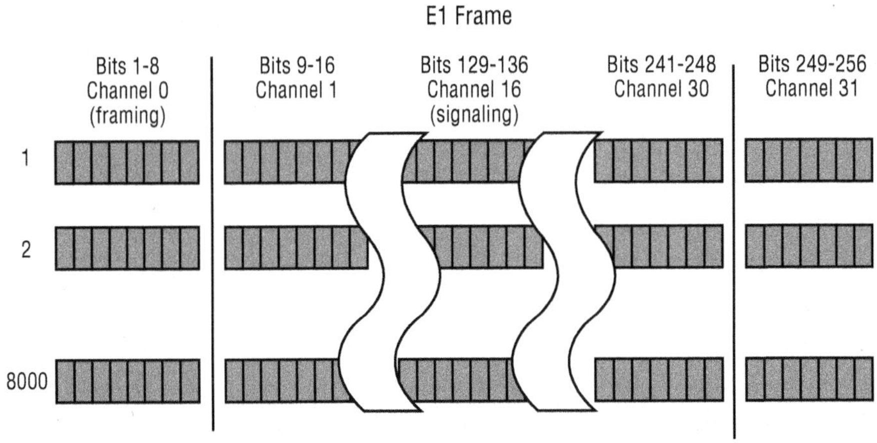

SONET/SDH

With the development of fiber optic transmission systems, a standard was required for the multiplexing and transport of TDM circuits. Again, two slightly different systems were developed in Europe and North America, although the two systems are very similar and use the same underlying technology. SONET is used in North America and SDH in Europe and most of the rest of the world.

The basic SONET signal is known as the synchronous transport signal (STS-1) and has a signaling rate of 51.84 Mbps. This includes a payload of 50.112 Mbps and an overhead of 1.728 Mbps. The STS-1 frame is 810 bytes in total and is transmitted in 125 microseconds, hence the bit rate of 51.84 Mbps. Each STS-1 frame can carry one DS3 or 28 DS1 frames. For higher data rates, the STS-1 signal is multiplexed at fixed levels to STS-3, STS-12, STS-48, and STS-192 (see Table 2.1).

Table 2.1 SONET/SDH Transmission Rates

	Bit Rate (Mbps)	SONET Frame	DS3s	DS1s	SDH Frame	E3s	E1s
OC-1	51.84	STS-1	1	28	STM-0	1	16
OC-3	155.52	STS-3	3	84	STM-1	4	64
OC-12	622	STS-12	12	336	STM-4	16	256
OC-48	2488	STS-48	48	1344	STM-16	64	1024
OC-192	9953	STS-192	192	5376	STM-64	256	4096

The STM-1 frame used by SDH is effectively an STS-3 frame with exactly the same signaling rate and the same size of payload and overhead. The STM-1 frame is designed to carry an E4 frame and can be multiplexed to higher levels in groups of four. Although the overhead is the same, the terminology and usage of the overhead bytes vary somewhat between SONET and SDH. A variety of different standards are also defined for the multiplexing of lower data rates within STS-1 or STM-1 frames.

Although SONET/SDH was designed for the transport of voice traffic, it is widely used for data as well. In the late 1980s, ATM was developed to support the provisioning of several different data service types over a SONET/SDH network. Later, POS was developed as a simpler method of encapsulating data traffic such as IP for transport over SONET/SDH.

Asynchronous Transfer Mode (ATM)

ATM was designed for the transport of a variety of data services over a SONET/SDH network. ATM uses fixed-size cells to simplify the high-speed switching required for optical interfaces. To minimize delay and jitter on lower-speed interfaces (especially important for voice applications), a small cell size is required. A 48-byte payload was chosen as a compromise to satisfy both those that wanted a 64-byte payload (more suitable for data applications) and those that wanted a 32-byte payload (more optimal for voice applications). A 5-byte header makes a total cell size of 53 bytes. Figure 2.16 shows the fields of the ATM header.

Figure 2.16 The ATM cell has a fixed payload of 48 bytes and a header of 4 bytes.

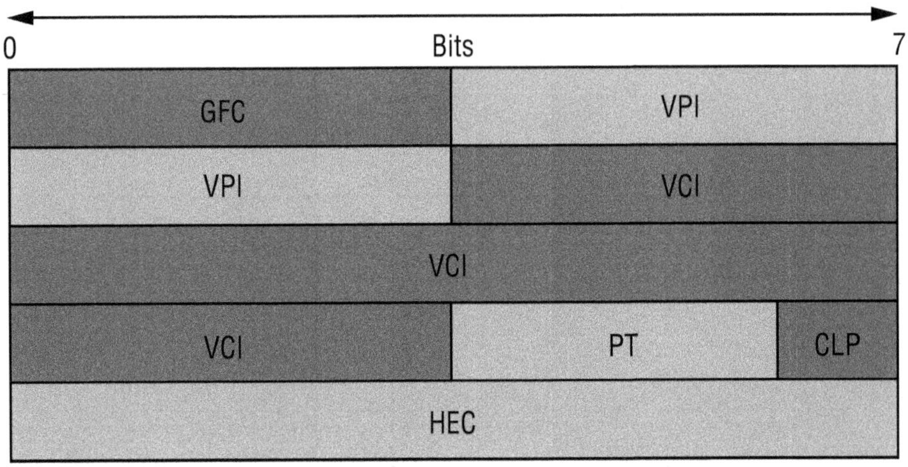

ATM includes quality of service (QoS) support and defines five different service classes to suit the requirements of different types of applications. ATM cells are transmitted on virtual circuits that are identified by a VPI/VCI value (Virtual Path Indicator/Virtual Circuit Indicator) in the cell header. Multiple virtual circuits supporting different service classes can be transmitted on the same physical connection.

To support the different service types, the ATM standards also define ATM adaptation layers (AALs). The adaptation layers define the service type provided by the network and the mapping of higher-layer data to the 53-byte ATM cells. Usually the following adaptation layers are mapped to the following classes of service:

- **AAL1–Constant bit rate service (CBR)**—Connection-oriented service with minimal delay, jitter, and data loss. Intended for the transport of traditional voice circuits.
- **AAL2–Variable bit rate service (VBR)**—Connection-oriented service with variable bit rates and a bounded delay. Intended for compressed voice or video traffic. May have real-time constraints (vbr-rt) or not (vbr-nrt).

- **AAL3/4–Available bit rate service (ABR)**—Connection-oriented data service, rarely used.
- **AAL5–Unspecified bit rate service (UBR)**—Connectionless data service for data such as IP packets. The majority of ATM traffic is AAL5.

AAL5 is the simplest and most efficient of the adaptation layers for the transport of connectionless, non-real-time data such as IP. The IP packet is encapsulated in an AAL5 SDU (Service Delivery Unit), which is always an even multiple of 48 bytes long. The AAL5 SDU is then transmitted as a group of ATM cells on a virtual circuit.

The AAL5 SDU (and its payload, the IP packet) is reconstructed from the stream of ATM cells at the egress of the ATM network. This function of the ATM adaptation layer is known as SAR (Segmentation and Reassembly). An AAL5 SDU is shown in Figure 2.17. Note that it has no header. The payload is first, followed by a trailer that includes a CRC (cyclic redundancy check) value that is used to verify integrity of the frame, similar to the Ethernet FCS field.

Figure 2.17 The AAL5 payload is encapsulated in an AAL5 SDU that is padded to have an even multiple of 48 bytes.

Variable length	0-47	1	1	2	4 Bytes
PDU payload	PAD	UU	CPI	LI	CRC-32

PDU - Variable length user information field (broken into 48 byte-segments)
PAD - Padding used to cell align the trailer between 0 and 47 bytes long
UU - CPCS user-to-user indication to transfer one byte of user information
CPI - Common Part Indication
LI - Length indicator

SAR is a relatively expensive process and difficult to do for higher-speed interfaces. Although ATM is occasionally used today in core networks, it is more often found at the service provider edge, such as for the aggregation of data from ADSL (Asymmetric Digital Subscriber Line) connections.

Packet over SONET/SDH (POS)

POS was developed as a simpler, cheaper, and more efficient method to encapsulate IP data for transmission over a SONET/SDH network. With POS, the IP packets are encapsulated in a PPP (Point-to-Point Protocol) frame and carried in the SONET/SDH payload. Figure 2.18 shows the structure of a PPP frame.

Figure 2.18 PPP defines a framing widely used for transmitting data over SONET/SDH circuits or over dial-up lines.

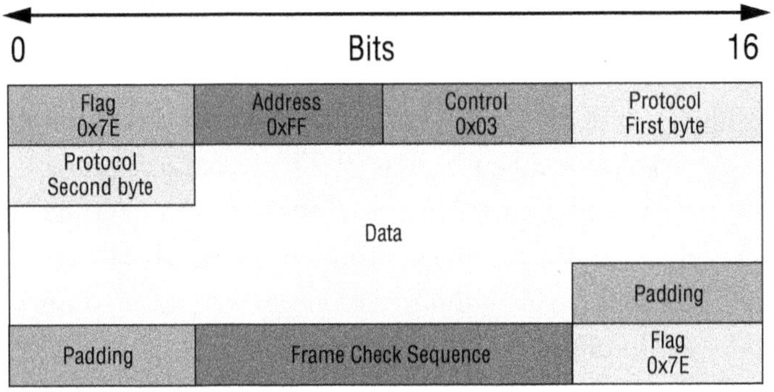

POS is widely used in the core of service provider networks where high-speed SONET/SDH links are common. PPP is also widely used for subscriber connections on dial-up lines and high-speed connections to the Internet.

2.5 Configuring Ports

On the 7750 SR, packet forwarding is handled by the IOM (Input/Output Module) and MDA (Media Dependent Adapter) cards. The IOM fits in one of the slots on the 7750 SR or 7450 ESS and supports two MDAs (see Figure 2.19). It is fairly accurate to say that the MDA handles the Layer 2 functions, and the IOM handles the Layer 3 functions.

Figure 2.19 An IOM card performs packet forwarding functions and can support up to 2 MDAs that perform media-specific functions.

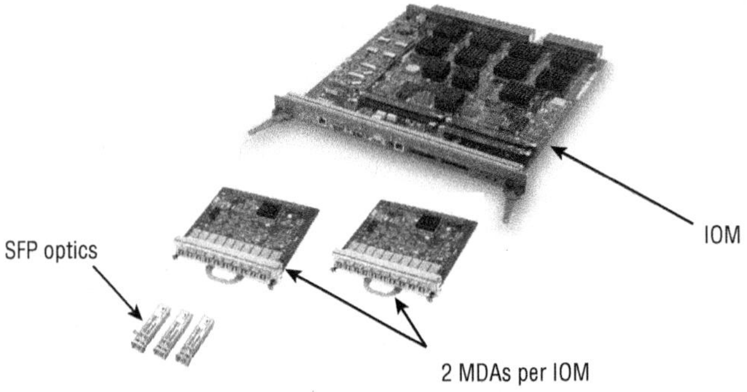

The first step in configuring ports on the 7750 SR is to configure the card with the appropriate `card-type`. Use the `show` command to see the type of card physically provisioned in the router (Listing 2.1).

Listing 2.1 Output of the show card command

```
*A:nrs2_r1# show card

===============================================================================
Card Summary
===============================================================================
Slot      Provisioned      Equipped        Admin   Operational        Comments
          Card-type        Card-type       State   State
-------------------------------------------------------------------------------
1                          iom-20g-b       up      unprovisioned
A         sfm-400g         sfm-400g        up      up/active
===============================================================================
```

From the `show` command you can see that the IOM in Slot 1 is an `iom-20g-b` card. Slot A shows the `sfm-400g` card. This is the SF/CPM (Switch Fabric/Control Processor Module) that is the control card for the router. Chapter 4 discusses the control plane and data plane of the router and describes this card in more detail. In a redundant system there will be a second SF/CPM in Slot B.

Based on the output of the `show card` command, you can use the `configure` command to configure the IOM appropriately, as shown in Listing 2.2.

Listing 2.2 Configuring the IOM card

```
*A:nrs2_r1# configure card 1 card-type "iom-20g-b"
*A:nrs2_r1# show card

===============================================================================
Card Summary
===============================================================================
Slot      Provisioned      Equipped        Admin   Operational        Comments
          Card-type        Card-type       State   State
-------------------------------------------------------------------------------
1         iom-20g-b        iom-20g-b       up      up
A         sfm-400g         sfm-400g        up      up/active
===============================================================================
```

Once the card is configured, you need to configure the MDA. Again, use the show command to see what type of MDAs are configured (Listing 2.3).

Listing 2.3 Output of the show mda command

```
*A:nrs2_r1# show mda

===============================================================================
MDA Summary
===============================================================================
Slot  Mda   Provisioned        Equipped          Admin     Operational
            Mda-type           Mda-type          State     State
-------------------------------------------------------------------------------
1     1                        m10-1gb-sfp-b     up        unprovisioned
===============================================================================
```

The MDA is configured in a similar manner as the IOM card (see Listing 2.4).

Listing 2.4 Configuring the MDA

```
*A:nrs2_r1# configure card 1 mda 1 mda-type "m10-1gb-sfp-b"
*A:nrs2_r1# show mda

===============================================================================
MDA Summary
===============================================================================
Slot  Mda   Provisioned        Equipped          Admin     Operational
            Mda-type           Mda-type          State     State
-------------------------------------------------------------------------------
1     1     m10-1gb-sfp-b      m10-1gb-sfp-b     up        up
===============================================================================
```

Once the IOM and MDA are configured, the ports can be brought up. A range of ports can be specified. Ports will only be operationally up if the port is connected to another active port (see Listing 2.5).

Listing 2.5 Configuring a range of ports

```
*A:nrs2_r1# configure port 1/1/[1..10] no shutdown
*A:nrs2_r1# show port

===============================================================================
Ports on Slot 1
===============================================================================
Port        Admin Link Port    Cfg  Oper LAG/ Port Port Port   SFP/XFP/
Id          State      State   MTU  MTU  Bndl Mode Encp Type   MDIMDX
-------------------------------------------------------------------------------
1/1/1       Up    Yes  Up      9212 9212    - netw null xcme
1/1/2       Up    Yes  Up      9212 9212    - netw null xcme
1/1/3       Up    Yes  Up      9212 9212    - netw null xcme
1/1/4       Up    Yes  Up      9212 9212    - netw null xcme
1/1/5       Up    No   Down    9212 9212    - netw null xcme
1/1/6       Up    No   Down    9212 9212    - netw null xcme
1/1/7       Up    No   Down    9212 9212    - netw null xcme
1/1/8       Up    No   Down    9212 9212    - netw null xcme
1/1/9       Up    No   Down    9212 9212    - netw null xcme
1/1/10      Up    No   Down    9212 9212    - netw null xcme

...output omitted...
```

The `show port` command can be used to show the configuration information for a specific port. `show port` *`port_num`* provides more detailed information, including port statistics (see Listing 2.6).

Listing 2.6 Detail output from the show port command

```
*A:nrs2_r1# show port 1/1/1

===============================================================================
Ethernet Interface
===============================================================================
Description        : 10/100/Gig Ethernet SFP
Interface          : 1/1/1                   Oper Speed       : 1 Gbps
Link-level         : Ethernet                Config Speed     : 1 Gbps
```

(continued)

Listing 2.6 *(continued)*

```
Admin State          : up                      Oper Duplex      : full
Oper State           : up                      Config Duplex    : full
Physical Link        : Yes                     MTU              : 9212
Single Fiber Mode    : No
IfIndex              : 35684352                Hold time up     : 0 seconds
Last State Change    : 07/30/2010 09:36:45     Hold time down   : 0 seconds
Last Cleared Time    : N/A                     DDM Events       : Enabled

Configured Mode      : network                 Encap Type       : null
Dot1Q Ethertype      : 0x8100                  QinQ Ethertype   : 0x8100
PBB Ethertype        : 0x88e7
Ing. Pool % Rate     : 100                     Egr. Pool % Rate : 100
Ing. Pool Policy     : n/a
Egr. Pool Policy     : n/a
Net. Egr. Queue Pol: default
Egr. Sched. Pol      : n/a
Auto-negotiate       : true                    MDI/MDX          : unknown
Accounting Policy    : None                    Collect-stats    : Disabled
Egress Rate          : Default                 Ingress Rate     : Default
Load-balance-algo    : default                 LACP Tunnel      : Disabled

Down-when-looped     : Disabled                  Keep-alive       : 10
Loop Detected        : False                     Retry            : 120
Use Broadcast Addr : False

Sync. Status Msg.    : Disabled                  Rx Quality Level : N/A

Configured Address : 8e:e6:01:01:00:01
Hardware Address     : 8e:e6:01:01:00:01
Cfg Alarm            :
Alarm Status         :

===============================================================================
Traffic Statistics
===============================================================================
                                           Input                  Output
-------------------------------------------------------------------------------
```

```
Octets                                          814                     0
Packets                                          11                     0
Errors                                            0                     0
===========================================================================

...output omitted...
```

The `configure port` command is also used to configure port parameters. The example in Listing 2.7 shows a change of the maximum transmission unit (MTU) for an Ethernet port to 5,000 bytes from its default value of 9,212.

Listing 2.7 Changing the Ethernet MTU

```
*A:nrs2_r1# configure port 1/1/1
*A:nrs2_r1>config>port# ethernet mtu 5000
*A:nrs2_r1>config>port# show port 1/1/1

===========================================================================
Ethernet Interface
===========================================================================
Description        : 10/100/Gig Ethernet SFP
Interface          : 1/1/1                Oper Speed       : 1 Gbps
Link-level         : Ethernet             Config Speed     : 1 Gbps
Admin State        : up                   Oper Duplex      : full
Oper State         : up                   Config Duplex    : full
Physical Link      : Yes                  MTU              : 5000
Single Fiber Mode  : No
IfIndex            : 35684352             Hold time up     : 0 seconds
Last State Change  : 07/30/2010 09:36:45  Hold time down   : 0 seconds
Last Cleared Time  : N/A                  DDM Events       : Enabled

...output omitted...
```

To configure a port for ATM traffic, the IOM and MDA must first be configured as above, and then the port configured with the ATM specific parameters.

Practice Lab: Configuring IOMs, MDAs, and Ports

The following lab is designed to reinforce your knowledge of the content in this chapter. Please review the instructions carefully, and perform the steps in the order in which they are presented. The practice labs require that you have access to six or more 7750 SRs or 7450 ESSs in a non-production environment.

These labs are designed to be used in a controlled lab environment. Please *do not* attempt to perform these labs in a production environment.

Alcatel-Lucent 7750/7450 products are modular for flexibility, upgradeability, and maintainability. A router is actually built from many modular components. None of the lab exercises in this book requires any configuration of the chassis, so exercises for this chapter deal with configuring everything from the IOM upward to the Layer 2 Ethernet ports.

Lab Section 2.1 Configuring IOMs

Objective In this exercise, you will become familiar with the different cards that fit into the chassis and be able to recognize and identify them from the CLI (command-line interface). This exercise also covers the steps required to configure an IOM card.

Validation You will know you have succeeded if you can display the state of IOMs and if the IOMs show an operational state of `Up`.

1. Display and examine the current card configuration with the `show card` command.

   a. In total, how many cards are physically present in the chassis? How many SF/CPMs? How many IOMs?

   b. What kind of labeling is used for the "two (2) card slots [...] dedicated for redundant SF/CPMs"?

   c. What kind of labeling is used for IOM card(s)?

   d. Is there any relationship between the first character of the prompt and any of the cards?

2. Configure the IOM card to the same type as `Equipped`.

The specific card type may be different on your router.

Wait a few moments, and repeat the `show card` command to see the IOM in its final state.

   a. Did the configuration command change the number of *physical* cards or the number of *available* cards?

   b. Why did the asterisk (*) appear in the command prompt? What will make it disappear again?

3. Have a look at the main log to see if anything has been recorded as a result of these last few configuration changes. Use the command `show log log-id 99`.

4. If your router has additional IOM cards and you want or need to use them for the exercises, you will need to repeat the configuration step for all additional IOM cards.

5. Repeat the preceding steps for each of the other routers.

Lab Section 2.2 Configuring MDAs

There are many MDAs available for the Alcatel-Lucent 7750/7450 products. The purpose of an MDA is to incorporate *all* circuitry that is specific to a particular type of Layer 2 connection, for example, Ethernet (both copper and fiber) and SONET/SDH (includes ATM). Within these broad categories, there are many different variations of MDAs to provide support for different speeds and numbers of connections. Having MDAs as a separate, modular component allows a customer to purchase and configure the right combination of connections required for any particular network node. Fortunately, the configuration process is very simple despite the large number of available MDAs.

Objective In this exercise, you will become familiar with recognizing, identifying, and configuring MDAs from the CLI.

Validation You will know you have succeeded if you display the state of MDAs and if the MDAs show an operational state of `Up`.

1. Display and examine the current MDA configuration using the `show mda` command. Note that the exact output will depend on your physical hardware.

   a. Can you see any MDAs for IOMs that are *not* configured?

   b. In total, how many MDAs are physically plugged into an IOM(s)?

   c. Which chassis slot/IOM is the MDA plugged into? Within that IOM, is the MDA plugged into the first or second MDA slot?

2. Generally, an MDA will always be configured to be the same as shown in the `Equipped Mda-type` column. Configure the available MDA(s). Note that the exact command will depend on your physical hardware; follow the rule of configuring the type to be the same as shown in the `show` command. What is the correspondence between the physical *location* of the MDA and the values specified in the above command?
3. Display and examine all MDAs that are now visible. Did the configuration command change the number of *physical* MDAs or the number of *available* MDAs?
4. Have a look at the main log to see what has been recorded as a result of this configuration change.
5. If your router has additional MDAs and you want or need to use them for the exercises, you will need to repeat the configuration step for all additional MDAs. Don't forget to save your configuration.
6. Repeat the preceding steps for each of the other routers.

Lab Section 2.3 Configuring Ports

The configuration process for the base hardware has a very definite hierarchy. First, the SF/CPM must be up and running in order to connect via the serial port or Ethernet management port. Next, the IOM(s) must be configured, followed by the MDA(s). An MDA will be neither visible nor configurable until its supporting IOM is fully configured; it is not possible to skip any preceding step. The same is true for individual ports: Everything in the hardware chain must be configured before ports become visible and configurable. Once they are configured, the raw hardware configuration is complete.

Objective In this exercise, you will become familiar with identifying and configuring ports from the CLI.

Validation You will know you have succeeded if you can display the state of the ports and if the (required) ports show an operational state of `Up`.

1. Display and examine the current port configuration (`show port` command). Note that the exact output will depend on your physical hardware.
   a. The output is split into three main sections. The first section is all the output for which (single) piece of hardware?
   b. How does the naming/labeling of the ports correspond with the SF/CPM, IOM, and MDA card numbering/labeling?

c. With default settings, are ports in an `Up` or a `Down` state? Is this consistent with other hardware (i.e., IOMs and MDAs)?

d. What is the default MTU for a 10/100 FastE port? For a GigE port?

2. Configure a single port to a functional state. With the port operationally `Up`, what new information is available?

3. Configure all ports `Up` that you need or want to use for the exercises. Configure the ports as a range, using a single command. Save your configuration.

4. Repeat the preceding steps for each of the other routers.

5. Is it possible to shut down/remove an MDA while ports are still active? Do the ports retain their previous state when the MDA is reconfigured? Try it!

6. If you have access to the physical hardware, try inserting and removing cables from a port and using a `show port` at each step to see the difference in the output.

Chapter Review

Now that you have completed this chapter, you should have a good understanding of the following topics:

- The purpose and scope of a Layer 2 protocol
- What the different types of Layer 2 protocols are
- How Ethernet frames are transmitted
- What the fields of the Ethernet header are used for
- How an Ethernet switch operates
- The purpose of a VLAN and the use of VLAN tags
- The structure and use of a basic TDM frame
- How SONET/SDH is used for data transmission
- The fundamental capabilities of ATM
- How to configure ports on the Alcatel-Lucent 7750 SR

Post-Assessment

The following questions will test your knowledge and prepare you for the Alcatel-Lucent NRS II Certification Exam. Compare your responses with the answers listed in Appendix A. You can also use the CD that accompanies this book to take all the assessment tests and review the answers.

1. Which of the following is a circuit switched protocol?
   - **A.** POS
   - **B.** ATM
   - **C.** IP
   - **D.** Ethernet

2. What does a switch do when it receives a frame with an unknown destination MAC address?
   - **A.** It sends an ICMP destination unreachable to the source.
   - **B.** It sends an ICMP redirect to the source.
   - **C.** It silently discards the frame.
   - **D.** It floods the frame to all ports except the one the frame was received on.
   - **E.** It holds the packet for the configured time-out value and discards it if the source is still not known.

3. How is communication accomplished between two users on separate VLANs?
   - **A.** The users must be relocated to the same VLAN.
   - **B.** A third VLAN must be created, and both users must be given membership.
   - **C.** A router must be used to route the packets at the IP layer.
   - **D.** The users on separate VLANs must use an IP address on the same subnet to trigger a direct VLAN transfer on the switch.
   - **E.** No special mechanism is required.

4. For what reason was TDM initially developed?
   - **A.** To support high-bandwidth video applications
   - **B.** As a technology to offer improvements over ATM with respect to QoS
   - **C.** To meet the demands of the emerging Internet
   - **D.** For the PSTN
   - **E.** To support the cellular network
5. Which ATM adaptation layer is used for connectionless non-real-time data such as IP?
   - **A.** AAL1
   - **B.** AAL2
   - **C.** AAL3
   - **D.** AAL4
   - **E.** AAL5
6. Which of the following is not an OSI Layer?
   - **A.** Application
   - **B.** Presentation
   - **C.** Establishment
   - **D.** Transport
   - **E.** Physical
7. How is a corrupted frame typically detected in Ethernet?
   - **A.** Using the framing information in the Layer 2 header
   - **B.** Using the FCS field in the Layer 2 header
   - **C.** By doing a reverse path forwarding check
   - **D.** Frame corruption is not typically detected at Layer 2, as it is handled by the higher-layer protocols.

8. Which of the following pieces of information is stored in the FDB when a frame arrives at an Ethernet switch?

A. The destination IP address

B. The source IP address

C. The source MAC address

D. The destination MAC address

9. What is the purpose of VLANs?

A. To allow more efficient use of the IPv4 address space

B. To separate broadcast domains

C. To allow direct routing between subnets

D. To separate collision domains

E. To provide full duplex functionality to a regular switch

10. What can be done when VLANs need to span more than one switch?

A. No special mechanism is required.

B. Signaling is used between switches for each destination MAC address in the FDB to build the correct VLAN-to-MAC associations.

C. Signaling is used between switches for each source MAC address in the FDB to build the correct VLAN-to-MAC associations.

D. A VLAN tag is attached to the Ethernet frame to indicate VLAN membership.

E. It's not possible for VLANs to span more than one switch.

11. Which statement is correct regarding the use of Ethernet Q-in-Q?

A. The outer tag is commonly used by the service provider, and the inner tag is commonly used by the customer.

B. The inner tag is commonly used by the service provider, and the outer tag is commonly used by the customer.

C. The service provider VLAN tag is identified with the SP field set to 1.

D. The customer VLAN tag is identified with the CE (customer equipment) field set to 1.

E. Service provider VLAN tags are identified with Ethertype 8100, and customer VLAN tags are identified with Ethertype 8200.

12. Which statement is correct regarding POS?

A. IP is encapsulated in an Ethernet frame and transported over SONET.

B. IP is encapsulated in PPP and transported over SONET.

C. IP is encapsulated in ATM and transported over SONET.

D. All the above variations are possible.

13. Which of the following is a reason for ATM's fixed 53-byte cell size?

A. To avoid data fragmentation

B. To minimize delay and jitter for voice services

C. To reduce the cell tax

D. To enable backward compatibility with TDM and Frame Relay

14. How many service classes are defined by ATM?

A. One

B. Three

C. Five

D. Seven

E. Eight

15. Which statement is correct regarding the required order for configuration of Alcatel-Lucent 7750 SR ports?

A. MDAs are configured first, followed by ports, followed by IOMs.

B. MDAs are configured first, followed by IOMs, followed by ports.

C. Ports are configured first, followed by MDAs, followed by IOMs.

D. Ports are configured first, followed by IOMs, followed by MDAs.

E. IOMs are configured first, followed by ports, followed by MDAs.

F. IOMs are configured first, followed by MDAs, followed by ports.

3 IP Networks

The Alcatel-Lucent NRS II exam topics covered in this chapter include the following:

- Summary of IP capabilities
- IP addressing review
- IP forwarding
- Configuring an IP interface
- Using and configuring static routes
- Other static-route options
- IPv6
- ICMPv6
- 6over4

This chapter provides an introduction to the Internet Protocol (IP)—both versions IPv4 and IPv6. We review the IPv4 addressing structure and the use of the subnet mask to divide the address into network and host components. We take a close look at how a router forwards IP packets and the difference between the data plane and the control plane. We work through an example of configuring the different types of IPv4 interfaces and the need for developing an address plan. This is followed by a thorough examination of static routes with examples of the different configuration options. The second part of the chapter covers IPv6 addressing and the IPv6 header. ICMPv6 and the process used for Neighbor Discovery (ND) in IPv6 are described. The chapter concludes with an example of a simple network configured for IPv6 and an example of how IPv6 traffic can be tunneled over an IPv4 network.

Pre-Assessment

The following assessment questions will help you understand what areas of the chapter you should review in more detail to prepare for the NRS II exam. You can also use the CD that accompanies this book to take all the assessment tests and review the answers.

1. Which statement is correct concerning the IP network 192.0.2.160 with a subnet mask of 255.255.255.224?
   - **A.** The host address range is 192.0.2.160–192.0.2.190.
   - **B.** The host address range is 192.0.2.161–192.0.2.190.
   - **C.** The host address range is 192.0.2.161–192.0.2.191.
   - **D.** The host address range is 192.0.2.160–192.0.2.191.
2. Which statement best describes the path of data traffic switched between two IOMs in an Alcatel-Lucent 7750 SR?
   - **A.** Data traffic will pass through the SF module.
   - **B.** Data traffic will pass through the SF module and then the CPM module.
   - **C.** Data traffic will pass through the CPM module and then the SF module.
   - **D.** Data traffic does not pass through either the SF or the CPM module.

3. If static routes are used for connectivity between a branch office and corporate headquarters, what is the most likely configuration?

A. Static route on the corporate router and a default route on the branch router

B. Default route on the corporate router and a static route on the branch router

C. Static route on the corporate and branch routers

D. Default route on the corporate and branch routers

4. An Alcatel-Lucent 7750 SR is configured with a default route and a static route for prefix 198.51.100.160/27. It has an OSPF route for 198.51.100.160/28. All routes are visible in the route-table and use default preference values. Which route will be used to forward an IP packet with the source address of 198.51.100.177?

A. Default route

B. Static route

C. OSPF route

D. There is not enough information to determine.

5. A router-interface on an Alcatel-Lucent 7750 SR is bound to a port and enabled with IPv6. An explicit IPv6 address is assigned to the interface. The port MAC address is 00:03:fa:ac:99:af, and the chassis MAC address is 00:03:fa:bf:b9:f8. Which statement below best describes the link-local address that will be assigned to the router interface?

A. The link-local interface address is FE80::203:FAFF:FEAC:99AF/64.

B. The link-local interface address is FC::3:FAFF:FEAC:99AF/64.

C. The link-local interface address is FC::203:FAFF:FEBF:B9F8/64.

D. The link-local interface address is FE80::3:FAFF:FEBF:B9F8/64.

E. A link-local address is not configured for the interface.

3.1 Summary of IP Capabilities

The Internet Protocol (IP) is the protocol of the Internet. By definition, a system is part of the Internet if it runs IP and is physically connected to the Internet. IP is often referred to as a Layer 3 protocol because it provides services similar to an OSI Network protocol, which is Layer 3 of the OSI seven-layer protocol model.

The major capabilities provided by the IP protocol are:

- Universal address plan
- Connectionless, unreliable datagram delivery service
- Consistent service interface for higher-level protocols

Universal Address Plan

The IP address is a logical address that differs from a Layer 2 address, such as the MAC address programmed into the device firmware. The IP address plan provides a unique identifier for every device on the Internet so that data sent from a source gets routed to the correct destination. The Internet Corporation for Assigned Names and Numbers (ICANN) operates the Internet Assigned Numbers Authority (IANA), which oversees the distribution of Internet addresses. IANA distributes blocks of addresses to the five Regional Internet Registries (RIRs). The RIRs further distribute these address blocks to the Local Internet Registries (LIRs) (usually service providers) which distribute addresses to end users or organizations. This process ensures that every Internet address is unique.

Datagram Delivery Service

IP provides an unreliable, connectionless datagram delivery service across the network. The service is considered *unreliable* because the network does not guarantee delivery or notify the end host system about packets that are lost through errors or network congestion. IP packets may be up to 65,535 bytes (octets) in length, although they are usually much smaller. There is no mechanism for flow control in IP.

IP is responsible for the routing of packets across the network. Routing is performed by the IP routers that connect the individual networks and forward packets hop by hop. In Figure 3.1, the source system with IP address 198.51.100.98 is sending data to the destination at IP address 192.0.2.4. Because the source and destination are on different networks, the IP packets must be sent to an IP router for routing.

Figure 3.1 IP packets are transmitted hop by hop across the Internet.

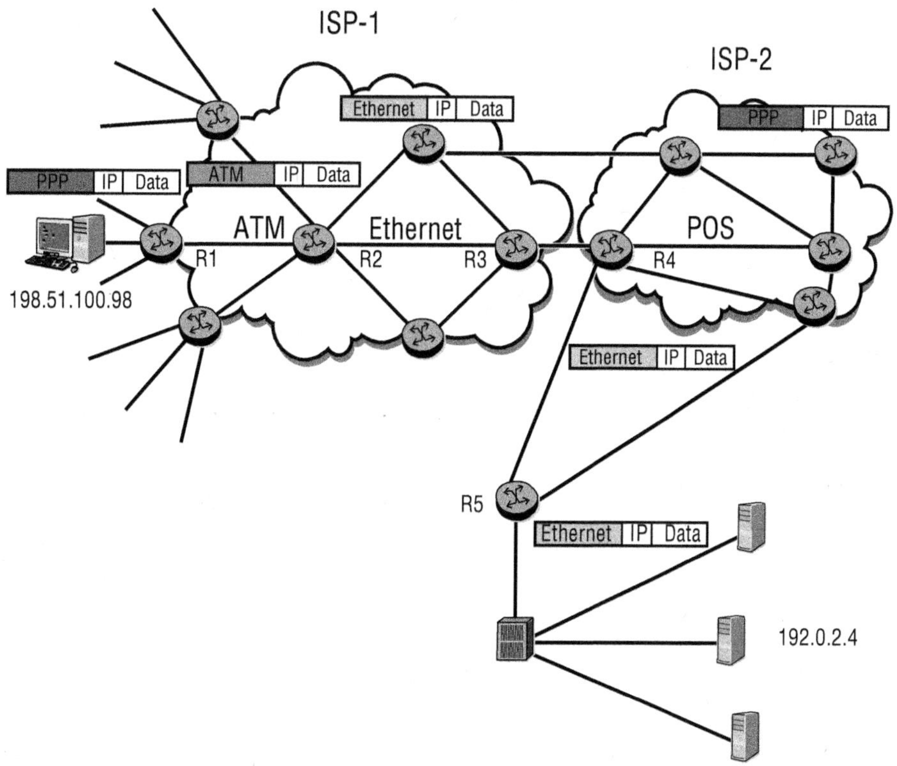

The IP packet is transmitted over the Layer 2 network (PPP in this example) to an IP router—R1. R1 transmits the packet to R2 using ATM, and R2 must decide which is the next best hop to reach the destination. R2 transmits the packet to R3 using Ethernet, and R3 transmits it to R4 in a PPP frame on a POS connection between them. R4 transmits the packet to R5 in an Ethernet frame, and R5 sends the packet to the final destination using Ethernet.

For the routers to decide which direction is the best path to the destination, they must have the appropriate information about the network. This information is exchanged using routing protocols that run on the routers. Every router on the network builds a routing table using the information that it receives from other routers. When a packet arrives at the router, it uses the routing table to determine the next-hop to the destination. The routing table contains a list of network destinations with the next-hop address to be used to reach each destination.

Consistent Service Interface

IP provides a consistent service interface for the higher-layer protocol (such as TCP or UDP) to communicate across the different physical networks. The data from every Internet application is transmitted across the network in an IP packet regardless of the nature of the application and regardless of the underlying Layer 2 protocol used for the actual transmission. An IP packet travels hop by hop between IP routers across the Internet—Layer 3 (IP) is responsible for the routing of the packet between the source and the destination.

3.2 IP Addressing Review

A key feature of IP is that it provides a globally unique address for every device attached to the Internet. A hierarchical structure is used for the addressing plan to increase organizational and routing efficiency of the network. The IP addressing plan includes a method of defining networks and subnetworks. IP routers perform the routing of packets between these IP networks and subnets.

IPv4 Address Structure

The current version of IP that is mainly in use on the Internet is IPv4. IPv4 uses a 32-bit address. IPv4 addresses are written using a dotted-decimal notation that divides the 32-bit IP address into four octets of 8 bits each. Each octet is written as a decimal number with a range from 0 to 255. As an example, 192.168.2.100 represents a 32-bit IPv4 address. The 32-bit address is obtained by converting each of the four decimal numbers to an 8-bit binary number—in this case 11000000 10101000 00000010 01100100.

> With the rapid growth of the Internet, the IPv4 address space is nearly exhausted, and a transition to IPv6 is necessary. IPv6 uses a 128-bit address which provides 3.4×10^{38} addresses.

IP unicast addresses are logically divided into two parts: the network and the host. The first part is the network number or network prefix, and identifies the network that a host resides in. The second part of the IP address is the host number, which uniquely identifies the host in the network. The network and host portions vary in size as described below. This creates a two-level hierarchy, as shown in Figure 3.2.

Figure 3.2 An IP address has two parts: the network prefix and the host number.

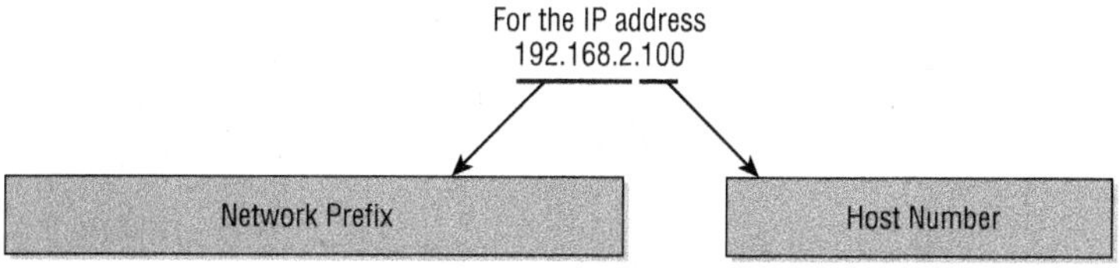

Classless Addressing

To support different network sizes, the unicast portion of the IP address space was originally divided into three classes: Class A, Class B, and Class C. However, *classful* addressing is restrictive and largely irrelevant today. Modern routing protocols use *classless* addressing.

With classless addressing, we exclusively use the subnet mask to indicate the size of an IP network. The *subnet mask* is a 32-bit long sequence of ones followed by a sequence of zeroes. The ones in the subnet mask correspond to the bits of the IP address that define the IP network. The zeroes in the subnet mask correspond to the bits of the IP address that identify the host on that network. The mask is used by the router to derive the network address from a given IP address. The router simply uses a logical AND between the address and the mask to derive the network address. This operation changes the host portion of the address to all zeroes and leaves the network portion intact.

In Figure 3.3, we see that the host address 192.168.2.132 with subnet mask 255.255.255.192 is part of the IP network that includes the address range from 192.168.2.128 through 192.168.2.191. The first and last addresses in an IP network are not used as host addresses but are reserved as the network address (192.168.2.128) and a broadcast address (192.168.1.191) for the network. This leaves 62 addresses ranging from 192.168.2.129 through 192.168.2.190 as host addresses for this network.

Figure 3.3 The subnet mask defines the network address, host addresses, and broadcast address for the network.

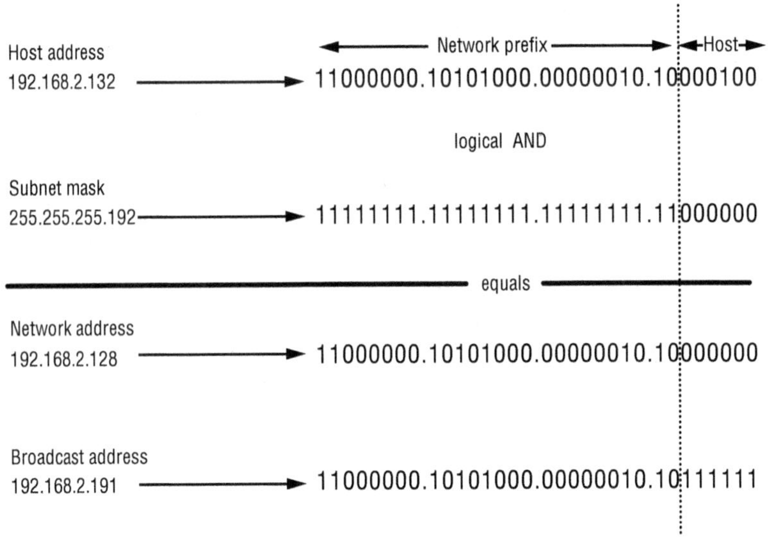

Although the subnet mask is always used for the internal representation by hosts and routers on the network, the network prefix notation is now widely used as a shorter way of expressing the address and subnet mask pair. For example, the network specified as address 172.16.64.0 and subnet mask 255.255.240.0 can be written in network prefix notation as 172.16.64.0/20. The traditional subnet mask is a sequence of 20 ones followed by 12 zeroes. The prefix notation simply indicates the number of ones in the subnet mask. For this prefix, the network address is 172.16.64.0, and the broadcast address is 172.16.79.255. The host addresses are the 4,094 values within this range, from 172.16.64.1 through 172.16.79.254.

The importance of network prefixes is seen in the next section when we look at the IP forwarding process. Network prefixes are the information collected and exchanged by IP routers that allow them to find the destination for packets they receive for forwarding across the network.

3.3 IP Forwarding

IP forwarding refers to the process used by an IP router when it receives a packet for forwarding through the network. The term is often used interchangeably with the term *IP routing*, but in this book, we use the term *IP forwarding* exclusively to refer to the processing of packets by the router to send them to the next-hop router. We use the term *IP routing* in a more general sense to describe the exchange of routing information that enables IP routers to build their IP forwarding tables.

Forwarding Information Base (FIB)

On the Alcatel-Lucent 7750 SR, each Input/Output Module (IOM) card contains a copy of the router's forwarding table, which contains the information the router needs to perform the forwarding process. Listing 3.1 shows the forwarding table (usually known as the *forwarding information base*, or FIB) from IOM 1 on an 7750 SR.

Listing 3.1 Forwarding information base (FIB) used by the IOM for packet forwarding

```
*A:R1# show router fib 1

===============================================================================
FIB Display
===============================================================================
Prefix                                                        Protocol
    NextHop
-------------------------------------------------------------------------------
10.1.2.0/27                                                   LOCAL
    10.1.2.0 (toR2)
10.1.3.0/27                                                   LOCAL
    10.1.3.0 (toR3)
10.1.5.0/27                                                   LOCAL
    10.1.5.0 (toR5)
10.2.6.0/27                                                   OSPF
    10.1.2.2 (toR2)
10.10.10.1/32                                                 LOCAL
    10.10.10.1 (system)
10.10.10.2/32                                                 OSPF
    10.1.2.2 (toR2)
10.20.1.0/24                                                  STATIC
    10.1.2.2 (toR2)
-------------------------------------------------------------------------------
Total Entries : 7
-------------------------------------------------------------------------------
===============================================================================
*A:R1#
```

In Listing 3.1, note that:

- The prefix column indicates the destinations in the network to which the router is capable of routing.
- The prefixes indicated as `LOCAL` correspond to networks to which the router is directly connected—the ones for which it has a local network interface.
- The prefixes indicated as `OSPF` are remote destinations the router has learned through the dynamic routing protocol OSPF.
- The `NextHop` entry tells the router the IP address of the router that should be used to forward a packet toward that specific destination. For a remote destination, the `NextHop` entry must be an address on a directly connected network. The router will use the appropriate Layer 2 network to transmit the packet to the next-hop for forwarding.

The IP forwarding table is essentially a copy of the IP routing table. The question of how the IP routing and forwarding tables are built is the subject of this and the next seven chapters.

IP Forwarding Process

Putting aside the question of how the forwarding table is built, we will first discuss how the router uses the forwarding table to forward IP packets. The forwarding steps are described below and shown in Figure 3.4:

1. The IP packet arrives at the ingress (incoming) MDA (Media Dependent Adapter) encapsulated in a Layer 2 frame. The MDA performs the Layer 2–specific functions for receiving the packet. In the case of an Ethernet frame, the MDA first determines if the frame is addressed to it by looking at the destination MAC (Media Access Control) address in the frame. If the frame is not addressed to the MDA, it is discarded.

   As the frame is received, the MDA performs the standard cyclic redundancy check (CRC) calculation on the incoming data. The calculated value is compared to the value in the Frame Check Sequence (FCS) field at the end of the Ethernet frame. If the two values do not match, the frame is discarded. Otherwise, the payload (in this case, the IP packet) is extracted from the frame and passed to the IOM.

2. The IOM performs the Layer 3 functions, which might include accounting, filtering, and quality of service (QoS; not covered here), but most importantly, making the IP forwarding decision. The IP header contents are validated against the header checksum, and if the checksum does not match, the packet

is discarded. If the time to live (TTL) value is one or zero, the packet is considered to have expired and is discarded.

Figure 3.4 Processing of an IP packet through the router.

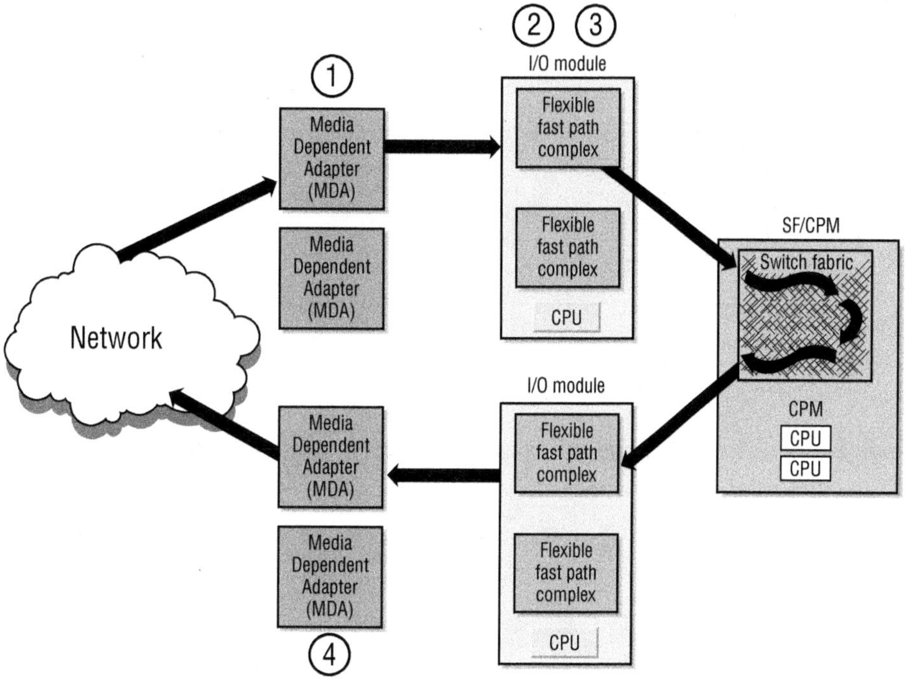

3. To make the forwarding decision, the destination address is compared to the IP forwarding table to find a prefix that matches the destination address. If multiple matching prefixes are found, the longest matching prefix is used. As an example, a packet with destination 172.16.65.227 matches both the prefixes 172.16.0.0/16 and 172.16.64.0/20. 172.16.64.0/20 is used for forwarding because it is the longest match. If no matching prefix is found, the packet cannot be forwarded and is discarded.
4. Once the prefix has been matched, the next-hop for the packet is known. Since the next-hop is directly connected, the router now knows the egress interface for the packet. The packet is switched through the router to the IOM with the egress MDA. The egress MDA encapsulates the packet in the appropriate Layer 2 frame and transmits it to the next-hop router.

On an Ethernet interface, the IPv4 router will use the Address Resolution Protocol (ARP) at the egress interface to find the MAC address to which the packet should be sent.

IP Header

We've discussed the forwarding of IP packets and have seen that this process depends entirely on the destination IP address. The address is one field in the IP header, but there are others, as shown in Figure 3.5. These are briefly described below:

Figure 3.5 IPv4 header.

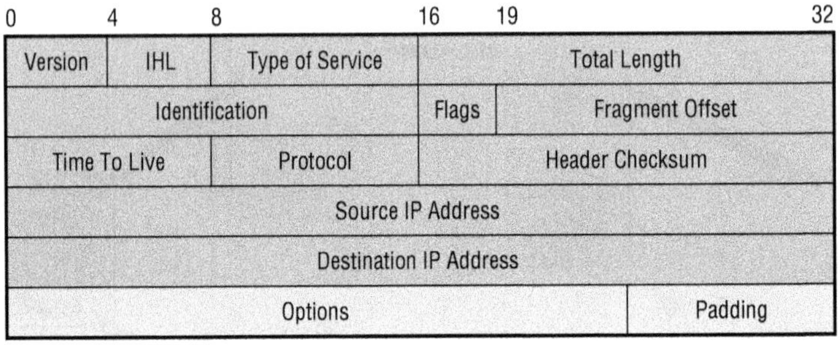

- **Version**—This header corresponds to IP version 4, thus the value is 4. IP version 6 has also been defined and has a different header.
- **IHL (IP header length)**—The number of 32-bit words that form the IP header. The value is 5, unless the Options field is used.
- **TOS (type of service)**—This is also known as the differentiated services code point (DSCP). The TOS byte can be used to specify quality of service parameters for the packet.
- **Total length**—The combined length of the header and the data, in bytes. The maximum value is 65,535.
- **Identification**—Together with the source address, this 16-bit number uniquely identifies the packet. The number is used during the reassembly of fragmented packets.
- **Flags**—Three bits used for the fragmentation of packets. The first bit is unused. The second indicates DF, or "don't fragment," meaning that the packet must be discarded rather than fragmented. The third bit indicates MF, or "more fragments," meaning that this is not the last fragment.
- **Fragment offset**—A value that indicates which portion of the original packet this corresponds to. This is used during the reassembly of fragmented packets.
- **Time to live (TTL)**—The number of hops or links that the packet may be routed over. TTL is decremented by each router. If the value reaches 0, the packet is discarded. (This prevents infinite looping of packets.)

- **Protocol**—This identifier indicates the type of higher-layer protocol being carried (e.g., 1 = ICMP, 2 = IGMP, 6 = TCP, 17 = UDP).
- **Header checksum**—1s complement checksum that is inserted by the sender and updated whenever the IP header is modified by a router. Used to detect errors introduced into the IP header. Datagrams with an invalid header checksum are discarded by all nodes in an IP network.
- **Source IP address**—IP address of the original sender of the packet.
- **Destination IP address**—IP address of the final destination of the packet.
- **Options**—Not often used. If the options are used, the IP header length value will be greater than 5 to include the size of the Options field. The maximum value for header length is 15, which equates to 60 bytes. Thus the maximum size of the options field is 40 bytes because the mandatory fields use 20 bytes.

Comparing the Forwarding Plane and the Control Plane

The previous section described the forwarding of an IP packet through the router. In this section, we take a closer look at how the architecture of the router supports this process and how it is possible to forward packets arriving at all interfaces at wire speed.

Modern routers such as the 7750 SR have a distributed architecture that separates router functions into control plane and forwarding plane actions. In the 7750 SR, the control plane functions are performed by the SF/CPM (switch fabric/control processing module), and the forwarding plane functions are performed by the IOM cards.

The operation of the forwarding plane is described above. The IOM cards have the intelligence and information required to forward IP packets without any involvement of the control plane. The forwarding complex on the IOM contains memory and processors that enable it to receive, process, and transmit packets at wire speeds.

The control plane has two main functions:

1. Supporting the management functions of the router through the command-line interface (CLI) and network management capabilities. This includes configuration and administration of the router.
2. Building the forwarding table for the IOM. The forwarding table is constructed from the routing table, which is built through the operation of dynamic routing protocols and/or configured with static routes.

Figure 3.6 shows the forwarding of packets through the 7750 SR. Note that there are two data streams shown. The top, labeled data plane, corresponds to the stream of data forwarded by the router. The bottom, labeled control plane, corresponds to the routing updates received by the router that are used by the control plane to construct the routing table.

Figure 3.6 Flow of data plane packets and control plane packets through the Alcatel-Lucent 7750 SR.

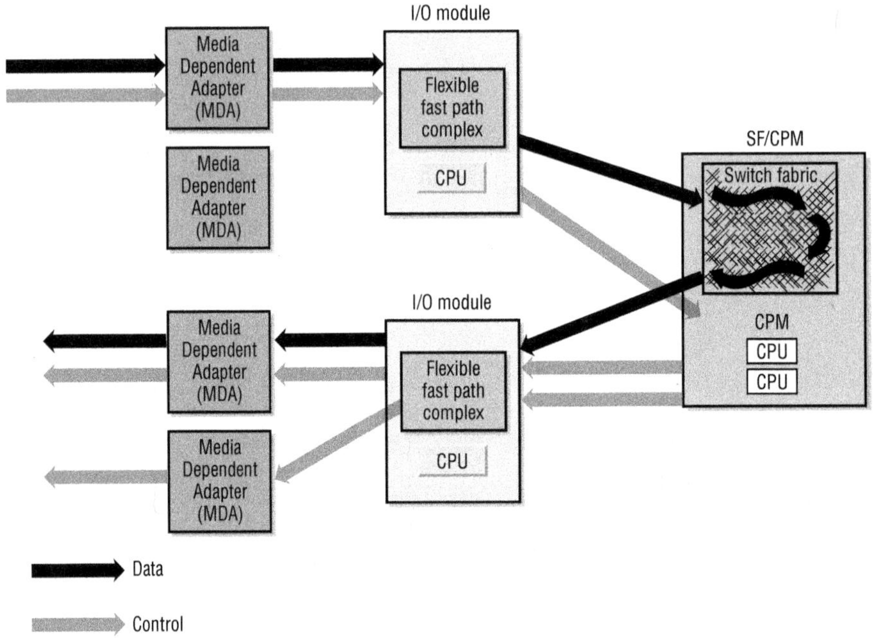

3.4 Configuring an IP Interface on the Alcatel-Lucent 7750 SR

An IP router forwards traffic between networks and therefore must have interfaces on at least two different networks. Three pieces of information are required to configure an interface for IP:

1. The physical port that is connected to the IP network
2. An IP address for the interface on the IP network
3. The subnet mask for the network

The address and subnet are specified in one command as a network prefix. For example, to configure an interface address of 10.1.2.1 on the network 10.1.2.0 with subnet mask of 255.255.255.0, the command is:

```
configure router interface address 10.1.2.1/24
```

Listing 3.2 shows the configuration of two interfaces on a 7750 SR.

Listing 3.2 Configuring two IP interfaces on the Alcatel-Lucent 7750 SR

```
*A:R1# configure router
*A:R1>config>router# interface toR2
*A:R1>config>router>if$ address 10.1.2.1/27
*A:R1>config>router>if$ port 1/1/1
*A:R1>config>router>if$ exit
*A:R1>config>router# interface toR3
*A:R1>config>router>if$ address 10.1.3.1/27
*A:R1>config>router>if$ port 1/1/3
*A:R1>config>router>if$ exit
*A:R1>config>router# show router interface

===============================================================================
Interface Table (Router: Base)
===============================================================================
Interface-Name                   Adm         Opr         Mode     Port/SapId
   IP-Address                                                     PfxState
-------------------------------------------------------------------------------
system                           Up          Down        Network system
   -                                                              -
toR2                             Up          Up          Network 1/1/1
   10.1.2.1/27                                                    n/a
toR3                             Up          Up          Network 1/1/3
   10.1.3.1/27                                                    n/a
-------------------------------------------------------------------------------
Interfaces : 3
===============================================================================
```

Note that there is a third interface defined, named `system`. The 7750 SR has this interface defined by default. You can think of it as an IP address for the entire router, instead of just for an interface. It's known as a loopback interface because it is not associated with any physical port. The system interface is down until an address is assigned to it. The system address is configured as a /32 (subnet mask of 255.255.255.255) because it is a host address and not associated with any network (Listing 3.3).

Listing 3.3 Configuring the system interface

```
*A:R1# configure router
*A:R1>config>router# interface "system"
*A:R1>config>router>if# address 10.10.10.1/32
*A:R1>config>router>if# exit
*A:R1>config>router# show router interface

===============================================================================
Interface Table (Router: Base)
===============================================================================
Interface-Name                   Adm         Opr(v4/v6)  Mode    Port/SapId
   IP-Address                                                    PfxState
-------------------------------------------------------------------------------
system                           Up          Up/Down     Network system
   10.10.10.1/32                                                 n/a
toR2                             Up          Up/Down     Network 1/1/1
   10.1.2.1/27                                                   n/a
toR3                             Up          Up/Down     Network 1/1/4
   10.1.3.1/27                                                   n/a
-------------------------------------------------------------------------------
Interfaces : 3
===============================================================================
```

Besides the system interface, additional loopback interfaces can be configured on the router. These are not associated with any specific physical port, but can be reached through any port on the router. You may not have any operational requirement to configure loopbacks; however, we will use loopback interfaces to represent networks attached to the router in later exercises. As with other IP interfaces, loopbacks are defined with an IP address and a subnet mask. Instead of a port, the keyword `loopback` is used to identify the interface as a loopback (Listing 3.4).

Listing 3.4 Loopback interfaces are defined like normal interfaces with the keyword loopback instead of the port number.

```
*A:R1# configure router
*A:R1>config>router# interface loopback_1
*A:R1>config>router>if$ address 10.0.253.1/24
*A:R1>config>router>if$ loopback
```

```
*A:R1>config>router>if$ exit
*A:R1>config>router# interface loopback_2
*A:R1>config>router>if$ address  10.0.254.1/24
*A:R1>config>router>if$ loopback
*A:R1>config>router>if$ exit
*A:R1>config>router# show router interface

===============================================================================
Interface Table (Router: Base)
===============================================================================
Interface-Name                   Adm         Opr(v4/v6)  Mode     Port/SapId
   IP-Address                                                     PfxState
-------------------------------------------------------------------------------
loopback_1                       Up          Up/--       Network loopback
   10.0.253.1/24                                                  n/a
loopback_2                       Up          Up/--       Network loopback
   10.0.254.1/24                                                  n/a
system                           Up          Up/--       Network system
   10.10.10.1/32                                                  n/a
toR2                             Up          Up/--       Network 1/1/1
   10.1.2.1/27                                                    n/a
toR3                             Up          Up/--       Network 1/1/3
   10.1.3.1/27                                                    n/a
-------------------------------------------------------------------------------
Interfaces : 5
===============================================================================
*A:R1>config>router#
```

Once we've defined the interfaces, we can look at the routing table (Listing 3.5). The router is now able to route between the two locally attached networks. However, any traffic the router receives for a destination other than these networks will be dropped because it does not have a route for any other destinations.

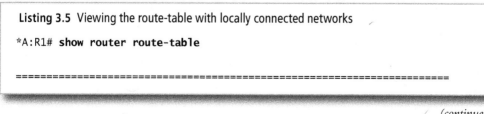

Listing 3.5 Viewing the route-table with locally connected networks

```
*A:R1# show router route-table

===============================================================================
```

(continued)

Listing 3.5 *(continued)*

```
Route Table (Router: Base)
===============================================================================
Dest Prefix                                   Type    Proto    Age        Pref
      Next Hop[Interface Name]                                       Metric
-------------------------------------------------------------------------------
10.0.253.0/24                                 Local   Local    00h04m33s  0
      loopback-1                                                     0
10.0.254.0/24                                 Local   Local    00h04m07s  0
      loopback-2                                                     0
10.1.2.0/27                                   Local   Local    00h03m40s  0
      toR2                                                           0
10.1.3.0/27                                   Local   Local    00h03m13s  0
      toR3                                                           0
10.10.10.1/32                                 Local   Local    00h04m10s  0
      system                                                         0
-------------------------------------------------------------------------------
No. of Routes: 5
===============================================================================
```

3.5 Using and Configuring Static Routes

In order to forward packets to destinations beyond the locally connected networks, additional entries are required in the routing table. These entries can be manually configured, or they can be learned through a dynamic routing protocol. If they are manually configured, they are known as *static routes*. Dynamic routing protocols are described in the following chapters. As with all entries in the routing table, static routes describe the remote destination network and the next-hop to which a packet must be forwarded in order to reach the destination. The destination is given as a network prefix (network address and subnet mask).

Consider the topology shown in Figure 3.7. Router R1 is not directly connected to network 10.20.1.0/24 and therefore does not have a route to this destination. However, the network administrator can configure a static routing table entry that will enable the router to forward packets to the remote network.

Listing 3.6 shows the commands required to configure the static route and the contents of the routing table afterward. The next-hop is the address of the directly connected router that is the next-hop toward the destination. If the router can reach the next-hop, it can forward the packet toward the destination.

Figure 3.7 Using a static route.

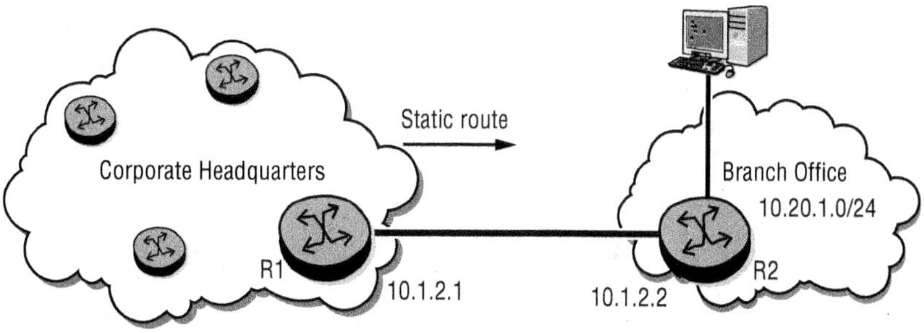

Listing 3.6 Configuring a static route

```
*A:R1# configure router
*A:R1>config>router# static-route 10.20.1.0/24 next-hop 10.1.2.2
*A:R1>config>router# show router route-table

===============================================================================
Route Table (Router: Base)
===============================================================================
Dest Prefix                                     Type    Proto    Age         Pref
       Next Hop[Interface Name]                                     Metric
-------------------------------------------------------------------------------
10.1.2.0/27                                     Local   Local    00h07m24s   0
       toR2                                                         0
10.20.1.0/24                                    Remote  Static   00h00m03s   5
       10.1.2.2                                                     1
10.10.10.1/32                                   Local   Local    00h03m53s   0
       system                                                       0
-------------------------------------------------------------------------------
No. of Routes: 4
===============================================================================
```

Note that for a bidirectional data flow, a route needs to be configured on both routers. After the static route is added, router R1 can forward traffic toward network 10.20.1.0/24 by sending it to router R2. If router R2 is to forward return traffic from network 10.20.1.0/24 to the corporate networks, it must have a routing table entry for those networks.

In the topology shown in Figure 3.8, router R2 is a router at one of the branch offices. The branch office at R2 connects to the central corporate network through a connection to router R1. A network like this that just connects to one larger network is often known as a *stub network*.

Figure 3.8 Using a default route.

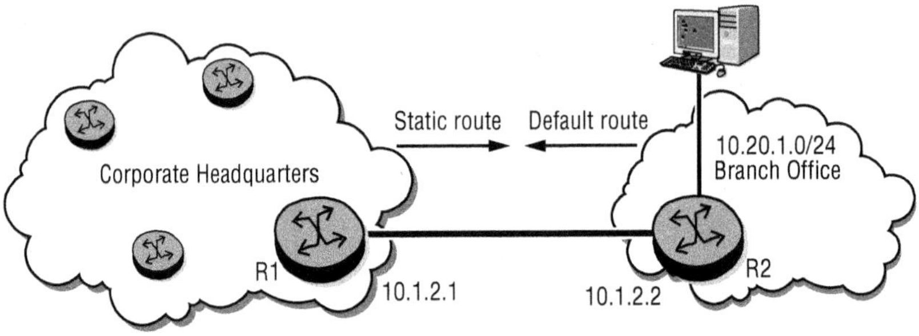

Instead of programming router R2 with all the destinations beyond router R1, it is simpler to program a default route to router R1 because the branch office is a stub and all traffic leaving it has to go to R1. A default route matches any destination that is not matched by another specific entry in the routing table. Remember that in IP forwarding, the most specific entry is always chosen first, so the default route is always the last one chosen. However, a router with a default route is always able to forward packets because it always has a next-hop router to forward them to. The default route is programmed like any other static route and is referred to as 0.0.0.0/0 (Listing 3.7).

Listing 3.7 Configuring a default static route

```
*A:R2# configure router
*A:R2>config>router# static-route 0.0.0.0/0 next-hop 10.1.2.1
*A:R2>config>router# show router route-table

===============================================================================
Route Table (Router: Base)
===============================================================================
Dest Prefix                                Type    Proto     Age          Pref
       Next Hop[Interface Name]                                    Metric
```

```
-------------------------------------------------------------------------
0.0.0.0/0                                       Remote  Static    00h00m20s   5
       10.1.2.1                                                   1
10.1.2.0/27                                     Local   Local     00h03m00s   0
       toR1                                                       0
10.10.10.2/32                                   Local   Local     00h03m50s   0
       system                                                     0
-------------------------------------------------------------------------
No. of Routes: 3
=========================================================================
```

The default route allows router R2 to reach destinations beyond router R1. However, remember that there must also be a route from the remote destinations back to router R2 in order to send data back.

3.6 Other Static Route Options

Besides the simple static route configuration above, there are several other options possible for static routes. A second alternative route can be configured to be used as a backup if the first fails, and bidirectional forwarding detection (BFD) can be used to help detect failures on the link. In some cases, static routes may be configured with `black-hole` as the next-hop or with an indirect next-hop.

Floating Static Routes

A disadvantage of using static routes is the inability to adapt to changes in the network topology. However, it is possible to create additional static routes to a destination that can be used as a backup to the original route. These are sometimes known as *floating static routes*.

In Figure 3.9, there is an alternate route to the branch office through router R3. A second static route is configured through R3 using a higher preference value, as shown in Listing 3.8. When the router has two routes to the same destination, the one with a higher preference is not installed in the route-table, but it is available as an alternate if the first route fails. This process is described in more detail in the section on the Route Table Manager (RTM).

Figure 3.9 Using a floating static route.

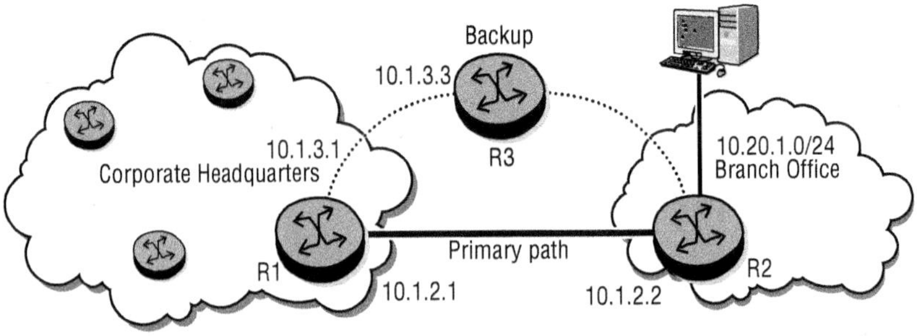

Listing 3.8 Configuring a floating static route. The inactive route does not appear in the route-table, but can be seen with show router static route.

```
*A:R1# configure router
*A:R1>config>router# static-route 10.20.1.0/24 next-hop 10.1.2.2
*A:R1>config>router# static-route 10.20.1.0/24 next-hop 10.1.3.3
preference 200
*A:R1>config>router# show router route-table

===============================================================================
Route Table (Router: Base)
===============================================================================
Dest Prefix                                 Type      Proto     Age         Pref
      Next Hop[Interface Name]                                    Metric
-------------------------------------------------------------------------------
10.1.2.0/27                                 Local     Local     00h27m16s   0
      toR2                                                          0
10.1.3.0/27                                 Local     Local     00h26m44s   0
      toR3                                                          0
10.10.10.1/32                               Local     Local     00h28m18s   0
      system                                                        0
10.20.1.0/24                                Remote    Static    00h00m54s   5
      10.1.2.2                                                      1
-------------------------------------------------------------------------------
No. of Routes: 4
===============================================================================
*A:R1#
*A:R1>config>router# show router static-route
```

```
===============================================================================
Static Route Table (Router: Base)  Family: IPv4
===============================================================================
Prefix                                 Tag         Met    Pref Type Act
   Next Hop                             Interface
-------------------------------------------------------------------------------
10.20.1.0/24                           0           1      5    NH   Y
   10.1.2.2                             toR2
10.20.1.0/24                           0           1      200  NH   N
   10.1.3.3                             n/a
-------------------------------------------------------------------------------
No. of Static Routes: 2
===============================================================================
```

In Listing 3.8, the second static route is configured using a higher preference. In this situation, the same effect could be achieved using a higher metric value.

You can see from Listing 3.8 that the alternate static route has been configured but does not appear in the route-table. However, when the original route becomes unavailable, as shown in Listing 3.9, the alternate route becomes active.

Listing 3.9 The second static route becomes active when the first goes down

```
*A:R1# configure port 1/1/1 shutdown
*A:R1# show router route-table


===============================================================================
Route Table (Router: Base)
===============================================================================
Dest Prefix                            Type    Proto    Age         Pref
       Next Hop[Interface Name]                           Metric
-------------------------------------------------------------------------------
10.1.3.0/27                            Local   Local    00h27m44s   0
       toR3                                               0
10.10.10.1/32                          Local   Local    00h29m18s   0
       system                                             0
10.20.1.0/24                           Remote  Static   00h00m04s   200
```

(continued)

Listing 3.9 *(continued)*

```
        10.1.3.3                                                  1
-------------------------------------------------------------------------------
No. of Routes: 3
===============================================================================
```

Remember that you always need a route in both directions; thus you will also need to configure a floating static default route on R2 through R3 in order to make communication successful when the link between R1 and R2 is down.

Bidirectional Forwarding Detection (BFD)

A static route might also be configured with bidirectional forwarding detection (BFD) enabled. BFD is used to detect failures on the link and can be enabled on the static route. If the link is operationally up but BFD discovers that data is not being transmitted across the link, it will make the static route inactive (Figure 3.10). This will cause the alternate static route to become active in the routing table.

Figure 3.10 BFD detects the loss of packet forwarding between two nodes.

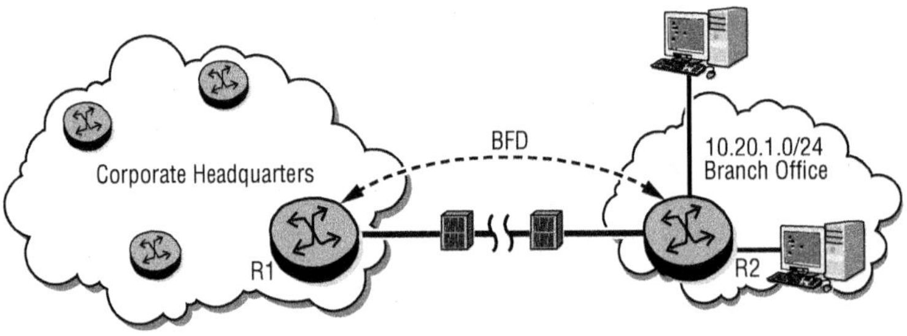

Two steps are required to enable BFD on the static route: First, the BFD session is configured on the interface; and second, BFD is enabled on the static route. The key parameters for the BFD session on the interface are the transmit interval, the receive interval, and the multiplier. An interface with BFD enabled transmits UDP (User Datagram Protocol) packets at the transmit interval and expects to receive them at the receive interval. These values are specified in milliseconds. The *multiplier* is the number of successive packets that can be missed before the interface is considered down (Listing 3.10).

Listing 3.10 BFD is enabled on the interface toR2, with a BFD packet transmitted 10 times per second and the default multiplier of 3.

```
*A:R1# configure router interface "toR2"
*A:R1>config>router>if# bfd 100 receive 100
*A:R1>config>router>if# info
----------------------------------------------
            address 10.1.2.1/27
            port 1/1/1
            bfd 100 receive 100 multiplier 3
----------------------------------------------
```

Once BFD is enabled on the interface, it can be enabled in a static route. BFD becomes active and begins transmitting its keep-alive packets when BFD is enabled on a static route or dynamic routing protocol on each end of the link (Listing 3.11).

Listing 3.11 After the BFD session is configured on the interface, it can be enabled on a static route or in a dynamic routing protocol.

```
*A:R1# configure router static-route 10.20.1.0/24 next-hop 10.1.2.2
bfd-enable
*A:R1# show router bfd session

===============================================================================
BFD Session
===============================================================================
Interface                State                      Tx Intvl  Rx Intvl  Multipl
  Remote Address         Protocols                  Tx Pkts   Rx Pkts   Type
-------------------------------------------------------------------------------
toR2                     Up (3)                     100       100       3
   10.1.2.2              static                     896       803       iom
-------------------------------------------------------------------------------
No. of BFD sessions: 1
===============================================================================
*A:R1#
```

Black-Hole Routes

Another option for a static route is `black-hole`. The black-hole option is used when creating a route-table entry for a route that does not actually exist. For example, a summarized route might be created on a router to be advertised using the dynamic routing protocol. Any traffic that matches the black-hole entry is silently dropped. This prevents looping in certain circumstances. It will be seen again in the description of summarization in OSPF (Open Shortest Path First) and IS-IS (Intermediate System to Intermediate System).

In Figure 3.11, router R1 has static routes to the networks used at the branch office. A single summary black-hole route is created on router R1 that will be advertised to the corporate network using a dynamic routing protocol. Any data sent to this address that does not match one of the networks at the branch office will be dropped by router R1 (e.g., a packet sent to 10.20.254.254).

Figure 3.11 Using a black-hole route.

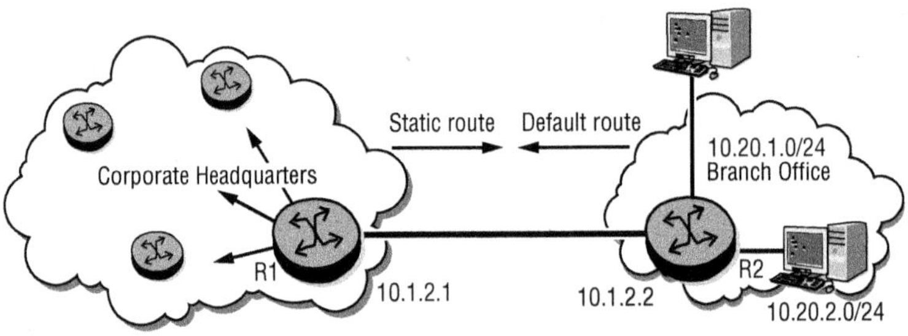

The configuration of the black-hole route is shown in Listing 3.12.

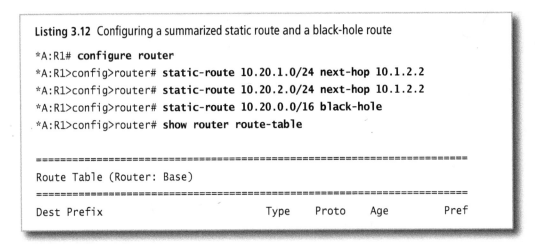

Listing 3.12 Configuring a summarized static route and a black-hole route

```
*A:R1# configure router
*A:R1>config>router# static-route 10.20.1.0/24 next-hop 10.1.2.2
*A:R1>config>router# static-route 10.20.2.0/24 next-hop 10.1.2.2
*A:R1>config>router# static-route 10.20.0.0/16 black-hole
*A:R1>config>router# show router route-table

===============================================================================
Route Table (Router: Base)
===============================================================================
Dest Prefix                                     Type     Proto     Age         Pref
```

```
        Next Hop[Interface Name]                                    Metric
-------------------------------------------------------------------------
10.1.2.0/27                                 Local    Local    00h46m47s   0
        toR2                                                       0
10.1.3.0/27                                 Local    Local    01h14m55s   0
        toR3                                                       0
10.10.10.1/32                               Local    Local    01h16m29s   0
        system                                                     0
10.20.0.0/16                                Remote   Static   00h00m05s   5
        Black Hole                                                 1
10.20.1.0/24                                Remote   Static   00h46m52s   5
        10.1.2.2                                                   1
10.20.2.0/24                                Remote   Static   00h00m27s   5
        10.1.2.2                                                      1
-------------------------------------------------------------------------
No. of Routes: 6
=========================================================================
```

Indirect Routes

In order for a static route to be accepted as valid and made active in the route-table, the next-hop address must be reachable on a directly connected interface. In some cases, it may be desirable to use a next-hop address that is not directly connected. In this case, the route can be defined as `indirect`. For an indirect static route to be active, the next-hop address must be learned through a dynamic routing protocol.

3.7 IPv6

IPv6 was developed in the 1990s (RFC 2460) as a replacement for IPv4, primarily because of the limited address size of IPv4. IPv6 uses a 128-bit address, which provides for 3.4×10^{38} addresses—a nearly limitless number of addresses. Aside from ensuring that there is no limitation on addresses, this large address space allows for a more flexible hierarchy that simplifies addressing of hosts, particularly for mobile devices.

IPv6 defines three different types of addresses:

- **Unicast**—A unicast address provides an address for a single host.
- **Multicast**—A multicast address provides an address for a group of hosts.

- **Anycast**—An anycast address is a unicast address used by more than one host. A packet addressed to an anycast address is delivered to the nearest host as determined by the routing protocol.

IPv6 does not define broadcast addresses. There is a link-local multicast address for all nodes on the link (ff02::1) and solicited-node multicast addresses that replaces the IPv4 ARP protocol.

Since the IPv6 address is 128 bits, there are several conventions used to shorten them as much as possible:

- Addresses are written in groups of four hex digits, separated by a single colon: for example, 2001:0db8:0000:0000:0021:0000:4ab9:0300.
- One or more groups of zeroes can be replaced by two colons. The number above becomes 2001:0db8::0021:0000:4ab9:0300.
- Only one group of zeroes can be replaced with double colons. Otherwise, it would not be possible to tell where the zeroes are located. However, leading zeroes in a group can also be omitted. The address above becomes 2001:db8::21:0:4ab9:300.

Unicast Addressing

Regular IPv6 unicast addressing uses a fixed structure in which 64 bits are defined as the routing prefix and 64 bits are defined as the interface identifier (Figure 3.12).

Figure 3.12 The standard IPv6 unicast address is divided into 64 bits for routing and 64 bits for the interface identifier.

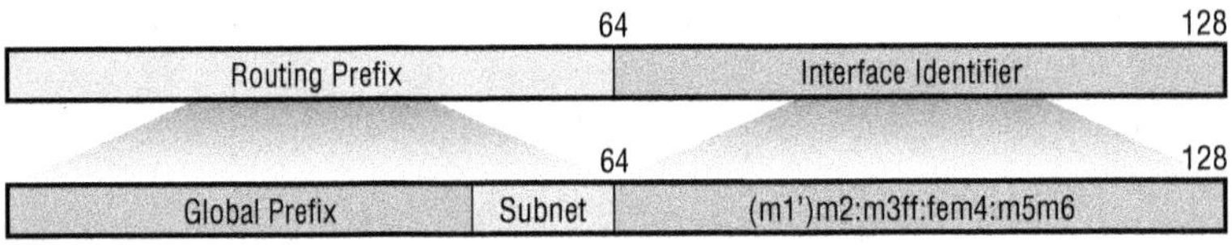

The allocation for globally routed IPv6 addresses is the address space 2000::/3. This represents one-eighth of the entire address space and is all addresses beginning with the bit pattern 001. An Internet service provider (ISP) is typically allocated a network assignment of /32 or shorter (shorter means a smaller prefix such as /31 or /30 and hence a larger network range). The ISP allocates longer prefixes from their range to their customers.

The interface ID portion of the address is locally assigned but can be automatically derived from the 48-bit MAC address. It might also be assigned from a DHCPv6 server, through an auto-discovery mechanism or manually assigned.

To derive an IPv6 interface ID from the MAC address, the approach is to create a modified EUI-64 (Extended Unique Identifier-64). This involves flipping the seventh most significant bit of the OUI (Organizationally Unique Identifier) and inserting the hex string `ff:fe` between the 3 bytes of the OUI and the 3 bytes of the NIC-specific component.

As an example, assume that an organization is assigned the prefix 2001:db8/48. The organization has 16 bits for subnetting. Perhaps they have 30 locations and decide to assign the first 8 bits based on the location and the next 8 on the subnet at that location. Subnet 10 at location 3 gives a subnet value of 030a, for a routing prefix of 2001:db8:0:30a::/64. With the modified EUI-64 assignment, the host with MAC address 00:16:4d:13:5c:ae has an interface ID of 0216:4dff:fe13:5cae. The resulting IPv6 address is 2001:db8::30a:216:4dff:fe13:5cae (Figure 3.13).

Figure 3.13 An IPv6 unicast address composed of the global routing prefix, the subnet, and the interface ID created from the system MAC address.

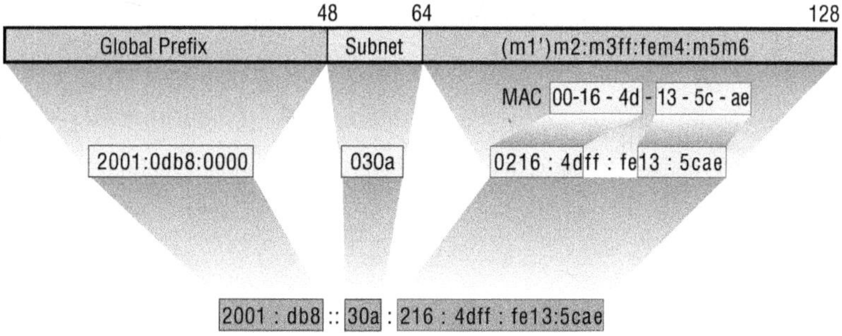

Other Unicast Addresses

There are a number of other unicast addresses in IPv6 that have special meaning:

- **::/128**—::/128 is the unspecified host address (all zeroes). This address might be used until an address is assigned to the device.
- **::1/128**—::1/128 is the loopback address (all zeroes except the last bit). This corresponds to the address 127.0.0.1 in IPv4.
- **::/0**—::/0 is the default unicast route (the same as 0.0.0.0/0 in IPv4).
- **fe80::/10**—fe80::/10 is the prefix for the link-local address (binary 1111111010 followed by 54 zeroes). IPv6 requires that every IPv6 interface have a link-local address. This is not a valid routing prefix and is only used for communications on the local link.

Typically, the link-local interface ID is assigned the same value as the global interface ID, which means using the modified EUI-64 address. For the global address 200 1:db8:0:30a:216:4dff:fe13:5cae, the link-local address would be fe80::216:4dff:fe13:5cae.

- **fc00::/7**—fc00::/7 defines a range known as Unique Local Addresses (ULA; RFC 4193). These are addresses intended to be used on a private network and not routed on the global Internet (similar to private addresses in IPv4). The ULA range is split into two ranges, depending on the value of the eighth bit:
    - **fd00::/8**—fd00::/8 is intended to be used as a 48-bit prefix with the remaining 40 bits self-assigned using a pseudo-random generator. This means that even though addresses are self-assigned, the probability of two networks sharing the same prefix is very small. This is intended to make it easier to interconnect privately addressed networks.
    - **fc00::/8**—fc00::/8 addresses are intended to have the remaining 40 bits allocated by a registrar to provide globally unique private addresses, although the mechanism is yet to be defined (draft-hain-ipv6-ulac-02) at the time of writing.
- **::ffff:0:0/96**—::ffff:0:0/96 is a prefix for IPv4-mapped IPv6 addresses. This provides an IPv6 address space that can be used by native IPv4 applications. It is acceptable to use the standard IPv4 notation for the low-order 32 bits of the address. For example, 192.168.0.1 is mapped to the IPv6 address ::ffff:0:0:192.168.0.1.

Multicast Addresses

All IPv6 multicast addresses have an 8-bit prefix of all ones (ff00::/8) followed by 4 flag bits and 4 bits that define the multicast scope. For general multicast addresses, the remaining 112 bits define the multicast group (Figure 3.14).

Figure 3.14 Format of the IPv6 general multicast address.

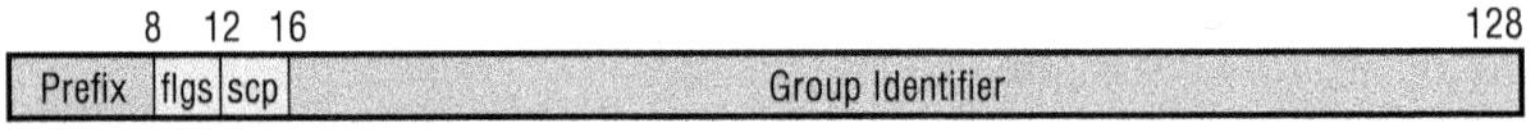

Some well-known IPv6 multicast addresses are:

- **ff02::1**—All nodes on the local link
- **ff02::2**—All routers on the local link
- **ff02::1:2**—All DHCPv6 servers and relays on the local link

IPv6 also defines a group of multicast addresses called *solicited-node multicast*. The 16 bits of the prefix, flags, and scope are followed by 79 zeroes and nine ones. The remaining 24 bits are taken from the last 24 bits of the unicast address (or addresses) that is being solicited. If the destination node has the address 2001:db8::30a:216:4dff:fe13:5cae, then the solicited-node multicast address becomes ff02::1:ff13:5cae (see Figure 3.15).

The IEEE provides the range of multicast addresses of 03-03-*xx-xx-xx-xx* for IPv6, where the *xx-xx-xx-xx* string is the 32 low-order bits of the multicast IP address. Each IPv6 node on Ethernet automatically joins the multicast groups corresponding to their solicited-node address and the all-nodes address. Thus, the host in this example will receive the Ethernet multicast groups:

- 03-03-ff-13-5c-ae
- 03-03-00-00-00-01

Figure 3.15 The solicited-node multicast address is formed using the last 24 bits of the unicast address. The MAC multicast address is formed using the last 32 bits of the IPv6 multicast address.

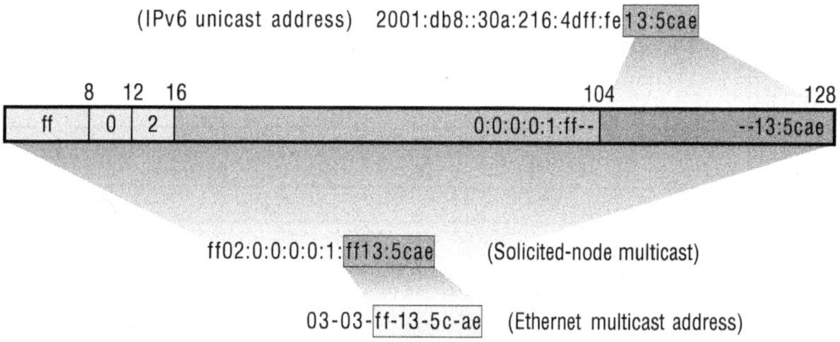

The use of solicited-node multicast for host address resolution is described later in this chapter, in the ICMPv6 section.

Anycast Addresses

Anycast addresses are used in limited situations in IPv4, but IPv6 formally incorporates the concept of an anycast address. Think of an anycast address as a virtual unicast address shared by multiple hosts. An IPv6 packet sent to an anycast address is routed to the nearest reachable host assigned the anycast address. This is a useful mechanism for providing a redundant service, such as a DNS server.

An anycast address can be formed from any unicast address. In addition, RFC 2526 defines a range of anycast addresses to be reserved on every subnet for well-known services. This range is the highest 128 interface addresses on the subnet. These addresses must never be assigned as unicast addresses. It's similar to the concept in IPv4 of reserving the highest address as the broadcast address on a subnet, except that a range of 128 addresses (from 0 to 127) is reserved for anycast in IPv6. To date, only one address in this range has been assigned—the value 126, for Mobile IPv6 Home Agents.

IPv6 Header

Despite the significant differences in addressing, IPv6 has many similarities to IPv4—it's actually a fairly conservative revision of the protocol. The forwarding mechanism is essentially the same as in IPv4. Packets are forwarded hop by hop based on a lookup in the forwarding table for the longest prefix match. This provides the next-hop for forwarding the packet. In fact, the IPv6 header has two significant changes that simplify the forwarding process compared to IPv4. These are:

- No fragmentation by routers
- No header checksum

The IPv6 header is shown in Figure 3.16. The meaning of each field is described below.

Figure 3.16 The fields of the IPv6 header.

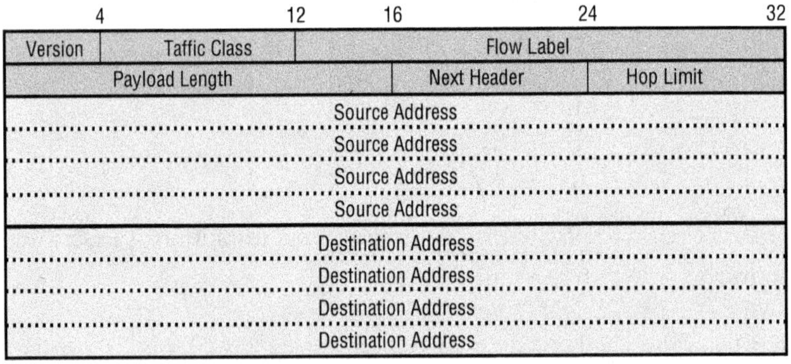

- **Version**—As in IPv4, this field contains the protocol version number—in this case, the value 6.
- **Traffic class**—Similar to the TOS field in IPv4, this value is used for prioritizing the treatment of traffic. The first 6 bits are to be interpreted as the DSCP defined in RFC 2474 and the last two as the Explicit Congestion Notification (ECN) defined in RFC 3168.

- **Flow label**—This field has no counterpart in IPv4. It can be used to indicate that this packet belongs to a specific data flow of an upper-layer protocol or application. This could be used as a simple classification mechanism by an intermediate router to identify all the packets belonging to a specific application, for example. The use of this field is defined in RFC 3697.
- **Payload length**—This field is similar to the IPv4 total length field except that it indicates payload length only. Since this is a 16-bit field, the maximum size of a regular size IPv6 packet is 65,535 bytes plus headers. A larger size field in the hop-by-hop options extension header provides for "jumbograms" up to a maximum of $2^{32} - 1$ bytes.
- **Next header**—This corresponds to the Protocol field in IPv4. In IPv6 it is also used to indicate that there are extension headers in use. An IPv6 packet may have 0 or multiple extension headers. The value in this field in the last extension header indicates the upper-layer protocol carried in the packet.
- **Hop limit**—This is the same as the TTL field in IPv4, although it is considered strictly a hop count in IPv6. The value is decremented by each router. If the value reaches zero, the packet is discarded and an ICMPv6 message is sent to the source.
- **Source address and destination address**—These fields have the same meaning as in IPv4, except that each requires 128 bits in IPv6.

You can see that the IPv6 header is simplified from IPv4; the forwarding process is simplified as well. The main changes in the forwarding process are:

- No header length field to process because the IPv6 header is a fixed length.
- No checksum calculations. In IPv4 the header checksum is verified and recalculated at each hop because the TTL value changes at each hop. IPv6 relies on the error checking performed by Layer 2 and the error checking of upper-layer protocols.
- No fragmentation operations to perform.

Although the IPv6 header is simplified, IPv6 provides more capabilities and protocol flexibility by defining extension headers, which can be used to provide additional capabilities. Table 3.1 shows the extension headers defined to date, as well as some common upper-layer protocols.

Table 3.1 Values for IPv6 Extension Headers and Upper-Layer Protocols

Value	Description
0	IPv6 Hop-by-hop options
6	Upper-layer protocol–TCP

(continued)

Table 3.1 Values for IPv6 Extension Headers and Upper-Layer Protocols *(continued)*

Value	Description
17	Upper-layer protocol–UDP
41	IPv6 Encapsulation header (tunneling)
43	Routing extension header
44	Fragment extension header
50	Encapsulating Security Payload (ESP)
51	Authentication Header (AH)
58	ICMPv6
59	IPv6 No next header
60	Destination options

In general, only the IPv6 header is used by intermediate nodes for forwarding, and the extension headers are only processed at the destination. The exception is the hop-by-hop options header, which must be processed by each intermediate node. Therefore, if it exists, it must be the first extension header after the IPv6 header. The extension headers described below must be supported by all IPv6 nodes:

- **Hop-by-hop options**—These are a grouping of options that must be processed by intermediate nodes. These include the option for jumbograms (RFC 2675) and the Router Alert option (RFC 2711).
- **Routing extension header**—This provides the ability for source routing. RFC 2460 defines a Type 0 routing header (RH0) for loose source, but this was deprecated in RFC 5095 because of security concerns. Mobility support in IPv6 (RFC 3775) defines a Type 2 routing header (RH2).
- **Fragment extension header**—IPv6 routers do not fragment IPv6 packets, but the fragment extension header allows the source node to fragment packets in case the payload supplied by the upper-layer protocol is too large for the link or path MTU. This should not be a common occurrence.
- **ESP header**—The ESP header (RFC 2402) is an IPsec header that provides security for IPv6 and IPv4. ESP provides authentication, data integrity, and data confidentiality for all fields after the ESP header, but not for the IPv6 header.
- **AH header**—The AH header (RFC 2406) is an IPsec header that provides authentication for IPv6 and IPv4. AH provides authentication and data integrity services for the entire packet, except for the fields of the header that might change in transit (traffic class, flow label, and hop limit).

- **Destination options**—The destination extension header defines options that are to be examined only by the destination node. Mobility support in IPv6 (RFC 3775) defines a Type 201 destination option for carrying the Home Address of a mobile node.

Except for the hop-by-hop options header, the extension headers have no impact on the forwarding of IPv6 packets and are not discussed any further in this book.

3.8 ICMPv6

Although many of the upper-layer protocols used in the Internet are relatively unaffected by the change to IPv6, a new version of ICMP is required and is defined in RFC 4443. ICMPv6 provides the functions of an echo service and reporting of delivery errors similar to those provided in IPv4. However, ICMPv6 also provides quite a lot of new functionality, including the Neighbor Discovery (ND) capability, which replaces the Address Resolution Protocol (ARP) of IPv4; and Multicast Listener Discovery (MLD), which replaces the Internet Group Management Protocol (IGMP).

ICMPv6 Header and Messages

The ICMPv6 header is similar to ICMPv4 (Figure 3.17). The meaning of each field is described below.

Figure 3.17 The fields of the ICMPv6 header.

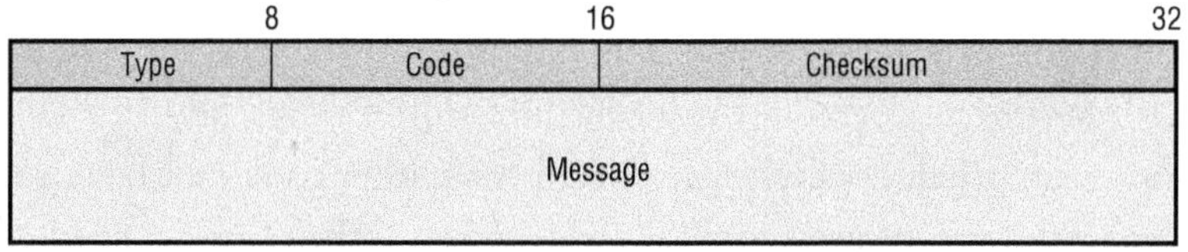

- **Type**—The 8-bit Type field indicates the type of ICMPv6 message. Some of the different types are listed in Table 3.2.
- **Code**—Similar to IPv4, a specific ICMPv6 message type may (or may not) have several codes defined to further define the nature of the message.
- **Checksum**—A 16-bit checksum of the ICMPv6 message, plus the IPv6 pseudo-header (includes the source address, destination address, length, and next header fields of the IPv6 header)
- **Message**—The content of the message body varies, depending on the type of message.

For the Type value, the range 0 to 127 (high order bit zero) is used for error messages. The range 128 to 255 (high order bit one) is used for informational messages (anything other than an error message). Table 3.2 shows some of the different ICMPv6 message types. At the time of writing, the IANA has allocated all the values from 128 thru 154.

Table 3.2 Some ICMPv6 Message Types

Type Value	Message
1	Destination unreachable
2	Packet too big
3	Time exceeded
4	Parameter error
127	Reserved for expansion of ICMPv6 error messages
128	Echo request
129	Echo reply
130	Multicast listener query
131	Multicast listener report
132	Multicast listener done
133	Router solicitation
134	Router advertisement
135	Neighbor solicitation
136	Neighbor advertisement
137	Redirect message
255	Reserved for expansion of ICMPv6 informational messages

Some of the ICMPv6 message types are described in more detail below:

- **Destination unreachable**—Generated when the packet could not be routed to the destination or the upper-layer protocol. Code values 0 thru 6 are defined.
- **Packet too big**—Generated when the maximum transmission unit (MTU) of the forwarding interface is too small for the packet to be forwarded. This message is used for path MTU discovery, which should be supported by IPv6 nodes.

  A sender will initially choose its link MTU as the path MTU. If this is too large for transmission to the destination, the sender will receive a "Packet too big" message with the MTU of the smaller link. The sender will reset the path MTU to the MTU of the smaller link and will continue in this way until no more "Packet too big" messages are received. If the path to the destination changes during a session and a "Packet too big" message is received, the sender resets the path MTU to this value.

When the path MTU is smaller than the local link MTU, the sender may periodically (every 10 minutes recommended) send a packet at the size of the link MTU to determine whether the path MTU can be increased. A sender that does not support path MTU discovery should always use the minimum IPv6 MTU of 1,280 for its transmissions.

- **Time exceeded**—Generated if the hop limit is exceeded or the time to reassemble a packet at the destination is exceeded (60 seconds).
- **Parameter error**—Generated if an unknown or illegal parameter is found in the header, such as an unknown value in the Next header field.
- **Echo request, echo reply**—A program such as `ping` will send an Echo request to a destination node. The destination should respond with an "Echo reply" message.

Neighbor Discovery (ND)

The Neighbor Discovery protocol for IPv6 (RFC 4861) provides the capabilities handled in IPv4 by ARP, Router Discovery and Router Redirect, and quite a few additional capabilities as well. The functions handled by ND are:

- **Router discovery**—Finds routers on a link.
- **Prefix discovery**—Finds the address prefixes for a link.
- **Parameter discovery**—Finds link parameters such as MTU or Hop Limit.
- **Address autoconfiguration**—Mechanism that allows an interface to configure its own address (defined in RFC 4862).
- **Address resolution**—Resolves a destination IP address to a link layer address.
- **Next-hop determination**—Maps an IP address into the next-hop address that the packet should be sent to.
- **Neighbor unreachability detection**—Mechanism to determine that the neighbor is no longer reachable. If this is the default router, the host can change its default to another router.
- **Duplicate address detection**—Mechanism to identify duplicate addresses on the link
- **Redirect**—Allows a router to inform a host of a better next-hop to a destination.

ND uses five different ICMPv6 messages to perform these functions. The messages are:

- **Router Solicitation (Type 133)**—When a host becomes active on a link, it can send a Router Solicitation to ask for a Router Advertisement immediately.

- **Router Advertisement (Type 134)**—Routers advertise their presence and link parameters periodically with Router Advertisement messages. This information can include link MTU, link prefixes, and route information.
- **Neighbor Solicitation (Type 135)**—Used by a node to determine the link address on a neighbor, or to verify that the neighbor is still reachable. If the link address is unknown, the message is sent to the solicited node multicast address. Because this address is formed with the last 24 bits of the IP address, it is unlikely that there will be more than one node with the address. This makes the protocol much less disruptive than ARP. If the node is verifying a known link address, the message is sent to the unicast address.
- **Neighbor Advertisement (Type 136)**—Response to a Neighbor Solicitation sent to the unicast address. A node may also send an unsolicited Neighbor Advertisement to announce a link address change.
- **Redirect (Type 137)**—Sent by a router to inform a host of a better next-hop address.

ND replaces the ARP protocol in IPv4. A host that wants to resolve an IPv6 address to a MAC address sends a Neighbor Solicitation message containing the IPv6 address. This message is sent to the solicited-node multicast address formed from the desired unicast address. The neighbor that has this unicast address is likely the only one listening to this multicast group. It responds with a Neighbor Advertisement message containing its MAC address (Figure 3.18). ND is more efficient than ARP because other hosts on the network do not have to process a broadcast message.

The flags in the Neighbor Advertisement message have the following meaning:

- **Router**—The advertisement message was sent by a router.
- **Solicited**—The advertisement was sent in response to a Neighbor Solicitation message.
- **Override**—The advertisement should override an existing cache entry.

3.9 Configuring IPv6

Configuring IPv6 interfaces and routing for IPv6 is very similar to configuration of IPv4. The most obvious difference is the use of IPv6 addresses. IPv6 and IPv4 can be configured in parallel on the same network. In this example, we will configure IPv6 on the same network that we used for the IPv4 example.

Figure 3.18 To resolve an IPv6 address to a Layer 2 address, the host sends a Neighbor Solicitation to the solicited-node multicast address. The neighbor with the unicast address responds with a Neighbor Advertisement message.

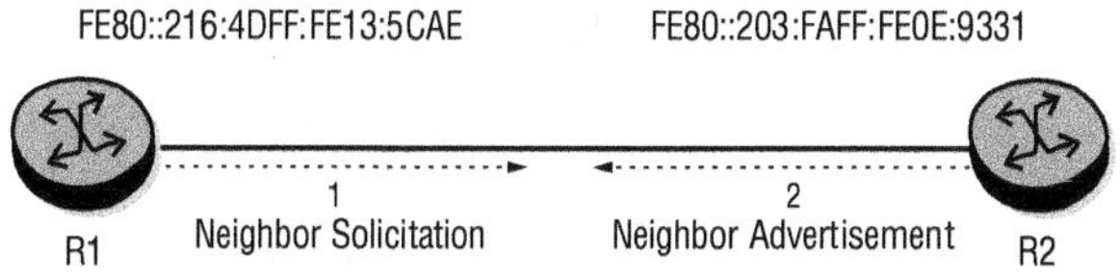

1

```
30 2010/10/26 12:20:43.10 UTC MINOR: DEBUG #2001 Base TIP
"TIP: ICMP6_PKT
ICMP6 egressing on toR2:
 FE80::216:4DFF:FE13:5CAE > FF02::1:FF0E:9331
 Type: Neighbor Solicitation (135)
 Code: No Code (0)
   Tgt Addr: FE80::203:FAFF:FE0E:9331
   Option  : Src Link Layer Addr 00:16:4d:13:5c:ae
```

2

```
31 2010/10/26 12:20:43.10 UTC MINOR: DEBUG #2001 Base TIP
"TIP: ICMP6_PKT
ICMP6 ingressing on toR2:
 FE80::203:FAFF:FE0E:9331  > FE80::216:4DFF:FE13:5CAE
 Type: Neighbor Advertisement (136)
 Code: No Code (0)
   Tgt Addr: FE80::203:FAFF:FE0E:9331
   Flags   : Router Solicited Override
   Option  : Tgt Link Layer Addr 00:03:fa:0e:93:31
```

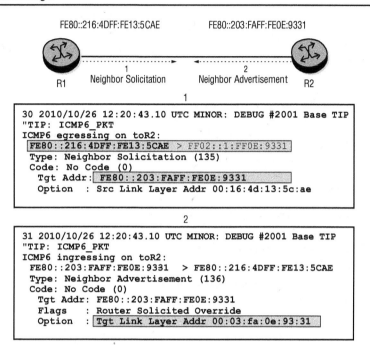

In our example, the enterprise has been allocated a prefix from their service provider, 2001:db8:1::/48. The enterprise decides to subnet the prefix using the first 8 bits to identify a specific location and the second 8 bits to identify subnets at that location. In our example, corporate headquarters is location 01 and subnet 01. The branch office is location 02 and subnet 01. System interfaces are addressed using subnet 00 at all locations. The topology is shown in Figure 3.19.

The interfaces have already been configured with IPv4 addresses. In order to use IPv6 on the 7750 SR, you must first enable chassis mode "c." As soon as we enable IPv6 on the interface, a link-local address is automatically assigned based on the modified EUI-64 address (Listing 3.13). If it's not necessary to route to the interfaces, we don't need to assign them global routing addresses—we can simply use the link-local addresses.

Figure 3.19 Topology for IPv6 configuration.

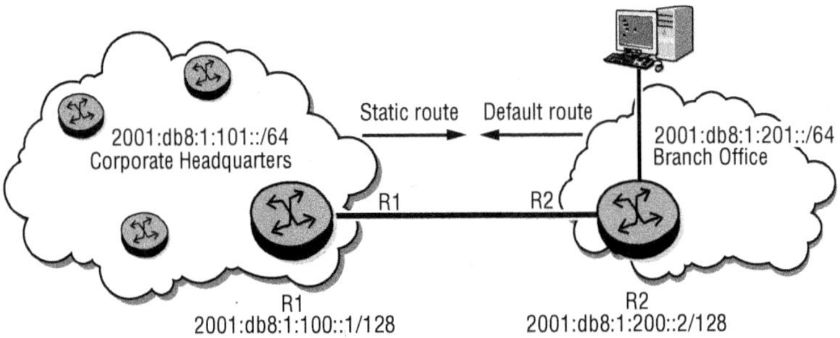

Listing 3.13 Configuring interfaces for IPv6

```
*A:R1# configure system chassis-mode c force
*A:R1# configure router
*A:R1>config>router# interface "toR2" ipv6
*A:R1>config>router# exit
*A:R1>config>router# interface "toR3" ipv6
*A:R1>config>router# show router interface

===============================================================================
Interface Table (Router: Base)
===============================================================================
Interface-Name              Adm         Opr(v4/v6)  Mode    Port/SapId
   IP-Address                                               PfxState
-------------------------------------------------------------------------------
loopback_1                  Up          Up/Down     Network loopback
   10.0.253.1/24                                            n/a
loopback_2                  Up          Up/Down     Network loopback
   10.0.254.1/24                                            n/a
system                      Up          Up/Down     Network system
   10.10.10.1/32                                            n/a
toR2                        Up          Up/Up       Network 1/1/1
   10.1.2.1/27                                              n/a
   FE80::225:BAFF:FE30:7908/64                              PREFERRED
toR3                        Up          Up/Up       Network 1/1/3
   10.1.3.1/27                                              n/a
   FE80::225:BAFF:FE30:790A/64                              PREFERRED
-------------------------------------------------------------------------------
Interfaces : 5
```

You can see that the link-local address was formed from the MAC address of the interface toR2 (Listing 3.14).

Listing 3.14 The link-local address is formed as a modified EUI-64 address from the interface MAC address.

```
*A:R1>config>router# show port 1/1/1

===============================================================================
Ethernet Interface
===============================================================================
Description          : 1-Gig Ethernet SFP
Interface            : 1/1/1                  Oper Speed        : 1 Gbps
Link-level           : Ethernet               Config Speed      : N/A
Admin State          : up                     Oper Duplex       : full
Oper State           : up                     Config Duplex     : N/A
Physical Link        : Yes                    MTU               : 9212
Single Fiber Mode    : No
IfIndex              : 35684352               Hold time up      : 0 seconds
Last State Change    : 10/05/2010 11:24:08    Hold time down    : 0 seconds
Last Cleared Time    : N/A                    DDM Events        : Enabled

Configured Mode      : network                Encap Type        : null
Dot1Q Ethertype      : 0x8100                 QinQ Ethertype    : 0x8100
PBB Ethertype        : 0x88e7
Ing. Pool % Rate     : 100                    Egr. Pool % Rate : 100
Ing. Pool Policy     : n/a
Egr. Pool Policy     : n/a
Net. Egr. Queue Pol: default
Egr. Sched. Pol      : n/a
Auto-negotiate       : true                   MDI/MDX           : N/A
Accounting Policy    : None                   Collect-stats     : Disabled
Egress Rate          : Default                Ingress Rate      : Default
Load-balance-algo    : default                LACP Tunnel       : Disabled

Down-when-looped     : Disabled               Keep-alive        : 10
Loop Detected        : False                  Retry             : 120
Use Broadcast Addr : False
```

(continued)

Listing 3.14 *(continued)*

```
Sync. Status Msg.  : Disabled                 Rx Quality Level : N/A

Configured Address : 00:25:ba:30:79:08
Hardware Address   : 00:25:ba:30:79:08
Cfg Alarm          :
Alarm Status       :

... output omitted ...
```

We will next configure an IPv6 address for the system interface and loopback interfaces (Listing 3.15). The link-local address for the loopbacks is formed from the chassis MAC address.

Listing 3.15 Configuring IPv6 on the system interface

```
*A:R1# configure router
*A:R1>config>router# interface "system" ipv6
*A:R1>config>router>if>ipv6# address 2001:db8:1:100::1/128
*A:R1>config>router>if>ipv6# exit
*A:R1>config>router# interface "loopback_1" ipv6
*A:R1>config>router>if>ipv6# address 2001:db8:1:1f1::/64 eui-64
*A:R1>config>router>if>ipv6# exit
*A:R1>config>router# interface "loopback_2" ipv6
*A:R1>config>router>if>ipv6# address 2001:db8:1:1f2::/64 eui-64
*A:R1>config>router>if>ipv6# exit
*A:R1>config>router# show router interface

===============================================================================
Interface Table (Router: Base)
===============================================================================
Interface-Name                   Adm         Opr(v4/v6)  Mode     Port/SapId
   IP-Address                                                     PfxState
-------------------------------------------------------------------------------
loopback_1                       Up          Up/Up       Network loopback
   10.0.253.1/24                                                  n/a
   2001:DB8:1:1F1:225:BAFF:FE7E:2BD0/64                           PREFERRED
   FE80::225:BAFF:FE7E:2BD0/64                                    PREFERRED
loopback_2                       Up          Up/Up       Network loopback
   10.0.254.1/24                                                  n/a
```

```
   2001:DB8:1:1F2:225:BAFF:FE7E:2BD0/64                            PREFERRED
   FE80::225:BAFF:FE7E:2BD0/64                                     PREFERRED
system                       Up           Up/Up        Network system
   10.10.10.1/32                                                   n/a
   2001:DB8:1:100::1/128                                           PREFERRED
toR2                         Up           Up/Up        Network 1/1/1
   10.1.2.1/27                                                     n/a
   FE80::225:BAFF:FE30:7908/64                                     PREFERRED
toR3                         Up           Up/Up        Network 1/1/3
   10.1.3.1/27                                                     n/a
   FE80::225:BAFF:FE30:790A/64                                     PREFERRED
-------------------------------------------------------------------------------
Interfaces : 5
===============================================================================
```

The router can now route IPv6 as well as IPv4 (Listing 3.16). The link-local addresses do not show in the route-table but can still be used. Since they are local to the link, the interface must also be specified when the address is used.

Listing 3.16 Viewing the IPv6 route-table

```
*A:R1>config>router# show router route-table ipv6

===============================================================================
IPv6 Route Table (Router: Base)
===============================================================================
Dest Prefix                            Type     Proto     Age          Pref
       Next Hop[Interface Name]                                 Metric
-------------------------------------------------------------------------------
2001:DB8:1:100::1/128                  Local    Local     00h08m56s    0
       system                                                    0
2001:DB8:1:1F1::/64                    Local    Local     00h06m00s    0
       loopback_1                                                0
2001:DB8:1:1F2::/64                    Local    Local     00h05m23s    0
       loopback_2                                                0
-------------------------------------------------------------------------------
No. of Routes: 3
===============================================================================
*A:R1>config>router#
```

The next step is to configure a route to the branch office (Listing 3.17). Our address plan gives each location 8 bits for subnetting, thus the prefix of the branch office is 2001:db8:1:200::/56.

Listing 3.17 Static route to reach the branch office networks

```
*A:R1# configure router
*A:R1>config>router# static-route 2001:db8:1:200::/56 next-hop
FE80::225:BAFF:FE30:94E3-toR2
*A:R1>config>router# show router route-table ipv6

========================================================================
IPv6 Route Table (Router: Base)
========================================================================
Dest Prefix                              Type     Proto     Age         Pref
         Next Hop[Interface Name]                              Metric
------------------------------------------------------------------------
2001:DB8:1:100::1/128                    Local    Local     00h58m51s   0
         system                                                 0
2001:DB8:1:1F1::/64                      Local    Local     00h55m55s   0
         loopback_1                                             0
2001:DB8:1:1F2::/64                      Local    Local     00h55m18s   0
         loopback_2                                             0
2001:DB8:1:200::/56                      Remote   Static    00h00m20s   5
         FE80::225:BAFF:FE30:94E3-"toR2"                        1
------------------------------------------------------------------------
No. of Routes: 4
========================================================================
```

On router R2 at the branch office, we will configure the interface to R1, the system interface, and a default route toward the corporate network. We should then be able to ping the system address of R1 (Listing 3.18).

Listing 3.18 Configuring a static route from the branch office to corporate headquarters

```
*A:R2# configure router
*A:R2>config>router# interface "system" ipv6 address
2001:db8:1:200::2/128
```

```
*A:R2>config>router# interface "toR1" ipv6
*A:R2>config>router>if>ipv6# exit
*A:R2>config>router# static-route ::/0 next-hop
FE80::225:BAFF:FE30:7908-toR1
*A:R2>config>router# show router route-table ipv6

===============================================================================
IPv6 Route Table (Router: Base)
===============================================================================
Dest Prefix                             Type    Proto     Age          Pref
       Next Hop[Interface Name]                                Metric
-------------------------------------------------------------------------------
::/0                                    Remote  Static    00h01m19s    5
       FE80::225:BAFF:FE30:7908-"toR1"                             1
2001:DB8:1:200::2/128                   Local   Local     00h00m23s    0
       system                                                      0
-------------------------------------------------------------------------------
No. of Routes: 2
===============================================================================
*A:R2>config>router# ping 2001:DB8:1:100::1
PING 2001:DB8:1:100::1 56 data bytes
64 bytes from 2001:DB8:1:100::1 icmp_seq=1 hlim=64 time=1.63ms.
64 bytes from 2001:DB8:1:100::1 icmp_seq=2 hlim=64 time=1.20ms.
64 bytes from 2001:DB8:1:100::1 icmp_seq=3 hlim=64 time=1.21ms.
64 bytes from 2001:DB8:1:100::1 icmp_seq=4 hlim=64 time=1.19ms.
64 bytes from 2001:DB8:1:100::1 icmp_seq=5 hlim=64 time=1.21ms.

---- 2001:DB8:1:100::1 PING Statistics ----
5 packets transmitted, 5 packets received, 0.00% packet loss
round-trip min = 1.19ms, avg = 1.29ms, max = 1.63ms, stddev = 0.173ms
*A:R2>config>router#
```

6over4

6over4 refers to the tunneling of IPv6 packets over an IPv4 network as defined in RFC 2529. IPv6 packets are encapsulated in IPv4 with a protocol ID value of 41 and routed across the IPv4 network. Figure 3.20 shows a topology similar to the topology in Figure 3.19. The difference in this example is that the customer branch office is connected to the corporate headquarters by an IPv4 network.

Figure 3.20 Branch office IPv6 network connected to corporate network over IPv4.

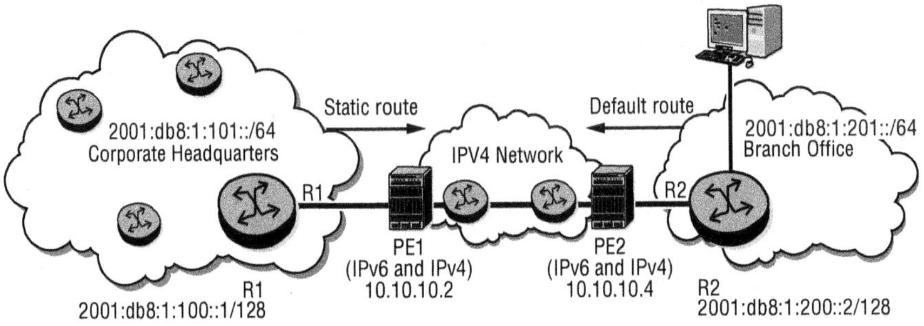

The configuration of the router R1 at corporate headquarters is the same as the in the previous example—a static route to the branch office network. In this case the next hop is the router PE1 (see Listing 3.19). R1 is completely IPv6 and knows nothing about the IPv4 network between it and R2.

Listing 3.19 Static route towards branch office on R1

```
*A:R1# show router interface

===============================================================================
Interface Table (Router: Base)
===============================================================================
Interface-Name                   Adm         Opr(v4/v6)  Mode    Port/SapId
   IP-Address                                                    PfxState
-------------------------------------------------------------------------------
corp-net                         Up          Down/Up     Network loopback
   2001:DB8:1:101::1/64                                          PREFERRED
   FE80::8CEA:FFFF:FE00:0/64                                     PREFERRED
system                           Up          Down/Up     Network system
   2001:DB8:1:100::1/128                                         PREFERRED
toPE1                            Up          Down/Up     Network 1/1/2
   FE80::216:4DFF:FE13:5CAF/64                                   PREFERRED
-------------------------------------------------------------------------------
Interfaces : 3
===============================================================================
```

```
*A:R1# show router route-table ipv6

===============================================================================
IPv6 Route Table (Router: Base)
===============================================================================
Dest Prefix                                   Type    Proto     Age         Pref
       Next Hop[Interface Name]                                    Metric
-------------------------------------------------------------------------------
2001:DB8:1:100::1/128                         Local   Local     17h11m41s   0
       system                                                      0
2001:DB8:1:101::/64                           Local   Local     00h08m04s   0
       corp-net                                                    0
2001:DB8:1:200::/56                           Remote  Static    00h09m52s   5
       FE80::203:FAFF:FE0E:9332-"toPE1"                           1
-------------------------------------------------------------------------------
No. of Routes: 3
===============================================================================
```

The PE router is running a dual stack of IPv4 and IPv6. To configure the tunnel, it is only necessary to configure an IPv6 static route with an IPv4 indirect next-hop. The router makes the IPv6 route active and will tunnel traffic using IPv4 to the next-hop. In order to handle return traffic from the branch office, the PE router must also have an IPv6 static route towards the corporate network (see Listing 3.20).

Listing 3.20 Configuration of PE1 for 6over4 tunneling

```
*A:PE1>config>router# info
----------------------------------------------
#--------------------------------------------------
echo "IP Configuration"
#--------------------------------------------------
        interface "system"
            address 10.10.10.2/32
        exit
        interface "toR1"
            port 1/1/2
            ipv6
            exit
```

(continued)

Listing 3.20 *(continued)*

```
        exit
        interface "toR3"
            address 10.2.3.2/27
            port 1/1/4
        exit
#--------------------------------------------------
echo "Static IPv6 Route Configuration"
#--------------------------------------------------
        static-route 2001:DB8:1:100::/56 next-hop
FE80::216:4DFF:FE13:5CAF-"toR1"
        static-route 2001:DB8:1:200::/56 indirect 10.10.10.4
#--------------------------------------------------
... output omitted ...
```

PE1 now has a mixture of IPv4 and IPv6 interfaces and routes, as shown in Listing 3.21. The next-hop for the branch office is the IPv4 system address of router PE2. From the IPv4 route table, we see that it was learned through OSPF and has a metric of 300. From this we can surmise that it is three hops away.

Listing 3.21 IPv4 and IPv6 routes on PE1

```
*A:PE1# show router interface

===============================================================================
Interface Table (Router: Base)
===============================================================================
Interface-Name                   Adm       Opr(v4/v6)  Mode    Port/SapId
   IP-Address                                                  PfxState
-------------------------------------------------------------------------------
system                           Up        Up/Down     Network system
   10.10.10.2/32                                               n/a
toR1                             Up        Down/Up     Network 1/1/2
   FE80::203:FAFF:FE0E:9332/64                                 PREFERRED
toR3                             Up        Up/Down     Network 1/1/4
   10.2.3.2/27                                                 n/a
-------------------------------------------------------------------------------
Interfaces : 3
```

```
==============================================================================
*A:PE1# show router route-table ipv6

==============================================================================
IPv6 Route Table (Router: Base)
==============================================================================
Dest Prefix                                    Type     Proto    Age          Pref
      Next Hop[Interface Name]                                       Metric
------------------------------------------------------------------------------
2001:DB8:1:100::/56                            Remote   Static   16h54m09s    5
      FE80::216:4DFF:FE13:5CAF-"toR1"                               1
2001:DB8:1:200::/56                            Remote   Static   17h01m26s    5
      10.10.10.4                                                    1
------------------------------------------------------------------------------
No. of Routes: 2
==============================================================================
*A:PE1# show router route-table ipv4

==============================================================================
Route Table (Router: Base)
==============================================================================
Dest Prefix                                    Type     Proto    Age          Pref
      Next Hop[Interface Name]                                       Metric
------------------------------------------------------------------------------
10.2.3.0/27                                    Local    Local    17d00h53m    0
      toR3                                                          0
10.3.5.0/27                                    Remote   OSPF     03d23h23m    10
      10.2.3.3                                                      200
10.4.5.0/27                                    Remote   OSPF     01d14h16m    10
      10.2.3.3                                                      300
10.10.10.2/32                                  Local    Local    43d03h32m    0
      system                                                        0
10.10.10.3/32                                  Remote   OSPF     16d17h37m    10
      10.2.3.3                                                      100
10.10.10.4/32                                  Remote   OSPF     01d14h16m    10
      10.2.3.3                                                      300
10.10.10.5/32                                  Remote   OSPF     01d14h16m    10
      10.2.3.3                                                      200
------------------------------------------------------------------------------
No. of Routes: 7
==============================================================================
```

A similar configuration is required on router PE2. In this case PE2 is configured with a default route towards the corporate network (see Listing 3.22).

Listing 3.22 Configuration of 6over4 on router PE2

```
*A:PE2>config>router# info
----------------------------------------------
#--------------------------------------------------
echo "IP Configuration"
#--------------------------------------------------
        interface "system"
            address 10.10.10.4/32
        exit
        interface "toR2"
            port 1/1/1
            ipv6
            exit
        exit
        interface "toR5"
            address 10.4.5.4/27
            port 1/1/4
        exit
#--------------------------------------------------
echo "Static IPv6 Route Configuration"
#--------------------------------------------------
        static-route ::/0 indirect 10.10.10.2
        static-route 2001:DB8:1:200::/56
next-hop FE80::203:FAFF:FEAC:B826-"toR2"
#--------------------------------------------------
```

The branch office router is completely IPv6 with a static route toward the corporate network. Once the static route is added to R2 it is possible to ping router R1 and the corporate network to demonstrate that the path has been successfully established (See Listing 3.23)

Listing 3.23 Default static route on R2

```
*A:R2# show router route-table ipv6
```

```
===============================================================================
IPv6 Route Table (Router: Base)
===============================================================================
Dest Prefix                                   Type     Proto    Age          Pref
      Next Hop[Interface Name]                                      Metric
-------------------------------------------------------------------------------
::/0                                          Remote   Static   00h03m15s    5
      FE80::216:4DFF:FE13:63C0-"toPE2"                              1
2001:DB8:1:200::2/128                         Local    Local    17h40m10s    0
      system                                                        0
2001:DB8:1:201::/64                           Local    Local    00h40m29s    0
      branch-net                                                    0
-------------------------------------------------------------------------------
No. of Routes: 3
===============================================================================
*A:R2# ping 2001:DB8:1:100::1 count 1
PING 2001:DB8:1:100::1 56 data bytes
64 bytes from 2001:DB8:1:100::1 icmp_seq=1 hlim=62 time=4.24ms.

---- 2001:DB8:1:100::1 PING Statistics ----
1 packet transmitted, 1 packet received, 0.00% packet loss
round-trip min = 4.24ms, avg = 4.24ms, max = 4.24ms, stddev = 0.000ms
*A:R2# ping 2001:DB8:1:101::1 source 2001:DB8:1:201::1 count 1
PING 2001:DB8:1:101::1 56 data bytes
64 bytes from 2001:DB8:1:101::1 icmp_seq=1 hlim=62 time=4.23ms.

---- 2001:DB8:1:101::1 PING Statistics ----
1 packet transmitted, 1 packet received, 0.00% packet loss
round-trip min = 4.23ms, avg = 4.23ms, max = 4.23ms, stddev = 0.000ms
*A:R2#
```

Practice Lab: Configuring IP Interfaces and Static Routes

The following lab is designed to reinforce your knowledge of the content in this chapter. Please review the instructions carefully, and perform the steps in the order in which they are presented. The practice labs require that you have access to six or more 7750 SR or 7450 ESS in a non-production environment.

These labs are designed to be used in a controlled lab environment. Please *do not* attempt to perform these labs in a production environment.

Lab Section 3.1: Configuring a Layer 3 Interface

One of the first steps in provisioning a router for service is to configure the required IP interfaces. You must be able to provision the system interface, loopback interfaces, and physical interfaces. This lab investigates the configuration and behavior of IP interfaces on the 7750 SR using the topology shown in Figure 3.21.

Figure 3.21 Topology used for Lab 3 exercises.

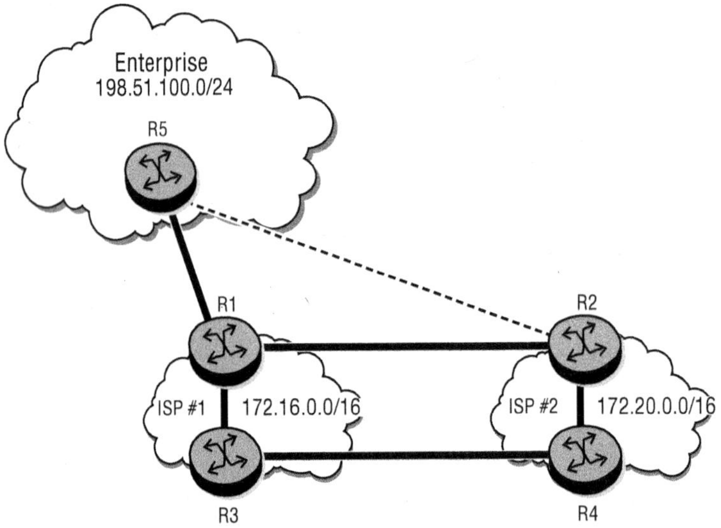

Objective In this exercise, you will configure the 7750 SR with Layer 3 interfaces.

Validation You will know you have succeeded if each configured router interface shows an operational state of Up.

1. Configure the system IP addresses of all five routers in the topology. Use the system IP address of 10.10.10.*x*, where *x* is the router number for routers R1, R2, R3, and R4. For example, R3 will have a system interface with IP address 10.10.10.3. Choose an address from the enterprise address space (198.51.100.0/24) for R5.

a. Does the system interface need to be explicitly created?

b. Can the system interface be removed?

c. What is the administrative status of the system interface before and after an IP address is assigned?

d. What is the operational status of the system interface before and after an IP address is assigned?

e. What port should be assigned to the system interface?

2. Configure all the router interfaces required for the point-to-point links in the topology (i.e., R1–R5, R3–R4, etc.). Point-to-point links generally use /30 subnet masks for efficient use of IP address space. Devise an address plan for all router links where ISP #2's address space is used for the R2–R4 and R2–R5 links and ISP #1's address space is used for all other link IP addresses.

   a. What is the admin status of the router interface before and after an IP address is assigned?

   b. What is the operational status of the router interface before and after an IP address is assigned?

   c. What else needs to be done to the router interface to ensure it is operationally up?

3. We will configure loopback interfaces on R3 and R4 to simulate locally attached networks at these routers. Configure a loopback interface with a /24 mask on R3 from the ISP #1 range. Configure a similar loopback on R4 from the ISP #2 range.

   a. Are the loopback interfaces administratively and operationally up after assigning an IP address to them? If not, what has to be done?

   b. Make sure that all the interfaces configured so far in the lab are operationally up before proceeding to the next step.

4. Verify connectivity between R5 and R1 by pinging the far-end interface IP address from each router.

   a. Is the ping successful? Explain.

   b. From R5, can you ping the system IP address of R1? Explain.

   c. From R5, can you ping the loopback interface on R3? Explain.

Lab Section 3.2: Configuring Static Routes

In the previous exercise, you provisioned the router to be able to ping directly connected interfaces. However, for useful router operations, you must be able to reach remote destinations other than directly connected interfaces. This lab exercise investigates the use of static routes to populate the route-table.

Objective In this exercise, you will configure static routes to enable the enterprise to reach various destinations in each ISP.

Validation You will know you have succeeded if the static routes are in the route-table and the required destinations are reachable with ping.

1. Configure a default static route on R5 toward R1.
   a. Verify that the static route is active.
   b. Does the static route appear in the route-table? If so, how is a default route indicated?
   c. What is the preference of the route?
   d. What is the metric of the route?
2. Try to ping the system IP address of R1 from R5.
   a. Is the ping successful? Explain.
   b. Ping the system IP address of R1 from R5 using the local interface address as the source for the ping. Is the ping successful? Explain.
   c. Add the necessary static routes to make the ping successful without specifying a source address.
3. Try to ping the loopback addresses of R3.
   a. Is the ping successful? Explain.
   b. Add the necessary static routes to make the ping successful.
   c. Use the `traceroute` command to determine the path taken.
   d. If a different path is required, what must be done?
4. *Optional:* For some extra practice, repeat the previous step to get reachability to R4's loopback IP address from R5 using the same ISP (i.e., through R1).

Lab Section 3.3: Configuring Floating Static Routes

The previous exercise used static routes for connectivity to various networks in the topology. However, the static nature of the routes offers no failover mechanism in case of a physical link failure. This lab exercise investigates the use of floating static routes as a failover mechanism.

Objective In this exercise, you will configure a floating static route on R5 toward ISP #2. This route can be used by the enterprise when the link to ISP #1 goes down.

Validation You will know you have succeeded if the floating static routes have the correct operational states and you can ping the required destinations when one or both links between the enterprise and the ISPs are up.

1. Configure a floating default route on R5 toward R2 to be used in case the link to R1 goes down.
   a. What preference needs to be used for the floating default route?
   b. How is the floating default route indicated when the `show router static-route` command is used?
   c. How is the floating static route displayed in the route-table?
2. Shut down the port on R5 that is connected to R1. How are the static routes displayed with the `show router static-route` command?
3. If you shut down the port on a router that is directly connected to another router, the port on the other router will also become operationally down. However, if the other router is not directly connected (e.g., both router ports connected to a switch), the other router port may remain up.
   a. What is the impact if the port on R1 remains up when you shut down the port on R5?
   b. What additional static routes are required on R1, R2, and R3 for R5 to be able to ping R3 through the alternate route?
4. In order to ensure that the floating static route will work correctly when the port on R5 is shut down, configure BFD on the link between R5 and R1. Set BFD to send a packet once a second on each interface.
   a. Make sure the physical ports between R5 and R1 are up, and then verify that the BFD session is operational.

b. Add the necessary static routes to make the ping successful between R5 and the loopback on R3.

c. Use the `traceroute` command to determine the path taken.

5. Bring the port on R5 that is connected to R1 down.

a. Which default route is now active?

b. Perform another `traceroute` to determine the new path taken.

6. What can be said about the static-route solutions investigated in this lab?

7. Bring all ports back up before proceeding to the next section.

Lab Section 3.4: Configuring IPv6

In the lab sections above, the network was configured for IPv4. This lab investigates the configuration and behavior of IPv6 on the 7750 SR using the topology shown in Figure 3.22.

Figure 3.22 Topology used for IPv6 exercise.

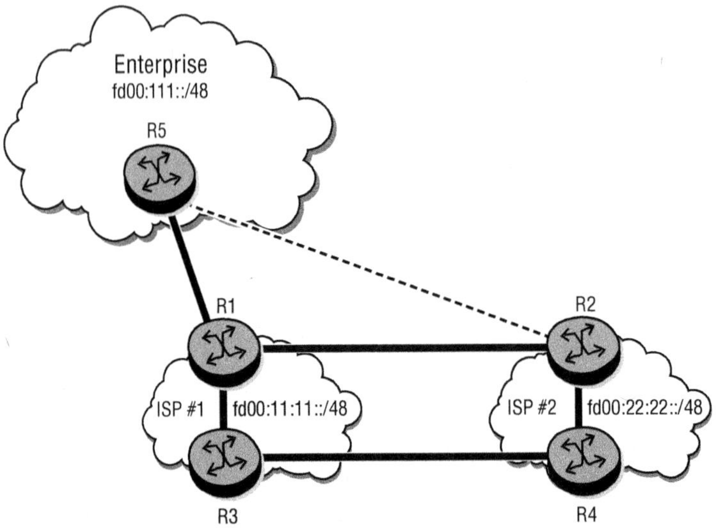

Objective In this exercise, you will configure the 7750 SR with IPv6 interfaces.

Validation You will know you have succeeded if each configured router interface shows an operational state of Up for IPv6.

1. Configure the system IP addresses of all five routers in the topology. The ISPs and enterprise are all using Unique Local Address space fc00::/7, with a self-assigned prefix (although it is not exactly random). Use the system IP address of *prefix::x*, where *prefix* is the 48-bit prefix of the ISP or enterprise, local subnet 0, and x is the router number for routers R1, R2, R3, and R4. For example, R3 will have a system interface with IP address fd00:11:11::3/128.
   a. What is the operational status of the system interface before an IPv6 address is assigned?
   b. What happens to an existing IPv4 address when an IPv6 address is assigned to the system interface?
2. Configure all the router interfaces for IPv6, but do not assign addresses.
   a. What is the operational status of the router interfaces?
   b. What IP address has been assigned to the router interfaces by default? How has this address been derived?
3. We will configure loopback interfaces on R3 and R4 to simulate locally attached networks at these routers. Configure a loopback interface with a /64 mask on R3 from the ISP #1 range. Configure a similar loopback on R4 from the ISP #2 range.
   a. What is the operational status of the loopback interfaces?
   b. How many IP addresses are assigned to each loopback interface?
4. Verify connectivity between the enterprise router R5 and the routers in ISP #1.
   a. From R5, can you ping the directly connected interface of R1? Explain.
   b. From R5, can you ping the system interface of R1? Explain.
   c. From R5, can you ping the loopback interface of R3? Explain.

Lab Section 3.5: Configuring Static Routes for IPv6

In the previous exercise, you provisioned the router to be able to ping directly connected interfaces. For useful router operations, however, you must be able to reach remote destinations other than directly connected interfaces. This lab exercise investigates the use of static routes to populate the route-table.

Objective In this exercise, you will configure static routes to enable the enterprise to reach various destinations in each ISP.

Validation You will know you have succeeded if the static routes are in the route-table and the required destinations are reachable by ping.

1. Configure a default static route on R5 toward R1.
   a. Verify that the static route is active.
   b. Does the static route appear in the route-table? If so, how is a default route indicated?
   c. What is the preference of the route?
   d. What is the metric of the route?
2. Try to ping the system IP address of R1 from R5.
   a. Is the ping successful? Explain.
   b. Ping the system IP address of R1 from R5 using the local interface address as the source for the ping. Is the ping successful? Explain.
   c. Add the necessary static routes to make the ping successful without specifying a source address.
3. Try to ping the loopback addresses of R3 from R5.
   a. Is the ping successful? Explain.
   b. Add the necessary static routes to make the ping successful.
4. *Optional:* For some extra practice, repeat the previous step to get reachability to R4's loopback IP address from R5 using the same ISP (i.e., through R1).

Chapter Review

Now that you have completed this chapter, you should be able to:

- Describe the fundamental capabilities of IP.
- Analyze the structure of an IP address.
- Perform IP subnet calculations.
- Decode the meaning of the fields in the IP route-table.
- Describe the forwarding of an IP packet on the 7750 SR.
- Explain the purpose of the different fields of the IP header.
- Explain the difference between the forwarding plane and control plane in an IP router.
- Configure IP interfaces on the 7750 SR.
- Configure and verify floating static routes.
- Configure BFD for a static route.
- Describe how IPv6 addresses are constructed and allocated.
- List the fields of the IPv6 header.
- Explain the purpose of ICMPv6.
- Describe the basic operation of ICMPv6 Neighbor Discovery.
- Configure IPv6 interfaces.
- Configure and verify an IPv6 static route.
- Describe the purpose and operation of 6over4.
- Configure a 7750 SR for 6over4 tunneling.

Post-Assessment

1. Which statement is correct concerning the IP network 192.0.2.160 with a subnet mask of 255.255.255.224?

   A. The host address range is 192.0.2.160–192.0.2.190.

   B. The host address range is 192.0.2.161–192.0.2.190.

   C. The host address range is 192.0.2.161–192.0.2.191.

   D. The host address range is 192.0.2.160–192.0.2.191.

2. Which statement best describes the path of data traffic switched between two IOMs in an Alcatel-Lucent 7750 SR?

   A. Data traffic will pass through the SF module.

   B. Data traffic will pass through the SF module and then the CPM module.

   C. Data traffic will pass through the CPM module and then the SF module.

   D. Data traffic does not pass through either the SF or the CPM module.

3. If static routes are used for connectivity between a branch office and corporate headquarters, what is the most likely configuration?

   A. Static route on the corporate router and a default route on the branch router

   B. Default route on the corporate router and a static route on the branch router

   C. Static route on the corporate and branch routers

   D. Default route on the corporate and branch routers

4. An Alcatel-Lucent 7750 SR is configured with a default route and a static route for prefix 198.51.100.160/27. It has an OSPF route for 198.51.100.160/28. All routes are visible in the route-table and use default preference values. Which route will be used to forward an IP packet with the source address of 198.51.100.177?

   A. Default route

   B. Static route

   C. OSPF route

   D. There is not enough information to determine

5. A router-interface on an Alcatel-Lucent 7750 SR is bound to a port and enabled with IPv6. An explicit IPv6 address is assigned to the interface. The port MAC address is 00:03:fa:ac:99:af, and the chassis MAC address is 00:03:fa:bf:b9:f8. Which statement below best describes the link-local address that will be assigned to the router interface?

   A. The link-local interface address is FE80::203:FAFF:FEAC:99AF/64.

   B. The link-local interface address is FC::3:FAFF:FEAC:99AF/64.

   C. The link-local interface address is FC::203:FAFF:FEBF:B9F8/64.

   D. The link-local interface address is FE80::3:FAFF:FEBF:B9F8/64.

   E. A link-local address is not configured for the interface.

6. Which of the following is a capability provided by IP?

   A. Connection-oriented, unreliable datagram delivery service

   B. Connectionless, unreliable datagram delivery service

   C. Connection-oriented, reliable datagram delivery service

   D. Connectionless, reliable datagram delivery service

7. Which of the following is *not* contained in the route-table maintained by the Alcatel-Lucent 7750 SR CPM?

   A. Preference

   B. Metric

   C. Layer 2 information of the next-hop

   D. Protocol used to learn the routes

8. Which command can be used on the CLI to view the FIB stored on the IOM in Slot 1 of an Alcatel-Lucent 7750 SR?

   A. `show router route-table`

   B. `show router 1 route-table`

   C. `show router iom 0`

   D. `show router iom 1`

   E. `show router fib 0`

   F. `show router fib 1`

9. Which of the following fields in the IPv4 header identifies that the IP packet is carrying ICMP data?

   A. Version

   B. IHL

   C. IP source address

   D. IP destination address

   E. Protocol

10. Which of the following is *not* part of the Alcatel-Lucent 7750 SR IP interface configuration?

   A. IP address

   B. Subnet mask

   C. Layer 2 media type

   D. Port number

11. Which statement is correct regarding the system interface on the Alcatel-Lucent 7750 SR?

   A. It always has an operational state of Up.

   B. It needs to be explicitly configured as a loopback.

   C. It assumes an IP address of the last four octets of the chassis MAC address if one is not configured.

   D. It always has an admin state of Up.

   E. It cannot be removed.

12. What is the correct syntax to configure a default route on an Alcatel-Lucent 7750 SR assuming that the local router interface to be used has an IP address of 10.1.1.1/30?

   A. `configure router default-route 0.0.0.0/0 next-hop 10.1.1.1`

   B. `configure router default-route 0.0.0.0/0 next-hop 10.1.1.2`

   C. `configure router static-route 0.0.0.0/0 next-hop 10.1.1.1`

   D. `configure router static-route 0.0.0.0/0 next-hop 10.1.1.2`

   E. `configure router static-route * next-hop 10.1.1.1`

   F. `configure router static-route * next-hop 10.1.1.2`

13. Which statement is true concerning floating static routes?

A. The floating static route is configured with the keyword `floating`.

B. The floating static route is used if the active route becomes too congested.

C. The route with the higher preference is active.

D. Floating static routes are only beneficial when the physical topology offers more than one next-hop to a prefix.

E. BFD must be used on the active static route to detect failures.

14. An Alcatel-Lucent 7750 SR is configured with the following routes:

```
configure router static-route 0.0.0.0/0 next-hop 10.1.1.1
configure router static-route 172.16.14.64/27 next-hop 10.1.2.2
  preference 200
configure router static-route 172.16.14.64/28 next-hop 10.1.3.3
```

The router also learns the route 172.16.14.0/24 from OSPF with a next-hop of 10.1.4.4. What is the next-hop for the packet with destination address 172.16.14.82?

A. 10.1.1.1

B. 10.1.2.2

C. 10.1.3.3

D. 10.1.4.4

E. The packet is discarded

15. Two Alcatel-Lucent 7750 SRs named R1 and R2 are directly connected. The MAC address of the port on R1 is 00:16:4d:13:63:cf, and the MAC address of the port on R2 is 00:16:4d:13:63:c1. The system IP address of R2 is fd00:33:33::1/128, and all interface names follow the convention "toR*x*," where *x* is the router number. Which of the following commands can be used on R1 to create a static route to R2's system interface address?

A. `configure router static-route fd00:33:33::1/128 next-hop FE80::216:4DFF:FE13:63C1`

B. `configure router static-route fd00:33:33::1/128 next-hop FE80::216:4DFF:FE13:63C1-toR2`

C. `configure router static-route fd00:33:33::1/128 next-hop FE80::216:4DFF:FE13:63CF-toR1`

D. `configure router static-route fd00:33:33::1/128 next-hop FE80::216:4DFF:FE13:63CF`

E. Static routes cannot be created until a global IPv6 address is assigned to the router interfaces

4 Dynamic Routing Protocols

The Alcatel-Lucent NRS II exam topics covered in this chapter include the following:

- Overview of dynamic routing
- Dynamic routing protocols
- Link-state routing protocols
- Role of BGP in Internet routing
- RTM and route selection

This chapter introduces the key concept of dynamic routing protocols—the protocols that make the Internet possible. A brief description of the different types of routing protocols is followed by a comparison of distance-vector and link-state routing protocols. We examine all the important operating characteristics of link-state routing protocols including the shortest path first (SPF) algorithm and the flooding of link-state information. To complete the story of routing in the Internet, we provide an overview of BGP (Border Gateway Protocol) and an example of configuring BGP on the Alcatel-Lucent 7750 SR. We conclude with a look at the route table manager (RTM) and how it selects the active routes for the route-table.

Pre-Assessment

The following assessment questions will help you understand what areas of the chapter you should review in more detail to prepare for the NRS II exam. You can also use the CD that accompanies this book to take all the assessment tests and review the answers.

1. Which of the following is the primary goal of an IGP?

- **A.** To facilitate load balancing
- **B.** To provide the lowest-cost route to networks within an autonomous system
- **C.** To provide the best route to Internet destinations considering policy rules and cost
- **D.** To distribute aggregate routes

2. Which statement is true about link-state protocols?

- **A.** Sequence numbers are incremented as the updates are passed from router to router.
- **B.** Updates and Hello messages are sent to a broadcast address so they can be seen by all routers running the protocol.
- **C.** When an interface changes state, a routing update is flooded to all routers in the domain.
- **D.** Routing tables are periodically sent between neighbors.

3. What action is taken when a router receives a new LSP from a neighbor?

   A. Run SPF on the LSDB and flood a SYNC message to all routers to start a query and reply process.

   B. Run SPF on the LSDB and send the results of the SPF calculation to its neighbors.

   C. Run an SPF calculation to update the route table and send incremental updates to the routers in its adjacency database.

   D. Flood the LSP to all its neighbors and then run an SPF calculation to update the route table.

4. Which statement is correct regarding the age and sequence number of an LSP as it is flooded throughout a network?

   A. The sequence number and age are increased.

   B. The sequence number and age are not changed.

   C. The sequence number is not changed, but the age is changed.

   D. The sequence number is increased, but the age is held constant.

5. Which statement is true regarding BGP?

   A. BGP discovers its neighbors through the use of Hello messages.

   B. BGP is a path-vector protocol that selects the route that is the least number of hops between autonomous systems.

   C. A BGP policy may cause BGP to choose a route that is not the shortest path to the destination.

   D. BGP routers are always directly connected to their neighbors.

   E. The primary objective of BGP is to offer the lowest-cost route to destination networks.

4.1 Overview of Dynamic Routing

In the preceding chapter, we have seen the mechanism that an IP router uses for forwarding datagrams over the network. When an IP datagram arrives, the router looks up the destination address in its forwarding table. This tells it the next-hop for forwarding and the egress interface to use. We have seen that entries are made in the routing table for directly connected networks and that we can also administratively configure static routes.

In this chapter, we look at how IP routers also use dynamic routing protocols to exchange information about the network and add more entries to the routing table. IP routing can be divided into two types—static and dynamic. Dynamic routing protocols can be further divided into two main categories—Interior Gateway Protocols (IGPs) and Exterior Gateway Protocols (EGPs).

Comparing IGPs and EGPs

IGPs such as RIP (Routing Information Protocol), OSPF (Open Shortest Path First), and IS-IS (Intermediate System to Intermediate System) are used for routing within an autonomous system. An autonomous system is defined as the networks and routers that are under the control of one entity or administrative authority. The purpose of an IGP is to find the best route to every destination in the network. Based on their method of determining this best route, routing protocols can also be divided into distance-vector and link-state protocols.

The goal of an EGP is to exchange routing information between autonomous systems. The EGP must also consider policy rules that may exist between the autonomous systems. As a result, an EGP protocol may not always choose the lowest-cost route to the destination. BGPv4 (Border Gateway Protocol version 4) is the current EGP used in the Internet (Figure 4.1).

Figure 4.1 An IGP distributes routing information within an autonomous system; BGP distributes routing information between autonomous systems.

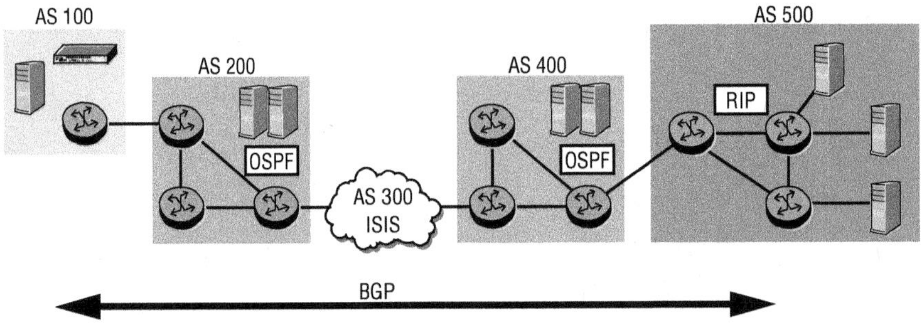

Understanding the IP Routing Table

Whether it's an IGP or EGP, the purpose of a dynamic routing protocol is to react dynamically to changes in the network topology and add or remove destinations from the route-table as the topology changes. An example of the routing table from the Alcatel-Lucent 7750 SR is shown in Listing 4.1 with a description of the fields below.

Listing 4.1 The routing table from the Alcatel-Lucent 7750 SR

```
*A:R1>config>router# show router route-table

========================================================================
Route Table (Router: Base)
========================================================================
Dest Prefix                              Type    Proto    Age         Pref
       Next Hop[Interface Name]                               Metric
------------------------------------------------------------------------
10.1.2.0/27                              Local   Local    06d08h01m   0
       toR2                                                    0
10.1.3.0/27                              Local   Local    06d08h29m   0
       toR3                                                    0
10.2.4.0/27                              Remote  OSPF     00h00m08s   10
       10.1.2.2                                                200
10.3.4.0/27                              Remote  OSPF     00h00m00s   10
       10.1.3.3                                                200
10.10.10.1/32                            Local   Local    06d08h31m   0
       system                                                  0
10.10.10.2/32                            Remote  OSPF     06d07h38m   10
       10.1.2.2                                                100
10.10.10.3/32                            Remote  OSPF     00h01m25s   10
       10.1.3.3                                                100
------------------------------------------------------------------------
No. of Routes: 7
========================================================================
```

- **Dest prefix**—The destination network. The prefix defines the network and subnet mask.
- **Type**—Indicates whether the destination prefix represents a locally attached network or a remote network.

- **Proto**—If the prefix type is `Remote`, this indicates how the router learned the prefix. This field can be RIP, OSPF, IS-IS, BGP, or static.
- **Age**—How long this entry has been in the routing table
- **Pref**—A unit of measurement that indicates the preference for one protocol over another
- **Next-Hop**—The IP address of the neighbor to which a datagram should be forwarded to reach this destination
- **Metric**—The numerical value used by the routing protocol to calculate the best route to a destination. Depending on the routing protocol, the metric is usually a hop count or a cost assigned to the network link.

From the routing table, the router Control Processor Module (CPM) constructs the forwarding table, which is loaded on the Input/Output Modules (IOMs) to forward packets.

4.2 Dynamic Routing Protocols

The purpose of a dynamic routing protocol is to find the best route to the different destinations in the network. Current IP routing protocols make a fairly simplistic assessment of the "best route." It is generally based on the number of hops to a destination, with possibly the bandwidth of the links being considered. Other factors, such as physical distance, delay, or congestion on the links, are not considered by the routing protocol.

The earliest routing protocols use a simple algorithm that simply finds the route with the lowest hop count—these are the distance-vector protocols. Later protocols such as OSPF and IS-IS use a more complex algorithm to map the network topology and find the lowest-cost route to each destination. This section provides an introductory look at the two approaches used by dynamic routing protocols to find the best routes.

Operation of Distance-Vector Routing Protocols

In a distance-vector routing algorithm (also known as the Bellman-Ford algorithm), a router passes a copy of its routing table periodically to all its neighbors. The routing table contains a metric that indicates the hop count. From its neighbor's routing tables, the router selects the route with the lowest metric as the best route to each remote destination.

With a distance-vector routing protocol, the routers do not have a complete topological view of the network; they only know the best next-hop to the destination.

Figure 4.2 shows the basic operation of a distance-vector protocol such as the RIP. There are several additional refinements that improve convergence, which are not discussed here.

Figure 4.2 Distance-vector routers periodically exchange their routing tables with their neighbors and use that information to update their route-tables.

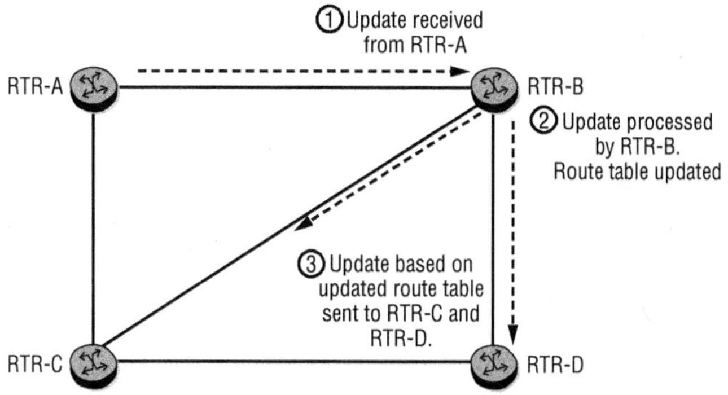

The steps as shown in Figure 4.2 are as follows:

1. RTR-B receives a routing update from RTR-A.
2. RTR-B uses the information received from RTR-A to update its routing table.
3. RTR-B then sends its routing table to RTR-D.

This process occurs in each direction between all directly connected routers.

RIPv2 is considered a modern distance-vector protocol, but is no longer widely used. The remainder of this book focuses on link-state protocols, specifically OSPF and IS-IS, the most widely used IGPs.

Operation of Link-State Routing Protocols

In a link-state routing protocol, each router distributes information about its local topology. This information includes the destination networks that are directly attached to the router and its links to other routers. There is a metric (or cost) associated with each of these links that usually represents the physical bandwidth of the interface.

In this chapter we use the term *link-state packet* (LSP) to describe the packet that carries the local topology information for a router. In OSPF, the topology information is contained in a *link-state advertisement* (LSA) which is transmitted in a *link-state update* (LSU) message. In IS-IS, the information is carried in a *link-state PDU* (protocol data unit).

When a router has received topology information from all other routers in the network, it has complete topology information about the network and can calculate the shortest path to every destination. This calculation is performed using the shortest path first (SPF) algorithm or the Dijkstra algorithm (after its inventor, Edsger W. Dijkstra).

OSPF and IS-IS are the two commonly used link-state routing protocols in IP networks. They have the following common attributes:

- An update is triggered when a link (interface) changes state. A router connected to the link sends an update to its neighbors, notifying them of the change in the topology.
- When the network is stable and no changes in state are detected, the routers send periodic Hello messages to maintain connectivity.
- Route information is classless because updates contain the subnet mask of each network being advertised.
- Summarization can be used to reduce the size and frequency of update messages.
- Authentication can be used to validate updates sent between neighbors. This ensures that accurate network topologies are created without false information.
- Updates and Hello messages are sent to a multicast address. Devices in the network that are not running the routing protocol ignore these messages.

Link-state protocols maintain three common databases. The purpose of these databases is described below:

1. The *adjacency database*, sometimes called the neighbor database, is used to keep track of all other directly connected routers. The adjacency database is built and maintained through the exchange of periodic Hello messages.
2. The *link-state database* (LSDB, or topology database) stores the most recent topology information sent by all the routers in the network. The LSDB is used to calculate the SPF tree that is used to create the routing table. The LSDB must be the same for all routers in the routing domain.
3. The *forwarding database* (the routing table) is used by the router to forward IP datagrams to the destination network.

The basic operation of a router running a link-state protocol (either OSPF or IS-IS) is shown in Figure 4.3 and described below.

- Send Hello messages out each interface to discover directly attached neighbors and build the adjacency database.

Figure 4.3 Basic operation of a link-state routing protocol on router R1.

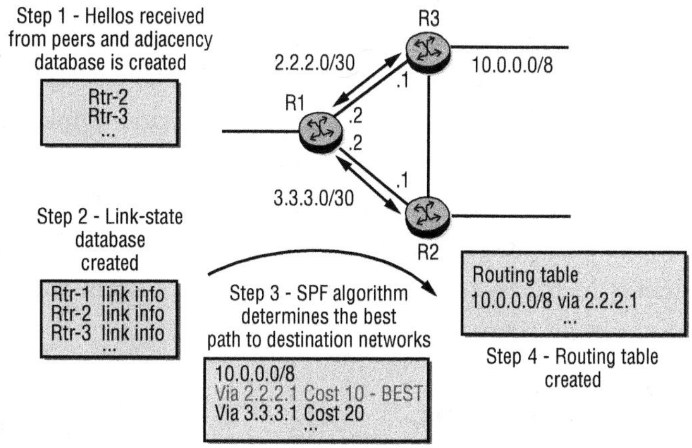

- Create a link-state packet (LSP) describing the router's local topology. This contains information about directly connected networks, links to neighbors, and their cost. Send the LSP and any other LSPs the router has received to its adjacent neighbors.
- Collect all the LSPs in the LSDB and run the SPF algorithm to build the forwarding database.
- Any time there is a change in the local topology, create a new LSP and flood it to all other routers. Rerun SPF and rebuild the forwarding database.
- When a new LSP is received from a neighbor, update the LSDB, flood the LSP to its neighbors, and rerun SPF to rebuild the forwarding database.

Comparing Distance-Vector and Link-State Protocols

An important characteristic of a routing protocol is its *convergence time*. This is the length of time from when there is a change in the network topology to the point when all of the routers in the network have updated their routing tables to reflect the new topology.

A key disadvantage of distance-vector protocols is that their convergence times are generally much greater than for link-state protocols. When a destination disappears from a distance-vector network, it may take many seconds or even minutes before the network has converged. A distance-vector network may also experience looping during this period.

Another disadvantage of distance-vector protocols is that an individual router does not have complete topology information, making distance-vector protocols unsuitable for traffic engineering.

Link-state routers have a complete and accurate topology of the network and can reliably construct the shortest path tree without routing loops. When a topology change occurs, they immediately flood updated LSPs throughout the network and rebuild the forwarding database. Convergence occurs quickly—within a few seconds even in large networks. Because each router has complete topology information, link-state routing protocols are useful for traffic engineering applications.

The primary disadvantage of link-state protocols is their scalability, as memory and processing requirements increase rapidly with network size. Both IS-IS and OSPF implement a system of hierarchy to address the scalability problem and are therefore preferred to distance-vector protocols such as RIP.

4.3 Link-State Routing Protocols

There are two important characteristics of link-state protocols that are described in more detail in the following sections. These are the SPF algorithm and the process used to reliably flood link-state information throughout the routing domain.

SPF Algorithm

Figure 4.4 shows a network topology and the LSDB associated with this topology. Each router floods information about its directly connected networks and links (with their associated costs) to all other routers. This information constitutes the LSDB. Although each router performs the SPF calculation from its own location in the network, the LSDB is identical for all routers in the network.

Figure 4.4 Network topology and its associated link-state database.

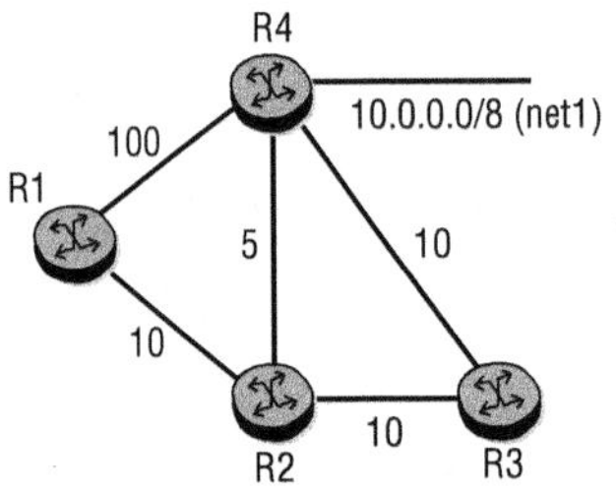

R1 LSDB	
Link	Cost
R1-R2	10
R1-R4	100
R2-R1	10
R2-R3	10
R2-R4	5
R3-R2	10
R3-R4	10
R4-R1	100
R4-R2	5
R4=R3	10
R4-net1	0

> Although Figure 4.4 shows the cost of each link, the cost, or metric, is assigned to the interface. The value can be configured to be different on each end of the link.

Once a router has an up-to-date LSDB, the SPF algorithm constructs the SPF tree, which contains the shortest path (lowest cost) to each destination in the network. The creation of the routing table from the SPF tree is straightforward.

The steps for calculating the SPF tree on R1 are shown in Figure 4.5 and occur as follows:

1. R1 puts itself as the root of the SPF tree.
2. Neighbors of R1 that are not already in the SPF tree are added to the candidate list.
3. The candidate neighbor {R1, R2, 10} with the lowest cost to the root (R2) is added to the SPF tree.
4. Neighbors of R2 that are not in the SPF tree are added to the candidate list.
5. The candidate {R2, R4, 5} with the lowest cost to the root is moved to the SPF tree. All the neighbors of R4 are moved to the candidate list. {R1, R4, 100} is removed from the candidate list because there is already a lower-cost path to R4 in the SPF tree.

Figure 4.5 The SPF calculation builds the SPF tree that contains the shortest route to every destination in the network.

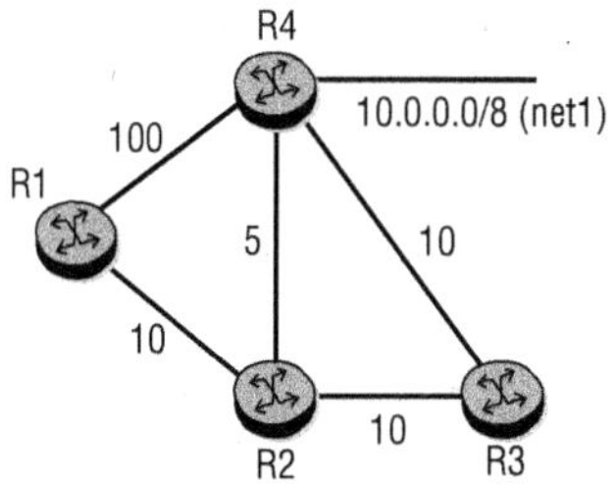

Step	Candidate links (cost)	Cost to root	SPF tree
1	—	—	R1
2	R1-R2 (10) R1-R4 (100)	10 100	R1
3	R1-R4 (100)	100	R1 —10— R2
4	R1-R4 (100) R2-R4 (5) R2-R3 (10)	100 15 20	R1 —10— R2
5	~~R1-R4 (100)~~ R2-R3 (10) R4-net1 (0) R4-R3 (10)	10 20 15 25	R1 —10— R2 —5— R4
6	R2-R3 (10) R4-R3 (10)	20 25	R1 —10— R2 —5— R4 — net1
7	~~R4-R3 (10)~~	20	R1 —10— R2 —5— R4 — net1; R2 —10— R3

6. {R4, net-1, 0} is the candidate with the lowest cost to the root and is moved to the SPF tree.
7. {R2, R3, 10} is the candidate with the lowest cost to the root and is moved to the SPF tree. {R4, R3, 10} is removed because there is already a lower-cost path to R3 in the SPF tree. All the neighbors of R3 are in the SPF tree, and because there are no more candidates in the list, the algorithm is terminated. The SPF tree is complete, and the forwarding database can be constructed.

Flooding, Sequence Numbers, and Aging

When a router recognizes a topology change (link down, neighbor down, new link, or new neighbor), it must notify its neighbors so that they can update their LSDBs, rerun the SPF calculation, and update their forwarding databases (see Figure 4.6).

Figure 4.6 After a topology change, new information is flooded to all routers, which rerun the SPF calculation to update their forwarding tables.

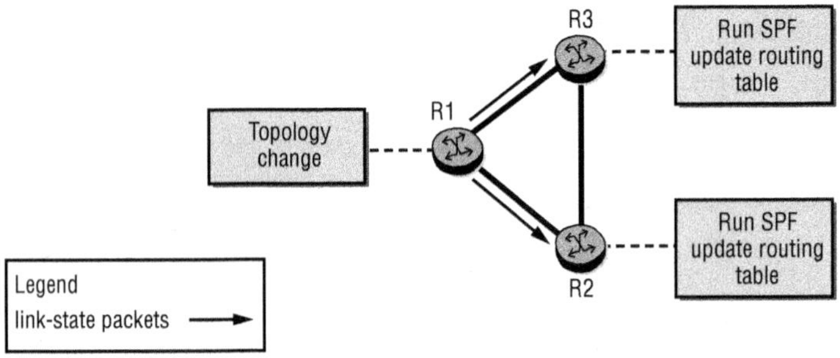

Routers must have a reliable method of flooding link-state information through the network to maintain a consistent LSDB. Routers must be able to tell if the link-state information they are receiving is more recent than the information they already have in their LSDBs. There must also be a mechanism to determine if the link-state information should be forwarded to neighbors or dropped. Otherwise, the link-state information could be flooded indefinitely (Figure 4.7).

Link-state protocols use sequence numbers to make the flooding procedure reliable and to ensure that the LSDB is up to date. The link-state packets always contain a sequence number that is maintained by the router that created the information. The sequence number remains the same from router to router during the flooding process.

Figure 4.7 Link-state information must be reliably flooded to all routers in the network.

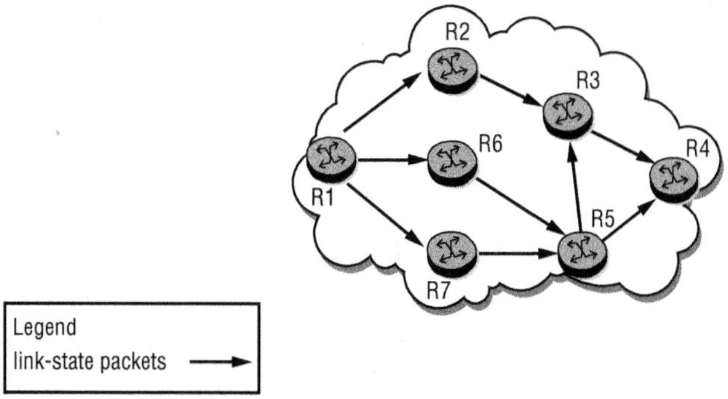

Based on the sequence number, the router follows the process below when it receives a link-state update:

- If the sequence number is lower than the one in the database, the link-state information is out of date and is discarded. Updated link-state information is transmitted to the sending router.
- If the sequence number is the same as the one in the database, the link-state information is acknowledged, then discarded.
- If the sequence number is higher than the one in the database, the link-state information is added to the LSDB, an acknowledgement is sent, and the router forwards the link-state information to its neighbors.

In Figure 4.8, R1 generates new link-state information for network A. It increments the sequence number and sends the link-state information to its neighbors.

Upon receiving the link-state information, the neighbors check the sequence number and see that it is newer. They acknowledge receipt of the information, update their LSDBs, and flood the link-state information to their neighbors (Figure 4.9). This process continues until the new information is flooded throughout the network.

In Figure 4.10, network Z connected to R4 has become unreachable. This represents a topology change, so R4 floods new link-state information with a higher sequence number. The link-state information generated by R4 is received at R1 from both R2 and R6. Assume that R1 receives the update from R2 before R6. When R1 receives the update from R2, the sequence number is higher than the one in the database, so the database is updated. When it receives the update from R6, the sequence number of the update matches the sequence number in the database, and the information is ignored.

Figure 4.8 After a topology change, new link-state information with a higher sequence number is sent to neighbors.

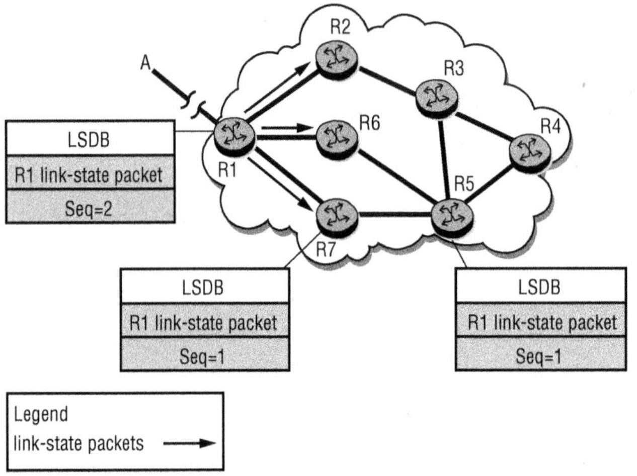

Figure 4.9 After receiving new information, routers R2, R6, and R7 acknowledge receipt, update their LSDBs, and flood the new information to their neighbors.

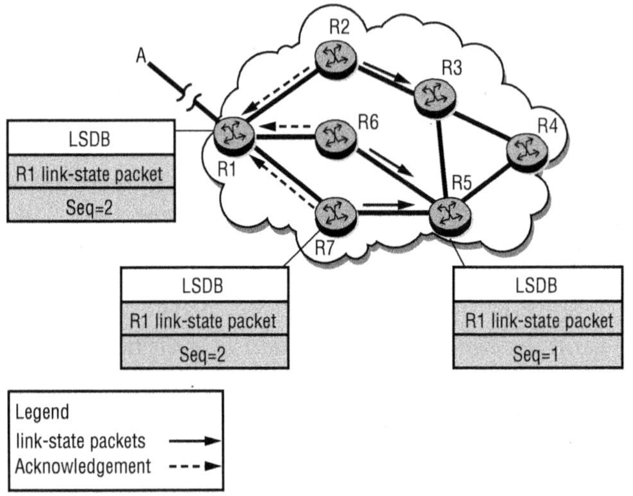

If network Z goes down and then comes back up soon afterward, R4 will generate two successive link-state updates. If R1 receives the older information from R6 after it has already received the newer information from R2, the older information will be ignored because the sequence number is lower.

Figure 4.10 Router R1 examines the sequence number on updates to discover which contain new information.

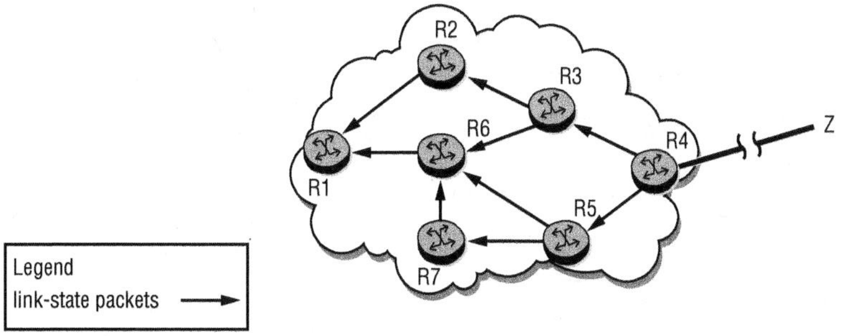

Link-state information also includes an age field. The age is changed as the information is flooded and while it is held in the LSDB. When the link-state information reaches its maximum age, it is no longer considered valid and is removed from the LSDB. However, the router that generated the information will always generate new link-state information with a higher sequence number before the maximum age is reached. Aging ensures that information from routers that are no longer part of the topology is eventually removed from the database. A router can also use maximum age to force the other routers to remove link-state information from their databases.

To summarize, the reliable flooding of link-state information is critical for the proper operation of a link-state network. Figure 4.11 summarizes the algorithm used to ensure reliable flooding. Note that IS-IS routers do not always generate an acknowledgement for information updates, but use another mechanism to ensure that the topological database is always up to date.

4.4 Role of BGP in Internet Routing

Although this book is primarily concerned with routing within a single service provider or enterprise network (IGP routing), an overview of BGP is included to complete the picture of routing on the Internet and to provide a contrast with the IGP protocols.

Figure 4.11 The algorithm that describes the processing that occurs when link-state updates are received.

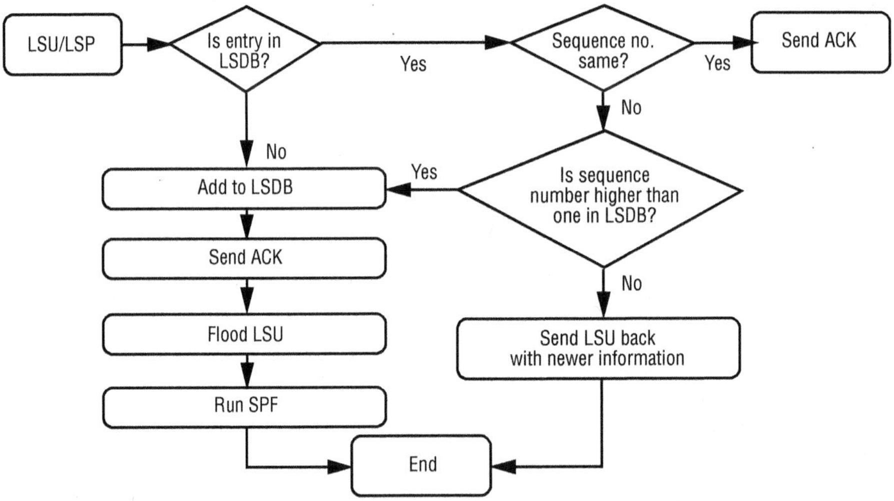

The IGP is designed to route between networks within an organization. Network topology information from within one organization is typically not advertised to other organizations. However, some routing information must be exchanged between organizations in order to support the flow of data between them. More control is required over the way that traffic flows between organizations—it is not always the shortest path that is preferred. BGPv4 provides many features to control traffic flows between organizations and is the EGP used on the Internet. BGPv4 is also able to scale to very large networks, which is an important requirement in order to manage the 300,000+ routes of the Internet!

BGP is a path-vector protocol (similar to distance-vector) that uses several criteria to choose a preferred path, including the number of autonomous systems that must be traversed. We say that BGP performs policy-based routing because policies can be used in many different ways to influence the route chosen as the preferred route.

Autonomous Systems

Figure 4.12 shows an enterprise network, content provider, and several ISPs—a typical configuration that would make up a small part of the Internet. Note that each separate network uses a different IGP for routing within the network. BGP is the protocol that allows for the exchange of route information between these diverse networks.

Figure 4.12 Different IGPs control routing within a network; BGP distributes routing information between networks.

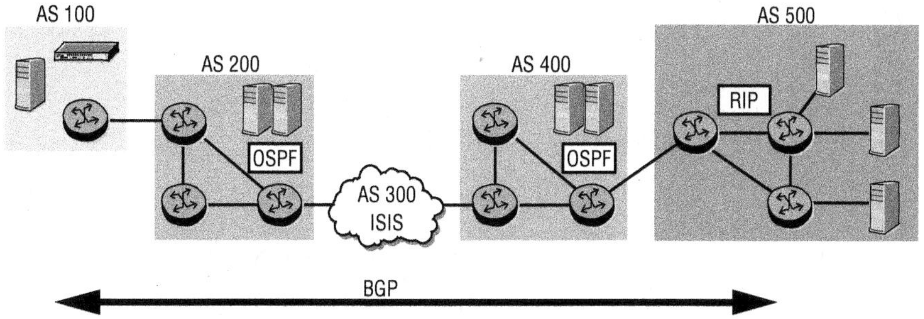

In BGP routing, we define an *autonomous system* (AS) as a network or group of networks and networking equipment under a common administration. An IGP (such as OSPF) is used to exchange routing information within the AS, whereas BGP is used to exchange routing information between ASs.

BGP sessions between routers in different ASs are known as *external BGP sessions* (EBGP), whereas sessions between routers in the same AS are known as *internal BGP sessions* (IBGP). Regardless of the type, a BGP session between two devices is referred to as a *neighbor* or *peer* session. A BGP router is also referred to as a *BGP speaker.*

BGP is not a discovery protocol, and BGP routers are not always directly connected to their neighbors. Each router must be manually configured to connect to other BGP routers using TCP/IP (Transmission Control Protocol/Internet Protocol). For example, two routers on different edges of a large service provider network may form an IBGP peering session. An IGP is required for the TCP/IP sessions between the BGP peers and to route traffic through the AS (Figure 4.13).

Operation of BGP

BGP is administratively much more complex than the IGPs because the route selected is not simply the one with the shortest path. Adding to the complexity of BGP is the fact that the number of routes exchanged is much larger than in an IGP environment. The increased size of the tables means that factors such as CPU loading, memory utilization, update generation, and route processing have greater implications in BGP. These factors affect convergence time, and, as a result, the convergence time for BGP in a large service provider network may be as long as several minutes.

Figure 4.13 BGP peering sessions between routers in the same AS are IBGP sessions; peering sessions between routers in different ASs are EBGP sessions.

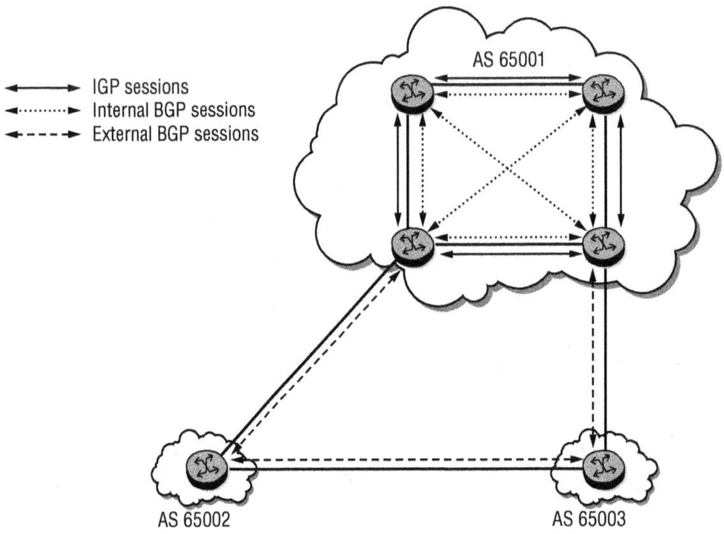

The criteria that BGP uses for route selection are very different from an IGP. In an IGP environment, the routes are selected based on one metric such as cost or hop count. However, in BGP the choice may not be solely based on the shortest path; it may be made for financial, security, or geographical reasons. For example, in the topology in Figure 4.14, it may be desired that all traffic enter and leave AS 65200 by router A and the path from router B be used as backup. This type of rule can be enforced through a BGP policy.

BGP Topologies

Owing to the administrative complexity of BGP, it is not generally recommended to run BGP unless necessary. Whether you choose to run BGP or not depends to a large extent on your network topology. There are three different network topologies to consider in BGP:

- **Stub**—A stub network has a single connection to the service provider and Internet.
- **Multi-homed stub**—A multi-homed stub has multiple connections to the service provider and Internet but does not carry any transit traffic.
- **Transit**—A transit network carries traffic that neither originates in nor is destined for the local network.

Figure 4.14 BGP policies can enforce which routes are used for traffic entering and leaving an AS.

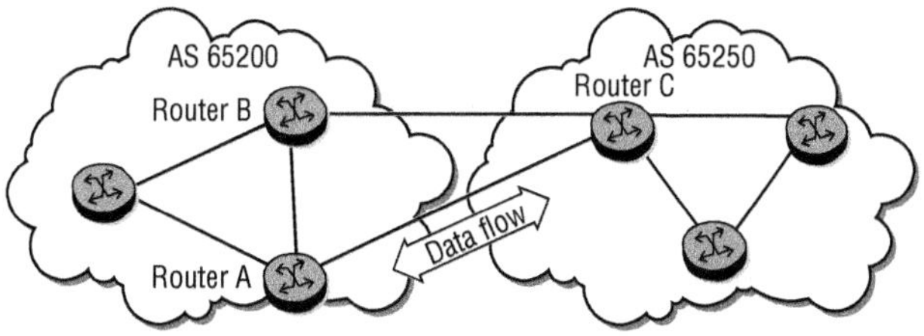

Typically, a stub network does not require BGP for routing to the Internet and will simply use a default route to the externally connected router (enterprise customer 1 in Figure 4.15). Even if the enterprise has multiple connection points to its external service provider, it may not need BGP. It can simply use a default route to the nearest exit point.

However, it is increasingly more common for an enterprise to have external connections to more than one external service provider, and it may be desirable to use BGP to manage the distribution of routes and traffic between the different providers. In this situation, a key policy requirement is usually that the enterprise is not used to route traffic between the service provider networks. All traffic that crosses the links to the external networks should either originate from or be destined for the enterprise network. This topology is known as a multi-homed stub network (Figure 4.15).

Service providers use BGP to exchange routes and thus control traffic flow among themselves. When an AS is carrying traffic that neither originates from, nor is destined for that network, it is known as a *transit network* (see Figure 4.16). Service providers often charge their customers (enterprises or other service providers) to provide transit services. The exchange of traffic between two service providers is usually governed by a peering arrangement. A service provider may have several peering arrangements with different service providers and a need to control their traffic flow accordingly.

This overview of BGP is intended to complete the picture of routing on the Internet and to provide a contrast with the IGP protocols. Table 4.1 shows the differences and similarities of the routing protocols supported on the 7750 SR platforms. RIP, OSPF, and IS-IS are the IGPs; BGP is the EGP.

Table 4.1 Comparison of Common Routing Protocols

Feature	BGP	OSPF/IS-IS	RIPv2
Updates	Incremental	Incremental	Periodic
Update type	Unicast	Multicast	Broadcast/Multicast
Authentication	MD5	Simple and MD5	Simple and MD5
Metric	Multiple	Cost	Hop
Metric type	Path vector	Link-state	Distance-vector
Topology size	Very large	Large	Small
Transport protocol	TCP	IP/Layer 2	UDP

Figure 4.15 Enterprise 1 has only one connection to its ISP and uses a default route. Enterprise 2 is multi-homed to two different ISPs and uses BGP to direct traffic entering and leaving its network.

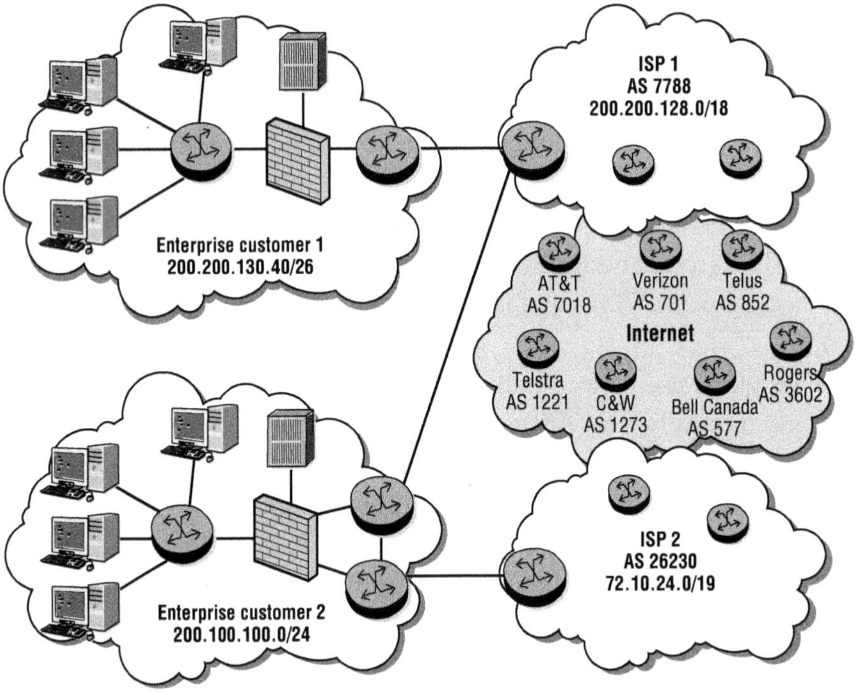

Configuring BGP

Before moving on to our in-depth look at IGPs, we will work through an example showing the configuration of BGP on the 7750 SR, using the topology in Figure 4.17.

Figure 4.16 Traffic that neither originates in nor is destined for a specific network is transit traffic. Network service providers usually charge for carrying transit traffic.

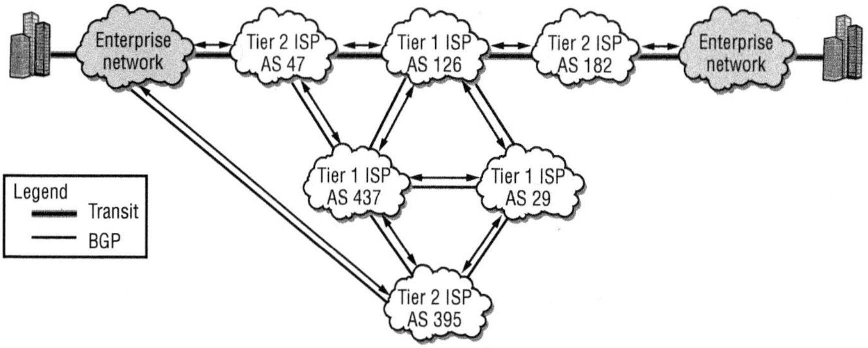

Figure 4.17 Configuring BGP between three autonomous systems.

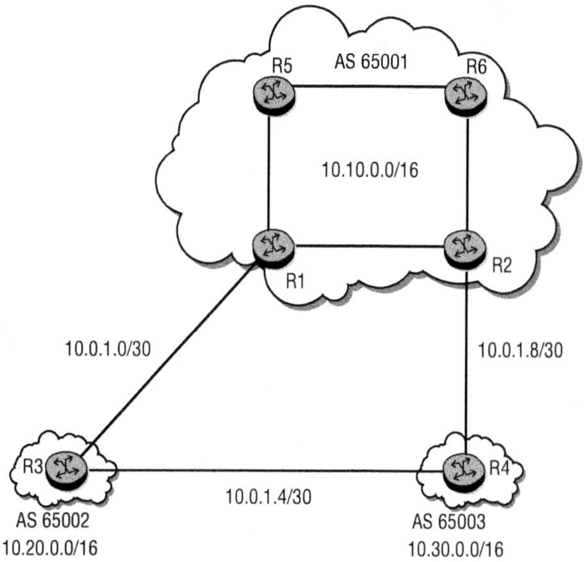

Our configuration example focuses on router R1 in autonomous system 65001. BGP requires an IGP for distribution of routing information within the autonomous system. We'll use OSPF as our IGP and show the basic configuration on R1 in Listing 4.2. The other routers of AS 65001 are configured in a similar manner.

Listing 4.2 R1 is configured to exchange routes with its neighbors R2 and R5. The route-table contains all the internal routes from AS 65001.

```
*A:R1# configure router ospf area 0
*A:R1>config>router>ospf>area$ interface "system"
*A:R1>config>router>ospf>area>if$ exit
*A:R1>config>router>ospf>area# interface "toR2"
interface-type point-to-point
*A:R1>config>router>ospf>area# interface "toR5"
interface-type point-to-point
*A:R1>config>router>ospf>area# exit all
*A:R1# show router route-table

========================================================================
Route-Table (Router: Base)
========================================================================
Dest Prefix                                 Type     Proto    Age          Pref
       Next Hop[Interface Name]                                  Metric
------------------------------------------------------------------------
10.0.1.0/30                                 Local    Local    00h05m25s    0
       toR3                                                      0
10.1.2.0/27                                 Local    Local    03d04h00m    0
       toR2                                                      0
10.1.5.0/27                                 Local    Local    03d04h00m    0
       toR5                                                      0
10.2.6.0/27                                 Remote   OSPF     00h10m18s    10
       10.1.2.2                                                  200
10.5.6.0/27                                 Remote   OSPF     00h08m07s    10
       10.1.5.5                                                  200
10.10.10.1/32                               Local    Local    03d04h00m    0
       system                                                    0
10.10.10.2/32                               Remote   OSPF     00h12m24s    10
       10.1.2.2                                                  100
10.10.10.5/32                               Remote   OSPF     00h08m28s    10
       10.1.5.5                                                  100
10.10.10.6/32                               Remote   OSPF     00h07m19s    10
       10.1.2.2                                                  200
------------------------------------------------------------------------
No. of Routes: 9
========================================================================
*A:R1#
```

Once OSPF is operational in the AS, BGP peering sessions can be established with the other routers of the AS. It is standard practice to peer with all transit routers in the AS—in this case, routers R2, R5, and R6. Note that the system addresses are used for IBGP peers (Listing 4.3).

Listing 4.3 Create peering sessions with all BGP routers in AS 65001

```
*A:R1# configure router autonomous-system 65001
*A:R1# configure router bgp
*A:R1>config>router>bgp$ group Internal_peers
*A:R1>config>router>bgp>group$ peer-as 65001
*A:R1>config>router>bgp>group$ neighbor 10.10.10.2
*A:R1>config>router>bgp>group>neighbor$ exit
*A:R1>config>router>bgp>group# neighbor 10.10.10.5
*A:R1>config>router>bgp>group>neighbor$ exit
*A:R1>config>router>bgp>group# neighbor 10.10.10.6
*A:R1>config>router>bgp>group>neighbor$ exit
*A:R1>config>router>bgp>group# show router bgp summary
===============================================================================
 BGP Router ID:10.10.10.1       AS:65001       Local AS:65001
===============================================================================
BGP Admin State         : Up          BGP Oper State              : Up
Total Peer Groups       : 1           Total Peers                 : 3
Total BGP Paths         : 6           Total Path Memory           : 720
Total IPv4 Remote Rts   : 0           Total IPv4 Rem. Active Rts  : 0
Total IPv6 Remote Rts   : 0           Total IPv6 Rem. Active Rts  : 0
Total Supressed Rts     : 0           Total Hist. Rts             : 0
Total Decay Rts         : 0

Total VPN Peer Groups   : 0           Total VPN Peers             : 0
Total VPN Local Rts     : 0
Total VPN-IPv4 Rem. Rts : 0           Total VPN-IPv4 Rem. Act. Rts: 0
Total VPN-IPv6 Rem. Rts : 0           Total VPN-IPv6 Rem. Act. Rts: 0
Total L2-VPN Rem. Rts   : 0           Total L2VPN Rem. Act. Rts   : 0
Total VPN Supp. Rts     : 0           Total VPN Hist. Rts         : 0
Total VPN Decay Rts     : 0
Total MVPN-IPv4 Rem Rts : 0           Total MVPN-IPv4 Rem Act Rts : 0
Total MDT-SAFI Rem Rts  : 0           Total MDT-SAFI Rem Act Rts  : 0
```

(continued)

Listing 4.3 *(continued)*

```
===============================================================================
BGP Summary
===============================================================================
Neighbor
                AS PktRcvd InQ  Up/Down   State|Rcv/Act/Sent (Addr Family)
                   PktSent OutQ
-------------------------------------------------------------------------------
10.10.10.2
                   65001       3    0 00h00m46s 0/0/0 (IPv4)
                               5    0
10.10.10.5
                   65001       2    0 00h00m27s 0/0/0 (IPv4)
                               2    0
10.10.10.6
                   65001       2    0 00h00m13s 0/0/0 (IPv4)
                               2    0
===============================================================================
*A:R1>config>router>bgp>group#
```

The next step is to establish peering sessions with the EBGP peers, in this case, R3. External peers are usually directly connected, and the interface address is used for peering (Listing 4.4).

Listing 4.4 Create the peering session with external peers

```
*A:R1>config>router>bgp>group# exit
*A:R1>config>router>bgp# group External_peers
*A:R1>config>router>bgp>group$ peer-as 65002
*A:R1>config>router>bgp>group$ neighbor 10.0.1.2
*A:R1>config>router>bgp>group>neighbor$ exit
*A:R1>config>router>bgp>group#
*A:R1>config>router>bgp>group# show router bgp summary
===============================================================================
 BGP Router ID:10.10.10.1       AS:65001       Local AS:65001
===============================================================================
BGP Admin State         : Up          BGP Oper State              : Up
Total Peer Groups       : 2           Total Peers                 : 4
Total BGP Paths         : 6           Total Path Memory           : 720
```

```
Total IPv4 Remote Rts    : 0          Total IPv4 Rem. Active Rts  : 0
Total IPv6 Remote Rts    : 0          Total IPv6 Rem. Active Rts  : 0
Total Supressed Rts      : 0          Total Hist. Rts             : 0
Total Decay Rts          : 0

Total VPN Peer Groups    : 0          Total VPN Peers             : 0
Total VPN Local Rts      : 0
Total VPN-IPv4 Rem. Rts  : 0          Total VPN-IPv4 Rem. Act. Rts: 0
Total VPN-IPv6 Rem. Rts  : 0          Total VPN-IPv6 Rem. Act. Rts: 0
Total L2-VPN Rem. Rts    : 0          Total L2VPN Rem. Act. Rts   : 0
Total VPN Supp. Rts      : 0          Total VPN Hist. Rts         : 0
Total VPN Decay Rts      : 0
Total MVPN-IPv4 Rem Rts  : 0          Total MVPN-IPv4 Rem Act Rts : 0
Total MDT-SAFI Rem Rts   : 0          Total MDT-SAFI Rem Act Rts  : 0

===============================================================================
BGP Summary
===============================================================================
Neighbor
                AS PktRcvd InQ  Up/Down   State|Rcv/Act/Sent (Addr Family)
                   PktSent OutQ
-------------------------------------------------------------------------------
10.0.1.2
                   65002       2    0 00h00m11s 0/0/0 (IPv4)
                               2    0
10.10.10.2
                   65001      36    0 00h17m27s 0/0/0 (IPv4)
                              39    0
10.10.10.5
                   65001      35    0 00h17m08s 0/0/0 (IPv4)
                              36    0
10.10.10.6
                   65001      35    0 00h16m54s 0/0/0 (IPv4)
                              35    0
===============================================================================
*A:R1>config>router>bgp>group#
```

Listing 4.4 shows that R1 has established four BGP peering sessions, but as you see in Listing 4.5, R1 is not learning or advertising any BGP routes.

Listing 4.5 By default, only routes learned through BGP are advertised to BGP peers.

```
*A:R1# show router bgp routes
===============================================================================
 BGP Router ID:10.10.10.1       AS:65001       Local AS:65001
===============================================================================
 Legend -
 Status codes  : u - used, s - suppressed, h - history, d - decayed,
 * - valid
 Origin codes  : i - IGP, e - EGP, ? - incomplete, > - best

===============================================================================
BGP IPv4 Routes
===============================================================================
Flag  Network                                            LocalPref   MED
      Nexthop                                                        VPNLabel
      As-Path
-------------------------------------------------------------------------------
No Matching Entries Found
===============================================================================
*A:R1#
```

By default on the 7750 SR, only routes that were learned through BGP are advertised to BGP neighbors. An export policy is required to have routes be advertised by BGP.

Configuring Export Policies

By default, the 7750 SR does not advertise routes learned through one routing protocol to another routing protocol. In the situation above, R1 has learned several routes through OSPF, but none of these routes is advertised to its BGP neighbors. Likewise, any routes learned through BGP would not be advertised in OSPF. To change this default behavior, we need an export policy. Export and import policies are often confused, but it is export policies that are used to export routes from one protocol into another. Import policies are used less frequently and are used only to restrict the routes that are learned from a neighbor.

On the 7750 SR, an export policy is configured in the `configure router policy-options` context. The statement `begin` is required to begin the policy configuration, and then the `commit` statement to cause the changes to take effect.

Policies are defined as templates and then applied with the `export` statement in the `configure router bgp` context.

In our example in Listing 4.6, we create a static route to summarize our local networks and then advertise it to our external neighbors using an export policy. The `prefix-list` is used to control precisely what routes are exported to BGP. It is possible to export all the OSPF routes from the AS to the external peers, but best practice is to create a summarized route to advertise to the neighbors. Advertising a summarized route reduces the number of advertisements and also reduces the effect that local topology changes will have on BGP.

Listing 4.6 An export policy is used to advertise a summarized route to BGP peers.

```
*A:R1# configure router
*A:R1>config>router# static-route 10.10.0.0/16 black-hole
*A:R1>config>router# policy-options
*A:R1>config>router>policy-options# begin
*A:R1>config>router>policy-options# prefix-list Summary
*A:R1>config>router>policy-options>prefix-list$ prefix 10.10.0.0/16 exact
*A:R1>config>router>policy-options>prefix-list$ exit
*A:R1>config>router>policy-options# policy-statement Advertise_summary
*A:R1>config>router>policy-options>policy-statement$ entry 10
*A:R1>config>router>policy-options>policy-statement>entry$ from
prefix-list"Summary"
*A:R1>config>router>policy-options>policy-statement>entry# action accept
*A:R1>config>router>policy-options>policy-statement>entry>action# exit
*A:R1>config>router>policy-options>policy-statement>entry# exit
*A:R1>config>router>policy-options>policy-statement# exit
*A:R1>config>router>policy-options# commit
*A:R1>config>router>policy-options# exit
*A:R1>config>router# bgp
*A:R1>config>router>bgp# group "External_peers"
*A:R1>config>router>bgp>group# export "Advertise_summary"
*A:R1>config>router>bgp>group# exit all
*A:R1# show router bgp neighbor 10.0.1.2 advertised-routes
===============================================================================
 BGP Router ID:10.10.10.1         AS:65001         Local AS:65001
===============================================================================
 Legend -
```

(continued)

Listing 4.6 *(continued)*

```
 Status codes  : u - used, s - suppressed, h - history, d - decayed,
 * - valid
 Origin codes  : i - IGP, e - EGP, ? - incomplete, > - best

===============================================================================
BGP IPv4 Routes
===============================================================================
Flag  Network                                          LocalPref   MED
      Nexthop                                                      VPNLabel
      As-Path
-------------------------------------------------------------------------------
?     10.10.0.0/16                                     n/a         None
      10.0.1.1                                                     -
      65001
-------------------------------------------------------------------------------
Routes : 1
===============================================================================
*A:R1#
```

If we create similar policies in the other two autonomous systems and create EBGP peering sessions for R2 and R4, we will see route advertisements for their networks as well. Listing 4.7 shows that R1 receives advertisements for both external networks from its EBGP peer, R3, and from its IBGP peer, R2.

Listing 4.7 AS 65002 and AS 65003 are advertising their summarized networks. R1 learns about these networks from both R3 and R2.

```
*A:R1# show router bgp routes
===============================================================================
 BGP Router ID:10.10.10.1       AS:65001       Local AS:65001
===============================================================================
 Legend -
 Status codes  : u - used, s - suppressed, h - history, d - decayed,
 * - valid
 Origin codes  : i - IGP, e - EGP, ? - incomplete, > - best

===============================================================================
BGP IPv4 Routes
===============================================================================
```

```
Flag  Network                                          LocalPref   MED
      Nexthop                                                      VPNLabel
      As-Path
-----------------------------------------------------------------------
u*>?  10.20.0.0/16                                     None        None
      10.0.1.2                                                     -
      65002
*?    10.20.0.0/16                                     100         None
      10.10.10.2                                                   -
      65003 65002
u*>?  10.30.0.0/16                                     100         None
      10.10.10.2                                                   -
      65003
*?    10.30.0.0/16                                     None        None
      10.0.1.2                                                     -
      65002 65003
-----------------------------------------------------------------------
Routes : 4
=======================================================================
```

The routes marked with a "u" in Listing 4.7 are those that are chosen by R1 as the active routes. These appear in the route-table seen in Listing 4.8. The choice of which routes are used is controlled by the BGP route selection process and the use of BGP policies. In this example, the routes chosen are those with the shortest number of AS hops.

Listing 4.8 R1 selects R3 as the next-hop for 10.20.0.0/16 and R2 as the next-hop for 10.30.0.0/16. This selection can be controlled through BGP policies.

```
*A:R1# show router route-table

=======================================================================
Route-Table (Router: Base)
=======================================================================
Dest Prefix                             Type    Proto    Age         Pref
       Next Hop[Interface Name]                                Metric
-----------------------------------------------------------------------
10.0.1.0/30                             Local   Local    02h51m46s   0
       toR3                                                    0
```

(continued)

Listing 4.8 *(continued)*

```
10.1.2.0/27                                   Local   Local    03d06h47m   0
       toR2                                                    0
10.1.5.0/27                                   Local   Local    03d06h47m   0
       toR5                                                    0
10.2.6.0/27                                   Remote  OSPF     02h56m40s   10
       10.1.2.2                                                200
10.5.6.0/27                                   Remote  OSPF     02h54m29s   10
       10.1.5.5                                                200
10.10.0.0/16                                  Remote  Static   02h00m16s   5
       Black Hole                                              1
10.10.10.1/32                                 Local   Local    03d06h47m   0
       system                                                  0
10.10.10.2/32                                 Remote  OSPF     02h58m46s   10
       10.1.2.2                                                100
10.10.10.5/32                                 Remote  OSPF     02h54m35s   10
       10.1.5.5                                                100
10.10.10.6/32                                 Remote  OSPF     02h53m26s   10
       10.1.2.2                                                200
10.20.0.0/16                                  Remote  BGP      00h05m39s   170
       10.0.1.2                                                0
10.30.0.0/16                                  Remote  BGP      00h01m28s   170
       10.1.2.2                                                0
-------------------------------------------------------------------------------
No. of Routes: 12
===============================================================================
*A:R1#
```

4.5 RTM and Route Selection

We have seen that there are several different ways by which a router can learn of network destinations in an IP network:

- Directly attached networks (Local)
- Administratively configured networks (Static)
- Dynamically learned networks (RIP, IS-IS, OSPF, BGP)

The output of a 7750 SR routing table in Listing 4.9 is an example in which the router has learned its routes from different sources. What happens if a router learns the same prefix from two different sources? How does it decide which one to use in the routing table? This question is especially important if the two entries have a different next-hop for the same prefix.

Listing 4.9 A prefix may be learned from several different routing protocols, but the prefix only appears once in the route-table.

```
*A:R1>config>router>bgp>group# show router route-table

==========================================================================
Route Table (Router: Base)
==========================================================================
Dest Prefix                             Type    Proto   Age         Pref
       Next Hop[Interface Name]                              Metric
--------------------------------------------------------------------------
0.0.0.0/0                               Remote  Static  00h06m00s   5
       10.1.2.2                                              1
10.1.2.0/27                             Local   Local   06d08h18m   0
       toR2                                                  0
10.1.3.0/27                             Local   Local   06d08h46m   0
       toR3                                                  0
10.10.10.1/32                           Local   Local   06d08h48m   0
       system                                                0
10.10.10.2/32                           Remote  OSPF    06d07h55m   10
       10.1.2.2                                              100
10.10.10.3/32                           Remote  OSPF    00h18m26s   10
       10.1.3.3                                              100
10.20.0.0/16                            Remote  BGP     00h00m19s   170
       10.1.2.2                                              0
10.30.0.0/16                            Remote  BGP     00h00m23s   170
       10.1.2.2                                              0
--------------------------------------------------------------------------
No. of Routes: 8
==========================================================================
```

The answer to this question can be found in the "`Pref`" (short for preference) field of the route table. Each routing protocol in operation on the router uses its standard algorithm (link-state or distance-vector) to find the best route to all the destinations in the routing domain. The routing protocol presents these routes to a process known as the route table manager (RTM). The RTM chooses from the prefixes offered by each routing protocol and adds those routes to the route-table, which is then used to build the FIB (forwarding information base), as shown in Figure 4.18.

Figure 4.18 Each routing protocol offers its routes to the RTM. The RTM selects routes based on the preference value for the protocol.

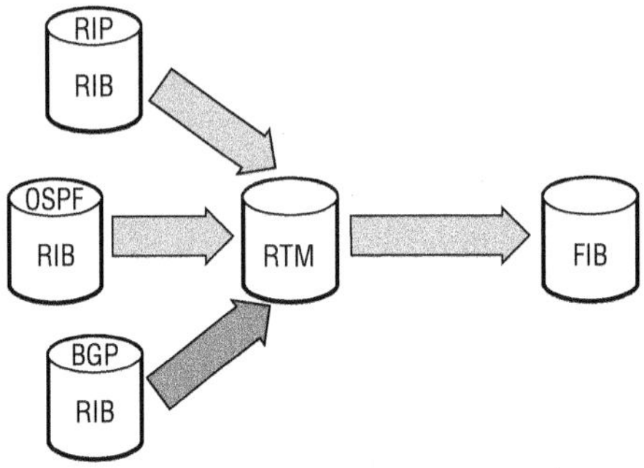

To chose the route, the RTM uses *protocol preference*, which is a value associated with each routing protocol. The default values for protocol preference on the 7750 SR are shown in Table 4.2. Note that the lower the value, the more the protocol is preferred.

Table 4.2 Routing Protocols with Default Preference Values

Route Type	Preference	Configurable?
Directly attached	0	No
Static	5	Yes
OSPF internal	10	Yes
IS-IS Level 1 internal	15	Yes
IS-IS Level 2 internal	18	Yes
RIP	100	Yes
OSPF external	150	Yes
IS-IS Level 1 external	160	Yes
IS-IS Level 2 external	165	Yes
BGP	170	Yes

From Table 4.2, you can see that a directly attached network is the most preferred with a value of zero and that this value cannot be changed. Static networks are the next most preferred, although this value can be changed. The preference value can be set for an entire protocol, so that IS-IS is always preferred over OSPF, for example.

It is important to remember that preference is used to select a route only when two *identical* prefixes are available from different protocols. For example, if 10.0.0.0/24 is learned through RIP and 10.0.0.0/16 is learned through OSPF, they will *both* appear in the routing table because they are different prefixes (the subnet mask, or number of matching bits, is different). Furthermore, a packet to destination 10.0.0.10 will be forwarded using the RIP route, even though OSPF is more preferred than RIP. This is because the RIP route is a more specific match than the OSPF route (24 bits instead of 16).

Chapter Review

Now that you have completed this chapter, you should be able to:

- Describe the difference between an IGP and an EGP.
- Describe the difference between a distance-vector and a link-state routing protocol.
- Explain the different fields in the route-table.
- Describe how a distance vector builds its route-table.
- List the common attributes of link-state routing protocols.
- Describe the basic operation of a link-state protocol.
- Explain how the SPF algorithm operates to build the route-table.
- Describe the flooding mechanism used to flood link-state information.
- Explain the purpose of BGP and autonomous systems.
- List the different BGP topologies.
- Explain the difference between IBGP and EBGP sessions.
- Configure and verify IBGP and EBGP peering sessions.
- Create and apply an export policy to advertise a static route in BGP.
- Verify the exchange and selection of BGP routes between peers.
- Describe the operation of the RTM.

Post-Assessment

The following questions will test your knowledge and prepare you for the Alcatel-Lucent NRS II Certification Exam. Compare your response with the answers listed in Appendix A. You can also use the CD that accompanies this book to take all the assessment tests and review the answers.

1. Which of the following is the primary goal of an IGP?
   - **A.** To facilitate load balancing
   - **B.** To provide the lowest-cost route to networks within an autonomous system
   - **C.** To provide the best route to Internet destinations considering policy rules and cost
   - **D.** To distribute aggregate routes
2. Which statement is true about link-state protocols?
   - **A.** Sequence numbers are incremented as the updates are passed from router to router.
   - **B.** Updates and Hello messages are sent to a broadcast address so they can be seen by all routers running the protocol.
   - **C.** When an interface changes state, a routing update is flooded to all routers in the domain.
   - **D.** Routing tables are periodically sent between neighbors.
3. What action is taken when a router receives a new LSP from a neighbor?
   - **A.** Run SPF on the LSDB and flood a SYNC message to all routers to start a query and reply process.
   - **B.** Run SPF on the LSDB and send the results of the SPF calculation to its neighbors.
   - **C.** Run an SPF calculation to update the route table and send incremental updates to the routers in its adjacency database.
   - **D.** Flood the LSP to all its neighbors and then run an SPF calculation to update the route table.

4. Which statement is correct regarding the age and sequence number of an LSP as it is flooded throughout a network?

   A. The sequence number and age are increased.

   B. The sequence number and age are not changed.

   C. The sequence number is not changed, but the age is changed.

   D. The sequence number is increased, but the age is held constant.

5. Which statement is true regarding BGP?

   A. BGP discovers its neighbors through the use of Hello messages.

   B. BGP is a path-vector protocol that selects the route that is the least number of hops between autonomous systems.

   C. A BGP policy may cause BGP to choose a route that is not the shortest path to the destination.

   D. BGP routers are always directly connected to their neighbors.

   E. The primary objective of BGP is to offer the lowest-cost route to destination networks.

6. Which of the following is an exterior gateway routing protocol?

   A. OSPF

   B. BGP

   C. IS-IS

   D. RIP

7. Which of the following is a link-state routing protocol?

   A. LDP

   B. BGP

   C. IS-IS

   D. RSVP-TE

   E. RIP

8. What does the `Type` field indicate in the Alcatel-Lucent 7750 SR route table?

A. The protocol used to learn the route

B. Whether the prefix is internal or external

C. Whether the route represents a locally attached network or a remote network

D. Relative weight of a route that can be used as a tie breaker

E. Whether the route is active or not

9. Which field is *not* present in the Alcatel-Lucent 7750 SR route-table?

A. Protocol

B. Source address

C. Age

D. Preference

E. Next-hop

10. Which statement is true about distance-vector protocols?

A. Each router is aware of the entire network topology.

B. Updates received by a router must be used to update its routing table before an update can be sent to other neighbors.

C. Routing updates are flooded throughout the network.

D. Traffic engineering is an option.

E. Routing updates are flooded throughout an area.

11. Which of the following is *not* a database required by a link-state protocol?

A. Adjacency database

B. Link-state database

C. Metric database

D. Forwarding database

12. What action is taken when a router receives an LSP with a lower sequence number than an LSP already in the LSDB?

   A. An ACK is sent to the sending router, and the LSP is discarded.

   B. The received LSP is discarded, and an updated LSP is transmitted to the sending router.

   C. The received LSP is discarded, and a SYNC message is sent to all neighbors.

   D. The received LSP is silently discarded.

13. What action is taken when an LSP is received with the same sequence number as one already in the database?

   A. An ACK is sent to the sending router, and the LSP is discarded.

   B. The received LSP is discarded, and the LSP in the database is sent to the sender.

   C. The received LSP is discarded, and a SYNC message is sent to all neighbors.

   D. The received LSP is silently discarded.

14. An Alcatel-Lucent 7750 SR with default settings has the following routes in its route table:

```
Dest Prefix         Proto    Pref        Next Hop[Interface Name]
192.168.0.0/16      OSPF     10          toR2
192.168.0.0/20      ISIS     18          toR3
192.168.100.0/24    BGP      170         toR4
0.0.0.0/0           Static   5           toR5
```

   A packet with destination address 192.168.10.111 is forwarded by the router. Which router is the next hop for this packet?

   A. Next hop is R2.

   B. Next hop is R3.

   C. Next hop is R4.

   D. Next hop is R5.

   E. The packet is discarded.

15. A router (R1) with default configuration is running OSPF and IS-IS and learns a network prefix through both protocols. OSPF has two paths to the destination, through R2 with a metric of 200 and through R3 with a metric of 1,000. IS-IS has one path to the destination, through R4 with a metric of 100. What will be the next-hop chosen for this destination, and what will become the next-hop if this path fails?

A. R2 will be the next-hop, and R3 will become the next-hop if R2 fails.

B. R2 will be the next-hop, and R4 will become the next-hop if R2 fails.

C. R4 will be the next-hop, and R2 will become the next-hop if R4 fails.

D. R3 will be the next-hop, and R4 will become the next-hop if R3 fails.

E. R3 will be the next-hop, and R2 will become the next-hop if R3 fails.

5 Introduction to OSPF

The Alcatel-Lucent NRS II exam topics covered in this chapter include the following:

- Overview of OSPF operation
- The OSPF database
- OSPF messages
- Establishing an adjacency
- Flooding LSAs
- Router LSA details
- The designated router and Network LSAs
- Configuring OSPF
- Other OSPF features

This chapter introduces the fundamental operation and components of a single-area Open Shortest Path First (OSPF) network. The contents of the OSPF database are described as well as the method used for flooding link-state advertisements (LSAs) to keep the database up to date. We look at the steps that occur in the formation of the OSPF adjacency and the messages that are exchanged in this process. To fully understand the behavior of OSPF, it's useful to look carefully at the contents of the LSAs. We examine the fields of the Router LSA and the Network LSA and the process for choosing the designated router on a broadcast link. We conclude with an example of configuring and verifying OSPF in a network of Alcatel-Lucent 7750 SRs.

Pre-Assessment

The following assessment questions will help you understand what areas of the chapter you should review in more detail to prepare for the NRS II exam. You can also use the CD that accompanies this book to take all the assessment tests and review the answers.

1. What is the cost value of an OSPF interface on the Alcatel-Lucent 7750 SR?

- **A.** It is based on the configuration of the global OSPF cost variable, which has a default value of 10.
- **B.** It is based on the configuration of the global OSPF cost variable, which has a default value of 100.
- **C.** It is based on a reference bandwidth, which has a default value of 10 Gbps.
- **D.** It is based on a reference bandwidth, which has a default value of 100 Gbps.

2. A router has an OSPF broadcast interface declared as passive. How will this be represented in the Router LSA originated by the router?

- **A.** The Router LSA will contain a stub network link type to describe the interface.
- **B.** The Router LSA will contain a transit link type to describe the interface.
- **C.** The Router LSA will contain a point-to-point link type to describe the interface.
- **D.** The Router LSA will contain a point-to-point link type and a stub network link type to describe the interface.
- **E.** The Router LSA will not describe the interface.

3. Which statement is *not* correct regarding an OSPF Type 1 LSA?

A. An OSPF Type 1 LSA is originated by every OSPF router.

B. An OSPF Type 1 LSA is called a *Router LSA*.

C. The OSPF Type 1 LSA is flooded throughout the autonomous system.

D. The OSPF Type 1 LSA describes the router's directly connected links.

E. The OSPF Type 1 LSA contains an age field.

4. An Alcatel-Lucent 7750 SR has an OSPF adjacency with its neighbor using a router ID derived from the last four octets of the chassis MAC address. The system interface IP address, `router-id`, and `ospf router-id` are then configured. Assuming that these are the only commands executed, what router ID will be seen by the OSPF neighbor?

A. The router ID seen by the neighbor will be derived from the last four octets of the chassis MAC address.

B. The router ID seen by the neighbor will be derived from the system interface address.

C. The router ID seen by the neighbor will be derived from the configured `router-id`.

D. The router ID seen by the neighbor will be derived from the configured `ospf router-id`.

5. Which of the following is not a field in an OSPF Hello packet that must match for a successful state transition to the 2-Way state?

A. Dead Interval

B. Authentication Type

C. MTU

D. Area ID

E. Stub Flag

5.1 Overview of OSPF Operation

Open Shortest Path First (OSPF) is a link-state routing protocol developed in the late 1980s specifically for IP routing. It was the first routing protocol widely deployed in IP networks that provided a convergence time of a few seconds, with no routing loops. IS-IS (Intermediate System to Intermediate System) was developed as an OSI routing protocol around the same time and later modified to support IP routing. Today, nearly all IP networks run either OSPF or IS-IS as their interior routing protocol (IRP).

To improve its efficiency and increase its scalability, OSPF supports hierarchy by allowing the definition of different OSPF areas. This chapter considers OSPF routing only within a single area. The exchange of routing information between OSPF areas is discussed in a later chapter.

Some of the key milestones in the development of OSPF are as follows:

- OSPFv1 defined in RFC 1131, October 1989
- OSPFv2 defined in RFC 1247, July 1991
- OSPFv3 created to support IPv6 and defined in RFC 2740, December 1999
- Traffic engineering extensions defined in RFC 3630, September 2003

Over the years, there have been many other RFCs defining enhancements and revisions to OSPF, including support for Classless Interdomain Routing (CIDR), authentication, and multicast support.

OSPF is a hierarchical link-state protocol used as an Interior Gateway Protocol (IGP) in networks ranging from small enterprise networks to large autonomous systems (ASs). OSPF routers exchange state, cost, and other relevant interface information with their neighbors. The information exchange enables all participating routers to establish a network topology map. Each router applies the Dijkstra shortest path first (SPF) algorithm to calculate the shortest path to each destination in the network. The resulting OSPF forwarding table is submitted to the route table manager (RTM) to calculate the routing table.

When a router is started with OSPF configured, the OSPF process is initialized and waits for an indication that its interfaces are functional. Alcatel-Lucent's implementation of OSPF conforms to the OSPFv2 specifications presented in RFC 2328.

OSPF Operation

The steps below list the major aspects of OSPF operation:

1. A router with OSPF configured sends Hello messages out every OSPF-enabled interface. If the router receives a valid Hello message on an OSPF interface, it proceeds to establish an adjacency with any OSPF routers on that network.
2. If the interface is a broadcast network, such as Ethernet, the routers use the Hello packets to establish a designated router (DR) and a backup designated router (BDR) on the network.
3. The routers exchange Database Description packets. These are essentially an index of all link-state advertisements (LSAs) the router has in its topology database.
4. Based on the contents of the Database Description packets, each router requests the LSAs it needs to bring its topology database up to date. The request is made with a link-state request (LSR) packet.
5. As requested, the router sends a link-state update (LSU) containing the LSAs requested by the neighbor. Each LSU is acknowledged with a link-state acknowledgment.
6. Once the exchange of LSUs is complete, the routers are fully adjacent. They continue to exchange periodic Hello messages to maintain the adjacency.
7. If there is a topology change, the affected routers transmit an updated LSA to reflect the change. Every OSPF router updates its link-state database (LSDB), floods the new LSA to its neighbors, and runs shortest path first (SPF) to recalculate its forwarding database.
8. LSAs age in the LSDB and are considered obsolete after 3,600 seconds (1 hour). The originating router will reflood an LSA after it reaches an age of ~1,800 seconds to refresh it in the LSDB.

OSPF Metrics and Topologies

As shown in Figure 5.1, all OSPF interfaces have a cost value used as the routing metric in the SPF calculation. This cost, or metric, is used to determine the best path to a particular destination: the lower the metric value, the more likely the interface will be used to forward data traffic.

Figure 5.1 Every interface in an OSPF network has a metric that is based on the interface bandwidth by default.

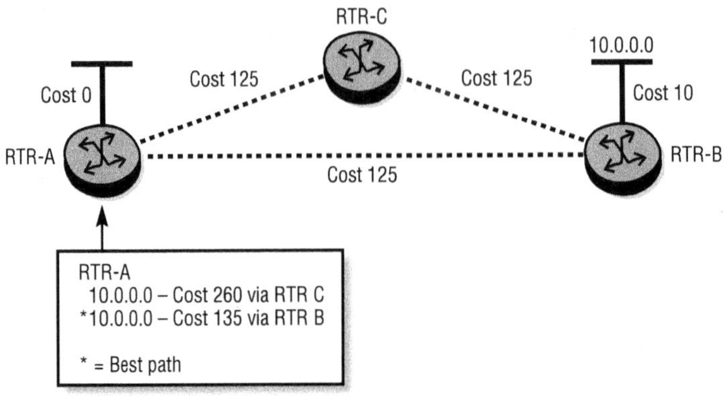

The metric is calculated using a reference bandwidth, defined in bits per second. The default interface metric is calculated as follows:

$$\frac{\text{Interface metric} = (\text{reference bandwidth})}{(\text{interface bandwidth})}$$

Interface metric = (reference bandwidth)/(interface bandwidth)

Because the default reference bandwidth on the Alcatel-Lucent 7750 SR is 100 Gbps, the default metrics for various link speeds are as follows:

- 10-Mbps link default metric of 10,000
- 100-Mbps link default metric of 1,000
- 1-Gbps link default metric of 100
- 10-Gbps link default metric of 10

This metric is a default metric and can be changed on any interface.

Reference bandwidth is not defined by the OSPF standard; thus, other routers may use a different reference bandwidth, leading to different metrics for the same speed interface. It is important to ensure that all routers are using consistent metrics in a mixed-vendor OSPF network.

OSPF on the 7750 SR supports two types of network topology—broadcast and point-to-point as described below:

- **Multi-access (broadcast)**—This topology is typically an Ethernet segment in which multiple routers are connected and actively exchanging OSPF updates. On a broadcast network, a DR and a BDR are elected.
- **Point-to-point**—A point-to-point connection is defined as a connection in which there is only one neighbor and the routers are actively exchanging OSPF updates.

The two topologies are illustrated in Figure 5.2.

Figure 5.2 Two types of network topologies are recognized by the Alcatel-Lucent 7750 SR.

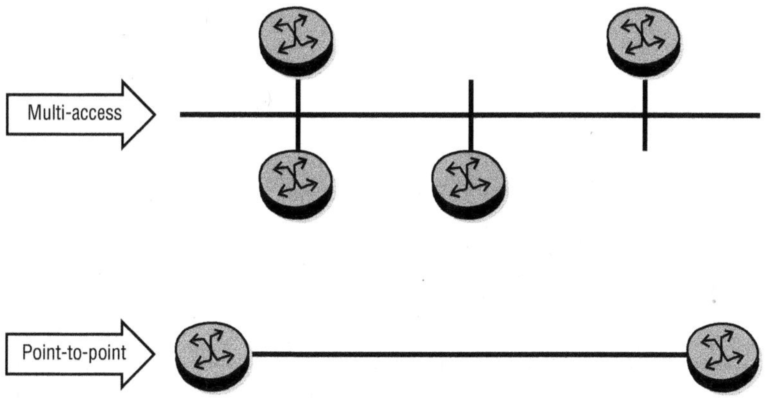

5.2 The OSPF Database and OSPF Messages

The OSPF LSDB contains the information used for the SPF calculation. The five different types of OSPF messages are used to establish OSPF adjacencies and exchange the LSAs that make up the database.

Link-State Database

The LSDB contains the complete topology information for the OSPF routing domain. Every router in an OSPF area contains an identical LSDB and uses it to calculate the best path to every destination in the network. The LSDB is kept up to date by flooding

LSAs throughout the routing domain. Listing 5.1 shows the output of the command `show router ospf database` for the topology in Figure 5.3. This output is essentially an index of all LSAs in the database.

Figure 5.3 Example topology with one broadcast link and three point-to-point links.

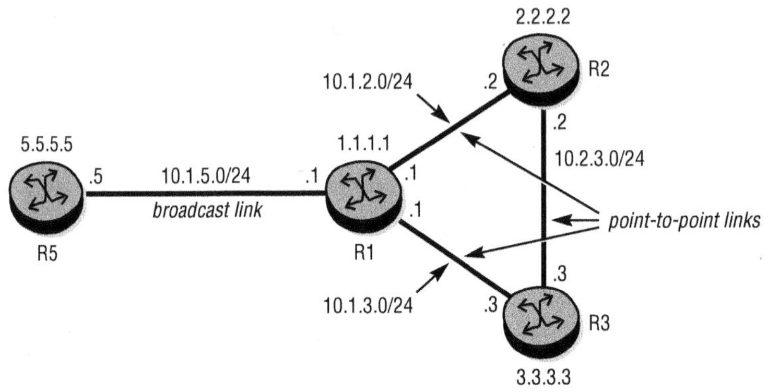

Listing 5.1 show router ospf database lists all the LSAs for the topology.

```
*A:R2# show router ospf database

===============================================================================
OSPF Link State Database (Type : All)
===============================================================================
Type    Area Id      Link State Id   Adv Rtr Id  Age  Sequence   Cksum
-------------------------------------------------------------------------------
Router  0.0.0.0      1.1.1.1         1.1.1.1     187  0x800008f2 0xfaf8
Router  0.0.0.0      2.2.2.2         2.2.2.2     197  0x800008d3 0x54d3
Router  0.0.0.0      3.3.3.3         3.3.3.3     190  0x800008d1 0x928b
Router  0.0.0.0      5.5.5.5         5.5.5.5     192  0x800008c9 0xee32
Network 0.0.0.0      10.1.5.5        5.5.5.5     192  0x80000001 0xcf49
-------------------------------------------------------------------------------
No. of LSAs: 5
===============================================================================
*A:R2#
```

The output of the command `show router ospf database 1.1.1.1 detail` shows the contents of the LSA with link-state ID of **1.1.1.1** as shown in Listing 5.2. This contains the topology information required by OSPF. The diagram shows the basic OSPF

LSA, known as the Type 1, or Router LSA. A Type 1 LSA is originated by every router and describes that router's directly connected links. The fields of the Type 1 LSA are described in more detail later in the chapter.

Listing 5.2 A detailed look at the Router LSA

```
*A:R1# show router ospf database 1.1.1.1 detail

===============================================================================
OSPF Link State Database (Type : All) (Detailed)
===============================================================================
-------------------------------------------------------------------------------
Router LSA for Area 0.0.0.0
-------------------------------------------------------------------------------
Area Id              : 0.0.0.0            Adv Router Id      : 1.1.1.1
Link State Id        : 1.1.1.1 (16843009)
LSA Type             : Router
Sequence No          : 0x800008f2         Checksum           : 0xfaf8
Age                  : 1048               Length             : 96
Options              : E
Flags                : None               Link Count         : 6
Link Type (1)        : Stub Network
Network (1)          : 1.1.1.1            Mask (1)           : 255.255.255.255
No of TOS (1)        : 0                  Metric-0 (1)       : 0
Link Type (2)        : Point To Point
Nbr Rtr Id (2)       : 2.2.2.2            I/F Address (2)    : 10.1.2.1
No of TOS (2)        : 0                  Metric-0 (2)       : 1000
Link Type (3)        : Stub Network
Network (3)          : 10.1.2.0           Mask (3)           : 255.255.255.0
No of TOS (3)        : 0                  Metric-0 (3)       : 1000
Link Type (4)        : Point To Point
Nbr Rtr Id (4)       : 3.3.3.3            I/F Address (4)    : 10.1.3.1
No of TOS (4)        : 0                  Metric-0 (4)       : 1000
Link Type (5)        : Stub Network
Network (5)          : 10.1.3.0           Mask (5)           : 255.255.255.0
No of TOS (5)        : 0                  Metric-0 (5)       : 1000
Link Type (6)        : Transit Network
DR Rtr Id (6)        : 10.1.5.5           I/F Address (6)    : 10.1.5.1
No of TOS (6)        : 0                  Metric-0 (6)       : 1000
===============================================================================
```

OSPF Messages

All communications between routers in an OSPF network happen through the exchange of OSPF messages. OSPF does not use a transport protocol; instead, the messages are transmitted in IP datagrams with IP protocol ID 89. OSPF messages are sent to an IP multicast addresses (224.0.0.5 or 224.0.0.6) or to a unicast address, depending on the message. Figure 5.4 shows the format of an OSPF message in a Layer 2 frame.

Figure 5.4 OSPF messages are carried in raw IP datagrams with a protocol number of 89.

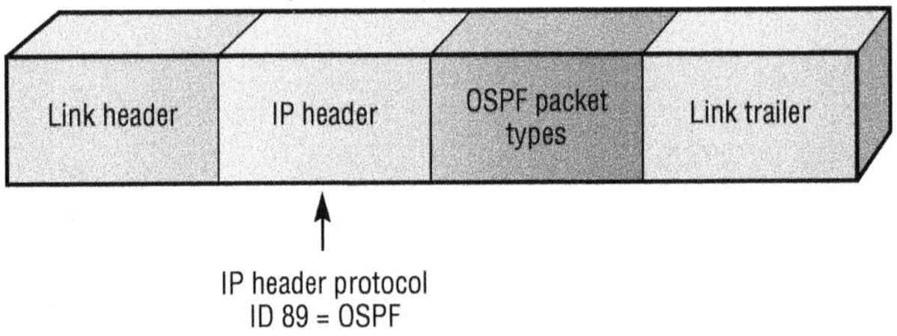

There are five different OSPF messages that are described in the following sections of this chapter. These are:

- OSPF Hello
- OSPF Database Description
- OSPF link-state request
- OSPF link-state update
- OSPF link-state acknowledgment

All messages share a common OSPF header as shown in Figure 5.5.

Figure 5.5 All OSPF messages share a common header.

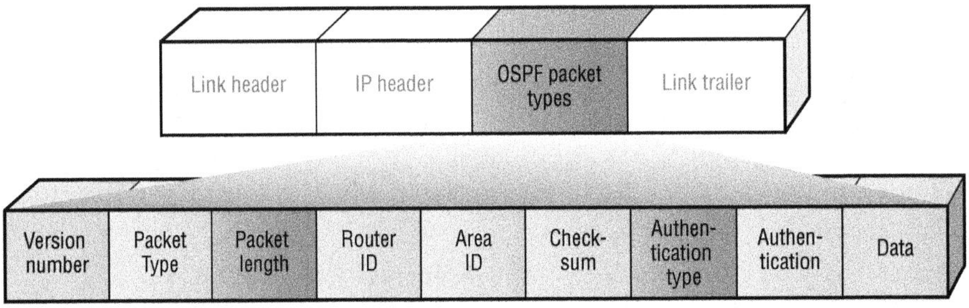

The data field is different depending on the message type.

Router ID

A unique router ID (RID) is required by the SPF algorithm to uniquely identify each router in the routing domain. The RID is a 32-bit value that is typically set to the system address. The algorithm for deriving the OSPF RID on the 7750 SR is described below:

1. Value explicitly set in the `config>router>ospf router-id` context
2. Value explicitly set in the `config>router router-id` context
3. Value set for the system interface address in the `config>router>interface system` context, if the system interface is up
4. Value derived from the last 4 bytes of the chassis MAC address

Although the RID is displayed in the same dotted-decimal format as an IP address, it is important to realize that the RID is not actually an IP address and is not necessarily a reachable destination in the OSPF domain. If the RID is derived from the system interface address and the system interface is included in an OSPF area, then the RID will be a reachable address.

When a new RID is configured, OSPF is not automatically restarted with the new RID. The next time OSPF is initialized or reinitialized, the new RID is used. To force the use of the new RID, issue the `shutdown` and `no shutdown` commands for OSPF, or restart the entire router.

5.3 Establishing OSPF Adjacencies

Before exchanging any topology information or updating the route table, an OSPF router must form adjacencies with its neighbors. In OSPF, two routers are considered adjacent only when they have completed the full process described below and are exchanging topology information.

OSPF Neighbor Discovery

OSPF is a discovery protocol in that it will discover its neighbors. A *neighbor* is an OSPF router that is configured with an interface to a common network. The router sends OSPF Hello packets on the network and receives Hello packets in return. The Hello packets are sent to a multicast address (224.0.0.5). Figure 5.6 shows the exchange of Hello packets between two routers.

When a router receives a Hello packet on an OSPF-enabled interface, the parameters are compared with the configuration of the interface. Certain values must match or the Hello is considered invalid and is ignored. The values that must match are as follows:

- Area ID
- AuType and authentication password
- Network mask
- Hello interval
- Stub flag (options field)
- Router dead interval

Figure 5.6 OSPF routers exchange Hello messages to discover their neighbors.

Once a router sees its own RID in the Hello received from a neighbor, it transitions to the 2-Way state and can elect a DR and BDR if it is on a broadcast network. Figure 5.7 shows the state transitions for two routers exchanging Hello packets.

Figure 5.7 A router transitions to the 2-Way state when it sees its own RID in a Hello from a neighbor.

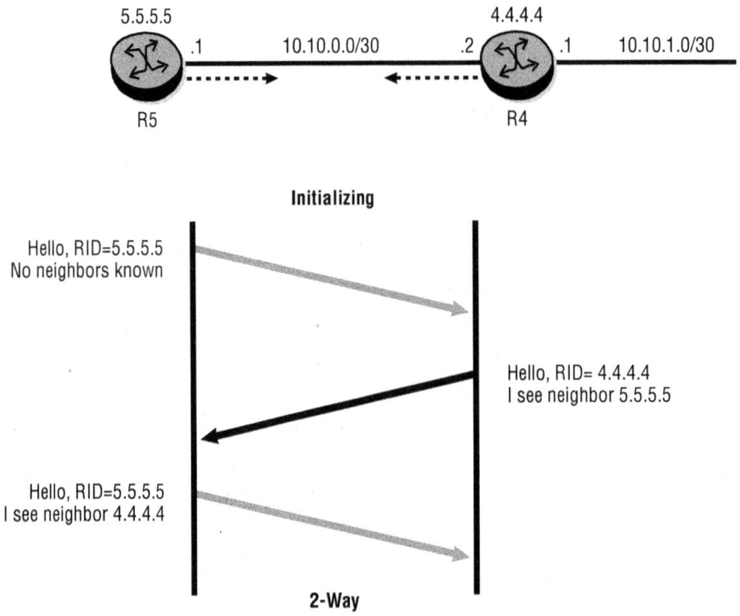

Hello Packet

The OSPF Hello packet (shown in Figure 5.8) consists of the following fields:

- **Header**—The OSPF header is the same for all five types of OSPF messages. In the Hello packet the type field has the value of "1."
- **Network mask**—The network mask field contains the network mask for the interface that the packet is being sent on.
- **Hello interval**—The Hello interval is the interval at which Hello packets are sent on the interface. The 7750 SR uses a 10-second Hello interval by default. The Hello interval must match for all neighbors on the interface.
- **Options**—The options field contains several flags, including the E bit. The E bit is set to indicate that the router interface is not in a stub area. It is 0 (cleared) if the interface is in a stub area. This value must match for all neighbors on the interface.

Figure 5.8 The Hello message. The shaded fields are specific to the Hello.

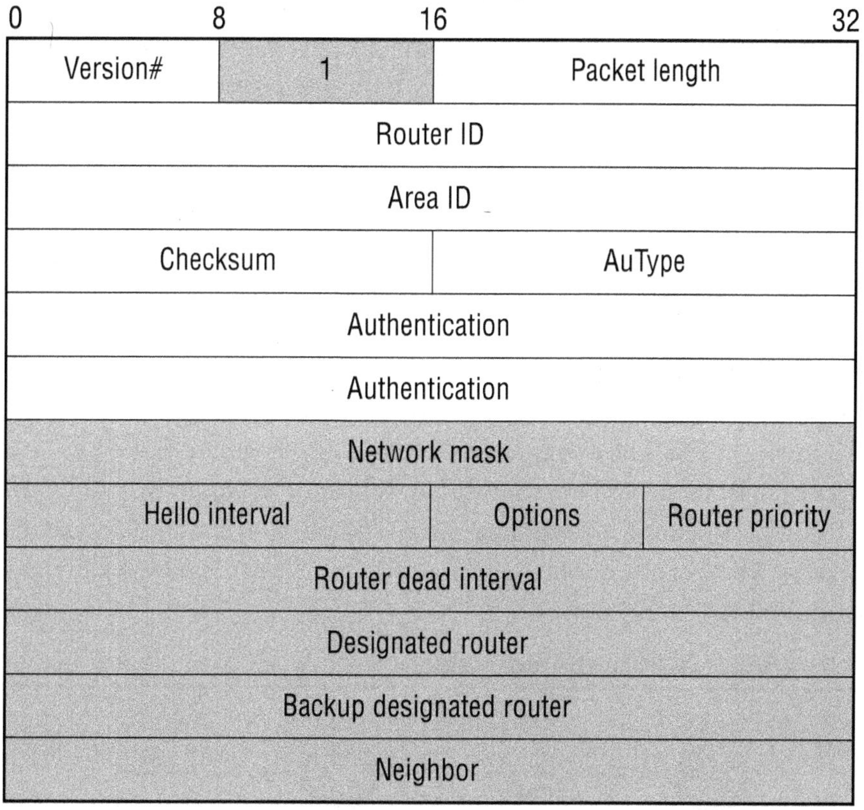

- **Router priority**—The router priority field denotes the priority value used when electing the DR and BDR. The default on the 7750 SR is a priority of 1. A priority of 0 means that the router can never be a DR or BDR on the network connected to this interface.
- **Router dead interval**—If a neighbor does not send a Hello packet within the dead interval, the router assumes that the neighbor is not active and purges all information from that neighbor. On the 7750 SR, the default value is 40 seconds, or four times the update interval. This value must match for all neighbors on the interface.
- **Designated router**—This field denotes the elected DR.
- **Backup designated router**—This field denotes the elected BDR.
- **Neighbor**—This field varies depending on the number of neighbors the router has learned of on the interface. The RID of all neighbors seen on this interface is carried in this field. A router looks for its own RID in the Hello, to know that it is seen by its neighbors.

Electing the Designated Router (DR)

On a multi-access, or broadcast interface, a DR and a BDR are elected. The DR is the router with the highest priority set in the Hello. If there is a tie, the router with the highest RID is chosen. The BDR is the router with the second highest value. The router waits for the router dead interval before selecting the DR. If there is an existing DR on the network, it is not preempted by a router with a higher priority but remains as the DR.

On the 7750 SR, an Ethernet interface is broadcast by default, even if it has a direct point-to-point connection with its neighbor. When two routers are directly connected by Ethernet, it is preferable to configure the interface as point-to-point because no DR is required and the adjacency can be formed more quickly.

Let's examine the packets exchanged between two routers as they exchange Hello packets and elect a DR. The example uses the topology shown in Figure 5.9.

In the example, R5 and R4 are reset. When R5 comes up, it sends an OSPF Hello packet. The RID is set to `5.5.5.5`. There are no neighbors in this Hello packet because it does not yet know of any neighbors on the segment. Also, there is no DR chosen yet (see Figure 5.10).

Figure 5.9 Election of the DR on a broadcast network

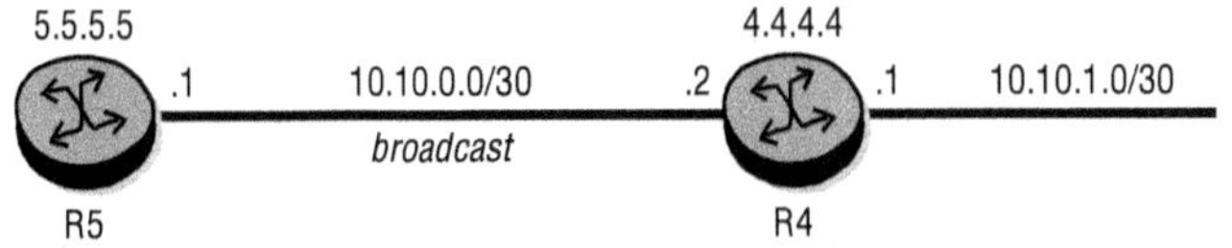

Figure 5.10 The first Hello sent shows no DR, and no neighbors are seen yet.

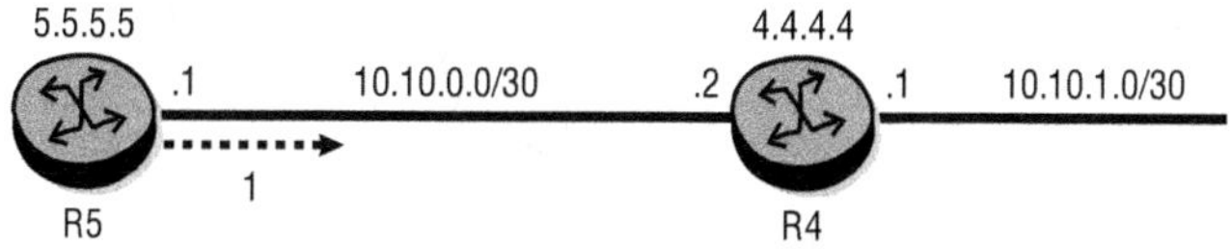

1

```
OSPF Version         : 2
Router Id            : 5.5.5.5
Area Id              : 0.0.0.0
Checksum             : f198
Authentication       : Null
Authentication Key: 00 00 00 00 00 00 00 00
Packet Type          : HELLO
Packet Length        : 44

Network Mask         : 255.255.255.252
Hello Interval       : 10
Options              : 02
Rtr Priority         : 1
Dead Interval        : 40
Designated Router : 0.0.0.0
Backup Router        : 0.0.0.0
"
```

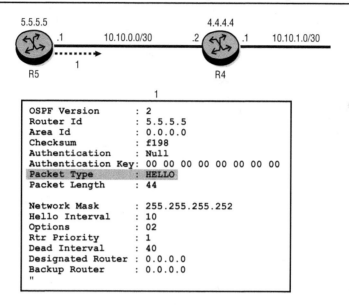

The next packet R5 receives is an OSPF Hello packet sent by R4. The RID is set to `4.4.4.4`, and because R4 has received a Hello packet from R5, it indicates this with RID `5.5.5.5 in` the neighbor field. R5 does the same when it receives the Hello from R4 (Figure 5.11). When both routers have sent a Hello packet with the neighbor address populated, the adjacency state changes to 2-Way.

Figure 5.11 Each router sees its own RID in the Hello from its neighbor.

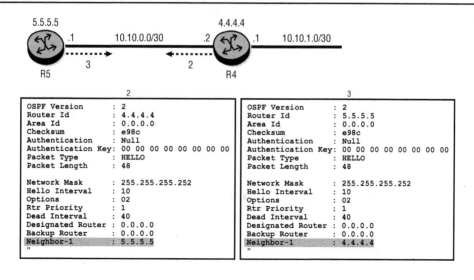

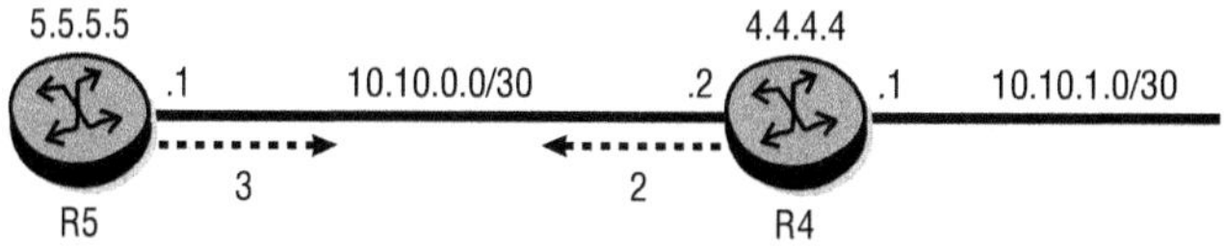

2

```
OSPF Version         : 2
Router Id            : 4.4.4.4
Area Id              : 0.0.0.0
Checksum             : e98c
Authentication       : Null
Authentication Key: 00 00 00 00 00 00 00 00
Packet Type          : HELLO
Packet Length        : 48

Network Mask         : 255.255.255.252
Hello Interval       : 10
Options              : 02
Rtr Priority         : 1
Dead Interval        : 40
Designated Router : 0.0.0.0
Backup Router        : 0.0.0.0
Neighbor-1           : 5.5.5.5
"
```

3

```
OSPF Version         : 2
Router Id            : 5.5.5.5
Area Id              : 0.0.0.0
Checksum             : e98c
Authentication       : Null
Authentication Key: 00 00 00 00 00 00 00 00
Packet Type          : HELLO
Packet Length        : 48

Network Mask         : 255.255.255.252
Hello Interval       : 10
Options              : 02
Rtr Priority         : 1
Dead Interval        : 40
Designated Router : 0.0.0.0
Backup Router        : 0.0.0.0
Neighbor-1           : 4.4.4.4
"
```

Both router priorities are the same, and there is no router already elected as the DR on the network. In this case, the router with the highest RID will be elected as the DR. In Figure 5.12, R4 sends a Hello packet with both the DR and the BDR set to `10.10.0.1`. The Hello packet sent from R5 has the DR set to `10.10.0.1` and the BDR set to `10.10.0.2`.

It is important to emphasize that it is an interface that is elected as the DR, rather than the router. A DR and a BDR are elected on each broadcast interface. A router may be a DR on some interfaces, a BDR on other interfaces, and neither on yet other interfaces.

Once the DR and the BDR are elected, the router can proceed to the next state in forming an adjacency, ExStart.

Figure 5.12 Since priorities are at their default, the router with the highest RID becomes the DR. The other becomes the BDR.

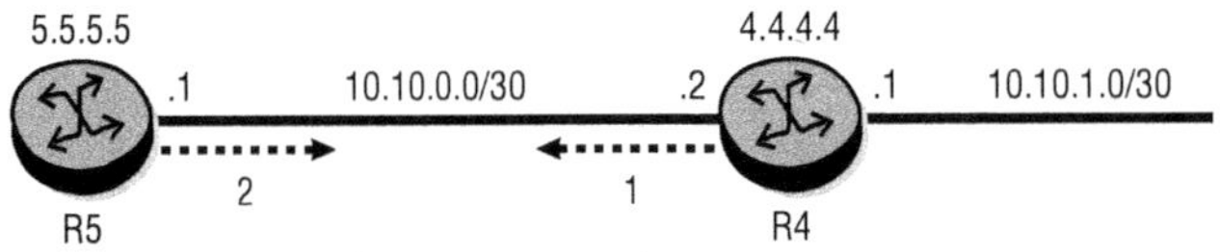

1

```
OSPF Version       : 2
Router Id          : 4.4.4.4
Area Id            : 0.0.0.0
Checksum           : d576
Authentication     : Null
Authentication Key: 00 00 00 00 00 00 00 00
Packet Type        : HELLO
Packet Length      : 48

Network Mask       : 255.255.255.252
Hello Interval     : 10
Options            : 02
Rtr Priority       : 1
Dead Interval      : 40
Designated Router  : 10.10.0.1
Backup Router      : 10.10.0.1
Neighbor-1         : 5.5.5.5
"
```

2

```
OSPF Version       : 2
Router Id          : 5.5.5.5
Area Id            : 0.0.0.0
Checksum           : d575
Authentication     : Null
Authentication Key: 00 00 00 00 00 00 00 00
Packet Type        : HELLO
Packet Length      : 48

Network Mask       : 255.255.255.252
Hello Interval     : 10
Options            : 02
Rtr Priority       : 1
Dead Interval      : 40
Designated Router  : 10.10.0.1
Backup Router      : 10.10.0.2
Neighbor-1         : 4.4.4.4
"
```

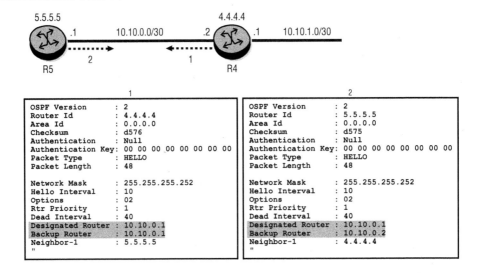

OSPF Exchange and the Database Description Packet

In Figure 5.13, the two routers have exchanged Hellos, elected the DR, and are in the ExStart state. The following are the next steps in the formation of the adjacency:

1. The neighboring routers establish a master/slave relationship. The routers exchange database description (DBD) packets with a sequence number only to determine the initial DBD sequence number for the exchange state.
2. The R4 sends its DBD sequence number. R5 has a higher RID, thus it becomes the master for the exchange, and its initial sequence number is used.

3. The slave (R4) router sends its DBD packet, describing its LSDB. The sequence number negotiated in Steps 1 and 2 is used.
4. The master (R5) router increments the sequence number and sends a DBD packet, describing its LSDB.

The DBD packet advertises a summary of all LSAs that the advertising router has in its LSDB. It is essentially an index of the LSDB (see Figure 5.14).

Figure 5.13 The routers exchange DBD messages, first to establish the sequence number and then to list the LSAs in their LSDBs.

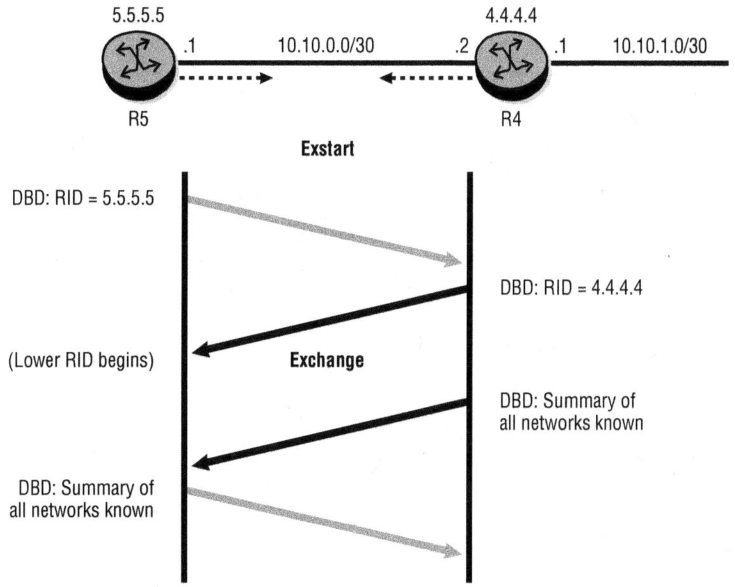

For each of the LSAs listed in the DBD packet, the receiving router compares the LSA sequence number with its existing LSDB entries:

- If an LSA is unknown or if it is known but the advertised sequence number is higher, the receiving router requests the LSA in an LSR.
- If the network is already known and the sequence number is lower, the receiving router sends back an LSU with the up-to-date information.
- If the network is already in the database and the sequence numbers are identical, the receiving router discards the information.

We next examine the exchange of DBD packets. Figure 5.15 shows the two DBDs used to negotiate the sequence number. The router with the higher RID becomes the master, and its sequence number (77793, in this example) is used.

One of the fields of the DBD packet is the interface MTU (maximum transmission unit). If this value does not match for the two routers, they will remain in the ExStart state and will not form an adjacency. The value is determined by the port MTU but can be modified in the `configure router ospf area 0 interface` context.

Figure 5.14 Database description (DBD) message. The shaded fields are specific to the DBD message.

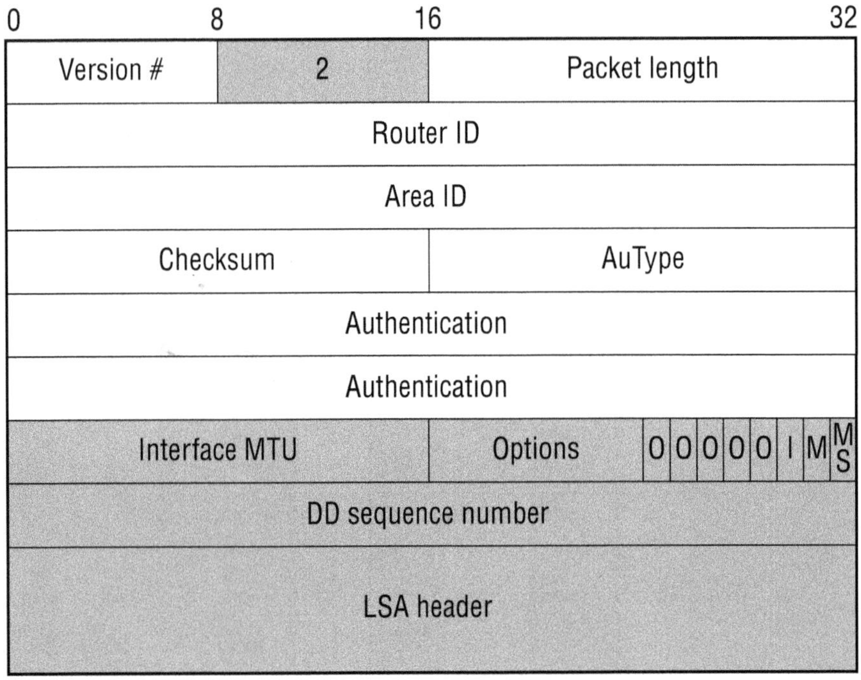

R4 sends its DBD with the database summary and the sequence number set by R5 (see Figure 5.16).

R5 sends its DBD with its database summary and the incremented sequence number (see Figure 5.17).

Establishing the Adjacency

After the exchange of DBD packets, the routers continue to form their adjacency by requesting the LSAs they need to bring their LSDBs up to date (Figure 5.18).

1. Based on the DBD received from R5, R4 requests the LSAs it needs to update its database by sending LSRs to R5.

2. Based on the DBD received from R4, R5 requests the LSAs it needs to update its database by sending LSRs to R4.
3. R5 sends an LSU containing the requested LSAs to R4.
4. R4 sends an LSU containing the requested LSAs to R5.

Figure 5.15 Both routers send DBDs to establish the starting sequence number.

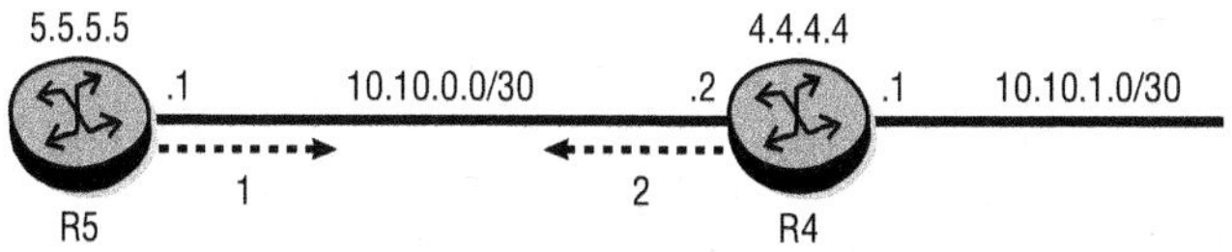

1

```
OSPF Version        : 2
Router Id           : 5.5.5.5
Area Id             : 0.0.0.0
Checksum            : 7c0e
Authentication      : Null
Authentication Key: 00 00 00 00 00 00 00 00
Packet Type         : DB_DESC
Packet Length       : 32

Interface MTU       : 1500
Options             : 000042
Flags               : 7
Sequence Num        : 77793
"
```

2

```
OSPF Version        : 2
Router Id           : 4.4.4.4
Area Id             : 0.0.0.0
Checksum            : 865e
Authentication      : Null
Authentication Key: 00 00 00 00 00 00 00 00
Packet Type         : DB_DESC
Packet Length       : 32

Interface MTU       : 1500
Options             : 000042
Flags               : 7
Sequence Num        : 75667
"
```

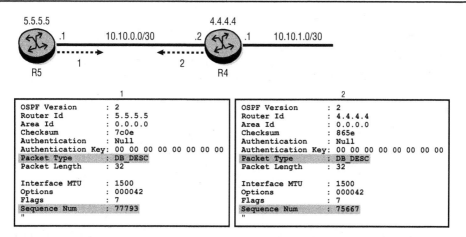

Figure 5.16 R4 sends a DBD describing the LSAs in its database.

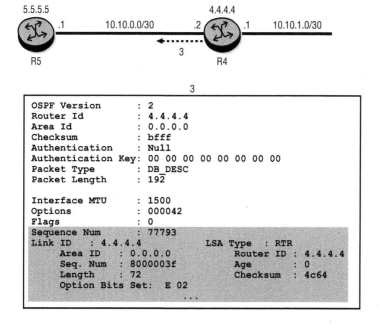

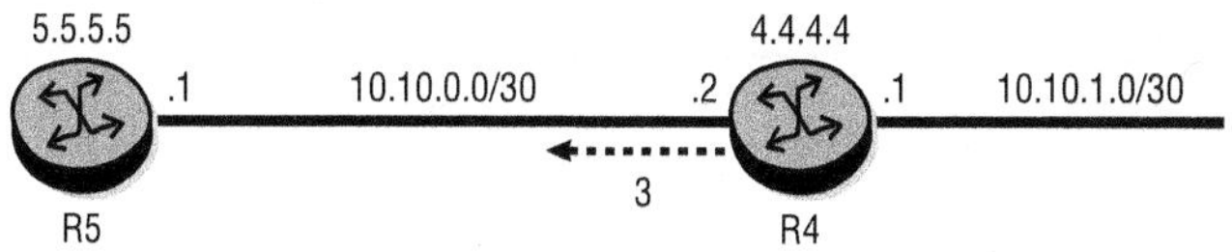

3

```
OSPF Version        : 2
Router Id           : 4.4.4.4
Area Id             : 0.0.0.0
Checksum            : bfff
Authentication      : Null
Authentication Key: 00 00 00 00 00 00 00 00
Packet Type         : DB_DESC
Packet Length       : 192

Interface MTU       : 1500
Options             : 000042
Flags               : 0
Sequence Num        : 77793
Link ID    : 4.4.4.4                LSA Type    : RTR
     Area ID    : 0.0.0.0               Router ID : 4.4.4.4
     Seq. Num   : 8000003f              Age       : 0
     Length     : 72                    Checksum  : 4c64
     Option Bits Set:   E 02
                              ...
```

Figure 5.17 DBD from R5 with database summary and incremented sequence number.

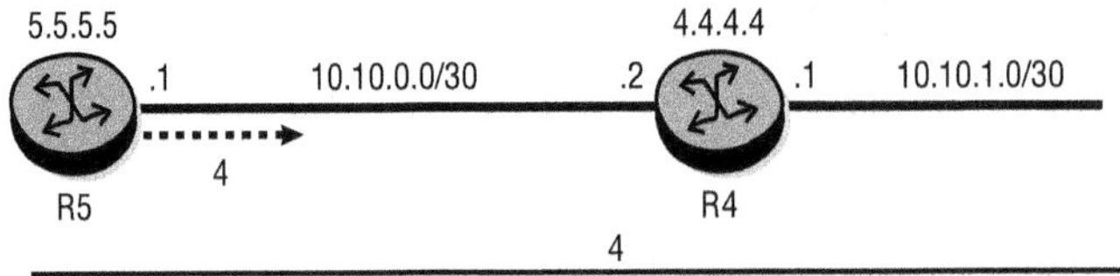

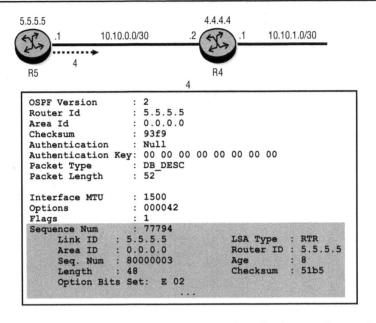

```
OSPF Version          : 2
Router Id             : 5.5.5.5
Area Id               : 0.0.0.0
Checksum              : 93f9
Authentication        : Null
Authentication Key: 00 00 00 00 00 00 00 00
Packet Type           : DB_DESC
Packet Length         : 52

Interface MTU         : 1500
Options               : 000042
Flags                 : 1
Sequence Num          : 77794
     Link ID     : 5.5.5.5                    LSA Type    : RTR
     Area ID     : 0.0.0.0                    Router ID : 5.5.5.5
     Seq. Num    : 80000003                   Age         : 8
     Length      : 48                         Checksum    : 51b5
     Option Bits Set:   E 02
                               ...
```

Figure 5.18 Based on the DBDs, the routers request updates for the LSAs they need to bring their databases up to date.

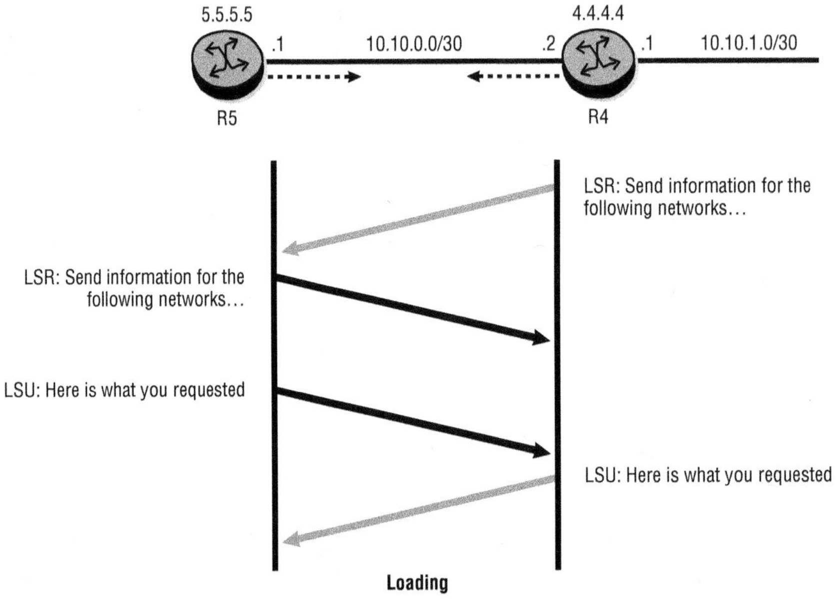

Link-State Request and Link-State Update Packets

Figure 5.19 shows the fields of the LSR packet. One LSR may request multiple LSAs.

Figure 5.19 The LSR packet. Shaded fields are specific to the LSR packet.

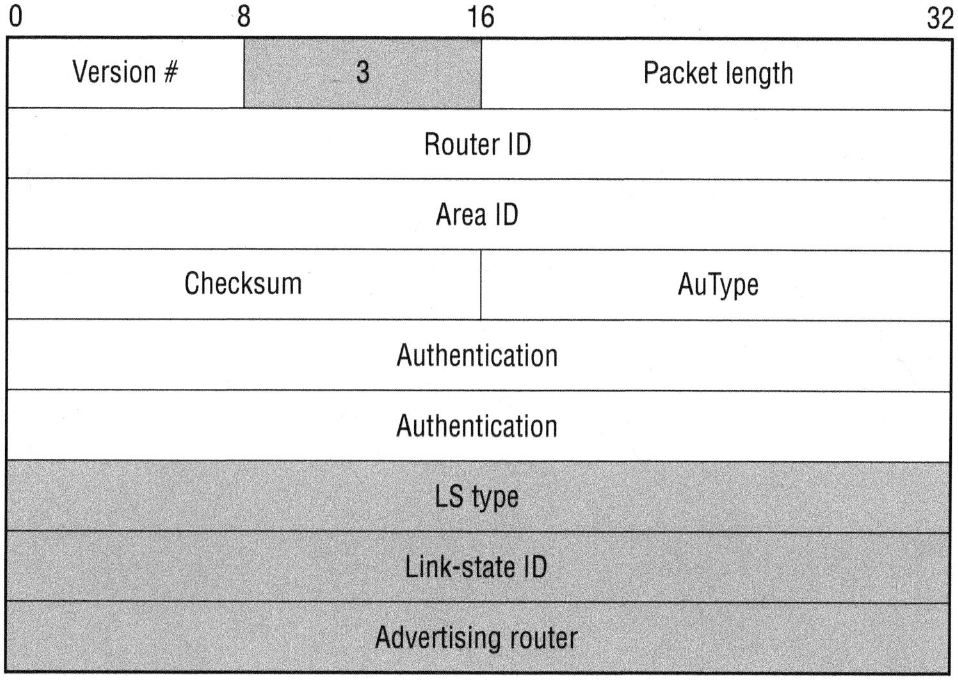

When it receives an LSR packet, the receiving router sends back an LSU packet with the full LSDB entries for the requested LSAs. The size of the LSU depends on the interface MTU and administrator settings. By default, the 7750 SR sends as many LSAs in the LSU as the network link can support. Figure 5.20 shows the fields of the LSU packet.

We next examine the exchange of packets as the routers bring their databases up to date. R5 sends an LSR to R4 (Figure 5.21) for any LSA that it does not have, and R4 does the same.

R4 responds with an LSU for the requested LSAs. At the same time, R5 responds to R4's request (see Figure 5.22).

Link-State Acknowledgment Packet

In OSPF, LSUs are always acknowledged with link-state acknowledgments to inform the sender that the LSU has been received. After the exchange of LSRs and LSUs, both LSDBs are completely up to date, and the routers have formed a full adjacency. The final steps are shown in Figure 5.23 and described below:

1. R4 acknowledges the LSU received from R5.
2. R5 acknowledges the LSU received from R4, and the state changes from Loading to Full.
3. To maintain the adjacency, the routers send periodic Hellos to each other. The default interval is 10 seconds.

Figure 5.20 The LSU packet. The shaded fields are specific to the LSU packet.

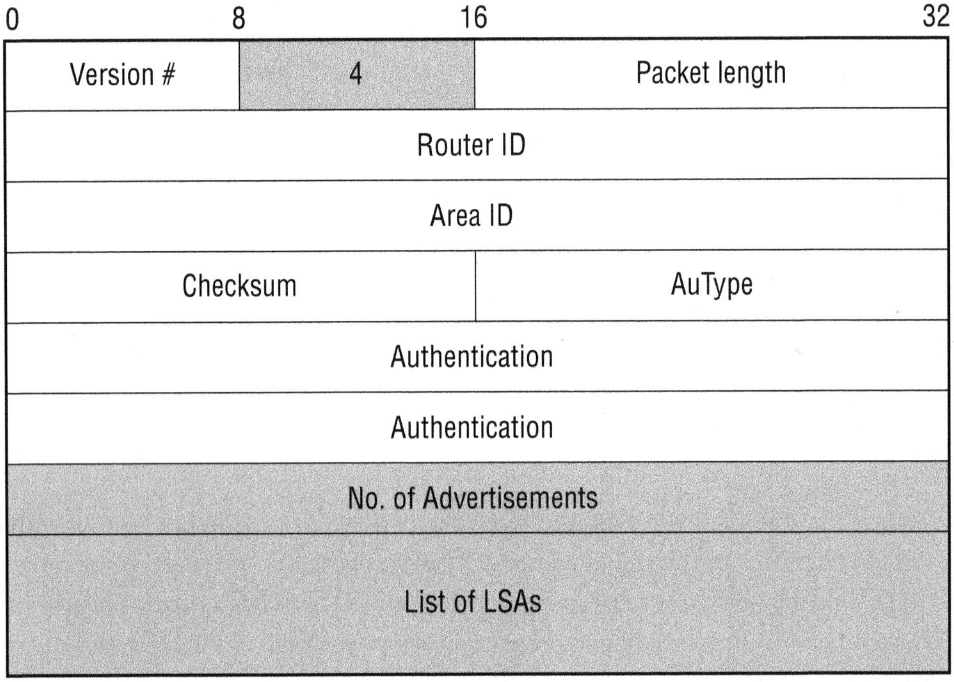

Figure 5.24 shows the link-state acknowledgment sent by R5. R4 also acknowledges the LSU received from R5. The adjacency state is now Full.

5.4 Flooding LSAs

The reliable flooding of topology information throughout the routing domain is a critical aspect of OSPF's operation. In OSPF, each router constructs a Router (or Type 1) LSA that describes the local topology as seen by the router. There may also be other types of LSAs generated to carry other topology details, as shown in Table 5.1.

Figure 5.21 R5 sends an LSR to R4 requesting an update.

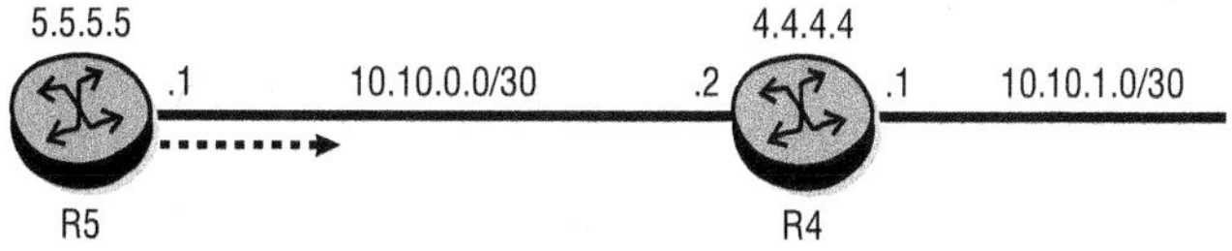

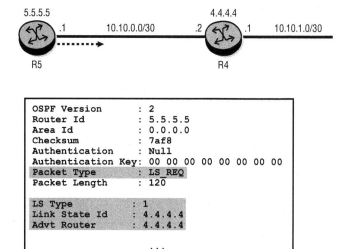

```
OSPF Version          : 2
Router Id             : 5.5.5.5
Area Id               : 0.0.0.0
Checksum              : 7af8
Authentication        : Null
Authentication Key: 00 00 00 00 00 00 00 00
Packet Type           : LS_REQ
Packet Length         : 120

LS Type              : 1
Link State Id        : 4.4.4.4
Advt Router          : 4.4.4.4

                     ...
```

Figure 5.22 R5 sends an LSU with the requested update to R4.

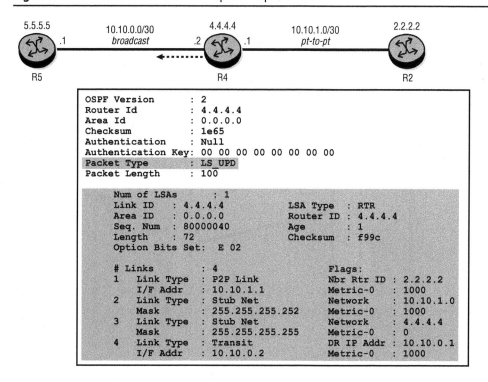

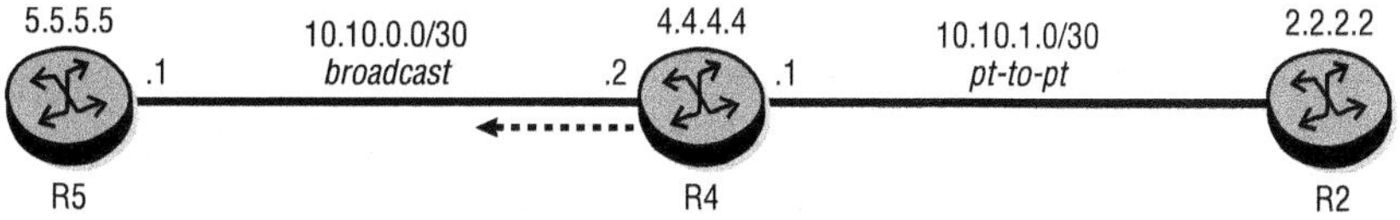


```
OSPF Version          : 2
Router Id             : 4.4.4.4
Area Id               : 0.0.0.0
Checksum              : 1e65
Authentication        : Null
Authentication Key: 00 00 00 00 00 00 00 00
Packet Type           : LS_UPD
Packet Length         : 100

     Num of LSAs        : 1
     Link ID   : 4.4.4.4                LSA Type  : RTR
     Area ID   : 0.0.0.0                Router ID : 4.4.4.4
     Seq. Num  : 80000040               Age       : 1
     Length    : 72                     Checksum  : f99c
     Option Bits Set:  E 02

     # Links          : 4                      Flags:
     1   Link Type    : P2P Link               Nbr Rtr ID  : 2.2.2.2
         I/F Addr     : 10.10.1.1              Metric-0    : 1000
     2   Link Type    : Stub Net               Network     : 10.10.1.0
         Mask         : 255.255.255.252        Metric-0    : 1000
     3   Link Type    : Stub Net               Network     : 4.4.4.4
         Mask         : 255.255.255.255        Metric-0    : 0
     4   Link Type    : Transit                DR IP Addr  : 10.10.0.1
         I/F Addr     : 10.10.0.2              Metric-0    : 1000
```

Table 5.1 OSPF LSA Types

LSA Type	OSPF LSA Name
1	Router LSA
2	Network LSA
3	Summary LSA
4	ASBR LSA
5	External summary LSA
7	NSSA summary LSA
8	External attributes for BGP
9, 10, 11	Opaque LSAs

Figure 5.23 The two routers acknowledge the received LSRs and continue to transmit Hello messages to maintain the adjacency.

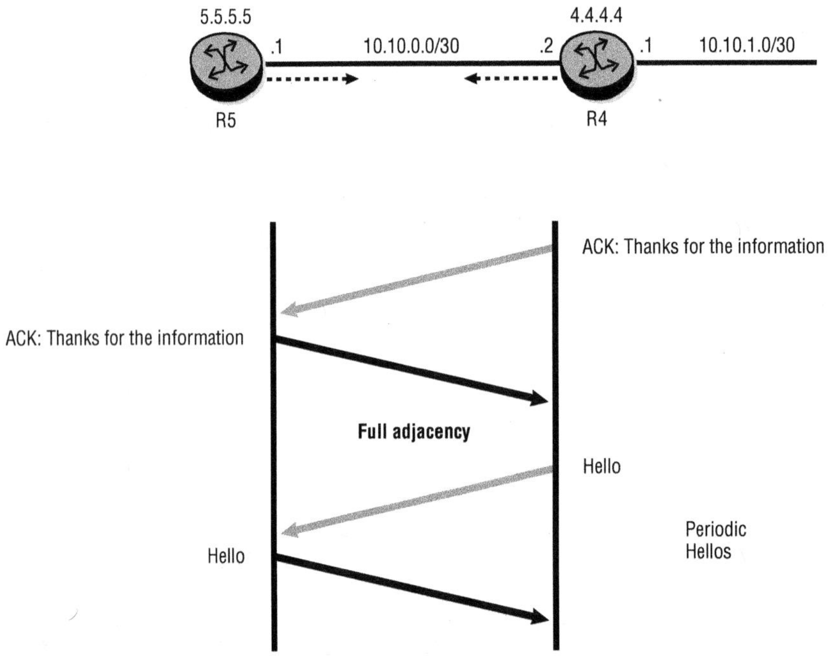

Listing 5.3 shows the contents of the OSPF database and the fields relevant to the flooding operation. This information is carried in the header of every LSA.

Figure 5.24 R5 sends a link-state acknowledgment to R4. They now have a full adjacency.

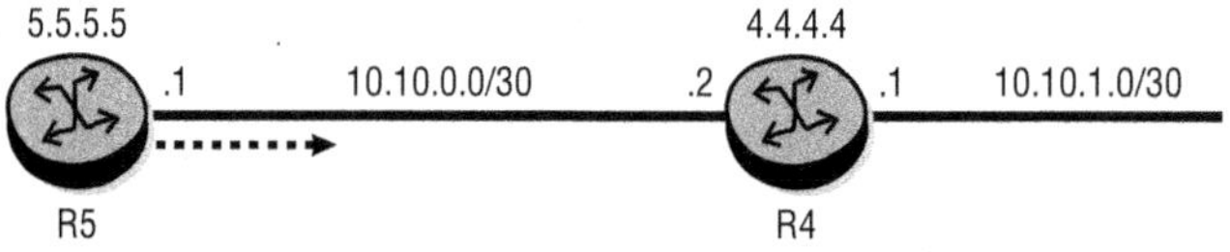


```
OSPF Version        : 2
Router Id           : 5.5.5.5
Area Id             : 0.0.0.0
Checksum            : 678d
Authentication      : Null
Authentication Key: 00 00 00 00 00 00 00 00
Packet Type         : LS_ACK
Packet Length       : 44

     Link ID    : 4.4.4.4              LSA Type   : RTR
     Area ID    : 0.0.0.0              Router ID  : 4.4.4.4
     Seq. Num   : 80000040             Age        : 1
     Length     : 72                   Checksum   : f99c
     Option Bits Set:  E 02
                            ...
```

Listing 5.3 The link-state database

```
*A:R2# show router ospf database

===============================================================================
OSPF Link State Database (Type : All)
===============================================================================
Type    Area Id      Link State Id   Adv Rtr Id   Age  Sequence   Cksum
-------------------------------------------------------------------------------
Router  0.0.0.0      1.1.1.1         1.1.1.1      187  0x800008f2 0xfaf8
Router  0.0.0.0      2.2.2.2         2.2.2.2      197  0x800008d3 0x54d3
Router  0.0.0.0      3.3.3.3         3.3.3.3      190  0x800008d1 0x928b
Router  0.0.0.0      5.5.5.5         5.5.5.5      192  0x800008c9 0xee32
Network 0.0.0.0      10.1.5.5        5.5.5.5      192  0x80000001 0xcf49
-------------------------------------------------------------------------------
No. of LSAs: 5
===============================================================================
*A:R2#
```

The combination of the four fields—Type, Area Id, Link State Id, and Adv Rtr Id—uniquely identifies every LSA in the network. The meaning of these fields is as follows:

- **Type**—LSA type. In this example, they are all Router and Network LSAs. The other types are introduced below.
- **Area Id**—This relates to hierarchy and is discussed below. Since this is a single area network, the Area Id is `0.0.0.0` for all LSAs.
- **Link State Id**—A value set by the advertising router to help identify the LSA
- **Adv Rtr Id**—Router ID of the advertising router

The sequence number is managed by the advertising router and is not modified by the other routers as the LSA is flooded. The age is originally set to 0 and incremented as it is flooded through the network and in the LSDB. `Cksum` is a checksum calculated on the LSA contents and used to validate its integrity. An LSA with an invalid checksum is discarded.

All LSAs are flooded using the algorithm described in Chapter 4. The advertising router creates the LSA, assigns a sequence number, sets the age to 0, and floods the LSA to all its neighbors. The neighboring routers process the LSA according to the following algorithm:

- If the sequence number is less than the value in the database, the LSA is discarded. The receiving router sends a copy of the LSA from its database to update its neighbor.
- If the sequence number is equal to the value in the database, the LSA is discarded. The router sends an acknowledgment to its neighbor.
- If the sequence number is greater than the value in the database or the LSA is unknown, the database is updated with the new LSA. The age is increased, but the sequence number is not changed. The LSA is flooded to its neighbors, and an acknowledgment is sent to the neighbor that sent the LSA.

LSA Aging

In OSPF, LSAs are considered valid until they reach the age of 3,600 (1 hour). At the age of 3,600, LSAs are removed from the database. When the age reaches ~1,800, the advertising router increments the sequence number and floods the LSA throughout the network. Although there has been no topology change, this refreshes the LSA in all the LSDBs.

5.5 Router LSA Details

Type 1 (Router) LSAs are generated by each OSPF router. Together with Type 2 (Network) LSAs, Router LSAs contain the basic topology information of the area. Router LSAs are flooded to all the routers in the local area but are not forwarded between OSPF areas (see Figure 5.25).

Figure 5.25 Each router floods a Router LSA to all the routers in the area.

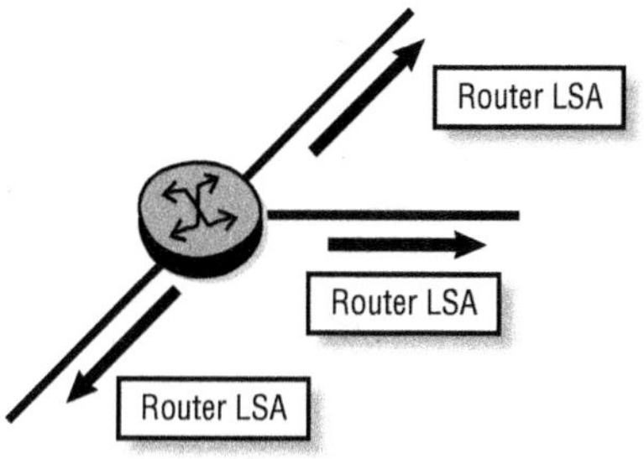

The fields of the Router LSA are shown in Figure 5.26. Remember that the Router LSA is transmitted to the neighboring routers in an LSU. The advertising router's RID is used as the link-state Id for the Router LSA.

At first glance, the Router LSA appears somewhat confusing. However, the structure of the LSA is fairly straightforward. It begins with the standard header of all LSAs—sequence number, age, and so on. This is followed by the status bits (V, E, and B) and the number of links that are described by the LSA. The V, E, and B bits all relate to multiple area networks that are described below. The remaining fields in the LSA describe each of the interfaces (links) in the area.

If a router has interfaces in multiple areas, the router generates a Router LSA for each area. The links described in a Router LSA are all the interfaces that are in the specific OSPF area and that are not down. OSPF defines four different types of links, identified in the Type field, as shown in Figure 5.27.

OSPF Link Types

There are four different link types defined for OSPF. The Type field identifies which of the four types of links the entry describes. Depending on the type of link, the Link ID and Link data fields have different meanings, as described below. All link types have a metric value, which is the cost assigned to the interface for the SPF calculation. OSPF also has the capability to carry TOS information, but this is not used. Therefore, you can expect the "`# ToS`" field to be 0 and the "`ToS`" and "`ToS metric`" fields to be missing from the LSA.

Figure 5.26 The Router (Type 1) LSA. Fields in white are common to all LSA types. Shaded fields are specific to the Router LSA. The link-state ID is set to the RID.

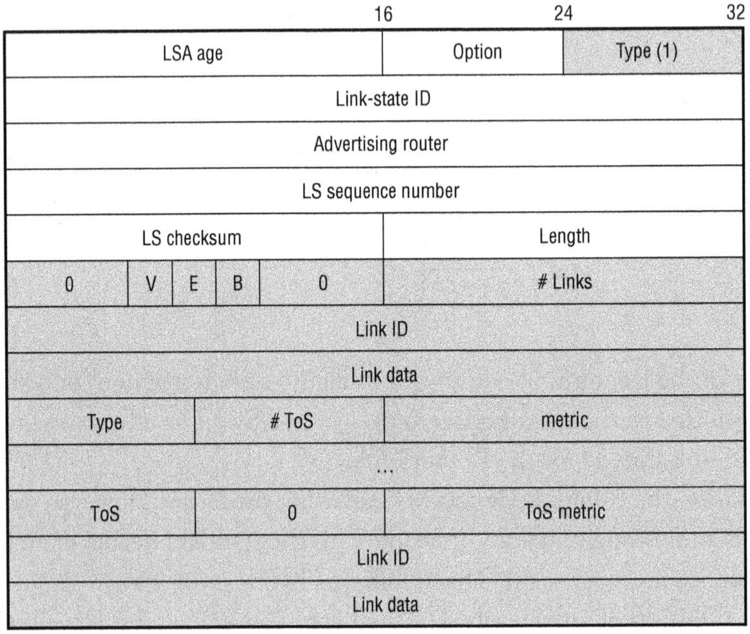

Remember, there is a link entry for each interface in the OSPF area. (In fact, there are two link entries created for each point-to-point interface in the area). The four different link types are:

- **Type 1 (point-to-point link)**—This entry is created for any point-to-point interface on which there is an adjacency with another OSPF router. (This includes an Ethernet interface that has been specifically configured as point-to-point.) The `Link ID` contains the RID of the neighbor, and the `Link data` field contains the IP interface address for the link. If the link is unnumbered (no IP address assigned), the `Link data` contains the interface index value. For each Type 1 entry, a Type 3 (stub network) entry is also created to describe the subnet.

Figure 5.27 There are four different link types that can be described in the Router LSA. All the router's active links in OSPF are described here.

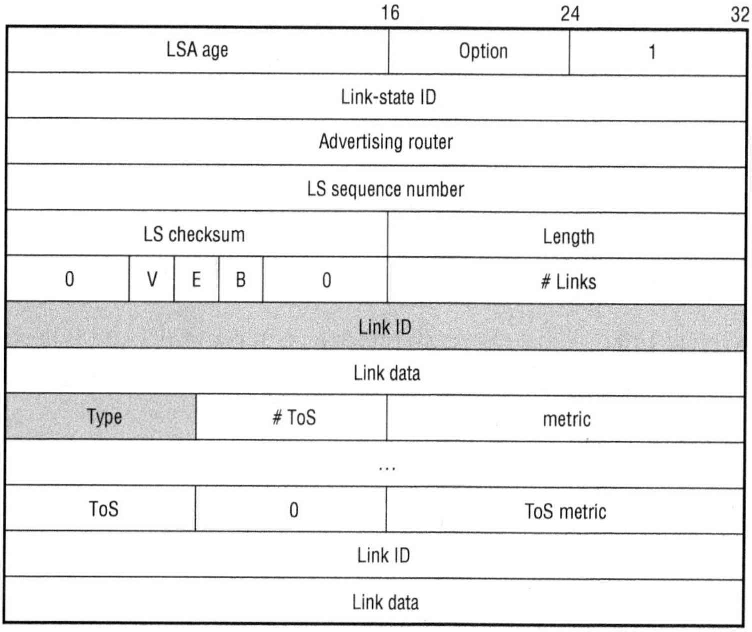

- **Type 2 (transit link)**—This entry is created for any broadcast interface, such as Ethernet, on which there is an adjacency with another OSPF router. On a transit link, there is an election of a designated router (described below), and the adjacency is formed with the DR. Until the adjacency is formed, the link is considered a stub and only a Type 3 entry is advertised for the interface.

  In a Type 2 entry, the `Link ID` field contains the interface address of the DR. The `Link data` field contains the IP interface address for the link. The DR advertises a Network LSA that contains the subnet address and subnet mask for this network. (This is similar to the way a second, Type 3 entry is created for point-to-point links. However, for a transit network, the information is advertised in a second LSA, the Network LSA.)

- **Type 3 (link to stub network)**—Do not confuse this with an OSPF stub area (described in Chapter 7). In this context, a stub network refers to any active interface in the OSPF area that does *not* have an adjacency with another OSPF router. Type 3 entries are created for these types of interfaces:

    - System interface or other loopback interfaces
    - Interfaces defined as passive in OSPF
    - Point-to-point or broadcast interfaces on which the OSPF adjacency has not yet formed
    - Type 3 entries also created for each Type 1 (point-to-point) entry

  In a Type 3 entry, the `Link ID` contains the subnet address and the `Link data` field contains the subnet mask.

- **Type 4 (virtual link)**—This relates to multiple area networks and is described in Chapter 7. For a virtual link, the `Link ID` field contains the RID of the neighbor, and the `Link data` field contains the interface IP address.

In OSPF, any interface included in the area is described in the Router LSA. An interface on which there is an adjacency with another OSPF router is described by a Type 2 or Type 1 plus Type 3 entry. If there is no OSPF adjacency on the interface, it is described by a Type 3 entry. Since they are virtual interfaces, the system interface and loopback interfaces are always described by Type 3 entries.

If you explicitly do not wish to form an OSPF adjacency on a specific interface, you can describe the interface as passive. In that case, OSPF will not transmit or accept Hello messages on that interface. The passive interface is described using a Type 3 entry. Table 5.2 summarizes the different link types as described in a Router LSA.

Table 5.2 Different Link Types Described in the Router LSA

Link Type	Description	Link ID Meaning	Link Data Meaning
1	Point-to-point	Neighbor router ID	Interface IP address
2	Transit	Interface address of DR	Interface IP address
3	Stub	IP subnet address	IP subnet mask
4	Virtual	Neighbor router ID	Interface IP address

For the topology shown in Figure 5.28, see Listing 5.4 for an examination of the Router LSA to see the different link types.

Figure 5.28 OSPF network with broadcast and point-to-point links.

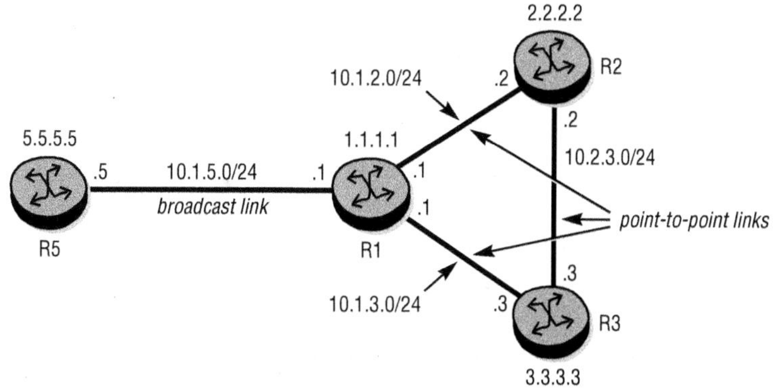

Listing 5.4 Detailed view of a Router LSA showing three of the four link types

```
*A:R1# show router ospf database 1.1.1.1 detail

======================================================================
OSPF Link State Database (Type : All) (Detailed)
======================================================================
----------------------------------------------------------------------
Router LSA for Area 0.0.0.0
----------------------------------------------------------------------
Area Id           : 0.0.0.0              Adv Router Id     : 1.1.1.1
Link State Id     : 1.1.1.1 (16843009)
LSA Type          : Router
Sequence No       : 0x800008f2        Checksum          : 0xfaf8
Age               : 1048              Length            : 96
Options           : E
Flags             : None              Link Count        : 6
Link Type (1)     : Stub Network
Network (1)       : 1.1.1.1           Mask (1)          : 255.255.255.255
No of TOS (1)     : 0                 Metric-0 (1)      : 0
Link Type (2)     : Point To Point
Nbr Rtr Id (2)    : 2.2.2.2           I/F Address (2)   : 10.1.2.1
No of TOS (2)     : 0                 Metric-0 (2)      : 1000
Link Type (3)     : Stub Network
```

(continued)

Listing 5.4 *(continued)*

```
Network (3)       : 10.1.2.0          Mask (3)          : 255.255.255.0
No of TOS (3)     : 0                 Metric-0 (3)      : 1000
Link Type (4)     : Point To Point
Nbr Rtr Id (4)    : 3.3.3.3           I/F Address (4)   : 10.1.3.1
No of TOS (4)     : 0                 Metric-0 (4)      : 1000
Link Type (5)     : Stub Network
Network (5)       : 10.1.3.0          Mask (5)          : 255.255.255.0
No of TOS (5)     : 0                 Metric-0 (5)      : 1000
Link Type (6)     : Transit Network
DR Rtr Id (6)     : 10.1.5.5          I/F Address (6)   : 10.1.5.1
No of TOS (6)     : 0                 Metric-0 (6)      : 1000
======================================================================
```

In the Router LSA shown in Listing 5.4, there are six link descriptions, as follows:

1. Stub link for the system interface
2. Point-to-point for the link to R2
3. Stub link to describe the network connecting to R2
4. Point-to-point for the link to R3
5. Stub link to describe the network connecting to R3
6. Transit network to R5

5.6 The Designated Router and Network LSAs

On a broadcast network such as Ethernet, a DR and a BDR are elected. The router with the highest priority on the interface is selected as DR and the one with the second highest priority becomes BDR. The default value is one, and if priority values are equal, the highest router ID is selected. Note that priority values are assigned to the interface, so a router may be DR on one broadcast network, but not on others. If the priority value is zero, the router will not become DR or BDR. DR election in OSPF is non-preemptive so if a DR already exists on the network a new router will not become DR even if it has a higher priority.

The DR is responsible for sending a Network LSA that describes the broadcast network and reduces the amount of network traffic (see Figure 5.29). The BDR monitors the transmissions of the DR and takes over if the DR fails.

Figure 5.29 The DR forms adjacencies with the other routers on the broadcast network and floods a Network LSA to represent the network.

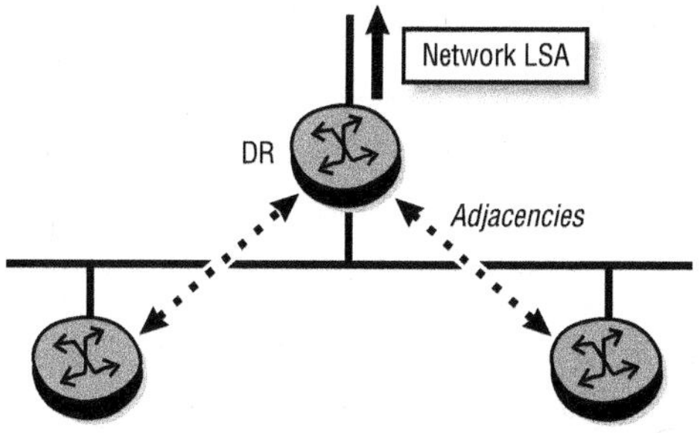

A DR and a BDR are elected for each broadcast network in the routing domain. One Network LSA is flooded for each broadcast network.

Forming an Adjacency with the DR

As seen in the section above, "OSPF Neighbor Discovery," when an OSPF router with broadcast interfaces starts up, it transmits Hello packets with `0.0.0.0` in the DR and BDR fields. If a DR has already been chosen on the network, the new router will discover the DR and BDR in the Hello packets from the other neighbors and will accept them. In Figure 5.30, all routers have the same priority. Router R5 is the DR, and Router R4 is the BDR. Routers R1 and R2 will only form adjacencies with Router R5 and Router R4, not with each other.

Figure 5.30 Router R5 has the highest RID and becomes the DR on the network.

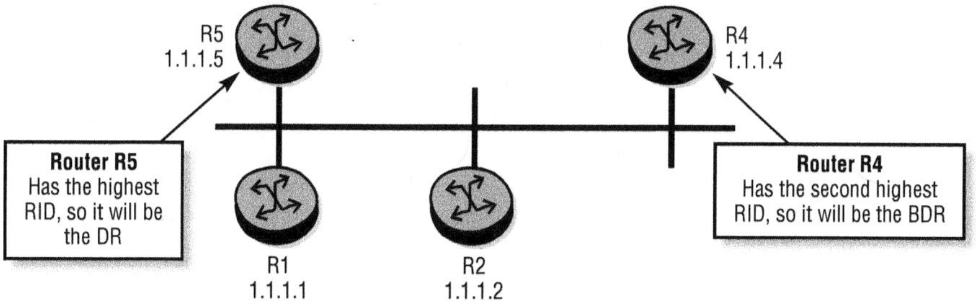

When a new router becomes active in a broadcast topology, it generates a Hello packet. The multicast address used is `224.0.0.5`, which is the "all OSPF routers" address.

The new router's Hello does not contain any neighbor RIDs because it has not yet seen any neighbors on the link (see Figure 5.31).

Figure 5.31 The new router generates a Hello message on the broadcast network. R3 lists no neighbors.

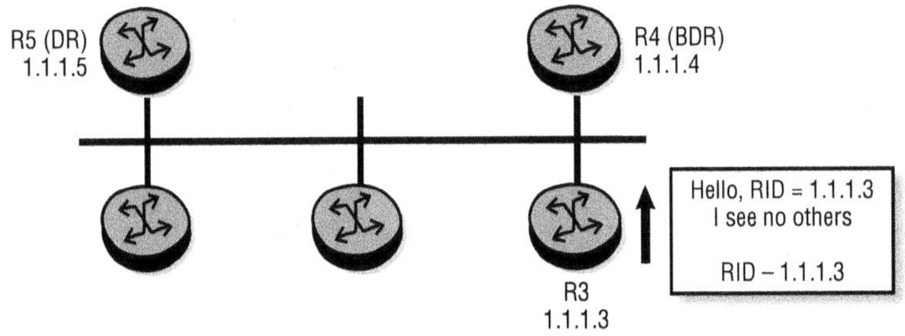

One of the already active routers (in this case, the DR) generates a periodic Hello. This Hello also uses the IP multicast address `224.0.0.5`. The new router not only sees its RID in the Hello, but it also learns of the other devices on the segment based on their RIDs. In addition, the Hello packet identifies the active DR and BDR for the link (see Figure 5.32).

Figure 5.32 Another router generates a Hello, listing the routers seen on the network segment, as well as the DR and BDR.

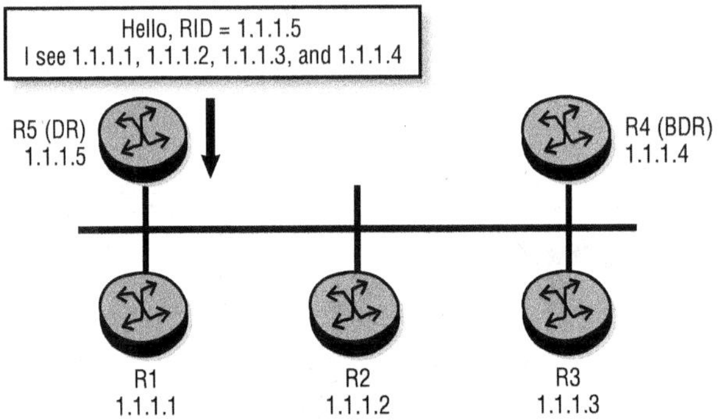

Because a DR and BDR already exist, the new router forms an adjacency with the DRs and advertises its networks to them by using the IP multicast address `224.0.0.6` (all DRs). The routers that are not DRs ignore this update because they are only listening to the `224.0.0.5` IP multicast address (see Figure 5.33).

Figure 5.33 The new router transmits its LSA to the DR and BDR using the DR multicast address.

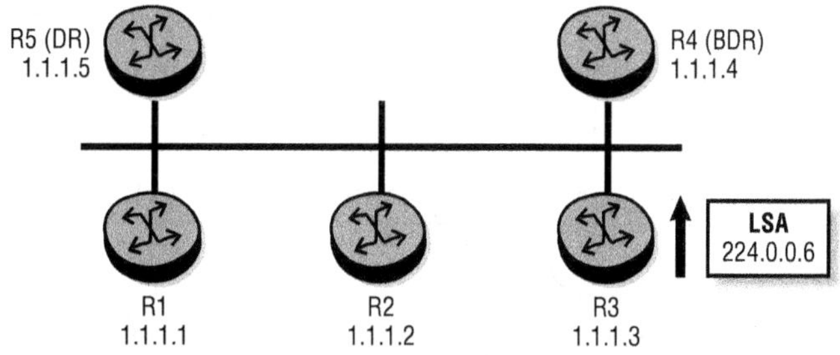

When the DR receives an LSA and determines that it represents a new entry in its topological database, it sends an update to all devices on the segment using the IP multicast address `224.0.0.5` (all OSPF routers) (see Figure 5.34). The BDR does not send an update because it sees the update sent by the DR. All routers send a link-state acknowledgment packet back to the DR to acknowledge receipt of the LSA. This includes the BDR and the new router that created the LSA.

Figure 5.34 The DR transmits an updated LSA to all routers on the network. They acknowledge receipt of the update.

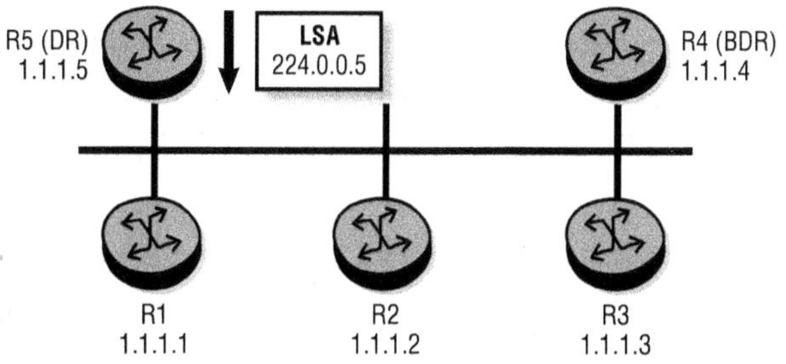

To improve operational efficiency and network convergence time, Ethernet interfaces should be configured as point-to-point if they are directly connected to another router, as is often the case in modern networks. When starting up, the routers will not have to wait for the DR election as they form their adjacency, and they will not generate Network LSAs (described below).

Since the DR election is non-preemptive, the DR on a network is usually not the one with the highest priority, but the one that has been operational for the longest time.

Network LSA Details

Besides forming adjacencies with the other routers on the broadcast network and handling the flooding of updates, the DR is responsible for generating the Network LSA (or Type 2 LSA) that represents the broadcast network. The format is shown in Figure 5.35.

Figure 5.35 The Network (Type 2) LSA. Shaded fields are specific to this LSA.

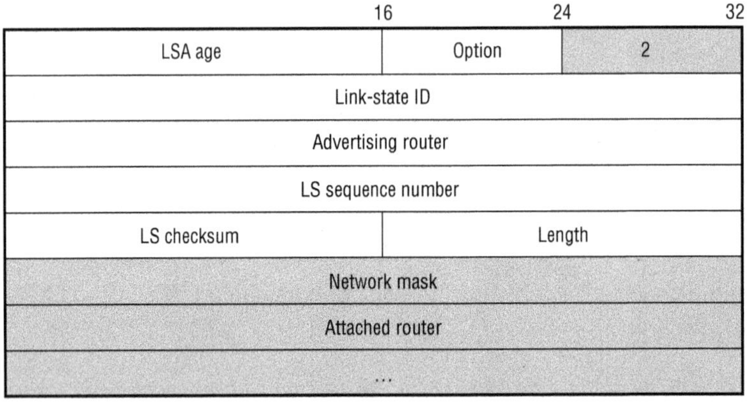

The DR creates a Network LSA only if it is fully adjacent to at least one other router on the broadcast network. The Network LSA is flooded throughout the local OSPF area, but not to other areas. The Network LSA lists the routers that are fully adjacent to the DR; each fully adjacent router is identified by its OSPF RID. The DR includes itself in this list.

The Network LSA contains an age, option, sequence number, and checksum like any LSA. The values in the other fields are:

- **Link-state ID**—Contains the IP address of the DR's interface on the broadcast network. With the subnet mask, the network address can be derived from this value.
- **Advertising router**—The RID of the DR
- **Network mask**—The subnet mask for the broadcast network
- **Attached router**—A list of the RIDs of all the routers with interfaces on the broadcast network that have formed an adjacency with the DR. The DR includes itself in the list.

Given the topology in Figure 5.36, R6 will become the DR if all routers start OSPF at the same time.

Figure 5.36 Broadcast network topology with four routers on a broadcast network segment

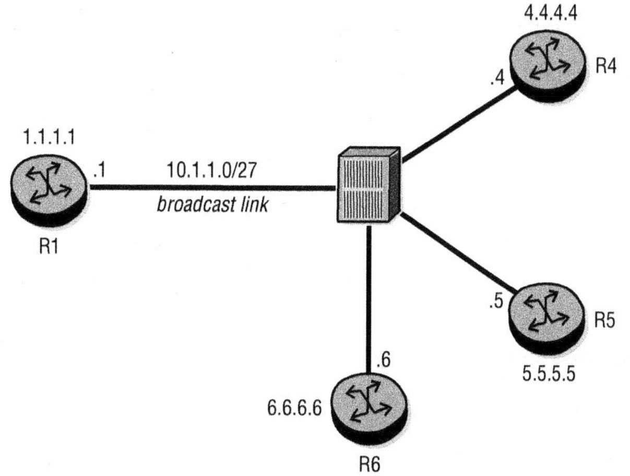

The Network LSA produced by R6 is shown in Listing 5.5. Notice that all four routers on the broadcast network are listed as adjacent routers.

Listing 5.5 Detailed view of the Network LSA

```
*A:R6>config>router>ospf# show router ospf database 10.1.1.6 detail

===============================================================================
OSPF Link State Database (Type : All) (Detailed)
===============================================================================
-------------------------------------------------------------------------------
Network LSA for Area 0.0.0.0
-------------------------------------------------------------------------------
Area Id          : 0.0.0.0              Adv Router Id     : 10.10.10.6
Link State Id    : 10.1.1.6 (167837958)
LSA Type         : Network
Sequence No      : 0x80000004           Checksum          : 0x7d32
Age              : 1084                 Length            : 40
Options          : E
Network Mask     : 255.255.255.224      No of Adj Rtrs    : 4
Router Id (1)    : 10.10.10.6           Router Id (2)     : 10.10.10.1
Router Id (3)    : 10.10.10.4           Router Id (4)     : 10.10.10.5
===============================================================================
```

5.7 Configuring and Verifying OSPF

The following characteristics relate to the configuration of OSPF on the 7750 SR:

- All OSPF routers must have a unique router ID. By default, the system interface is used as the router ID on the 7750 SR.
- Once the OSPF context is entered, OSPF is administratively enabled on the router. When an area is created and interfaces are added, the router is operational in the OSPF routing domain.
- Interfaces must be configured in an OSPF area:
    - By default, interfaces in an area are advertised by OSPF.
    - Routes received through OSPF are advertised by OSPF.
    - No other routes are advertised.

Configuring OSPF

Consider the topology shown in Figure 5.37. In Listing 5.6, we demonstrate the configuration of OSPF for this network on one router.

Figure 5.37 Topology used for sample configuration

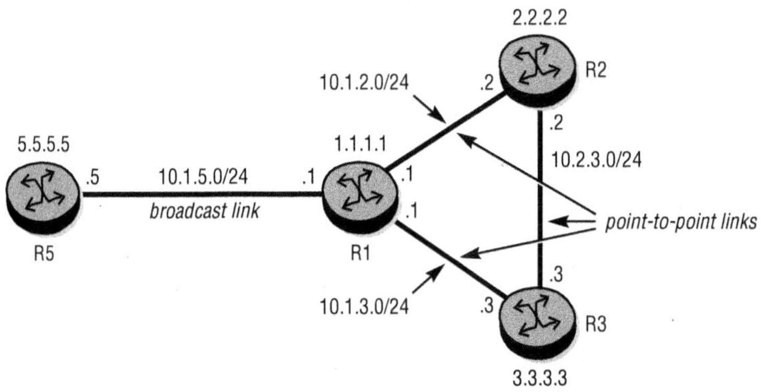

Listing 5.6 Configure the Layer 3 interfaces

```
*A:R1# configure router
*A:R1>config>router# interface system
```

```
*A:R1>config>router>if# address 1.1.1.1/32
*A:R1>config>router>if# exit
*A:R1>config>router# interface toR2
*A:R1>config>router>if$ address 10.1.2.1/24
*A:R1>config>router>if$ port 1/1/2
*A:R1>config>router>if$ exit
*A:R1>config>router# interface toR3
*A:R1>config>router>if$ address 10.1.3.1/24
*A:R1>config>router>if$ port 1/1/3
*A:R1>config>router>if$ exit
*A:R1>config>router# interface toR5
*A:R1>config>router>if$ address 10.1.5.1/24
*A:R1>config>router>if$ port 1/1/1
*A:R1>config>router>if$ exit
*A:R1>config>router# show router interface

========================================================================
Interface Table (Router: Base)
========================================================================
Interface-Name                Adm         Opr(v4/v6)  Mode    Port/SapId
   IP-Address                                                 PfxState
------------------------------------------------------------------------
system                      Up          Up/--       Network system
   1.1.1.1/32                                                 n/a
toR2                        Up          Up/--       Network 1/1/2
   10.1.2.1/24                                                n/a
toR3                        Up          Up/--       Network 1/1/3
   10.1.3.1/24                                                n/a
toR5                        Up          Up/--       Network 1/1/1
   10.1.5.1/24                                                n/a
```

1. On R1, first configure the Layer 3 interfaces.
2. Verify connectivity and check the routing table. It's possible to ping the interface of a neighboring router, but not the system address (it's not directly connected). Since there is no dynamic routing protocol running, only directly connected networks are in the routing table (Listing 5.7).

Listing 5.7 Verify reachability of directly connected networks

```
*A:R1>config>router# ping 10.1.2.2
PING 10.1.2.2 56 data bytes
64 bytes from 10.1.2.2: icmp_seq=1 ttl=64 time<1ms.
64 bytes from 10.1.2.2: icmp_seq=2 ttl=64 time<1ms.
64 bytes from 10.1.2.2: icmp_seq=3 ttl=64 time<1ms.
64 bytes from 10.1.2.2: icmp_seq=4 ttl=64 time<1ms.
64 bytes from 10.1.2.2: icmp_seq=5 ttl=64 time<1ms.

---- 10.1.2.2 PING Statistics ----
5 packets transmitted, 5 packets received, 0.00% packet loss
round-trip min < 1ms, avg < 1ms, max < 1ms, stddev < 1ms
*A:R1>config>router#
*A:R1>config>router# ping 2.2.2.2
PING 2.2.2.2 56 data bytes
No route to destination. Address: 2.2.2.2, Router: Base
No route to destination. Address: 2.2.2.2, Router: Base
No route to destination. Address: 2.2.2.2, Router: Base
No route to destination. Address: 2.2.2.2, Router: Base
No route to destination. Address: 2.2.2.2, Router: Base

---- 2.2.2.2 PING Statistics ----
5 packets transmitted, 0 packets received, 100% packet loss
*A:R1>config>router#
*A:R1>config>router# show router route-table

===============================================================================
Route Table (Router: Base)
===============================================================================
Dest Prefix                               Type    Proto    Age           Pref
      Next Hop[Interface Name]                                 Metric
-------------------------------------------------------------------------------
1.1.1.1/32                                Local   Local    54d08h43m     0
      system                                                   0
10.1.2.0/24                               Local   Local    00h15m57s     0
      toR2                                                     0
10.1.3.0/24                               Local   Local    00h15m12s     0
      toR3                                                     0
10.1.5.0/24                               Local   Local    00h14m43s     0
```

```
    toR5                                                  0
-------------------------------------------------------------------------------
No. of Routes: 4
===============================================================================
```

3. Start OSPF, and since this is a single area network, create all interfaces in area 0. The interface to R5 is a broadcast network. The others are configured as point-to-point interfaces (Listing 5.8).

Listing 5.8 Configure the interfaces in OSPF

```
*A:R1# configure router
*A:R1>config>router# ospf
*A:R1>config>router>ospf# area 0
*A:R1>config>router>ospf>area# interface system
*A:R1>config>router>ospf>area>if# exit
*A:R1>config>router>ospf>area# interface toR2
*A:R1>config>router>ospf>area>if$ interface-type point-to-point
*A:R1>config>router>ospf>area>if$ exit
*A:R1>config>router>ospf>area# interface toR3
*A:R1>config>router>ospf>area>if$ interface-type point-to-point
*A:R1>config>router>ospf>area>if$ exit
*A:R1>config>router>ospf>area# interface toR5
*A:R1>config>router>ospf>area>if$ exit
*A:R1>config>router>ospf>area#
*A:R1>config>router>ospf>area# show router ospf interface

===============================================================================
OSPF Interfaces
===============================================================================
If Name          Area Id       Designated Rtr  Bkup Desig Rtr  Adm  Oper
-------------------------------------------------------------------------------
system           0.0.0.0       1.1.1.1         0.0.0.0         Up   DR
toR2             0.0.0.0       0.0.0.0         0.0.0.0         Up   PToP
toR3             0.0.0.0       0.0.0.0         0.0.0.0         Up   PToP
toR5             0.0.0.0       5.5.5.5         1.1.1.1         Up   BDR
-------------------------------------------------------------------------------
No. of OSPF Interfaces: 4
===============================================================================
```

Verifying OSPF Operation

Because OSPF has already been configured on the other routers in the network, R1 forms adjacencies with them and updates its LSDB (Listing 5.9).

Listing 5.9 Verify the OSPF neighbors and the OSFP database

```
*A:R1>config>router>ospf>area# show router ospf neighbor

===============================================================================
OSPF Neighbors
===============================================================================
Interface-Name                   Rtr Id           State        Pri  RetxQ   TTL
-------------------------------------------------------------------------------
toR2                           2.2.2.2          Full         1    0        36
toR3                           3.3.3.3          Full         1    0        34
toR5                           5.5.5.5          Full         1    0        34
-------------------------------------------------------------------------------
No. of Neighbors: 3
===============================================================================
*A:R1>config>router>ospf>area#
*A:R1>config>router>ospf>area# show router ospf database

===============================================================================
OSPF Link State Database (Type : All)
===============================================================================
Type    Area Id      Link State Id   Adv Rtr Id   Age  Sequence    Cksum
-------------------------------------------------------------------------------
Router  0.0.0.0      1.1.1.1         1.1.1.1      179  0x800008f2 0xfaf8
Router  0.0.0.0      2.2.2.2         2.2.2.2      190  0x800008d3 0x54d3
Router  0.0.0.0      3.3.3.3         3.3.3.3      183  0x800008d1 0x928b
Router  0.0.0.0      5.5.5.5         5.5.5.5      184  0x800008c9 0xee32
Network 0.0.0.0      10.1.5.5        5.5.5.5      184  0x80000001 0xcf49
-------------------------------------------------------------------------------
No. of LSAs: 5
===============================================================================
```

If we check the database on R2, it should be identical—all routers in the area must have the same LSDB. The ages may differ by a few seconds, but sequence numbers and checksums must be the same. Listing 5.10 shows that the database on R2 is the same as the one on R1 (Listing 5.9).

Listing 5.10 The LSDB on R2 is identical to the LSDB on the other routers in the network

```
*A:R2# show router ospf database

===============================================================================
OSPF Link State Database (Type : All)
===============================================================================
Type     Area Id         Link State Id   Adv Rtr Id      Age  Sequence   Cksum
-------------------------------------------------------------------------------
Router   0.0.0.0         1.1.1.1         1.1.1.1         187  0x800008f2 0xfaf8
Router   0.0.0.0         2.2.2.2         2.2.2.2         197  0x800008d3 0x54d3
Router   0.0.0.0         3.3.3.3         3.3.3.3         190  0x800008d1 0x928b
Router   0.0.0.0         5.5.5.5         5.5.5.5         192  0x800008c9 0xee32
Network  0.0.0.0         10.1.5.5        5.5.5.5         192  0x80000001 0xcf49
-------------------------------------------------------------------------------
No. of LSAs: 5
===============================================================================
*A:R2#
```

Analyzing an LSA

As expected, there are four Router LSAs (one for each router) and one Network LSA (for the single broadcast network). The Router LSA from R1 contains all its directly connected networks (Listing 5.11). The different link types were described above.

Listing 5.11 The Router LSA from R1 describes three different link types.

```
*A:R1# show router ospf database 1.1.1.1 detail

===============================================================================
OSPF Link State Database (Type : All) (Detailed)
===============================================================================
-------------------------------------------------------------------------------
Router LSA for Area 0.0.0.0
-------------------------------------------------------------------------------
```

(continued)

Listing 5.11 *(continued)*

```
Area Id            : 0.0.0.0            Adv Router Id      : 1.1.1.1
Link State Id      : 1.1.1.1 (16843009)
LSA Type           : Router
Sequence No        : 0x800008f2         Checksum           : 0xfaf8
Age                : 1048               Length             : 96
Options            : E
Flags              : None               Link Count         : 6
Link Type (1)      : Stub Network
Network (1)        : 1.1.1.1            Mask (1)           : 255.255.255.255
No of TOS (1)      : 0                  Metric-0 (1)       : 0
Link Type (2)      : Point To Point
Nbr Rtr Id (2)     : 2.2.2.2            I/F Address (2)    : 10.1.2.1
No of TOS (2)      : 0                  Metric-0 (2)       : 1000
Link Type (3)      : Stub Network
Network (3)        : 10.1.2.0           Mask (3)           : 255.255.255.0
No of TOS (3)      : 0                  Metric-0 (3)       : 1000
Link Type (4)      : Point To Point
Nbr Rtr Id (4)     : 3.3.3.3            I/F Address (4)    : 10.1.3.1
No of TOS (4)      : 0                  Metric-0 (4)       : 1000
Link Type (5)      : Stub Network
Network (5)        : 10.1.3.0           Mask (5)           : 255.255.255.0
No of TOS (5)      : 0                  Metric-0 (5)       : 1000
Link Type (6)      : Transit Network
DR Rtr Id (6)      : 10.1.5.5           I/F Address (6)    : 10.1.5.1
No of TOS (6)      : 0                  Metric-0 (6)       : 1000
===============================================================================
```

In addition to the Router LSAs, R5 (the DR for this link) advertises a Network LSA for the broadcast network (Listing 5.12). Remember, the network address for this network is derived from the link-state ID.

Listing 5.12 Router R5 broadcasts the Network LSA for the broadcast network.

```
*A:R1# show router ospf database 10.1.5.5 detail

===============================================================================
OSPF Link State Database (Type : All) (Detailed)
===============================================================================
```

```
-------------------------------------------------------------------------
Network LSA for Area 0.0.0.0
-------------------------------------------------------------------------
Area Id          : 0.0.0.0              Adv Router Id    : 5.5.5.5
Link State Id    : 10.1.5.5 (167838981)
LSA Type         : Network
Sequence No      : 0x80000001           Checksum         : 0xcf49
Age              : 1311                 Length           : 32
Options          : E
Network Mask     : 255.255.255.0        No of Adj Rtrs   : 2
Router Id (1)    : 5.5.5.5              Router Id (2)    : 1.1.1.1
=========================================================================
```

Now that the network is fully converged, all routes are in the route table, and it is possible to reach any address in the network (Listing 5.13).

Listing 5.13 All OSPF enabled networks are seen in the route table.

```
*A:R1# show router route-table

=========================================================================
Route Table (Router: Base)
=========================================================================
Dest Prefix                               Type    Proto    Age         Pref
       Next Hop[Interface Name]                                Metric
-------------------------------------------------------------------------
1.1.1.1/32                                Local   Local    54d09h25m   0
       system                                                  0
2.2.2.2/32                                Remote  OSPF     00h25m36s   10
       10.1.2.2                                                1000
3.3.3.3/32                                Remote  OSPF     00h25m28s   10
       10.1.3.3                                                1000
5.5.5.5/32                                Remote  OSPF     00h25m28s   10
       10.1.5.5                                                1000
10.1.2.0/24                               Local   Local    00h57m54s   0
       toR2                                                    0
10.1.3.0/24                               Local   Local    00h57m09s   0
       toR3                                                    0
10.1.5.0/24                               Local   Local    00h56m39s   0
```

(continued)

Listing 5.13 *(continued)*

```
        toR5                                              0
10.2.3.0/24                          Remote  OSPF      00h25m28s   10
        10.1.3.3                                          2000
-------------------------------------------------------------------------------
No. of Routes: 8
===============================================================================
*A:R1#
*A:R1# ping 2.2.2.2
PING 2.2.2.2 56 data bytes
64 bytes from 2.2.2.2: icmp_seq=1 ttl=64 time<1ms.
64 bytes from 2.2.2.2: icmp_seq=2 ttl=64 time<1ms.
64 bytes from 2.2.2.2: icmp_seq=3 ttl=64 time<1ms.
64 bytes from 2.2.2.2: icmp_seq=4 ttl=64 time<1ms.
64 bytes from 2.2.2.2: icmp_seq=5 ttl=64 time<1ms.

---- 2.2.2.2 PING Statistics ----
5 packets transmitted, 5 packets received, 0.00% packet loss
round-trip min < 1ms, avg < 1ms, max < 1ms, stddev < 1ms
```

5.8 Other OSPF Features

Several additional features are described below. These include the ability to define a passive interface, overload on boot, authentication between OSPF neighbors, and bidirectional forwarding detection (BFD).

Passive Interface

An interface can be configured as passive when it is desirable to have the network advertised in OSPF, but the interface is not part of the OSPF routing domain, as seen in the topology in Figure 5.38.

The configuration of the passive interface on R5 is shown in Listing 5.14.

Listing 5.14 Configuring a passive interface

```
*A:R5# show router interface
```

```
===============================================================================
Interface Table (Router: Base)
===============================================================================
Interface-Name                   Adm         Opr(v4/v6)  Mode    Port/SapId
   IP-Address                                                    PfxState
-------------------------------------------------------------------------------
system                           Up          Up/--       Network system
   10.10.10.5/32                                                 n/a
toR1                             Up          Up/--       Network 1/1/3
   10.1.5.5/24                                                   n/a
to_External                      Up          Up/--       Network 1/1/1
   10.20.5.5/24                                                  n/a
-------------------------------------------------------------------------------
Interfaces : 3
===============================================================================
*A:R5# configure router ospf area 0
*A:R5>config>router>ospf>area# interface "to_External" passive
```

Figure 5.38 Topology with an external network to be configured as a passive interface

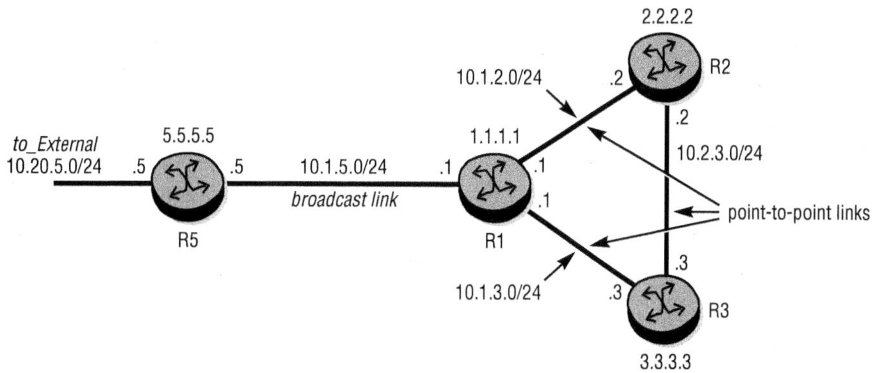

After the passive interface is configured, the network is described in the Router LSA as a stub link and is advertised throughout the OSPF domain (Listing 5.15).

Listing 5.15 The passive interface is listed in the Router LSA as a link type stub.

```
*A:R5>config>router>ospf>area# show router ospf database
10.10.10.5 detail
```

(continued)

Listing 5.15 *(continued)*

```
===============================================================================
OSPF Link State Database (Type : All) (Detailed)
===============================================================================
-------------------------------------------------------------------------------
Router LSA for Area 0.0.0.0
-------------------------------------------------------------------------------
Area Id          : 0.0.0.0            Adv Router Id     : 10.10.10.5
Link State Id    : 10.10.10.5 (168430085)
LSA Type         : Router
Sequence No      : 0x80000009         Checksum          : 0x6349
Age              : 117                Length            : 60
Options          : E
Flags            : None               Link Count        : 3
Link Type (1)    : Transit Network
DR Rtr Id (1)    : 10.1.5.5           I/F Address (1)   : 10.1.5.5
No of TOS (1)    : 0                  Metric-0 (1)      : 100
Link Type (2)    : Stub Network
Network (2)      : 10.10.10.5         Mask (2)          : 255.255.255.255
No of TOS (2)    : 0                  Metric-0 (2)      : 0
Link Type (3)    : Stub Network
Network (3)      : 10.20.5.0          Mask (3)          : 255.255.255.0
No of TOS (3)    : 0                  Metric-0 (3)      : 100
===============================================================================
```

Overload on Boot

Overload on boot is configured to avoid having the router used as a route for forwarding data immediately after the router has booted. The router's links will be advertised with the maximum metric value in the Router LSA. This is useful when the router is a transit router in a BGP (Border Gateway Protocol) autonomous system and needs additional time to process the BGP routes it is receiving. When the router is rebooted, OSPF will converge in a matter of seconds, whereas BGP might take much longer if there are a large number of routes. Packets to external destinations will be dropped if they are forwarded to this router before it has the external BGP routes in its route table.

In some special circumstances, a router may be configured in a permanent overload. In this case, it is part of the topology and able to exchange routes with the other routers but is not used for traffic forwarding. The topology in Figure 5.39 shows R2 configured in the permanent overload state. Note the metric of the links in the Router LSA shown in Listing 5.16.

Figure 5.39 Router R2 is configured in a permanent overload.

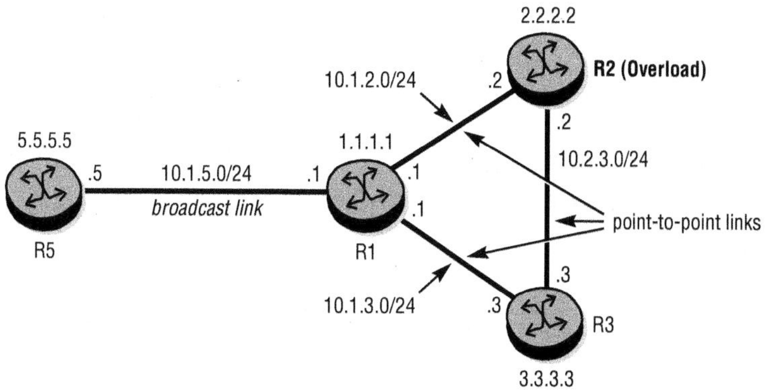

Listing 5.16 R2 configured in permanent overload

```
*A:R2# configure router ospf
*A:R2>config>router>ospf# overload
*A:R2>config>router>ospf# show router ospf database 10.10.10.2 detail

===============================================================================
OSPF Link State Database (Type : All) (Detailed)
===============================================================================
-------------------------------------------------------------------------------
Router LSA for Area 0.0.0.0
-------------------------------------------------------------------------------
Area Id           : 0.0.0.0              Adv Router Id     : 10.10.10.2
Link State Id     : 10.10.10.2 (168430082)
LSA Type          : Router
Sequence No       : 0x80000005         Checksum          : 0xacc0
Age               : 14                 Length            : 84
Options           : E
Flags             : None               Link Count        : 5
Link Type (1)     : Stub Network
```

(continued)

Listing 5.16 *(continued)*

```
Network (1)       : 10.10.10.2        Mask (1)          : 255.255.255.255
No of TOS (1)     : 0                 Metric-0 (1)      : 0
Link Type (2)     : Point To Point
Nbr Rtr Id (2)    : 10.10.10.3        I/F Address (2)   : 10.2.3.2
No of TOS (2)     : 0                 Metric-0 (2)      : 65535
Link Type (3)     : Stub Network
Network (3)       : 10.2.3.0          Mask (3)          : 255.255.255.0
No of TOS (3)     : 0                 Metric-0 (3)      : 100
Link Type (4)     : Point To Point
Nbr Rtr Id (4)    : 10.10.10.1        I/F Address (4)   : 10.1.2.2
No of TOS (4)     : 0                 Metric-0 (4)      : 65535
Link Type (5)     : Stub Network
Network (5)       : 10.1.2.0          Mask (5)          : 255.255.255.0
No of TOS (5)     : 0                 Metric-0 (5)      : 100
===============================================================================
```

Authentication

In a public network, it is simple for an unauthorized device to emulate an OSPF router and potentially disrupt network operation by presenting false information. To provide protection from this situation, two options are available—simple and MD5 authentication. The levels of security supported by OSPF are as follows:

- **No authentication**—OSPF does not do any authentication and therefore provides no security. This is the default value.
- **Simple authentication**—Provides password authentication between OSPF neighbors. This is less secure than MD5 because the password is transmitted in plaintext.
- **MD5 authentication**—Provides password authentication between OSPF neighbors using an MD5 hashed key. This is the most secure and recommended configuration.

The output in Listing 5.17 shows the configuration of authentication for the adjacency between R1 and R2. Note that the key is stored in its hashed form.

Listing 5.17 Configuring authentication on the OSPF interface

```
*A:R1# configure router ospf area 0
*A:R1>config>router>ospf>area# interface "toR2"
```

```
*A:R1>config>router>ospf>area>if# authentication-type message-digest
*A:R1>config>router>ospf>area>if# message-digest-key 1 md5
"Alcatel-Lucent"
*A:R1>config>router>ospf>area>if# info
----------------------------------------------
                    interface-type point-to-point
                    authentication-type message-digest
                    message-digest-key 1 md5
"wcQxCDYefsIJNA9t//sKYQvPFs2cPDgA/rpMiYe3glItnDy3YW.nFU" hash2
----------------------------------------------
*A:R1>config>router>ospf>area>if# show router ospf interface
"toR2" detail

===============================================================================
OSPF Interface (Detailed) :  toR2
===============================================================================
-------------------------------------------------------------------------------
Configuration
-------------------------------------------------------------------------------
IP Address        : 10.1.2.1
Area Id           : 0.0.0.0                Priority          : 1
Hello Intrvl      : 10 sec                 Rtr Dead Intrvl   : 40 sec
Retrans Intrvl    : 5 sec                  Poll Intrvl       : 120 sec
Cfg Metric        : 0                      Advert Subnet     : True
Transit Delay     : 1                      Auth Type         : MD5
Passive           : False                  Cfg MTU           : 0
IPsec In Stat SA  :                        IPsec Out Stat SA:
IPsec In Stat SA*:
-------------------------------------------------------------------------------
State
...output omitted...
```

If the key is not correctly configured on one side of the adjacency, expect to find an entry in log 99 (Listing 5.18).

Listing 5.18 Check log 99 for authentication problems.

```
*A:R1# show log log-id 99
```

(continued)

Listing 5.18 *(continued)*

```
===============================================================================
Event Log 99
===============================================================================
Description : Default System Log
Memory Log contents  [size=500   next event=301  (not wrapped)]

300 2010/08/26 13:22:43.60 UTC WARNING: OSPF #2006 Base VR:
  1 OSPFv2 (0)
"LCL_RTR_ID 10.10.10.1: Packet failed authFailure authentication on
 interface toR2 from 10.1.2.2 in hello"
```

Bidirectional Forwarding Detection

When an OSPF interface goes down, OSPF immediately recognizes this as a topology change and generates a new Router LSA reflecting the new topology. This includes a physical failure of the link or anything else that causes the port to go down. In such a situation, the router detects the failure immediately, and OSPF converges within a few seconds.

However, Figure 5.40 shows two routers connected by two Ethernet switches. OSPF will not detect a failure between the two switches until the dead router timer has expired (40 seconds by default). It is possible to decrease the Hello interval for OSPF sessions, but the processing of these messages increases the overhead within the OSPF process on the CPM (Control Processor Module). BFD provides a lightweight network protocol that operates at the level of the physical interface to detect the loss of packet forwarding capabilities on the link. BFD establishes a session between the two OSPF neighbors, as shown in Figure 5.40.

Figure 5.40 BFD establishes a lightweight session to quickly detect failures on the link.

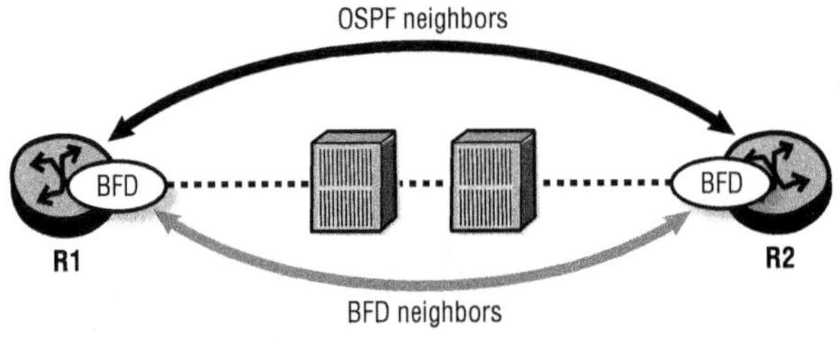

Because the processing of BFD packets is handled by the IOM (Input/Output Module) and does not have an impact on the CPM, the transmission rate can be much higher and the failure detected much more quickly. When a BFD failure is detected on the interface, the routing protocol is signaled and responds immediately to the failure (Figure 5.41).

Figure 5.41 When a BFD failure is detected, the OSPF process is notified and immediately responds to the topology change.

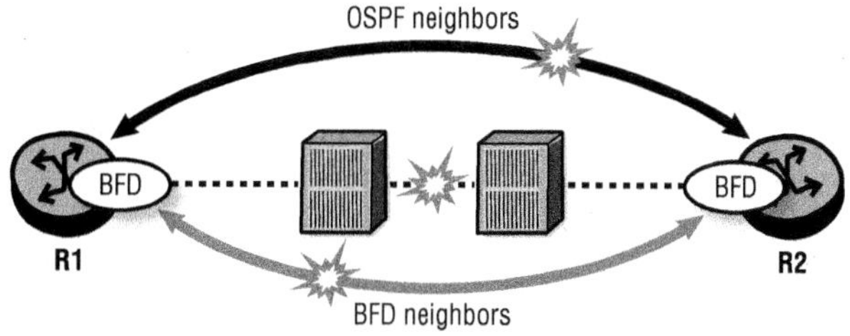

The BFD session is configured on the interface and enabled in the routing protocol (Listing 5.19). An interface with BFD enabled transmits UDP (User Datagram Protocol) packets at the transmit interval and expects to receive them at the receive interval. The transmit interval for BFD can be set as low as 10 milliseconds with a multiplier of 3, meaning that failures can be detected within 30 milliseconds.

Listing 5.19 BFD is configured on the IP interface and enabled in the OSPF interface.

```
*A:R1# show router ospf neighbor

===============================================================================
OSPF Neighbors
===============================================================================
Interface-Name                  Rtr Id           State        Pri  RetxQ   TTL
-------------------------------------------------------------------------------
toR2                            10.10.10.2       Full         1    0       39
toR3                            10.10.10.3       Full         1    0       39
toR5                            10.10.10.5       Full         1    0       30
-------------------------------------------------------------------------------
No. of Neighbors: 3
===============================================================================
*A:R1# configure router interface "toR2"
```

(continued)

Listing 5.19 *(continued)*

```
*A:R1>config>router>if# bfd 100 receive 100 multiplier 3
*A:R1>config>router>if# exit
*A:R1# configure router ospf area 0 interface "toR2" bfd-enable
*A:R1>config>router>if# show router bfd session
===============================================================================
BFD Session
===============================================================================
Interface                   State               Tx Intvl  Rx Intvl  Multipl
  Remote Address            Protocols           Tx Pkts   Rx Pkts   Type
-------------------------------------------------------------------------------
toR2                        Up (3)              100       100       3
   10.1.2.2                 ospf2               276       189       iom
-------------------------------------------------------------------------------
No. of BFD sessions: 1
===============================================================================
*A:R1>config>router>if#
```

In our example, the interface remains up, but the interface on R2 is no longer responding. Instead of waiting for the OSPF session to time out, the BFD session on R1 signals OSPF that the adjacency should be brought down (Listing 5.20).

Listing 5.20 The interface is still up, but the OSPF adjacency is down.

```
*A:R1>config>router>if# show router ospf interface

===============================================================================
OSPF Interfaces
===============================================================================
If Name              Area Id         Designated Rtr  Bkup Desig Rtr  Adm  Oper
-------------------------------------------------------------------------------
system               0.0.0.0         10.10.10.1      0.0.0.0         Up   DR
toR2                 0.0.0.0         0.0.0.0         0.0.0.0         Up   PToP
toR3                 0.0.0.0         0.0.0.0         0.0.0.0         Up   PToP
toR5                 0.0.0.0         10.10.10.1      10.10.10.5      Up   DR
-------------------------------------------------------------------------------
No. of OSPF Interfaces: 4
```

```
===========================================================================
*A:R1>config>router>if# show router ospf neighbor

===========================================================================
OSPF Neighbors
===========================================================================
Interface-Name                  Rtr Id          State      Pri  RetxQ   TTL
---------------------------------------------------------------------------
toR3                            10.10.10.3      Full       1    0       38
toR5                            10.10.10.5      Full       1    0       36
---------------------------------------------------------------------------
No. of Neighbors: 2
===========================================================================
```

Because the interface is still up, OSPF includes the network in its topology. However, since there is no longer an adjacency on this link, OSPF creates only a stub entry for the network in the Router LSA. There is no point-to-point entry (Listing 5.21).

Listing 5.21 The entry in the Router LSA lists the network as a stub type.

```
*A:R1>config>router>if# show router ospf database 10.10.10.1 detail

===========================================================================
OSPF Link State Database (Type : All) (Detailed)
===========================================================================
---------------------------------------------------------------------------
Router LSA for Area 0.0.0.0
---------------------------------------------------------------------------
Area Id            : 0.0.0.0              Adv Router Id     : 10.10.10.1
Link State Id      : 10.10.10.1 (168430081)
LSA Type           : Router
Sequence No        : 0x8000025f        Checksum           : 0xc6d0
Age                : 66                Length             : 84
Options            : E
Flags              : None              Link Count         : 5
Link Type (1)      : Stub Network
Network (1)        : 10.1.2.0          Mask (1)           : 255.255.255.224
No of TOS (1)      : 0                 Metric-0 (1)       : 100
```

(continued)

Listing 5.21 *(continued)*

```
Link Type (2)     : Point To Point
Nbr Rtr Id (2)    : 10.10.10.3        I/F Address (2)  : 10.1.3.1
No of TOS (2)     : 0                 Metric-0 (2)     : 100
Link Type (3)     : Stub Network
Network (3)       : 10.1.3.0          Mask (3)         : 255.255.255.224
No of TOS (3)     : 0                 Metric-0 (3)     : 100
Link Type (4)     : Stub Network
Network (4)       : 10.10.10.1        Mask (4)         : 255.255.255.255
No of TOS (4)     : 0                 Metric-0 (4)     : 0
Link Type (5)     : Transit Network
DR Rtr Id (5)     : 10.1.5.1          I/F Address (5)  : 10.1.5.1
No of TOS (5)     : 0                 Metric-0 (5)     : 100
===============================================================================
```

Practice Lab: Configuring OSPF in a Single Area Network

The following lab is designed to reinforce your knowledge of the content in this chapter. Please review the instructions carefully and perform the steps in the order in which they are presented. The practice labs require that you have access to six or more 7750 SRs or 7450 ESSs in a non-production environment.

These labs are designed to be used in a controlled lab environment. Please *do not* attempt to perform these labs in a production environment.

Lab Section 5.1: Configuring an OSPF Point-to-Point Interface

Point-to-point OSPF interfaces are configured when there are only two routers on a segment, also known as a point-to-point link.

Objective In this exercise, you will configure two 7750 SRs with OSPF point-to-point interfaces to form an OSPF adjacency, as shown in Figure 5.42.

Validation You will know you have succeeded if the OSPF adjacency between the routers is up.

1. Configure system interfaces on all four routers in the topology shown in Figure 5.42. Use the convention `10.10.10.x/32`, where `x` is the router number. For example, R2 will have the system interface address `10.10.10.2/32`.

Figure 5.42 Topology used to configure an OSPF single area network.

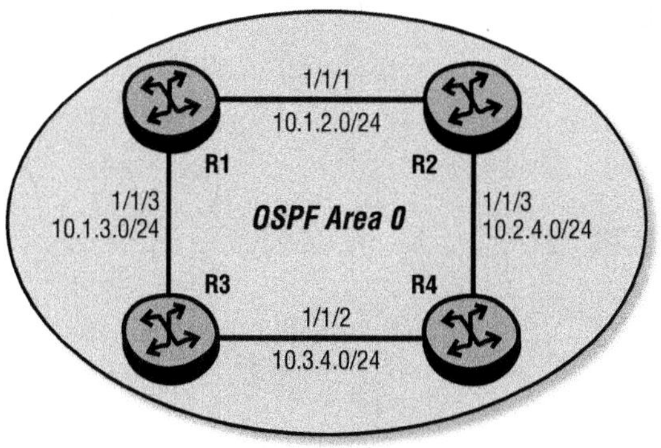

2. Configure a router interface on R1 toward R2, and include it in OSPF Area 0 as a point-to-point interface. Do not configure a router interface on R2 toward R1 yet. Use the IP networks given in Figure 5.42. Note that the convention for each router interface address is `10.x.y.z/24`, where `x` is the lower router number on the link, `y` is the higher router number on the link, and `z` is the router number on which the address is being configured. Thus the router interface on R1 toward R2 will have the address `10.1.2.1/24`. This IP addressing scheme will be used for this and subsequent lab sections for simplicity; however, note that typical real-world addressing schemes are likely to use /30 or /31 addresses for point-to-point links.
   - **a.** Is the OSPF adjacency up? Explain why or why not.
   - **b.** Are there any LSAs in R1's database? If so, what kind of LSAs and what can you observe about their contents?
   - **c.** Are there any LSAs in R2's database? Why or why not?
3. Configure an OSPF interface on R2 toward R1.
   - **a.** What type of OSPF interface needs to be configured on R2?
   - **b.** Which router is the DR?
   - **c.** Are there any LSAs in R1's database? If so, how have they changed since before the adjacency was up?
   - **d.** How many routes are in the route table of R1? How many OSPF routes? Explain.

4. From R1 try and ping the system interface of R2.
   a. Does the ping work? Explain and make the ping work if required.
   b. How is the system interface represented in the LSA on each node?
5. What is the OSPF MTU on the interface between R1 and R2, and how has it been derived?
   a. Change the OSPF MTU on R1 only. What is the state of the adjacency on each router? Explain.
   b. Change the OSPF MTU back so that the adjacency between R1 and R2 is up before proceeding to the next section.

Lab Section 5.2: Configuring an OSPF Broadcast Interface

When there are more than two routers on the same network segment, OSPF broadcast interfaces must be used to form an adjacency.

Objective In this exercise, you will configure an OSPF broadcast adjacency between two routers. Although there are only two routers on the segment, OSPF broadcast interfaces can still be used to illustrate the concept.

Validation You will know you have succeeded if the OSPF broadcast adjacency is established.

1. Configure a router interface on R3 toward R1, and add it to OSPF as a broadcast interface. Do not configure an interface on R1 to R3 yet.
   a. Is an adjacency formed between R1 and R3? Explain.
   b. Are there any LSAs in R3's database? If so, what type and how are the interfaces represented?
2. Complete the adjacency by configuring the interface on R1 toward R3.
   a. Which router is the DR? Explain why. How can you change the DR? Ensure that R3 is the DR (you may have to restart OSPF to force this).
   b. Examine the LSAs that R3 originates. How have the LSAs changed from before the adjacency was up?
   c. Force R1 to be the DR for the broadcast link (you may have to restart OSPF to force this). How have the LSAs originated by R3 changed?
   d. Does R3 have any of the LSAs originated by R2? Explain.

e. Examine the LSAs on R2. Which router (R1 or R3) originates the LSA that describes the broadcast network between R1 and R3? Why? What type of LSA is this? Does R2 have LSAs from both R1 and R3? What type of LSAs?

3. From R3 try to ping the system interface of R2.

a. Does the ping work? Why or why not? If not, make the ping work.

b. How many routes should you see in the route table of each router?

c. How many LSAs are in the database of each router? Describe the LSAs.

Lab Section 5.3: Configuring OSPF Passive Interfaces and Loopbacks

It is often desirable to include directly connected routes in OSPF for the purpose of communicating their prefixes to other routers. OSPF adjacencies are not established on these interfaces, but they are advertised throughout the network.

Objective In this exercise, you will configure physical and loopback interfaces and include them in the OSPF routing protocol.

Validation You will know you have succeeded if the other routers in the topology become aware of these interfaces through OSPF route exchange.

1. Configure a router interface on R3 toward R4, and add it to OSPF as a point-to-point passive interface. Do not make an interface on R4 toward R3 yet.

a. How is the interface represented in the LSA on R3?

b. Examine the route tables on R1 and R2. Are they aware of the passive interface on R3? Explain why or why not.

2. Configure a router interface on R4 toward R3, and add it to OSPF as a point-to-point interface (not passive).

a. Does the adjacency between R3 and R4 come up? Explain why or why not.

3. Configure a loopback interface on R3 with address `10.99.3.3/24`, and add it to OSPF.

a. Can you configure the loopback interface as passive? Explain.

b. How is the loopback interface represented in the LSA originated by R3?

c. Verify that you can ping the loopback interface on R3 from R2.

Lab Section 5.4: Configuring Authentication

OSPF authentication adds security to OSPF adjacencies. There are two types of security supported in OSPF. You will configure both types in this exercise.

Objective In this exercise, you will configure both simple password and MD5 authentication on an OSPF adjacency.

Validation You will know you have succeeded if the adjacencies come up after authentication is configured.

1. Configure an OSPF point-to-point adjacency between R2 and R4.
2. On R2 add simple password authentication using the password "**nrs2-pwd**."
   a. Does the adjacency stay up? Explain.
   b. Add password authentication to R4. Is the adjacency up? If not, fix the problem.
   c. What is the limitation of this type of simple password authentication?
3. Change the authentication type to MD5 authentication.
   a. Why is this type of authentication better than simple password authentication?
   b. How many routes are in each router's route table?
   c. Describe the LSAs in each router's database.

Chapter Review

Now that you have completed this chapter, you should have a good understanding of the following topics:

- The main steps that OSPF routers go through to form an adjacency
- How metrics are assigned to interfaces in OSPF and used in the SPF calculation
- The differences between a point-to-point and a broadcast network in OSPF
- The purpose of the OSPF link-state database and how to view its contents
- The five different OSPF messages and their purposes
- The importance of the OSPF router ID and how it is determined
- How OSPF uses Hello messages to discover its neighbors
- The fields that must match in OSPF Hello messages
- How the DR and BDR are elected on a broadcast network
- How DBD messages are used to synchronize databases between neighbors
- How OSPF routers use LSR and LSU, and messages to update their databases.
- The details of LSA flooding and aging in OSPF
- The purpose of the Router LSA and the meaning of its fields
- The role of the DR and the details of the Network LSA
- How to configure OSPF in a single area network
- Verifying the operation and the database in a single area OSPF network
- The purpose and behavior of a passive interface
- The purpose and operation of overload on boot
- The use of authentication in OSPF
- The purpose and operation of BFD

Post-Assessment

The following questions will test your knowledge and prepare you for the Alcatel-Lucent NRS II Certification Exam. Compare your response with the answers listed in Appendix A. You can also use the CD that accompanies this book to take all the assessment tests and review the answers.

1. What is the cost value of an OSPF interface on the Alcatel-Lucent 7750 SR?
   - **A.** It is based on the configuration of the global OSPF cost variable, which has a default value of 10.
   - **B.** It is based on the configuration of the global OSPF cost variable, which has a default value of 100.
   - **C.** It is based on a reference bandwidth, which has a default value of 10 Gbps.
   - **D.** It is based on a reference bandwidth, which has a default value of 100 Gbps.
2. A router has an OSPF broadcast interface declared as passive. How will this be represented in the Router LSA originated by the router?
   - **A.** The Router LSA will contain a stub network link type to describe the interface.
   - **B.** The Router LSA will contain a transit link type to describe the interface.
   - **C.** The Router LSA will contain a point-to-point link type to describe the interface.
   - **D.** The Router LSA will contain a point-to-point link type and a stub network link type to describe the interface.
   - **E.** The Router LSA will not describe the interface.
3. Which statement is *not* correct regarding an OSPF Type 1 LSA?
   - **A.** An OSPF Type 1 LSA is originated by every OSPF router.
   - **B.** An OSPF Type 1 LSA is called a Router LSA.
   - **C.** The OSPF Type 1 LSA is flooded throughout the autonomous system.
   - **D.** The OSPF Type 1 LSA describes the router's directly connected links.
   - **E.** The OSPF Type 1 LSA contains an age field.

4. A 7750 SR has an OSPF adjacency with its neighbor using a router ID derived from the last four octets of the chassis MAC address. The system interface IP address, RID, and OSPF RID are then configured. Assuming these are the only commands executed, what RID will be seen by the OSPF neighbor?

   A. The RID seen by the neighbor will be derived from the last four octets of the chassis MAC address.

   B. The RID seen by the neighbor will be derived from the system interface address.

   C. The RID seen by the neighbor will be derived from the configured RID.

   D. The RID seen by the neighbor will be derived from the configured OSPF RID.

5. Which of the following is not a field in an OSPF Hello packet that must match for a successful state transition to the 2-Way state?

   A. Dead Interval

   B. Authentication Type

   C. MTU

   D. Area ID

   E. Stub Flag

6. When does an OSPF router transition to the 2-Way state?

   A. After a LSR is received from a neighbor

   B. After the first LSU is received from a neighbor

   C. After a Hello packet that contains its own RID is received from a neighbor

   D. After the first LSA is received from a neighbor

   E. After a DBD message is received from a neighbor

7. Two routers, R1 and R2, have a point-to-point OSPF adjacency. R1 has a priority of 15 and an OSPF router ID of `10.10.10.10`. R2 has a priority of 25 and an OSPF router ID of `5.5.5.5`. Which router will be the DR?

   A. R1 will be the DR.

   B. R2 will be the DR.

   C. The first router to initialize will be the DR.

   D. There will be no DR.

8. When two routers are in the OSPF ExStart state, how is the initial DBD sequence number determined?

   A. Both routers send a DBD packet with an initial sequence number, and the highest is used.

   B. The sequence number of the router with the highest priority is used.

   C. The sequence number of the router that sends the first DBD packet is used.

   D. The sequence number of the router with the highest Router ID is used.

9. R1 and R2 are directly connected to each other and running OSPF on the link. The OSPF interface MTU of both routers is different, but the port MTU of each router is the same. What state will the adjacency be in?

   A. The adjacency will be in the Init state.

   B. The adjacency will be in the 2-Way state.

   C. The adjacency will be in the ExStart state.

   D. The adjacency will be in the Full state.

   E. It cannot be determined without details of the DR/BDR election.

10. What is the main purpose of the DBD packet?

   A. The DBD packet is used to carry LSAs between routers.

   B. The DBD packet is used in the OSPF neighbor discovery mechanism.

   C. The DBD packet is used to provide summary LSA information to each router so that specific LSAs can be requested.

   D. The DBD packet is used to withdraw LSA information when there is a topology change.

11. Which statement is correct regarding OSPF LSA exchange between routers?

   A. A router requests one LSA at a time using an LSR.

   B. A router can request multiple LSAs using a single LSR. The size of the LSR is dependent on the MTU settings.

   C. A router can request multiple LSAs using a single LSR. The size of the LSR is dependent on the value of the maximum LSA size parameter.

   D. A router never requests LSAs; they are always flooded.

12. Which statement best describes what happens when an OSPF receives an LSA with a higher sequence number than the LSA in its database?

A. The router acknowledges the LSA but does not add it to its LSDB and does not flood it to its neighbors.

B. The router does not acknowledge the LSA but sends a copy of the LSA from its database to the neighbor from which it received the LSA.

C. The router acknowledges the LSA and floods it to its neighbors but does not add it to its LSDB.

D. The router acknowledges the LSA, adds it to its own database, and floods it to its neighbors.

13. A router has four interfaces that are added to OSPF. Two point-to-point interfaces are in Area 1. There is one point-to-point interface in Area 2 and one broadcast interface in Area 3. How many Network LSAs will be originated by the router?

A. The router will not originate any Network LSAs.

B. The router will originate one Network LSA.

C. The router will originate two Network LSAs.

D. The router will originate four Network LSAs.

E. It is not possible to determine with the given information.

14. Which of the following best describes the election of the DR on a broadcast interface in OSPF when all routers have the same priority value?

A. The router with the lowest router ID is always the DR.

B. The router with the highest router ID is always the DR.

C. The router with the highest IP address on the broadcast interface is always the DR.

D. The router with the lowest IP address on the broadcast interface is always the DR.

E. The router that has been up the longest is usually the DR, since DR election is non-preemptive.

15. A router has been elected the DR on a broadcast OSPF interface on a subnet with three other routers. How will the link-state topology be described by routers on the subnet? Choose the best statement.

  A. The DR originates a Router LSA that includes the broadcast interface. The other routers on the subnet do not originate any LSAs that include the broadcast interface.

  B. The DR originates only a Network LSA that describes the broadcast network.

  C. The DR originates a Router LSA that includes the broadcast interface and a Network LSA that includes the broadcast interface. The other routers on the subnet do not originate any LSAs that include the broadcast interface.

  D. All routers on the subnet originate a Router LSA that includes the broadcast interface and a Network LSA that describes the broadcast network.

  E. All routers on the subnet originate a Router LSA that includes the broadcast interface. Only the DR originates a Network LSA that describes the broadcast network.

6 OSPF Multi-Area Networks

The Alcatel-Lucent NRS II exam topics covered in this chapter include the following:

- Requirements for multiple areas
- Area border routers (ABRs)
- Details of the Summary LSA
- Creation and flooding of Summary LSAs
- Route summarization
- Virtual links
- Exporting routes to OSPF
- Stub areas
- Configuring export policies
- Opaque LSAs

This chapter describes the implementation of multiple areas in OSPF (Open Shortest Path First) and the inclusion of external prefixes in OSPF. Hierarchy is required to improve the scalability of the protocol for large networks. To implement multiple areas, OSPF defines several different types of routers, which are described here. Routing information between areas is flooded using Summary LSAs. We look at the contents of the Summary LSA and the rules for flooding between areas. We also examine route summarization—an important tool for improving the efficiency and scalability of large networks.

A router participating in an OSPF network may also run other dynamic routing protocols, such as BGP (Border Gateway Protocol). An OSPF router that is going to exchange routes between OSPF and another routing protocol is an ASBR (autonomous system boundary router) in OSPF. A policy is required on the ASBR to export external routes into OSPF. The routes are flooded throughout the routing domain as AS External Summary (Type 5) LSAs, similar to the Summary LSAs used for inter-area routing. If it is not desirable to flood these routes into some areas, they can be configured as stubs or NSSAs (not so stubby areas). Finally, we look at opaque LSAs that have been defined for the flooding of information other than basic topology information.

Pre-Assessment

The following assessment questions will help you understand what areas of the chapter you should review in more detail to prepare for the NRS II exam. You can also use the CD that accompanies this book to take all the assessment tests and review the answers.

1. Which of the following is the definition of an ASBR?

- **A.** An OSPF router that routes in the backbone network
- **B.** An OSPF router that routes in a stub network
- **C.** An OSPF router that connects two or more different OSPF areas
- **D.** An OSPF router that connects to an external routing domain
- **E.** An OSPF router that connects to a BGP network

2. A router has four interfaces configured in OSPF. Two point-to-point interfaces are in Area 0, one point-to-point interface in Area 1, and one broadcast interface in Area 2. How many Router LSAs will be originated by the router?

A. The router will originate one Router LSA.

B. The router will originate two Router LSAs.

C. The router will originate three Router LSAs.

D. The router will originate four Router LSAs.

E. It is not possible to determine with the given information.

3. What is the default behavior of multi-area OSPF with respect to originating Type 3 Summary LSAs?

A. Every backbone router originates a Summary LSA for each prefix in its Router LSA.

B. Every ABR originates a Summary LSA for each Router LSA in its database.

C. Every backbone router originates a Summary LSA for every prefix listed in the LSDB.

D. Every ABR originates a Summary LSA for every prefix listed in the LSDB.

E. Summary LSAs are only originated by backbone routers when manual summarization is configured.

4. R1 is an ABR with an interface connected to R2 that is an Area 1 intra-area router. The network operator wants to summarize the backbone area networks `192.168.1.0/24` and `192.168.2.0/24` routes with the summary route `192.168.0.0/16`. Which statement below is correct regarding the Summary LSA flooded throughout Area 1?

A. It will have its metric set to the highest cost of the component networks, and the Adv Router ID set to R1's router ID.

B. It will have its metric set to the highest cost of the component networks, and the Adv Router ID set to R2's router ID.

C. It will have its metric set to the lowest cost of the component networks, and the Adv Router ID set to R1's router ID.

D. It will have its metric set to the lowest cost of the component networks, and the Adv Router ID set to R2's router ID.

5. Consider an OSPF network topology with Area 0, Area 1, and Area 2. An ASBR in Area 1 is configured to redistribute external routes into OSPF using a policy. Which statement below correctly describes how external routes are advertised to Area 0 and Area 2?

   A. The ASBR originates Router LSAs with the ASBR flag set that are flooded throughout Area 1. The external routes are not learned in Area 0 or Area 2 without additional policy on the ABRs.

   B. The ASBR originates Router LSAs that are flooded throughout Area 1. Area 1 ABRs originate Summary LSAs that are flooded throughout Area 0. The ABRs between Area 0 and Area 2 originate Summary LSAs that are flooded throughout Area 2.

   C. The ASBR originates Router LSAs with the ASBR flag set that are flooded throughout the autonomous system.

   D. The ASBR originates ASBR Summary LSAs that are flooded throughout the autonomous system.

   E. The ASBR originates AS External LSAs that are flooded throughout the autonomous system.

6.1 OSPF Multi-Area Networks

As mentioned in Chapter 5, the link-state protocols OSPF (Open Shortest Path First) and IS-IS (Intermediate System to Intermediate System) both support hierarchy to improve their scalability. Hierarchy is implemented by allowing the autonomous system (AS) to be divided into multiple areas. Routing within an area is exactly as defined in Chapter 5, by flooding Router and Network LSAs throughout the area with every router performing the shortest path first (SPF) calculation. However, routing between areas is handled differently, with only limited (or summary) routing information distributed between areas.

Reasons for Multi-Area Networks

In the early days of OSPF (early 1990s), routers had very limited processing and memory capacity compared to modern routers. Performing the SPF algorithm could be a very taxing process in a network of 20 to 30 routers. As the size of the network grows, the size of the databases and the complexity of the SPF algorithm grows significantly. Also, a topology change anywhere in the network results in a flooding of new LSAs (link-state advertisements) and a recalculation of the SPF algorithm. The larger the network, the more frequent the topology changes will be. Early routers had a single processor that handled both control and forwarding operations. Thus, while the router was performing an SPF calculation or processing LSAs, it might not have the capacity to forward packets, resulting in the loss of data.

The size of the link-state database (LSDB), and complexity of the SPF calculation, is reduced by a design that segregates the network into multiple areas. Performing the SPF calculation for multiple smaller networks requires much less processing than performing the calculation for one large network.

It is important to have a design and address plan that matches the physical topology and allows for summarization between network areas. A topology change in a remote area has a lesser impact on the local area if routing information is summarized between areas.

The disadvantage of multiple areas is a greater complexity in design, configuration, and troubleshooting. Often the route to a destination outside the area takes the shortest path to the exit point of the area, which may not be the shortest path to the destination overall. Thus, hierarchy can lead to suboptimal routing between areas.

Finally, there is currently no mechanism to make traffic engineering calculations across a multi-area network. Modern routers have greatly increased processing capabilities and can handle link-state networks of several hundred routers. Thus, the need for multiple areas is much less than it used to be.

6.2 Backbone Network and ABRs

In an OSPF multi-area network, all areas are connected to the OSPF backbone area, which has Area ID `0.0.0.0`. The backbone area must be contiguous, and all other areas must be connected to it. The backbone distributes routing information among areas. If it is not practical to connect an area directly to the backbone, it may be connected using a virtual link.

The other areas are connected to the backbone by area border routers (ABRs). Besides the backbone, an area may be a normal area, a stub area, or an NSSA (not so stubby area).

A *stub area* is an area that does not allow external route advertisements. Routers in a stub area have a default route to an ABR instead of having the external prefixes. Defining an area as a stub area reduces topological database sizes as well as OSPF protocol traffic, memory usage, and route-calculation CPU time.

NSSAs are similar to stub areas in that no external prefixes are imported into the area from other OSPF areas. However, some routers in the area may be learning external prefixes from another routing protocol.

Types of OSPF Routers

In OSPF, router interfaces are configured to be in a specific area, but the router may have interfaces in multiple areas (ABR). As shown in Figure 6.1, when an OSPF router has interfaces in multiple areas, it sets the "B" bit in its Router LSA to indicate that it is an ABR.

There are several terms used to define the types of routers in an OSPF topology. The following definitions are based on the position of the router in the topology and not on the size or model of the router:

- **Backbone router**—A router that has at least one interface in Area 0 (backbone area). Backbone routers may be intra-area routers (only Area 0) or ABRs.
- **Area border router (ABR)**—A router that has interfaces configured in more than one area. Often, this is between the backbone area and one other area; however, it is possible that an ABR connects to multiple other areas.
- **Intra-area router**—A router that only has neighbors in its area (all its interfaces are in the same area). Its neighbors may include other intra-area routers or ABRs.
- **Autonomous system boundary router (ASBR)**—A router that connects the OSPF routing domain with other routing domains. An ASBR may or may not also be an ABR.

Figure 6.1 ABRs set the "B" bit in their Router LSAs.

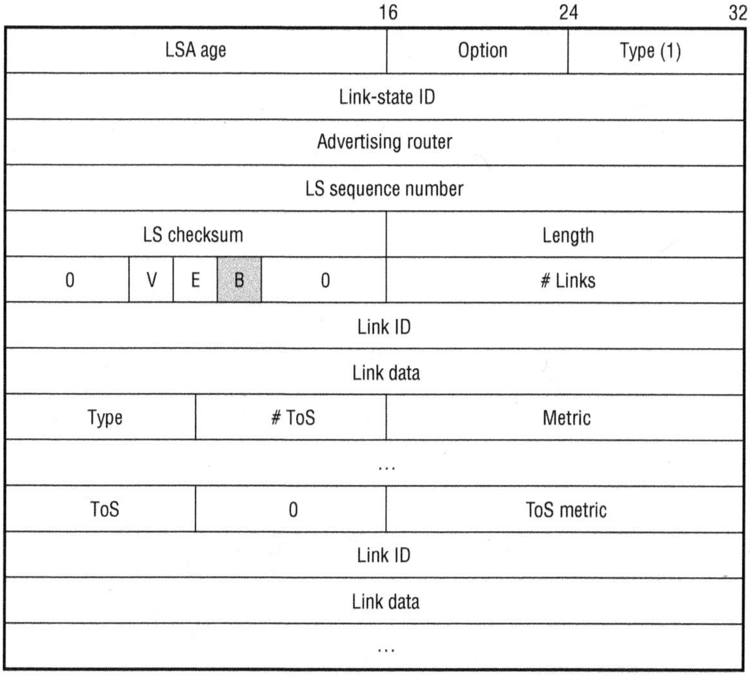

In Figure 6.2, R1, R2, and R3 are backbone routers. R1, R4, and R5 are intra-area routers. R2 and R3 are ABRs. There are no ASBRs shown in the diagram.

6.3 Summary LSA Details

In an OSPF multi-area network, each router generates a Router LSA (and possibly Network LSAs) for every area to which it is connected. An ABR generates multiple Router LSAs, with each one describing only the interfaces defined in that specific area.

Creation and Flooding of Summary LSAs

Routing information is distributed between areas using Summary (Type 3) LSAs. Summary LSAs are always created by an ABR and are flooded into neighboring areas. For example, in Figure 6.2, R2 creates Summary LSAs to describe the prefixes from Area 1 and floods them into the backbone. By default, it will also create Summary LSAs to describe the prefixes from the backbone area and flood them into Area 1.

A Summary LSA is generated for every prefix listed in the LSDB for the area. Each Summary LSA describes only one destination, thus an ABR can generate many Summary LSAs if there are many prefixes in the LSDB. By design, the Summary LSA should be a true summary network advertisement rather than just a repetition of the individual prefixes from that area. This requires the configuration of manual summarization on the router by the network administrator.

Figure 6.2 Backbone routers, intra-area routers, and ABRs in an OSPF routing domain.

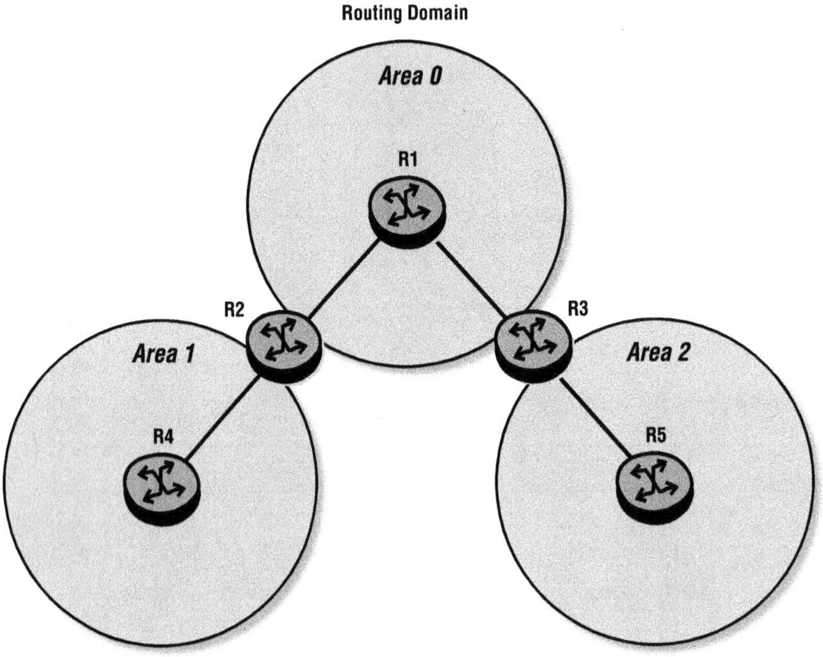

Contents of the Summary LSA

Figure 6.3 shows the fields of a Summary LSA. The white fields are those seen in all LSAs. The link-state ID is set to the network's address, and the metric is set to the cost to the destination from the route table.

Summary LSA Example

Consider the topology shown in Figure 6.4.

R1 is an intra-area, backbone router. Its database contains Router LSAs only from Area 0, as shown in Listing 6.1. (All links are configured as point-to-point in Area 0, thus there are no Network LSAs.) All other LSAs are Summary LSAs. Note that there is a Summary LSA for every prefix in the network outside Area 0. There is no summarization done by the ABR, thus there are individual entries for each of the 172.10 networks.

Figure 6.3 Summary LSA.

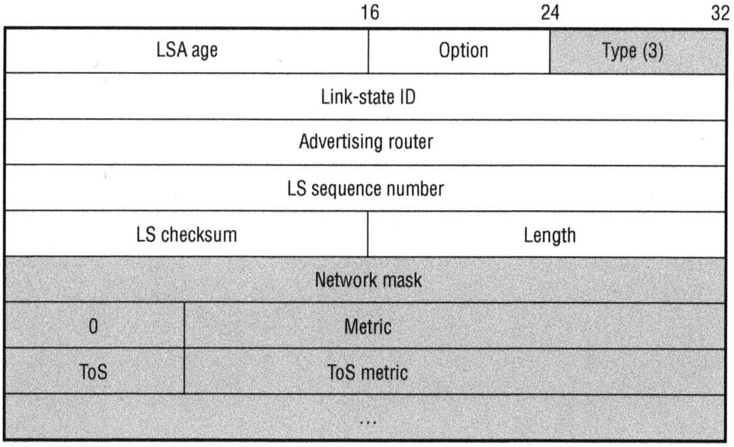
16
24
32
LSA age
Option
Type (3)
Link-state ID
Advertising router
LS sequence number
LS checksum
Length
Network mask
0
Metric
ToS
ToS metric
...

Figure 6.4 Multi-area OSPF topology.

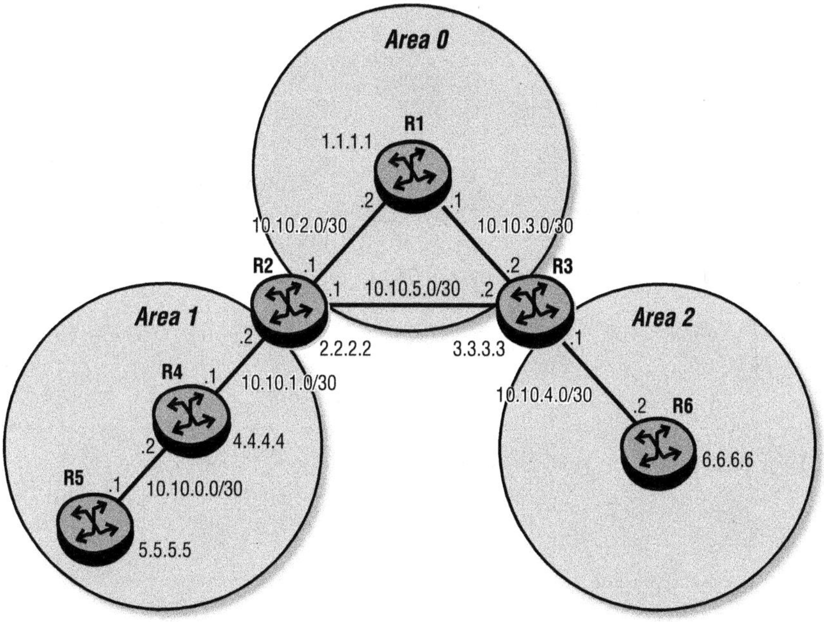


```
R5 has other links to the following networks:
172.10.1.0/24
172.10.2.0/24
172.10.3.0/24
```

Listing 6.1 R1 receives Summary LSAs describing networks in other areas

```
A:R1# show router ospf database

===============================================================================
OSPF Link State Database (Type : All)
===============================================================================
Type    Area Id    Link State Id   Adv Rtr Id   Age  Sequence   Cksum
-------------------------------------------------------------------------------
Router  0.0.0.0    1.1.1.1         1.1.1.1      460  0x8000009c 0x74de
Router  0.0.0.0    2.2.2.2         2.2.2.2      615  0x80000074 0xf975
Router  0.0.0.0    3.3.3.3         3.3.3.3      208  0x80000091 0x69dc
Summary 0.0.0.0    4.4.4.4         2.2.2.2      761  0x80000002 0xb2a4
Summary 0.0.0.0    5.5.5.5         2.2.2.2      824  0x80000002 0xb7af
Summary 0.0.0.0    6.6.6.6         3.3.3.3      1982 0x80000001 0x3a12
Summary 0.0.0.0    10.10.0.0       2.2.2.2      473  0x80000002 0x87e3
Summary 0.0.0.0    10.10.1.0       2.2.2.2      1323 0x80000002 0x490d
Summary 0.0.0.0    10.10.4.0       3.3.3.3      401  0x80000002 0xa45
Summary 0.0.0.0    172.10.1.0      2.2.2.2      423  0x80000002 0x566d
Summary 0.0.0.0    172.10.2.0      2.2.2.2      744  0x80000002 0x4b77
Summary 0.0.0.0    172.10.3.0      2.2.2.2      2114 0x80000001 0x4280
-------------------------------------------------------------------------------
No. of LSAs: 12
===============================================================================
```

R2 is an ABR for Area 0 and Area 1, thus it has the complete LSDB for both areas to which it belongs. Listing 6.2 shows the configuration of R2 as an ABR. The system interface can be configured in either area.

Listing 6.2 Router R2 is configured as an ABR with interfaces in two areas

```
*A:R2>config>router>ospf# info
----------------------------------------------
            area 0.0.0.0
                exit
                interface "system"
                    interface-type point-to-point
                exit
                interface "toR1"
```

```
                interface-type point-to-point
            exit
            interface "toR3"
                interface-type point-to-point
            exit
        exit
        area 0.0.0.1
            interface "toR4"
                interface-type point-to-point
            exit
        exit
----------------------------------------------
```

You can tell from the LSDB that the R2 system interface was configured in Area 0, because the router creates a Summary LSA for the system interface (`2.2.2.2`) in Area 1 (Listing 6.3).

Listing 6.3 The ABR R2 contains the LSDB for both areas it is connected to

```
A:R2# show router ospf database

=======================================================================
OSPF Link State Database (Type : All)
=======================================================================
Type    Area Id    Link State Id   Adv Rtr Id   Age  Sequence   Cksum
-----------------------------------------------------------------------
Router  0.0.0.0    1.1.1.1         1.1.1.1      570  0x8000009c 0x74de
Router  0.0.0.0    2.2.2.2         2.2.2.2      723  0x80000074 0xf975
Router  0.0.0.0    3.3.3.3         3.3.3.3      317  0x80000091 0x69dc
Summary 0.0.0.0    4.4.4.4         2.2.2.2      870  0x80000002 0xb2a4
Summary 0.0.0.0    5.5.5.5         2.2.2.2      933  0x80000002 0xb7af
Summary 0.0.0.0    6.6.6.6         3.3.3.3      100  0x80000002 0x3813
Summary 0.0.0.0    10.10.0.0       2.2.2.2      582  0x80000002 0x87e3
Summary 0.0.0.0    10.10.1.0       2.2.2.2      1432 0x80000002 0x490d
Summary 0.0.0.0    10.10.4.0       3.3.3.3      510  0x80000002 0xa45
Summary 0.0.0.0    172.10.1.0      2.2.2.2      532  0x80000002 0x566d
Summary 0.0.0.0    172.10.2.0      2.2.2.2      853  0x80000002 0x4b77
Summary 0.0.0.0    172.10.3.0      2.2.2.2      2223 0x80000001 0x4280
Router  0.0.0.1    2.2.2.2         2.2.2.2      922  0x80000004 0x9d82
```

(continued)

Listing 6.3 *(continued)*

```
Router  0.0.0.1    4.4.4.4          4.4.4.4         1118 0x80000007 0x6a5a
Router  0.0.0.1    5.5.5.5          5.5.5.5         605  0x8000000d 0xcfb0
Summary 0.0.0.1    1.1.1.1          2.2.2.2         870  0x80000005 0x3729
Summary 0.0.0.1    2.2.2.2          2.2.2.2         1225 0x80000003 0xd871
Summary 0.0.0.1    3.3.3.3          2.2.2.2         1111 0x80000003 0xde7b
Summary 0.0.0.1    6.6.6.6          2.2.2.2         541  0x80000002 0x89d9
Summary 0.0.0.1    10.10.2.0        2.2.2.2         856  0x80000005 0x381a
Summary 0.0.0.1    10.10.3.0        2.2.2.2         890  0x80000003 0x6403
Summary 0.0.0.1    10.10.4.0        2.2.2.2         313  0x80000002 0x5b0c
Summary 0.0.0.1    10.10.5.0        2.2.2.2         998  0x80000003 0x1b36
-------------------------------------------------------------------------------
No. of LSAs: 23
===============================================================================
```

The database for R4 contains Router LSAs from Area 1 and Summary LSAs for prefixes in Area 0 and Area 2 (Listing 6.4). Note that Summary LSAs for all the prefixes are generated by R2, even destinations in Area 2 such as `6.6.6.6` (R6).

Listing 6.4 The LSDB for intra-area router R4 contains Summary LSAs for destinations in other areas

```
A:R4# show router ospf database


===============================================================================
OSPF Link State Database (Type : All)
===============================================================================
Type    Area Id    Link State Id    Adv Rtr Id      Age  Sequence   Cksum
-------------------------------------------------------------------------------
Router  0.0.0.1    2.2.2.2          2.2.2.2         801  0x80000005 0x9b83
Router  0.0.0.1    4.4.4.4          4.4.4.4         1016 0x80000008 0x685b
Router  0.0.0.1    5.5.5.5          5.5.5.5         15   0x8000000e 0xcdb1
Summary 0.0.0.1    1.1.1.1          2.2.2.2         98   0x80000006 0x352a
Summary 0.0.0.1    2.2.2.2          2.2.2.2         626  0x80000004 0xd672
Summary 0.0.0.1    3.3.3.3          2.2.2.2         676  0x80000004 0xdc7c
Summary 0.0.0.1    6.6.6.6          2.2.2.2         1897 0x80000002 0x89d9
Summary 0.0.0.1    10.10.2.0        2.2.2.2         24   0x80000006 0x361b
Summary 0.0.0.1    10.10.3.0        2.2.2.2         581  0x80000004 0x6204
Summary 0.0.0.1    10.10.4.0        2.2.2.2         1669 0x80000002 0x5b0c
```

```
Summary 0.0.0.1    10.10.5.0       2.2.2.2      992  0x80000004 0x1937
-------------------------------------------------------------------------------
No. of LSAs: 11
===============================================================================
```

Listing 6.5 shows a Summary LSA from Area 1. It describes the system address of R1, `1.1.1.1/32`. Note that it was created by the ABR, R2 (Adv Router ID is `2.2.2.2`).

Listing 6.5 Summary LSA in Area 1 for system address of R1

```
A:R4# show router ospf database 1.1.1.1 detail

===============================================================================
OSPF Link State Database (Type : All) (Detailed)
===============================================================================
-------------------------------------------------------------------------------
Summary LSA for Area 0.0.0.1
-------------------------------------------------------------------------------
Area Id          : 0.0.0.1             Adv Router Id     : 2.2.2.2
Link State Id    : 1.1.1.1             LSA Type          : Summary
Sequence No      : 0x80000008          Checksum          : 0x312c
Age              : 84                  Length            : 28
Options          : E
Network Mask     : 255.255.255.255     Metric-0          : 1001
===============================================================================
```

6.4 Route Summarization

Ideally, the network topology and address plan will be designed to allow one entry to describe a range of prefixes when they are advertised by the ABR. This is known as *summarization*. If summarization is configured, a Summary LSA is generated with the link-state ID set to the range's address. The metric is set to the highest cost of the component networks. Summarization is configured on the ABR in the area that is being summarized. Figure 6.5 shows the use of summarization to describe the 172.10 prefixes.

The three Summary LSAs for `172.10.1.0`, `172.10.2.0`, and `172.10.3.0` have now been summarized and advertised with a single Summary LSA of `172.10.0.0/16`

(Listing 6.6). Note that the statement to perform the summarization is configured in Area 1 (location of the summarized networks). When summarizing, the link-state ID is the configured area-range. The prefixes that are in Area 1 but not included in the area-range statement continue to be advertised.

Figure 6.5 The area-range statement is used to create one Summary LSA that describes a range of prefixes.

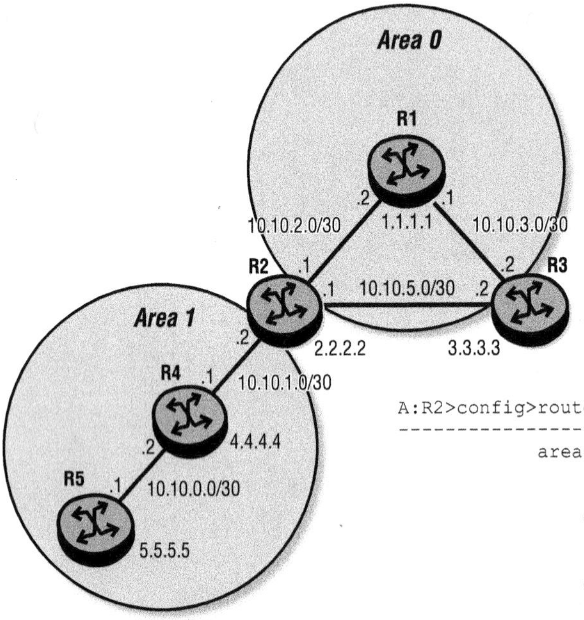

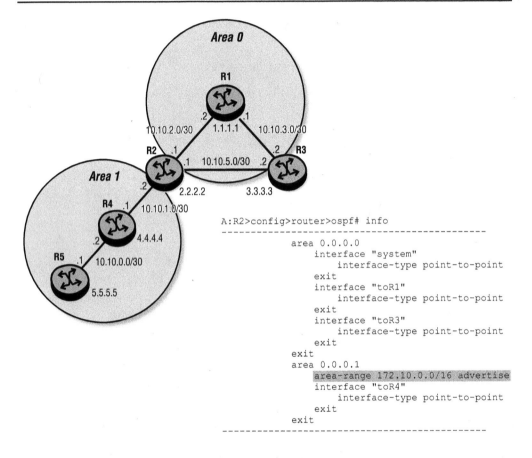

```
A:R2>config>router>ospf# info
----------------------------------------------
            area 0.0.0.0
                interface "system"
                    interface-type point-to-point
                exit
                interface "toR1"
                    interface-type point-to-point
                exit
                interface "toR3"
                    interface-type point-to-point
                exit
            exit
            area 0.0.0.1
                area-range 172.10.0.0/16 advertise
                interface "toR4"
                    interface-type point-to-point
                exit
            exit
----------------------------------------------
```

Listing 6.6 Only a single summarized entry for the local networks is advertised into Area 0

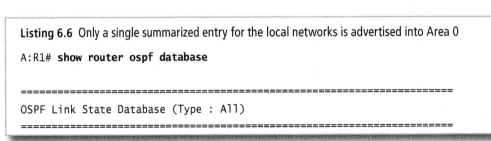

```
A:R1# show router ospf database

===============================================================
OSPF Link State Database (Type : All)
===============================================================
```

```
Type     Area Id    Link State Id   Adv Rtr Id   Age  Sequence   Cksum
-----------------------------------------------------------------------
Router  0.0.0.0    1.1.1.1         1.1.1.1      533  0x8000009f 0x6ee1
Router  0.0.0.0    2.2.2.2         2.2.2.2      756  0x80000077 0xf378
Router  0.0.0.0    3.3.3.3         3.3.3.3      410  0x80000094 0x63df
Summary 0.0.0.0    4.4.4.4         2.2.2.2      1414 0x80000005 0xaca7
Summary 0.0.0.0    5.5.5.5         2.2.2.2      7    0x80000006 0xafb3
Summary 0.0.0.0    6.6.6.6         3.3.3.3      104  0x80000005 0x3216
Summary 0.0.0.0    10.10.0.0       2.2.2.2      661  0x80000005 0x81e6
Summary 0.0.0.0    10.10.1.0       2.2.2.2      1171 0x80000005 0x4310
Summary 0.0.0.0    10.10.4.0       3.3.3.3      65   0x80000005 0x448
Summary 0.0.0.0    172.10.0.0      2.2.2.2      1796 0x80000002 0x6163
-----------------------------------------------------------------------
No. of LSAs: 10
=======================================================================
```

The summarized prefix that is being advertised is derived from the link-state ID and network mask (Listing 6.7).

Listing 6.7 Summarized prefix advertised into Area 0

```
A:R1# show router ospf database 172.10.0.0 detail

=======================================================================
OSPF Link State Database (Type : All) (Detailed)
=======================================================================
-----------------------------------------------------------------------
Summary LSA for Area 0.0.0.0
-----------------------------------------------------------------------
Area Id          : 0.0.0.0             Adv Router Id     : 2.2.2.2
Link State Id    : 172.10.0.0          LSA Type          : Summary
Sequence No      : 0x80000003          Checksum          : 0x5f64
Age              : 289                 Length            : 28
Options          : E
Network Mask     : 255.255.0.0         Metric-0          : 2001
=======================================================================
```

The Black-Hole Entry

When router R2 advertises a summarized route from Area 1 into Area 0, it is effectively advertising some prefixes for which it does not actually have a route (Figure 6.6). In this situation, R2 has routes for networks `172.10.1.0/24`, `172.10.2.0/24`, and `172.10.3.0/24`, but if it receives a datagram destined to `172.10.254.1`, it does not have a route to this destination. To prevent situations that could lead to an infinite looping of packets, the router installs a black-hole route for the summarized prefix in the route-table by default. Any packet that matches the black-hole entry is silently discarded.

In Figure 6.6, the three routes are known in Area 1 but summarized for Area 0. The route-table on R2 shows that it knows the three prefixes, but because it is advertising a summary, it creates a black-hole entry in the route-table (Listing 6.8). This will cause it to silently drop any packets that do not match the specific, known routes. Note that the preference value for this route is set to 255, the lowest possible preference.

Figure 6.6 A summarized route is advertised into Area 0.

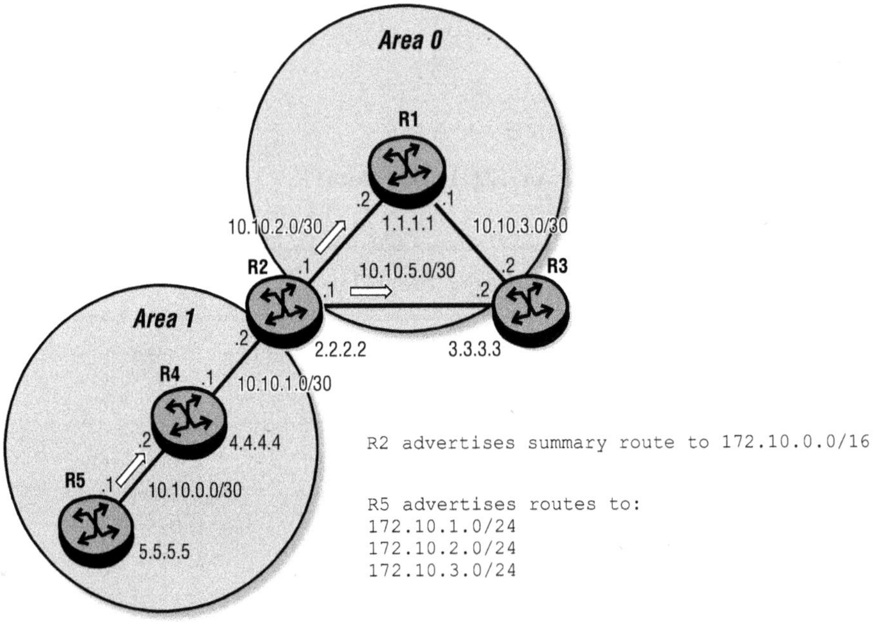

Listing 6.8 The ABR that is advertising the summarized route creates a black-hole entry in its route-table

```
*A:R2>config>router>ospf# show router route-table
```

```
===============================================================================
Route Table (Router: Base)
===============================================================================
Dest Prefix                                    Type     Proto     Age          Pref
       Next Hop[Interface Name]                                     Metric
-------------------------------------------------------------------------------
1.1.1.1/32                                     Remote   OSPF      00h36m55s    10
       10.10.2.2                                                    100
2.2.2.2/32                                     Local    Local     00h52m12s    0
       system                                                       0
3.3.3.3/32                                     Remote   OSPF      00h37m05s    10
       10.10.5.2                                                    100
4.4.4.4/32                                     Remote   OSPF      00h29m41s    10
       10.10.1.1                                                    100
5.5.5.5/32                                     Remote   OSPF      00h27m40s    10
       10.10.1.1                                                    200
10.10.0.0/30                                   Remote   OSPF      00h29m41s    10
       10.10.1.1                                                    200
10.10.1.0/30                                   Local    Local     00h33m54s    0
       toR4                                                         0
10.10.2.0/30                                   Local    Local     00h52m30s    0
       toR1                                                         0
10.10.3.0/30                                   Remote   OSPF      00h37m09s    10
       10.10.5.2                                                    200
10.10.5.0/30                                   Local    Local     00h51m03s    0
       toR3                                                         0
172.10.0.0/16                                  Remote   OSPF      00h00m36s    255
       Black Hole                                                   200
172.10.1.0/24                                  Remote   OSPF      00h00m37s    10
       10.10.1.1                                                    200
172.10.2.0/24                                  Remote   OSPF      00h00m37s    10
       10.10.1.1                                                    200
172.10.3.0/24                                  Remote   OSPF      00h00m32s    10
       10.10.1.1                                                    200
-------------------------------------------------------------------------------
No. of Routes: 14
===============================================================================
```

6.5 Virtual Links

The backbone area in an OSPF AS must be contiguous, and all other areas must be connected to the backbone area. Sometimes this is not practical or is unreasonably expensive to implement. Virtual links can be used to connect an area to the backbone through a non-backbone area.

Figure 6.7 shows that Area 111 is not directly connected to the backbone. Routers R2 and R5 are the endpoints of a virtual link, and Area 1 is the transit area. The transit area must have full routing information and therefore cannot be a stub area or an NSSA.

Virtual links are considered part of the backbone and behave as if they were unnumbered point-to-point networks between the two routers. When a router is fully adjacent to its neighbor over a virtual link, it sets the V bit in its Router LSA (Figure 6.8).

Figure 6.7 Area 111 is not directly connected to Area 0. It can be connected by a virtual link through Area 1.

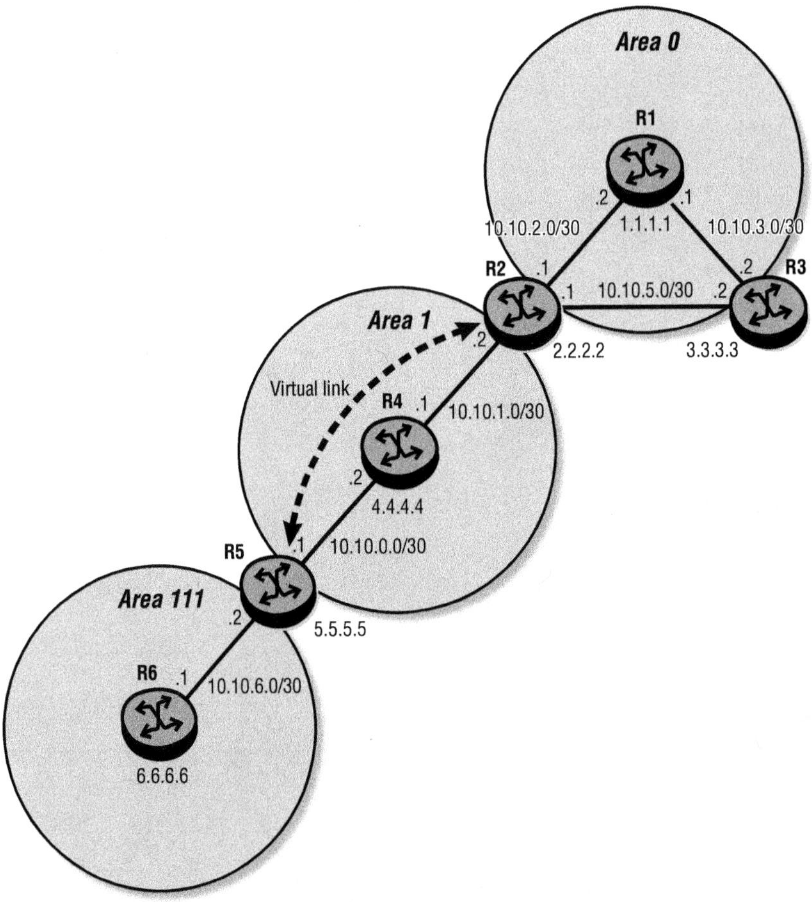

Figure 6.8 The V bit is set in the Router LSA of the transit area.

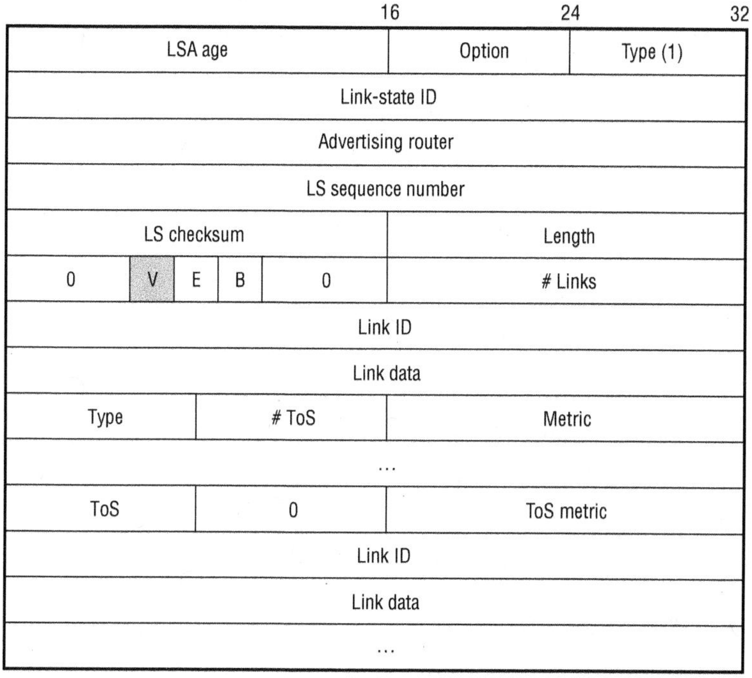

The virtual link is configured on both endpoints—in this case, R2 and R5. Router R5 is configured to include Area 0—connected by the virtual link. The virtual link is identified by the RID (router ID) of the other endpoint. These two endpoint routers must both be attached to the common transit area. Listing 6.9 shows the configuration of the virtual link on R5. There is a similar configuration of the virtual link in Area 0 of R2.

Listing 6.9 Router R5 is configured with a virtual link to Area 0

```
*A:R5>config>router>ospf# info
----------------------------------------------
            area 0.0.0.0
                virtual-link 2.2.2.2 transit-area 0.0.0.1
                exit
            exit
            area 0.0.0.1
                interface "system"
                    interface-type point-to-point
                exit
```

(continued)

Listing 6.9 *(continued)*

```
            interface "toR4"
                interface-type point-to-point
            exit
        exit
        area 0.0.0.111
            interface "toR6"
                interface-type point-to-point
            exit
        exit
----------------------------------------------
```

Because R5 is part of Area 0, its database contains the LSAs for all three areas (Listing 6.10).

Listing 6.10 Router R5 contains the LSAs from Area 111, Area 1, and Area 0

```
*A:R5# show router ospf database

===============================================================================
OSPF Link State Database (Type : All)
===============================================================================
Type    Area Id     Link State Id   Adv Rtr Id    Age  Sequence   Cksum
-------------------------------------------------------------------------------
Router  0.0.0.0     1.1.1.1         1.1.1.1       1582 0x80000025 0x5495
Router  0.0.0.0     2.2.2.2         2.2.2.2       435  0x80000030 0x28a5
Router  0.0.0.0     3.3.3.3         3.3.3.3       965  0x8000002a 0x8944
Router  0.0.0.0     5.5.5.5         5.5.5.5       1093 0x80000021 0x76ac
Summary 0.0.0.0     4.4.4.4         2.2.2.2       1544 0x80000022 0x209f
Summary 0.0.0.0     5.5.5.5         2.2.2.2       1240 0x80000023 0xdb7a
Summary 0.0.0.0     10.10.0.0       2.2.2.2       555  0x80000024 0xb3a4
Summary 0.0.0.0     10.10.1.0       2.2.2.2       690  0x80000024 0xbcfe
Summary 0.0.0.0     4.4.4.4         5.5.5.5       1184 0x80000022 0xc5ed
Summary 0.0.0.0     5.5.5.5         5.5.5.5       933  0x80000022 0xab68
Summary 0.0.0.0     6.6.6.6         5.5.5.5       1468 0x80000021 0x6b41
Summary 0.0.0.0     10.10.0.0       5.5.5.5       810  0x80000022 0x7141
Summary 0.0.0.0     10.10.1.0       5.5.5.5       285  0x80000023 0x50fb
Summary 0.0.0.0     10.10.6.0       5.5.5.5       830  0x80000022 0x2f7d
Router  0.0.0.1     2.2.2.2         2.2.2.2       1376 0x8000002d 0xf30e
```

```
Router  0.0.0.1     4.4.4.4         4.4.4.4       224  0x80000027 0x2d96
Router  0.0.0.1     5.5.5.5         5.5.5.5       1783 0x80000035 0xe8d7
Summary 0.0.0.1     1.1.1.1         2.2.2.2       1205 0x80000026 0xa225
Summary 0.0.0.1     2.2.2.2         2.2.2.2       1202 0x80000024 0x8c9d
Summary 0.0.0.1     3.3.3.3         2.2.2.2       670  0x80000025 0x4878
Summary 0.0.0.1     10.10.2.0       2.2.2.2       676  0x80000023 0xb308
Summary 0.0.0.1     10.10.3.0       2.2.2.2       1428 0x80000025 0x90c3
Summary 0.0.0.1     10.10.5.0       2.2.2.2       9    0x80000026 0x8c29
Summary 0.0.0.1     6.6.6.6         5.5.5.5       751  0x80000020 0x6d40
Summary 0.0.0.1     10.10.6.0       5.5.5.5       422  0x80000022 0x2f7d
Router  0.0.0.111   5.5.5.5         5.5.5.5       659  0x80000026 0xffe2
Router  0.0.0.111   6.6.6.6         6.6.6.6       1741 0x80000022 0x8537
Summary 0.0.0.111   1.1.1.1         5.5.5.5       808  0x80000020 0x2bcd
Summary 0.0.0.111   2.2.2.2         5.5.5.5       367  0x80000021 0x1048
Summary 0.0.0.111   3.3.3.3         5.5.5.5       1656 0x80000022 0xca24
Summary 0.0.0.111   4.4.4.4         5.5.5.5       80   0x80000022 0xc5ed
Summary 0.0.0.111   5.5.5.5         5.5.5.5       59   0x80000023 0xa969
Summary 0.0.0.111   10.10.0.0       5.5.5.5       257  0x80000023 0x6f42
Summary 0.0.0.111   10.10.1.0       5.5.5.5       1040 0x80000022 0x52fa
Summary 0.0.0.111   10.10.2.0       5.5.5.5       1254 0x80000021 0x34b4
Summary 0.0.0.111   10.10.3.0       5.5.5.5       2179 0x80000020 0x176d
Summary 0.0.0.111   10.10.5.0       5.5.5.5       1879 0x8000001f 0x17d0
-------------------------------------------------------------------------------
No. of LSAs: 37
===============================================================================
```

The R5 Router LSA for Area 0 contains a description of the virtual link (Listing 6.11).

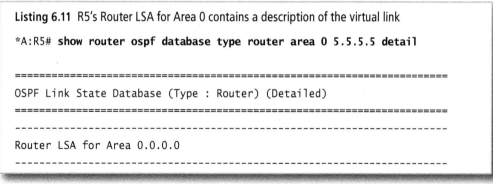

Listing 6.11 R5's Router LSA for Area 0 contains a description of the virtual link

```
*A:R5# show router ospf database type router area 0 5.5.5.5 detail

===============================================================================
OSPF Link State Database (Type : Router) (Detailed)
===============================================================================
-------------------------------------------------------------------------------
Router LSA for Area 0.0.0.0
-------------------------------------------------------------------------------
```

(continued)

Listing 6.11 *(continued)*

```
Area Id            : 0.0.0.0              Adv Router Id     : 5.5.5.5
Link State Id      : 5.5.5.5 (84215045)
LSA Type           : Router
Sequence No        : 0x80000021           Checksum          : 0x76ac
Age                : 1396                 Length            : 36
Options            : E
Flags              : ABR                  Link Count        : 1
Link Type (1)      : Virtual Link
Nbr Rtr Id (1)     : 2.2.2.2              I/F Address (1)   : 10.10.0.1
No of TOS (1)      : 0                    Metric-0 (1)      : 200
===============================================================================
```

The R5 Router LSA for Area 1 has the V bit set to describe the virtual link across the transit area (Listing 6.12). The R2 Router LSA in Area 1 will also have the V bit set.

Listing 6.12 The Router LSA for Area 1 has the V bit set to indicate a virtual link.

```
*A:R5# show router ospf database type router area 1 5.5.5.5 detail

===============================================================================
OSPF Link State Database (Type : Router) (Detailed)
===============================================================================
-------------------------------------------------------------------------------
Router LSA for Area 0.0.0.1
-------------------------------------------------------------------------------
Area Id            : 0.0.0.1           Adv Router Id     : 5.5.5.5
Link State Id      : 5.5.5.5 (84215045)
LSA Type           : Router
Sequence No        : 0x80000037        Checksum          : 0xe4d9
Age                : 113               Length            : 60
Options            : E
Flags              : ABR Virt          Link Count        : 3
Link Type (1)      : Stub Network
Network (1)        : 5.5.5.5           Mask (1)          : 255.255.255.255
No of TOS (1)      : 0                 Metric-0 (1)      : 0
```

```
Link Type (2)       : Point To Point
Nbr Rtr Id (2)      : 4.4.4.4            I/F Address (2)   : 10.10.0.1
No of TOS (2)       : 0                  Metric-0 (2)      : 100
Link Type (3)       : Stub Network
Network (3)         : 10.10.0.0          Mask (3)          : 255.255.255.252
No of TOS (3)       : 0                  Metric-0 (3)      : 100
=======================================================================
```

6.6 Exporting Routes to OSPF

In its default configuration, an OSPF router advertises any interface defined in OSPF to its neighbors. To advertise prefixes that are not part of the OSPF routing topology, an export policy is required. Export policies are implemented on the ASBR.

The ASBR

Routes in the route-table that have been learned through other means, such as another routing protocol or static routes, are not advertised in OSPF by default. If it is desired to route data to these external destinations from the OSPF network, the OSPF routers must have routing information about these prefixes. If a router is to advertise externally learned prefixes to its neighbors, it must be explicitly configured as an ASBR. Secondly, an export policy is required to identify exactly which prefixes are to be advertised into OSPF. These routes must be active in the route-table.

A router informs its neighbors that it is an ASBR by setting the E bit in its Router LSA (capable of handling external routes) (Figure 6.9).

In Figure 6.10, R4 is exchanging prefixes with R5 using a protocol other than OSPF (IS-IS in this example). The routes learned by R4 through IS-IS are to be advertised in the OSPF routing domain. To do this, R4 must be configured as an ASBR and an export policy applied to OSPF.

Route Export Policies

To advertise externally learned prefixes, a route policy is required. A route policy is shown in Listing 6.13. Any route learned from IS-IS will be distributed into OSPF with the metric set to 2000.

Figure 6.9 The E bit is set in the Router LSA by an ASBR.

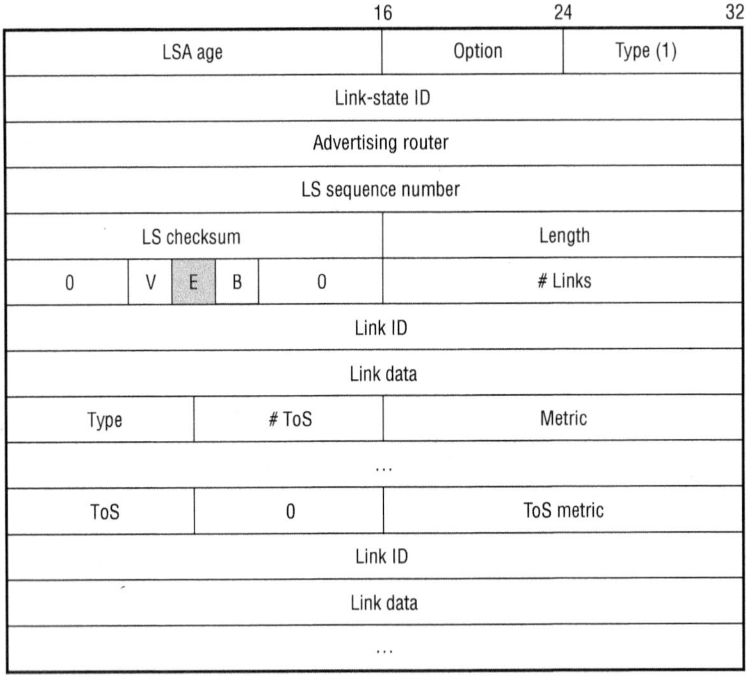

Listing 6.13 Policy to export IS-IS routes. This has been applied on the ASBR (R4).

```
A:R4>config>router>policy# info
----------------------------------------------
policy-statement "redist"
                entry 10
                    from
                        protocol isis
                    exit
                    action accept
                        metric set 2000
                    exit
                exit
            exit
----------------------------------------------
```

Figure 6.10 Router R4 configured as an ASBR with an export policy in OSPF.

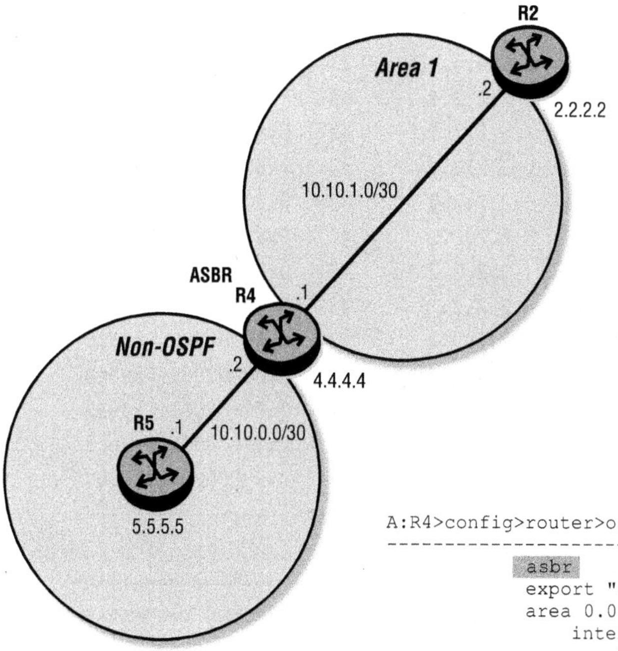

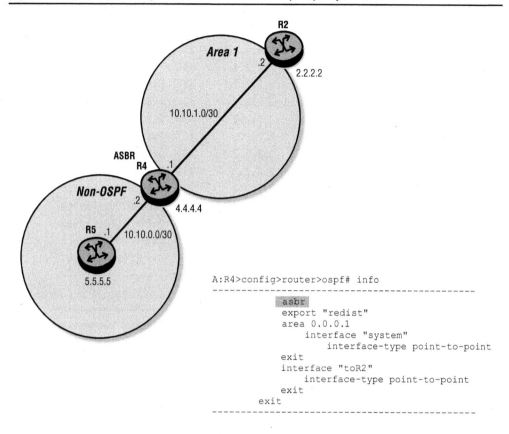

```
A:R4>config>router>ospf# info
----------------------------------------------
            asbr
            export "redist"
            area 0.0.0.1
                interface "system"
                    interface-type point-to-point
                exit
                interface "toR2"
                    interface-type point-to-point
                exit
            exit
----------------------------------------------
```

Once R4 is configured as an ASBR with an export policy, it produces AS External Summary LSAs (also known as Type 5 LSAs) as seen in the topological database in Listing 6.14. Notice that there is an LSA for each of the external prefixes the router has learned.

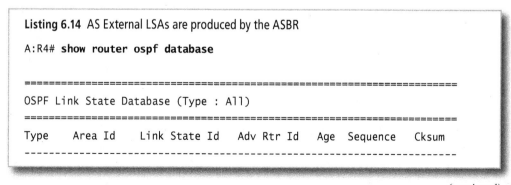

Listing 6.14 AS External LSAs are produced by the ASBR

```
A:R4# show router ospf database

===============================================================================
OSPF Link State Database (Type : All)
===============================================================================
Type     Area Id      Link State Id    Adv Rtr Id    Age  Sequence    Cksum
-------------------------------------------------------------------------------
```

(continued)

Listing 6.14 *(continued)*

```
Router  0.0.0.1   2.2.2.2       2.2.2.2      29    0x80000003 0x9f81
Router  0.0.0.1   4.4.4.4       4.4.4.4      23    0x80000002 0x8177
Summary 0.0.0.1   1.1.1.1       2.2.2.2      43    0x80000002 0x3d26
Summary 0.0.0.1   2.2.2.2       2.2.2.2      43    0x80000002 0xda70
Summary 0.0.0.1   3.3.3.3       2.2.2.2      43    0x80000002 0xe07a
Summary 0.0.0.1   6.6.6.6       2.2.2.2      43    0x80000002 0x89d9
Summary 0.0.0.1   10.10.2.0     2.2.2.2      43    0x80000002 0x3e17
Summary 0.0.0.1   10.10.3.0     2.2.2.2      43    0x80000002 0x6602
Summary 0.0.0.1   10.10.4.0     2.2.2.2      43    0x80000002 0x5b0c
Summary 0.0.0.1   10.10.5.0     2.2.2.2      43    0x80000002 0x1d35
AS Ext  n/a       5.5.5.5       4.4.4.4      27    0x80000001 0xeaeb
AS Ext  n/a       172.10.1.0    4.4.4.4      27    0x80000001 0x89a9
AS Ext  n/a       172.10.2.0    4.4.4.4      27    0x80000001 0x7eb3
AS Ext  n/a       172.10.3.0    4.4.4.4      27    0x80000001 0x73bd
-------------------------------------------------------------------------
No. of LSAs: 14
=========================================================================
```

External LSA Details

Externally learned prefixes are advertised as AS External (Type 5) LSAs (Figure 6.11). Their content is very similar to Summary LSAs. The link-state ID is the network address being advertised. The Adv Router ID is the router ID of the ASBR. AS External LSAs are not associated with a specific area and therefore have no Area ID.

Unlike the Summary LSA, the AS External LSA carries some additional fields: Fwding Address, Metric Type, and Ext Route Tag. Fwding Address is set if it is desired to have traffic for this prefix forwarded to another router than this one. By default, the value is 0, which means that traffic will be forwarded to this router.

Metric Type can be Type 1 or 2 and is 2 by default. A Metric Type of 1 means that the Metric value should be added to the cost to reach the ASBR when calculating the cost to the destination. Metric Type 2 means that only the Metric value should be used as the cost to the destination. An LSA with Metric Type 1 is preferred over one with Metric Type 2.

Ext Route Tag values are used to carry information for use by another external routing protocol—typically for setting BGP attributes. Listing 6.15 shows an AS External LSA generated by R4, the ASBR.

Figure 6.11 Format of the AS External (Type 5) LSA.

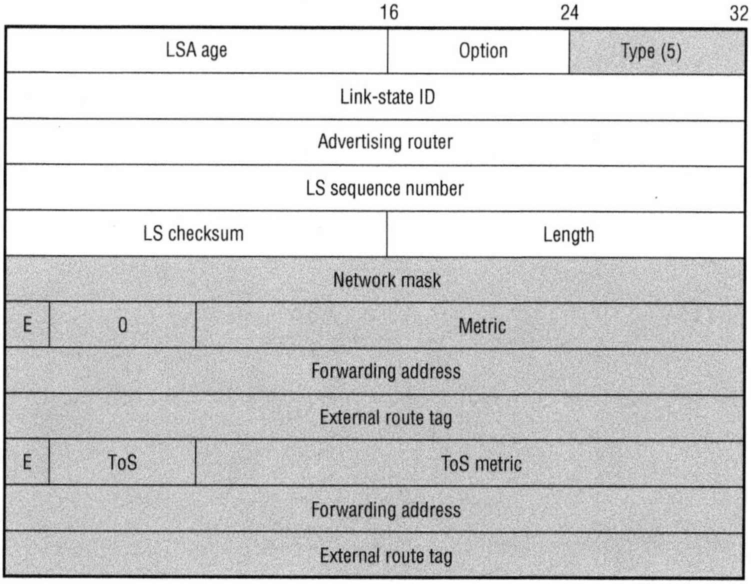

Listing 6.15 Details of an AS External LSA

```
A:R4# show router ospf database 5.5.5.5 detail

===============================================================================
OSPF Link State Database (Type : All) (Detailed)
===============================================================================
-------------------------------------------------------------------------------
AS Ext LSA for Network 5.5.5.5
-------------------------------------------------------------------------------
Area Id          : N/A                  Adv Router Id     : 4.4.4.4
Link State Id    : 5.5.5.5              LSA Type          : AS Ext
Sequence No      : 0x80000001           Checksum          : 0xeaeb
Age              : 231                  Length            : 36
Options          : E
Network Mask     : 255.255.255.255      Fwding Address    : 0.0.0.0
Metric Type      : Type 2               Metric-0          : 2000
Ext Route Tag    : 0
===============================================================================
```

ASBR Summary LSA Details

AS External LSAs are flooded unchanged throughout the OSPF routing domain. In Figure 6.12, R2 is an ABR and floods the AS External LSAs into the backbone area. The advertising router ID remains unchanged in the AS External LSAs. However, the ASBR is not known in the backbone area because R4 is located entirely within Area 1. Therefore, the ABR also floods an ASBR Summary (Type 4) LSA into the backbone area.

Figure 6.12 Type 4 and 5 LSAs are flooded into the backbone area by the ABR (R2).

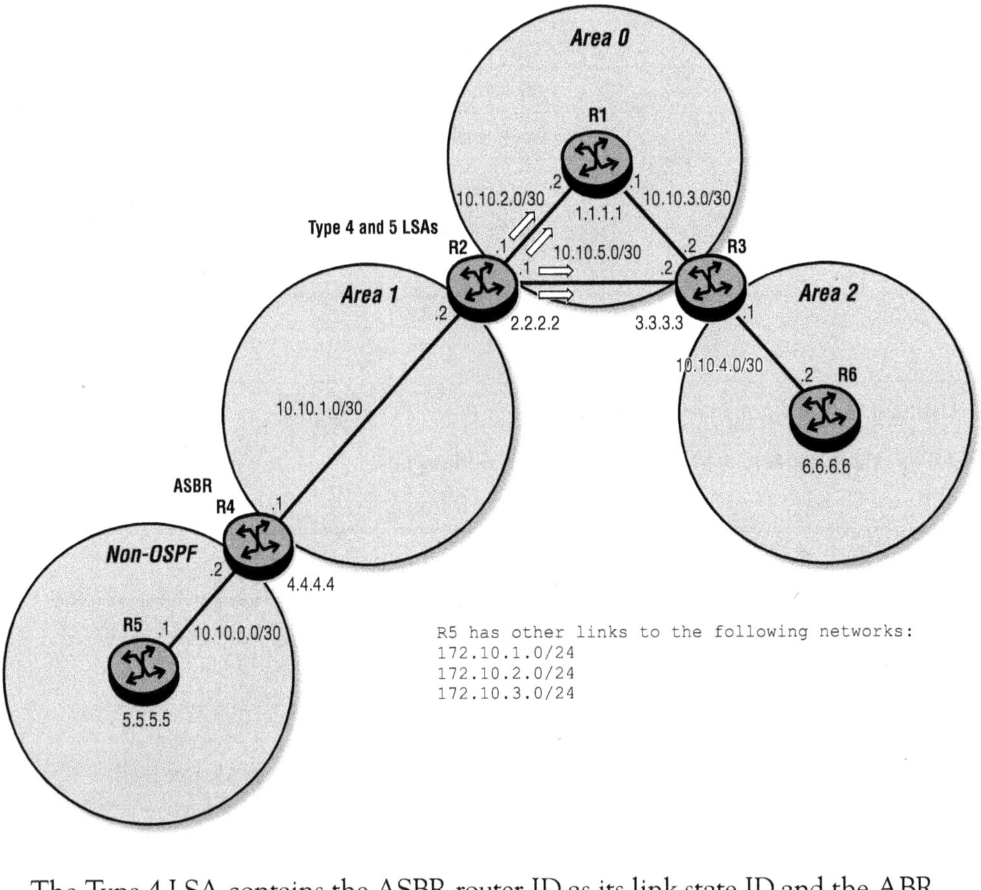

The Type 4 LSA contains the ASBR router ID as its link-state ID and the ABR as the advertising router ID. This informs routers in Area 1 that they should forward traffic for the external prefixes to the ASBR (R4), by first forwarding it to this ABR (R2). In the Type 4 LSA, the network mask is meaningless and always set to 0. The metric is the cost to reach the ASBR from the ABR (Figure 6.13).

Listing 6.16 shows the topological database on R1 in the backbone area. Notice that it contains the AS External LSAs, which advertise the external prefixes as advertised by R4, and the ASBR Summary LSA, which says that to reach R4, traffic should be forwarded to R2.

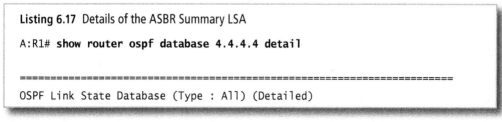

Listing 6.16 The Area 0 database includes the ASBR Summary (Type 4) LSA

```
A:R1# show router ospf database

===============================================================================
OSPF Link State Database (Type : All)
===============================================================================
Type     Area Id     Link State Id    Adv Rtr Id     Age  Sequence    Cksum
-------------------------------------------------------------------------------
Router   0.0.0.0     1.1.1.1          1.1.1.1        717  0x800000de 0xef21
Router   0.0.0.0     2.2.2.2          2.2.2.2        745  0x800000b4 0x79b5
Router   0.0.0.0     3.3.3.3          3.3.3.3        913  0x800000d1 0xe81d
Summary  0.0.0.0     4.4.4.4          2.2.2.2        721  0x80000001 0xb4a3
Summary  0.0.0.0     6.6.6.6          3.3.3.3        1298 0x80000002 0x3813
Summary  0.0.0.0     10.10.1.0        2.2.2.2        1408 0x80000034 0xe43f
Summary  0.0.0.0     10.10.4.0        3.3.3.3        935  0x80000033 0xa776
AS Summ  0.0.0.0     4.4.4.4          2.2.2.2        722  0x80000001 0x9cbb
AS Ext   n/a         5.5.5.5          4.4.4.4        729  0x80000001 0xeaeb
AS Ext   n/a         172.10.1.0       4.4.4.4        729  0x80000001 0x89a9
AS Ext   n/a         172.10.2.0       4.4.4.4        729  0x80000001 0x7eb3
AS Ext   n/a         172.10.3.0       4.4.4.4        729  0x80000001 0x73bd
-------------------------------------------------------------------------------
No. of LSAs: 12
===============================================================================
```

The important information in the ASBR Summary (Type 4) LSA is the router ID of the ASBR (as the link-state ID), the address of the ABR as the advertising router ID, and the metric to reach the ABR (Listing 6.17).

Listing 6.17 Details of the ASBR Summary LSA

```
A:R1# show router ospf database 4.4.4.4 detail

===============================================================================
OSPF Link State Database (Type : All) (Detailed)
```

(continued)

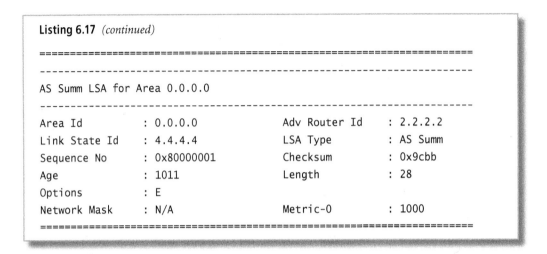

Listing 6.17 *(continued)*

```
===============================================================================
-------------------------------------------------------------------------------
AS Summ LSA for Area 0.0.0.0
-------------------------------------------------------------------------------
Area Id          : 0.0.0.0              Adv Router Id    : 2.2.2.2
Link State Id    : 4.4.4.4              LSA Type         : AS Summ
Sequence No      : 0x80000001           Checksum         : 0x9cbb
Age              : 1011                 Length           : 28
Options          : E
Network Mask     : N/A                  Metric-0         : 1000
===============================================================================
```

Figure 6.13 Format of the ASBR Summary (Type 4) LSA.

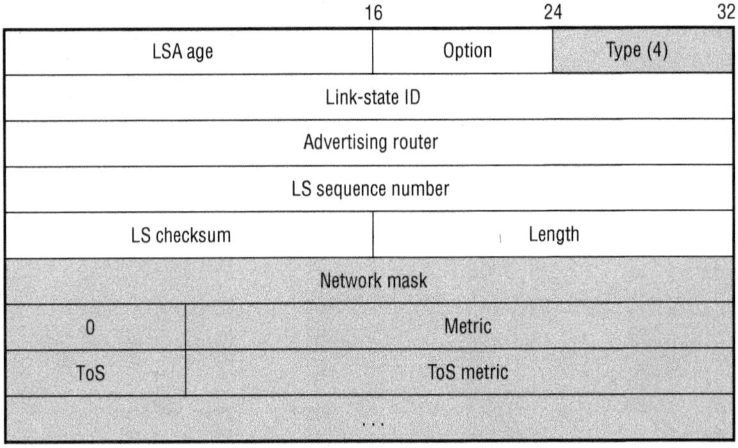

In the topology of Figure 6.12, R3 floods the AS External LSAs unchanged into Area 2 and also creates an ASBR Summary LSA to tell routers in Area 2 to forward traffic to R3 in order to reach the external prefixes advertised by R4.

6.7 Stub Areas

Consider the topology in Figure 6.14 (the same topology as Figure 6.12).

R4 is an ASBR generating AS External LSAs, which are flooded throughout the routing domain. R3 is the only ABR connecting Area 2 to the backbone. Therefore, there is not much value in flooding the external LSAs into Area 2, and this area can be configured as a stub area. All the routers in Area 2 must be configured as stubs. The configuration on R3 is shown in Figure 6.15.

Figure 6.14 Multi-area topology to be used for stub networks.

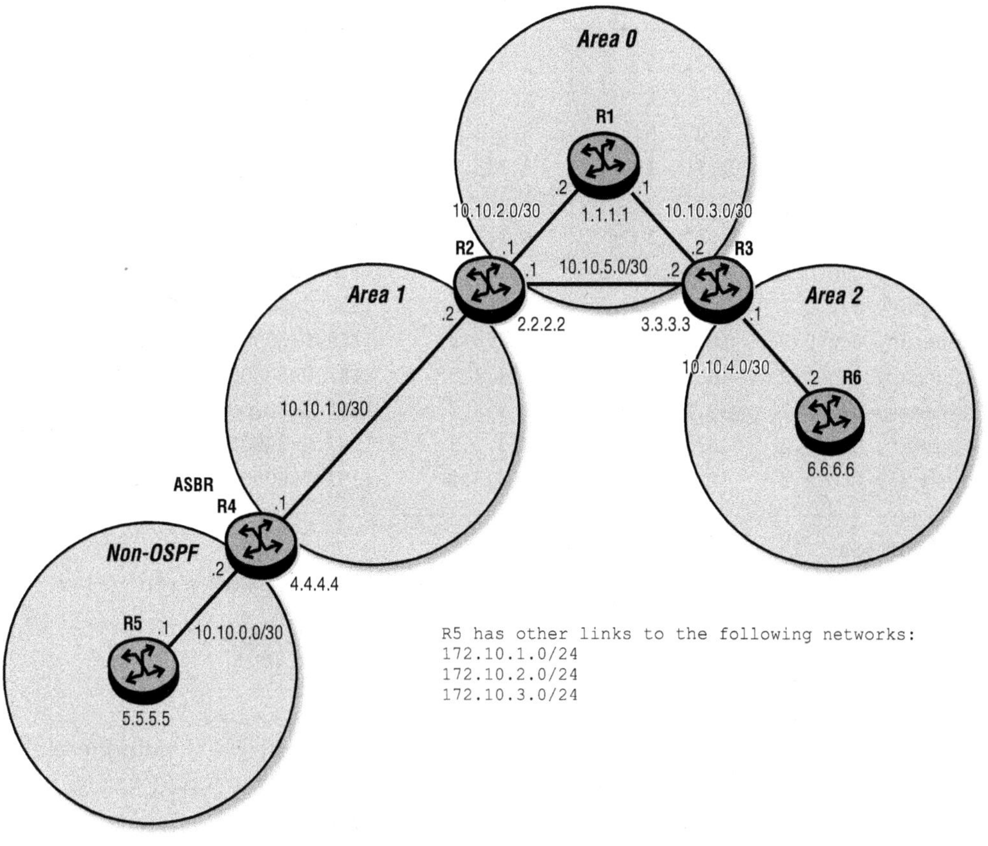

A stub area must not contain Type 4 or Type 5 LSAs. The ABR does not flood these LSAs into the area. Instead, a Summary LSA for the default route is flooded into the area and is installed in the route-table of the intra-area routers in the stub. Listing 6.18 shows the database of router R6 in the stub area.

Listing 6.18 OSPF database in Area 2, configured as a stub

```
A:R6# show router ospf database
```

(continued)

Listing 6.18 *(continued)*

```
===============================================================================
OSPF Link State Database (Type : All)
===============================================================================
Type    Area Id    Link State Id    Adv Rtr Id    Age  Sequence    Cksum
-------------------------------------------------------------------------------
Router  0.0.0.2    3.3.3.3          3.3.3.3       1188 0x80000002  0x10fe
Router  0.0.0.2    6.6.6.6          6.6.6.6       1192 0x80000003  0xdcb
Summary 0.0.0.2    0.0.0.0          3.3.3.3       1187 0x80000002  0x371a
Summary 0.0.0.2    1.1.1.1          3.3.3.3       1187 0x80000002  0x3d24
Summary 0.0.0.2    2.2.2.2          3.3.3.3       1187 0x80000002  0xf4e
Summary 0.0.0.2    3.3.3.3          3.3.3.3       1187 0x80000002  0xac98
Summary 0.0.0.2    4.4.4.4          3.3.3.3       1150 0x80000001  0xe782
Summary 0.0.0.2    5.5.5.5          3.3.3.3       1150 0x80000001  0xec8d
Summary 0.0.0.2    10.10.0.0        3.3.3.3       1150 0x80000001  0xbcc1
Summary 0.0.0.2    10.10.1.0        3.3.3.3       1187 0x80000002  0x7ceb
Summary 0.0.0.2    10.10.2.0        3.3.3.3       1187 0x80000002  0x71f5
Summary 0.0.0.2    10.10.3.0        3.3.3.3       1187 0x80000002  0x331f
Summary 0.0.0.2    10.10.5.0        3.3.3.3       1187 0x80000002  0x1d33
-------------------------------------------------------------------------------
No. of LSAs: 13
```

Totally Stubby Areas

Because there is only one exit point from the area, the Summary LSAs are not useful in the stub area either. It is possible to have the ABR filter the Summary LSAs as well by configuring `no summaries`. Such an area is often referred to as a *totally stubby* area (Figure 6.16).

In a totally stubby area, the link-state database contains only Router and Network LSAs from the area and a Summary LSA with the default route from the ABR (Listing 6.19).

Listing 6.19 OSPF database in totally stubby Area 2

```
A:R6# show router ospf database
```

```
==========================================================================
OSPF Link State Database (Type : All)
==========================================================================
Type     Area Id     Link State Id   Adv Rtr Id   Age  Sequence   Cksum
--------------------------------------------------------------------------
Router   0.0.0.2     3.3.3.3         3.3.3.3      854  0x80000003 0xeff
Router   0.0.0.2     6.6.6.6         6.6.6.6      536  0x80000004 0xbcc
Summary  0.0.0.2     0.0.0.0         3.3.3.3      9    0x80000004 0x331c
--------------------------------------------------------------------------
No. of LSAs: 3
==========================================================================
```

Figure 6.15 Area 2 configured as a stub on R3.

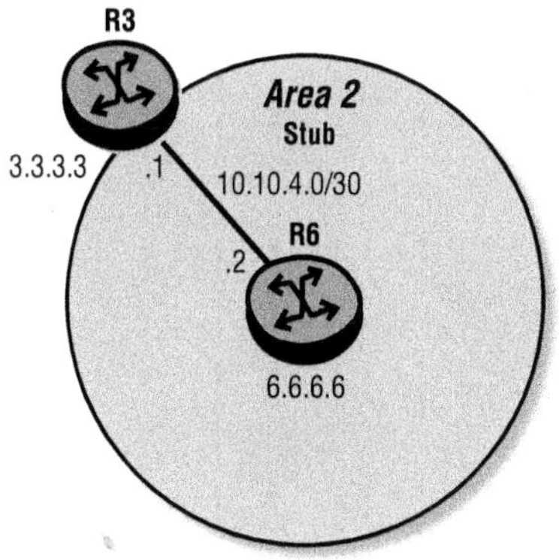


```
A:R3>config>router>ospf# info
----------------------------------------------
            area 0.0.0.0
                interface "system"
                    interface-type point-to-point
                exit
                interface "toR1"
                    interface-type point-to-point
                exit
                interface "toR2"
                    interface-type point-to-point
                exit
            exit
            area 0.0.0.2
                stub
                exit
                interface "toR6"
                    interface-typr point-to-point
                exit
            exit
----------------------------------------------
```

Not-So-Stubby-Areas (NSSAs)

A stub area may not contain any Type 4 or Type 5 LSAs. However, in some cases, it may be desirable to configure a stub area that contains an ASBR. In that case, the area may be configured as an NSSA (not-so-stubby area) (Figure 6.17). In an NSSA, the ASBR generates NSSA (Type 7) LSAs instead of Type 5 LSAs.

Figure 6.16 Area 2 configured as totally stubby (no Type 3, 4, or 5 LSAs).

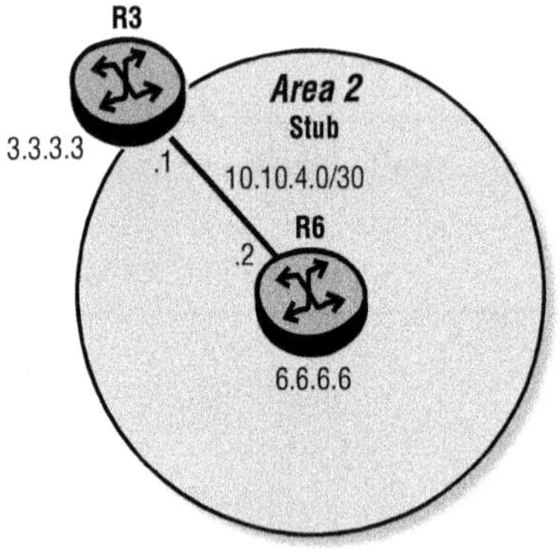

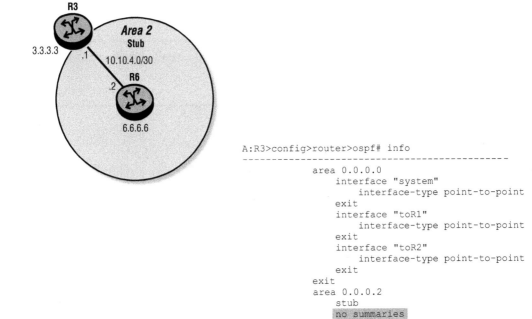

```
A:R3>config>router>ospf# info
----------------------------------------------
            area 0.0.0.0
                interface "system"
                    interface-type point-to-point
                exit
                interface "toR1"
                    interface-type point-to-point
                exit
                interface "toR2"
                    interface-type point-to-point
                exit
            exit
            area 0.0.0.2
                stub
                no summaries
                exit
                interface "toR6"
                    interface-typr point-to-point
                exit
            exit
----------------------------------------------
```

Note that R4 is configured as an ASBR with an export policy and Area 1 is configured as NSSA. Type 7 (NSSA) LSAs are created instead of Type 5 LSAs (Listing 6.20).

Listing 6.20 The external routes in an NSSA are flooded as Type 7 LSAs

```
A:R4# show router ospf database

===============================================================================
OSPF Link State Database (Type : All)
```

```
================================================================================
Type     Area Id     Link State Id    Adv Rtr Id     Age   Sequence     Cksum
--------------------------------------------------------------------------------
Router   0.0.0.1     2.2.2.2          2.2.2.2        1089  0x8000002a   0x7584
Router   0.0.0.1     4.4.4.4          4.4.4.4        509   0x8000002b   0x4d84
Summary  0.0.0.1     0.0.0.0          2.2.2.2        1136  0x80000026   0xd24
NSSA     0.0.0.1     5.5.5.5          4.4.4.4        398   0x80000001   0x3d81
NSSA     0.0.0.1     172.10.1.0       4.4.4.4        398   0x80000001   0xdb3f
NSSA     0.0.0.1     172.10.2.0       4.4.4.4        398   0x80000001   0xd049
NSSA     0.0.0.1     172.10.3.0       4.4.4.4        398   0x80000001   0xc553
--------------------------------------------------------------------------------
No. of LSAs: 7
================================================================================
```

Figure 6.17 All the routers in an NSSA must be configured as NSSA. The ASBR generates Type 7 LSAs for external prefixes.

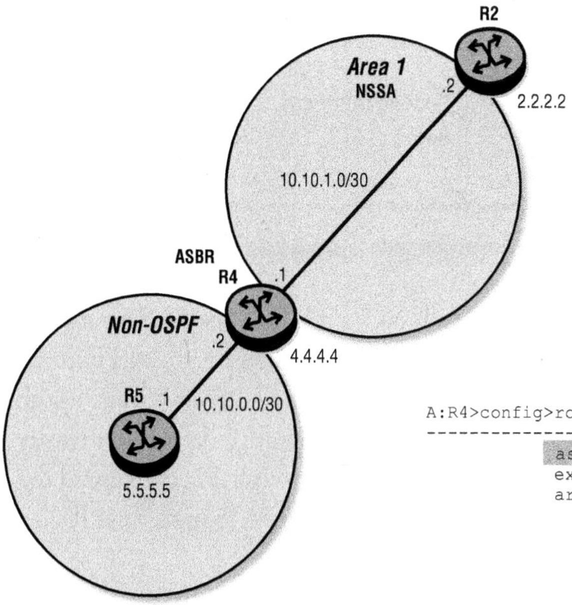

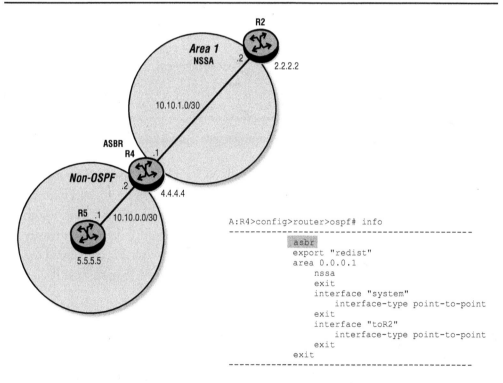

```
A:R4>config>router>ospf# info
----------------------------------------------
            asbr
            export "redist"
            area 0.0.0.1
                nssa
                exit
                interface "system"
                    interface-type point-to-point
                exit
                interface "toR2"
                    interface-type point-to-point
                exit
            exit
----------------------------------------------
```

The NSSA LSA is very similar to the AS External (Type 5) LSA (Listing 6.21). All routers in the NSSA must have the N option set to indicate that they are configured for an NSSA. The P option indicates that the Type 7 LSA should be flooded to other areas by the ABR as a Type 5 LSA.

Listing 6.21 The NSSA LSA contains the same information as the AS External LSA

```
A:R4# show router ospf database 5.5.5.5 detail

===============================================================================
OSPF Link State Database (Type : All) (Detailed)
===============================================================================
-------------------------------------------------------------------------------
NSSA LSA for Area 0.0.0.1
-------------------------------------------------------------------------------
Area Id            : 0.0.0.1              Adv Router Id      : 4.4.4.4
Link State Id      : 5.5.5.5              LSA Type           : NSSA
Sequence No        : 0x80000005           Checksum           : 0x3585
Age                : 362                  Length             : 36
Options            : NP
Network Mask       : 255.255.255.255      Fwding Address     : 4.4.4.4
Metric Type        : Type 2               Metric-0           : 2000
Ext Route Tag      : 0
===============================================================================
```

The ABR connecting to an NSSA converts Type 7 LSAs to Type 5 LSAs and floods them into other areas. Because the ABR is the advertising router for the AS External LSAs and is known in the other areas, it does not create Type 4 LSAs. Unlike a stub network, the ABR for an NSSA does not automatically generate a default route into the area. On the Alcatel-Lucent 7750 SR, the ABR must be explicitly configured to `originate-default-route` if a default route is desired. In Figure 6.18, note that R2 is also configured to summarize some of the external networks.

Totally Stubby NSSA

An NSSA can also be configured with `no summaries`, in which case it becomes a *totally stubby* NSSA (Figure 6.19). No Type 3, 4, or 5 LSAs are flooded into the area by the ABR.

Figure 6.18 The ABR converts Type 7 LSAs to Type 5 LSAs for flooding into other areas. It may also originate a default route into the NSSA.

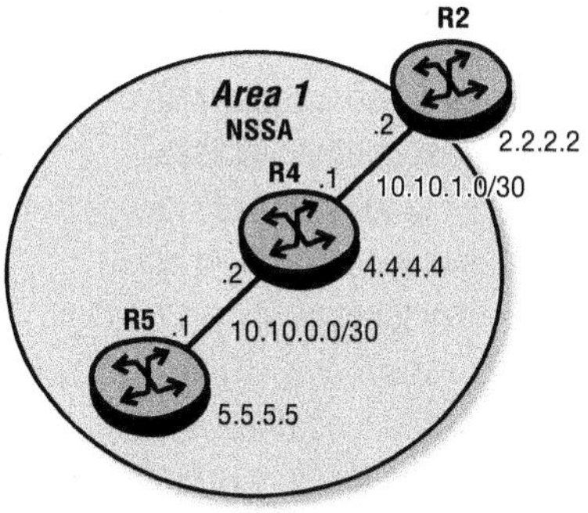

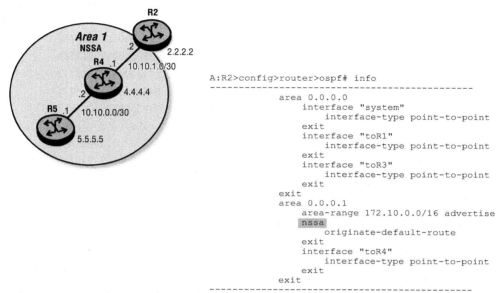

```
A:R2>config>router>ospf# info
----------------------------------------------
            area 0.0.0.0
                interface "system"
                    interface-type point-to-point
                exit
                interface "toR1"
                    interface-type point-to-point
                exit
                interface "toR3"
                    interface-type point-to-point
                exit
            exit
            area 0.0.0.1
                area-range 172.10.0.0/16 advertise
                nssa
                    originate-default-route
                exit
                interface "toR4"
                    interface-type point-to-point
                exit
            exit
----------------------------------------------
```

Because R2 is the ABR between Areas 1 and 0, it contains both the Type 7 and corresponding Type 5 LSAs in its database (Listing 6.22). The only Summary LSA in Area 1 is one for the default route.

Listing 6.22 The ABR has LSAs from both areas

```
A:R2# show router ospf database

===============================================================================
OSPF Link State Database (Type : All)
===============================================================================
Type    Area Id    Link State Id   Adv Rtr Id    Age  Sequence    Cksum
-------------------------------------------------------------------------------
Router  0.0.0.0    1.1.1.1         1.1.1.1       176  0x800000dd 0xf718
Router  0.0.0.0    2.2.2.2         2.2.2.2       174  0x800000b1 0x85aa
Router  0.0.0.0    3.3.3.3         3.3.3.3       178  0x800000d0 0xea1c
Summary 0.0.0.0    4.4.4.4         2.2.2.2       176  0x80000001 0xb4a3
Summary 0.0.0.0    6.6.6.6         3.3.3.3       258  0x80000001 0x3a12
Summary 0.0.0.0    10.10.1.0       2.2.2.2       184  0x80000033 0xe63e
Summary 0.0.0.0    10.10.4.0       3.3.3.3       266  0x80000032 0xa975
```

(continued)

Listing 6.22 *(continued)*

```
Router  0.0.0.1    2.2.2.2          2.2.2.2          179   0x8000000f 0xab69
Router  0.0.0.1    4.4.4.4          4.4.4.4          180   0x8000000c 0x8b65
Summary 0.0.0.1    0.0.0.0          2.2.2.2          97    0x80000001 0x57fe
NSSA    0.0.0.1    5.5.5.5          4.4.4.4          224   0x80000005 0x3585
NSSA    0.0.0.1    172.10.1.0       4.4.4.4          224   0x80000005 0xd343
NSSA    0.0.0.1    172.10.2.0       4.4.4.4          224   0x80000005 0xc84d
NSSA    0.0.0.1    172.10.3.0       4.4.4.4          224   0x80000005 0xbd57
AS Ext  n/a        5.5.5.5          2.2.2.2          173   0x80000003 0xebe0
AS Ext  n/a        172.10.1.0       2.2.2.2          173   0x80000003 0x8a9e
AS Ext  n/a        172.10.2.0       2.2.2.2          173   0x80000003 0x7fa8
AS Ext  n/a        172.10.3.0       2.2.2.2          173   0x80000003 0x74b2
-------------------------------------------------------------------------------
No. of LSAs: 22
===============================================================================
```

Figure 6.19 No Type 3, 4, or 5 LSAs are flooded into a totally stubby NSSA.

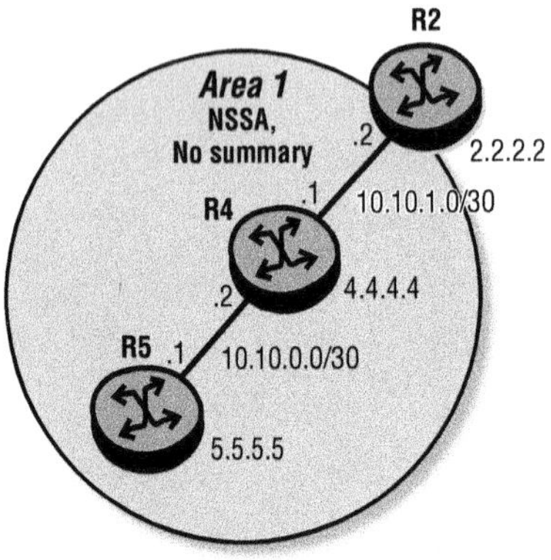

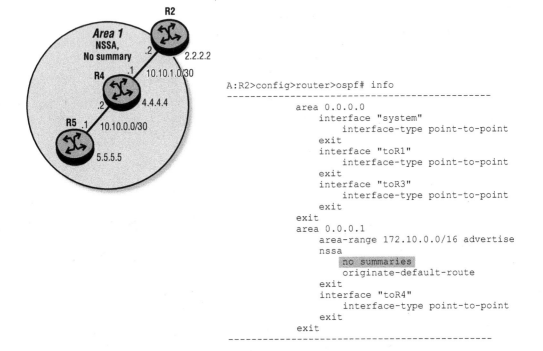

```
A:R2>config>router>ospf# info
----------------------------------------------
            area 0.0.0.0
                interface "system"
                    interface-type point-to-point
                exit
                interface "toR1"
                    interface-type point-to-point
                exit
                interface "toR3"
                    interface-type point-to-point
                exit
            exit
            area 0.0.0.1
                area-range 172.10.0.0/16 advertise
                nssa
                    no summaries
                    originate-default-route
                exit
                interface "toR4"
                    interface-type point-to-point
                exit
            exit
----------------------------------------------
```

Note the similarity between the Type 7 and Type 5 LSAs (Listing 6.23). Remember, the ASBR is the advertising router for the NSSA LSA, and the ABR is the advertising router of the AS External and Summary LSAs.

Listing 6.23 The OSPF database on the ABR has both the Type 7 and Type 5 LSAs, which are nearly identical

```
A:R2# show router ospf database 5.5.5.5 detail

=======================================================================
OSPF Link State Database (Type : All) (Detailed)
=======================================================================
-----------------------------------------------------------------------
NSSA LSA for Area 0.0.0.1
-----------------------------------------------------------------------
Area Id          : 0.0.0.1            Adv Router Id     : 4.4.4.4
Link State Id    : 5.5.5.5            LSA Type          : NSSA
Sequence No      : 0x80000005         Checksum          : 0x3585
Age              : 627                Length            : 36
Options          : NP
Network Mask     : 255.255.255.255    Fwding Address    : 4.4.4.4
Metric Type      : Type 2             Metric-0          : 2000
Ext Route Tag    : 0
-----------------------------------------------------------------------
AS Ext LSA for Network 5.5.5.5
-----------------------------------------------------------------------
Area Id          : N/A                Adv Router Id     : 2.2.2.2
Link State Id    : 5.5.5.5            LSA Type          : AS Ext
Sequence No      : 0x80000004         Checksum          : 0xe9e1
Age              : 117                Length            : 36
Options          : E
Network Mask     : 255.255.255.255    Fwding Address    : 4.4.4.4
Metric Type      : Type 2             Metric-0          : 2000
Ext Route Tag    : 0
=======================================================================
```

6.8 Flooding Rules Summary

The rules to remember for flooding of LSAs are the following (Figure 6.20):

- An ABR creates Summary (Type 3) LSAs to represent all prefixes in an area and floods these to other areas.
- An ASBR creates AS External (Type 5) LSAs to represent external prefixes. These are flooded to all areas.
- When flooding a Type 5 LSA to a different area, the ABR creates an ASBR Summary (Type 4) LSA to represent the ASBR in the other area.
- An NSSA is a stub area with one or more ASBRs. NSSA (Type 7) LSAs are created instead of Type 5 LSAs. They are converted to Type 5 LSAs by the ABR for flooding to neighboring areas.
- The ABR for a stub or NSSA area does not flood any Type 4 or 5 LSAs into the area.
- A Summary LSA for the default route is flooded into a stub area. By default, the default route is not flooded into an NSSA.
- If the stub or NSSA area is configured `no summaries`, no Summary (Type 3) LSAs are flooded into the area either.

An OSPF router could potentially learn a specific prefix through several different types of LSAs. OSPF applies its own preference rules to select the route when this occurs. From most preferred to least preferred, the prefix that will be selected is:

- An OSPF prefix advertised by a router in the same area
- An OSPF prefix advertised by a router in another area (learned through a Summary LSA)
- An external prefix (learned through an AS External LSA) with a Type 1 metric
- An external prefix (learned through an AS External LSA) with a Type 2 metric

These rules govern the selection of the route even if the metric of another route is lower.

6.9 Opaque LSAs

In addition to the LSA types described above, there is another class of LSAs, known as Opaque LSAs. These LSAs were defined in RFC 2370 to support extensions to the OSPF protocol. For example, RFC 3630 defines extensions to allow OSPF to calculate the best path to a destination based on traffic engineering criteria. Three different Opaque LSAs are defined in RFC 2370, each with a different flooding behavior. The RFC does not define the use of the LSAs, only their behavior.

Figure 6.20 Flooding rules for different LSA types.

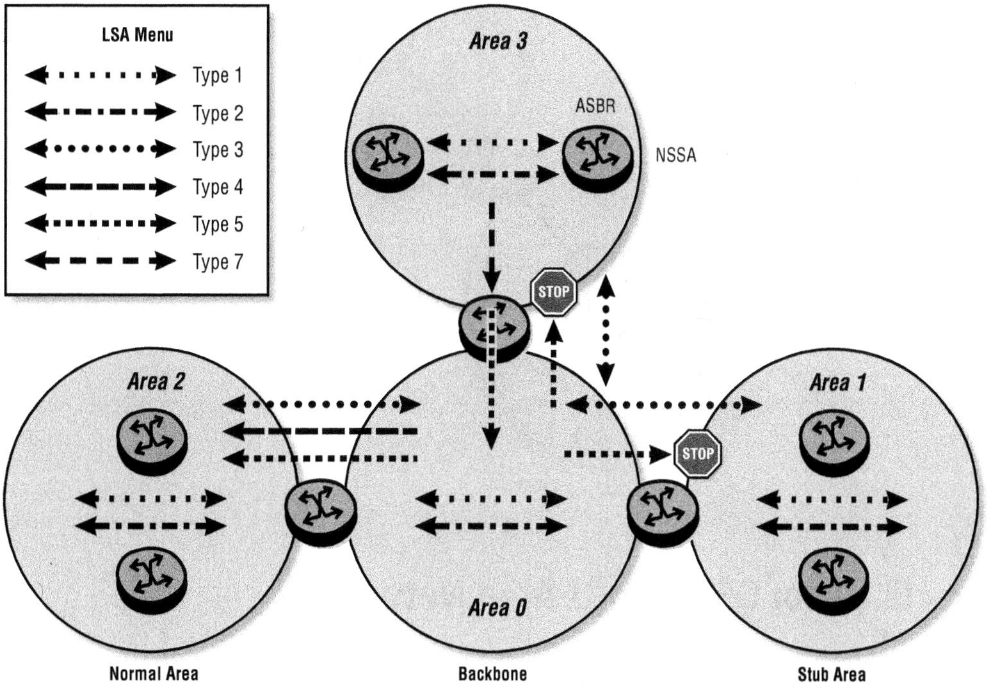

Type 9 (link-local) LSAs are not flooded beyond the local link on which they are created.

Type 10 (intra-area) LSAs are flooded throughout the area but are not forwarded by the ABR beyond the area in which they are created.

Type 11 (network) LSAs are flooded throughout the entire OSPF routing domain.

Figure 6.21 illustrates the flooding behavior of the Opaque LSAs.

As an example, Type 9 LSAs are used for bidirectional forwarding detection (BFD), and Type 10 LSAs are used for flooding traffic engineering information. An OSPF router might not support traffic engineering but still support the flooding of Type 10 LSAs.

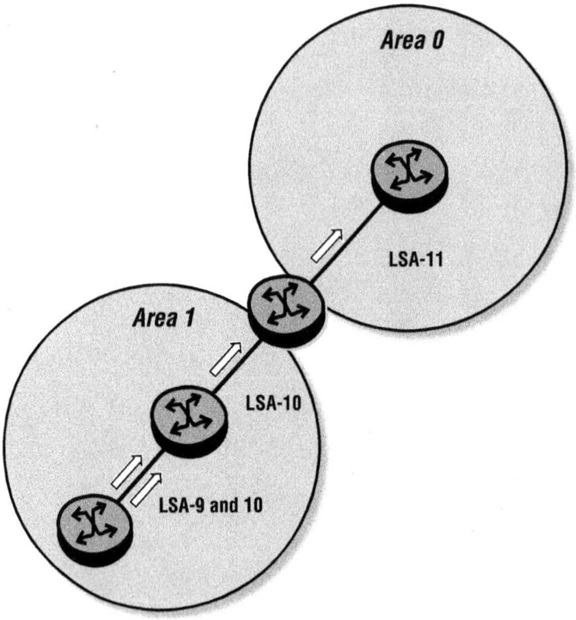

Figure 6.21 Flooding scope of OSPF Opaque LSAs.

Practice Lab: OSPF Multi-Area Networks

The following lab is designed to reinforce your knowledge of the content in this chapter. Please review the instructions carefully, and perform the steps in the order in which they are presented. The practice labs require that you have access to six or more 7750 SRs or Alcatel-Lucent 7450 ESSs in a non-production environment.

These labs are designed to be used in a controlled lab environment. Please *do not* attempt to perform these labs in a production environment.

Lab Section 6.1: Configuring Multi-Area OSPF

Multiple OSPF areas can be used to improve scalability and convergence time.

Objective In this exercise, you will configure a topology of six Alcatel-Lucent 7750 SRs with three OSPF areas (Figure 6.22).

Validation You will know you have succeeded if the OSPF adjacencies between the routers are up and all the routers have routes to all the network destinations.

1. Configure R1–R4 as OSPF routers. This may already be partially configured if you have just completed the practice lab in Chapter 5. Throughout this lab, configure all OSPF interfaces as point-to-point.
2. Configure Area 1 to contain R5 with R1 as the ABR. Advertise the system interface of R5 in OSPF.
   - **A.** Is the OSPF adjacency up? Explain.
   - **B.** Examine the route-table on R5. How does it compare with the route-table on a backbone router such as R3?
   - **C.** Examine the LSDB on R5. How are the LSAs in the LSDB on R5 different from the LSAs on R2?
3. Configure Area 2 to contain R6 with R2 as the ABR. Advertise the system interface of R6 in OSPF.
   - **A.** Examine the route-table on R6. How does it compare with the route-tables on the backbone and Area 1 routers?
   - **B.** Examine the LSDB on R6. Does R6 contain LSAs from both Area 0 and Area 1? If so, describe how they are propagated to Area 2.
   - **C.** From R6 try and ping the system IP address of R5. Is the ping successful? Explain.
   - **D.** How many routes are in the route-tables of R1, R2, R5, and R6? Explain.

Lab Section 6.2: Configuring OSPF Route Summarization

Route summarization is used in conjunction with a multi-area OSPF design to reduce the size of the database and simplify the SPF calculations. In this and the following exercises, you will configure loopback addresses to simulate other networks that might be connected to the router. Normally, you may not have much cause to use loopbacks, but they are useful to simulate other networks to observe how they are handled by the routing protocol.

Objective In this exercise, you will configure route summarization so that OSPF Areas 1 and 2 are only aware of summary routes to the backbone area.

Figure 6.22 Multi-area OSPF topology.

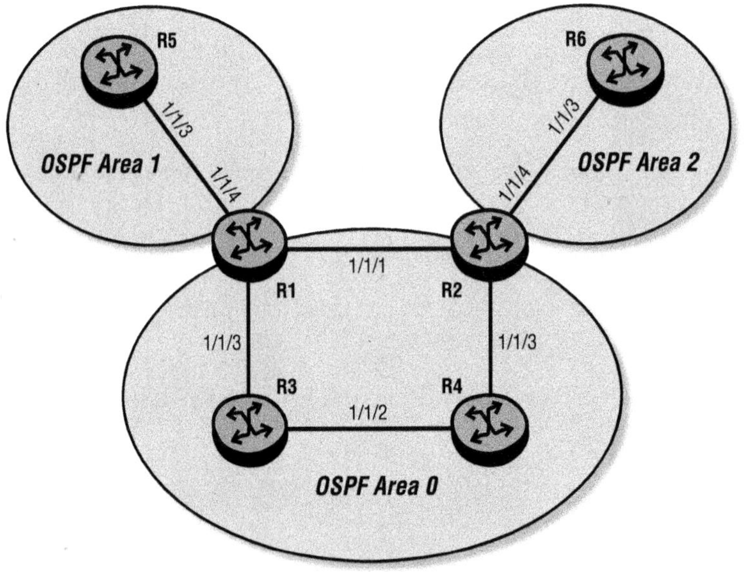

Validation You will know you have succeeded if the non-backbone areas only contain summary routes for the specified networks but can still reach all destinations.

1. Configure R3 with three loopback addresses `192.168.3.1/32`, `192.168.3.2/32`, and `192.168.3.3/32` and advertise the routes in OSPF.
   - **A.** Are the loopback prefixes advertised to the other routers in the backbone area? If so what type of LSA is used to propagate the routes?
   - **B.** Are the prefixes advertised to the other routers in Areas 1 and 2? If so what type of LSA is used to propagate the routes to those areas? Explain.
2. Configure summarization so that Area 1 is only aware of the summary route `192.168.3.0/24`.
   - **A.** After summarization is configured, examine the route-tables of the backbone routers. How have they changed after summarization? Explain.
   - **B.** How has the route-table of R5 changed after summarization?
   - **C.** How do the LSAs originated by R3 change after summarization is configured on R1?
   - **D.** How have the LSAs originated by R1 changed after summarization has been configured?

E. Ping `192.168.3.3` from R5. Does the ping work? Explain.

F. Ping `192.168.3.4` from R5. Does the ping work? Explain.

3. Configure summarization so that the loopback interfaces of R3 are *not* advertised in Area 2.

   A. How have the route-table and LSDB on R2 changed after summarization?

   B. How have the route-table and LSDB on R6 changed after summarization?

   C. From R6 try and ping one of the loopback interfaces on R3. Is the ping successful? Explain. How has the route-table and LSDB on R6 changed after summarization?

Lab Section 6.3: Configuring OSPF Route Redistribution

Prefixes that were not learned through OSPF can be exported into the OSPF routing domain. Known as *route redistribution*, this process allows other routers in the OSPF domain to learn the external prefixes. You will simulate the external routes using loopback addresses.

Objective In this exercise, you will configure route redistribution in Area 1 and observe how external prefixes are propagated to the other OSPF areas.

Validation You will know you have succeeded if the external prefixes are propagated as expected to other routers in the topology.

1. Configure R5 as an ASBR.

   A. How has the LSDB of R1 changed? Explain.

   B. How has the LSDB of R5 changed? Explain.

   C. How has the LSDB of R6 changed? Explain.

2. Configure three loopback interfaces on R5: `192.168.5.1/32`, `192.168.5.2/32`, and `192.168.5.3/32`. Use a policy to redistribute these loopback interfaces into OSPF.

   A. Describe the LSAs used to propagate the loopback routes in Area 1.

   B. Are these routes learned in the backbone area? If so describe the LSAs used to propagate the routes and which routers originate them.

   C. Are these routes learned in Area 2? If so what type of LSAs are used to propagate the routes and which routers originate them?

Lab Section 6.4: Configuring OSPF Stub Areas

In some cases, it is not desirable or necessary to flood external routing information into an area. In this case, the area should be configured as a stub.

Objective In this exercise, you will configure OSPF Area 2 as a stub area (Figure 6.23) and examine the differences in the database.

Validation You will know you have succeeded if the OSPF adjacency forms between R2 and R6 and the external prefixes are replaced by a default route in Area 2.

1. On R2, configure Area 2 as a stub.
   - **A.** Does the OSPF adjacency stay up? Explain, and fix any problems required to bring the adjacency up.
   - **B.** How have the route-table and LSDB on R6 changed?
   - **C.** How have the route-table and LSDB on R2 changed?
2. From R6 try and ping one of the loopbacks redistributed by R5, `192.168.5.1/32`.
   - **A.** Is the ping successful? Explain.
   - **B.** Try and ping the system IP address of R3 (`10.10.10.3`). Is this ping successful? Explain.

Figure 6.23 OSPF network with stub area.

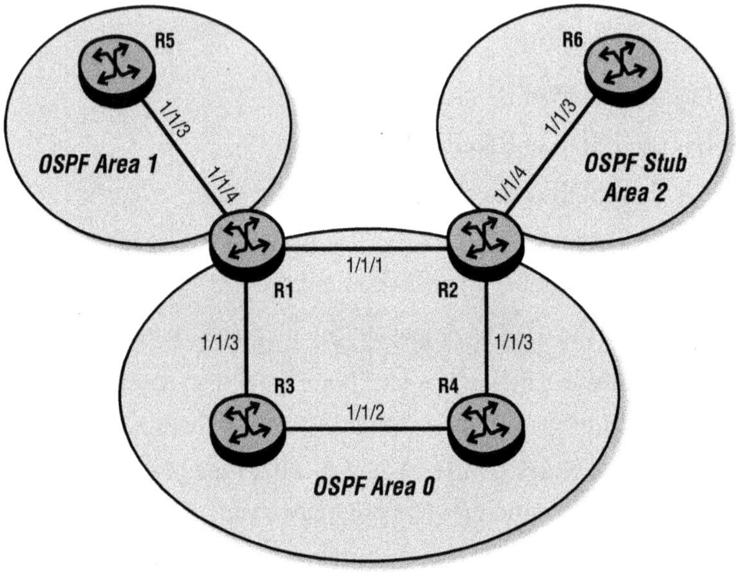

3. Configure Area 2 so that it does not contain Type 3 Summary LSAs.
   A. Which router needs to be configured for this to take effect?
   B. Are there any Type 3 Summary LSAs still in the LSDB of R6?
   C. Try to ping the system IP address of R3 (`10.10.10.3`). Is this ping successful? Explain.

Lab Section 6.5: Configuring OSPF Not So Stubby Areas

If it is necessary to have an ASBR in a stub area, the area can be made into an NSSA. The external prefixes are flooded through the NSSA as Type 7 LSAs and converted to Type 5 LSAs by the ABR.

Objective In this exercise, you will configure OSPF Area 1 as an NSSA (Figure 6.24) and verify the expected changes in the databases in Area 1 and Area 0.

Validation You will know you have succeeded if the OSPF adjacency forms between R1 and R5 and the Type 7 and Type 5 LSAs are produced as expected.

1. Configure Area 1 as an NSSA without Summary LSAs.
   A. Examine the route-table on R5 and R1. How have they changed?
   B. Examine the LSDB on R5, R1, and R3. How have they changed? Explain.
2. Try and ping the system interface of R3 (`10.10.10.3`).
   A. Is the ping successful? Explain, and fix any problems.

Figure 6.24 OSPF network with NSSA.

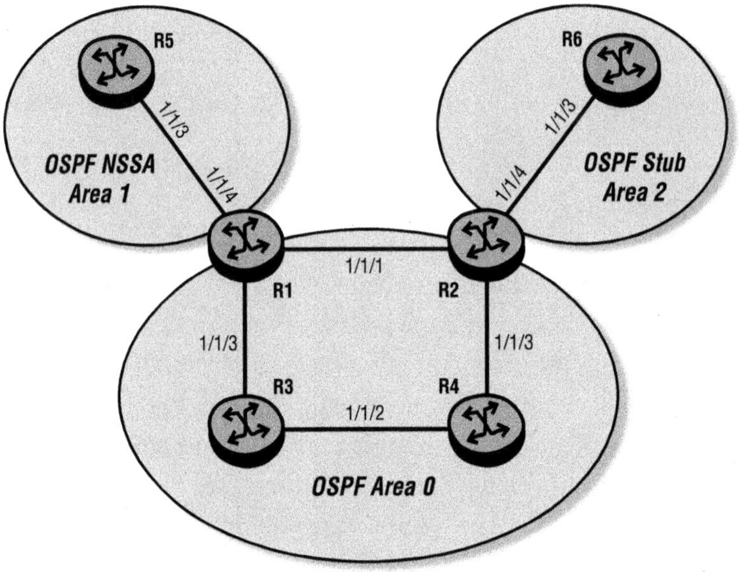

Chapter Review

Now that you have completed this chapter, you should have a good understanding of the following topics:

- The reasons for multi-area networks
- What are the different types of OSPF areas
- What are the different types of OSPF routers
- The purpose and operation of the ABR
- The purpose and operation of an ASBR
- The purpose and flooding behaviors of Summary LSAs
- The contents of the Summary LSA
- The importance of route summarization and how it is implemented
- The significance of the black-hole entry
- The purpose and configuration of virtual links
- The ASBR and reason for exporting routes to OSPF
- How to configure route export policies
- The contents of the External LSA
- The purpose and contents of the ASBR Summary LSA
- The behavior and configuration of a stub area
- The behavior and configuration of a totally stubby area
- The behavior and configuration of an NSSA
- The contents of a Type 7 LSA
- The behavior and configuration of a totally stubby NSSA
- The purpose and flooding behavior of opaque LSAs

Post-Assessment

The following questions will test your knowledge and prepare you for the Alcatel-Lucent NRS II Certification Exam. Compare your response with the answers listed in Appendix A. You can also use the CD that accompanies this book to take all the assessment tests and review the answers.

1. Which of the following is the definition of an ASBR?
   - **A.** An OSPF router that routes in the backbone network
   - **B.** An OSPF router that routes in a stub network
   - **C.** An OSPF router that connects two or more different OSPF areas
   - **D.** An OSPF router that connects to an external routing domain
   - **E.** An OSPF router that connects to a BGP network

2. A router has four interfaces configured in OSPF. Two point-to-point interfaces are in Area 0, one point-to-point interface is in Area 1, and one broadcast interface is in Area 2. How many Router LSAs will be originated by the router?
   - **A.** The router will originate one Router LSA.
   - **B.** The router will originate two Router LSAs.
   - **C.** The router will originate three Router LSAs.
   - **D.** The router will originate four Router LSAs.
   - **E.** It is not possible to determine with the given information.

3. What is the default behavior of multi-area OSPF with respect to originating Type 3 Summary LSAs?
   - **A.** Every backbone router originates a Summary LSA for each prefix in its Router LSA.
   - **B.** Every ABR originates a Summary LSA for each Router LSA in its database.
   - **C.** Every backbone router originates a Summary LSA for every prefix listed in the LSDB.
   - **D.** Every ABR originates a Summary LSA for every prefix listed in the LSDB.
   - **E.** Summary LSAs are only originated by backbone routers when manual summarization is configured.

4. R1 is an ABR with an interface connected to R2 that is an Area 1 intra-area router. The network operator wants to summarize the backbone area networks `192.168.1.0/24` and `192.168.2.0/24` routes with the summary route `192.168.0.0/16`. Which statement below is correct regarding the Summary LSA flooded throughout Area 1?

   A. It will have its metric set to the highest cost of the component networks, and the Adv Router ID set to R1's router ID.

   B. It will have its metric set to the highest cost of the component networks, and the Adv Router ID set to R2's router ID.

   C. It will have its metric set to the lowest cost of the component networks, and the Adv Router ID set to R1's router ID.

   D. It will have its metric set to the lowest cost of the component networks, and the Adv Router ID set to R2's router ID.

5. Consider an OSPF network topology with Area 0, Area 1, and Area 2. An ASBR in Area 1 is configured to redistribute external routes into OSPF using a policy. Which statement below correctly describes how external routes are advertised to Area 0 and Area 2?

   A. The ASBR originates Router LSAs with the ASBR flag set that are flooded throughout Area 1. The external routes are not learned in Area 0 or Area 2 without additional policy on the ABRs.

   B. The ASBR originates Router LSAs that are flooded throughout Area 1. Area 1 ABRs originate Summary LSAs that are flooded throughout Area 0. The ABRs between Area 0 and Area 2 originate Summary LSAs that are flooded throughout Area 2.

   C. The ASBR originates Router LSAs with the ASBR flag set that are flooded throughout the autonomous system.

   D. The ASBR originates ASBR Summary LSAs that are flooded throughout the autonomous system.

   E. The ASBR originates AS External LSAs that are flooded throughout the autonomous system.

6. Select the *incorrect* statement about multi-area OSPF networks.

   A. Suboptimal routing may occur in a multi-area network.

   B. Traffic engineering calculations cannot be made across a multi-area network.

   C. Troubleshooting of routing issues in a multi-area network is usually more difficult than in a single area network.

   D. The large number of Summary LSAs makes the SPF calculation more complex in a multi-area network.

7. Which of the following is NOT an OSPF area type?

   A. Backbone Area

   B. Virtual Area

   C. Stub Area

   D. Not So Stubby Area

   E. Totally Stubby Area

8. Consider an OSPF network with Area 0, Area 1, and Area 2. R1 is an ABR for Area 1, and R2 is an ABR for Area 2. If default OSPF configurations are used, which statement below is correct?

   A. Area 1 routes are advertised to Area 2 using Router LSAs originated by R1.

   B. Area 1 routes are advertised to Area 2 using Router LSAs originated by R2.

   C. Area 1 routes are advertised to Area 2 using Summary LSAs originated by R1.

   D. Area 1 routes are advertised to Area 2 using Summary LSAs originated by R2.

9. Router R1 is an ABR connected to R2 that is an Area 1 intra-area router. The network operator wants to configure OSPF summarization to reduce routing table sizes of Area 1 routers. Which statement below is correct about the required configuration?

A. R1 needs to be configured with the `area-range` command in the `configure router OSPF area 0` context.

B. R1 needs to be configured with the `area-range` command in the `configure router OSPF area 1` context.

C. R1 needs to be configured with the `aggregate` command in the `configure router` context.

D. R2 needs to be configured with the `area-range` command in the `configure router OSPF area 1` context.

E. R2 needs to be configured with the `aggregate` command in the `configure router` context.

10. R1 is an ABR with an interface connected to R2 that is an Area 1 intra-area router. The network operator uses the OSPF `area-range` command to summarize the backbone area networks `192.168.1.0/24` and `192.168.2.0/24` with the summary prefix `192.168.0.0/16`. Which statement below is correct?

A. R1 will contain entries in its route table for both the /24 networks and for the summarized /16 network.

B. R2 will contain entries in its route table for both the /24 networks and for the summarized /16 network

C. R2 will contain entries in its route table for only the /24 networks.

D. Both answers A and B are correct.

11. Consider an OSPF network topology with Area 0, Area 1, and Area 2, all configured as normal areas. R1 is the only ABR between Area 0 and Area 1. R2 is the only ABR between Area 0 and Area 2. R3 is in Area 1 and is the only router in the entire network configured as an ASBR. Which statement below is correct?

   A. Only Area 1 routers have an ASBR Summary LSA with Adv Rtr-ID of R3.

   B. Only Area 0 routers have an ASBR Summary LSA with Adv Rtr-ID of R1.

   C. Area 0 and Area 2 routers have an ASBR Summary LSA with Adv Rtr-ID of R1.

   D. Area 0 routers have an ASBR Summary LSA with Adv Rtr-id of R1. Area 2 routers have an ASBR Summary LSA with Adv Rtr-ID of R2.

   E. All routers in the autonomous system have an ASBR Summary LSA with Adv Rtr-ID of R3.

   F. Area 1 routers have an ASBR Summary LSA with Adv Rtr-ID of R3. Area 0 routers have an ASBR Summary LSA with Adv Rtr-ID of R1. Area 2 routers have an ASBR Summary LSA with Adv Rtr-ID of R2.

12. Consider an OSPF network topology with Area 0, Area 1, and Area 2. Area 2 is a simple stub area. Area 1 contains an ASBR that redistributes external routes into OSPF. Which LSA types listed below will *not* be contained in the LSDB of the Area 2 routers?

   A. A Summary LSA describing the default route

   B. AS External LSAs originated by the ASBR in Area 1

   C. Summary LSAs describing Area 0 internal networks

   D. Summary LSAs describing Area 1 internal networks

   E. Router LSAs originated by Area 2 routers

13. An OSPF network consists of Area 0, Area 1, and Area 2. Area 1 contains an ASBR that originates AS External LSAs. Area 2 is initially declared as a simple stub area. An operator changes the Area 2 intra-area router to be a totally stubby area. How does the configuration change the LSDB of the Area 2 routers?

   A. AS External LSAs will be blocked.

   B. Summary LSAs will be blocked.

   C. Router LSAs originated by Area 2 will not be flooded throughout Area 2.

   D. There will not be a Summary LSA to describe a default route.

   E. There will be no change.

14. An OSPF network is designed to include Area 0, Area 1, and Area 2. Area 2 is not required to learn any specific routes from the other areas but should use a default route to its ABR instead. Area 2 contains an ASBR that redistributes external routes into the network. Which of the configurations below would be the most likely choice for the Area 2 ABR if it is an Alcatel-Lucent 7750 SR?

   A. It should be configured as a `stub` area with the parameter `originate-default-route`.

   B. It should be configured as a `stub` area with the parameters `no summaries` and `originate-default-route`.

   C. It should be configured as an `nssa` area with the parameter `no summaries`.

   D. It should be configured as an `nssa` area with the parameter `originate-default-route`.

   E. It should be configured as an `nssa` area with the parameters `no summaries` and `originate-default-route`.

15. Consider an OSPF network topology with Area 0, Area 1, and Area 2. Area 2 is configured as an NSSA area and contains Router R10, which is an ASBR redistributing external routes into the OSPF network, but not an ABR. Which statement below is *not* correct?

A. The LSDB of routers in Area 2 contains an NSSA LSA with an advertising router-id of R10.

B. The LSDB of routers in Area 0 contains AS External LSAs with an advertising router-ID of R10.

C. The LSDB of routers in Area 1 contains an ASBR Summary LSA with an advertising router-ID of the ABR between Area 0 and Area 1.

D. The LSDB of routers in Area 1 contains an AS External LSA with an advertising router-ID of the ABR between Area 0 and Area 2.

E. The LSDB of routers in Area 1 does not contain NSSA LSAs from Area 2.

7 OSPFv3

The Alcatel-Lucent NRS II exam topics covered in this chapter include the following:

- OSPFv3 overview
- Router and Network LSAs
- Intra-Area Prefix LSAs
- Link LSAs
- Multi-area networks and Inter-Area Prefix LSAs
- External prefixes

OSPF was designed to carry routing information for IPv4. To support IPv6, a new version was defined, OSPFv3. In this chapter, we describe the enhancements made in OSPFv3 that allow it to support the exchange of IPv6 routing information. The most significant difference is that Router and Network LSAs (link-state advertisements) no longer carry any address or prefix information. This information is carried in a new LSA, the Intra-Area Prefix LSA. We also look at the differences in the other LSAs that are used in multi-area networks and to carry external prefixes. We show some examples of how to configure an IPv6 network to use OSPFv3 to distribute routing information.

Pre-Assessment

The following assessment questions will help you understand what areas of the chapter you should review in more detail to prepare for the NRS II exam. You can also use the CD that accompanies this book to take all the assessment tests and review the answers.

1. When only IPv6 is configured, how is the OSPFv3 router ID derived on an Alcatel-Lucent 7750 SR?

A. The router ID is derived from the system interface address if it is assigned; otherwise, it defaults to the last four octets of the chassis MAC (Media Access Control) address.

B. The router ID is derived from the system interface address if it is assigned; otherwise, it defaults to `0.0.0.0`.

C. The router ID is derived from an explicitly configured router ID if there is one assigned; otherwise, it defaults to the system interface address.

D. The router ID is derived from an explicitly configured router ID if there is one assigned; otherwise, it defaults to the last four octets of the chassis MAC address.

E. The router ID is derived from an explicitly configured router ID. OSPFv3 does not become active until the router ID is configured.

2. Two routers, R1 and R2, have an OSPFv3 adjacency between them. Both routers are configured with a system interface address, and their directly connected links are configured with a global IPv6 address. When R2 learns routes from R1, which next-hop will be used in R2's routing table? Assume that the OSPFv3 routes from R1 are the best routes received by R2.

   A. The link-local interface address of R2 will be used for the next-hop.

   B. The link-local interface address of R1 will be used for the next-hop.

   C. The global interface address of R2 will be used for the next-hop.

   D. The global interface address of R1 will be used for the next-hop.

   E. The system interface address of R1 will be used for the next-hop.

3. An OSPFv3 router has a system interface, a loopback interface, and a router interface in Area 0. Global IPv6 addresses are assigned only to the system interface and the router interface. Which of the prefixes will appear in the IAP LSA originated by the router?

   A. The loopback and router link-local prefixes will appear in the IAP LSA along with the two global prefixes.

   B. The system interface and loopback prefixes will appear in the IAP LSA.

   C. The loopback prefixes and both router interface prefixes will appear in the IAP LSA.

   D. The system interface prefix and the global router interface prefix will appear in the IAP LSA.

   E. The loopback prefix and the link-local router interface prefix will appear in the IAP LSA.

4. What is the flooding scope of an OSPFv3 Inter-Area Prefix LSA?

   A. Link-local scope

   B. External scope

   C. Area scope

   D. Autonomous System scope

   E. None of the above

5. Which of the following statements about OSPFv3 is *not* correct?

   A. OSPFv3 supports the equivalent of OSPFv2 stub areas.

   B. OSPFv3 does not require global IPv6 addresses for router interfaces.

   C. OSPFv3 uses the same authentication mechanisms as OSPFv2.

   D. OSPFv3 Router LSAs do not carry IPv6 prefix information.

   E. An OSPFv3 router-id is 32 bits long.

7.1 OSPFv3

OSPFv3 is defined in RFC 5340 and was developed specifically for routing IPv6. The basic mechanisms of OSPFv2 are unchanged: flooding mechanism, hierarchy, designated router (DR) election, and shortest path first (SPF) calculation. The five Open Shortest Path First (OSPF) message types are also relatively unchanged. However, new LSAs are required to support IPv6 addresses and hence a new version of the protocol.

The significant changes in OSPFv3 are as follows:

- IPv4 address characteristics are removed from basic LSAs.
- New LSAs are defined to carry IPv6 addresses.
- Network prefix information is carried as a prefix length and prefix address instead of network address and subnet mask.
- A generalized flooding scope is defined.
- OSPFv3 runs on a per-link rather than per-IP-subnet basis.
- Support for multiple instances per link.
- Authentication is removed. OSPFv3 relies on the AH (Authentication Header) and ESP (Encapsulating Security Payload) capabilities of IPv6.
- Option handling is made more flexible.
- Optional features of OSPFv2 are supported (NSSA [not so stubby area], etc.).

One of the most significant differences with OSPFv3 is that Router and Network LSAs do not carry any IPv6 addresses or prefix information. They only carry protocol-independent topology information. Router IDs, area IDs, and LSA link-state IDs are still 32 bits but have no relationship to IPv6 addresses.

Flooding scope has been generalized in OSPFv3 and three different scopes defined (similar to the scope of opaque LSAs):

- **Link-local scope**—LSAs are flooded on the local link only.
- **Area scope**—LSAs are flooded throughout the area, but not beyond.
- **AS scope**—LSAs are flooded throughout the entire OSPF routing domain.

Another noticeable difference is the use of link-local addresses. All IPv6 interfaces are expected to have a link-local address assigned. OSPFv3 uses the link-local unicast address as the source of messages sent to neighbors. A router learns its neighbor's link-local addresses and uses them as the next-hop address for its prefixes. However, link-local addresses are never carried as prefix information in other LSAs.

Single Area Network in OSPFv3

As in OSPFv2, OSPFv3 floods Router and Network LSAs throughout an area. However, in OSPFv3, these LSAs do not carry any network prefixes. Prefix information is carried in Intra-Area Prefix LSAs. In this section, we examine the LSAs generated in the single area network shown in Figure 7.1.

Figure 7.1 Single area network topology for OSPFv3.

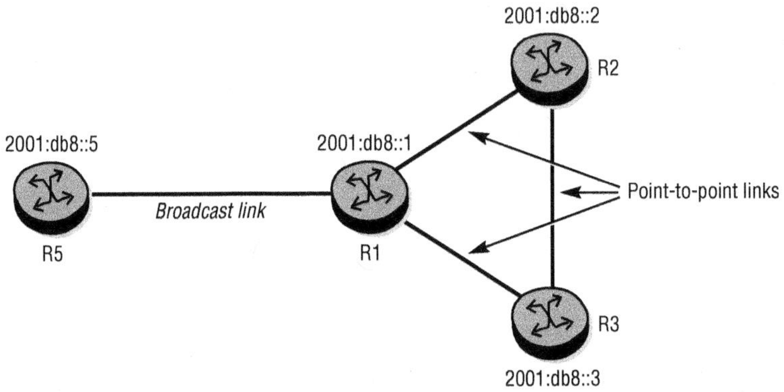

The first step is to configure the Layer 3 interfaces. Because we do not care about routing to the interfaces, we only use global IPv6 addresses for the system address. The interface configuration is very simple and is shown in Listing 7.1.

Listing 7.1 Configuring the IPv6 interfaces on R1

```
*A:R1# configure router
*A:R1>config>router# info
----------------------------------------------
#--------------------------------------------------
echo "IP Configuration"
#--------------------------------------------------
        interface "system"
            ipv6
                address 2001:DB8::1/128
            exit
        exit
        interface "toR2"
            port 1/1/1
```

```
            ipv6
            exit
        exit
        interface "toR3"
            port 1/1/4
            ipv6
            exit
        exit
        interface "toR5"
            port 1/1/3
            ipv6
            exit
        exit
        ----------------------------------------------
```

The interfaces are addressed using link-local addresses (Listing 7.2).

Listing 7.2 Link-local addresses are used on all interfaces except the system interface

```
*A:R1>config>router# show router interface

===============================================================================
Interface Table (Router: Base)
===============================================================================
Interface-Name                   Adm       Opr(v4/v6)  Mode    Port/SapId
   IP-Address                                                  PfxState
-------------------------------------------------------------------------------
system                           Up        Down/Up     Network system
   2001:DB8::1/128                                             PREFERRED
toR2                             Up        Down/Up     Network 1/1/1
   FE80::216:4DFF:FE13:5CAE/64                                 PREFERRED
toR3                             Up        Down/Up     Network 1/1/4
   FE80::216:4DFF:FE13:5CB1/64                                 PREFERRED
toR5                             Up        Down/Up     Network 1/1/3
   FE80::216:4DFF:FE13:5CB0/64                                 PREFERRED
-------------------------------------------------------------------------------
Interfaces : 4
===============================================================================
```

The OSPFv3 configuration is similar to that of OSPFv2 (Listing 7.3). Because the Alcatel-Lucent 7750 SR does not create a router ID from the IPv6 system address, a specific `router-id` value is assigned. Otherwise the router ID is formed from the chassis MAC (Media Access Control) address.

Listing 7.3 OSPFV3 configuration on R1—essentially the same as an OSPFv2 configuration

```
*A:R1# configure router
*A:R1>config>router# info
----------------------------------------------
... output omitted ...

        router-id 1.1.1.1
#--------------------------------------------------
echo "OSPFv3 Configuration"
#--------------------------------------------------
        ospf3
            area 0.0.0.0
                interface "system"
                exit
                interface "toR2"
                    interface-type point-to-point
                exit
                interface "toR3"
                    interface-type point-to-point
                exit
                interface "toR5"
                exit
            exit
        exit
----------------------------------------------
```

Once OSPFv3 has been configured on the neighbors, we can view the link-state database (LSDB). As we would expect in an IPv4 network, there are four Router LSAs and one Network LSA for the broadcast network. There are also an additional five Intra-Area Prefix LSAs that carry the actual IPv6 prefixes (Listing 7.4).

Listing 7.4 Besides the Router and Network LSAs, an OSPFv3 area also contains Intra-Area Prefix LSAs

```
*A:R1# show router ospf3 database

===============================================================================
OSPF Link State Database (Type : All)
===============================================================================
Type    Area Id    Link State Id  Adv Rtr Id  Age  Sequence   Cksum
-------------------------------------------------------------------------------
Router  0.0.0.0    0.0.0.0        1.1.1.1     768  0x80000010 0xe4af
Router  0.0.0.0    0.0.0.0        2.2.2.2     442  0x80000010 0x5bba
Router  0.0.0.0    0.0.0.0        3.3.3.3     1326 0x8000000c 0xc454
Router  0.0.0.0    0.0.0.0        5.5.5.5     1706 0x8000000c 0x5240
Network 0.0.0.0    0.0.0.4        1.1.1.1     1849 0x80000009 0xf60a
IA Pfx  0.0.0.0    0.0.0.0        1.1.1.1     888  0x80000010 0x5627
IA Pfx  0.0.0.0    0.0.117.52     1.1.1.1     509  0x8000000a 0x1c38
IA Pfx  0.0.0.0    0.0.0.0        2.2.2.2     713  0x80000010 0x8ce7
IA Pfx  0.0.0.0    0.0.0.0        3.3.3.3     192  0x8000000d 0xc8a5
IA Pfx  0.0.0.0    0.0.0.0        5.5.5.5     1504 0x8000000c 0x3726
-------------------------------------------------------------------------------
No. of LSAs: 10
===============================================================================
```

OSPFv3 Router LSA

The Router LSA in Listing 7.5 shows that there is considerable similarity to the OSPFv2 Router LSA. One difference is that the Type field in an OSPFv3 LSA is 16 bits instead of the 8 bits in OSPFv2. The three high-order bits are used to define flooding scope. The highest bit (U bit) indicates what to do with unknown LSA types, and the next two indicate the flooding scope. A Router LSA has an area flooding scope, and its hex value is `0x2001`. The other differences between OSPFv3 and OSPFv2 are described below.

Listing 7.5 OSPFv3 Router LSA

```
*A:R1# show router ospf3 database type router adv-router 1.1.1.1 detail
```

(continued)

Listing 7.5 *(continued)*

```
===============================================================================
OSPF Link State Database (Type : Router) (Detailed)
===============================================================================
-------------------------------------------------------------------------------
Router LSA for Area 0.0.0.0
-------------------------------------------------------------------------------
Area Id           : 0.0.0.0              Adv Router Id     : 1.1.1.1
Link State Id     : 0.0.0.0 (0)
LSA Type          : Router
Sequence No       : 0x80000010           Checksum          : 0xe4af
Age               : 995                  Length            : 72
Options           : --R--EV6
Flags             :                      Link Count        : 3
Link Type (1)     : P2P Link             Nbr Rtr ID (1)    : 2.2.2.2
I/F Index (1)     : 2                    Nbr I/F Index (1): 2
Metric (1)        : 100
Link Type (2)     : P2P Link             Nbr Rtr ID (2)    : 3.3.3.3
I/F Index (2)     : 3                    Nbr I/F Index (2): 2
Metric (2)        : 100
Link Type (3)     : Transit Network      DR Rtr ID (3)     : 1.1.1.1
I/F Index (3)     : 4                    DR I/F Index (3) : 4
Metric (3)        : 100
===============================================================================
*A:R1#
```

- The link-state ID is no longer the router ID and is a value chosen by the router.
- The Options field is 24 bits long. The bits are set in this Router LSA as described below. In the case of normal IPv6 routing, the R and the V6 bits will always be on:
  - The E bit indicates that the network is not a stub network.
  - The R bit indicates that the router is routing packets.
  - The V6 bit indicates that the router is routing IPv6 packets.
- The links are described as Type 1, 2, or 4 as in OSPFv3. Type 3 links (for stub networks) are not used because they are not part of the topology used for SPF. No addresses are used in any of the fields. Router IDs are used to describe neighbors.

- The I/F index, or interface ID, is a unique value assigned by the router to each interface. This is used instead of an IP address to identify the individual interfaces.
- The interface cost is carried as the link metric for each link. There is no TOS information.

OSPFv3 Network LSA

The Type value for the OSPFv3 Network LSA is `0x2002`. The OSPFv3 Network LSA is generated by the DR and is very similar to the OSPFv2 Network LSA, except that no address information is carried (Listing 7.6).

Listing 7.6 OSPFv3 Network LSA

```
*A:R1# show router ospf3 database type network adv-router 1.1.1.1 detail

===============================================================================
OSPF Link State Database (Type : Network) (Detailed)
===============================================================================
-------------------------------------------------------------------------------
Network LSA for Area 0.0.0.0
-------------------------------------------------------------------------------
Area Id          : 0.0.0.0              Adv Router Id     : 1.1.1.1
Link State Id    : 0.0.0.4 (4)
LSA Type         : Network
Sequence No      : 0x80000009           Checksum          : 0xf60a
Age              : 2133                 Length            : 32
Options          : --R--EV6             No of Adj Rtrs    : 2
Router Id (1)    : 1.1.1.1              Router Id (2)     : 5.5.5.5
===============================================================================
*A:R1#
```

- The link-state ID is the interface ID of the DR's interface to the broadcast network.
- The Options field is set as in the Router LSA.
- As in the OSPFv2 Network LSA, the routers on the broadcast network are listed by router ID.

Intra-Area Prefix LSAs

Intra-Area Prefix (IAP) LSAs are a new type of LSA defined in OSPFv3 with a Type value of `0x2009`. Router and Network LSAs now carry only topology information—IAP LSAs carry all the IPv6 prefix information for the area. Each router generates an IAP LSA for its reachable destinations, and the DR generates one to carry the prefix information for a broadcast link. The IAP LSA generated by R1 is shown in Listing 7.7.

Listing 7.7 Intra-Area Prefix LSA

```
*A:R1# show router ospf3 database 0.0.0.0 type intra-area-pfx adv-router
 1.1.1.1 detail

===============================================================================
OSPF Link State Database (Type : IA Pfx) (Detailed)
===============================================================================
-------------------------------------------------------------------------------
IA Pfx LSA for Area 0.0.0.0
-------------------------------------------------------------------------------
Area Id            : 0.0.0.0              Adv Router Id     : 1.1.1.1
Link State Id      : 0.0.0.0 (0)
LSA Type           : IA Pfx
Sequence No        : 0x80000011           Checksum          : 0x5428
Age                : 330                  Length            : 52
Ref Ls Type        : 2001                 Ref Ls Id         : 0
Ref Adv Rtr        : 1.1.1.1              No of Pfxs        : 1
Prefix (1)         : 2001:DB8::1/128
Options (1)        : LA                   Metric (1)        : 0
===============================================================================
```

Because the router interfaces have not been given global IPv6 addresses, the only prefix information in the IAP LSAs in the IAP LSA is the global prefix assigned to the system interface. In the IAP LSA, the Ref Ls Type, Ref Ls Id, and Ref Adv Rtr fields refer to the Router or Network LSA that this IAP LSA corresponds to.

The IAP LSA for the Network LSA from the DR (router R1 in this example) is shown in Listing 7.8. Because there are no prefixes associated with the broadcast link, there are no prefixes carried in this LSA. RFC 5340 does not specify how the link-state

ID should be chosen, except that each IAP LSA originated by a router must have a unique address.

Listing 7.8 Intra-Area Prefix LSA that references a Network LSA

```
*A:R1# show router ospf3 database 0.0.117.52 type
intra-area-pfx adv-router 1.1.1.1 detail

===============================================================================
OSPF Link State Database (Type : IA Pfx) (Detailed)
===============================================================================
-------------------------------------------------------------------------------
IA Pfx LSA for Area 0.0.0.0
-------------------------------------------------------------------------------
Area Id             : 0.0.0.0               Adv Router Id     : 1.1.1.1
Link State Id       : 0.0.117.52 (30004)
LSA Type            : IA Pfx
Sequence No         : 0x8000000b            Checksum          : 0x1a39
Age                 : 93                    Length            : 32
Ref Ls Type         : 2002                  Ref Ls Id         : 4
Ref Adv Rtr         : 1.1.1.1               No of Pfxs        : 0
===============================================================================
*A:R1#
```

Because we have used global IPv6 addresses only for the system interfaces, there is little prefix information in our network. Here we configure two loopback interfaces on R5 and add them to OSPF. The prefixes are `2001:db8:0:ff01::/64` and `2001:db8:0:ff02::/64`. They appear in the IAP LSA from R5 as seen in Listing 7.9. However, they have no effect on the Router LSA from R5.

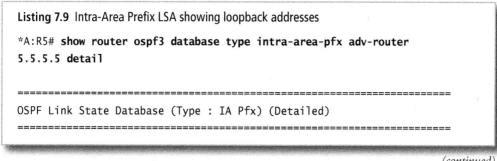

Listing 7.9 Intra-Area Prefix LSA showing loopback addresses

```
*A:R5# show router ospf3 database type intra-area-pfx adv-router
5.5.5.5 detail

===============================================================================
OSPF Link State Database (Type : IA Pfx) (Detailed)
===============================================================================
```

(continued)

Listing 7.9 *(continued)*

```
-------------------------------------------------------------------------
IA Pfx LSA for Area 0.0.0.0
-------------------------------------------------------------------------
Area Id           : 0.0.0.0               Adv Router Id     : 5.5.5.5
Link State Id     : 0.0.0.0 (0)
LSA Type          : IA Pfx
Sequence No       : 0x8000005b            Checksum          : 0xbfe2
Age               : 22                    Length            : 76
Ref Ls Type       : 2001                  Ref Ls Id         : 0
Ref Adv Rtr       : 5.5.5.5               No of Pfxs        : 3
Prefix (1)        : 2001:DB8::5/128
Options (1)       : LA                    Metric (1)        : 0
Prefix (2)        : 2001:DB8::FF01:0:0:0:0/64
Options (2)       :                       Metric (2)        : 0
Prefix (3)        : 2001:DB8::FF02:0:0:0:0/64
Options (3)       :                       Metric (3)        : 0
=========================================================================
```

Link LSAs

Another new LSA in OSPFv3 is the Link LSA (Type value `0x0008`). The Link LSA has only link-local scope and is used to exchange information about the link between neighbors. The information exchanged includes:

- The router's link-local address, to be used as the next-hop address by its neighbors
- Other IPv6 addresses associated with the link
- Option values indicating the router's capabilities on the link

Because the Link LSA has link-local scope, it is not flooded beyond the link. On the 7750 SR, Link LSAs are not shown in the OSPF database. Use the command `show router ospf3 interface` *`interface_name`* `database detail` to display the Link LSAs.

If we assign the global address `2001:db8:111::1/64` to the interface `toR5` on router R1, the Link LSAs exchanged between routers R1 and R5 are as shown in Listing 7.10. The link-state ID of the Link LSA is set to the value of the interface ID on the link.

Listing 7.10 Link LSAs

```
*A:R1# show router ospf3 interface "toR5" database detail

===============================================================================
OSPF Link State Database (Detailed)
===============================================================================
-------------------------------------------------------------------------------
Link LSA
-------------------------------------------------------------------------------
Interface Address: 0.0.0.0                  Adv Router Id      : 1.1.1.1
Link State Id     : 4                       LSA Type           : Link
Sequence No       : 0x80000055              Checksum           : 0xe5fc
Age               : 91                      Length             : 44
Options           : --R--EV6                Rtr Priority       : 1
Link Local Addr   : FE80::216:4DFF:FE13:5CB1
No of Pfxs        : 1
Prefix (1)        : 2001:DB8:111::/64
Options (1)       :
-------------------------------------------------------------------------------
Link LSA
-------------------------------------------------------------------------------
Interface Address: 0.0.0.0                  Adv Router Id      : 5.5.5.5
Link State Id     : 2                       LSA Type           : Link
Sequence No       : 0x80000056              Checksum           : 0x9f32
Age               : 1972                    Length             : 44
Options           : --R--EV6                Rtr Priority       : 1
Link Local Addr   : FE80::203:FAFF:FEAC:99B0
No of Pfxs        : 0
===============================================================================
```

OSPFv3 Multi-Area Networks

OSPFv3 supports hierarchy in the same way as OSPFv2, including features such as stub areas, NSSAs, and virtual links. ABRs join areas and flood summary information into neighboring areas. Type 3 LSAs and Type 4 LSAs have been renamed and the Type values changed as shown in Table 7.1.

Table 7.1 Name and Type Values of OSPFv3 LSAs

OSPFv2 LSA	OSPFv3 Type Value (hex)	OSPFv3 LSA Name
Type 1	0x2001	Router
Type 2	0x2002	Network
Type 3	0x2003	Inter-Area Prefix
Type 4	0x2004	Inter-Area Router
Type 5	0x4005	AS External
Type 7	0x2007	NSSA
n/a	0x0008	Link
n/a	0x2009	Intra-Area Prefix

You might think that the Inter-Area Prefix and Router LSAs would have AS flooding scope, but really they are created by the ABR and flooded into the neighboring area and thus have only area scope.

We look at the LSAs generated for the network topology shown in Figure 7.2.

Figure 7.2 Multi-area topology for OSPFv3.

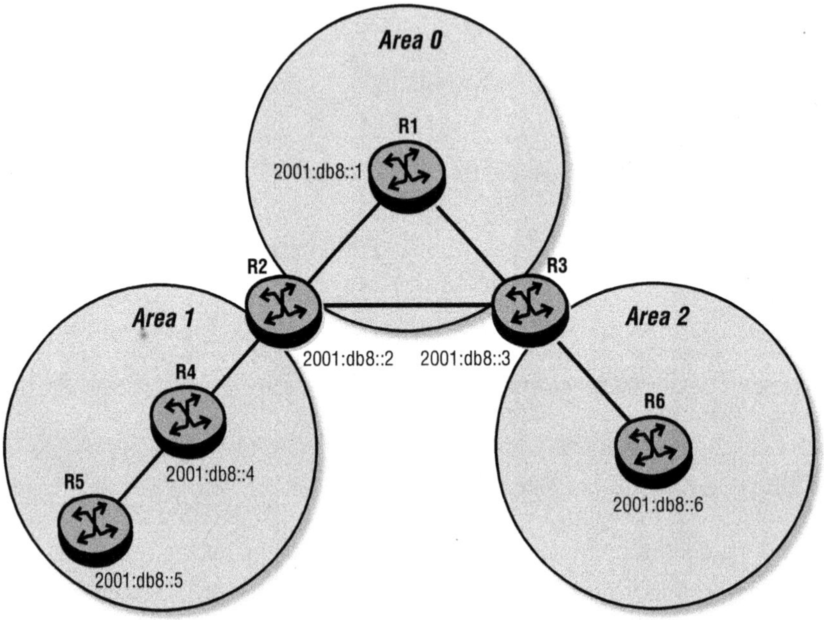


```
R5 has other links to the following networks:
2001:db8:0:ff01/64
2001:db8:0:ff02/64
2001:db8:0:ff03/64
```

Inter-Area Prefix LSAs

Like the OSPFv2 Type 3 LSA, the Inter-Area Prefix (IEP) LSA contains summary information that is flooded by the ABR into a neighboring area. After the topology above is configured with point-to-point links between all routers, the LSDB is as shown in Listing 7.11.

Listing 7.11 OSPFv3 database in a multi-area network

```
*A:R1# show router ospf3 database

===============================================================================
OSPF Link State Database (Type : All)
===============================================================================
Type    Area Id    Link State Id   Adv Rtr Id   Age  Sequence   Cksum
-------------------------------------------------------------------------------
Router  0.0.0.0    0.0.0.0         1.1.1.1      2042 0x8000006f 0xeacc
Router  0.0.0.0    0.0.0.0         2.2.2.2      1686 0x80000072 0x9919
Router  0.0.0.0    0.0.0.0         3.3.3.3      862  0x8000006d 0x5b1
IE Pfx  0.0.0.0    0.0.0.7         2.2.2.2      1641 0x80000002 0xba94
IE Pfx  0.0.0.0    0.0.0.8         2.2.2.2      918  0x80000003 0x23c4
IE Pfx  0.0.0.0    0.0.0.12        2.2.2.2      327  0x80000001 0xbc75
IE Pfx  0.0.0.0    0.0.0.13        2.2.2.2      280  0x80000001 0xc46b
IE Pfx  0.0.0.0    0.0.0.14        2.2.2.2      259  0x80000001 0xcc61
IE Pfx  0.0.0.0    0.0.0.1         3.3.3.3      228  0x80000003 0xb43
IA Pfx  0.0.0.0    0.0.0.0         1.1.1.1      1852 0x80000070 0x9587
IA Pfx  0.0.0.0    0.0.0.0         2.2.2.2      336  0x8000006f 0xcd47
IA Pfx  0.0.0.0    0.0.0.0         3.3.3.3      910  0x8000006b 0xc04
-------------------------------------------------------------------------------
No. of LSAs: 12
===============================================================================
```

The Inter-Area Prefix LSAs each contains information for one prefix. As can be seen by the LSAs shown in Listing 7.12, the IEP LSAs are very similar to Type 3 Summary LSAs.

Listing 7.12 Inter-Area Prefix LSAs

```
*A:R1# show router ospf3 database type inter-area-pfx adv-router
2.2.2.2 detail

===============================================================================
OSPF Link State Database (Type : IE Pfx) (Detailed)
===============================================================================
-------------------------------------------------------------------------------
IE Pfx LSA for Area 0.0.0.0
-------------------------------------------------------------------------------
Area Id          : 0.0.0.0              Adv Router Id     : 2.2.2.2
Link State Id    : 0.0.0.7 (7)
LSA Type         : IE Pfx
Sequence No      : 0x80000002           Checksum          : 0xba94
Age              : 1724                 Length            : 44
Options          :                      Metric            : 100
Dest Prefix      : 2001:DB8::4/128
-------------------------------------------------------------------------------
IE Pfx LSA for Area 0.0.0.0
-------------------------------------------------------------------------------
Area Id          : 0.0.0.0              Adv Router Id     : 2.2.2.2
Link State Id    : 0.0.0.8 (8)
LSA Type         : IE Pfx
Sequence No      : 0x80000003           Checksum          : 0x23c4
Age              : 1001                 Length            : 44
Options          :                      Metric            : 200
Dest Prefix      : 2001:DB8::5/128
-------------------------------------------------------------------------------
IE Pfx LSA for Area 0.0.0.0
-------------------------------------------------------------------------------
Area Id          : 0.0.0.0              Adv Router Id     : 2.2.2.2
Link State Id    : 0.0.0.12 (12)
LSA Type         : IE Pfx
Sequence No      : 0x80000001           Checksum          : 0xbc75
Age              : 418                  Length            : 36
Options          :                      Metric            : 200
Dest Prefix      : 2001:DB8::FF01:0:0:0:0/64
... output omitted ...
===============================================================================
```

Summarization can be configured as in OSPFv2. When router R2 is configured with the statement `configure router area 1 area-range 2001:db8:0:ff00::/56 advertise`, the three IEP LSAs for the individual networks are replaced by a single LSA summarizing the networks (Listing 7.13). A black-hole entry for the summarized network is created by default on R2.

Listing 7.13 IEP LSA for summarized routes

```
*A:R2# configure router ospf3 area 1
*A:R2>config>router>ospf3>area# area-range 2001:db8:0:ff00::/56 advertise
*A:R2>config>router>ospf3>area# show router ospf3 database 0.0.0.15 detail

===============================================================================
OSPF Link State Database (Type : All) (Detailed)
===============================================================================
-------------------------------------------------------------------------------
IE Pfx LSA for Area 0.0.0.0
-------------------------------------------------------------------------------
Area Id          : 0.0.0.0                Adv Router Id    : 2.2.2.2
Link State Id    : 0.0.0.15 (15)
LSA Type         : IE Pfx
Sequence No      : 0x80000001             Checksum         : 0x54e3
Age              : 547                    Length           : 36
Options          :                        Metric           : 200
Dest Prefix      : 2001:DB8::FF00:0:0:0:0/56
===============================================================================
```

OSPFv3 AS External and Inter-Area Router LSAs

External networks can be exported into an OSPFv3 network in the same way as in OSPFv2. In the topology in Figure 7.3, routers R4 and R5 are exchanging route information using IS-IS. R4 is configured as an ASBR with a policy to export IS-IS routes to OSPF.

Listing 7.14 shows the LSDB at router R1.

Figure 7.3 Multi-area topology including non-OSPF networks.

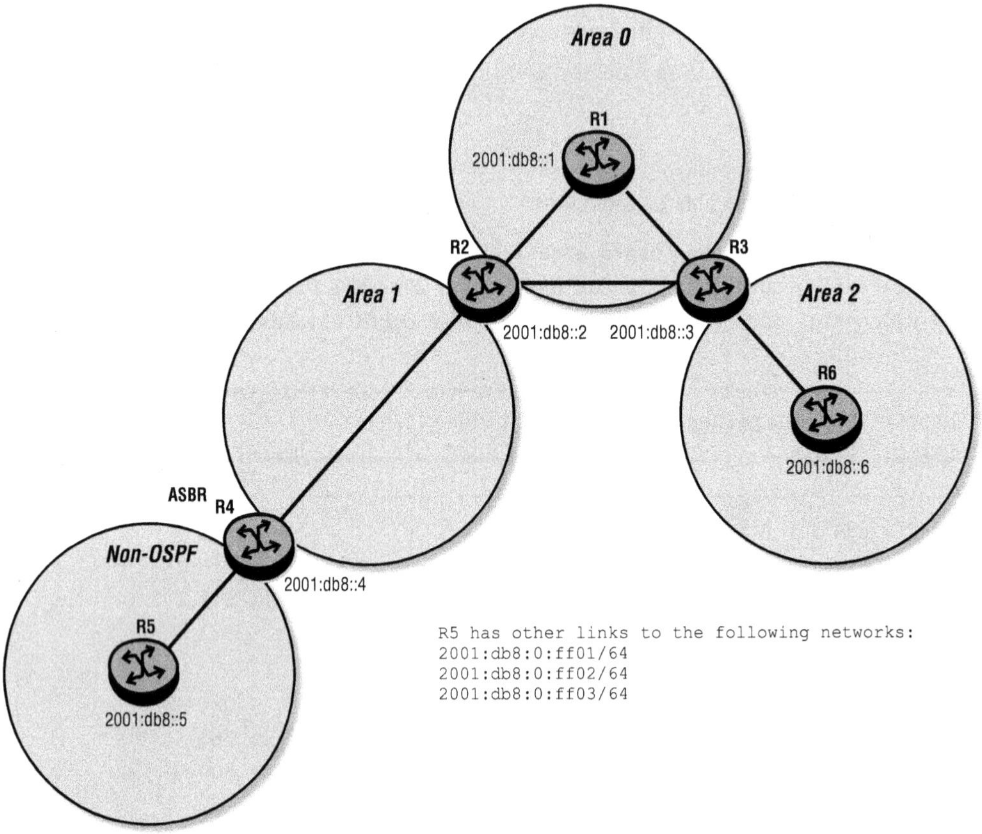

Listing 7.14 Link-state database including AS External and Inter-Area Router LSAs

```
*A:R1# show router ospf3 database

===============================================================================
OSPF Link State Database (Type : All)
===============================================================================
Type    Area Id    Link State Id   Adv Rtr Id   Age  Sequence   Cksum
-------------------------------------------------------------------------------
Router  0.0.0.0    0.0.0.0         1.1.1.1      1230 0x80000071 0xe6ce
Router  0.0.0.0    0.0.0.0         2.2.2.2      873  0x80000074 0x951b
```

```
Router  0.0.0.0    0.0.0.0         3.3.3.3      9    0x8000006f 0x1b3
IE Pfx  0.0.0.0    0.0.0.7         2.2.2.2      908  0x80000004 0xb696
IE Pfx  0.0.0.0    0.0.0.1         3.3.3.3      1782 0x80000004 0x944
IE Rtr  0.0.0.0    4.4.4.4         2.2.2.2      60   0x80000001 0xd3c6
IA Pfx  0.0.0.0    0.0.0.0         1.1.1.1      976  0x80000072 0x9189
IA Pfx  0.0.0.0    0.0.0.0         2.2.2.2      1450 0x80000070 0xcb48
IA Pfx  0.0.0.0    0.0.0.0         3.3.3.3      222  0x8000006d 0x806
AS Ext  n/a        0.0.0.2         4.4.4.4      59   0x80000001 0x358c
AS Ext  n/a        0.0.0.3         4.4.4.4      59   0x80000001 0xe824
AS Ext  n/a        0.0.0.4         4.4.4.4      59   0x80000001 0xf01a
AS Ext  n/a        0.0.0.5         4.4.4.4      59   0x80000001 0xf810
-------------------------------------------------------------------------------
No. of LSAs: 13
===============================================================================
```

Listing 7.15 shows the contents of an AS External LSA.

Listing 7.15 OSPFv3 AS External LSA

```
*A:R1# show router ospf3 database 0.0.0.2 detail

===============================================================================
OSPF Link State Database (Type : All) (Detailed)
===============================================================================
-------------------------------------------------------------------------------
AS Ext LSA (0.0.0.2 (2))
-------------------------------------------------------------------------------
Area Id          : N/A                  Adv Router Id     : 4.4.4.4
Link State Id    : 0.0.0.2 (2)
LSA Type         : AS Ext
Sequence No      : 0x80000001           Checksum          : 0x358c
Age              : 754                  Length            : 44
Options          :                      E2-Metric         : 200
Dest Prefix      : 2001:DB8::5/128
===============================================================================
```

In the same way that router R2 would generate a Type 4 LSA in an OSPFv2 network, R2 generates the Inter-Area Router (IER) LSA to identify the ASBR (router R4). Listing 7.16 shows the contents of the IER LSA.

Listing 7.16 Inter-Area Router LSA

```
*A:R1# show router ospf3 database 4.4.4.4 detail

===============================================================================
OSPF Link State Database (Type : All) (Detailed)
===============================================================================
-------------------------------------------------------------------------------
IE Rtr LSA for Area 0.0.0.0
-------------------------------------------------------------------------------
Area Id            : 0.0.0.0                 Adv Router Id     : 2.2.2.2
Link State Id      : 4.4.4.4 (67372036)
LSA Type           : IE Rtr
Sequence No        : 0x80000001              Checksum          : 0xd3c6
Age                : 791                     Length            : 32
Options            : --R--EV6                Metric            : 100
ASB Rtr Id         : 4.4.4.4
===============================================================================
```

OSPFv3 Stub and NSSAs

OSPFv3 areas can be defined as stubs or NSSAs and have the same behavior as OSPFv2. AS External and Inter-Area Router LSAs are not flooded into a stub or NSSA area. If the ABR is configured with `no summaries`, then Inter-Area Prefix LSAs are also filtered by the ABR. An IEP LSA for the default route is automatically originated in a stub network and in an NSSA if configured for `originate-default-route`.

Listing 7.17 shows the database on R2 when Area 1 is configured as an NSSA. Because this is the ABR, it shows both the NSSA LSAs and the corresponding AS External LSAs.

Listing 7.17 OSPFv3 database for the ABR connected to the NSSA

```
*A:R2# show router ospf3 database

===============================================================================
OSPF Link State Database (Type : All)
===============================================================================
Type    Area Id    Link State Id    Adv Rtr Id    Age   Sequence    Cksum
-------------------------------------------------------------------------------
Router  0.0.0.0    0.0.0.0          1.1.1.1       464   0x800000c1 0x461f
Router  0.0.0.0    0.0.0.0          2.2.2.2       74    0x800000c4 0xfa63
Router  0.0.0.0    0.0.0.0          3.3.3.3       529   0x800000bf 0x6004
IE Pfx  0.0.0.0    0.0.0.16         2.2.2.2       49    0x80000001 0x62e4
IE Pfx  0.0.0.0    0.0.0.1          3.3.3.3       1507  0x80000050 0x7090
IA Pfx  0.0.0.0    0.0.0.0          1.1.1.1       96    0x800000c3 0xeeda
IA Pfx  0.0.0.0    0.0.0.0          2.2.2.2       1589  0x800000c2 0x279a
IA Pfx  0.0.0.0    0.0.0.0          3.3.3.3       1953  0x800000be 0x6557
Router  0.0.0.1    0.0.0.0          2.2.2.2       49    0x80000001 0x87d
Router  0.0.0.1    0.0.0.0          4.4.4.4       51    0x80000002 0xf99b
IE Pfx  0.0.0.1    0.0.0.12         2.2.2.2       74    0x80000002 0x3a13
IE Pfx  0.0.0.1    0.0.0.13         2.2.2.2       74    0x80000002 0xefbf
IE Pfx  0.0.0.1    0.0.0.14         2.2.2.2       74    0x80000002 0x5aee
IE Pfx  0.0.0.1    0.0.0.15         2.2.2.2       74    0x80000002 0xf8e7
NSSA    0.0.0.1    0.0.0.1          4.4.4.4       46    0x80000001 0xb328
NSSA    0.0.0.1    0.0.0.2          4.4.4.4       51    0x80000001 0x1017
NSSA    0.0.0.1    0.0.0.3          4.4.4.4       51    0x80000001 0x180d
NSSA    0.0.0.1    0.0.0.4          4.4.4.4       51    0x80000001 0x2003
IA Pfx  0.0.0.1    0.0.0.0          4.4.4.4       51    0x80000002 0x155b
AS Ext  n/a        0.0.0.1          2.2.2.2       48    0x80000001 0xe9e3
AS Ext  n/a        0.0.0.2          2.2.2.2       48    0x80000001 0x46d2
AS Ext  n/a        0.0.0.3          2.2.2.2       48    0x80000001 0x4ec8
AS Ext  n/a        0.0.0.4          2.2.2.2       48    0x80000001 0x56be
-------------------------------------------------------------------------------
No. of LSAs: 23
===============================================================================
```

Listing 7.18 shows an NSSA LSA from Area 1.

Listing 7.18 OSPFv3 NSSA LSA

```
*A:R2# show router ospf3 database 0.0.0.1 adv-router 4.4.4.4 detail

===============================================================================
OSPF Link State Database (Type : All) (Detailed)
===============================================================================
-------------------------------------------------------------------------------
NSSA LSA for Area 0.0.0.1
-------------------------------------------------------------------------------
Area Id          : 0.0.0.1             Adv Router Id     : 4.4.4.4
Link State Id    : 0.0.0.1 (1)
LSA Type         : NSSA
Sequence No      : 0x80000001          Checksum          : 0xb328
Age              : 459                 Length            : 60
Options          : P                   N2-Metric         : 200
Dest Prefix      : 2001:DB8::5/128
Nexthop          : 2001:DB8::4
===============================================================================
```

When the ABR is configured with `originate-default-route`, R2 creates an IEP for the default route (Listing 7.19).

Listing 7.19 Inter-Area Prefix for the default route that is flooded into the NSSA

```
*A:R2# show router ospf3 database 0.0.0.0 type
inter-area-pfx adv-router 2.2.2.2 detail

===============================================================================
OSPF Link State Database (Type : IE Pfx) (Detailed)
===============================================================================
-------------------------------------------------------------------------------
IE Pfx LSA for Area 0.0.0.1
-------------------------------------------------------------------------------
Area Id          : 0.0.0.1             Adv Router Id     : 2.2.2.2
Link State Id    : 0.0.0.0 (0)
LSA Type         : IE Pfx
Sequence No      : 0x80000001          Checksum          : 0x71c4
Age              : 210                 Length            : 28
```

```
Options             :                    Metric          : 1
Dest Prefix         : ::/0
===============================================================================
```

OSPFv3 Authentication

OSPFv3 uses IPsec for authentication, which requires a different configuration than for OSPFv2. In order to enable OSPF3 authentication on the 7750 SR, you first manually configure an IPsec security association (SA). In the example in Listing 7.20 we specify the Authentication Header (AH) to enable authentication only. We must also configure a Security Parameter Index (SPI) that must be the same on both sides.

Listing 7.20 Authentication configuration for OSPFv3

```
*A:R1# configure ipsec
*A:R1>config>ipsec# static-sa ospf-peers create
*A:R1>config>ipsec>static-sa# authentication sha1
ascii-key NRS_IISelfStudyGuide
*A:R1>config>ipsec>static-sa# protocol ah
*A:R1>config>ipsec>static-sa# direction bidirectional
*A:R1>config>ipsec>static-sa# spi 256
*A:R1>config>ipsec>static-sa# info
----------------------------------------------
            protocol ah
            authentication sha1 hex-key
0xce89c543ad4257eaa020c4d1f0dbb647981354d5b4238154891450707eb98f741b8
c9cdb71ccede9 hash2
            spi 256
----------------------------------------------
*A:R1>config>ipsec>static-sa# exit all
*A:R1# configure router ospf3 area 0 interface "toR2"
*A:R1>config>router>ospf3>area>if# authentication bidirectional
"ospf-peers"
*A:R1>config>router>ospf3>area# show ipsec static-sa

===============================================================================
IPsec Static Security Associations
```

(continued)

Listing 7.20 *(continued)*

```
===============================================================================
Name                            Dir   Proto Auth SPI   Description
-------------------------------------------------------------------------------
ospf-peers                      bidir ah    sha1 256
-------------------------------------------------------------------------------
No. of IPsec Static Security Associations: 1
===============================================================================
*A:R1>config>router>ospf3>area# show router ospf3 neighbor

===============================================================================
OSPF Neighbors
===============================================================================
Interface-Name             Rtr Id           State      Pri  RetxQ   TTL
-------------------------------------------------------------------------------
toR2                       2.2.2.2          Full       1    0       39
-------------------------------------------------------------------------------
No. of Neighbors: 1
===============================================================================
```

The keys used for the SA can be changed by configuring a new SA with a new SPI. The old SA is removed and the routers will change to the new SA without dropping the OSPF3 adjacency.

Practice Lab: OSPFv3

The following lab is designed to reinforce your knowledge of the content in this chapter. Please review the instructions carefully, and perform the steps in the order in which they are presented. The practice labs require that you have access to six or more 7750 SRs or Alcatel-Lucent 7450 ESSs in a non-production environment.

These labs are designed to be used in a controlled lab environment. Please *do not* attempt to perform these labs in a production environment.

Lab Section 7.1: Configuring OSPFv3

OSPFv2 was designed to carry routing information for IPv4. To support IPv6, a new version was defined, OSPFv3.

Objective In this exercise, you will configure OSPFv3 between the backbone area routers as shown in Figure 7.4.

Figure 7.4 Topology for Lab 7.1.

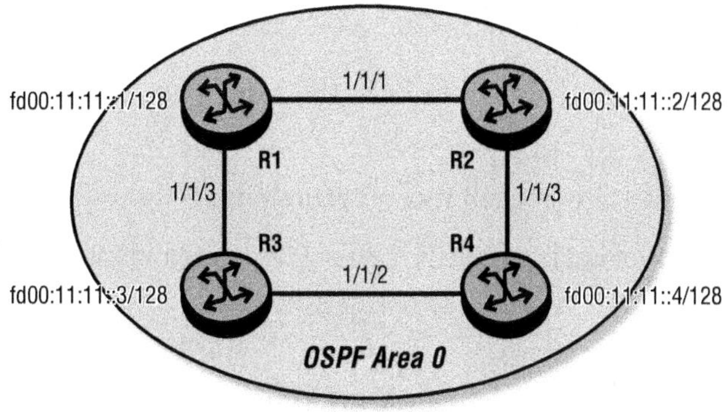

Validation You will know you have succeeded if the OSPF adjacencies between the routers are operationally up and the routing tables and LSDBs on each router are populated as expected.

1. Configure the system IP addresses of the four backbone area routers R1 through R4. Use the addressing scheme shown in Figure 7.4.
2. Configure all interfaces between the routers to be IPv6-capable. Use link-local addresses for the router interfaces.
3. Configure the router interfaces between R1 and R2 as OSPF point-to-point interfaces. Use an OSPF router ID of `10.10.10.x`, where `x` is the router number. For example, R2 will have a router ID of `10.10.10.2`.
   a. Is the OSPF adjacency up? Explain and correct any problems as required.
   b. Examine the route tables on R1 and R2. How many routes have been learned by OSPFv3?
   c. Make sure the system interface addresses are propagated between each router.
   d. Examine the LSDB on R5 and contrast the contents to what was observed in the OSPFv2 labs.
3. Configure the R3–R4 link in the backbone area as an OSPFv3 broadcast interface. Ensure that the system address of each router is included in OSPF and the router IDs are set appropriately.

a. Examine the route-tables on R3 and R4. How many routes are in each route-table?

b. Which router is the DR/BDR? Explain.

c. Examine the LSDB on R3 and R4. Contrast the contents to what was observed in the OSPFv2 labs.

4. Configure the R1–R3 and R2–R4 links in the backbone area as OSPFv3 point-to-point interfaces.

   a. How many routes are in each router's route-table?

   b. Are the LSDBs of each router in the backbone area identical? Describe the contents.

Lab Section 7.2: Configuring Multi-Area OSPFv3

OSPFv3 supports multi-area networks to support hierarchy and scalability for IPv6 implementations. Although the operation is similar to OSPFv2, there are some differences in the LSAs used for route advertisement.

Objective In this exercise, you will configure a multi-area OSPFv3 network as shown in Figure 7.5.

Figure 7.5 Topology for Lab 7.2.

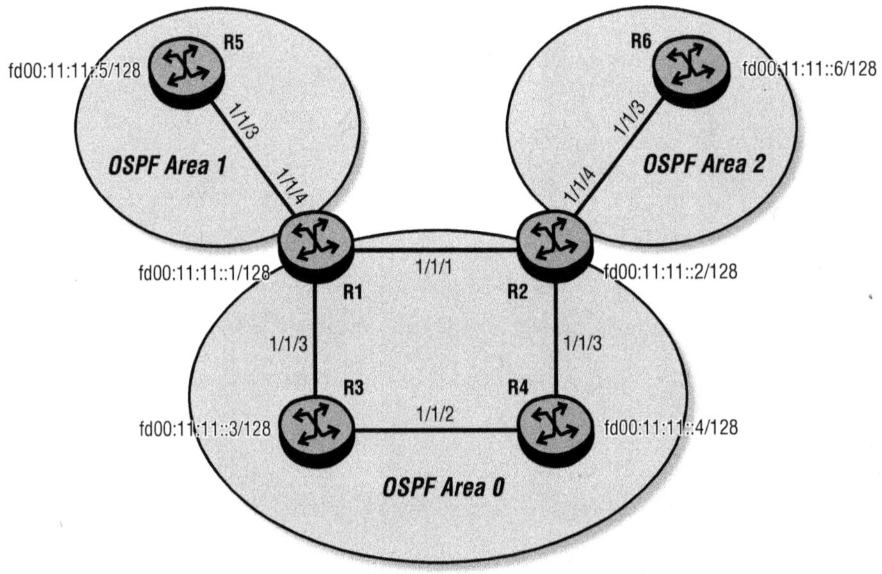

Validation You will know you have succeeded if all adjacencies betwee are up and the routing tables and LSDBs of each router are populated corr

1. Configure the R1–R5 link in Area 1 as an OSPFv3 point-to-point inteı sure to include R5's system interface address in Area 1.
   a. Verify that the adjacency is operationally up.
   b. Examine the route-table of R5. Does it contain routes from the backbone area?
   c. Examine the LSDB of R5. Is the LSDB of R5 identical to the LSDB of the backbone area routers? Explain.
   d. Examine the route-table of R3. Is R3 aware of the routes in Area 1? If so which LSAs in R3's LSDB are used to construct the routes?
2. Configure the link between R2 and R6 in Area 2 as a point-to-point OSPFv3 interface. Be sure to include R6's system interface address in Area 2.
   a. Verify that the adjacency is operationally up.
   b. Examine the route-table of R6. Does it contain routes from Area 1? If so which LSAs in R6's database were used to construct the routes?

Lab Section 7.3: Configuring OSPFv3 Route Summarization

Route summarization in OSPFv3 is done in a very similar manner to the way it is done in OSPFv2.

Objective In this exercise, you will configure route summarization for backbone area routes (Figure 7.6) and observe how the summary routes are propagated to other areas.

Validation You will know you have succeeded if the backbone summary routes are propagated as expected to other areas in the topology.

1. Configure a single loopback interface on R3 and advertise it into the OSPF backbone area. As shown in Figure 7.6, bind the following three IPv6 addresses to the loopback interface:

   `fd00:11:11:1000::1/128`

   `fd00:11:11:1000::2/128`

   `fd00:11:11:1000::3/128.`

   a. Using the `show router interface` command, how many IP addresses appear to be bound to the loopback interface? Explain.

b. Which of the prefixes bound to the loopback interface are advertised to the other backbone area routers, and what types of LSAs are used to propagate the routes?

c. Verify that the loopback prefixes are seen on the Area 1 and Area 2 routers. Which LSA types are used to propagate the routes to these non-backbone areas?

Figure 7.6 Topology for Lab 7.3.

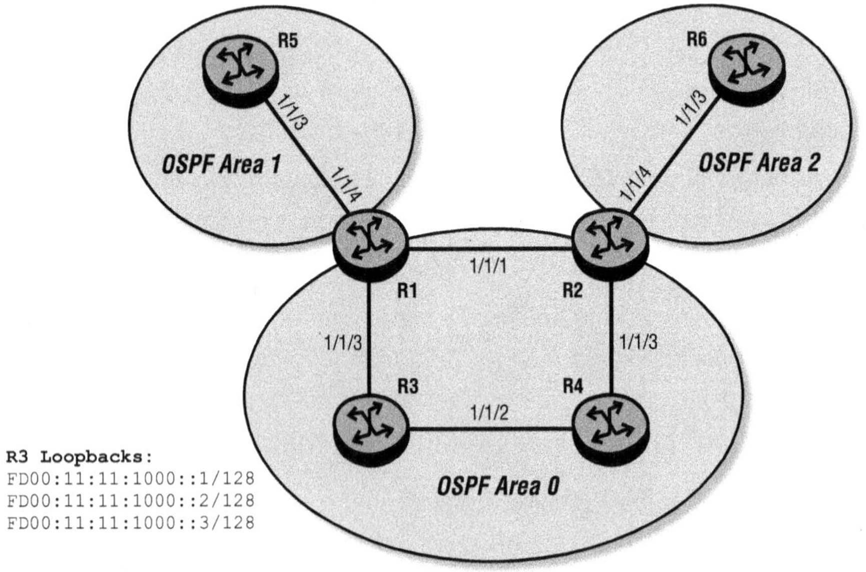

2. Configure summarization so that routers in Area 1 only see the summarized route `fd00:11:11:1000::/56`.

   a. Verify the route-table and LSDB on R5.

   b. Verify the route-table and LSDB on R1.

3. Configure summarization so that routers in Area 2 are not aware of R3's loopback interfaces.

   a. Verify the route-table and LSDB on R6.

Lab Section 7.4: OSPFv3 External Routes

OSPFv3 supports advertisement of external routes in a similar way to OSPFv2.

Objective In this exercise, you will configure R5 in Area 1 to distribute its loopback interfaces as external networks (Figure 7.7).

Figure 7.7 Topology for Lab 7.4.

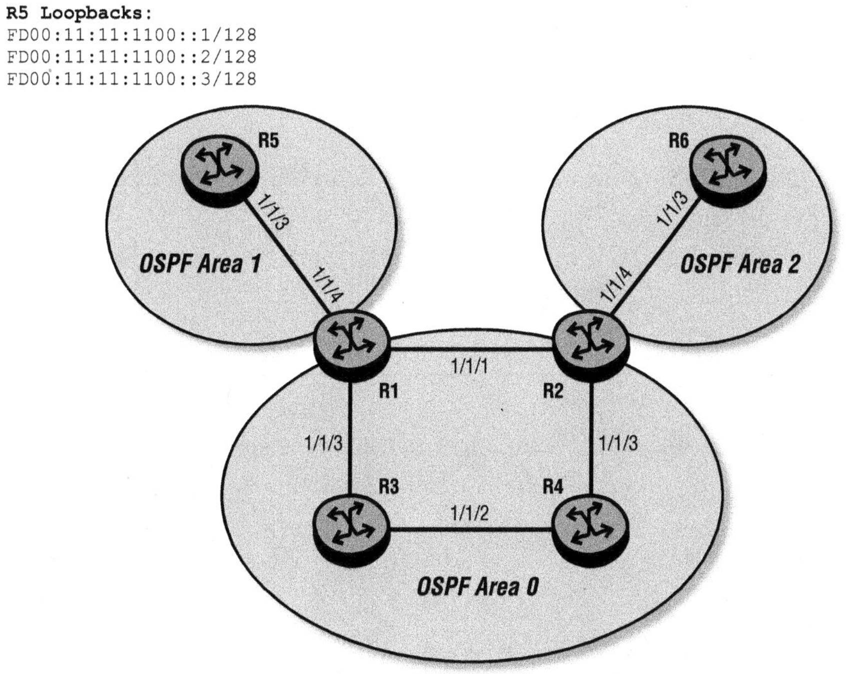

Validation You will know you have succeeded if the routing tables and LSDBs of the other areas are correctly populated.

1. Configure R5 as an ASBR.
   a. How has the LSDB of R5 changed? Explain.
   b. How has the LSDB of R1 changed? Explain.
   c. How has the LSDB of R2 changed? Explain.
2. Configure a single loopback interface on R5 as shown in Figure 7.7. Bind the following three addresses to the interface and use a policy to redistribute the loopback interface into OSPF:

   `fd00:11:11:1100::1/128`

   `fd00:11:11:1100::2/128`

   `fd00:11:11:1100::3/128`

a. Describe the LSAs that R5 originates to advertise the prefixes to Area 1.

b. Are the prefixes learned in the backbone area? If so describe the LSAs used to propagate the routes into the backbone area.

c. Are the prefixes learned in Area 2? If so describe the LSAs used to propagate the routes into Area 2.

Lab Section 7.5: Configuring OSPFv3 Stub Areas

Stub areas in OSPFv3 behave the same way as they do in OSPFv2; external routes are not flooded into the stub area.

Objective In this exercise, you will configure OSPF Area 1 as a stub area (Figure 7.8) and verify the expected behavior.

Figure 7.8 Topology for Lab 7.5.

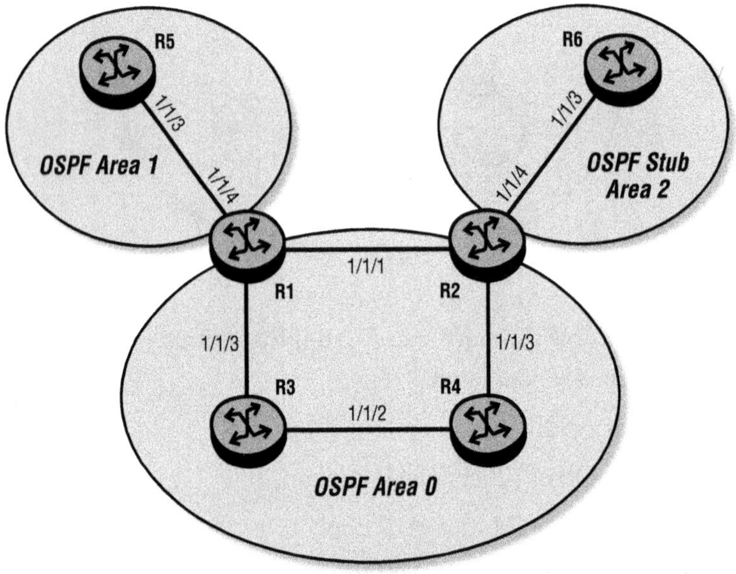

Validation You will know you have succeeded if the OSPF adjacency forms between R2 and R6 and the routing tables and LSDB of the routers are populated as expected.

1. Configure Area 2 as an OSPF stub area.

   a. How has the route-table and LSDB on R6 changed?

   b. How has the route-table and LSDB on R2 changed?

2. From R6 try to ping one of the loopbacks redistributed by R5.
   a. Is the ping successful? Explain.
   b. Try to ping the system IP address of R3. Is this ping successful? Explain.
3. Configure Area 2 so that it does not contain Inter-Area Prefix LSAs.
   a. Which router needs to be configured for this to take effect?
   b. How has the route-table and LSDB on R6 changed?
   c. Try to ping the system IP address of R3. Is this ping successful? Explain.

Chapter Review

Now that you have completed this chapter, you should have a good understanding of the following topics:

- What the main differences are between OSPFv2 and OSPFv3
- What the requirements are to configure the Alcatel-Lucent 7750 SR for OSPFv3
- How the Router and Network LSAs are different in OSPFv3
- The purpose and contents of the IAP LSA
- The purpose and contents of the Link LSA
- How the IEP LSA compares to the Type 3 Summary LSA and how to perform summarization
- How the AS External and IER LSAs compare to the Type 5 and Type 4 LSAs
- How stub and NSSA areas are handled in OSPFv3

Post-Assessment

The following questions will test your knowledge and prepare you for the Alcatel-Lucent NRS II Certification Exam. Compare your response with the answers listed in Appendix A. You can also use the CD that accompanies this book to take all the assessment tests and review the answers.

1. When only IPv6 is configured, how is the OSPFv3 router ID derived on an Alcatel-Lucent 7750 SR?
   - **A.** The router ID is derived from the system interface address if it is assigned; otherwise, it defaults to the last four octets of the chassis MAC address.
   - **B.** The router ID is derived from the system interface address if it is assigned; otherwise, it defaults to `0.0.0.0`.
   - **C.** The router ID is derived from an explicitly configured router ID if there is one assigned; otherwise, it defaults to the system interface address.
   - **D.** The router ID is derived from an explicitly configured router ID if there is one assigned; otherwise, it defaults to the last four octets of the chassis MAC address.
   - **E.** The router ID is derived from an explicitly configured router ID. OSPFv3 does not become active until the router ID is configured.

2. Two routers, R1 and R2, have an OSPFv3 adjacency between them. Both routers are configured with a system interface address, and their directly connected links are configured with a global IPv6 address. When R2 learns routes from R1, which next-hop will be used in R2's routing table? Assume that the OSPFv3 routes from R1 are the best routes received by R2.
   - **A.** The link-local interface address of R2 will be used for the next-hop.
   - **B.** The link-local interface address of R1 will be used for the next-hop.
   - **C.** The global interface address of R2 will be used for the next-hop.
   - **D.** The global interface address of R1 will be used for the next-hop.
   - **E.** The system interface address of R1 will be used for the next-hop.

3. An OSPFv3 router has a system interface, a loopback interface, and a router interface in Area 0. Global IPv6 addresses are assigned only to the system interface and the router interface. Which of the prefixes will appear in the IAP LSA originated by the router?

   A. The loopback and router link-local prefixes will appear in the IAP LSA along with the two global prefixes.

   B. The system interface and loopback prefixes will appear in the IAP LSA.

   C. The loopback prefixes and both router interface prefixes will appear in the IAP LSA.

   D. The system interface prefix and the global router interface prefix will appear in the IAP LSA.

   E. The loopback prefix and the link-local router interface prefix will appear in the IAP LSA.

4. What is the flooding scope of an OSPFv3 Inter-Area Prefix LSA?

   A. Link-local scope

   B. External scope

   C. Area scope

   D. Autonomous System scope

   E. None of the above

5. Which of the following statements about OSPFv3 is *not* correct?

   A. OSPFv3 supports the equivalent of OSPFv2 stub areas.

   B. OSPFv3 does not require global IPv6 addresses for router interfaces.

   C. OSPFv3 uses the same authentication mechanisms as OSPFv2.

   D. OSPFv3 Router LSAs do not carry IPv6 prefix information.

   E. An OSPFv3 router-id is 32 bits long.

6. Consider an OSPFv3 network topology with three normal areas; Area 0, Area 1, and Area 2. An ASBR in Area 1 is configured to redistribute external routes into OSPFv3. Which statement below correctly describes how external routes are advertised to Area 2?

   A. The ASBR in Area 1 originates AS External LSAs that are flooded throughout the AS to describe external routes. The Area 2 ABR originates an Inter-Area Router LSA to describe the ASBR.

   B. The ASBR in Area 1 originates AS External LSAs that are flooded throughout the AS to describe the external routes. The Area 1 ABR originates an Inter-Area Router LSA that is flooded throughout the AS to describe the ASBR.

   C. The ASBR in Area 1 originates AS External LSAs that are flooded throughout the AS to describe the external routes. The Area 2 ABR originates an Intra-Area Router LSA that is flooded throughout the AS to describe the ASBR.

   D. The ASBR in Area 1 originates Inter-Area Router LSAs that are flooded throughout the AS to describe the external routes. The ABR for Area 2 originates an Intra-Area Router LSA to describe the ASBR.

   E. The ASBR in Area 1 originates Inter-Area Router LSAs that are flooded throughout the AS to describe the external routes. The ABR for Area 1 originates an AS External LSA that is flooded throughout the AS to describe the ASBR.

7. Two routers, R1 and R2, have an OSPFv3 broadcast adjacency between them. R1 has a system interface address of `FD00:11:11::1`. R2 has a system interface address of `FD00:11:11::2`. Which of the following LSA types is *not* originated by R1?

   A. Router LSA

   B. Network LSA

   C. Intra-Area Prefix LSA

   D. There is not enough information to determine

8. Which of the following commands can be used on an Alcatel-Lucent 7750 SR to view Link LSAs?

   A. `show router ospf3 database`

   B. `show router ospf3 database detail`

   C. `show router ospf3 database type link-local detail`

   D. `show router ospf3 interface <interface> database detail`

   E. None of the above

9. Two routers, R1 and R2, are directly connected and actively exchanging routes over an OSPFv3 broadcast adjacency. How does R1 learn about R2's link-local interface address?

   A. From the Router LSA

   B. From the Network LSA

   C. From the IAP LSA

   D. From the Link LSAs

   E. R2 is not aware of R1's link-local interface address

10. What value is used for the link-state ID of an OSPFv3 Network LSA?

    A. The router ID of the DR on the broadcast network.

    B. The router ID of the first OSPFv3 router to initialize on the link.

    C. The interface ID of the DR's interface to the broadcast network.

    D. It is set to match the link-state ID of the Router LSA it refers to.

    E. It is derived from the DR's current sequence number and router ID.

11. Each of the following statements compares an OSPv3 LSA with a corresponding OSPFv2 LSA. Which statement is *incorrect*?

    A. An IAP LSA is comparable to a Type 1 LSA in OSPFv2.

    B. An IEP LSA is comparable to a Type 3 LSA in OSPFv2.

    C. An IER LSA is comparable to a Type 4 LSA in OSPFv2.

    D. An AS External LSA is comparable to a Type 5 LSA in OSPFv2.

    E. An NSSA LSA is comparable to a Type 7 LSA in OSPFv2.

12. Which command can be used on an Alcatel-Lucent 7750 to display the link-local addresses associated with its router interfaces?

- **A.** `show router ospf3 interface`
- **B.** `show router ospf interface detail`
- **C.** `show router route-table`
- **D.** `show router route-table ipv6`
- **E.** `show router interface`

13. Which OSPFv3 LSA has a similar function to the OSPFv2 Type 3 Summary LSA?

- **A.** Inter-Area Router LSA
- **B.** Inter-Area Prefix LSA
- **C.** Intra-Area Prefix LSA
- **D.** AS External LSA
- **E.** None of the above

14. Consider an OSPFv3 network topology with Area 0, Area 1, and Area 2. Area 1 contains an intra-area router that advertises a prefix in OSPFv3. There is a single Area 1 ABR that advertises a prefix in Area 0. There are two ABRs for Area 2. Assuming that manual summarization is not configured, how are the prefix in Area 0 and the prefix in Area 1 represented in the LSDB of Area 2 intra-area routers?

- **A.** There are two IEP LSAs. The Area 1 prefix is described by an IEP LSA originated by the Area 1 ABR. The Area 2 prefix is described by an IEP LSA originated by the Area 2 ABR with the least cost to each router.
- **B.** There are three IEP LSAs. The Area 1 prefix is described by an IEP LSA originated by the Area 1 ABR. Each Area 2 ABR originates an IEP LSA for the Area 0 prefix.
- **C.** There is one IEP LSA to describe both prefixes. The IEP LSA is originated by the Area 2 ABR with the least cost to each router.
- **D.** There are two IEP LSAs. Each Area 2 ABR originates an IEP LSA for each prefix; however, only the LSAs to the least-cost ABR are stored in each router's LSDB.
- **E.** There are four IEP LSAs. Each Area 2 ABR originates one IEP LSA for each prefix.

15. Consider an OSPF network topology with Area 0 and Area 1. Area 1 is configured as a totally stubby area. Which LSA type is used to propagate a default route into Area 1?

A. Intra-Area Router LSA

B. Inter-Area Router LSA

C. AS External LSA

D. Intra-Area Prefix LSA

E. Inter-Area Prefix LSA

8 Introduction to IS-IS

- Overview of IS-IS operation
- Comparison of IS-IS to OSPF
- IS-IS metrics and topologies
- The IS-IS database and IS-IS PDUs
- IS-IS addressing
- Establishing IS-IS adjacencies
- IS-IS Neighbor Discovery and Hello PDU
- Use of the CSNP and PSNP
- The IS-IS link-state PDU
- Flooding LSPs
- The Designated IS
- Configuring and verifying IS-IS
- Other IS-IS features

This chapter introduces the fundamental operation and components of a single-area IS-IS (Intermediate System to Intermediate System) network. The contents of the IS-IS database are described as well as the method used for flooding LSPs (link-state PDUs) to keep the database up to date. We look at the steps that occur in the formation of the IS-IS adjacency and the PDUs (protocol data units) that are exchanged in this process. We examine the fields of the LSPs used for exchanging link-state information and the process for choosing the DIS (Designated Intermediate System) on a broadcast link. We conclude with an example of configuring and verifying IS-IS in a network of Alcatel-Lucent 7750 SRs.

Pre-Assessment

The following assessment questions will help you understand what areas of the chapter you should review in more detail to prepare for the NRS II exam. You can also use the CD that accompanies this book to take all the assessment tests and review the answers.

1. Which of the following statements comparing IS-IS and OSPF on the Alcatel-Lucent 7750 SR is false?

A. OSPF and IS-IS are both link-state routing protocols.

B. OSPF uses a reference bandwidth and the bandwidth of an interface to calculate the metric for the link. IS-IS always uses the value of 10 as a metric.

C. Both protocols support hierarchy. In OSPF, an ABR joins different areas; in IS-IS, L2 routers join the different areas.

D. OSPF uses IP to send its messages, whereas IS-IS uses the Layer 2 protocol.

E. OSPF was developed specifically for routing IP, whereas IS-IS was originally developed as an OSI protocol.

F. All of the above statements are true.

2. Which of the following statements best describes the election of the DIS on a broadcast network where all routers have the same priority?

   A. The DIS is the router with the highest interface MAC address.

   B. The DIS is the router with the highest system IP address.

   C. If there is no DIS, the router with the highest interface MAC address is selected; otherwise, the existing DIS continues as DIS.

   D. If there is no DIS, the router with the highest system IP address is selected; otherwise, the existing DIS continues as DIS.

   E. The first router active on the broadcast network becomes the DIS.

3. Which of the following statements best describes how IS-IS routers ensure that their LSDBs are always up to date?

   A. Routers periodically exchange Hello PDUs to ensure that their LSDBs are up to date.

   B. Routers periodically exchange CSNPs that list the LSPs in their LSDBs.

   C. Routers acknowledge any new LSPs received. If an LSP is not acknowledged, the router retransmits the LSP.

   D. When the age of an LSP in the LSDB reaches zero, the originating router floods a new LSP to ensure that all of the LSDBs are kept up to date.

   E. No special mechanism is required because new LSPs are flooded anytime there is a topology change.

4. Which of the following statements about the flooding of IS-IS LSPs is false?

   A. An L1/L2 capable router floods both an L1 and an L2 LSP.

   B. A router only floods an LSP when there is a topology change or when it receives an updated LSP from a neighbor.

   C. The sequence number of the LSP is set by the originating router and used by other routers to tell if the LSP is an update to their LSDBs.

   D. On point-to-point links, LSPs are acknowledged with a PSNP.

   E. All of the above statements are true.

5. Which of the following statements about the IS-IS metric is false?
   - **A.** The interface metric can be set to different values for Level 1 and Level 2.
   - **B.** On the 7750 SR the default metric for an IS-IS interface is 10.
   - **C.** IS-IS can be configured on the 7750 SR with a reference bandwidth and wide metrics so that it calculates the link metric the same way that OSPF does.
   - **D.** If an IS-IS router does not use wide metrics, the maximum metric is 63.
   - **E.** All of the above statements are true.

8.1 Overview of IS-IS Operation

IS-IS is a link-state routing protocol that was developed around the same time as OSPF (late 1980s), primarily by Digital Equipment Corporation, as the network routing protocol for DECnet Phase V. It was standardized as the interior routing protocol for use in OSI (Open System Interconnect) networks as International Organization for Standardization (ISO) 10589. IS-IS was later modified to distribute Internet Protocol (IP) routing information, and today nearly all IP networks run either OSPF or IS-IS as their interior routing protocol.

Some of the key milestones in the development of IS-IS are the following:

- IS-IS was published as ISO standard 10589 in 1990 and republished in RFC 1142.
- RFC 1195, known as *Integrated IS-IS*, was released in 1990. It described the use of IS-IS to route TCP/IP (Transmission Control Protocol/Internet Protocol) and OSI simultaneously.
- RFC 1629 was released in 1994 to describe NSAP (Network Service Access Point) addressing.
- RFC 3359 was published in 2002 to formally define the code values used for IS-IS TLVs (type–length–values).
- Traffic engineering (TE) extensions were described in RFC 3784, published in 2004.
- TE extensions were formally standardized in 2008 in RFC 5305.
- RFC 5308 was published in 2008 to describe the routing of IPv6 with IS-IS.

To improve its efficiency and increase its scalability, IS-IS supports hierarchy, by allowing the definition of different areas similar to OSPF. This chapter considers IS-IS routing only within a single area. The exchange of routing information between areas is discussed in Chapter 9.

IS-IS is a hierarchical link-state protocol most often found as the IGP (interior gateway protocol) for large service provider networks. Like OSPF, IS-IS routers exchange link-state and cost information with their neighbors. Each router builds a complete topology map of the local routing area and calculates the shortest path to each destination in the network. The resulting IS-IS forwarding table is submitted to the Route Table Manager (RTM) to calculate the routing table. On the Alcatel-Lucent 7750 SR, the protocol preference value for IS-S is higher than for OSPF by default, thus the RTM prefers OSPF routes over IS-IS routes to the same prefix.

Comparison of IS-IS to OSPF

IS-IS and OSPF are both hierarchical, link-state routing protocols and share many similarities. Both protocols use a similar mechanism for flooding and aging link-state information, and both use the Dijkstra SPF algorithm to find the shortest path to all destinations in the network. The two most substantial differences between the protocols are the following:

- IS-IS was designed for OSI routing, whereas OSPF was specifically designed for routing IPv4 packets. As a result, IS-IS uses terminology and constructs that are unfamiliar in the IPv4 world. However, it is also more extensible than OSPF.
- IS-IS and OSPF both implement hierarchy for scalability but take a different approach.

The most immediately noticeable difference with IS-IS is the different terminology used. This is one of the more difficult obstacles to understanding for those otherwise familiar with IPv4. Table 8.1 summarizes some common terms used in IS-IS and compares them with their counterparts in OSPF.

Table 8.1 Comparison of OSPF and IS-IS Terminology

OSPF Term	IS-IS Term
Host	End system
Router	Intermediate system
Subnet	Circuit
Link-state advertisement (LSA)	Link-state PDU (LSP)
Database Description packet	Complete Sequence Number PDU (CSNP)
ACK	Partial Sequence Number PDU (PSNP)
Designated router	Designated IS
Interface address	Network Service Access Point (NSAP)

Hierarchy is implemented differently in IS-IS than in OSPF. Unlike OSPF, an IS-IS router is fully within an area, and area boundaries occur between routers. Routers that exchange routes within an area are Level 1 routers, and routers that exchange routes between areas are Level 2. Hierarchy is described in detail in Chapter 9. Preference values are different for Level 1 and Level 2 by default; Level 1 is 15, and Level 2 is 18. The value is set in the `configure router level 1` or `level 2` context. The default preference value for OSPF routes is 10 and is set in the `configure router ospf` or `ospf3` context.

IS-IS Operation

The steps below list the major aspects of IS-IS operation.

1. A router with IS-IS configured sends Hello PDUs out every IS-IS-enabled interface.
2. Based on configuration, Level 1 and/or Level 2 adjacencies are formed with neighbors. A router considers the adjacency up when it sees its identifier in a neighbor's Hello PDU.
3. On broadcast networks, the Designated IS (DIS) is chosen.
4. Routers exchange CSNPs that describe their link-state databases.
5. Based on the contents of the CSNP received, neighbors send LSPs (link-state PDUs) to update their neighbors' databases.
6. On point-to-point networks, a PSNP is sent to acknowledge LSPs.
7. Routers periodically exchange CSNPs to maintain database synchronization.
8. Routers periodically exchange Hello PDUs to maintain adjacencies.
9. When there is a topology change, the affected routers transmit an updated LSP that reflects the change. Every router updates its link-state database, floods the new LSP to its neighbors, and runs shortest path first (SPF) to recalculate its forwarding database.
10. LSPs age in the link-state database for 1,200 seconds. At approximately half the age, the LSP is reflooded to refresh the LSDB.

IS-IS Metrics and Topologies

In IS-IS, the default metric for an interface is 10, regardless of the bandwidth of the interface. To operate in a similar manner to OSPF, IS-IS can be configured on the 7750 SR to use a reference bandwidth to calculate the interface metric. The default value in OSPF is 100,000,000. When that value is configured as the reference bandwidth for IS-IS, the interface metric is calculated using the same formula:

$$\frac{\text{Interface metric} = \text{(reference bandwidth)}}{\text{(interface bandwidth)}}$$

With a value of 100,000,000, the metric for a 1 Gb/s link is 100. However, the original version of IS-IS had only a 6-bit field in the LSP for carrying the metric value, giving a maximum value of 63. This was changed in RFC 5305 when IS-IS was updated for TE enhancements. Wide metrics are enabled on the 7750 SR at Level 1 or Level 2. The command to use wide metrics at Level 2 is `configure router is-is level 2 wide-metrics-only`. Wide metrics are not enabled by default. However, wide metrics have been enabled for all of the examples in this book.

Similar to OSPF, IS-IS on the 7750 SR supports two types of network topology—broadcast and point-to-point, as described below:

- **Multi-access (broadcast)**—This topology is typically an Ethernet segment in which multiple routers are connected and actively exchanging IS-IS updates. On a broadcast network, a DIS is elected. The DIS originates an LSP describing the broadcast network as a *pseudonode*.
- **Point-to-point**—A point-to-point connection is defined as a connection in which there is only one neighbor and the routers are actively exchanging IS-IS updates.

8.2 The IS-IS Database and IS-IS PDUs

There are four different types of IS-IS PDUs used to establish IS-IS adjacencies and exchange the LSPs that make up the IS-IS databases used for the SPF calculation. IS-IS maintains two link-state databases, one for the Level 1 topology and one for the Level 2 topology. The differences between Level 1 and Level 2 are described in Chapter 9. In this chapter, we examine IS-IS in a single area. All routers will be configured as Level 1, and we will only be concerned with the Level 1 database.

Best practice is to configure all routers as Level 2–capable in a single-area IS-IS network. The Level 1 database is the same as the Level 2 database in a single-area network and therefore not necessary. If the network is eventually changed to a multi-area network, the migration is less disruptive if all existing routers are Level 2–capable to begin with.

Link-State Database

The link-state database (LSDB) contains the topology information for the IS-IS routing domain. Every router in an IS-IS area contains an identical LSDB and uses it to calculate the best path to every destination in the network. The LSDB is kept up to date by flooding LSPs throughout the routing domain. Listing 8.1 shows the output of the command `show router isis database` for the topology in Figure 8.1. This output is essentially an index of all LSPs in the database. Each router generates an LSP to describe its topology, and one additional LSP (LSP ID R1.03-00) is generated to describe the broadcast link. These are discussed in more detail below in the chapter. Point-to-point links would normally be configured using `/30` or `/31` addresses, but in this network are configured as `/27` to simplify the addressing plan.

Figure 8.1 Example topology with one broadcast link and three point-to-point links.

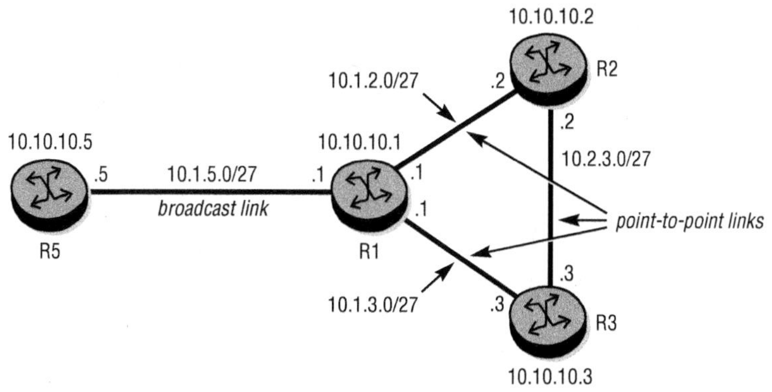

Listing 8.1 IS-IS database lists all of the LSPs for the topology.

```
*A:R1# show router isis database

===============================================================================
ISIS Database
===============================================================================
LSP ID                          Sequence Checksum Lifetime Attributes
-------------------------------------------------------------------------------

Displaying Level 1 database
-------------------------------------------------------------------------------
R2.00-00                        0x82     0x9253   1190     L1
R3.00-00                        0xae     0xebc3   717      L1
R1.00-00                        0xd1     0x1eb8   1168     L1
R1.03-00                        0x5a     0x415    952      L1
R5.00-00                        0x67     0xec60   852      L1
```

(continued)

Listing 8.1 *(continued)*

```
Level (1) LSP Count : 5

Displaying Level 2 database
-------------------------------------------------------------------------------
Level (2) LSP Count : 0
===============================================================================
```

The output of the command `show router isis database R1.00-00 detail` shows the contents of the LSP with link-state ID of R1.00-00, as shown in Listing 8.2. This contains the topology information generated by router R1. It has been configured as a Level 2 router with wide metrics specified. These options and the fields of the LSP are described in more detail below in the chapter.

Listing 8.2 A detailed look at an IS-IS LSP

```
*A:R1# show router isis database R1.00-00 detail

===============================================================================
ISIS Database
===============================================================================


Displaying Level 1 database
-------------------------------------------------------------------------------
LSP ID     : R1.00-00                                     Level     : L1
Sequence   : 0xd1                 Checksum   : 0x1eb8     Lifetime  : 967
Version    : 1                    Pkt Type   : 18         Pkt Ver   : 1
Attributes: L1                    Max Area   : 3
SysID Len  : 6                    Used Len   : 169        Alloc Len : 1492

TLVs :
  Area Addresses:
    Area Address : (1) 49
  Supp Protocols:
    Protocols      : IPv4
  IS-Hostname    : R1
  Router ID    :
    Router ID    : 10.10.10.1
  I/F Addresses :
    I/F Address    : 10.10.10.1
```

```
    I/F Address   : 10.1.3.1
    I/F Address   : 10.1.5.1
    I/F Address   : 10.1.2.1
  TE IS Nbrs   :
    Nbr   : R1.03
    Default Metric  : 10
    Sub TLV Len     : 6
    IF Addr   : 10.1.5.1
  TE IS Nbrs   :
    Nbr   : R2.00
    Default Metric  : 10
    Sub TLV Len     : 12
    IF Addr   : 10.1.2.1
    Nbr IP    : 0.0.0.0
  TE IS Nbrs   :
    Nbr   : R3.00
    Default Metric  : 10
    Sub TLV Len     : 12
    IF Addr   : 10.1.3.1
    Nbr IP    : 10.1.3.3
  TE IP Reach   :
    Default Metric  : 0
    Control Info:    , prefLen 32
    Prefix   : 10.10.10.1
    Default Metric  : 10
    Control Info:    , prefLen 27
    Prefix   : 10.1.3.0
    Default Metric  : 10
    Control Info:    , prefLen 27
    Prefix   : 10.1.5.0
    Default Metric  : 10
    Control Info:    , prefLen 27
    Prefix   : 10.1.2.0

Level (1) LSP Count : 1

Displaying Level 2 database
-----------------------------------------------------------------------
Level (2) LSP Count : 0
=======================================================================
```

IS-IS Addressing

One of the first differences you will notice with IS-IS is that routers are identified with an OSI NSAP (Network Service Access Point) address. Figure 8.2 shows the fields of an NSAP address. The fields of the NSAP are the following:

Figure 8.2 Structure of the NSAP address.

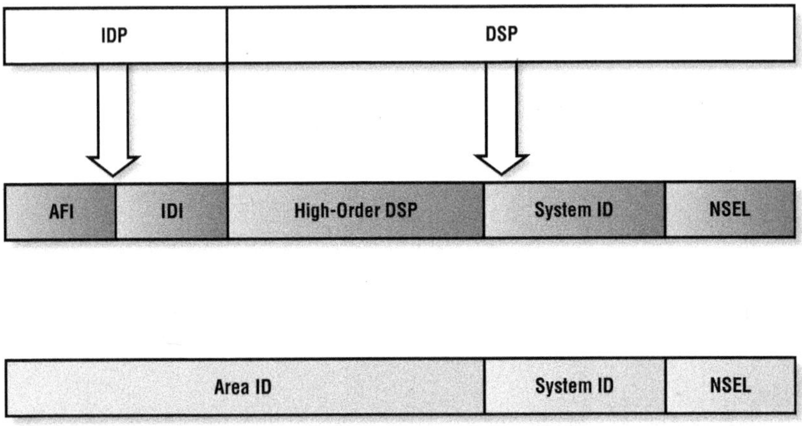

- **IDP**—The initial domain part (IDP) is composed of the AFI and IDI fields.
- **AFI**—The area format and identifier (AFI) is 1 byte long and indicates the type of authority through which the address was assigned. Common values for the AFI are:
  - 39—Single country authority such as ANSI (American National Standards Institute)
  - 47—International authority such as ISO
  - 49—Privately assigned address
- **IDI**—The initial domain identifier (IDI) is variable length and identifies the actual authority that assigned the address.
- **DSP**—The domain-specific part (DSP) is the portion of the address managed by the network operator. It is comprised of the HO-DSP, System ID, and NSEL.
- **HO-DSP**—The high-order domain-specific part (HO-DSP) allows the hierarchical delegation of addresses within the routing domain.

- **System ID**—The system ID is 6 bytes long and identifies the network device. It is generally expected to be a MAC (Media Access Control) address or router ID.
- **NSEL**—The NSAP selector (NSEL) allows multiplexing of network services to a single system ID. The NSEL must be zero for a router.

The 7750 SR uses a simplified form of the standard NSAP address in which the IDP and HO-DSP are assigned as the area ID, as shown in Figure 8.2. This value must be 1 to 13 bytes long. The 6-byte system ID is assigned from the router ID, and the NSEL is zero. To simplify output in `show router isis` commands, the system name is often used for the system ID. Listing 8.3 shows the mapping of system IDs to hostnames for the routers shown in Figure 8.1.

Listing 8.3 Mapping of system ID values to hostnames

```
*A:R1>config>router>isis# show router isis hostname

===============================================================================
Hosts
===============================================================================
System Id                  Hostname
-------------------------------------------------------------------------------
0100.1001.0001             R1
0100.1001.0002             R2
0100.1001.0003             R3
0100.1001.0005             R5
===============================================================================
```

Notice how the router ID of `10.10.10.1` is transformed into a 6-byte value of `0100.1001.0001`. The transformation is done by using each of the four parts of the router ID as three digits. (Think of it as `010.010.010.001` divided into three instead of four parts.)

IS-IS PDUs

IS-IS routers do not use IP to exchange messages but rather the underlying Layer 2 protocol. In the case of Ethernet, IEEE 802.3 is used instead of the Ethernet II format used for IP packets. IS-IS messages are carried in IS-IS PDUs. The IS-IS PDU format is shown in Figure 8.3.

Figure 8.3 Format of the IS-IS PDU.

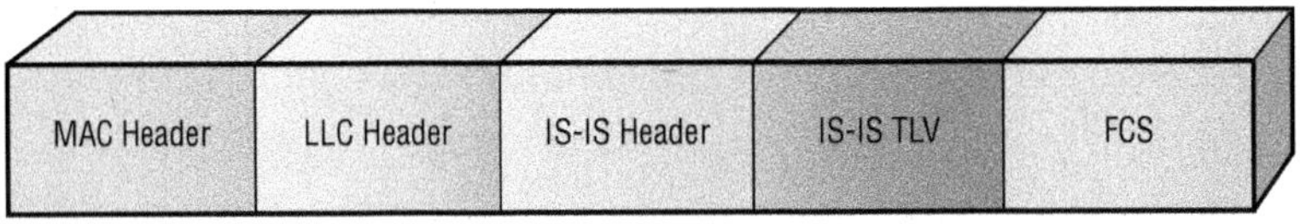

The data fields of IS-IS PDUs are described using the TLV construct. TLVs provide a flexible and extensible method of defining data fields in protocol messages. The structure of a TLV is shown in Figure 8.4. The purpose of the fields are as follows:

Figure 8.4 Format of the TLV construct.

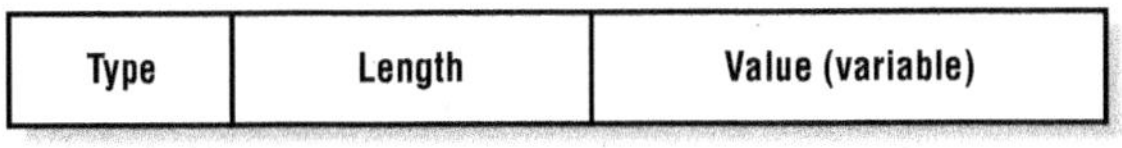

- **Type**—Identifies the specific data field that the TLV contains.
- **Length**—Specifies the length in bytes of the TLV and thus permits a variable length value field.
- **Value**—Contains the actual data to be carried in the TLV. The format of this field is determined by the protocol definition for the specific type.

All IS-IS PDUs share a common format as shown in Figure 8.5. The protocol discriminator is assigned by the ISO to identify IS-IS and contains the decimal value 131. The PDU type field identifies the IS-IS PDU type.

Figure 8.5 IS-IS PDU format.

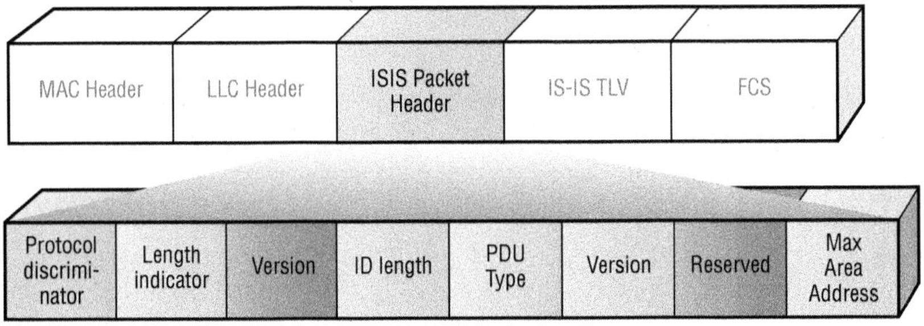

The four types of IS-IS PDUs are introduced below and described in detail in the following section of this chapter.

- **Hello**—Used to establish and maintain adjacencies.
- **Link-state PDU (LSP)**—Used to distribute link-state information.
- **Partial Sequence Number PDU (PSNP)**—Used to request and acknowledge link-state information.
- **Complete Sequence Number PDU (CSNP)**—Used to describe a router's complete link-state database.

8.3 Establishing IS-IS Adjacencies

Similar to OSPF, IS-IS routers first exchange Hello PDUs to form an adjacency before exchanging any topology information. Unlike OSPF, an IS-IS adjacency is considered to be formed as soon as they have successfully exchanged Hello PDUs.

IS-IS Neighbor Discovery and the Hello PDU

In IS-IS, neighbors are routers that are directly connected to a common network. Routers that are configured as Level 1 form adjacencies with neighboring Level 1 routers that have a common area ID. (An IS-IS router can be configured with up to three area IDs.) Routers configured for Level 2 form an adjacency with any neighboring Level 2 router. A router configured as Level 1 and Level 2 will form two adjacencies (Level 1 and Level 2) if they have a common area ID.

IS-IS uses three different types of Hello PDUs to form adjacencies between routers:

- **Level 1 LAN Hello**—Used to form Level 1 adjacencies on a broadcast network. These are sent to the all Level 1 routers multicast address `01-80-C2-00-00-14`.
- **Level 2 LAN Hello**—Used to form Level 2 adjacencies on a broadcast network. These are sent to the all Level 2 routers multicast address `01-80-C2-00-00-15`.
- **Point-to-point Hello**—Used to form Level 1 and Level 2 adjacencies on a point-to-point network. These are sent to the all IS-IS routers multicast address `09-00-2B-00-00-05`.

Figure 8.6 shows the generalized format of the IS-IS Hello messages. The use of the fields varies slightly between the different types of messages:

Figure 8.6 IS-IS Hello PDU.

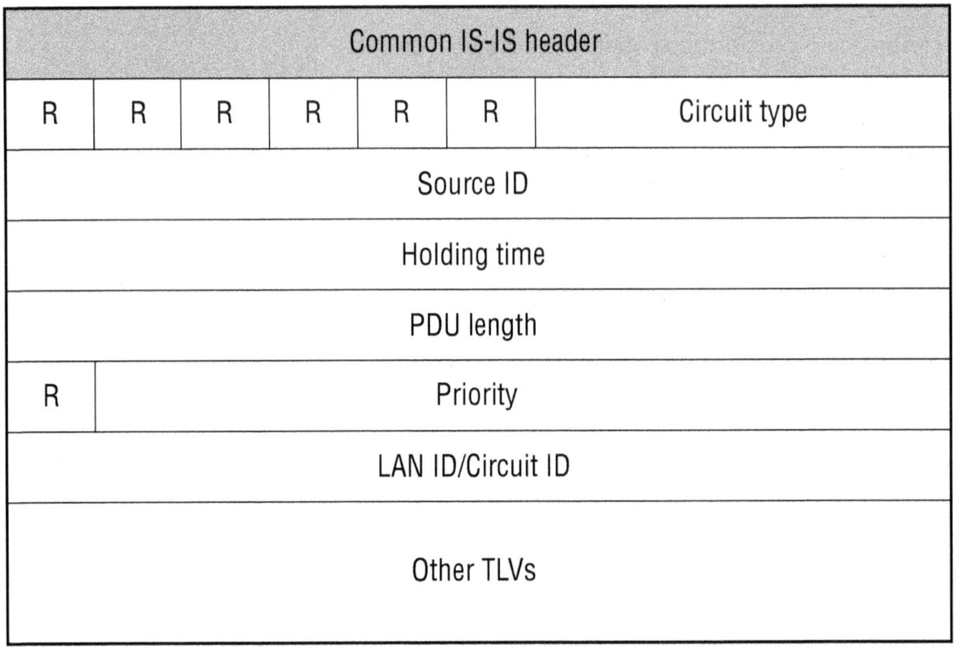

- **Circuit type**—Indicates whether the interface is Level 1, Level 2, or both.
- **Source ID**—Contains the system ID of the sending router.
- **Holding time**—Is the length of time the recipient should wait for a Hello PDU before considering the adjacency to be down. Unlike OSPF, holding time does not have to match on both ends of the link.
- **Priority**—Is the priority for DIS election on a broadcast network. The router with the highest priority on the LAN is chosen as DIS. This field does not appear in the point-to-point Hello.
- **LAN ID/circuit ID**—Is the LAN ID used in broadcast Hellos and is the system ID of the DIS plus a locally assigned, 1-byte identifier. The circuit ID is used in point-to-point Hellos and is a locally assigned 1-byte identifier.
- **Other TLVs**—This field contains additional information carried in the Hello PDU, including:
    - **Area addresses**—Up to three areas can be defined. These are carried in area address TLVs.

- **IS neighbors TLV**—Used in broadcast Hellos, this TLV lists the interface MAC addresses of systems seen on the LAN. A router considers the adjacency up when it sees its MAC address in a neighbor's Hello.
- **Supported protocols**—Defines the protocols supported by this router. On the 7750 SR this will be either IPv4, IPv6, or both.
- **I/F addresses**—These are Layer 3 addresses of the interface.
- **3Way adjacency**—Defined in RFC 3373, this TLV is used on point-to-point Hellos and contains information about the state of the adjacency.

Listing 8.4 shows the point-to-point Hello PDU transmitted between Routers R1 and R2 in the topology of Figure 8.1.

Listing 8.4 Debug output showing point-to-point Hello

```
*A:R1# configure log log-id 11
*A:R1>config>log>log-id$ from debug-trace
*A:R1>config>log>log-id$ to session
*A:R1>config>log>log-id$ exit
*A:R1# debug router isis packet ptop-hello detail
37 2011/02/15 15:24:53.15 UTC MINOR: DEBUG #2001 Base ISIS PKT
"ISIS PKT:
TX ISIS PDU ifId 2 len 67:
  DMAC           : 09:00:2b:00:00:05
  Proto Disc     : 131
  Header Len     : 20
  Version PID    : 1
  ID Length      : 0
  Version        : 1
  Reserved       : 0
  Max Area Addr  : 3
  PDU Type       : (11) Point-2-Point IS-IS Hello Pdu
  Circuit Type   : L1L2
  Source Id      : 01 00 10 01 00 01
  Hold Time      : 27
  Packet length  : 50
  Circuit Id     : 0
  Area Addresses:
    Area Address : (1) 49
```

(continued)

Listing 8.4 *(continued)*

```
  Supp Protocols:
    Protocols      : IPv4
  I/F Addresses :
    I/F Address    : 10.1.2.1
  3Way Adjacency    :
    State           : UP
    Ext ckt ID      : 2
    NbrSysID        : 01 00 10 01 00 02
    Nbr ext ckt ID : 2
```

Electing the Designated IS (DIS)

IS-IS routers on a broadcast network elect a DIS to simplify the SPF calculation and reduce the number of adjacencies required, like the election of a designated router (DR) in OSPF. Routers on the broadcast LAN form an adjacency with the DIS and not with each other. The DIS represents the broadcast network as a pseudonode and generates an LSP to represent the pseudonode in the network topology (see Figure 8.7).

Figure 8.7 DIS generates an LSP for the broadcast network pseudonode.

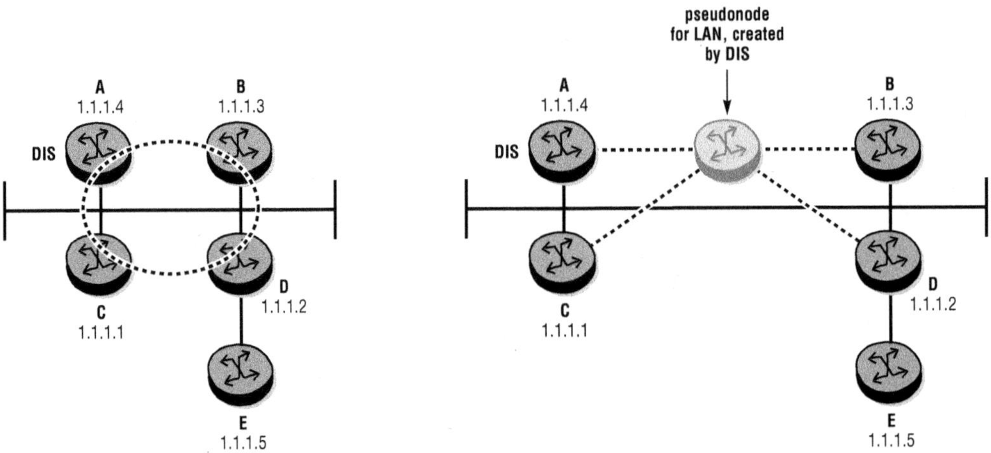

The router elected as the DIS is the router with the highest-priority interface on the broadcast LAN. The highest interface MAC address on the LAN is used as a tie-breaker. Unlike OSPF, DIS election is preemptive, thus a new router with a higher priority immediately becomes the DIS and generates a new LSP for the LAN. There is no backup DIS; if the DIS disappears, there is a new DIS election. Listing 8.5 shows the Hello PDU sent by router R1 in Figure 8.8. R1 and R5 both have the default priority of 64, and because R1 has the higher MAC address, it is the DIS. We know that R1 is the DIS because its system ID is used for the LAN ID.

Figure 8.8 Broadcast network between R1 and R5.

Listing 8.5 Hello PDU with R1 as DIS

```
171 2011/02/15 22:38:26.63 UTC MINOR: DEBUG #2001 Base ISIS PKT
"ISIS PKT:
TX ISIS PDU ifId 3 len 65:
  DMAC           : 01:80:c2:00:00:15
  Proto Disc     : 131
  Header Len     : 27
  Version PID    : 1
  ID Length      : 0
  Version        : 1
  Reserved       : 0
  Max Area Addr  : 3
  PDU Type       : (10) Level 2 LAN IS-IS Hello Pdu
  Circuit Type   : L1L2
  Source Id      : 01 00 10 01 00 01
  Hold Time      : 9
  Packet length  : 48
  Priority       : 64
  LAN Id         : 01 00 10 01 00 01 04
  Area Addresses:
    Area Address : (1) 49
  Neighbors MACs:
    Neighbor       : 0003faacb826
  Supp Protocols:
    Protocols      : IPv4
  I/F Addresses :
    I/F Address    : 10.1.5.1
```

If we change the priority on R5 to 100, R5 immediately becomes the DIS for the LAN (see Listing 8.6). It has taken only a few seconds for the change to occur. We can see that the priority is now 100, and the LAN ID shows that R5 is now the DIS. By default, the DIS transmits a Hello every 3 seconds and advertises a 9-second hold time. The other routers on the LAN transmit every 9 seconds and advertise a 27-second hold time.

Listing 8.6 Hello PDU with R5 as DIS

```
175 2011/02/15 22:38:31.73 UTC MINOR: DEBUG #2001 Base ISIS PKT
"ISIS PKT:
RX ISIS PDU ifId 3 len 44:
  DMAC           : 01:80:c2:00:00:15
  Proto Disc     : 131
  Header Len     : 27
  Version PID    : 1
  ID Length      : 0
  Version        : 1
  Reserved       : 0
  Max Area Addr  : 3
  PDU Type       : (10) Level 2 LAN IS-IS Hello Pdu
  Circuit Type   : L1L2
  Source Id      : 01 00 10 01 00 05
  Hold Time      : 9
  Packet length  : 44
  Priority       : 100
  LAN Id         : 01 00 10 01 00 05 01
  Neighbors MACs:
    Neighbor       : 00164d135cae
  Supp Protocols:
    Protocols      : IPv4
  I/F Addresses  :
    I/F Address    : 10.1.5.5
```

After two IS-IS routers have established an adjacency, there is an exchange of CSNPs, PSNPs, and LSPs to bring their databases up to date.

The CSNP and PSNP and Their Use

The CSNP and PSNP are similar to the OSPF database description message in that they list several LSPs in the router's database. The format of the CSNP is shown in Figure 8.9.

Figure 8.9 Format of the CSNP.

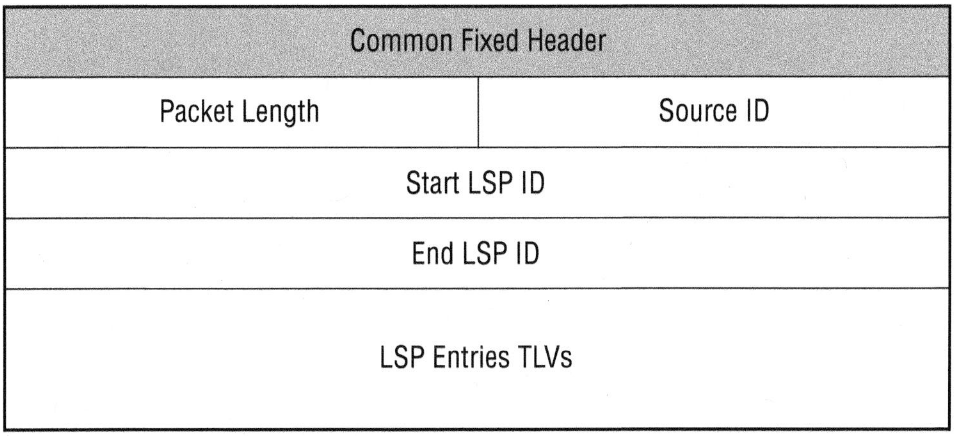

The *Start LSP ID* and *End LSP ID* fields indicate the range of LSP IDs carried in the PDU. The *TLV* field contains a list of LSP Entries TLVs that describe the LSPs. Its format is shown in Figure 8.10. The *LSP Entries TLV* contains the remaining lifetime, sequence number, and the checksum for an individual LSP.

Figure 8.10 Format of the LSP Entries TLV.

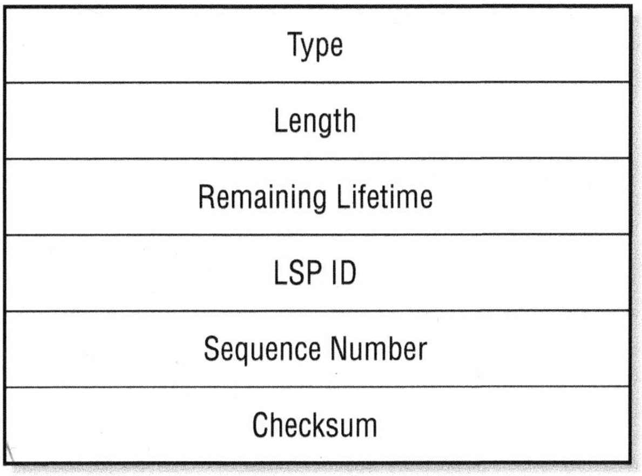

When IS-IS is enabled on router R5 with the broadcast interface shown in Figure 8.1, routers R1 and R5 first form an adjacency through the exchange of Hello PDUs. In this example, router R1 is the DIS. It sends a CSNP with the list of LSPs in its database, as shown in Listing 8.7.

Listing 8.7 CSNP sent by R1 to describe its link-state database

```
11 2011/02/20 10:12:11.49 UTC MINOR: DEBUG #2001 Base ISIS PKT
"ISIS PKT:
TX ISIS PDU ifId 4 len 100:
  Proto Disc     : 131
  Header Len     : 33
  Version PID    : 1
  ID Length      : 0
  Version        : 1
  Reserved       : 0
  Max Area Addr : 3
  PDU Type       : (19) Level 2 CSNP PDU
  Packet length : 83
  Source Id      : 01 00 10 01 00 01 00
  Start LSP Id   : 00 00 00 00 00 00 00 00
  End LSP Id     : FF FF FF FF FF FF FF FF
  LSP Entries    :
    Remaining Life: 1200
    LSP ID         : 01 00 10 01 00 01 00 00
    Sequence Num   : 000005c6
    Checksum       : 4ed7
    Remaining Life: 720
    LSP ID         : 01 00 10 01 00 02 00 00
    Sequence Num   : 000005a7
    Checksum       : 7a35
    Remaining Life: 897
    LSP ID         : 01 00 10 01 00 03 00 00
    Sequence Num   : 00000058
    Checksum       : e89c
```

Router R5 uses a PSNP to request the LSPs that it is missing or that are out of date in its database. Figure 8.11 shows the format of the PSNP. It is the same as the CSNP without the Start LSP ID and End LSP ID fields.

Figure 8.11 Format of the PSNP.

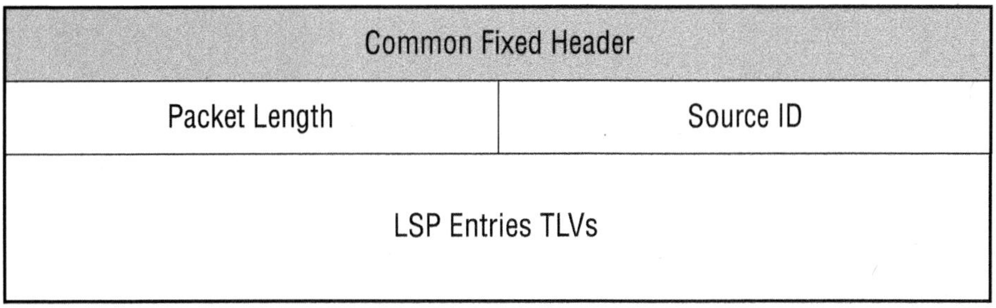

When a new router appears on a broadcast network, the DIS sends a CSNP with a complete list of the LSPs in the network. The new router can use a PSNP to request the LSPs it needs to bring its database up to date. The DIS for a broadcast network periodically sends a CSNP on the LAN (every 10 seconds by default). If a router on the broadcast LAN has an LSP that is out of date or is missing an LSP, it can request an update with a PSNP. If a router on the LAN sees that the DIS has an out-of-date LSP or is missing one, it transmits an update.

The CSNP and PSNP are used on a point-to-point network as well but in a slightly different way. When the interface between R1 and R3 in Figure 8.1 is enabled for IS-IS, the routers first establish an adjacency with Hello PDUs, and then each transmits CSNPs to describe their respective link-state databases. Because this represents a topology change, they also flood an updated LSP to describe the new topology. On point-to-point links, LSPs are acknowledged with a PSNP. Listing 8.8 shows the PSNP sent by R3 to acknowledge the updated LSP sent by R1.

Listing 8.8 PSNP sent by R3 to acknowledge LSP sent by R1

```
28 2011/02/20 15:37:31.96 UTC MINOR: DEBUG #2001 Base ISIS PKT
"ISIS PKT:
TX ISIS PDU ifId 2 len 52:
  DMAC          : 09:00:2b:00:00:05
  Proto Disc    : 131
  Header Len    : 17
  Version PID   : 1
  ID Length     : 0
  Version       : 1
  Reserved      : 0
```

(continued)

Listing 8.8 *(continued)*

```
  Max Area Addr : 3
  PDU Type      : (1b) Level 2 PSNP Pdu
  Packet length : 35
  Source Id     : 01 00 10 01 00 03 00
  LSP Entries   :
    Remaining Life: 1198
    LSP ID        : 01 00 10 01 00 01 00 00
    Sequence Num  : 000005e9
    Checksum      : 4577
```

Based on the CSNPs sent by their neighbors, a router can either send a PSNP to request an up-to-date LSP or send an LSP to update its neighbor as required. Each end of the point-to-point link continues to send CSNPs to ensure synchronization of the databases (sent every 10 seconds by default). Listing 8.9 shows the CSNP sent by R3 to maintain synchronization.

Listing 8.9 CSNP sent periodically to maintain link-state database synchronization

```
31 2011/02/20 15:37:37.96 UTC MINOR: DEBUG #2001 Base ISIS PKT
"ISIS PKT:
TX ISIS PDU ifId 2 len 132:
  Proto Disc    : 131
  Header Len    : 33
  Version PID   : 1
  ID Length     : 0
  Version       : 1
  Reserved      : 0
  Max Area Addr : 3
  PDU Type      : (19) Level 2 CSNP PDU
  Packet length : 115
  Source Id     : 01 00 10 01 00 03 00
  Start LSP Id  : 00 00 00 00 00 00 00 00
  End LSP Id    : FF FF FF FF FF FF FF FF
  LSP Entries   :
    Remaining Life: 1192
    LSP ID        : 01 00 10 01 00 01 00 00
    Sequence Num  : 000005e9
```

```
    Checksum        : 4577
    Remaining Life: 949
    LSP ID          : 01 00 10 01 00 01 03 00
    Sequence Num    : 00000022
    Checksum        : 5cfb
    Remaining Life: 623
    LSP ID          : 01 00 10 01 00 02 00 00
    Sequence Num    : 000005c8
    Checksum        : 3856
    Remaining Life: 1193
    LSP ID          : 01 00 10 01 00 03 00 00
    Sequence Num    : 0000007b
    Checksum        : fed6
    Remaining Life: 674
    LSP ID          : 01 00 10 01 00 05 00 00
    Sequence Num    : 00000023
    Checksum        : 839e
```

The following points summarize the default IS-IS behavior between two 7750 SR routers on an interface:

- Routers exchange Hello PDUs to form an adjacency and to elect the DIS on a broadcast network. The DIS election is preemptive and is the router with the highest priority, or the highest interface MAC address as a tiebreaker.
- Routers use CSNPs to announce the contents of their link-state databases.
- Routers use PSNPs to request up-to-date LSPs. Routers send LSPs to neighbors with out-of-date LSPs.
- Received LSPs are acknowledged with PSNPs on point-to-point networks.
- On a broadcast network, the DIS transmits a CSNP every 10 seconds. Routers on the LAN request up-to-date LSPs using PSNPs or update the DIS with an LSP as required. The DIS transmits a Hello PDU every 3 seconds to maintain the adjacencies. Other routers transmit Hellos every 9 seconds.
- On a point-to-point network, each router transmits a CSNP every 10 seconds. Up-to-date LSPs are requested or transmitted as required. Each router transmits a Hello PDU every 9 seconds.

The IS-IS Link-State PDU (LSP)

The link-state PDU (LSP) is the IS-IS PDU that actually contains the topology and reachability information. Because all of the data fields in IS-IS PDUs are defined using TLVs, there is considerable flexibility and variance in the data seen in LSPs. Some of the different variations include the following:

- LSPs in the original RFC 1195 format with the IP Internal Reachability and IP External Reachability TLVs
- LSPs in the RFC 5305 format for wide metrics using the Extended IP Reachability TLV
- LSPs carrying traffic engineering (TE) TLVs as described in RFC 5305
- LSPs carrying IPv6 Reachability TLVs as described in RFC 5308

In addition to the different TLVs, there are also Level 1 and Level 2 LSPs. The examples in this section use wide metrics and Level 2 LSPs. The format of the LSP is shown in Figure 8.12.

Figure 8.12 IS-IS link-state PDU.

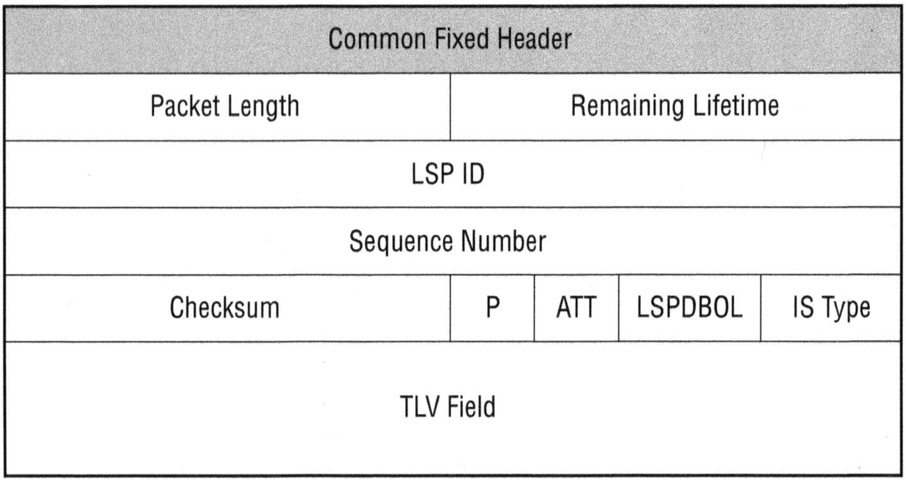

The default maximum size for an LSP is 1,492 bytes. If the LSP is larger than this, it can be split and carried in multiple LSPs, identified by the LSP ID. The fields of the LSP in Figure 18.12 are the following:

- **LSP ID**—Created by the system that originates the link-state information and comprised of three parts. The first part is 6 bytes and contains the system ID of the originating system. The second field is the pseudonode identifier. If the LSP represents a pseudonode, it contains the 1-byte circuit ID for the broadcast network; otherwise, it is zero. The last byte is non-zero if the LSP is the continuation of another LSP.

- **Sequence number**—This is a 4-byte field used to identify the different versions of the LSP. The initial value is 1 and is incremented by the originator every time the LSP must be updated.
- **Checksum**—This is a checksum used to validate the integrity of the LSP contents.
- **P**—This is the Partition Repair bit and is not normally used.
- **ATT**—This is the Attached bit (although the field is actually 4 bits). It is used by Level 2 routers to inform Level 1 routers that it is capable of routing to other areas.
- **LSPDBOL**—This is the Database Overload bit, used to indicate an overload condition. Its use is described below.
- **LS type**—This field indicates whether the LSP is a Level 1 or Level 2 LSP.
- **TLV fields**—These are the TLVs that carry interface and reachability information. The most significant TLVs are described in more detail below.

When `wide-metrics-only` is specified as an option in the IS-IS configuration, the LSP contains only the TLVs defined in RFC 5305. The format of the LSP generated by R1 in the topology of Figure 8.1 is shown in Listing 8.10. Note that the LSP ID is given as `R1.00-00`. The hostname (R1) is used to represent the 6 bytes of the system ID in a more human-friendly format. The first `00` means that the LSP was not generated for a pseudonode. The second `00` means that the LSP is not a continuation of another LSP. After the standard LSP header fields are the TLVs. The first four are self-explanatory, and the others are described below.

- **I/F addresses**—This lists the Layer 3 addresses assigned to the router interfaces. It is required for TE calculations.
- **TE IS Nbrs**—Also known as the Extended IS Reachability TLV (Type 22), this TLV provides the information about neighbors required to define the topology used for the SPF calculation. The default metric is the metric assigned to the interface and is a 24-bit field. The neighbor's address is included when it is on a point-to-point link. On a broadcast link, the pseudonode is shown as the neighbor.
- **TE IP Reachability**—Also known as the Extended IP Reachability TLV (Type 135), this contains the actual IP reachability information. The network address is included as well as the prefix length. The default metric is the cost to the network and is a 32-bit field.

Listing 8.10 LSP generated by R1 when wide-metrics-only is specified

```
*A:R1>config>router>isis# show router isis database R1.00-00 detail

===============================================================================
ISIS Database
===============================================================================

Displaying Level 1 database
-------------------------------------------------------------------------------
Level (1) LSP Count : 0

Displaying Level 2 database
-------------------------------------------------------------------------------
LSP ID    : R1.00-00                                  Level     : L2
Sequence  : 0x5fa                 Checksum  : 0xd4d6  Lifetime  : 1195
Version   : 1                     Pkt Type  : 20      Pkt Ver   : 1
Attributes: L1L2                  Max Area  : 3
SysID Len : 6                     Used Len  : 169     Alloc Len : 1492

TLVs :
  Area Addresses:
    Area Address : (1) 49
  Supp Protocols:
    Protocols     : IPv4
  IS-Hostname   : R1
  Router ID   :
    Router ID   : 10.10.10.1
  I/F Addresses :
    I/F Address   : 10.10.10.1
    I/F Address   : 10.1.5.1
    I/F Address   : 10.1.2.1
    I/F Address   : 10.1.3.1
  TE IS Nbrs   :
    Nbr   : R1.03
    Default Metric  : 10
    Sub TLV Len     : 6
    IF Addr   : 10.1.5.1
  TE IS Nbrs   :
    Nbr   : R3.00
```

```
    Default Metric  : 10
    Sub TLV Len     : 12
    IF Addr   : 10.1.3.1
    Nbr IP    : 10.1.3.3
  TE IS Nbrs   :
    Nbr   : R2.00
    Default Metric  : 10
    Sub TLV Len     : 12
    IF Addr   : 10.1.2.1
    Nbr IP    : 10.1.2.2
  TE IP Reach   :
    Default Metric  : 0
    Control Info:    , prefLen 32
    Prefix   : 10.10.10.1
    Default Metric  : 10
    Control Info:    , prefLen 27
    Prefix   : 10.1.5.0
    Default Metric  : 10
    Control Info:    , prefLen 27
    Prefix   : 10.1.2.0
    Default Metric  : 10
    Control Info:    , prefLen 27
    Prefix   : 10.1.3.0

Level (2) LSP Count : 1
=======================================================================
```

When `wide-metrics-only` is not specified in the IS-IS configuration, the LSP also contains the older fields specified in RFC 1195. A portion of the LSP from router R1 in Figure 8.1 is shown in Listing 8.11. The additional fields carried in this case include the following:

- **IS neighbors**—This provides the topology information about the neighbors for the SPF calculation. IS-IS was defined to carry four different types of metric information, but only the default metric is used. Each metric is only a 6-bit field. The TE IS Nbrs TLV (see Listing 8.10) is a newer version with only the default metric, but carried in a 24-bit field.

- **Internal Reachability**—This carries the IP reachability information, including the four different metric types. The metrics are 6-bit fields, and the IP mask contains the full 32-bit subnet mask. This TLV corresponds to the newer TE IP Reachability TLV (see Listing 8.10), which has only the default metric carried in a 32-bit field.
- **External Reachability**—This TLV is not shown in Listing 8.11. It is similar to the Internal Reachability TLV but carries information about externally reachable routes and was also replaced by the TE IP Reachability TLV (see Listing 8.10) in RFC 5305.

The other TLVs from RFC 5305 are also carried in the LSP, including the I/F Addresses, TE IS Nbrs, and TE IP Reachability.

Listing 8.11 Older TLVs carried in an IS-IS LSP

```
*A:R1>config>router>isis# show router isis database R1.00-00 detail

===============================================================================
ISIS Database
===============================================================================

Displaying Level 1 database
-------------------------------------------------------------------------------
Level (1) LSP Count : 0

Displaying Level 2 database
-------------------------------------------------------------------------------
LSP ID     : R1.00-00                                    Level      : L2
Sequence   : 0x601                 Checksum   : 0x2fa7   Lifetime   : 1074
Version    : 1                     Pkt Type   : 20       Pkt Ver    : 1
Attributes: L1L2                   Max Area   : 3
SysID Len : 6                      Used Len   : 261      Alloc Len : 1492

TLVs :
  Area Addresses:
    Area Address : (1) 49
  Supp Protocols:
    Protocols      : IPv4
  IS-Hostname    : R1
  Router ID    :
    Router ID    : 10.10.10.1
```

```
IS Neighbors  :
  Virtual Flag  : 0
  Default Metric: (I) 10
  Delay Metric  : (I) 0
  Expense Metric: (I) 0
  Error Metric  : (I) 0
  Neighbor      : R1.03
IS Neighbors  :
  Virtual Flag  : 0
  Default Metric: (I) 10
  Delay Metric  : (I) 0
  Expense Metric: (I) 0
  Error Metric  : (I) 0
  Neighbor      : R3.00
IS Neighbors  :
  Virtual Flag  : 0
  Default Metric: (I) 10
  Delay Metric  : (I) 0
  Expense Metric: (I) 0
  Error Metric  : (I) 0
  Neighbor      : R2.00
Internal Reach:
  Default Metric: (I) 10
  Delay Metric  : (I) 0
  Expense Metric: (I) 0
  Error Metric  : (I) 0
  IP Address    : 10.1.2.0
  IP Mask       : 255.255.255.224
  Default Metric: (I) 10
  Delay Metric  : (I) 0
  Expense Metric: (I) 0
  Error Metric  : (I) 0
  IP Address    : 10.1.3.0
  IP Mask       : 255.255.255.224
  Default Metric: (I) 10
  Delay Metric  : (I) 0
  Expense Metric: (I) 0
  Error Metric  : (I) 0
  IP Address    : 10.1.5.0
```

(continued)

Listing 8.11 *(continued)*

```
    IP Mask        : 255.255.255.224
    Default Metric: (I) 0
    Delay Metric  : (I) 0
    Expense Metric: (I) 0
    Error Metric  : (I) 0
    IP Address     : 10.10.10.1
    IP Mask        : 255.255.255.255
  I/F Addresses :
    I/F Address    : 10.10.10.1
    I/F Address    : 10.1.5.1
    I/F Address    : 10.1.3.1
    I/F Address    : 10.1.2.1
... output omitted ...
```

8.4 Flooding LSPs

As in OSPF, the reliable flooding of topology information is critical to the correct operation of IS-IS. Topology information must be flooded across a single area (Level 1) and, in the case of a multi-area network, across the entire network (Level 2). The distinctions between Level 1 and Level 2 are described in Chapter 9. The basic flooding mechanism is the same and is described here.

Listing 8.12 shows the IS-IS link-state database from the topology in Figure 8.1. The key fields relevant to flooding are the following:

- **LSP ID**—Uniquely identifies the LSP in the routing domain
- **Sequence**—Sequence number that is incremented by the originating router when it floods an updated LSP
- **Lifetime**—Remaining life of the LSP. Initially set to `lsp-lifetime`, which is 1,200 seconds by default

The sequence number is managed by the advertising router. The initial sequence number of 1 is incremented every time the LSP is updated. If a router receives an LSP with a higher sequence number than the one in its database, the database is updated and the LSP flooded to its neighbors. If the sequence number is lower, the router sends an LSP to update its neighbors. If the sequence number is the same, the LSP is ignored.

Listing 8.12 IS-IS link-state database

```
*A:R1# show router isis database

===============================================================================
ISIS Database
===============================================================================
LSP ID                          Sequence Checksum Lifetime Attributes
-------------------------------------------------------------------------------

Displaying Level 1 database
-------------------------------------------------------------------------------
Level (1) LSP Count : 0

Displaying Level 2 database
-------------------------------------------------------------------------------
R1.00-00                        0xc4b    0xddbd   1185     L1L2
R1.04-00                        0x4      0x91e3   1185     L1L2
R2.00-00                        0xbfa    0xf8a0   1086     L1L2
R3.00-00                        0xa      0x928c   1079     L1L2
R5.00-00                        0x75     0xd594   1151     L1L2
Level (2) LSP Count : 5
===============================================================================
```

The lifetime is initially set to 1,200 seconds and is decremented in the database. When the LSP's lifetime reaches approximately half, the originating router increments the sequence number and floods the LSP to refresh it in the database. If the LSP lifetime reaches zero in the database, it is kept as a zero-age LSP for a period and then removed from the database. The 7750 SR keeps zero-age LSPs for `lsp-lifetime`.

In Listing 8.13, priority was increased for R5 so that it became the DIS. Because the pseudonode LSP is no longer valid, R1 floods a zero-age LSP that shows a negative age (1167).

LSP lifetime is a configurable parameter on the 7750 SR with a default value of 1200. This gives IS-IS a slight advantage over OSPF in a large, stable network because the value can be increased to a much higher value to reduce the periodic flooding of LSPs.

Listing 8.13 LSDB with a zero-age LSP

```
*A:R1# show router isis database

===============================================================================
ISIS Database
===============================================================================
LSP ID                                  Sequence  Checksum Lifetime Attributes
-------------------------------------------------------------------------------

Displaying Level 1 database
-------------------------------------------------------------------------------
Level (1) LSP Count : 0

Displaying Level 2 database
-------------------------------------------------------------------------------
R1.00-00                                0xc4d     0x860d   1173     L1L2
R1.04-00                                0x4       0x0      (1167)   L1L2
R2.00-00                                0xbfa     0xf8a0   912      L1L2
R3.00-00                                0xa       0x928c   905      L1L2
R5.00-00                                0x76      0xcc96   1166     L1L2
R5.03-00                                0x1       0x4a2b   1166     L1L2
Level (2) LSP Count : 6
===============================================================================
```

8.5 The Designated IS (DIS)

On a broadcast network such as Ethernet, a DIS is elected. The DIS creates an LSP for the pseudonode. The pseudonode is an imaginary router on the broadcast LAN that is a neighbor of all other routers on the LAN. IS-IS treats the broadcast LAN as a series of point-to-point links between each router on the LAN and the pseudonode. The cost to the pseudonode is the cost of the interface on the LAN, and the cost from the pseudonode to the other routers is zero. Figure 8.13 shows a broadcast LAN with four IS-IS routers attached. The link-state database for the network is shown in Listing 8.14.

Figure 8.13 Broadcast LAN with four IS-IS routers.

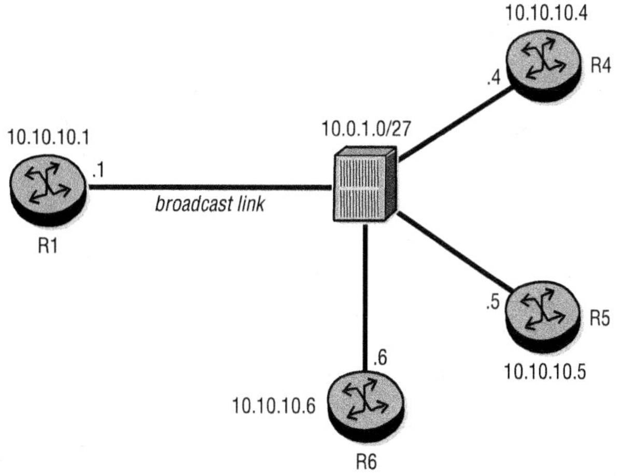

Listing 8.14 LSDB for broadcast network

```
*A:R1# show router isis database

===============================================================================
ISIS Database
===============================================================================
LSP ID                              Sequence Checksum Lifetime Attributes
-------------------------------------------------------------------------------

Displaying Level 1 database
-------------------------------------------------------------------------------
Level (1) LSP Count : 0

Displaying Level 2 database
-------------------------------------------------------------------------------
R1.00-00                            0x66f    0xbf38   712      L1L2
R4.00-00                            0x632    0x55ca   833      L1L2
R4.03-00                            0x9      0x7b82   757      L1L2
R5.00-00                            0x9c     0x466e   1149     L1L2
R6.00-00                            0xb      0x1d22   748      L1L2
Level (2) LSP Count : 5
===============================================================================
```

The database in Listing 8.14 shows the four LSPs generated by each of the routers, plus the additional LSP generated for the pseudonode (`R4.03-00`). All routers have the same priority, thus R4 is chosen as the DIS because it has the highest interface MAC address. Listing 8.15 shows the contents of the LSP advertised by R1. Notice that it lists one neighbor, the pseudonode, and the cost to that neighbor is the metric of the interface.

Listing 8.15 LSP generated by R1 showing pseudonode as its neighbor

```
*A:R1# show router isis database R1.00-00 detail

===============================================================================
ISIS Database
===============================================================================

Displaying Level 1 database
-------------------------------------------------------------------------------
Level (1) LSP Count : 0

Displaying Level 2 database
-------------------------------------------------------------------------------
LSP ID     : R1.00-00                                  Level     : L2
Sequence   : 0x672                Checksum  : 0xb93b   Lifetime  : 1186
Version    : 1                    Pkt Type  : 20       Pkt Ver   : 1
Attributes: L1L2                  Max Area  : 3
SysID Len : 6                     Used Len  : 93       Alloc Len : 1492

TLVs :
  Area Addresses:
    Area Address : (1) 49
  Supp Protocols:
    Protocols      : IPv4
  IS-Hostname    : R1
  Router ID    :
    Router ID    : 10.10.10.1
  I/F Addresses :
    I/F Address    : 10.10.10.1
    I/F Address    : 10.0.1.1
  TE IS Nbrs    :
```

```
    Nbr   : R4.03
    Default Metric  : 10
    Sub TLV Len     : 6
    IF Addr   : 10.0.1.1
  TE IP Reach   :
    Default Metric  : 0
    Control Info:    , prefLen 32
    Prefix   : 10.10.10.1
    Default Metric  : 10
    Control Info:    , prefLen 27
    Prefix   : 10.0.1.0

Level (2) LSP Count : 1
===============================================================================
```

The pseudonode LSP shown in Listing 8.16 shows that the pseudonode lists all four routers as its neighbors with a metric of 0 to all of them. Routers R1 and R4 are directly connected with a metric of 10, although IS-IS represents the connection as R1 to the pseudonode with a metric of 10 and from the pseudonode to R4 with a metric of 0.

Listing 8.16 Pseudonode LSP showing four neighbors with a cost of 0 to all

```
*A:R1# show router isis database R4.03-00 detail

===============================================================================
ISIS Database
===============================================================================

Displaying Level 1 database
-------------------------------------------------------------------------------
Level (1) LSP Count : 0

Displaying Level 2 database
-------------------------------------------------------------------------------
LSP ID    : R4.03-00                                 Level     : L2
Sequence  : 0xc                  Checksum  : 0x7585  Lifetime  : 667
```

(continued)

Listing 8.16 *(continued)*

```
Version    : 1                        Pkt Type   : 20       Pkt Ver    : 1
Attributes: L1L2                      Max Area   : 3
SysID Len : 6                         Used Len   : 79       Alloc Len : 135

TLVs :
  TE IS Nbrs    :
    Nbr    : R4.00
    Default Metric  : 0
    Sub TLV Len     : 0
  TE IS Nbrs    :
    Nbr    : R1.00
    Default Metric  : 0
    Sub TLV Len     : 0
  TE IS Nbrs    :
    Nbr    : R5.00
    Default Metric  : 0
    Sub TLV Len     : 0
  TE IS Nbrs    :
    Nbr    : R6.00
    Default Metric  : 0
    Sub TLV Len     : 0

Level (2) LSP Count : 1
===============================================================================
```

On the 7750 SR, Ethernet interfaces are broadcast by default. To avoid the extra overhead in generating and processing the pseudonode LSP, it is recommended that Ethernet interfaces be specifically configured as point-to-point in IS-IS when they are physically configured as point-to-point links.

8.6 Configuring and Verifying IS-IS

The following characteristics relate to the default behavior of IS-IS on the 7750 SR:

- All IS-IS routers must have a unique router ID. By default, the system interface is used as the router ID.

- Once the IS-IS context is entered, IS-IS is administratively enabled on the router. When interfaces are added to IS-IS, the router is operational in the IS-IS routing domain.
- Routers and interfaces have Level 1 and Level 2 capability.
- The metric on all interfaces is 10. Wide metrics are not enabled.
- The default behavior for advertising routes is as follows:
    - Interfaces included in IS-IS are advertised in IS-IS.
    - Routes received through IS-IS are advertised by IS-IS.
    - No other routes are advertised.

Configuring IS-IS

Consider the topology shown in Figure 8.14. In the section below we demonstrate the configuration of IS-IS for this network on one router, R1.

Figure 8.14 Topology used for sample configuration.

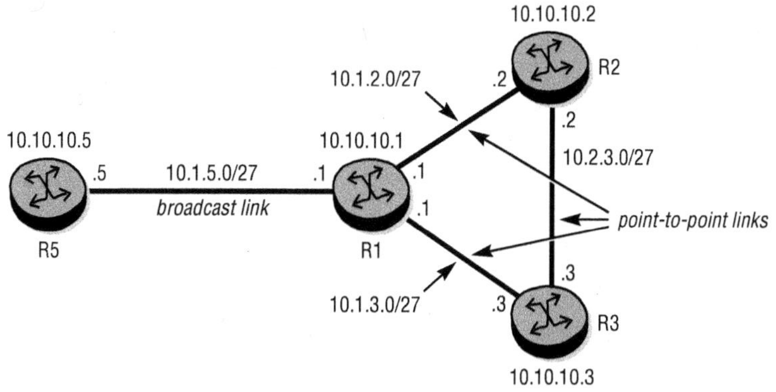

On R1, verify that the Layer 3 interfaces have been configured as shown in Listing 8.17.

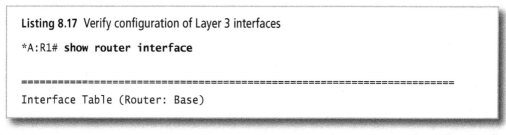

Listing 8.17 Verify configuration of Layer 3 interfaces

```
*A:R1# show router interface

===============================================================================
Interface Table (Router: Base)
```

(continued)

Listing 8.17 *(continued)*

```
===============================================================================
Interface-Name                   Adm         Opr(v4/v6)  Mode    Port/SapId
   IP-Address                                                    PfxState
-------------------------------------------------------------------------------
system                           Up          Up/--       Network system
   10.10.10.1/32                                                 n/a
toR2                             Up          Up/--       Network 1/1/1
   10.1.2.1/27                                                   n/a
toR3                             Up          Up/--       Network 1/1/2
   10.1.3.1/27                                                   n/a
toR5                             Up          Up/--       Network 1/1/3
   10.1.5.1/27                                                   n/a
-------------------------------------------------------------------------------
Interfaces : 4
===============================================================================
```

Verify connectivity and check the routing table. It's possible to ping the interface of a neighboring router, but not the system address (it's not directly connected). Because there is no dynamic routing protocol running, only directly connected networks are in the routing table (Listing 8.18).

Listing 8.18 Verify reachability of directly connected networks

```
*A:R1# ping 10.1.2.2 count 2
PING 10.1.2.2 56 data bytes
64 bytes from 10.1.2.2: icmp_seq=1 ttl=64 time=1.26ms.
64 bytes from 10.1.2.2: icmp_seq=2 ttl=64 time=1.09ms.

---- 10.1.2.2 PING Statistics ----
2 packets transmitted, 2 packets received, 0.00% packet loss
round-trip min = 1.09ms, avg = 1.17ms, max = 1.26ms, stddev = 0.084ms
*A:R1# ping 10.10.10.2 count 2
PING 10.10.10.2 56 data bytes
No route to destination. Address: 10.10.10.2, Router: Base
No route to destination. Address: 10.10.10.2, Router: Base

---- 10.10.10.2 PING Statistics ----
```

```
2 packets transmitted, 0 packets received, 100% packet loss
*A:R1# show router route-table

===============================================================================
Route Table (Router: Base)
===============================================================================
Dest Prefix                                     Type    Proto     Age         Pref
      Next Hop[Interface Name]                                         Metric
-------------------------------------------------------------------------------
10.1.2.0/27                                     Local   Local     00h20m10s   0
      toR2                                                             0
10.1.3.0/27                                     Local   Local     00h23m18s   0
      toR3                                                             0
10.1.5.0/27                                     Local   Local     00h16m36s   0
      toR5                                                             0
10.10.10.1/32                                   Local   Local     01d16h03m   0
      system                                                           0
-------------------------------------------------------------------------------
No. of Routes: 4
===============================================================================
```

Start IS-IS and define the global IS-IS parameters:

- Configure the area address.
- Configure the router as Level 2 only.
- Configure wide metrics.
- Configure a reference bandwidth.

Add the interfaces to IS-IS. R5 is a broadcast interface, and the other two are point-to-point (see Listing 8.19).

Listing 8.19 Configuring R1 for IS-IS

```
*A:R1# configure router isis
*A:R1>config>router>isis# area-id 49
*A:R1>config>router>isis# reference-bandwidth 100000000
*A:R1>config>router>isis# level-capability level-2
*A:R1>config>router>isis# level 2 wide-metrics-only
```

(continued)

Listing 8.19 *(continued)*

```
*A:R1>config>router>isis# interface "toR2" interface-type point-to-point
*A:R1>config>router>isis# interface "toR3" interface-type point-to-point
*A:R1>config>router>isis# interface "toR5"
*A:R1>config>router>isis>if# exit all
*A:R1# show router isis interface

===============================================================================
ISIS Interfaces
===============================================================================
Interface                          Level CircID  Oper State    L1/L2 Metric
-------------------------------------------------------------------------------
system                             L1L2  1       Up            0/0
toR3                               L1L2  2       Up            100/100
toR5                               L1L2  4       Up            100/100
toR2                               L1L2  5       Up            100/100
-------------------------------------------------------------------------------
Interfaces : 4
===============================================================================
```

Verifying IS-IS Operation

Because IS-IS has already been configured on the other routers in the network, R1 forms adjacencies with them and updates its LSDB (see Listing 8.20).

Listing 8.20 Verify the IS-IS neighbors and the IS-IS database

```
*A:R1# show router isis adjacency

===============================================================================
ISIS Adjacency
===============================================================================
System ID              Usage State Hold Interface                     MT Enab
-------------------------------------------------------------------------------
R3                     L2    Up    24   toR3                          No
R5                     L2    Up    19   toR5                          No
R2                     L2    Up    27   toR2                          No
-------------------------------------------------------------------------------
```

```
Adjacencies : 3
===============================================================================
*A:R1# show router isis database

===============================================================================
ISIS Database
===============================================================================
LSP ID                                  Sequence Checksum Lifetime Attributes
-------------------------------------------------------------------------------

Displaying Level 1 database
-------------------------------------------------------------------------------
Level (1) LSP Count : 0

Displaying Level 2 database
-------------------------------------------------------------------------------
R1.00-00                                0x67d    0xc95b   905      L1L2
R1.03-00                                0x1      0x9eda   904      L1L2
R2.00-00                                0x84     0x1356   882      L1L2
R5.00-00                                0xab     0x7227   904      L1L2
R3.00-00                                0x1c     0x2699   897      L1L2
Level (2) LSP Count : 5
===============================================================================
```

If we check the database on R2, it should be identical—all routers in the area must have the same LSDB. The ages may differ by a few seconds, but sequence numbers and checksums must be the same. Listing 8.21 shows that the database on R2 is the same as the one on R1 (Listing 8.19).

Listing 8.21 The LSDB on R2 is identical to the LSDB on the other routers in the network.

```
*A:R2# show router isis database

===============================================================================
ISIS Database
===============================================================================
LSP ID                                  Sequence Checksum Lifetime Attributes
```

(continued)

Listing 8.21 *(continued)*

```
------------------------------------------------------------------------


Displaying Level 1 database
------------------------------------------------------------------------
Level (1) LSP Count : 0

Displaying Level 2 database
------------------------------------------------------------------------
R1.00-00                              0x67d    0xc95b   892      L1L2
R1.03-00                              0x1      0x9eda   891      L1L2
R2.00-00                              0x84     0x1356   872      L1L2
R5.00-00                              0xab     0x7227   892      L1L2
R3.00-00                              0x1c     0x2699   886      L1L2
Level (2) LSP Count : 5
========================================================================
```

Analyzing an LSP

As expected, there are five LSPs (one for each router and one for the pseudonode for the broadcast network between R1 and R5). R1's LSP contains all the relevant information for its topology (see Listing 8.22):

- Area address
- Layer 3 interface addresses
- Neighbors
- IP reachability information

Listing 8.22 The LSP from R1 describes its topology

```
*A:R1# show router isis database R1.00-00 detail

========================================================================
ISIS Database
========================================================================


Displaying Level 1 database
------------------------------------------------------------------------
```

```
Level (1) LSP Count : 0

Displaying Level 2 database
-----------------------------------------------------------------------
LSP ID    : R1.00-00                                   Level     : L2
Sequence  : 0x67d                  Checksum  : 0xc95b  Lifetime  : 700
Version   : 1                      Pkt Type  : 20      Pkt Ver   : 1
Attributes: L1L2                   Max Area  : 3
SysID Len : 6                      Used Len  : 169     Alloc Len : 1492

TLVs :
  Area Addresses:
    Area Address : (1) 49
  Supp Protocols:
    Protocols     : IPv4
  IS-Hostname   : R1
  Router ID   :
    Router ID   : 10.10.10.1
  I/F Addresses :
    I/F Address   : 10.10.10.1
    I/F Address   : 10.1.2.1
    I/F Address   : 10.1.3.1
    I/F Address   : 10.1.5.1
  TE IS Nbrs   :
    Nbr   : R2.00
    Default Metric  : 100
    Sub TLV Len     : 12
    IF Addr   : 10.1.2.1
    Nbr IP    : 10.1.2.2
  TE IS Nbrs   :
    Nbr   : R3.00
    Default Metric  : 100
    Sub TLV Len     : 12
    IF Addr   : 10.1.3.1
    Nbr IP    : 10.1.3.3
  TE IS Nbrs   :
    Nbr   : R1.03
    Default Metric  : 100
    Sub TLV Len     : 6
    IF Addr   : 10.1.5.1
```

(continued)

Listing 8.22 *(continued)*

```
  TE IP Reach    :
    Default Metric  : 0
    Control Info:    , prefLen 32
    Prefix    : 10.10.10.1
    Default Metric  : 100
    Control Info:    , prefLen 27
    Prefix    : 10.1.2.0
    Default Metric  : 100
    Control Info:    , prefLen 27
    Prefix    : 10.1.3.0
    Default Metric  : 100
    Control Info:    , prefLen 27
    Prefix    : 10.1.5.0

Level (2) LSP Count : 1
===============================================================================
```

Now that the network is fully converged, all routes are in the route table, and it is possible to reach any address in the network (see Listing 8.23).

Listing 8.23 All IS-IS-enabled networks are seen in the route table.

```
*A:R1# show router route-table

===============================================================================
Route Table (Router: Base)
===============================================================================
Dest Prefix                             Type    Proto    Age          Pref
       Next Hop[Interface Name]                                Metric
-------------------------------------------------------------------------------
10.1.2.0/27                             Local   Local    00h41m34s    0
       toR2                                                    0
10.1.3.0/27                             Local   Local    00h44m42s    0
       toR3                                                    0
10.1.5.0/27                             Local   Local    00h38m01s    0
       toR5                                                    0
```

```
10.2.3.0/27                                Remote  ISIS     00h14m35s    18
       10.1.2.2                                                  200
10.10.10.1/32                              Local   Local    01d16h24m    0
       system                                                    0
10.10.10.2/32                              Remote  ISIS     00h14m35s    18
       10.1.2.2                                                  100
10.10.10.3/32                              Remote  ISIS     00h14m16s    18
       10.1.3.3                                                  100
10.10.10.5/32                              Remote  ISIS     00h14m15s    18
       10.1.5.5                                                  100
-----------------------------------------------------------------------
No. of Routes: 8
=======================================================================
*A:R1# ping 10.10.10.2 count 2
PING 10.10.10.2 56 data bytes
64 bytes from 10.10.10.2: icmp_seq=1 ttl=64 time=1.25ms.
64 bytes from 10.10.10.2: icmp_seq=2 ttl=64 time=1.09ms.

---- 10.10.10.2 PING Statistics ----
2 packets transmitted, 2 packets received, 0.00% packet loss
round-trip min = 1.09ms, avg = 1.17ms, max = 1.25ms, stddev = 0.085ms
```

8.7 Configuring Other IS-IS Features

Several additional features are described below. These include the ability to define a passive interface, overload-on-boot, authentication between IS-IS neighbors, and bidirectional forwarding detection (BFD).

Passive Interface

An interface can be configured as passive when it is desirable to have the network advertised in IS-IS, but the interface is not part of the IS-IS routing domain, as seen in the topology in Figure 8.15.

The configuration of the passive interface on R5 is shown in Listing 8.24.

Listing 8.24 Configuring a passive interface

```
*A:R5# show router interface

===============================================================================
Interface Table (Router: Base)
===============================================================================
Interface-Name                   Adm         Opr(v4/v6)  Mode    Port/SapId
   IP-Address                                                    PfxState
-------------------------------------------------------------------------------
system                           Up          Up/Down     Network system
   10.10.10.5/32                                                 n/a
toR1                             Up          Up/Down     Network 1/1/3
   10.1.5.5/27                                                   n/a
to_External                      Up          Up/Down     Network 1/1/1
   10.20.5.5/24                                                  n/a
-------------------------------------------------------------------------------
Interfaces : 3
===============================================================================
*A:R5# configure router isis
*A:R5>config>router>isis# interface "to_External" passive
```

Figure 8.15 Topology with an external network to be configured as a passive interface.

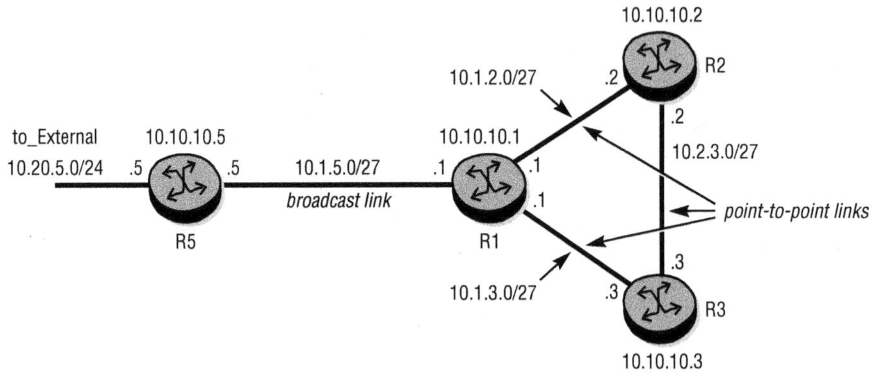

After the passive interface is configured, the interface is listed in the Interface Addresses TLVs but does not appear as an IS neighbor. IS-IS Hello PDUs will not be sent or responded to on this interface. However, the network is listed in the IP Reachability TLV (see Listing 8.25), and thus it will appear in the route tables of other IS-IS routers in the domain.

Listing 8.25 The IP reachability information for the passive interface is listed in the LSP.

```
*A:R1# show router isis database R5.00-00 detail

===============================================================================
ISIS Database
===============================================================================

Displaying Level 1 database
-------------------------------------------------------------------------------
Level (1) LSP Count : 0

Displaying Level 2 database
-------------------------------------------------------------------------------
LSP ID     : R5.00-00                                  Level     : L2
Sequence   : 0xae               Checksum   : 0xe13b   Lifetime  : 1121
Version    : 1                  Pkt Type   : 20       Pkt Ver   : 1
Attributes: L1L2                Max Area   : 3
SysID Len : 6                   Used Len   : 105      Alloc Len : 105

TLVs :
  Area Addresses:
    Area Address : (1) 49
  Supp Protocols:
    Protocols     : IPv4
  IS-Hostname    : R5
  Router ID    :
    Router ID    : 10.10.10.5
  I/F Addresses :
    I/F Address    : 10.10.10.5
    I/F Address    : 10.1.5.5
    I/F Address    : 10.20.5.5
  TE IS Nbrs    :
    Nbr    : R1.03
    Default Metric   : 100
    Sub TLV Len      : 6
```

(continued)

Listing 8.25 *(continued)*

```
    IF Addr    : 10.1.5.5
  TE IP Reach    :
    Default Metric  : 0
    Control Info:    , prefLen 32
    Prefix   : 10.10.10.5
    Default Metric  : 100
    Control Info:    , prefLen 27
    Prefix   : 10.1.5.0
    Default Metric  : 100
    Control Info:    , prefLen 24
    Prefix   : 10.20.5.0

Level (2) LSP Count : 1
=========================================================================
*A:R1#  show router route-table 10.20.5.0/24

=========================================================================
Route Table (Router: Base)
=========================================================================
Dest Prefix                             Type    Proto    Age          Pref
       Next Hop[Interface Name]                               Metric
-------------------------------------------------------------------------
10.20.5.0/24                            Remote  ISIS     00h06m25s    18
       10.1.5.5                                               200
-------------------------------------------------------------------------
No. of Routes: 1
=========================================================================
```

Overload-on-Boot

Overload-on-boot is configured to avoid having the router used as a route for forwarding data immediately after the router has booted. During the overload period, the router's LSP is advertised with the overload attribute set. A router with overload set will not be used as a route unless there is no other option. When IS-IS was developed, this feature was designed to accommodate the limited processing capabilities of the routers of the day. When the router rebooted, it might initially be very busy processing routing information. If other routers considered it to be a part of the topology, they could forward traffic that might be dropped if the router did not yet have a route to the destination.

Today overload-on-boot is useful when the router is a transit router in a BGP autonomous system and needs additional time to process the BGP routes it is receiving. When the router is rebooted, IS-IS will converge in a matter of seconds, whereas BGP might take much longer (especially if receiving the 300,000+ routes of today's Internet). Packets to external destinations will be dropped if they are forwarded to this router before it has the external BGP routes in its route table.

In some special circumstances a router may be configured in a permanent overload. In this case, it is part of the topology and able to exchange routes with the other routers but is not used for traffic forwarding. This is the case when routers are configured exclusively as route reflectors or for analytical purposes such as CPAM (Control Plane Assurance Manager). The topology in Figure 8.16 shows R2 configured in the permanent overload state, and the configuration is shown in Listing 8.26. The overload attribute is shown in the database.

Figure 8.16 Router R2 is configured in a permanent overload.

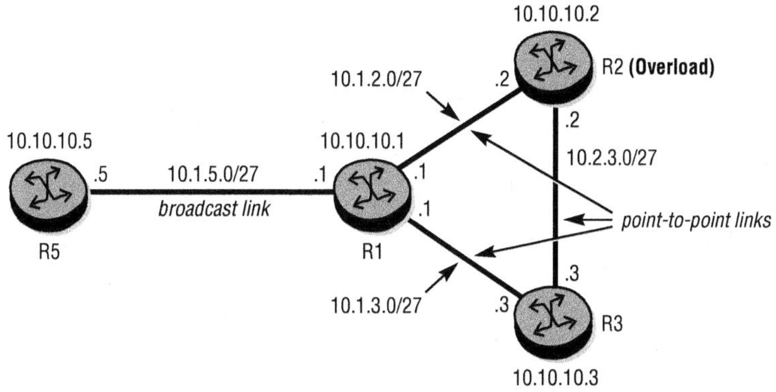

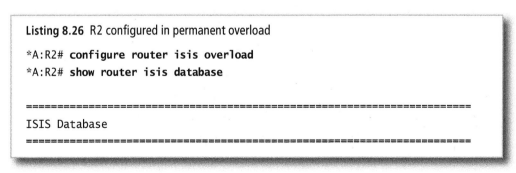

Listing 8.26 R2 configured in permanent overload

```
*A:R2# configure router isis overload
*A:R2# show router isis database

===============================================================================
ISIS Database
===============================================================================
```

(continued)

Listing 8.26 *(continued)*

```
LSP ID                                 Sequence Checksum Lifetime Attributes
-------------------------------------------------------------------------------


Displaying Level 1 database
-------------------------------------------------------------------------------
Level (1) LSP Count : 0

Displaying Level 2 database
-------------------------------------------------------------------------------
R1.00-00                               0x680    0xc35e   1063     L1L2
R1.03-00                               0x4      0x98dd   962      L1L2
R2.00-00                               0x88     0xf52    1171     L1L2 OV
R5.00-00                               0xaf     0xdf3c   1135     L1L2
R3.00-00                               0x1f     0x209c   1114     L1L2
Level (2) LSP Count : 5
===============================================================================
```

Authentication

IS-IS has several different options for authenticating PDUs. By default, authentication is not used on PDUs. When authentication is configured, the authentication TLV is included in the PDU, and the receiving router rejects the PDU if it does not match its authentication configuration. Characteristics of authentication on IS-IS are the following:

- Authentication options are no authentication, simple password, and MD5. Simple password is transmitted as plaintext. MD5 is the most secure and recommended option.
- Authentication can be configured globally at the `configure router isis` context or at a specific level. In this case, all PDUs are authenticated.
- Authentication can also be configured at the IS-IS interface. This overrides the global configuration.
- IS-IS can be configured to individually authenticate Hello, CSNP, or PSNP packets.

Listing 8.27 shows the configuration of MD5 authentication on router R2.

Listing 8.27 MD5 configuration

```
*A:R2# configure router isis
*A:R2>config>router>isis# authentication-key Alcatel-Lucent
*A:R2>config>router>isis# authentication-type message-digest
*A:R2>config>router>isis# info
----------------------------------------------
        level-capability level-2
        area-id 49
        reference-bandwidth 100000000
        authentication-key
"uFvoZORQPaWUGUPOQU2W9gNQe3Nuo2J0676/wUXeKxY" hash2
        authentication-type message-digest
        level 2
            wide-metrics-only
        exit
        interface "system"
            interface-type point-to-point
        exit
        interface "toR1"
            interface-type point-to-point
        exit
        interface "toR3"
            interface-type point-to-point
        exit
----------------------------------------------
```

Once authentication is configured, the authentication TLV is included in all PDUs. Listing 8.28 shows a Hello PDU received on R3 from R2. Because the adjacency is up, we know that authentication is also configured correctly on R3.

Listing 8.28 Hello PDU with authentication configured

```
45 2011/02/21 18:49:26.62 UTC MINOR: DEBUG #2001 Base ISIS PKT
"ISIS PKT:
RX ISIS PDU ifId 3 len 69:
  DMAC          : 09:00:2b:00:00:05
  Proto Disc    : 131
```

(continued)

Listing 8.28 *(continued)*

```
Header Len    : 20
Version PID   : 1
ID Length     : 0
Version       : 1
Reserved      : 0
Max Area Addr : 3
PDU Type      : (11) Point-2-Point IS-IS Hello Pdu
Circuit Type  : L1L2
Source Id     : 01 00 10 01 00 02
Hold Time     : 27
Packet length : 69
Circuit Id    : 0
Area Addresses:
  Area Address : (1) 49
Supp Protocols:
  Protocols     : IPv4
I/F Addresses :
  I/F Address   : 10.2.3.2
3Way Adjacency   :
  State          : UP
  Ext ckt ID     : 5
  NbrSysID       : 01 00 10 01 00 03
  Nbr ext ckt ID : 4
Authentication:
  Auth Type     : MD5(54) (16 bytes)
  Auth Info     : e1df57324d10524218b470133aecbaa0
```

Bidirectional Forwarding Detection (BFD)

Chapter 5 describes the use of BFD to quickly detect the loss of an OSPF neighbor on the link. BFD can be used the same way in IS-IS to detect the loss of an adjacency. This is generally preferred to reducing the Hello timer because BFD messages are handled by the IOM (Input/Output Module) and do not have an impact on the CPM (Control Processing Module) as Hello PDUs do. Figure 8.17 shows two routers connected by two switches. A failure between the two switches will not be detected until the hold time expires (27 seconds by default on a point-to-point link).

Figure 8.17 BFD establishes a lightweight session to quickly detect failures on the link.

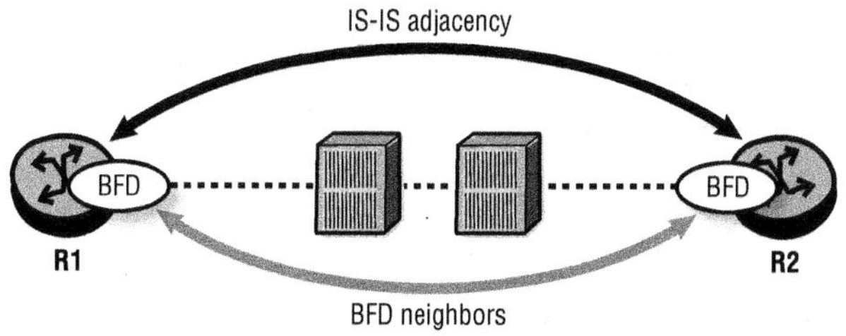

The configuration of IS-IS to use BFD is the same as that of OSPF, and an example similar to the one in Chapter 5 is shown here for IS-IS. The BFD session is configured on the interface and enabled in the routing protocol (see Listing 8.29). An interface with BFD enabled transmits UDP packets at the transmit interval and expects to receive them at the receive interval. The transmit interval for BFD can be set as low as 10 milliseconds with a multiplier of 3, meaning that failures can be detected within 30 milliseconds.

Listing 8.29 BFD is configured on the IP interface and enabled in the IS-IS interface.

```
*A:R1# show router isis adjacency

===============================================================================
ISIS Adjacency
===============================================================================
System ID                Usage State Hold Interface                     MT Enab
-------------------------------------------------------------------------------
R3                       L2    Up    19   toR3                          No
R5                       L2    Up    23   toR5                          No
R2                       L2    Up    23   toR2                          No
-------------------------------------------------------------------------------
Adjacencies : 3
===============================================================================
*A:R1# configure router interface "toR2"
*A:R1>config>router>if# bfd 100 receive 100 multiplier 3
*A:R1>config>router>if# exit
*A:R1# configure router isis interface "toR2" bfd-enable ipv4
```

(continued)

Listing 8.29 *(continued)*

```
*A:R1# show router bfd session

===============================================================================
BFD Session
===============================================================================
Interface                     State              Tx Intvl  Rx Intvl  Multipl
  Remote Address              Protocols          Tx Pkts   Rx Pkts   Type
-------------------------------------------------------------------------------
toR2                          Up (3)             100       100       3
   10.1.2.2                   isis               623       500       iom
-------------------------------------------------------------------------------
No. of BFD sessions: 1
===============================================================================
```

In our example, the interface remains up, but the interface on R2 is no longer responding. Instead of waiting for the IS-IS session to time out, the BFD session on R1 signals IS-IS that the adjacency should be brought down (Listing 8.30).

Listing 8.30 The interface is still up, but the IS-IS adjacency is down.

```
*A:R1# show router interface


===============================================================================
Interface Table (Router: Base)
===============================================================================
Interface-Name                 Adm         Opr(v4/v6)  Mode    Port/SapId
   IP-Address                                                  PfxState
-------------------------------------------------------------------------------
system                         Up          Up/--       Network system
   10.10.10.1/32                                               n/a
toR2                           Up          Up/--       Network 1/1/1
   10.1.2.1/27                                                 n/a
toR3                           Up          Up/--       Network 1/1/2
   10.1.3.1/27                                                 n/a
toR5                           Up          Up/--       Network 1/1/3
   10.1.5.1/27                                                 n/a
-------------------------------------------------------------------------------
```

```
Interfaces : 4
===============================================================================
*A:R1# show router isis adjacency

===============================================================================
ISIS Adjacency
===============================================================================
System ID                Usage State Hold Interface                     MT Enab
-------------------------------------------------------------------------------
R3                       L2    Up    23   toR3                          No
R5                       L2    Up    27   toR5                          No
-------------------------------------------------------------------------------
Adjacencies : 2
===============================================================================
```

Because the interface is still up, IS-IS includes the network in its topology, but there is no adjacency formed on the link.

Practice Lab: Introduction to IS-IS

The following lab is designed to reinforce your knowledge of the content in this chapter. Please review the instructions carefully, and perform the steps in the order in which they are presented. The practice labs require that you have access to six or more Alcatel-Lucent 7750 SRs or Alcatel-Lucent 7450 ESSs in a non-production environment.

These labs are designed to be used in a controlled lab environment. Please *do not* attempt to perform these labs in a production environment.

Lab Section 8.1: Configuring an IS-IS Point-to-Point Interface

Point-to-point IS-IS interfaces are configured when there are only two routers on a segment, also known as a point-to-point link.

Objective In this exercise you will configure two Alcatel-Lucent 7750 SRs with IS-IS point-to-point interfaces to form a Level 2 IS-IS adjacency in the network of Figure 8.18.

Figure 8.18 IS-IS single-area topology.

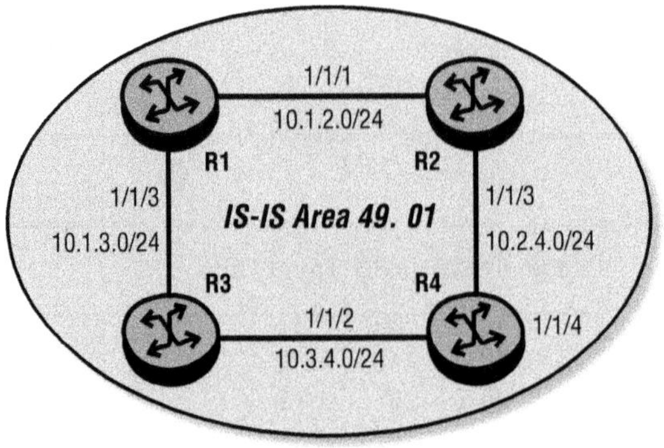

Validation You will know you have succeeded if the Level 2 IS-IS adjacency between the routers is up.

1. Configure system interfaces and network interfaces of all four routers in the topology as indicated in Figure 8.18. If you have just completed previous labs, this step may already be done.
2. Configure R1's interface to R2 into IS-IS area 49.01 as a Level 2 point-to-point interface. Do not configure a router interface on R2 toward R1 yet.
   a. Is the IS-IS adjacency up? Explain why or why not.
   b. Are there any LSPs in R1's database? If so, describe the contents.
   c. Are there any LSAs in R2's database? Explain.
3. Configure an IS-IS interface on R2 toward R1.
   a. What type of IS-IS interface needs to be configured on R2?
   b. Which router is the DIS?
   c. Are there any LSPs in R1's database? If so, how have they changed since before the adjacency was up?
   d. How many routes are in the route table of R1? How many IS-IS routes? Explain.
   e. What is the metric of each route in the route table? What metrics have been exchanged in the LSPs? Explain.
   f. Configure wide metrics and reference bandwidths on all routers so that IS-IS metrics are derived in a similar way to OSPF metrics.
   g. What metrics are now in the LSPs exchanged between R1 and R2? Explain.

4. From R1 try to ping the system interface of R2.
    a. Does the ping work? Explain, and make the ping work if required.

Lab Section 8.2: Configuring an IS-IS Broadcast Interface

When there are more than two routers on the same network segment, IS-IS broadcast interfaces must be used to form an adjacency.

Objective In this exercise, you will configure an IS-IS broadcast adjacency between two routers. Although there are only two routers on the segment, IS-IS broadcast interfaces can still be used to illustrate the concept.

Validation You will know you have succeeded if the IS-IS broadcast adjacency is established.

1. Configure an IS-IS Level 2 broadcast adjacency between R1 and R3. Use priority settings to ensure that R3 will be the DIS.
    a. Verify that the adjacency between R1 and R3 is up.
    b. Verify that R3 is the DIS.
    c. Describe the LSPs in R3's database.
    d. Describe the LSP originated by the DIS.
    e. Which router is the backup DIS for the broadcast network between R1 and R3?
2. Force R1 to be the DIS for the broadcast link by adjusting the priority settings. Do you have to restart IS-IS?
    a. How have the LSPs originated by R3 changed?
    b. Does R3 have any of the LSPs originated by R2? Explain.
    c. Examine the LSPs on R2. Which router (R1 or R3) originates the LSP that describes the broadcast network between R1 and R3? Why? Does R2 have LSPs from both R1 and R3?
3. From R3 try to ping the system interface of R2.
    a. Does the ping work? Why or why not? If not, make the ping work.
    b. How many routes should you see in the route table of each router?
    c. How many LSPs are in the database of each router? Describe the LSPs.

Lab Section 8.3: Configuring IS-IS Passive Interfaces and Loopbacks

It is often desirable to include directly connected routes in IS-IS for the purpose of communicating their prefixes to other routers. IS-IS adjacencies are not established on these interfaces, but they are advertised throughout the network.

Objective In this exercise, you will configure physical and loopback interfaces and include them in the IS-IS routing protocol.

Validation You will know you have succeeded if the other routers in the topology become aware of these interfaces through IS-IS route exchange.

1. Configure R3's interface toward R4 in IS-IS as a point-to-point passive L2 interface. Do not make an interface on R4 toward R3 yet.
   a. How is the interface represented in the LSP on R3?
   b. Examine the route tables on R1 and R2. Are they aware of the passive interface on R3? Explain why or why not.
   c. Configure R4's interface to R3 in IS-IS. Does the adjacency between R3 and R4 come up? Explain.
2. Configure a loopback interface on R3 with address `10.99.3.3/24` and add it to IS-IS.
   a. How is the loopback interface represented in the LSP originated by R3?

b. Verify that you can ping the loopback interface on R3 from R2.

Lab Section 8.4: Configuring IS-IS Authentication

IS-IS authentication adds security to IS-IS adjacencies. There are two types of security supported in IS-IS. You will configure both types in this exercise.

Objective In this exercise, you will configure both simple password and MD5 authentication on an IS-IS adjacency.

Validation You will know you have succeeded if the IS-IS adjacencies come up after authentication is configured.

1. Configure an IS-IS Level 2 point-to-point adjacency between R2 and R4.
   a. Verify that the IS-IS adjacency is up before proceeding.

2. On R2 add simple password authentication to all IS-IS messages for all IS-IS interfaces using the password `nrs2-pwd`.
   a. Does the adjacency stay up? Explain.
   b. Add password authentication to R4, and verify that the adjacency is up.
   c. What is the limitation of this type of simple password authentication?
3. Change the authentication type to MD5 authentication on R2 using the same key.
   a. Is the adjacency still up? Explain.
   b. Change the authentication type on R4 to MD5, and verify that the adjacency is up.
   c. Why is this type of authentication better than simple password authentication?
   d. Change the configuration of R2 and R4 to only authenticate IS-IS Hello messages on the interface.

Chapter Review

Now that you have completed this chapter, you should have a good understanding of the following topics:

- The similarities and differences between IS-IS and OSPF
- The main steps IS-IS routers go through to form an adjacency
- How metrics are assigned to interfaces in IS-IS
- The purpose of Level 1 and Level 2 routers in an IS-IS network
- The differences between a point-to-point and a broadcast network in IS-IS
- The purpose of the IS-IS link-state database and how to view its contents
- The four different IS-IS PDUs and their purposes
- How NSAP addresses are used in IS-IS
- How IS-IS uses Hello PDUs to discover its neighbors
- How the DIS is elected on a broadcast network
- How IS-IS routers use CSNPs and PSNPs to keep their databases up to date
- The details of LSP flooding and aging in IS-IS
- The format of the LSP and the meaning of its fields
- The role of the DIS and the details of the pseudonode LSP
- How to configure IS-IS in a single-area network
- Verifying the operation and the database in a single-area IS-IS network
- The purpose and behavior of a passive interface
- The purpose and operation of overload-on-boot
- The use of authentication in IS-IS
- The purpose and operation of BFD

Post-Assessment

The following questions will test your knowledge and prepare you for the Alcatel-Lucent NRS II Certification Exam. Compare your responses with the answers listed in Appendix A. You can also use the CD that accompanies this book to take all the assessment tests and review the answers.

1. Which of the following statements comparing IS-IS and OSPF on the Alcatel-Lucent 7750 SR is false?
   - **A.** OSPF and IS-IS are both link-state routing protocols.
   - **B.** OSPF uses a reference bandwidth and the bandwidth of an interface to calculate the metric for the link. IS-IS always uses the value of 10 as a metric.
   - **C.** Both protocols support hierarchy. In OSPF, an ABR joins different areas; in IS-IS, L2 routers join the different areas.
   - **D.** OSPF uses IP to send its messages, whereas IS-IS uses the Layer 2 protocol.
   - **E.** OSPF was developed specifically for routing IP, whereas IS-IS was originally developed as an OSI protocol.
   - **F.** All of the above statements are true.

2. Which of the following statements best describes the election of the DIS on a broadcast network where all routers have the same priority?
   - **A.** The DIS is the router with the highest interface MAC address.
   - **B.** The DIS is the router with the highest system IP address.
   - **C.** If there is no DIS, the router with the highest interface MAC address is selected; otherwise, the existing DIS continues as DIS.
   - **D.** If there is no DIS, the router with the highest system IP address is selected; otherwise, the existing DIS continues as DIS.
   - **E.** The first router active on the broadcast network becomes the DIS.

3. Which of the following statements best describes how IS-IS routers ensure that their LSDB is always up to date?
   - **A.** Routers periodically exchange Hello PDUs to ensure that the LSDB is up to date.
   - **B.** Routers periodically exchange CSNPs that list the LSPs in their LSDBs.
   - **C.** Routers acknowledge any new LSPs received. If an LSP is not acknowledged, the router retransmits the LSP.
   - **D.** When the age of an LSP in the LSDB reaches zero, the originating router floods a new LSP to ensure that all of the LSDBs are kept up to date.
   - **E.** No special mechanism is required because new LSPs are flooded anytime there is a topology change.
4. Which of the following statements about the flooding of IS-IS LSPs is false?
   - **A.** An L1/L2-capable router floods both an L1 and an L2 LSP.
   - **B.** A router only floods an LSP when there is a topology change or when it receives an updated LSP from a neighbor.
   - **C.** The sequence number of the LSP is set by the originating router and used by other routers to tell if the LSP is an update to their LSDBs.
   - **D.** On point-to-point links, LSPs are acknowledged with a PSNP.
   - **E.** All of the above statements are true.
5. Which of the following statements about the IS-IS metric is false?
   - **A.** The interface metric can be set to different values for Level 1 and Level 2.
   - **B.** On the 7750 SR the default metric for an IS-IS interface is 10.
   - **C.** IS-IS can be configured on the 7750 SR with a reference bandwidth and wide metrics so that it calculates the link metric the same way that OSPF does.
   - **D.** If an IS-IS router does not use wide metrics, the maximum metric is 63.
   - **E.** All of the above statements are true.

6. Which of the following is not a valid IS-IS PDU type?
   A. Hello
   B. LSP
   C. ACK
   D. PSNP
   E. CSNP
   F. All of the above are valid IS-IS PDUs.
7. Which of the following statements about the NSAP address is false?
   A. The AFI indicates the authority through which the address was assigned.
   B. On the 7750 SR, the IDP and high-order DSP are assigned as the area ID.
   C. The system ID is always 4 bytes long.
   D. The NSAP selector is always zero for a router.
   E. All of the above statements are true.
8. Which of the following best describes the CSNP?
   A. The CSNP is used to discover neighbors and establish adjacencies.
   B. The CSNP is an index that lists all of the LSPs in the LSDB.
   C. The CSNP is an index that lists some of the LSPs in the LSDB.
   D. The CSNP is the PDU that carries the router's link-state information.
   E. The CNSP is not a valid IS-IS PDU.
9. Which of the following statements about IS-IS adjacencies is incorrect?
   A. There are three types of Hello messages used to form an adjacency: the Level 1 LAN Hello, the Level 2 LAN Hello, and the point-to-point Hello.
   B. An IS-IS router may form both L1 and L2 adjacencies.
   C. L1 adjacencies are only formed if both routers have the same area ID.
   D. In IS-IS, an adjacency is considered to be established after the successful exchange of Hello PDUs.
   E. All of the above statements are correct.

10. Which of the following best describes how the IS-IS system ID is created on the 7750 SR?

A. The four numbers of the router ID are each represented using three digits to create a 6-byte system ID.

B. The 4-byte router ID is directly copied to the system ID, and the two NSAP selector bytes are added to create a 6-byte system ID.

C. The hexadecimal value of the router ID is converted to a decimal number to create the 6-byte system ID.

D. The chassis MAC address is used to create a 6-byte system ID.

E. None of the above statements describes the creation of the IS-IS system ID.

11. An extract from an IS-IS LSP on the 7750 SR is shown below. Which of the TLVs contains the information used to create the entry in the route table for the subnet corresponding to the interface with IP address `10.1.5.1/27`?

```
*A:R1>config>router>isis# show router isis database R1.00-00 detail
  Router ID   :
    Router ID    : 10.10.10.1
  I/F Addresses :
    I/F Address    : 10.10.10.1
    I/F Address    : 10.1.5.1
  TE IS Nbrs    :
    Nbr    : R1.03
    Default Metric   : 10
    Sub TLV Len      : 6
    IF Addr    : 10.1.5.1
  TE IP Reach    :
    Default Metric   : 0
    Control Info:     , prefLen 32
    Prefix    : 10.10.10.1
    Default Metric   : 10
    Control Info:     , prefLen 27
    Prefix    : 10.1.5.0
```

A. Router ID TLV

B. I/F Addresses TLV

C. TE IS Nbrs TLV

D. TE IP Reach TLV

E. None of the above. The output shown is from a Traffic Engineering LSP. The prefix information is actually carried in another PDU.

12. The neighbors listed in an LSP are all shown as having a metric of 0. Which of the following is a true statement?

   A. All neighbors are connected on point-to-point links.

   B. All neighbors are connected on broadcast links.

   C. The LSP is the pseudonode LSP.

   D. The LSP is from a router that has only the system interface defined in IS-IS.

   E. The LSP described is not a valid IS-IS LSP.

13. Given the output from `show router isis database` on router R1 shown below, which of the following is not necessarily a true statement? Assume that all routers in the network have formed adjacencies with all their neighbors.

```
*A:R1# show router isis database

===============================================================================
ISIS Database
===============================================================================
LSP ID                                  Sequence Checksum Lifetime Attributes
-------------------------------------------------------------------------------

Displaying Level 1 database
-------------------------------------------------------------------------------
Level (1) LSP Count : 0

Displaying Level 2 database
-------------------------------------------------------------------------------
R1.00-00                                0x67d    0xc95b   905      L1L2
R1.03-00                                0x1      0x9eda   904      L1L2
R2.00-00                                0x84     0x1356   882      L1L2
R5.00-00                                0xab     0x7227   904      L1L2
R3.00-00                                0x1c     0x2699   897      L1L2
Level (2) LSP Count : 5
===============================================================================
```

   A. There are four routers in the network that are L2-capable.

   B. At least one of the interfaces in the network is a broadcast network.

   C. R1 does not have any L1 adjacencies.

   D. All routers in the network have the same Area ID.

   E. All of the above statements must be true statements.

14. Which of the following statements about a passive interface in IS-IS is false?

  A. The passive interface is listed in the I/F Addresses TLV.

  B. The passive interface is listed in the TE IS Nbrs TLV.

  C. The passive interface is listed in the TE IP Reach TLV.

  D. All of the above statements are true.

15. An interface is configured for BFD using a transmit and receive interval of 100 milliseconds and a multiplier of 5. The interface is BFD-enabled in IS-IS. What is the maximum length of time it will take after loss of forwarding on the interface to notify IS-IS of the failure?

  A. 5 milliseconds

  B. 10 milliseconds

  C. 100 milliseconds

  D. 500 milliseconds

  E. 5 seconds

  F. 10 seconds

9 IS-IS Multi-Area Networks

The Alcatel-Lucent NRS II exam topics covered in this chapter include the following:

- Hierarchy in IS-IS
- Level 1 and Level 2 topologies
- Suboptimal routing and asymmetric paths
- Level 1 database
- Level 2 database
- Configuring a multi-area network
- Configuring route summarization
- Route leaking
- External routes
- Administrative route tags

This chapter describes the implementation of hierarchy in IS-IS (Intermediate System to Intermediate System). To improve scalability, IS-IS supports two levels of hierarchy: Level 1 and Level 2. Level 1 LSPs (link-state PDUs) are used to build a link-state database (LSDB) for a single area, and the Level 1 routers in that area perform the SPF (shortest path first) algorithm on this database. Level 2 LSPs are used to build a link-state database for the Level 2 topology, which is used to route between Level 1 networks. This chapter examines the contents and use of the Level 1 and Level 2 LSPs.

To help manage the size of the LSDB and the route table, IS-IS allows for the summarization of prefixes. We show an example of summarization in this chapter. The loss of routing information that can result from hierarchy can be managed through the use of route leaking policies. We show an example of a suboptimal route and how route leaking can be used to solve this problem.

Pre-Assessment

The following assessment questions will help you understand what areas of the chapter you should review in more detail to prepare for the NRS II exam. You can also use the CD that accompanies this book to take all the assessment tests and review the answers.

1. Which of the following best describes the implementation of hierarchy in IS-IS?
   - **A.** L1 routers perform the SPF calculation over their local area. L2 routers connect to L1 routers in different areas and exchange routes between the different areas.
   - **B.** L1 routers perform the SPF calculation over their local area. L2 routers perform the SPF calculation over the L2 topology and route between the different areas.
   - **C.** L1 routers exchange routes only with other L1 routers. L2 routers exchange routes only with other L2 routers.
   - **D.** L1 routers route only in their own area. L2 routers create tunnels between different areas.
2. What is the most likely cause of asymmetric routing in a multi-area IS-IS network?
   - **A.** Asymmetric routing can occur because L1 routers can only forward traffic to other L1 routers and L2 routers can only forward traffic to other L2 routers.
   - **B.** In an IS-IS multi-area network, all traffic between areas must pass through the backbone area.

C. A prefix learned from an L1 LSP is preferred over one learned from an L2 LSP even if it is not the most direct route.

D. A prefix learned from an L2 LSP is preferred over one learned from an L1 LSP even if it is not the most direct route.

E. L1 routers only have a default route to an L1/L2 router, which may not be the most direct route to the destination.

3. Which of the following best describes the advantage of using summarization?

A. Summarization provides more accurate routing information to routers outside the area.

B. Summarization simplifies the configuration required on the L2 routers.

C. Summarization eliminates the possibility of asymmetric routing and suboptimal routing.

D. Summarization reduces the size of the LSP and of the route table of routers outside the area.

E. Summarization is not supported in IS-IS because it was not designed as an IP routing protocol.

4. Which of the following statements best describes route leaking in IS-IS?

A. Route leaking allows prefixes from outside an L1 area to be known inside the area.

B. Route leaking reduces the number of routes in the route table by replacing a group of prefixes with one less specific prefix.

C. Route leaking allows prefixes from outside the IS-IS routing domain to be known in the IS-IS domain.

D. Route leaking allows prefixes from the IS-IS routing domain to be advertised in another routing protocol such as BGP.

5. What is the likely result if there is a break in the L2 backbone?

A. Some destinations in the network will be unreachable.

B. Some routes will have an asymmetric path.

C. Some routes will not take the most optimal path.

D. The network will take longer to converge after a topology change.

E. All of the above conditions are likely to occur.

9.1 Hierarchy in an IS-IS Network

As mentioned in the previous chapter, IS-IS supports hierarchy to improve its scalability in a large routing domain. Hierarchy is implemented by splitting the routing domain into distinct topologies: multiple Level 1 topologies and a single Level 2 topology. Level 1 topologies are composed of the routers in a single common area. The Level 2 topology is the backbone that connects the Level 1 topologies. A separate link-state database is maintained for each topology. Every IS-IS router participates in either a Level 1 topology, the Level 2 topology, or both (see Figure 9.1).

Figure 9.1 IS-IS routers are either Level 1, Level 2, or both.

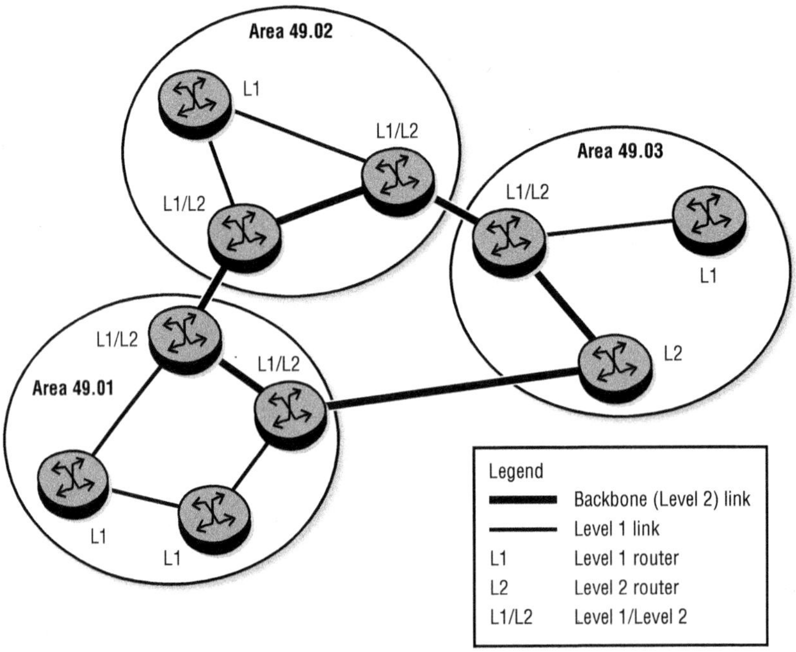

Level 1 and Level 2 Topologies

A weakness of link-state routing protocols is that they do not scale especially well for large networks. Splitting the network into smaller areas reduces the size of the LSDB and the complexity of the SPF calculation. In IS-IS, the Level 1 routers in a single area have the same database that represents the topology of the area. They perform the SPF calculation for the local topology only and use a default route to a Level 2–capable router for destinations outside the local area.

Level 2 routers share the same Level 2 topology database describing all of the Level 2 routers. This allows them to route between areas. Level 2 routers are usually also Level 1–capable, in which case they are part of the local Level 1 topology and have the Level 1 LSDB as well (see Figure 9.2). Notice that routers are always contained within an area, unlike OSPF (Open Shortest Path First).

Figure 9.2 Level 1 routers perform the SPF calculation over a single area. Level 2 routers perform the SPF calculation over the Level 2 topology.

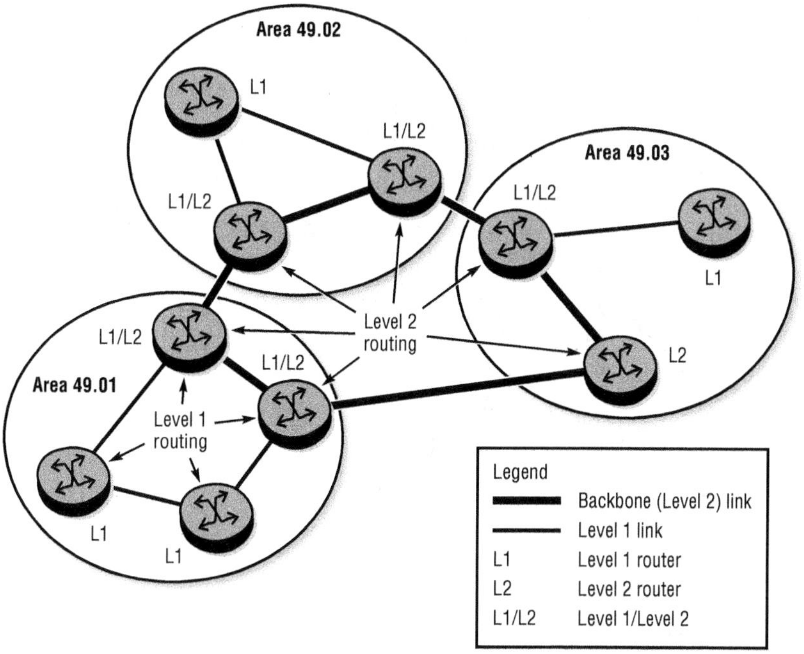

Level 2 routers must be connected in a contiguous backbone. If the Level 2 topology is not contiguous, there will likely be destinations in the network that are unreachable from some locations.

Suboptimal Routing and Asymmetric Paths

The default behavior of IS-IS is that Level 1 routers install a default route to the nearest Level 1/Level 2–capable router in their area. They do not have specific routes for prefixes outside the area. This simplifies the route table of Level 1 routers but can result in suboptimal routing or asymmetric routing paths. Figure 9.3 shows a topology in which some routing paths are suboptimal and in which asymmetric paths will be used for bidirectional data flows. An asymmetric path is a path between two endpoints where the data traveling in one direction follows a different path from the data flowing in the other direction. This is not necessarily a problem, but a significant difference in latency between the two directions may adversely affect some applications.

Figure 9.3 Routing topology with suboptimal and asymmetric paths.

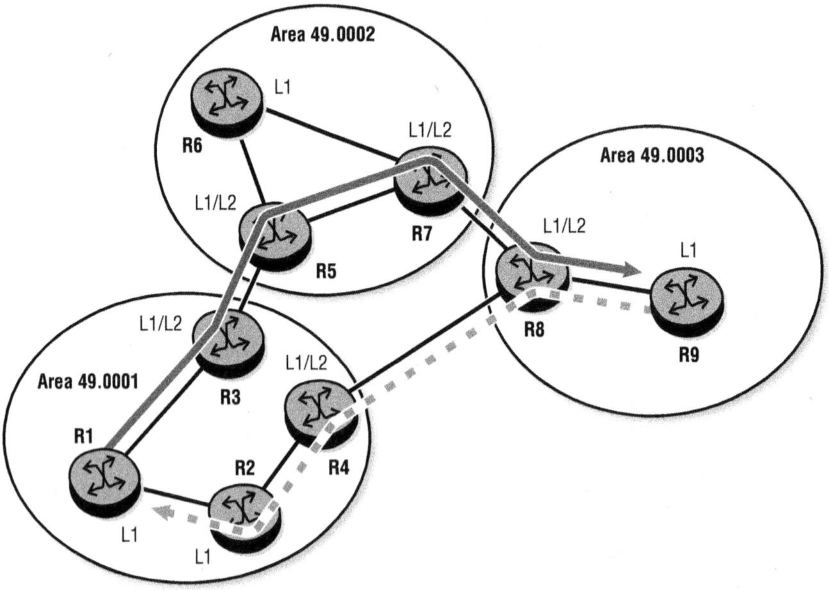

In Figure 9.3, all links have the same cost of 10. The L1 router R1 forwards data destined to R9 to its nearest L1/L2 router, R3, which forwards the data using its shortest path to R9. The total cost of the route is 50. R9 forwards data destined to R1 to its L1/L2 router, R8, which forwards the data using its shortest path to R1. The total cost of the path from R9 to R1 is 40 and the path is different from the one from R1 to R9.

This situation occurs because routers in a hierarchical network do not have complete topology information. This is the primary disadvantage of hierarchy in a link-state network. It is important to note that this is not a problem particular to IS-IS. This topology is essentially the same as an OSPF network with totally stubby areas. Below in this chapter, we examine *route leaking*, which is used to flood routing information into Level 1 areas and can be used to improve this type of situation.

9.2 Implementing a Multi-Area IS-IS Network

IS-IS implements hierarchy by dividing the routing domain into Level 1 and Level 2 topologies. A separate LSDB is maintained for each topology. Topology information is flooded between neighboring routers using the same mechanism whether it is a Level 1 or Level 2 area. Figure 9.4 shows a topology with two areas and a mixture of L1, L2, and L1/L2 routers.

Figure 9.4 Multi-area IS-IS topology.

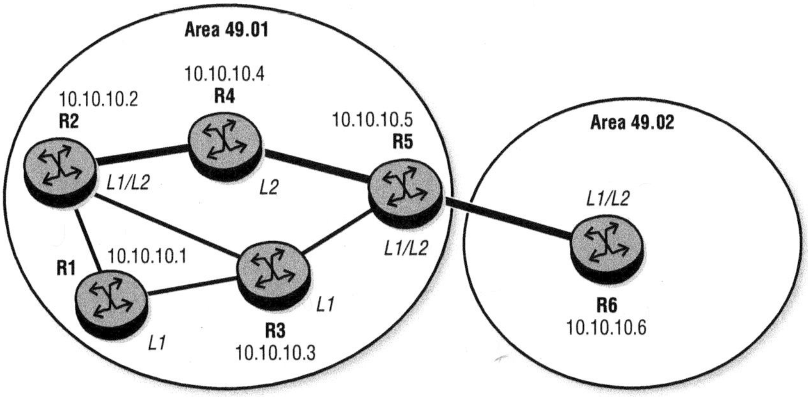

Level 1 Database

In the network of Figure 9.4, routers R1, R2, R3, and R5 comprise the Level 1 topology. They form Level 1 adjacencies with each other and flood Level 1 LSPs (see Listing 9.1).

Listing 9.1 R1 adjacencies and the Level 1 database

```
A:R1# show router isis adjacency

===============================================================================
ISIS Adjacency
===============================================================================
System ID                Usage State Hold Interface                     MT Enab
-------------------------------------------------------------------------------
R2                       L1    Up    23   toR2                          No
```

(continued)

Listing 9.1 *(continued)*

```
R3                    L1    Up    26   toR3                        No
----------------------------------------------------------------------
Adjacencies : 2
======================================================================
A:R1# show router isis database level 1

======================================================================
ISIS Database
======================================================================
LSP ID                            Sequence Checksum Lifetime Attributes
----------------------------------------------------------------------

Displaying Level 1 database
----------------------------------------------------------------------
R1.00-00                          0x84     0x7305   1111     L1
R2.00-00                          0x84     0x654f   1096     L1L2 ATT
R3.00-00                          0x82     0xe8d0   1122     L1
R5.00-00                          0x80     0x94ca   1139     L1L2 ATT
Level (1) LSP Count : 4
======================================================================
```

As seen, each of the four routers in the Level 1 topology floods an LSP that describes their local topology. Listing 9.2 shows the LSP flooded by R1. The Level 1 routers in the area perform the SPF calculation on the Level 1 database to find the shortest route to every destination in the Level 1 topology.

Listing 9.2 LSP flooded by R1

```
A:R1# show router isis database R1.00-00 detail level 1

======================================================================
ISIS Database
======================================================================

Displaying Level 1 database
----------------------------------------------------------------------
LSP ID    : R1.00-00                                Level     : L1
Sequence  : 0x84                 Checksum  : 0x7305  Lifetime  : 1059
```

```
Version    : 1                        Pkt Type  : 18      Pkt Ver   : 1
Attributes: L1                        Max Area  : 3
SysID Len : 6                         Used Len  : 138     Alloc Len : 1492

TLVs :
  Area Addresses:
    Area Address : (2) 49.01
  Supp Protocols:
    Protocols     : IPv4
  IS-Hostname    : R1
  Router ID    :
    Router ID    : 10.10.10.1
  I/F Addresses :
    I/F Address    : 10.10.10.1
    I/F Address    : 10.1.2.1
    I/F Address    : 10.1.3.1
  TE IS Nbrs    :
    Nbr    : R3.00
    Default Metric  : 100
    Sub TLV Len      : 12
    IF Addr    : 10.1.3.1
    Nbr IP     : 10.1.3.3
  TE IS Nbrs    :
    Nbr    : R2.00
    Default Metric  : 100
    Sub TLV Len      : 12
    IF Addr    : 10.1.2.1
    Nbr IP     : 10.1.2.2
  TE IP Reach    :
    Default Metric  : 0
    Control Info:     , prefLen 32
    Prefix    : 10.10.10.1
    Default Metric  : 100
    Control Info:     , prefLen 27
    Prefix    : 10.1.2.0
    Default Metric  : 100
    Control Info:     , prefLen 27
    Prefix    : 10.1.3.0

Level (1) LSP Count : 1
===============================================================================
```

We can see the following main TLVs in the LSP:

- **Area addresses**—Contains the area address of `49.01`.
- **I/F addresses**—Contains the IP addresses for all the interfaces in the Level 1 topology.
- **TE IS neighbors**—Lists the neighbors with which the router has formed a Level 1 adjacency.
- **TE IP reachability**—Contains the local prefixes that are reachable in the Level 1 topology.

In the Level 1 database shown in Listing 9.1, the LSPs from routers R2 and R5 have the ATT bit set in the Attributes field. The ATT bit indicates that the routers are attached to the Level 2 topology (they have L1/L2 capability). The L1-only routers (R1 and R3 in this network) install a default route toward the closest L1/L2 router in the topology. As seen in Listing 9.3, R1 does not have a route to either `10.10.10.4` or `10.10.10.6` because neither of these is part of the local Level 1 topology. The router uses the default route to reach these destinations.

Listing 9.3 The R1 route table contains a default route toward the nearest L1/L2 router.

```
A:R1# show router route-table

===============================================================================
Route Table (Router: Base)
===============================================================================
Dest Prefix                                Type    Proto    Age          Pref
      Next Hop[Interface Name]                                 Metric
-------------------------------------------------------------------------------
0.0.0.0/0                                  Remote  ISIS     00h03m54s    15
      10.1.2.2                                                 100
10.1.2.0/27                                Local   Local    19h57m18s    0
      toR2                                                     0
10.1.3.0/27                                Local   Local    19h56m11s    0
      toR3                                                     0
10.2.3.0/27                                Remote  ISIS     00h03m42s    15
      10.1.2.2                                                 200
10.2.4.0/27                                Remote  ISIS     00h03m54s    15
      10.1.2.2                                                 200
```

```
10.3.5.0/27                                   Remote  ISIS     00h03m42s   15
       10.1.3.3                                                    200
10.4.5.0/27                                   Remote  ISIS     00h03m25s   15
       10.1.3.3                                                    300
10.5.6.0/27                                   Remote  ISIS     00h03m26s   15
       10.1.3.3                                                    300
10.10.10.1/32                                 Local   Local    20h01m40s   0
       system                                                      0
10.10.10.2/32                                 Remote  ISIS     00h03m55s   15
       10.1.2.2                                                    100
10.10.10.3/32                                 Remote  ISIS     00h03m55s   15
       10.1.3.3                                                    100
10.10.10.5/32                                 Remote  ISIS     00h03m43s   15
       10.1.3.3                                                    200
------------------------------------------------------------------------
No. of Routes: 12
========================================================================
```

The use of the default route leads to the possibility of asymmetric routes. Listing 9.4 shows the results of two `traceroute` commands in the network: one from R3 to R6 and the other from R6 to R3. Because R3 is Level 1-only, it uses a default route to leave the Level 1 topology and takes four hops to reach R6 (R3–R2–R4–R5–R6). R6 has Level 2 routing information and therefore can reach R3 in two hops (R6–R5–R3).

Listing 9.4 The route from R3 to R6 is four hops; the route from R6 to R3 is only two hops.

```
A:R3# traceroute 10.10.10.6
traceroute to 10.10.10.6, 30 hops max, 40 byte packets
  1  10.2.3.2 (10.2.3.2)    4.06 ms  1.73 ms  1.72 ms
  2  10.2.4.4 (10.2.4.4)    2.41 ms  2.33 ms  2.33 ms
  3  10.4.5.5 (10.4.5.5)    6.44 ms  2.35 ms  2.42 ms
  4  10.10.10.6 (10.10.10.6)    4.95 ms  2.90 ms  2.80 ms

A:R6# traceroute 10.10.10.3
traceroute to 10.10.10.3, 30 hops max, 40 byte packets
  1  10.5.6.5 (10.5.6.5)    2.04 ms  1.72 ms  1.70 ms
  2  10.10.10.3 (10.10.10.3)    2.81 ms  2.81 ms  2.99 ms
```

Level 2 Database

IS-IS uses a separate topology, the Level 2 topology, to perform routing between the Level 1 topologies. In many cases, a Level 2 router is also part of a Level 1 topology and may be the default router for some of the Level 1 routers. However, a router may also be a Level 2 router only. Listing 9.5 shows the adjacencies formed by R2: two Level 1 adjacencies and one Level 2 adjacency with router R4.

Listing 9.5 Adjacencies formed by router R2

```
*A:R2>config>router>isis# show router isis adjacency

===============================================================================
ISIS Adjacency
===============================================================================
System ID                Usage State Hold Interface                     MT Enab
-------------------------------------------------------------------------------
R1                       L1    Up    22   toR1                          No
R3                       L1    Up    23   toR3                          No
R4                       L2    Up    19   toR4                          No
-------------------------------------------------------------------------------
Adjacencies : 3
===============================================================================
```

The Level 2 database shows the LSPs flooded by all of the Level 2 routers in the network (see Listing 9.6).

Listing 9.6 Level 2 database has LSPs from all Level 2 routers.

```
*A:R2# show router isis database level 2

===============================================================================
ISIS Database
===============================================================================
LSP ID                                 Sequence Checksum Lifetime Attributes
-------------------------------------------------------------------------------

Displaying Level 2 database
```

```
------------------------------------------------------------------------
R2.00-00                            0x8a     0x3d24   936      L1L2
R4.00-00                            0x87     0x3cf7   923      L1L2
R5.00-00                            0x8e     0x6c5    936      L1L2
R6.00-00                            0x7c     0x9036   940      L1L2
Level (2) LSP Count : 4
========================================================================
```

A Level 2 LSP contains the local Level 2 topology information as well as the prefixes the router learned from the Level 1 topology if it is a L1/L2 router (see Listing 9.7).

Listing 9.7 Level 2 LSP originated by router R2

```
*A:R2# show router isis database level 2 R2.00-00 detail

========================================================================
ISIS Database
========================================================================

Displaying Level 2 database
------------------------------------------------------------------------
LSP ID     : R2.00-00                                  Level     : L2
Sequence   : 0x8a                 Checksum  : 0x3d24   Lifetime  : 886
Version    : 1                    Pkt Type  : 20       Pkt Ver   : 1
Attributes: L1L2                  Max Area  : 3
SysID Len : 6                     Used Len  : 189      Alloc Len : 1492

TLVs :
  Area Addresses:
    Area Address : (2) 49.01
  Supp Protocols:
    Protocols     : IPv4
  IS-Hostname    : R2
  Router ID    :
    Router ID    : 10.10.10.2
  I/F Addresses :
    I/F Address   : 10.1.2.2
    I/F Address   : 10.2.3.2
```

(continued)

Listing 9.7 *(continued)*

```
    I/F Address    : 10.2.4.2
    I/F Address    : 10.10.10.2
  TE IS Nbrs    :
    Nbr    : R4.00
    Default Metric  : 100
    Sub TLV Len     : 12
    IF Addr    : 10.2.4.2
    Nbr IP     : 10.2.4.4
  TE IP Reach    :
    Default Metric  : 100
    Control Info:     , prefLen 27
    Prefix    : 10.1.2.0
    Default Metric  : 100
    Control Info:     , prefLen 27
    Prefix    : 10.2.3.0
    Default Metric  : 200
    Control Info:     , prefLen 27
    Prefix    : 10.1.3.0
    Default Metric  : 200
    Control Info:     , prefLen 27
    Prefix    : 10.3.5.0
    Default Metric  : 100
    Control Info:     , prefLen 32
    Prefix    : 10.10.10.1
    Default Metric  : 100
    Control Info:     , prefLen 32
    Prefix    : 10.10.10.3
    Default Metric  : 300
    Control Info:     , prefLen 27
    Prefix    : 10.4.5.0
    Default Metric  : 200
    Control Info:     , prefLen 32
    Prefix    : 10.10.10.5
    Default Metric  : 300
    Control Info:     , prefLen 27
    Prefix    : 10.5.6.0
    Default Metric  : 100
    Control Info:     , prefLen 27
    Prefix    : 10.2.4.0
```

```
    Default Metric   : 0
    Control Info:     , prefLen 32
    Prefix    : 10.10.10.2

Level (2) LSP Count : 1
===============================================================================
```

Note the similarity to the Level 1 LSP. All three interfaces plus the system interface are shown, even though two interfaces are connected to Level 1 routers only (R1 and R3). Interfaces are defined as Level 1– and 2–capable by default and are thus included in both topologies. The router has one Level 2 neighbor, router R4, which is shown in the LSP.

Level 2 routers have routes to all of the destinations in the network, including destinations in other areas (see Listing 9.8). By default, routes learned through the Level 1 topology have a preference value of 15. Routes learned through the Level 2 topology have a preference value of 18. When a route is learned through both topologies, such as the one to `10.10.10.5`, the Level 1 route is always preferred even if the Level 1 route is higher cost because Level 1 has a lower preference value than Level 2.

Listing 9.8 Route table on R2 showing routes learned through Level 1 and Level 2

```
*A:R2# show router route-table

===============================================================================
Route Table (Router: Base)
===============================================================================
Dest Prefix                                 Type    Proto     Age         Pref
       Next Hop[Interface Name]                                 Metric
-------------------------------------------------------------------------------
10.1.2.0/27                                 Local   Local     19h54m09s   0
       toR1                                                     0
10.1.3.0/27                                 Remote  ISIS      00h06m16s   15
       10.1.2.1                                                 200
10.2.3.0/27                                 Local   Local     19h53m51s   0
       toR3                                                     0
10.2.4.0/27                                 Local   Local     19h53m39s   0
       toR4                                                     0
10.3.5.0/27                                 Remote  ISIS      00h06m16s   15
```

(continued)

Listing 9.8 *(continued)*

```
        10.2.3.3                                          200
10.4.5.0/27                          Remote  ISIS     00h06m00s   15
        10.2.3.3                                          300
10.5.6.0/27                          Remote  ISIS     00h06m00s   15
        10.2.3.3                                          300
10.10.10.1/32                        Remote  ISIS     00h06m44s   15
        10.1.2.1                                          100
10.10.10.2/32                        Local   Local    20h03m30s   0
        system                                            0
10.10.10.3/32                        Remote  ISIS     00h06m44s   15
        10.2.3.3                                          100
10.10.10.4/32                        Remote  ISIS     00h06m44s   18
        10.2.4.4                                          100
10.10.10.5/32                        Remote  ISIS     00h06m17s   15
        10.2.3.3                                          200
10.10.10.6/32                        Remote  ISIS     00h06m00s   18
        10.2.4.4                                          300
-------------------------------------------------------------------------------
No. of Routes: 13
===============================================================================
```

Configuring a Multi-Area Network

On the Alcatel-Lucent 7750 SR, IS-IS routers and their interfaces all have Level 1 and Level 2 capability by default. Routers such as R1 and R3 that are Level 1 only must be explicitly configured as such (see Listing 9.9). Notice that the routers have been configured to use wide metrics and a reference bandwidth so that the interface bandwidth is used to calculate the metric.

Listing 9.9 IS-IS configuration on router R1

```
A:R1# configure router isis
A:R1>config>router>isis# info
----------------------------------------------
        level-capability level-1
        area-id 49.01
```

```
        reference-bandwidth 100000000
        level 1
            wide-metrics-only
        exit
        interface "system"
        exit
        interface "toR2"
            interface-type point-to-point
        exit
        interface "toR3"
            interface-type point-to-point
        exit
----------------------------------------------
```

R1 will form an adjacency with any other L1–capable router with the same area address. It will not form any L2 adjacencies. Listing 9.10 shows that R2 is configured as a Level 1/Level 2–capable router (by default). It forms L1 adjacencies with R2 and R3 and an L2 adjacency with R4.

Listing 9.10 Configuration of R2 as an L1/L2 router

```
*A:R2# configure router isis
*A:R2>config>router>isis# info
----------------------------------------------
        area-id 49.01
        reference-bandwidth 100000000
        level 1
            wide-metrics-only
        exit
        level 2
            wide-metrics-only
        exit
        interface "system"
        exit
        interface "toR1"
            interface-type point-to-point
        exit
        interface "toR3"
```

(continued)

Listing 9.10 *(continued)*

```
            interface-type point-to-point
        exit
        interface "toR4"
            interface-type point-to-point
        exit
----------------------------------------------
```

R6 is in a different area and is configured as an L1/L2 router. There are no other L1 routers in that area, but the router still originates an L1 LSP for its local topology as well as an L2 LSP (see Listing 9.11).

Listing 9.11 Configuration of R6 and its LSDB

```
*A:R6# configure router isis
*A:R6>config>router>isis# info
----------------------------------------------
        area-id 49.02
        reference-bandwidth 100000000
        level 1
            wide-metrics-only
        exit
        level 2
            wide-metrics-only
        exit
        interface "system"
        exit
        interface "toR5"
            interface-type point-to-point
        exit
----------------------------------------------
*A:R6>config>router>isis# show router isis database

===============================================================================
ISIS Database
===============================================================================
LSP ID                              Sequence Checksum Lifetime Attributes
-------------------------------------------------------------------------------
```

```
Displaying Level 1 database
-----------------------------------------------------------------------
R6.00-00                         0x72      0xf8d7   1190      L1L2
Level (1) LSP Count : 1

Displaying Level 2 database
-----------------------------------------------------------------------
R2.00-00                         0x8b      0x3b25   922       L1L2
R4.00-00                         0x88      0x3af8   910       L1L2
R5.00-00                         0x8f      0x4c6    863       L1L2
R6.00-00                         0x7e      0xdde6   1190      L1L2
Level (2) LSP Count : 4
=======================================================================
```

9.3 Route Summarization and Route Leaking

The examples in the "Configuring a Multi-Area Network" section earlier in this chapter show the configuration for the routers in the network. As for OSPF, an important part of the network plan is designing an address plan that allows for summarization between areas to reduce the size of the LSDB and route table. In Figure 9.5, loopback prefixes have been added to demonstrate route summarization.

Figure 9.5 Network topology with additional loopback prefixes.

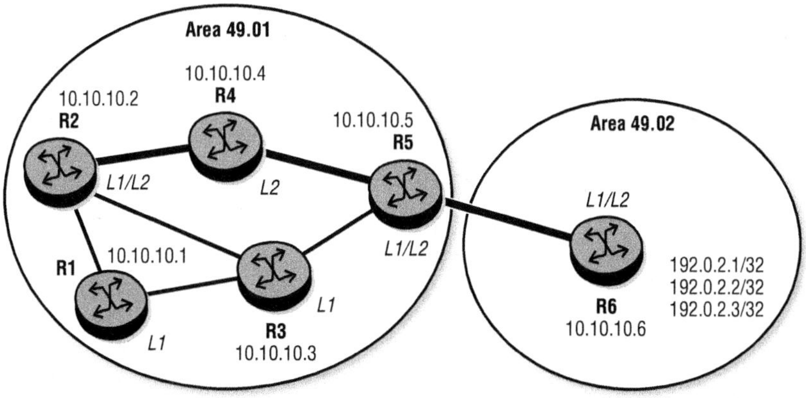

Configuring Route Summarization

In Figure 9.5, router R6 is configured with an additional three loopback interfaces that have also been added to IS-IS. Listing 9.12 shows the L2 LSP originated by R6 with the loopback prefixes. (The L1 LSP will contain the loopbacks as well.)

Listing 9.12 Level 2 LSP showing loopback prefixes

```
*A:R6# show router isis database R6.00-00 detail level 2

===============================================================================
ISIS Database
===============================================================================

Displaying Level 2 database
-------------------------------------------------------------------------------
LSP ID    : R6.00-00                                    Level     : L2
Sequence  : 0x82                   Checksum  : 0xaaf1    Lifetime  : 1173
Version   : 1                      Pkt Type  : 20        Pkt Ver   : 1
Attributes: L1L2                   Max Area  : 3
SysID Len : 6                      Used Len  : 139       Alloc Len : 1492

TLVs :
  Area Addresses:
    Area Address : (2) 49.02
  Supp Protocols:
    Protocols     : IPv4
  IS-Hostname   : R6
  Router ID   :
    Router ID   : 10.10.10.6
  I/F Addresses :
    I/F Address   : 10.5.6.6
    I/F Address   : 10.10.10.6
    I/F Address   : 192.0.2.1
    I/F Address   : 192.0.2.2
    I/F Address   : 192.0.2.3
  TE IS Nbrs   :
    Nbr   : R5.00
    Default Metric  : 100
    Sub TLV Len     : 12
```

```
    IF Addr   : 10.5.6.6
    Nbr IP    : 10.5.6.5
  TE IP Reach   :
    Default Metric  : 100
    Control Info:    , prefLen 27
    Prefix   : 10.5.6.0
    Default Metric  : 0
    Control Info:    , prefLen 32
    Prefix   : 10.10.10.6
    Default Metric  : 0
    Control Info:    , prefLen 32
    Prefix   : 192.0.2.1
    Default Metric  : 0
    Control Info:    , prefLen 32
    Prefix   : 192.0.2.2
    Default Metric  : 0
    Control Info:    , prefLen 32
    Prefix   : 192.0.2.3

Level (2) LSP Count : 1
===============================================================================
```

As expected, the routes are visible in the route table on R2 (see Listing 9.13).

Listing 9.13 Individual routes visible on router R2

```
*A:R2# show router route-table 192.0.2.0/24 longer

===============================================================================
Route Table (Router: Base)
===============================================================================
Dest Prefix                               Type    Proto    Age         Pref
       Next Hop[Interface Name]                                Metric
-------------------------------------------------------------------------------
192.0.2.1/32                              Remote  ISIS     00h12m38s   18
       10.2.4.4                                                 300
192.0.2.2/32                              Remote  ISIS     00h12m34s   18
       10.2.4.4                                                 300
192.0.2.3/32                              Remote  ISIS     00h12m29s   18
```

(continued)

Listing 9.13 *(continued)*

```
      10.2.4.4                                           300
-------------------------------------------------------------------------------
No. of Routes: 3
===============================================================================
```

Summarization in IS-IS is configured using the `summary-address` command. The level at which the command is applied is specified as either Level 1, Level 2, or both. Listing 9.14 shows R6 configured to summarize the loopback addresses as a single address.

Listing 9.14 Configuration of R6 to summarize loopbacks

```
*A:R6# configure router isis
*A:R6>config>router>isis# info
----------------------------------------------
        area-id 49.02
        reference-bandwidth 100000000
        summary-address 192.0.2.0/24 level-2
        level 1
            wide-metrics-only
        exit
        level 2
            wide-metrics-only
        exit
        interface "system"
        exit
        interface "toR5"
            interface-type point-to-point
        exit
        interface "loop1"
        exit
        interface "loop2"
        exit
        interface "loop3"
        exit
----------------------------------------------
```

Once summarization is configured, the L2 LSP contains only the summarized prefix (see Listing 9.15). The L1 LSP still contains the individual prefixes.

Listing 9.15 Level 2 LSP showing summarized address

```
*A:R6# show router isis database R6.00-00 detail level 2

===============================================================================
ISIS Database
===============================================================================

Displaying Level 2 database
-------------------------------------------------------------------------------
LSP ID     : R6.00-00                                   Level     : L2
Sequence   : 0x84                 Checksum  : 0x6d14    Lifetime  : 957
Version    : 1                    Pkt Type  : 20        Pkt Ver   : 1
Attributes: L1L2                  Max Area  : 3
SysID Len : 6                     Used Len  : 120       Alloc Len : 1492

TLVs :
  Area Addresses:
    Area Address : (2) 49.02
  Supp Protocols:
    Protocols     : IPv4
  IS-Hostname    : R6
  Router ID   :
    Router ID    : 10.10.10.6
  I/F Addresses :
    I/F Address    : 10.5.6.6
    I/F Address    : 10.10.10.6
    I/F Address    : 192.0.2.1
    I/F Address    : 192.0.2.2
    I/F Address    : 192.0.2.3
  TE IS Nbrs    :
    Nbr   : R5.00
    Default Metric  : 100
    Sub TLV Len     : 12
    IF Addr   : 10.5.6.6
    Nbr IP    : 10.5.6.5
  TE IP Reach   :
```

(continued)

Listing 9.15 *(continued)*

```
    Default Metric  : 100
    Control Info:    , prefLen 27
    Prefix   : 10.5.6.0
    Default Metric  : 0
    Control Info:    , prefLen 32
    Prefix   : 10.10.10.6
    Default Metric  : 0
    Control Info:    , prefLen 24
    Prefix   : 192.0.2.0

Level (2) LSP Count : 1
===============================================================================
```

When summarization is configured, the router creates a black-hole entry for the summarized route by default (see Listing 9.16). This is to prevent the possibility of looping packets in certain situations.

Listing 9.16 Black-hole entry added to R6's route table

```
*A:R6# show router route-table 192.0.2.0/24 longer

===============================================================================
Route Table (Router: Base)
===============================================================================
Dest Prefix                                 Type    Proto    Age         Pref
       Next Hop[Interface Name]                                Metric
-------------------------------------------------------------------------------
192.0.2.0/24                                Remote  ISIS     00h47m13s   255
       Black Hole                                              1
192.0.2.1/32                                Local   Local    06h20m14s   0
       loop1                                                   0
192.0.2.2/32                                Local   Local    06h20m00s   0
       loop2                                                   0
192.0.2.3/32                                Local   Local    06h19m47s   0
       loop3                                                   0
-------------------------------------------------------------------------------
No. of Routes: 4
===============================================================================
```

Only the summarized prefix is seen on router R2 and the other routers in the Level 2 topology (see Listing 9.17).

Listing 9.17 Summarized prefix in the route table on R2

```
*A:R2# show router route-table 192.0.2.0/24 longer

===============================================================================
Route Table (Router: Base)
===============================================================================
Dest Prefix                                  Type    Proto     Age         Pref
      Next Hop[Interface Name]                                       Metric
-------------------------------------------------------------------------------
192.0.2.0/24                                 Remote  ISIS      00h02m23s   18
      10.2.4.4                                                       300
-------------------------------------------------------------------------------
No. of Routes: 1
===============================================================================
```

Route Leaking

Route leaking is configured by creating a policy on the router where it is desired to leak the routes into another topology. For example, if it is desirable to leak routes from the Level 2 topology into the Level 1 topology of Area `49.01` from Figure 9.5, a policy can be configured on R5 as shown in Listing 9.18. This policy leaks all Level 2 routes; a prefix list can be used to make the policy more selective.

Listing 9.18 Route leaking configured on R5

```
*A:R5# configure router policy-options
*A:R5>config>router>policy-options# begin
*A:R5>config>router>policy-options# policy-statement route-leak
*A:R5>config>router>policy-options>policy-statement$ entry 10
*A:R5>config>router>policy-options>policy-statement>entry$ from level 2
*A:R5>config>router>policy-options>policy-statement>entry# to level 1
*A:R5>config>router>policy-options>policy-statement>entry# action accept
*A:R5>config>router>policy-options>policy-statement>entry>action# exit
```

(continued)

Listing 9.18 *(continued)*

```
*A:R5>config>router>policy-options>policy-statement>entry# exit
*A:R5>config>router>policy-options>policy-statement# exit
*A:R5>config>router>policy-options# commit
*A:R5>config>router>policy-options# exit
*A:R5# configure router isis export "route-leak"
```

Once route leaking is configured, the Level 1 LSP contains the routes from the Level 2 topology (see Listing 9.19).

Listing 9.19 Level 1 LSP showing routes leaked from Level 2

```
*A:R5# show router isis database R5.00-00 detail level 1

===============================================================================
ISIS Database
===============================================================================

Displaying Level 1 database
-------------------------------------------------------------------------------
LSP ID    : R5.00-00                                    Level     : L1
Sequence  : 0xa6                  Checksum  : 0x8d81   Lifetime  : 1166
Version   : 1                     Pkt Type  : 18       Pkt Ver   : 1
Attributes: L1L2 ATT              Max Area  : 3
SysID Len : 6                     Used Len  : 152      Alloc Len : 1492

TLVs :
  Area Addresses:
    Area Address : (2) 49.01
  Supp Protocols:
    Protocols     : IPv4
  IS-Hostname   : R5
  Router ID   :
    Router ID   : 10.10.10.5
  I/F Addresses :
    I/F Address   : 10.10.10.5
    I/F Address   : 10.3.5.5
    I/F Address   : 10.4.5.5
```

```
    I/F Address   : 10.5.6.5
  TE IS Nbrs   :
    Nbr   : R3.00
    Default Metric  : 100
    Sub TLV Len     : 12
    IF Addr   : 10.3.5.5
    Nbr IP    : 10.3.5.3
  TE IP Reach   :
    Default Metric  : 0
    Control Info:    , prefLen 32
    Prefix   : 10.10.10.5
    Default Metric  : 100
    Control Info:    , prefLen 27
    Prefix   : 10.3.5.0
    Default Metric  : 100
    Control Info:    , prefLen 27
    Prefix   : 10.4.5.0
    Default Metric  : 100
    Control Info:    , prefLen 27
    Prefix   : 10.5.6.0
    Default Metric  : 100
    Control Info: D  , prefLen 32
    Prefix   : 10.10.10.4
    Default Metric  : 100
    Control Info: D  , prefLen 32
    Prefix   : 10.10.10.6
    Default Metric  : 100
    Control Info: D  , prefLen 24
    Prefix   : 192.0.2.0

Level (1) LSP Count : 1
===============================================================================
```

Router R1 still contains a default route to its nearest L1/L2 router, but now also contains the prefixes from Level 2 (see Listing 9.20).

Listing 9.20 Route table on R1 with route leaking

```
*A:R1# show router route-table
```

(continued)

Listing 9.20 *(continued)*

```
===============================================================================
Route Table (Router: Base)
===============================================================================
Dest Prefix                                 Type    Proto    Age         Pref
      Next Hop[Interface Name]                                 Metric
-------------------------------------------------------------------------------
0.0.0.0/0                                   Remote  ISIS     06h19m45s   15
      10.1.2.2                                                  100
10.1.2.0/27                                 Local   Local    01d02h13m   0
      toR2                                                      0
10.1.3.0/27                                 Local   Local    01d02h12m   0
      toR3                                                      0
10.2.3.0/27                                 Remote  ISIS     06h19m33s   15
      10.1.2.2                                                  200
10.2.4.0/27                                 Remote  ISIS     06h19m45s   15
      10.1.2.2                                                  200
10.3.5.0/27                                 Remote  ISIS     06h19m33s   15
      10.1.3.3                                                  200
10.4.5.0/27                                 Remote  ISIS     06h19m16s   15
      10.1.3.3                                                  300
10.5.6.0/27                                 Remote  ISIS     06h19m18s   15
      10.1.3.3                                                  300
10.10.10.1/32                               Local   Local    01d02h17m   0
      system                                                    0
10.10.10.2/32                               Remote  ISIS     06h19m48s   15
      10.1.2.2                                                  100
10.10.10.3/32                               Remote  ISIS     06h19m48s   15
      10.1.3.3                                                  100
10.10.10.4/32                               Remote  ISIS     00h01m56s   15
      10.1.2.2                                                  200
10.10.10.5/32                               Remote  ISIS     06h19m35s   15
      10.1.3.3                                                  200
10.10.10.6/32                               Remote  ISIS     00h07m32s   15
      10.1.3.3                                                  300
192.0.2.0/24                                Remote  ISIS     00h07m32s   15
      10.1.3.3                                                  300
-------------------------------------------------------------------------------
No. of Routes: 15
===============================================================================
```

Route leaking policies must be carefully planned. The route to the Level 2 router, R4 (`10.10.10.4`), is now through R5 (see Figure 9.6 and Listing 9.21), because R5 is the one leaking the route into the Level 1 topology.

Figure 9.6 Route leaking by R5 influences route to R4.

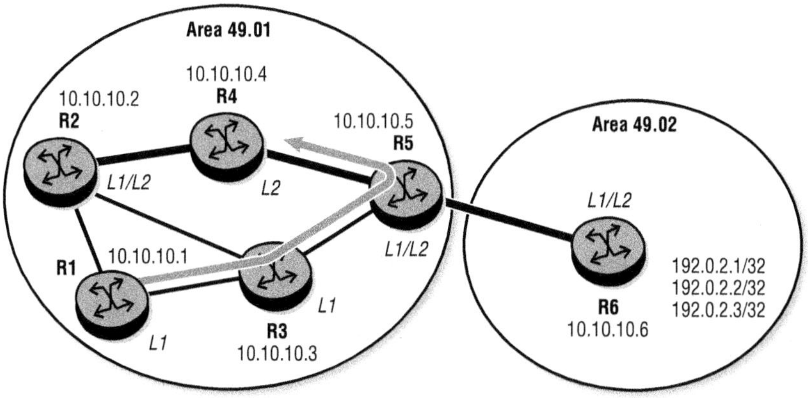

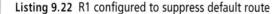

Listing 9.21 Route from R1 to R4 is through R5.

```
*A:R1# traceroute 10.10.10.4
traceroute to 10.10.10.4, 30 hops max, 40 byte packets
  1  10.1.3.3 (10.1.3.3)     3.98 ms  1.74 ms  1.76 ms
  2  10.3.5.5 (10.3.5.5)     4.24 ms  2.33 ms  2.33 ms
  3  10.10.10.4 (10.10.10.4)    6.73 ms  3.08 ms  2.68 ms
```

If the network administrator intends to leak all the routes from Level 2 into the Level 1 topology, he or she may want to suppress the creation of the default route. In Listing 9.22, R1 is configured to suppress the default route, and R2 and R5 have been configured to leak the Level 2 routes. The IS-IS Level 1 Area `49.01` is now configured like a normal (non-stub) OSPF area.

Listing 9.22 R1 configured to suppress default route

```
*A:R1>config>router>isis# info
---------------------------------------------
        level-capability level-1
```

(continued)

Listing 9.22 *(continued)*

```
        area-id 49.01
        reference-bandwidth 100000000
        suppress-default
        level 1
            wide-metrics-only
        exit
        interface "system"
        exit
        interface "toR2"
            interface-type point-to-point
        exit
        interface "toR3"
            interface-type point-to-point
        exit
----------------------------------------------
*A:R1>config>router>isis# show router route-table

========================================================================
Route Table (Router: Base)
========================================================================
Dest Prefix                           Type    Proto   Age         Pref
       Next Hop[Interface Name]                           Metric
------------------------------------------------------------------------
10.1.2.0/27                           Local   Local   03d22h06m   0
       toR2                                                0
10.1.3.0/27                           Local   Local   03d22h05m   0
       toR3                                                0
10.2.3.0/27                           Remote  ISIS    03d02h13m   15
       10.1.2.2                                            200
10.2.4.0/27                           Remote  ISIS    03d02h13m   15
       10.1.2.2                                            200
10.3.5.0/27                           Remote  ISIS    03d02h13m   15
       10.1.3.3                                            200
10.4.5.0/27                           Remote  ISIS    03d02h12m   15
       10.1.3.3                                            300
10.5.6.0/27                           Remote  ISIS    03d02h12m   15
```

```
        10.1.3.3                                              300
    10.10.10.1/32                            Local   Local    03d22h11m   0
        system                                                0
    10.10.10.2/32                            Remote  ISIS     03d02h13m   15
        10.1.2.2                                              100
    10.10.10.3/32                            Remote  ISIS     03d02h13m   15
        10.1.3.3                                              100
    10.10.10.4/32                            Remote  ISIS     00h00m31s   15
        10.1.2.2                                              200
    10.10.10.5/32                            Remote  ISIS     03d02h13m   15
        10.1.3.3                                              200
    10.10.10.6/32                            Remote  ISIS     02d20h01m   15
        10.1.3.3                                              300
    192.0.2.0/24                             Remote  ISIS     00h00m08s   15
        10.1.3.3                                              300
    -------------------------------------------------------------------------------
    No. of Routes: 14
    ===============================================================================
```

9.4 Exporting Routes to IS-IS

In its default configuration, an IS-IS router advertises any interface defined in IS-IS to its neighbors. To advertise prefixes that are not part of the IS-IS routing topology, an export policy is required. Routes can be exported into either the Level 1 or Level 2 topology, or both.

IS-IS Export Policies

In Figure 9.7, router R2 has several external routes that are to be exported into IS-IS. An export policy will add these routes to both the Level 1 and Level 2 LSPs by default. If it is desirable to have these routes known only at Level 2, this can be specified in the export policy (see Listing 9.23).

Figure 9.7 Exporting external routes known on router R2.

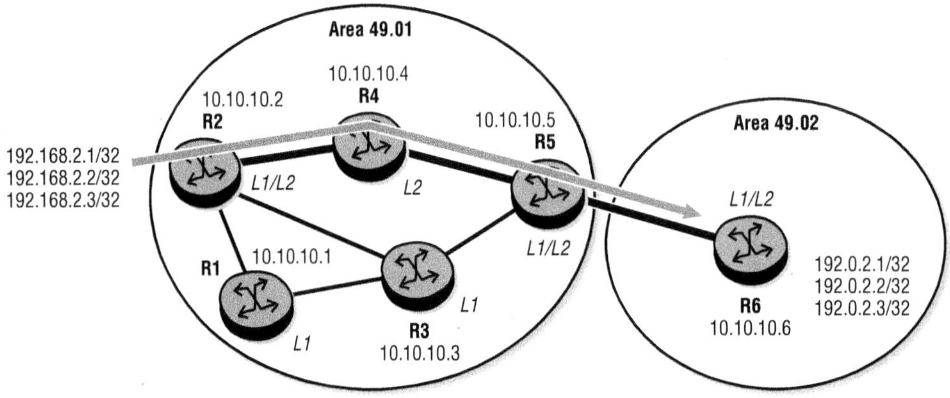

Listing 9.23 External routes exported to IS-IS by R2

```
*A:R2# configure router policy-options
*A:R2>config>router>policy-options# info
----------------------------------------------
            prefix-list "external_nets"
                prefix 192.168.2.0/24 longer
            exit
            policy-statement "externals"
                entry 10
                    from
                        prefix-list "external_nets"
                    exit
                    to
                        level 2
                    exit
                    action accept
                    exit
                exit
            exit
----------------------------------------------
*A:R2>config>router>policy-options# exit
*A:R2# configure router isis export "externals"
*A:R2# show router isis database R2.00-00 detail level 2
```

```
===============================================================================
ISIS Database
===============================================================================

Displaying Level 2 database
-------------------------------------------------------------------------------
LSP ID    : R2.00-00                                   Level     : L2
Sequence  : 0x24e                  Checksum  : 0x8552  Lifetime  : 1093
Version   : 1                      Pkt Type  : 20      Pkt Ver   : 1
Attributes: L1L2                   Max Area  : 3
SysID Len : 6                      Used Len  : 216     Alloc Len : 1492

TLVs :
  Area Addresses:
    Area Address : (2) 49.01
  Supp Protocols:
    Protocols     : IPv4
  IS-Hostname   : R2
  Router ID   :
    Router ID   : 10.10.10.2
  I/F Addresses :
    I/F Address   : 10.1.2.2
    I/F Address   : 10.2.3.2
    I/F Address   : 10.2.4.2
    I/F Address   : 10.10.10.2
  TE IS Nbrs   :
    Nbr   : R4.00
    Default Metric  : 100
    Sub TLV Len     : 12
    IF Addr   : 10.2.4.2
    Nbr IP    : 10.2.4.4
  TE IP Reach   :
    Default Metric  : 100
    Control Info:    , prefLen 27
    Prefix   : 10.1.2.0
    Default Metric  : 100
    Control Info:    , prefLen 27
    Prefix   : 10.2.3.0
    Default Metric  : 200
```

(continued)

Listing 9.23 *(continued)*

```
    Control Info:     , prefLen 27
    Prefix    : 10.1.3.0
    Default Metric  : 200
    Control Info:     , prefLen 27
    Prefix    : 10.3.5.0
    Default Metric  : 100
    Control Info:     , prefLen 32
    Prefix    : 10.10.10.1
    Default Metric  : 100
    Control Info:     , prefLen 32
    Prefix    : 10.10.10.3
    Default Metric  : 300
    Control Info:     , prefLen 27
    Prefix    : 10.4.5.0
    Default Metric  : 200
    Control Info:     , prefLen 32
    Prefix    : 10.10.10.5
    Default Metric  : 300
    Control Info:     , prefLen 27
    Prefix    : 10.5.6.0
    Default Metric  : 100
    Control Info:     , prefLen 27
    Prefix    : 10.2.4.0
    Default Metric  : 0
    Control Info:     , prefLen 32
    Prefix    : 10.10.10.2
    Default Metric  : 0
    Control Info:     , prefLen 32
    Prefix    : 192.168.2.1
    Default Metric  : 0
    Control Info:     , prefLen 32
    Prefix    : 192.168.2.2
    Default Metric  : 0
    Control Info:     , prefLen 32
    Prefix    : 192.168.2.3

Level (2) LSP Count : 1
===============================================================================
```

Administrative Route Tags

RFC 5130 defines the ability to add an additional attribute to IS-IS routes—the *administrative route tag*. This can be used to identify certain routes that are to receive some special treatment at another point in the network. This might be for routes that are to be exported to another protocol such as BGP (Border Gateway Protocol) or to control leaking between levels in IS-IS.

In the example in Listing 9.23, router R2 is exporting external routes into the Level 2 topology. There is also a policy in place to leak routes from Level 2 into Level 1 on router R5. The result is that the external routes from R2 are leaked as well. Listing 9.24 shows that R1 has a route for these prefixes. Because they were leaked by R5, the route is through R5.

Listing 9.24 All Level 2 routes are leaked into Level 1.

```
*A:R1# show router route-table

=========================================================================
Route Table (Router: Base)
=========================================================================
Dest Prefix                               Type     Proto    Age          Pref
       Next Hop[Interface Name]                                Metric
-------------------------------------------------------------------------
0.0.0.0/0                                 Remote   ISIS     04h48m20s    15
       10.1.2.2                                                100
10.1.2.0/27                               Local    Local    04d03h24m    0
       toR2                                                    0
10.1.3.0/27                               Local    Local    04d03h23m    0
       toR3                                                    0
10.2.3.0/27                               Remote   ISIS     03d07h31m    15
       10.1.2.2                                                200
10.2.4.0/27                               Remote   ISIS     03d07h31m    15
       10.1.2.2                                                200
10.3.5.0/27                               Remote   ISIS     03d07h31m    15
       10.1.3.3                                                200
10.4.5.0/27                               Remote   ISIS     03d07h30m    15
       10.1.3.3                                                300
10.5.6.0/27                               Remote   ISIS     03d07h30m    15
       10.1.3.3                                                300
```

(continued)

Listing 9.24 *(continued)*

```
10.10.10.1/32                                    Local   Local     04d03h29m   0
         system                                                       0
10.10.10.2/32                                    Remote  ISIS      03d07h31m   15
         10.1.2.2                                                     100
10.10.10.3/32                                    Remote  ISIS      03d07h31m   15
         10.1.3.3                                                     100
10.10.10.4/32                                    Remote  ISIS      04h51m44s   15
         10.1.3.3                                                     300
10.10.10.5/32                                    Remote  ISIS      03d07h31m   15
         10.1.3.3                                                     200
10.10.10.6/32                                    Remote  ISIS      03d01h19m   15
         10.1.3.3                                                     300
192.0.2.0/24                                     Remote  ISIS      05h18m03s   15
         10.1.3.3                                                     300
192.168.2.1/32                                   Remote  ISIS      04h43m39s   15
         10.1.3.3                                                     400
192.168.2.2/32                                   Remote  ISIS      04h43m39s   15
         10.1.3.3                                                     400
192.168.2.3/32                                   Remote  ISIS      04h43m39s   15
         10.1.3.3                                                     400
-------------------------------------------------------------------------------
No. of Routes: 18
===============================================================================
```

Route tags can be used in a situation like this to control the routes leaked into the Level 1 topology (see Figure 9.8). Route tags can be added at several different places:

- On the IS-IS interface
- On an IS-IS summary address
- In a policy redistributing the route from another protocol
- In a policy redistributing the route between IS-IS levels
- On a static route

Listing 9.25 shows a policy on R2 that tags routes with a value of 111. Notice the additional sub-TLV carrying the route tag in the LSP that carries the prefix. The "`S`" in the `Control Info` indicates that the TLV contains a sub-TLV.

Figure 9.8 Block tagged routes from being leaked into Level 1 Area 49.01.

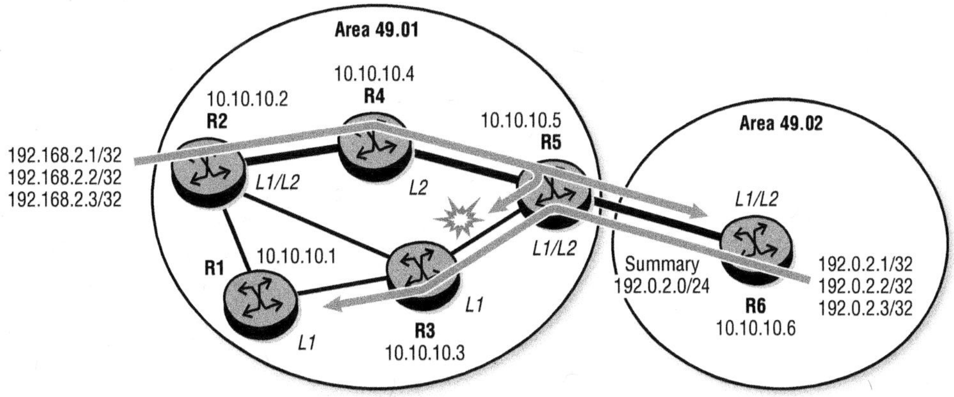

Listing 9.25 Policy to tag routes exported on R2

```
*A:R2# configure router policy-options
*A:R2>config>router>policy-options# info
----------------------------------------------
            prefix-list "external_nets"
                prefix 192.168.2.0/24 longer
            exit
            policy-statement "externals"
                entry 10
                    from
                        prefix-list "external_nets"
                    exit
                    to
                        level 2
                    exit
                    action accept
                        tag 0x6f
                    exit
                exit
            exit
----------------------------------------------
*A:R2# show router isis database R2.00-00 detail level 2
```

(continued)

Listing 9.25 *(continued)*

```
===============================================================================
ISIS Database
===============================================================================

Displaying Level 2 database
-------------------------------------------------------------------------------
LSP ID    : R2.00-00                                   Level     : L2
Sequence  : 0x26d                 Checksum  : 0xf77b   Lifetime  : 1069
Version   : 1                     Pkt Type  : 20       Pkt Ver   : 1
Attributes: L1L2                  Max Area  : 3
SysID Len : 6                     Used Len  : 237      Alloc Len : 1492

TLVs :
  Area Addresses:
    Area Address : (2) 49.01
  Supp Protocols:
    Protocols      : IPv4
  IS-Hostname    : R2
  Router ID    :
    Router ID    : 10.10.10.2
  I/F Addresses :
    I/F Address    : 10.1.2.2
    I/F Address    : 10.2.3.2
    I/F Address    : 10.2.4.2
    I/F Address    : 10.10.10.2
  TE IS Nbrs    :
    Nbr    : R4.00
    Default Metric  : 100
    Sub TLV Len     : 12
    IF Addr    : 10.2.4.2
    Nbr IP     : 10.2.4.4
  TE IP Reach    :
    Default Metric  : 100
    Control Info:    , prefLen 27
    Prefix    : 10.1.2.0
    Default Metric  : 100
    Control Info:    , prefLen 27
    Prefix    : 10.2.3.0
```

```
Default Metric  : 200
Control Info:    , prefLen 27
Prefix   : 10.1.3.0
Default Metric  : 200
Control Info:    , prefLen 27
Prefix   : 10.3.5.0
Default Metric  : 100
Control Info:    , prefLen 32
Prefix   : 10.10.10.1
Default Metric  : 100
Control Info:    , prefLen 32
Prefix   : 10.10.10.3
Default Metric  : 300
Control Info:    , prefLen 27
Prefix   : 10.4.5.0
Default Metric  : 200
Control Info:    , prefLen 32
Prefix   : 10.10.10.5
Default Metric  : 300
Control Info:    , prefLen 27
Prefix   : 10.5.6.0
Default Metric  : 100
Control Info:    , prefLen 27
Prefix   : 10.2.4.0
Default Metric  : 0
Control Info:    , prefLen 32
Prefix   : 10.10.10.2
Default Metric  : 0
Control Info:   S, prefLen 32
Prefix   : 192.168.2.1
Sub TLV   :
  AdminTag(32bit): 111
Default Metric  : 0
Control Info:   S, prefLen 32
Prefix   : 192.168.2.2
Sub TLV   :
  AdminTag(32bit): 111
Default Metric  : 0
Control Info:   S, prefLen 32
Prefix   : 192.168.2.3
```

(continued)

Listing 9.25 *(continued)*

```
    Sub TLV   :
      AdminTag(32bit): 111

Level (2) LSP Count : 1
========================================================================
```

The route leaking policy on R5 is modified so that tagged routes are not leaked into Level 1 (see Listing 9.26).

Listing 9.26 Tagged routes are filtered from route leaking policy on R5.

```
*A:R5# configure router policy-options
*A:R5>config>router>policy-options# info
----------------------------------------------
            policy-statement "route-leak"
                entry 5
                    from
                        tag 111
                    exit
                    action reject
                exit
                entry 10
                    from
                        level 2
                    exit
                    to
                        level 1
                    exit
                    action accept
                    exit
                exit
            exit
----------------------------------------------
```

The route table on R1 (see Listing 9.27) verifies that the routes are not received by the Level 1 routers. R1 and R3 will reach these destinations using their default route. They are still receiving the route for `192.0.2.0/24`.

Listing 9.27 Filtered routes are not received by Level 1 router

```
*A:R1# show router route-table

===============================================================================
Route Table (Router: Base)
===============================================================================
Dest Prefix                                 Type    Proto    Age         Pref
      Next Hop[Interface Name]                                  Metric
-------------------------------------------------------------------------------
0.0.0.0/0                                   Remote  ISIS     05h20m30s   15
      10.1.2.2                                                    100
10.1.2.0/27                                 Local   Local    04d03h56m   0
      toR2                                                        0
10.1.3.0/27                                 Local   Local    04d03h55m   0
      toR3                                                        0
10.2.3.0/27                                 Remote  ISIS     03d08h03m   15
      10.1.2.2                                                    200
10.2.4.0/27                                 Remote  ISIS     03d08h03m   15
      10.1.2.2                                                    200
10.3.5.0/27                                 Remote  ISIS     03d08h03m   15
      10.1.3.3                                                    200
10.4.5.0/27                                 Remote  ISIS     03d08h03m   15
      10.1.3.3                                                    300
10.5.6.0/27                                 Remote  ISIS     03d08h03m   15
      10.1.3.3                                                    300
10.10.10.1/32                               Local   Local    04d04h01m   0
      system                                                      0
10.10.10.2/32                               Remote  ISIS     03d08h03m   15
      10.1.2.2                                                    100
10.10.10.3/32                               Remote  ISIS     03d08h03m   15
      10.1.3.3                                                    100
10.10.10.4/32                               Remote  ISIS     05h23m54s   15
      10.1.3.3                                                    300
10.10.10.5/32                               Remote  ISIS     03d08h03m   15
      10.1.3.3                                                    200
10.10.10.6/32                               Remote  ISIS     03d01h51m   15
      10.1.3.3                                                    300
192.0.2.0/24                                Remote  ISIS     05h50m13s   15
      10.1.3.3                                                    300
-------------------------------------------------------------------------------
No. of Routes: 15
===============================================================================
```

Although it is possible to perform this operation using just prefix lists, in more complex situations, route tags provide an additional tool to the administrator to simplify routing policies.

Practice Lab: IS-IS Multi-Area Networks

The following lab is designed to reinforce your knowledge of the content in this chapter. Please review the instructions carefully, and perform the steps in the order in which they are presented. The practice labs require that you have access to six or more Alcatel-Lucent 7750 SRs or Alcatel-Lucent 7450 ESSs in a non-production environment.

These labs are designed to be used in a controlled lab environment. Please *do not* attempt to perform these labs in a production environment.

Lab Section 9.1: Configuring Multi-Area IS-IS

Multiple IS-IS areas can be used to improve scalability and convergence time.

Objective In this exercise you will configure a topology of six Alcatel-Lucent 7750 SRs with three IS-IS areas as shown in Figure 9.9.

Figure 9.9 IS-IS multi-area topology.

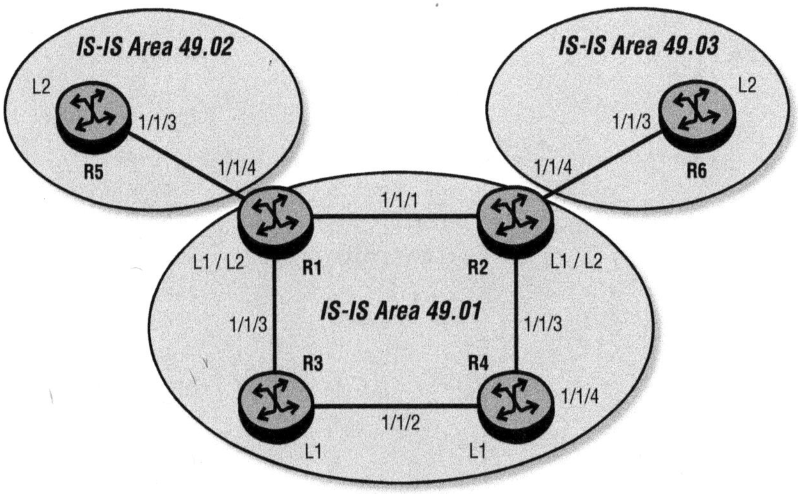

Validation You will know you have succeeded if the IS-IS adjacencies between the routers are up and all the routers have routes to all of the network destinations.

1. Configure IS-IS Area `49.01` as shown in Figure 9.9. Throughout this lab, configure all interfaces as point-to-point. Be sure to configure R3 and R4 as Level 1 routers and R1 and R2 as Level 1/2 routers, and make sure that each router advertises its system interface into IS-IS. If you have just finished a previous lab, part of this configuration may already be done.
    a. Add each router's system interface to IS-IS so that every router in the area is aware of it.
    b. Configure each router to use wide metrics and a reference bandwidth so that IS-IS computes link metrics the same way as OSPF.
    c. How do R1's LSDB and route table compare to R2's LSDB and route table? Explain.
    d. How do R1's LSDB and route table compare to R3's LSDB and route table? Explain.
2. Configure R5 in IS-IS Area `49.02` as an L1 router. Enable wide metrics on R5 with the same configuration as R1–R4, and include its system interface in IS-IS.
    a. Complete the corresponding configuration on R1.
    b. Is the IS-IS adjacency up? Explain.
    c. Configure R5 as an L1/L2 router.
    d. How many IS-IS adjacencies are there between R1 and R5? Explain.
    e. Configure R5 as an L2 router. How many IS-IS adjacencies between R1 and R5 are up?
    f. How many LSPs are in R5's LSDB? Explain.
    g. How do R5's LSDB and route table compare to R1's LSDB and route table?
    h. How do R5's LSDB and route table compare to R3's LSDB and route table?
    i. How have R3's LSPs changed after R5 was configured in IS-IS Area `49.02`?
3. Configure R6 in IS-IS Area `49.03` as an L2 router. Enable wide metrics on R6 with the same configuration as R1–R5. In addition, complete the corresponding configuration on R2.
    a. Verify that the adjacency is up before proceeding.

b. How do R6's LSDB and route table compare to R5's LSDB and route table? Explain.
c. Can R6 ping R2's system interface?
d. Can R6 ping R5's system interface?
e. Can R6 ping R4's system interface?

Lab Section 9.2: Configuring IS-IS Route Summarization

Route summarization is used in conjunction with a multi-area IS-IS design to reduce the size of the database and simplify the SPF calculations. In this and the following exercises, you will configure loopback addresses to simulate other networks that might be connected to the router. Normally you may not have much cause to use loopbacks, but they are useful in this case to simulate other networks to observe how they are handled by the routing protocol.

Objective In this exercise, you will configure route summarization so that routers in IS-IS Areas `49.02` and `49.03` are only aware of summary routes to networks advertised by R3.

Validation You will know you have succeeded if routers outside Area `49.01` only contain summary routes for the specified networks but can still reach all destinations.

1. Configure R3 with three loopback addresses, `192.168.3.1/32`, `192.168.3.2/32`, and `192.168.3.3/32`, and advertise the routes in IS-IS.
   a. Are the loopback routes advertised to the other routers in Area `49.01`? If so, what type of LSP is used to propagate the routes?
   b. Are the routes advertised to the other routers in Areas `49.02` and `49.03`? If so, what type of LSP is used to propagate the routes to those areas? Explain.
2. Configure R1 to summarize R3's loopback interfaces as `192.168.3.0/24`.
   a. Verify that R1's L2 LSP only contains a summary address of `192.168.3.0/24`.
   b. How has the route table of R1 changed? Explain.
   c. How has the route table of R5 changed? Explain.
   d. Configure the network so that R5 is only aware of a single summarized route to `192.168.3.0/24`.
   e. Ping `192.168.3.3` from R5. Does the ping work? Explain.

Lab Section 9.3: Configuring IS-IS Route Redistribution and Route Tagging

Routes that were not learned through IS-IS can be exported into the IS-IS routing domain. Known as *route redistribution*, this process allows other routers in the IS-IS domain to learn the external routes. You will simulate the external routes using loopback addresses.

Objective In this exercise, you will configure route redistribution in Area `49.02` and observe how external routes are propagated to the other IS-IS areas.

Validation You will know you have succeeded if the external routes are propagated as expected to other routers in the topology.

1. Configure three loopback interfaces on R5: `192.168.5.1/32`, `192.168.5.2/32`, and `192.168.5.3/32`. Use a policy to redistribute these loopback interfaces into IS-IS.
   a. Describe the LSPs used to propagate the loopback routes in Area `49.02`.
   b. Are these routes learned in Areas `49.01` and `49.03`? If so, describe the LSPs used to propagate the routes and which routers originate them.
2. Configure a route tag on the loopback interfaces on R5.
   a. How is the route tag information propagated in the LSPs?

Lab Section 9.4: Configuring IS-IS Route Leaking

In some cases, it may be desirable to leak L2 routes to L1 routers to avoid asymmetrical or suboptimal routing.

Objective In this exercise, you will configure metrics in the network in a way that illustrates asymmetrical or suboptimal routing and then use route leaking to change the forwarding behavior. The network used is shown in Figure 9.10.

Validation You will know you have succeeded if the forwarding path of traffic changes after route leaking is configured.

1. For the purposes of this exercise, adjust the metrics on the links R1–R2, R1–R5, and R2–R6 to be 200. (*Hint:* Be sure to change the L1 and L2 metrics on routers that have an L1/L2 adjacency.)
   a. On R4, perform a `traceroute` to R5's loopback interface `192.168.5.1`. What path does traffic between R4 and R5 take? Is this the most optimal route?
   b. On R5, perform a `traceroute` to R4's system interface. What path does traffic between R5 and R4 take? Is this the most optimal route?

Figure 9.10 Asymmetric routing.

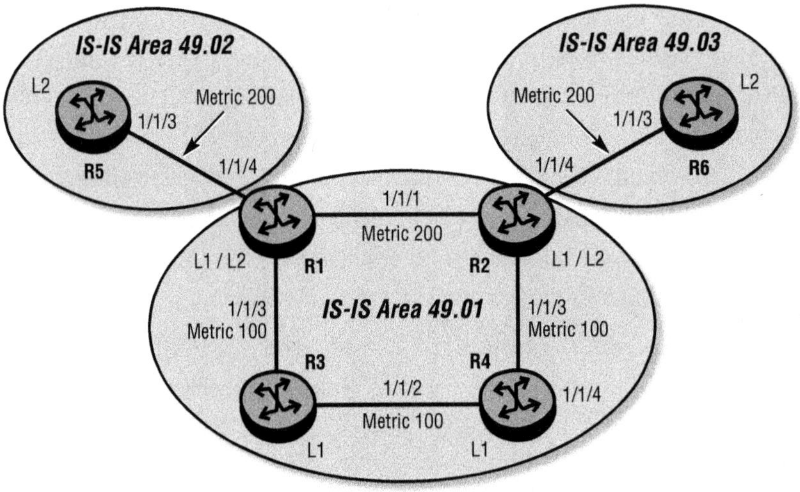

2. Configure route leaking to avoid asymmetrical routing in the network for R5's loopback interfaces only. Make use of the Admin Tag that was configured in the previous section.
   a. Which routers need to be configured with route leaking? Explain.
   b. What path does R4 now use to reach R5's loopback address?
   c. How has the route table on R4 changed?
   d. Has the configuration fixed the asymmetrical routing problem for all prefixes in the network? Explain.
   e. Configure route leaking to avoid asymmetrical routing for all prefixes in the network.

Chapter Review

Now that you have completed this chapter, you should be able to:

- Describe the advantage of splitting an IS-IS network into multiple areas.
- Explain the problem of suboptimal routing in a hierarchical network.
- Describe how IS-IS uses Level 1 and Level 2 topologies to implement hierarchy.
- Describe and compare the contents of L1 and L2 LSPs.
- Explain the purpose of the ATT bit.
- Configure Alcatel-Lucent 7750 SRs to operate in an IS-IS multi-area network.
- Configure a 7750 SR for summarization in an IS-IS network.
- Configure route leaking for IS-IS on a 7750 SR.
- Configure a policy to export external routes to IS-IS.
- Use route tags to control route leaking in IS-IS.

Post-Assessment

The following questions will test your knowledge and prepare you for the Alcatel-Lucent NRS II Certification Exam. Compare your responses with the answers listed in Appendix A. You can also use the CD that accompanies this book to take all the assessment tests and review the answers.

1. Which of the following best describes the implementation of hierarchy in IS-IS?
   - **A.** L1 routers perform the SPF calculation over their local area. L2 routers connect to L1 routers in different areas and exchange routes between the different areas.
   - **B.** L1 routers perform the SPF calculation over their local area. L2 routers perform the SPF calculation over the L2 topology and route between the different areas.
   - **C.** L1 routers exchange routes only with other L1 routers. L2 routers exchange routes only with other L2 routers.
   - **D.** L1 routers route only in their own area. L2 routers create tunnels between different areas.

2. What is the most likely cause of asymmetric routing in a multi-area IS-IS network?
   - **A.** Asymmetric routing can occur because L1 routers can only forward traffic to other L1 routers and L2 routers can only forward traffic to other L2 routers.
   - **B.** In an IS-IS multi-area network, all traffic between areas must pass through the backbone area.
   - **C.** A prefix learned from an L1 LSP is preferred over one learned from an L2 LSP even if it is not the most direct route.
   - **D.** A prefix learned from an L2 LSP is preferred over one learned from an L1 LSP even if it is not the most direct route.
   - **E.** L1 routers only have a default route to an L1/L2 router, which may not be the most direct route to the destination.

3. Which of the following best describes the advantage of using summarization?
   - **A.** Summarization provides more accurate routing information to routers outside the area.
   - **B.** Summarization simplifies the configuration required on the L2 routers.
   - **C.** Summarization eliminates the possibility of asymmetric routing and suboptimal routing.
   - **D.** Summarization reduces the size of the LSP and of the route table of routers outside the area.
   - **E.** Summarization is not supported in IS-IS because it was not designed as an IP routing protocol.

4. Which of the following statements best describes route leaking in IS-IS?
   - **A.** Route leaking allows prefixes from outside an L1 area to be known inside the area.
   - **B.** Route leaking reduces the number of routes in the route table by replacing a group of prefixes with one less specific prefix.
   - **C.** Route leaking allows prefixes from outside the IS-IS routing domain to be known in the IS-IS domain.
   - **D.** Route leaking allows prefixes from the IS-IS routing domain to be advertised in another routing protocol such as BGP.

5. What is the likely result if there is a break in the L2 backbone?
   - **A.** Some destinations in the network will be unreachable.
   - **B.** Some routes will have an asymmetric path.
   - **C.** Some routes will not take the most optimal path.
   - **D.** The network will take longer to converge after a topology change.
   - **E.** All of the above conditions are likely to occur.

6. Which of the following best describes the purpose of hierarchy in an IS-IS network?
   - **A.** Hierarchy improves the efficiency of packet forwarding through the network.
   - **B.** Hierarchy eliminates the possibility of asymmetric routing in the network.
   - **C.** Hierarchy simplifies the configuration and troubleshooting of routers.
   - **D.** Hierarchy is required in order to implement traffic engineering.
   - **E.** None of the above statements describes the purpose of hierarchy in IS-IS.

7. Which of the following statements is false?
   A. The L1 LSDB is the same for all L1 and L1/L2 routers in the same area.
   B. The L2 LSDB is the same for all L1/L2 and L2 routers in the network.
   C. An L1/L2 router has one LSDB with both L1 and L2 LSPs.
   D. An L1/L2 router has both an L1 and an L2 LSDB.
   E. Both A and B are false.

8. The command `summary-address 192.0.2.0/24 level-2` is used on an L1/L2 router to summarize several `/28` prefixes in the area. Which of the following statements is false?
   A. The L2 LSP originated by the router will contain only the summarized prefix.
   B. The L1 LSP originated by the router will contain a black-hole prefix for the summarized prefix.
   C. The individual prefixes will be seen in the L1 LSDB for the area.
   D. The router will have a black-hole entry in its route table for the summary prefix.
   E. All of the above statements are true.

9. IS-IS routes are being leaked into an L1 area, and the network operator does not want to have the default route used in the area. Where does the operator configure `suppress-default` to accomplish this?
   A. The command is configured on any L1/L2 router that is leaking routes into the area.
   B. The command is configured on all L1/L2 or L2 routers in the area.
   C. The command is configured on all L1/L2 or L2 routers in the IS-IS routing domain.
   D. The command is configured on all L1 routers in the area.
   E. The command is configured on all routers in the area.

10. Which of the following statements about IS-IS export policies is false?

A. By default, an IS-IS router only advertises interfaces that are defined in IS-IS.

B. An export policy must be applied in IS-IS to advertise routes from another routing domain.

C. By default, routes exported to IS-IS from another routing protocol are always advertised in the L2 LSP only.

D. The metric for the route can be set in the export policy.

E. All of the above statements are true.

11. Which of the following statements about route tags is incorrect?

A. A route tag can be assigned on an IS-IS interface.

B. A route tag can be assigned on an IS-IS summary address.

C. A route tag can be assigned in a route leaking policy.

D. A route tag can be used in a policy to control route leaking.

E. All of the above statements are correct.

12. Router R1 learns a route to `10.10.0.0/20` with next-hop R2 from OSPF, a route to `10.10.10.0/24` with next-hop R3 from an L1 LSP, and a route to `10.10.10.0/24` with next-hop R4 from an L2 LSP, and has a static route to `10.10.0.0/16` with next-hop R5. What will be the next-hop for a packet destined to `10.10.10.10`?

A. The next-hop is R2.

B. The next-hop is R3.

C. The next-hop is R4.

D. The next-hop is R5.

E. The packet is discarded.

13. Which of the following statements is false?

    A. Routing in an IS-IS L1 area is similar to routing in an OSPF stub area with no summaries.

    B. Routing in a normal OSPF area is similar to routing in an IS-IS L1 area with all of the L2 routes leaked by the L1/L2 routers in the area.

    C. The IS-IS routing protocol is more likely to create asymmetric routes than OSPF.

    D. IS-IS can be configured to calculate the interface bandwidth the same way as OSPF.

    E. All of the above statements are true.

14. Which of the following statements is false?

    A. An L1 router forms adjacencies with all neighbors in the same area.

    B. An L2 router forms adjacencies with all neighbors regardless of area.

    C. An L1/L2 router forms adjacencies only with other L1 and L1/L2 neighbors in the same area.

    D. Answers A–C are true.

    E. Answers A–C are false.

15. Which of the following best describes the use of the ATT bit in IS-IS?

    A. The ATT bit indicates that the router is in the overload state.

    B. The ATT bit is set by a router to indicate that it is configured for route leaking.

    C. The ATT bit is set by a router that is exporting external routes to IS-IS.

    D. The ATT bit is set by an L1/L2 router to indicate that it can be used for a default route by L1 routers in the area.

10 IS-IS for IPv6

The Alcatel-Lucent NRS II exam topics covered in this chapter include the following:

- IPv6 TLVs for IS-IS
- Multi-topology IS-IS
- Multi-area IS-IS for IPv6

This chapter describes the implementation of IS-IS (Intermediate System to Intermediate System) for IPv6 on the Alcatel-Lucent 7750 SR. Additional TLVs (type–length–values) have been defined to support IPv6. These can be used together with IPv4 to implement a mixed network of IPv4 and IPv6 routing, but it is usually desirable to treat the IPv6 network as separate from the IPv4 network. This is handled by additional extensions to IS-IS to support multi-topology (MT) operation. MT configuration and operation are also described in this chapter. Finally, multi-area operation for IPv6 is examined.

Pre-Assessment

The following assessment questions will help you understand what areas of the chapter you should review in more detail to prepare for the NRS II exam. You can also use the CD that accompanies this book to take all the assessment tests and review the answers.

1. Which of the following statements about the operation of IS-IS for IPv6 is false?
   - **A.** Two separate instances of IS-IS must operate on the router in order to support both IPv4 and IPv6 routing.
   - **B.** Operating with IPv4 and IPv6 in a single routing topology could lead to holes in either IPv4 or IPv6 routing.
   - **C.** IS-IS can be configured to exchange IPv6 routes with OSPFv3.
   - **D.** IS-IS can operate on the Alcatel-Lucent 7750 SR with a mix of IPv4 and IPv6 interfaces.
   - **E.** All of the above statements are true.

2. The complete output of the `show router isis database detail level 2` command is shown below. Which of the following statements about router R1 is true?

```
Displaying Level 2 database
-------------------------------------------------------------------------
LSP ID     : R1.00-00                                 Level      : L2
Sequence   : 0xae7                Checksum  : 0x4a18   Lifetime   : 1014
Version    : 1                    Pkt Type  : 20       Pkt Ver    : 1
Attributes: L1L2                  Max Area  : 3
```

```
SysID Len : 6                    Used Len  : 81      Alloc Len : 1492

TLVs :
  Area Addresses:
    Area Address : (1) 49
  Supp Protocols:
    Protocols     : IPv4
    Protocols     : IPv6
  MT Topology:
    MT ID           : 0                    No Flags
    MT ID           : 2                    No Flags
  IS-Hostname   : R1
  Router ID   :
    Router ID   : 10.10.10.1
  I/F Addresses :
    I/F Address   : 10.10.10.1
    I/F Address   : 10.1.2.1
  TE IP Reach   :
    Default Metric  : 0
    Control Info:     , prefLen 32
    Prefix   : 10.10.10.1
    Default Metric  : 10
    Control Info:     , prefLen 27
    Prefix   : 10.1.2.0

Level (2) LSP Count : 1
=======================================================================
```

A. The router is configured for IPv4 operation only.

B. The router is configured for IPv6 operation only.

C. The router is configured for single-topology IPv4 and IPv6.

D. The router is configured for multi-topology IPv4 and IPv6.

E. There is not enough information to select from the above statements.

3. Given the following extract from the `show router isis database` command, what is the most likely IPv6 system address for router R1?

```
Displaying Level 2 database
-----------------------------------------------------------------------
LSP ID    : R1.00-00                                   Level     : L2

TLVs :
  Supp Protocols:
    Protocols      : IPv4
    Protocols      : IPv6
  I/F Addresses :
    I/F Address    : 10.10.10.1
    I/F Address    : 10.1.2.1
    I/F Address    : 10.1.3.1
  I/F Addresses IPv6 :
    IPv6 Address     : 2001:DB8::1
    IPv6 Address     : 2001:DB8::12:0:0:0:1
  TE IP Reach    :
    Default Metric  : 0
    Control Info:     , prefLen 32
    Prefix    : 10.10.10.1
    Default Metric  : 100
    Control Info:     , prefLen 27
    Prefix    : 10.1.2.0
    Default Metric  : 100
    Control Info:     , prefLen 27
    Prefix    : 10.1.3.0
  IPv6 Reach:
    Metric: ( I ) 0
    Prefix    : 2001:DB8::1/128
    Metric: ( I ) 100
    Prefix    : 2001:DB8::12:0:0:0:0/64
```

A. `2001:DB8::1`

B. `2001:DB8::12:0:0:0:1`

C. An IPv6 address is not assigned to the system interface.

D. It is not possible to tell which is the system address.

E. IPv6 is not enabled on the router.

4. Which of the following best describes how multi-topology capabilities are implemented in IS-IS?
   - **A.** No changes are required to the protocol. The IS-IS process on the router is enhanced to support multi-topologies.
   - **B.** The existing TLVs are used with an additional sub-TLV added to indicate the topology to which it applies.
   - **C.** New TLVs are defined that contain a field identifying the topology to which it applies.
   - **D.** Multiple IS-IS instances are implemented on each router to support each of the topologies.
   - **E.** The Alcatel-Lucent 7750 SR does not support MT IS-IS for IPv6.
5. Which of the following statements about IPv6 for IS-IS on the 7750 SR is false?
   - **A.** Routers can be configured to leak IPv6 prefixes in a similar manner to route leaking for IPv4.
   - **B.** An L1 router creates an IPv6 default route to the nearest L1/L2 router in the IPv6 topology.
   - **C.** Export policies can be configured on routers to bring IPv6 prefixes from other IPv6 routing protocols into IS-IS.
   - **D.** IPv6 global addresses do not necessarily need to be configured on interfaces because routers use the link-local addresses to form their adjacency.
   - **E.** Statements A–D are true.
   - **F.** Statements A–D are false.

10.1 IPv6 in an IS-IS Network

IS-IS was designed as an OSI (Open System Interconnect) routing protocol, not specifically for IP (Internet Protocol) as OSPF (Open Shortest Path First) was. The result is that it is simpler to modify IS-IS for use as an IPv6 routing protocol. RFC 5308 defines two new TLVs to be used for IPv6 routing:

- **IPv6 Reachability TLV** (Type 236)—This TLV carries the prefix and metric information for IPv6 prefixes.
- **IPv6 Interface Address TLV** (Type 232)—This TLV contains up to 15 IPv6 addresses.

IPv6 TLVs for IS-IS

With the addition of the two new TLVs for IPv6, it is possible for IS-IS to support the distribution of IPv6 routing information. However, if the router also supports IPv4, by default the IPv4 and IPv6 information is considered as if it were a single topology. One SPF calculation is performed for all prefixes. Figure 10.1 shows a topology with a combination of IPv4 and IPv6 prefixes. All routers are Level 2.

Figure 10.1 IPv4 and IPv6 network topology.

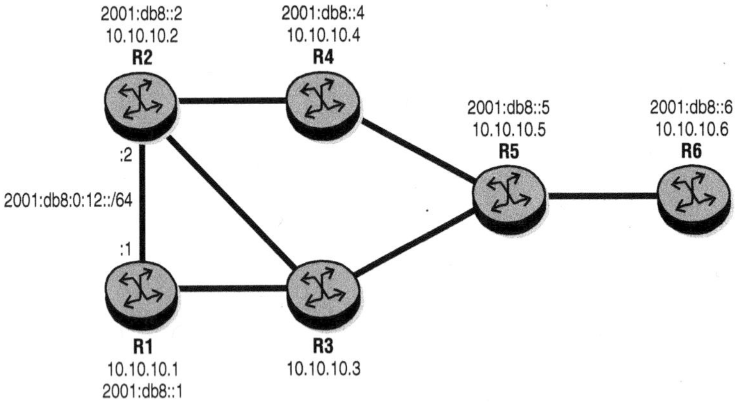

On router R1, the IPv6 interfaces have been created and IPv6 routing has been enabled (see Listing 10.1). IPv6 has been enabled in a similar manner on the other routers in the network except for R3.

Listing 10.1 R1 configured for IPv6

```
*A:R1# configure router isis
*A:R1>config>router>isis# info
----------------------------------------------
        level-capability level-2
        area-id 49.01
        reference-bandwidth 100000000
        ipv6-routing native
        level 2
            wide-metrics-only
        exit
        interface "system"
        exit
        interface "toR2"
            interface-type point-to-point
        exit
        interface "toR3"
            interface-type point-to-point
        exit
----------------------------------------------
```

The IS-IS database does not look much different with the addition of IPv6. If we look at an LSP in detail (see Listing 10.2), we can see that it contains the new IPv6 TLVs for the IPv6 interface addresses and the IPv6 reachability information.

Listing 10.2 LSP containing IPv6 TLVs

```
*A:R1# show router isis database

===============================================================================
ISIS Database
===============================================================================
LSP ID                            Sequence Checksum Lifetime Attributes
-------------------------------------------------------------------------------

Displaying Level 1 database
-------------------------------------------------------------------------------
```

(continued)

Listing 10.2 *(continued)*

```
Level (1) LSP Count : 0

Displaying Level 2 database
-------------------------------------------------------------------------
R1.00-00                          0x68     0xf30d   777      L1L2
R2.00-00                          0x7a     0xd56c   755      L1L2
R3.00-00                          0x67     0xbc36   825      L1L2
R4.00-00                          0x64     0x8ee6   661      L1L2
R5.00-00                          0x35d    0x2b7e   1196     L1L2
R6.00-00                          0x346    0xe42f   1184     L1L2
Level (2) LSP Count : 6
=========================================================================
*A:R1# show router isis database R1.00-00 detail level 2

=========================================================================
ISIS Database
=========================================================================


Displaying Level 2 database
-------------------------------------------------------------------------
LSP ID    : R1.00-00                                  Level     : L2
Sequence  : 0x68                  Checksum  : 0xf30d  Lifetime  : 764
Version   : 1                     Pkt Type  : 20      Pkt Ver   : 1
Attributes: L1L2                  Max Area  : 3
SysID Len : 6                     Used Len  : 211     Alloc Len : 1492

TLVs :
  Area Addresses:
    Area Address : (2) 49.01
  Supp Protocols:
    Protocols     : IPv4
    Protocols     : IPv6
  IS-Hostname   : R1
  Router ID   :
    Router ID   : 10.10.10.1
  I/F Addresses :
    I/F Address   : 10.10.10.1
    I/F Address   : 10.1.2.1
```

```
    I/F Address    : 10.1.3.1
  I/F Addresses IPv6 :
    IPv6 Address     : 2001:DB8::1
    IPv6 Address     : 2001:DB8::12:0:0:0:1
  TE IS Nbrs    :
    Nbr    : R2.00
    Default Metric  : 100
    Sub TLV Len     : 12
    IF Addr    : 10.1.2.1
    Nbr IP     : 10.1.2.2
  TE IS Nbrs    :
    Nbr    : R3.00
    Default Metric  : 100
    Sub TLV Len     : 12
    IF Addr    : 10.1.3.1
    Nbr IP     : 10.1.3.3
  TE IP Reach    :
    Default Metric  : 0
    Control Info:     , prefLen 32
    Prefix    : 10.10.10.1
    Default Metric  : 100
    Control Info:     , prefLen 27
    Prefix    : 10.1.2.0
    Default Metric  : 100
    Control Info:     , prefLen 27
    Prefix    : 10.1.3.0
  IPv6 Reach:
    Metric: ( I ) 0
    Prefix    : 2001:DB8::1/128
    Metric: ( I ) 100
    Prefix    : 2001:DB8::12:0:0:0:0/64

Level (2) LSP Count : 1
===============================================================================
```

When IS-IS is configured for native IPv6 routing, IPv6 and IPv4 are considered as a single topology with both types of prefixes. If the IPv6 and IPv4 topologies are not congruent—if they are actually different—routing holes may occur. For example, in Figure 10.1, R3 is not configured for IPv6. Although there is a valid route from R1 to

R5, the SPF (shortest path first) algorithm selects the route through R3 that is not valid for IPv6. R1 does not have an IPv6 route to R3, R5, or R6 (see Listing 10.3).

Listing 10.3 Hole in IPv6 routing

```
*A:R1>config>router>isis# show router route-table ipv6

===============================================================================
IPv6 Route Table (Router: Base)
===============================================================================
Dest Prefix                              Type     Proto    Age          Pref
       Next Hop[Interface Name]                                Metric
-------------------------------------------------------------------------------
2001:DB8::1/128                          Local    Local    00h51m29s    0
       system                                                  0
2001:DB8::2/128                          Remote   ISIS     00h10m56s    18
       FE80::203:FAFF:FE0E:9332-"toR2"                          100
2001:DB8::4/128                          Remote   ISIS     00h10m51s    18
       FE80::203:FAFF:FE0E:9332-"toR2"                          200
2001:DB8::12:0:0:0:0/64                  Local    Local    00h51m01s    0
       toR2                                                    0
-------------------------------------------------------------------------------
No. of Routes: 4
===============================================================================
```

In most cases, it is desirable to treat the IPv6 network as a completely separate topology from the IPv4 topology. Because OSPFv3 is implemented on the Alcatel-Lucent 7750 SR completely separately from the IPv4 version of OSPFv2, IPv4 and IPv6 are separate. Multiple topologies for IS-IS are also supported on the 7750 SR as described in the next section.

Multi-Topology IS-IS

RFC 5120 describes extensions to IS-IS to support multi-topology (MT) routing. This enables the use of one routing protocol instance to support multiple, distinct topologies. This could be used to implement distinct IPv4 and IPv6 routing topologies, distinct unicast and multicast routing topologies, or even distinct IPv4 routing topologies. When a router implements MT routing, it maintains a separate Routing Information Base (RIB) for each of the topologies.

Several TLVs are defined for multi-topology routing. These additions are required to specify an MT ID that identifies to which topology the prefix belongs. The four new TLVs defined in RFC 5120 are the following:

- **MT TLV** (Type 229)—Is used in Hello messages and LSPs to identify the supported topologies.
- **MT Intermediate System TLV** (Type 222)—Similar to the Extended IS Reachability TLV (Type 22), this TLV identifies IS neighbors. There are an extra 2 bytes at the start of the TLV to identify the MT.
- **MT Reachable IPv4 Prefixes TLV** (Type 235)—Similar to the Extended IP Reachability TLV (Type 135), this TLV identifies IPv4 prefixes. There are an extra 2 bytes at the start of the TLV to identify the MT.
- **MT Reachable IPv6 Prefixes TLV** (Type 237)—Similar to the IPv6 Reachability TLV (Type 236), this TLV identifies IPv6 prefixes. There are an extra 2 bytes at the start of the TLV to identify the MT.

The MT TLV in Figure 10.2 is composed of up to 127 MT identifiers, each one 2 bytes long. The first 4 bits are flags, followed by the MT ID:

Figure 10.2 Multi-topology (MT) TLV.

O	A	R	R	Multi-Topology ID (12 bits)

- **O**—Indicates whether the overload bit is set for this topology.
- **A**—Indicates whether the ATT bit is set for this topology.
- **R**—Third and fourth bits are reserved and should be set to zero.
- **MT ID**—12 bits that identify the specific multi-topology.

RFC 5120 defines specific values for MT IDs, listed in Table 10.1.

Table 10.1 Values for MT ID

MT ID	Purpose
0	"Standard" topology (IPv4)
1	IPv4 in-band management
2	IPv6 routing
3	IPv4 multicast routing
4	IPv6 multicast routing

(continued)

Table 10.1 *(continued)*

MT ID	Purpose
5	IPv6 in-band management
6–3995	Reserved for IETF
3996–4095	Reserved for experimental and proprietary use

If a router does not include the MT TLV in its Hello and LSPs, it should be included in topology 0.

To use MT IS-IS, two commands are required in the `configure router isis` context (see Listing 10.4):

- `ipv6-routing mt`

  and

- `multi-topology ipv6-unicast`

Listing 10.4 Configuration of R1 for MT IS-IS

```
*A:R1# configure router isis
*A:R1>config>router>isis# info
----------------------------------------------
        level-capability level-2
        area-id 49.01
        reference-bandwidth 100000000
        ipv6-routing mt
        multi-topology
            ipv6-unicast
        exit
        level 2
            wide-metrics-only
        exit
        interface "system"
        exit
        interface "toR2"
            interface-type point-to-point
        exit
        interface "toR3"
            interface-type point-to-point
        exit
----------------------------------------------
```

After enabling MT IS-IS, the LSP contains the MT TLVs described above as shown in Listing 10.5:

- **MT Topology**—Shows that two topologies are supported on this router, 0 and 2.
- **MT IS Nbrs**—Shows the IS neighbors for topology 2 (IPv6). Note that only one neighbor is shown (R2), because R3 is not enabled for IPv6.
- **MT IPv6 Reach**—Shows the IPv6 reachability prefixes for topology 2.

Listing 10.5 LSP containing MT TLVs

```
*A:R1# show router isis database R1.00-00 detail level 2

===============================================================================
ISIS Database
===============================================================================

Displaying Level 2 database
-------------------------------------------------------------------------------
LSP ID    : R1.00-00                                   Level     : L2
Sequence  : 0x22                  Checksum  : 0x6b84   Lifetime  : 1094
Version   : 1                     Pkt Type  : 20       Pkt Ver   : 1
Attributes: L1L2                  Max Area  : 3
SysID Len : 6                     Used Len  : 234      Alloc Len : 1492

TLVs :
  Area Addresses:
    Area Address : (2) 49.01
  Supp Protocols:
    Protocols     : IPv4
    Protocols     : IPv6
  MT Topology:
    MT ID          : 0                      No Flags
    MT ID          : 2                      No Flags
  IS-Hostname    : R1
  Router ID    :
    Router ID    : 10.10.10.1
  I/F Addresses :
    I/F Address    : 10.10.10.1
    I/F Address    : 10.1.2.1
   I/F Address    : 10.1.3.1
```

(continued)

Listing 10.5 *(continued)*

```
  I/F Addresses IPv6 :
    IPv6 Address    : 2001:DB8::1
    IPv6 Address    : 2001:DB8::12:0:0:0:1
  TE IS Nbrs   :
    Nbr   : R2.00
    Default Metric  : 100
    Sub TLV Len     : 12
    IF Addr   : 10.1.2.1
    Nbr IP    : 10.1.2.2
  MT IS Nbrs     :
    MT ID           : 2
    Nbr   : R2.00
    Default Metric  : 100
    Sub TLV Len     : 0
  TE IS Nbrs   :
    Nbr   : R3.00
    Default Metric  : 100
    Sub TLV Len     : 12
    IF Addr   : 10.1.3.1
    Nbr IP    : 10.1.3.3
  TE IP Reach   :
    Default Metric  : 0
    Control Info:    , prefLen 32
    Prefix   : 10.10.10.1
    Default Metric  : 100
    Control Info:    , prefLen 27
    Prefix   : 10.1.2.0
    Default Metric  : 100
    Control Info:    , prefLen 27
    Prefix   : 10.1.3.0
  MT IPv6 Reach.  :
    MT ID           : 2
    Metric: ( I ) 0
    Prefix   : 2001:DB8::1/128
    Metric: ( I ) 100
    Prefix   : 2001:DB8::12:0:0:0:0/64

Level (2) LSP Count : 1
===============================================================================
```

In Figure 10.1, router R3 is not configured as an IPv6 router. When IPv6 is considered as a distinct topology with a separate SPF calculation, there is a route from R1 to routers R5 and R6, as shown in Listing 10.6.

Listing 10.6 R1 has routes to R5 and R6 in the IPv6 topology.

```
*A:R1# show router route-table ipv6

===============================================================================
IPv6 Route Table (Router: Base)
===============================================================================
Dest Prefix                                  Type    Proto    Age         Pref
       Next Hop[Interface Name]                                    Metric
-------------------------------------------------------------------------------
2001:DB8::1/128                              Local   Local    01h45m03s   0
       system                                                      0
2001:DB8::2/128                              Remote  ISIS     00h26m11s   18
       FE80::203:FAFF:FE0E:9332-"toR2"                             100
2001:DB8::4/128                              Remote  ISIS     00h26m03s   18
       FE80::203:FAFF:FE0E:9332-"toR2"                             200
2001:DB8::5/128                              Remote  ISIS     00h26m03s   18
       FE80::203:FAFF:FE0E:9332-"toR2"                             300
2001:DB8::6/128                              Remote  ISIS     00h26m03s   18
       FE80::203:FAFF:FE0E:9332-"toR2"                             400
2001:DB8::12:0:0:0:0/64                      Local   Local    01h44m35s   0
       toR2                                                           0
-------------------------------------------------------------------------------
No. of Routes: 6
===============================================================================
*A:R1# ping 2001:DB8::5 count 1
PING 2001:DB8::5 56 data bytes
64 bytes from 2001:DB8::5 icmp_seq=1 hlim=62 time=2.93ms.

---- 2001:DB8::5 PING Statistics ----
1 packet transmitted, 1 packet received, 0.00% packet loss
round-trip min = 2.93ms, avg = 2.93ms, max = 2.93ms, stddev = 0.000ms
```

Multi-Area IS-IS for IPv6

Implementing IPv6 in an IS-IS multi-area network is no different from IPv4. Routing is segregated into Level 1 and Level 2 topologies as shown in Figure 10.3.

Figure 10.3 Multi-area IS-IS topology with IPv6.

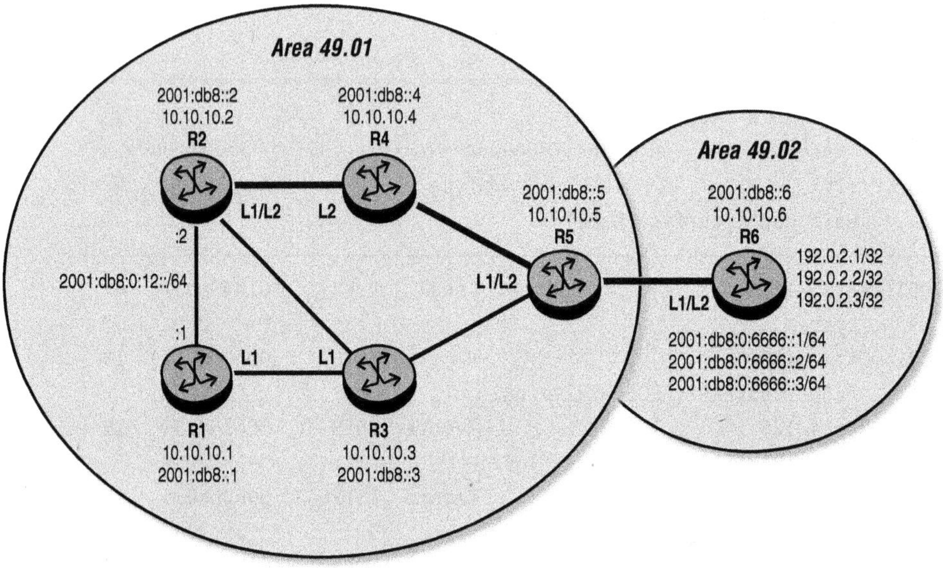

Listing 10.7 shows R6 configured with three loopback addresses in IS-IS that are summarized in Level 2.

Listing 10.7 Summarization of IPv6 routes on R6

```
*A:R6# configure router isis
*A:R6>config>router>isis# info
----------------------------------------------
        area-id 49.02
        reference-bandwidth 100000000
        ipv6-routing mt
        multi-topology
            ipv6-unicast
        exit
        summary-address 192.0.2.0/24 level-2
        summary-address 2001:DB8::6666:0:0:0:0/64 level-2
```

```
        level 1
            wide-metrics-only
        exit
        level 2
            wide-metrics-only
        exit
        interface "system"
        exit
        interface "toR5"
            interface-type point-to-point
        exit
        interface "loop1"
        exit
        interface "loop2"
        exit
        interface "loop3"
        exit
----------------------------------------------
*A:R6>config>router>isis# show router route-table ipv6

========================================================================
IPv6 Route Table (Router: Base)
========================================================================
Dest Prefix                             Type    Proto    Age         Pref
       Next Hop[Interface Name]                               Metric
------------------------------------------------------------------------
2001:DB8::1/128                         Remote  ISIS     12h23m44s   18
       FE80::216:4DFF:FE13:5CB0-"toR5"                         300
2001:DB8::2/128                         Remote  ISIS     12h27m17s   18
       FE80::216:4DFF:FE13:5CB0-"toR5"                         300
2001:DB8::3/128                         Remote  ISIS     12h23m44s   18
       FE80::216:4DFF:FE13:5CB0-"toR5"                         200
2001:DB8::4/128                         Remote  ISIS     12h27m17s   18
       FE80::216:4DFF:FE13:5CB0-"toR5"                         200
2001:DB8::5/128                         Remote  ISIS     12h27m20s   18
       FE80::216:4DFF:FE13:5CB0-"toR5"                         100
2001:DB8::6/128                         Local   Local    01d14h18m   0
       system                                                 0
2001:DB8::12:0:0:0:0/64                 Remote  ISIS     12h27m17s   18
```

(continued)

Listing 10.7 *(continued)*

```
       FE80::216:4DFF:FE13:5CB0-"toR5"                       400
2001:DB8::6666:0:0:0:0/64             Remote  ISIS      00h09m40s   255
       Black Hole                                            1
2001:DB8::6666:0:0:0:1/128            Local   Local     12h12m36s   0
       loop1                                                 0
2001:DB8::6666:0:0:0:2/128            Local   Local     12h12m27s   0
       loop2                                                 0
2001:DB8::6666:0:0:0:3/128            Local   Local     12h12m19s   0
       loop3                                                        0
-------------------------------------------------------------------------
No. of Routes: 11
=========================================================================
```

R5 is configured with a policy to leak Level 2 routes into Level 1 (see Listing 10.8).

Listing 10.8 Route leaking configured on R5

```
*A:R5# configure router isis
*A:R5>config>router>isis# info
----------------------------------------------
        area-id 49.01
        export "route-leak"
        reference-bandwidth 100000000
        ipv6-routing mt
        multi-topology
            ipv6-unicast
        exit
        level 1
            wide-metrics-only
        exit
        level 2
            wide-metrics-only
        exit
        interface "system"
            interface-type point-to-point
        exit
        interface "toR3"
            interface-type point-to-point
```

```
        exit
        interface "toR4"
            interface-type point-to-point
        exit
        interface "toR6"
            interface-type point-to-point
        exit
----------------------------------------------
*A:R5>config>router>isis# show router policy "route-leak"
    entry 10
        from
            level 2
        exit
        to
            level 1
        exit
        action accept
        exit
    exit
```

As expected, the summarized route is seen on router R1 (see Listing 10.9). Note that R1 also has a default route, as expected.

Listing 10.9 IPv6 route table on R1

```
*A:R1# show router route-table ipv6

========================================================================
IPv6 Route Table (Router: Base)
========================================================================
Dest Prefix                          Type    Proto    Age         Pref
       Next Hop[Interface Name]                             Metric
------------------------------------------------------------------------
::/0                                 Remote  ISIS     12h31m59s   15
       FE80::203:FAFF:FE0E:9332-"toR2"                        100
2001:DB8::1/128                      Local   Local    14h21m47s   0
       system                                         0
2001:DB8::2/128                      Remote  ISIS     12h31m59s   15
```

(continued)

Listing 10.9 *(continued)*

```
        FE80::203:FAFF:FE0E:9332-"toR2"                         100
2001:DB8::3/128                          Remote   ISIS      12h30m19s    15
        FE80::203:FAFF:FEAC:B826-"toR3"                         100
2001:DB8::4/128                          Remote   ISIS      12h26m07s    15
        FE80::203:FAFF:FE0E:9332-"toR2"                         200
2001:DB8::5/128                          Remote   ISIS      12h30m19s    15
        FE80::203:FAFF:FEAC:B826-"toR3"                         200
2001:DB8::6/128                          Remote   ISIS      00h43m25s    15
        FE80::203:FAFF:FEAC:B826-"toR3"                         300
2001:DB8::12:0:0:0:0/64                  Local    Local     14h21m20s    0
        toR2                                          0
2001:DB8::6666:0:0:0:0/64                Remote   ISIS      00h16m04s    15
        FE80::203:FAFF:FEAC:B826-"toR3"                         300
-------------------------------------------------------------------------------
No. of Routes: 9
===============================================================================
```

Practice Lab: IS-IS for IPv6

The following lab is designed to reinforce your knowledge of the content in this chapter. Please review the instructions carefully, and perform the steps in the order in which they are presented. The practice labs require that you have access to six or more Alcatel-Lucent 7750 SRs or Alcatel-Lucent 7450 ESSs in a non-production environment.

These labs are designed to be used in a controlled lab environment. Please *do not* attempt to perform these labs in a production environment.

Lab Section 10.1: Configuring Multi-Area IS-IS for IPv6

IS-IS was designed as an OSI routing protocol and not specifically for IP as OSPF was. The result is that it is simpler to modify IS-IS for use as an IPv6 routing protocol. This lab repeats some of the same steps as the Chapter 9 lab but uses IPv6 rather than IPv4. For a more detailed investigation of IS-IS, it is recommended that you complete the Chapter 9 lab before this lab.

Objective In this exercise, you will configure a topology of six Alcatel-Lucent 7750 SRs with three IS-IS areas as shown in Figure 10.4.

Figure 10.4 Multi-area IS-IS topology for IPv6.

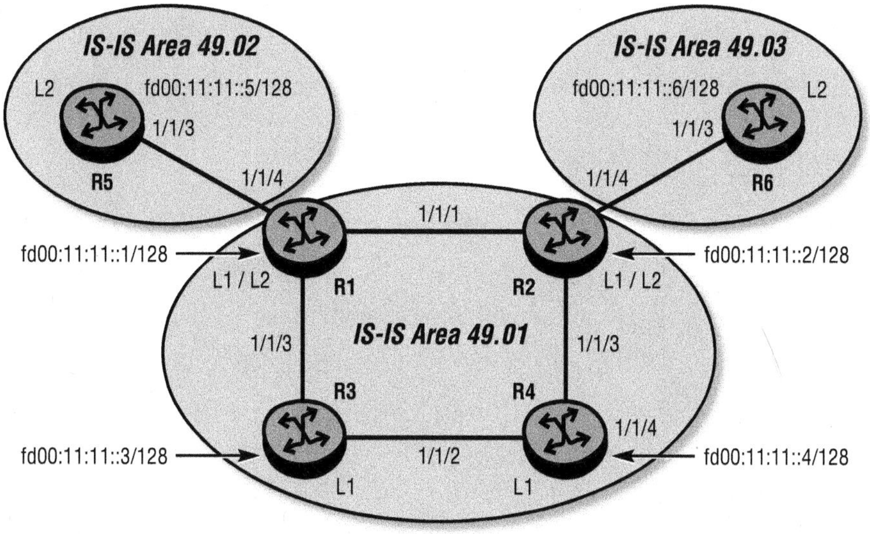

Validation You will know you have succeeded if the IS-IS adjacencies between the routers are up and all the routers have routes to all the network destinations.

1. Configure IS-IS area 49.01 as shown in Figure 10.4. Throughout this lab, configure IS-IS interfaces as point-to-point, and use IPv6 link-local addresses for all network interfaces. Configure R3 and R4 as Level 1 routers and R1 and R2 as Level 1/2 routers, and make sure that each router advertises its IPv6 system interface in IS-IS. If you have just finished the Chapter 9 lab, much of this configuration will be completed, but be sure to remove any export policies, explicit metrics, and interfaces to Areas `49.02` and `49.03`.

   a. Configure each router's system interface in IS-IS so that every router in the area is aware of it.

   b. Configure each router to use wide metrics and a reference bandwidth so that IS-IS computes link metrics the same way as OSPF.

   c. Ensure that the IPv6 network is treated as a completely separate topology from the IPv4 topology.

   d. How do R1's LSDB and IPv6 route table compare with R3's LSDB and route table? Explain.

2. Configure R5 into IS-IS Area `49.02` as an L2 router. Enable wide metrics on R5 with the same configuration as R1–R4, and include its system interface in IS-IS.

   a. Complete the corresponding configuration on R1.

   b. Ensure that the IPv6 network is treated as a completely separate topology from the IPv4 topology.

   c. How many LSPs are in R5's LSDB? Explain.

   d. How do R5's LSDB and IPv6 route table compare with R1's LSDB and IPv6 route table?

   e. How do R5's LSDB and route table compare with R3's LSDB and route table?

   f. How have R3's LSPs changed after R5 was configured in IS-IS Area `49.02`?

3. Configure R6 in IS-IS Area `49.03` as an L2 router. Enable wide metrics on R6 with the same configuration as R1–R5. Also complete the corresponding configuration on R2.

   a. Ensure that the IPv6 network is treated as a completely separate topology from the IPv4 topology.

   b. How do R6's LSDB and route table compare with R5's LSDB and route table? Explain.

   c. Can R6 ping R2's system interface?

   d. Can R6 ping R5's system interface?

   e. Can R6 ping R4's system interface?

Chapter Review

Now that you have completed this chapter, you should be able to:

- Describe the use of the IPv6 Reachability TLV.
- Describe the use of the IPv6 Interface Address TLV.
- Explain the potential problems of combining IPv4 and IPv6 routing.
- List the four new TLVs defined for MT IS-IS.
- Configure MT IS-IS on the Alcatel-Lucent 7750 SR.
- Configure a multi-area IPv6 network in IS-IS.

Post-Assessment

The following questions will test your knowledge and prepare you for the Alcatel-Lucent NRS II Certification Exam. Compare your responses with the answers listed in Appendix A. You can also use the CD that accompanies this book to take all the assessment tests and review the answers.

1. Which of the following statements about the operation of IS-IS for IPv6 is false?
   - **A.** Two separate instances of IS-IS must operate on the router in order to support both IPv4 and IPv6 routing.
   - **B.** Operating with IPv4 and IPv6 in a single routing topology could lead to holes in either IPv4 or IPv6 routing.
   - **C.** IS-IS can be configured to exchange IPv6 routes with OSPFv3.
   - **D.** IS-IS can operate on the 7750 SR with a mix of IPv4 and IPv6 interfaces.
   - **E.** All of the above statements are true.

2. The complete output of the `show router isis database detail level 2` is shown below. Which of the following statements about router R1 is true?

```
Displaying Level 2 database
-----------------------------------------------------------------------
LSP ID     : R1.00-00                                    Level      : L2
Sequence   : 0xae7                  Checksum  : 0x4a18   Lifetime   : 1014
Version    : 1                      Pkt Type  : 20       Pkt Ver    : 1
Attributes: L1L2                    Max Area  : 3
SysID Len : 6                       Used Len  : 81       Alloc Len : 1492

TLVs :
  Area Addresses:
    Area Address : (1) 49
  Supp Protocols:
    Protocols      : IPv4
    Protocols      : IPv6
  MT Topology:
    MT ID            : 0                        No Flags
    MT ID            : 2                        No Flags
  IS-Hostname    : R1
  Router ID    :
    Router ID    : 10.10.10.1
  I/F Addresses :
    I/F Address    : 10.10.10.1
    I/F Address    : 10.1.2.1
  TE IP Reach    :
    Default Metric  : 0
    Control Info:     , prefLen 32
    Prefix    : 10.10.10.1
    Default Metric  : 10
    Control Info:     , prefLen 27
    Prefix    : 10.1.2.0

Level (2) LSP Count : 1
=======================================================================
```

A. The router is configured for IPv4 operation only.

B. The router is configured for IPv6 operation only.

C. The router is configured for single-topology IPv4 and IPv6.

D. The router is configured for multi-topology IPv4 and IPv6.

E. There is not enough information to select from the above statements.

3. Given the following extract from the `show router isis database` command, what is the most likely IPv6 system address for router R1?

```
Displaying Level 2 database
-----------------------------------------------------------------------
LSP ID    : R1.00-00                                  Level     : L2

TLVs :
  Supp Protocols:
    Protocols      : IPv4
    Protocols      : IPv6
  I/F Addresses :
    I/F Address    : 10.10.10.1
    I/F Address    : 10.1.2.1
    I/F Address    : 10.1.3.1
  I/F Addresses IPv6 :
    IPv6 Address    : 2001:DB8::1
    IPv6 Address    : 2001:DB8::12:0:0:0:1
  TE IP Reach   :
    Default Metric  : 0
    Control Info:    , prefLen 32
    Prefix   : 10.10.10.1
    Default Metric  : 100
    Control Info:    , prefLen 27
    Prefix   : 10.1.2.0
    Default Metric  : 100
    Control Info:    , prefLen 27
    Prefix   : 10.1.3.0
  IPv6 Reach:
    Metric: ( I ) 0
    Prefix   : 2001:DB8::1/128
    Metric: ( I ) 100
    Prefix   : 2001:DB8::12:0:0:0:0/64
```

A. 2001:DB8::1

B. 2001:DB8::12:0:0:0:1

C. An IPv6 address is not assigned to the system interface.

D. It is not possible to tell which is the system address.

E. IPv6 is not enabled on the router.

4. Which of the following best describes how multi-topology capabilities are implemented in IS-IS?

   A. No changes are required to the protocol. The IS-IS process on the router is enhanced to support multi-topologies.

   B. The existing TLVs are used with an additional sub-TLV added to indicate the topology to which it applies.

   C. New TLVs are defined that contain a field identifying the topology to which it applies.

   D. Multiple IS-IS instances are implemented on each router to support each of the topologies.

   E. The Alcatel-Lucent 7750 SR does not support MT IS-IS for IPv6.

5. Which of the following statements about IPv6 for IS-IS on the 7750 SR is false?

   A. Routers can be configured to leak IPv6 prefixes in a similar manner to route leaking for IPv4.

   B. An L1 router creates an IPv6 default route to the nearest L1/L2 router in the IPv6 topology.

   C. Export policies can be configured on routers to bring IPv6 prefixes from other IPv6 routing protocols into IS-IS.

   D. IPv6 global addresses do not necessarily need to be configured on interfaces because routers use the link-local addresses to form their adjacency.

   E. Statements A–D are true.

   F. Statements A–D are false.

6. Which of the following is the TLV that carries the information about IPv6 destinations in the network?

   A. Extended IS Reachability TLV (Type 22)

   B. Extended IP Reachability TLV (Type 135)

   C. IPv6 Interface Address TLV (Type 232)

   D. IPv6 Reachability TLV (Type 236)

   E. None of the above

7. What is meant by multi-topology IS-IS?

   A. Multi-topology means that there are multiple address families supported in the same topology.

   B. Multi-topology means that the router maintains different LSDBs and route tables for distinct topologies such as IPv4 and IPv6.

   C. Multi-topology means that the routing domain is split into multiple areas to provide better scalability in a large network.

   D. Multi-topology means that the router is learning routes from multiple different routing protocols.

   E. None of the above statements describe a multi-topology network.

8. An extract from the `show routerisis database detail` command is shown below. How many interfaces are enabled for IPv4 and IPv6 in IS-IS? Assume that an adjacency is formed on all enabled interfaces.

```
Displaying Level 2 database
-----------------------------------------------------------------------
LSP ID     : R1.00-00                                     Level      : L2

TLVs :
  TE IS Nbrs    :
    Nbr    : R2.00
    Default Metric  : 100
    Sub TLV Len     : 12
    IF Addr    : 10.1.2.1
    Nbr IP     : 10.1.2.2
  MT IS Nbrs      :
    MT ID           : 2
    Nbr    : R2.00
    Default Metric  : 100
    Sub TLV Len     : 0
  TE IS Nbrs    :
    Nbr    : R3.00
    Default Metric  : 100
    Sub TLV Len     : 12
    IF Addr    : 10.1.3.1
    Nbr IP     : 10.1.3.3
```

A. There are no interfaces in either IPv4 or IPv6.

B. There is one IPv4 interface and two IPv6 interfaces.

C. There are two IPv4 interfaces and one IPv6 interface.

D. There are three IPv4 interfaces and three IPv6 interfaces.

E. It is not possible to tell from this output.

9. Given the output below from the `show router route-table ipv6` command, which of the following statements is most likely true?

```
IPv6 Route Table (Router: Base)
===============================================================================
Dest Prefix                                     Type    Proto   Age         Pref
      Next Hop[Interface Name]                                    Metric
-------------------------------------------------------------------------------
2001:DB8::1/128                                 Remote  ISIS    12h23m44s   18
      FE80::216:4DFF:FE13:5CB0-"toR5"                              300
2001:DB8::5/128                                 Remote  ISIS    12h27m20s   18
      FE80::216:4DFF:FE13:5CB0-"toR5"                              100
2001:DB8::6/128                                 Local   Local   01d14h18m   0
      system                                                      0
2001:DB8::12:0:0:0:0/64                         Remote  ISIS    12h27m17s   18
      FE80::216:4DFF:FE13:5CB0-"toR5"                              400
2001:DB8::6666:0:0:0:0/64                       Remote  ISIS    00h09m40s   255
      Black Hole                                                  1
2001:DB8::6666:0:0:0:1/128                      Local   Local   12h12m36s   0
      loop1                                                       0
2001:DB8::6666:0:0:0:2/128                      Local   Local   12h12m27s   0
      loop2                                                       0
2001:DB8::6666:0:0:0:3/128                      Local   Local   12h12m19s   0
      loop3                                                       0
-------------------------------------------------------------------------------
No. of Routes: 8
```

A. The router does not have any interfaces configured for IPv4.

B. The system address of the router is `2001:DB8::5/128`.

C. The router is a Level 1 router.

D. The router is summarizing its local loopback interfaces as `2001:DB8::6666:0:0:0:0/64`.

E. None of the above statements is likely to be true.

10. Which of the following is *not* one of the MT topologies defined in RFC 5120?

A. IPv4 in-band management

B. IPv6 routing

C. IPv4 multicast routing

D. IPv6 multicast routing

E. Answers C and D are not valid MT topologies.

F. Answers A, B, C, and D are all valid MT topologies.

II

Multiprotocol Label Switching

11 Introduction to Multiprotocol Label Switching (MPLS)

The Alcatel-Lucent NRS II exam topics covered in this chapter include the following:

- Applications of MPLS
- MPLS concepts and components
- FECs and LSPs
- Label switching operations
- MPLS label structure
- Label values and label space
- Reserved labels and penultimate hop popping
- Configuring and verifying static LSPs
- Dynamic label distribution protocols
- Downstream and upstream flows
- Label distribution modes
- Downstream unsolicited and downstream on demand
- Ordered versus independent control mode
- Label retention modes

Multiprotocol Label Switching (MPLS) enables routers to forward traffic based on a simple label embedded in the packet header. It's known as multiprotocol because it can be used to transport any type of packet payload across any Layer 2 network protocol using a simple label switching approach. The MPLS architecture is described in RFC 3031.

In MPLS, specific paths known as label switched paths (LSPs) are established for different forwarding destinations. At ingress, each packet is assigned a label based on its destination. An MPLS router examines the label to determine the next-hop for the packet. This simplifies the forwarding process and separates it from the routing protocol and the nature of the data. MPLS networks use IP for internal communication and to help establish the LSPs, but forwarding along an LSP is not dependent on the packet's protocol or content.

This chapter introduces the purpose and concepts of an MPLS network as well as the basic label switching operations. The fields of the MPLS label are also described in detail.

Finally, in this chapter, we see how labels can be assigned manually to form a static LSP. We also introduce dynamic label distribution protocols and describe their use in an MPLS network. We finish the chapter with a look at the different modes of distributing and managing labels.

Pre-Assessment

The following assessment questions will help you understand what areas of the chapter you should review in more detail to prepare for the NRS II exam. You can also use the CD that accompanies this book to take all the assessment tests and review the answers.

1. Which protocol cannot be transported in MPLS?

- **A.** IP
- **B.** Ethernet
- **C.** ATM
- **D.** Frame Relay
- **E.** All of the above protocols can be transported in MPLS

2. What is the primary purpose of using MPLS for IGP shortcuts?

   A. To provide the shortest path possible for forwarding data across the network

   B. To reduce the number of EBGP sessions required

   C. To reduce the number of IBGP sessions required

   D. To eliminate the use of an IGP in the carrier network

   E. None of the above

3. Which statement is correct regarding the definition of a P router?

   A. P routers are service-aware.

   B. P routers are typically LERs.

   C. P routers perform label push and pop operations.

   D. P routers have all their interfaces inside the service provider domain.

   E. None of the above.

4. When is a packet assigned to an FEC in an MPLS network?

   A. The FEC is assigned at each LSR in the MPLS network.

   B. The FEC is assigned at the ingress LER.

   C. The FEC is assigned at the ingress LER and at each LSR in the MPLS network.

   D. The FEC is assigned at the ingress LER and the egress LER.

   E. There is not enough information provided.

5. Which of the following MPLS signaling protocols are used to signal transport labels?

   A. Multiprotocol BGP

   B. Targeted LDP

   C. GRE

   D. RSVP-TE

   E. All of the above

11.1 Applications of MPLS

Multiprotocol Label Switching (MPLS) originated as IP switching or tag switching and was intended as a simplified forwarding mechanism to replace the more complex IP forwarding mechanism. However, once hardware was developed that could perform IP forwarding at line rates, MPLS evolved as a method for forwarding packets independently of their content, making it ideal as a base for implementing VPN (Virtual Private Network) technology.

MPLS is a tunneling technology. In a data communications network, *tunneling* is a method of data transport in which the data arriving at the edge of the tunneling network is encapsulated in another protocol for transport across the network. The data being carried through the tunnel could be in any form: an IP datagram, an Ethernet frame, or ATM (Asynchronous Transfer Mode) cells, for example.

The format of the tunneled data is not important because the forwarding of data across the tunneled network is controlled by the tunneling protocol. There are many different technologies that can be used for tunneling, including IP itself. In an MPLS network, the MPLS label and the label switched path create the tunnel across the network.

Limitations of IP Forwarding

The fantastic growth of the Internet is evidence of the effectiveness of IP as a simple and powerful networking technology. What, then, is the reason for increasing the overall complexity of an IP network by adding MPLS tunnels? Despite its significant advantages, however, IP does have some serious limitations. These are summarized in Figure 11.1.

Figure 11.1 Benefits and limitations of basic IP routing.

IP Benefits	IP Limitations
Scalability	Hyper aggregation
Overall network resiliency	End-to-end service level limitations
Simple addressing scheme	Address-based forwarding is limiting

Traditional routing protocols route IP packets across the path with the lowest metric. These are simple and very scalable protocols but do not provide routers with any visibility into the state of the network. They often do not make use of all available network resources because of their limited mechanism for selection of the best path. This results in link congestion for some paths and link underutilization for other paths through the network, a condition known as *hyperaggregation*. Distributing the aggregate network traffic load over all available resources is difficult to achieve in conventional IP routing.

Packets in an IP network are transported across the network on a hop-by-hop basis, with an independent routing decision made at every node based on the destination IP address of a packet's header. This provides a simple, resilient forwarding mechanism but makes it very difficult to provide any end-to-end service guarantees.

The IP address plan is very simple to use and provides some basic hierarchy. However, all users of a public network are required to follow specific addressing rules and address allocations. For example, if a service provider has two customers both using private addressing, the service provider must maintain a completely separate infrastructure for these customers.

MPLS provides a mechanism to address these limitations while easily interoperating with existing IP networks and striving to maintain the simplicity and resiliency that have contributed to the success of IP networks.

MPLS Tunneling

Creating tunnels across an IP network with MPLS resolves some of the limitations of IP routing while providing a simple base for adding new services. A forwarding decision is made for data when it arrives at the edge of the MPLS network, and it is then forwarded across the network on a label switched path (LSP). Data can be classified and transported across the network using criteria other than the traditional IP forwarding mechanisms.

IP packets arrive at an MPLS network. They are assigned to an LSP for transport and are tunneled across the network using an MPLS label for switching. When they arrive at the egress of the MPLS network, the label is removed, and the data is forwarded again as an IP datagram (Figure 11.2).

Some of the applications of MPLS are listed and described in more detail in the following sections:

- Virtual Private Network services (VPNs)
- High availability and redundancy
- Traffic engineering
- Provides service guarantees and resource reservations
- IGP (interior gateway protocol) shortcuts to reduce the requirement for full IBGP (Internal Border Gateway Protocol) mesh
- Any other tunneling requirements

Figure 11.2 Forwarding of IP packets across an MPLS network.

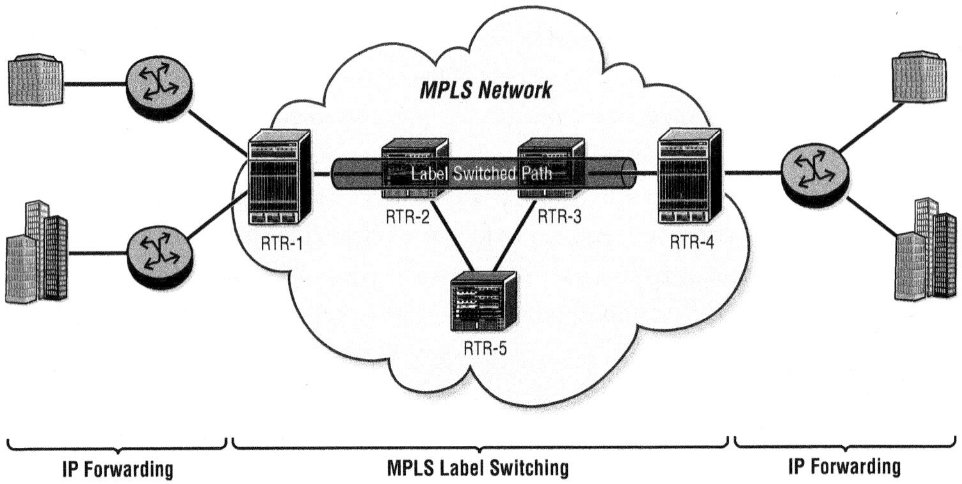

MPLS for VPNs

Because data in an MPLS network is transported in LSP tunnels, MPLS provides an ideal foundation for the construction of Virtual Private Networks (VPNs). Customer traffic is identified as it enters the service provider's network and is assigned to the appropriate LSP for transport across the network. At the egress side of the network, the traffic is delivered to the appropriate customer. From the customer's perspective, it appears as if their data is transported over a private network.

This configuration allows a service provider to use a common infrastructure for multiple customers while maintaining complete separation between between them. Because customer data is encapsulated in an MPLS labeled packet, the type of packet and its addressing are irrelevant to the core network.

MPLS VPNs can support Layer 2 Virtual Private Wire Services (VPWS) that emulate a point-to-point connection for ATM, Frame Relay, Ethernet, and TDM (Time Division Multiplexing) networks. MPLS VPNs can also support the Virtual Private LAN Service (VPLS), which emulates a switched Ethernet service as shown in Figure 11.3.

An MPLS VPN can be used to provide a Layer 3 Virtual Private Routed Network (VPRN) service on the same infrastructure. From the customer's perspective, the VPRN service appears to be a router participating in their private routed network (Figure 11.4).

Figure 11.3 A VPLS emulates a switched Ethernet network over an MPLS network.

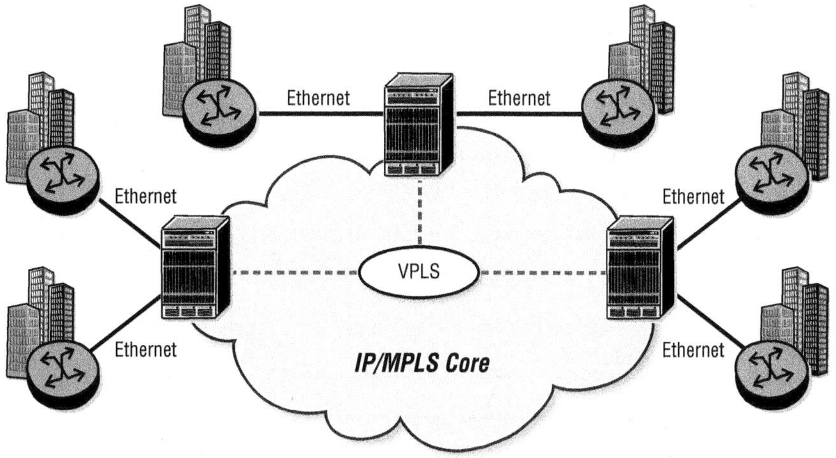

Figure 11.4 A VPRN emulates a private Layer 3 routed network.

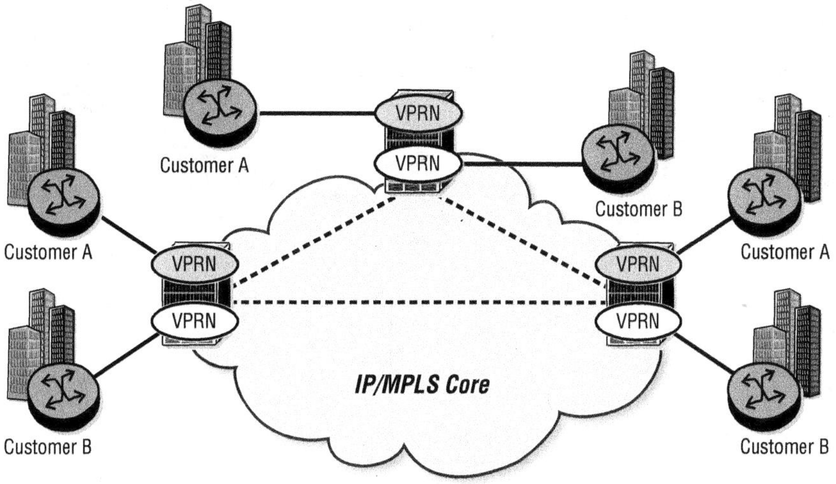

In this chapter, we describe the MPLS technology. The use of MPLS for deploying service VPNs is described later, starting in Chapter 17.

MPLS for High Availability

Resiliency is one of the strengths of IP routing protocols. Modern link-state routing protocols typically converge within a few seconds of a topology change. However, some current applications such as real-time voice or video demand much higher availability—on the order of 50-millisecond recovery from failures. In an MPLS network, alternate paths can be established in advance. If there is a failure on the primary path, data can immediately be switched to an alternate path.

Figure 11.5 shows an MPLS network in which data is transported on the primary LSP (R1–R2–R4–R6–R8) during normal operation. The primary LSP is protected with fast reroute detours and a secondary LSP. If a node on the primary LSP detects the failure of a downstream node or link, it can immediately switch the traffic to an alternate route with minimal delay and loss of data.

Figure 11.5 With MPLS, alternate paths can be established in advance. Traffic can be switched to these as soon as a failure is detected.

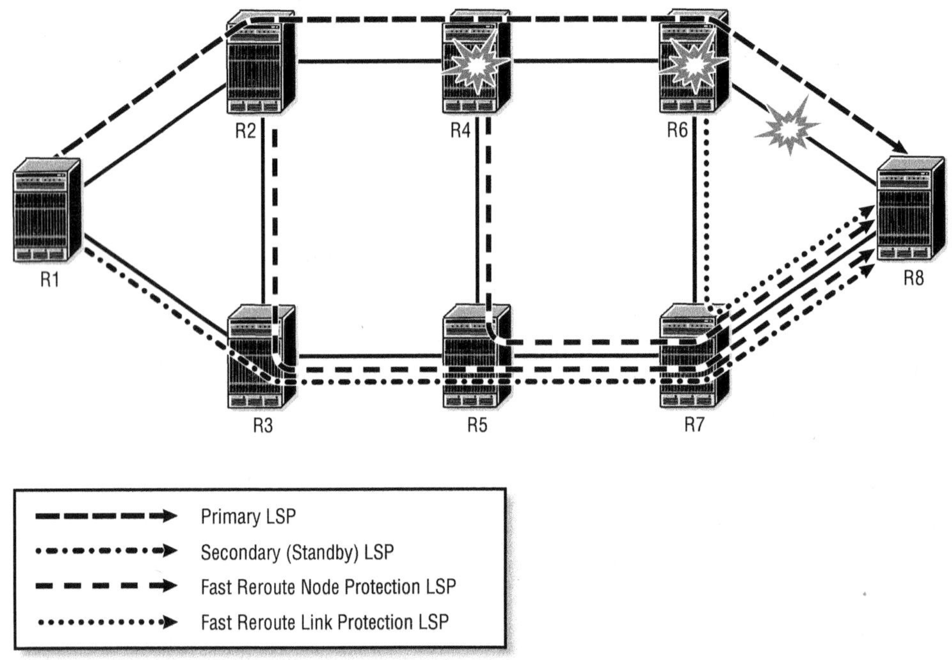

MPLS for Traffic Engineering

MPLS is widely used for traffic engineering, which means the routing of traffic using more sophisticated criteria than those offered by traditional routing protocols. A traditional

IP routing protocol selects the best route solely on metric. A traffic-engineering routing protocol may apply additional criteria for choosing the best path across the network:

- Use or avoid specific links.
- Use links that have specific amounts of bandwidth available.
- Choose a path with a limited hop count.

Because the routing of packets in an MPLS network is not done hop-by-hop, alternate paths across the network can be created as required. Besides relieving congestion on oversubscribed links, alternately routed paths can be used to meet other constraints such as quality of service requirements. As shown in Figure 11.6, the path chosen across the network may differ from that chosen by the IGP, depending on the constraints on the traffic-engineered path.

Figure 11.6 Comparison of path chosen by IGP versus traffic-engineered path.

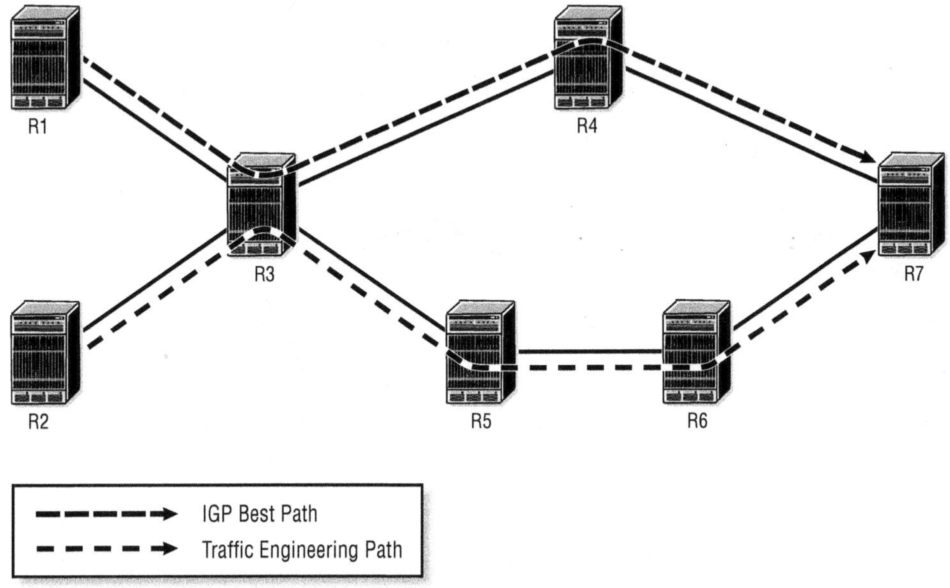

MPLS for IGP Shortcuts

IGP shortcuts enable a service provider to reduce the requirement for a full mesh of peering sessions for IBGP. With IGP shortcuts, a full mesh of peering sessions and LSPs is established between all the edge BGP (Border Gateway Protocol) routers (those with

EBGP [External Border Gateway Protocol] sessions to other autonomous systems), as shown in Figure 11.7. The edge router then defines the peer at the other end of the LSP as the next-hop and sends its packet flow through the LSP tunnel. Because the packets are transmitted in an LSP tunnel, the core routers do not perform any IP forwarding and thus do not need to participate in the IBGP mesh.

Figure 11.7 BGP routers with external connections form a full mesh and send transit data through MPLS tunnels.

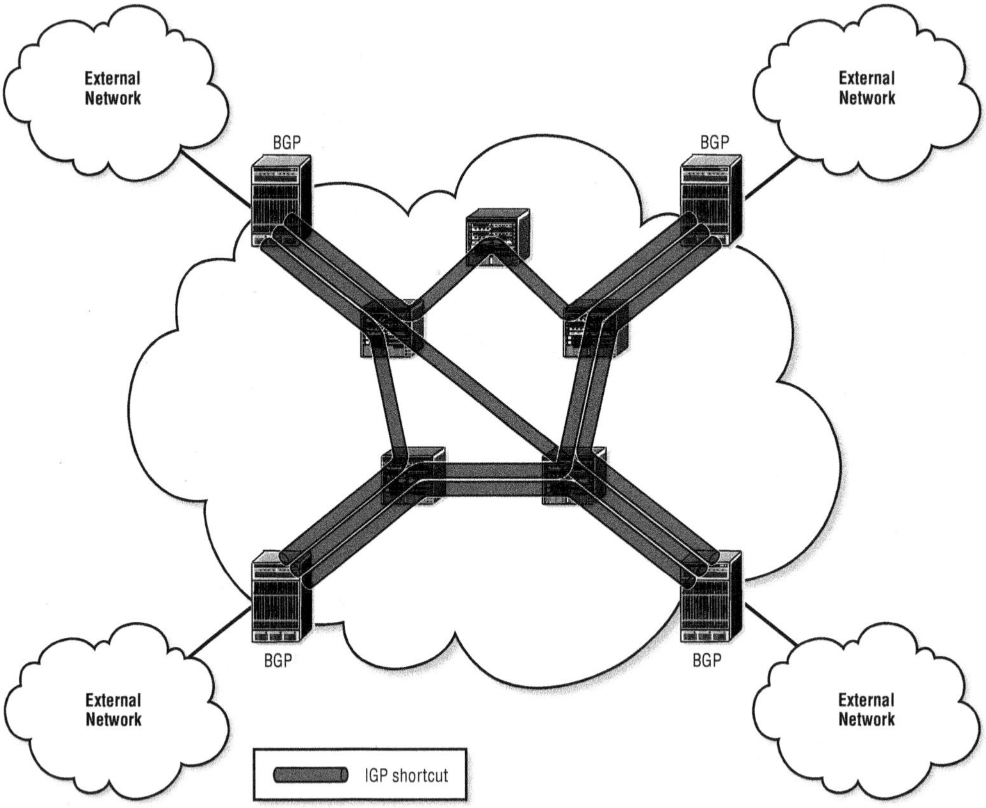

Consolidation of Services

There are other technologies and protocols that can be used to provide the services described above. However, MPLS leverages the ubiquitous technologies of IP and Ethernet to provide a cost-effective core network technology that can be used by service providers and telecommunication carriers to deploy a wide range of services, as shown in Figure 11.8.

Figure 11.8 Service providers and carriers can offer a wide range of services over a highly available IP/MPLS core.

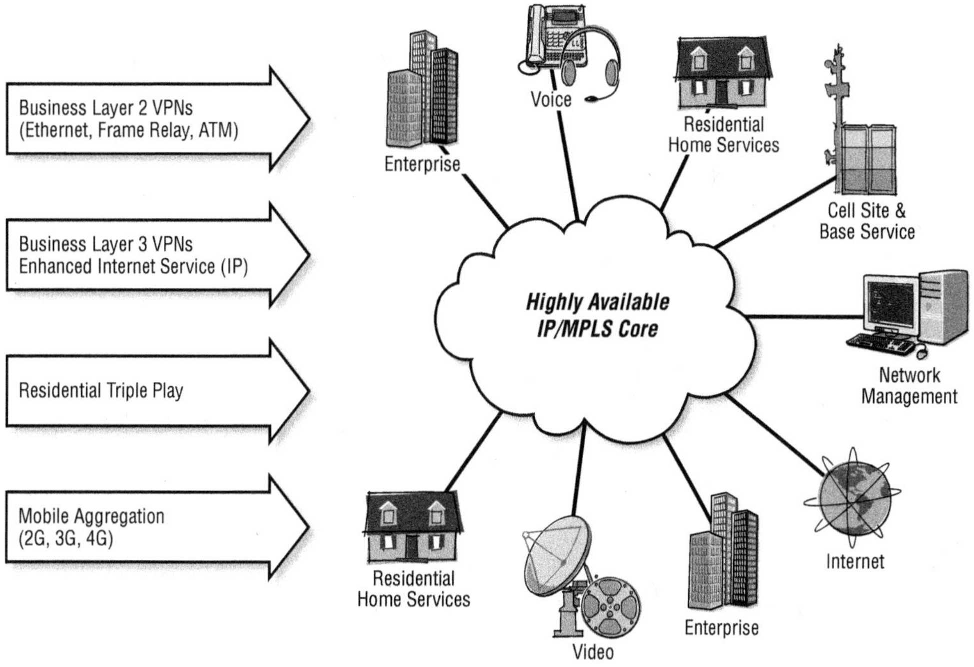

11.2 MPLS Concepts and Components

An MPLS network is made up of label switch routers (LSRs) that have the capability of labeling packets and forwarding them based on their labels. Labeled packets are forwarded along a label switched path (LSP) to their destination.

LSPs and LSRs

MPLS is a tunneling technology with the tunnels known as LSPs. Packets arriving at the edge of the MPLS network are assigned a label associated with the LSP and forwarded across the network based on the label. The forwarding operation and distribution of labels are described in more detail below.

Routers that forward MPLS labeled packets are known as LSRs. When they are at the edge of the MPLS network and have to add or remove labels, they are known as edge LSRs or Label Edge Routers (LERs). An LER has one or more interfaces outside the MPLS domain and is capable of handling labeled and unlabeled packets.

LSPs are unidirectional, and a router is defined as an LER based on its position relative to a specific LSP. The MPLS router at the start of an LSP is called the *ingress Label Edge Router* (iLER), and the router at the end of the LSP is called the *egress Label Edge Router* (eLER). An iLER receives unlabeled packets from outside the MPLS domain, applies an MPLS label (or labels) to the packets, and forwards the labeled packets into the MPLS domain. An eLER receives labeled packets from the MPLS domain, removes the labels, and forwards the unlabeled packets outside the MPLS domain. In practice, LERs always perform the ingress and egress roles because two unidirectional LSPs are required for bidirectional traffic flows.

An LSR switches labeled packets in the core of the network. The LSR ignores any headers below the MPLS label, such as the packet's IP header, and simply forwards the packet using the MPLS label switching mechanism.

To summarize, the MPLS routers along an LSP perform one of the following tasks (Figure 11.9):

Figure 11.9 An LSP is defined by its ingress LER, transit LSRs, and egress LER.

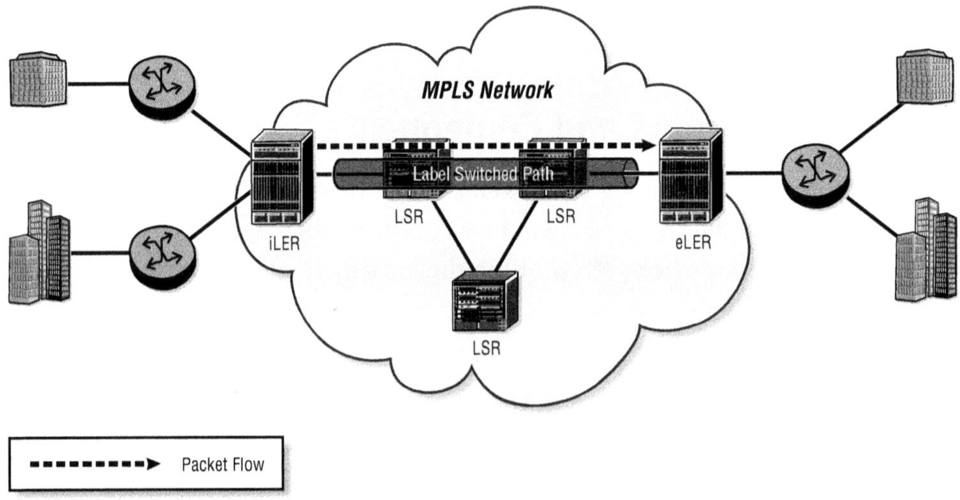

- **iLER**—The iLER encapsulates a packet with an MPLS header and forwards it to the next router along the LSP.
- **Transit LSR**—A *transit LSR* is any intermediate router in the MPLS network between the ingress and egress LERs. The transit router swaps the incoming label for an outgoing label and forwards the labeled packet to the next router along the LSP. An LSP may have any number of transit LSRs from 0 to 253.
- **eLER**—The eLER strips the MPLS header, which changes it from an MPLS packet to its original form. The packet is then forwarded according to the original protocol of the packet.

Often, a given router in an MPLS network functions as both an LER and an LSR. It may be an LER for some LSPs and an LSR for others.

In a service provider network, routers are usually described as Provider Edge (PE) routers and Provider (P) routers. PE routers connect to customer equipment and have at least one interface *outside* the provider domain. P routers are part of the provider core and have their interfaces *inside* the provider domain.

This corresponds closely to the routers in an MPLS domain. The PE routers at the edge of the provider network are MPLS LERs, and the P routers at the core of the provider network are LSRs (Figure 11.10).

Figure 11.10 In a service provider MPLS network, PE routers are LERs, and P routers are LSRs.

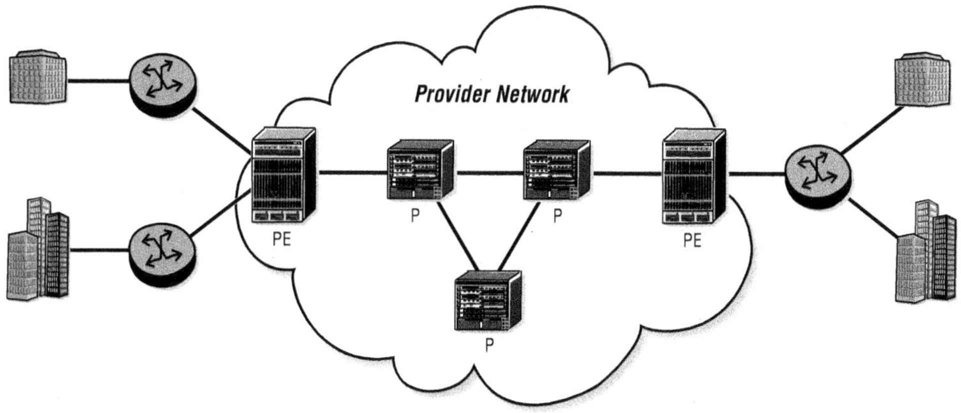

Table 11.1 summarizes the characteristics of the different MPLS routers and makes a comparison with service provider terminology.

Table 11.1 MPLS Service Provider Terminology

Terminology	Role
PE router	• Router at the edge of the service provider network • Faces the customer router and provides services • Typically an LER
P router	• Router in the core of the service provider network • Normally not service-aware • Typically an LSR
LSR	• Router in the MPLS domain responsible for swapping labels • An intermediate router along an LSP • Typically a P router
iLER	• Router at the edge of the MPLS domain responsible for pushing labels • The router at the ingress (head end) of an LSP • Typically a PE router
eLER	• Router at the edge of the MPLS domain responsible for popping labels • The router at the egress (tail end) of an LSP • Typically a PE router

Forwarding Equivalence Class (FEC)

We've introduced LSPs as the paths along which data is forwarded in an MPLS network, but have not explicitly defined the LSP. In MPLS, an LSP is created to carry the data for a Forwarding Equivalence Class (FEC). An FEC defines a group of packets to be forwarded over the same path with the same forwarding treatment. Typically, an FEC corresponds to a network destination but is not necessarily restricted to that.

FEC in a Traditional IP Network

In a traditional IP network, an FEC corresponds to an entry in the IP route table. Any packet that matches a specific entry is forwarded to the given next-hop address. In conventional IP routing, a packet is assigned to an FEC each time a Layer 3 routing lookup is performed (i.e., at each hop).

Figure 11.11 shows that a packet with a destination IP address of `10.2.1.1` matches IP prefix `10.2.0.0/16` at Router A. A packet with destination IP address of `10.2.2.1` will also match IP prefix `10.2.0.0/16`. Both these IP packets belong to the same FEC, and both receive the same forwarding treatment.

Figure 11.11 In traditional IP forwarding, an FEC corresponds to an entry in the route table.

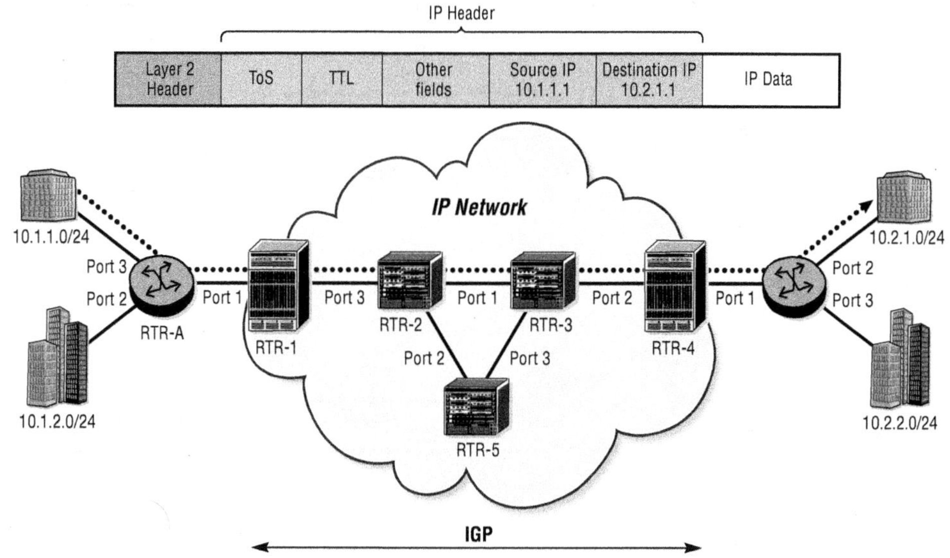

Rtr-A FIB	Prefix	Via
	10.1.1.0/24	Port 3
	10.1.2.0/24	Port 2
	10.2.0.0/16	Port 1

Rtr-2 FIB	Prefix	Via
	10.1.0.0/16	Port 3
	10.2.0.0/16	Port 1

Rtr-4 FIB	Prefix	Via
	10.1.0.0/16	Port 2
	10.2.0.0/16	Port 1

FEC in an MPLS Network

In MPLS, an FEC also defines a group of packets to be forwarded on the same path with the same forwarding treatment. An FEC may correspond simply to an entry in the IP routing table, or it may be defined by other criteria such as packet header information or the incoming port. However, the packet is assigned to an FEC only at the network ingress, as opposed to assignment at each hop in conventional IP forwarding. Once an incoming packet is classified to an FEC, it is transported on an LSP bound to that FEC using the label and next-hop address assigned to that LSP (Figure 11.12).

The benefit of label switching is that user traffic can be mapped to an LSP that has been specifically engineered to satisfy their traffic and service requirements. MPLS offers service providers more control over the flow of traffic in their networks and enables them to offer a variety of services over a common infrastructure.

Figure 11.12 An unlabeled packet is assigned to an FEC at network ingress. The packet is forwarded over the LSP for that FEC using the label and next-hop address for the LSP.

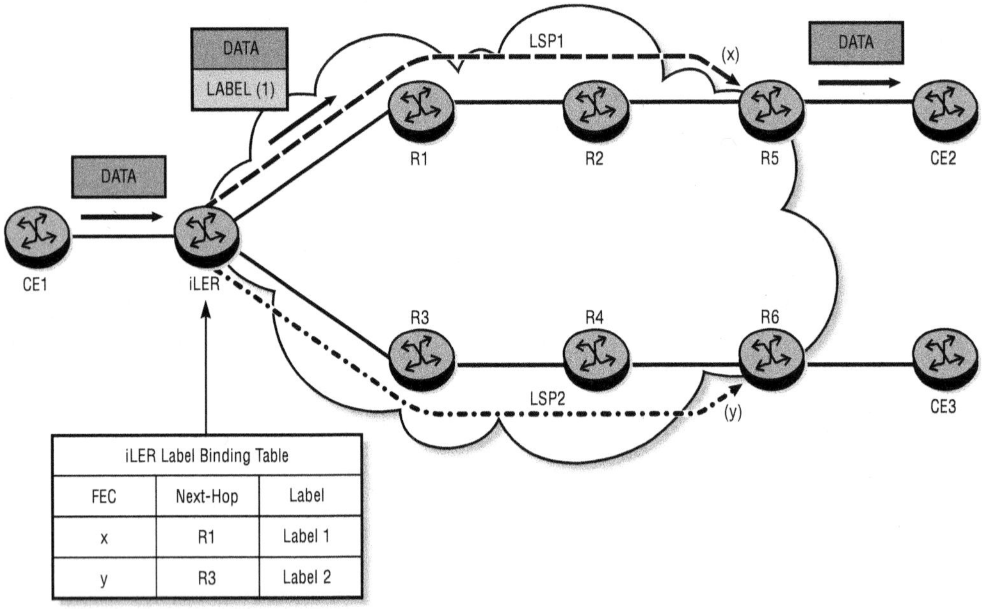

FEC	Next-Hop	Label
x	R1	Label 1
y	R3	Label 2

11.3 Label Switching and Label Operations

An MPLS label is a 20-bit field contained in the MPLS header. The MPLS header, when present in a frame, occurs immediately after the frame header. The original use of MPLS was to encapsulate IP packets, and thus MPLS is often described as Layer 2.5 (Figure 11.13). However, more recent specifications describe the encapsulation of Layer 2 frames as well.

Figure 11.13 The MPLS label can be used to encapsulate IP packets as well as Layer 2 frames.

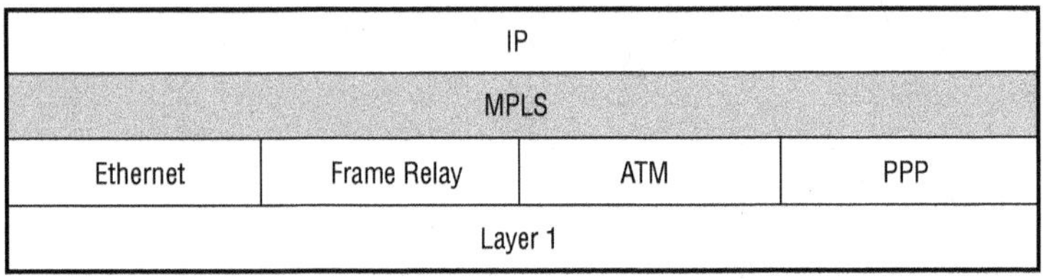

Label Switching

MPLS is based on a label swapping mechanism for forwarding labeled packets across the network. This is similar to the mechanism used to forward data in ATM and Frame Relay switches. As a result, the MPLS label itself is very similar in function to the ATM VPI/VCI or a Frame Relay DLCI.

When a packet enters the network, it is classified into an FEC that is bound to an LSP. An MPLS header containing the label for that LSP is added (PUSH operation), and the packet is transmitted to the next-hop. As the packet traverses the MPLS domain, forwarding decisions are made by looking up the received MPLS label, exchanging it for a new MPLS label (SWAP operation), and then forwarding the packet. When the packet leaves the MPLS network, all labels are removed (POP operation). Figure 11.14 shows the process of forwarding traffic across an MPLS domain.

Figure 11.14 Packets are forwarded across an MPLS network using PUSH, POP, and SWAP operations.

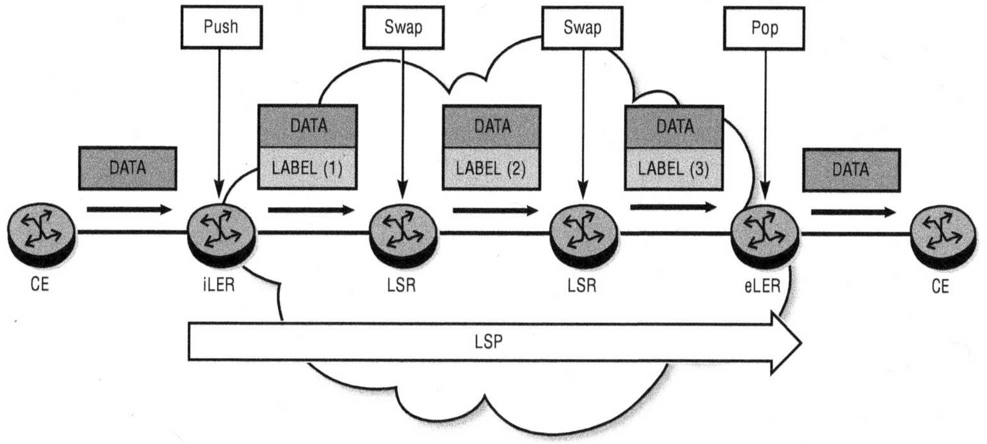

On the end-to-end path between two host systems, part of the network may be a traditional IP network and part of the network an MPLS domain. In the part of the network that is not MPLS, traditional IP forwarding methods are used. Figure 11.15 shows a service provider's MPLS network with a customer's network attached. Routers Rtr A, Rtr B, and Rtr C are the customer routers. Rtr A has a packet destined to the `10.2.1.0/24` network and forwards it to RTR-1 as a normal IP packet. The customer has no knowledge of the MPLS network.

Figure 11.15 Rtr A forwards a normal IP packet to RTR-1. Rtr A has no knowledge of the MPLS network.

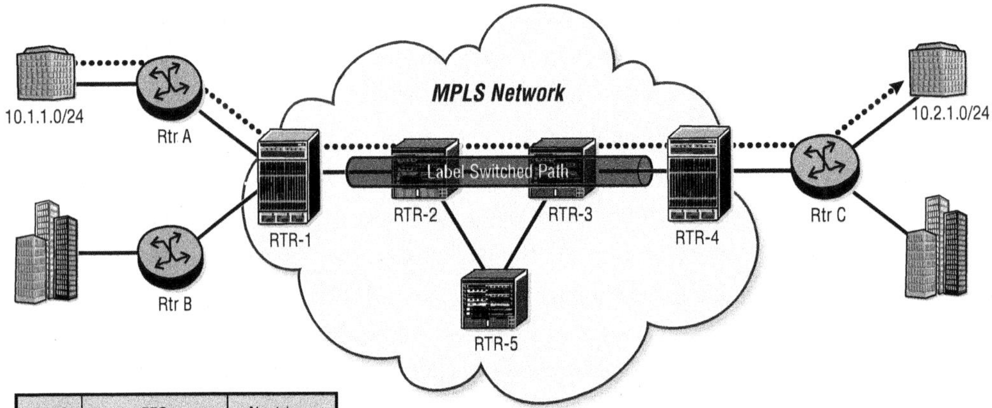

Rtr A	FEC	Next-hop
	10.2.1.0/24	RTR-1

IP Forward

The PE router, RTR-1, is the ingress LER to the MPLS domain for this packet. RTR-1 assigns the incoming packet to an FEC that is bound to an LSP that defines the path the packet will follow across the MPLS network. The ingress MPLS router adds an MPLS header with the label for the LSP (label `100`) to the original IP packet. This is known as a label PUSH operation. The labeled packet is forwarded to the next-hop, RTR-2 (Figure 11.16).

RTR-2 and RTR-3 are transit LSRs for this LSP. RTR-2 receives the packet with label `100` and does a table lookup, which says that the outgoing packet should use label `300` and be transmitted to RTR-3 as the next-hop (Figure 11.17). This is known as a SWAP operation. RTR-3 also performs a SWAP operation and uses label `200` for the outgoing packet.

RTR-4 is a PE router and is the egress LER for this LSP. RTR-4 receives a labeled packet with the label value `200`. A table lookup tells RTR-4 that the label should be removed and the packet forwarded as a normal IP datagram (Figure 11.18). This is known as a POP operation.

When the packet reaches Rtr C, it is no longer labeled and is handled like any other IP packet. Rtr C forwards the packet based on the longest prefix match from the IP routing table (Figure 11.19). Rtr C has no knowledge of the MPLS network.

Figure 11.16 The packet is classified to an FEC and labeled for the LSP bound to the FEC. This is a PUSH operation.

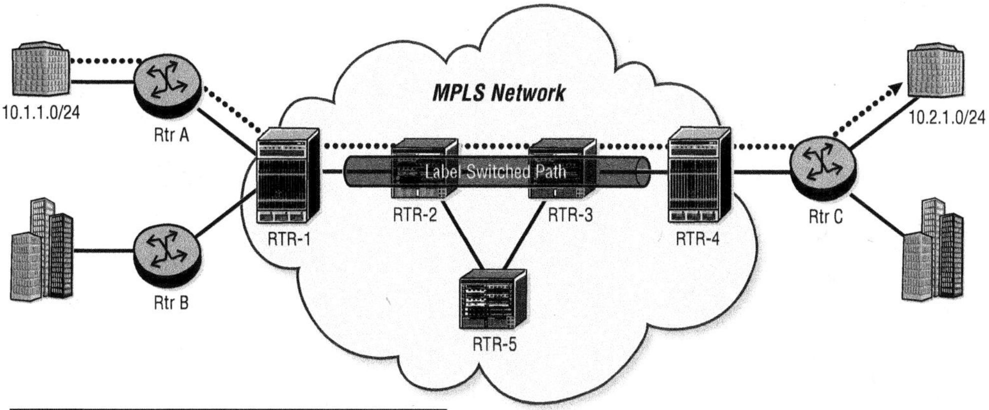

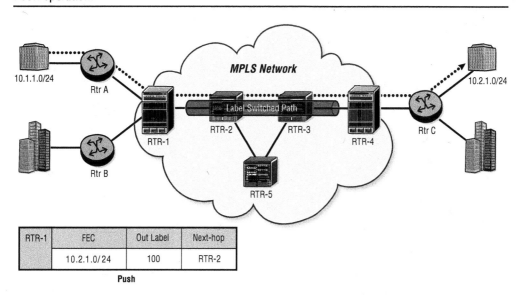

RTR-1	FEC	Out Label	Next-hop
	10.2.1.0/24	100	RTR-2

Push

Figure 11.17 RTR-2 and RTR-3 are transit routers. They SWAP the incoming label and forward the packet with a new label.

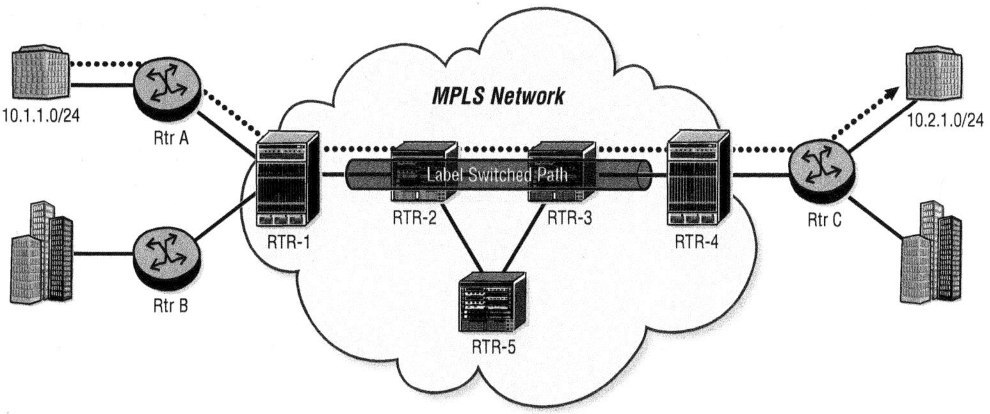

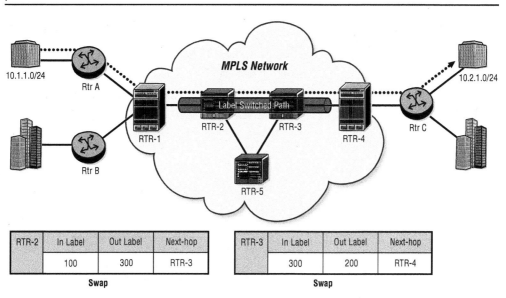

RTR-2	In Label	Out Label	Next-hop
	100	300	RTR-3

Swap

RTR-3	In Label	Out Label	Next-hop
	300	200	RTR-4

Swap

Figure 11.18 RTR-4 removes the label and forwards the unlabeled packet to Rtr C. This is a POP operation.

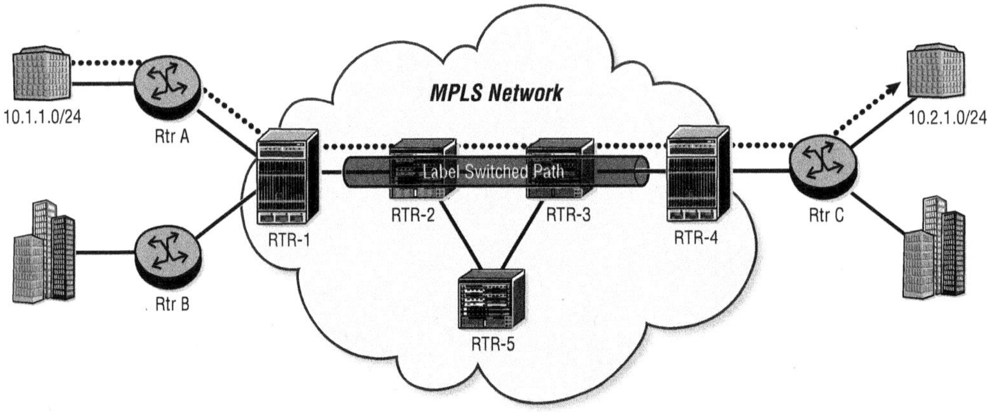

RTR-4	In Label	Next-hop
	200	Rtr C

Pop

Figure 11.19 Rtr C forwards the packet as a normal IP packet. It has no knowledge of the MPLS network.

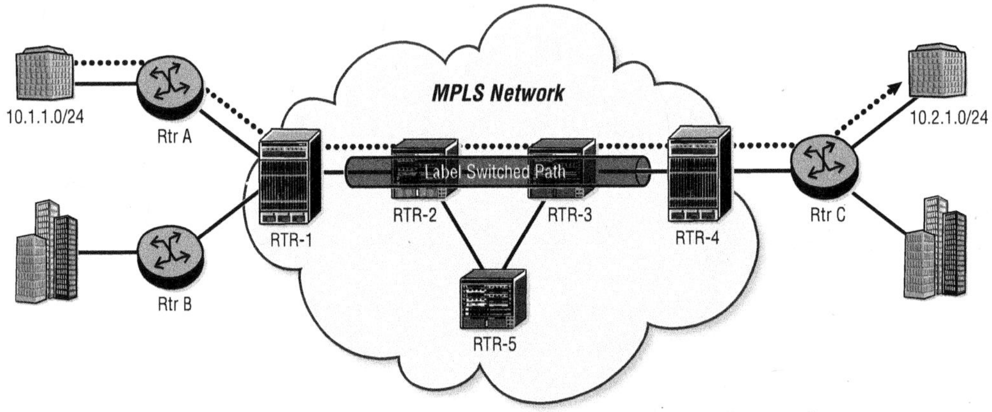

Rtr C	Prefix	Next-hop
	10.2.1.0./24	Direct

IP Forward

The example above illustrates the basic operation of an MPLS network. In fact, a packet may have more than one label, known as a *label stack*. Label operations are always performed on the outermost label; inner labels remain unchanged until the outer label is popped.

In a VPN services network, every packet has two labels. The outer label is used to forward the packet on an LSP to the egress PE router (MPLS transport tunnel). The inner label identifies the service that the packet belongs to (service tunnel). The use of two labels means that one MPLS transport tunnel can be used to carry the data for many different services (Figure 11.20). This is described in detail in Chapter 17.

Figure 11.20 VPN services use two labels: the outer one for the LSP to the egress PE and the inner one to identify the service.

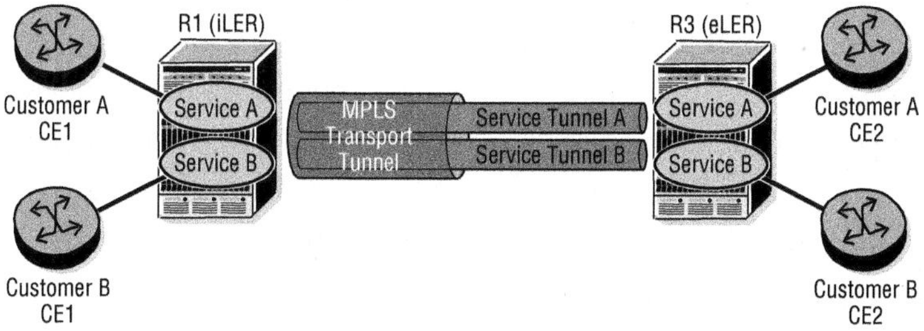

Label Distribution

To create an LSP, it is necessary to define the labels to be used for the path. Labels for an FEC are always generated by the router that will receive the labeled packet, and this label is always local to the router that generates it. When the router receives a packet using the label, it knows which FEC it belongs to because it generated the label for it.

There are several different protocols used for label distribution. These are introduced here and discussed in detail in later chapters:

- **LDP (Label Distribution Protocol)**—LDP can be thought of as a label distribution protocol that works in conjunction with the network IGP. As routers become aware of new destination networks through their IGP, they use LDP to advertise labels that allow their neighbors to reach the destination. LSPs signaled with LDP always follow the path determined by the IGP.
- **RSVP-TE (Resource Reservation Protocol–Traffic Engineering)**—RSVP-TE can also be used to signal LSPs across the network. RSVP-TE is used for traffic

engineering when the ingress router wishes to create an LSP with specific constraints beyond the route chosen by the IGP. RSVP-TE specifies the path desired for the LSP and may include resource requirements or other constraints for the path. RSVP-TE is also used for high-availability LSPs.

- **Targeted LDP**—This is an extended version of LDP that is used by the two end points of a Layer 2 VPN service to exchange labels for that service.
- **Multiprotocol BGP**—This is an enhanced version of standard BGP that is used by the two end points of a Layer 3 VPN service to exchange labels for that service.

MPLS Data Plane versus Control Plane

An MPLS router is composed of two distinct functional components (or planes)—the control component (control plane) and the forwarding component (data plane). The data plane is responsible for forwarding packets based on its forwarding tables. The control plane is responsible for building the forwarding tables. In the Alcatel-Lucent 7750 SR, these components are also physically separate. The CPM (Control Processing Module) performs the functions of the control plane; data plane functions are handled by the IOMs (Input/Output Modules).

The MPLS control plane uses:

- Standard routing protocols to exchange information with other LSRs to build and maintain forwarding tables; and
- Label distribution, or signaling protocols to communicate label binding information with other LSRs.

An IP router forwards only unlabeled packets. It participates in the routing domain, exchanging routing updates with its neighbors. The best routes for each routing protocol are stored in the Routing Information Base (RIB) as shown in Figure 11.21.

Figure 11.21 Routers exchange routing updates to build the RIB and route table.

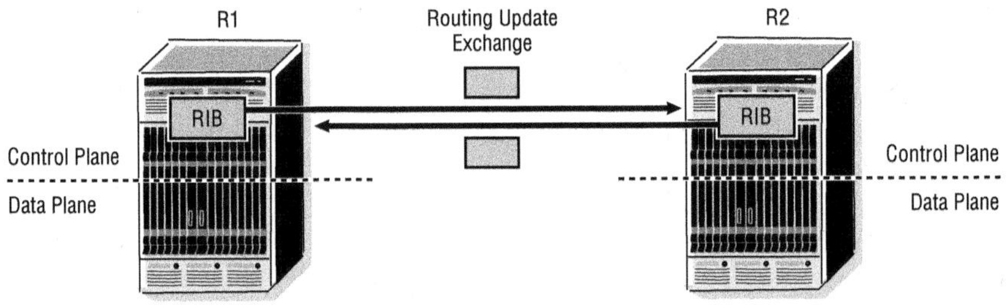

The Route Table Manager (RTM) selects the routes to be used for forwarding and propagates them to the Forwarding Information Base (FIB), where they become the active routes. The FIB is used to perform IP forwarding of unlabeled packets (Figure 11.22).

Figure 11.22 The FIB is used in the data plane for the forwarding of unlabeled IP packets.

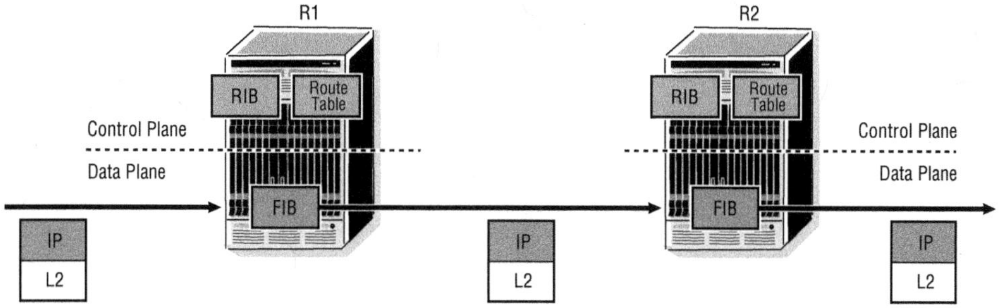

An MPLS router has another component in the control plane—the label control plane. MPLS enabled devices generate labels for selected FECs and exchange them with other MPLS enabled devices, similar to the exchange of routing information by an IGP. The locally generated labels and those received from other devices are stored in the Label Information Base (LIB) as shown in Figure 11.23.

Figure 11.23 MPLS routers exchange label information and store these labels in the LIB.

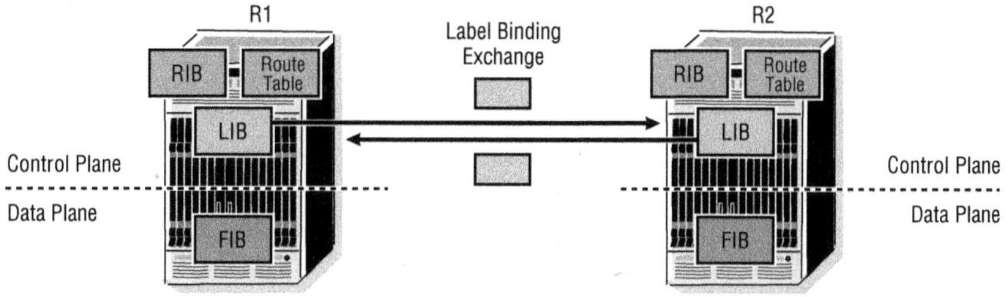

A selection is made from those labels, and the labels that will be used for switching packets are propagated from the LIB to the Label Forwarding Information Base (LFIB). These labels are used to forward labeled packets. Figure 11.24 shows the forwarding of unlabeled and labeled packets using the FIB and LFIB.

To summarize, there are multiple tables maintained by a router in an MPLS enabled network, as shown in Table 11.2. These tables are populated through control plane functions, with the FIB and LFIB used by the data plane to forward packets.

Figure 11.24 Unlabeled packets are forwarded based on the FIB. Labeled packets are forwarded based on the LFIB.

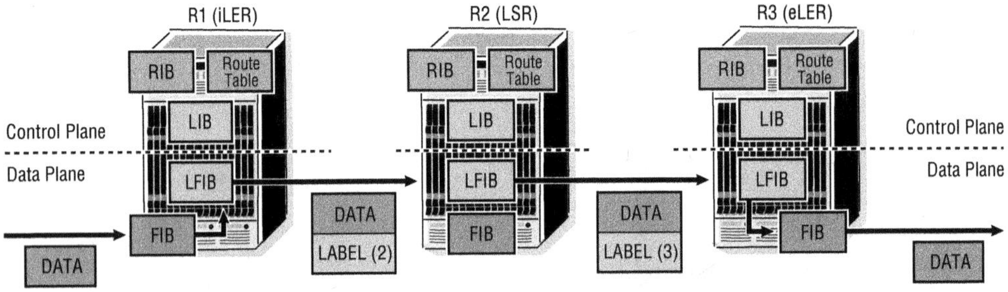

Table 11.2 Summary of Tables Maintained on the Router

Table Name	Meaning	Contents	Populated by
RIB	Routing Information Base	Routing information	Routing protocol exchange (OSPF or IS-IS)
FIB	Forwarding Information Base	Active routes	Active routes selected by RTM
LIB	Label Information Base	Locally generated and received labels	Label exchange by label distribution protocol (LDP or RSVP-TE)
LFIB	Label Forwarding Information Base	Labels used for forwarding by the LSR	Labels received for active routes

11.4 MPLS Label Structure

A *label* is a 20-bit identifier applied to each packet. The label applied to a particular packet depends on the Forwarding Equivalence Class (FEC) to which that packet is assigned. Often a packet is assigned to an FEC based on an IP destination address. However, the label is never an encoding of that address. The label is an arbitrarily assigned, locally significant value that identifies the FEC or LSP.

Frame Mode and Cell Mode Labeling

A *labeled packet* is a packet into which an MPLS label has been encoded. Two techniques are used to encode the MPLS label in the frame: frame mode and cell mode:

- **Frame mode MPLS**—In frame mode MPLS, the label is part of the MPLS encapsulation header. It is sometimes referred to as a *shim header* because it is inserted into the frame between the Layer 2 header and the Layer 3 header.

- **Cell mode MPLS**—Cell mode is used on ATM or Frame Relay connections. In cell mode, the circuit ID in the existing data link layer header is mapped to the MPLS label information. In the case of ATM, the VPI/VCI field in the cell header is used as the MPLS label. For Frame Relay, the DLCI is used.

Figure 11.25 shows the two types of MPLS label implementations with a comparison to an unlabeled IP packet. The 7750 SR does not use cell mode—only frame mode is supported.

Figure 11.25 An unlabeled IP packet, frame mode with an MPLS header, and cell mode using the existing header.

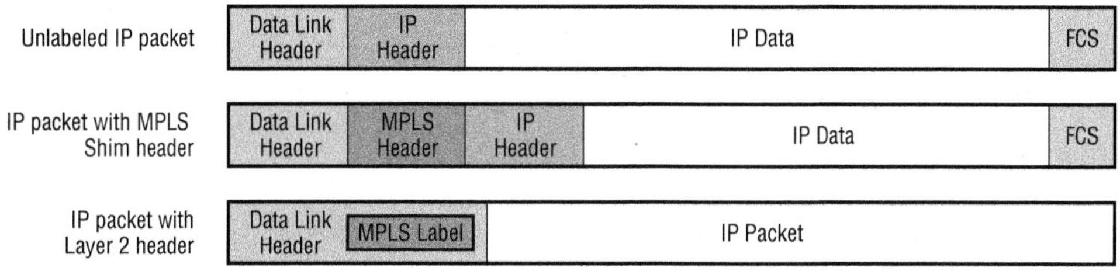

MPLS Label Encapsulation

As defined by IANA (`http://www.iana.org/assignments/ethernet-numbers`), the Ethertype (type) field of an Ethernet frame must use the Type values shown in Table 11.3 to identify the payload of the frame.

Table 11.3 Ethertype Values for MPLS

Ethertype Value	Description
0x0800	IPv4
0x8847	MPLS unicast
0x8848	MPLS multicast

Figure 11.26 shows two Ethernet frames, one with an IP packet and the other with a unicast MPLS packet.

MPLS implements a general model in which a labeled packet may carry multiple labels, organized as a last-in, first-out sequence. This sequence is referred to as an *MPLS label stack*. An MPLS frame with a single label is said to have a label stack of 1. An MPLS frame with two labels has a label stack of 2, etc. Multiple entry label stacks are used in the implementation of MPLS-based services such as VPLS, VPRN, and fast reroute. The 7750 SR supports a maximum of five labels in the MPLS label stack.

Figure 11.26 Two Ethernet frames. The top frame carries an IP packet, and the lower frame carries a unicast MPLS packet.

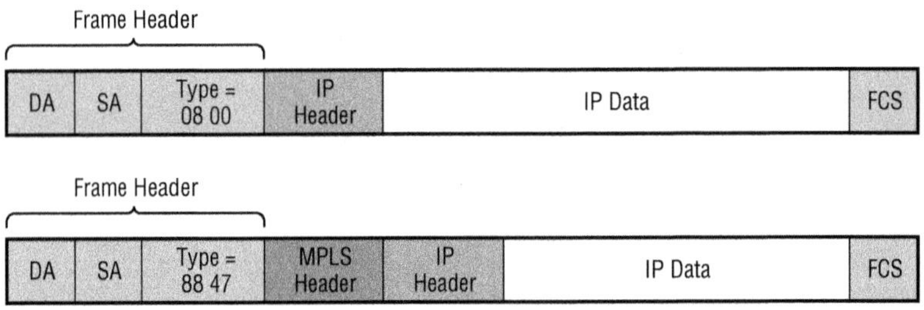

MPLS Label Structure

The structure of the MPLS header is shown in Figure 11.27. Each MPLS header is a fixed length of 4 bytes (32 bits) in size. Table 11.4 describes the fields of the header.

Figure 11.27 MPLS header.

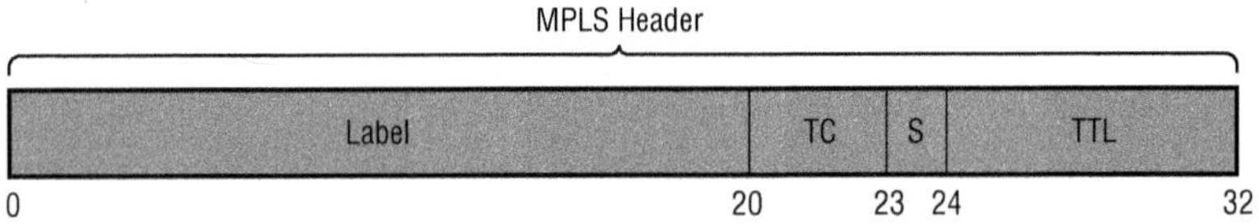

Table 11.4 Fields of the MPLS Header

Field	Description	Size (bits)	Purpose
Label	MPLS label	20	Contains label value.
TC	Traffic class	3	Indicates QoS handling.
S	Bottom of stack	1	A value of 1 indicates the last label in the stack.
TTL	Time to live	8	Hop count.

The fields of the header are described in more detail below:

- **Label field**—The primary field of the MPLS header is the MPLS label itself. The label field carries the label used to forward the packet inside and is 20 bits long. The range of label values is 0 through 1,048,575. Label values are discussed in more detail in the next section.

- **Traffic Class (TC) Field**—The Traffic Class field was renamed from the Experimental (EXP) field in RFC 5462. It was always intended for carrying quality of service (QoS) information but was not considered to be sufficiently well defined when the MPLS standards were developed. The use of this field to support Differentiated Services is described in RFC 3270 and its use for Explicit Congestion Notification in RFC 5129.
- **Bottom of Stack (S) field**—The S field is 1 bit in length and indicates that the bottom or last entry of the MPLS label stack has been reached and that the payload header immediately follows. The S bit is set to 1 for the last entry in the label stack (the bottom of the stack), and 0 for all other label stack entries. The use of the S bit is shown in Figure 11.28.

Figure 11.28 All labels in the MPLS label stack have the S bit set to 0, except the last one before the payload header.

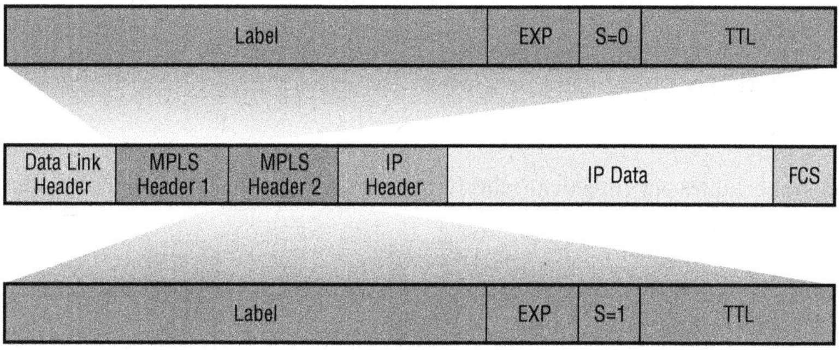

- **TTL field**—The MPLS TTL field is used as a control mechanism over the packet lifetime similar to IP TTL, to prevent packets looping in the network. Label processing is always based on the outer label in the stack, which includes information about the operations to perform on the packet's label stack, including modification to the MPLS TTL header field.

Pipe and Uniform Mode

There are two approaches to the handling of the TC and TTL fields in the MPLS header. These are known as pipe and uniform mode:

- **Uniform mode**—In uniform mode, the MPLS routers act as if they were routers in the overall end-to-end connection (think of uniform behavior by the MPLS routers).

- **Pipe mode**—In pipe mode, the MPLS routers are effectively invisible from the perspective of the end-to-end connection (think of the LSP appearing simply as a pipe between the edge routers).

Uniform mode is really only meaningful for an MPLS network in which the payload is IP packets. In a network providing Layer 2 services such as VPLS, the payload is an Ethernet frame, and pipe mode is the only feasible method. The 7750 SR uses pipe mode exclusively for managing the TC and TTL fields in the MPLS network.

RFC 3270 describes how the TC field is used to specify QoS treatment for packets in an MPLS network. In uniform mode, the TC value is determined by the DSCP (differentiated services code point) value of the ingress IP packet. The first 3 bits of the DSCP value are copied into the TC field at the iLER, as shown in Figure 11.29. Within the MPLS network, the TC value may be modified depending on the QoS configuration of the network. At the eLER, the value of the TC field is copied back into the DSCP field of the IP header. Therefore, if the TC value was modified within the MPLS network, this new value is used in the DSCP field of the IP packet at the egress of the MPLS network.

Figure 11.29 DSCP values are copied into the TC field of the MPLS header in uniform mode.

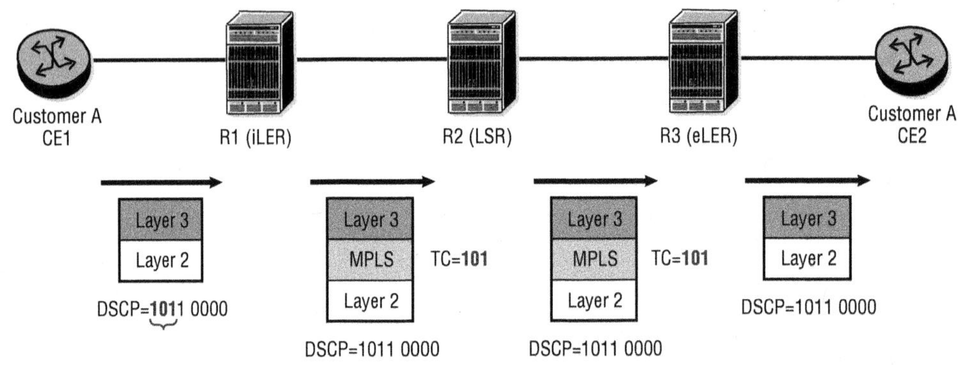

In pipe mode, the iLER applies a specific value for the TC field. This value may depend on the DSCP value of the IP packet or on other classification criteria. The TC value may be modified as the packet traverses the MPLS network, depending on the QoS configuration. However, the use of the TC field is independent of the payload DSCP value. At the eLER, the MPLS header is popped, and the original DSCP value of the IP header is maintained.

The 7750 SR uses pipe mode, and the TC value is explicitly set by a QoS policy at the iLER. If the label stack contains multiple labels, the TC value of the inner labels is set to the same value as the outer label (Figure 11.30).

Figure 11.30 TC values are set by a QoS policy at ingress in pipe mode. The value used for the TC field has no effect on the DSCP value of the payload.

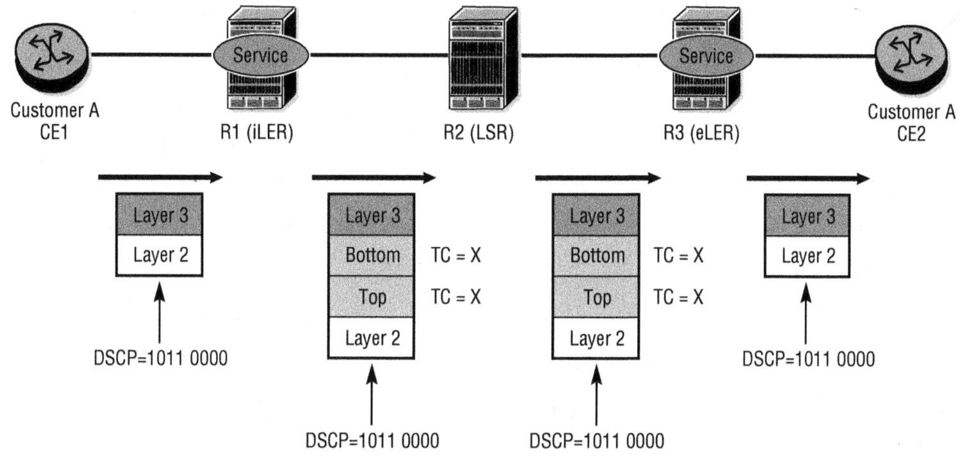

Within the MPLS domain, the LSRs copy the TC value into any new MPLS header that is swapped or pushed onto the stack. If an outer MPLS header is popped, then its TC value is copied into the newly revealed inner MPLS header.

RFC 3443 defines time to live (TTL) processing in MPLS networks. TTL handling is also described in terms of uniform mode and pipe mode. In uniform mode, the MPLS network is "visible" from the outside, and thus MPLS nodes decrement the same TTL value as the non-MPLS nodes. In pipe mode, the MPLS network is "invisible" from the outside in the sense that the network appears as a single pipe between the ingress and egress LER. TTL handling in the pipe mode MPLS network is independent of the IP TTL.

An unlabeled IP packet received by the iLER undergoes standard TTL treatment upon ingress (as per RFC 1812). If the resulting TTL is non-zero, the packet is accepted for processing by the iLER.

In uniform mode, the TTL value is set to the TTL value of the arriving IP packet, minus one. The TTL value in the MPLS header is decremented by one at each MPLS router. Upon egress from the MPLS network, the TTL value in the MPLS header is decremented and copied to the TTL field of the IP packet. Thus, in uniform mode, the TTL value reflects the number of hops from source to destination, including all MPLS routers (Figure 11.31).

Figure 11.31 TTL handling in uniform mode. The TTL value is decremented by the number of MPLS and non-MPLS nodes traversed.

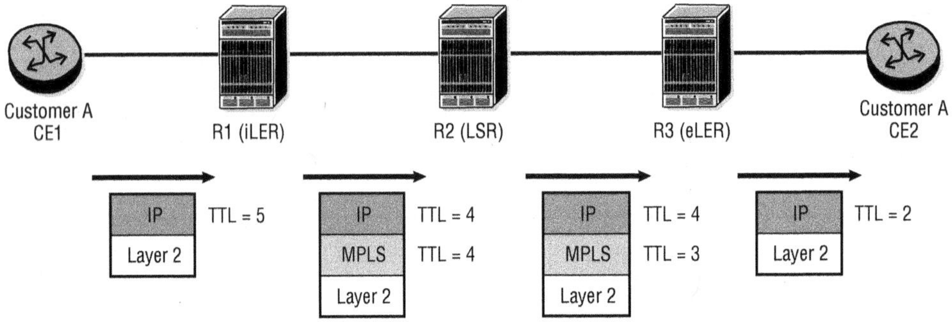

In pipe mode for a Layer 3 service (payload is an IP packet), the TTL value of the arriving packet is decremented at the iLER and encapsulated with an MPLS header. The 7750 SR sets the TTL value to 255 in the outer MPLS (transport) header and sets the value in the inner (service) header to the payload TTL, as shown in Figure 11.32. The TTL value of the outer header is decremented at each hop as the packet traverses the network. Upon egress, the MPLS label is popped, and the TTL value of the IP payload is decremented. The result is that the payload TTL is decremented once for the iLER and once for the eLER, but not for the transit LSRs.

Figure 11.32 TTL handling in pipe mode for a Layer 3 service. The TTL value of the IP payload is decremented at the iLER and eLER. The TTL in the outer MPLS header is set to 255 at ingress.

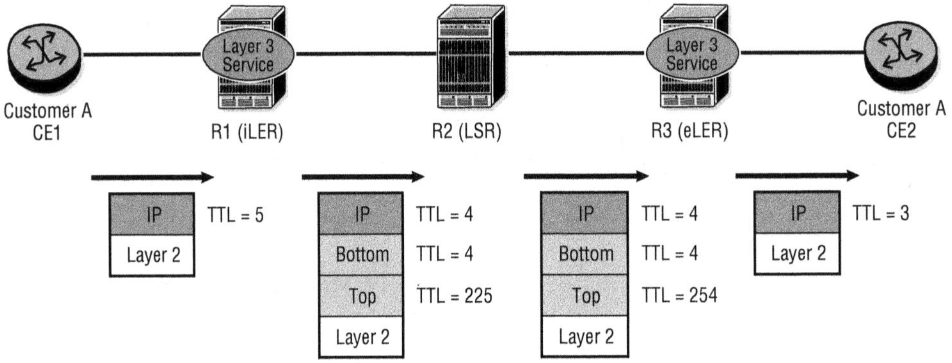

When the MPLS network is used to provide a Layer 2 service, the entire MPLS network is invisible to the IP path because it is part of the Layer 2 path. In this case, if the Layer 2 frames are carrying IP, the TTL value is not changed. The TTL value is set to 255 in both the outer (transport) and the inner (service) label (Figure 11.33).

Figure 11.33 TTL handling in pipe mode for a Layer 2 service. TTL is set to 255 in all MPLS labels at ingress. TTL in the payload is unaffected.

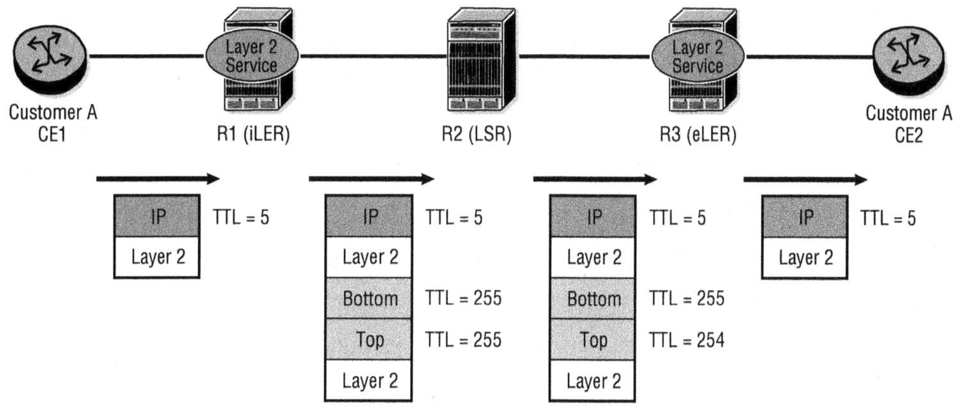

In either mode, the MPLS TTL is decremented at each LSR. If the value reaches zero, the packet is discarded. Operations on the TTL and the TC field are always performed on the outermost (top) label in the stack. These fields in any inner labels remain untouched.

11.5 Label Values and Label Space

The MPLS label field is 20 bits in length and carries the label used to forward the packet inside an MPLS domain. The range of possible label values is 0 through 1,048,575.

Label Values

Label values 0–15 are reserved in the MPLS standard. The use of these reserved labels is described below. On the 7750 SR, the label space is further divided, as shown in Table 11.5.

Table 11.5 MPLS Label Space on the 7750 SR

Label Range	Label Usage
0–15	Reserved by the MPLS standard
16–31	Reserved for future use
32–1,023	Statically assigned LSPs
1,024–2,047	Reserved for future use
2,048–18,431	Statically assigned for services
18,432–32,767	Reserved for future use
32,768–131,071	Dynamically assigned for LSPs and services
131,072–1,048,575	Reserved for future use

Per-Platform and Per-Interface Label Space

The concept of label space is useful for discussing the assignment and distribution of labels. There are two types of label space defined in the MPLS standard: per platform and per interface.

- **Per-platform**—Per-platform label space assigns a single label to each FEC per router and uses the same label on all interfaces of that router.
- **Per-interface**—Per-interface label space assigns a unique label to each FEC per interface. Per-interface label space is typically used with cell mode MPLS such as Frame Relay or ATM because the labels they use are local to the interface.

Per-platform label space uses fewer label resources than per-interface label space because the same label is advertised on all interfaces. The 7750 SR implements per-platform label space. Figure 11.34 shows the difference between per-platform and per-interface label space. The labels from the ATM router (per-interface label space) are the VPI/VCI (Virtual Path Identifier/Virtual Channel Identifier) value for the circuit.

Reserved Labels and Penultimate Hop Popping

In MPLS, there are several reserved label values with special handling required for these labels. The reserved values are:

- 0—IPv4 explicit null
- 1—Router alert
- 2—IPv6 explicit null
- 3—IPv4 implicit null

Figure 11.34 A comparison of per-platform and per-interface label space.

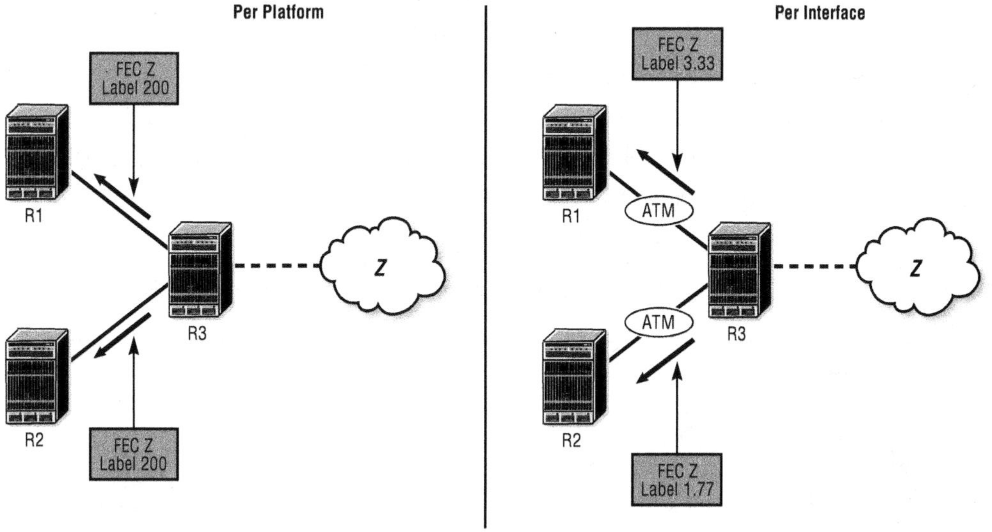

The remaining values reserved by MPLS (4 through 15) have not been defined to date.

Router Alert Label

The router alert label (value of 1) indicates that the packet is intended for the next-hop router and should be examined by that router. Typically the router alert label is used for OAM (operations, administration, and maintenance) functions, such as testing reachability.

Implicit Null and Penultimate Hop Popping

The implicit null label (value of 3) is signaled only by an egress LER. It is a request to the upstream router (the penultimate, or second last router) to pop the label and forward the packet. Because the egress router would normally pop the label and forward the packet as an unlabeled packet, the label is not actually necessary for the last hop. This is known as *penultimate hop popping* (PHP) because the label is popped by the second last router on the LSP instead of the last router.

Normally, the MPLS egress router performs two lookups: first a label lookup, and then an IP forwarding lookup to forward the unlabeled packet. Penultimate hop popping is used by an egress router that suffers a performance penalty for doing two lookups. With penultimate hop popping there is no label for the egress router to look up, and it simply forwards the unlabeled packet. To request penultimate hop popping, the egress router signals a label value of 3 to its neighbors. This value will never occur as an MPLS label in a data packet. It is a way of signaling the neighbors to pop the label before forwarding, instead of swapping the label.

Figure 11.35 shows an LSP with R1 as the ingress router and R3 as the egress. R3 requests PHP by signaling a label value of 3 to R2. When R2 receives a packet with a label of 200, the LFIB indicates an egress label of 3. This value is not used for the label; rather, the label is popped, and the unlabeled packet is forwarded to R3.

Figure 11.35 R3 requests penultimate hop popping from its upstream router by signaling a label value of 3.

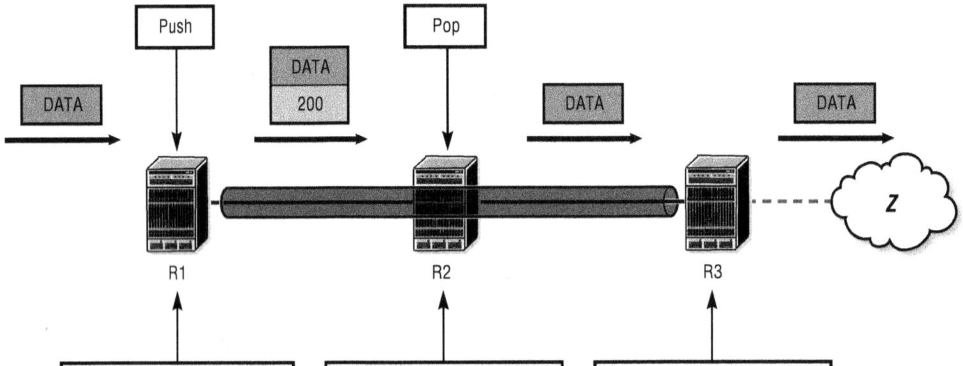

R1 Label Forwarding Table

FEC	Ingress Label	Egress Label	Next Hop
Z	-	200	R2

R2 Label Forwarding Table

FEC	Ingress Label	Egress Label	Next Hop
Z	200	3	R3

R3 Label Forwarding Table

(Not relevant for FEC Z)

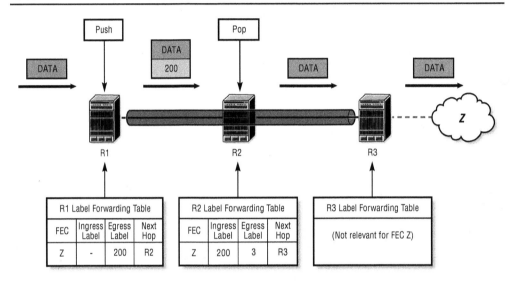

The disadvantage of PHP is that because the label has been popped by the penultimate router, the TC and TTL information in the label have been lost. As a result, there is no way to signal the QoS handling that should be applied to the packet. When information in the label is required at egress, the explicit null label is used.

Explicit Null Label

The explicit null label (value of 0 or 2) is similar to the implicit null label and is signaled only by an egress LER. Because this is the last hop on the MPLS network, this label can be simply POPped by the egress router without any lookup. Again, this label is used by routers that suffer performance penalties from a double lookup. The difference is that the explicit null label is used to encapsulate the data packet, whereas the implicit null label (value of 3) is not. The explicit null label is typically used if it is desired to carry the other information in the MPLS label (TC bits and TTL) to the egress router.

In Figure 11.36, R3 is the egress router for the LSP and has signaled a label of 0 to its upstream router. When R2 receives a packet with a label of 200, the LFIB indicates that it should be forwarded to R3 with a label of 0. When R3 sees the value 0 in the label, it does not perform a lookup and immediately pops the label. The TC and TTL values can be processed from the label if desired.

Figure 11.36 R3 requests a label of 0 from its upstream router so that the label can be popped without a lookup.

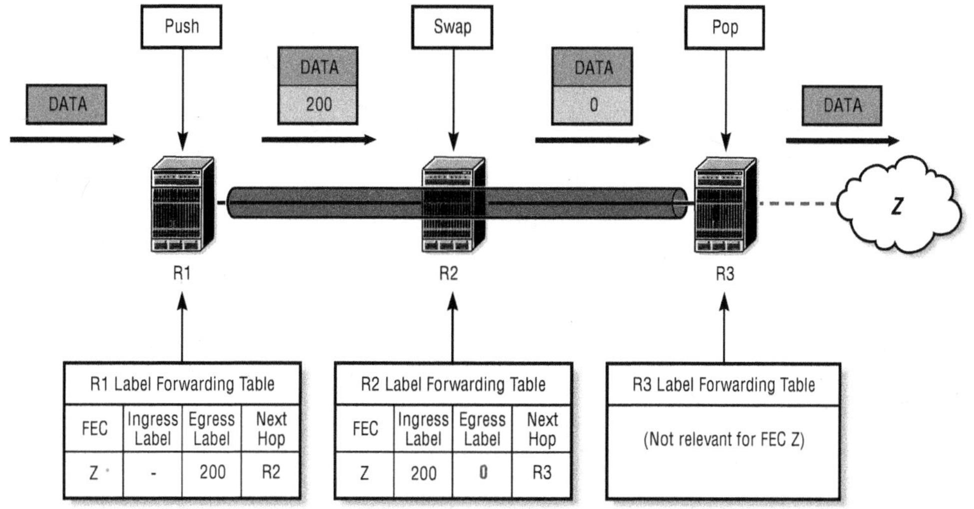

11.6 Static LSPs

A static LSP is a manually configured LSP in which the next-hop IP address, the outgoing label, and the label action are explicitly specified. These parameters must be configured on every node along the path.

To enable a bidirectional flow of traffic, two LSPs must be created, one in each direction across the provider core. Dynamic label signaling protocols such as LDP or RSVP-TE may be shut down or may coexist with static label mappings.

Manual label definition provides the following benefits:

- High degree of control over each static LSP—allows you to manually define each path.
- Does not require dynamic label signaling protocols or their associated configuration.

However, the following caveats must be considered:

- Every node in the network must be manually configured.
- Changes or modifications must be manually implemented.
- There are no dynamic redundancy features.
- Label stacking is not supported.

Although static label assignment does provide a high degree of control, you can see there are limited benefits to using them. Typically, static label assignment is used only in a vendor interoperation situation when there are problems with getting a dynamic signaling protocol to work. The dynamic signaling protocol RSVP-TE allows complete control over the path used; thus, there is really no benefit to using static LSPs in general.

Static LSP Configuration Requirements

To configure a static LSP to be used to transport a service, the following steps must be performed:

1. **Configure interface**—The Layer 2 and Layer 3 parameters required for the interface must first be configured.
2. **Enable interface for MPLS**—Any interface used by the static LSP must be added into the MPLS protocol instance. Even though RSVP-TE is not actually used to signal labels, MPLS must be enabled to perform label operations.
3. **Verify label space**—Verify the acceptable label range for use with static configurations and the labels already in use.
4. **Configure the iLER**—The configuration of the static LSP on the ingress router is notably different from a transit or egress device.
5. **Configure the label maps**—The transit routers on the LSP are configured with a SWAP operation and the eLER with a POP operation.
6. **Configure an LSP in the opposite direction**—To support a service, LSPs must be configured in both directions.

Configuring a Static LSP

The following example shows the steps to configuring a static LSP for the network in Figure 11.37 from the ingress PE (PE-1), across three transit LSRs (LSR 1, LSR 2, and LSR 3) to the egress PE (PE-2).

Figure 11.37 Configuring a static LSP across an MPLS network.

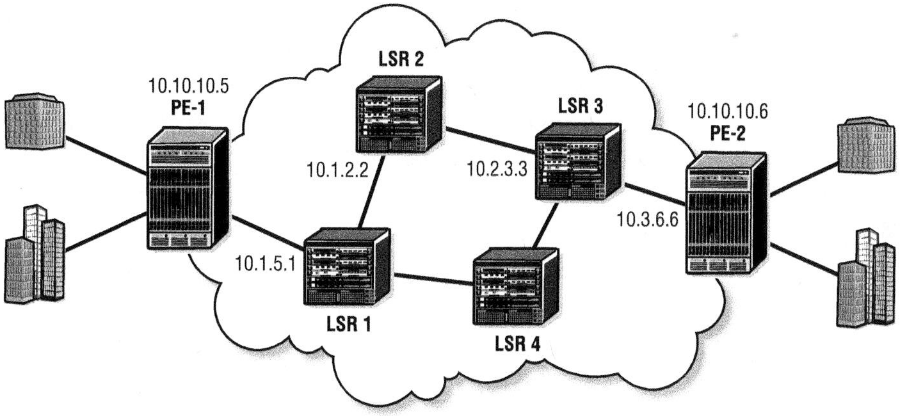

The `show router mpls label-range` command displays the total number of available labels on the router per defined range (Listing 11.1). Static LSPs should be configured using labels in the range of 32 through 1023.

Listing 11.1 MPLS label ranges available on the router

```
A:P1# show router mpls label-range

=========================================================================
Label Ranges
=========================================================================
Label Type     Start Label    End Label     Aging        Total Available
-------------------------------------------------------------------------
Static-lsp     32             1023          -            991
Static-svc     2048           18431         -            16384
Dynamic        32768          131071        0            98304
=========================================================================
```

Use the `show router mpls label` command on each router along the LSP to display the contents of the LIB (Listing 11.2). This way you can be sure that the labels have not already been used in another configuration.

Listing 11.2 MPLS label values in use on the router

```
A:P1# show router mpls label 32 131071 in-use

===============================================================
MPLS Labels from 32 to 131071 (In-use)
===============================================================
Label                Label Type           Label Owner
---------------------------------------------------------------
598                  static-lsp           RSVP
999                  static-lsp           RSVP
131069               dynamic              ILDP
131070               dynamic              ILDP
131071               dynamic              ILDP
---------------------------------------------------------------
In-use labels (Owner: All) in specified range    : 5
In-use labels in entire range                    : 5
===============================================================
```

On the ingress router the static LSP is configured in the `config>router>mpls` context (Listing 11.3). Two items must be specified in the configuration:

- **System IP address of the egress node**—If the LSP is used as a transport tunnel for a VPN service, it will not be operationally up unless this value matches the far end value of the tunnel.
- **Label operation and next-hop for the LSP**—Because it's the ingress, the label operation is a `push` with the value to be pushed on the stack. `Next-hop` is the interface address of the next-hop. The static LSP will be operationally up if the router has an ARP entry for this address. If not, the router will make the LSP operationally down and continue to ARP for the address.

Listing 11.3 Configuration of a static LSP on the ingress router

```
A:PE-1# configure router
A:PE-1>config>router# mpls
A:PE-1>config>router>mpls# static-lsp "PE-1 to PE-2"
A:PE-1>config>router>mpls>static-lsp$ to 10.10.10.6
A:PE-1>config>router>mpls>static-lsp$ push 999 nexthop 10.1.5.1
A:PE-1>config>router>mpls>static-lsp$ no shutdown
A:PE-1>config>router>mpls>static-lsp$ exit all
```

On the transit LSRs the static LSP is configured in the `mpls interface` context of the ingress interface with the `label-map` command. We specify a label-map for the ingress label to define the label operation (`swap`), the egress label, and the next-hop for the LSP. Configuration of the three transit LSRs is shown in Listings 11.4 through 11.6.

Listing 11.4 Configuration of the label-map on the first transit LSR (LSR 1)

```
A:LSR-1>config>router# mpls
A:LSR-1>config>router>mpls# interface "to PE-1"
A:LSR-1>config>router>mpls>if$ label-map 999
A:LSR-1>config>router>mpls>if>label-map$ swap 998 nexthop 10.1.2.2
A:LSR-1>config>router>mpls>if>label-map$ no shutdown
```

Listing 11.5 Configuration of the label-map on LSR 2

```
A:LSR-2>config>router# mpls
A:LSR-2>config>router>mpls# interface "to LSR 1"
A:LSR-2>config>router>mpls>if$ label-map 998
A:LSR-2>config>router>mpls>if>label-map$ swap 997 nexthop 10.2.3.3
A:LSR-2>config>router>mpls>if>label-map$ no shutdown
```

Listing 11.6 Configuration of the label-map on LSR 3

```
A:LSR-3>config>router# mpls
A:LSR-3>config>router>mpls# interface "to LSR 2"
```

(continued)

Listing 11.6 *(continued)*

```
A:LSR-3>config>router>mpls>if$ label-map 997
A:LSR-3>config>router>mpls>if>label-map$ swap 996 nexthop 10.3.6.6
A:LSR-3>config>router>mpls>if>label-map$ no shutdown
```

The final step in the configuration is the `label-map` on the egress router. The operation is now a `pop` operation, and there is no next-hop required (Listing 11.7).

Listing 11.7 Configuration of the label-map on the egress router (PE-2)

```
A:PE-2>config>router# mpls
A:PE-2>config>router>mpls# interface "to LSR 3"
A:PE-2>config>router>mpls>if$ label-map 996
A:PE-2>config>router>mpls>if>label-map$ pop
A:PE-2>config>router>mpls>if>label-map$ no shutdown
```

Notice how the label values match across the LSP:

- The egress label on PE-1 matches the ingress label on LSR 1.
- The egress label on LSR 1 matches the ingress label on LSR 2.
- The egress label on LSR 2 matches the ingress label on LSR 3.
- The egress label on LSR 3 matches the ingress label on PE-2.

If for some reason the label values do not match in this way, then, of course, the LSP will not function. The LSP may show as operationally up at all hops, but if the label values do not match, the LSP cannot transmit data.

This completes the configuration of one LSP in one direction. If the LSP was correctly configured and the next-hop is reachable at each step from ingress to egress, the LSP will be up and functioning. To verify this, we must check the LSP at each hop. In addition, if we wish to use the LSP for a service, we must also configure one in the opposite direction.

Verifying the Static LSP

There is a different command for displaying the status on each of the different types of LSRs: ingress, transit, and egress. The verification is shown in Listings 11.8 through 11.10.

Listing 11.8 Verify static LSP on the ingress router

```
A:PE-1# show router mpls static-lsp

===============================================================================
MPLS Static LSPs (Originating)
===============================================================================
LSP Name      To             Next Hop    Out Label Up/Down Time    Adm  Opr
  ID                                      Out Port
-------------------------------------------------------------------------------
PE-1 to PE-2 10.10.10.6     10.1.2.2    999       0d 00:11:34     Up   Up
  2                                       1/1/1
-------------------------------------------------------------------------------
LSPs : 1
===============================================================================
```

Listing 11.9 Verify static LSP on a transit router

```
A:LSR-1# show router mpls static-lsp transit

===============================================================================
MPLS Static LSPs (Transit)
===============================================================================
In Label    In Port     Out Label    Out Port    Next Hop        Adm    Opr
-------------------------------------------------------------------------------
999         1/1/1       998          1/1/3       10.2.3.3        Up     Up
-------------------------------------------------------------------------------
LSPs : 1
===============================================================================
```

Listing 11.10 Verify static LSP on the egress router

```
A:PE-2# show router mpls static-lsp terminate

===============================================================================
MPLS Static LSPs (Terminate)
===============================================================================
In Label    In Port     Out Label    Out Port     Next Hop       Adm    Opr
-------------------------------------------------------------------------------
```

(continued)

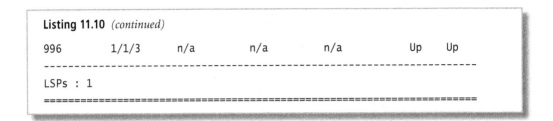

Listing 11.10 *(continued)*

```
996         1/1/3       n/a          n/a          n/a             Up     Up
-------------------------------------------------------------------------------
LSPs : 1
===============================================================================
```

If the "to" address configured on the ingress LER is the correct system address of the egress LER, the LSP is up at each hop, and if you have an LSP configured for the reverse direction, you can configure a service to use the LSP as a transport tunnel. As you can see, the process is labor-intensive and error-prone, and thus the use of a dynamic label distribution protocol is always preferred.

11.7 Dynamic Label Distribution

In a typical IP/MPLS network used for VPN services, information about destinations and the labels to reach these destinations are exchanged using an IGP and a dynamic label distribution protocol. A typical IGP would be OSPF or IS-IS, and a typical label distribution protocol would be LDP or RSVP-TE.

The IGP is used to distribute information about FECs that are reachable in the network. In a services network of 7750 SRs, the FECs that we are interested in are usually the system addresses of the PE routers in the domain.

The purpose of the Label Distribution Protocol is to provide a label binding for the FECs in the network. A label binding associates an FEC to a locally significant label. These label bindings represent the LSP itself. There will be multiple LSPs established, typically one per FEC.

Label Distribution Protocols define the procedures and messages by which MPLS LSRs inform each other of the label bindings they have made. Label distribution is done before the forwarding of any data. Once label assignment and distribution are complete, data traffic can be forwarded across the MPLS network. Based on the destination FEC, a label is assigned to a packet upon network ingress, gets swapped inside the network, and is then removed upon egress from the MPLS network.

It should be clearly stated that MPLS itself does not provide any advantage in convergence time over a simple IP network with dynamic routing. MPLS is dependent on the IGP for establishing the path in most cases, as well as the signaling of labels. Thus, when there is a topology change, forwarding cannot occur until the IGP has converged *and* labels have been signaled for the LSPs.

The advantage of MPLS is in the separation of the forwarding mechanism from the control plane. This provides the ability to transport data other than normally addressed IP data on paths other than the one chosen through the IGP. MPLS can also provide higher availability by allowing alternative paths to be established so that when a failure is detected, traffic can be immediately switched to the alternate path without waiting for the IGP to converge.

Label Distribution Protocols

When an IP/MPLS network is used to provide VPN services, two labels are used to transport user data across the network (Figure 11.38). The outer label is used to label-switch the user packet across the MPLS network and is known as the *transport label.* The inner label is used between the endpoints (the ingress and egress PE routers) to identify the VPN service to which the packet belongs. This is known as the *service label.* Different protocols are used for signaling the transport and service labels.

Figure 11.38 Transport labels define the transport tunnel across the network; service labels identify the service between the endpoints (PE routers).

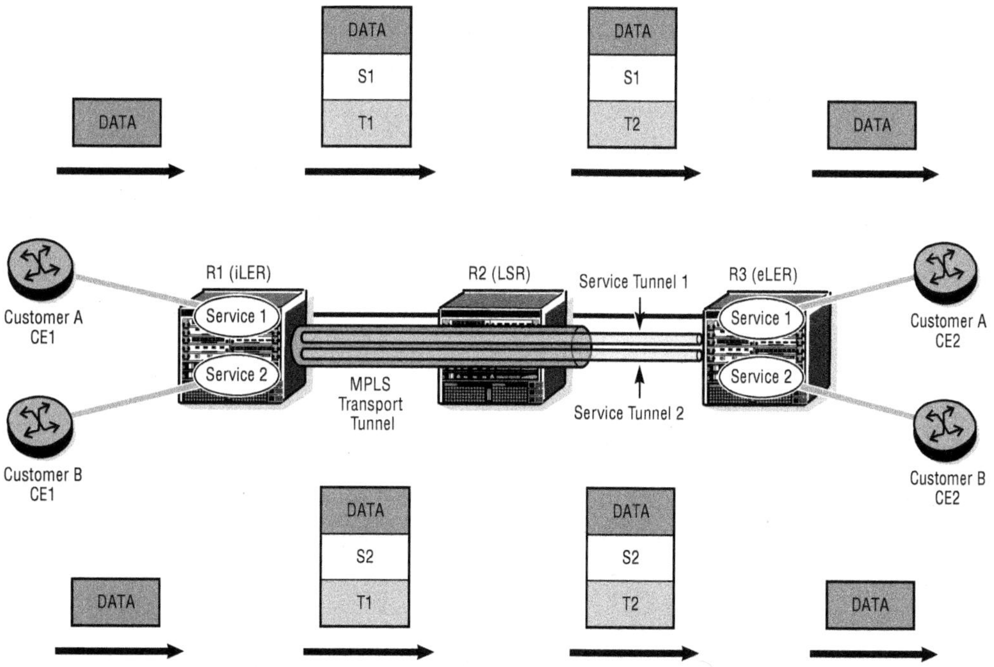

The two protocols used for distribution of the transport labels in an IP/MPLS network are LDP and RSVP-TE. LDP provides a simple and efficient mechanism for label distribution, but LSPs always follow the path selected by the IGP. RSVP-TE is more complex to configure and operate but provides much more control over the path followed by the LSP. It is used for traffic engineering and for provisioning highly available and redundant LSPs.

The two protocols used for distribution of service labels are T-LDP (targeted LDP) and MP-BGP (Multiprotocol BGP). T-LDP is used to signal service labels for Layer 2 services (VPWS and VPLS) and MP-BGP is used to signal service labels for Layer 3 VPRN services.

The MPLS chapters in this book are primarily concerned with the signaling and use of transport labels. Service labels are described in more detail in Chapter 17.

Downstream and Upstream

Downstream and *upstream* are terms relative to each FEC or LSP. The terms *ingress* and *egress* (as used with "ingress LER" and "egress LER") always refer to the direction of data flow. Data packets flow in the downstream direction, from ingress to egress. Label bindings are distributed in the upstream direction, from egress to ingress.

Figure 11.39 shows two FECs in an MPLS network, `10.10.10.5/32` and `10.10.10.6/32`. Data destined to `10.10.10.5` flows in the downstream direction along the LSP from LER 2 to LER 1 (right to left). However, labels are distributed in the upstream direction. LER 1 provides a label for its FEC (`10.10.10.5/32`) to its upstream neighbor LSR 1. LSR 1 provides a label for the FEC to its upstream neighbor LSR 2, and LSR 2 provides a label for the FEC to LER 2. Once LER 2 has a label for the FEC, it can transmit data using that label. The same process works in reverse for the FEC `10.10.10.6/32`. You can see that labels are originated from the LSR "attached" to the FEC in much the same way that routing information is distributed into the IGP from the router that is attached to the destination.

11.8 Label Distribution Modes

Three pairs of attributes are defined for label distribution in MPLS (Figure 11.40). In theory, any combination of the three attributes is possible. In practice, only specific combinations are used.

Figure 11.39 Data flows in the downstream direction; labels are distributed in the upstream direction.

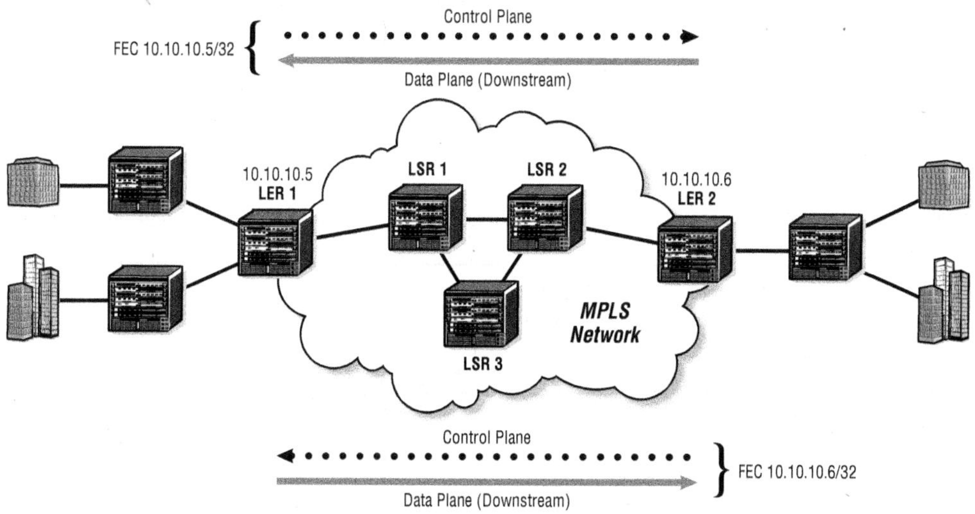

Figure 11.40 Matrix of MPLS label distribution modes.

Label Distribution Modes		
Distribution	Downstream On Demand	Downstream Unsolicited
Control	Ordered Control	Independent Control
Retention	Conservative Retention	Liberal Retention

The 7750 SR uses two modes:

- Downstream unsolicited, ordered control with liberal retention (method used by LDP)
- Downstream on demand, ordered control with conservative retention (method used by RSVP-TE)

Downstream Unsolicited

The MPLS architecture allows an LSR to generate and distribute label bindings to other LSRs without receiving an explicit request for a label. This is known as downstream unsolicited label distribution. In downstream unsolicited mode, an LSR generates label mappings for local FECs and advertises them to all peers for which it might be a next-hop for these FECs.

In Figure 11.41, R3 generates a label (value 100) for its FEC Z, even though it has not received an explicit request to do so. R2 receives the label from R3 and installs it in its LIB. R2 then generates a label (value 200) for the FEC and sends it to R1.

Figure 11.41 In downstream unsolicited mode, labels are distributed to upstream neighbors without any specific request.

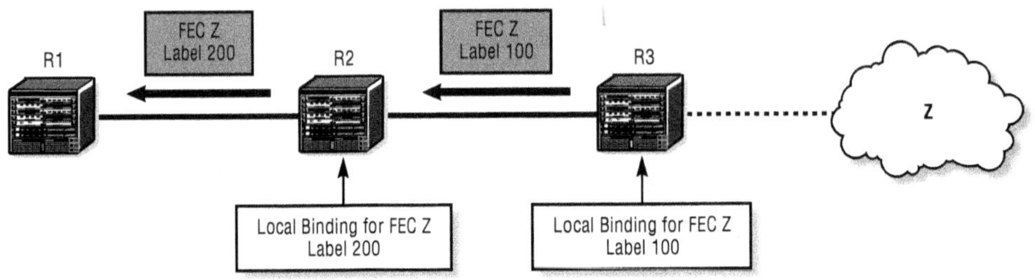

Downstream on Demand

In downstream-on-demand mode, label mappings are provided to an upstream LSR only when requested by that LSR. In Figure 11.42, the R1 does not have a valid label mapped to the FEC Z and requests it from its downstream neighbor. The request travels downstream until it reaches the destination FEC.

Figure 11.42 Labels must be explicitly requested in downstream-on-demand mode.

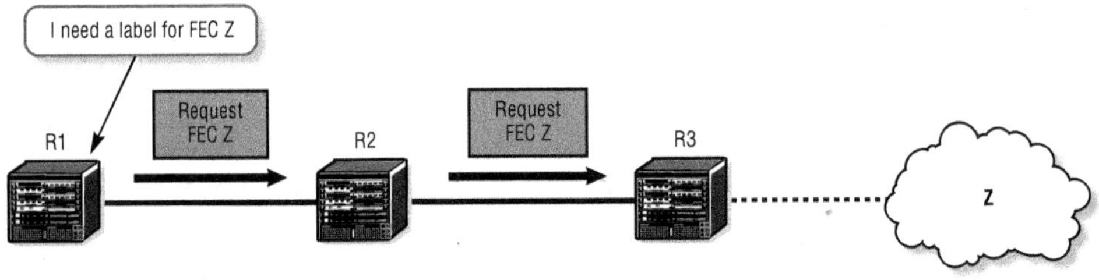

When the request for a label reaches the destination FEC, the egress router generates a label for this FEC and sends it to the upstream neighbor that requested the label. In Figure 11.43, R3 generates a label (value 100) for the FEC Z and sends it to R2. R2 installs this in its LIB and generates a label (value 200) that is sent upstream to R1.

Figure 11.43 The egress router (R3) generates a label and sends it to the upstream neighbor that requested the label. The process repeats until the ingress router (R1) receives a label for the FEC.

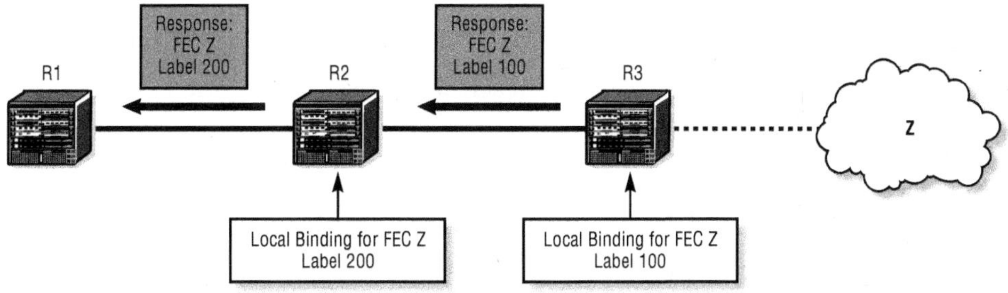

Although it is the ingress router that initially requests the label for the FEC in downstream on demand, labels are always signaled in the upstream direction. This is true for both downstream on demand and downstream unsolicited label distribution modes.

Ordered versus Independent Control Mode

In a downstream unsolicited mode of operation (used by LDP), a router could conceivably generate a label for an FEC as soon as it becomes aware of the FEC through its IGP. This behavior is known as independent control mode. In ordered control mode, a router does not generate a label for an FEC until it has received a valid label from its downstream neighbor (Figure 11.44).

Figure 11.44 Behavior of ordered control mode versus independent control mode.

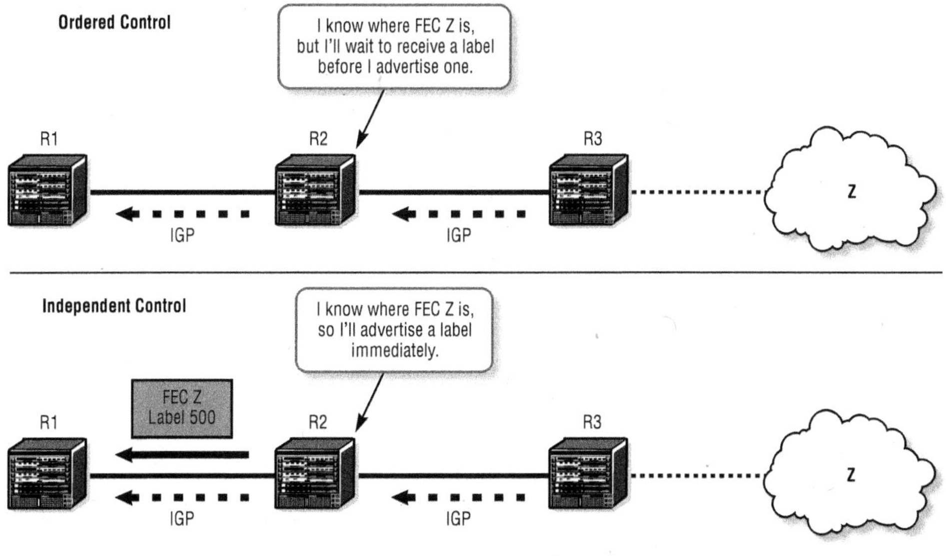

The 7750 SR always operates in ordered control mode. In LDP a label is not generated for a downstream FEC until the router has a valid label for it. A valid label is a label from the router that is the next-hop for the FEC. This means that label mappings always proceed from the egress router in an ordered upstream direction to the ingress router. It may take a little longer for the LSP label to reach the ingress with ordered control, but the ingress is assured that it has a path to the egress when it receives the label.

Label Retention Modes

There are two modes of operation for label retention: liberal retention and conservative retention. With liberal label retention, every label received from neighbors is stored in the LIB. One label is chosen for each FEC to be used for forwarding. This is known as the active label and is stored in the LFIB. With conservative label retention, only the active label is kept in the LIB, and thus there is no difference between the LIB and LFIB.

In LDP, an MPLS router receives a label for a given FEC from every neighbor that has a path to the FEC. However, only one router is the next-hop for the FEC. The label received from the next-hop router is the one that becomes the active label. If there is a change in the next-hop router, there may already be a label in the LIB from that router, and this now becomes the active label.

RSVP-TE operates in downstream-on-demand mode, and thus the only label it receives for an FEC is from the next-hop router. Therefore, the LIB and LFIB are the same, and RSVP-TE uses conservative label retention.

The advantage of liberal label retention is that the router may react more quickly to a topology change because it already has a label from the new next-hop neighbor. The disadvantage is that the router uses more memory resources to store the labels received from all of its neighbors.

Chapter Review

Now that you have completed this chapter, you should have a good understanding of the following topics:

- The benefits provided by MPLS tunneling and its common applications
- Terminology used in MPLS networks
- The meaning of an FEC and its relationship to an LSP
- How packets are label switched across an MPLS network
- The difference between the MPLS control plane and data plane
- The meaning of the fields in the MPLS header
- The mapping of the MPLS label space and the use of the reserved label values
- Requirements for configuring a static LSP
- Steps to configure a static LSP at the ingress, transit, and egress routers
- How to verify the status of a static LSP
- The purpose of a dynamic label distribution protocol
- The difference between the transport label and the service label
- The meaning of *downstream* and *upstream* in an MPLS network
- The difference between downstream unsolicited and downstream-on-demand label distribution
- The difference between independent and ordered control mode
- The difference between conservative and liberal label retention

Post-Assessment

The following questions will test your knowledge and prepare you for the Alcatel-Lucent NRS II Certification Exam. Compare your responses with the answers listed in Appendix A. You can also use the CD that accompanies this book to take all the assessment tests and review the answers.

1. Which protocol cannot be transported in MPLS?
   - **A.** IP
   - **B.** Ethernet
   - **C.** ATM
   - **D.** Frame Relay
   - **E.** All of the above protocols can be transported in MPLS

2. What is the primary purpose of using MPLS for IGP shortcuts?
   - **A.** To provide the shortest path possible for forwarding data across the network
   - **B.** To reduce the number of EBGP sessions required
   - **C.** To reduce the number of IBGP sessions required
   - **D.** To eliminate the use of an IGP in the carrier network
   - **E.** None of the above.

3. Which statement is correct regarding the definition of a P router?
   - **A.** P routers are service-aware.
   - **B.** P routers are typically LERs.
   - **C.** P routers perform label PUSH and POP operations.
   - **D.** P routers have all their interfaces inside the service provider domain.
   - **E.** None of the above.

4. When is a packet assigned to an FEC in an MPLS network?
   - **A.** The FEC is assigned at each LSR in the MPLS network.
   - **B.** The FEC is assigned at the ingress LER.
   - **C.** The FEC is assigned at the ingress LER and at each LSR in the MPLS network.
   - **D.** The FEC is assigned at the ingress LER and the egress LER.
   - **E.** There is not enough information provided.

5. Which of the following MPLS signaling protocols are used to signal transport labels?
   - **A.** Multiprotocol BGP
   - **B.** Targeted LDP
   - **C.** GRE
   - **D.** RSVP-TE
   - **E.** All of the above
6. Which of the following is *not* a current application of MPLS today?
   - **A.** Virtual Private Networks
   - **B.** Traffic engineering
   - **C.** Enabling line rate forwarding
   - **D.** High availability and redundancy
   - **E.** All of the above
7. Which of the following statements about Label Distribution Protocols is correct?
   - **A.** Label bindings are distributed in the downstream direction.
   - **B.** A router using ordered control mode will not generate a label until it receives one from its upstream neighbor.
   - **C.** A router using liberal label retention will have the same contents in its LIB and LFIB.
   - **D.** Answers A and B are correct.
   - **E.** None of the above answers are correct.
8. Consider a network that is used to provide MPLS VPN services. Which statement best describes the packets that egress a CE router that is directly connected to a PE?
   - **A.** The packets are unlabeled.
   - **B.** The packets have one outer transport label and one inner service label.
   - **C.** The packets have one inner transport label and one outer service label.
   - **D.** There is not enough information to answer the question.

9. Which MPLS construct is used to store the active MPLS labels used for switching packets?

A. RIB

B. Route table

C. LIB

D. FIB

E. LFIB

10. Consider a network topology with three Alcatel-Lucent 7750 SR routers, R1, R2, and R3. R1 and R3 are PE routers, and R2 is a P router. An operator wants to configure a static LSP for a particular FEC to have a path of R1–R2–R3. Which statement below is correct?

A. The FEC needs to be configured on all three routers.

B. R2 needs to have its interface to R1 and its interface to R3 configured with label swap operations.

C. The same MPLS label must be used for the LSP on all three routers.

D. None of the above answers are correct.

11. Consider a network with an ingress PE, five P routers, and an egress PE that are all Alcatel-Lucent 7750 SRs used to provide a VPN service. When an unlabeled packet enters the ingress PE, it has an IP TTL of 10. What will the IP TTL be when the packet leaves the egress PE?

A. 255

B. 10

C. 9

D. 8

E. 3

F. There is not enough information to determine

12. Consider a network topology that contains three Alcatel-Lucent 7750 SRs: R1, R2, and R3. R3 is connected to R1 with port `1/1/1` and to R2 with port `1/1/2`. R3 advertises label 32,800 for a particular FEC to R1. What label will be advertised to R2 for the same FEC assuming that R3 is not advertising any other FECs?

   A. 32,800

   B. 32,799

   C. 32,801

   D. There is not enough information to determine

13. An MPLS router is signaled a label of 3 from its downstream router. What will the router do when it receives a data packet for this LSP from an upstream router?

   A. It will perform label swapping and transmit the packet with an MPLS label of 3.

   B. It will push the label of 3 and transmit the packet.

   C. It will silently discard the packet.

   D. It will extract the packet to the CPM for OAM options.

   E. It will pop the outer label and forward the packet to the next-hop.

14. Which statement is correct regarding an Alcatel-Lucent 7750 SR VPN services network?

   A. An IGP such as OSPF or IS-IS is required inside the carrier network.

   B. All user data traffic that traverses the carrier network contains an MPLS transport label that is held constant through the carrier network.

   C. All user data traffic that traverses the carrier network contains an MPLS service label that is swapped at each P router.

   D. None of the above statements are correct.

15. Which statement is correct concerning label distribution modes on the Alcatel-Lucent 7750 SR?

   A. RSVP-TE uses downstream unsolicited mode.

   B. LDP uses downstream-on-demand mode.

   C. RSVP-TE and LDP use conservative label retention.

   D. RSVP-TE and LDP use ordered control.

   E. None of the above statements are correct.

12 Label Distribution Protocol (LDP)

The Alcatel-Lucent NRS II exam topics covered in this chapter include the following:

- LDP PDUs and TLVs
- LDP messages
- Neighbor Discovery
- LDP session establishment
- LDP label generation
- LDP label propagation
- LDP and IGP interaction
- Controlling label distribution with policies

LDP (Label Distribution Protocol) is a protocol for distributing MPLS (Multiprotocol Label Switching) labels defined in RFC 5036. Routers configured for LDP establish an LDP session and become peers. The LDP sessions allow for the exchange of label to FEC (Forwarding Equivalence Class) binding information.

The LDP protocol in the Alcatel-Lucent 7750 SR is used for:

- Establishing transport tunnel LSPs (label switched paths) Establishing transport tunnel LSPs (label switched paths) to transport VPN data across the MPLS network. The labels are known as *transport labels.*
- Establishing Targeted LDP (T-LDP) sessions between directly or indirectly connected peers (used to signal labels and parameters for establishing a VPN service). These labels are known as *service labels.*

This chapter describes the operation of LDP as used to establish MPLS transport tunnels. This includes the type and format of LDP messages, the formation of LDP sessions, and the exchange of labels. Targeted LDP is essentially the same protocol, but used to exchange service labels. It is described in Chapter 17. We'll use the terms *LDP* or *Link LDP* to describe sessions established for the exchange of transport labels and *Targeted LDP* (or T-LDP) for sessions used to exchange service labels.

Pre-Assessment

The following assessment questions will help you understand what areas of the chapter you should review in more detail to prepare for the NRS II exam. You can also use the CD that accompanies this book to take all the assessment tests and review the answers.

1. Which of the following statements about LDP are correct?

A. Link LDP is used to exchange service labels.

B. Targeted LDP is used to exchange transport labels.

C. Link LDP peers are always directly connected.

D. Targeted LDP is required to provide L3 VPN services.

E. None of the above statements are correct.

2. What is the purpose of an LDP Notification message?
   - **A.** To create, change, and delete label mappings for FECs
   - **B.** To signal errors and other notable events
   - **C.** To establish LDP sessions between neighbors
   - **D.** To announce and maintain the presence of an LSR in a network
   - **E.** None of the above

3. Which statement below best describes the default behavior of LDP label advertisement on the Alcatel-Lucent 7750 SR?
   - **A.** Advertise a label for the system address.
   - **B.** Advertise labels for reachable FECs for which a label has been received.
   - **C.** Advertise a label for the system address and for reachable FECs for which a label has been received.
   - **D.** Do not advertise any labels unless an LDP export policy is configured.
   - **E.** Do not advertise any labels unless an LDP import policy is configured.

4. When an operator uses the `show router ldp bindings active` command on an Alcatel-Lucent 7750 SR, which construct is viewed?
   - **A.** RIB
   - **B.** FIB
   - **C.** LIB
   - **D.** LFIB
   - **E.** RTM

5. Consider a network topology that includes four Alcatel-Lucent 7750 SRs. An IGP (interior gateway protocol) is running in the network, and each router advertises its system interface into the IGP. Assuming that export policies are not configured and LDP is converged, how many label prefix bindings are seen on each router when the `show router ldp bindings` command is used?
   - **A.** 4
   - **B.** 8
   - **C.** 12
   - **D.** 16
   - **E.** There is not enough information to determine the answer.

12.1 LDP Operation and Messages

The process followed by routers configured for LDP can be described generally as:

1. **Discovery**—LDP routers discover their neighbors through the exchange of Hello messages.
2. **Session establishment**—LDP routers establish a TCP session with their neighbors for the reliable exchange of messages. They then establish an LDP session using the LDP Initialization message.
3. **Label exchange**—Once the LDP session is established, routers exchange labels for the FECs that they are aware of.

Link LDP peers are always directly connected, sharing a common data link. When LDP is enabled in a network of routers, LDP peering sessions are established between all neighboring LDP routers (Figure 12.1).

Figure 12.1 LDP routers form peering sessions with all their neighbors.

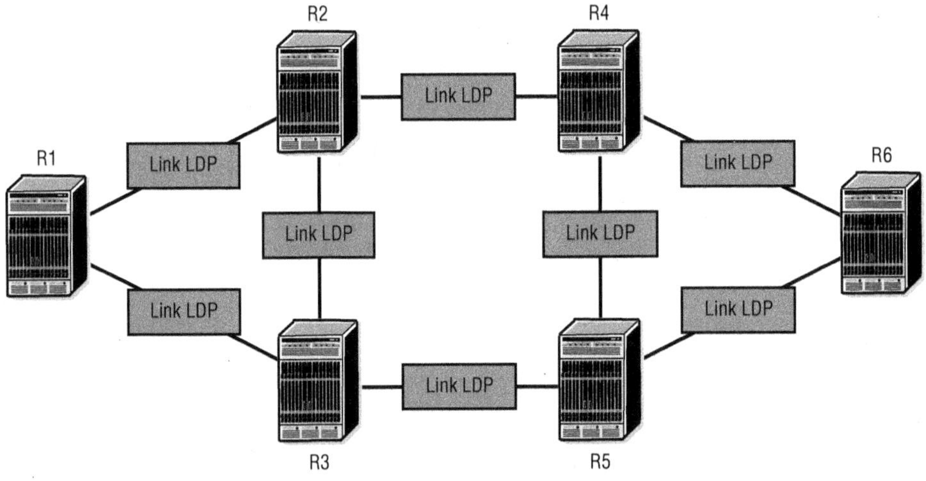

In a network of Alcatel-Lucent 7750 SRs enabled for LDP, the routers will establish peering sessions with their neighbors and exchange labels for their system addresses. The net result is a full mesh of LDP transport tunnels between all the routers.

LDP PDUs

All LDP messages are sent in LDP protocol data units (PDUs). Each PDU contains a header followed by one or more LDP messages. The LDP header is shown in Figure 12.2. The fields are described below.

Figure 12.2 Fields of the LDP header.

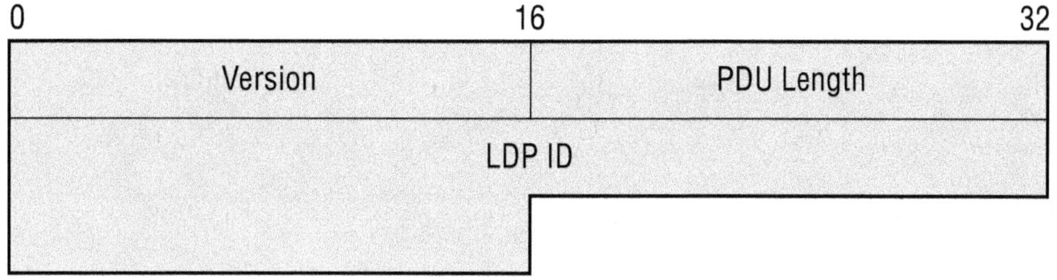

- **Version**—A 2-byte unsigned integer containing the version number of the protocol. The current version is 1.
- **PDU Length**—A 2-byte integer specifying the total length of this PDU in bytes, excluding the Version and PDU Length fields.
- **LDP Identifier**—A 6-byte field that uniquely identifies the label space of the sending LSR (label switch router). The first 4 bytes identify the LSR and must be a globally unique value, such as a 32-bit router ID. The last 2 bytes identify a specific label space within the LSR (Figure 12.3). If the router uses a per-platform label space, this value is zero. The 7750 SR uses a per-platform label space.

Figure 12.3 Fields of the LDP Identifier.

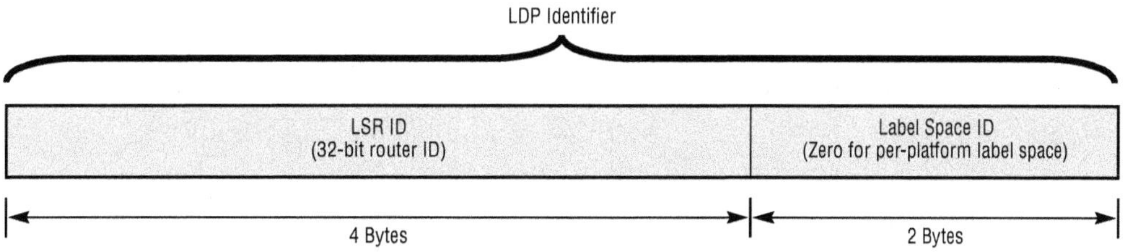

LDP Message Format

After the common LDP header, all messages have the format shown in Figure 12.4. The optional and mandatory parameters are encoded using a TLV (type–length–value) scheme. The fields of the LDP message are described below.

Figure 12.4 Fields of the LDP message.

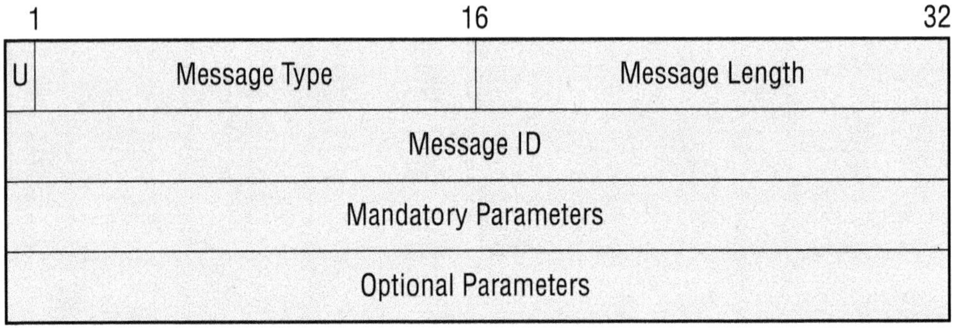

- **U bit**—(Unknown message bit) Upon receipt of an unknown message type, a notification is returned to the message originator if U is clear (0). The unknown message is silently ignored if U is set (1).
- **Message Type**—Identifies the type of message.
- **Message Length**—Specifies the cumulative length in bytes of the Message ID, Mandatory Parameters, and Optional Parameters.
- **Message ID**—A 32-bit value used to identify this message. An LSR sending a notification in response to this message should include this Message ID in the Status TLV of the notification message.
- **Mandatory Parameters**—Variable length set of required message parameters. Some messages have no required parameters.
- **Optional Parameters**—Variable length set of optional message parameters. Many messages have no optional parameters.

LDP TLVs

All LDP messages use a TLV encoding scheme to encode their mandatory and optional parameters (Figure 12.5). Every LDP TLV has a 2-byte Type field followed by a 2-byte Length field, and then a variable-length Value field. The Value field of any TLV may itself contain additional TLVs. This provides a very flexible and extensible way to encode the fields of the LDP messages. The components of a TLV are described below.

Figure 12.5 Fields of an LDP TLV.

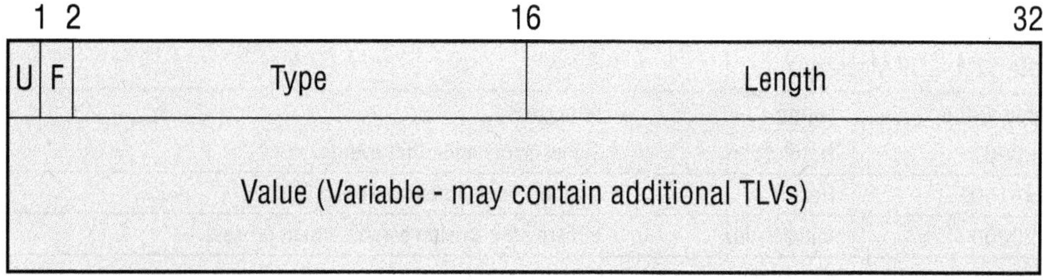

- **Type**—The first 2 bits are the U and F bits, which tell the recipient how to handle the TLV if the Type is unknown. The remaining 14 bits specify the Type that determines how the Value field is to be interpreted.
- **U bit**—(Unknown TLV bit) The U bit applies only if the Type value is unknown by the recipient of the TLV. If U is clear (0) in the unknown TLV, a notification is returned to the sender and the entire message is ignored. If U is set (1), the unknown TLV is silently ignored and the rest of the message is processed as if the unknown TLV did not exist.
- **F bit**—(Forward unknown TLV bit) The F bit applies only when the U bit is set and the LDP message containing the unknown TLV is to be forwarded. If F is clear (0), the message is forwarded without the unknown TLV; and if F is set (1), the message is forwarded with the unknown TLV.
- **Length**—The length of the Value field in bytes.
- **Value**—The actual information that is being carried in the message.

The TLV format provides a generalized and flexible method of describing the data fields of a message. Most fields in an LDP PDU are encoded as TLVs including an FEC, a label, or a hop count.

LDP Message Categories

There are four categories of LDP messages described below. The LDP messages are listed in Table 12.1:

- **Discovery messages**—Used to periodically announce and maintain the presence of an LSR in a network.

- **Session messages**—Used to establish, maintain, and terminate sessions between LDP peers.
- **Advertisement messages**—Used to create, change, and delete label mappings for FECs.
- **Notification messages**—Used to signal errors and other events of note.

Table 12.1 LDP Messages

Type Value	Name	Function
0x0001	Notification	Signal errors and other events.
0x0100	Hello	Announces the presence of an LSR.
0x0200	Initialization	Initiates the session establishment process.
0x0201	KeepAlive	Monitors the integrity of the LDP session transport connection.
0x0300	Address	Advertises the interface addresses to an LDP peer.
0x0301	Address Withdraw	Withdraws a previously advertised interface address.
0x0400	Label Mapping	Advertises an FEC-label binding to an LDP peer.
0x0401	Label Request	Requests an FEC-label binding from an LDP peer.
0x0402	Label Withdraw	Signals the peer that the previously advertised FEC-label mapping may no longer be used.
0x0403	Label Release	Signals the peer that the LSR no longer needs specific FEC-label mappings previously requested of and/or advertised by the peer.
0x0404	Label Abort Request	Aborts an outstanding Label Request message.
0x3E00–0x3EFF	Vendor Private	Used to convey vendor-private information between LSRs.
0x3F00–0x3FFF	Experimental	LDP Experimental Extensions.

Correct operation of LDP requires a reliable and ordered delivery of messages. To satisfy these requirements, LDP uses TCP (Transmission Control Protocol) as a transport protocol for Session, Advertisement, and Notification messages (everything except Link Hellos, which use UDP [User Datagram Protocol]).

12.2 LDP Sessions

There are four phases to the establishment and maintenance of an LDP session:

1. Neighbor Discovery
2. LDP session establishment
3. Label exchange
4. Session maintenance

These are further described below.

Neighbor Discovery

Two LDP routers use LDP discovery to discover potential LDP peers. Discovery makes it unnecessary to explicitly configure an LSR's label switching peers.

To perform LDP discovery, an LSR periodically sends LDP Link Hello messages out each LDP enabled interface. LDP Link Hello messages are sent in LDP PDUs as UDP packets addressed to the all-routers multicast group address of `224.0.0.2` and the well-known LDP discovery port (`646`) as shown in Figure 12.6. The source IP address of the LDP Hello is the egress interface of the router.

Receipt of an LDP Link Hello on an interface identifies a Hello adjacency with a potential LDP peer, as well as the label space the peer intends to use for the interface. Figure 12.7 shows the format of the LDP Hello message.

Figure 12.6 LDP peers exchange Hello messages to establish a link adjacency.

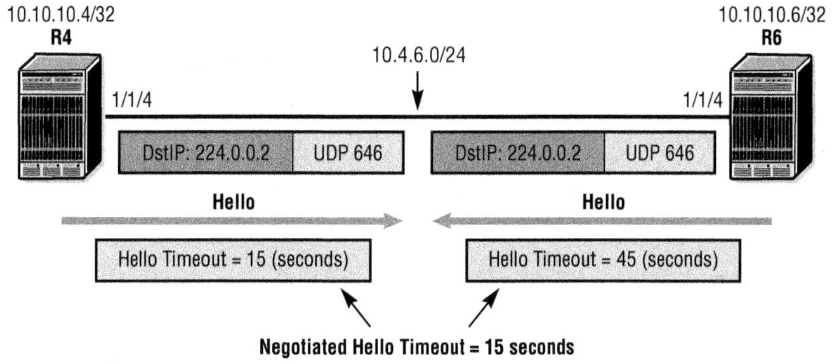

Figure 12.7 Fields of the LDP Hello message.

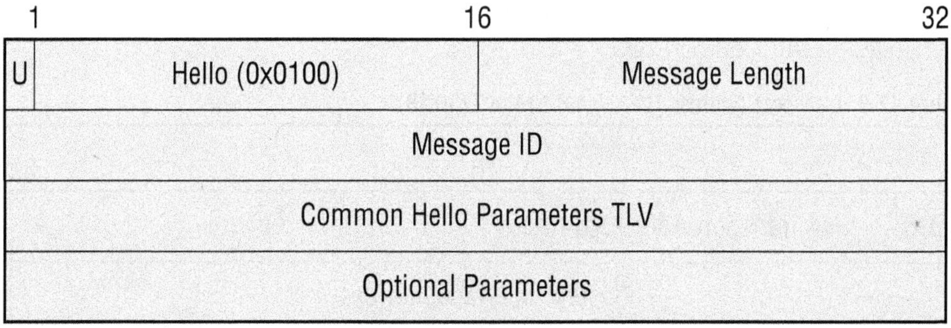

The mandatory parameters for the Hello message are carried in the Common Hello Parameters TLV shown in Figure 12.8. The fields are described below:

Figure 12.8 Fields of the Common Hello Parameters.

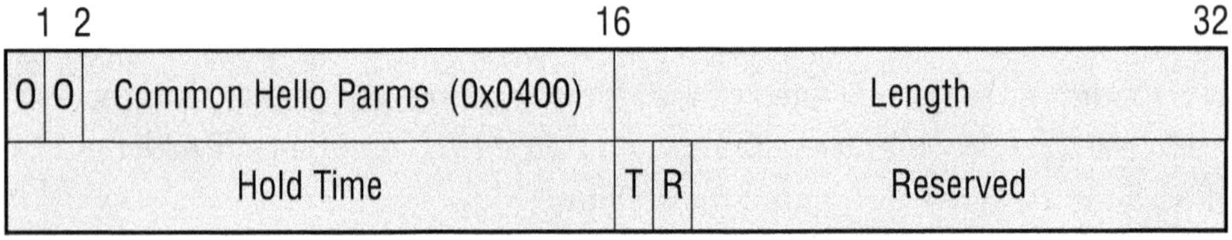

- **Hold Time**—The time an LSR will wait for a Hello from a peer LSR before declaring the adjacency down. The Hello hold time value used is the smaller of the two. The Hello hold timer is reset each time a Hello is received from the peer.
- **T (Targeted Hello)**—A value of 1 specifies a Targeted Hello, and a value of 0 specifies a Link Hello.
- **R (Request Send Targeted Hello)**—The sender sets a value of 1 to request that the receiver send periodic Targeted Hellos.

After the Common Hello Parameters TLV are the Optional Parameters. The optional parameters sent by the 7750 SR are:

- **Transport Address**—The IPv4 (or IPv6) address to be used to open the TCP connection between the peers (Figure 12.9). If this TLV is not included, the transport address used is the source address of the Hello message (address of the egress interface). The 7750 SR specifies the system address as the transport address by default.
- **Configuration Sequence Number**—A 4-byte number to identify the configuration state of the sending LSR so that the receiving LSR can detect configuration changes on the sending LSR.

Figure 12.9 Transport Address TLV as sent by the 7750 SR.

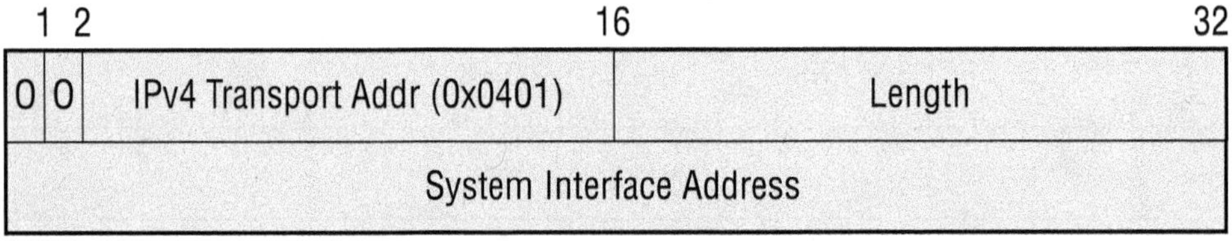

After the exchange of Hello messages, the routers are considered to have formed a link adjacency (see Listing 12.1).

Listing 12.1 Details of link adjacency between LDP peers

```
A:R6# show router ldp discovery interface "toR4" detail

===============================================================================
LDP Hello Adjacencies (Detail)
===============================================================================
-------------------------------------------------------------------------------
Interface "toR4"
-------------------------------------------------------------------------------
Local Address       : 10.10.10.6         Peer Address          : 10.10.10.4
Adjacency Type      : Link               State                 : Established
Up Time             : 0d 19:43:37        Hold Time Remaining : 11
Hello Mesg Recv     : 17757              Hello Mesg Sent       : 17756
Local IP Address    : 10.4.6.6           Remote IP Address     : 10.4.6.4
Local Hello Timeout: 15                  Remote Hello Timeout: 15
Local Cfg Seq No    : 4174193241         Remote Cfg Seq No     : 4010425649

===============================================================================
```

Once a link adjacency has been established, the routers proceed to form an LDP session.

LDP Session Establishment

TCP is used for all LDP message exchanges other than the Hello messages. Therefore, the first step in LDP session establishment is to open a TCP connection as the transport session. Once the transport session has been established, the LDP session can be established. Routers using a per-interface label space establish one LDP session for each interface. The 7750 SR uses per-platform label space, which requires only one session between peers. The 7750 SR uses its system address as the transport address in its Hello by default to ensure that only one LDP session is established, even if there are multiple links between the peers (Figure 12.10).

The routers determine the transport address through the exchange of Hello messages. The router with the higher transport address is considered the active router and the other the passive router for session establishment. The active router opens the TCP connection.

Figure 12.10 LDP peers with multiple links establish only one LDP session for per-platform label space.

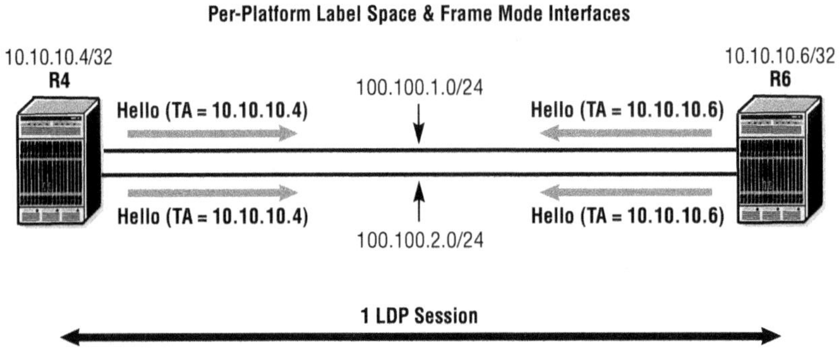

Once the TCP session is established, the active router initiates the opening of the LDP session by sending an LDP Initialization message. This contains LDP session parameters including the keep-alive timer value and maximum PDU size.

The passive router examines the session parameters, and, if it agrees, transmits Initialization and KeepAlive messages. If it does not agree to the session parameters, it sends a Notification message to indicate an error and closes the TCP connection. Upon receipt of the Initialization message, if the active router does not agree to the session parameters, it sends a Notification message, and the passive router closes the TCP connection.

If the active router agrees to the session parameters, it sends a KeepAlive message. Upon receipt of the KeepAlive message, the passive router enters the Operational state. It transmits a KeepAlive message, and upon receipt of this message, the active router enters the Operational state. LDP Address and Label Mapping messages can now be exchanged between the routers. Figure 12.11 shows the packets exchanged in the establishment of an LDP session. Listing 12.2 shows the condition of an LDP router in its normal operational state.

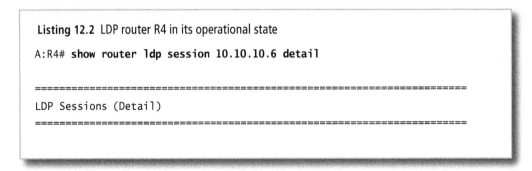

Listing 12.2 LDP router R4 in its operational state

```
A:R4# show router ldp session 10.10.10.6 detail

===============================================================================
LDP Sessions (Detail)
===============================================================================
```

```
Legend:  DoD - Downstream on Demand (for address FEC's only)
         DU  - Downstream Unsolicited
===============================================================================
-------------------------------------------------------------------------------
Session with Peer 10.10.10.6:0
-------------------------------------------------------------------------------
Adjacency Type     : Link          State                    : Established
Up Time            : 0d 19:52:49
Max PDU Length     : 4096          KA/Hold Time Remaining: 26
Link Adjacencies   : 1             Targeted Adjacencies  : 0
Local Address      : 10.10.10.4    Peer Address             : 10.10.10.6
Local TCP Port     : 646           Peer TCP Port            : 49873
Local KA Timeout   : 30            Peer KA Timeout          : 30
Mesg Sent          : 25852         Mesg Recv                : 25853
FECs Sent          : 5             FECs Recv                : 5
GR State           : Capable       Label Distribution       : DU
Nbr Liveness Time  : 0             Max Recovery Time        : 0
Number of Restart  : 0             Last Restart Time        : Never
Advertise          : Address

===============================================================================
```

12.3 Label Distribution with LDP

LDP will establish one session per label space advertised by the router. Because the 7750 SR uses per-platform label space, there should be only one LDP session between any two peers. The primary purpose of the LDP session is for the exchange of FEC/label binding information. Label bindings received from other LDP peers are stored in the Label Information Base (LIB).

As seen from the output of `show router ldp parameters` in Listing 12.3, LDP on the 7750 SR operates in downstream unsolicited, ordered control mode with liberal label retention. These parameters are fixed and cannot be modified.

Figure 12.11 Packets exchanged to form an LDP session.

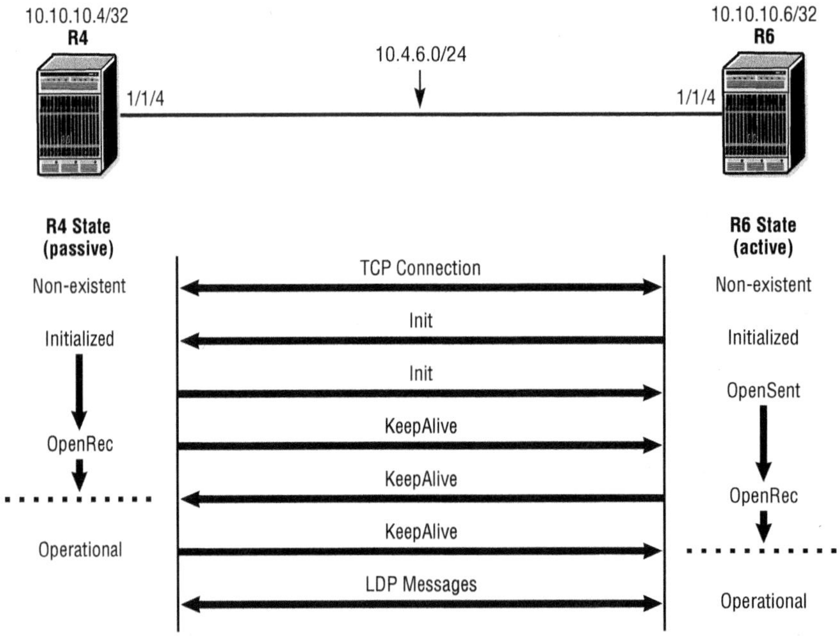

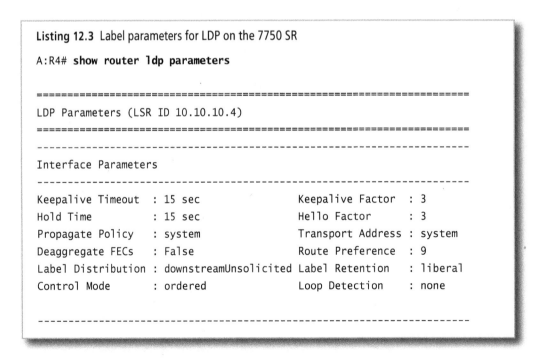

Listing 12.3 Label parameters for LDP on the 7750 SR

```
A:R4# show router ldp parameters

===============================================================================
LDP Parameters (LSR ID 10.10.10.4)
===============================================================================
-------------------------------------------------------------------------------
Interface Parameters
-------------------------------------------------------------------------------
Keepalive Timeout  : 15 sec                Keepalive Factor  : 3
Hold Time          : 15 sec                Hello Factor      : 3
Propagate Policy   : system                Transport Address : system
Deaggregate FECs   : False                 Route Preference  : 9
Label Distribution : downstreamUnsolicited Label Retention   : liberal
Control Mode       : ordered               Loop Detection    : none

-------------------------------------------------------------------------------
```

Generation of LDP Labels

Once an LDP session has been established, the routers exchange LDP Address messages. These contain the LDP interfaces for each router.

After the exchange of Address messages, the LDP routers send Label Mapping messages that contain labels for each of the FECs the routers are advertising (Figure 12.3). The default behavior of the 7750 SR is to advertise a label only for its system address and for any other reachable FEC for which it has received a label. Figure 12.12 shows the format of the LDP Label Mapping message.

Figure 12.13 shows the format of the Generic Label TLV, one of the TLVs that can be used in the Label TLV field of the Label Mapping message. This TLV is used for labels on links where label values are independent of the underlying link technology. This includes links such as PPP and Ethernet.

Figure 12.12 LDP Label Mapping message.

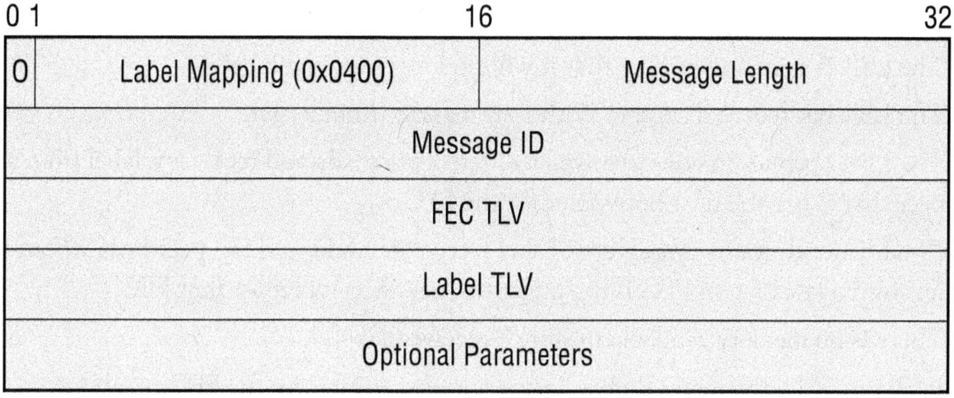

Figure 12.13 LDP Generic Label TLV.

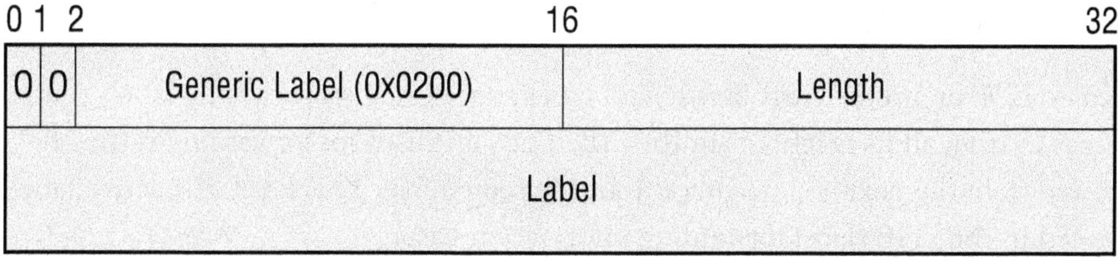

Label Withdraw and Label Release Messages

The label for a given FEC may be withdrawn, and as a result invalidated, if any of the following actions occur. In these situations a Label Withdraw message is issued.

- **Interface MTU (maximum transmission unit) changes**—LDP withdraws the previously assigned label and resignals the FEC with the new MTU in the interface parameter.
- **Network topology change**—A network topology change occurs causing the router to no longer recognize a FEC for which it had previously advertised a label.
- **Router configured**—The router is configured to cease the generation of labels for specified FECs.
- **Configuration command issued**—A configuration command is issued to clear the labels. Labels are withdrawn, and new label mappings are issued.

An LDP Label Release message may be generated if one of the following conditions occurs:

- The LSR is signaling its peer that it will no longer use the label.
- The LSR has received a Label Withdraw message from a peer.
- The LSR operates in conservative label retention mode and receives a label from a peer that is not the next-hop router for the FEC.
- The LSR operates in conservative label retention mode, and the peer from whom it received a label for an FEC is no longer the next-hop router for that FEC.
- There is no memory available to store a received label.

In Figure 12.14, the router R6 has been advertising a label for the FEC `192.168.6.1/32` when this destination becomes unreachable. R6 issues a Label Withdraw message to its upstream neighbor R4, which responds with a Label Release message.

The LIB and the LFIB

Because LDP on the 7750 SR uses liberal label retention, it stores all the labels that it receives from all its neighbors in the LIB. The label used for forwarding is the one received from the next-hop neighbor from the route table. This label, the active label, is stored in the LFIB (label forwarding information base).

The LIB is analogous to the RIB (routing information base) for a routing protocol such as BGP (Border Gateway Protocol) or RIP (Routing Information Protocol). The RIB contains all the routing information that the router has received. Only routes that are chosen by the RTM (Route Table Manager) as active routes are used to populate the FIB (forwarding information base) or routing table. In the same way, the LIB contains all labels received from LDP neighbors, but the LFIB contains only the active labels to be used for forwarding. Figure 12.15 and Table 12.2 show the relationship between the RIB, FIB, LIB, and LFIB.

Figure 12.14 Label Withdraw and Label Release messages exchanged when an FEC becomes unreachable.

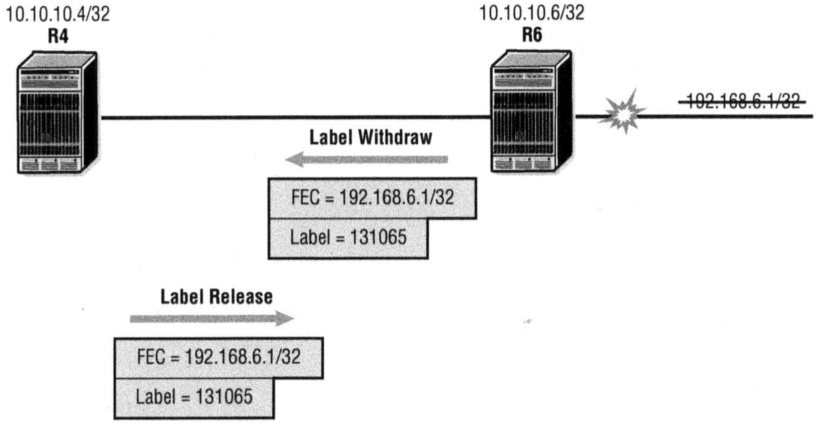

Figure 12.15 The RIB and LIB collect the routes in the control plane, and the FIB and LFIB are used for forwarding in the data plane.

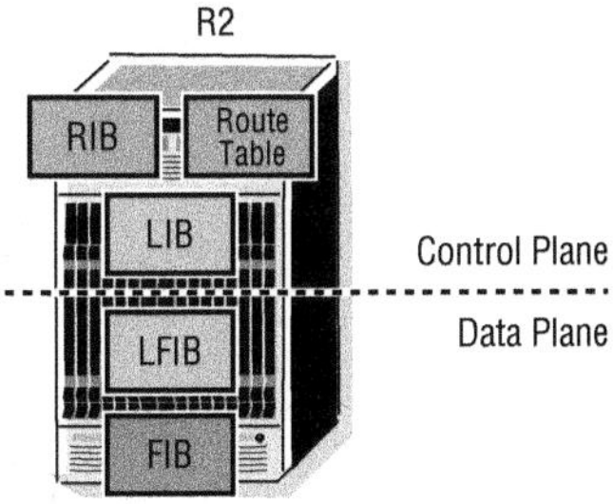

Table 12.2 Comparison of RIB, FIB, LIB, and LFIB

Table	Meaning	Contents	Populated by
RIB	Routing Information Base	All routing updates received from neighbors	Routing protocol exchange (each routing protocol has a separate RIB)

(continued)

Table 12.2 *(continued)*

FIB	Forwarding Information Base	Active routes used by the router for forwarding	RTM selects the active routes from all protocol "best" routes
LIB	Label Information Base	All locally generated and received MPLS labels	MPLS label exchange
LFIB	Label Forwarding Information Base	Active labels used by the LSR for forwarding	Label received from next-hop neighbor

If the LSR does not have a next-hop for an FEC in the FIB or there is a next-hop but the LSR has not received a label from that router, there will be no label stored in the LFIB. Even if there are labels for the FEC in the LIB, the router does not forward packets to the FEC unless it has a label from the next-hop router as determined by the IGP (interior gateway protocol). Thus, the LSPs in LDP always follow the path selected by the IGP.

LDP Label Propagation

The default behavior of the 7750 SR is to generate an LDP label for its system address and for any other FEC for which it receives a label. By default, the 7750 SR does not generate labels for any other FECs.

As an example, we will examine how labels are propagated through the topology shown in Figure 12.16. We will look at the isolated case of how a label generated by R6 for its system address is propagated through the network so that R1 has a label it can use for traffic that will flow from ingress (R1) to egress (R6). The addressing is as shown, and the fourth digit of the IP address is the same as the router number for all addresses on all nodes.

The configuration of LDP is very simple—the interfaces to be used for LDP must simply be added in the `config router ldp context`. The configuration for R6 is shown in Listing 12.4. The router will form LDP adjacencies with other LDP routers that it discovers on its LDP interfaces.

Listing 12.4 Interfaces are simply added to the config router ldp context to enable LDP on the router

```
*A:R6# configure router ldp
*A:R6>config>router>ldp$ interface-parameters interface "toR4"
*A:R6>config>router>ldp>if-params>if$ exit
*A:R6>config>router>ldp# interface-parameters interface "toR5"
*A:R6>config>router>ldp>if-params>if$ exit
```

Figure 12.16 Labels distributed across an LDP network from R6 to R1 enable data flow from R1 to R6.

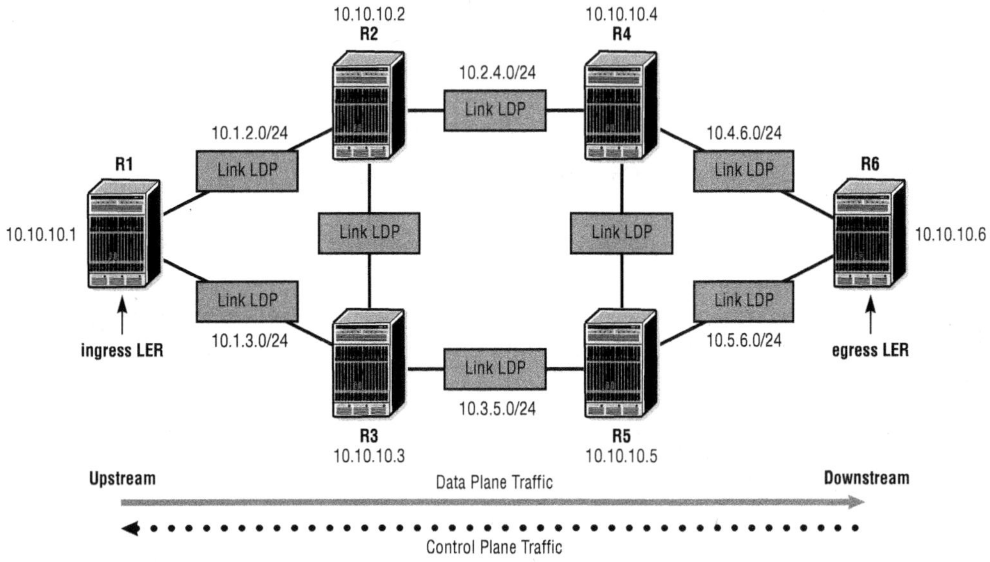

Once the router interfaces are enabled for LDP and adjacencies formed with LDP neighbors, R6 sends a Label Mapping message for its system address to its two neighbors (Figure 12.17). Because LDP is operating in downstream unsolicited mode, the label is sent immediately. Because the 7750 SR uses per-platform label space, the same label value, `131071`, is sent to both neighbors, and the LDP-ID is `10.10.10.6:0`.

Figure 12.17 R6 originates a label for its system address and advertises it in a Label Mapping message to both its neighbors.

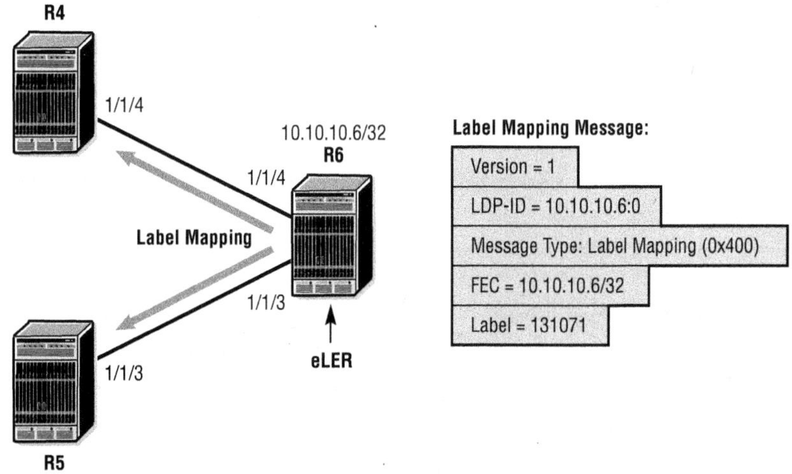

Listing 12.5 shows the LIB and the label generated by R6 and sent to its neighbors. The label is an ingress label because R6 expects to receive incoming packets from its neighbors with this label.

Listing 12.5 Label generated by R6 for its system address

```
*A:R6# show router ldp bindings prefix 10.10.10.6/32

=======================================================================
LDP LSR ID: 10.10.10.6
=======================================================================
Legend: U - Label In Use,  N - Label Not In Use, W - Label Withdrawn
    WP - Label Withdraw Pending
=======================================================================
LDP Prefix Bindings
=======================================================================
Prefix             Peer            IngLbl    EgrLbl EgrIntf    EgrNextHop
-----------------------------------------------------------------------
10.10.10.6/32      10.10.10.4      131071U     --     --          --
10.10.10.6/32      10.10.10.5      131071U     --     --          --
-----------------------------------------------------------------------
No. of Prefix Bindings: 2
=======================================================================
```

There is no egress label because R6 is the destination for this FEC. We can see from the FIB in Listing 12.6 that the FEC is local to R6.

Listing 12.6 View of the FIB shows that R6 is the destination for this FEC

```
*A:R6# show router route-table 10.10.10.6/32

=======================================================================
Route Table (Router: Base)
=======================================================================
Dest Prefix                           Type     Proto     Age         Pref
       Next Hop[Interface Name]                             Metric
-----------------------------------------------------------------------
10.10.10.6/32                         Local    Local     00h27m36s   0
```

```
        system                                                      0
-------------------------------------------------------------------------------
No. of Routes: 1
===============================================================================
```

Because R6 is the destination for the FEC, the operation in the LFIB is a POP, as shown in Listing 12.7.

Listing 12.7 LFIB shows a POP operation for the FEC

```
*A:R6# show router ldp bindings active prefix 10.10.10.6/32

===============================================================================
Legend:  (S) - Static
===============================================================================
LDP Prefix Bindings (Active)
===============================================================================
Prefix               Op   IngLbl    EgrLbl    EgrIntf/LspId  EgrNextHop
-------------------------------------------------------------------------------
10.10.10.6/32        Pop  131071      --          --              --
-------------------------------------------------------------------------------
No. of Prefix Bindings: 1
```

Figure 12.18 shows what happens on R4 after it receives the label mapping from R6. R4 generates its own label and sends it to its neighbors.

The upstream neighbors from R4 all generate labels for the FEC as shown in Figure 12.19. R4 also receives labels from these neighbors.

Listing 12.8 shows the contents of the LIB on router R4 after it has generated labels for the FEC to its two neighbors, R2 and R5, and after they have also generated labels for the FEC. The ingress label, 131070, was generated by R4 and sent to its neighbors R2 and R5. R4 received a label of 131068 from R2 and a label of 131069 from R5, which are recorded as the egress labels for these next-hops. The label received from R6, 131071, is the active label that is used for forwarding. Notice that there is an egress interface and next-hop defined for this label entry.

Figure 12.18 Labels for the FEC are propagated to R4's neighbors.

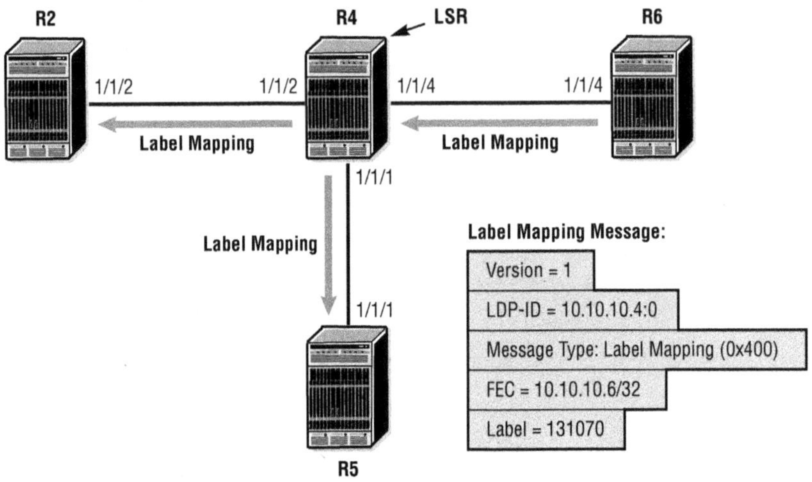

Figure 12.19 Upstream routers generate labels for the FEC, and R4 receives labels from these neighbors as well.

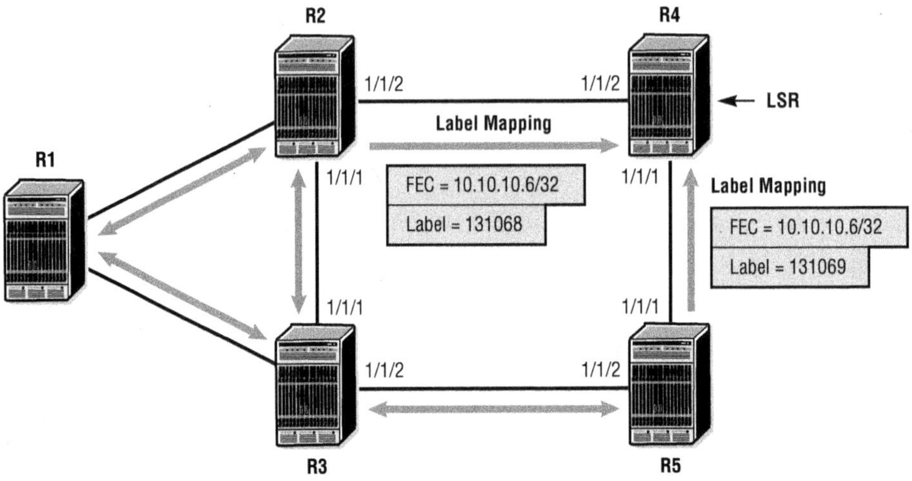

Listing 12.8 R4 FIB after generating labels for the FEC 10.10.10.6/32

```
*A:R4>config>router# show router ldp bindings prefix 10.10.10.6/32
```

```
===============================================================================
LDP LSR ID: 10.10.10.4
===============================================================================
Legend: U - Label In Use,  N - Label Not In Use, W - Label Withdrawn
    WP - Label Withdraw Pending
===============================================================================
LDP Prefix Bindings
===============================================================================
Prefix            Peer            IngLbl     EgrLbl EgrIntf      EgrNextHop
-------------------------------------------------------------------------------
10.10.10.6/32     10.10.10.2      131070U    131068   --             --
10.10.10.6/32     10.10.10.5      131070U    131069   --             --
10.10.10.6/32     10.10.10.6        --       131071 1/1/4        10.4.6.6
-------------------------------------------------------------------------------
No. of Prefix Bindings: 3
===============================================================================
```

Listing 12.9 shows the contents of the FIB on R4. R6 is the next-hop for the FEC `10.10.10.6/32`, which is what we expect because we saw from the LIB that the label from R6 was the one being used for forwarding.

Listing 12.9 FIB on R4 shows that R6 is the next-hop for the FEC 10.10.10.6/32

```
*A:R4# show router fib 1 10.10.10.6/32

===============================================================================
FIB Display
===============================================================================
Prefix                                                          Protocol
    NextHop
-------------------------------------------------------------------------------
10.10.10.6/32                                                   OSPF
    10.4.6.6 (toR6)
-------------------------------------------------------------------------------
Total Entries : 1
-------------------------------------------------------------------------------
===============================================================================
```

The command `show router ldp bindings active` displays the content of the LFIB. Listing 12.10 shows that on router R4, an incoming packet with the label `131070` belongs to FEC `10.10.10.6/32` and is swapped for label `131071` and transmitted to the next-hop, R6. Router R4 could also be the ingress for the FEC, thus the entry with a PUSH operation.

Listing 12.10 LFIB shows that an incoming packet with label 131070 is swapped for label 131071 and transmitted to R6

```
*A:R4# show router ldp bindings active prefix 10.10.10.6/32

===============================================================================
Legend:  (S) - Static
===============================================================================
LDP Prefix Bindings (Active)
===============================================================================
Prefix                 Op    IngLbl     EgrLbl     EgrIntf/LspId  EgrNextHop
-------------------------------------------------------------------------------
10.10.10.6/32          Push    --       131071     1/1/4          10.4.6.6
10.10.10.6/32          Swap 131070      131071     1/1/4          10.4.6.6
-------------------------------------------------------------------------------
No. of Prefix Bindings: 2
```

R1 receives labels for the FEC from both its downstream neighbors, R2 and R3 (Figure 12.20).

Figure 12.20 R1 receives labels from both R2 and R3 for the FEC 10.10.10.6/32.

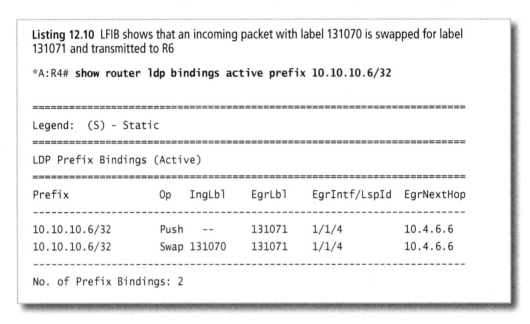

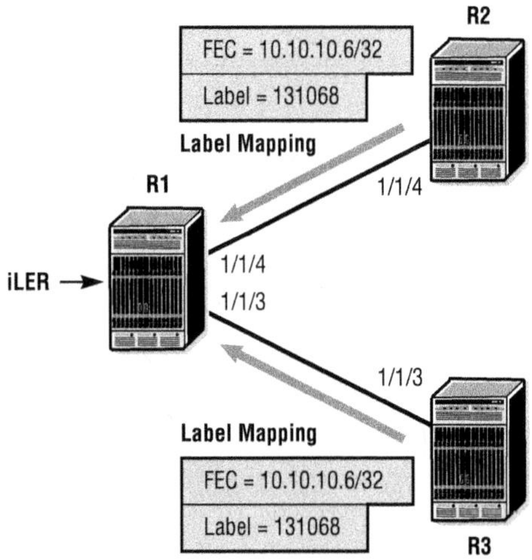

Listing 12.11 shows that the LIB on R1 contains the two labels received from its neighbors for `10.10.10.6/32`. By chance, they both have the same value, `131068`. Because the egress next-hop is R2, we deduce that this is the active label and that R2 is the next-hop selected by the IGP.

Listing 12.11 Labels received for FEC 10.10.10.6/32 from R1's neighbors

```
*A:R1# show router ldp bindings prefix 10.10.10.6/32

=======================================================================
LDP LSR ID: 10.10.10.1
=======================================================================
Legend: U - Label In Use,  N - Label Not In Use, W - Label Withdrawn
    WP - Label Withdraw Pending
=======================================================================
LDP Prefix Bindings
=======================================================================
Prefix           Peer           IngLbl    EgrLbl EgrIntf     EgrNextHop
-----------------------------------------------------------------------
10.10.10.6/32    10.10.10.2     131066N   131068 1/1/4       10.1.2.2
10.10.10.6/32    10.10.10.3     131066U   131068   --          --
-----------------------------------------------------------------------
No. of Prefix Bindings: 2
=======================================================================
```

Listing 12.12, showing R1's route table, confirms that R2 is the next-hop selected by OSPF (Open Shortest Path First) for the destination `10.10.10.6/32`.

Listing 12.12 R2 has been selected by OSPF as the next-hop for the FEC 10.10.10.6/32

```
*A:R1# show router route-table 10.10.10.6/32

=======================================================================
Route Table (Router: Base)
=======================================================================
Dest Prefix                          Type    Proto    Age         Pref
       Next Hop[Interface Name]                             Metric
-----------------------------------------------------------------------
10.10.10.6/32                        Remote  OSPF     01h01m40s   10
```

(continued)

Listing 12.12 *(continued)*

```
        10.1.2.2                                                   300
-------------------------------------------------------------------------------
No. of Routes: 1
===============================================================================
```

Viewing the LFIB in Listing 12.13 shows that R1 is an ingress router for the FEC `10.10.10.6/32` with a PUSH operation and next-hop of R2. It has also generated a label for the FEC and could be used as a transit router.

Listing 12.13 R1 is an ingress for the FEC 10.10.10.6/32 with a PUSH operation and next-hop of R2

```
*A:R1# show router ldp bindings active prefix 10.10.10.6/32

===============================================================================
Legend:  (S) - Static
===============================================================================
LDP Prefix Bindings (Active)
===============================================================================
Prefix                Op   IngLbl    EgrLbl    EgrIntf/LspId  EgrNextHop
-------------------------------------------------------------------------------
10.10.10.6/32         Push   --      131068    1/1/4          10.1.2.2
10.10.10.6/32         Swap 131066    131068    1/1/4          10.1.2.2
-------------------------------------------------------------------------------
No. of Prefix Bindings: 2
```

Once labels have been propagated from egress to ingress, R1 is able to forward labeled packets to R6 (Figure 12.21). A label is PUSHed on by R1, SWAPped by R2 and R4, and POPped by R6.

In the example above, we isolated the propagation of the label for the FEC `10.10.10.6/32`. In reality, all the routers in the network advertise labels for their system addresses, thus the full LIB on R1 is as shown in Listing 12.14. There are two entries for each FEC because R1 has two neighbors to advertise (ingress) labels to and receive (egress) labels from. Some of the labels are marked N (not in use), the label for `10.10.10.6/32` received from R2, for example. This is because R1 does not expect to receive a labeled packet from R2 for this FEC because R2 is the downstream next-hop.

Figure 12.21 Forwarding of a labeled packet from ingress (R1) to egress (R6).

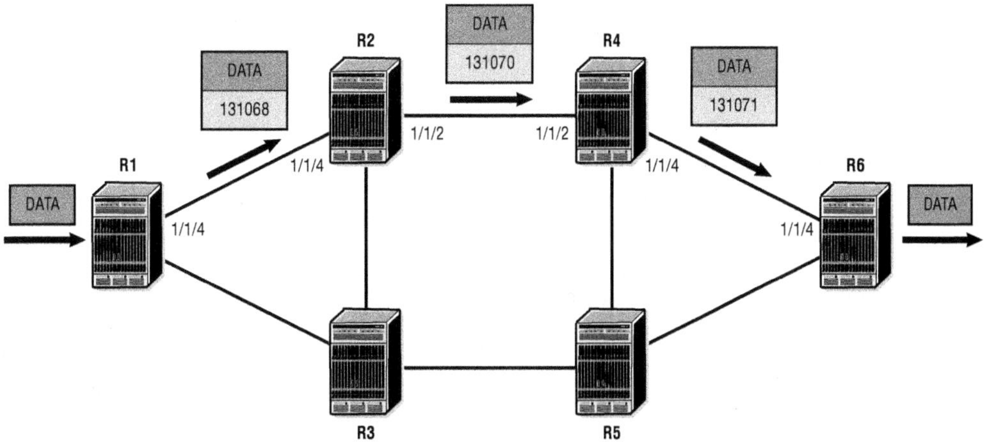

Listing 12.14 LIB of R1 contains two entries for each FEC in the network

```
*A:R1# show router ldp bindings fec-type prefixes

===============================================================================
LDP LSR ID: 10.10.10.1
===============================================================================
Legend: U - Label In Use,  N - Label Not In Use, W - Label Withdrawn
    WP - Label Withdraw Pending
===============================================================================
LDP Prefix Bindings
===============================================================================
Prefix            Peer            IngLbl     EgrLbl EgrIntf/     EgrNextHop
                                                    LspId
-------------------------------------------------------------------------------
10.10.10.1/32     10.10.10.2      131071U      --     --            --
10.10.10.1/32     10.10.10.3      131071U      --     --            --
10.10.10.2/32     10.10.10.2        --       131071 1/1/4        10.1.2.2
10.10.10.2/32     10.10.10.3      131070U    131067   --            --
10.10.10.3/32     10.10.10.2      131069U    131067   --            --
10.10.10.3/32     10.10.10.3        --       131071 1/1/3        10.1.3.3
10.10.10.4/32     10.10.10.2      131068N    131070 1/1/4        10.1.2.2
10.10.10.4/32     10.10.10.3      131068U    131070   --            --
10.10.10.5/32     10.10.10.2      131067U    131069   --            --
```

(continued)

Listing 12.14 *(continued)*

```
10.10.10.5/32     10.10.10.3      131067N    131069 1/1/3         10.1.3.3
10.10.10.6/32     10.10.10.2      131066N    131068 1/1/4         10.1.2.2
10.10.10.6/32     10.10.10.3      131066U    131068    --           --
-----------------------------------------------------------------------
No. of Prefix Bindings: 12
=======================================================================
```

Listing 12.15 shows the LFIB on R1. There are two operations, PUSH and SWAP, for each FEC, except for `10.10.10.1/32`. This is because in this topology, R1 could be the ingress or a transit router for all of these destinations. In either case, the egress label is the same. There is only one operation for `10.10.10.1/32` (system address of R1) because R1 is the egress for this FEC, and therefore the operation must be a POP.

Listing 12.15 LFIB on R1 with two operations for each FEC, except for the system address of R1

```
*A:R1# show router ldp bindings active

=======================================================================
Legend:  (S) - Static
=======================================================================
LDP Prefix Bindings (Active)
=======================================================================
Prefix              Op   IngLbl    EgrLbl    EgrIntf/LspId  EgrNextHop
-----------------------------------------------------------------------
10.10.10.1/32       Pop  131071      --          --             --
10.10.10.2/32       Push   --      131071    1/1/4          10.1.2.2
10.10.10.2/32       Swap 131070    131071    1/1/4          10.1.2.2
10.10.10.3/32       Push   --      131071    1/1/3          10.1.3.3
10.10.10.3/32       Swap 131069    131071    1/1/3          10.1.3.3
10.10.10.4/32       Push   --      131070    1/1/4          10.1.2.2
10.10.10.4/32       Swap 131068    131070    1/1/4          10.1.2.2
10.10.10.5/32       Push   --      131069    1/1/3          10.1.3.3
10.10.10.5/32       Swap 131067    131069    1/1/3          10.1.3.3
10.10.10.6/32       Push   --      131068    1/1/4          10.1.2.2
10.10.10.6/32       Swap 131066    131068    1/1/4          10.1.2.2
-----------------------------------------------------------------------
No. of Prefix Bindings: 11
```

In the example above, we considered R1 as the ingress for the FEC `10.10.10.6/32`. If the topology changes to the one shown in Figure 12.22, R1 becomes a transit LSR for traffic from R3. No changes in the LFIB on R1 are required—if R1 receives a packet from R3 with the label `131066`, it will simply swap the label for `131068` and forward the packet to R2.

Figure 12.22 A topology change makes R1 a transit LSR for FEC 10.10.10.6/32. No change is required in the LFIB.

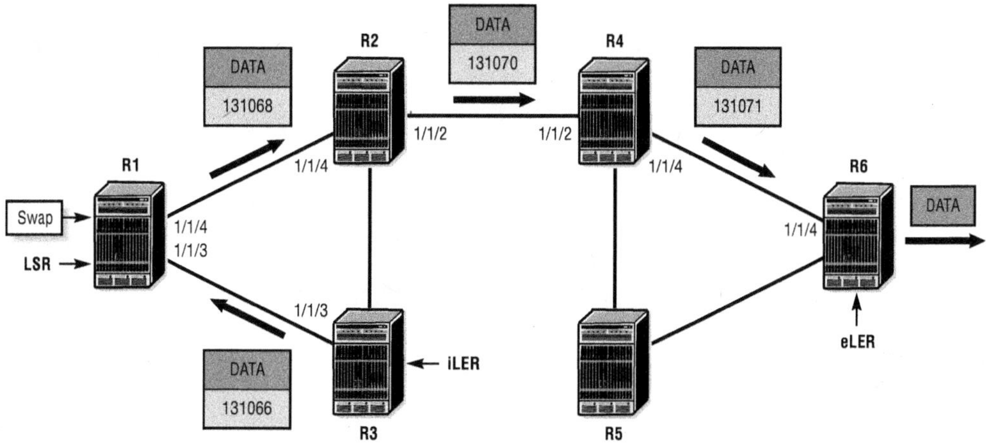

To summarize, when LDP is enabled in the network, all routers generate a label binding for their own system address and distribute it to their peers. The labels are flooded throughout the network, and eventually all the routers have an LSP to all the other routers. Thus a full mesh of tunnels is created (Figure 12.23).

The `show router tunnel-table` command in Listing 12.16 shows the tunnels on router R1 that have been created by LDP label distribution. A tunnel exists from router R1 to the system address of all of the other routers. The same command would show similar tunnels on all other routers in the network.

Listing 12.16 Each LSR in the network has a tunnel to all other FECs in the network

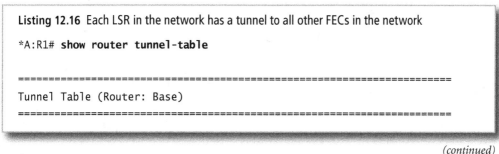

```
*A:R1# show router tunnel-table

===============================================================================
Tunnel Table (Router: Base)
===============================================================================
```

(continued)

Listing 12.16 *(continued)*

```
Destination          Owner Encap TunnelId  Pref     Nexthop          Metric
---------------------------------------------------------------------------
10.10.10.2/32        ldp   MPLS   -         9        10.1.2.2         100
10.10.10.3/32        ldp   MPLS   -         9        10.1.3.3         100
10.10.10.4/32        ldp   MPLS   -         9        10.1.2.2         200
10.10.10.5/32        ldp   MPLS   -         9        10.1.3.3         200
10.10.10.6/32        ldp   MPLS   -         9        10.1.2.2         300
===========================================================================
```

Figure 12.23 LDP automatically creates a full mesh of LSP tunnels to every FEC in the network.

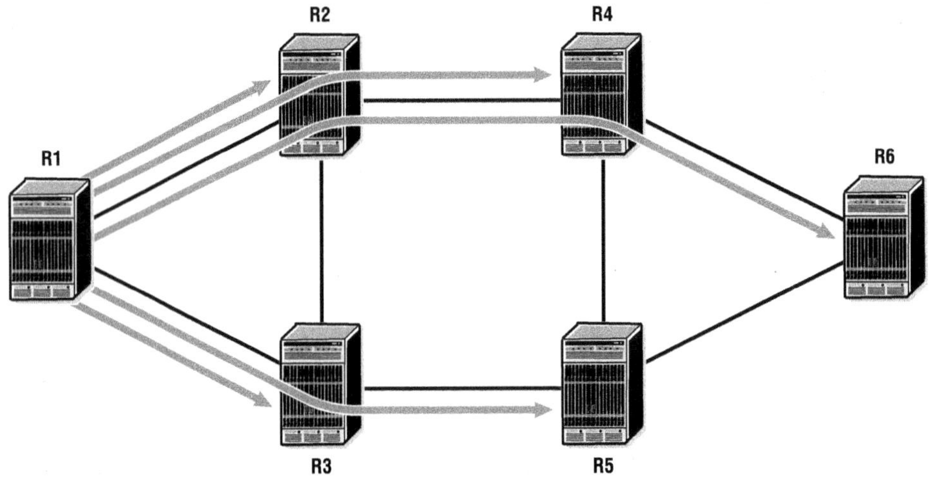

With LDP, the router does not have an end-to-end view of its tunnels. As seen from the LIB and LFIB displays, an LDP router only knows the egress label and the next-hop router to reach the tunnel destination. The consistent sequence of labels and their associated label actions from ingress to egress point constitute the tunnel. When using LDP-signaled transport tunnels, an LSP is more of a logical construct than an actual end-to-end tunnel.

12.4 LDP and IGP Interaction

The default settings for LDP are downstream unsolicited and liberal label retention. In a converged LDP network, an LDP router will have labels for all FECs from all of its LDP peers. Listing 12.17 shows the labels received on R1 from R2 and R3 for the FEC `10.10.10.6/32` in the topology of Figure 12.24.

Figure 12.24 LDP network topology.

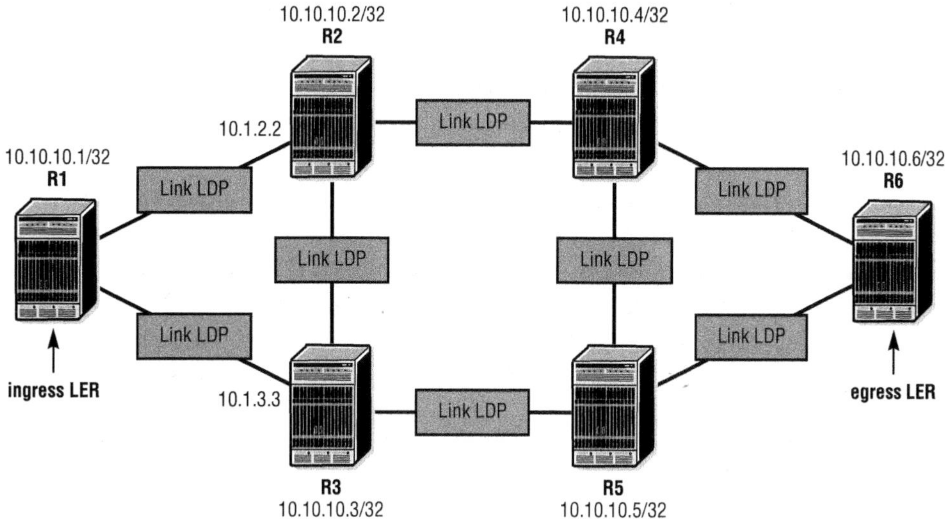

Listing 12.17 R1 LIB shows labels received for all FECs from both neighbors

```
*A:R1# show router ldp bindings prefix 10.10.10.6/32

===============================================================================
LDP LSR ID: 10.10.10.1
===============================================================================
Legend: U - Label In Use,  N - Label Not In Use, W - Label Withdrawn
    WP - Label Withdraw Pending
===============================================================================
LDP Prefix Bindings
===============================================================================
Prefix          Peer            IngLbl    EgrLbl EgrIntf     EgrNextHop
-------------------------------------------------------------------------------
10.10.10.6/32   10.10.10.2      131066N   131068 1/1/4       10.1.2.2
10.10.10.6/32   10.10.10.3      131066U   131068   --          --
-------------------------------------------------------------------------------
No. of Prefix Bindings: 2
===============================================================================
```

We can see from Listing 12.18 that R2 is the next-hop for the FEC `10.10.10.6/32`, and Listing 12.19 shows that the active label is the one received from R2.

Listing 12.18 R1 route table shows R2 as the next-hop for the FEC

```
*A:R1# show router route-table 10.10.10.6/32

===============================================================================
Route Table (Router: Base)
===============================================================================
Dest Prefix                                     Type    Proto    Age         Pref
       Next Hop[Interface Name]                                    Metric
-------------------------------------------------------------------------------
10.10.10.6/32                                   Remote  OSPF     10h54m19s   10
       10.1.2.2                                                    300
-------------------------------------------------------------------------------
No. of Routes: 1
===============================================================================
```

Listing 12.19 R1 LFIB shows that the active label is the one from R2

```
*A:R1# show router ldp bindings active prefix 10.10.10.6/32

===============================================================================
Legend:  (S) - Static
===============================================================================
LDP Prefix Bindings (Active)
===============================================================================
Prefix                Op    IngLbl    EgrLbl    EgrIntf/LspId  EgrNextHop
-------------------------------------------------------------------------------
10.10.10.6/32         Push    --      131068    1/1/4          10.1.2.2
10.10.10.6/32         Swap  131066    131068    1/1/4          10.1.2.2
-------------------------------------------------------------------------------
No. of Prefix Bindings: 2
```

If there is a link failure between R2 and R4, this represents a topology change in the network (Figure 12.25).

Figure 12.25 Link down between R2 and R4 causes a network topology change.

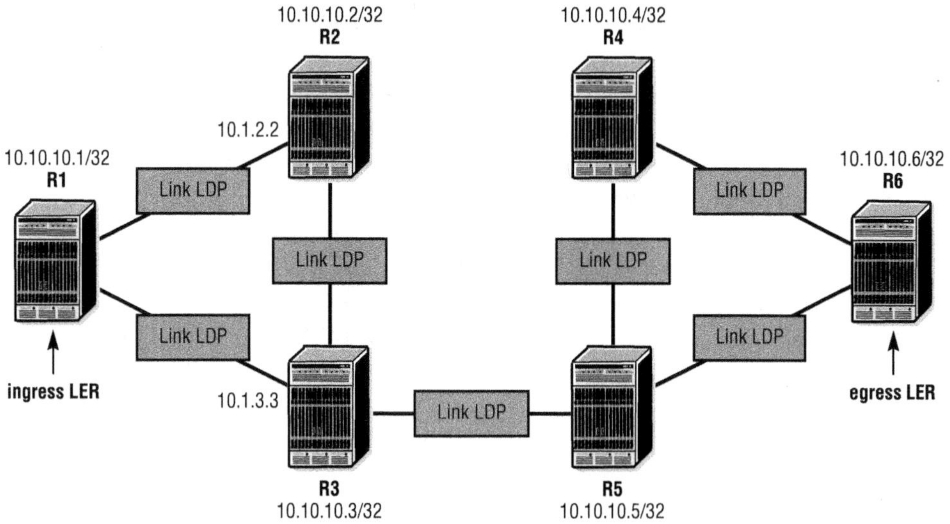

The topology change is detected by the IGP, and within a few seconds the route table has changed to reflect the new topology (Listing 12.20). The next-hop for `10.10.10.6/32` is now router R3, and we see in the LFIB that the label from R3 is now the active label (Listing 12.21).

Listing 12.20 The router table shows that R3 is now the next-hop

```
*A:R1# show router route-table 10.10.10.6/32

===============================================================================
Route Table (Router: Base)
===============================================================================
Dest Prefix                                 Type    Proto    Age         Pref
      Next Hop[Interface Name]                                     Metric
-------------------------------------------------------------------------------
10.10.10.6/32                               Remote  OSPF     00h00m38s   10
      10.1.3.3                                                     300
-------------------------------------------------------------------------------
No. of Routes: 1
===============================================================================
```

Listing 12.21 The LFIB shows that the active label is now the label from R3

```
*A:R1# show router ldp bindings active prefix 10.10.10.6/32

===============================================================================
Legend:  (S) - Static
===============================================================================
LDP Prefix Bindings (Active)
===============================================================================
Prefix              Op   IngLbl    EgrLbl    EgrIntf/LspId  EgrNextHop
-------------------------------------------------------------------------------
10.10.10.6/32       Push   --      131068    1/1/3          10.1.3.3
10.10.10.6/32       Swap 131066    131068    1/1/3          10.1.3.3
-------------------------------------------------------------------------------
No. of Prefix Bindings: 2
```

There is no change in the LIB, and labels do not have to be re-advertised. Listing 12.22 shows that R1 still has labels from R2 and R3, although the egress interface is now toward R3. If the link from R2 to R4 comes back up, the IGP will converge again. When R2 becomes the next-hop to the FEC, the label from R2 becomes the active label.

Listing 12.22 R1 still has labels for the FEC from both neighbors

```
*A:R1# show router ldp bindings prefix 10.10.10.6/32

===============================================================================
LDP LSR ID: 10.10.10.1
===============================================================================
Legend: U - Label In Use,  N - Label Not In Use, W - Label Withdrawn
    WP - Label Withdraw Pending
===============================================================================
LDP Prefix Bindings
===============================================================================
Prefix           Peer           IngLbl    EgrLbl EgrIntf     EgrNextHop
-------------------------------------------------------------------------------
10.10.10.6/32    10.10.10.2     131066U   131068   --           --
10.10.10.6/32    10.10.10.3     131066N   131068 1/1/3       10.1.3.3
-------------------------------------------------------------------------------
No. of Prefix Bindings: 2
===============================================================================
```

LDP forwarding always follows the IGP. It would be a mistake to think that there is any improvement in convergence time with LDP. In fact, convergence is never faster than the IGP convergence time and could possibly be longer. After the IGP converges, if a router does not have a label from its next-hop neighbor, it cannot forward traffic until it receives one.

Different LDP and IGP Topologies

It is essential that the LDP and IGP topologies always be the same. In Figure 12.26, OSPF is enabled on all the links of the network, but LDP is not enabled on R4's interface to R2. As a result, there is no LDP adjacency between R2 and R4. Listing 12.23 shows that there is no Hello adjacency and no LDP session between R2 and R4.

Figure 12.26 No LDP adjacency between R2 and R4.

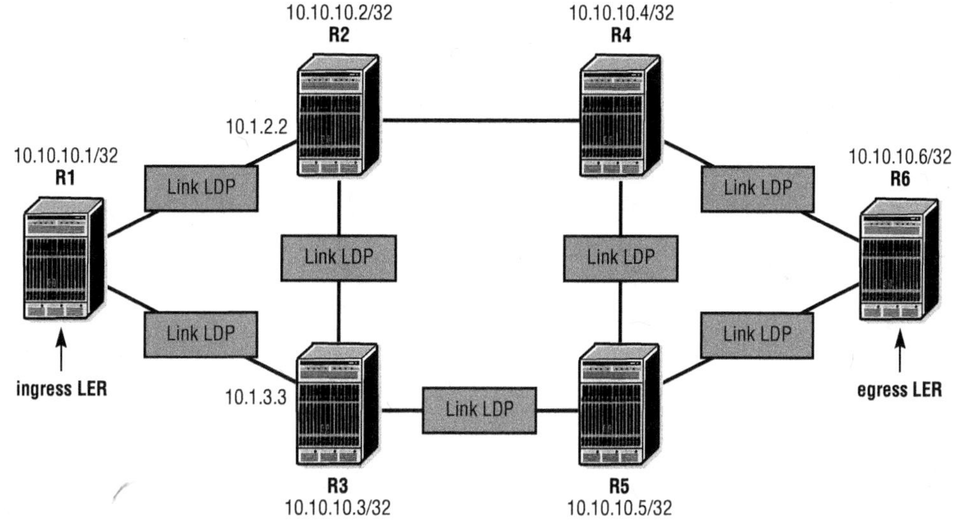

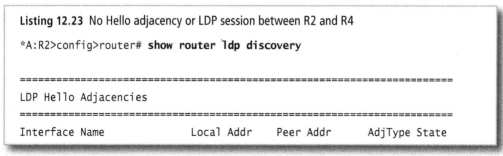

Listing 12.23 No Hello adjacency or LDP session between R2 and R4

```
*A:R2>config>router# show router ldp discovery

===============================================================================
LDP Hello Adjacencies
===============================================================================
Interface Name                Local Addr      Peer Addr       AdjType State
```

(continued)

Listing 12.23 *(continued)*

```
-------------------------------------------------------------------------
toR3                          10.10.10.2     10.10.10.3      Link     Estab
toR4                          10.2.4.2       224.0.0.2       Link     Trying
toR1                          10.10.10.2     10.10.10.1      Link     Estab
-------------------------------------------------------------------------
No. of Hello Adjacencies: 3
=========================================================================
*A:R2>config>router# show router ldp session

=========================================================================
LDP Sessions
=========================================================================
Peer LDP Id      Adj Type    State         Msg Sent  Msg Recv  Up Time
-------------------------------------------------------------------------
10.10.10.1:0     Link        Established  13506     13504     0d 10:22:32
10.10.10.3:0     Link        Established  13633     13632     0d 10:28:34
-------------------------------------------------------------------------
No. of Sessions: 2
=========================================================================
```

R2's route table in Listing 12.24 shows that R4 is the next-hop for `10.10.10.6/32`. R2's LIB in Listing 12.25 shows that R2 has a label from R3, but none from R4. Because R4 is the next-hop, R2 does not have an active label for the FEC, as shown in Listing 12.26.

Listing 12.24 The R2 route table shows the next-hop for the FEC to be R4

```
*A:R2>config>router# show router route-table 10.10.10.6/32

=========================================================================
Route Table (Router: Base)
=========================================================================
Dest Prefix                                 Type     Proto    Age          Pref
       Next Hop[Interface Name]                                  Metric
-------------------------------------------------------------------------
10.10.10.6/32                               Remote   OSPF     00h06m43s    10
       10.2.4.4                                                  200
-------------------------------------------------------------------------
No. of Routes: 1
=========================================================================
```

Listing 12.25 R2 has a label for the FEC from R3, but none from R4

```
*A:R2>config>router# show router ldp bindings prefix 10.10.10.6/32

===============================================================================
LDP LSR ID: 10.10.10.2
===============================================================================
Legend: U - Label In Use,  N - Label Not In Use, W - Label Withdrawn
    WP - Label Withdraw Pending
===============================================================================
LDP Prefix Bindings
===============================================================================
Prefix           Peer            IngLbl    EgrLbl EgrIntf     EgrNextHop
-------------------------------------------------------------------------------
10.10.10.6/32    10.10.10.3        --      131068   --            --
-------------------------------------------------------------------------------
No. of Prefix Bindings: 1
===============================================================================
```

Listing 12.26 R2 has no active label for the FEC

```
*A:R2>config>router# show router ldp bindings prefix 10.10.10.6/32
active

===============================================================================
Legend:  (S) - Static
===============================================================================
LDP Prefix Bindings (Active)
===============================================================================
Prefix                Op   IngLbl    EgrLbl    EgrIntf/LspId  EgrNextHop
-------------------------------------------------------------------------------
No Matching Entries Found
```

Furthermore, R2 does not generate a label for the FEC because it has no active label (ordered control). R1 does not receive a label from R2 and thus has no active label either (Listing 12.27). This situation can be difficult to troubleshoot because `10.10.10.6/32` is reachable through IP routing, but not through an MPLS tunnel. Even though labels are being generated and LDP appears to be functioning properly,

R1 does not have a tunnel to `10.10.10.6/32`, as shown in Listing 12.28. It does still have tunnels to the FECs where the labels received match the IGP topology (routers R2, R3, and R5).

Listing 12.27 R1 has not received a label from R2 and thus has no active label

```
*A:R1# show router ldp bindings prefix 10.10.10.6/32

===============================================================================
LDP LSR ID: 10.10.10.1
===============================================================================
Legend: U - Label In Use,  N - Label Not In Use, W - Label Withdrawn
    WP - Label Withdraw Pending
===============================================================================
LDP Prefix Bindings
===============================================================================
Prefix           Peer           IngLbl    EgrLbl EgrIntf      EgrNextHop
-------------------------------------------------------------------------------
10.10.10.6/32    10.10.10.3       --       131068   --           --
-------------------------------------------------------------------------------
No. of Prefix Bindings: 1
===============================================================================
*A:R1# show router ldp bindings active prefix 10.10.10.6/32

===============================================================================
Legend:  (S) - Static
===============================================================================
LDP Prefix Bindings (Active)
===============================================================================
Prefix                Op   IngLbl    EgrLbl    EgrIntf/LspId  EgrNextHop
-------------------------------------------------------------------------------
No Matching Entries Found
```

Listing 12.28 R1 has no tunnel to R4 or R6 in the topology

```
*A:R1# show router tunnel-table

===============================================================================
Tunnel Table (Router: Base)
```

```
===============================================================================
Destination        Owner Encap TunnelId  Pref     Nexthop          Metric
-------------------------------------------------------------------------------
10.10.10.2/32      ldp   MPLS   -         9        10.1.2.2         100
10.10.10.3/32      ldp   MPLS   -         9        10.1.3.3         100
10.10.10.5/32      ldp   MPLS   -         9        10.1.3.3         200
===============================================================================
```

LDP-IGP Synchronization

Figure 12.27 shows an LDP network in normal operation. R1 is sending data to R4 and has two labels (from R2 and R3) in its LIB. Because R2 is the next-hop in the route table, the label from R2 is installed in the LFIB as the active label for forwarding. Listing 12.29 shows the route table, LIB, and FIB on R1 for R4's system prefix.

Figure 12.27 LDP network, normal operation.

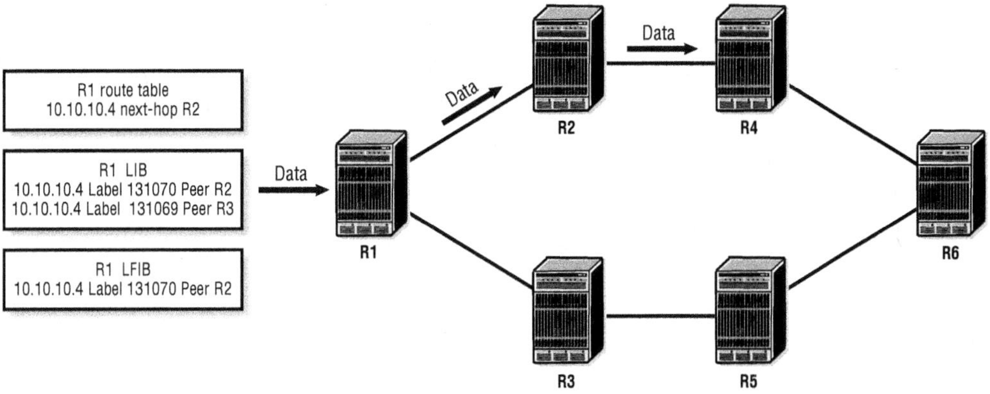

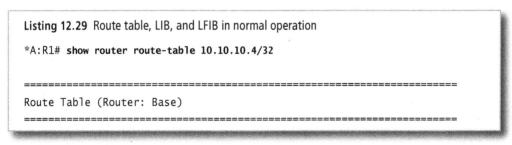

Listing 12.29 Route table, LIB, and LFIB in normal operation

```
*A:R1# show router route-table 10.10.10.4/32

===============================================================================
Route Table (Router: Base)
===============================================================================
```

(continued)

Listing 12.29 *(continued)*

```
Dest Prefix                               Type     Proto     Age          Pref
       Next Hop[Interface Name]                                     Metric
-------------------------------------------------------------------------------
10.10.10.4/32                             Remote   OSPF      00h01m12s    10
       10.1.2.2                                                     200
-------------------------------------------------------------------------------
No. of Routes: 1
===============================================================================
*A:R1# show router ldp bindings prefix 10.10.10.4/32

===============================================================================
LDP LSR ID: 10.10.10.1
===============================================================================
Legend: U - Label In Use,  N - Label Not In Use, W - Label Withdrawn
    WP - Label Withdraw Pending
===============================================================================
LDP Prefix Bindings
===============================================================================
Prefix              Peer           IngLbl     EgrLbl EgrIntf      EgrNextHop
-------------------------------------------------------------------------------
10.10.10.4/32       10.10.10.2     131069N    131070 1/1/3        10.1.2.2
10.10.10.4/32       10.10.10.3     131069U    131069   --           --
-------------------------------------------------------------------------------
No. of Prefix Bindings: 2
===============================================================================
*A:R1# show router ldp bindings active prefix 10.10.10.4/32

===============================================================================
Legend:  (S) - Static
===============================================================================
LDP Prefix Bindings (Active)
===============================================================================
Prefix              Op   IngLbl     EgrLbl     EgrIntf/LspId  EgrNextHop
-------------------------------------------------------------------------------
10.10.10.4/32       Push   --       131070     1/1/3          10.1.2.2
10.10.10.4/32       Swap 131069     131070     1/1/3          10.1.2.2
-------------------------------------------------------------------------------
No. of Prefix Bindings: 2
*A:R1#
```

When a link failure occurs between R2 and R4, traffic is routed in the opposite direction around the ring (see Figure 12.28). Because LDP uses liberal label retention, R1's LIB already contains a label for R4 from R3. R1 can start using the label from R3 as soon as it is installed in the LFIB (when R3 becomes the next-hop in the route table). Therefore, network convergence is dependent on the IGP convergence. Listing 12.30 shows the FIB, LIB, and LFIB after network convergence.

Figure 12.28 LDP network convergence.

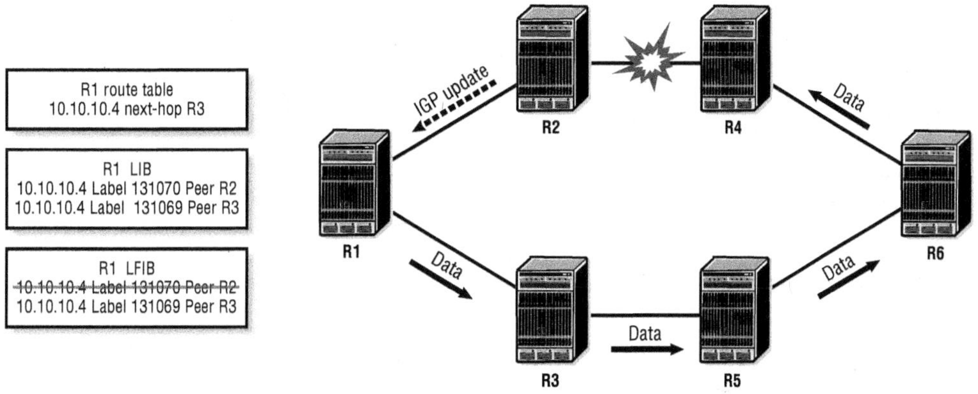

Listing 12.30 LDP network convergence, FIB, LIB, and LFIB

```
*A:R1# show router route-table 10.10.10.4/32

===============================================================================
Route Table (Router: Base)
===============================================================================
Dest Prefix                                   Type    Proto    Age         Pref
       Next Hop[Interface Name]                                      Metric
-------------------------------------------------------------------------------
10.10.10.4/32                                 Remote  OSPF     00h00m16s   10
       10.1.3.3                                                      400
-------------------------------------------------------------------------------
No. of Routes: 1
===============================================================================
*A:R1# show router ldp bindings prefix 10.10.10.4/32
```

(continued)

Listing 12.30 *(continued)*

```
===============================================================================
LDP LSR ID: 10.10.10.1
===============================================================================
Legend: U - Label In Use,  N - Label Not In Use, W - Label Withdrawn
    WP - Label Withdraw Pending
===============================================================================
LDP Prefix Bindings
===============================================================================
Prefix           Peer           IngLbl    EgrLbl EgrIntf     EgrNextHop
-------------------------------------------------------------------------------
10.10.10.4/32    10.10.10.2     131068U   131069   --          --
10.10.10.4/32    10.10.10.3     131068N   131069 1/1/2       10.1.3.3
-------------------------------------------------------------------------------
No. of Prefix Bindings: 2
===============================================================================
*A:R1# show router ldp bindings active prefix 10.10.10.4/32

===============================================================================
Legend:  (S) - Static
===============================================================================
LDP Prefix Bindings (Active)
===============================================================================
Prefix                Op   IngLbl    EgrLbl     EgrIntf/LspId  EgrNextHop
-------------------------------------------------------------------------------
10.10.10.4/32         Push   --      131069     1/1/2          10.1.3.3
10.10.10.4/32         Swap 131068    131069     1/1/2          10.1.3.3
-------------------------------------------------------------------------------
No. of Prefix Bindings: 2
*A:R1#
```

When planning resilient networks, it is equally important to consider the behavior of network protocols when failures are resolved. This is known as their *revertive* behavior. The revertive behavior of LDP is more complex than its behavior after the original link failure. After the link is repaired, we expect R1 to send traffic for R4 toward R2. This depends not only on IGP convergence, but also on the routers having labels to forward on the new path. IGP and LDP convergence must be in sync for efficient reversion to the optimal path.

Figure 12.29 illustrates a problem that arises when IGP convergence is reached before R2 has a label from R4. Because LDP always follows the IGP, R1 replaces the label from R3 with the one from R2 in the LFIB as soon as IGP convergence is reached. If R2 has not yet received a label from R4, it will discard any traffic it receives from R1 for R4.

Figure 12.29 LDP link recovery.

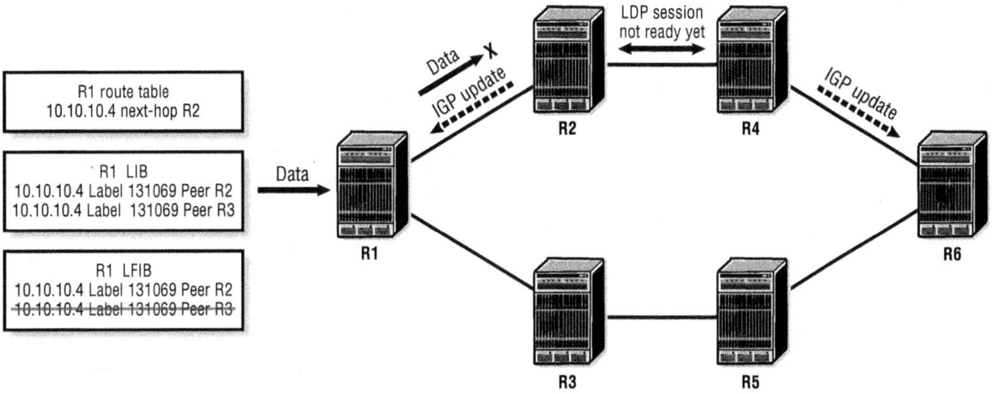

A solution to this problem is the LDP–IGP sync feature of the 7750 SR. When LDP–IGP sync is enabled, R2 still sends an IGP notification when the link is recovered, but with the maximum metric for the restored interfaces. This means that R3 remains the next-hop for R4, and traffic is still forwarded toward R3 while the new LDP labels are signaled. When the sync timer elapses, R2 floods new information with the proper metric. The expectation is that LDP labels will have been signaled by this time. LDP–IGP sync can also be used to reduce the effects of flapping links. The LDP–IGP sync solution is shown in Figure 12.30.

LDP–IGP sync is enabled in OSPF and IS-IS by default, but each router interface must be configured with an appropriate value for the sync timer. Listing 12.31 shows the configuration on R2 for the interface toward R4. The configuration should be applied consistently network wide.

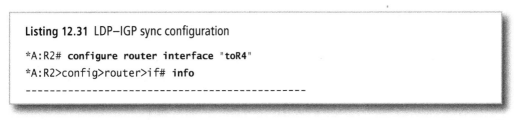

Listing 12.31 LDP–IGP sync configuration

```
*A:R2# configure router interface "toR4"
*A:R2>config>router>if# info
----------------------------------------------
```

(continued)

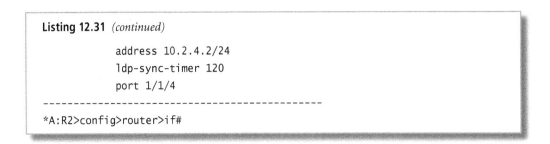

Listing 12.31 *(continued)*

```
            address 10.2.4.2/24
            ldp-sync-timer 120
            port 1/1/4
----------------------------------------------
*A:R2>config>router>if#
```

Figure 12.30 LDP–IGP sync.

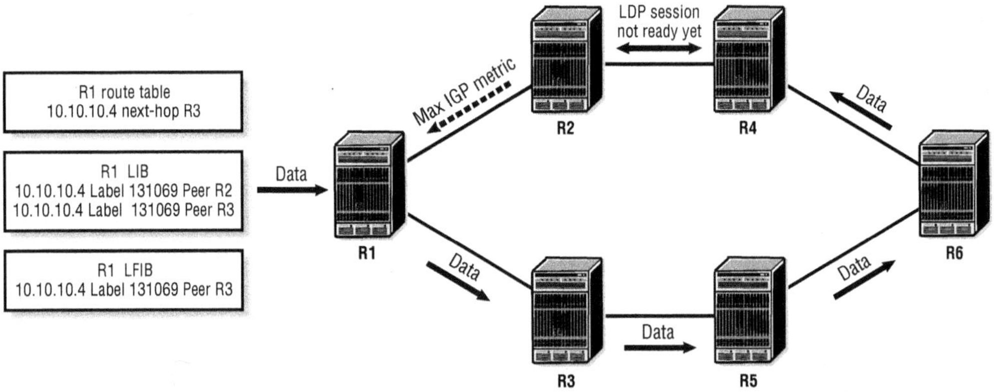

Listing 12.32 shows the maximum metric advertisement in the IGP database before the LDP sync timer expires.

Listing 12.32 LDP–IGP sync, RIB, LIB, and LFIB

```
*A:R1# show router route-table 10.10.10.4/32

=======================================================================
Route Table (Router: Base)
=======================================================================
Dest Prefix                          Type    Proto    Age         Pref
       Next Hop[Interface Name]                            Metric
-----------------------------------------------------------------------
10.10.10.4/32                        Remote  OSPF     00h25m33s   10
       10.1.3.3                                            400
-----------------------------------------------------------------------
```

```
No. of Routes: 1
===============================================================================
*A:R1#
*A:R1# show router ospf database adv-router 10.10.10.2 detail

===============================================================================
OSPF Link State Database (Type : All) (Detailed)
===============================================================================
-------------------------------------------------------------------------------
Router LSA for Area 0.0.0.0
-------------------------------------------------------------------------------
Area Id          : 0.0.0.0            Adv Router Id    : 10.10.10.2
Link State Id    : 10.10.10.2 (168430082)
LSA Type         : Router
Sequence No      : 0x8000017b         Checksum         : 0xc72b
Age              : 3                  Length           : 84
Options          : E
Flags            : None               Link Count       : 5
Link Type (1)    : Stub Network
Network (1)      : 10.10.10.2         Mask (1)         : 255.255.255.255
No of TOS (1)    : 0                  Metric-0 (1)     : 0
Link Type (2)    : Point To Point
Nbr Rtr Id (2)   : 10.10.10.1         I/F Address (2)  : 10.1.2.2
No of TOS (2)    : 0                  Metric-0 (2)     : 100
Link Type (3)    : Stub Network
Network (3)      : 10.1.2.0           Mask (3)         : 255.255.255.0
No of TOS (3)    : 0                  Metric-0 (3)     : 100
Link Type (4)    : Point To Point
Nbr Rtr Id (4)   : 10.10.10.4         I/F Address (4)  : 10.2.4.2
No of TOS (4)    : 0                  Metric-0 (4)     : 65535
Link Type (5)    : Stub Network
Network (5)      : 10.2.4.0           Mask (5)         : 255.255.255.0
No of TOS (5)    : 0                  Metric-0 (5)     : 65535
===============================================================================
*A:R1# show router ldp bindings prefix 10.10.10.4/32

===============================================================================
LDP LSR ID: 10.10.10.1
===============================================================================
```

(continued)

Listing 12.32 *(continued)*

```
Legend: U - Label In Use,  N - Label Not In Use, W - Label Withdrawn
    WP - Label Withdraw Pending
========================================================================
LDP Prefix Bindings
========================================================================
Prefix            Peer          IngLbl    EgrLbl EgrIntf     EgrNextHop
------------------------------------------------------------------------
10.10.10.4/32     10.10.10.2    131068U   131069   --           --
10.10.10.4/32     10.10.10.3    131068N   131069 1/1/2       10.1.3.3
------------------------------------------------------------------------
No. of Prefix Bindings: 2
========================================================================
*A:R1# show router ldp  bindings active prefix 10.10.10.4/32

========================================================================
Legend:  (S) - Static
========================================================================
LDP Prefix Bindings (Active)
========================================================================
Prefix              Op   IngLbl    EgrLbl    EgrIntf/LspId  EgrNextHop
------------------------------------------------------------------------
10.10.10.4/32       Push   --      131069    1/1/2          10.1.3.3
10.10.10.4/32       Swap 131068    131069    1/1/2          10.1.3.3
------------------------------------------------------------------------
No. of Prefix Bindings: 2
*A:R1#
```

Once the sync timer expires, the proper IGP metric is advertised, and the network returns to its normal state, as shown in Figure 12.31 and Listing 12.33.

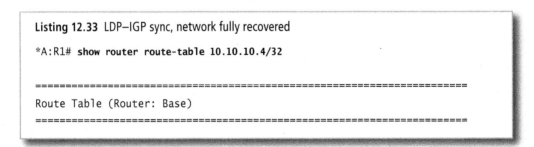

Listing 12.33 LDP–IGP sync, network fully recovered

```
*A:R1# show router route-table 10.10.10.4/32

========================================================================
Route Table (Router: Base)
========================================================================
```

```
Dest Prefix                              Type     Proto    Age          Pref
       Next Hop[Interface Name]                                   Metric
-----------------------------------------------------------------------
10.10.10.4/32                            Remote  OSPF     00h01m30s    10
       10.1.2.2                                                   200
-----------------------------------------------------------------------
No. of Routes: 1
=======================================================================
*A:R1# show router ospf database adv-router 10.10.10.2 detail

=======================================================================
OSPF Link State Database (Type : All) (Detailed)
=======================================================================
-----------------------------------------------------------------------
Router LSA for Area 0.0.0.0
-----------------------------------------------------------------------
Area Id          : 0.0.0.0            Adv Router Id     : 10.10.10.2
Link State Id    : 10.10.10.2 (168430082)
LSA Type         : Router
Sequence No      : 0x8000017c         Checksum          : 0xd454
Age              : 99                 Length            : 84
Options          : E
Flags            : None               Link Count        : 5
Link Type (1)    : Stub Network
Network (1)      : 10.10.10.2         Mask (1)          : 255.255.255.255
No of TOS (1)    : 0                  Metric-0 (1)      : 0
Link Type (2)    : Point To Point
Nbr Rtr Id (2)   : 10.10.10.1         I/F Address (2)   : 10.1.2.2
No of TOS (2)    : 0                  Metric-0 (2)      : 100
Link Type (3)    : Stub Network
Network (3)      : 10.1.2.0           Mask (3)          : 255.255.255.0
No of TOS (3)    : 0                  Metric-0 (3)      : 100
Link Type (4)    : Point To Point
Nbr Rtr Id (4)   : 10.10.10.4         I/F Address (4)   : 10.2.4.2
No of TOS (4)    : 0                  Metric-0 (4)      : 100
Link Type (5)    : Stub Network
Network (5)      : 10.2.4.0           Mask (5)          : 255.255.255.0
No of TOS (5)    : 0                  Metric-0 (5)      : 100
=======================================================================
```

(continued)

Listing 12.33 *(continued)*

```
*A:R1# show router ldp bindings prefix 10.10.10.4/32

===============================================================================
LDP LSR ID: 10.10.10.1
===============================================================================
Legend: U - Label In Use,  N - Label Not In Use, W - Label Withdrawn
    WP - Label Withdraw Pending
===============================================================================
LDP Prefix Bindings
===============================================================================
Prefix            Peer            IngLbl     EgrLbl EgrIntf      EgrNextHop
-------------------------------------------------------------------------------
10.10.10.4/32     10.10.10.2      131068N    131069 1/1/3        10.1.2.2
10.10.10.4/32     10.10.10.3      131068U    131069   --           --
-------------------------------------------------------------------------------
No. of Prefix Bindings: 2
===============================================================================
*A:R1# show router ldp  bindings active prefix 10.10.10.4/32

===============================================================================
Legend:  (S) - Static
===============================================================================
LDP Prefix Bindings (Active)
===============================================================================
Prefix                 Op   IngLbl     EgrLbl     EgrIntf/LspId  EgrNextHop
-------------------------------------------------------------------------------
10.10.10.4/32          Push   --       131069     1/1/3          10.1.2.2
10.10.10.4/32          Swap 131068     131069     1/1/3          10.1.2.2
-------------------------------------------------------------------------------
No. of Prefix Bindings: 2
*A:R1#
```

ECMP

Equal cost multi-path routing (ECMP) is a standard feature of most IP routing protocols that allows traffic to be distributed across multiple paths when there are more than one path of equal cost. As seen in Figure 12.32, without ECMP the IGP chooses a single route, and thus the same LSP is used for all traffic. R1's route table has a single entry for the FEC and one active label in its LFIB.

Figure 12.31 LDP–IGP sync, full recovery.

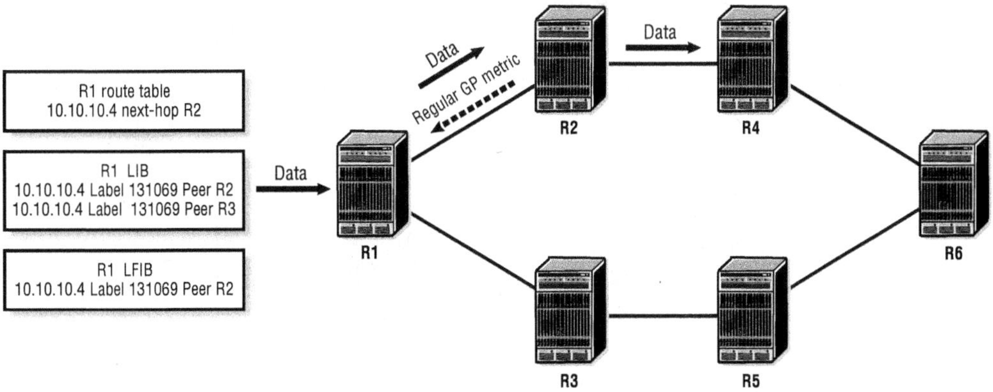

Figure 12.32 Normal IGP operation chooses a single best route for all traffic to the same destination.

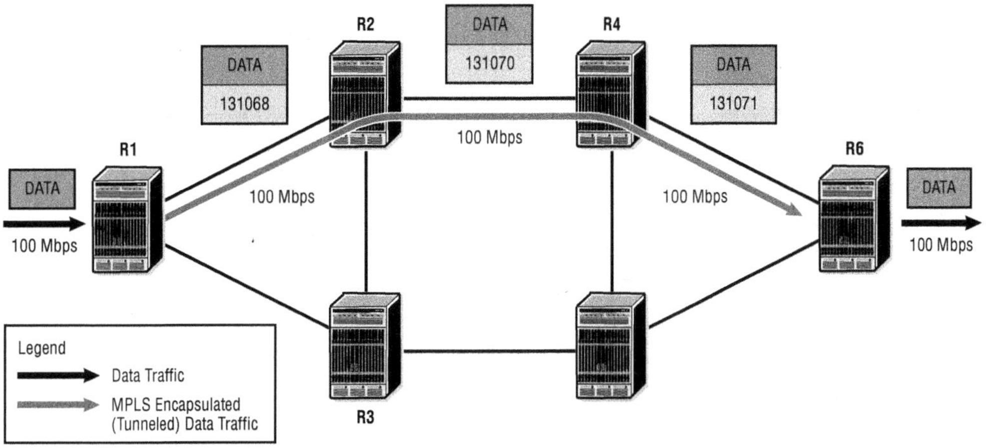

You can see that this may result in inefficient use of network resources when there are additional paths that are underutilized. In IP routing, ECMP allows us to distribute traffic between these two routes. ECMP is also supported in LDP. In the ECMP topology of Figure 12.33, there are two tunnels from R1 to R6, and traffic is distributed between them (Listing 12.34).

Figure 12.33 With ECMP enabled, traffic can be shared between the two paths.

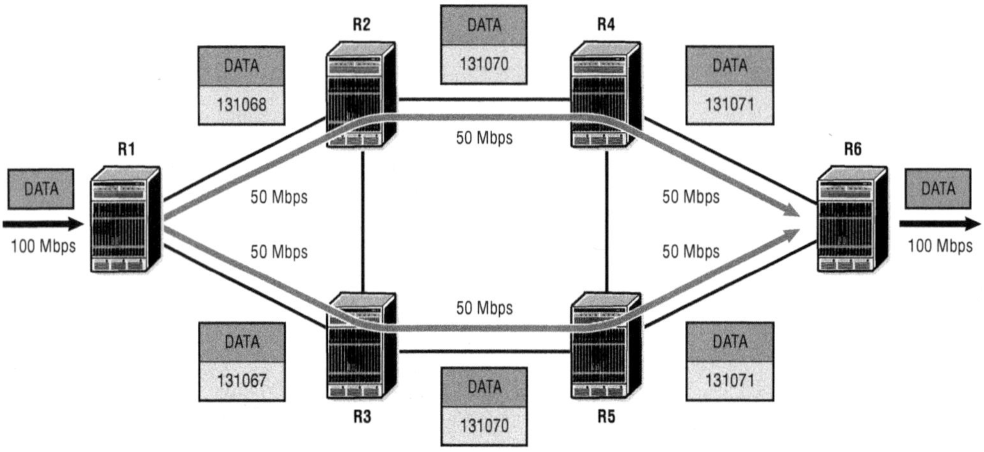

Listing 12.34 With ECMP, R1 has two tunnels to R6

```
*A:R1# show router tunnel-table

===============================================================================
Tunnel Table (Router: Base)
===============================================================================
Destination         Owner Encap TunnelId  Pref     Nexthop          Metric
-------------------------------------------------------------------------------
10.10.10.2/32       ldp   MPLS    -         9        10.1.2.2         100
10.10.10.3/32       ldp   MPLS    -         9        10.1.3.3         100
10.10.10.4/32       ldp   MPLS    -         9        10.1.2.2         200
10.10.10.5/32       ldp   MPLS    -         9        10.1.3.3         200
10.10.10.6/32       ldp   MPLS    -         9        10.1.2.2         300
10.10.10.6/32       ldp   MPLS    -         9        10.1.3.3         300
===============================================================================
```

ECMP is disabled by default, but only needs to be enabled in the `config router` context. After ECMP is enabled, there are two entries for the FEC in R1's route table and FIB (Listing 12.35). There are also two active labels in the LFIB (Listing 12.36).

Listing 12.35 With ECMP, R1 has two entries for the FEC in its route table

```
*A:R1# show router route-table 10.10.10.6/32

===============================================================================
Route Table (Router: Base)
===============================================================================
Dest Prefix                                  Type    Proto    Age         Pref
      Next Hop[Interface Name]                                    Metric
-------------------------------------------------------------------------------
10.10.10.6/32                                Remote  OSPF     00h02m28s   10
      10.1.2.2                                                    300
10.10.10.6/32                                Remote  OSPF     00h02m28s   10
      10.1.3.3                                                    300
-------------------------------------------------------------------------------
No. of Routes: 2
===============================================================================
```

Listing 12.36 With ECMP and LDP, R1 also has two active labels for the FEC

```
*A:R1# show router ldp bindings active prefix 10.10.10.6/32

===============================================================================
Legend:  (S) - Static
===============================================================================
LDP Prefix Bindings (Active)
===============================================================================
Prefix               Op   IngLbl    EgrLbl    EgrIntf/LspId  EgrNextHop
-------------------------------------------------------------------------------
10.10.10.6/32        Push   --      131068    1/1/4          10.1.2.2
10.10.10.6/32        Push   --      131068    1/1/3          10.1.3.3
-------------------------------------------------------------------------------
No. of Prefix Bindings: 2
```

When there are multiple paths to an FEC, the 7750 SR uses a hashing algorithm to distribute traffic between the multiple paths. If the split between paths occurs at ingress to the MPLS network, the hashing algorithm uses the source and destination IP addresses to choose the path. (MAC [Media Access Control] addresses are used for non-IP traffic.) If a split occurs at a transit LSR, the router uses the label stack for hashing. Although hashing does not always provide an equal division of traffic, it will not divide the traffic from a single data flow between different paths.

Controlling Label Distribution with Policies

As stated above, when LDP is enabled on the 7750 SR, it generates a label for its system address and for any FEC for which it has an active label. This default behavior can be modified through the use of export and import policies. The approach is very similar to routing protocol policies; export policies are used to advertise additional labels, and import policies are used to restrict the labels that are accepted from neighbors.

Export policies can be used to have the router advertise labels for FECs that are local to the router or FECs for which this router would be the egress LER. Below we look at an example in which we generate labels for loopback interfaces that simulate directly connected networks (Figure 12.34).

Figure 12.34 R6 is configured with two loopback interfaces for which LDP will generate labels.

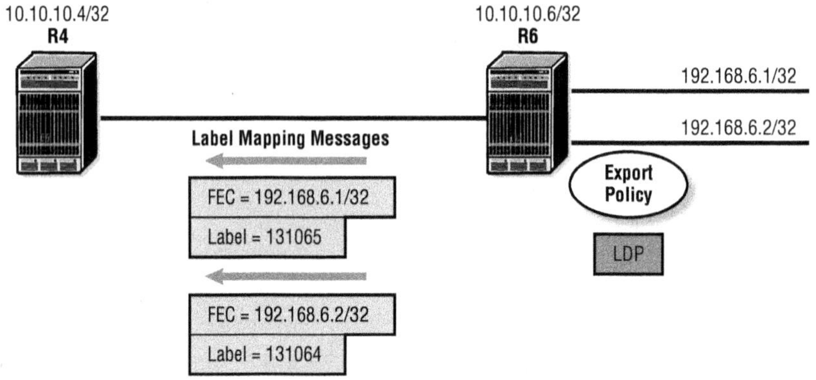

The first step is to configure the loopback interfaces, verify that they are in the route table, and then advertise them in OSPF (Listing 12.37). Although they are locally attached interfaces, LDP will not generate labels for these FECs by default.

Listing 12.37 Configure two loopback interfaces on R6

```
*A:R6# configure router
*A:R6>config>router# interface loopback-1
```

```
*A:R6>config>router>if$ address 192.168.6.1/32
*A:R6>config>router>if$ loopback
*A:R6>config>router>if$ exit
*A:R6>config>router# interface loopback-2
*A:R6>config>router>if$ address 192.168.6.2/32
*A:R6>config>router>if$ loopback
*A:R6>config>router>if# exit
*A:R6>config>router# ospf area 0
*A:R6>config>router>ospf>area# interface "loopback-1"
*A:R6>config>router>ospf>area>if$ exit
*A:R6>config>router>ospf>area# interface "loopback-2"
*A:R6>config>router>ospf>area>if$ exit all
*A:R6# show router route-table

========================================================================
Route Table (Router: Base)
========================================================================
Dest Prefix                                 Type    Proto    Age         Pref
       Next Hop[Interface Name]                                Metric
------------------------------------------------------------------------
... output omitted ...
192.168.6.1/32                              Local   Local    00h01m43s   0
       loopback-1                                              0
192.168.6.2/32                              Local   Local    00h01m23s   0
       loopback-2                                              0
------------------------------------------------------------------------
No. of Routes: 17
========================================================================
```

Once the loopbacks exist in the FIB, we create a prefix list that matches these addresses and then use that prefix list in the export policy. As with any policy, we first create the policy and then apply it to LDP (Listing 12.38).

Listing 12.38 Create a prefix list and an export policy and then apply it to LDP

```
*A:R6# configure router policy-options
*A:R6>config>router>policy-options# info
----------------------------------------------
```

(continued)

Listing 12.38 *(continued)*

```
            prefix-list "loopbacks"
                prefix 192.168.6.0/24 longer
            exit
            policy-statement "LDP_export"
                entry 10
                    from
                        prefix-list "loopbacks"
                    exit
                    action accept
                    exit
                exit
            exit
----------------------------------------------
*A:R6# configure router ldp export "LDP_export"
```

Once the policy is applied, the router generates labels for the FECs that match the prefix list (Listing 12.39). Because these interfaces were added to OSPF, the other routers in the network know these FECs and will also generate labels for them. Their default behavior is to generate labels to FECs for which they have an active label themselves. Listing 12.40 shows the LFIB on R1. Because ECMP is still enabled in our network, there are two active labels for both these FECs.

Listing 12.39 R6 has generated labels for the two loopback addresses

```
*A:R6# show router ldp bindings fec-type prefixes

===============================================================================
LDP LSR ID: 10.10.10.6
===============================================================================
Legend: U - Label In Use,  N - Label Not In Use, W - Label Withdrawn
    WP - Label Withdraw Pending
===============================================================================
LDP Prefix Bindings
===============================================================================
Prefix                Peer            IngLbl     EgrLbl EgrIntf/     EgrNextHop
                                                        LspId
```

```
--------------------------------------------------------------------------------
10.10.10.1/32     10.10.10.4     131066N    131068 1/1/4          10.4.6.4
10.10.10.1/32     10.10.10.5     131066N    131066 1/1/3          10.5.6.5
10.10.10.2/32     10.10.10.4     131068N    131066 1/1/4          10.4.6.4
10.10.10.2/32     10.10.10.5     131068U    131068   --             --
10.10.10.3/32     10.10.10.4     131067U    131067   --             --
10.10.10.3/32     10.10.10.5     131067N    131067 1/1/3          10.5.6.5
10.10.10.4/32     10.10.10.4       --       131071 1/1/4          10.4.6.4
10.10.10.4/32     10.10.10.5     131070U    131070   --             --
10.10.10.5/32     10.10.10.4     131069U    131069   --             --
10.10.10.5/32     10.10.10.5       --       131071 1/1/3          10.5.6.5
10.10.10.6/32     10.10.10.4     131071U      --     --             --
10.10.10.6/32     10.10.10.5     131071U      --     --             --
192.168.6.1/32    10.10.10.4     131065U      --     --             --
192.168.6.1/32    10.10.10.5     131065U      --     --             --
192.168.6.2/32    10.10.10.4     131064U      --     --             --
192.168.6.2/32    10.10.10.5     131064U      --     --             --
--------------------------------------------------------------------------------
No. of Prefix Bindings: 16
================================================================================
```

Listing 12.40 Labels for the new FECs are distributed throughout the network

```
*A:R1# show router ldp bindings active

================================================================================
Legend:  (S) - Static
================================================================================
LDP Prefix Bindings (Active)
================================================================================
Prefix                  Op   IngLbl     EgrLbl     EgrIntf/LspId  EgrNextHop
--------------------------------------------------------------------------------
10.10.10.1/32           Pop  131071       --          --             --
10.10.10.2/32           Push   --       131071     1/1/4          10.1.2.2
10.10.10.2/32           Swap 131070     131071     1/1/4          10.1.2.2
10.10.10.3/32           Push   --       131071     1/1/3          10.1.3.3
10.10.10.3/32           Swap 131069     131071     1/1/3          10.1.3.3
10.10.10.4/32           Push   --       131070     1/1/4          10.1.2.2
```

(continued)

Listing 12.40 *(continued)*

```
10.10.10.4/32        Swap 131068    131070     1/1/4          10.1.2.2
10.10.10.5/32        Push   --      131069     1/1/3          10.1.3.3
10.10.10.5/32        Swap 131067    131069     1/1/3          10.1.3.3
10.10.10.6/32        Push   --      131068     1/1/4          10.1.2.2
10.10.10.6/32        Push   --      131068     1/1/3          10.1.3.3
192.168.6.1/32       Push   --      131065     1/1/4          10.1.2.2
192.168.6.1/32       Push   --      131065     1/1/3          10.1.3.3
192.168.6.2/32       Push   --      131064     1/1/4          10.1.2.2
192.168.6.2/32       Push   --      131064     1/1/3          10.1.3.3
------------------------------------------------------------------------
No. of Prefix Bindings: 15
```

As with routing protocols, import policies are used to restrict the number of labels accepted by the router. Most often, this would be a situation in which a network of 7750 SRs is interoperating with another type of LDP router that has a more promiscuous policy of generating labels for every local FEC. If these labels are of no interest, an import policy can be used to filter some of the incoming labels (Figure 12.35).

Figure 12.35 Import policies are used to restrict the number of active labels on a router.

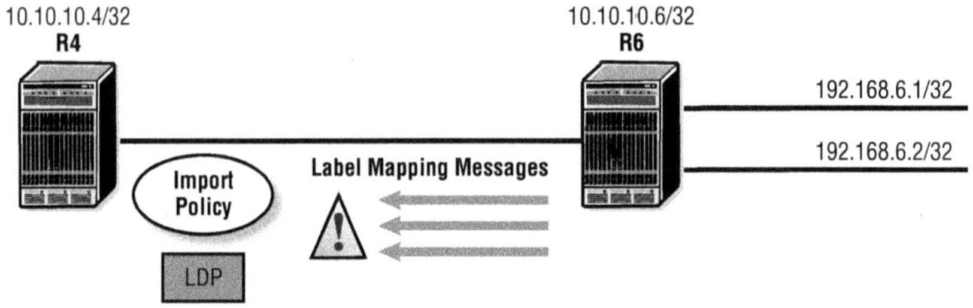

Listing 12.41 shows a simple example of an import policy that rejects all labels received from its neighbors. A more sophisticated policy might use a prefix list to reject labels selectively.

Listing 12.41 A simple import policy to filter all learned labels

```
A:R4# configure router policy-options
A:R4>config>router>policy-options# info
```

```
---------------------------------------------
            policy-statement "LDP_import"
                entry 10
                    action reject
                exit
            exit
---------------------------------------------
*A:R4>configure router ldp import "LDP_import"
```

Once the policy is applied, we see from Listing 12.42 that only the label for the system address is in the LFIB. The import policy does not affect this label because it is locally generated, but filters all other labels. Labels received from neighbors are still stored in the LIB, but do not become active.

Listing 12.42 After the import policy is applied, the router filters all learned labels

```
A:R4# show router ldp bindings active
=========================================================================
LDP Prefix Bindings (Active)
=========================================================================
Prefix                 Op   IngLbl    EgrLbl    EgrIntf/LspId  EgrNextHop
-------------------------------------------------------------------------
10.10.10.4/32          Pop  131071      --         --             --
-------------------------------------------------------------------------
No. of Prefix Bindings: 1
*A:R4# show router ldp bindings fec-type prefixes


=========================================================================
LDP LSR ID: 10.10.10.4
=========================================================================
Legend: U - Label In Use,  N - Label Not In Use, W - Label Withdrawn
    WP - Label Withdraw Pending
=========================================================================
LDP Prefix Bindings
=========================================================================
Prefix           Peer           IngLbl    EgrLbl EgrIntf/    EgrNextHop
                                                 LspId
-------------------------------------------------------------------------
```

(continued)

Listing 12.42 *(continued)*

```
10.10.10.1/32    10.10.10.2        --       131066   --         --
10.10.10.1/32    10.10.10.6        --       131066   --         --
10.10.10.2/32    10.10.10.2        --       131071   --         --
10.10.10.3/32    10.10.10.2        --       131067   --         --
10.10.10.3/32    10.10.10.6        --       131067   --         --
10.10.10.4/32    10.10.10.2    131071U        --     --         --
10.10.10.4/32    10.10.10.6    131071U        --     --         --
10.10.10.5/32    10.10.10.2        --       131069   --         --
10.10.10.5/32    10.10.10.6        --       131069   --         --
10.10.10.6/32    10.10.10.6        --       131071   --         --
192.168.6.1/32   10.10.10.6        --       131065   --         --
192.168.6.2/32   10.10.10.6        --       131064   --         --
-------------------------------------------------------------------------------
No. of Prefix Bindings: 12
===============================================================================
```

Multi-Area IGP with Summarization

We have seen the very tight relationship between the IGP and the LDP. If a router receives a label for a given FEC but does not have a route table entry for that FEC, it will not install an active label and thus will not forward traffic to that FEC. When LDP is used in a multi-area network in which destination prefixes are being summarized, a router may receive labels for FECs that do not exactly match entries in the route table. In Figure 12.36, there are individual entries in the route table on R6 for destinations `192.168.6.1/32` and `192.168.6.2/32` with labels for these FECs as well. At R4, the ABR (area border router), the routes are summarized as `192.168.6.0/24` (Listing 12.43).

Listing 12.43 Individual routes are summarized on R4

```
*A:R4>config>router>ospf# info
----------------------------------------------
            area 0.0.0.0
                interface "system"
                exit
                interface "toR2"
```

```
                interface-type point-to-point
            exit
        exit
        area 0.0.0.1
            area-range 192.168.6.0/24 advertise
            interface "toR6"
                interface-type point-to-point
            exit
        exit
----------------------------------------------
```

Figure 12.36 After summarization into Area 0, labels do not match the routes in the route table.

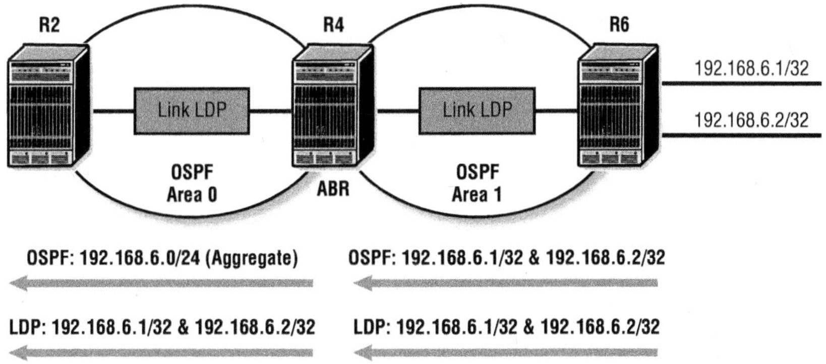

Router R2 in Area 0 receives the summarized route for `192.168.6.0/24` (Listing 12.44) and labels for the individual FECs `192.168.6.1/32` and `192.168.6.2/32` (Listing 12.45). Because the individual routes are not in the route table, these labels are not installed in the LFIB on R2.

Listing 12.44 R2 receives a summarized route

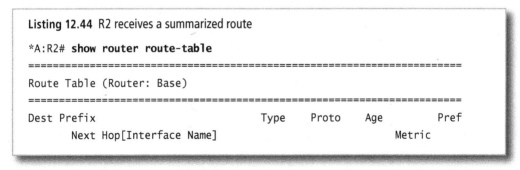

```
*A:R2# show router route-table
===============================================================================
Route Table (Router: Base)
===============================================================================
Dest Prefix                                    Type     Proto    Age          Pref
       Next Hop[Interface Name]                                       Metric
```

(continued)

Listing 12.44 *(continued)*

```
-------------------------------------------------------------------------
10.1.2.0/24                                   Local   Local    15h21m08s   0
       toR1                                                         0
10.2.3.0/24                                   Local   Local    15h23m02s   0
       toR3                                                         0
10.2.4.0/24                                   Local   Local    01h36m36s   0
       toR4                                                         0
10.4.6.0/24                                   Remote  OSPF     00h09m30s   10
       10.2.4.4                                                     200
10.10.10.2/32                                 Local   Local    15h22m07s   0
       system                                                       0
10.10.10.4/32                                 Remote  OSPF     00h09m55s   10
       10.2.4.4                                                     100
10.10.10.6/32                                 Remote  OSPF     00h08m43s   10
       10.2.4.4                                                     200
192.168.6.0/24                                Remote  OSPF     00h09m06s   10
       10.2.4.4                                                     200
-------------------------------------------------------------------------
No. of Routes: 8
=========================================================================
```

Listing 12.45 R2 has labels for the individual FECs and thus no active labels

```
*A:R2# show router ldp bindings fec-type prefixes

=========================================================================
LDP LSR ID: 10.10.10.2
=========================================================================
Legend: U - Label In Use,  N - Label Not In Use, W - Label Withdrawn
    WP - Label Withdraw Pending
=========================================================================
LDP Prefix Bindings
=========================================================================
Prefix            Peer            IngLbl     EgrLbl EgrIntf/    EgrNextHop
                                                    LspId
-------------------------------------------------------------------------
10.10.10.2/32     10.10.10.4      131071U    --     --          --
```

```
10.10.10.4/32     10.10.10.4          --       131071 1/1/2          10.2.4.4
10.10.10.6/32     10.10.10.4      131066N      131066 1/1/2          10.2.4.4
192.168.6.1/32    10.10.10.4          --       131065   --             --
192.168.6.2/32    10.10.10.4          --       131064   --             --
-----------------------------------------------------------------------------
No. of Prefix Bindings: 5
=============================================================================
*A:R2# show router ldp bindings active

=============================================================================
Legend:  (S) - Static
=============================================================================
LDP Prefix Bindings (Active)
=============================================================================
Prefix                 Op   IngLbl    EgrLbl    EgrIntf/LspId  EgrNextHop
-----------------------------------------------------------------------------
10.10.10.2/32          Pop  131071      --          --            --
10.10.10.4/32          Push   --      131071    1/1/2          10.2.4.4
10.10.10.6/32          Push   --      131066    1/1/2          10.2.4.4
-----------------------------------------------------------------------------
No. of Prefix Bindings: 3
```

The `aggregate-prefix-match` command can be used to override the default requirement for an exact prefix match. Listing 12.46 shows the configuration on router R2 and the LFIB that results.

Listing 12.46 With aggregate-prefix-match, more specific FECs match the aggregate

```
*A:R2# configure router ldp aggregate-prefix-match

*A:R2# show router route-table

=============================================================================
Route Table (Router: Base)
=============================================================================
Dest Prefix                             Type    Proto     Age          Pref
       Next Hop[Interface Name]                                Metric
-----------------------------------------------------------------------------
```

(continued)

Listing 12.46 *(continued)*

```
10.1.2.0/24                                Local    Local     15h33m02s   0
       toR1                                                       0
10.2.3.0/24                                Local    Local     15h34m55s   0
       toR3                                                       0
10.2.4.0/24                                Local    Local     01h48m29s   0
       toR4                                                       0
10.4.6.0/24                                Remote   OSPF      00h21m24s   10
       10.2.4.4                                                   200
10.10.10.2/32                              Local    Local     15h34m01s   0
       system                                                     0
10.10.10.4/32                              Remote   OSPF      00h21m49s   10
       10.2.4.4                                                   100
10.10.10.6/32                              Remote   OSPF      00h20m36s   10
       10.2.4.4                                                   200
192.168.6.0/24                             Remote   OSPF      00h21m00s   10
       10.2.4.4                                                   200
-----------------------------------------------------------------------
No. of Routes: 8
=======================================================================
*A:R2# show router ldp bindings active

=======================================================================
Legend:  (S) - Static
=======================================================================
LDP Prefix Bindings (Active)
=======================================================================
Prefix              Op   IngLbl    EgrLbl    EgrIntf/LspId  EgrNextHop
-----------------------------------------------------------------------
10.10.10.2/32       Pop  131071      --         --             --
10.10.10.4/32       Push   --      131071    1/1/2          10.2.4.4
10.10.10.6/32       Push   --      131066    1/1/2          10.2.4.4
192.168.6.1/32      Push   --      131065    1/1/2          10.2.4.4
192.168.6.2/32      Push   --      131064    1/1/2          10.2.4.4
-----------------------------------------------------------------------
No. of Prefix Bindings: 5
```

Practice Lab: Configuring and Verifying LDP

The following lab is designed to reinforce your knowledge of the content in this chapter. Please review the instructions carefully, and perform the steps in the order in which they are presented. The practice labs require that you have access to six or more 7750 SRs or Alcatel-Lucent 7450 ESSs in a non-production environment.

These labs are designed to be used in a controlled lab environment. Please *do not* attempt to perform these labs in a production environment.

Lab Section 12.1: Configuring LDP

LDP is a protocol for distributing MPLS labels. Routers configured for the LDP protocol establish an LDP session and become peers.

Objective In this exercise you will configure a topology of four Alcatel-Lucent 7750 SRs to run LDP (see Figure 12.37) and investigate the label distributions.

Figure 12.37 Lab topology for single-area LDP configuration.

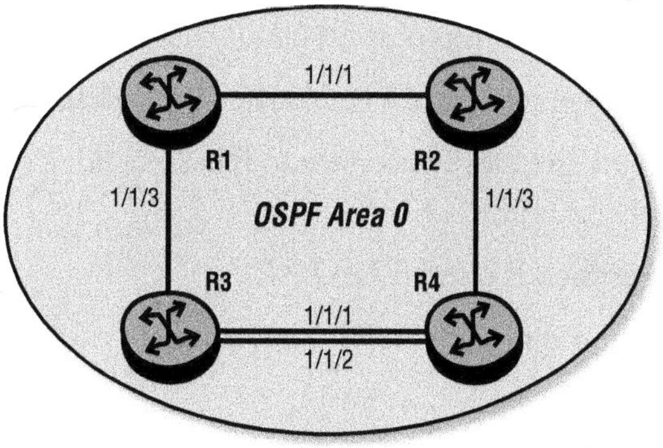

Validation You will know you have succeeded if you see the LDP sessions established between the routers and correct LDP label bindings on each router.

1. Configure an IGP to run between the backbone routers R1, R2, R3, and R4. OSPF is shown as the IGP, but you can use IS-IS if you prefer. Note the additional link between R3 and R4. Follow the regular IP addressing scheme on one of the links (`10.3.4.0/24` network) and use the `10.33.44.0/24` network on the other link. Make sure all router interfaces are distributed into the IGP.

2. Add the router interface on R1 toward R2 to LDP.
   a. Check the LDP status on R1. How many active interfaces and adjacencies exist? Explain.
   b. How many LDP label bindings exist on R1? Explain.
   c. Add the router interface on R2 toward R1 to LDP.
   d. How many LDP label bindings exist on R2? How many of the label bindings are active? Explain.
3. Add one of the links between R3 and R4 to LDP.
   a. How many label bindings exist on R3? How many of the label bindings are active?
   b. How many LDP sessions exist on R3?
   c. Add the second link between R3 and R4 to LDP. How many LDP sessions exist on R3?
   d. How many label bindings exist on R3 now? How many are active?
4. Add the interfaces between R2 and R4 to LDP.
   a. Does R4 have a label binding for R2's system address? Does R1 have a label binding for R2? What do you observe about these label bindings?
   b. Does R1 have a label binding for R3? Is the label binding active?
   c. On R3, shut down the OSPF interface to R1. Does R1 have a label binding to R3? Is the label binding active?
   d. Add the link between R1 and R3 to LDP.
   e. How many label bindings are on R1? How many of the bindings are active?

Lab Section 12.2: ECMP for LDP

ECMP is a standard feature of most IP routing protocols that allows traffic to be distributed across multiple paths when there are more than one path of equal cost.

Objective In this exercise, you will configure ECMP and investigate its effects.

Validation You will know that you have succeeded if the required prefixes have more than one active label binding with different label values and egress interfaces.

1. How many active LDP label bindings does R3 have for R4's system address?

2. Configure ECMP on R3 so that it will accept at least two active LDP bindings.
    a. How many active LDP bindings does R3 have for R4's system address? How has this changed from before the ECMP configuration?
    b. How many active LDP bindings does R3 have for R2? Contrast the result when ECMP is enabled and disabled.
    c. How many active LDP bindings does R2 have for R3?
3. Configure the metric of the link between R2 and R4 to a high value such as 2000.
    a. How many LDP bindings does R3 have for R2? How many are active? Explain.
    b. What side effect has this configuration had on R4?
    c. How could the network be configured so that R1 has two active LDP bindings with different label values to R2?
4. Remove the ECMP configuration on R3, and return all the link metrics to default values before proceeding to the next section.

Lab Section 12.3: Multi-Area LDP and LDP Export Policies

LDP can be used in a network with a multi-area IGP; however, some extra configuration may be required. Export policies can be used to modify LDP's default behavior on the Alcatel-Lucent 7750 SR.

Objective The objective of this lab is to investigate the use of LDP in a multi-area IGP network and the use of LDP export policies (see Figure 12.38).

Figure 12.38 Multi-area topology with LDP.

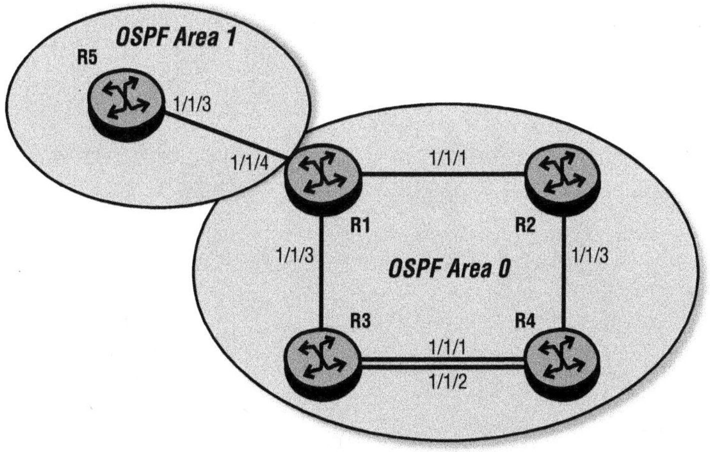

Validation You will know you have succeeded if the additional prefixes specified in the LDP export policy are propagated through different areas of the network.

1. Ensure that your IGP is configured as shown in Figure 12.38 with R5 in Area 1.
2. Configure LDP on R5 and R1.
   a. Does R1 have a label binding to R5?
   b. How many label bindings are now seen on R1? How many are active?
   c. Does R5 have a label binding to R1?
   d. How many label bindings are on R5? How many are active? Explain.
3. Configure three loopback interfaces on R5 with the addresses `192.168.55.1/32`, `192.168.55.2/32`, and `192.168.55.3/32`. Distribute the loopback interfaces into OSPF.
   a. Does R1's route table contain the loopback prefixes from R5?
   b. Does R1 have label bindings to the loopback prefixes from R5? Why or why not? Ensure that R1 has label bindings for the loopback prefixes before continuing.
   c. How many label bindings are now on R5? How many are active? Explain.
   d. Does R4 have active label bindings to the loopback prefixes from R5? Are they active? Why or why not?
4. Perform route summarization so that only a summarized route of `192.168.55.0/24` is advertised into Area 0.
   a. Ensure that the summarized route is seen on R2, R3, and R4 but that the individual loopback prefixes are not.
   b. How many active LDP bindings are now on R1?
   c. Do R2 and R3 have label bindings for the loopback prefixes from R5? Are they active?
   d. Does R4 have label bindings for the loopback prefixes from R5? Are they active?
   e. Perform any configuration required to ensure that all the Area 0 routers have an LDP label binding for the loopback prefixes from Area 1. Which routers require specific configuration for this?

Chapter Review

Now that you have completed this chapter, you should have a good understanding of the following topics:

- The format of an LDP PDU
- The use of TLVs for encoding LDP messages
- How Hello messages are used for neighbor discovery
- The process for establishing an LDP session
- How the Label Mapping message is used to generate labels
- The use of Label Withdraw and Label Release messages
- The operation of the LIB and the LFIB
- How LDP labels are propagated across the network
- What is required for convergence in an LDP network
- The effect of ECMP on LDP label generation
- How to use export policies to generate labels for additional FECs
- How to use import policies to reduce the number of active labels
- Label generation in a multi-area IGP network with summarization

Post-Assessment

The following questions will test your knowledge and prepare you for the Alcatel-Lucent NRS II Certification Exam. Compare your responses with the answers listed in Appendix A. You can also use the CD that accompanies this book to take all the assessment tests and review the answers.

1. Which of the following statements about LDP are correct?
   - **A.** Link LDP is used to exchange service labels.
   - **B.** Targeted LDP is used to exchange transport labels.
   - **C.** Link LDP peers are always directly connected.
   - **D.** Targeted LDP is required to provide L3 VPN services.
   - **E.** None of the above statements are correct.
2. What is the purpose of an LDP Notification message?
   - **A.** To create, change, and delete label mappings for FECs
   - **B.** To signal errors and other notable events
   - **C.** To establish LDP sessions between neighbors
   - **D.** To announce and maintain the presence of an LSR in a network
   - **E.** None of the above
3. Which statement below best describes the default behavior of LDP label advertisement on the Alcatel-Lucent 7750 SR?
   - **A.** Advertise a label for the system address.
   - **B.** Advertise labels for reachable FECs for which a label has been received.
   - **C.** Advertise a label for the system address and for reachable FECs for which a label has been received.
   - **D.** Do not advertise any labels unless an LDP export policy is configured.
   - **E.** Do not advertise any labels unless an LDP import policy is configured.

4. When an operator uses the `show router ldp bindings active` command on an Alcatel-Lucent 7750 SR, which construct is viewed?

   A. RIB

   B. FIB

   C. LIB

   D. LFIB

   E. RTM

5. Consider a network topology that includes four Alcatel-Lucent 7750 SRs. An IGP is running in the network, and each router advertises its system interface into the IGP. Assuming that export policies are not configured and LDP is converged, how many label prefix bindings are seen on each router when the `show router ldp bindings` command is used?

   A. 4

   B. 8

   C. 12

   D. 16

   E. There is not enough information to determine the answer

6. Which of the following is *not* a function of LDP?

   A. Discovery

   B. Flow control

   C. Session establishment

   D. Label exchange

   E. All of the above are functions of LDP

7. Which LDP message type does *not* use TCP as a transport protocol?

   A. Notification

   B. Label Mapping

   C. Keep Alive

   D. Hello

   E. All of the above messages use TCP as a transport protocol

8. Which of the statements below is correct regarding Link LDP adjacencies on an Alcatel-Lucent 7750 SR?

   A. A non-zero label space is indicated in each Hello message.

   B. The source IP address in each Hello message is the system interface address of the originating router.

   C. The destination IP address in each Hello message is the interface address of the destination router.

   D. The Hello time-out value must match between routers for the LDP adjacency to come up.

   E. By default, the egress interface address of the originating router is used for the transport address in Hello messages.

   F. None of the above statements are correct.

9. Consider a network that contains three Alcatel-Lucent 7750 SRs—R1, R2, and R3. The network is used to provide MPLS VPN services. R1 has two links to R2 and a single link to R3. R2 and R3 do not have a link between them. If Link LDP is used to distribute labels between all three routers, how many LDP sessions will R2 have?

   A. 1

   B. 2

   C. 3

   D. 4

   E. There is not enough information to determine the answer

10. Two Alcatel-Lucent 7750 SRs are configured to use Link LDP. R1 has a system interface address of `10.0.0.5`, and R2 has a system interface address of `10.0.0.12`. Which of the following statements is correct regarding LDP session establishment between the routers?

    A. R1 is considered the active router for session establishment.

    B. R1 does not send any LDP Initialization messages for session establishment.

    C. R2 initiates the opening of the LDP session by sending an LDP Notification message.

    D. Both routers will attempt to open a TCP connection.

    E. LDP Address and Label Mapping messages cannot be exchanged until the active router reaches the operational state.

11. Consider two routers, R1 and R2, running a Link LDP session between them. R2 has a label binding for an FEC that it received from R1; however, a network topology change occurs that causes R1 to no longer recognize the FEC. Which statement best characterizes the LDP message sequence used to indicate the change on R1?

   A. R1 sends a Label Withdraw message to R2.

   B. R1 sends a Label Release message to R2.

   C. R1 sends a Label Withdraw message to R2, and R2 sends a Label Release message to R1.

   D. R1 sends a Label Release message to R2, and R2 sends a Label Release message to R1.

12. Consider a network topology that contains three Alcatel-Lucent 7750 SRs—R1, R2, and R3—running Link LDP. R1 is connected to both R2 and R3. Assuming that an export policy is not configured on R1, which statement best describes R1's actions as soon as the LDP adjacencies are established with both routers?

   A. R1 originates a Label Mapping message for its system address to R1 and R2. Both Label Mapping messages contain the same label value.

   B. R1 originates a Label Mapping message for its system address to R1 and R2. The Label Mapping messages contain different label values.

   C. R1 originates a Notification message for its system address to R1 and R2. Both Notification messages contain the same label value.

   D. R1 originates a Notification message for its system address to R1 and R2. The Notification messages contain different values.

   E. There is not enough information to determine R1's actions.

13. Consider a network topology of three Alcatel-Lucent 7750 SRs in which each router has a single connection to the other two routers. An IGP is running in the network, and each router advertises its system interface into the IGP. All router links in the network are equal cost, and ECMP is configured throughout the network. How many prefix bindings are seen on each router when the `show router ldp bindings active` command is used?

   A. 3

   B. 5

   C. 6

   D. 9

   E. There is not enough information to determine the answer

14. Consider a network of Alcatel-Lucent 7750 SRs with two OSPF Area 1 ABRs. Both Area 1 ABRs receive the prefixes `192.168.3.0/24` and `192.168.4.0/24` from Area 1 and summarize them as `192.168.0.0/16` toward Area 0. What configuration is required in the network to ensure that Area 0 routers have active LDP bindings for the FECs `192.168.3.0/24` and `192.168.4.0/24`?

   A. The `aggregate-prefix-match` command has to be used on one of the ABRs.

   B. The `aggregate-prefix-match` command has to be used on both of the ABRs.

   C. The `aggregate-prefix-match` command has to be used on Area 0 routers that are directly connected to either of the Area 1 ABRs.

   D. The `aggregate-prefix-match` command has to be used on all Area 0 routers.

   E. No specific configuration is required.

15. Consider a network topology of three Alcatel-Lucent 7750 SRs. Each router has a connection to the other two routers. An IGP is running in the network, and each router advertises its system interface into the IGP. An operator intends to configure the router interfaces between all three routers into LDP but forgets an interface on one of the routers. How many active LDP prefix bindings are on the router that the operator mistakenly configured with only one LDP interface? Assume that all the router links have the same cost.

   A. 0

   B. 1

   C. 2

   D. 3

   E. 5

   F. 6

13 RSVP-TE Operation

The Alcatel-Lucent NRS II exam topics covered in this chapter include the following:

- Configuring RSVP
- RSVP-TE operation and messages
- Path and Resv messages
- RSVP-TE tunnels and LSP::Paths
- Other RSVP messages
- RSVP-TE path selection
- MPLS shortcuts for BGP
- MPLS shortcuts for IGP
- 6PE - IPv6 tunnels

Originally the Resource Reservation Protocol (RSVP) was developed as a network control protocol to be used by a host to request specific qualities of service from the network for an application data stream or flow. RSVP is used by routers to deliver quality of service (QoS) requests to all nodes along the path(s) of the flows and to establish and maintain a state to provide the requested service level. An RSVP request results in resources being reserved by each node along the data path.

In RFC 3209, RSVP was enhanced as RSVP-TE (Resource Reservation Protocol–Traffic Engineering) for use with MPLS (Multiprotocol Label Switching) to set up traffic-engineered LSPs (label switched paths). When used for signaling an LSP, RSVP-TE also returns a label for the LSP path. RSVP-TE can be used to signal LSPs that either include or don't include resiliency options, bandwidth reservations, or other options.

This chapter examines how LSPs are signaled using Path and Resv messages, as well as the other messages used in maintaining an LSP. We take a detailed look at the format of the messages and the operation of routers using RSVP-TE. We also provide an example configuration of an RSVP-TE LSP. The method that RSVP-TE uses to select the path for the LSP is described, although not for traffic-engineered paths. Constraint-based routing and traffic-engineered paths are covered in Chapter 14.

Pre-Assessment

The following assessment questions will help you understand what areas of the chapter you should review in more detail to prepare for the NRS II exam. You can also use the CD that accompanies this book to take all the assessment tests and review the answers.

1. Which statement is correct regarding RSVP-TE messages used for setting up an LSP?

- **A.** The destination IP address of a Path message is always the next-hop neighbor.
- **B.** Resv messages must contain an RRO so that they can be forwarded appropriately.
- **C.** Label binding information is carried in Path messages.
- **D.** The head end signals LSP label values to be used by all other routers in a Path trigger message.
- **E.** None of the above statements are correct.

2. Consider an operationally up LSP that has a strict path of R1 ➪ R2 ➪ R3 ➪ R4. A link failure occurs between R2 and R3. Which statement best describes the RSVP-TE message sequence that follows?

   A. R1 detects the IGP topology change and sends a Path Tear message downstream.

   B. R1 detects the IGP topology change and sends a Resv Tear message downstream.

   C. R2 sends a Path Error message upstream, and R3 sends a Resv Error message downstream.

   D. R2 sends a Path Tear message upstream, and R3 sends a Resv Tear message downstream.

   E. R2 sends a Resv Tear message upstream, and R3 sends a Path Tear message downstream.

3. Consider an established LSP with a path traversing four routers. There are six routers in the IGP domain, and all routers have operational RSVP-TE interfaces. Which routers will have an RSVP-TE session for this LSP?

   A. Only the head end router will have an RSVP-TE session for the LSP.

   B. The head end router and the tail end router will have an RSVP-TE session for the LSP.

   C. All routers in the LSP path will have an RSVP-TE session for the LSP.

   D. All routers in the IGP domain will have an RSVP-TE session for the LSP.

   E. There is not enough information to answer the question.

4. Which statement is correct concerning RSVP Error messages?

   A. Path Error messages travel upstream and are addressed to the head end router.

   B. Resv Error messages travel downstream and are addressed to the tail end router.

   C. Resv Error messages modify the RSB on RSVP routers.

   D. Path Error messages do not modify the PSB on RSVP routers.

   E. None of the above answers are correct.

5. Consider a network that has four routers with EBGP peers and five core routers that only have IBGP peers. A service provider wants to start using MPLS shortcuts for BGP. Which routers need to be provisioned with MPLS shortcuts?

A. MPLS shortcuts need to be provisioned on the routers that only have IBGP peers.

B. MPLS shortcuts need to be provisioned on the routers that have EBGP peers.

C. MPLS shortcuts need to be provisioned on all routers in the autonomous system.

D. MPLS shortcuts need to be provisioned on all routers that have EBGP connections and their peers in other autonomous systems.

E. There is not enough information to answer the question.

13.1 Overview of RSVP-TE

RSVP-TE (Resource Reservation Protocol–Traffic Engineering) operates in downstream-on-demand mode for signaling LSP labels. A request for a label is signaled in a Path message sent from the head end of the LSP (label switched path) (iLER [ingress LER, Label Edge Router]). Labels are signaled from the tail end (eLER [egress LER]) using Resv messages. The Path message may or may not contain an explicit route to be followed and may or may not contain specific bandwidth reservation requests.

RSVP-TE is not a routing protocol. It requests resources and a label for a unidirectional flow; that is, it requests resources only in one direction. A bidirectional flow requires two LSPs—one to carry traffic in each direction. In the description of the protocol, *downstream* and *upstream* indicate the direction of data flow in the LSP.

Setting Up an LSP with Path and Resv Messages

RSVP-TE uses two message types to set up an LSP—the Path and Resv messages.

The head end sends a Path message toward the tail end indicating the FEC (Forwarding Equivalence Class) for which a label binding is desired and any resource requirements. Each LSR (label switch router) verifies that it can provide the resources requested and sends the Path message to the next downstream hop toward the eLER (see Figure 13.1).

The tail end sends label binding information in a Resv message in response to the received Path message. The Resv message is sent back along the same LSP path of the Path message. Each router makes the necessary resource reservations and provides a label binding to the upstream router (Figure 13.2).

Figure 13.1 The ingress router sends a Path message requesting a label binding for FEC 10.10.10.6.

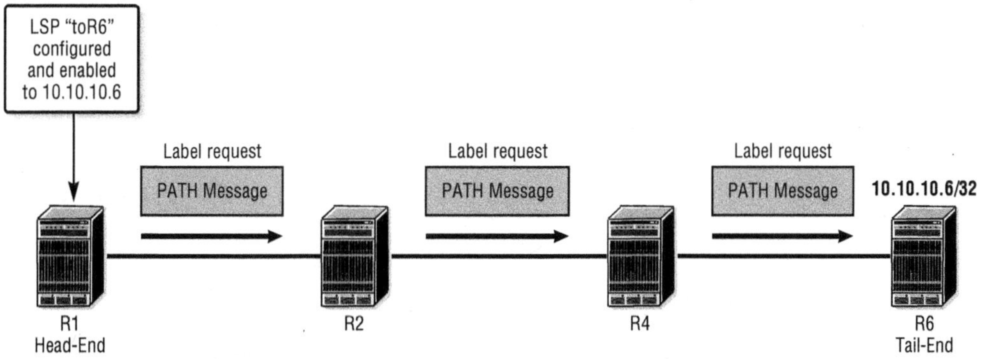

Figure 13.2 The egress router sends a Resv message upstream with a label binding.

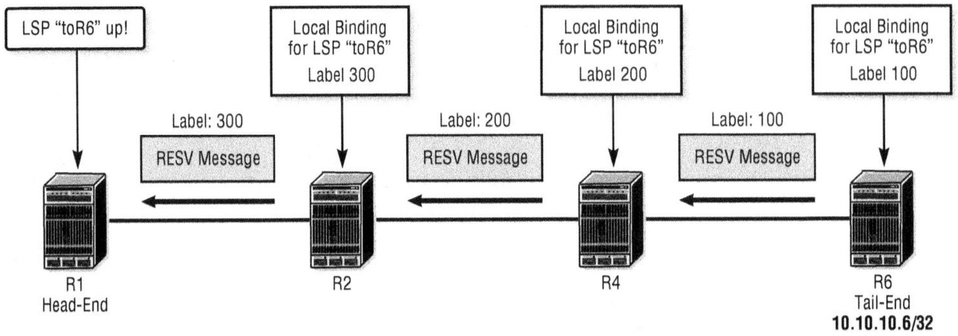

The LSP becomes operational when the head end receives the label binding information for the FEC, via the Resv message. At this point, every router along the LSP path has received a label and made a bandwidth reservation for the FEC.

Configuring RSVP-TE

RSVP-TE provides more control over the definition of LSPs than LDP (Label Distribution Protocol). As a result, the configuration is a little more complex than for LDP. Below we show the simple configuration of an LSP from router R1 to R6 in the topology shown in Figure 13.3.

Figure 13.3 Topology used to illustrate RSVP-TE LSP creation and message signaling.

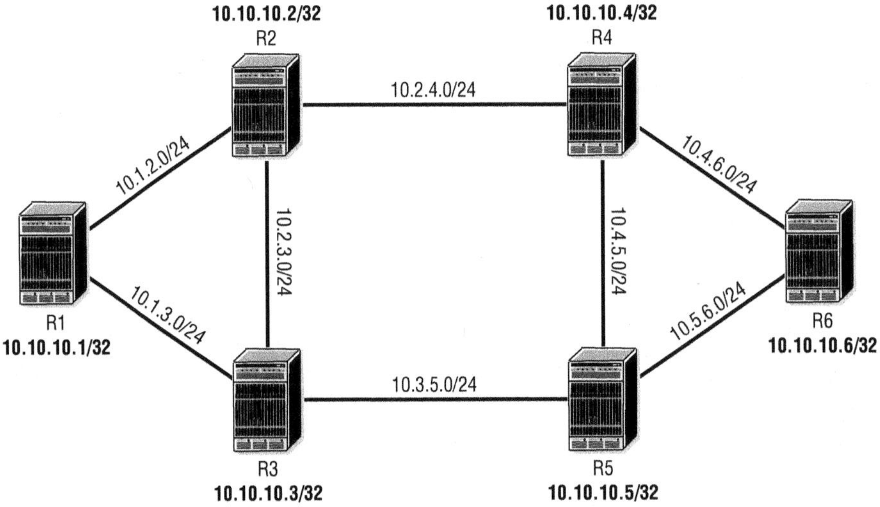

Although an operational IGP (interior gateway protocol) is not strictly required as a prerequisite for creating RSVP-TE LSPs, in practice, an IGP is always enabled. Once the Layer 3 infrastructure is in place, all interfaces in the MPLS (Multiprotocol Label Switching) domain must be enabled for MPLS. When interfaces are added to the MPLS context on the Alcatel-Lucent 7750 SR, they are automatically added to the RSVP-TE context, as shown in Listing 13.1. Note that the system interface is already included in the MPLS and RSVP-TE contexts. Both MPLS and RSVP-TE are administratively down by default.

Listing 13.1 All interfaces are added to MPLS

```
*A:R1# configure router mpls
*A:R1>config>router>mpls# interface "toR2"
*A:R1>config>router>mpls>if$ exit
*A:R1>config>router>mpls# interface "toR3"
*A:R1>config>router>mpls>if$ exit
*A:R1>config>router>mpls# info
----------------------------------------------
            shutdown
            interface "system"
            exit
            interface "toR2"
            exit
            interface "toR3"
            exit
----------------------------------------------
*A:R1>config>router>mpls# no shutdown
*A:R1>config>router>mpls# exit
*A:R1# configure router rsvp
*A:R1>config>router>rsvp# info
----------------------------------------------
            shutdown
            interface "system"
            exit
            interface "toR2"
            exit
            interface "toR3"
            exit
----------------------------------------------
```

(continued)

Listing 13.1 *(continued)*

```
*A:R1>config>router>rsvp# no shutdown
*A:R1>config>router>rsvp# show router rsvp interface

=========================================================================
RSVP Interfaces
=========================================================================
Interface                Total    Active   Total BW  Resv BW   Adm Opr
                         Sessions Sessions (Mbps)    (Mbps)
-------------------------------------------------------------------------
system                   -        -        -         -         Up  Up
toR2                     0        0        1000      0         Up  Up
toR3                     0        0        1000      0         Up  Up
-------------------------------------------------------------------------
Interfaces : 3
=========================================================================
*A:R1>config>router>rsvp#
```

Once the interfaces are enabled for RSVP-TE, the LSP is created in the `config>router>mpls>` context. First, any LSP must have a path defined. The path is essentially a way of putting constraints on the LSP; thus if we want the LSP to simply follow the route of the IGP, then the path is empty. To define the LSP, we only need to specify the path that is to be used and the egress node of the LSP. Listing 13.2 shows the path defined with the name `loose`. This path is then selected in the definition of the LSP `toR6` with the keyword `primary`. The use of the path is discussed in more detail below in this chapter and in Chapter 14.

Listing 13.2 Declaration of an LSP with no path constraints

```
*A:R1>config>router>mpls# path loose
*A:R1>config>router>mpls>path$ no shutdown
*A:R1>config>router>mpls>path$ exit
*A:R1>config>router>mpls# lsp toR6
*A:R1>config>router>mpls>lsp$ to 10.10.10.6
*A:R1>config>router>mpls>lsp$ primary "loose"
*A:R1>config>router>mpls>lsp>primary$ exit
*A:R1>config>router>mpls>lsp# no shutdown
```

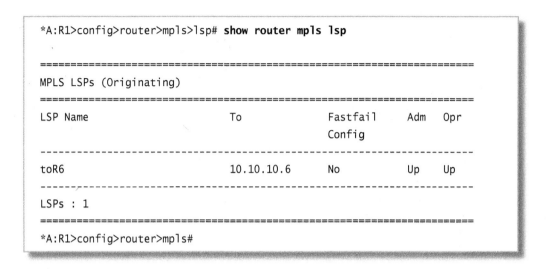

```
*A:R1>config>router>mpls>lsp# show router mpls lsp

===============================================================================
MPLS LSPs (Originating)
===============================================================================
LSP Name                          To              Fastfail      Adm   Opr
                                                  Config
-------------------------------------------------------------------------------
toR6                              10.10.10.6      No            Up    Up
-------------------------------------------------------------------------------
LSPs : 1
===============================================================================
*A:R1>config>router>mpls#
```

When you configure an LSP, do not expect it to be operationally up immediately. The LSP must be signaled, and this can take several seconds. Once the LSP is up, you can see the path that it has taken and the labels signaled at each hop in the actual hops field (see Listing 13.3). In this case, it must follow the path chosen by the IGP, and this is confirmed by the output of the `traceroute` command.

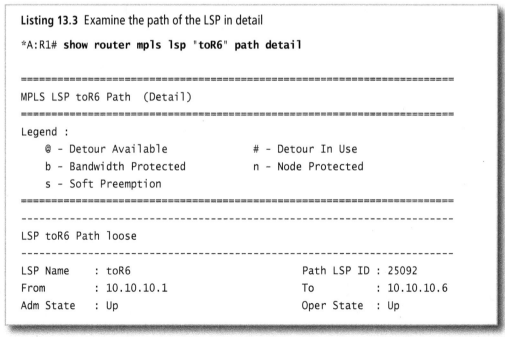

Listing 13.3 Examine the path of the LSP in detail

```
*A:R1# show router mpls lsp "toR6" path detail

===============================================================================
MPLS LSP toR6 Path  (Detail)
===============================================================================
Legend :
    @ - Detour Available              # - Detour In Use
    b - Bandwidth Protected           n - Node Protected
    s - Soft Preemption
===============================================================================
-------------------------------------------------------------------------------
LSP toR6 Path loose
-------------------------------------------------------------------------------
LSP Name     : toR6                          Path LSP ID : 25092
From         : 10.10.10.1                    To          : 10.10.10.6
Adm State    : Up                            Oper State  : Up
```

(continued)

Listing 13.3 *(continued)*

```
Path Name    : loose                         Path Type    : Primary
Path Admin   : Up                            Path Oper    : Up
OutInterface: 1/1/2                          Out Label    : 131065
Path Up Time: 0d 00:00:12                    Path Dn Time: 0d 00:00:00
Retry Limit : 0                              Retry Timer : 30 sec
RetryAttempt: 0                              NextRetryIn : 0 sec
SetupPriori*: 7                              Hold Priori*: 0
Preference  : n/a
Bandwidth    : No Reservation                Oper Bw      : 0 Mbps
Hop Limit    : 255                           Class Type   : 0
Backup CT    : None
MainCT Retry: n/a                            MainCT Retry: 0
    Rem      :                                   Limit    :
Oper CT      : 0
Record Route: Record                         Record Label: Record
Oper MTU     : 9198                          Neg MTU      : 9198
Adaptive     : Enabled                       Oper Metric : 300
Include Grps:                                Exclude Grps:
None                                       None
Path Trans   : 3                             CSPF Queries: 0
Failure Code: noError                        Failure Node: n/a
ExplicitHops:
    No Hops Specified
Actual Hops :
    10.1.2.1(10.10.10.1)                     Record Label    : N/A
 -> 10.1.2.2(10.10.10.2)                     Record Label    : 131065
 -> 10.2.4.4(10.10.10.4)                     Record Label    : 131065
 -> 10.4.6.6(10.10.10.6)                     Record Label    : 131065
ResigEligib*: False
LastResignal: n/a                            CSPF Metric : 0
===============================================================================
* indicates that the corresponding row element may have been truncated.
*A:R1#
*A:R1# traceroute 10.10.10.6
traceroute to 10.10.10.6, 30 hops max, 40 byte packets
  1  10.1.2.2 (10.1.2.2)    2.11 ms  1.73 ms  1.71 ms
  2  10.2.4.4 (10.2.4.4)    2.31 ms  2.36 ms  2.32 ms
  3  10.10.10.6 (10.10.10.6)    2.82 ms  2.74 ms  2.77 ms
```

13.2 RSVP-TE Operation and Messages

When discussing RSVP-TE, we will use the term *tunnel* to describe the LSP used for transporting data. An RSVP-TE tunnel is identified by its Tunnel ID. It may comprise several distinct LSPs, possibly following different paths (see Figure 13.4). In this book, we refer to these individual LSPs as *LSP::Paths* to distinguish them from the RSVP-TE tunnel. These LSP::Paths each have a unique LSP ID but share the same Tunnel ID. The LSP::Paths are used to provide redundancy and are also created whenever a new LSP is signaled for the tunnel.

Figure 13.4 One RSVP-TE tunnel may include several LSP::Paths.

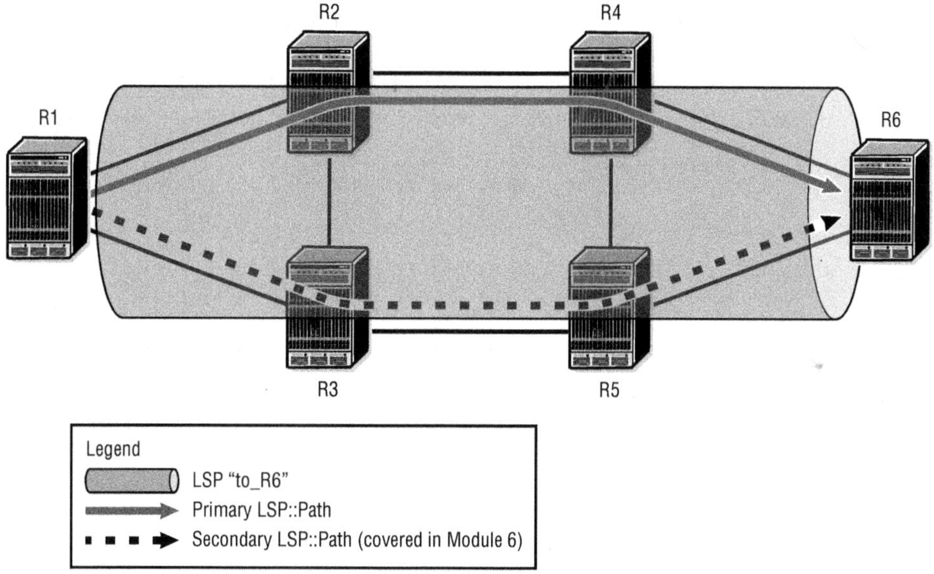

This section describes the Path and Resv messages that are used to signal all LSP::Paths. All RSVP-TE messages are carried in raw IP packets, with IP protocol value 46 (hex 0x2E). We will show the signaling of Path and Resv messages for the topology in Figure 13.3.

Path Message

When an RSVP-TE LSP is to be established, the requirements are signaled in a Path message. The Path message is composed of several different objects. The most important ones are described in Table 13.1.

Table 13.1 Objects in the Path Message

Object Name	Description
SESSION	The SESSION object uniquely identifies the RSVP-TE tunnel. All LSPs belonging to the same tunnel have the same SESSION object. It contains the destination IP address of the tunnel, the Tunnel ID, and the extended-tunnel-id (system IP address of the tunnel head end).
HOP	Contains the IP address of the egress interface used to send the Path message to the next-hop downstream router.
TIME_VALUE	The expected refresh interval for the RSVP-TE session
SENDER_TEMPLATE	The SESSION object and SENDER_TEMPLATE object uniquely identify the individual LSP::Path. SENDER_TEMPLATE contains the sender system IP address and the LSP ID. Each LSP::Path within an RSVP-TE tunnel has a unique LSP ID.
SENDER_TSPEC	Contains traffic engineering parameters for the LSP, such as bandwidth required or fast reroute options. These are described in more detail in Chapters 14, 15, and 16.
LABEL REQUEST	Requests a label for the LSP.
EXPLICIT ROUTE (ERO)	ERO is optional and contains a list of strict or loose hops to be followed by the LSP.
RECORD ROUTE (RRO)	RRO is optional and contains a list of the hops that the Path message has traversed. By default, the RRO is always used on the 7750 SR.

The source IP address of the Path message is the system address of the head end router. The destination is the system address of the tail end router. However, the Router Alert option is used in the IP header. This tells the next-hop router that it must process the message, even if it is not the ultimate destination for the message (Figure 13.5).

Figure 13.5 The Path message is addressed to the tail end router with the Router Alert option set.

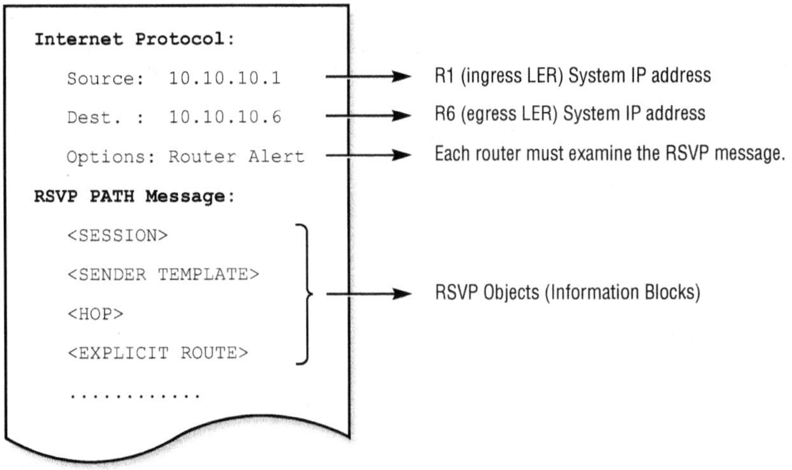

RSVP-TE can signal an LSP to follow the path chosen by the IGP (similar to LDP) or may apply some constraints to the route to be followed. These constraints are listed in the ERO (EXPLICIT_ROUTE object) as either strict or loose hops. Constraints on an RSVP-TE LSP are described in more detail below in this chapter and in Chapter 14. If there are no constraints (LSP to follow the path of the IGP), there is no ERO in the Path message, and the message is sent to the next-hop for the tail end router as selected by the IGP (Figure 13.6).

Figure 13.6 The Path message is sent to the next-hop specified by the ERO or the next-hop selected by IGP.

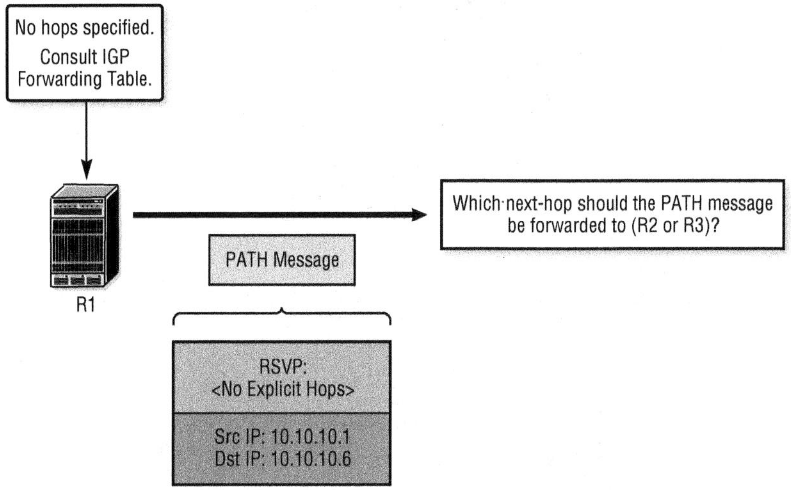

Each router on the path of an RSVP-TE LSP maintains a Path State Block (PSB) for the LSP. The PSB contains the RSVP-TE session information as well as the original Path message used to signal the LSP. The SESSION and SENDER_TEMPLATE in each PSB identify the specific RSVP-TE session (or LSP::Path) and will be the same on each router along the path.

When a router receives a Path message for a new RSVP-TE session, this is known as a Path *trigger* message because it triggers the creation of a new PSB for the session. The router verifies that it has resources available to satisfy the resource request in the Path message. If the requirements can be met, it adds the interface IP address to the RRO (RECORD_ROUTE object), changes the HOP address to the IP address of the egress interface and transmits the Path message to the next-hop router (Figure 13.7).

Figure 13.7 Arrival of a Path message for a new RSVP-TE session triggers the creation of the PSB.

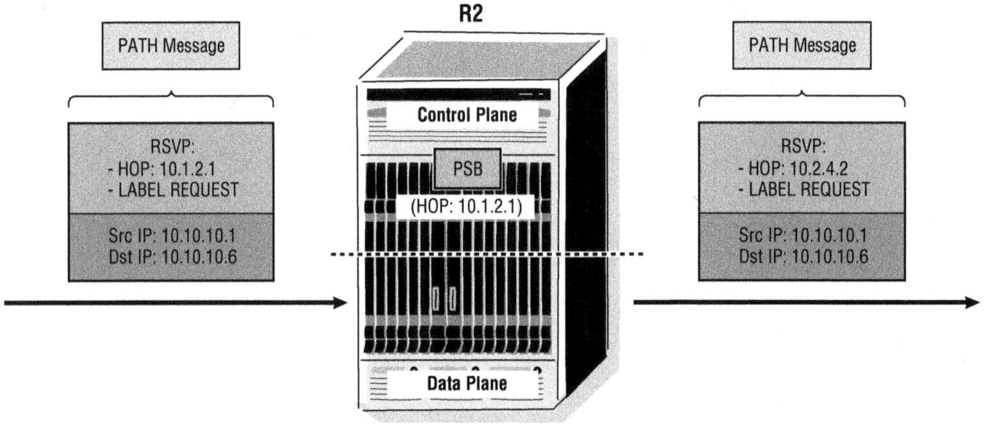

The process continues until the message reaches the tail end with the creation of a PSB at each node (Figure 13.8). The arrival of the Path message at the tail end results in the transmission of a Resv message in the upstream direction.

Figure 13.8 The Path message is transmitted to the tail end with the creation of a PSB at each node.

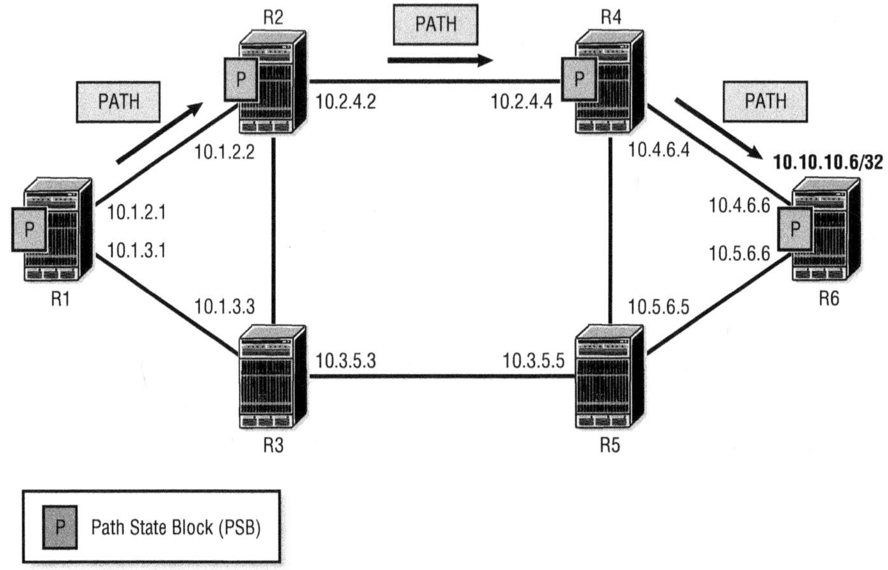

Resv Message

The Resv message is used to signal labels and confirm the reservation of the resources along the nodes that carry the LSP from the tail end to the head end. The important objects of the Resv message are listed in Table 13.2.

Table 13.2 Objects of the Resv Message

Object Name	Description
SESSION	The SESSION object identifying the RSVP-TE tunnel as in the Path message. It contains the destination IP of the tunnel, the Tunnel ID, and the extended-tunnel-id (system address of the tunnel head end).
HOP	Contains the IP address of the egress interface on which the Resv message is sent to the next-hop upstream router.
TIME_VALUE	The expected refresh interval for the RSVP-TE session
STYLE	Contains the RSVP-TE reservation style. This can be Shared Explicit (SE) or Fixed Filter (FF).
FLOW_SPEC	Corresponds to the SENDER_TSPEC from the Path message. It contains traffic engineering parameters, such as the bandwidth reserved for the LSP.
FILTER_SPEC	This corresponds to the SENDER_TEMPLATE of the Path message. It contains the sender's system IP and the LSP ID.
LABEL	LSP label signaled by this router to the next-hop upstream router.
RECORD ROUTE (RRO)	RRO is optional and contains a list of the hops that the Path message traversed. In the Resv message the RRO also contains the label assigned for each hop that has been signaled. By default, the RRO is always used on the 7750.

When the tail end receives the Path message, it creates a PSB but does not need to allocate bandwidth resources because it is the egress for the tunnel. It allocates a label and creates a Resv message for transmission in the upstream direction.

Unlike the Path message, which is addressed to the tail end router with the Router Alert set, the Resv message is addressed to the next-hop router in the upstream direction. The address of the next-hop router is taken from the PSB. It does not come from the RRO (remember that this is an optional field in the Resv and Path messages). The HOP object and the source of the Resv message are set to the IP address of the egress interface (Figure 13.9).

The tail end router also creates a Resv State Block (RSB) when it generates the Resv message (see Figure 13.10). The RSB stores the Resv message and the label allocated for the LSP. The Resv message is sent to the next upstream hop as stored in the PSB.

Figure 13.9 The Resv message is sent to the next-hop upstream using the IP address from the HOP object in the PSB.

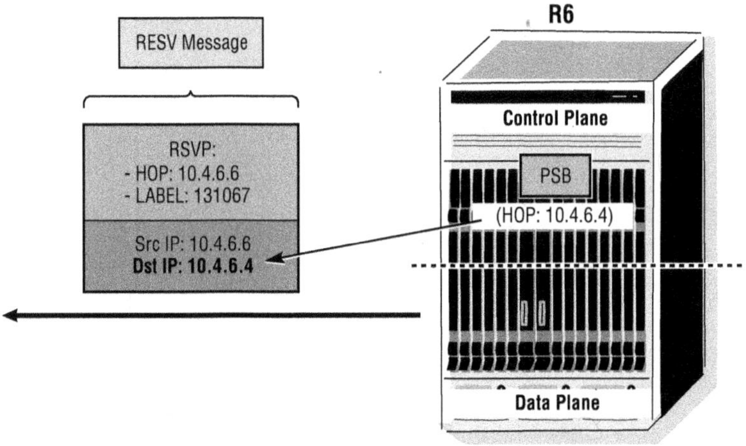

Figure 13.10 RSB created on the tail end router and Resv message transmitted upstream.

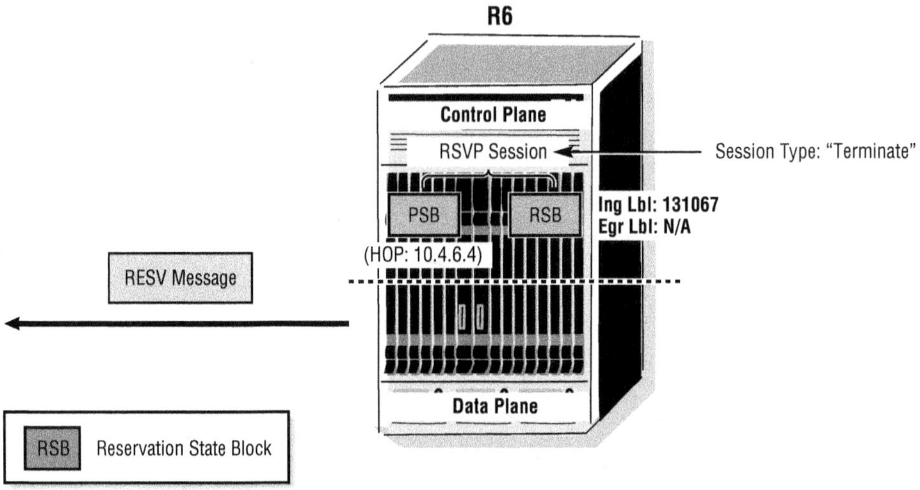

The reception of a Resv message at the upstream router triggers the allocation of resources and a label. The RSB is created to manage the reservation state, and a Resv message is created for the next-hop. The Resv is sent to the next upstream hop using the address from the HOP object stored in the PSB (Figure 13.11).

Figure 13.11 Receipt of a Resv message triggers creation of the RSB, resource reservation, allocation of a label, and a Resv message to the next upstream hop.

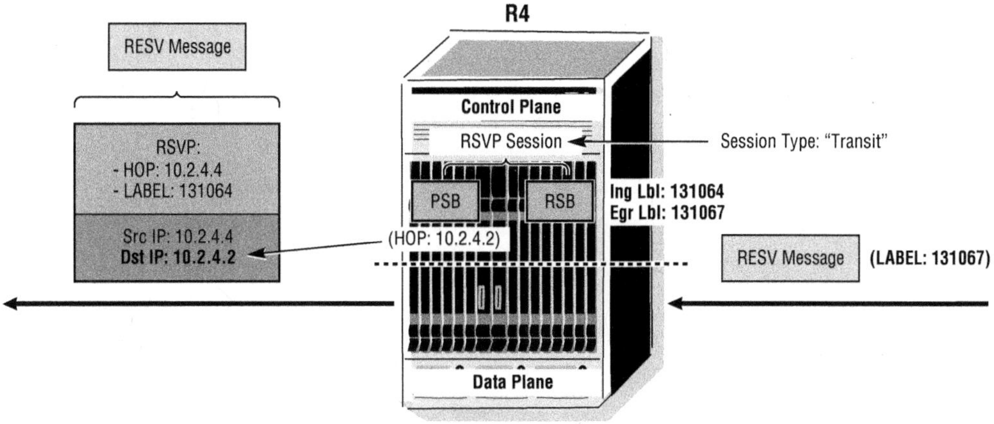

The process of creating the RSB and allocating labels continues in the upstream direction until the head end router is reached. The LSP is now created and operational (see Figure 13.12).

Figure 13.12 The Resv message propagates upstream until it reaches the head end and the LSP is created.

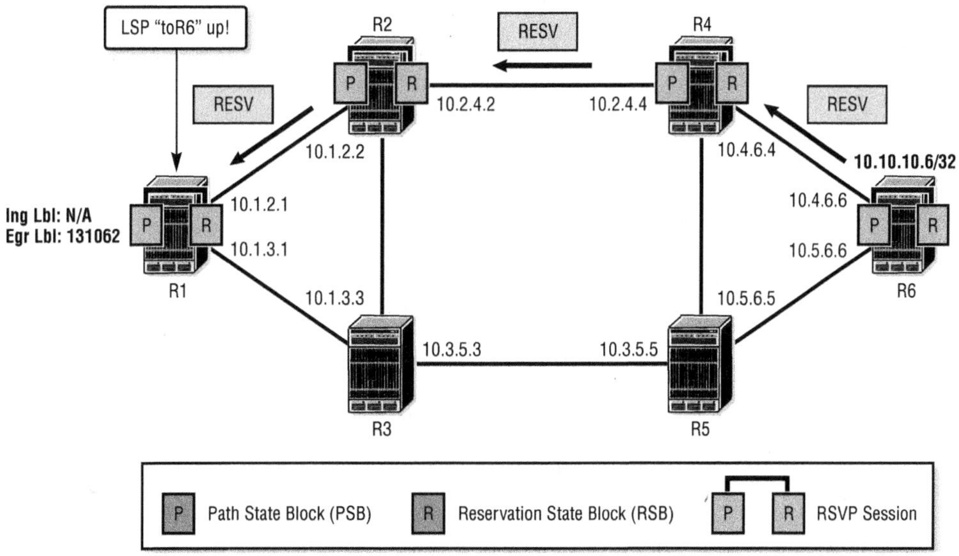

RSVP-TE Tunnels and LSP::Paths

An RSVP-TE tunnel may have more than one LSP::Path associated with it (see Figure 13.4). For example, in Chapter 16, we see how secondary paths are used for LSP redundancy. A secondary path uses a separate LSP::Path but belongs to the same RSVP-TE tunnel. When an RSVP-TE tunnel has more than one LSP::Path, each LSP::Path is really a distinct LSP and is signaled separately.

In our simple example below, the RSVP-TE tunnel has only one LSP::Path. The RSVP-TE Tunnel ID is contained in the `SESSION` object. The LSP::Path is identified by the LSP ID. In a Path message the LSP ID is contained in the `SENDER_TEMPLATE` object. In a Resv message the LSP ID is contained in the `FILTER_SPEC` object. Listing 13.4 shows the Tunnel ID and LSP ID values for the LSP created above.

Listing 13.4 Information that uniquely identifies an LSP (RSVP-TE tunnel)

```
*A:R1# show router rsvp session originate

=======================================================================
RSVP Sessions
=======================================================================
From            To              Tunnel LSP   Name                State
                                ID     ID
-----------------------------------------------------------------------
10.10.10.1      10.10.10.6      2      25092 toR6::loose         Up
-----------------------------------------------------------------------
Sessions : 1
=======================================================================
```

Listing 13.5 shows the debug output from the 7750 SR containing a Path and a Resv message for this LSP. You can see that the Tunnel ID is carried in the `SESSION` object and identifies the RSVP-TE tunnel. The LSP ID is carried in the `SENDER_TEMPLATE` and `FILTER_SPEC` objects and identifies the specific LSP::Path within that RSVP-TE tunnel.

Listing 13.5 Path and Resv messages carrying Tunnel ID and LSP ID

```
*A:R1# configure log log-id 11
*A:R1>config>log>log-id$ from debug-trace
```

```
*A:R1>config>log>log-id$ to session
*A:R1>config>log>log-id$ exit
*A:R1# debug router rsvp tunnel-id 2 packet
*A:R1>debug>router>rsvp>packet# path
*A:R1>debug>router>rsvp>packet# resv
*A:R1>debug>router>rsvp>packet# exit all
*A:R1#22 2010/12/15 10:19:08.03 UTC MINOR: DEBUG #2001 Base RSVP
"RSVP: PATH Msg
Send PATH From:10.10.10.1, To:10.10.10.6
          TTL:255, Checksum:0x1213, Flags:0x0
Session     - EndPt:10.10.10.6, TunnId:2, ExtTunnId:10.10.10.1
SendTempl   - Sender:10.10.10.1, LspId:25092
"


24 2010/12/15 10:19:09.72 UTC MINOR: DEBUG #2001 Base RSVP
"RSVP: RESV Msg
Recv RESV From:10.1.2.2, To:10.1.2.1
          TTL:255, Checksum:0xc673, Flags:0x0
Session     - EndPt:10.10.10.6, TunnId:2, ExtTunnId:10.10.10.1
FlowSpec    - Ctype:QOS, CDR:0.000 bps, PBS:0.000 bps, PDR:infinity
              MPU:20, MTU:9198, RSpecRate:0, RSpecSlack:0
FilterSpec - Sender:10.10.10.1, LspId:25092, Label:131065
  RRO       - IpAddr:10.1.2.2, Flags:0x0
              Label:131065, Flags:0x1
              IpAddr:10.2.4.4, Flags:0x0
              Label:131065, Flags:0x1
              IpAddr:10.4.6.6, Flags:0x0
              Label:131065, Flags:0x1
"
```

RSVP-TE Soft State and Path Refresh

RSVP-TE takes a "soft state" approach to managing the reservation state in routers and hosts. This means that the RSVP-TE state must be periodically refreshed by Path and Resv messages. The state is deleted if no refresh messages arrive before the expiration of the time-out interval. The LSP state may also be deleted by an explicit teardown message.

At the expiration of each refresh time-out period or after a state change, the RSVP-TE process in a router scans its records of RSVP-TE sessions to build and forward Path and Resv refresh messages to neighboring routers (see Figure 13.13). The default for the time-out period is 30 seconds on the 7750 SR.

Figure 13.13 Path and Resv messages are sent independently at the end of each time-out period.

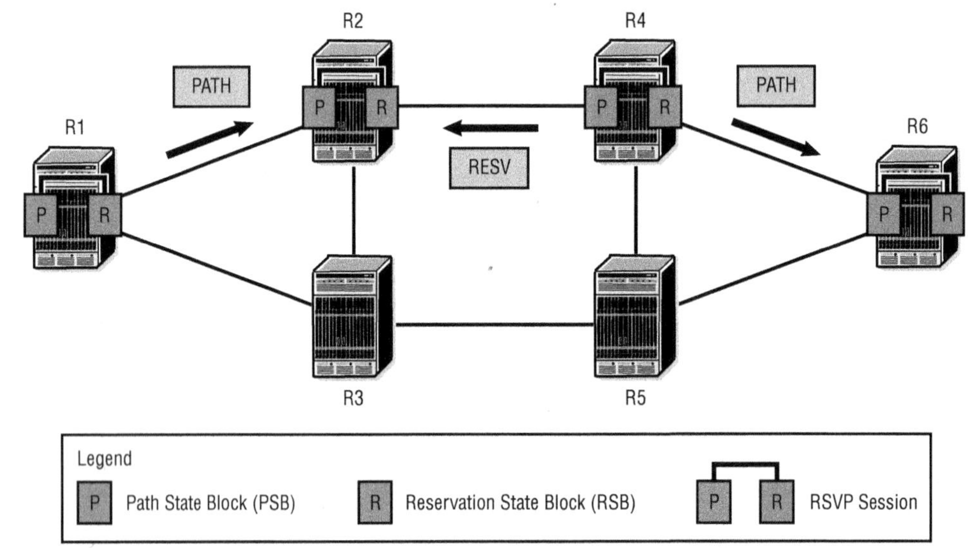

Whether a message is *new* or a *refresh* is determined separately at each node, depending on the existence of the RSVP-TE state at that node. If a Path message is received and the `SESSION` and `SENDER_TEMPLATE` objects match the values in an existing PSB, then the Path message is treated as a refresh. The Resv message is treated in a similar manner. If the `SESSION` and `FILTER_SPEC` objects match the values in an existing RSB, the message acts as a refresh message. When a router receives a Path or Resv refresh message, it updates the PSB or RSB and resets the lifetime timer to 0.

Each router is programmed with an RSVP-TE keep-alive multiplier (default value of 3). If the lifetime timer reaches a value equal to the (time interval) * (keep-alive multiplier), the corresponding Path or Resv state is cleared and a PathTear or ResvTear message is sent to clear the state on other routers.

Tearing Down an LSP with PathTear and ResvTear Messages

PathTear and ResvTear messages are used to explicitly clear the reservation state for an LSP. A PathTear message travels downstream and is routed along the exact path as the corresponding Path message. That is, the PathTear is addressed to the tail end router with the Router Alert option set so that it is processed by each node. The source address is the address of the head end router, even if sent by an intermediate node. A ResvTear travels upstream and is routed along the same path as the corresponding Resv message. Each ResvTear message is addressed to the next upstream node.

In Figure 13.14 the LSP is administratively shut down. This initiates the transmission of a PathTear message from the head end to the tail end. The LSP is identified by the SESSION and SENDER_TEMPLATE objects in the PathTear message. The PSBs and RSBs corresponding to the LSP are cleared at each node.

Figure 13.14 A PathTear is sent by the head end to clear the state for the LSP.

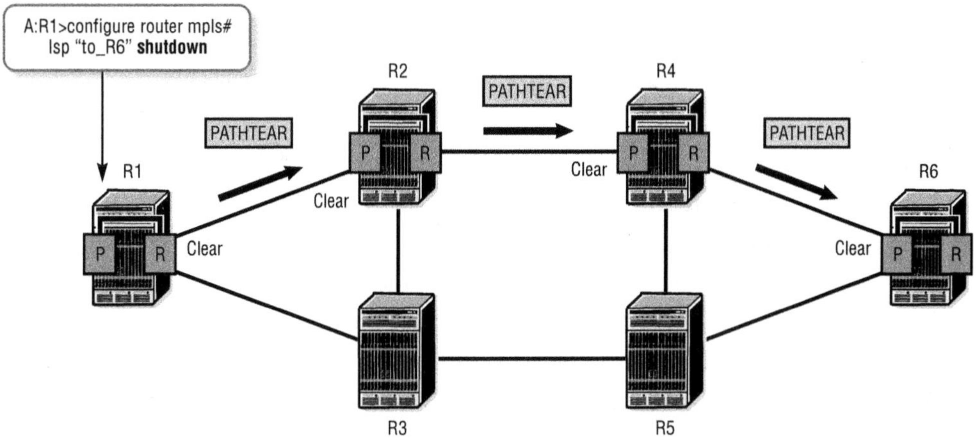

Listing 13.6 shows the PathTear message sent by R1 when the LSP is shut down. Note that the LSP is identified by the SESSION object and the SENDER_TEMPLATE.

Listing 13.6 PathTear message sent by R1 when the LSP to R6 is shut down

```
*A:R6# show debug
debug
    router "Base"
        rsvp tunnel-id 2
            packet
                patherr
                pathtear
                resverr
```

(continued)

Listing 13.6 *(continued)*

```
                    resvtear
                exit
            exit
        exit
exit
*A:R6#
1 2010/12/19 12:36:53.19 UTC MINOR: DEBUG #2001 Base RSVP
"RSVP: PATHTEAR Msg
Recv PATHTEAR From:10.10.10.1, To:10.10.10.6
              TTL:255, Checksum:0x36e, Flags:0x0
Session     - EndPt:10.10.10.6, TunnId:2, ExtTunnId:10.10.10.1
SendTempl   - Sender:10.10.10.1, LspId:25092
"
```

PathTear or ResvTear messages are also initiated by path or reservation state time-out in any router. Figure 13.15 illustrates a loss of connectivity on the link between adjacent routers R2 and R4. This results in R2 failing to receive Resv messages from R4. The Resv state will time out, and a ResvTear message will be sent upstream by R2. Likewise, the Path state will time out on R4, and a PathTear will be sent downstream by R4 to clear the LSP state. If the messages are not successfully reached on the other nodes, the LSP state will eventually time out at the other nodes.

Figure 13.15 If the Resv and Path states time out on R2 and R4, PathTear and ResvTear messages are sent to clear the LSP state.

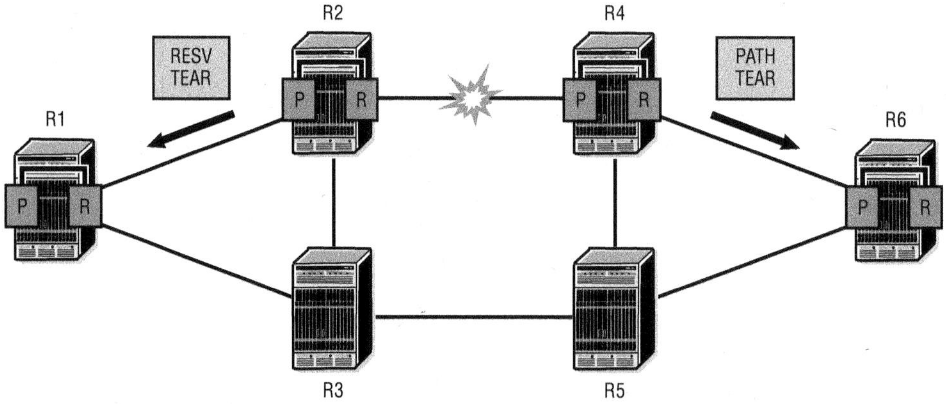

To illustrate the effect of a loss of connectivity between R4 and R2, we shut down MPLS on the interface `toR2` on router R4. Listing 13.7 shows the PathTear message received at R6 after the interface is shut down. As in the Path message, the LSP is identified by the `SESSION` and `SENDER_TEMPLATE` objects.

Listing 13.7 PathTear message received at R6

```
3 2010/12/19 11:55:39.25 UTC MINOR: DEBUG #2001 Base RSVP
"RSVP: PATHTEAR Msg
Recv PATHTEAR From:10.10.10.1, To:10.10.10.6
              TTL:255, Checksum:0x366, Flags:0x0
Session     - EndPt:10.10.10.6, TunnId:2, ExtTunnId:10.10.10.1
SendTempl   - Sender:10.10.10.1, LspId:25094
"
```

Below we see that RSVP-TE uses Hello messages to maintain adjacencies. When R2 discovers that the MPLS adjacency with R4 is down, it sends a ResvTear to R1 as shown in Listing 13.8. Just as in the Resv message, the LSP is identified by the `SESSION` and `FILTER_SPEC` objects. After R1 receives the ResvTear message, the LSP is made operationally down.

Listing 13.8 ResvTear message received at R1

```
13 2010/12/19 11:55:44.47 UTC MINOR: DEBUG #2001 Base RSVP
"RSVP: RESVTEAR Msg
Recv RESVTEAR From:10.1.2.2, To:10.1.2.1
              TTL:255, Checksum:0xff47, Flags:0x0
Session     - EndPt:10.10.10.6, TunnId:2, ExtTunnId:10.10.10.1
FlowSpec    - Ctype:QOS, CDR:0.000 bps, PBS:0.000 bps, PDR:infinity
              MPU:20, MTU:9198, RSpecRate:0, RSpecSlack:0
FilterSpec - Sender:10.10.10.1, LspId: 25094
"
```

In the examples above, the LSP ID changes while the Tunnel ID remains the same. A new LSP ID is used anytime the LSP is shut down and brought back up to distinguish the new LSP::Path from the old one.

When an RSVP-TE tunnel is shut down as a result of a PathTear or ResvTear message, the related reservation state is also adjusted to maintain consistency in the local router. This adjustment depends on the reservation style being used (discussed in Chapter 15).

RSVP-TE Error Messages

RSVP-TE error conditions are signaled using PathErr and ResvErr messages. These messages contain the ERROR object, which contains an error code and an error value to indicate the cause of the error as well as the node where the error occurred. PathErr messages travel upstream to the head end and are addressed hop by hop. ResvErr messages are also addressed hop by hop and travel downstream to the tail end. It is important to note that PathErr and ResvErr messages do not modify the LSP state at any of the nodes; they only report the error condition.

In Figure 13.16, a Path message is sent to set up an LSP. The signaling of the Path message cannot be completed because an intermediate router does not have a route to the next-hop. A PathErr is sent upstream to the head end from the node that cannot forward the Path message. The head end router sets the LSP to be operationally down and sends a PathTear message downstream along the LSP to release the associated state for the LSP and thus release any reserved resources along the LSP::Path.

Figure 13.16 An error occurs on the sending of a Path message.

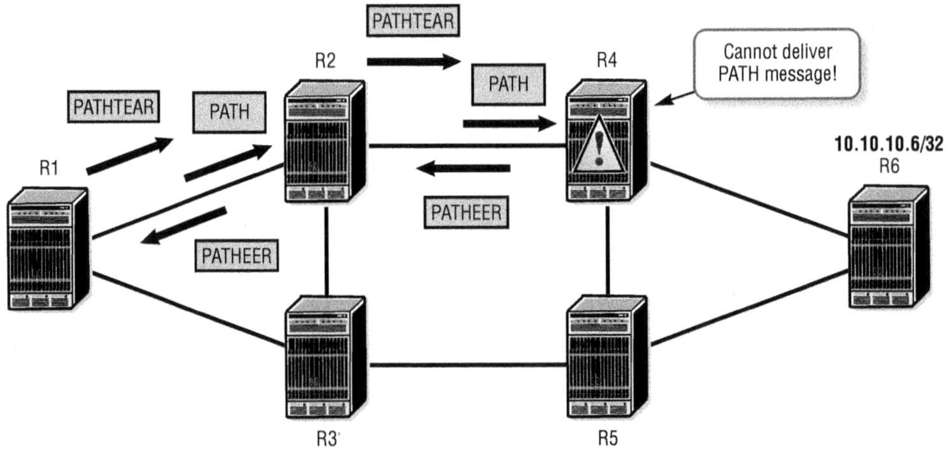

In Figure 13.17, an LSP is being established. A Path message is sent successfully downstream to the tail end router. The LSP::Path state is created along the path through the creation of a PSB at each node. The tail end router sends a Resv message hop by hop toward the head end router. Resources are allocated at each node and a label allocated for the LSP. In this example, an intermediate node is unable to allocate a label for the LSP. A ResvErr is sent downstream to the tail end router, which then sends a ResvTear message upstream toward the head end router. The ResvTear clears the RSB and PSB and releases the allocated label at each intermediate node.

Figure 13.17 A ResvErr message is sent downstream when an error occurs with a Resv message.

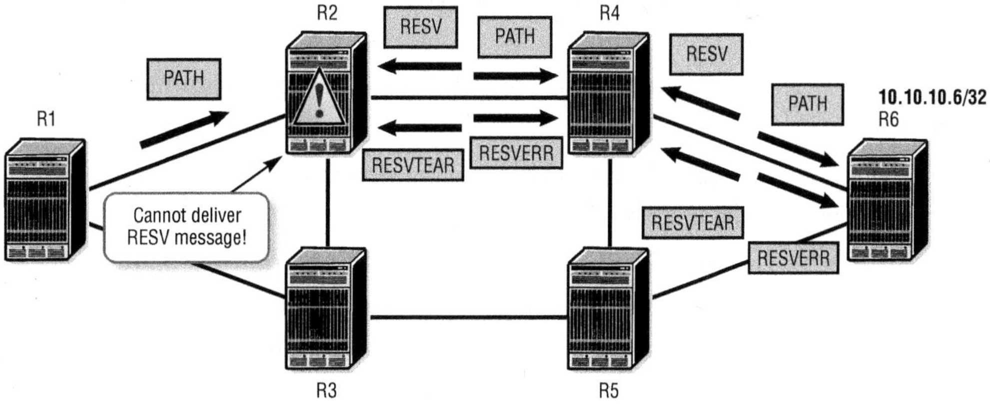

13.3 RSVP-TE Adjacencies and the Hello Message

In its original form, RSVP did not use the concept of an RSVP adjacency, or RSVP neighbor. RSVP was only concerned with the state of its paths, which are continuously refreshed. However, the refresh interval is typically fairly long (30 seconds by default), and it can take a relatively long time to discover the loss of an RSVP neighbor or the failure of the associated LSPs. Shortening the refresh timer leads to excessive overhead because the router might need to refresh a large number of LSPs.

To improve the scalability of RSVP-TE and improve convergence time after failure, Hello messages were added to the RSVP-TE standard (RFC 3209). Hello messages monitor the RSVP-TE state between two adjacent routers and thus, indirectly, the state of LSPs between them.

Hello Message

The Hello message has two objects, the `REQUEST` and `ACKNOWLEDGEMENT` objects. A Hello message is sent with a `REQUEST` object, and a Hello message with an `ACKNOWLEDGEMENT` object is expected in return. Each side independently maintains a 4-byte session identifier to ensure that the RSVP-TE state has not changed on either side. These identifiers are generated at the start of the Hello adjacency and do not change throughout the session.

Because there is only one adjacency required between two routers, Hello messages can be sent much more frequently than Path refresh messages. The default interval for Hello messages is 3 seconds. The adjacency between two RSVP-TE routers is considered to be down when:

- Consecutive Hello messages are not received on the interface within the Hello interval; OR
- A Hello message is received whose destination session identifier does not match the expected value on the neighbor.

When the adjacency to an RSVP-TE neighbor is lost, the states of all RSVP-TE sessions to the neighbor are cleared, and PathTear and ResvTear messages are sent as necessary. Path messages continue to be sent by the LSP head end to try and reestablish the LSPs.

Refresh Reduction

The state of every LSP must be refreshed at every router through the exchange of Path and Resv messages. In a network with hundreds or even thousands of LSPs, this can represent a significant signaling and control processing overhead. Listing 13.9 shows three transit LSPs on R3 in the topology of Figure 13.17. Two LSPs are established from R1 to R5 and a third to R6 passing through R3.

Listing 13.9 Transit LSPs through R3

```
*A:R3# show router rsvp session transit

===============================================================================
RSVP Sessions
===============================================================================
```

```
From            To              Tunnel LSP   Name                          State
                                ID     ID
-------------------------------------------------------------------------------
10.10.10.1      10.10.10.5      26     17934 toR5::loose                   Up
10.10.10.1      10.10.10.6      27     15872 toR6::r3_loose                Up
10.10.10.1      10.10.10.6      28     8192  toR6-2::r3_loose              Up
-------------------------------------------------------------------------------
Sessions : 3
===============================================================================
```

Listing 13.10 shows the debug output from the interface toward R1. In 30 seconds we can expect to see three Path messages received. Three Resv messages will also be sent on that interface to refresh the LSPs.

Listing 13.10 Path and Resv messages on the R3 interface toward R1

```
*A:R3>config>log>log-id# show debug
debug
    router "Base"
        rsvp interface "toR5"
            packet
                path
            exit
        exit
    exit
exit
1 2011/01/23 12:45:40.74 UTC MINOR: DEBUG #2001 Base RSVP
"RSVP: PATH Msg
Recv PATH From:10.10.10.1, To:10.10.10.5
         TTL:255, Checksum:0xb9ac, Flags:0x0
Session     - EndPt:10.10.10.5, TunnId:26, ExtTunnId:10.10.10.1
SendTempl   - Sender:10.10.10.1, LspId:17934
"

11
*A:R3#
2 2011/01/23 12:45:44.74 UTC MINOR: DEBUG #2001 Base RSVP
"RSVP: PATH Msg
Recv PATH From:10.10.10.1, To:10.10.10.6
```

(continued)

Listing 13.10 *(continued)*

```
          TTL:255, Checksum:0xdbb, Flags:0x0
Session    - EndPt:10.10.10.6, TunnId:28, ExtTunnId:10.10.10.1
SendTempl  - Sender:10.10.10.1, LspId:8192
"


4 2011/01/23 12:45:54.74 UTC MINOR: DEBUG #2001 Base RSVP
"RSVP: PATH Msg
Recv PATH From:10.10.10.1, To:10.10.10.6
          TTL:255, Checksum:0x1cf8, Flags:0x0
Session    - EndPt:10.10.10.6, TunnId:27, ExtTunnId:10.10.10.1
SendTempl  - Sender:10.10.10.1, LspId:15872
"
```

RFC 2961 ("RSVP Refresh Overhead Reduction Extensions") defines extensions to RSVP to reduce the number of messages required to refresh LSPs. It defines several new objects and RSVP messages, including the `MESSAGE_ID` object and the Summary Refresh message. Refresh reduction is enabled on the 7750 SR by configuring it on the RSVP-TE interface, as shown in Listing 13.11.

Listing 13.11 Configuring refresh reduction on R1

```
*A:R1>config>router>rsvp# info
----------------------------------------------
            interface "system"
            exit
            interface "toR2"
            exit
            interface "toR3"
                refresh-reduction
                exit
            exit
            no shutdown
----------------------------------------------
```

When an RSVP-TE interface is configured for refresh reduction, it adds a `MESSAGE_ID` to Path and Resv messages sent on that interface. The router also sets the lowest bit of the `Flags` field in the RSVP-TE header to inform its neighbor that it is capable of refresh reduction. Listing 13.12 shows the Path messages received on R3 from R1 with the `MESSAGE_ID` object. Note that the value of the `Flags` field in the header has changed to `0x1`.

Listing 13.12 MESSAGE_ID in Path messages received on R3 from R1

```
23 2011/01/23 12:47:35.74 UTC MINOR: DEBUG #2001 Base RSVP
"RSVP: PATH Msg
Recv PATH From:10.10.10.1, To:10.10.10.6
          TTL:255, Checksum:0x55a8, Flags:0x1
MSG ID      - Flags:0x0, Epoch:14528088, MsgId:1
Session     - EndPt:10.10.10.6, TunnId:27, ExtTunnId:10.10.10.1
SendTempl   - Sender:10.10.10.1, LspId:15872
"

24 2011/01/23 12:47:40.74 UTC MINOR: DEBUG #2001 Base RSVP
"RSVP: PATH Msg
Recv PATH From:10.10.10.1, To:10.10.10.5
          TTL:255, Checksum:0xf25b, Flags:0x1
MSG ID      - Flags:0x0, Epoch:14528088, MsgId:2
Session     - EndPt:10.10.10.5, TunnId:26, ExtTunnId:10.10.10.1
SendTempl   - Sender:10.10.10.1, LspId:17934
"

25 2011/01/23 12:47:41.74 UTC MINOR: DEBUG #2001 Base RSVP
"RSVP: PATH Msg
Recv PATH From:10.10.10.1, To:10.10.10.6
          TTL:255, Checksum:0x4669, Flags:0x1
MSG ID      - Flags:0x0, Epoch:14528088, MsgId:3
Session     - EndPt:10.10.10.6, TunnId:28, ExtTunnId:10.10.10.1
SendTempl   - Sender:10.10.10.1, LspId:8192
"
```

When the interfaces on both sides of an adjacency are configured for refresh reduction, the routers will send a Summary Refresh message listing the LSPs that it wishes to refresh, instead of many Path and Resv messages. The individual LSPs are uniquely identified by the sending router's IP address and the Message ID values. Listing 13.13 shows the Summary Refresh message sent by R1 to replace the three Path messages and refresh the three LSPs in Listing 13.12.

Listing 13.13 Summary Refresh message sent from R1 to R3

```
48 2011/01/23 12:50:26.74 UTC MINOR: DEBUG #2001 Base RSVP
"RSVP: SREFRESH Msg
Recv SREFRESH From:10.1.3.1, To:10.1.3.3
              TTL:1, Checksum:0x2584, Flags:0x1
MSG ID LIST: Flags:0x0, Epoch:14528088
  0000000001,  0000000002,  0000000003
Total Message Ids: 3
"
```

When R1 receives this Summary Refresh message, it searches the PSBs and RSBs it has for those with Path or Resv messages received from R1 corresponding to these Message ID values. The state for these LSPs is then refreshed as if a regular Path or Resv message had been received.

If the router does not find a message corresponding to one of the Message ID values, it sends its neighbor a Summary Refresh message with a `MESSAGE_ID_NACK` object that indicates the unknown Message ID. The neighbor will then transmit the regular Path or Resv message corresponding to the unknown Message ID.

RSVP-TE Timers

There are a number of timers that control the operation of RSVP-TE. Two that are often confused are the *retry* and *resignal* timers.

The *retry* timer is set on individual LSPs and controls the interval at which the router tries to bring up an LSP. If an operational LSP goes down, or fails to come up in the first place, the router will try to establish the LSP at the interval set by the retry timer.

The default value for the retry timer on the 7750 SR is 30 seconds, with a possible range of 1 to 600. The `retry-limit` parameter is also set on the individual LSP and determines how many times the router will try to establish an LSP that is down. The default value is zero, which means that there is no limit; the router will continue to try to signal the LSP indefinitely every time the retry timer expires.

The *resignal* timer only applies to LSPs that are operationally up. It controls the interval at which the router tries to find a more optimal path for established LSPs. Traffic-engineered LSPs do not automatically change their path if a better one becomes available. The LSP continues to follow the path along which it was originally established regardless of topology changes or changes in IGP costs. At the interval of the resignal timer, the router checks to see if there is a better path for all LSPs that are operationally up. An LSP will be signaled on the new path if a better one is found. Traffic is switched from the old (less optimal) LSP::Path to the new one in a make-before-break fashion. The newly signaled LSP::Path uses the same Tunnel ID but a new LSP-ID.

The resignal timer is disabled by default and is enabled in the `configure router mpls` context. Its value is specified in minutes and can range from 30 to 10,080 (7 days). The network operator can manually force an LSP to be resignaled using the `tools perform router mpls resignal` command.

13.4 RSVP-TE Path Selection

Until now we've discussed the operation of RSVP-TE without concern regarding how the path of the LSP is determined. One of the main reasons for using RSVP-TE instead of LDP is that it provides the ability to select paths that do not follow the IGP. The key component of path selection in RSVP-TE is the `EXPLICIT_ROUTE` object (`ERO`), which is carried in the Path message. The `ERO` contains a list of IP addresses that specify some or all of the hops that the LSP must traverse.

The methods of path selection fall into three general categories:

1. The path is determined completely by the IGP with no constraints.
2. The path is determined by the IGP but subject to the constraint that it must pass through specific nodes.
3. The path is subject to traffic-engineering constraints such as hop count, admin groups, or bandwidth requirements.

We examine each of these three cases in turn.

Choosing the Path with the IGP

In the simplest case, an RSVP-TE LSP follows the path chosen by the IGP. In this case, there is no `ERO` in the Path message. The head end router selects the next downstream router based on the next-hop for the FEC in the route table and sends the Path message out the interface connecting to the next downstream router. The next downstream node repeats the process, and the Path message travels hop by hop to the tail end router. Listing 13.14 shows the configuration of an LSP on a 7750 SR. Note that the path is first defined and then referenced in the LSP configuration with the keyword `primary`. The fact that the path is empty indicates that there are no constraints and the path is to be determined by the IGP.

Listing 13.14 Configuration of a simple LSP that follows the IGP

```
*A:R1>config>router>mpls# info
----------------------------------------------
            interface "system"
            exit
            interface "toR2"
            exit
            interface "toR3"
            exit
            path "loose"
                no shutdown
            exit
            lsp "toR6"
                to 10.10.10.6
                primary "loose"
                exit
                no shutdown
            exit
            no shutdown
----------------------------------------------
```

Once the LSP is defined, it can be verified with the `show router mpls path detail` command. The output shows that there were no explicit hops defined and also shows the actual hops that were signaled. These are the hops returned in the RRO (Listing 13.15).

Listing 13.15 Detailed information about the LSP after it is signaled

```
*A:R1>config>router>mpls# show router mpls lsp "toR6" path detail

===============================================================================
MPLS LSP toR6 Path  (Detail)
===============================================================================
Legend :
    @ - Detour Available                 # - Detour In Use
    b - Bandwidth Protected              n - Node Protected
    s - Soft Preemption
```

```
===============================================================================
-------------------------------------------------------------------------------
LSP toR6 Path loose
-------------------------------------------------------------------------------
LSP Name     : toR6                        Path LSP ID : 25280
From         : 10.10.10.1                  To          : 10.10.10.6
Adm State    : Up                          Oper State  : Up
Path Name    : loose                       Path Type   : Primary
Path Admin   : Up                          Path Oper   : Up
OutInterface: 1/1/2                        Out Label   : 131067
Path Up Time: 0d 00:01:06                  Path Dn Time: 0d 00:00:00
Retry Limit : 0                            Retry Timer : 30 sec
RetryAttempt: 0                            NextRetryIn : 0 sec
SetupPriori*: 7                            Hold Priori*: 0
Preference  : n/a
Bandwidth    : No Reservation              Oper Bw     : 0 Mbps
Hop Limit    : 255                         Class Type  : 0
Backup CT    : None
MainCT Retry: n/a                          MainCT Retry: 0
    Rem     :                                  Limit   :
Oper CT      : 0
Record Route: Record                       Record Label: Record
Oper MTU     : 9198                        Neg MTU     : 9198
Adaptive     : Enabled                     Oper Metric : 300
Include Grps:                              Exclude Grps:
None                                       None
Path Trans   : 1                           CSPF Queries: 0
Failure Code: noError                      Failure Node: n/a
ExplicitHops:
    No Hops Specified
Actual Hops :
    10.1.2.1(10.10.10.1)                   Record Label    : N/A
 -> 10.1.2.2(10.10.10.2)                   Record Label    : 131067
 -> 10.2.4.4(10.10.10.4)                   Record Label    : 131070
 -> 10.4.6.6(10.10.10.6)                   Record Label    : 131067
ResigEligib*: False
LastResignal: n/a                          CSPF Metric : 0
===============================================================================
* indicates that the corresponding row element may have been truncated.
```

Path Selection with Strict and Loose Hops

The LSP may follow the IGP but be constrained by having to pass through specific nodes. These nodes are specified as strict or loose hops and are carried in the `ERO`. A path can contain a mixture of strict and loose hops. If the hop entry specified in the path is `strict`, it means that the address the Path message is sent to must be the immediate next-hop. If the hop entry is `loose`, the Path message is routed to the specified hop using the IGP and may traverse several intermediate nodes. If the Path message has not reached the tail end after all the hops have been traversed, it is routed to the tail end as if it were a loose hop. Listing 13.16 shows a path that specifies the node `10.10.10.5` as a loose hop. This means that RSVP-TE will use the IGP to reach node `10.10.10.5` and then continue to the tail end following the IGP.

Listing 13.16 Path with a loose hop that must traverse Router R5

```
*A:R1>config>router>mpls# info
----------------------------------------------
            interface "system"
            exit
            interface "toR2"
            exit
            interface "toR3"
            exit
            exit
            path "one_loose"
                hop 1 10.10.10.5 loose
                no shutdown
            exit
            lsp "toR6"
                to 10.10.10.6
                primary "one_loose"
                exit
                no shutdown
            exit
            no shutdown
----------------------------------------------
```

Notice that the output of the path detail command in Listing 13.17 now shows an explicit hop immediately before the list of actual hops traversed by the path.

Listing 13.17 Path detail showing explicit hop to be traversed

```
*A:R1>config>router>mpls# show router mpls lsp path detail

===============================================================================
MPLS LSP  Path  (Detail)
===============================================================================
Legend :
    @ - Detour Available              # - Detour In Use
    b - Bandwidth Protected           n - Node Protected
    s - Soft Preemption
===============================================================================
-------------------------------------------------------------------------------
LSP toR6 Path one_loose
-------------------------------------------------------------------------------
LSP Name     : toR6                    Path LSP ID : 25284
From         : 10.10.10.1              To          : 10.10.10.6
Adm State    : Up                      Oper State  : Up
Path Name    : one_loose               Path Type   : Primary
Path Admin   : Up                      Path Oper   : Up
OutInterface: 1/1/1                    Out Label   : 131067
Path Up Time: 0d 00:00:08              Path Dn Time: 0d 00:00:00

... output omitted ...

Failure Code: noError                  Failure Node: n/a
ExplicitHops:
    10.10.10.5
Actual Hops :
    10.1.3.1(10.10.10.1)               Record Label    : N/A
 -> 10.1.3.3(10.10.10.3)               Record Label    : 131071
 -> 10.3.5.5(10.10.10.5)               Record Label    : 131071
 -> 10.5.6.6(10.10.10.6)               Record Label    : 131069
ResigEligib*: False
LastResignal: n/a                      CSPF Metric : 0
===============================================================================
* indicates that the corresponding row element may have been truncated.
```

When the hop in a path is defined as a strict hop, it must be adjacent to the previous hop. Listing 13.18 shows a path defined with a strict hop that is not the next adjacent hop.

Listing 13.18 Path with a strict hop that is not adjacent

```
*A:R1>config>router>mpls# info
----------------------------------------------
... output omitted...

            path "one_strict"
                hop 1 10.10.10.3 loose
                hop 2 10.10.10.6 strict
                no shutdown
            exit
            lsp "toR6"
                to 10.10.10.6
                primary "one_strict"
                exit
                no shutdown
            exit
            no shutdown
----------------------------------------------
*A:R1>config>router>mpls>lsp# show router mpls lsp "toR6" path  detail

=======================================================================
MPLS LSP toR6 Path  (Detail)
=======================================================================
Legend :
    @ - Detour Available               # - Detour In Use
    b - Bandwidth Protected            n - Node Protected
    s - Soft Preemption
=======================================================================
-----------------------------------------------------------------------
LSP toR6 Path one_strict
-----------------------------------------------------------------------
LSP Name     : toR6                    Path LSP ID : 25356
From         : 10.10.10.1              To          : 10.10.10.6
Adm State    : Up                      Oper State  : Down
Path Name    : one_strict              Path Type   : Primary
Path Admin   : Up                      Path Oper   : Down
OutInterface: n/a                      Out Label   : n/a
Path Up Time: 0d 00:00:00              Path Dn Time: 0d 00:01:28

... output omitted ...
```

```
Failure Code: badNode                       Failure Node: 10.1.3.3
ExplicitHops:
    10.10.10.3      -> 10.10.10.6
Actual Hops :
    No Hops Specified
ResigEligib*: False
LastResignal: n/a                          CSPF Metric : 0
===============================================================================
* indicates that the corresponding row element may have been truncated.
```

Because the strict hop cannot be reached from the previous node, the constraints of the LSP are not met and the LSP cannot be established. Listing 13.19 shows the PathErr message received when the path is signaled.

Listing 13.19 PathErr received when the LSP cannot be signaled

```
*A:R1>debug>router>rsvp>packet# show debug
debug
    router "Base"
        rsvp tunnel-id 2
            packet
                path
                patherr detail
            exit
        exit
    exit
exit
9 2010/12/21 21:56:24.02 UTC MINOR: DEBUG #2001 Base RSVP
"RSVP: PATH Msg
Send PATH From:10.10.10.1, To:10.10.10.6
          TTL:255, Checksum:0x8544, Flags:0x0
Session    - EndPt:10.10.10.6, TunnId:2, ExtTunnId:10.10.10.1
SendTempl  - Sender:10.10.10.1, LspId:25356
"


10 2010/12/21 21:56:24.03 UTC MINOR: DEBUG #2001 Base RSVP
"RSVP: PATHERR Msg
```

(continued)

Listing 13.19 *(continued)*

```
Recv PATHERR From:10.1.3.3, To:10.1.3.1
             TTL:255, Checksum:0x263, Flags:0x0
Session    - EndPt:10.10.10.6, TunnId:2, ExtTunnId:10.10.10.1
ErrorSpec  - ErrNode:10.1.3.3, Flags:0x0, ErrCode:24, ErrValue:2
SendTempl  - Sender:10.10.10.1, LspId:25356
SendTSpec  - Ctype:QOS, CDR:0.000 bps, PBS:0.000 bps, PDR:infinity
             MPU:20, MTU:9198
"
```

Note that the `ERROR_SPEC` object provides an `ErrorCode` and `ErrorValue` as well as the `ErrorNode` on which the error occurred, `10.1.3.3`.

Path Selection with Traffic-Engineering Constraints

Besides the constraints of strict and loose hops, a path may also be subject to other traffic-engineering constraints. These constraints—hop count, admin groups, and bandwidth requirements—are discussed in Chapters 14 and 15. If traffic-engineered LSPs are to be created, traffic engineering must be enabled in the IGP for the RSVP-TE domain, and CSPF (Constrained Shortest Path First) must be enabled on the LSP.

For a traffic-engineered LSP, the head end router performs the CSPF calculation to find a path that meets the constraints. If there is none, the LSP stays operationally down. If a path is found from the head end to the tail end that meets all the constraints, the path is put in the `ERO` as a list of strict hops, and the Path message is signaled with this `ERO`. Traffic-engineered LSPs are discussed in more detail in the next two chapters.

13.5 MPLS Shortcuts

Most of our attention in this book is on the use of MPLS networks as a platform for deploying VPN (Virtual Private Network) services such as VPLS (Virtual Private LAN Service) and VPRN (Virtual Private Routed Network). However, MPLS is a tunneling technology that can be used in other parts of an IP network where tunneling is appropriate. One of these situations is for sending regular IP traffic through an MPLS tunnel instead of using the standard IP forwarding mechanism. We call these MPLS shortcuts and describe this in detail in this section.

MPLS Shortcuts for BGP

Consider the BGP (Border Gateway Protocol) network shown in Figure 13.18. AS 200 and AS 300 are exchanging routes with AS 100, and AS 100 is carrying transit traffic for these two ASs (autonomous systems). The routes learned by R6 from AS 200 are propagated to R1 through an IBGP session (internal BGP session) and then passed on to AS 300. As seen in Listing 13.20 from R1, the BGP routes have a next-hop of R6 that is resolved by the IGP to R2 as the next-hop for transit traffic.

Figure 13.18 BGP transit AS.

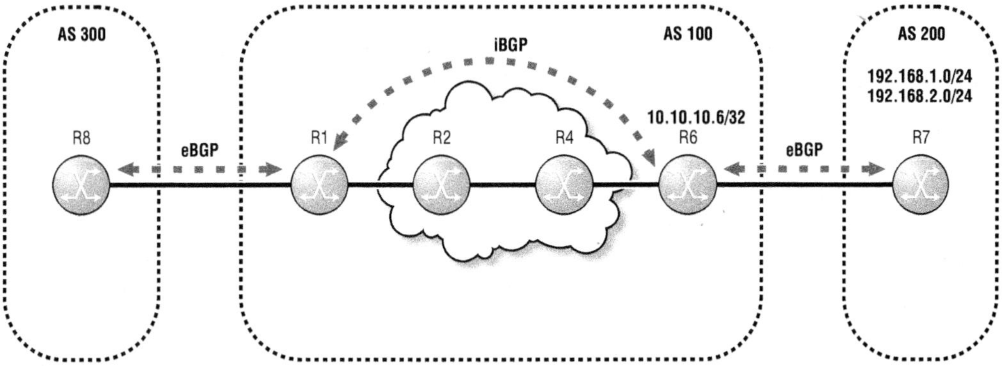

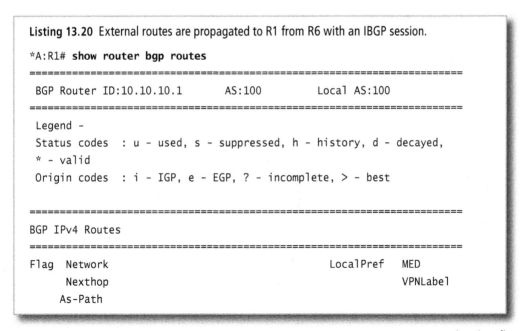

Listing 13.20 External routes are propagated to R1 from R6 with an IBGP session.

```
*A:R1# show router bgp routes
===============================================================================
 BGP Router ID:10.10.10.1       AS:100          Local AS:100
===============================================================================
 Legend -
 Status codes  : u - used, s - suppressed, h - history, d - decayed,
 * - valid
 Origin codes  : i - IGP, e - EGP, ? - incomplete, > - best

===============================================================================
BGP IPv4 Routes
===============================================================================
Flag  Network                                          LocalPref   MED
      Nexthop                                                      VPNLabel
     As-Path
```

(continued)

Listing 13.20 *(continued)*

```
-------------------------------------------------------------------------------
u*>?  192.168.1.0/24                                    100          None
      10.10.10.6                                                     -
      200
u*>?  192.168.2.0/24                                    100          None
      10.10.10.6                                                     -
      200
-------------------------------------------------------------------------------
*A:R1# show router route-table

===============================================================================
Route Table (Router: Base)
===============================================================================
Dest Prefix                              Type    Proto     Age          Pref
      Next Hop[Interface Name]                                 Metric
-------------------------------------------------------------------------------
10.1.2.0/27                              Local   Local     19d07h28m    0
      toR2                                                     0
10.1.8.0/27                              Local   Local     00h34m57s    0
      toR8                                                     0
10.2.4.0/27                              Remote  ISIS      01d03h06m    18
      10.1.2.2                                                 20
10.4.6.0/27                              Remote  ISIS      00h31m03s    18
      10.1.2.2                                                 30
10.10.10.1/32                            Local   Local     19d07h28m    0
      system                                                   0
10.10.10.2/32                            Remote  ISIS      01d03h06m    18
      10.1.2.2                                                 10
10.10.10.4/32                            Remote  ISIS      00h31m03s    18
      10.1.2.2                                                 20
10.10.10.6/32                            Remote  ISIS      00h30m03s    18
      10.1.2.2                                                 30
192.168.1.0/24                           Remote  BGP       00h05m11s    170
      10.1.2.2                                                 0
192.168.2.0/24                           Remote  BGP       00h05m11s    170
      10.1.2.2                                                 0
-------------------------------------------------------------------------------
No. of Routes: 10
===============================================================================
```

This configuration allows the external route information to be propagated across the network to AS 300, but AS 100 cannot forward transit data traffic across the network. Traffic from R1 destined to `192.168.1.0/24` will be forwarded to R2, but R2 does not have a route to the external destination.

Although there are only a few routes in this example, in practice you would not inject external routes learned from BGP into your IGP. Instead, all transit routers (R2 and R4, in this case) would run BGP to learn the external destinations (see Figure 13.19). This substantially increases the control processing requirements for the transit routers and in a large network requires many more IBGP peering sessions.

Figure 13.19 A full mesh of IBGP peering sessions is required for distributing external routes to transit routers.

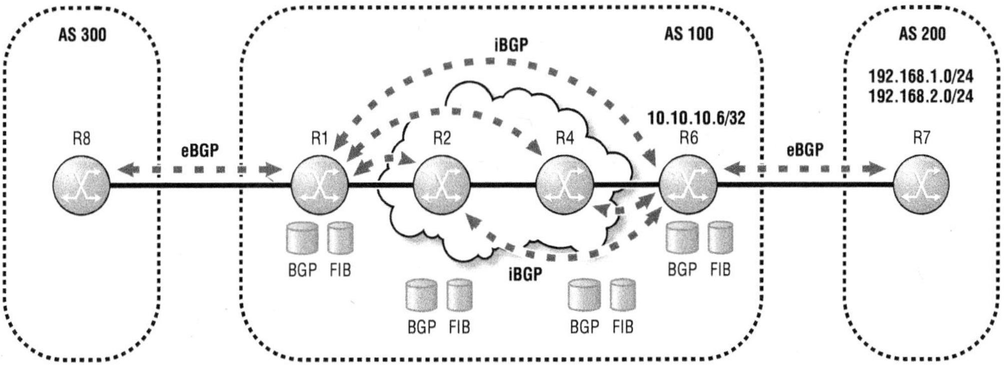

With MPLS shortcuts for BGP, we use MPLS tunnels to forward transit traffic across the network (see Figure 13.20). In this case, only the external facing routers need to run BGP and have knowledge of the external routes. Transit traffic is sent in an MPLS tunnel to the next-hop BGP router and is label-switched across the AS. The transit routers do not need to know the external routes—they only label-switch the transit traffic.

Figure 13.20 shows only one MPLS tunnel—in reality, there will be a full mesh of LSPs between all external facing routers that have the full BGP routes. These LSPs can be signaled with either LDP (Label Distribution Protocol) or RSVP-TE.

Two steps are required to configure BGP to use MPLS tunnels:

1. Configure LDP or the RSVP-TE LSPs on all routers to be used for the transit traffic.
2. Configure BGP to use MPLS shortcuts on the external facing routers.

Figure 13.20 MPLS tunnels are used to carry transit traffic across the network.

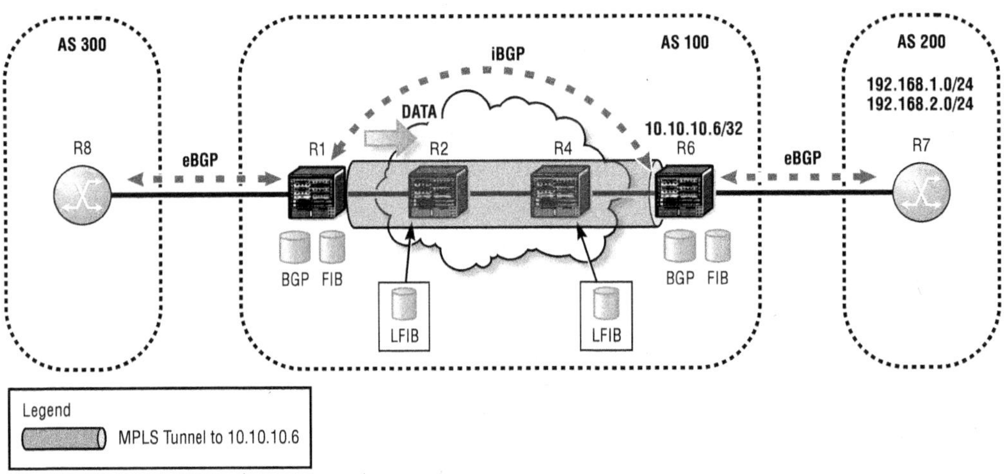

The `configure router bgp igp-shortcut` command specifies one of three options:

- `ldp`—Use the active LDP label for the next-hop.
- `rsvp-te`—Use an RSVP-TE LSP to the next-hop.
- `mpls`—Use an RSVP-TE LSP if one exists; otherwise, use an active LDP label.

In any case, if there is no valid tunnel or label, the router will use native IP forwarding unless the `disallow-igp` option is specified.

Listing 13.21 shows the configuration on Router R1 to use MPLS shortcuts. LDP has been enabled in AS 100. Notice that the next-hop in the route table for the external routes is now `10.10.10.6` and that traffic will be tunneled. The display of the FIB (forwarding information base) shows that LDP transport tunnels are used for forwarding.

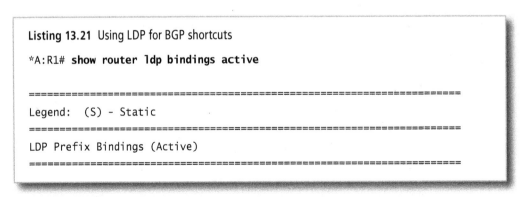

Listing 13.21 Using LDP for BGP shortcuts

```
*A:R1# show router ldp bindings active

===============================================================================
Legend:  (S) - Static
===============================================================================
LDP Prefix Bindings (Active)
===============================================================================
```

```
Prefix              Op   IngLbl    EgrLbl    EgrIntf/LspId  EgrNextHop
-----------------------------------------------------------------------
10.10.10.1/32       Pop  131071     --         --              --
10.10.10.2/32       Push   --      131071    1/1/2           10.1.2.2
10.10.10.4/32       Push   --      131068    1/1/2           10.1.2.2
10.10.10.6/32       Push   --      131070    1/1/2           10.1.2.2
-----------------------------------------------------------------------
No. of Prefix Bindings: 4
*A:R1# configure router bgp igp-shortcut mpls
*A:R1# show router route-table

=======================================================================
Route Table (Router: Base)
=======================================================================
Dest Prefix                           Type    Proto    Age         Pref
       Next Hop[Interface Name]                          Metric
-----------------------------------------------------------------------
10.1.2.0/27                           Local   Local    19d08h41m   0
       toR2                                             0
10.1.8.0/27                           Local   Local    01h48m11s   0
       toR8                                             0
10.2.4.0/27                           Remote  ISIS     01d04h19m   18
       10.1.2.2                                         20
10.4.6.0/27                           Remote  ISIS     01h44m17s   18
       10.1.2.2                                         30
10.10.10.1/32                         Local   Local    19d08h41m   0
       system                                           0
10.10.10.2/32                         Remote  ISIS     01d04h20m   18
       10.1.2.2                                         10
10.10.10.4/32                         Remote  ISIS     01h44m17s   18
       10.1.2.2                                         20
10.10.10.6/32                         Remote  ISIS     01h43m17s   18
       10.1.2.2                                         30
10.10.10.8/32                         Remote  BGP      00h04m41s   170
       10.1.8.8                                         0
192.168.1.0/24                        Remote  BGP      00h04m41s   170
       10.10.10.6 (tunneled)                            0
192.168.2.0/24                        Remote  BGP      00h04m41s   170
       10.10.10.6 (tunneled)                            0
```

(continued)

Listing 13.21 *(continued)*

```
-------------------------------------------------------------------------
No. of Routes: 11
=========================================================================
*A:R1#
*A:R1# show router fib 1

=========================================================================
FIB Display
=========================================================================
Prefix                                                          Protocol
    NextHop
-------------------------------------------------------------------------
... output omitted ...

192.168.1.0/24                                                  BGP
    10.10.10.6 (Transport:LDP)
192.168.2.0/24                                                  BGP
    10.10.10.6 (Transport:LDP)
-------------------------------------------------------------------------
Total Entries : 11
-------------------------------------------------------------------------
=========================================================================
```

If an RSVP-TE LSP is configured to the next-hop address, the 7750 SR will prefer the RSVP-established LSP over an active LDP label. If there are multiple RSVP-TE tunnels to the destination, the one with the lower metric is preferred. Listing 13.22 shows the configuration with an RSVP-TE LSP.

Listing 13.22 BGP shortcut using RSVP-TE tunnel

```
*A:R1>config>router>mpls# info
----------------------------------------------
            interface "system"
            exit
            interface "toR2"
```

```
            exit
            path "loose"
                no shutdown
            exit
            lsp "bgp_shortcut"
                to 10.10.10.6
                primary "loose"
                exit
                no shutdown
            exit
            no shutdown
----------------------------------------------
*A:R1# show router route-table

===============================================================================
Route Table (Router: Base)
===============================================================================
Dest Prefix                          Type    Proto    Age         Pref
       Next Hop[Interface Name]                            Metric
-------------------------------------------------------------------------------
... output omitted ...

192.168.1.0/24                       Remote  BGP      00h01m40s   170
       10.10.10.6 (tunneled:RSVP:5)                         0
192.168.2.0/24                       Remote  BGP      00h01m40s   170
       10.10.10.6 (tunneled:RSVP:5)                         0
-------------------------------------------------------------------------------
No. of Routes: 11
===============================================================================
*A:R1# show router tunnel-table

===============================================================================
Tunnel Table (Router: Base)
===============================================================================
Destination        Owner Encap TunnelId  Pref     Nexthop        Metric
-------------------------------------------------------------------------------
10.10.10.2/32      ldp   MPLS   -         9        10.1.2.2       10
10.10.10.4/32      ldp   MPLS   -         9        10.1.2.2       20
```

(continued)

Listing 13.22 *(continued)*

```
10.10.10.6/32       rsvp  MPLS  5         7         10.1.2.2        30
10.10.10.6/32       ldp   MPLS   -        9         10.1.2.2        30
========================================================================
*A:R1#
```

When MPLS shortcuts are used for BGP or IGP, the 7750 SR operates in uniform mode instead of pipe mode (described in Chapter 11). In uniform mode, the TTL (time to live) value is copied from the IP packet into the MPLS header, and the `traceroute` shows the intermediate LSRs in the path.

Listing 13.23 shows the result of a `traceroute` on R8 to the loopback address on R7 that is advertised through BGP. The intermediate LSR nodes are shown as address `0.0.0.0`.

Listing 13.23 Traceroute across transit network using MPLS shortcuts

```
*A:R8# traceroute 192.168.1.1
traceroute to 192.168.1.1, 30 hops max, 40 byte packets
  1  10.1.8.1 (10.1.8.1)    2.09 ms  1.82 ms  1.78 ms
  2  0.0.0.0  * * *
  3  0.0.0.0  * * *
  4  10.4.6.6 (10.4.6.6)    3.63 ms  3.40 ms  3.45 ms
  5  192.168.1.1 (192.168.1.1)    4.39 ms  4.25 ms  4.51 ms
*A:R8#
```

MPLS Shortcuts for IGP

MPLS can also be used for forwarding native IP traffic with the use of IGP shortcuts. This can be done using LDP or RSVP-TE tunnels.

To use RSVP-TE LSPs for IGP shortcuts, configure `rsvp-shortcut` in the routing protocol context. If there is an LSP to the destination node, it will be used as the next-hop for the destination. The LSP cannot have a loose path; it must either have explicit hops configured or use CSPF and traffic engineering. Traffic-engineered LSPs are covered in more detail in Chapters 14 and 15. In Figure 13.21, router R6 is exporting some specific routes learned from BGP into IS-IS (Intermediate System to Intermediate System). The configuration is shown below in Listing 13.24.

Figure 13.21 Topology used for IGP shortcuts

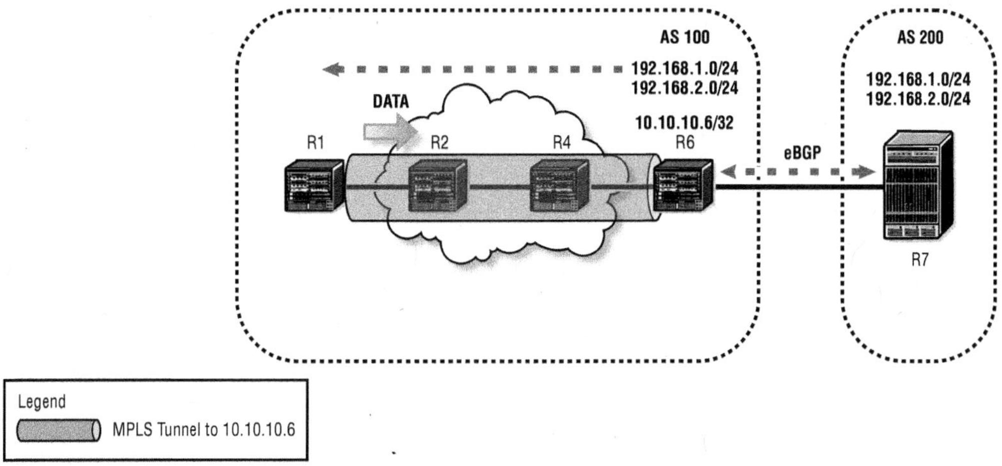

Listing 13.24 BGP routes exported to IS-IS on R6

```
*A:R6>config>router# policy-options
*A:R6>config>router>policy-options# info
----------------------------------------------
            prefix-list "192_168_pref"
                prefix 192.168.0.0/16 longer
            exit
            policy-statement "exports"
                entry 10
                    from
                        protocol bgp
                        prefix-list "192_168_pref"
                    exit
                    action accept
                    exit
                exit
            exit
----------------------------------------------
*A:R6>config>router>policy-options# exit
```

(continued)

Listing 13.24 *(continued)*

```
*A:R6>config>router# isis
*A:R6>config>router>isis# info
----------------------------------------------
        level-capability level-2
        area-id 49
        export "exports"
        traffic-engineering
        interface "system"
            interface-type point-to-point
        exit
        interface "toR4"
            interface-type point-to-point
        exit
----------------------------------------------
```

As seen in Listing 13.25, an LSP is configured on R1 to R6 with CSPF enabled. To use CSPF in an LSP, traffic engineering must be enabled in the IGP on all the routers in the network. When `rsvp-shortcut` is enabled in the IGP, the router uses the LSP as the next-hop for destinations on R6.

Listing 13.25 Configuration of R6 for IGP shortcuts using RSVP-TE

```
*A:R1>config>router>mpls# info
----------------------------------------------
            interface "system"
            exit
            interface "toR2"
            exit
            path "loose"
                no shutdown
            exit
            lsp "toR6"
                to 10.10.10.6
                cspf
                primary "loose"
                exit
                no shutdown
            exit
```

```
            no shutdown
----------------------------------------------
*A:R1>config>router>mpls# exit
*A:R1# configure router isis
*A:R1>config>router>isis# info
----------------------------------------------
        level-capability level-2
        area-id 49
        traffic-engineering
        rsvp-shortcut
        interface "system"
            interface-type point-to-point
        exit
        interface "toR2"
            interface-type point-to-point
        exit
----------------------------------------------
```

Listing 13.26 shows that the RSVP-TE tunnel is being used for destinations at R6.

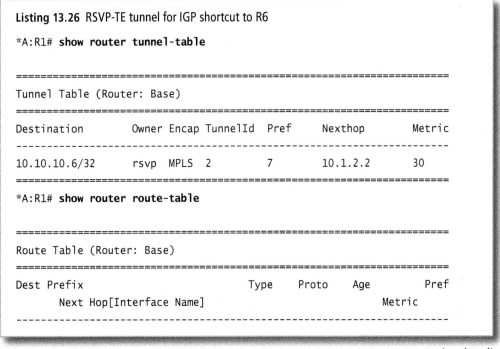

Listing 13.26 RSVP-TE tunnel for IGP shortcut to R6

```
*A:R1# show router tunnel-table

=======================================================================
Tunnel Table (Router: Base)
=======================================================================
Destination        Owner Encap TunnelId  Pref     Nexthop        Metric
-----------------------------------------------------------------------
10.10.10.6/32      rsvp  MPLS  2         7        10.1.2.2       30
=======================================================================
*A:R1# show router route-table

=======================================================================
Route Table (Router: Base)
=======================================================================
Dest Prefix                          Type    Proto    Age          Pref
       Next Hop[Interface Name]                            Metric
-----------------------------------------------------------------------
```

(continued)

Listing 13.26 *(continued)*

```
10.1.2.0/27                                  Local    Local     20d08h35m    0
       toR2                                                         0
10.1.8.0/27                                  Local    Local     01d01h41m    0
       toR8                                                         0
10.2.4.0/27                                  Remote   ISIS      00h12m37s    18
       10.1.2.2                                                     20
10.4.6.0/27                                  Remote   ISIS      00h12m33s    18
       10.1.2.2                                                     30
10.10.10.1/32                                Local    Local     20d08h34m    0
       system                                                       0
10.10.10.2/32                                Remote   ISIS      00h12m37s    18
       10.1.2.2                                                     10
10.10.10.4/32                                Remote   ISIS      00h12m33s    18
       10.1.2.2                                                     20
10.10.10.6/32                                Remote   ISIS      00h02m52s    18
       10.10.10.6 (tunneled:RSVP:2)                                 30
192.168.1.0/24                               Remote   ISIS      00h02m52s    18
       10.10.10.6 (tunneled:RSVP:2)                                 30
192.168.2.0/24                               Remote   ISIS      00h02m52s    18
       10.10.10.6 (tunneled:RSVP:2)                                 30
-------------------------------------------------------------------------------
No. of Routes: 10
===============================================================================
```

6PE–IPv6 Tunneling over MPLS

There are many issues involved in interconnecting IPv4 and IPv6 networks and many strategies for transitioning to IPv6. One useful technology that makes use of MPLS tunnels is known as 6PE and involves tunneling IPv6 traffic over an IPv4/MPLS core. In the 6PE architecture, the PE routers of the IPv4/MPLS core run a dual stack of IPv4/IPv6 and exchange the IPv6 routes using MP-BGP (Multiprotocol BGP). IPv6 packets are label-switched across the IPv4/MPLS core network. Two labels are used:

- **Inner label**—The inner label has the IPv6 explicit null value of 2 to indicate that the payload is a native IPv6 packet.
- **Outer label**—The outer label is the MPLS transport label used for switching across the network.

Figure 13.22 shows a topology with a customer IPv6 network (routers R7 and R8) connected by the service provider IPv4/MPLS network. Routers R1 and R6 are the PE routers that run a dual IPv4/IPv6 stack and exchange IPv6 routes using MP-BGP. Routers R2 and R4 are service provider core routers that are only IPv4 MPLS–capable and do not run BGP.

Figure 13.22 6PE topology.

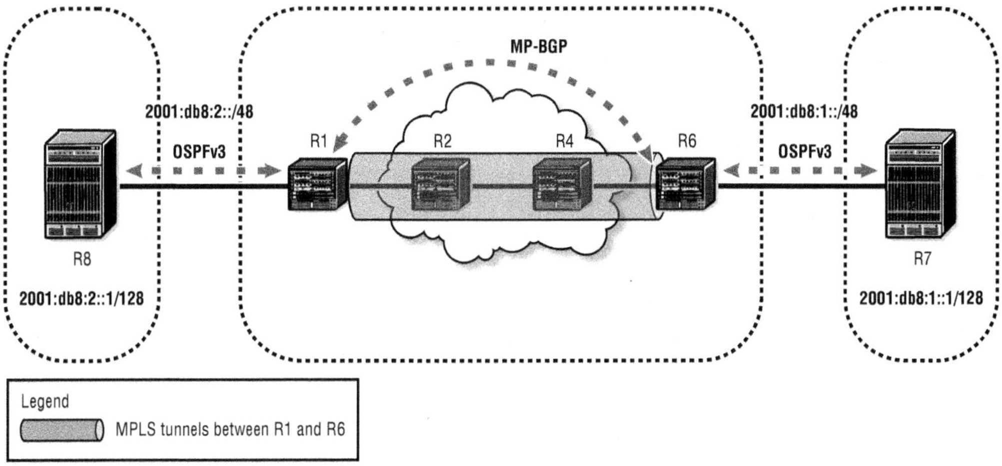

The steps to configure and operate 6PE over an IP/MPLS network can be summarized as follows:

1. PE routers run a dual stack of IPv4 and IPv6 with IPv6 interfaces toward the customer network and IPv4 interfaces toward the service provider core.
2. PE routers use MP-BGP to exchange IPv6 routes learned from customer networks across the core network.
3. IPv6 routes learned through MP-BGP on the PE routers have their next-hop resolved through an LDP tunnel.
4. PE routers are configured with static routes or an IPv6 IGP such as OSPFv3 or IS-IS to exchange routes with customer routers. Routes learned through MP-BGP are exported to the customer network.
5. IPv6 data received by the PE routers is encapsulated with two MPLS labels for transmission across the core network. The inner label has the value of 2 for IPv6 explicit null.

Listing 13.27 shows the configuration on R1 with the dual IPv4/IPv6 stack. The interface toward R8 is IPv6; the system interface and the interface toward the MPLS core are IPv4. R1 is configured with a policy to export the IPv6 routes learned from BGP into the IPv6 network with OSPFv3 (Open Shortest Path First version 3).

Listing 13.27 Configuration of R1 for 6PE

```
*A:R1# show router interface

===============================================================================
Interface Table (Router: Base)
===============================================================================
Interface-Name              Adm         Opr(v4/v6)  Mode    Port/SapId
   IP-Address                                               PfxState
-------------------------------------------------------------------------------
system                      Up          Up/Down     Network system
   10.10.10.1/32                                            n/a
toR2                        Up          Up/Down     Network 1/1/2
   10.1.2.1/27                                              n/a
toR8                        Up          Down/Up     Network 1/1/1
   FE80::216:4DFF:FE13:5CAE/64                              PREFERRED
-------------------------------------------------------------------------------
Interfaces : 3
===============================================================================
*A:R1# configure router ospf3
*A:R1>config>router>ospf3# info
----------------------------------------------
            asbr
            export "bgp_6pe"
            area 0.0.0.0
                interface "toR8"
                    interface-type point-to-point
                exit
            exit
----------------------------------------------
*A:R1>config>router>ospf3# show router policy "bgp_6pe"
    entry 10
        from
            protocol bgp
```

```
            family ipv6
        exit
        action accept
        exit
    exit
```

We see in Listing 13.27 that R1 is configured with a policy to export the IPv6 routes learned through BGP to OSPFv3. The routers are actually using MP-BGP to exchange the IPv6 routes. MP-BGP is an extended version of regular BGP that allows it to carry other address families than simply IPv4. It is typically used for carrying IPv6 or VPRN routes (as described in Chapter 20). The configuration and operation of MP-BGP are the same as "classic" BGP. On the 7750 SR we simply specify the address family to be carried, as shown in Listing 13.28. IPv4 is the default address family. Notice that the neighbor statement for R6 also specifies advertise-label. This causes R1 to add the IPv6 explicit null label so that the recipient (R6) knows it is receiving tunneled IPv6 data.

Listing 13.28 BGP configuration on the PE router

```
*A:R1# configure router bgp
*A:R1>config>router>bgp# info
----------------------------------------------
            group "internals"
                family ipv6
                export "ospf_6pe"
                peer-as 100
                neighbor 10.10.10.6
                    advertise-label ipv6
                exit
            exit
----------------------------------------------
*A:R1>config>router>bgp# show router policy "ospf_6pe"
    entry 10
        from
            protocol ospf3
        exit
        action accept
        exit
    exit
```

Listing 13.29 shows the peering of R1 with R6 and the route for R7's system address learned through BGP. Note that the resolved next-hop for the prefix is through LDP to the next downstream router, R2.

Listing 13.29 Remote IPv6 route learned through BGP

```
*A:R1# show router bgp summary
===============================================================================
 BGP Router ID:10.10.10.1       AS:100         Local AS:100
===============================================================================
BGP Admin State         : Up         BGP Oper State              : Up
Total Peer Groups       : 1          Total Peers                 : 1
Total BGP Paths         : 8          Total Path Memory           : 960
Total IPv4 Remote Rts   : 0          Total IPv4 Rem. Active Rts  : 0
Total IPv6 Remote Rts   : 1          Total IPv6 Rem. Active Rts  : 1
Total Supressed Rts     : 0          Total Hist. Rts             : 0
Total Decay Rts         : 0

... output omitted ...
===============================================================================
BGP Summary
===============================================================================
Neighbor
           AS PktRcvd InQ  Up/Down   State|Rcv/Act/Sent (Addr Family)
              PktSent OutQ
-------------------------------------------------------------------------------
10.10.10.6
               100      1543     0 10h51m28s 1/1/1 (IPv6)
                        1556     0
===============================================================================
*A:R1# show router bgp routes ipv6 2001:DB8:1::1/128 hunt
===============================================================================
 BGP Router ID:10.10.10.1       AS:100         Local AS:100
===============================================================================
 Legend -
 Status codes  : u - used, s - suppressed, h - history, d - decayed,
 * - valid
 Origin codes  : i - IGP, e - EGP, ? - incomplete, > - best
```

```
===============================================================================
BGP IPv6 Routes
===============================================================================
-------------------------------------------------------------------------------
RIB In Entries
-------------------------------------------------------------------------------
Network         : 2001:DB8:1::1/128
Nexthop         : ::FFFF:A0A:A06
From            : 10.10.10.6
Res. Nexthop    : 10.1.2.2 (LDP)
Local Pref.     : 100                    Interface Name : toR2
Aggregator AS   : None                   Aggregator     : None
Atomic Aggr.    : Not Atomic             MED            : 100
Community       : No Community Members
Cluster         : No Cluster Members
Originator Id   : None                   Peer Router Id : 10.10.10.6
6PE Label       : 2 (Ipv6 Explicit-Null)
Flags           : Used  Valid  Best  IGP
AS-Path         : No As-Path

-------------------------------------------------------------------------------
RIB Out Entries
-------------------------------------------------------------------------------
-------------------------------------------------------------------------------
Routes : 1
===============================================================================
```

Once learned through BGP and installed in the route table, the route is exported to OSPFv3 and thus to its neighbor, R8 (Listing 13.30).

Listing 13.30 IPv6 route exported to OSPFv3

```
*A:R1# show router ospf3 neighbor

===============================================================================
OSPF Neighbors
===============================================================================
Interface-Name                Rtr Id           State       Pri  RetxQ   TTL
```

(continued)

Listing 13.30 *(continued)*

```
-------------------------------------------------------------------------
toR8                         10.10.10.8      Full        1    0        33
-------------------------------------------------------------------------
No. of Neighbors: 1
=========================================================================
*A:R1# show router ospf3 database

=========================================================================
OSPF Link State Database (Type : All)
=========================================================================
Type    Area Id    Link State Id    Adv Rtr Id     Age  Sequence    Cksum
-------------------------------------------------------------------------
Router  0.0.0.0    0.0.0.0          10.10.10.1     481  0x80000035 0x4feb
Router  0.0.0.0    0.0.0.0          10.10.10.8     483  0x80000001 0xf47c
IA Pfx  0.0.0.0    0.0.0.0          10.10.10.8     477  0x8000003a 0xd636
AS Ext  n/a        0.0.0.6          10.10.10.1     536  0x80000002 0xd93b
-------------------------------------------------------------------------
No. of LSAs: 4
=========================================================================
*A:R1# show router ospf3 database 0.0.0.6 detail

=========================================================================
OSPF Link State Database (Type : All) (Detailed)
=========================================================================
-------------------------------------------------------------------------
AS Ext LSA (0.0.0.6 (6))
-------------------------------------------------------------------------
Area Id          : N/A                  Adv Router Id    : 10.10.10.1
Link State Id    : 0.0.0.6 (6)
LSA Type         : AS Ext
Sequence No      : 0x80000002           Checksum         : 0xd93b
Age              : 543                  Length           : 44
Options          :                      E2-Metric        : 100
Dest Prefix      : 2001:DB8:1::1/128
=========================================================================
```

Router R8 receives the route and is able to ping the system address of the remote IPv6 router (R7) through the MPLS tunnel (Listing 13.31).

Listing 13.31 Remote IPv6 route available on R8

```
*A:R8# show router route-table ipv6

===============================================================================
IPv6 Route Table (Router: Base)
===============================================================================
Dest Prefix                           Type    Proto    Age         Pref
       Next Hop[Interface Name]                               Metric
-------------------------------------------------------------------------------
2001:DB8:1::1/128                     Remote  OSPF3    00h22m21s   150
       FE80::216:4DFF:FE13:5CAE-"toR1"                         100
2001:DB8:2::1/128                     Local   Local    01d02h38m   0
       system                                                  0
-------------------------------------------------------------------------------
No. of Routes: 2
===============================================================================
*A:R8# ping 2001:DB8:1::1 count 1
PING 2001:DB8:1::1 56 data bytes
64 bytes from 2001:DB8:1::1 icmp_seq=1 hlim=62 time=4.20ms.

---- 2001:DB8:1::1 PING Statistics ----
1 packet transmitted, 1 packet received, 0.00% packet loss
round-trip min = 4.20ms, avg = 4.20ms, max = 4.20ms, stddev = 0.000ms
```

Listing 13.32 shows the very simple configuration of the provider's core P routers, R2 and R4. They have no IPv6 or BGP configuration. They are configured as pure IPv4/MPLS routers with IS-IS for the provider's core and LDP for the transport tunnels.

Listing 13.32 Core routers are configured with IPv4 and LDP only

```
*A:R2>config>router# info
----------------------------------------------
#--------------------------------------------------
echo "IP Configuration"
#--------------------------------------------------
        interface "system"
            address 10.10.10.2/32
```

(continued)

Listing 13.32 *(continued)*

```
        exit
        interface "toR1"
            address 10.1.2.2/27
            port 1/1/2
        exit
        interface "toR4"
            address 10.2.4.2/27
            port 1/1/3
        exit
#---------------------------------------------------
echo "ISIS Configuration"
#---------------------------------------------------
        isis
            level-capability level-2
            area-id 49
            interface "system"
                interface-type point-to-point
            exit
            interface "toR1"
                interface-type point-to-point
            exit
            interface "toR4"
                interface-type point-to-point
            exit
        exit
#---------------------------------------------------
echo "LDP Configuration"
#---------------------------------------------------
        ldp
            interface-parameters
                interface "toR1"
                exit
                interface "toR4"
                exit
            exit
            targeted-session
            exit
        exit
 ----------------------------------------------
```

Practice Lab: RSVP-TE Operation and 6PE

The following lab is designed to reinforce your knowledge of the content in this chapter. Please review the instructions carefully, and perform the steps in the order in which they are presented. The practice labs require that you have access to six or more Alcatel-Lucent 7750 SRs or Alcatel-Lucent 7450 ESSs in a non-production environment.

These labs are designed to be used in a controlled lab environment. Please *do not* attempt to perform these labs in a production environment.

Lab Section 13.1: Configuring RSVP-TE LSPs

RSVP-TE is an MPLS label distribution protocol that operates in downstream-on-demand mode. A major advantage of RSVP-TE is that it provides more control over the definition of LSPs than LDPs.

Objective In this exercise you will configure a topology of four Alcatel-Lucent 7750 SRs (see Figure 13.23) with both strict and loose hop RSVP-TE LSPs and investigate their behavior.

Figure 13.23 Topology for configuring RSVP-TE LSPs.

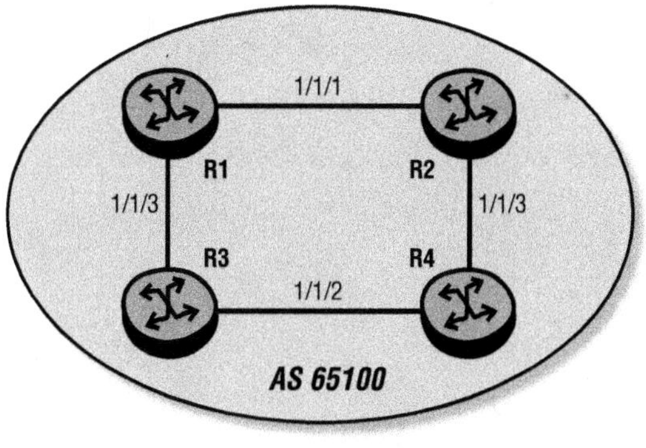

Validation You will know you have succeeded if the LSPs are operationally up and the behavior described in the lab exercise is observed.

1. For the first few tasks of this lab, shut down any IGP that you may have running in the network of four routers shown in Figure 13.23.
   a. Verify the route tables to make sure that each router does not have a route to any of the other routers' system addresses.

2. On R1, configure a strict-path LSP R1–R2–R4–R3. Do not perform any other configurations yet.

   a. Is the LSP operationally up? If not, what failure code is given?

   b. Add R1's interface to R2 into MPLS, and activate RSVP-TE (do not configure the other routers yet). Is the LSP operationally up? If not, what failure code is given?

   c. Add R2's interface to R1 to MPLS, and activate RSVP-TE. What failure code is given now?

   d. Add R2's interface to R4 to MPLS. What failure code is given now?

   e. Perform any remaining configuration required to get the LSP operationally up. In addition, make sure that the infrastructure can support additional LSPs between the four routers.

   f. How many RSVP-TE sessions are on R1? How many RSVP-TE sessions are on the other routers? Compare the Tunnel ID and LSP ID between the routers.

   g. Describe the MPLS label operations required by R4 to support the data path for this LSP.

3. Disable RSVP-TE Hello messages on R4, and enable debug trace for all RSVP-TE control traffic.

   a. What types of RSVP-TE messages are sent and received by R4? How often do they occur?

   b. Shut down the LSP on R1. What kind of RSVP-TE message is received by R4? What kind of RSVP-TE message is sent by R4?

   c. Shut down the RSVP-TE interface on R4 toward R3. What kind of RSVP-TE messages are sent by R4? Bring the RSVP-TE interface on R4 toward R3 back up before proceeding.

   d. Shut down the RSVP-TE interface on R4 toward R2. What kind of RSVP-TE messages are sent by R4? Bring the RSVP-TE interface back up before proceeding.

4. Configure another strict-path LSP R1–R2–R4–R3.

   a. How many RSVP-TE sessions exist on each router? Compare the Tunnel IDs and LSP IDs of the RSVP-TE sessions.

5. Configure a totally loose path LSP from R1 to R3.
    a. Is the LSP operationally up? If not, what is the failure code? Explain.
    b. Complete all configurations so that the LSP goes operationally up.
    c. What path does the LSP follow? Explain.
    d. How many RSVP-TE sessions now exist on each of the routers? Explain.
6. Turn on debug trace on R1, and view RSVP-TE Path messages only.
    a. What major difference do you see between the RSVP-TE Path messages sent to R2 and the ones sent to R3? Explain.
    b. How do the Tunnel ID and LSP ID of these paths relate to each other?

Lab Section 13.2: RSVP-TE Hello Messages and Timers

There are a few configurable timers on the Alcatel-Lucent 7750 SR that determine how quickly an LSP failure can be detected, how often an attempt is made to reestablish operationally down LSPs, and how often operational LSPs are optimized.

Objective In this lab you will observe the effect of Hello messages on detecting a failure on an LSP::Path. You will also examine the retry timer and resignal timer on the Alcatel-Lucent 7750 SR.

Validation You will know you have succeeded if you observe improved detection times when Hello messages are disabled and if you can explain the role of the retry timer and resignal timer in establishing LSPs.

1. Ensure that RSVP-TE Hello messages are disabled on R1, R2, R3, and R4. This may already be done from Lab Section 13.1.
2. Shut down the RSVP-TE interface on R3 toward R4.
    a. How long does it take for one of the strict-path LSPs to become operationally down on R1? Explain.
    b. Will both strict-path LSPs always become operationally down on R1 at the exact same time?
    c. Bring the RSVP-TE interface on R3 back up. View the RSVP-TE sessions. How do the Tunnel ID and LSP ID values compare to earlier results?
3. Enable RSVP-TE Hello messages between R3 and R4 only. Use default values.
    a. Enable debug trace on R4, and view RSVP-TE Hello messages only.

b. How often are Hello messages sent and received by R4?

c. If an LSP from R3 to R4 was added to the network, how would you expect the Hello messages to change?

d. Shut down the RSVP-TE interface on R3 toward R4.

e. How long does it take for one of the strict-path LSPs to become operationally down on R1? How does this compare to the previous result?

f. If RSVP-TE Hello messages were enabled in the entire network, would the detection time on R1 be quicker for this particular case? Explain.

g. How often does R1 attempt to reestablish the LSPs? How long will this process continue? Can these values be configured? Explain.

h. Bring the RSVP-TE interface on R3 back up, and ensure that all LSPs are operationally up. In addition, set the default Hello timers throughout the entire network before proceeding to the next step.

4. Shut down the RSVP-TE interface on R3 toward R1.

a. What happens to the loose LSP? Does it take a new path? If so, how long does it take for the LSP to be established over a new path? Explain.

b. Shut down the RSVP-TE interface on R1 toward R3. What happens to the loose LSP?

c. Bring the RSVP-TE interface on R1 and R3 back up.

d. Shut down the physical port of R3 that is connected to R1. What happens to the loose LSP? Explain.

e. Bring the port on R3 back up, and wait for the IGP to converge. Does the LSP revert to its original path from R1 to R3? Explain.

Lab Section 13.3: MPLS Shortcuts for BGP

MPLS can be used to avoid running BGP on all core routers in a service provider's network. This reduces the burden of all core routers requiring a full Internet routing table and reduces the number of IBGP sessions.

Objective In this lab you will configure MPLS shortcuts to avoid running a full mesh of IBGP in the provider core (see Figure 13.24).

Figure 13.24 Service provider topology for MPLS shortcuts.

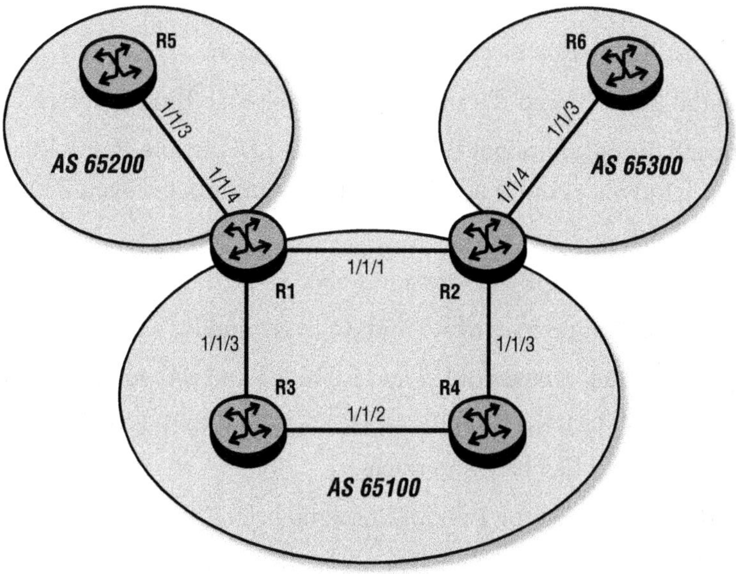

Validation You will know you have succeeded if you can ping between autonomous systems even when there are link failures in AS 65100.

1. Configure the autonomous systems as shown in Figure 13.24.
2. Configure EBGP sessions between R1 and R5 and between R2 and R6.
3. Configure an IBGP session between R1 and R2.
4. Configure a loopback interface with an address of `192.168.55.5/32` on R5 and a loopback interface with an address of `192.168.66.6/32` on R6. Distribute both loopback interfaces into BGP.

Private addresses are not normally distributed to BGP. It is done here for illustrative purposes only.

   a. Verify that R5 and R6 can ping each other's loopback interfaces.
   b. Are the loopback prefixes from R5 and R6 in the route tables of R1 and R2? Explain.
   c. Are the loopback prefixes from R5 and R6 in the route tables of R3 and R4? Explain.

d. Shut down the physical link between R1 and R2.

e. Can R1 still ping R2's system interface address? Explain.

f. Can R5 still ping R6's loopback interface? Explain.

g. Bring the link between R1 and R2 up before proceeding to the next step.

5. Without configuring additional BGP sessions or LDP, ensure that R1 can reach the loopback interfaces of R5 and R6 if the physical link between R1 and R2 is down.

   a. Which LSP does R1 use to shortcut to R2?

   b. Are the loopback prefixes of R5 and R6 in R1 and R2's route table? Explain.

   c. Are the loopback prefixes of R5 and R6 in R3 and R4's route table? Explain.

   d. Shut down the link between R1 and R2, and ensure that R5 and R6 can still ping each other's loopback interfaces.

   e. Bring the link between R1 and R2 back up before proceeding to the next step.

6. Configure R1 and R2 to use RSVP-TE or LDP shortcuts.

   a. Configure LDP on all interfaces within AS 65100.

   b. Will R1 use its LDP binding or its RSVP-TE LSP to forward traffic destined to R6's loopback interface?

   c. Verify that R5 and R6 can ping each other's loopback interfaces.

   d. Shut down RSVP-TE on R1. How has R1's route table changed? Can R5 still ping R6's loopback interface? Explain.

Lab Section 13.4: 6PE

6PE is a technology used for interconnecting IPv4 and IPv6 networks. It tunnels IPv6 traffic over an IPv4 core using MPLS and MP-BGP.

Objective In this lab exercise you will tunnel IPv6 traffic from Routers R5 and R6 over an IPv4 core. R1 and R2 will be dual-stacked, and R2 and R3 will only run IPv4 (see Figure 13.25).

Validation You will know you have succeeded if R5 and R6 can ping each other's IPv6 system interface addresses.

1. Remove the BGP sessions between R1 and R5 and between R2 and R6, and ensure that all routers in your network use the same autonomous system.

Figure 13.25 Topology for 6PE exercise.

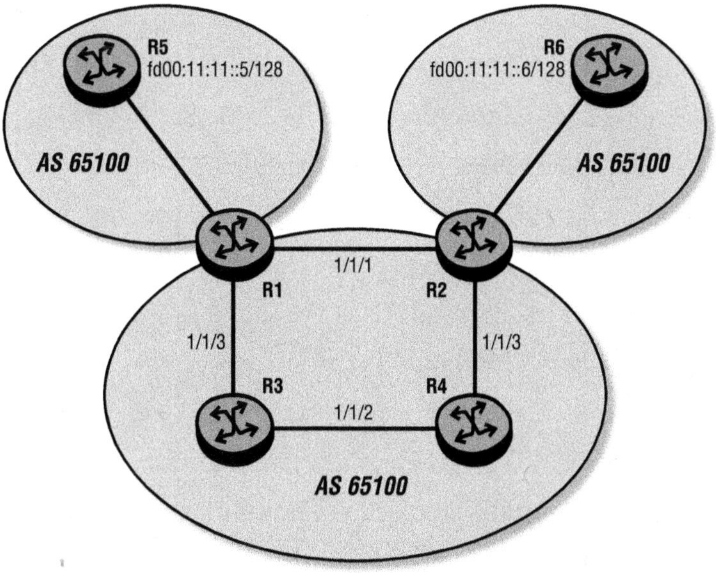

2. Configure R5 and R6 with the IPv6 system interface addresses shown in Figure 13.25.
3. Run OSPFv3 between R1 and R5 and between R2 and R6. Configure all routers to be in area 0.
4. Configure R1 and R2 so that they export any IPv6 routes learned from the provider core to their OSPFv3 neighbors.
5. Configure the existing BGP session between R1 and R2 to use 6PE to tunnel IPv6 traffic over the existing IPv4 infrastructure.
   a. Can R5 ping R6's system interface address? Explain, and correct any problems before proceeding.
   b. Are the system interface addresses of R5 and R6 in the route tables of R1 and R2?
   c. Are the system interface addresses of R5 and R6 in the route tables of R3 and R4? Explain.
   d. Shut down the port between R1 and R2. Can R5 still ping R6's system interface address? Explain.
   e. Bring the port between R1 and R2 back up.

Chapter Review

Now that you have completed this chapter, you should be able to:

- Describe how the Path and Resv messages are used to establish an LSP.
- Configure RSVP-TE LSPs on the Alcatel-Lucent 7750 SR.
- Explain how an RSVP-TE tunnel can contain multiple LSP::Paths.
- List the key fields in the Path message, and explain their use.
- List the key fields in the Resv message, and explain their use.
- Describe the purpose of the PSB and RSB.
- Explain how RSVP-TE uses Path and Resv messages to refresh an LSP.
- Explain how PathTear and ResvTear messages are used to tear down an LSP.
- Describe when and how RSVP-TE error messages are used.
- Explain how and why RSVP-TE uses Hello messages to maintain adjacencies.
- Explain how refresh reduction operates and reduces the overhead necessary to maintain multiple LSPs.
- Explain the purpose and operation of the RSVP-TE retry and resignal timers.
- Describe the purpose and operation of loose and strict hops in the LSP::Path.
- Configure a network to use MPLS shortcuts for BGP.
- Configure a network to use MPLS shortcuts for IGP.
- Describe how an IPv4/MPLS network can be used to tunnel IPv6 traffic.
- Configure an MPLS network for 6PE tunneling.

Post-Assessment

The following questions will test your knowledge and prepare you for the Alcatel-Lucent NRS II Certification Exam. Compare your responses with the answers listed in Appendix A. You can also use the CD that accompanies this book to take all the assessment tests and review the answers.

1. Which statement is correct regarding RSVP-TE messages used for setting up an LSP?
   - **A.** The destination IP address of a Path message is always the next-hop neighbor.
   - **B.** Resv messages must contain an RRO so that they can be forwarded appropriately.
   - **C.** Label binding information is carried in Path messages.
   - **D.** The head end signals LSP label values to be used by all other routers in a Path trigger message.
   - **E.** None of the above statements are correct.
2. Consider an operationally up LSP that has a strict path of R1 ⇨ R2 ⇨ R3 ⇨ R4. A link failure occurs between R2 and R3. Which statement best describes the RSVP-TE message sequence that follows?
   - **A.** R1 detects the IGP topology change and sends a Path Tear message downstream.
   - **B.** R1 detects the IGP topology change and sends a Resv Tear message downstream.
   - **C.** R2 sends a Path Error message upstream, and R3 sends a Resv Error message downstream.
   - **D.** R2 sends a Path Tear message upstream, and R3 sends a Resv Tear message downstream.
   - **E.** R2 sends a Resv Tear message upstream, and R3 sends a Path Tear message downstream.
3. Consider an established LSP with a path traversing four routers. There are six routers in the IGP domain, and all routers have operational RSVP-TE interfaces. Which routers will have an RSVP-TE session for this LSP?
   - **A.** Only the head end router will have an RSVP-TE session for the LSP.
   - **B.** The head end router and the tail end router will have an RSVP-TE session for the LSP.
   - **C.** All routers in the LSP::Path will have an RSVP-TE session for the LSP.
   - **D.** All routers in the IGP domain will have an RSVP-TE session for the LSP.
   - **E.** There is not enough information to answer the question.

4. Which statement is correct concerning RSVP Error messages?
   A. Path Error messages travel upstream and are addressed to the head end router.
   B. Resv Error messages travel downstream and are addressed to the tail end router.
   C. Resv Error messages modify the RSB on RSVP routers.
   D. Path Error messages do not modify the PSB on RSVP routers.
   E. None of the above answers are correct.

5. Consider a network that has four routers with EBGP peers and five core routers that only have IBGP peers. A service provider wants to start using MPLS shortcuts for BGP. Which routers need to be provisioned with MPLS shortcuts?
   A. MPLS shortcuts need to be provisioned on the routers that only have IBGP peers.
   B. MPLS shortcuts need to be provisioned on the routers that have EBGP peers.
   C. MPLS shortcuts need to be provisioned on all routers in the autonomous system.
   D. MPLS shortcuts need to be provisioned on all routers that have EBGP connections and their peers in other autonomous systems.
   E. There is not enough information to answer the question.

6. Consider an RSVP-TE LSP that is operationally up. An operator administratively shuts down the LSP at the head end. Which statement best describes the sequence of messages that follows?
   A. A Path Tear message is sent from the head end router to the tail end, intercepted by each router along the path of the LSP.
   B. A Path Tear message is tunneled from the head end router to the tail end. Upon reception of the Path Tear, the tail end originates a Resv Tear message that travels back to the head end, intercepted at each hop.
   C. A Resv Tear message is sent from the head end router toward the tail end, intercepted by each router in the Path.
   D. A Path Error message is tunneled from the head end router to the tail end. The tail end then originates a Resv Tear message that travels back to the head end, intercepted at each hop.
   E. A Resv Error message is sent from the head end router toward the tail end, intercepted by each router in the path.

7. A router is the ingress LER for three RSVP-TE–signaled LSPs, the egress LER for two RSVP-TE–signaled LSPs, and the transit LSR for four RSVP-TE–signaled LSPs. The router has 10 Layer 2 VPN service instances configured. How many RSVP-TE sessions exist on the node?

A. 2

B. 3

C. 4

D. 5

E. 9

F. 19

8. An operator mistakenly does an admin shutdown on an operationally up LSP and later brings it back up. How do the Tunnel ID and LSP ID compare before and after the LSP was shut down?

A. The Tunnel ID and LSP ID remain unchanged.

B. The Tunnel ID changes, but the LSP ID stays constant.

C. The Tunnel ID stays constant, but the LSP ID changes.

D. The Tunnel ID and the LSP ID change.

E. There is not enough information to determine the answer.

9. An operationally up LSP in an Alcatel-Lucent 7750 SR network has a totally loose path. CSPF is not configured on the LSP, and the resignal timer has not been changed from default settings. A link failure in the network causes a topology change that affects the path of the LSP. The link is later repaired. Which statement best describes the LSP ID before and after the link failure?

A. The LSP ID stays constant through the network changes.

B. The LSP ID changes when the link goes down. It does not change again until the resignal timer expires or the LSP is manually resignaled.

C. The LSP ID changes when the link goes down and changes again when the link is restored.

D. There is not enough information to determine the answer.

10. Consider two routers, R1 and R2. There are two LSPs that originate on R1 and terminate on R2. There are two LSPs that originate on R2 and terminate on R1. R1 is a transit LSR for seven LSPs, and three of these also transit R2. Assuming that these are the only LSPs in the network, how many Hello messages will R1 send to R2 at every Hello interval?

A. 2

B. 4

C. 7

D. 11

E. None of the above answers are correct.

11. Which statement is correct regarding RSVP-TE refresh reduction?

A. A summary refresh message is sent to indicate that a router can support refresh reduction.

B. A summary refresh message lists the tunnel IDs that the router is refreshing.

C. A summary refresh message lists the LSP IDs that the router is refreshing.

D. If a router receives an unknown Message ID, it sends a Path Tear message downstream and a Resv Tear message upstream.

E. If a router receives an unknown Message ID, it sends a Path Tear message upstream and a Resv Tear message downstream.

F. Message ID values are included in Path and Resv messages when RSVP-TE refresh is enabled on an interface.

12. Consider a totally loose LSP that is established over a network of Alcatel-Lucent 7750 SRs. The LSP is not enabled with CSPF. Routers are added to the network in such a way that the original path of the LSP is not affected but a more optimal path becomes available. The resignal timer is set to 30 minutes, and the retry timer has default settings. How long after IGP convergence does it take for the LSP to take the more optimal path?

   A. It takes 30 seconds to start establishing a new path.

   B. It takes 30 minutes to start establishing a new path.

   C. A new path starts to be established at the next resignal timer interval, which could be as long as 30 minutes.

   D. The LSP will not be optimized until it is manually resignaled.

   E. There is not enough information to determine the answer.

13. Consider a totally loose LSP that traverses four routers in the order R1, R2, R3, and R4. CSPF is not configured on the LSP. Which statement below describes the `ERO` in the Path message sent by R1?

   A. There will not be an `ERO` in the Path message.

   B. The `ERO` only contains the system address of R4.

   C. The `ERO` contains the system address of R1 and the system address of R4.

   D. The `ERO` contains the router interface addresses of each router along the Path followed by the system interface of R4.

   E. There is not enough information to answer the question.

14. An Alcatel-Lucent 7750 SR is provisioned with MPLS shortcuts for BGP. The command `configure router bgp igp-shortcut mpls` is used on the router. If a prefix has both an LDP label binding and an RSVP-TE LSP to the next-hop, which will be used?

   A. The RSVP-TE LSP will be used.

   B. The LDP label binding will be used.

   C. The tunnel that gives the shortest path through the network will be used.

   D. Native IP forwarding will be used.

   E. The tunnel that became available first will be used.

15. Which statement is correct regarding 6PE networks running over Alcatel-Lucent 7750 SRs?

- **A.** The outer label is an MPLS transport label, and the inner label is an IPv6 implicit null label.
- **B.** The outer label is an MPLS transport label, and the inner label is an IPv4 explicit null label.
- **C.** 6PE is used by a service provider that wants to tunnel IPv6 traffic over an IPv4 core.
- **D.** 6PE is used by a service provider that wants to tunnel IPv4 traffic over an IPv6 core.

14 Constraint-Based Routing and TE-LSPs

The Alcatel-Lucent NRS II exam topics covered in this chapter include the following:

- Traffic-engineered LSPs
- CSPF algorithm
- Traffic-engineering database
- Traffic engineering in OSPF
- Traffic engineering in IS-IS
- Controlling the LSP Path with specific hops
- The explicit route object
- Use of CSPF in the LSP
- Using tools perform to troubleshoot LSPs
- Specifying hop limits as a constraint
- Configuring a TE metric
- Using administrative groups
- Using admin groups to create a ring topology
- Failures on TE-LSPs
- LDP-over-RSVP

Standard routing in an IP network involves determining the shortest path to all the possible destinations in the network. With distance vector protocols, this is achieved by having the routers exchange their routing tables with their neighbors. Thus, a router learns about remote destinations from its neighbors and chooses the neighbor with the least number of hops to the destination as the best route.

In a link-state routing protocol such as OSPF (Open Shortest Path First) or IS-IS (Intermediate System to Intermediate System), routers exchange their local topology information so that every router can build a complete topology map of the network. From this they can calculate the best path to all destinations.

Constraint-based routing involves finding the best route to a destination, *subject to some specific constraints.* As we see in upcoming chapters, these constraints often involve a requirement to use or to avoid specific links or nodes in the network—a capability that does not exist in classic IGP protocols. Constraint-based routing requires extensions to a link-state routing protocol. Both OSPF and IS-IS support these extensions, known as the *traffic-engineering extensions.*

In this chapter, we see how OSPF and IS-IS have been modified to carry traffic-engineering information and the ways that RSVP-TE (Resource Reservation Protocol–Traffic Engineering) uses this information to signal LSPs (label switched paths) that satisfy a variety of constraints.

After we examine the enhancements to the IGP to support traffic engineering, we look at how this information can be used to signal traffic-engineered LSPs (TE-LSPs). Constraints can be relatively simple, such as a requirement to pass through a specific node or to avoid a specific node, or they can involve more sophisticated capabilities such as traffic-engineering metrics and the use of administrative groups.

Pre-Assessment

The following assessment questions will help you understand what areas of the chapter you should review in more detail to prepare for the NRS II exam. You can also use the CD that accompanies this book to take all the assessment tests and review the answers.

1. Which statement is correct regarding constraint-based routing?

A. TE-LSPs always follow the best IGP route.

B. LDP is commonly used for constraint-based routing applications.

C. Constraint-based routing can be used to provide QoS functions in the data plane.

D. The route for a TE-LSP is calculated at the head end router.

E. None of the above statements are correct.

2. An operationally up LSP in a network of Alcatel-Lucent 7750 SRs has a totally loose path and is following the shortest route from the IGP. CSPF is configured on the LSP, and the resignal timer has not been changed from default settings. A link failure in the network causes a topology change that affects the path of the LSP. The link is later repaired. Which statement best describes the LSP ID before and after the link failure?

   A. The LSP ID stays constant.

   B. The LSP ID changes when the link goes down. It will not change again until the resignal timer expires or the LSP is manually resignaled.

   C. The LSP ID changes when the link goes down and changes again when the link is restored.

   D. There is not enough information to determine the answer.

3. Which statement is *not* correct regarding the processing of the `ERO` and `RRO` on a CSPF-enabled router?

   A. Each transit LSR removes the first hop from the `ERO` in the path message and builds a new Path message for the next-hop LSR.

   B. The head end router fills the `ERO` according to the CSPF calculation results.

   C. Each LSR in the LSP path helps to build the `RRO` by adding the IP address of the interface on which it transmits the Path message.

   D. When CSPF is enabled, the `ERO` can contain strict or loose hops.

   E. All of the above statements are correct.

4. Consider an Alcatel-Lucent 7750 SR that has three MPLS interfaces. One interface is configured with the admin group gold, one with the admin group silver, and one with the admin group bronze. These are the only interfaces in the entire network configured with admin groups. An established LSP is configured to exclude the admin group gold; however, an operator decides to change the LSP to include the admin group bronze. No other routers are changed. Assuming that the ingress LER and egress LER of the LSP are not directly connected, which statement best describes the resulting behavior?

   A. The LSP becomes operationally down until the retry timer expires and then becomes established.

   B. The LSP becomes operationally down and stays in this state until a configuration change is made.

C. The LSP path does not change until it is manually resignaled or the resignal timer expires.
D. The LSP path changes to use the interface with admin group bronze.
E. None of the above statements are correct.

5. Which statement is not correct regarding the use of LDP-over-RSVP on a network of Alcatel-Lucent 7750 SRs?
    A. CSPF is not required on RSVP-TE LSPs used for LDP-over-RSVP.
    B. For the purposes of LDP-over-RSVP, T-LDP is only required on the ABRs.
    C. Data travels across an area with an outer MPLS label signaled with RSVP-TE, an inner MPLS label signaled with LDP, and possibly a VPN service label.
    D. The IGP must be configured to support LDP-over-RSVP.
    E. All of the above statements are correct.

14.1 Purpose of Constraint-Based Routing

Constraint-based routing is used to provide more control over the paths that an LSP will take through the network. It allows an operator to specify more criteria than simply "choose the best route from the IGP (interior gateway protocol)." There are several criteria that can be used to constrain the route. These are described in this chapter.

LDP (Label Distribution Protocol) and RSVP-TE are label distribution protocols and are used in conjunction with an IGP but do not replace normal IGP routing. As we have seen in our study of LDP, each LSR (Label Switch Router) uses the IP routing table to choose which label to install in the LFIB (label forwarding information base) for a specific FEC (Forwarding Equivalence Class). Thus, the LSPs in an LDP network *always* follow the path chosen by the IGP.

When we use RSVP-TE for signaling an LSP, we have more control over the path selection process for the LSP than with LDP. When traffic engineering (TE) is enabled in the IGP, the routers not only distribute the normal topological information, but also additional TE information. This is maintained in a separate database: the traffic-engineering database (TED).

When we configure an RSVP-TE LSP with TE constraints, RSVP-TE requests a path that meets the constraints from the TE-enabled IGP. The IGP uses the link-state database (LSDB) and the TED to find the shortest route that satisfies the constraints. RSV-TE then signals the LSP along this path. This is the advantage that a TE-capable network provides over a normal IGP routed network. To have a TE-capable network we must have routers with a TE-capable IGP (OSPF-TE or IS-IS-TE) and a TE-capable label signaling protocol (RSVP-TE).

Constraint-Based Routed LDP (CR-LDP) was defined in RFC 3212 as a TE-capable label signaling protocol but was deprecated in 2003 because only one traffic-engineering signaling protocol is really necessary and RSVP-TE had wider industry acceptance.

Constraint-Based Routing Examples

RSVP-TE defines a mechanism for reserving bandwidth from the routers along a specific LSP path. The TE-enabled IGP uses a constraint-based routing algorithm (CSPF) to find the best path through the network such that every link on the path has the requisite bandwidth available, if there is one. In Figure 14.1, constraint-based routing can be used to find the route with 10 Gb/s bandwidth available on each link.

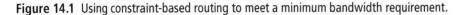

Figure 14.1 Using constraint-based routing to meet a minimum bandwidth requirement.

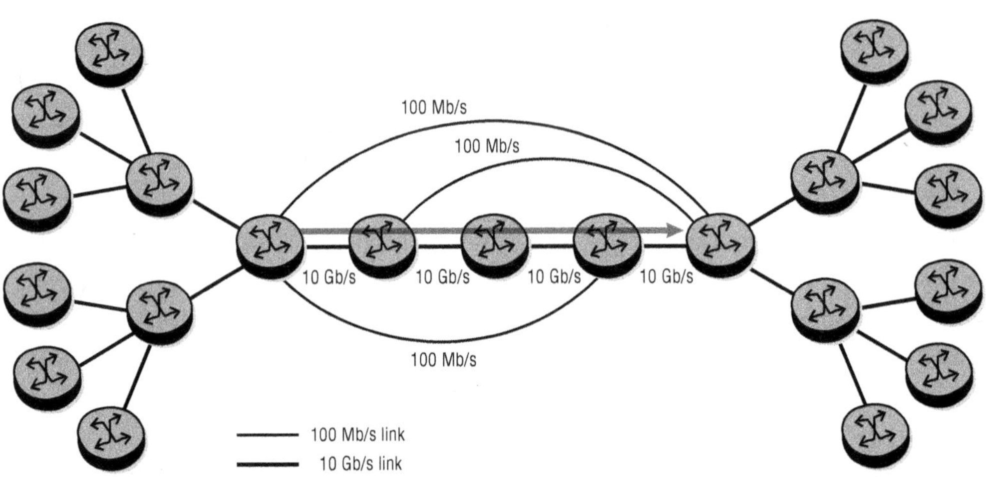

RSVP-TE also supports a technique called *link coloring* to identify specific links and then ask for a route that includes only links of a specific color or one that avoids links of a specific color. For example, we might identify the satellite links in our network as "satellite." When choosing the path for a voice over IP service, we could specify the constraint to exclude any satellite links. Our constraint-based routing algorithm will then choose the shortest path that does not include any satellite links (Figure 14.2).

Figure 14.2 Using constraint-based routing to select or avoid specific types of links.

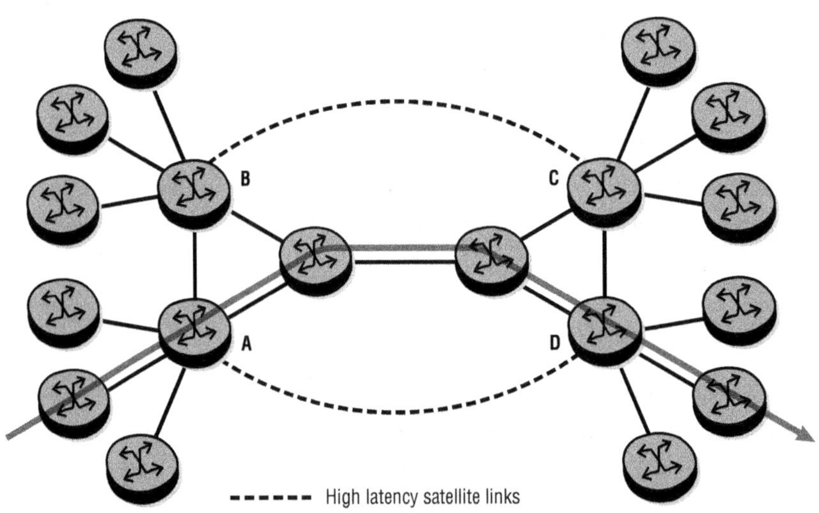

Another example of a constraint-based route is one that excludes a specific node or a specific link. We use this form of constraint-based routing in calculating the detour LSPs used by fast reroute—a capability of RSVP-TE that is discussed in Chapter 16. As an example, consider Figure 14.3, where we know that the link between A and E is frequently congested or prone to failure. A route chosen to avoid the link between A and E is a constraint-based route.

Figure 14.3 Using constraint-based routing to exclude specific nodes or links.

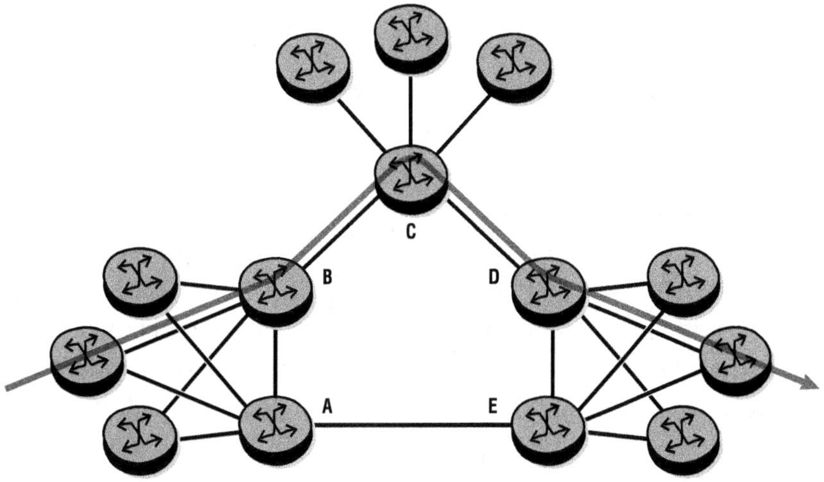

Traffic-Engineered LSPs

If we use constraint-based routing to choose the path followed by an LSP, we say that it is a traffic-engineered LSP (TE-LSP). LDP does not provide any mechanism for building TE-LSPs because it can only follow the IGP, but RSVP-TE *does* provide such a mechanism.

RSVP-TE requests the IGP to calculate the best route through the network that meets the administratively defined constraints. Using the TED and the LSDB, the TE-enabled IGP calculates the best path and then RSVP-TE signals for an LSP along this specific path. This is a TE-LSP. It is common that the TE-LSP will follow a different path across the network than the route selected as the best route by the IGP.

Like any other LSP, a TE-LSP is a path through an MPLS network. For a TE-LSP, the route of the LSP is always calculated by the head end router. RSVP-TE includes the path as a series of strict hops in the `EXPLICIT_ROUTE` object (`ERO`) carried in the

Path message. The TE-LSP is then signaled along the selected path to the egress node. A TE-LSP is created on the Alcatel-Lucent 7750 SR by using the `cspf` command in the LSP definition.

If `cspf` is not configured, the LSP is not a TE-LSP. In this case the downstream path is selected at each hop from the information in the IGP route-table, subject to any constraints in the ERO.

14.2 CSPF Algorithm

Constraint-based routing with OSPF and IS-IS involves the flooding of additional information that is collected in the traffic-engineering database (TED). Unlike the regular link-state information in the link-state database (LSDB), the information in the TED is not used to build the IP forwarding table. Traffic-engineering information is only used when a TE-LSP is required. At that time, the constrained shortest path first (CSPF) algorithm operates on the TED to find the shortest route to the destination that meets the given constraints.

The CSPF algorithm is very similar to the regular SPF (shortest path first) algorithm except that in the CSPF calculation, any links in the TED that do not meet the given constraints are disregarded. You can think of them as being discarded, although they are still maintained in the TED, just not used in the calculation for the constraint-based route. Constraints are based on the unreserved bandwidth available, administrative groups, hop count, or a requirement to include or bypass a specific node or link.

Review of the SPF Calculation

Figure 14.4 shows a network topology and the link-state database for the topology.

Remember the steps of the SPF algorithm:

1. Add the root node to the SPF tree. Add all the links from the root node to the candidate list.
2. Remove the link in the candidate list with the lowest cost to the root and add it to the SPF tree. Remove any other higher-cost links to this node from the candidate list.
3. Find all the links from the latest node in the SPF tree to any node not yet in the tree, and add them to the candidate list. Repeat Steps 2 and 3 until the candidate list is empty.

Figure 14.4 Network topology with associated LSDB.

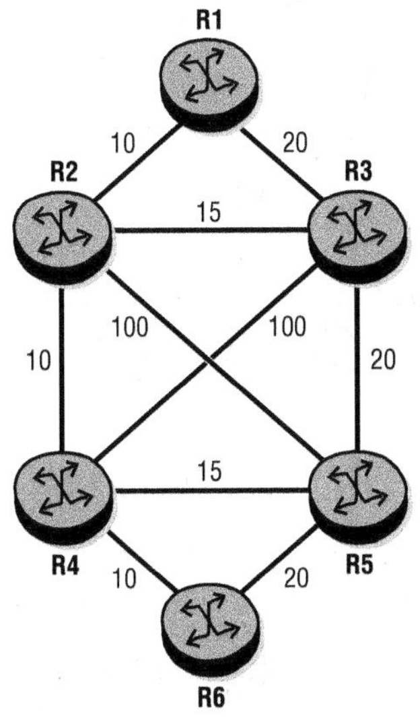

R1 LSDB	
Link	**Cost**
R1-R2	10
R1-R3	20
R2-R1	10
R2-R3	15
R2-R4	10
R2-R5	100
R3-R1	20
R3-R2	15
R3-R4	100
R3-R5	20
R4-R2	10
R4-R3	100
R4-R5	15
R4-R6	10
R5-R2	100
R5-R3	20
R5-R4	15
R5-R6	20
R6-R4	10
R6-R5	20

Figure 14.5 provides an example of the regular SPF calculation that OSPF would perform on router R1 to populate its IP forwarding table.

The steps of the SPF algorithm are as follows:

1. R1 puts itself in the SPF tree as the root.
2. R1 adds all the links from R1 to the candidate list.
3. Node R2 has the shortest cost to the root and is therefore added to the SPF tree.
4. All of the links from R2 are added to the candidate list. (The link from R2 to R1 is not added because the SPF tree already contains R1.)
5. There are two links with the lowest cost to the root (R1–R3 and R2–R4). Either one can be added to the tree—we chose the link R2–R4.
6. The links from R4 are added to the candidate list. (R4–R2 is not added because R2 is already in the SPF tree.)

Figure 14.5 SPF algorithm used to calculate LSDB.

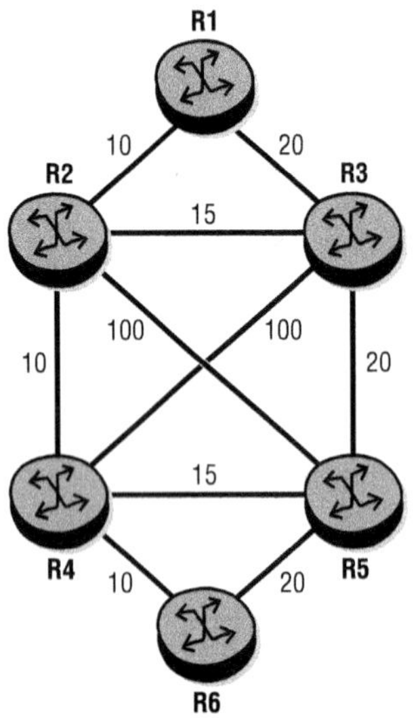

Step	Candidate links [cost]	Cost to root	SPF tree
1	-	-	R1-R1 [0]
2	R1-R2 [10] R1-R3 [20]	10 20	R1-R1 [0]
3	R1-R3 [20]	20	R1-R1 [0] R1-R2 [10]
4	R1-R3 [20] R2-R4 [10] R2-R3 [15] R2-R5 [100]	20 20 25 110	R1-R1 [0] R1-R2 [10]
5	R1-R3 [20] R2-R3 [15] R2-R5 [100]	20 25 110	R1-R1 [0] R1-R2 [10] R2-R4 [10]
6	R1-R3 [20] R2-R3 [15] R2-R5 [100] R4-R3 [100] R4-R5 [15] R4-R6 [10]	20 25 110 120 35 30	R1-R1 [0] R1-R2 [10] R2-R4 [10]
7	~~R2-R3 [15]~~ R2-R5 [100] ~~R4-R3 [100]~~ R4-R5 [15] R4-R6 [10]	~~25~~ 110 ~~120~~ 35 30	R1-R1 [0] R1-R2 [10] R2-R4 [10] R1-R3 [20]
8	R2-R5 [100] R4-R5 [15] R4-R6 [10] R3-R5 [20]	110 35 30 40	R1-R1 [0] R1-R2 [10] R2-R4 [10] R1-R3 [20]
9	R2-R5 [100] R4-R5 [15] R3-R5 [20] R6-R5 [20]	110 35 40 55	R1-R1 [0] R1-R2 [10] R2-R4 [10] R1-R3 [20] R4-R6 [10]
10	~~R2-R5 [100]~~ ~~R3-R5 [20]~~ ~~R6-R5 [20]~~	~~110~~ ~~40~~ ~~55~~	R1-R1 [0] R1-R2 [10] R2-R4 [10] R1-R3 [20] R4-R6 [10] R4-R5 [15]

7. The link with the lowest cost to the root (R1–R3) is added to the SPF tree. The other, higher-cost links to R3 are removed from the candidate list.
8. The remaining links from R3 are added to the candidate list.
9. The lowest-cost link in the candidate list (R4–R6) is added to the SPF tree. The remaining links from R6 are added to the candidate list.

10. The lowest-cost link in the candidate list (R4–R5) is added to the SPF tree. The other links to R5 are removed, and the candidate list is empty. The SPF tree is complete and contains the shortest path from R1 to all the destinations in the network.

Example of the CSPF Calculation

Now imagine the same network, but using constraint-based routing for traffic engineering. For our example, consider that all links in the network have 100 Mbps unreserved, except the link R2–R4 and the link R4–R6, which have only 50 Mbps unreserved. We would like to find the shortest route between R1 and R6 that has 100 Mbps unreserved bandwidth. The TED is shown in Figure 14.6. It's similar to the LSDB except that it also contains the unreserved bandwidth value for each link. The TED actually contains more information, including the administrative group and traffic-engineering metric, but we will only consider unreserved bandwidth for simplicity.

Figure 14.6 Topology and TED used for CSPF calculation.

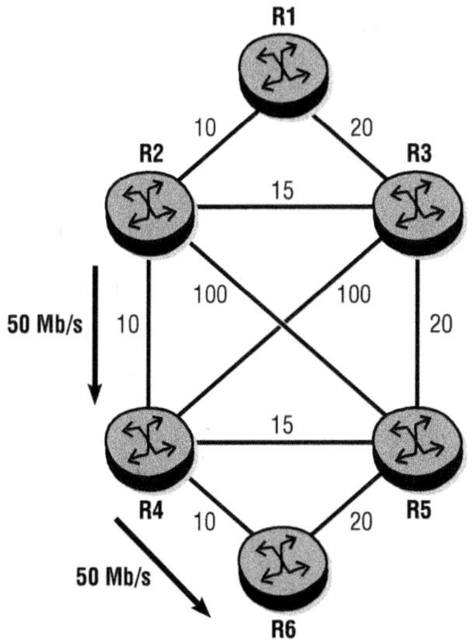

R1 TED		
Link	**Cost**	**BW (Mb/s)**
R1-R2	10	100
R1-R3	20	100
R2-R1	10	100
R2-R3	15	100
R2-R4	10	50
R2-R5	100	100
R3-R1	20	100
R3-R2	15	100
R3-R4	100	100
R3-R5	20	100
R4-R2	10	100
R4-R3	100	100
R4-R5	15	100
R4-R6	10	50
R5-R2	100	100
R5-R3	20	100
R5-R4	15	100
R5-R6	20	100
R6-R4	10	100
R6-R5	20	100

The CSPF algorithm is the same as the SPF algorithm except that we disregard any link that does not meet the specified constraint. In this case, the constraint is that the link must have 100 Mbps unreserved bandwidth. Figure 14.7 shows the CSPF calculation made without the two links that do not meet the constraint. Note that although the links R2–R4 and R4–R6 have only 50 Mbps unreserved, the links in the reverse direction have 100 Mbps unreserved. Thus, the shortest constraint-based route from R6 to R1 could follow a different path. The CSPF calculation is complete when we have added R6 to the SPF tree. We have now found the shortest path from R1 to R6 that meets the constraint.

Following are the steps taken to perform the CSPF calculation:

1. R1 puts itself in the SPF tree as the root.
2. R1 adds all the links from R1 to the candidate list.
3. Node R2 has the shortest cost to the root and is therefore added to the SPF tree.
4. All of the links from R2 are added to the candidate list. (R2–R4 is not added because it does not meet the constraint.)
5. R1–R3 has the lowest cost to the root and is added to the SPF tree. R2–R3 is removed because it is not required.
6. The links from R3 are added to the candidate list.
7. The link with the lowest cost to the root (R3–R5) is added to the SPF tree. The other, higher-cost link to R5 is removed from the candidate list.
8. The remaining links from R5 are added to the candidate list.
9. The lowest-cost link in the candidate list (R5–R4) is added to the SPF tree. R4–R6 is not added to the candidate list because it does not meet the constraint.
10. The remaining link in the candidate list (R5–R6) is added to the SPF tree. Once R6 is added to the SPF tree, the path from R1 to R6 has been calculated and the algorithm can be halted. In this case, R6 is the farthest from R1; thus, it is the last node in the topology and the candidate list is now empty.

Figure 14.7 CSPF algorithm used to calculate constrained path to router R6.

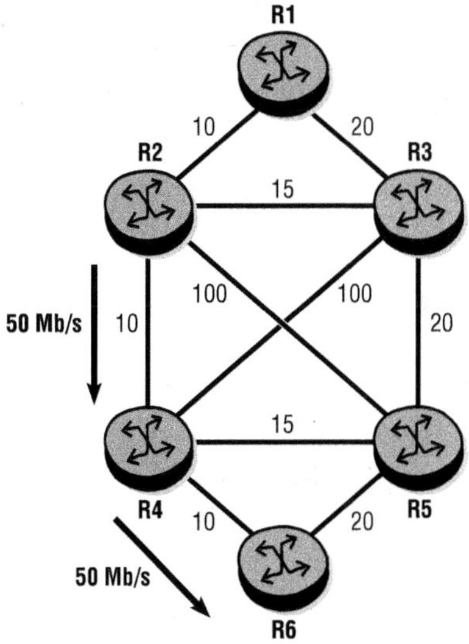

Step	Candidate links [cost]	Cost to root	SPF tree
1	-	-	R1-R1 [0]
2	R1-R2 [10] R1-R3 [20]	10 20	R1-R1 [0]
3	R1-R3 [20]	20	R1-R1 [0] R1-R2 [10]
4	R1-R3 [20] R2-R3 [15] R2-R5 [100]	20 25 110	R1-R1 [0] R1-R2 [10]
5	~~R2-R3 [15]~~ R2-R5 [100]	~~25~~ 110	R1-R1 [0] R1-R2 [10] R1-R3 [20]
6	R2-R5 [100] R3-R4 [100] R3-R5 [20]	110 120 40	R1-R1 [0] R1-R2 [10] R1-R3 [20]
7	~~R2-R5 [100]~~ R3-R4 [100]	~~110~~ 120	R1-R1 [0] R1-R2 [10] R1-R3 [20] R3-R5 [20]
8	R3-R4 [100] R5-R4 [15] R5-R6 [20]	120 55 60	R1-R1 [0] R1-R2 [10] R1-R3 [20] R3-R5 [20]
9	~~R3-R4 [100]~~ R5-R6 [20]	~~120~~ 60	R1-R1 [0] R1-R2 [10] R1-R3 [20] R3-R5 [20] R5-R4 [15]
10			R1-R1 [0] R1-R2 [10] R1-R3 [20] R3-R5 [20] R5-R4 [15] R5-R6 [20]

14.3 Traffic-Engineering Extensions

RSVP-TE is not a routing protocol but, rather, a signaling protocol used to signal and allocate resource requirements and to request labels for an LSP. In the case of a TE-LSP, the path is determined through a constraint-based routing protocol. Both OSPF and IS-IS have been adapted for traffic engineering by adding constraint-based routing capabilities. There is no traffic-engineering capability in RIP (Routing Information Protocol). With distance vector protocols an individual router does not have a full topology view of the network; thus, the constraint-based routing method used in MPLS is not possible with RIP.

Traffic-Engineering Database

OSPF and IS-IS have both been enhanced in a very similar manner to support constraint-based routing. The traffic-engineering enhancements to OSPF are described in RFC 3630 and the enhancements to IS-IS in RFC 3784. These enhancements describe additional link-state information that is flooded by the routing protocols. This information is collected in the traffic-engineering database (TED). Each router capable of traffic engineering maintains two databases, as shown in Figure 14.8.

Figure 14.8 Traffic-engineering–capable network with LSDB and TED.

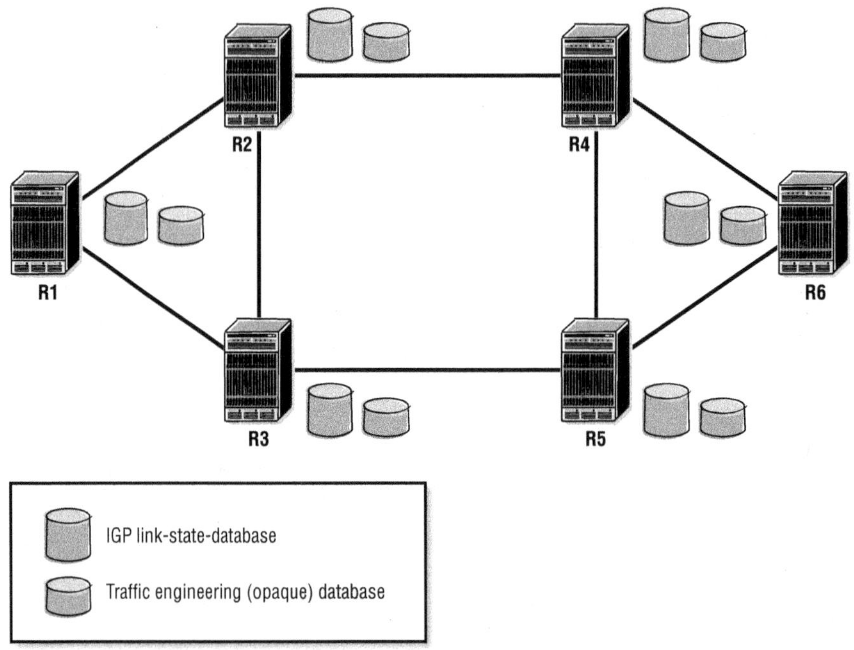

Whereas the link-state database contains the link metric, the TED contains additional information associated with the link. For both OSPF and IS-IS, the important traffic-engineering information is carried in sub-TLVs in the link-state packets. These are as follows:

- **Traffic-engineering metric**—This may be the same as the link-state metric, or may be different.
- **Maximum bandwidth**—True capacity of the link. The unit for all bandwidth information is bytes per second.
- **Maximum reservable bandwidth**—Amount of bandwidth that can be reserved on this link. It may exceed maximum bandwidth (oversubscription). On the 7750 SR, the maximum reservable bandwidth is expressed as a percentage of maximum bandwidth and may exceed maximum bandwidth by a factor of 10.
- **Unreserved bandwidth**—Bandwidth that has not yet been reserved. Bandwidth can be reserved at one of eight different priority levels. The amount of unreserved bandwidth is carried for each priority level. The initial value for all eight priority levels is the maximum reservable bandwidth.
- **Administrative group**—A 32-bit mask assigned by the network administrator. When the bit is set, it indicates membership of that group. The least significant bit is known as group 0; the most significant as group 31. A link may be a member of multiple groups (multiple bits set). An administrative group is also known as a resource class or color.

In addition to the TE information described above, OSPF and IS-IS have been further modified to carry information relating to shared risk link groups (SRLG). SRLGs are defined for OSPF in RFC 4203 and for IS-IS in RFC 5307. SRLG information is used to calculate diverse paths for redundancy and is described in more detail in Chapter 16.

The TE information is flooded throughout the network in the same manner as the flooding of link-state information and is collected in the TED. Any change of traffic-engineering information for a specific link represents a topology change; hence, the information is reflooded. Although the traffic-engineering information and the TED are the same for both OSPF and IS-IS, the format and mechanism for transmitting this information are somewhat different in the two protocols and are described in more detail below.

At present, traffic engineering is only performed in single-area networks. In hierarchical, multi-area networks, one area does not have complete topology information about its neighboring areas. The CSPF algorithm described above can only be used when a node has complete topology information about the network.

14.4 OSPF-TE

Both OSPF and IS-IS have been extended for traffic engineering (TE) and carry essentially the same TE information as described above. They also both maintain a TED and perform the CSPF algorithm as described. In this section, we look at the additions to OSPF that support traffic engineering. The next section looks at additions to IS-IS.

The Type 10 LSA

OSPF uses a new type of LSA (link state advertisement), the Type 10 Opaque LSA for carrying traffic-engineering information. The Opaque LSAs (Type 9, Type 10, and Type 11) are defined in RFC 2370. This RFC describes the flooding behavior of these LSAs but does not define how they are to be used. The Type 10 LSA is the area local opaque LSA that is flooded within a single area (Figure 14.9). RFC 3630 describes the traffic-engineering extensions for OSPF and uses Type 10 LSAs to flood the traffic-engineering information. If there are non-TE-capable routers in an area, they must flood the TE LSAs that they receive.

Figure 14.9 Type 10 LSAs have area flooding scope.

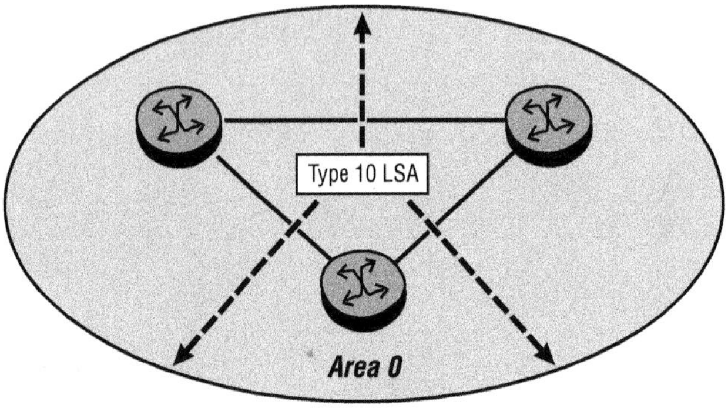

The opaque LSAs are defined using a TLV (type–length–value) approach as is standard in modern protocols. The Type 10 LSA carries the same OSPF header as the other LSAs as shown in Figure 14.10.

The initial field in the data component of the LSA contains two fields. The first defines the type of Type 10 LSA, in this case, a traffic-engineering LSA, which has a type value of 1. The second is an arbitrary value that defines the LSA instance. This 24-bit field allows a router to originate a maximum of 16,777,216 Type 10 TE LSAs.

Figure 14.10 OSPF header for Type 10 LSAs.

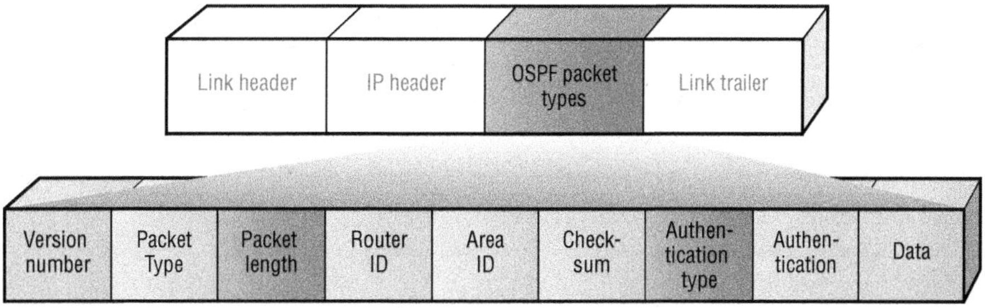

The Two Type 10 LSA Subtypes

Following the initial field are additional TLVs that define the traffic-engineering data. There are two top-level subtypes of the Type 10 TE LSA, Type 1 and Type 2. The Type 1 LSA contains router information. The Type 2 LSA carries the TE information for a single link. Each TE LSA contains only one of the two top-level TLVs.

The Type 1 TLV of the TE LSA contains the router IP address. This is an address that is always reachable on the router, typically implemented as a loopback address. On the 7750 SR, this is the system address, and the LSA is generated as soon as traffic engineering is enabled on the router. Listing 14.1 shows the Type 1 TLV (the Router-ID TLV) generated by router R1 in the topology shown in Figure 14.11. LSA `1.0.0.1` is the Type 1 TLV. LSA `1.0.0.2` and LSA `1.0.0.3` are the Type 2 LSAs.

Figure 14.11 Topology for traffic-engineering TLVs.

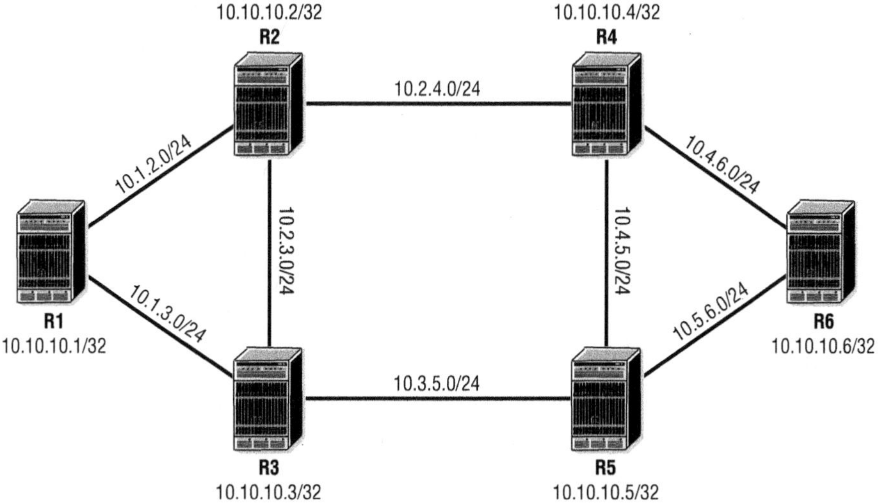

Listing 14.1 TE Router-ID TLV

```
*A:R1# configure router ospf
*A:R1>config>router>ospf# traffic-engineering
*A:R1>config>router>ospf# show router ospf opaque-database

===============================================================================
OSPF Opaque Link State Database (Type : All)
===============================================================================
Type  Id           Link State Id    Adv Rtr Id     Age  Sequence    Cksum
-------------------------------------------------------------------------------
Area  0.0.0.0      1.0.0.1          10.10.10.1     14   0x80000001 0x12fe
Area  0.0.0.0      1.0.0.2          10.10.10.1     14   0x80000001 0x81ca
Area  0.0.0.0      1.0.0.3          10.10.10.1     14   0x80000001 0xf551
-------------------------------------------------------------------------------
No. of Opaque LSAs: 3
===============================================================================
*A:R1>config>router>ospf# show router ospf opaque-database 1.0.0.1 detail

===============================================================================
OSPF Opaque Link State Database (Type : All) (Detailed)
===============================================================================
-------------------------------------------------------------------------------
Opaque LSA
-------------------------------------------------------------------------------
Area Id          : 0.0.0.0             Adv Router Id     : 10.10.10.1
Link State Id    : 1.0.0.1             LSA Type          : Area Opaque
Sequence No      : 0x80000001          Checksum          : 0x12fe
Age              : 117                 Length            : 28
Options          :  E
Advertisement    :
     ROUTER-ID TLV  (0001) Len   4 : 10.10.10.1
===============================================================================
*A:R1>config>router>ospf#
```

Fields of the TE Link LSA

The Type 2 TLV of the TE LSA contains the traffic-engineering information for individual links. There is one Type 2 LSA generated for each link. On the 7750 SR, Type 2

LSAs are generated for each link when traffic engineering is enabled and the link is enabled for MPLS. The Type 2 (Link) LSA contains up to nine sub-TLVs. They are the traffic-engineering TLVs described above, plus the additional fields described below:

- **Link type (1 octet)**—Type of link, point-to-point or multi-access (mandatory TLV).
- **Link ID (4 octets)**—Identifies the other end of the link. This is the router ID of the neighbor for point-to-point links and the interface address of the DR on multi-access links. (mandatory TLV).
- **Local interface IP address (4 octets)**—Interface address or addresses for this link. If there are multiple addresses, they are all listed.
- **Remote interface IP address (4 octets)**—Interface address or addresses for the neighbor's interface on point-to-point links. Set to `0.0.0.0` on multi-access networks, or, alternatively, the TLV may not be sent at all.

Table 14.1 summarizes the sub-TLVs defined for the traffic-engineering Link LSA.

Table 14.1 OSPF TE TLV Types

Sub-TLV Type	Length (Octets)	Name
1	1	Link type
2	4	Link ID
3	4	Local interface IP address
4	4	Remote interface IP address
5	4	TE metric
6	4	Maximum link bandwidth
7	4	Reservable bandwidth
8	32	Unreserved bandwidth
9	4	Administrative group
16	Variable	SRLG

Listing 14.2 shows the contents of the TE Type 2 Link TLV. Note that OSPF advertises a Type 10 LSA containing one Link TLV for each interface on the router.

Listing 14.2 Details of TE Link TLV

```
*A:R1# show router ospf opaque-database 1.0.0.2 detail
```

(continued)

Listing 14.2 *(continued)*

```
===========================================================================
OSPF Opaque Link State Database (Type : All) (Detailed)
===========================================================================
---------------------------------------------------------------------------
Opaque LSA
---------------------------------------------------------------------------
Area Id          : 0.0.0.0              Adv Router Id    : 10.10.10.1
Link State Id    : 1.0.0.2              LSA Type         : Area Opaque
Sequence No      : 0x80000002           Checksum         : 0x7fcb
Age              : 10                   Length           : 124
Options          :  E
Advertisement    :
     LINK INFO TLV  (0002) Len 100 :
       Sub-TLV: 1     Len: 1     LINK_TYPE    : 1
       Sub-TLV: 2     Len: 4     LINK_ID      : 10.10.10.2
       Sub-TLV: 3     Len: 4     LOC_IP_ADDR  : 10.1.2.1
       Sub-TLV: 4     Len: 4     REM_IP_ADDR  : 10.1.2.2
       Sub-TLV: 5     Len: 4     TE_METRIC    : 100
       Sub-TLV: 6     Len: 4     MAX_BDWTH    : 1000000 Kbps
       Sub-TLV: 7     Len: 4     RSRVBL_BDWTH : 1000000 Kbps
       Sub-TLV: 8     Len: 32    UNRSRVD_CLS0 :
         P0: 1000000 Kbps P1: 1000000 Kbps P2: 1000000 Kbps P3:
 1000000 Kbps
         P4: 1000000 Kbps P5: 1000000 Kbps P6: 1000000 Kbps P7:
 1000000 Kbps
       Sub-TLV: 9     Len: 4     ADMIN_GROUP  : 0 None

===========================================================================
```

14.5 IS-IS TE

The addition of traffic-engineering capabilities to IS-IS is a little simpler than for OSPF because the IS-IS LSPs (link-state PDUs—not to be confused with label switched paths!) that are used for flooding topology information are defined in a more extensible manner than the OSPF LSAs. In IS-IS, traffic-engineering information is added by defining new TLVs and adding the concept of sub-TLVs. If a router does not understand the TLV or sub-TLV, it will be ignored, although the LSP will still be flooded to the neighbors as usual. TE extensions to IS-IS are defined in RFC 3784.

RFC 3784 replaces some of the existing TLVs defined in RFC 1195 with the new TLVs as shown in Table 14.2. The new TLVs are defined using sub-TLVs for flexibility and add the ability to carry TE information, as well as the wide metric (maximum value 4,261,412,864 instead of 63). The new Extended IP Reachability TLV (135) does not distinguish between externally and internally originated routes.

Table 14.2 Comparison of TLVs between RFC 1195 and RFC 3784

1195 TLV	Name	3784 TLV	Name
2	IS Reachability	22	Extended IS Reachability
128	IP Internal Reachability	135	Extended IP Reachability
130	IP External Reachability	135	Extended IP Reachability
n/a	N/A	134	Traffic-Engineering Router ID

The IS Reachability TLV is the TLV containing the information about the router's neighbors used to build the topology tree. The new Extended IS Reachability TLV (TLV 22) removes the TOS routing information (for delay, monetary cost, and reliability) that was carried in the original TLV 2. The metric is increased to a 24-bit field, and sub-TLVs are defined to carry the traffic-engineering information.

The fields of TLV 22 are described in Table 14.3.

Table 14.3 Fields of TLV 22

Field	Length (Octets)
System ID and pseudonode number	7
Metric	3
Sub-TLV length	1
Sub-TLVs	0–244

The sub-TLV fields carry the TE information. Besides the TE information described above, the additional sub-TLVs defined for this TLV are as follows:

- **IPv4 interface address**—Mandatory for traffic engineering, optional otherwise. May occur several times.
- **IPv4 neighbor address**—Mandatory for traffic engineering on point-to-point interfaces, optional otherwise. May occur several times.

Table 14.4 summarizes the sub-TLVs defined for TLV 22.

Table 14.4 Sub-TLVs Used for TE Information in TLV 22

Sub-TLV Type	Length (Octets)	Name
3	4	Administrative group
6	4	IPv4 interface
8	4	IPv4 neighbor
9	4	Maximum link bandwidth
10	4	Reservable bandwidth
11	32	Unreserved bandwidth
18	3	TE default metric

The IP Reachability TLVs carry the prefix information about IP networks that can be reached by the advertising router. In RFC 1195, two different types of TLV were defined, but these have been replaced by a single TLV in RFC 3784, the Extended IP Reachability TLV (TLV 135). A side effect of this new TLV is that it is no longer possible to know if the route was generated from an external network or not.

The fields of TLV 135 are as follows:

- **Metric (4 octets)**—Note that this is larger than the 24-bit link metric in TLV 22 to ensure that it is large enough to carry the entire path metric.
- **Control (1 octet)**
- **1 bit for up/down flag**
- **1 bit to identify sub-TLVs**
- **6 bits for prefix length (max value 32)**
- **Prefix (0 to 4 octets)**—Length of the prefix depends on the value of prefix length. Unnecessary zeroes in the prefix are not carried.
- **Sub-TLVs (0 to 250 octets)**—If the sub-TLV bit is set, the first octet after the prefix is interpreted as the length of the sub-TLVs. RFC 3784 does not define any sub-TLVs for TLV 135.

Besides TLV 135, a completely new TLV is defined for traffic engineering; the traffic-engineering router ID (TLV 134). This TLV carries a reachable IP address for the router, typically a loopback address. On the 7750 SR it would usually be the system address. TLV 134 is mandatory for traffic engineering and optional otherwise. It corresponds to the Type 1 TLV (router address) of the traffic-engineering LSA in OSPF.

Listing 14.3 shows the configuration of IS-IS for traffic engineering. The router is configured as Level 2 only for simplicity.

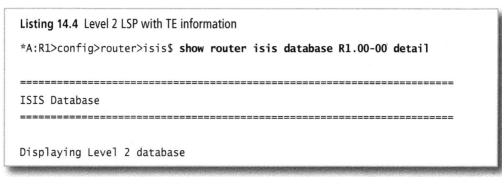

Listing 14.3 Configuration of IS-IS for traffic engineering

```
*A:R1# configure router isis
*A:R1>config>router>isis$ traffic-engineering
*A:R1>config>router>isis$ level-capability level-2
*A:R1>config>router>isis$ show router isis database

===============================================================================
ISIS Database
===============================================================================
LSP ID                                  Sequence Checksum Lifetime Attributes
-------------------------------------------------------------------------------

Displaying Level 1 database
-------------------------------------------------------------------------------
Level (1) LSP Count : 0

Displaying Level 2 database
-------------------------------------------------------------------------------
R1.00-00                                0xa      0x964b   1196     L1L2
R2.00-00                                0xf      0xd91a   1195     L1L2
R3.00-00                                0xb      0x7e66   1197     L1L2
Level (2) LSP Count : 3
===============================================================================
```

Listing 14.4 shows the Level 2 LSP for the topology in Figure 14.11. The detailed LSP listing on the 7750 SR shows output from the fields of both the older TLVs and the newer TE TLVs. The older TLVs are not relevant in a TE network and are omitted from the output.

Listing 14.4 Level 2 LSP with TE information

```
*A:R1>config>router>isis$ show router isis database R1.00-00 detail

===============================================================================
ISIS Database
===============================================================================

Displaying Level 2 database
```

(continued)

Listing 14.4 *(continued)*

```
-----------------------------------------------------------------------
LSP ID    : R1.00-00                                    Level     : L2
Sequence  : 0xa                    Checksum  : 0x964b   Lifetime  : 1162
Version   : 1                      Pkt Type  : 20       Pkt Ver   : 1
Attributes: L1L2                   Max Area  : 3
SysID Len : 6                      Used Len  : 317      Alloc Len : 1492

TLVs :
  Area Addresses:
    Area Address : (1) 49
  Supp Protocols:
    Protocols     : IPv4
  IS-Hostname   : R1
  Router ID   :
    Router ID   : 10.10.10.1

... output omitted ...

  TE IS Nbrs    :
    Nbr   : R2.00
    Default Metric  : 10
    Sub TLV Len     : 69
    IF Addr   : 10.1.2.1
    Nbr IP    : 10.1.2.2
    MaxLink BW: 1000000 kbps
    Resvble BW: 1000000 kbps
    Unresvd BW:
        BW[0] : 1000000 kbps
        BW[1] : 1000000 kbps
        BW[2] : 1000000 kbps
        BW[3] : 1000000 kbps
        BW[4] : 1000000 kbps
        BW[5] : 1000000 kbps
        BW[6] : 1000000 kbps
        BW[7] : 1000000 kbps
    Admin Grp : 0x0
    TE Metric : 10
  TE IS Nbrs    :
    Nbr   : R3.00
```

```
    Default Metric  : 10
    Sub TLV Len     : 69
    IF Addr   : 10.1.3.1
    Nbr IP    : 10.1.3.3
    MaxLink BW: 1000000 kbps
    Resvble BW: 1000000 kbps
    Unresvd BW:
        BW[0] : 1000000 kbps
        BW[1] : 1000000 kbps
        BW[2] : 1000000 kbps
        BW[3] : 1000000 kbps
        BW[4] : 1000000 kbps
        BW[5] : 1000000 kbps
        BW[6] : 1000000 kbps
        BW[7] : 1000000 kbps
    Admin Grp : 0x0
    TE Metric : 10
  TE IP Reach   :
    Default Metric  : 0
    Control Info:    , prefLen 32
    Prefix   : 10.10.10.1
    Default Metric  : 10
    Control Info:    , prefLen 27
    Prefix   : 10.1.2.0
    Default Metric  : 10
    Control Info:    , prefLen 27
    Prefix   : 10.1.3.0

Level (2) LSP Count : 1
=======================================================================
```

SRLG information is carried in another optional TLV, Type 138, defined in RFC 5307. SRLGs are described in Chapter 16.

14.6 Traffic-Engineered LSPs

There are a variety of different applications of the general term *traffic engineering.* Ultimately, it means exercising control over the path that data takes through the network beyond the simple shortest path first algorithm used by a typical routing protocol. In general, traffic-engineering applications fall into three broad categories:

- Manually controlling the path to create a specific topology or accommodate known characteristics of the network such as congestion, latency, or reliability
- Signaling paths with defined bandwidth requirements and making bandwidth reservations for each link of the path
- Signaling paths that provide redundancy and path diversity for deploying highly available services

This chapter describes the first two applications of traffic engineering in detail. Redundancy and path diversity are described in Chapter 16.

Controlling the LSP Path with Specific Hops

The simplest approach to controlling the LSP path is through the use of the `path` attribute of the LSP. This provides a mechanism very similar to the use of static routes in IP. The path can be controlled to follow a manually configured route. This provides a high degree of control but results in a loss of flexibility. The path may not be able to accommodate changes in the network topology and may need to be manually reconfigured.

Figure 14.12 shows a simple approach to forcing a specific path for an LSP from R1 to R6. By specifying a loose hop of R3 or R5, the resulting LSP follows the best path chosen by the IGP, which is R1–R3–R5–R6. Listing 14.5 shows the configuration and status of the path with R3 included as a single loose hop.

Figure 14.12 LSP path forced through node R3.

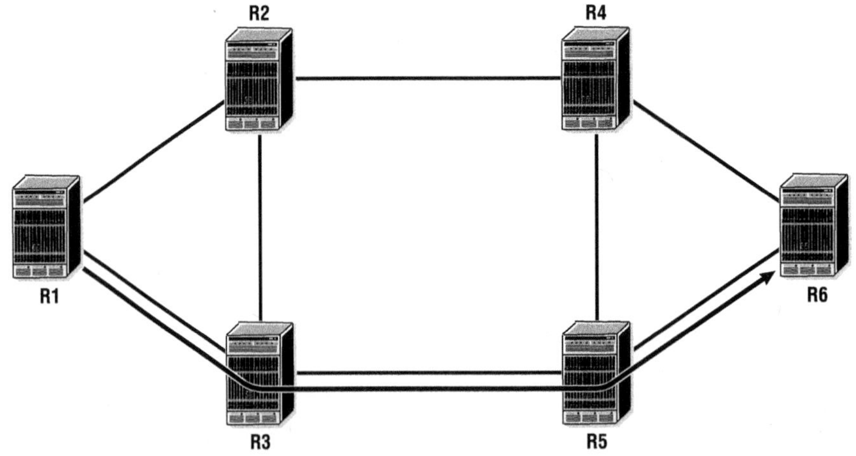

Listing 14.5 LSP path with a single loose hop

```
*A:R1>config>router>mpls# info
----------------------------------------------
            interface "system"
            exit
            interface "toR2"
            exit
            interface "toR3"
            exit
            path "one_loose"
                hop 5 10.10.10.3 loose
                no shutdown
            exit
            lsp "toR6"
                to 10.10.10.6
                primary "one_loose"
                exit
                no shutdown
            exit
            no shutdown
----------------------------------------------
*A:R1>config>router>mpls# show router mpls lsp "toR6" path detail

=======================================================================
MPLS LSP toR6 Path  (Detail)
=======================================================================
Legend :
    @ - Detour Available              # - Detour In Use
    b - Bandwidth Protected           n - Node Protected
    s - Soft Preemption
=======================================================================
-----------------------------------------------------------------------
LSP toR6 Path one_loose
-----------------------------------------------------------------------
LSP Name     : toR6                          Path LSP ID : 36494
From         : 10.10.10.1                    To          : 10.10.10.6
Adm State    : Up                            Oper State  : Up
Path Name    : one_loose                     Path Type   : Primary
Path Admin   : Up                            Path Oper   : Up
```

(continued)

Listing 14.5 *(continued)*

```
OutInterface: 1/1/1                          Out Label     : 131070
Path Up Time: 0d 00:00:20                    Path Dn Time: 0d 00:00:00
Retry Limit : 0                              Retry Timer : 30 sec
RetryAttempt: 0                              NextRetryIn : 0 sec
SetupPriori*: 7                              Hold Priori*: 0
Preference  : n/a
Bandwidth   : No Reservation                 Oper Bw     : 0 Mbps
Hop Limit   : 255                            Class Type  : 0
Backup CT   : None
MainCT Retry: n/a                            MainCT Retry: 0
    Rem     :                                    Limit   :
Oper CT     : 0
Record Route: Record                         Record Label: Record
Oper MTU    : 9198                           Neg MTU     : 9198
Adaptive    : Enabled                        Oper Metric : 65535
Include Grps:                                Exclude Grps:
None                                        None
Path Trans  : 3                              CSPF Queries: 0
Failure Code: noError                        Failure Node: n/a
ExplicitHops:
    10.10.10.3
Actual Hops :
    10.1.3.1(10.10.10.1)                     Record Label    : N/A
 -> 10.1.3.3(10.10.10.3)                     Record Label    : 131070
 -> 10.3.5.5(10.10.10.5)                     Record Label    : 131070
 -> 10.5.6.6(10.10.10.6)                     Record Label    : 131064
ResigEligib*: False
LastResignal: n/a                            CSPF Metric : 0
===============================================================================
* indicates that the corresponding row element may have been truncated.
```

The *Actual Hops* field of the output in Listing 14.5 shows the path that was taken by the LSP. This information is taken from the record route object (RRO) from the Resv message that defines the LSP. *Explicit Hops* contains the hops that were specified for the path.

In this example, only one node, R3, was specified as a loose hop. This means that the Path message is free to take the best route to R3 as selected by the IGP and then the best route from R3 to the LSP egress. If the network topology changes, the path will be resignaled along the new path determined by the IGP. The only constraint is that the path must travel through node R3. If this is not possible in the topology, the path will not become operational.

The path can be as strictly or loosely defined as desired. It is not necessary to specify the egress node in the path—the Path message will be routed to the egress from the last hop specified in the path. Also, because the path parameter really represents constraints on the LSP, it is possible to use the same path to define multiple LSPs, even if they do not share the same egress. Listing 14.6 shows a second LSP to router R4 defined using the same path.

Listing 14.6 Two different LSPs using the same path definition

```
*A:R1>config>router>mpls# info
----------------------------------------------
            interface "system"
            exit
            interface "toR2"
            exit
            interface "toR3"
            exit
            path "one_loose"
                hop 5 10.10.10.3 loose
                no shutdown
            exit
            lsp "toR6"
                to 10.10.10.6
                primary "one_loose"
                exit
                no shutdown
            exit
            lsp "toR4"
                to 10.10.10.4
                primary "one_loose"
                exit
                no shutdown
            exit
            no shutdown
----------------------------------------------
```

(continued)

Listing 14.6 *(continued)*

```
*A:R1>config>router>mpls# show router mpls lsp

===============================================================================
MPLS LSPs (Originating)
===============================================================================
LSP Name                    To                  Fastfail     Adm    Opr
                                                Config
-------------------------------------------------------------------------------
toR6                        10.10.10.6          No           Up     Up
toR4                        10.10.10.4          No           Up     Up
-------------------------------------------------------------------------------
LSPs : 2
===============================================================================
```

Explicit Route Object

When an LSP path contains specific hops, the head end router creates an EXPLICIT_ROUTE object (ERO) in the Path message that carries the constraints for the path. Listing 14.7 shows the output of a debug capture of the Path message sent from R1. The router has also specified the next downstream hop (as chosen by the IGP) in the ERO and the tail end node of the LSP.

Listing 14.7 Path message sent by R1 with one loose hop defined

```
*A:R1# configure log log-id 11
*A:R1>config>log>log-id$ from debug-trace
*A:R1>config>log>log-id$ to session
*A:R1>config>log>log-id$ exit
*A:R1# debug router rsvp packet path detail

74 2011/01/11 12:33:46.02 UTC MINOR: DEBUG #2001 Base RSVP
"RSVP: PATH Msg
Send PATH From:10.10.10.1, To:10.10.10.6
          TTL:255, Checksum:0xe239, Flags:0x0
Session     - EndPt:10.10.10.6, TunnId:2, ExtTunnId:10.10.10.1
SessAttr    - Name:toR6::one_loose
```

```
               SetupPri:7, HoldPri:0, Flags:0x6
RSVPHop      - Addr:10.1.3.1, LIH:3
TimeValue    - RefreshPeriod:30
SendTempl    - Sender:10.10.10.1, LspId:36494
SendTSpec    - Ctype:QOS, CDR:0.000 bps, PBS:0.000 bps, PDR:infinity
               MPU:20, MTU:9198
LabelReq     - IfType:General, L3ProtID:2048
RRO          - IpAddr:10.1.3.1, Flags:0x0
ERO          - Prefix:10.1.3.3/32, Type:Loose
               Prefix:10.10.10.3/32, Type:Loose
               Prefix:10.10.10.6/32, Type:Loose
"
```

Router R3 removes the first hop from the ERO and creates a new Path message with a new ERO to transmit to R5, as shown in Listing 14.8.

Listing 14.8 Path message from R3 containing ERO

```
11 2011/01/11 12:49:38.74 UTC MINOR: DEBUG #2001 Base RSVP
"RSVP: PATH Msg
Send PATH From:10.10.10.1, To:10.10.10.6
          TTL:254, Checksum:0x6438, Flags:0x0
Session      - EndPt:10.10.10.6, TunnId:2, ExtTunnId:10.10.10.1
SessAttr     - Name:toR6::one_loose
               SetupPri:7, HoldPri:0, Flags:0x6
RSVPHop      - Addr:10.3.5.3, LIH:4
TimeValue    - RefreshPeriod:30
SendTempl    - Sender:10.10.10.1, LspId:36494
SendTSpec    - Ctype:QOS, CDR:0.000 bps, PBS:0.000 bps, PDR:infinity
               MPU:20, MTU:9198
LabelReq     - IfType:General, L3ProtID:2048
RRO          - IpAddr:10.3.5.3, Flags:0x0
               IpAddr:10.1.3.1, Flags:0x0
ERO          - Prefix:10.3.5.5/32, Type:Loose
               Prefix:10.10.10.6/32, Type:Loose
"
```

R5 also removes the first hop from the ERO and builds a Path message for transmission to R6 (Listing 14.9). Notice how the RRO is also being built as the Path message progresses on the LSP path.

Listing 14.9 Path message from R5 with ERO

```
14 2011/01/11 13:03:13.85 UTC MINOR: DEBUG #2001 Base RSVP
"RSVP: PATH Msg
Send PATH From:10.10.10.1, To:10.10.10.6
          TTL:253, Checksum:0x3210, Flags:0x0
Session     - EndPt:10.10.10.6, TunnId:2, ExtTunnId:10.10.10.1
SessAttr    - Name:toR6::one_loose
              SetupPri:7, HoldPri:0, Flags:0x6
RSVPHop     - Addr:10.5.6.5, LIH:3
TimeValue   - RefreshPeriod:30
SendTempl   - Sender:10.10.10.1, LspId:36494
SendTSpec   - Ctype:QOS, CDR:0.000 bps, PBS:0.000 bps, PDR:infinity
              MPU:20, MTU:9198
LabelReq    - IfType:General, L3ProtID:2048
RRO         - IpAddr:10.5.6.5, Flags:0x0
              IpAddr:10.3.5.3, Flags:0x0
              IpAddr:10.1.3.1, Flags:0x0
ERO         - Prefix:10.5.6.6/32, Type:Loose
              Prefix:10.10.10.6/32, Type:Loose
"
```

Use of Strict Hops in the Path

A loose hop means that the path must traverse the specified hop but will take the best route chosen by the IGP to get there. A strict hop means that the hop must be the next immediate downstream hop. A path with strict hops from ingress to egress does not actually require an IGP, because all the hops are specified. However, if a strict hop is not the next downstream hop, the LSP will not become operational. Listing 14.10 shows an LSP from R1 with a loose hop to R3 and a strict hop to R4 in the topology of Figure 14.12. Because R4 is not immediately downstream from R3, the LSP is operationally down. If the first hop in a path is strict, it must be adjacent to the ingress node.

Listing 14.10 LSP with an unreachable strict hop

```
*A:R1>config>router>mpls# info
----------------------------------------------
            interface "system"
            exit
            interface "toR2"
            exit
            interface "toR3"
            exit
            path "one_loose-one_strict"
                hop 5 10.10.10.3 loose
                hop 10 10.10.10.4 strict
                no shutdown
            exit
            lsp "toR6"
                to 10.10.10.6
                primary "one_loose-one_strict"
                exit
                no shutdown
            exit
----------------------------------------------
*A:R1>config>router>mpls# show router mpls lsp "toR6" path detail

===============================================================================
MPLS LSP toR4 Path  (Detail)
===============================================================================
Legend :
    @ - Detour Available              # - Detour In Use
    b - Bandwidth Protected           n - Node Protected
    s - Soft Preemption
===============================================================================
-------------------------------------------------------------------------------
LSP toR6 Path one_loose-one_strict
-------------------------------------------------------------------------------
LSP Name    : toR6                               Path LSP ID : 2566
From        : 10.10.10.1                         To          : 10.10.10.6
Adm State   : Up                                 Oper State  : Down
Path Name   : one_loose-one_strict               Path Type   : Primary
Path Admin  : Up                                 Path Oper   : Down
OutInterface: n/a                                Out Label   : n/a
```

(continued)

Listing 14.10 *(continued)*

```
Path Up Time: 0d 00:00:00                        Path Dn Time: 0d 00:01:35

... output omitted ...

Failure Code: badNode                               Failure Node: 10.1.3.3
ExplicitHops:
    10.10.10.3      -> 10.10.10.4
Actual Hops :
    No Hops Specified
ResigEligib*: False
LastResignal: n/a                                   CSPF Metric : 0
==============================================================================
* indicates that the corresponding row element may have been truncated.
```

The show router mpls lsp path detail command shows a *Failure Code* and a *Failure Node* that are taken from the ERROR object in the PathErr message. Listing 14.11 contains debug output showing the Path message sent by R1 and the PathErr message it receives from R3.

Listing 14.11 Path and PathErr messages from a bad path

```
22 2011/01/11 18:18:00.02 UTC MINOR: DEBUG #2001 Base RSVP
"RSVP: PATH Msg
Send PATH From:10.10.10.1, To:10.10.10.6
          TTL:255, Checksum:0xe5e8, Flags:0x0
Session     - EndPt:10.10.10.6, TunnId:9, ExtTunnId:10.10.10.1
SessAttr    - Name:toR6-2::one_loose-one_strict
              SetupPri:7, HoldPri:0, Flags:0x6
RSVPHop     - Addr:10.1.3.1, LIH:3
TimeValue   - RefreshPeriod:30
SendTempl   - Sender:10.10.10.1, LspId:2566
SendTSpec   - Ctype:QOS, CDR:0.000 bps, PBS:0.000 bps, PDR:infinity
              MPU:20, MTU:9198
LabelReq    - IfType:General, L3ProtID:2048
RRO         - IpAddr:10.1.3.1, Flags:0x0
ERO         - Prefix:10.1.3.3/32, Type:Loose
              Prefix:10.10.10.3/32, Type:Loose
```

```
            Prefix:10.10.10.4/32, Type:Strict
            Prefix:10.10.10.6/32, Type:Loose
"

23 2011/01/11 18:18:00.03 UTC MINOR: DEBUG #2001 Base RSVP
"RSVP: PATHERR Msg
Recv PATHERR From:10.1.3.3, To:10.1.3.1
            TTL:255, Checksum:0x5b62, Flags:0x0
Session     - EndPt:10.10.10.6, TunnId:9, ExtTunnId:10.10.10.1
ErrorSpec   - ErrNode:10.1.3.3, Flags:0x0, ErrCode:24, ErrValue:2
SendTempl   - Sender:10.10.10.1, LspId:2566
SendTSpec   - Ctype:QOS, CDR:0.000 bps, PBS:0.000 bps, PDR:infinity
            MPU:20, MTU:9198
"
```

Use of CSPF in the LSP

In most applications of traffic engineering, the constrained shortest path first (CSPF) algorithm is an important tool in the calculation of the path of the LSP. When `cspf` is specified in the `configure router mpls lsp` context, the router will first use the CSPF algorithm to calculate a path for the LSP that meets the constraints. The path is then encoded in the ERO as a series of strict hops.

If CSPF is unable to find a route to the destination, the Path message is never sent. Listing 14.12 shows the configuration of the LSP from Listing 14.10 with CSPF enabled.

Listing 14.12 CSPF enabled on a path with strict hops

```
*A:R1>config>router>mpls# info
----------------------------------------------
            interface "system"
            exit
            interface "toR2"
            exit
            interface "toR3"
            exit
            path "one_loose-one_strict"
```

(continued)

Listing 14.12 *(continued)*

```
                hop 5 10.10.10.3 loose
                hop 10 10.10.10.4 strict
                no shutdown
            exit
            lsp "toR6"
                to 10.10.10.6
                cspf
                primary "one_loose-one_strict"
                exit
                no shutdown
            exit
            no shutdown
----------------------------------------------
```

In the example, R4 is specified as a strict hop that is not reachable from the previous node. The CSPF calculation on the head end fails, and no Path message is sent. As seen in Listing 14.13, the *Failure Code* is `noCspfRouteToDestination`, and the *Failure Node* is the head end router.

Listing 14.13 Path error on a strict hop LSP with CSPF

```
*A:R1>config>router>mpls# show router mpls lsp "toR6" path detail

===============================================================================
MPLS LSP toR6 Path  (Detail)
===============================================================================
Legend :
    @ - Detour Available              # - Detour In Use
    b - Bandwidth Protected           n - Node Protected
    s - Soft Preemption
===============================================================================
-------------------------------------------------------------------------------
LSP toR6 Path one_loose-one_strict
-------------------------------------------------------------------------------
LSP Name     : toR6                         Path LSP ID : 58882
From         : 10.10.10.1                   To          : 10.10.10.6
Adm State    : Up                           Oper State  : Down
Path Name    : one_loose-one_strict         Path Type   : Primary
```

```
Path Admin   : Up                                 Path Oper    : Down
OutInterface: n/a                                 Out Label    : n/a
Path Up Time: 0d 00:00:00                         Path Dn Time: 0d 00:00:29

... output omitted ...

Failure Code: noCspfRouteToDestination            Failure Node: 10.10.10.1
ExplicitHops:
    10.10.10.3      -> 10.10.10.4
Actual Hops :
    No Hops Specified
ComputedHops:
    No Hops Specified
ResigEligib*: False
LastResignal: n/a                                    CSPF Metric : 0
=======================================================================
* indicates that the corresponding row element may have been truncated.
```

The topology for the above examples is shown in Figure 14.13. Listing 14.14 shows the LSP configured with another strict hop so that there is a valid route to the destination.

Figure 14.13 Network with a strict hop LSP.

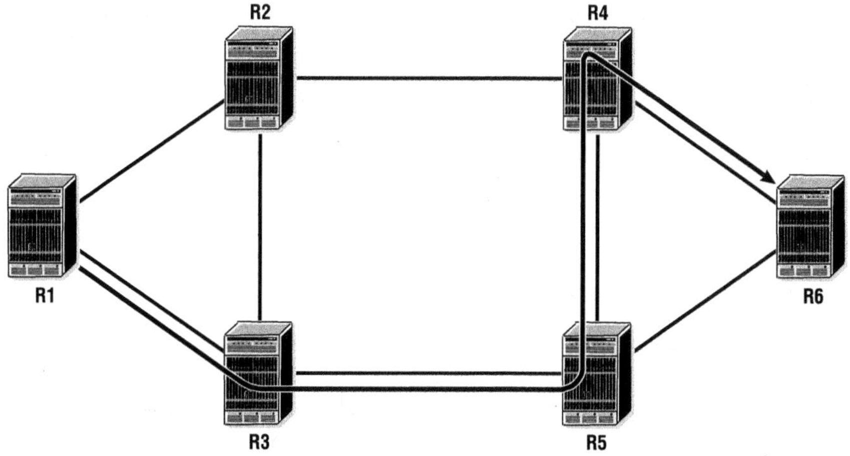

Listing 14.14 Valid path with strict hops

```
*A:R1>config>router>mpls# info
----------------------------------------------
            interface "system"
            exit
            interface "toR2"
            exit
            interface "toR3"
            exit
            path "one_loose-one_strict"
                hop 5 10.10.10.3 loose
                hop 7 10.10.10.5 strict
                hop 10 10.10.10.4 strict
                no shutdown
            exit
            lsp "toR6"
                to 10.10.10.6
                cspf
                primary "one_loose-one_strict"
                exit
                no shutdown
            exit
            no shutdown
----------------------------------------------
```

In the output of the `show router mpls lsp path detail` command shown in Listing 14.15, the different hops fields have the following meaning:

- **Explicit Hops**—Specific hops included in the path configuration
- **Computed Hops**—Hops calculated by the CSPF algorithm and used in the ERO
- **Actual Hops**—Hops traversed by the Path and Resv messages as recorded in the RRO

Listing 14.15 Path detail

```
*A:R1>config>router>mpls# show router mpls lsp "toR6" path detail

===============================================================================
MPLS LSP toR6 Path  (Detail)
```

```
===============================================================================
Legend :
    @ - Detour Available                # - Detour In Use
    b - Bandwidth Protected             n - Node Protected
    s - Soft Preemption
===============================================================================
-------------------------------------------------------------------------------
LSP toR6 Path one_loose-one_strict
-------------------------------------------------------------------------------
LSP Name     : toR6                         Path LSP ID : 58882
From         : 10.10.10.1                   To          : 10.10.10.6
Adm State    : Up                           Oper State  : Up
Path Name    : one_loose-one_strict         Path Type   : Primary
Path Admin   : Up                           Path Oper   : Up
OutInterface: 1/1/1                         Out Label   : 131071

... output omitted ...

Failure Code: noError                       Failure Node: n/a
ExplicitHops:
    10.10.10.3      -> 10.10.10.5      -> 10.10.10.4
Actual Hops :
    10.1.3.1(10.10.10.1)                    Record Label    : N/A
 -> 10.1.3.3(10.10.10.3)                    Record Label    : 131071
 -> 10.3.5.5(10.10.10.5)                    Record Label    : 131071
 -> 10.4.5.4(10.10.10.4)                    Record Label    : 131068
 -> 10.4.6.6(10.10.10.6)                    Record Label    : 131065
ComputedHops:
    10.1.3.1        -> 10.1.3.3        -> 10.3.5.5        -> 10.4.5.4
 -> 10.4.6.6
ResigEligib*: False
LastResignal: n/a                             CSPF Metric : 400
===============================================================================
* indicates that the corresponding row element may have been truncated.
```

Listing 14.16 shows the debug message of the Path message sent from R1. Note that even though the first hop, `10.10.10.3`, is defined as a loose hop, only strict hops appear in the ERO. This is because CSPF is used on the LSP to calculate the route beforehand, and all hops in the ERO are specified as strict as a result.

Listing 14.16 Path message containing ERO from CSPF LSP

```
*A:R1# show debug
debug
    router "Base"
        rsvp
            packet
                path detail
            exit
        exit
    exit
exit
3 2011/01/14 11:36:41.02 UTC MINOR: DEBUG #2001 Base RSVP
"RSVP: PATH Msg
Send PATH From:10.10.10.1, To:10.10.10.6
          TTL:255, Checksum:0xc535, Flags:0x0
Session     - EndPt:10.10.10.6, TunnId:14, ExtTunnId:10.10.10.1
SessAttr    - Name:toR6::one_loose-one_strict
              SetupPri:7, HoldPri:0, Flags:0x6
RSVPHop     - Addr:10.1.3.1, LIH:3
TimeValue   - RefreshPeriod:30
SendTempl   - Sender:10.10.10.1, LspId:58882
SendTSpec   - Ctype:QOS, CDR:0.000 bps, PBS:0.000 bps, PDR:infinity
              MPU:20, MTU:9198
LabelReq    - IfType:General, L3ProtID:2048
RRO         - IpAddr:10.1.3.1, Flags:0x0
ERO         - Prefix:10.1.3.3/32, Type:Strict
              Prefix:10.3.5.5/32, Type:Strict
              Prefix:10.4.5.4/32, Type:Strict
              Prefix:10.4.6.6/32, Type:Strict
"
```

Using tools perform to Troubleshoot LSPs

We have seen how the CSPF calculation is used to create a path of strict hops in the ERO message for setting up an LSP path. The `tools perform router mpls cspf` command is a useful tool to validate a TE configuration and troubleshoot problems establishing a CSPF LSP.

The `tools perform` command can be used with many of the constraints that can be applied to an LSP to determine the path that will be taken by the LSP. Listing 14.17 shows the use of `tools perform` to find the path from R1 to R5 that does not include node R3.

Listing 14.17 Use of tools perform to exclude a specific node

```
*A:R1# tools perform router mpls cspf to 10.10.10.5
exclude-node 10.10.10.3
Req CSPF for all ECMP paths
    from: this node to: 10.10.10.5 w/(no Diffserv) class: 0 ,
    setup Priority 7, Hold Priority 0 TE Class: 7

CSPF Path
To          : 10.10.10.5
Path 1      : (cost 300)
    Start: 10.10.10.1
    Egr:   10.1.2.1        -> Ingr:   10.1.2.2         (met 100)
    Egr:   10.2.4.2        -> Ingr:   10.2.4.4         (met 100)
    Egr:   10.4.5.4        -> Ingr:   10.4.5.5         (met 100)
    End:   10.10.10.5
```

Because the CSPF calculation uses the TE database shared by all routers in the network, the command can be used on one node to find the route that would be chosen between two remote nodes. In Listing 14.18 `tools perform` is used on router R1 to find the route for an LSP between R3 and R4.

Listing 14.18 Using tools perform to find the route between R3 and R4

```
*A:R1# tools perform router mpls cspf to 10.10.10.4 from 10.10.10.3
Req CSPF for all ECMP paths
    from: 10.10.10.3 to: 10.10.10.4 w/(no Diffserv) class: 0 ,
    setup Priority 7, Hold Priority 0 TE Class: 7
```

(continued)

Listing 14.18 *(continued)*

```
CSPF Path
To        : 10.10.10.4
From      : 10.10.10.3
Path 1    : (cost 200)
    Start: 10.10.10.3
    Egr:   10.2.3.3      -> Ingr:   10.2.3.2      (met 100)
    Egr:   10.2.4.2      -> Ingr:   10.2.4.4      (met 100)
    End:   10.10.10.4
```

14.7 More Control over Path Selection

We've seen how the path attribute can be used to control the path of an LSP. There are additional tools that can be used in conjunction with CSPF calculation to influence path selection. The techniques described in this section include:

- Specifying a hop limit for the LSP
- Using TE metrics to influence route selection
- Using administrative groups

For all of these TE techniques, `cspf` must be specified on the LSP. CSPF is used to calculate the route that is included in the ERO as a series of strict hops. The Path message must then be signaled along this path.

Specifying Hop Limits

One tool for traffic engineering is the ability to specify the maximum number of hops for the path. This is useful in a situation such as the one shown in Figure 14.14. The path desired for the LSP is not necessarily the best path chosen by the IGP but is one that satisfies the requirement of a maximum of three hops. The path can be selected by specifying a hop count limit in the LSP, as shown in Listing 14.19. The `hop-limit` really indicates the number of routers on the path, and the ingress and egress LERs are included in the hop count. Notice that the CSPF metric value is `1100`, as expected.

Figure 14.14 LSP signaled on a path with a hop-limit of 3.

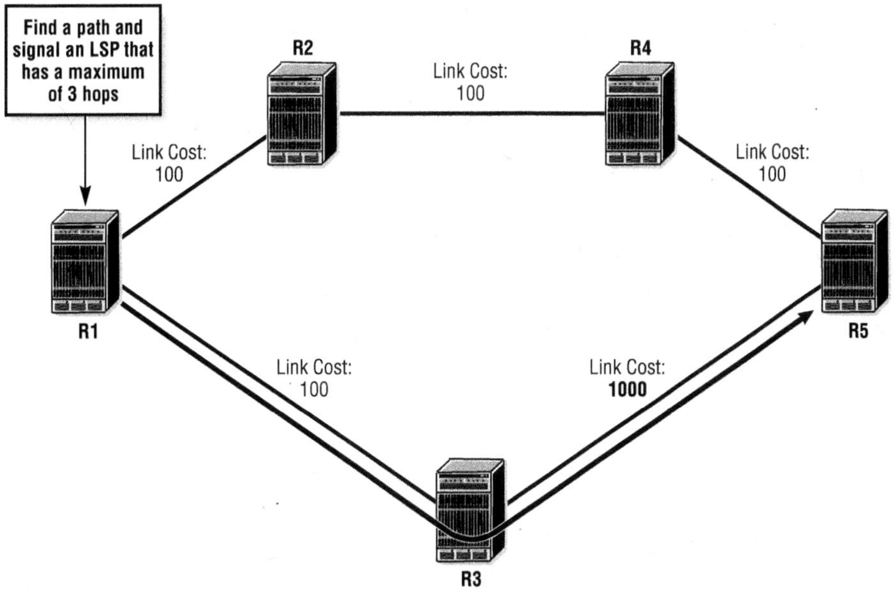

Listing 14.19 LSP defined with a hop limit

```
*A:R1>config>router>mpls# info
----------------------------------------------
            interface "system"
            exit
            interface "toR2"
            exit
            interface "toR3"
            exit
            path "loose"
                no shutdown
            exit
            lsp "toR5"
                to 10.10.10.5
                cspf
                hop-limit 3
                primary "loose"
                exit
```

(continued)

Listing 14.19 *(continued)*

```
                no shutdown
            exit
            no shutdown
----------------------------------------------
*A:R1>config>router>mpls# show router mpls lsp "toR5" path detail

========================================================================
MPLS LSP toR5 Path  (Detail)
========================================================================
Legend :
    @ - Detour Available              # - Detour In Use
    b - Bandwidth Protected           n - Node Protected
    s - Soft Preemption
========================================================================
------------------------------------------------------------------------
LSP toR5 Path loose
------------------------------------------------------------------------
LSP Name    : toR5                           Path LSP ID : 40492
From        : 10.10.10.1                     To          : 10.10.10.5
Adm State   : Up                             Oper State  : Up
Path Name   : loose                          Path Type   : Primary
Path Admin  : Up                             Path Oper   : Up
OutInterface: 1/1/1                          Out Label   : 131070
Path Up Time: 0d 00:00:21                    Path Dn Time: 0d 00:00:00

... output omitted ...

Record Route: Record                         Record Label: Record
Oper MTU    : 9198                           Neg MTU     : 9198
Adaptive    : Enabled                        Oper Metric : 1100
Include Grps:                                Exclude Grps:
None                                       None
Path Trans  : 21                             CSPF Queries: 97
Failure Code: noError                        Failure Node: n/a
ExplicitHops:
    No Hops Specified
Actual Hops :
    10.1.3.1(10.10.10.1)                     Record Label    : N/A
```

```
 -> 10.1.3.3(10.10.10.3)                          Record Label    : 131070
 -> 10.3.5.5(10.10.10.5)                          Record Label    : 131070
ComputedHops:
    10.1.3.1         -> 10.1.3.3        -> 10.3.5.5
ResigEligib*: False
LastResignal: n/a                                    CSPF Metric : 1100
===============================================================================
* indicates that the corresponding row element may have been truncated.
```

From the `route-table` and a `traceroute` as shown in Listing 14.20, it can be seen that a different route with four hops is chosen by the IGP.

Listing 14.20 Four-hop route selected by the IGP

```
*A:R1>config>router>mpls# show router route-table 10.10.10.5

===============================================================================
Route Table (Router: Base)
===============================================================================
Dest Prefix                                  Type     Proto    Age          Pref
       Next Hop[Interface Name]                                    Metric
-------------------------------------------------------------------------------
10.10.10.5/32                                Remote   OSPF     01d12h58m    10
       10.1.2.2                                                    300
-------------------------------------------------------------------------------
No. of Routes: 1
===============================================================================
*A:R1>config>router>mpls>lsp# traceroute 10.10.10.5
traceroute to 10.10.10.5, 30 hops max, 40 byte packets
  1  10.1.2.2 (10.1.2.2)     2.00 ms  1.72 ms  1.69 ms
  2  10.2.4.4 (10.2.4.4)     2.36 ms  2.28 ms  2.30 ms
  3  10.10.10.5 (10.10.10.5)     4.52 ms  2.55 ms  2.54 ms
```

Configuring a TE Metric

Traffic engineering also provides the ability to configure a separate, TE metric on the interface. This can be used to define a distinct topology for a TE application. For example, if the intention is to avoid the path R1–R2–R4–R5 in Figure 14.15, a TE metric can be configured to influence route selection as shown in Listing 14.21.

Figure 14.15 Path selection using a TE metric.

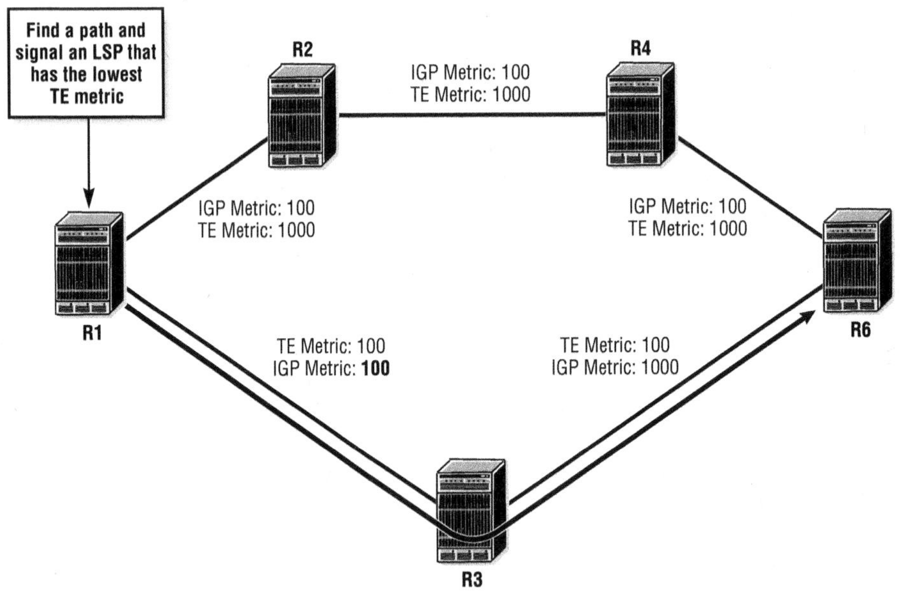

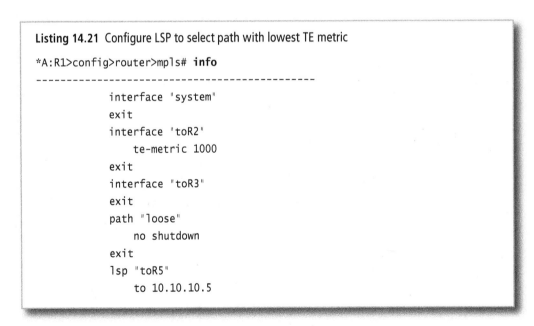

Listing 14.21 Configure LSP to select path with lowest TE metric

```
*A:R1>config>router>mpls# info
----------------------------------------------
            interface "system"
            exit
            interface "toR2"
                te-metric 1000
            exit
            interface "toR3"
            exit
            path "loose"
                no shutdown
            exit
            lsp "toR5"
                to 10.10.10.5
```

```
                cspf use-te-metric
                primary "loose"
                exit
                no shutdown
            exit
            no shutdown
----------------------------------------------
*A:R1>config>router>mpls# show router mpls lsp "toR5" path detail

=======================================================================
MPLS LSP toR5 Path  (Detail)
=======================================================================
Legend :
    @ - Detour Available              # - Detour In Use
    b - Bandwidth Protected           n - Node Protected
    s - Soft Preemption
=======================================================================
-----------------------------------------------------------------------
LSP toR5 Path loose
-----------------------------------------------------------------------
LSP Name     : toR5                          Path LSP ID : 40496
From         : 10.10.10.1                    To          : 10.10.10.5
Adm State    : Up                            Oper State  : Up
Path Name    : loose                         Path Type   : Primary
Path Admin   : Up                            Path Oper   : Up
OutInterface: 1/1/1                          Out Label   : 131071

... output omitted ...

Failure Code: noError                        Failure Node: n/a
ExplicitHops:
    No Hops Specified
Actual Hops :
    10.1.3.1(10.10.10.1)                     Record Label    : N/A
 -> 10.1.3.3(10.10.10.3)                     Record Label    : 131071
 -> 10.3.5.5(10.10.10.5)                     Record Label    : 131070
ComputedHops:
    10.1.3.1        -> 10.1.3.3        -> 10.3.5.5
ResigEligib*: False
```

(continued)

Listing 14.21 *(continued)*

```
LastResignal: n/a                               CSPF Metric : 200
===============================================================================
* indicates that the corresponding row element may have been truncated.

*A:R1>config>router>mpls# show router route-table 10.10.10.5

===============================================================================
Route Table (Router: Base)
===============================================================================
Dest Prefix                                Type    Proto    Age          Pref
       Next Hop[Interface Name]                                   Metric
-------------------------------------------------------------------------------
10.10.10.5/32                              Remote  OSPF     01d16h15m    10
       10.1.2.2                                                   300
-------------------------------------------------------------------------------
No. of Routes: 1
===============================================================================
*A:R1>config>router>mpls#
```

Notice that the TE metric is set on the interface in the `configure router mpls` context and that `use-te-metric` is a parameter on the `cspf` command. The LSP is set up on the path through R3 and shows a CSPF metric of 200. The IGP route is still through R2 and R4 and shows a metric of 300.

Looking at the LSAs in Listing 14.22, we can see from the Router LSA on R1 that the IGP metric is still 100 for the link to R2. However, the Type 10 LSA for that link shows a value of `1000` for the TE metric.

Listing 14.22 Metric in Type 10 LSA is different from metric in the Router LSA.

```
*A:R1>config>router>mpls# show router ospf database 10.10.10.1 detail

===============================================================================
OSPF Link State Database (Type : All) (Detailed)
===============================================================================
-------------------------------------------------------------------------------
Router LSA for Area 0.0.0.0
-------------------------------------------------------------------------------
```

```
Area Id              : 0.0.0.0              Adv Router Id      : 10.10.10.1
Link State Id        : 10.10.10.1 (168430081)
LSA Type             : Router
Sequence No          : 0x800000b2           Checksum           : 0x7ebc
Age                  : 1502                 Length             : 84
Options              : E
Flags                : None                 Link Count         : 5
Link Type (1)        : Point To Point
Nbr Rtr Id (1)       : 10.10.10.2           I/F Address (1)    : 10.1.2.1
No of TOS (1)        : 0                    Metric-0 (1)       : 100
Link Type (2)        : Stub Network
Network (2)          : 10.1.2.0             Mask (2)           : 255.255.255.224
No of TOS (2)        : 0                    Metric-0 (2)       : 100
Link Type (3)        : Point To Point
Nbr Rtr Id (3)       : 10.10.10.3           I/F Address (3)    : 10.1.3.1
No of TOS (3)        : 0                    Metric-0 (3)       : 100
Link Type (4)        : Stub Network
Network (4)          : 10.1.3.0             Mask (4)           : 255.255.255.224
No of TOS (4)        : 0                    Metric-0 (4)       : 100
Link Type (5)        : Stub Network
Network (5)          : 10.10.10.1           Mask (5)           : 255.255.255.255
No of TOS (5)        : 0                    Metric-0 (5)       : 0
========================================================================
*A:R1>config>router>mpls# show router ospf opaque-database 1.0.0.2
adv-router 10.10.10.1 detail

========================================================================
OSPF Opaque Link State Database (Type : All) (Detailed)
========================================================================
------------------------------------------------------------------------
Opaque LSA
------------------------------------------------------------------------
Area Id              : 0.0.0.0                 Adv Router Id     : 10.10.10.1
Link State Id        : 1.0.0.2                 LSA Type          : Area Opaque
Sequence No          : 0x800000b1              Checksum          : 0x779c
Age                  : 1354                    Length            : 124
Options              :  E
Advertisement        :
     LINK INFO TLV  (0002) Len 100 :
```

(continued)

Listing 14.22 *(continued)*

```
        Sub-TLV: 1      Len: 1      LINK_TYPE     : 1
        Sub-TLV: 2      Len: 4      LINK_ID       : 10.10.10.2
        Sub-TLV: 3      Len: 4      LOC_IP_ADDR   : 10.1.2.1
        Sub-TLV: 4      Len: 4      REM_IP_ADDR   : 10.1.2.2
        Sub-TLV: 5      Len: 4      TE_METRIC     : 1000
        Sub-TLV: 6      Len: 4      MAX_BDWTH     : 1000000 Kbps
        Sub-TLV: 7      Len: 4      RSRVBL_BDWTH  : 1000000 Kbps
        Sub-TLV: 8      Len: 32     UNRSRVD_CLS0  :
          P0: 1000000 Kbps P1: 1000000 Kbps P2: 1000000 Kbps P3:
 1000000 Kbps
          P4: 1000000 Kbps P5: 1000000 Kbps P6: 1000000 Kbps P7:
 1000000 Kbps
        Sub-TLV: 9      Len: 4      ADMIN_GROUP   : 0 None

===============================================================================
*A:R1>config>router>mpls#
```

Using Administrative Groups

Administrative groups (*admin groups*) provide an additional level of control over the selection of network links in the CSPF algorithm. Also known as *link coloring*, admin groups are assigned by the network administrator and can be used to categorize network interfaces in a wide variety of ways.

The `admin group` attribute is carried as a 32-bit mask in the OSPF Type 10 LSA or the IS-IS LSP. The bits in the mask are set depending on which admin group the interface is assigned to. An interface can be assigned to multiple admin groups, one admin group, or none (none by default). Although we often refer to the technique as link coloring, the assignment is actually made to the interface (the same as the TE metric). A link can thus be assigned to one set of admin groups at one end, and another set at the other end.

On the 7750 SR, admin groups are first defined in the `configure router mpls` context and then assigned to the interface in the `mpls` context, as shown in Listing 14.23. Any name can be used to identify the `admin-group`, and the value is 0 to 31. Zero corresponds to the lowest-order bit.

Listing 14.23 Definition of admin groups on MPLS interfaces

```
*A:R1>config>router>mpls# info
----------------------------------------------
            admin-group "blue" 1
            admin-group "green" 2
            admin-group "red" 0
            admin-group "yellow" 3
            interface "system"
            exit
            interface "toR2"
                admin-group "green"
            exit
            interface "toR3"
                admin-group "blue"
                admin-group "red"
                admin-group "yellow"
            exit
            no shutdown
----------------------------------------------
```

In the example shown in Listing 14.24, four groups are defined. The `admin-group "green"`, which has a value of `2`, is assigned to the interface `toR2`. Because this is the third lowest bit, the encoding in the LSA is binary 00000000 00000000 00000000 00000100, or decimal 4. The admin groups "red", "blue," and "yellow" are assigned to the interface `toR3`. These correspond to the first, second, and fourth bits. The binary value is 00000000 00000000 00000000 00001011, which is hexadecimal "b" or decimal 11. These values can be seen in the LSAs for the two interfaces in Listing 14.24. They are displayed as both hexadecimal and decimal values. Of course, it is essential that the use of admin groups be managed consistently across the network.

Listing 14.24 Admin group values in the Type 10 LSA

```
*A:R1>config>router>mpls# show router ospf opaque-database adv-router
10.10.10.1 detail

===============================================================================
OSPF Opaque Link State Database (Type : All) (Detailed)
```

(continued)

Listing 14.24 *(continued)*

```
===============================================================================
-------------------------------------------------------------------------------
Opaque LSA
-------------------------------------------------------------------------------
Area Id          : 0.0.0.0              Adv Router Id    : 10.10.10.1
Link State Id    : 1.0.0.1              LSA Type         : Area Opaque
Sequence No      : 0x800000a1           Checksum         : 0xd09f
Age              : 864                  Length           : 28
Options          :  E
Advertisement    :
     ROUTER-ID TLV  (0001) Len   4 : 10.10.10.1
-------------------------------------------------------------------------------
Opaque LSA
-------------------------------------------------------------------------------
Area Id          : 0.0.0.0              Adv Router Id    : 10.10.10.1
Link State Id    : 1.0.0.2              LSA Type         : Area Opaque
Sequence No      : 0x800000be           Checksum         : 0xafda
Age              : 174                  Length           : 124
Options          :  E
Advertisement    :
     LINK INFO TLV  (0002) Len 100 :
       Sub-TLV: 1     Len: 1     LINK_TYPE    : 1
       Sub-TLV: 2     Len: 4     LINK_ID      : 10.10.10.2
       Sub-TLV: 3     Len: 4     LOC_IP_ADDR  : 10.1.2.1
       Sub-TLV: 4     Len: 4     REM_IP_ADDR  : 10.1.2.2
       Sub-TLV: 5     Len: 4     TE_METRIC    : 100
       Sub-TLV: 6     Len: 4     MAX_BDWTH    : 1000000 Kbps
       Sub-TLV: 7     Len: 4     RSRVBL_BDWTH : 1000000 Kbps
       Sub-TLV: 8     Len: 32    UNRSRVD_CLS0 :
         P0: 1000000 Kbps P1: 1000000 Kbps P2: 1000000 Kbps P3:
 1000000 Kbps
         P4: 1000000 Kbps P5: 1000000 Kbps P6: 1000000 Kbps P7:
 1000000 Kbps
       Sub-TLV: 9     Len: 4     ADMIN_GROUP  : 00000004 (4)

-------------------------------------------------------------------------------
Opaque LSA
-------------------------------------------------------------------------------
```

```
Area Id             : 0.0.0.0                Adv Router Id     : 10.10.10.1
Link State Id       : 1.0.0.3                LSA Type          : Area Opaque
Sequence No         : 0x8000013a             Checksum          : 0x13ee
Age                 : 49                     Length            : 124
Options             :  E
Advertisement       :
     LINK INFO TLV  (0002) Len 100 :
       Sub-TLV: 1     Len: 1     LINK_TYPE     : 1
       Sub-TLV: 2     Len: 4     LINK_ID       : 10.10.10.3
       Sub-TLV: 3     Len: 4     LOC_IP_ADDR   : 10.1.3.1
       Sub-TLV: 4     Len: 4     REM_IP_ADDR   : 10.1.3.3
       Sub-TLV: 5     Len: 4     TE_METRIC     : 100
       Sub-TLV: 6     Len: 4     MAX_BDWTH     : 1000000 Kbps
       Sub-TLV: 7     Len: 4     RSRVBL_BDWTH  : 1000000 Kbps
       Sub-TLV: 8     Len: 32    UNRSRVD_CLS0  :
         P0: 1000000 Kbps P1: 1000000 Kbps P2: 1000000 Kbps P3:
 1000000 Kbps
         P4: 1000000 Kbps P5: 1000000 Kbps P6: 1000000 Kbps P7:
 1000000 Kbps
       Sub-TLV: 9     Len: 4     ADMIN_GROUP   : 0000000b (11)

===============================================================================
*A:R1>config>router>mpls#
```

Admin groups give the network administrator extensive control over the path that will be chosen for an LSP. In Figure 14.16, the interface on R2 to R4 and the interface on R5 to R6 have been assigned to the admin group `green`.

Once the interfaces are assigned to admin groups, LSPs can be defined to either include or exclude one or more admin groups. If an LSP includes an admin group, all interfaces used for the LSP must be assigned to the group. If an LSP excludes an admin group, no links assigned to that group or groups can be used for the LSP.

The LSP in Figure 14.17 has been defined to exclude any links in the admin group `green`. In the CSPF calculation, any links belonging to this admin group are excluded, and the best path is calculated from the remaining topology.

Note that the admin group is assigned to the interface and thus can be different at either end of the link. If the interface on R5 to R3 was assigned to the `green` admin group, it would have no effect on this LSP because it goes in the other direction, from R3 to R5.

Figure 14.16 Network with admin groups assigned on two interfaces.

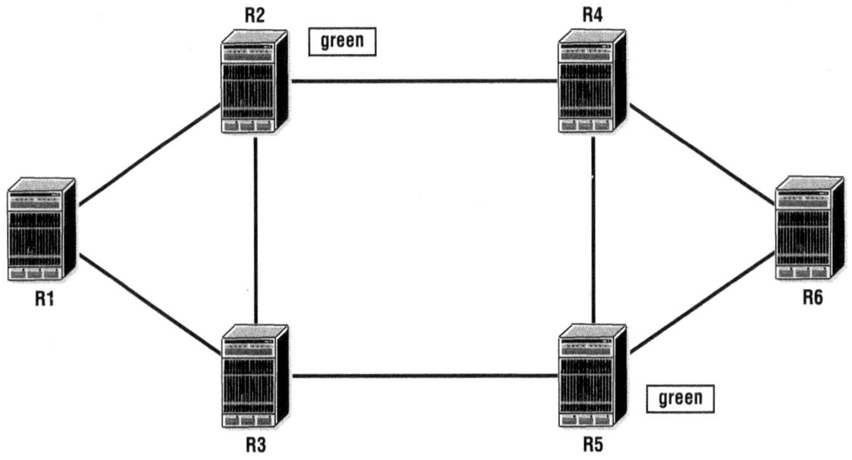

Figure 14.17 LSP that excludes "green" links.

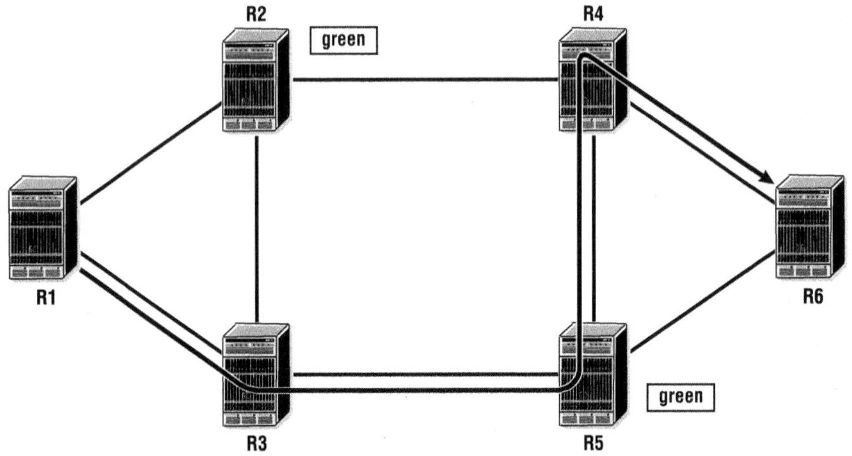

Care must be taken in the definition and use of admin groups. If a path cannot be found that meets the constraint, the LSP will not come up. Figure 14.18 shows the topology used for the CSPF calculation when an LSP is configured to include admin group `green`. Although the routers are all physically connected, the diagram shows only the links that match the constraint. Obviously, there is no possible path from R1 to R6 that satisfies this constraint.

Figure 14.18 Topology of links that include admin group "green."

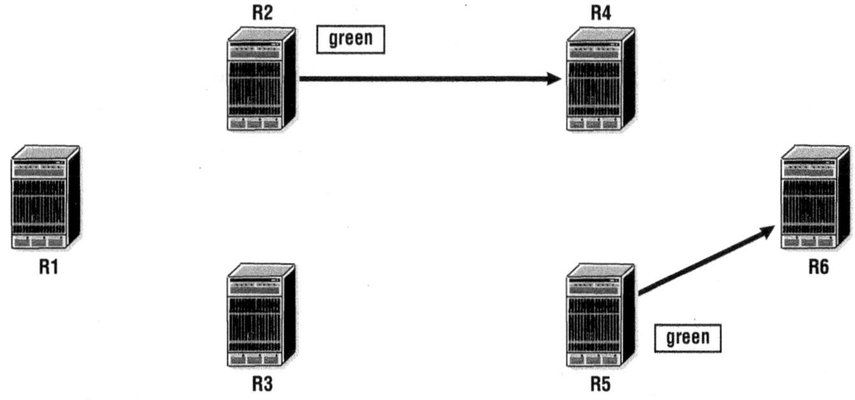

Using Admin Groups in a Ring Topology

A common use of admin groups is to create LSPs in a specific direction on a ring. For example, in the topology of Figure 14.19, all interfaces in the clockwise direction can be assigned to one admin group and the interfaces in the counterclockwise direction assigned to another. To force all LSPs in a clockwise direction, `include` or `exclude` the appropriate admin group in the configuration of the LSPs.

Figure 14.19 Ring topology created using admin groups.

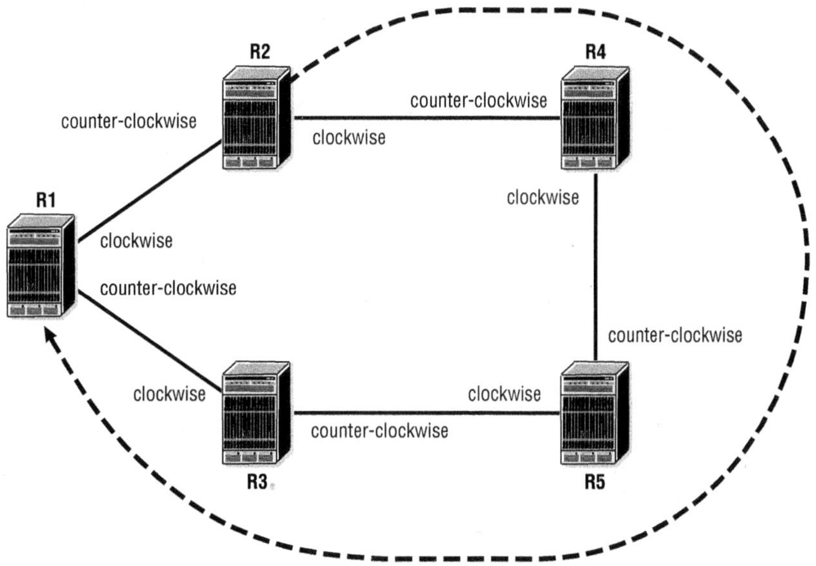

Listing 14.25 shows the configuration of the admin groups and LSP on router R1. Often, in more complex configurations, it is easier to achieve the desired behavior using `exclude` rather than `include`; therefore, we have used `exclude` in this example. Each router in the ring must have the same admin-group definition and have the appropriate interfaces assigned to the `clockwise` and `counter-clockwise` admin groups. The admin group `clockwise` could be used to define a secondary LSP (described in Chapter 16) traveling counterclockwise around the ring.

Listing 14.25 Configuration of admin groups to define a ring LSP

```
*A:R2# configure router mpls
*A:R2>config>router>mpls# info
----------------------------------------------
            admin-group "clockwise" 0
            admin-group "counter-clockwise" 1
            interface "system"
            exit
            interface "toR1"
                admin-group "counter-clockwise"
            exit
            interface "toR4"
                admin-group "clockwise"
            exit
            path "loose"
                no shutdown
            exit
            lsp "ring_toR1"
                to 10.10.10.1
                cspf
                primary "loose"
                    exclude "counter-clockwise"
                exit
                no shutdown
            exit
            no shutdown
----------------------------------------------
*A:R2>config>router>mpls# show router mpls lsp "ring_toR1" path detail

===============================================================================
```

```
MPLS LSP ring_toR1 Path  (Detail)
===============================================================================
Legend :
    @ - Detour Available                  # - Detour In Use
    b - Bandwidth Protected               n - Node Protected
    s - Soft Preemption
===============================================================================
-------------------------------------------------------------------------------
LSP ring_toR1 Path loose
-------------------------------------------------------------------------------
LSP Name     : ring_toR1                           Path LSP ID : 15362
From         : 10.10.10.2                          To          : 10.10.10.1
Adm State    : Up                                  Oper State  : Up
Path Name    : loose                               Path Type   : Primary
Path Admin   : Up                                  Path Oper   : Up
OutInterface: 1/1/3                                Out Label   : 131071

... output omitted ...

Include Grps:                                      Exclude Grps:
None                                             counter-clockwise
Path Trans   : 3                                   CSPF Queries: 1
Failure Code: noError                              Failure Node: n/a
ExplicitHops:
    No Hops Specified
Actual Hops :
    10.2.4.2(10.10.10.2)                           Record Label    : N/A
 -> 10.2.4.4(10.10.10.4)                           Record Label    : 131071
 -> 10.4.5.5(10.10.10.5)                           Record Label    : 131071
 -> 10.3.5.3(10.10.10.3)                           Record Label    : 131071
 -> 10.1.3.1(10.10.10.1)                           Record Label    : 131070
ComputedHops:
    10.2.4.2        -> 10.2.4.4        -> 10.4.5.5        -> 10.3.5.3
 -> 10.1.3.1
ResigEligib*: False
LastResignal: n/a                                    CSPF Metric : 400
===============================================================================
* indicates that the corresponding row element may have been truncated.
```

This type of ring could certainly be defined using only strict hops. The disadvantage is that there is less flexibility than with admin groups. If the topology changes—such as the addition or removal of a node—all the LSPs must be reconfigured. If the rings are defined with admin groups, it is possible to add a node without changing the LSP configuration or disrupting any services or traffic using the LSP.

Figure 14.20 shows a commonly deployed ring topology. R1 is a provider edge (PE) router in the central office (CO) that aggregates rings connecting smaller customer premise equipment (CPE) routers in remote locations. The CPE routers have two high-speed uplink ports and are connected in a ring for redundancy. Often they will connect to two PE routers in different COs, but in our example, we use only one PE router for simplicity.

Figure 14.20 Ring topology with LSPs to PE router.

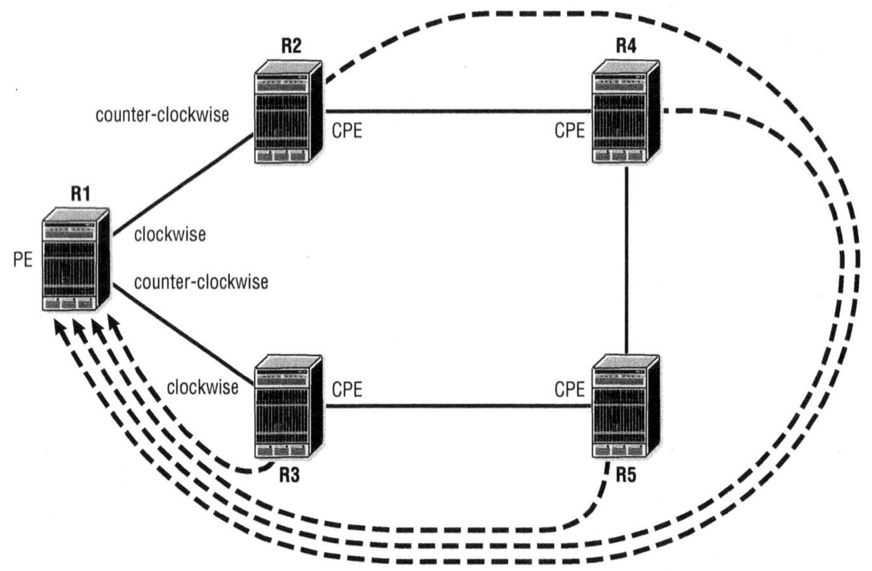

In this example, LSPs have been configured from the CPE routers to the PE router in a clockwise direction. There will also be LSPs from the PE router to the CPE routers, but these have been omitted for simplicity because the principle for managing these is the same. Admin groups are configured on the link between the PE router and the first and last CPE routers. These are used to force the LSPs to travel in the desired direction. The configuration on R2 is shown in Listing 14.26.

Listing 14.26 LSP traveling clockwise to R1

```
*A:R2# configure router mpls
*A:R2>config>router>mpls# info
----------------------------------------------
            admin-group "clockwise" 0
            admin-group "counter-clockwise" 1
            interface "system"
            exit
            interface "toR1"
                admin-group "counter-clockwise"
            exit
            interface "toR4"
            exit
            path "loose"
                no shutdown
            exit
            lsp "ring_toR1"
                to 10.10.10.1
                cspf
                primary "loose"
                    exclude "counter-clockwise"
                exit
                no shutdown
            exit
            no shutdown
----------------------------------------------
```

It is necessary to add a node between R4 and R5, and desirable to perform this operation without affecting existing services. It can be seen from Figure 14.20 that the LSPs from R2 and R4 will be affected when the link between R4 and R5 is broken to insert the new router. Listing 14.27 shows that there are two RSVP-TE tunnels on this interface.

Listing 14.27 RSVP-TE tunnels from R4 to R5

```
*A:R4# show router rsvp interface "toR5"

=======================================================================
```

(continued)

Listing 14.27 *(continued)*

```
RSVP Interface : toR5
===============================================================================
Interface                  Total    Active    Total BW  Resv BW   Adm Opr
                           Sessions Sessions  (Mbps)    (Mbps)
-------------------------------------------------------------------------------
toR5                       2        2         1000      0         Up  Up
===============================================================================
*A:R4# show router rsvp session

===============================================================================
RSVP Sessions
===============================================================================
From           To              Tunnel LSP   Name                      State
                               ID     ID
-------------------------------------------------------------------------------
10.10.10.2     10.10.10.1      1      15378 ring_toR1::loose          Up
10.10.10.4     10.10.10.1      1      18440 ring_toR1::loose          Up
-------------------------------------------------------------------------------
Sessions : 2
===============================================================================
```

To add node R6 without affecting services and data using the link, the two LSPs must first be changed to go counterclockwise to R1. This can be done by removing the admin group `counter-clockwise` on the link from R2 to R1 and then manually resignaling the LSP. To ensure that the R4–R5 link is not used, we can also set the IGP metric to a high value on the link if necessary. Note that it is not the configuration of the LSP that changes; we're actually changing the TE topology of the network by removing the admin group. If we change the configuration of the LSP itself, the LSP will go down while the path is resignaled.

The `tools perform` command is used to force the head end node to recalculate the path and resignal the LSP. The head end uses a make-before-break (MBB) method to establish the new LSP.

MBB is described in more detail in Chapter 15. "Make-before-break" means that the new LSP is signaled and traffic is switched to it before the original LSP is torn down.

Listing 14.28 shows the use of `tools perform` and the new path of the LSP. There are two things to notice in the new LSP:

- The new LSP has a different LSP ID from before it was resignaled.
- The *Path Up Time* is not reset because the tunnel is never operationally down in the resignaling process.

Listing 14.28 Resignaling LSP on R2 to go counterclockwise

```
*A:R2>config>router>mpls# info
----------------------------------------------
            admin-group "clockwise" 0
            admin-group "counter-clockwise" 1
            interface "system"
            exit
            interface "toR1"
                admin-group "counter-clockwise"
            exit
            interface "toR4"
            exit
            path "loose"
                no shutdown
            exit
            lsp "ring_toR1"
                to 10.10.10.1
                cspf
                primary "loose"
                    exclude "counter-clockwise"
                exit
                no shutdown
            exit
*A:R2>config>router>mpls# interface "toR1" no admin-group
"counter-clockwise"
*A:R2>config>router>mpls# exit
*A:R2# tools perform router mpls resignal lsp "ring_toR1" path "loose"
*A:R2# show router mpls lsp "ring_toR1" path detail

===============================================================================
MPLS LSP ring_toR1 Path  (Detail)
```

(continued)

Listing 14.28 *(continued)*

```
===============================================================================
Legend :
    @ - Detour Available              # - Detour In Use
    b - Bandwidth Protected           n - Node Protected
    s - Soft Preemption
===============================================================================
-------------------------------------------------------------------------------
LSP ring_toR1 Path loose
-------------------------------------------------------------------------------
LSP Name    : ring_toR1                     Path LSP ID : 15380
From        : 10.10.10.2                    To          : 10.10.10.1
Adm State   : Up                            Oper State  : Up
Path Name   : loose                         Path Type   : Primary
Path Admin  : Up                            Path Oper   : Up
OutInterface: 1/1/2                         Out Label   : 131069
Path Up Time: 1d 17:44:36                   Path Dn Time: 0d 00:00:00

... output omitted ...

ExplicitHops:
    No Hops Specified
Actual Hops :
    10.1.2.2(10.10.10.2)                    Record Label    : N/A
 -> 10.1.2.1(10.10.10.1)                    Record Label    : 131069
ComputedHops:
    10.1.2.2        -> 10.1.2.1
ResigEligib*: False
LastResignal: n/a                           CSPF Metric : 100
Last MBB    :
 MBB Type   : ManualResignal                MBB State   : Success
 Ended At   : 02/12/2011 17:46:41           Old Metric  : 400
===============================================================================
* indicates that the corresponding row element may have been truncated.
```

We follow similar steps on R4 to resignal the LSP. Although not necessary in this topology, we set the metric high on the link between R4 and R5 (see Listing 14.29).

Listing 14.29 Resignaling the LSP on R4

```
*A:R4# configure router ospf area 0 interface "toR5" metric 10000
*A:R4# tools perform router mpls resignal lsp "ring_toR1" path "loose"
*A:R4# show router mpls lsp "ring_toR1" path detail

===============================================================================
MPLS LSP ring_toR1 Path  (Detail)
===============================================================================
Legend :
    @ - Detour Available              # - Detour In Use
    b - Bandwidth Protected           n - Node Protected
    s - Soft Preemption
===============================================================================
-------------------------------------------------------------------------------
LSP ring_toR1 Path loose
-------------------------------------------------------------------------------
LSP Name     : ring_toR1                     Path LSP ID : 18448
From         : 10.10.10.4                    To          : 10.10.10.1
Adm State    : Up                            Oper State  : Up
Path Name    : loose                         Path Type   : Primary
Path Admin   : Up                            Path Oper   : Up
OutInterface: 1/1/3                          Out Label   : 131071
Path Up Time: 1d 18:26:21                    Path Dn Time: 0d 00:00:00

... output omitted ...

ExplicitHops:
    No Hops Specified
Actual Hops :
    10.2.4.4(10.10.10.4)                     Record Label    : N/A
 -> 10.2.4.2(10.10.10.2)                     Record Label    : 131071
 -> 10.1.2.1(10.10.10.1)                     Record Label    : 131070
ComputedHops:
    10.2.4.4       -> 10.2.4.2        -> 10.1.2.1
ResigEligib*: False
LastResignal: n/a                            CSPF Metric : 200
Last MBB    :
 MBB Type    : ManualResignal                MBB State   : Success
 Ended At    : 02/12/2011 17:46:53           Old Metric  : 300
```

(continued)

Listing 14.29 *(continued)*

```
===============================================================================
* indicates that the corresponding row element may have been truncated.
*A:R4#
*A:R4# show router rsvp interface "toR5"

===============================================================================
RSVP Interface : toR5
===============================================================================
Interface                   Total    Active   Total BW  Resv BW   Adm Opr
                            Sessions Sessions (Mbps)    (Mbps)
-------------------------------------------------------------------------------
toR5                        0        0        1000      0         Up  Up
===============================================================================
```

If there were LSPs traveling in the counterclockwise direction from R5 to R4, we would perform similar operations to move them. After verifying on R5 that there are no LSPs between R4 and R5, our topology is now as shown in Figure 14.21.

Figure 14.21 LSPs moved from link between R4 and R5.

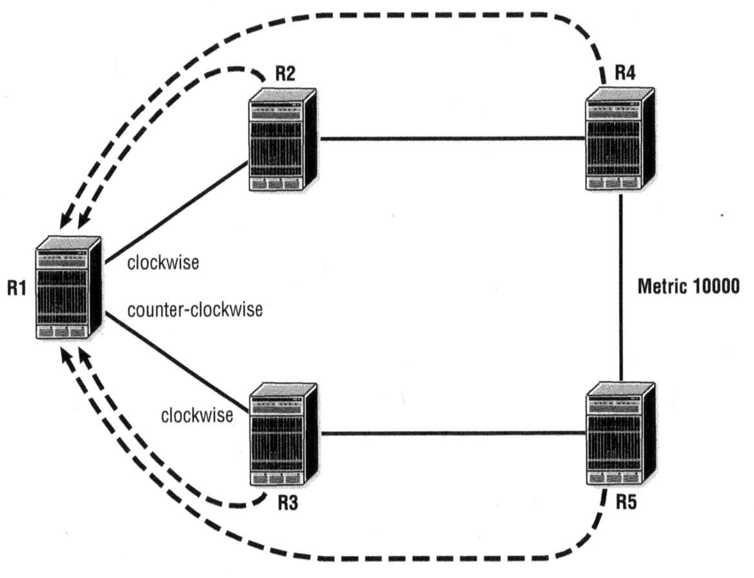

Now that there is no data traveling on the R4–R5 link, it can be connected to the new CPE router without affecting live traffic. Once the new node has been added, the admin group `counter-clockwise` is added to the R2–R1 link. The `tools perform` command can be used to verify that the correct path exists to the destination after the nodes have been configured. The value for the `include-bitmap` is specified as a decimal, binary, or hexadecimal value and is calculated based on the admin-group memberships. In this case, the calculation is simple because only two admin groups are defined using bits 0 and 1. The decimal values these two bits represent are 1 and 2. For more complex combinations, it may be desirable to find the value in the TE LSA or LSP. Listing 14.30 shows the configuration and resignaling of the LSP.

Listing 14.30 LSP resignaled on R2 to revert to clockwise direction

```
*A:R2# configure router mpls interface "toR1" admin-group
"counter-clockwise"
*A:R2# tools perform router mpls cspf to 10.10.10.1 exclude-bitmap 2
Req CSPF for all ECMP paths
    from: this node to: 10.10.10.1 w/(no Diffserv) class: 0 , setup
    Priority 7, Hold Priority 0 TE Class: 7

CSPF Path
To          : 10.10.10.1
Path 1      : (cost 500)
    Start: 10.10.10.2
    Egr:    10.2.4.2        -> Ingr:    10.2.4.4        (met 100)
    Egr:    10.4.6.4        -> Ingr:    10.4.6.6        (met 100)
    Egr:    10.5.6.6        -> Ingr:    10.5.6.5        (met 100)
    Egr:    10.3.5.5        -> Ingr:    10.3.5.3        (met 100)
    Egr:    10.1.3.3        -> Ingr:    10.1.3.1        (met 100)
    End:    10.10.10.1
*A:R2# tools perform router mpls resignal lsp "ring_toR1" path "loose"
*A:R2# show router mpls lsp "ring_toR1" path detail

===============================================================================
MPLS LSP ring_toR1 Path  (Detail)
===============================================================================
Legend :
    @ - Detour Available                # - Detour In Use
    b - Bandwidth Protected             n - Node Protected
    s - Soft Preemption
```

(continued)

Listing 14.30 *(continued)*

```
===============================================================================
-------------------------------------------------------------------------------
LSP ring_toR1 Path loose
-------------------------------------------------------------------------------
LSP Name     : ring_toR1                    Path LSP ID : 15382
From         : 10.10.10.2                   To          : 10.10.10.1
Adm State    : Up                           Oper State  : Up
Path Name    : loose                        Path Type   : Primary
Path Admin   : Up                           Path Oper   : Up
OutInterface: 1/1/3                         Out Label   : 131071
Path Up Time: 1d 18:18:26                   Path Dn Time: 0d 00:00:00

... output omitted ...

ExplicitHops:
    No Hops Specified
Actual Hops :
    10.2.4.2(10.10.10.2)                    Record Label    : N/A
 -> 10.2.4.4(10.10.10.4)                    Record Label    : 131071
 -> 10.4.6.6(10.10.10.6)                    Record Label    : 131071
 -> 10.5.6.5(10.10.10.5)                    Record Label    : 131071
 -> 10.3.5.3(10.10.10.3)                    Record Label    : 131071
 -> 10.1.3.1(10.10.10.1)                    Record Label    : 131071
ComputedHops:
    10.2.4.2        -> 10.2.4.4        -> 10.4.6.6        -> 10.5.6.5
 -> 10.3.5.3        -> 10.1.3.1
ResigEligib*: False
LastResignal: n/a                              CSPF Metric : 500
Last MBB    :
 MBB Type   : ManualResignal                   MBB State   : Success
 Ended At   : 02/12/2011 18:20:31              Old Metric  : 100
===============================================================================
* indicates that the corresponding row element may have been truncated.
```

Once the LSP on R4 is resignaled and a new LSP is added from R6, the topology is as shown in Figure 14.22. Listing 14.31 shows that there are five LSPs from R3 to R1 as expected.

Figure 14.22 LSPs are all clockwise with new node added.

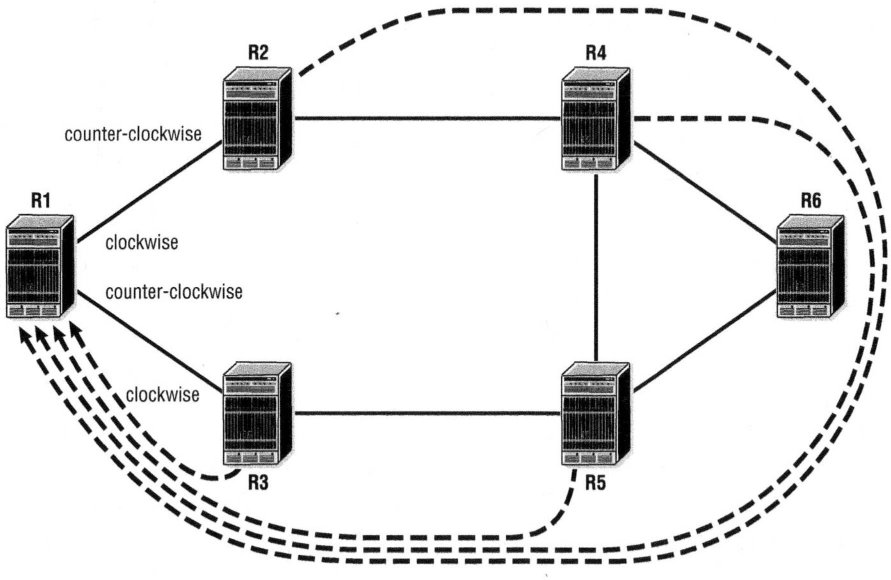

Listing 14.31 LSPs on CPE router R3

```
*A:R3# show router rsvp session

===========================================================================
RSVP Sessions
===========================================================================
From           To             Tunnel LSP   Name                      State
                              ID     ID
---------------------------------------------------------------------------
10.10.10.2     10.10.10.1     1      15382 ring_toR1::loose          Up
10.10.10.4     10.10.10.1     1      18450 ring_toR1::loose          Up
10.10.10.6     10.10.10.1     1      11264 ring_toR1::loose          Up
10.10.10.5     10.10.10.1     1      17408 ring_toR1::loose          Up
10.10.10.3     10.10.10.1     1      15872 ring_toR1::loose          Up
---------------------------------------------------------------------------
Sessions : 5
===========================================================================
*A:R3# show router rsvp interface "toR1"
```

(continued)

Listing 14.31 *(continued)*

```
===============================================================================
RSVP Interface : toR1
===============================================================================
Interface                    Total    Active   Total BW  Resv BW   Adm Opr
                             Sessions Sessions (Mbps)    (Mbps)
-------------------------------------------------------------------------------
toR1                         5        5        1000      0         Up  Up
===============================================================================
```

Failures on CSPF LSPs

When the head end router performs the CSPF calculation and does not find a valid route that meets the constraints, the output of `show router mpls lsp path detail` will show the *Failure Code* as `noCspfRouteToDestination` and the *Failure Node* as the head end because the Path message is never sent. In the topology of Figure 14.22, we accidentally configured the interface on R6 to R5 in admin group `counter-clockwise`. An LSP from R2 going clockwise to R1 does not come up as shown in Listing 14.32.

Listing 14.32 Troubleshooting problems with the CSPF calculation

```
*A:R2# configure router mpls lsp "ring_toR1"
*A:R2>config>router>mpls>lsp# info
----------------------------------------------
                to 10.10.10.1
                cspf
                primary "loose"
                    exclude "counter-clockwise"
                exit
                no shutdown
----------------------------------------------
*A:R2>config>router>mpls>lsp# exit
*A:R2# show router mpls lsp "ring_toR1" path detail

===============================================================================
MPLS LSP ring_toR1 Path  (Detail)
===============================================================================
```

```
Legend :
    @ - Detour Available              # - Detour In Use
    b - Bandwidth Protected           n - Node Protected
    s - Soft Preemption
=======================================================================
-----------------------------------------------------------------------
LSP ring_toR1 Path loose
-----------------------------------------------------------------------
LSP Name    : ring_toR1                         Path LSP ID : 15386
From        : 10.10.10.2                        To          : 10.10.10.1
Adm State   : Up                                Oper State  : Down
Path Name   : loose                             Path Type   : Primary
Path Admin  : Up                                Path Oper   : Down
OutInterface: n/a                               Out Label   : n/a
Path Up Time: 0d 00:00:00                       Path Dn Time: 0d 00:00:21

... output omitted ...

Include Grps:                                   Exclude Grps:
None                                          counter-clockwise
Path Trans  : 20                                CSPF Queries: 19
Failure Code: noCspfRouteToDestination          Failure Node: 10.10.10.2
ExplicitHops:
    No Hops Specified
Actual Hops :
    No Hops Specified
ComputedHops:
    No Hops Specified
ResigEligib*: False
LastResignal: n/a                               CSPF Metric : 0
=======================================================================
* indicates that the corresponding row element may have been truncated.
```

It is necessary to verify the path through each node to troubleshoot the problem. Again, `tools perform` can be helpful in troubleshooting the LSP. We use it to verify that the path is good to R6, but not beyond, thereby isolating the problem (Listing 14.33).

Listing 14.33 Use of tools perform to troubleshoot CSPF problems

```
*A:R2# tools perform router mpls cspf to 10.10.10.5 exclude-bitmap 2
Req CSPF for all ECMP paths
    from: this node to: 10.10.10.5 w/(no Diffserv) class: 0 , setup
    Priority 7, Hold Priority 0 TE Class: 7

MINOR: CLI No CSPF path to "10.10.10.5" with specified constraints.
*A:R2# tools perform router mpls cspf to 10.10.10.6 exclude-bitmap 2
Req CSPF for all ECMP paths
    from: this node to: 10.10.10.6 w/(no Diffserv) class: 0 ,
    setup Priority 7, Hold Priority 0 TE Class: 7

CSPF Path
To        : 10.10.10.6
Path 1    : (cost 200)
    Start: 10.10.10.2
    Egr:   10.2.4.2       -> Ingr:   10.2.4.4       (met 100)
    Egr:   10.4.6.4       -> Ingr:   10.4.6.6       (met 100)
    End:   10.10.10.6
```

14.8 LDP-over-RSVP

When RSVP-TE is deployed in very large networks (hundreds of LSRs), scalability becomes a concern. A large network with a full mesh of LSPs can require thousands of LSPs. Maintaining the state information and handling the signaling requirements may impose significant overhead, particularly on the core transit routers.

The solution for addressing the scalability problem in our IGPs is through the use of hierarchy. However, because traffic-engineering information is only distributed over a single area and the CSPF calculation is performed in a single area, this prevents us from having traffic-engineered LSPs across a multi-area network (see Figure 14.23).

One approach to solving this problem is to create traffic-engineered LSPs within the individual areas and then "stitch" them together to create an end-to-end LSP that provides some traffic-engineering capabilities. This is the solution offered by LDP-over-RSVP. In this case, RSVP-TE LSPs are created individually across each area. These can use CSPF or any other feature used on a normal RSVP-TE LSP. T-LDP sessions are then created between the routers at the edges of the areas to connect together the individual RSVP-TE LSPs (see Figure 14.24). We will see in Chapter 17 that T-LDP is used to exchange service labels between peers that are not directly connected. In this case T-LDP is being used to exchange transport labels that stitch together the RSVP-TE LSPs.

Figure 14.23 Traffic-engineering information is not distributed between areas.

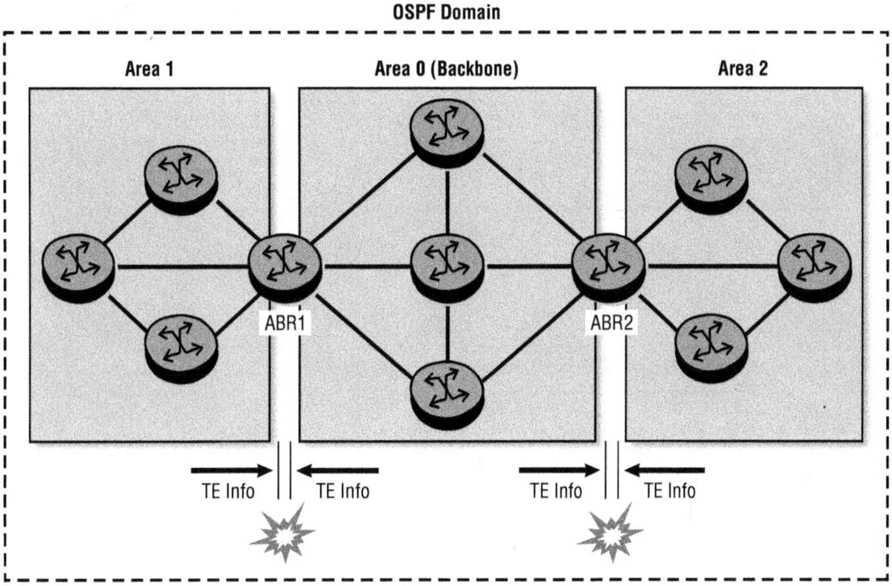

Figure 14.24 T-LDP used to stitch together RSVP-TE LSPs.

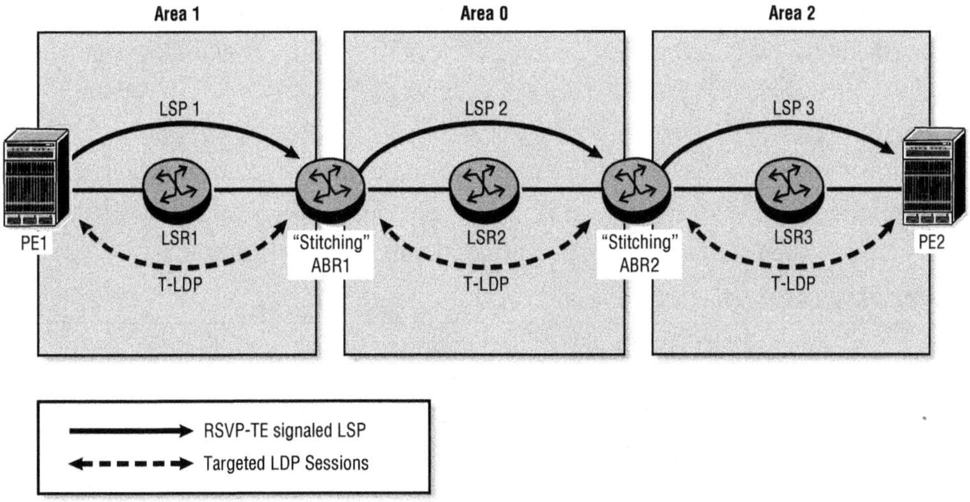

LDP alone does not provide any traffic-engineering capabilities, but LDP-over-RSVP can take advantage of the TE capabilities of RSVP-TE. Figure 14.25 shows that we can effectively create an end-to-end LDP tunnel that benefits from the TE capabilities of the underlying RSVP-TE LSPs.

Figure 14.25 End-to-end LDP tunnel comprised of interconnected RSVP-TE LSPs.

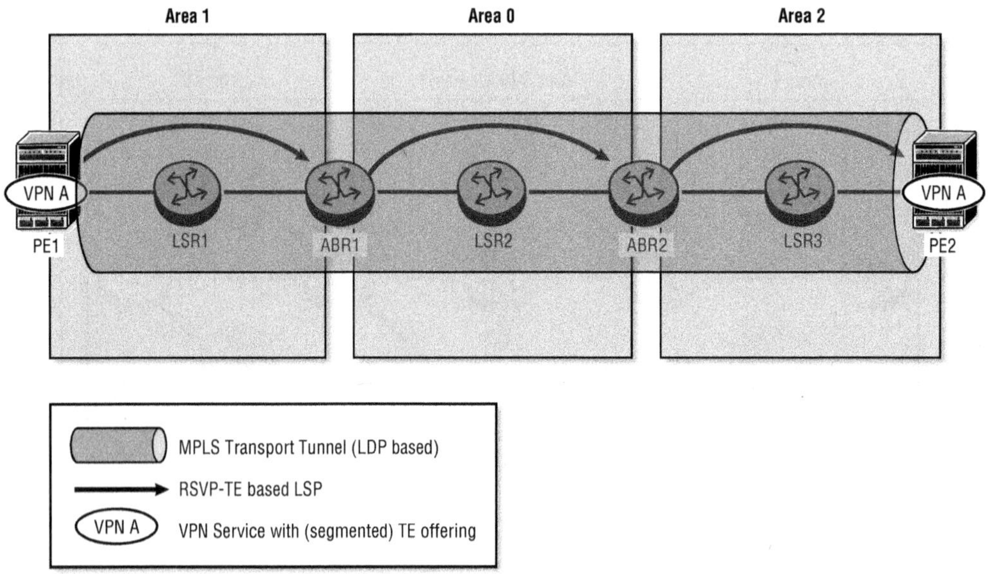

In later chapters, we examine how MPLS LSPs are used for the transport of VPN (Virtual Private Network) services such as VPLS (Virtual Private LAN Service) or VPRN (Virtual Private Routed Network). In this case, there is an inner service label that is signaled end-to-end between the PE routers. The outer label is the transport label that is used to switch the data end-to-end across the network. For LDP-over-RSVP, there is an additional label added to the label stack (see Figure 14.26). The inner label at the bottom of the stack is still the service label. The next outermost label is the one signaled by LDP that represents the FEC for the far-end PE router. The outer label is the RSVP-TE label that is used to switch the data on the LSP across the individual routing area.

Figure 14.26 Label stack for LDP-over-RSVP.

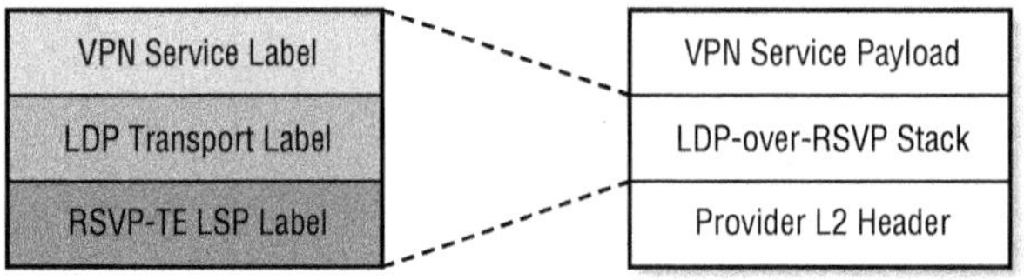

LDP-over-RSVP operates very much like a network with LDP as the transport protocol, except that in LDP-over-RSVP the next-hop resolved for the LDP label is actually an RSVP-TE tunnel instead of an adjacent router. Referring to Figure 14.27, the data flow for a packet that is part of the service VPN A would be as follows:

1. Unlabeled customer packet in VPN A arrives at PE1.
2. The service label that was signaled by PE2 corresponding to VPN A is pushed onto the label stack as the innermost label.
3. The LDP label for the FEC PE2 that was signaled by ABR1 is pushed onto the label stack.
4. The RSVP-TE label for the tunnel that is the next-hop for the LDP FEC is pushed onto the label stack.
5. The packet is label-switched across Area 1 using the outer, RSVP-TE label to ABR1 (Area Border Router 1).
6. ABR1 is the egress for the RSVP-TE LSP, and thus the label is popped. The LDP label for PE2 that was signaled by ABR2 is swapped for the ingress LDP label. The label for the RSVP-TE tunnel that is the next-hop for the LDP FEC is pushed on the label stack.
7. The packet is switched across the RSVP-TE LSP in Area 0 using the outer label until it reaches the LSP egress, ABR2.
8. The outer label is popped, and the LDP label is swapped for the label that was signaled by PE2. A new label is pushed for the RSVP-TE LSP to PE2.
9. The packet is switched across Area 2 to PE2 using the outer label.
10. All three labels are popped. The service label is used to identify the service to which the packet belongs and thus the egress interface for transmission of the unlabeled packet.

Configuring LDP-over-RSVP

Figure 14.28 shows the topology used to demonstrate the configuration of LDP-over-RSVP. The steps to be followed are:

1. Configure RSVP-TE LSPs to cross each area.
2. Configure Targeted-LDP (T-LDP) peering sessions between PEs and ABRs.
3. Configure IGP to accept RSVP-TE LSPs for next-hop addresses for LDP.
4. Verify the configuration.

Figure 14.27 Data plane for an LDP-over-RSVP LSP.

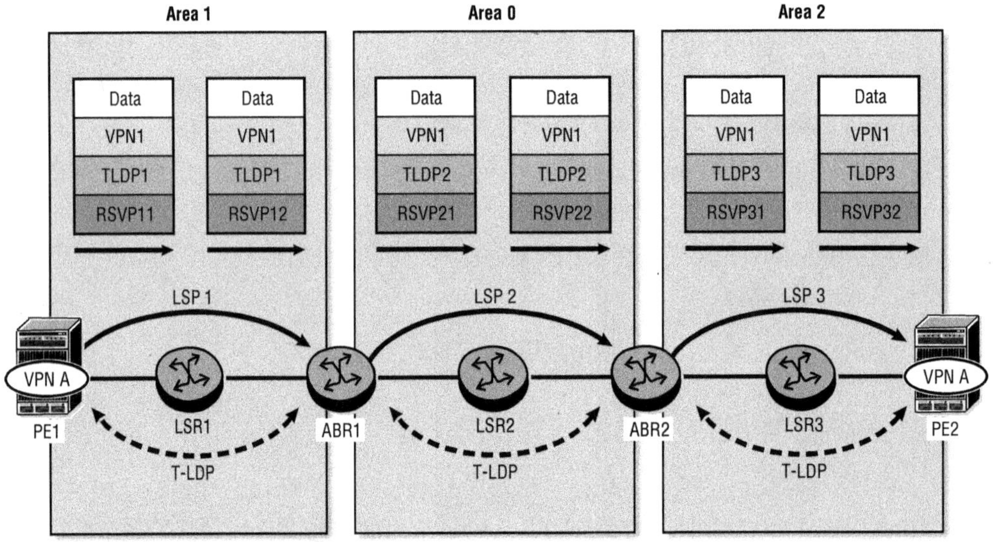

Figure 14.28 Three-area network for configuration of LDP-over-RSVP.

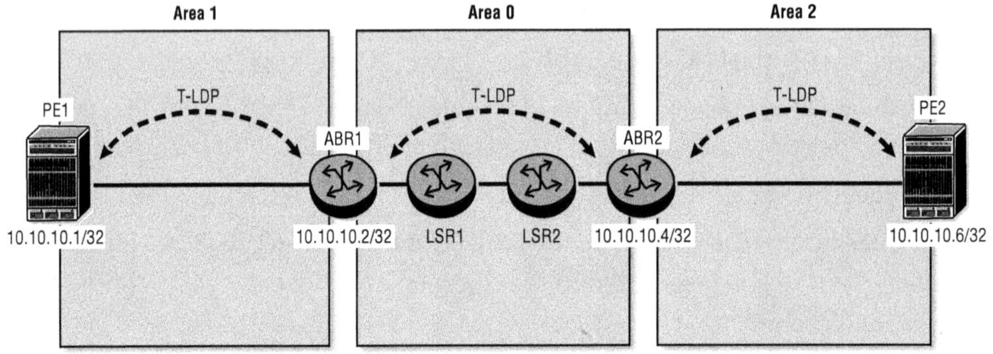

We first configure RSVP-TE LSPs to cross Areas 1, 0, and 2. For this example, all LSPs are defined as fully loose LSPs, although LSPs could be configured with any type of TE constraints. Listing 14.34 shows the configuration on ABR1 and the fact that the LSP from PE1 also terminates here.

Listing 14.34 RSVP-TE LSPs configured on ABR1

```
*A:ABR1>config>router>mpls# info
----------------------------------------------
            interface "system"
            exit
            interface "toPE1"
            exit
            interface "toLSR1"
            exit
            path "loose"
                no shutdown
            exit
            lsp "toABR2"
                to 10.10.10.4
                primary "loose"
                exit
                no shutdown
            exit
            no shutdown
----------------------------------------------
*A:ABR1>config>router>mpls# show router rsvp session

===============================================================================
RSVP Sessions
===============================================================================
From          To            Tunnel LSP   Name                                State
                            ID     ID
-------------------------------------------------------------------------------
10.10.10.2    10.10.10.4    1      42496 toABR2::loose                          Up
10.10.10.1    10.10.10.2    33     49152 toABR1::loose                          Up
-------------------------------------------------------------------------------
Sessions : 2
===============================================================================
```

Once the RSVP-TE LSPs are configured, T-LDP is configured to provide an end-to-end transport tunnel across the multi-area network. Because link LDP is not being used, the interfaces are not declared in LDP. Only the peers for T-LDP sessions are required and the fact that they are to be used for LDP-over-RSVP tunnels (see Listing 14.35). If link LDP is active, these labels will be preferred over those from the T-LDP sessions. To force the router to use LDP-over-RSVP when link LDP is active, the command `configure router ldp prefer-tunnel-in-tunnel` must be used.

Listing 14.35 Configuration of T-LDP peers on ABR1

```
*A:ABR1>config>router>ldp# info
----------------------------------------------
            prefer-tunnel-in-tunnel
            interface-parameters
            exit
            targeted-session
                peer 10.10.10.1
                    tunneling
                    exit
                exit
                peer 10.10.10.4
                    tunneling
                    exit
                exit
            exit
----------------------------------------------
*A:ABR1>config>router>ldp# show router ldp peer

==============================================================================
LDP Peers
==============================================================================
Peer            Adm  Opr  Hello   Hold   KA      KA      Passive  Auto
                          Factor  Time   Factor  Timeout Mode     Created
------------------------------------------------------------------------------
10.10.10.1      Up   Up   3       45     4       40      Disabled No
10.10.10.4      Up   Up   3       45     4       40      Disabled No
------------------------------------------------------------------------------
No. of Peers: 2
```

Once the T-LDP peering sessions are established across the network, labels are partially distributed. However, until the IGP is configured for `ldp-over-rsvp`, LDP does not install the remote labels as active. Once the IGP is configured on all the routers, as shown in Listing 14.36, the RSVP-TE tunnels can be used as the next-hop for LDP. Note that the Tunnel ID is shown for the LSP that will be used as the next-hop.

Listing 14.36 Configuration of IGP and verification of labels on PE1

```
*A:PE1# configure router ospf ldp-over-rsvp
*A:PE1# show router ldp bindings active

=======================================================================
Legend:  (S) - Static
=======================================================================
LDP Prefix Bindings (Active)
=======================================================================
Prefix                Op   IngLbl    EgrLbl    EgrIntf/LspId  EgrNextHop
-----------------------------------------------------------------------
10.10.10.1/32         Pop  131070      --          --             --
10.10.10.2/32         Push   --      131066    LspId 33       10.10.10.2
10.10.10.4/32         Push   --      131065    LspId 33       10.10.10.2
10.10.10.6/32         Push   --      131064    LspId 33       10.10.10.2
-----------------------------------------------------------------------
No. of Prefix Bindings: 4
*A:PE1# show router rsvp session

=======================================================================
RSVP Sessions
=======================================================================
From         To              Tunnel LSP   Name                     State
                             ID     ID
-----------------------------------------------------------------------
10.10.10.1   10.10.10.2      33     49152 toABR1::loose               Up
-----------------------------------------------------------------------
Sessions : 1
=======================================================================
```

For LDP-over-RSVP, LDP is only required on the PE and ABR routers. Listing 14.37 shows that LDP is not active on LSR1. Traffic passing through LSR1 is carried on an RSVP-TE LSP.

Listing 14.37 No LDP is active on LSR1

```
*A:LSR1# show router ldp status
MINOR: CLI LDP is not configured.
*A:LSR1# show router rsvp session

===============================================================================
RSVP Sessions
===============================================================================
From            To              Tunnel LSP   Name                        State
                                ID     ID
-------------------------------------------------------------------------------
10.10.10.2      10.10.10.4      1      42496 toABR2::loose                  Up
-------------------------------------------------------------------------------
Sessions : 1
===============================================================================
```

One of the reasons for using traffic-engineered LSPs is to provide redundancy using secondary paths and fast reroute. (These subjects are covered in detail in Chapter 16.) Although the individual RSVP-TEs in an LDP-over-RSVP solution can be configured fast reroute protection, the ABRs in this example represent a single point of failure. To provide redundancy, multiple ABRs can be used, as shown in Figure 14.29. In this situation, a full mesh of LSPs and T-LDP peering sessions is recommended between the ABRs.

Figure 14.29 LDP-over-RSVP with multiple ABRs for redundancy.

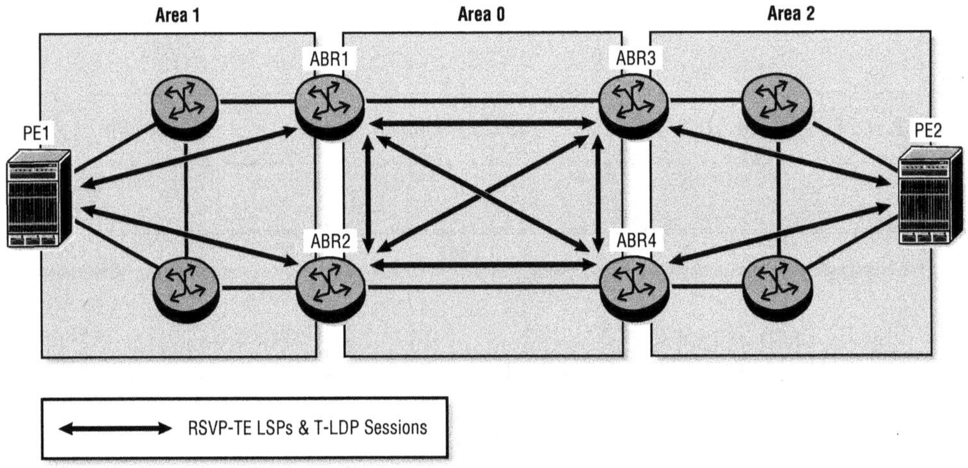

Summary

Constraint-based routing and TE-LSPs are used in two situations:

- Traffic engineering for resource reservation in LSPs
- Calculation of detours for fast reroute (FRR)

Figure 14.30 illustrates the algorithm that governs the signaling of TE-LSPs.

Figure 14.30 Process for signaling of TE-LSPs.

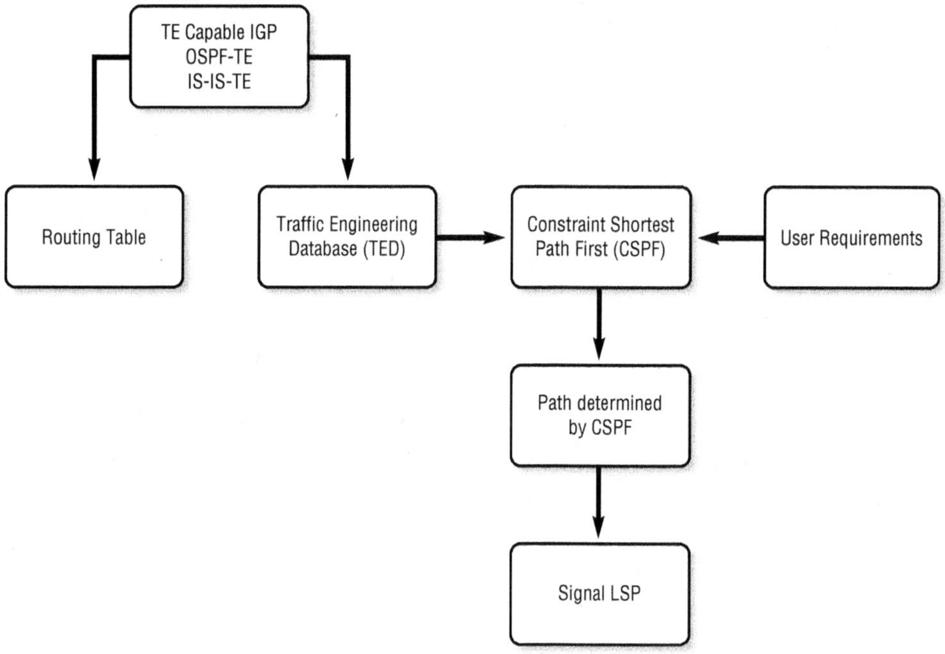

As shown in Figure 14.30, the steps in signaling TE-LSPs are as follows:

1. Traffic engineering is enabled in the IGP on the routers in the network.
2. The TE information is flooded in LSAs (OSPF) or LSPs (IS-IS) and collected in the TED.
3. User (or operator) requirements are such that a constraint-based route is required for an LSP.
4. The head end router calculates the route using the CSPF algorithm.
5. The LSP is signaled along the specific path calculated by the head end router.

Traffic engineering for resource reservation is described in detail in Chapter 15. The use of CSPF for calculating detours and redundancy in an MPLS network is described in Chapter 16.

Practice Lab: Constraint-Based Routing and TE-LSPs

The following lab is designed to reinforce your knowledge of the content in this chapter. Please review the instructions carefully and perform the steps in the order in which they are presented. The practice labs require that you have access to six or more 7750 SRs or Alcatel-Lucent 7450 ESSs in a non-production environment.

These labs are designed to be used in a controlled lab environment. Please *do not* attempt to perform these labs in a production environment.

Lab Section 14.1: Configuring CSPF RSVP-TE LSPs

To take full advantage of traffic engineering, RSVP-TE-signaled LSPs can be enabled with CSPF. This section investigates the behavior of CSPF-enabled RSVP-TE–signaled LSPs.

Objective In this exercise, you will configure a topology of four 7750 SRs with CSPF-enabled RSVP-TE LSPs (see Figure 14.31).

Figure 14.31 Topology for configured CSPF LSPs.

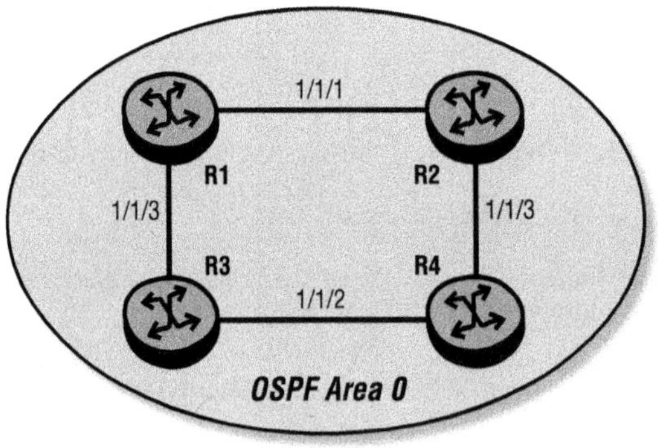

Validation You will know you have succeeded if the LSPs follow the specified constraints.

1. For the first few tasks of this lab, shut down any IGP that you may have running in the network of four routers shown in Figure 14.31.
2. Make sure that all RSVP-TE interfaces on the four routers are operationally up.
3. On R1, configure a strict-path LSP from R1 to R2 to R4 to R3. Do not enable CSPF yet.
   a. Is the LSP operationally up? If not, what *Failure Code* is given?
   b. Enable CSPF on the LSP. Is the LSP operationally up? If not what *Failure Code* is given?
   c. Enable OSPF (this lab uses OSPF, but you can use IS-IS if you desire) in the network, but do not enable traffic engineering. Is the LSP operationally up? If not, what *Failure Code* is given?
   d. Enable traffic engineering on R3 only. Is the LSP operationally up? If not what *Failure Code* is given?
   e. Does R2 have a copy of the Opaque LSAs originated by R3? Explain.
   f. Enable traffic engineering on R2 and R4. Is the LSP operationally up? If not, what *Failure Code* is given?
   g. Enable traffic engineering on R1. Is the LSP operationally up? If not, what *Failure Code* is given?
4. Configure a totally loose LSP from R1 to R2. Do not enable CSPF yet.
   a. Enable debug trace on R1 and examine the Path message for the LSP. Describe the contents of the ERO.
   b. Enable CSPF on the LSP and examine the Path message originated by R1. Describe the contents of the ERO.
   c. Examine the output of the `show router mpls lsp path detail command`. Explain the contents of the *Explicit Hops*, *Actual Hops*, and *Computed Hops* fields.
5. Force the LSP from R1 to R2 to use the path through R3 and R4 by specifying two strict hops (`10.1.3.3` and `10.3.4.4`) followed by a loose hop.
   a. Verify that the LSP is operationally up before proceeding.
   b. Are there any loose hops seen in the ERO of the Path message sent by R1? Explain.

c. Increase the metric of the link between R2 and R4 to a very high value like `2000`. Administratively shut down the LSP, and then bring it up again. Does the LSP still come up? If not, what *Failure Code* is given?

d. Disable CSPF on the LSP. Does the LSP still come up? If not, what *Failure Code* is given? Explain.

6. Enable CSPF and configure the LSP from R1 to R2 to use a totally loose path. Also, change the metric on the link from R4 to R2 back to its default value.

   a. Verify that the LSP is operationally up and is using the path directly to R2 before proceeding.

   b. Configure the LSP to use TE metrics, and change the TE metric on the link between R1 and R2 to a very high value like `2000`.

   c. What path is the LSP using now? Explain.

   d. Record the Tunnel ID and LSP ID of the LSP.

   e. Manually resignal the LSP. What path is the LSP using now? How do the Tunnel ID and LSP ID compare to the values before the LSP was resignaled?

   f. Examine the OSPF Router LSA originated by R1, and compare it to the OSPF Opaque LSAs originated by R1. What are some key differences?

   g. On R1, use the `tools perform cspf route` command with and without the `use-te-metric` flag, and compare it to the result of the `traceroute` command.

   h. Disable CSPF on the LSP. What path does the LSP use now? Explain.

7. Enable CSPF on the LSP from R1 to R2, and ensure that it is still using the path through R3 and R4 as it will be used in the next section.

Lab Section 14.2: More Constraints, Hop Limits, and Admin Groups

Constraints such as hop limits and admin groups can be used to further increase the applications of CSPF-enabled LSPs.

Objective In this lab, you will configure additional constraints such as hop limit and admin groups and observe the effect on the LSPs.

Validation You will know you have succeeded if you are successful in influencing the path of LSPs with the additional constraints.

1. Ensure that the LSP between R1 and R2 from the previous exercise is still using the path through R3 and R4.

2. Can you configure the LSP to use a hop limit of 1? Explain.

3. Configure the LSP to use a hop limit of 3. What path is taken by the LSP? Explain.

   a. Do you need to manually resignal the LSP for a change in hop limit to take effect? Explain.

   b. Remove the hop limit on the LSP and the TE metrics on the interfaces between R1 and R2 before proceeding.

4. Verify that the LSP between R1 and R2 is operationally up and using the path directly from R1 to R2. Do you need to resignal the LSP for the change in TE metrics to take effect?

5. Use an `exclude` admin group named `red` with a value of 1 to force the LSP to use the path through R3 and R4.

   a. Is a manual resignal required to force the LSP to take the `exclude` statement into consideration?

   b. Remove the admin group from the MPLS interface on R1 toward R2 (don't remove it from the LSP yet). What path is the LSP using? Explain.

   c. Without removing the `exclude` statement from the LSP, ensure that the path from R1 to R2 is in use before proceeding.

   d. Add the `red` admin group on R2's interface to R1 (make sure that the values are consistent with the definition on R1), and resignal the LSP. What path is the LSP using? Explain.

   e. View the Opaque LSA advertised by R2. How is the admin group represented?

   f. Add an admin group called `black` with a value of 3 to R2's interface to R1. How is the admin group represented in the Opaque LSA advertised by R2?

6. Configure R1's MPLS interface to R3 with an admin group named `green` with a value of 0. Configure the LSP from R1 to R2 to include the `green` admin group, and remove any other admin-group constraints.

   a. Is the LSP operationally up? If not, what is the *Failure Code*? Explain.

   b. Ensure that the LSP is operationally up using the `include` admin-group constraint before proceeding.

   c. Add an admin group named `yellow` with a value of 2 on R3's interface to R4. Remove the `green` admin group from the interface `toR4`. Is the `green` admin group still advertised in the Opaque LSA originated by R3?

d. Verify that the LSP from R1 to R2 is now operationally down.

e. Include the admin group `yellow` as a constraint in the LSP from R1 to R2. Is the LSP operationally up? Explain.

Lab Section 14.3: Inter-Area LSPs with Traffic Engineering

This section investigates the mechanisms required to support traffic engineering for inter-area LSPs.

Objective In this lab, you will configure LDP-over-RSVP to have a traffic-engineered LSP that traverses multiple areas (see Figure 14.32).

Figure 14.32 Topology for inter-area TE LSPs.

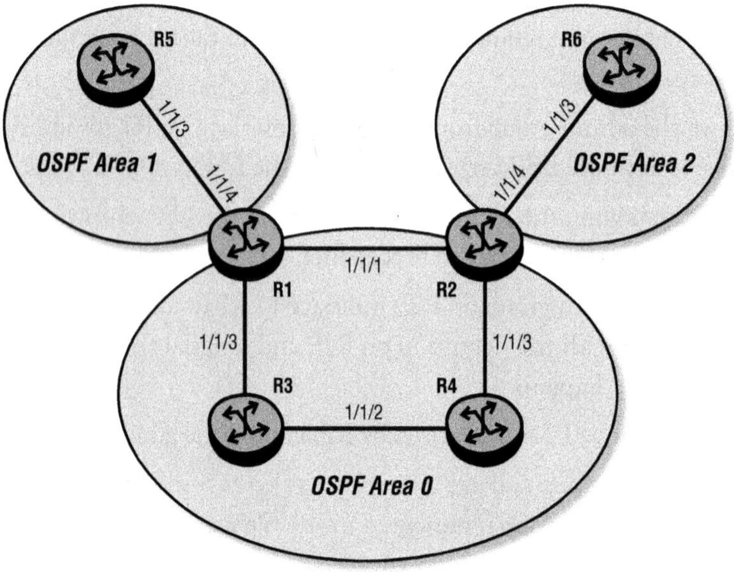

Validation You will know you have succeeded if your traffic-engineered LSPs are operationally up and can traverse multiple areas.

1. Configure your IGP with the OSPF areas as shown in Figure 14.32, and enable traffic engineering on all routers in the network. Also, make sure that RSVP-TE interfaces are operational between R1 and R5 and between R2 and R6.
2. Configure a totally loose path LSP from R5 to R6. Do not enable CSPF.
   a. Is the LSP operationally up? If not, what is the *Failure Code*?

3. Enable CSPF on the LSP from R5 to R6.
   a. Is the LSP operationally up? If not, what is the *Failure Code*?
   b. Perform a `traceroute` from R5 to R6. What path is taken?
   c. Is the `tools perform router mpls cspf to 10.10.10.6` command on R5 successful? Is it successful on R1? On R2?
   d. Are the traffic-engineering LSAs originated by R6 seen on R2? Are they seen on R1? Are they seen on R5? Explain.
4. Configure individual RSVP-TE LSPs in both directions across each area that can later be stitched together using LDP-over-RSVP.
   a. Does CSPF need to be configured on each LSP?
5. Configure LDP sessions as required to use LDP-over-RSVP in the network.
   a. Is Link LDP required? Explain.
   b. What routers required T-LDP configuration?
   c. Configure the IGP to use LDP-over-RSVP on each router.
   d. How many active LDP label bindings do you see on R5 and R6?
   e. How many active LDP label bindings do you see on R1 and R2?
   f. How many active LDP label bindings do you see on R3 and R4?
   g. An operator that is logged into a CLI (command line interface) session on R5 wants to know which RSVP-TE LSPs are used for traffic sent to R6. How would the operator deduce this information?

Chapter Review

Now that you have completed this chapter, you should be able to:

- Describe the purpose of constraint-based routing.
- Give examples that show the application of constraint-based routing.
- Explain how a TE-LSP is signaled across the network.
- Use the TED and CSPF algorithm to calculate the shortest, constrained path to a specific destination.
- Describe the information carried in traffic-engineering TLVs.
- Describe the OSPF Type 10 LSA.
- List the two Type 10 LSA TE subtypes.
- Describe the fields of the TE Link LSA.
- List the new TLVs defined for traffic engineering in IS-IS.
- Describe the fields of TLV 22 in IS-IS.
- Configure an LSP path to traverse specific nodes.
- Explain the purpose and operation of the explicit route object.
- Configure an LSP path with strict hops.
- Describe how CSPF is used in the LSP.
- Use `tools perform` to troubleshoot LSPs.
- Configure LSPs constrained by hop limits.
- Configure TE metrics and use them to control the LSP path.
- Configure administrative groups.
- Use admin groups to create a ring topology.
- Troubleshoot failures on CSPF LSPs.
- Describe the purpose and operation of LDP-over-RSVP.
- Configure LDP-over-RSVP.

Post-Assessment

1. Which statement is correct regarding constraint-based routing?
   - **A.** TE-LSPs always follow the best IGP route.
   - **B.** LDP is commonly used for constraint-based routing applications.
   - **C.** Constraint-based routing can be used to provide QoS functions in the data plane.
   - **D.** The route for a TE-LSP is calculated at the head end router.
   - **E.** None of the above statements are correct.
2. An operationally up LSP in a network of Alcatel-Lucent 7750 SRs has a totally loose path and is following the shortest route from the IGP. CSPF is configured on the LSP, and the resignal timer has not been changed from default settings. A link failure in the network causes a topology change that affects the path of the LSP. The link is later repaired. Which statement best describes the LSP ID before and after the link failure?
   - **A.** The LSP ID stays constant.
   - **B.** The LSP ID changes when the link goes down. It will not change again until the resignal timer expires or the LSP is manually resignaled.
   - **C.** The LSP ID changes when the link goes down and changes again when the link is restored.
   - **D.** There is not enough information to determine the answer.
3. Which statement is *not* correct regarding the processing of ERO and RRO messages on a CSPF-enabled router?
   - **A.** Each transit LSR removes the first hop from the ERO in the path message and builds a new Path message for the next-hop LSR.
   - **B.** The head end router fills the ERO according to the CSPF calculation results.
   - **C.** Each LSR in the LSP path helps to build the RRO by adding the IP address of the interface on which it transmits the Path message.
   - **D.** When CSPF is enabled, the ERO can contain strict or loose hops.
   - **E.** All of the above statements are correct.

4. Consider an Alcatel-Lucent 7750 SR that has three MPLS interfaces. One interface is configured with the admin group `gold`, one with the admin group `silver`, and one with the admin group `bronze`. These are the only interfaces in the entire network configured with admin groups. An established LSP is configured to exclude the admin group `gold`; however, an operator decides to change the LSP to include the admin group `bronze`. No other routers are changed. Assuming that the ingress LER and egress LER of the LSP are not directly connected, which statement best describes the resulting behavior?

   A. The LSP becomes operationally down until the retry timer expires and then becomes established.

   B. The LSP becomes operationally down and stays in this state until a configuration change is made.

   C. The LSP path does not change until it is manually resignaled or the resignal timer expires.

   D. The LSP path changes to use the interface with admin group `bronze`.

   E. None of the above statements are correct.

5. Which statement is not correct regarding the use of LDP-over-RSVP on a network of 7750 SRs?

   A. CSPF is not required on RSVP-TE LSPs used for LDP-over-RSVP.

   B. For the purposes of LDP-over-RSVP, T-LDP is only required on the ABRs.

   C. Data travels across an area with an outer MPLS label signaled with RSVP-TE, an inner MPLS label signaled with LDP, and possibly a VPN service label.

   D. The IGP must be configured to support LDP-over-RSVP.

   E. All of the above statements are correct.

6. Which statement is incorrect regarding CSPF calculations?

   A. The router doing the CSPF calculation puts itself as the root of the SPF tree.

   B. CSPF calculations are performed on the TED.

   C. Traffic-engineering metrics are stored in the LSDB.

   D. Hop count can be used as a constraint for a TE-LSP.

   E. All of the above statements are correct.

7. Which of the following attributes is not carried in link-state packets for traffic engineering?
   - **A.** Maximum bandwidth.
   - **B.** IGP metric.
   - **C.** Administrative groups.
   - **D.** Unreserved bandwidth.
   - **E.** Maximum reservable bandwidth.
   - **F.** All of the above parameters are carried in link-state packets.

8. What type of LSA does OSPF use for flooding traffic-engineering information?
   - **A.** Type 7 LSA
   - **B.** Type 8 LSA
   - **C.** Type 9 LSA
   - **D.** Type 10 LSA
   - **E.** None of the above

9. If a non-TE-capable OSPF router in an area receives a traffic-engineering LSA, what actions will it take?
   - **A.** It will flood the LSA.
   - **B.** It will silently discard the LSA.
   - **C.** It will discard the LSA and send an error to the originating router.
   - **D.** It will discard the LSA and send an error to the router from which it received the LSA.
   - **E.** It will not take any of the above actions.

10. Which of the following statements about the OSPF-TE Type 10 LSA is incorrect?
    - **A.** The Type 10 LSA has two subtypes.
    - **B.** The subtype 1 of the Type 10 LSA contains the router's IP address.
    - **C.** The subtype 2 of the Type 10 LSA contains TE information for all links on the router.
    - **D.** Each Type 10 LSA only contains one subtype.
    - **E.** All of the statements are correct.

11. An operator configures an LSP with CSPF on an Alcatel-Lucent 7750 SR and specifies a strict hop to an adjacent node followed by a loose hop to the destination node. The command `no record` is used to disable building of the RRO. The operator observes the output of the `show router mpls lsp <lsp-name> path detail` command. Assuming that the LSP is operationally up, which of the following statements is incorrect?

   A. The *Explicit Hops* field will list the IP address of the strict hop followed by the IP address of the loose hop.

   B. The *Actual Hops* field will list the hops along the entire LSP path.

   C. The *Computed Hops* field will list the hops along the entire LSP path.

   D. All of the above statements are correct.

12. Consider a network topology that contains four 7750 SRs. R1 is directly connected to R2. Another path from R1 to R2 exists through R3 and R4. The link from R1 to R2 has an IGP cost of 1,000, and all other links in the network have an IGP cost of 100. An LSP is configured from R1 to R2 with a hop limit of 3 and enabled with CSPF. Which path will be taken by the LSP?

   A. The path of the LSP will be directly from R1 to R2.

   B. The path of the LSP will be through R3 and R4.

   C. The LSP will be operationally down because a path that meets the constraint does not exist.

   D. There is not enough information to determine the answer.

13. An operator is trying to use traffic engineering to influence the path of a totally loose LSP on a network of 7750 SRs by changing the TE metrics of MPLS interfaces. The path of the LSP does not change. Which statements below could be a possible reason why the LSP path has not changed?

   A. A manual resignal is required to create an immediate change in the LSP's path.

   B. The operator may not have enabled CSPF on the LSP.

   C. The operator may not have explicitly configured the LSP to use TE metrics for its CSPF calculation.

   D. A, B, and C could all explain why the LSP path has not changed.

   E. None of the answers explain why the LSP path has not changed.

14. Which of the following statements is *not* correct regarding MPLS admin groups on the 7750 SR?

A. The use of admin groups is also known as link coloring.

B. The `admin group` attribute is carried as a 32-bit mask in OSPF LSAs.

C. IS-IS supports admin groups.

D. Only one admin group at a time can be bound to an MPLS interface.

E. All of the above statements are correct.

15. An admin group is configured with the command `admin-group "green" 2` and bound to an interface on a 7750 SR. If OSPF is the IGP in the network, which statement best describes how the admin group is advertised?

A. The Opaque LSA for the interface advertises a value of 0 for the admin group.

B. The Opaque LSA for the interface advertises a value of 1 for the admin group.

C. The Opaque LSA for the interface advertises a value of 2 for the admin group.

D. The Opaque LSA for the interface advertises a value of 3 for the admin group.

E. The Opaque LSA for the interface advertises a value of 4 for the admin group.

F. None of the above answers are correct.

15 RSVP-TE Resource Reservation

The Alcatel-Lucent NRS II exam topics covered in this chapter include the following:

- Signaling and reserving bandwidth requirements
- Threshold-triggered IGP TE updates
- Shared Explicit bandwidth reservation
- Fixed Filter bandwidth reservation
- Make-before-break behavior
- Least-fill bandwidth reservation
- LSP soft preemption
- DiffServ-Aware Traffic Engineering
- Understanding class types (CTs)
- Bandwidth constraints per class type
- DiffServ-TE examples

One special case of constraint-based routing is the reservation of bandwidth resources. The definition of bandwidth resources and the signaling of them are covered in detail in this chapter. We also look at the ability to specify priorities for LSPs (label switched paths) and how a higher-priority LSP preempts a lower-priority LSP to reserve bandwidth.

Finally, we look at the operation of Differentiated Services-Aware Traffic Engineering (DiffServ-TE) and how it is supported on the Alcatel-Lucent 7750 SR. DiffServ-TE provides more granular allocation of bandwidth resources by supporting the grouping of LSPs into class types.

Pre-Assessment

The following assessment questions will help you understand what areas of the chapter you should review in more detail to prepare for the NRS II exam. You can also use the CD that accompanies this book to take all the assessment tests and review the answers.

1. A router has just finished a CSPF (Constrained Shortest Path First) computation to find a route for a bandwidth-constrained LSP. Which statement best describes the next step for the head end router, assuming that a path is found for the LSP?

A. The head end router sends a CAC message to the next-hop router so that it can perform bandwidth reservation.

B. The head end router floods a TE LSA to all routers in the LSP path so that they can perform bandwidth reservation.

C. The head end router sends a Path message to the tail end router. The next-hop router intercepts the Path message and performs bandwidth reservation.

D. The head end router sends a Resv message to the tail end router. The next-hop router intercepts the Resv message and performs bandwidth reservation.

E. None of the statements above are correct.

2. Consider a network of Alcatel-Lucent 7750 SRs. An operator wants to provision a bandwidth-constrained LSP with a fully loose path. There are two paths between the head and tail end routers. One path has a lower IGP (interior gateway protocol) cost but has RSVP-TE (Resource Reservation Protocol–Traffic Engineering) interfaces that cannot meet the bandwidth requirement. The RSVP-TE interfaces of all routers along the path with the higher IGP metric can meet the bandwidth requirement. The operator forgets to enable the LSP with CSPF. Which statement below is correct?

A. The LSP is established and operationally up along the path with the lower IGP cost.

B. The LSP is established and operationally up along the path with the higher IGP cost.

C. The LSP is operationally down with the failure code `admissionControlError`.

D. The LSP is operationally down with the failure code `noCspfRouteToDestination`.

E. None of the above statements are correct.

3. Consider a network of 7750 SRs. All ports in the network are 1 Gb/s, and default subscription values are used. An operator provisions an LSP with a primary and hot standby secondary path between two nodes. Both paths have a bandwidth constraint of 800 Mb/s and are totally loose. Assume that there are no other RSVP-TE sessions in the network. Which statement below is correct?

A. If Shared Explicit mode is used, the primary and secondary paths will be established over different paths in the network.

B. The secondary LSP will not be signaled unless the primary path goes down.

C. If Fixed Filter mode is used and CSPF is enabled on the LSP, the primary and secondary LSPs will take separate paths through the network.

D. If Shared Explicit mode is used and CSPF is not enabled on the LSP, the secondary LSP will have a failure code of `admissionControlError`.

E. All of the above statements are incorrect.

4. Consider a network of 7750 SRs with three CSPF LSPs configured between the same head and tail end router. All ports in the network are 1 Gb/s. Two equal cost paths exist to the tail end router, but ECMP is not enabled on the IGP. The three CSPF LSPs are configured in the following order: a 300 Mb/s LSP, a 400 Mb/s LSP, and a 200 Mb/s LSP. The first and third LSPs have the least-fill option enabled, but the second LSP does not. Assuming that there are no other LSPs in the network, which statement below is correct?

A. The first and second LSPs will have the same path.

B. The first and third LSPs will have the same path.

C. The first and third LSPs will have different paths, but it is not possible to determine which path the second LSP will use.

D. There is not enough information to determine the path of the LSPs.

5. Which statement below is correct regarding DiffServ-aware traffic engineering on an Alcatel-Lucent 7750 SR?

A. An Alcatel-Lucent 7750 SR can be configured to use MAM for some LSPs and RDM for other LSPs.

B. RDM allows lower CTs to allocate the unused bandwidth from higher CTs.

C. RDM allocates bandwidth discretely to different CTs and bandwidth cannot be shared between CTs.

D. If an incorrect class type and priority pair is configured on an LSP the LSP stays operationally down with a failure code of `admissionControlError`.

E. None of the statements are correct.

15.1 RSVP-TE and Bandwidth Reservation

RSVP (Resource Reservation Protocol) was originally designed as a protocol for signaling routers to reserve network resources. In MPLS (Multiprotocol Label Switching), we use RSPVP-TE (Resource Reservation Protocol–Traffic Engineering) to not only signal labels, but also to reserve network bandwidth. As we have seen, the traffic engineering (TE) extensions to the IGP (interior gateway protocol) routing protocols include information regarding available bandwidth. We can use the TED (traffic engineering database) and the CSPF (constrained shortest path first) algorithm to find the best route through the network that has the necessary bandwidth available and then signal our LSP (label switched path) along that path. This is no different from using the constraints such as admin groups and hop limits that we discussed in Chapter 14.

It should be noted that the signaling of bandwidth reservations is purely at the control plane level. The router uses this information to keep track of the resource expectations of the LSPs signaled through the router. This has no impact on the data plane. In other words, there is no restriction on the data sent on an LSP that was signaled with a specific bandwidth requirement. There is nothing to prevent 100 Mb/s of data being sent on an LSP that was signaled with a bandwidth requirement of 1 Mb/s.

Control of the actual data traffic through the router must be managed through quality of service (QoS) policies. These must be designed to work in concert with the traffic engineering policies.

Signaling and Reserving Bandwidth Requirements

When specific bandwidth requirements are requested for an LSP, a CSPF calculation is performed at the head end to find the shortest path to the tail end that satisfies the bandwidth requirements and meets any other constraints on the path. If a path is found, it is signaled in the Path message using a series of strict hops in the `ERO` (`EXPLICIT_ROUTE` object).

Figure 15.1 shows a Path message requesting an LSP with a 600 Mb/s bandwidth reservation on a path of 1 Gb/s links. The CSPF calculation has selected this as the best path that meets the bandwidth constraint; however, it is possible that there have been changes in the network since the last update of the TED. For example, perhaps another LSP has requested resources on the same link. When each router receives the Path message, it first performs Connection Admission Control (CAC) to verify that the requested resources are actually available. If they are not, the Path message is not transmitted downstream, and a PathErr is sent back upstream. If the resources are available, a Path message is sent downstream. The Path message initiates a CAC operation but does not actually trigger the reservation of any bandwidth resources.

Figure 15.1 CAC is performed at each node when the Path message is received.

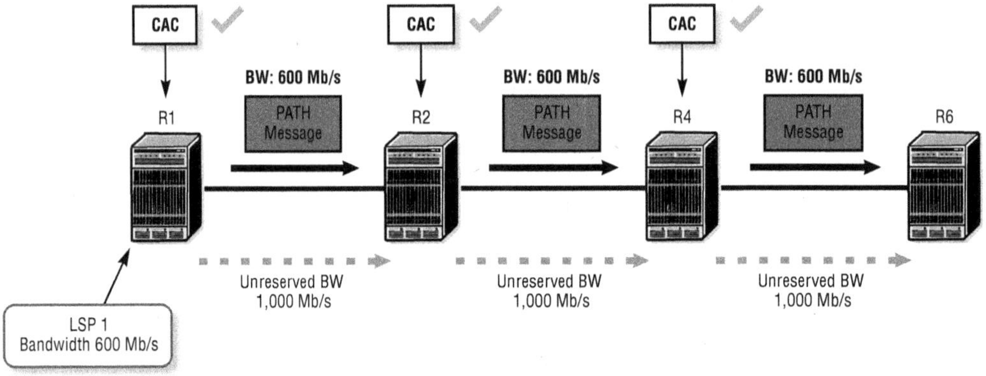

Once the Path message is received by the tail end router, a Resv message is sent upstream (see Figure 15.2). The routers on the path reserve the bandwidth when they receive the Resv message. If the bandwidth has become unavailable, a ResvErr message is sent to the tail end. The tail end will send a ResvTear to the head end to release any resources that have been reserved, and the LSP will remain operationally down.

Figure 15.2 Bandwidth reservations are made following receipt of the Resv message.

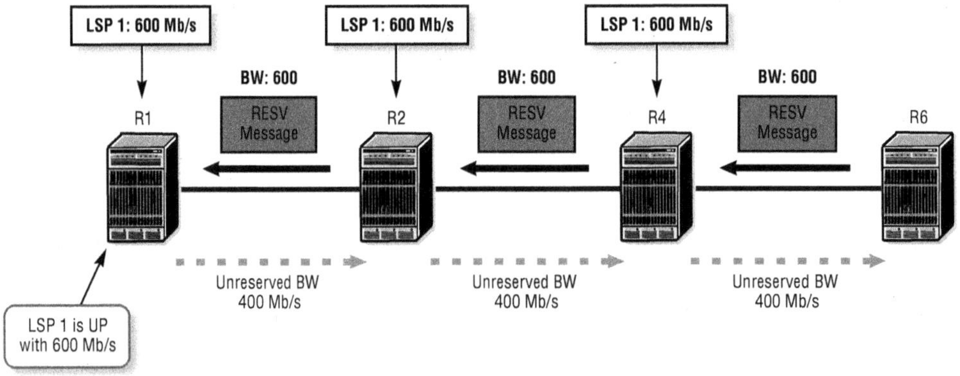

When the resource reservation is made, it changes the TE topology of the network because there is now less bandwidth available on the link. Therefore, each router floods an updated LSA (link-state advertisement) reflecting the change and updating the TED on the other routers in the network.

In Figure 15.3 we have configured the interface on R4 to R6 to be undersubscribed to demonstrate a CAC failure. Remember that an interface can be oversubscribed up to 1,000 percent of the actual bandwidth by specifying reservable bandwidth as a percentage of the actual bandwidth. In this case, we set it to 40 percent, or 400 Mb/s. Listing 15.1 shows the RSVP-TE configuration on R4 to set the subscription rate, or reservable bandwidth. A display of the database shows that LSA `1.0.0.3` advertised by `10.10.10.4` has a much younger age. Examining the LSA we see that reservable bandwidth is, in fact, 400 Mb/s.

Figure 15.3 Network with undersubscribed interface on R4.

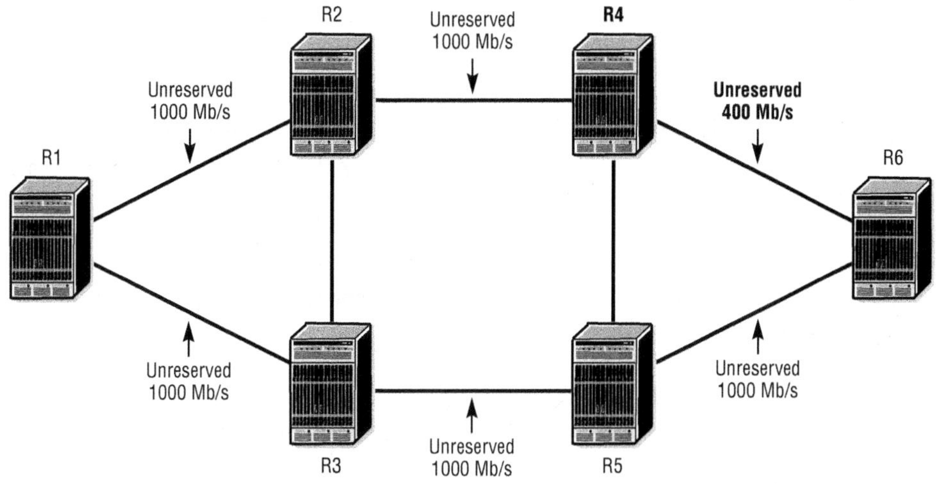

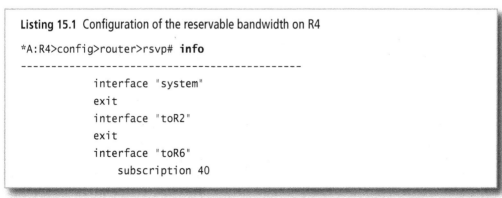

Listing 15.1 Configuration of the reservable bandwidth on R4

```
*A:R4>config>router>rsvp# info
----------------------------------------------
            interface "system"
            exit
            interface "toR2"
            exit
            interface "toR6"
                subscription 40
```

(continued)

Listing 15.1 *(continued)*

```
            exit
            interface "toR5"
            exit
            no shutdown
----------------------------------------------
*A:R4>config>router>rsvp>if# show router ospf opaque-database
adv-router 10.10.10.4

========================================================================
OSPF Opaque Link State Database (Type : All)
========================================================================
Type  Id           Link State Id   Adv Rtr Id     Age  Sequence   Cksum
------------------------------------------------------------------------
Area  0.0.0.0      1.0.0.1         10.10.10.4     749  0x800000fd 0x24e9
Area  0.0.0.0      1.0.0.2         10.10.10.4     992  0x80000200 0x5fdd
Area  0.0.0.0      1.0.0.3         10.10.10.4     15   0x800001fb 0x2d2
Area  0.0.0.0      1.0.0.4         10.10.10.4     689  0x80000171 0xeb2
------------------------------------------------------------------------
No. of Opaque LSAs: 4
========================================================================
*A:R4>config>router>rsvp>if# show router ospf  opaque-database
1.0.0.3 adv-router 10.10.10.4 detail

========================================================================
OSPF Opaque Link State Database (Type : All) (Detailed)
========================================================================
------------------------------------------------------------------------
Opaque LSA
------------------------------------------------------------------------
Area Id          : 0.0.0.0            Adv Router Id     : 10.10.10.4
Link State Id    : 1.0.0.3            LSA Type          : Area Opaque
Sequence No      : 0x800001fb         Checksum          : 0x2d2
Age              : 44                 Length            : 124
Options          :  E
Advertisement    :
     LINK INFO TLV  (0002) Len 100 :
       Sub-TLV: 1     Len: 1     LINK_TYPE    : 1
       Sub-TLV: 2     Len: 4     LINK_ID      : 10.10.10.6
```

```
        Sub-TLV: 3      Len: 4      LOC_IP_ADDR  : 10.4.6.4
        Sub-TLV: 4      Len: 4      REM_IP_ADDR  : 10.4.6.6
        Sub-TLV: 5      Len: 4      TE_METRIC    : 100
        Sub-TLV: 6      Len: 4      MAX_BDWTH    : 1000000 Kbps
        Sub-TLV: 7      Len: 4      RSRVBL_BDWTH : 400000 Kbps
        Sub-TLV: 8      Len: 32     UNRSRVD_CLS0 :
          P0:  400000 Kbps P1:  400000 Kbps P2:  400000 Kbps P3:
          400000 Kbps
          P4:  400000 Kbps P5:  400000 Kbps P6:  400000 Kbps P7:
          400000 Kbps
        Sub-TLV: 9      Len: 4      ADMIN_GROUP  : 00000001 (1)

===============================================================================
```

If we configure an LSP on R1 with a bandwidth reservation of 600 Mb/s but do not specify `cspf` in the LSP, it is signaled without performing the CSPF calculation. The Path message follows the IGP, and, as expected, the LSP fails at node R4 with a CAC failure (see Figure 15.4). Listing 15.2 shows the configuration of the LSP on R1 and the failed LSP.

Figure 15.4 LSP signaled without CSPF showing CAC failure.

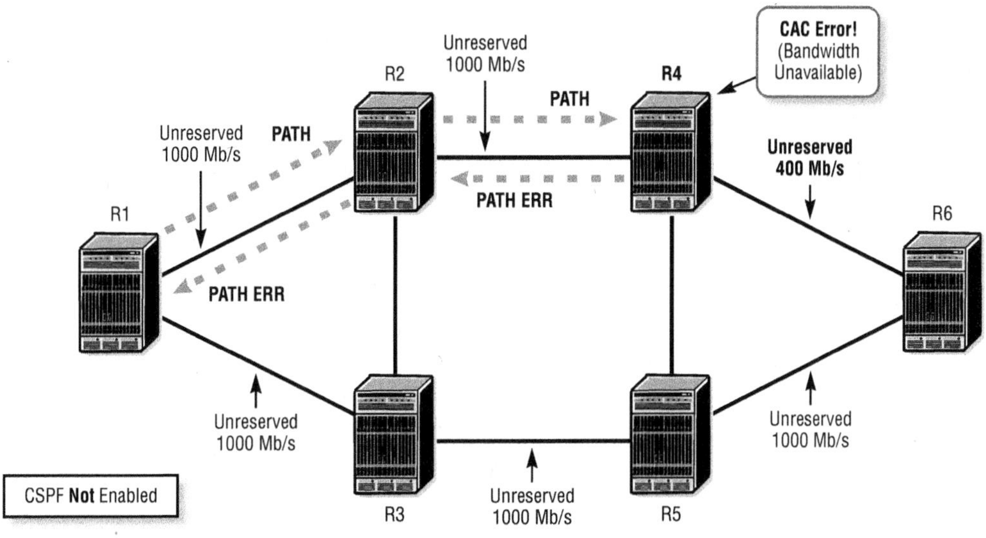

Listing 15.2 Configuring a bandwidth reservation without specifying CSPF

```
*A:R1>config>router>mpls# info
----------------------------------------------
            interface "system"
            exit
            interface "toR2"
            exit
            interface "toR3"
            exit
            path "loose"
                no shutdown
            exit
            lsp "toR6"
                to 10.10.10.6
                primary "loose"
                    bandwidth 600
                exit
                no shutdown
            exit
            no shutdown
----------------------------------------------
*A:R1>config>router>mpls# show router mpls lsp "toR6" path detail

=======================================================================
MPLS LSP toR6 Path  (Detail)
=======================================================================
Legend :
    @ - Detour Available              # - Detour In Use
    b - Bandwidth Protected           n - Node Protected
    s - Soft Preemption
=======================================================================
-----------------------------------------------------------------------
LSP toR6 Path loose
-----------------------------------------------------------------------
LSP Name     : toR6                         Path LSP ID : 58892
From         : 10.10.10.1                   To          : 10.10.10.6
Adm State    : Up                           Oper State  : Down
Path Name    : loose                        Path Type   : Primary
Path Admin   : Up                           Path Oper   : Down
```

```
OutInterface: n/a                          Out Label    : n/a
Path Up Time: 0d 00:00:00                  Path Dn Time: 0d 00:00:23
Retry Limit : 0                            Retry Timer : 30 sec
RetryAttempt: 1                            NextRetryIn : 14 sec
SetupPriori*: 7                            Hold Priori*: 0
Preference  : n/a
Bandwidth   : 600 Mbps                     Oper Bw     : 0 Mbps
Hop Limit   : 255                          Class Type  : 0

... output omitted ...

Failure Code: admissionControlError        Failure Node: 10.2.4.4
ExplicitHops:
    No Hops Specified
Actual Hops :
    No Hops Specified
ResigEligib*: False
LastResignal: n/a                          CSPF Metric : 0
=======================================================================
* indicates that the corresponding row element may have been truncated.
```

Listing 15.3 shows the Path and PathErr messages sent for the LSP. Because `cspf` is not specified and the path is completely loose, there is no `ERO` sent in the Path message.

Listing 15.3 Path and PathErr messages showing CAC failure

```
*A:R1# show debug
debug
    router "Base"
        rsvp
            packet
                path detail
                patherr detail
            exit
        exit
    exit
exit
*A:R1# configure log log-id 11
```

(continued)

Listing 15.3 *(continued)*

```
*A:R1>config>log>log-id$ from debug-trace
*A:R1>config>log>log-id$ to session
*A:R1>config>log>log-id$ exit
*A:R1#

2 2011/01/15 18:33:14.02 UTC MINOR: DEBUG #2001 Base RSVP
"RSVP: PATH Msg
Send PATH From:10.10.10.1, To:10.10.10.6
          TTL:255, Checksum:0xda9b, Flags:0x0
Session     - EndPt:10.10.10.6, TunnId:14, ExtTunnId:10.10.10.1
SessAttr    - Name:toR6::loose
              SetupPri:7, HoldPri:0, Flags:0x6
RSVPHop     - Addr:10.1.2.1, LIH:2
TimeValue   - RefreshPeriod:30
SendTempl   - Sender:10.10.10.1, LspId:58912
SendTSpec   - Ctype:QOS, CDR:600.000 Mbps, PBS:600.000 Mbps, PDR:infinity
              MPU:20, MTU:9198
LabelReq    - IfType:General, L3ProtID:2048
RRO         - IpAddr:10.1.2.1, Flags:0x0
"

3 2011/01/15 18:33:14.03 UTC MINOR: DEBUG #2001 Base RSVP
"RSVP: PATHERR Msg
Recv PATHERR From:10.1.2.2, To:10.1.2.1
              TTL:255, Checksum:0xcb08, Flags:0x0
Session     - EndPt:10.10.10.6, TunnId:14, ExtTunnId:10.10.10.1
ErrorSpec   - ErrNode:10.2.4.4, Flags:0x0, ErrCode:1, ErrValue:2
SendTempl   - Sender:10.10.10.1, LspId:58912
SendTSpec   - Ctype:QOS, CDR:600.000 Mbps, PBS:600.000 Mbps, PDR:infinity
              MPU:20, MTU:9198
"
```

Once `cspf` is configured on the LSP, the CSPF calculation is performed and chooses the path R1–R3–R5–R6, as shown in Figure 15.5. Listing 15.4 shows the Path message. Note that it now contains an `ERO` with strict hops for the entire path.

Figure 15.5 LSP with CSPF finds the best path to satisfy bandwidth requirements.

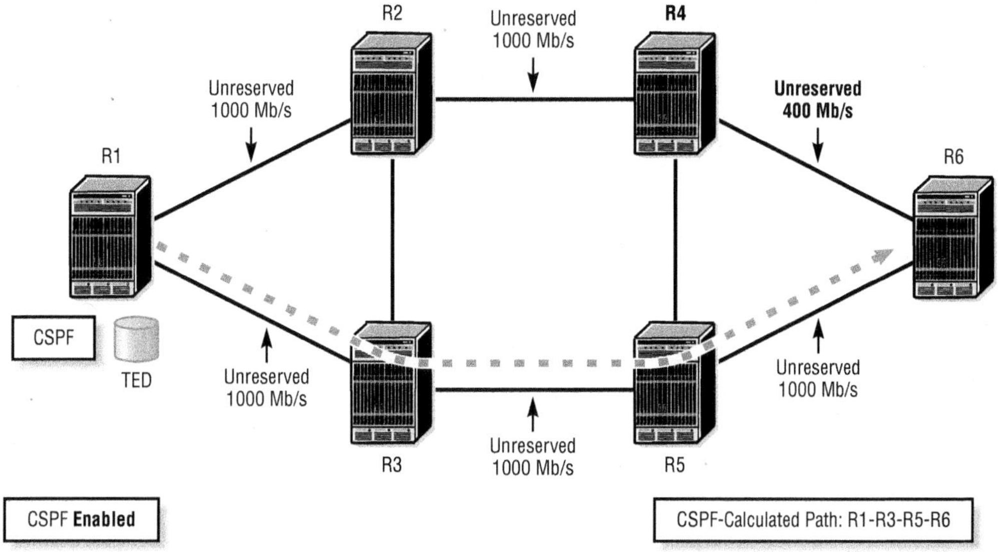

Listing 15.4 Path message with ERO created by CSPF calculation on the LSP

```
10 2011/01/15 18:41:35.02 UTC MINOR: DEBUG #2001 Base RSVP
"RSVP: PATH Msg
Send PATH From:10.10.10.1, To:10.10.10.6
          TTL:255, Checksum:0xf523, Flags:0x0
Session    - EndPt:10.10.10.6, TunnId:14, ExtTunnId:10.10.10.1
SessAttr   - Name:toR6::loose
             SetupPri:7, HoldPri:0, Flags:0x46
RSVPHop    - Addr:10.1.3.1, LIH:3
TimeValue  - RefreshPeriod:30
SendTempl  - Sender:10.10.10.1, LspId:58926
SendTSpec  - Ctype:QOS, CDR:600.000 Mbps, PBS:600.000 Mbps, PDR:infinity
             MPU:20, MTU:9198
LabelReq   - IfType:General, L3ProtID:2048
RRO        - IpAddr:10.1.3.1, Flags:0x0
ERO        - Prefix:10.1.3.3/32, Type:Strict
             Prefix:10.3.5.5/32, Type:Strict
             Prefix:10.5.6.6/32, Type:Strict
"
```

Once the path is established, the routers flood new LSAs to reflect the change in available network resources. Listing 15.5 shows the LSA flooded by R1 about its link to R3. The LSA shows only 400 Mb/s bandwidth available at all eight priority levels (P0–P7) because bandwidth is reserved at the highest priority (P0) by default. The use of priority levels for bandwidth reservations is described in more detail below in the chapter.

Listing 15.5 LSA from R1 showing only 400 Mb/s available

```
*A:R1# show router ospf opaque-database 1.0.0.3 adv-router 10.10.10.1
detail

===============================================================================
OSPF Opaque Link State Database (Type : All) (Detailed)
===============================================================================
-------------------------------------------------------------------------------
Opaque LSA
-------------------------------------------------------------------------------
Area Id          : 0.0.0.0              Adv Router Id    : 10.10.10.1
Link State Id    : 1.0.0.3              LSA Type         : Area Opaque
Sequence No      : 0x80000207           Checksum         : 0xf485
Age              : 1275                 Length           : 124
Options          :  E
Advertisement    :
     LINK INFO TLV  (0002) Len 100 :
       Sub-TLV: 1     Len: 1     LINK_TYPE     : 1
       Sub-TLV: 2     Len: 4     LINK_ID       : 10.10.10.3
       Sub-TLV: 3     Len: 4     LOC_IP_ADDR   : 10.1.3.1
       Sub-TLV: 4     Len: 4     REM_IP_ADDR   : 10.1.3.3
       Sub-TLV: 5     Len: 4     TE_METRIC     : 100
       Sub-TLV: 6     Len: 4     MAX_BDWTH     : 1000000 Kbps
       Sub-TLV: 7     Len: 4     RSRVBL_BDWTH : 1000000 Kbps
       Sub-TLV: 8     Len: 32    UNRSRVD_CLS0 :
         P0:  400000 Kbps P1:  400000 Kbps P2:  400000 Kbps P3:
         400000 Kbps
         P4:  400000 Kbps P5:  400000 Kbps P6:  400000 Kbps P7:
         400000 Kbps
       Sub-TLV: 9     Len: 4     ADMIN_GROUP  : 0 None

===============================================================================
```

Threshold-Triggered IGP TE Updates

Whenever an LSP is successfully signaled with bandwidth reservations or when one is torn down and resources are released, this represents a change in the TE topology of the network. As a result, the routers involved each flood new LSAs to reflect the change, and every router in the network must update its TE database. In a large network with many traffic-engineered LSPs, this can create a significant processing requirement in the control plane.

To reduce the number of updates flooded, the 7750 SR can be configured for threshold-triggered IGP TE updates. This means that the router does not immediately flood an updated LSA whenever there is a change in the reserved bandwidth, but, rather, it only sends updates when the reserved bandwidth crosses specific thresholds. The thresholds are specified as a percentage of maximum reservable bandwidth and are set in the up (reserved bandwidth increasing) and in the down (reserved bandwidth decreasing) directions (Figure 15.6). The values for up and down are set individually.

Figure 15.6 Values for threshold-triggered updates.

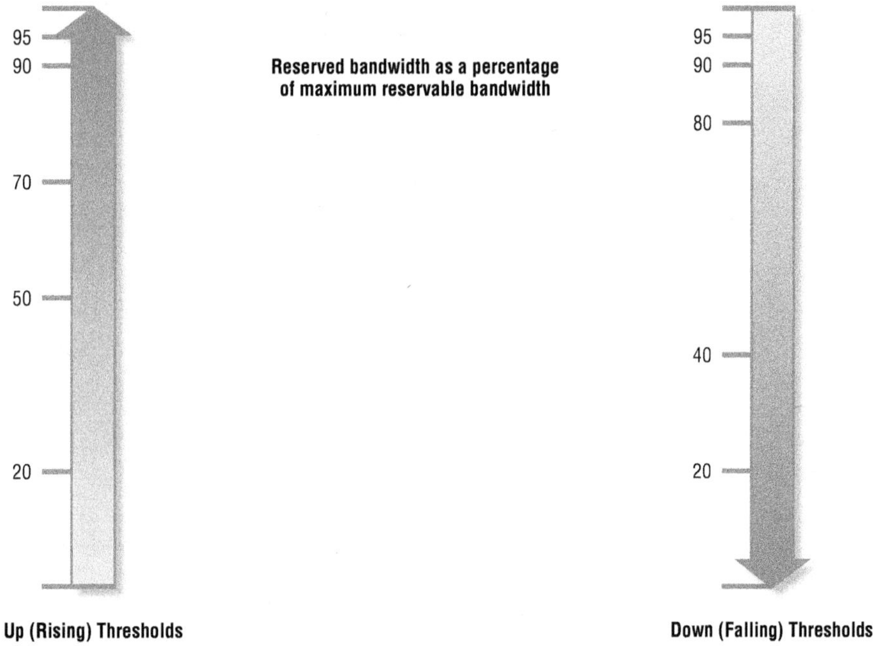

Listing 15.6 shows the activation of threshold-triggered updates with the `configure router rsvp te-threshold-update` command (not enabled by default). The default values for the thresholds are shown, although these can be modified by the user with a maximum of 16 values in each direction.

Listing 15.6 Configuring IGP TE update thresholds

```
*A:R1>config>router>rsvp# info
----------------------------------------------
            te-threshold-update
                on-cac-failure
            exit
            interface "system"
            exit
            interface "toR2"
            exit
            interface "toR3"
            exit
            no shutdown
----------------------------------------------
*A:R1>config>router>rsvp# show router rsvp status

===============================================================================
RSVP Status
===============================================================================
Admin Status        : Up                    Oper Status         : Up
Keep Multiplier     : 3                     Refresh Time        : 30 sec

... output omitted ...

IgpThresholdUpdate : Enabled
Up Thresholds(%)   : 0 15 30 45 60 75 80 85 90 95 96 97 98 99 100
Down Thresholds(%) : 100 99 98 97 96 95 90 85 80 75 60 45 30 15 0
Update Timer       : N/A
Update on CAC Fail : Enabled
===============================================================================
*A:R1>config>router>rsvp# te-up-threshold 50 60 80 90 95 98 99 100
*A:R1>config>router>rsvp# te-down-threshold 100 98 95 90 70 50
*A:R1>config>router>rsvp# show router rsvp status
```

```
=======================================================================
RSVP Status
=======================================================================
Admin Status        : Up                    Oper Status         : Up
Keep Multiplier     : 3                     Refresh Time        : 30 sec

... output omitted ...

IgpThresholdUpdate : Enabled
Up Thresholds(%)    : 50 60 80 90 95 98 99 100
Down Thresholds(%) : 100 98 95 90 70 50
Update Timer        : N/A
Update on CAC Fail : Enabled
=======================================================================
*A:R1>config>router>rsvp#
```

The disadvantage of using triggered updates is that the TE will be more out of date than if updates are flooded immediately. This means there is a greater chance of CAC failure upon signaling a new LSP. Notice that `te-threshold-update` was configured with the option `on-cac-failure`. This means that if there is a CAC failure when signaling a TE LSP, IGP updates will be flooded immediately (without waiting until the threshold is crossed).

15.2 Bandwidth Reservation Styles

Bandwidth reservation styles refer to the situation in which multiple LSP::Paths are defined for the same RSVP-TE tunnel. In Chapter 16 we will see that multiple secondary paths can be defined for the same RSVP-TE tunnel to provide redundancy. These represent distinct LSPs because they have different label mappings; however, they will all have the same Tunnel ID. Only one of the LSP::Paths will be transporting data at a given time.

The two methods of signaling bandwidth requirements are the Shared Explicit and Fixed Filter reservation styles. *Shared Explicit* means that any reserved bandwidth is shared by all of the LSP::Paths of a specific RSVP-TE tunnel. *Fixed Filter* means that each LSP::Path receives its own bandwidth allocation. On the Alcatel-Lucent 7750 SR, Shared Explicit is the default reservation style.

Reservation styles only apply to LSP::Paths that share the same Tunnel ID. LSPs with different Tunnel IDs are distinct LSPs and never share bandwidth.

Shared Explicit Bandwidth Reservation

Listing 15.7 shows the configuration of the LSP `toR6` with a secondary path defined (`standby` on the secondary means that the LSP::Path is signaled and active). Both the primary and secondary paths have bandwidth reservations.

Listing 15.7 Configuring an LSP with bandwidth reservations on primary and secondary paths

```
*A:R1>config>router>mpls# info
----------------------------------------------
            interface "system"
            exit
            interface "toR2"
            exit
            path "loose"
                no shutdown
            exit
            path "one_strict"
                hop 5 10.10.10.3 loose
                no shutdown
            exit
            lsp "toR6"
                to 10.10.10.6
                cspf
                primary "loose"
                    bandwidth 500
                exit
                secondary "one_strict"
                    standby
                    bandwidth 400
                exit
                no shutdown
            exit
            lsp "toR4"
                to 10.10.10.4
```

```
            cspf
            primary "loose"
                bandwidth 100
            exit
            no shutdown
        exit
        no shutdown
----------------------------------------------
```

Figure 15.7 shows the bandwidth requirements for the two LSPs. Although the primary path requests 500 Mb/s and the secondary path requests 400 Mb/s, the total bandwidth reserved on the interface toward R2 is still only 600 (the 500 Mb/s requested by `toR6` plus the 100 Mb/s requested by `toR4`). This is logical because data is not expected to be traveling on the primary and secondary paths at the same time. Notice that both LSP::Paths for the primary and secondary paths have the same Tunnel ID, whereas the Tunnel ID for `toR4` is different (see Listing 15.8).

Figure 15.7 Shared Explicit reservation style.

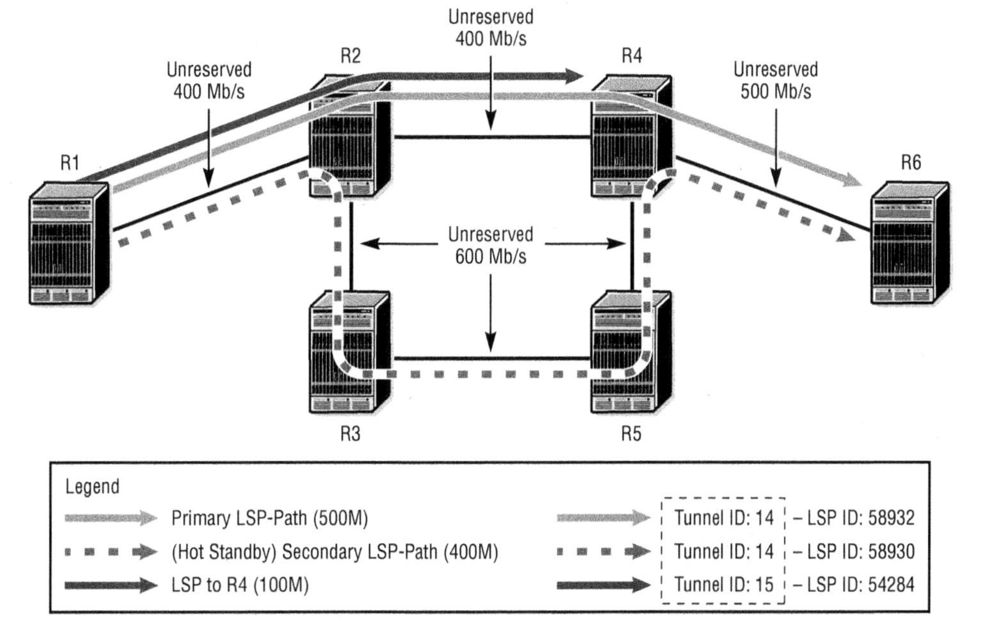

Listing 15.8 Bandwidth reserved with Shared Explicit style

```
*A:R1>config>router>mpls# show router rsvp session

==========================================================================
RSVP Sessions
==========================================================================
From          To            Tunnel LSP   Name                     State
                            ID     ID
--------------------------------------------------------------------------
10.10.10.1    10.10.10.6    14     58930 toR6::one_strict         Up
10.10.10.1    10.10.10.4    15     54284 toR4::loose              Up
10.10.10.1    10.10.10.6    14     58932 toR6::loose              Up
--------------------------------------------------------------------------
Sessions : 3
==========================================================================
*A:R1>config>router>mpls# show router rsvp interface

==========================================================================
RSVP Interfaces
==========================================================================
Interface               Total    Active   Total BW  Resv BW   Adm Opr
                        Sessions Sessions (Mbps)    (Mbps)
--------------------------------------------------------------------------
system                  -        -        -         -         Up  Up
toR2                    3        3        1000      600       Up  Up
--------------------------------------------------------------------------
Interfaces : 2
==========================================================================
```

Fixed Filter Bandwidth Reservation

With the *Fixed Filter* reservation style, each LSP::Path receives an individual bandwidth reservation. Therefore, the bandwidth consumed by the LSP tunnel is the sum of the bandwidth of all the LSP::Paths. Figure 15.8 shows the same LSPs, except that the Fixed Filter reservation style is used. Listing 15.9 shows that all the bandwidth on the interface toward R2 has been reserved (500 + 400 + 100 = 1,000 Mb/s). In most cases, this is a waste of bandwidth, and thus it is not the default behavior on the 7750 SR.

Figure 15.8 Fixed Filter reservation style.

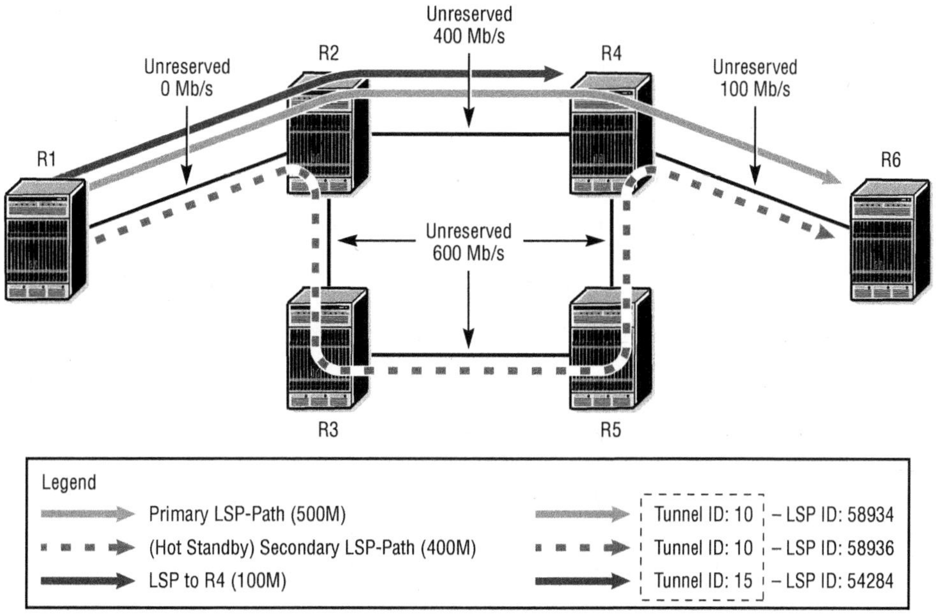

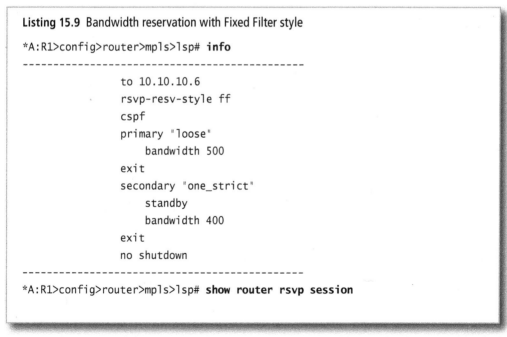

Listing 15.9 Bandwidth reservation with Fixed Filter style

```
*A:R1>config>router>mpls>lsp# info
----------------------------------------------
                to 10.10.10.6
                rsvp-resv-style ff
                cspf
                primary "loose"
                    bandwidth 500
                exit
                secondary "one_strict"
                    standby
                    bandwidth 400
                exit
                no shutdown
----------------------------------------------
*A:R1>config>router>mpls>lsp# show router rsvp session
```

(continued)

Listing 15.9 *(continued)*

```
===============================================================================
RSVP Sessions
===============================================================================
From            To              Tunnel LSP   Name                          State
                                ID     ID
-------------------------------------------------------------------------------
10.10.10.1      10.10.10.4      15     54284 toR4::loose                   Up
10.10.10.1      10.10.10.6      14     58936 toR6::one_strict              Up
10.10.10.1      10.10.10.6      14     58934 toR6::loose                   Up
-------------------------------------------------------------------------------
Sessions : 3
===============================================================================
*A:R1>config>router>mpls>lsp# show router rsvp interface

===============================================================================
RSVP Interfaces
===============================================================================
Interface                 Total    Active    Total BW   Resv BW    Adm Opr
                          Sessions Sessions  (Mbps)     (Mbps)
-------------------------------------------------------------------------------
system                    -        -         -          -          Up  Up
toR2                      3        3         1000       1000       Up  Up
-------------------------------------------------------------------------------
Interfaces : 2
===============================================================================
```

Make-Before-Break (MBB)

By default, RSVP-TE uses a strategy called *make-before-break* (MBB) in any situation that necessitates the resignaling of an existing LSP, for example, an increase in reserved bandwidth for the LSP. With MBB, traffic will continue to flow on the existing LSP::Path while the head end signals a new LSP::Path with the new requirements.

Figure 15.9 shows an LSP with a bandwidth reservation of 500 Mb/s. The bandwidth requirement is increased to 600 Mb/s; thus, a new LSP::Path is signaled with a request for 600 Mb/s. Because it is a Shared Explicit style LSP, only the incremental 100 Mb/s bandwidth needs to be available. Listing 15.10 shows the state of the LSP before the bandwidth is increased.

Figure 15.9 Increasing bandwidth reservation on a Shared Explicit LSP.

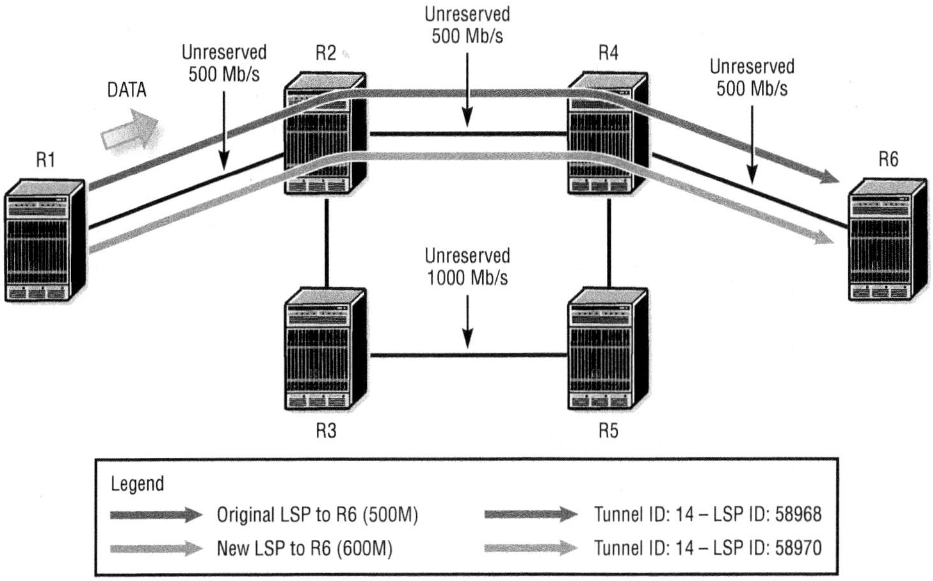

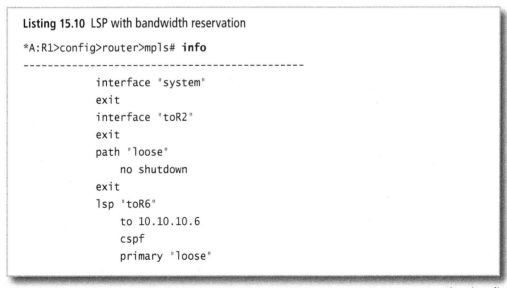

Listing 15.10 LSP with bandwidth reservation

```
*A:R1>config>router>mpls# info
----------------------------------------------
            interface "system"
            exit
            interface "toR2"
            exit
            path "loose"
                no shutdown
            exit
            lsp "toR6"
                to 10.10.10.6
                cspf
                primary "loose"
```

(continued)

Listing 15.10 *(continued)*

```
                bandwidth 500
            exit
            no shutdown
        exit
        no shutdown
----------------------------------------------
*A:R1>config>router>mpls>lsp# show router rsvp session

========================================================================
RSVP Sessions
========================================================================
From          To            Tunnel LSP   Name                      State
                            ID     ID
------------------------------------------------------------------------
10.10.10.1    10.10.10.6    14     58968 toR6::loose               Up
------------------------------------------------------------------------
Sessions : 1
========================================================================
*A:R1>config>router>mpls>lsp# show router rsvp interface

========================================================================
RSVP Interfaces
========================================================================
Interface                Total    Active   Total BW  Resv BW   Adm Opr
                         Sessions Sessions (Mbps)    (Mbps)
------------------------------------------------------------------------
system                   -        -        -         -         Up  Up
toR2                     1        1        1000      500       Up  Up
------------------------------------------------------------------------
Interfaces : 2
========================================================================
```

Once the new LSP is successfully signaled, traffic is switched to the new LSP::Path, and the original one is torn down with a PathTear message (Figure 15.10). No change is made to the data flow until the new LSP has been successfully signaled, to ensure that there is no loss of data. Listing 15.11 shows the LSP that was resignaled and the fact that the bandwidth was successfully increased using MBB behavior.

Figure 15.10 MBB behavior on a Shared Explicit LSP.

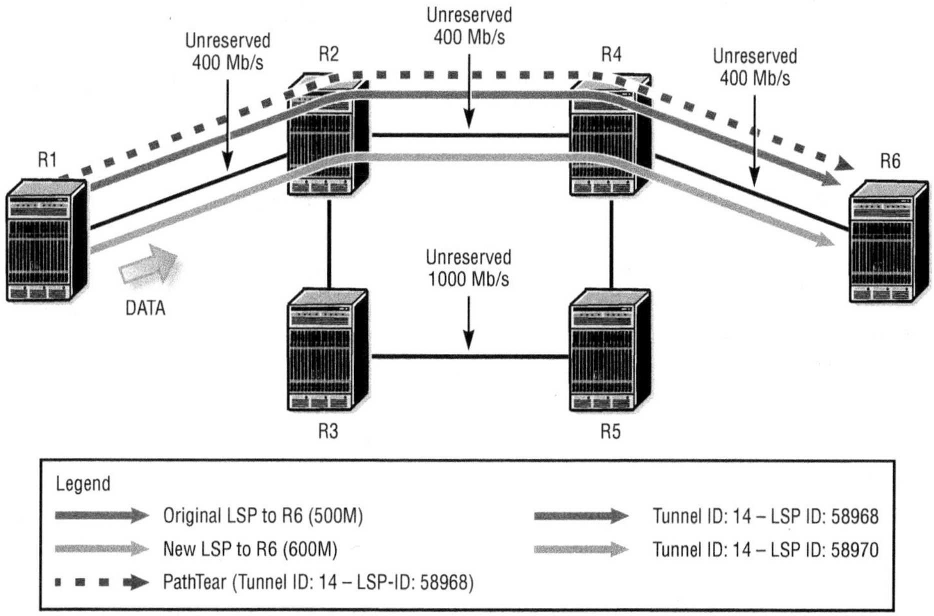

Listing 15.11 MBB used to increase bandwidth on an LSP

```
*A:R1>config>router>mpls>lsp# primary "loose" bandwidth 600
*A:R1>config>router>mpls>lsp# show router rsvp interface

===============================================================================
RSVP Interfaces
===============================================================================
Interface                Total    Active    Total BW  Resv BW   Adm Opr
                         Sessions Sessions  (Mbps)    (Mbps)
-------------------------------------------------------------------------------
system                   -        -         -         -         Up  Up
toR2                     1        1         1000      600       Up  Up
-------------------------------------------------------------------------------
Interfaces : 2
===============================================================================
*A:R1>config>router>mpls>lsp# show router mpls lsp "toR6" path detail
```

(continued)

Listing 15.11 *(continued)*

```
===============================================================================
MPLS LSP toR6 Path  (Detail)
===============================================================================
Legend :
    @ - Detour Available              # - Detour In Use
    b - Bandwidth Protected           n - Node Protected
    s - Soft Preemption
===============================================================================
-------------------------------------------------------------------------------
LSP toR6 Path loose
-------------------------------------------------------------------------------
LSP Name    : toR6                          Path LSP ID : 58970
From        : 10.10.10.1                    To          : 10.10.10.6
Adm State   : Up                            Oper State  : Up
Path Name   : loose                         Path Type   : Primary
Path Admin  : Up                            Path Oper   : Up
OutInterface: 1/1/2                         Out Label   : 131066
Path Up Time: 0d 00:02:11                   Path Dn Time: 0d 00:00:00
Retry Limit : 0                             Retry Timer : 30 sec
RetryAttempt: 0                             NextRetryIn : 0 sec
SetupPriori*: 7                             Hold Priori*: 0
Preference  : n/a
Bandwidth   : 600 Mbps                      Oper Bw     : 600 Mbps

... output omitted ...

ExplicitHops:
    No Hops Specified
Actual Hops :
    10.1.2.1(10.10.10.1)                    Record Label    : N/A
 -> 10.1.2.2(10.10.10.2)                    Record Label    : 131066
 -> 10.2.4.4(10.10.10.4)                    Record Label    : 131065
 -> 10.4.6.6(10.10.10.6)                    Record Label    : 131064
ComputedHops:
    10.1.2.1       -> 10.1.2.2       -> 10.2.4.4       -> 10.4.6.6
ResigEligib*: False
LastResignal: n/a                           CSPF Metric : 300
Last MBB    :
```

```
MBB Type    : ConfigChange                        MBB State    : Success
Ended At    : 01/16/2011 17:49:02                 Old Metric   : 300
===============================================================================
* indicates that the corresponding row element may have been truncated.
```

Listing 15.12 shows the debug output for the PathTear message sent after the new LSP has been successfully signaled.

Listing 15.12 PathTear message for old LSP after resignaling

```
*A:R1# show debug
debug
    router "Base"
        rsvp
            packet
                pathtear detail
            exit
        exit
    exit
exit
10 2011/01/16 17:49:05.02 UTC MINOR: DEBUG #2001 Base RSVP
"RSVP: PATHTEAR Msg
Send PATHTEAR From:10.10.10.1, To:10.10.10.6
              TTL:255, Checksum:0x13f5, Flags:0x0
Session     - EndPt:10.10.10.6, TunnId:14, ExtTunnId:10.10.10.1
RSVPHop     - Addr:10.1.2.1, LIH:2
SendTempl   - Sender:10.10.10.1, LspId:58968
SendTSpec   - Ctype:QOS, CDR:500.000 Mbps, PBS:500.000 Mbps, PDR:infinity
              MPU:20, MTU:9198
"
```

If the LSP is configured with a Fixed Filter reservation style, then the bandwidth available in the network must be the sum of the bandwidth reserved for the original LSP::Path plus the new LSP::Path. Listing 15.13 shows an LSP that is to be increased to 600 Mb/s bandwidth in the same topology as above.

Listing 15.13 Fixed Filter LSP

```
*A:R1>config>router>mpls>lsp# info
----------------------------------------------
              to 10.10.10.6
              rsvp-resv-style ff
              cspf
              primary "loose"
                  bandwidth 500
              exit
              no shutdown
----------------------------------------------
*A:R1>config>router>mpls>lsp# show router rsvp session

=======================================================================
RSVP Sessions
=======================================================================
From          To            Tunnel LSP   Name                    State
                            ID     ID
-----------------------------------------------------------------------
10.10.10.1    10.10.10.6    14     58974 toR6::loose             Up
-----------------------------------------------------------------------
Sessions : 1
=======================================================================
*A:R1>config>router>mpls>lsp# show router rsvp interface

=======================================================================
RSVP Interfaces
=======================================================================
Interface                Total    Active   Total BW  Resv BW   Adm Opr
                         Sessions Sessions (Mbps)    (Mbps)
-----------------------------------------------------------------------
system                   -        -        -         -         Up  Up
toR2                     1        1        1000      500       Up  Up
-----------------------------------------------------------------------
Interfaces : 2
=======================================================================
*A:R1>config>router>mpls>lsp#
```

A CSPF calculation is performed to find a path that provides the bandwidth. However, because the LSP is Fixed Filter, 1100 Mb/s is required but is not available. Because MBB is used, the old LSP is not torn down but continues to be used after the CSPF calculation fails. Listing 15.14 shows the status of the LSP after the attempt to increase the bandwidth. Note the following interesting details from the `show router mpls path detail` command:

- LSP ID has not changed because the original LSP::Path is still being used.
- Output shows a bandwidth of 600 Mb/s but an operational bandwidth of only 500 Mb/s.
- Output shows MBB as "in progress." The head end will continue to retry the CSPF calculation until it finds a path that satisfies the bandwidth requirements.

Listing 15.14 MBB behavior when new LSP cannot be signaled

```
*A:R1>config>router>mpls>lsp# primary "loose" bandwidth 600
*A:R1>config>router>mpls>lsp# show router mpls lsp "toR6" path detail

===============================================================================
MPLS LSP toR6 Path  (Detail)
===============================================================================
Legend :
    @ - Detour Available              # - Detour In Use
    b - Bandwidth Protected           n - Node Protected
    s - Soft Preemption
===============================================================================
-------------------------------------------------------------------------------
LSP toR6 Path loose
-------------------------------------------------------------------------------
LSP Name     : toR6                        Path LSP ID : 58974
From         : 10.10.10.1                  To          : 10.10.10.6
Adm State    : Up                          Oper State  : Up
Path Name    : loose                       Path Type   : Primary
Path Admin   : Up                          Path Oper   : Up
OutInterface: 1/1/2                        Out Label   : 131065
Path Up Time: 0d 00:05:08                  Path Dn Time: 0d 00:00:00
Retry Limit : 0                            Retry Timer : 30 sec
```

(continued)

Listing 15.14 *(continued)*

```
RetryAttempt: 0                          NextRetryIn : 0 sec
SetupPriori*: 7                          Hold Priori*: 0
Preference  : n/a
Bandwidth   : 600 Mbps                   Oper Bw     : 500 Mbps
Hop Limit   : 255                        Class Type  : 0
Backup CT   : None
MainCT Retry: n/a                        MainCT Retry: 0
    Rem     :                                Limit   :
Oper CT     : 0
Record Route: Record                     Record Label: Record
Oper MTU    : 9198                       Neg MTU     : 9198
Adaptive    : Enabled                    Oper Metric : 300
Include Grps:                            Exclude Grps:
None                                   None
Path Trans  : 35                         CSPF Queries: 24
Failure Code: noError                    Failure Node: n/a
ExplicitHops:
    No Hops Specified
Actual Hops :
    10.1.2.1(10.10.10.1)                 Record Label    : N/A
 -> 10.1.2.2(10.10.10.2)                 Record Label    : 131065
 -> 10.2.4.4(10.10.10.4)                 Record Label    : 131064
 -> 10.4.6.6(10.10.10.6)                 Record Label    : 131063
ComputedHops:
    10.1.2.1        -> 10.1.2.2        -> 10.2.4.4        -> 10.4.6.6
ResigEligib*: False
LastResignal: n/a                        CSPF Metric : 300
In Prog MBB :
 MBB Type   : ConfigChange               NextRetryIn : 13 sec
 Started At : 01/16/2011 18:23:19        RetryAttempt: 1
 FailureCode: noCspfRouteToDestination   Failure Node: 10.10.10.1
======================================================================
* indicates that the corresponding row element may have been truncated.
*A:R1>config>router>mpls>lsp#
```

Least-Fill Bandwidth Reservation

Figure 15.11 shows a network topology with two equal cost paths from R1 to R6 and two LSPs that have reserved bandwidth. Listing 15.15 shows the configuration of the LSPs.

Figure 15.11 Multiple bandwidth reservations.

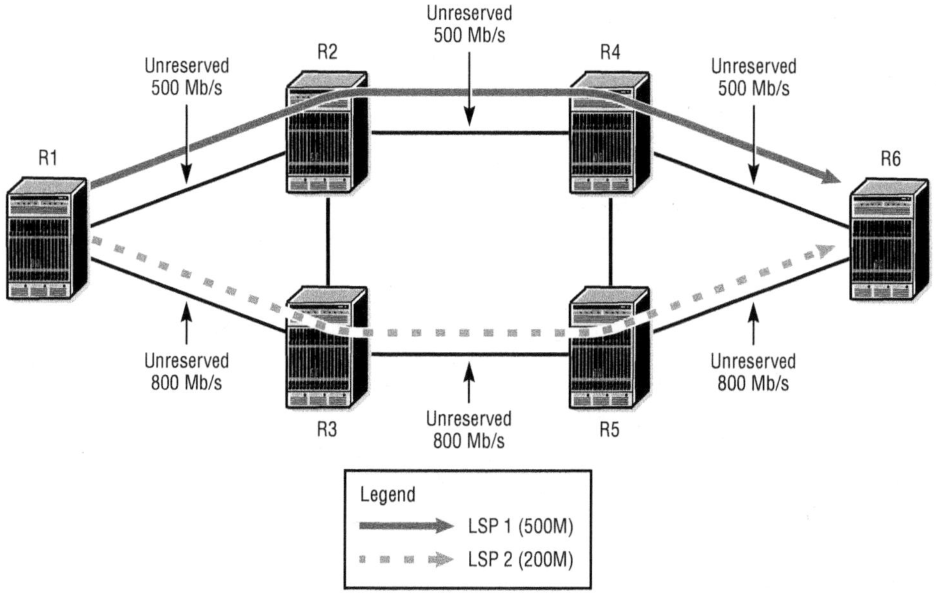

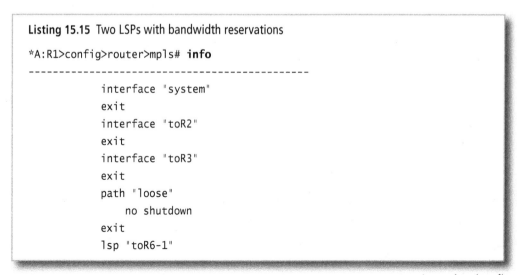

Listing 15.15 Two LSPs with bandwidth reservations

```
*A:R1>config>router>mpls# info
----------------------------------------------
            interface "system"
            exit
            interface "toR2"
            exit
            interface "toR3"
            exit
            path "loose"
                no shutdown
            exit
            lsp "toR6-1"
```

(continued)

Listing 15.15 *(continued)*

```
                to 10.10.10.6
                cspf
                primary "loose"
                    bandwidth 500
                exit
                no shutdown
            exit
            lsp "toR6-2"
                to 10.10.10.6
                cspf
                primary "loose"
                    bandwidth 200
                exit
                no shutdown
            exit
            no shutdown
---------------------------------------------
*A:R1>config>router>mpls# show router rsvp interface

======================================================================
RSVP Interfaces
======================================================================
Interface                Total    Active   Total BW  Resv BW   Adm Opr
                         Sessions Sessions (Mbps)    (Mbps)
----------------------------------------------------------------------
system                   -        -        -         -         Up  Up
toR2                     1        1        1000      500       Up  Up
toR3                     1        1        1000      200       Up  Up
----------------------------------------------------------------------
Interfaces : 3
======================================================================
```

When a new LSP is configured with a bandwidth reservation and there are multiple equal cost paths to the destination, the default behavior of CSPF is to randomly select any one of the paths that satisfies the bandwidth requirement. As a result, bandwidth usage might not be evenly distributed as seen in Figure 15.12. Listing 15.16 shows the change after the new LSP is configured.

Figure 15.12 Additional LSP with bandwidth reservation added.

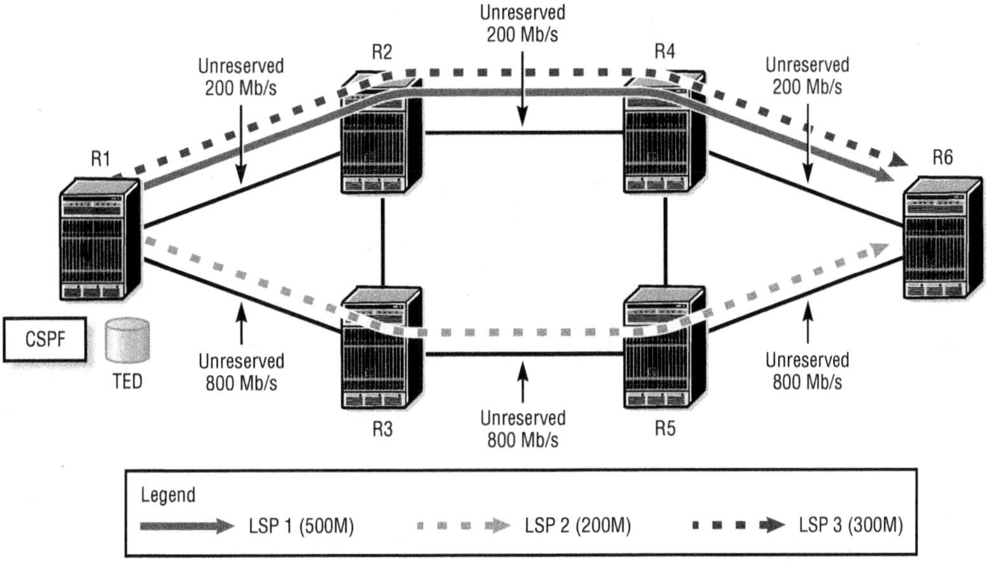

Listing 15.16 New LSP is added to path with less bandwidth available

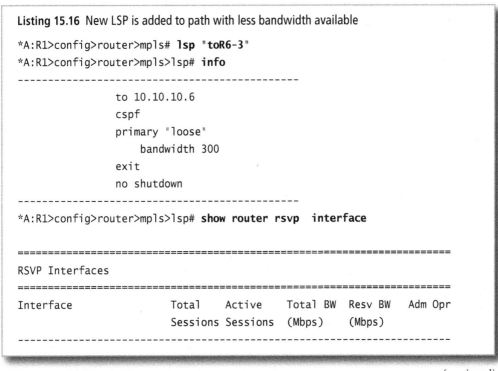

```
*A:R1>config>router>mpls# lsp "toR6-3"
*A:R1>config>router>mpls>lsp# info
----------------------------------------------
                to 10.10.10.6
                cspf
                primary "loose"
                    bandwidth 300
                exit
                no shutdown
----------------------------------------------
*A:R1>config>router>mpls>lsp# show router rsvp  interface

=======================================================================
RSVP Interfaces
=======================================================================
Interface                 Total    Active    Total BW  Resv BW   Adm Opr
                          Sessions Sessions  (Mbps)    (Mbps)
-----------------------------------------------------------------------
```

(continued)

(continued)

Listing 15.16 *(continued)*

```
system                        -     -     -       -      Up  Up
toR2                          2     2     1000    800    Up  Up
toR3                          1     1     1000    200    Up  Up
-----------------------------------------------------------------------
Interfaces : 3
=======================================================================
```

To force CSPF to choose a path that will more equally distribute the bandwidth reservations, the `least-fill` option can be used on the LSPs. If there are multiple equal cost paths to the destination, CSPF will choose the one that provides the most equal distribution of bandwidth. Equal cost multi-path routing (ECMP) is not required in the IGP, but CSPF must be enabled on the LSP. Figure 15.13 shows the result of configuring LSP 3 with the `least-fill` option. Listing 15.17 shows the configuration of the LSP.

Figure 15.13 Least-fill option on an LSP.

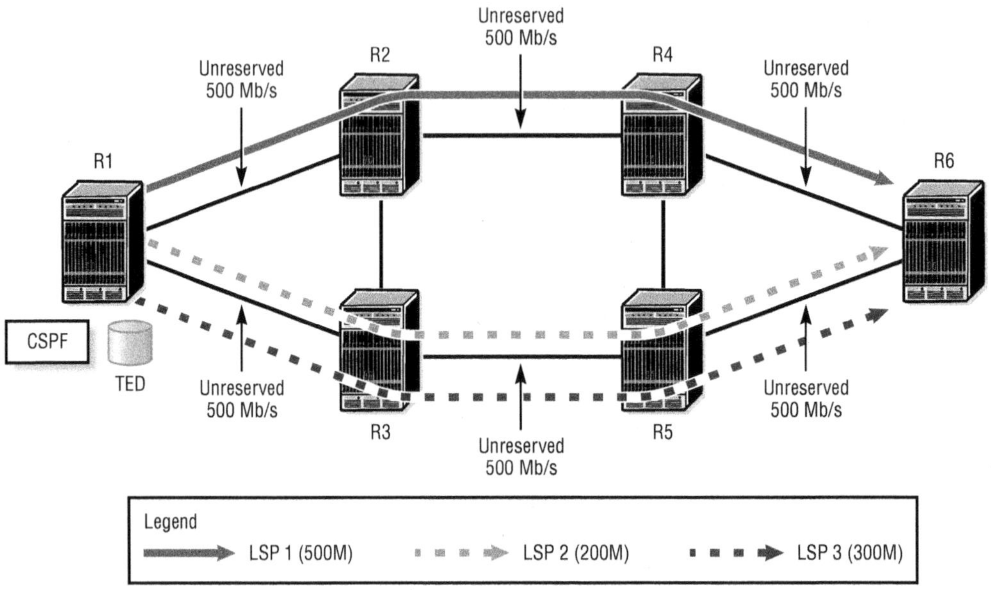

Listing 15.17 Configuring least fill on an LSP

```
*A:R1>config>router>mpls# lsp "toR6
*A:R1>config>router>mpls>lsp# info
----------------------------------------------
                to 10.10.10.6
                cspf
                least-fill
                primary "loose"
                    bandwidth 300
                exit
                no shutdown
----------------------------------------------
*A:R1>config>router>mpls>lsp# show router rsvp interface

===============================================================================
RSVP Interfaces
===============================================================================
Interface                Total    Active   Total BW  Resv BW   Adm Opr
                         Sessions Sessions (Mbps)    (Mbps)
-------------------------------------------------------------------------------
system                   -        -        -         -         Up  Up
toR2                     1        1        1000      500       Up  Up
toR3                     2        2        1000      500       Up  Up
-------------------------------------------------------------------------------
Interfaces : 3
===============================================================================
*A:R1>config>router>mpls>lsp#
```

15.3 LSP Soft Preemption

LSP soft preemption provides a method for prioritizing LSPs to determine their chance to obtain bandwidth reservations. Soft preemption allows a higher-priority LSP to preempt a lower-priority LSP in order to satisfy its bandwidth requirements. Preemption is done in a MBB manner to avoid disrupting services or data flows using the LSP.

LSPs are assigned two priority values from a range of 0 to 7:

- **Setup priority**—is the priority for setting up the LSP.
- **Hold priority**—is the priority an LSP has to maintain its resource reservation.

The lower the value, the higher the priority for the LSP. Setup priority cannot have a value lower than hold priority; otherwise, two LSPs could endlessly preempt each other. Recommended practice is to set the values equal for simplicity. The default values are 7 for setup and 0 for hold, which means that the LSP cannot preempt any others and cannot be preempted once established.

Soft Preemption Operation

When an LSP is signaled with a bandwidth reservation, the bandwidth available at each priority level is carried in the Unreserved Bandwidth TLV (type–length–value) as in Figure 15.14. In the `priority` command, the first value specifies the setup priority, the second value the hold priority. These are carried in the Path message for the LSP as shown in Listing 15.18.

Figure 15.14 Bandwidth reservations and priorities on an LSP.

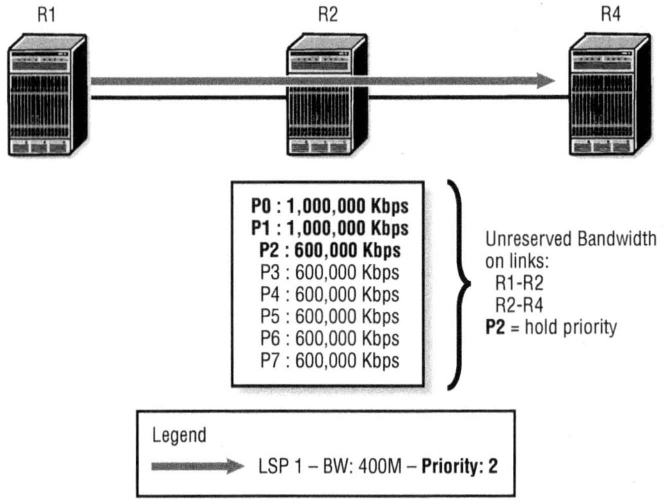

Listing 15.18 Bandwidth reservation in the TLV and in the Path message

```
*A:R1>config>router>mpls# lsp toR4-1
*A:R1>config>router>mpls>lsp# info
----------------------------------------------
                to 10.10.10.4
                cspf
                primary "loose"
                    bandwidth 400
```

```
                    priority 2 2
                exit
                no shutdown
----------------------------------------------
*A:R1>config>router>mpls>lsp# show router rsvp interface

===============================================================================
RSVP Interfaces
===============================================================================
Interface                  Total    Active   Total BW  Resv BW   Adm Opr
                           Sessions Sessions (Mbps)    (Mbps)
-------------------------------------------------------------------------------
system                     -        -        -         -         Up  Up
toR2                       1        1        1000      400       Up  Up
toR3                       0        0        1000      0         Up  Up
-------------------------------------------------------------------------------
Interfaces : 3
===============================================================================
*A:R1>config>router>mpls>lsp#
1 2011/01/16 21:31:21.94 UTC MINOR: DEBUG #2001 Base RSVP
"RSVP: PATH Msg
Send PATH From:10.10.10.1, To:10.10.10.4
          TTL:255, Checksum:0x6a03, Flags:0x0
Session     - EndPt:10.10.10.4, TunnId:21, ExtTunnId:10.10.10.1
SessAttr    - Name:toR4-1::loose
              SetupPri:2, HoldPri:2, Flags:0x46
RSVPHop     - Addr:10.1.2.1, LIH:2
TimeValue   - RefreshPeriod:30
SendTempl   - Sender:10.10.10.1, LspId:19970
SendTSpec   - Ctype:QOS, CDR:400.000 Mbps, PBS:400.000 Mbps, PDR:infinity
              MPU:20, MTU:9198
LabelReq    - IfType:General, L3ProtID:2048
RRO         - IpAddr:10.1.2.1, Flags:0x0
ERO         - Prefix:10.1.2.2/32, Type:Strict
              Prefix:10.2.4.4/32, Type:Strict
"
```

Once the path is successfully signaled and the bandwidth reserved, an updated LSA is flooded to advertise the change in the topology. Four hundred megabits per second has been reserved with a hold priority of 2. Thus, the TLV shows 600 Mb/s unreserved at priority levels 2 through 7 and 1,000 Mb/s unreserved at priority levels 0 and 1 (Listing 15.19).

Listing 15.19 Update showing bandwidth reserved at priority level 2

```
*A:R1>config>router>mpls>lsp# show router ospf opaque-database 1.0.0.2
adv-router 10.10.10.1 detail

===============================================================================
OSPF Opaque Link State Database (Type : All) (Detailed)
===============================================================================
-------------------------------------------------------------------------------
Opaque LSA
-------------------------------------------------------------------------------
Area Id           : 0.0.0.0                Adv Router Id     : 10.10.10.1
Link State Id     : 1.0.0.2                LSA Type          : Area Opaque
Sequence No       : 0x80000029             Checksum          : 0x678f
Age               : 106                    Length            : 124
Options           :  E
Advertisement     :
     LINK INFO TLV  (0002) Len 100 :
       Sub-TLV: 1     Len: 1     LINK_TYPE     : 1
       Sub-TLV: 2     Len: 4     LINK_ID       : 10.10.10.2
       Sub-TLV: 3     Len: 4     LOC_IP_ADDR   : 10.1.2.1
       Sub-TLV: 4     Len: 4     REM_IP_ADDR   : 10.1.2.2
       Sub-TLV: 5     Len: 4     TE_METRIC     : 100
       Sub-TLV: 6     Len: 4     MAX_BDWTH     : 1000000 Kbps
       Sub-TLV: 7     Len: 4     RSRVBL_BDWTH  : 1000000 Kbps
       Sub-TLV: 8     Len: 32    UNRSRVD_CLS0  :
         P0: 1000000 Kbps P1: 1000000 Kbps P2:  600000 Kbps P3:
         600000 Kbps
         P4:  600000 Kbps P5:  600000 Kbps P6:  600000 Kbps P7:
         600000 Kbps
       Sub-TLV: 9     Len: 4     ADMIN_GROUP   : 0 None

===============================================================================
```

In the following example, we show the establishment of several LSPs with different priority levels and different bandwidth requirements. The setup and hold priorities in each LSP are the same. The first is the LSP `toR4-1`, which was shown above. The topology is shown in Figure 15.15.

The LSP `toR4-2` requests 300 Mb/s at a priority of 5 and is successfully set up on the shortest IGP path to R4 (Figure 15.16).

Figure 15.15 Topology for preempting LSPs.

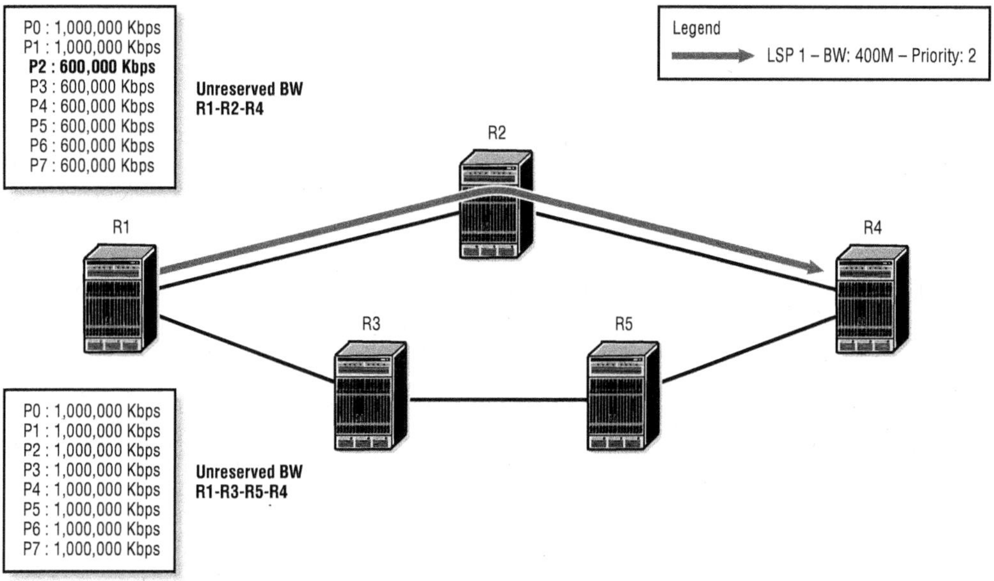

Figure 15.16 The second LSP reserves 300 Mb/s at a priority of 5.

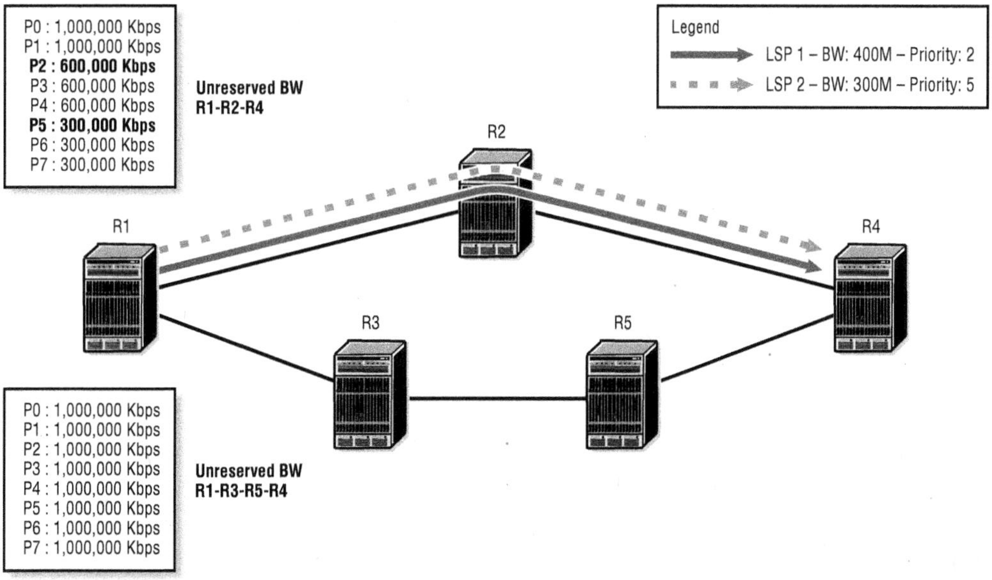

A third LSP requires 800 Mb/s of bandwidth at a priority level of 7. Because this bandwidth is not available on the shortest IGP path, the LSP is established on the other path (Figure 15.17).

If a fourth LSP were to request 600 Mb/s without specifying a priority level, it could not be set up. The default setup priority is 7, and neither path has 600 Mb/s at priority 7, as seen in the TE LSAs from router R1 shown in Listing 15.20.

Figure 15.17 The third LSP is established on an alternate path.

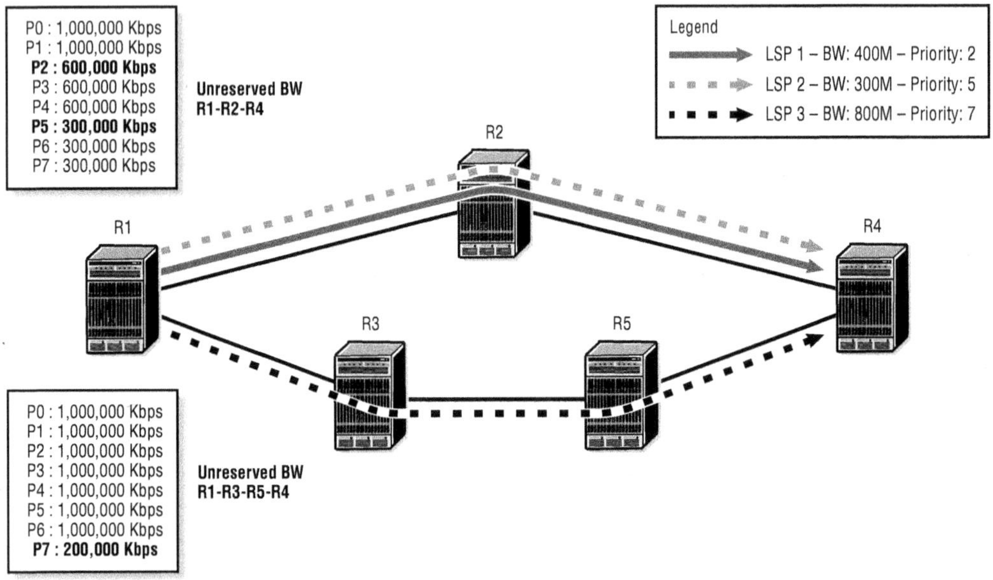

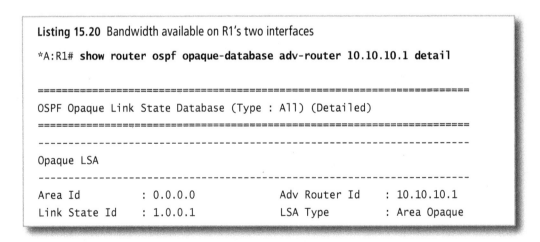

Listing 15.20 Bandwidth available on R1's two interfaces

```
*A:R1# show router ospf opaque-database adv-router 10.10.10.1 detail

===============================================================================
OSPF Opaque Link State Database (Type : All) (Detailed)
===============================================================================
-------------------------------------------------------------------------------
Opaque LSA
-------------------------------------------------------------------------------
Area Id          : 0.0.0.0             Adv Router Id      : 10.10.10.1
Link State Id    : 1.0.0.1             LSA Type           : Area Opaque
```

```
Sequence No      : 0x8000013b          Checksum         : 0x9a3b
Age              : 1314                Length           : 28
Options          :  E
Advertisement    :
     ROUTER-ID TLV  (0001) Len   4 : 10.10.10.1
-----------------------------------------------------------------------
Opaque LSA
-----------------------------------------------------------------------
Area Id          : 0.0.0.0             Adv Router Id    : 10.10.10.1
Link State Id    : 1.0.0.2             LSA Type         : Area Opaque
Sequence No      : 0x8000002e          Checksum         : 0xd2a0
Age              : 93                  Length           : 124
Options          :  E
Advertisement    :
     LINK INFO TLV  (0002) Len 100 :
       Sub-TLV: 1     Len: 1     LINK_TYPE    : 1
       Sub-TLV: 2     Len: 4     LINK_ID      : 10.10.10.2
       Sub-TLV: 3     Len: 4     LOC_IP_ADDR  : 10.1.2.1
       Sub-TLV: 4     Len: 4     REM_IP_ADDR  : 10.1.2.2
       Sub-TLV: 5     Len: 4     TE_METRIC    : 100
       Sub-TLV: 6     Len: 4     MAX_BDWTH    : 1000000 Kbps
       Sub-TLV: 7     Len: 4     RSRVBL_BDWTH : 1000000 Kbps
       Sub-TLV: 8     Len: 32    UNRSRVD_CLS0 :
         P0: 1000000 Kbps P1: 1000000 Kbps P2:  600000 Kbps P3:
         600000 Kbps
         P4:  600000 Kbps P5:  300000 Kbps P6:  300000 Kbps P7:
         300000 Kbps
       Sub-TLV: 9     Len: 4     ADMIN_GROUP  : 0 None

-----------------------------------------------------------------------
Opaque LSA
-----------------------------------------------------------------------
Area Id          : 0.0.0.0             Adv Router Id    : 10.10.10.1
Link State Id    : 1.0.0.3             LSA Type         : Area Opaque
Sequence No      : 0x8000001c          Checksum         : 0xb09
Age              : 34                  Length           : 124
Options          :  E
Advertisement    :
     LINK INFO TLV  (0002) Len 100 :
       Sub-TLV: 1     Len: 1     LINK_TYPE    : 1
```

(continued)

Listing 15.20 *(continued)*

```
        Sub-TLV: 2      Len: 4      LINK_ID      : 10.10.10.3
        Sub-TLV: 3      Len: 4      LOC_IP_ADDR  : 10.1.3.1
        Sub-TLV: 4      Len: 4      REM_IP_ADDR  : 10.1.3.3
        Sub-TLV: 5      Len: 4      TE_METRIC    : 100
        Sub-TLV: 6      Len: 4      MAX_BDWTH    : 1000000 Kbps
        Sub-TLV: 7      Len: 4      RSRVBL_BDWTH : 1000000 Kbps
        Sub-TLV: 8      Len: 32     UNRSRVD_CLS0 :
          P0: 1000000 Kbps P1: 1000000 Kbps P2: 1000000 Kbps P3:
          1000000 Kbps
          P4: 1000000 Kbps P5: 1000000 Kbps P6: 1000000 Kbps P7:
          200000 Kbps
        Sub-TLV: 9      Len: 4      ADMIN_GROUP  : 0 None

===========================================================================
```

If the fourth LSP requests 600 Mb/s bandwidth at priority 3, the LSP is established on the shortest IGP path because both have sufficient bandwidth at priority 3 (Figure 15.18).

Figure 15.18 The fourth LSP is successfully established at priority 3.

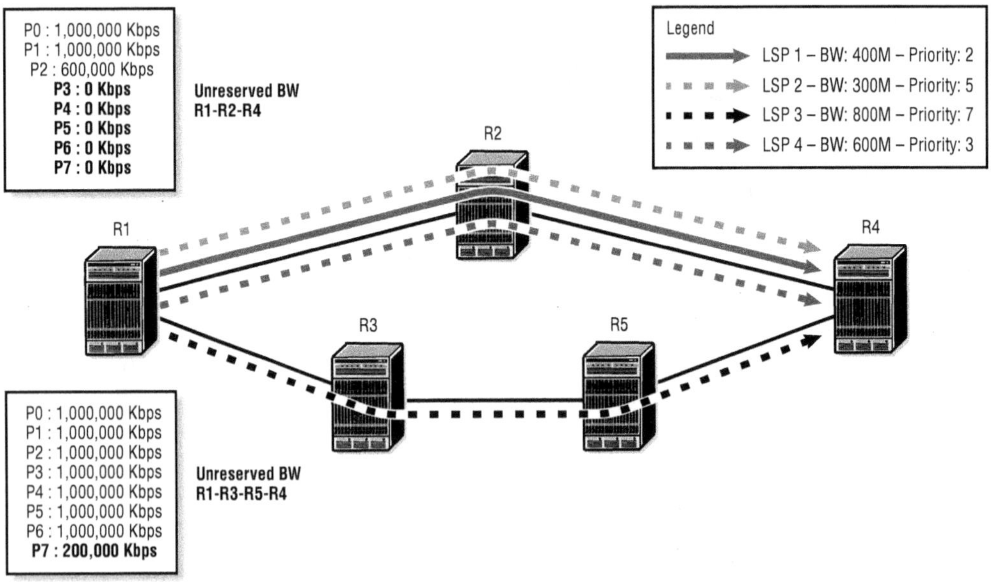

After the fourth LSP is established, there is no longer sufficient bandwidth for LSP 2 on this path. The head end performs a CSPF calculation and finds a path with sufficient bandwidth at priority 5 on the other path through R3. It resignals the LSP on this path and performs an MBB switchover to this path. However, there is now insufficient bandwidth for LSP 3 (see Figure 15.19).

Figure 15.19 LSP 2 moves and LSP 3 goes down.

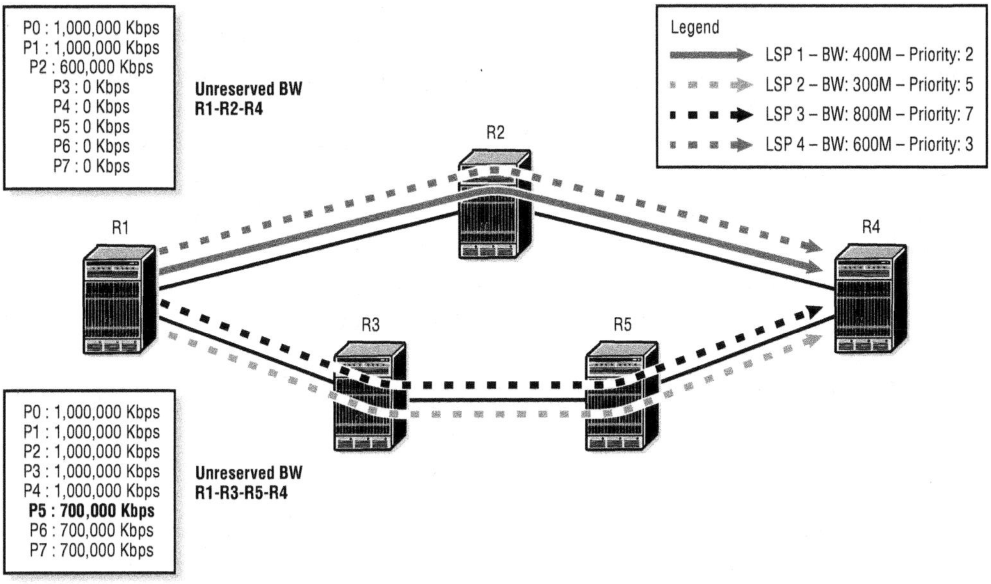

Listing 15.21 shows that the LSP is not immediately shut down. The head end attempts to find a path for the LSP until the preemption timer expires. This is set to 300 seconds by default, and the CSPF calculation is retried at the interval of the RSVP-TE retry timer, which is 30 seconds by default.

Listing 15.21 Preempted LSP is not down until the preemption timer expires

```
*A:R1>config>router>mpls>lsp# show router mpls lsp

===============================================================================
MPLS LSPs (Originating)
===============================================================================
LSP Name                       To                 Fastfail     Adm    Opr
                                                  Config
```

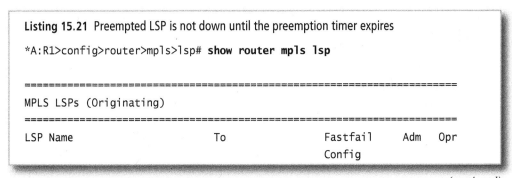

(continued)

Listing 15.21 *(continued)*

```
-------------------------------------------------------------------------------
toR4-1                         10.10.10.4        No            Up     Up
toR4-2                         10.10.10.4        No            Up     Up
toR4-3                         10.10.10.4        No            Up     Up
toR4-4                         10.10.10.4        No            Up     Up
-------------------------------------------------------------------------------
LSPs : 4
===============================================================================
*A:R1>config>router>mpls>lsp# show router mpls lsp "toR4-3" path detail

===============================================================================
MPLS LSP toR4-3 Path  (Detail)
===============================================================================
Legend :
    @ - Detour Available                 # - Detour In Use
    b - Bandwidth Protected              n - Node Protected
    s - Soft Preemption
===============================================================================
-------------------------------------------------------------------------------
LSP toR4-3 Path loose
-------------------------------------------------------------------------------
LSP Name     : toR4-3                        Path LSP ID : 13312
From         : 10.10.10.1                    To          : 10.10.10.4
Adm State    : Up                            Oper State  : Up
Path Name    : loose                         Path Type   : Primary
Path Admin   : Up                            Path Oper   : Up
OutInterface: 1/1/1                          Out Label   : 131071
Path Up Time: 0d 00:16:03                    Path Dn Time: 0d 00:00:00
Retry Limit : 0                              Retry Timer : 30 sec
RetryAttempt: 0                              NextRetryIn : 0 sec
SetupPriori*: 7                              Hold Priori*: 7
Preference   : n/a
Bandwidth    : 800 Mbps                      Oper Bw     : 800 Mbps
Hop Limit    : 255                           Class Type  : 0
Backup CT    : None
MainCT Retry: n/a                            MainCT Retry: 0
    Rem      :                                   Limit   :
Oper CT      : 0
```

```
Record Route: Record                             Record Label: Record
Oper MTU     : 9198                              Neg MTU      : 9198
Adaptive     : Enabled                           Oper Metric : 300
Include Grps:                                    Exclude Grps:
None                                           None
Path Trans   : 1                                 CSPF Queries: 10
Failure Code: softPreemption                     Failure Node: 10.4.5.5
ExplicitHops:
    No Hops Specified
Actual Hops :
    10.1.3.1(10.10.10.1) s                       Record Label     : N/A
 -> 10.1.3.3(10.10.10.3) s                       Record Label     : 131071
 -> 10.3.5.5(10.10.10.5) s                       Record Label     : 131071
 -> 10.4.5.4(10.10.10.4)                         Record Label     : 131064
ComputedHops:
    10.1.3.1        -> 10.1.3.3        -> 10.3.5.5        -> 10.4.5.4
ResigEligib*: False
LastResignal: n/a                                CSPF Metric : 300
In Prog MBB :
 MBB Type    : SoftPreemption                    NextRetryIn : 17 sec
 Started At : 01/16/2011 22:28:47                RetryAttempt: 9
 FailureCode: noCspfRouteToDestination           Failure Node: 10.10.10.1
===============================================================================
* indicates that the corresponding row element may have been truncated.
```

Once the preemption timer expires, the LSP becomes operationally down (Listing 15.22).

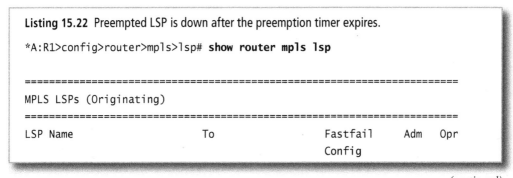

Listing 15.22 Preempted LSP is down after the preemption timer expires.

```
*A:R1>config>router>mpls>lsp# show router mpls lsp

===============================================================================
MPLS LSPs (Originating)
===============================================================================
LSP Name                      To                  Fastfail      Adm    Opr
                                                  Config
```

(continued)

Listing 15.22 *(continued)*

```
-----------------------------------------------------------------------
toR4-1                       10.10.10.4         No          Up     Up
toR4-2                       10.10.10.4         No          Up     Up
toR4-3                       10.10.10.4         No          Up     Dwn
toR4-4                       10.10.10.4         No          Up     Up
-----------------------------------------------------------------------
LSPs : 4
=======================================================================
```

15.4 DiffServ-Aware Traffic Engineering

RFC 2475 describes the architecture for Differentiated Services (DiffServ). This is a model widely used for implementing quality of service (QoS) in an IP/MPLS network. DiffServ groups traffic flows with similar QoS requirements into behavior aggregates (BA) that receive the same treatment by the network. This is the fundamental approach used to implement QoS in an IP/MPLS network.

RFC 3564 describes an architecture for DiffServ-aware traffic engineering (DiffServ-TE). It provides more granularity for bandwidth reservations and links to DiffServ-based QoS. DiffServ-TE is still strictly a control plane function; the appropriate QoS mechanisms are required to enforce these policies in the data plane.

Understanding Class Types (CTs)

DiffServ-TE introduces two new concepts:

- **Class type (CT)**—Allows the definition of an aggregate bandwidth allocated to LSPs of a specific CT. Values range from 0 to 7.
- **TE class**—Defines a specific pairing of a CT with a preemption priority. Up to eight TE classes can be defined.

A preemption priority can be assigned to each of the eight different class types. Because there are eight different preemption priorities, there are 64 different combinations possible, as shown in Figure 15.20. This assumes that the same priority is used for both the setup and hold priorities.

Figure 15.20 Sixty-four different combinations of CT and preemption priority are possible.

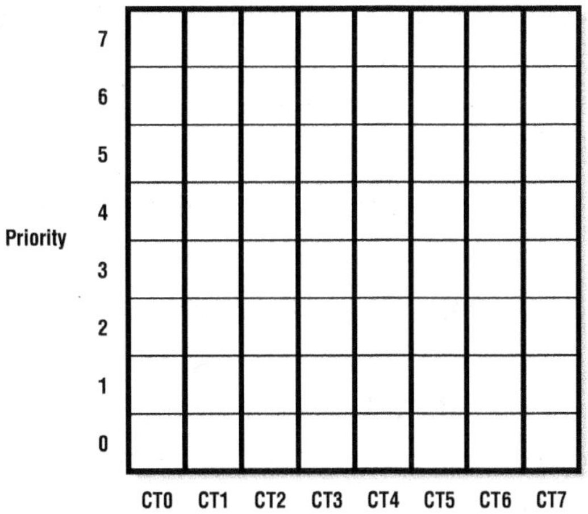

RFC 4124 ("Protocol Extensions for DiffServ-TE") defines the extensions that are required to the IGP and RSVP-TE in order to support DiffServ-TE. To simplify the information that needs to be carried by the IGP, RFC 4124 defines eight TE classes. These are the eight CT and preemption priority pairs that can be used out of the 64 possible combinations. They are chosen by the network operator and must be consistent throughout the network. Figure 15.21 shows an example of TE classes that could be chosen.

Figure 15.21 Example of CT and priority pairs mapped to TE classes.

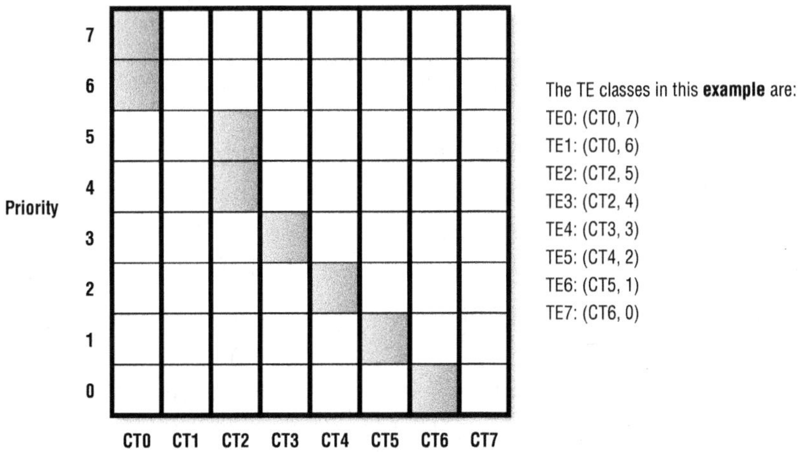

Bandwidth Constraints per Class Type

The purpose of the class type is to allow bandwidth to be collectively allocated to LSPs of that type. Thus, it is necessary to distribute the maximum reservable bandwidth between the different CTs. The allocation of bandwidth to a CT is called the bandwidth constraint (BC). There are two approaches to assigning the BC:

- **Maximum Allocation Model (MAM)**—Bandwidth is allocated discretely to different CTs and cannot be shared between CTs.
- **Russian Dolls Model (RDM)**—Unused bandwidth assigned to a higher CT can be used by a lower CT.

Figure 15.22 shows the use of MAM for assigning the BC. Bandwidth is assigned as a percentage of the maximum reservable bandwidth and cannot be shared between CTs. The sum of the assignments must not exceed 100.

Figure 15.22 MAM used to assign BCs.

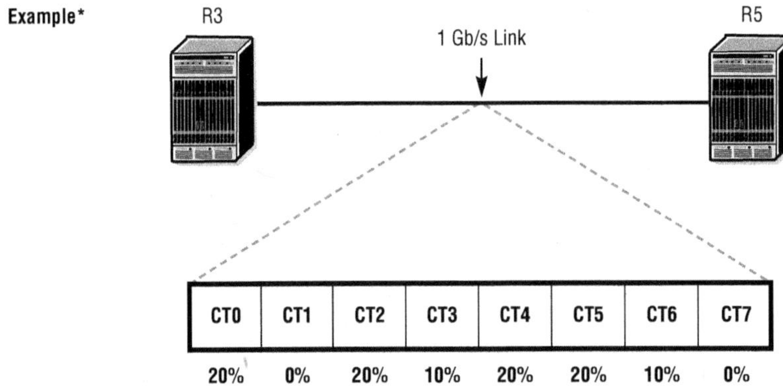

With RDM the lower CTs can allocate the unused bandwidth of the higher CTs. In a sense, the BC of the higher classes is nested within that of a lower CT, hence the term *Russian Dolls*. The expectation is that lower classes will have lower preemption priority. If they allocate bandwidth to an LSP from a higher CT and that CT needs the bandwidth, it will preempt the lower CT. Of course, priorities must be assigned carefully and consistently.

Figure 15.23 shows the nesting of three CTs. Note that the effective BC on CT0 is the sum of the bandwidth assigned to CT0, CT1, and CT2.

Figure 15.23 BC for the different CTs when using RDM.

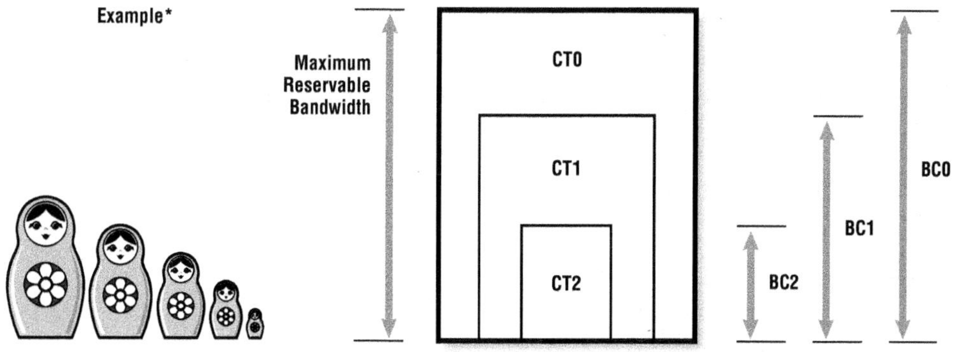

DiffServ-TE Example Using MAM

In this section, we provide an example of bandwidth assignment using MAM. For simplicity, we define only two TE classes (Figure 15.24). In this example, voice traffic is the most important and should never be preempted. For this reason, it is assigned priority 0 (we use the same values for setup and hold priority in this example). Data traffic is unable to preempt voice traffic, and a data LSP will never preempt another data LSP.

Figure 15.24 Definition of two TE classes.

Traffic Type	TE Class	Class Type	Preemption Priority	Bandwidth Constraint
Voice	1	CT1	0	20 (%)
Data	0	CT0	1	20 (%)

Before any LSPs can be configured to use DiffServ-TE, the following steps must be performed:

1. Shut down MPLS on the router.
2. In the `configure router rsvp` context, configure `diffserv-te` as either `mam` (default) or `rdm`.
3. In the `diffserv-te` context, configure the CTs with a BC value as a percentage of maximum reservable bandwidth.

4. In the `diffserv-te` context, configure the TE classes with the appropriate CT and preemption priority.
5. DiffServ-TE needs to be configured consistently on all routers in the network.

We will use the topology in Figure 15.25 for our example. The configuration is shown in Listing 15.23.

Figure 15.25 Example of DiffServ-TE using MAM.

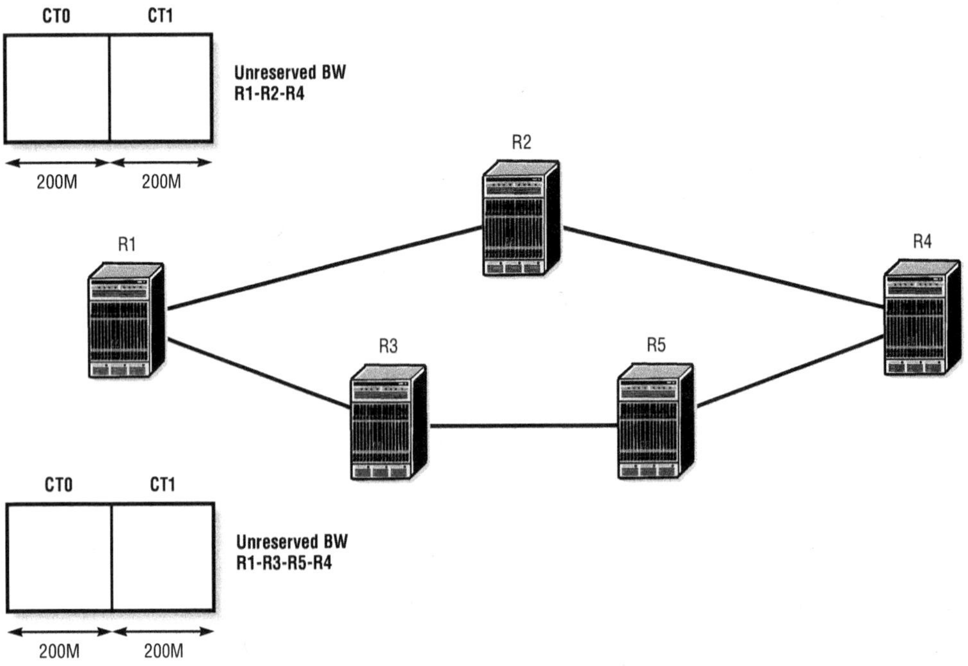

Listing 15.23 Configuration of RSVP-TE for DiffServ TE with two TE classes

```
*A:R1# configure router mpls shutdown
*A:R1# configure router rsvp
*A:R1>config>router>rsvp# diffserv-te mam
*A:R1>config>router>rsvp# info
----------------------------------------------
    diffserv-te mam
        class-type-bw ct0 20 ct1 20 ct2 0 ct3 0 ct4 0 ct5 0 ct6 0 ct7 0
        te-class 0 class-type 0 priority 1
```

```
        te-class 1 class-type 1 priority 0
    exit
    interface "system"
    exit
    interface "toR2"
    exit
    interface "toR3"
    exit
    no shutdown
----------------------------------------------
```

Once the DiffServ-TE parameters are configured, we can examine their effect on the RSVP-TE interface as shown in Listing 15.24.

Listing 15.24 DiffServ-TE parameters on the RSVP-TE interface

```
*A:R1# show router rsvp interface "toR2" detail

===============================================================================
RSVP Interface (Detailed) : toR2
===============================================================================
-------------------------------------------------------------------------------
Interface : toR2
-------------------------------------------------------------------------------
Interface            : toR2
Port ID              : 1/1/2
Admin State          : Up                    Oper State         : Up

... output omitted ...

Percent Link Bandwidth for Class Types*
Link Bw CT0          : 20                    Link Bw CT4        : 0
Link Bw CT1          : 20                    Link Bw CT5        : 0
Link Bw CT2          : 0                     Link Bw CT6        : 0
Link Bw CT3          : 0                     Link Bw CT7        : 0

Bandwidth Constraints for Class Types (Kbps)
BC0                  : 200000                BC4                : 0
BC1                  : 200000                BC5                : 0
```

(continued)

Listing 15.24 *(continued)*

```
BC2                 : 0                     BC6                 : 0
BC3                 : 0                     BC7                 : 0

Bandwidth for TE Class Types (Kbps)
TE0->  Resv. Bw   : 0                     Unresv. Bw          : 200000
TE1->  Resv. Bw   : 0                     Unresv. Bw          : 200000
TE2->  Resv. Bw   : 0                     Unresv. Bw          : 0
TE3->  Resv. Bw   : 0                     Unresv. Bw          : 0
TE4->  Resv. Bw   : 0                     Unresv. Bw          : 0
TE5->  Resv. Bw   : 0                     Unresv. Bw          : 0
TE6->  Resv. Bw   : 0                     Unresv. Bw          : 0
TE7->  Resv. Bw   : 0                     Unresv. Bw          : 0


... output omitted ...

===============================================================================
```

The IGP must carry new information relating to the BC and the bandwidth reserved per TE class. The bandwidth model and BC information is carried in the `TELK_BW_CONST` TLV, which contains the BC for each CT. The `UNRSRVD_CLS0` TLV now carries the bandwidth reserved per TE class as shown in Listing 15.25. The preemption priority fields are now used to carry the bandwidth for the TE classes: The `P0` field now represents TE0, `P1` represents TE1, and so on.

Listing 15.25 Changes in IGP to support DiffServ-TE

```
*A:R1# show router ospf opaque-database 1.0.0.2 adv-router 10.10.10.1
detail
===============================================================================
OSPF Opaque Link State Database (Type : All) (Detailed)
===============================================================================
-------------------------------------------------------------------------------
Opaque LSA
-------------------------------------------------------------------------------
Area Id             : 0.0.0.0               Adv Router Id       : 10.10.10.1
Link State Id       : 1.0.0.2               LSA Type            : Area Opaque
```

```
Sequence No       : 0x80000002             Checksum          : 0x6738
Age               : 233                    Length            : 164
Options           :  E
Advertisement     :
     LINK INFO TLV  (0002) Len 140 :
       Sub-TLV: 1      Len: 1     LINK_TYPE     : 1
       Sub-TLV: 2      Len: 4     LINK_ID       : 10.10.10.2
       Sub-TLV: 3      Len: 4     LOC_IP_ADDR   : 10.1.2.1
       Sub-TLV: 4      Len: 4     REM_IP_ADDR   : 10.1.2.2
       Sub-TLV: 5      Len: 4     TE_METRIC     : 100
       Sub-TLV: 6      Len: 4     MAX_BDWTH     : 1000000 Kbps
       Sub-TLV: 7      Len: 4     RSRVBL_BDWTH : 1000000 Kbps
       Sub-TLV: 8      Len: 32    UNRSRVD_CLS0 :
         P0:  200000 Kbps P1:  200000 Kbps P2:  0 Kbps P3:   0 Kbps
         P4:       0 Kbps P5:       0 Kbps P6:  0 Kbps P7:   0 Kbps
       Sub-TLV: 9      Len: 4     ADMIN_GROUP   : 0 None
       Sub-TLV: 17     Len: 36    TELK_BW_CONST:
         BW Model : MAM
         BC0:  200000 Kbps BC1:  200000 Kbps BC2:  0 Kbps BC3:   0 Kbps
         BC4:       0 Kbps BC5:       0 Kbps BC6:  0 Kbps BC7:   0 Kbps

===============================================================================
```

In our example, an LSP is configured for data traffic, as shown in Figure 15.26. It is essential that the priority and CT set for the LSP match one of the pairs specified as a TE class. In this case, we configured a priority of 2, which does not correspond to any TE class. As seen in Listing 15.26, the LSP does not come up.

Listing 15.26 LSP configured with incorrect CT, priority pair

```
*A:R1>config>router>mpls# lsp "toR4-1"
*A:R1>config>router>mpls>lsp# info
----------------------------------------------
                to 10.10.10.4
                cspf
                primary "loose"
                    bandwidth 200
                    priority 2 2
```

(continued)

Listing 15.26 *(continued)*

```
                    class-type 0
                exit
                no shutdown
----------------------------------------------
*A:R1>config>router>mpls>lsp# show router mpls lsp "toR4-1" path detail

===============================================================================
MPLS LSP toR4-1 Path  (Detail)
===============================================================================
Legend :
    @ - Detour Available              # - Detour In Use
    b - Bandwidth Protected           n - Node Protected
    s - Soft Preemption
===============================================================================
-------------------------------------------------------------------------------
LSP toR4-1 Path loose
-------------------------------------------------------------------------------
LSP Name     : toR4-1                          Path LSP ID : 25602
From         : 10.10.10.1                      To          : 10.10.10.4
Adm State    : Up                              Oper State  : Down

... output omitted ...

Failure Code: invCtAndSetupAndHoldPri          Failure Node: 10.10.10.1
ExplicitHops:
    No Hops Specified
Actual Hops :
    No Hops Specified
ComputedHops:
    No Hops Specified
ResigEligib*: False
LastResignal: n/a                                CSPF Metric : 0
===============================================================================
* indicates that the corresponding row element may have been truncated.
```

When the LSP is configured with the correct priority value of 1, the LSP becomes operational. Upon checking the interface to router R2, we find that 200 Mb/s has been reserved for TE class 1. The same information is reflected in the updated OSPF LSA that has been flooded; there is no bandwidth available for P0 (TE0) (Listing 15.27).

Figure 15.26 Data LSP configured for 200 Mb/s in CT0.

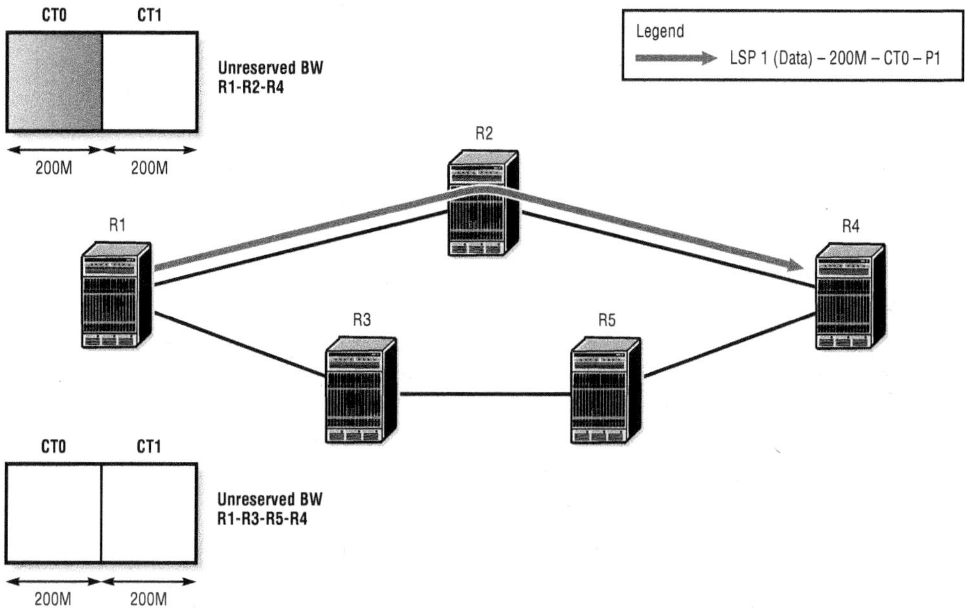

Listing 15.27 Bandwidth reserved

```
*A:R1# show router rsvp interface "toR2" detail

===============================================================================
RSVP Interface (Detailed) : toR2
===============================================================================
-------------------------------------------------------------------------------
Interface : toR2
-------------------------------------------------------------------------------
Interface              : toR2
Port ID                : 1/1/2
Admin State            : Up                    Oper State          : Up

... output omitted ...
```

(continued)

Listing 15.27 *(continued)*

```
Bandwidth for TE Class Types (Kbps)
TE0->  Resv. Bw   : 200000             Unresv. Bw       : 0
TE1->  Resv. Bw   : 0                  Unresv. Bw       : 200000
TE2->  Resv. Bw   : 0                  Unresv. Bw       : 0
TE3->  Resv. Bw   : 0                  Unresv. Bw       : 0
TE4->  Resv. Bw   : 0                  Unresv. Bw       : 0
TE5->  Resv. Bw   : 0                  Unresv. Bw       : 0
TE6->  Resv. Bw   : 0                  Unresv. Bw       : 0
TE7->  Resv. Bw   : 0                  Unresv. Bw       : 0

... output omitted ...

===============================================================================
*A:R1# show router ospf opaque-database 1.0.0.2 adv-router 10.10.10.1
detail

===============================================================================
OSPF Opaque Link State Database (Type : All) (Detailed)
===============================================================================
-------------------------------------------------------------------------------
Opaque LSA
-------------------------------------------------------------------------------
Area Id           : 0.0.0.0            Adv Router Id     : 10.10.10.1
Link State Id     : 1.0.0.2            LSA Type          : Area Opaque
Sequence No       : 0x8000000a         Checksum          : 0x502e
Age               : 469                Length            : 164
Options           :  E
Advertisement     :
     LINK INFO TLV  (0002) Len 140 :
       Sub-TLV: 1     Len: 1     LINK_TYPE    : 1
       Sub-TLV: 2     Len: 4     LINK_ID      : 10.10.10.2
       Sub-TLV: 3     Len: 4     LOC_IP_ADDR  : 10.1.2.1
       Sub-TLV: 4     Len: 4     REM_IP_ADDR  : 10.1.2.2
       Sub-TLV: 5     Len: 4     TE_METRIC    : 100
       Sub-TLV: 6     Len: 4     MAX_BDWTH    : 1000000 Kbps
       Sub-TLV: 7     Len: 4     RSRVBL_BDWTH : 1000000 Kbps
       Sub-TLV: 8     Len: 32    UNRSRVD_CLS0 :
```

```
      P0:        0 Kbps P1:  200000 Kbps P2:    0 Kbps P3:  0 Kbps
      P4:        0 Kbps P5:        0 Kbps P6:    0 Kbps P7:  0 Kbps
    Sub-TLV: 9      Len: 4     ADMIN_GROUP  : 0 None
    Sub-TLV: 17     Len: 36    TELK_BW_CONST:
      BW Model : MAM
      BC0:  200000 Kbps BC1:  200000 Kbps BC2:   0 Kbps BC3:  0 Kbps
      BC4:        0 Kbps BC5:        0 Kbps BC6:   0 Kbps BC7:  0 Kbps

===============================================================================
```

In Figure 15.27, another data LSP is configured (LSP 2), reserving 100 Mb/s of bandwidth. LSP 1 is using all of the CT0 bandwidth on the shortest IGP path, and we are using the MAM bandwidth model. The only path found by CSPF is the longer path through R3 and R5. Listing 15.28 shows 200 Mb/s reserved on one interface and 100 Mb/s on the other.

Listing 15.28 Bandwidth reserved on two interfaces

```
*A:R1# show router rsvp interface

===============================================================================
RSVP Interfaces
===============================================================================
Interface                 Total    Active   Total BW  Resv BW   Adm Opr
                          Sessions Sessions (Mbps)    (Mbps)
-------------------------------------------------------------------------------
system                    -        -        -         -         Up  Up
toR2                      1        1        1000      200       Up  Up
toR3                      1        1        1000      100       Up  Up
-------------------------------------------------------------------------------
Interfaces : 3
===============================================================================
```

When a third LSP is configured, this time for voice traffic, the bandwidth is allocated from the pool for CT1 (Figure 15.28; Listing 15.29).

Figure 15.27 The second LSP uses the longer IGP path.

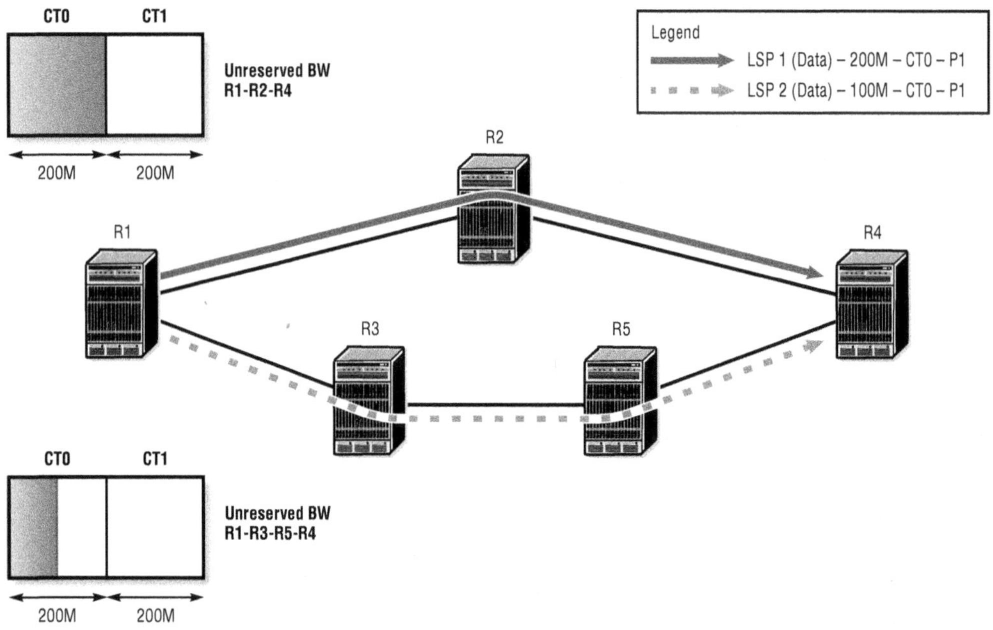

Figure 15.28 Bandwidth allocated for an LSP in CT1.

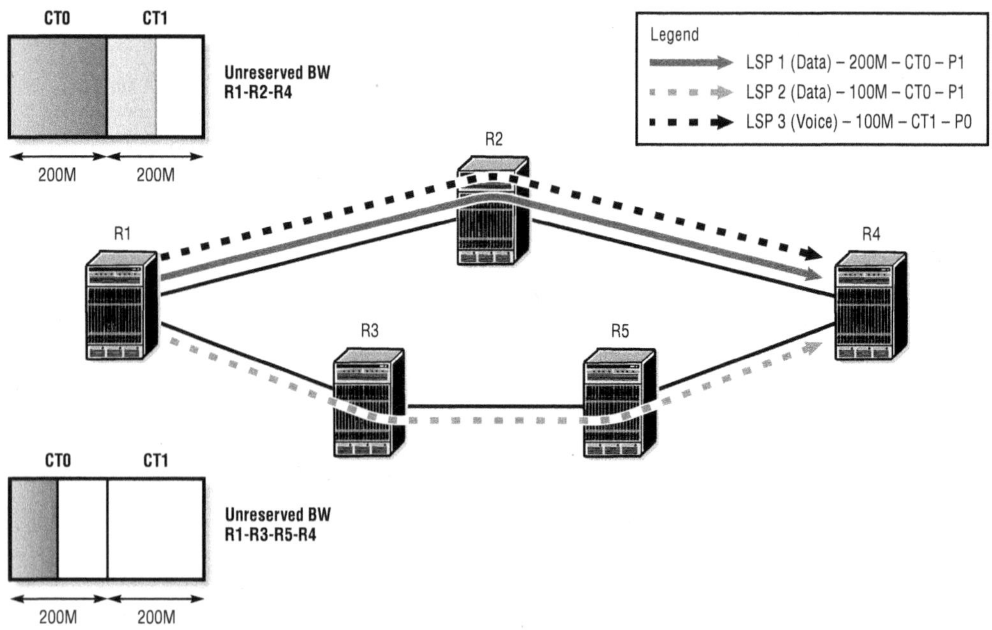

Listing 15.29 Configuration of an LSP in CT1 and resulting bandwidth reservation

```
*A:R1>config>router>mpls# lsp "toR4-3" primary "loose"
*A:R1>config>router>mpls>lsp>primary# info
----------------------------------------------
                    bandwidth 200
                    priority 0 0
                    class-type 1
----------------------------------------------
*A:R1>config>router>mpls>lsp# show router mpls lsp

=======================================================================
MPLS LSPs (Originating)
=======================================================================
LSP Name                    To                  Fastfail     Adm   Opr
                                                Config
-----------------------------------------------------------------------
toR4-1                      10.10.10.4          No           Up    Up
toR4-2                      10.10.10.4          No           Up    Up
toR4-3                      10.10.10.4          No           Up    Up
-----------------------------------------------------------------------
LSPs : 3
=======================================================================
*A:R1>config>router>mpls>lsp# show router rsvp interface

=======================================================================
RSVP Interfaces
=======================================================================
Interface                 Total    Active    Total BW  Resv BW    Adm Opr
                                 Sessions Sessions  (Mbps)    (Mbps)
-----------------------------------------------------------------------
system                    -        -         -         -          Up  Up
toR2                      2        2         1000      400        Up  Up
toR3                      1        1         1000      100        Up  Up
-----------------------------------------------------------------------
Interfaces : 3
=======================================================================
*A:R1>config>router>mpls>lsp#
```

DiffServ-TE Example Using RDM

In the next section, we look at the same configuration using RDM and compare the differences in behavior. In RDM, lower CTs can allocate unused bandwidth from higher CTs (Figure 15.29). The configuration is identical, except that we specify `diffserv-te rdm` as the bandwidth model (Listing 15.30).

Figure 15.29 Allocation of bandwidth using RDM.

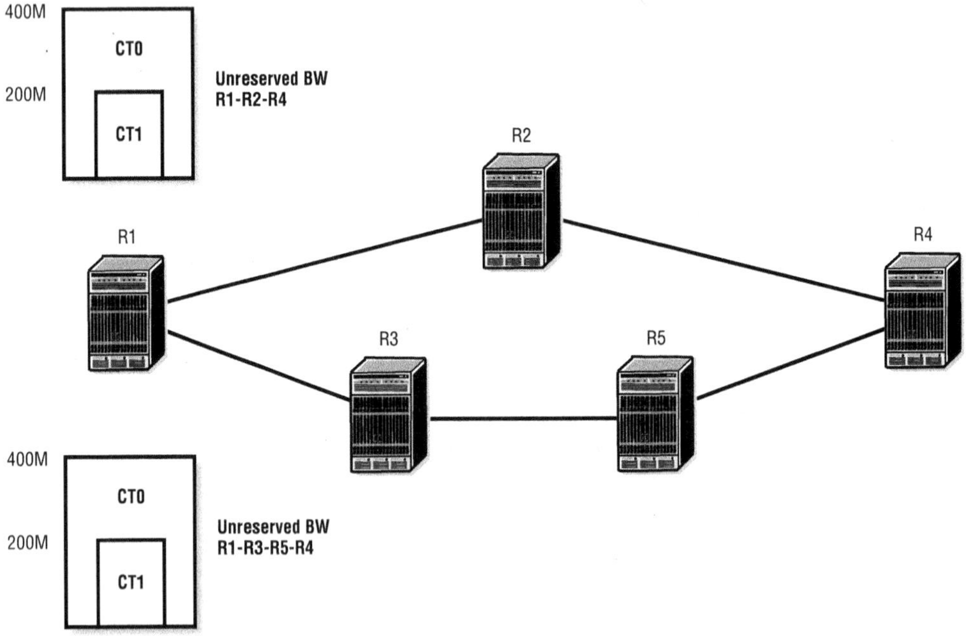

Listing 15.30 Configuration of DiffServ-TE for RDM

```
*A:R1# configure router rsvp
*A:R1>config>router>rsvp# info
----------------------------------------------
    diffserv-te rdm
        class-type-bw ct0 20 ct1 20 ct2 0 ct3 0 ct4 0 ct5 0 ct6 0 ct7 0
        te-class 0 class-type 0 priority 1
        te-class 1 class-type 1 priority 0
    exit
    interface "system"
    exit
```

```
    interface "toR2"
    exit
    interface "toR3"
    exit
    no shutdown
----------------------------------------------
```

The resulting change can be seen in the configuration of the interface (Listing 15.31).

Listing 15.31 Interface toR2 configured for RDM

```
*A:R1# show router rsvp interface "toR2" detail

===============================================================================
RSVP Interface (Detailed) : toR2
===============================================================================
-------------------------------------------------------------------------------
Interface : toR2
-------------------------------------------------------------------------------
Interface          : toR2
Port ID            : 1/1/2
Admin State        : Up                     Oper State         : Up

... output omitted ...

Percent Link Bandwidth for Class Types*
Link Bw CT0        : 20                     Link Bw CT4        : 0
Link Bw CT1        : 20                     Link Bw CT5        : 0
Link Bw CT2        : 0                      Link Bw CT6        : 0
Link Bw CT3        : 0                      Link Bw CT7        : 0

Bandwidth Constraints for Class Types (Kbps)
BC0                : 400000                 BC4                : 0
BC1                : 200000                 BC5                : 0
BC2                : 0                      BC6                : 0
BC3                : 0                      BC7                : 0

Bandwidth for TE Class Types (Kbps)
```

(continued)

Listing 15.31 *(continued)*

```
TE0->  Resv. Bw    : 0                Unresv. Bw        : 400000
TE1->  Resv. Bw    : 0                Unresv. Bw        : 200000
TE2->  Resv. Bw    : 0                Unresv. Bw        : 0
TE3->  Resv. Bw    : 0                Unresv. Bw        : 0
TE4->  Resv. Bw    : 0                Unresv. Bw        : 0
TE5->  Resv. Bw    : 0                Unresv. Bw        : 0
TE6->  Resv. Bw    : 0                Unresv. Bw        : 0
TE7->  Resv. Bw    : 0                Unresv. Bw        : 0

... output omitted ...

===============================================================================
```

Note that the BC for the CTs and the unreserved bandwidth for the TE class reflect the fact that a lower CT has a BC that is the sum of its own assignment and all of the other higher CT assignments. CT0 has a BC of 400 Mb/s even though it is only assigned 20 percent of the link bandwidth. This can also be seen in the OSPF LSA for the link (Listing 15.32).

Listing 15.32 BC and unreserved bandwidth in the TE LSA

```
*A:R1# show router ospf opaque-database 1.0.0.2 adv-router 10.10.10.1
detail

===============================================================================
OSPF Opaque Link State Database (Type : All) (Detailed)
===============================================================================
-------------------------------------------------------------------------------
Opaque LSA
-------------------------------------------------------------------------------
Area Id           : 0.0.0.0           Adv Router Id      : 10.10.10.1
Link State Id     : 1.0.0.2           LSA Type           : Area Opaque
Sequence No       : 0x80000018        Checksum           : 0x2663
Age               : 44                Length             : 164
Options           :  E
Advertisement     :
     LINK INFO TLV  (0002) Len 140 :
       Sub-TLV: 1     Len: 1     LINK_TYPE    : 1
```

```
        Sub-TLV: 2      Len: 4      LINK_ID       : 10.10.10.2
        Sub-TLV: 3      Len: 4      LOC_IP_ADDR   : 10.1.2.1
        Sub-TLV: 4      Len: 4      REM_IP_ADDR   : 10.1.2.2
        Sub-TLV: 5      Len: 4      TE_METRIC     : 100
        Sub-TLV: 6      Len: 4      MAX_BDWTH     : 1000000 Kbps
        Sub-TLV: 7      Len: 4      RSRVBL_BDWTH : 1000000 Kbps
        Sub-TLV: 8      Len: 32     UNRSRVD_CLS0 :
          P0:  400000 Kbps P1:  200000 Kbps P2:    0 Kbps P3:   0 Kbps
          P4:       0 Kbps P5:       0 Kbps P6:    0 Kbps P7:   0 Kbps
        Sub-TLV: 9      Len: 4      ADMIN_GROUP  : 0 None
        Sub-TLV: 17     Len: 36     TELK_BW_CONST:
          BW Model : RDM
          BC0:  400000 Kbps BC1:  200000 Kbps BC2:    0 Kbps BC3:   0 Kbps
          BC4:       0 Kbps BC5:       0 Kbps BC6:    0 Kbps BC7:   0 Kbps

=======================================================================
```

When the first two data LSPs are configured with 200 Mb/s and 100 Mb/s, they are allocated bandwidth from CT0 and CT1, and both follow the IGP shortest path (Figure 15.30). Listing 15.33 shows that the bandwidth is all allocated to TE class 0 and there is still 200 Mb/s available to TE class 1 (voice traffic).

Figure 15.30 LSPs assigned bandwidth using RDM.

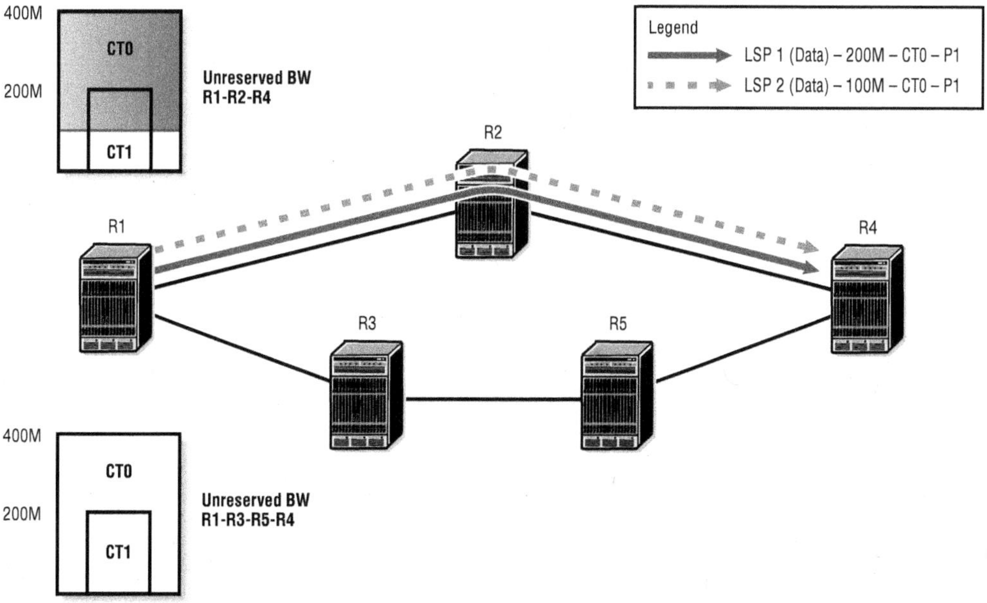

Listing 15.33 Allocation of bandwidth by TE class

```
*A:R1# show router rsvp interface "toR2" detail

===============================================================================
RSVP Interface (Detailed) : toR2
===============================================================================
-------------------------------------------------------------------------------
Interface : toR2
-------------------------------------------------------------------------------
Interface          : toR2
Port ID            : 1/1/2
Admin State        : Up                     Oper State         : Up
Active Sessions    : 2                      Active Resvs       : 2

... output omitted ...

Bandwidth for TE Class Types (Kbps)
TE0->  Resv. Bw    : 300000                 Unresv. Bw         : 100000
TE1->  Resv. Bw    : 0                      Unresv. Bw         : 200000
TE2->  Resv. Bw    : 0                      Unresv. Bw         : 0
TE3->  Resv. Bw    : 0                      Unresv. Bw         : 0
TE4->  Resv. Bw    : 0                      Unresv. Bw         : 0
TE5->  Resv. Bw    : 0                      Unresv. Bw         : 0
TE6->  Resv. Bw    : 0                      Unresv. Bw         : 0
TE7->  Resv. Bw    : 0                      Unresv. Bw         : 0

... output omitted ...

===============================================================================
```

When the third LSP is signaled for voice traffic with CT1, it has a higher priority and thus preempts the data LSP (see Figure 15.31). The bandwidth on the shortest IGP path is completely allocated for both TE classes. One hundred megabits per second is allocated from CT0 on the longer path (see Listing 15.34).

Figure 15.31 Higher-priority voice LSP preempts data LSP.

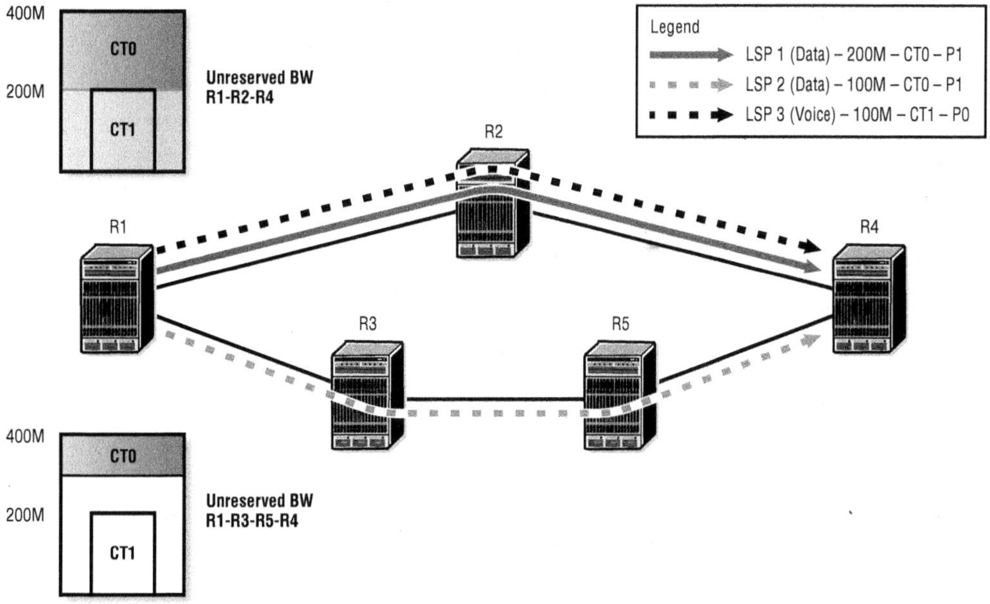

Listing 15.34 Bandwidth on the interface to R2 is completely allocated in both TE classes.

```
*A:R1# show router rsvp interface

===============================================================================
RSVP Interfaces
===============================================================================
Interface                   Total    Active   Total BW  Resv BW   Adm Opr
                            Sessions Sessions (Mbps)    (Mbps)
-------------------------------------------------------------------------------
system                      -        -        -         -         Up  Up
toR2                        3        3        1000      400       Up  Up
toR3                        1        1        1000      100       Up  Up
-------------------------------------------------------------------------------
Interfaces : 3
===============================================================================
*A:R1# show router ospf opaque-database 1.0.0.2 adv-router 10.10.10.1
detail
```

(continued)

Listing 15.34 *(continued)*

```
===============================================================================
OSPF Opaque Link State Database (Type : All) (Detailed)
===============================================================================
-------------------------------------------------------------------------------
Opaque LSA
-------------------------------------------------------------------------------
Area Id          : 0.0.0.0              Adv Router Id     : 10.10.10.1
Link State Id    : 1.0.0.2              LSA Type          : Area Opaque
Sequence No      : 0x8000001f           Checksum          : 0x4d83
Age              : 116                  Length            : 164
Options          :  E
Advertisement    :
     LINK INFO TLV  (0002) Len 140 :
       Sub-TLV: 1     Len: 1     LINK_TYPE    : 1
       Sub-TLV: 2     Len: 4     LINK_ID      : 10.10.10.2
       Sub-TLV: 3     Len: 4     LOC_IP_ADDR  : 10.1.2.1
       Sub-TLV: 4     Len: 4     REM_IP_ADDR  : 10.1.2.2
       Sub-TLV: 5     Len: 4     TE_METRIC    : 100
       Sub-TLV: 6     Len: 4     MAX_BDWTH    : 1000000 Kbps
       Sub-TLV: 7     Len: 4     RSRVBL_BDWTH : 1000000 Kbps
       Sub-TLV: 8     Len: 32    UNRSRVD_CLS0 :
         P0:       0 Kbps P1:       0 Kbps P2:    0 Kbps P3:   0 Kbps
         P4:       0 Kbps P5:       0 Kbps P6:    0 Kbps P7:   0 Kbps
       Sub-TLV: 9     Len: 4     ADMIN_GROUP  : 0 None
       Sub-TLV: 17    Len: 36    TELK_BW_CONST:
         BW Model : RDM
         BC0:  400000 Kbps BC1:  200000 Kbps BC2:    0 Kbps BC3:   0 Kbps
         BC4:       0 Kbps BC5:       0 Kbps BC6:    0 Kbps BC7:   0 Kbps

===============================================================================
```

Practice Lab: RSVP-TE Resource Reservation

The following lab is designed to reinforce your knowledge of the content in this chapter. Please review the instructions carefully, and perform the steps in the order in which they are presented. The practice labs require that you have access to six or more Alcatel-Lucent 7750 SRs or Alcatel-Lucent 7450 ESSs in a non-production environment.

These labs are designed to be used in a controlled lab environment. Please *do not* attempt to perform these labs in a production environment.

Lab Section 15.1: Bandwidth-Constrained LSPs

RSVP-TE supports bandwidth constraints so that bandwidth capacity can be distributed between LSPs.

Objective In this exercise, you will configure a topology of six Alcatel-Lucent 7750 SRs with RSVP-TE bandwidth-constrained LSPs (see Figure 15.32).

Validation You will know you have succeeded if the LSPs follow the specified bandwidth constraints.

1. Make sure that your IGP is configured as in Figure 15.32. This lab uses OSPF (Open Shortest Path First) for the IGP, but you can use IS-IS (Intermediate System to Intermediate System) if you prefer. Configure your IGP with traffic engineering. In addition, make sure that all RSVP-TE interfaces are functional.
2. Configure a totally loose CSPF-enabled LSP from R5 to R6.
   a. Verify that the LSP is operationally up before proceeding.
   b. What path does the LSP take?

Figure 15.32 Lab topology for bandwidth-constrained LSPs.

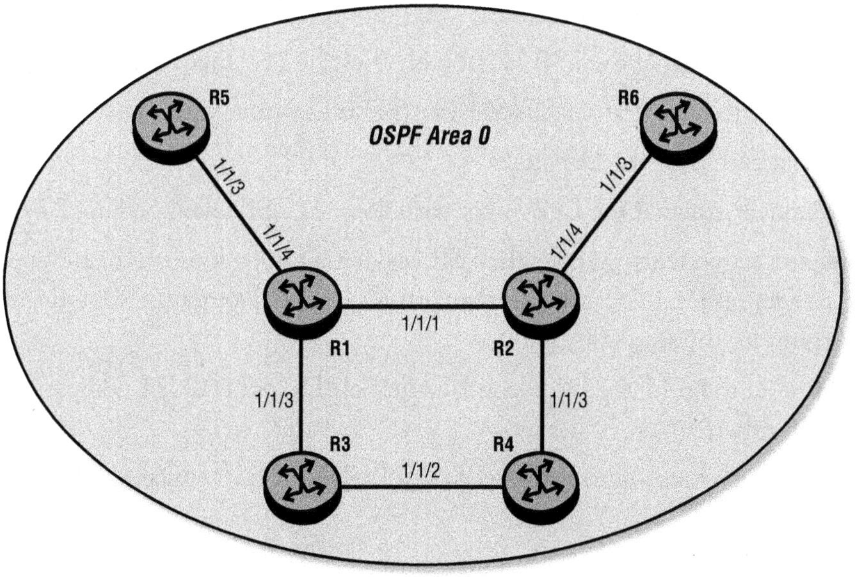

3. Change the subscription rate of the RSVP-TE interfaces between R1 and R2 to 50 percent.
   a. How many TE LSAs are originated in the network because of this configuration change?
   b. Describe the contents of the TE LSAs originated by R2 with respect to maximum bandwidth, reservable bandwidth, and unreserved bandwidth.
   c. What path does the LSP take now? Explain.
   d. Configure the LSP with a bandwidth constraint of 600 Mb/s. What path does the LSP take now? Does the LSP require a manual resignal? Explain.
   e. How many TE LSAs are originated in the network because a bandwidth constraint was added to the LSP? Explain.
   f. Describe the contents of the TE LSAs originated by R4 with respect to maximum bandwidth, reservable bandwidth, and unreserved bandwidth.
   g. Using the `show router rsvp interface` command, how much bandwidth is reserved on R5's interface to R1? What about R1's interface to R5? Explain.
   h. Disable CSPF on the LSP. Is the LSP operationally up? If not, what is the failure code? Explain.
   i. Enable CSPF on the LSP before proceeding.
4. Change the bandwidth constraint on the LSP to 400 Mb/s.
   a. What path does the LSP take?
   b. Manually resignal the LSP. What path does the LSP take? Explain.
   c. Change the LSP to use a Fixed Filter (FF) reservation style.
   d. What path does the LSP take?
   e. Manually resignal the LSP. What path does the LSP take? Explain.
5. Configure a secondary path for the LSP. Make it a totally loose path, and specify the `standby` option to ensure that the path is signaled. Do not use a bandwidth constraint for the secondary path.
   a. How do the primary and secondary tunnel IDs and LSP IDs compare to each other?
   b. How much bandwidth is reserved on R5's RSVP-TE interface to R1?

c. What path does the secondary LSP take?

d. Add a bandwidth constraint of 400 Mb/s on the secondary path. What path does the secondary LSP take now? Explain.

e. How much bandwidth is reserved on R5's RSVP-TE interface to R6? Explain.

f. Resignal the primary LSP. Is the MBB successful? What path is taken by the LSP? Explain.

6. Change the reservation style of the LSP to Shared Explicit (SE).

   a. How much bandwidth is reserved on R5's RSVP-TE interface to R1? Explain.

   b. What path do the primary and secondary LSPs take?

   c. Resignal the primary LSP. Is the MBB successful? What path is taken by the LSP? Explain.

   d. How practical is the secondary path configuration presented so far in this lab?

   e. Remove the secondary path before proceeding.

Lab Section 15.2: Soft Preemption

The previous section investigated how RSVP-TE LSPs can be configured with bandwidth constraints. This section investigates how setup and holding priorities can be applied to the LSPs to prioritize the allocation or resources between LSPs.

Objective This lab will investigate the setup and hold priorities associated with soft preemption.

Validation You will know you have succeeded if the high-priority LSPs preempt low-priority LSPs when there is bandwidth contention.

1. Examine the TE LSAs originated by R5. What can you deduce regarding the default holding and setup priorities of an LSP?

2. Configure the LSP from R5 to R6 with a setup priority of 3 and a hold priority of 4. Is the operation successful? Explain.

3. Configure the LSP with a setup priority of 4 and a hold priority of 3.

   a. How is this change reflected in the TE LSA originated by R5?

   b. Verify that the path of the LSP is through R1 and R2 before proceeding. You may need to resignal the LSP.

4. Configure a CSPF-enabled LSP reserving 500 Mb/s bandwidth with a totally loose path from R5 to R2. Assign setup and hold priorities of 2.
   a. What path does the LSP from R5 to R2 take?
   b. What path does the LSP from R5 to R6 take? Explain.
   c. Describe the contents of the TE LSA originated by R5 after the LSP from R5 to R2 is configured.
   d. How do the tunnel IDs and LSP IDs of both LSPs compare to each other?
5. Configure a CSPF-enabled LSP reserving 300 Mb/s bandwidth with a totally loose path from R5 to R3. Assign setup and hold priorities of 1.
   a. Is the LSP from R5 to R3 operationally up? If not, what is the failure code? Explain.
   b. Is the LSP from R5 to R2 operationally up? If not, what is the failure code? Explain.
   c. Is the LSP from R5 to R6 operationally up? If not, what is the failure code? Explain.
   d. Wait for 5 minutes, and then check the operational status of each LSP again. How do the results compare to before? Explain.
   e. Adjust the subscription rate on R1's interface to R5 to 150 percent. Are all LSPs operationally up? Explain.
   f. Adjust the subscription rate on R5's interface to R1 to 150 percent. Are all LSPs operationally up? Explain.
6. Configure a CSPF-enabled LSP reserving 900 Mb/s bandwidth with a totally loose path from R5 to R4. Assign a setup priority of 4 and a holding priority of 0.
   a. Is the LSP from R5 to R4 operationally up? If not, what is the failure code? Explain.
   b. Configure a CSPF-enabled LSP reserving 500 Mb/s bandwidth from R6 to R5. Assign the lowest possible setup and hold priorities. Is the LSP operationally up? If so, what path does the LSP take? Explain.

Lab Section 15.3: Diffserv Traffic Engineering

The previous lab sections investigated bandwidth-constrained LSPs and the setup and hold priorities that can be configured on an RSVP-TE LSP. This section investigates the use of the MAM and RDM DiffServ Traffic Engineering models that provide more granularity for bandwidth reservations.

Objective In this lab, you will configure MAM and RDM DiffServ-TE models and investigate the effect on different bandwidth-constrained LSPs.

Validation You will know you have succeeded if you can see the difference in the LSP operational status and path depending on which DiffServ-TE model is used (see Figure 15.33).

1. Set the link between R1 and R2 to use default subscription values. Leave the subscription value of the link between R1 and R5 at 150 percent. Administratively shut down all the LSPs on R5 and R6.

   a. Verify that there are no RSVP-TE sessions on R1–R4 before proceeding.

2. Configure the TE classes and class types according to the table in the figure using the DiffServ Memory Allocation Model. Which nodes require the DiffServ configuration?

   a. Explain the effect that the MAM configuration has had on the RSVP-TE interfaces of R1 (use the command `show router rsvp interfaces detail`).

3. Configure a 400 Mb/s LSP from R1 to R2 with the Bronze class type, but use a setup and hold priority of 3. Name the LSP *toR2-bronze-1*.

   a. Is the LSP operationally up? If not, what failure code is given?

   b. Change the setup and hold priority of the LSP to 2. Is the LSP operationally up? If not, what is the failure code?

Figure 15.33 TE class assignments for MAM and RDM lab.

Traffic Type	TE Class	Class Type	Preemption Priority	Bandwdith Constraint
Gold	2	CT2	0	40
Silver	1	CT1	1	30
Bronze	0	CT0	2	30

4. Leave the LSP from the previous step configured. Configure two additional LSPs from R1 to R2. Use the parameters required for a Bronze TE class and a bandwidth of 200 Mb/s. Name the first LSP *toR2-bronze-2* and the second LSP *toR2-bronze-3*.

    a. Are the LSPs operationally up? If so, what are the paths of the LSPs? Explain.

5. Configure a 300 Mb/s LSP from R1 to R2 that uses the Silver TE class. Name the LSP *toR2-silver-1*.

    a. Is the LSP operationally up? If so, what path does it take?

6. Configure a 500 Mb/s LSP from R1 to R2 that uses the Gold TE class. Name the LSP *toR2-gold-1*.

    a. Is the LSP operationally up? Explain.

7. Administratively shut down all the LSPs on R1, but leave them configured, as they will be used in the subsequent steps.

8. Change the DiffServ model from MAM to RDM. Use the same TE classes and related parameters.

    a. Explain the effect the RDM configuration has had on the RSVP-TE interface on R1 toward R2 (use the `show router rsvp interface detail` command).

    b. Administratively enable the LSP `toR2-gold-1`. Is the LSP operationally up? Explain.

    c. Administratively enable the LSP `toR2-bronze-1`. Is the LSP operationally up? If so, what path does the LSP use? Explain.

    d. Administratively enable the `toR2-bronze-2` and `toR2-bronze-3` LSPs. Are the LSPs operationally up? What path do the LSPs take?

    e. How much bandwidth is left on R1's RSVP-TE interface to R2?

9. Administratively enable the LSP `toR2-silver-1`.

    a. Is the LSP operationally up? What path does it take?

    b. Are the Bronze LSPs still operationally up? What paths do they take? Explain.

10. Configure a CSPF-enabled LSP on R1 to R2 that does not have a bandwidth constraint, class type, or priority.

    a. Is the LSP operationally up? Explain.

Chapter Review

Now that you have completed this chapter, you should be able to:

- Describe how bandwidth requirements are signaled and reserved.
- Explain threshold-triggered IGP TE updates.
- Describe the Shared Explicit bandwidth reservation style.
- Describe the Fixed Filter bandwidth reservation style.
- Explain the make-before-break behavior of LSPs.
- Explain least-fill bandwidth reservation.
- Describe LSP soft preemption.
- Explain the benefit of DiffServ-Aware Traffic Engineering.
- Configure class types (CTs) and TE classes.
- Configure bandwidth constraints per class type.
- Describe the operation DiffServ-TE with MAM using an example.
- Describe the operation DiffServ-TE with RDM using an example.

Post-Assessment

1. A router has just finished a CSPF computation to find a route for a bandwidth-constrained LSP. Which statement best describes the next step for the head end router, assuming a path is found for the LSP?

   A. The head end router sends a CAC message to the next-hop router so that it can perform bandwidth reservation.

   B. The head end router floods a TE LSA to all routers in the LSP path so that they can perform bandwidth reservation.

   C. The head end router sends a Path message to the tail end router. The next-hop router intercepts the Path message and performs bandwidth reservation.

   D. The head end router sends a Resv message to the tail end router. The next-hop router intercepts the Resv message and performs bandwidth reservation.

   E. None of the above statements are correct.

2. Consider a network of Alcatel-Lucent 7750 SRs. An operator wants to provision a bandwidth-constrained LSP with a fully loose path. There are two paths between the head and tail end routers. One path has a lower IGP cost but has RSVP-TE interfaces that cannot meet the bandwidth requirement. The RSVP-TE interfaces of all routers along the path with the higher IGP metric can meet the bandwidth requirement. The operator forgets to enable the LSP with CSPF. Which statement below is correct?

   A. The LSP is established and operationally up along the path with the lower IGP cost.

   B. The LSP is established and operationally up along the path with the higher IGP cost.

   C. The LSP is operationally down with the failure code `admissionControlError`.

   D. The LSP is operationally down with the failure code `noCspfRouteToDestination`.

   E. None of the above statements are correct.

3. Consider a network of 7750 SRs. All ports in the network are 1 Gb/s, and default subscription values are used. An operator provisions an LSP with a primary and hot standby secondary path between two nodes. Both paths have a bandwidth constraint of 800 Mb/s and are totally loose. Assume that there are no other RSVP-TE sessions in the network. Which statement below is correct?

   A. If Shared Explicit mode is used, the primary and secondary paths will be established over different paths in the network.

   B. The secondary LSP will not be signaled unless the primary path goes down.

   C. If Fixed Filter mode is used and CSPF is enabled on the LSP, the primary and secondary LSPs will take separate paths through the network.

   D. If Shared Explicit mode is used and CSPF is not enabled on the LSP, the secondary LSP will have a failure code of `admissionControlError`.

   E. All of the above statements are incorrect.

4. Consider a network of 7750 SRs with three CSPF LSPs configured between the same head and tail end router. All ports in the network are 1 Gb/s. Two equal cost paths exist to the tail end router, but ECMP is not enabled on the IGP. The three CSPF LSPs are configured in the following order: a 300 Mb/s LSP, a 400 Mb/s LSP, and a 200 Mb/s LSP. The first and third LSPs have the least-fill option enabled, but the second LSP does not. Assuming that there are no other LSPs in the network, which statement below is correct?

   A. The first and second LSPs will have the same path.

   B. The first and third LSPs will have the same path.

   C. The first and third LSPs will have different paths, but it is not possible to determine which path the second LSP will use.

   D. There is not enough information to determine the path of the LSPs.

5. Which statement below is correct regarding DiffServ-aware traffic engineering on an Alcatel-Lucent 7750 SR?

   A. An Alcatel-Lucent 7750 SR can be configured to use MAM for some LSPs and RDM for other LSPs.

   B. RDM allows lower CTs to allocate the unused bandwidth from higher CTs.

   C. RDM allocates bandwidth discretely to different CTs, and bandwidth cannot be shared between CTs.

   D. If an incorrect class type and priority pair is configured on an LSP, the LSP stays operationally down with a failure code of `admissionControlError`.

   E. None of the above statements are correct.

6. A router receives a Resv message but does not have the required bandwidth resources for the LSP. What action will the router take?

   A. It will flood an LSA to indicate that it cannot service the LSP.

   B. It will send a Path Error message upstream.

   C. It will send a ResvErr message downstream.

   D. It will send a PathTear message downstream and a ResvTear message upstream.

   E. None of the above statements are correct.

7. What is the maximum rate at which an interface can be oversubscribed to actual bandwidth on an Alcatel-Lucent 7750 SR?

   A. 50%

   B. 100%

   C. 1,000%

   D. 10,000%

   E. There is no oversubscription limit.

8. Consider an Alcatel-Lucent 7750 SR that is the head end for a bandwidth-constrained LSP of 600 Mb/s that is operationally up. All of the ports on the router have a speed of 1 Gb/s. The operator changes all RSVP-TE interfaces to have a subscription rate of 50 percent. Assume there is only one RSVP-TE session on the router. Which statement below is correct?

   A. There is no change to the LSP until the resignal timer expires or the LSP is manually resignaled.

   B. The LSA sent by the head end router for the interface the LSP uses has a maximum bandwidth of 500 Mb/s.

   C. The LSA sent by the head end router for the port the LSP uses has an unreserved bandwidth of 500 Mb/s.

   D. The LSA sent by the head end router for the port the LSP uses has a reservable bandwidth of 0 Mb/s.

   E. There is not enough information to answer the question.

9. A bandwidth-constrained CSPF-enabled LSP is successfully established and passes through two LSRs between the head and tail end routers. Threshold-triggered IGP TE updates are not configured. How many TE LSAs are expected to be flooded in the network because of this LSP establishment?

   A. 0

   B. 1

   C. 3

   D. 4

   E. 6

   F. 8

10. Consider a network of 7750 SRs in which all ports have a speed of 1 Gb/s. The RSVP-TE `te-down` thresholds are configured with a single value of 0 percent on every router. A physical link failure between two directly connected nodes in the network causes a CSPF-enabled LSP with a totally strict path and a bandwidth reservation of 500 Mb/s to go down. The LSP passes through a total of four routers (including head and tail end). Assuming that there are no other LSPs in the network, how many TE LSAs are generated in the network because of the link failure?

A. 1

B. 2

C. 3

D. 4

E. 6

F. 8

11. Consider a 7750 SR that is a transit LSR for three RSVP-TE tunnels each configured with a primary and a standby secondary path. All LSPs (primary and secondary) egress the same interface. One of the tunnels has an FF reservation style with a primary and secondary bandwidth constraint of 100 Mb/s. The second LSP uses an SE reservation style with a primary and secondary bandwidth constraint of 200 Mb/s. The third LSP uses an SE reservation style with a primary bandwidth constraint of 300 Mb/s and a secondary bandwidth constraint of 400 Mb/s. Assuming that these are the only RSVP-TE sessions on the router, what should an operator expect to see for the egress interface when they use the `show router rsvp interface` command?

A. The total *Resv BW* is 400 Mb/s.

B. The total *Resv BW* is 600 Mb/s.

C. The total *Resv BW* is 700 Mb/s.

D. The total *Resv BW* is 800 Mb/s.

E. None of the above answers are correct.

12. Consider a network of 7750 SRs. All ports in the network are 1 Gb/s, and all RSVP-TE interfaces have default subscription values. An LSP that is operationally up is configured with a bandwidth constraint of 600 Mb/s and has a Fixed Filter reservation style. There are two distinct paths through the network for the LSP. The LSP is manually resignaled. Assuming that there is no other bandwidth-constrained LSP in the network, which statement below is correct?

A. The LSP will be operationally down after it is resignaled.

B. The LSP will be operationally up and will take the same path as before it was resignaled.

C. The LSP will have the same LSP ID but a different Tunnel ID after it is resignaled.

D. The LSP will be operationally up but will take a different path through the network after it is resignaled.

E. None of the above answers are correct.

13. A CSPF LSP with a bandwidth constraint of 600 Mb/s is established with a setup priority of 4 and a hold priority of 3 on a 7750 SR. There are no other LSPs that use the same RSVP-TE interface on the head end router, all ports in the network have a speed of 1 Gb/s, and all RSVP-TE interfaces are configured with default subscription rates. Which statement below is correct regarding the TE LSA that is sent by the head end router as a result of the LSP becoming established?

A. The unreserved bandwidth for P0–P2 is 1 Gb/s, and the unreserved bandwidth for P3–P7 is 400 Mb/s.

B. The unreserved bandwidth for P3–P7 is 1 Gb/s, and the unreserved bandwidth for P0–P2 is 400 Mb/s.

C. The unreserved bandwidth for P3 and P4 is 400 Mb/s, and the rest of the priorities are 1 Gb/s.

D. The unreserved bandwidth for P3 is 400 Mb/s, and the rest of the priorities are 1 Gb/s.

E. The unreserved bandwidth for P4 is 400 Mb/s, and the rest of the priorities are 1 Gb/s.

F. None of the above statements are correct.

14. Consider a network of 7750 SRs. All ports in the network are 1 Gb/s, and all RSVP-TE interfaces have default subscription rates. There are exactly two unequal cost paths in the network between the head and tail end routers. An operator configures three CSPF-enabled totally loose LSPs between the two routers in the following order: an 800 Mb/s LSP with setup and hold priority of 3, a 400 Mb/s LSP with setup and hold priority of 1, and a 700 Mb/s LSP with a setup and hold priority of 2. The operator views the output of the `show router mpls lsp path detail` command immediately after the last LSP is configured. Which statement below is *not* correct?

A. The 400 Mb/s LSP is operationally up along the lowest-cost path.

B. The 700 Mb/s LSP is operationally up along the lowest-cost path.

C. The 800 Mb/s LSP is operationally up along the higher-cost path.

D. All of the above statements are correct.

15. Consider a 7750 SR in which all ports are 1 Gb/s and all RSVP-TE interfaces have a subscription rate of 200. The router is configured for DiffServ TE using the Russian Dolls Model. Class type 0 is assigned 20 percent of the reservable bandwidth, class type 1 is assigned 0 percent of the reservable bandwidth, and class type 2 is assigned 30 percent of the reservable bandwidth. Assuming that no LSPs are configured, what bandwidth constraints are expected to be in the Traffic Engineering LSAs originated by the router?

A. The BC0 value is 500 Mb/s, the BC1 value is 300 Mb/s, and the BC2 value is 300 Mb/s.

B. The BC0 value is 1 Gb/s, the BC1 value is 600 Mb/s, and and the BC2 value is 600 Mb/s.

C. The BC0 value is 300 Mb/s, the BC1 value is 500 Mb/s, and the BC2 value is 500 Mb/s.

D. The BC0 value is 600 Mb/s, the BC1 value is 1 Gb/s, and the BC2 value is 1 Gb/s.

E. None of the above answers are correct.

16 MPLS Resiliency

The Alcatel-Lucent NRS II exam topics covered in this chapter include the following:

- Network resiliency overview
- Non-standby secondary LSP::Paths
- Standby secondary LSP::Paths
- Using SRLG and admin groups with secondary LSP::Paths
- Secondary LSP::Path selection criteria
- RSVP-TE fast reroute
- One-to-one fast reroute method
- Facility backup fast reroute method
- Global revertive mode
- Using SRLG with fast reroute

We start the chapter with an overview of network resiliency and then proceed to discuss the resiliency features of RSVP-TE (Resource Reservation Protocol–Traffic Engineering). First, we discuss head end switching using secondary LSP::Paths. Then we investigate how fast reroute can be used to improve fail over times that are not dependent on the size of a network. Shared Risk Link groups are also covered in this chapter as they pertain to both secondary LSP::Paths and fast reroute (FRR).

Pre-Assessment

The following assessment questions will help you understand what areas of the chapter you should review in more detail to prepare for the NRS II exam. You can also use the CD that accompanies this book to take all the assessment tests and review the answers.

1. An operator configures an Alcatel-Lucent 7750 SR with a primary LSP::Path and a non-standby secondary LSP::Path. The operator mistakenly configures a strict hop in the secondary LSP::Path that does not exist. If the primary LSP::Path is operationally up and FRR is not configured, which statement below is false?
   - **A.** The primary LSP::Path will be active.
   - **B.** The secondary LSP::Path will be operationally down.
   - **C.** The secondary LSP::Path will have a failure code of `noCspfRouteToDestination`.
   - **D.** The secondary LSP::Path will not have any computed hops.
   - **E.** All of the above statements are true.
2. An LSP is configured with a totally loose primary LSP::Path and a totally loose standby secondary LSP::Path. If there are at least two unequal cost totally disjoint paths between the head and tail end router, which statement below is incorrect?
   - **A.** The LSP::Paths should be made disjoint by the use of strict hops, admin groups, or SRLGs.
   - **B.** The secondary LSP::Path is operationally up.
   - **C.** The secondary LSP::Path will take the second least cost path between the head and tail end routers.
   - **D.** If there is a link failure on the primary LSP::Path, there will be a traffic outage at least as long as the LSP retry interval.
   - **E.** All of the above statements are correct.

3. A 7750 SR is configured with three totally loose secondary LSP::Paths in the following order. The first secondary LSP::Path is non-standby, has no constraints, and has no configured path preference. The second secondary LSP::Path is declared standby, has admin group constraints to achieve path diversity, and has a path preference of 50. The third secondary LSP::Path is declared standby, uses SRLG to achieve path diversity, has no configured path preference, and has a lower CSPF metric than the second secondary LSP::Path. Which secondary LSP::Path will become active if the primary LSP::Path fails? Assume that the failure does not affect the standby LSP::Paths.

A. The first secondary LSP::Path will become active.

B. The second secondary LSP::Path will become active.

C. The third secondary LSP::Path will become active.

D. None of the secondary LSP::Paths will become active.

4. Consider a router that could be a PLR for two established protected LSPs that have the same tail end router. Which statement best describes the detour LSPs originated by the PLR?

A. The PLR originates one detour LSP that follows the shortest CSPF path to the destination.

B. If both protected LSPs have identical paths, the PLR originates one detour LSP; otherwise, two detour LSPs are originated.

C. If both protected LSPs have the same head end router, the PLR originates one detour LSP; otherwise, two detour LSPs are originated.

D. The PLR originates two detour LSPs that follow the shortest CSPF path to the destination.

E. None of the above statements are correct.

5. Consider an LSP protected with facility backup and a primary LSP::Path constrained with strict hops. The LSP also has a totally loose non-standby secondary. Assuming that the primary LSP::Path is operationally up and fully protected, which of the following statements is incorrect?

   A. After a link failure on the primary LSP::Path, the PLR will switch traffic to the bypass tunnel.

   B. After the head end node learns that local protection is in use, it signals the secondary LSP::Path and makes it active.

   C. FRR protection is attempted by every router on the secondary LSP::Path after it becomes active.

   D. The bypass tunnel remains up even if the secondary LSP::Path is active.

   E. All of the above statements are true.

16.1 Network Resiliency Overview

One of the key characteristics of a modern transport network is how quickly it can react to network failures and restore network services. The term *convergence* refers to the overall time that it takes to restore the services. Quick detection of network failures and short convergence times are crucial to a service provider's ability to meet the standards set in the Service Level Agreement (SLA).

Interior gateway protocols (IGPs) are reactionary. A new path is calculated only after the detection of a failure that affects the existing path. Although this is relatively fast, the convergence times might fall short of the increasing demands of emerging applications, such as video conferencing, voice, online gaming, and so on.

Using MPLS (Multiprotocol Label Switching) resiliency features, such as secondary LSP::Paths and fast reroute (FRR) with RSVP-TE signaling, protection tunnels can be created before failures occur. This is a proactive approach toward providing network resilience.

The primary aspects of network convergence are:

- **Failure detection**—Failures are identified by the neighboring network devices.
- **Failure propagation**—After a failure is detected, other devices in the network are notified of the problem. They exchange control messages to describe and recover from the failure.
- **Service recovery**—Customer services are recovered by directing traffic around the point of network failure.

In LDP (Label Distribution Protocol), resiliency is provided by the IGP, and the time to recover from a failure is never less than the IGP convergence time. An RSVP-TE LSP (label switched path) without CSPF (constrained shortest path first) enabled behaves very much like an LDP LSP. When there is a topology change, there is an outage until the LSP can be reestablished on the path that follows the IGP.

RSVP-TE with CSPF provides superior resiliency functions and is the focus of this chapter. The LSPs examined in this chapter are all configured with CSPF enabled.

16.2 RSVP-TE Secondary Paths

As shown in previous chapters, RSVP-TE can be used to provide traffic-engineering functions based on strict hops, admin groups, or bandwidth constraints. RSVP-TE also provides excellent failover and reversion mechanisms.

The first RSVP-TE resiliency mechanism we investigate is the use of secondary LSP::Paths.

Non-Standby Secondary LSP::Paths

To provide some motivation and insight into the use of secondary LSP::Paths, we first consider a case that uses only a single primary LSP::Path, as shown in Figure 16.1.

Figure 16.1 Primary LSP with a totally loose path.

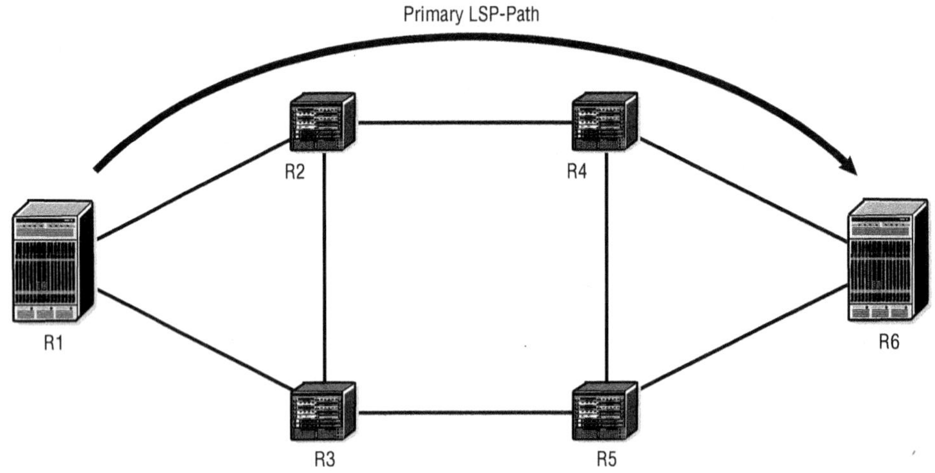

When a failure occurs between R4 and R6 (see Figure 16.2), the LSP is brought down, and the primary LSP is eventually established over the new IGP best path.

This example has the simplest possible configuration and *does* recover from the link failure, but has some significant limitations.

- When the head end router for a CSPF-enabled LSP receives the ResvTear message indicating the failure, it does not try to reestablish the LSP until the retry timer expires (default 30 seconds). This time, plus the time necessary to signal the ResvTear and the new LSP, can result in a significant traffic outage.
- If the LSP has traffic-engineering constraints, there may not be another path that satisfies the constraints. In Figure 16.3, the LSP is constrained to include the admin group `green`. If there is a failure on any link along the path, the LSP cannot be rerouted and is operationally down until the link is repaired.

Figure 16.2 Primary LSP with a totally loose path rerouted.

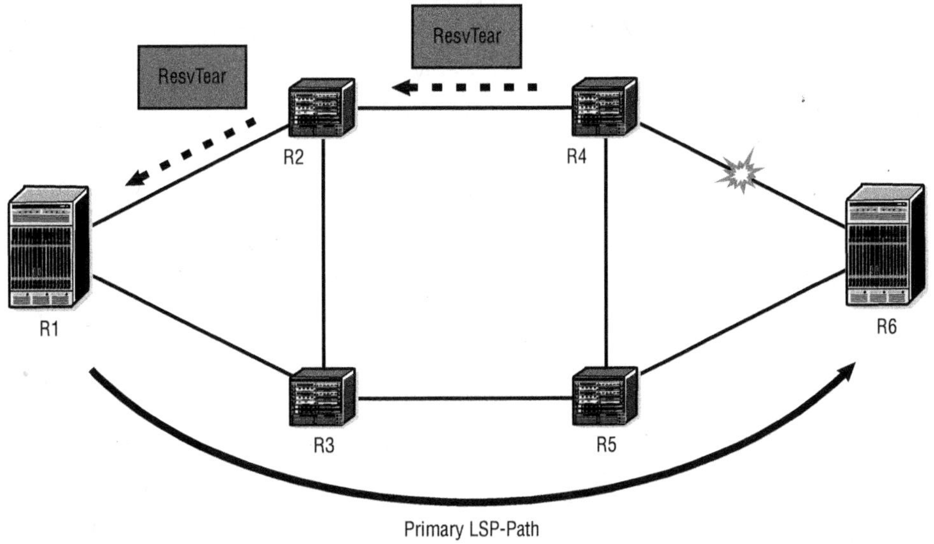

Figure 16.3 Constrained primary LSP operationally down.

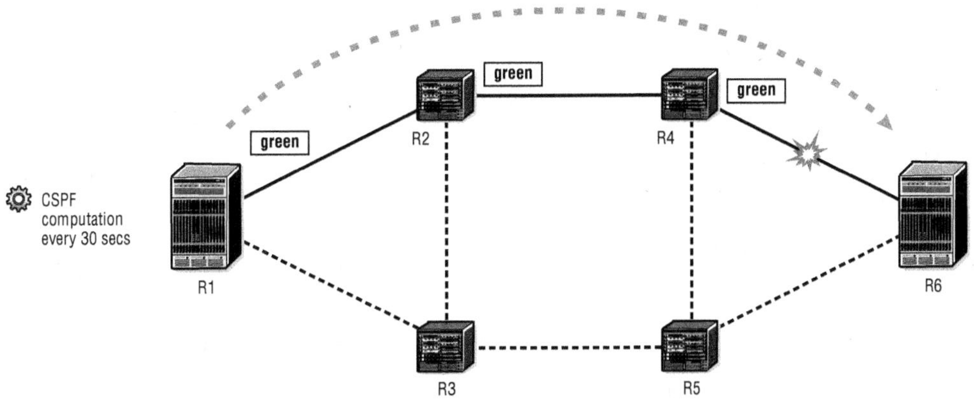

- Once the link failure is repaired, the LSP does not revert to the original path unless a manual resignal is performed or the resignal timer expires (disabled by default on the Alcatel-Lucent 7750 SR).

  The solution is to configure the LSP with one or more secondary paths.

The 7750 SR supports the definition of alternate paths for an LSP called *secondary* LSP::Paths. This allows the primary LSP::Path to be constrained for traffic-engineering purposes. The secondary LSP::Path can either be signaled when the LSP is created (standby) or after a failure causes the primary LSP::Path to become operationally down. We first look at non-standby secondaries and then at standby secondaries in the next section.

In the case of a non-standby secondary, when the head end detects the primary LSP::Path failure, it performs the CSPF computation and signals the secondary LSP. Traffic is switched to the secondary as soon as it comes up. When the retry timer expires, the head end performs the CSPF calculation and attempts to signal the primary. The head end tries to signal the primary every time the retry timer expires until it is successfully signaled. Once the primary is up again, traffic is switched back to it in a make-before-break (MBB) fashion.

The configuration of the secondary LSP::Path is similar to that of the primary LSP::Path with the exception of the keyword `secondary` (see Listing 16.1). The 7750 SR does not allow the same path to be bound to both the primary and secondary, thus we configure another loose path with a different name. We only show the admin group configuration on the head end router, but the admin group `green` will be configured on all egress router interfaces along the primary path.

Listing 16.1 Secondary path configuration with primary up (some output omitted)

```
*A:R1>config>router>mpls# info
----------------------------------------------
            admin-group "green" 3
            interface "toR2"
                admin-group "green"
            exit
            path "loose"
                no shutdown
            exit
            path "sec-loose"
                no shutdown
            exit
            lsp "toR6"
                to 10.10.10.6
                cspf
```

```
                primary "loose"
                    include "green"
                exit
                secondary "sec-loose"
                exit
                no shutdown
            exit
            no shutdown
----------------------------------------------
*A:R1>config>router>mpls
*A:R1# show router mpls lsp "toR6" path detail

=======================================================================
MPLS LSP toR6 Path  (Detail)
=======================================================================
Legend :
    @ - Detour Available              # - Detour In Use
    b - Bandwidth Protected           n - Node Protected
    s - Soft Preemption
=======================================================================
-----------------------------------------------------------------------
LSP toR6 Path loose
-----------------------------------------------------------------------
LSP Name     : toR6                         Path LSP ID : 55394
From         : 10.10.10.1                   To          : 10.10.10.6
Adm State    : Up                           Oper State  : Up
Path Name    : loose                        Path Type   : Primary
Path Admin   : Up                           Path Oper   : Up
OutInterface: 1/1/3                         Out Label   : 131071
Path Up Time: 0d 00:00:03                   Path Dn Time: 0d 00:00:00
Retry Limit : 0                             Retry Timer : 30 sec
RetryAttempt: 0                             NextRetryIn : 0 sec
SetupPriori*: 7                             Hold Priori*: 0
Preference   : n/a
Bandwidth    : No Reservation               Oper Bw     : 0 Mbps
Hop Limit    : 255                          Class Type  : 0
Backup CT    : None
MainCT Retry: n/a                           MainCT Retry: 0
    Rem      :                                  Limit   :
Oper CT      : 0
```

(continued)

Listing 16.1 *(continued)*

```
Record Route: Record                         Record Label: Record
Oper MTU    : 1564                           Neg MTU     : 1564
Adaptive    : Enabled                        Oper Metric : 30
Include Grps:                                Exclude Grps:
green                                       None
Path Trans  : 45                             CSPF Queries: 72
Failure Code: noError                        Failure Node: n/a
ExplicitHops:
    No Hops Specified
Actual Hops :
    10.1.2.1(10.10.10.1)                     Record Label    : N/A
 -> 10.1.2.2(10.10.10.2)                     Record Label    : 131071
 -> 10.2.4.4(10.10.10.4)                     Record Label    : 131071
 -> 10.4.6.6(10.10.10.6)                     Record Label    : 131071
ComputedHops:
    10.1.2.1        -> 10.1.2.2        -> 10.2.4.4        -> 10.4.6.6
ResigEligib*: False
LastResignal: n/a                            CSPF Metric : 30
-----------------------------------------------------------------------
LSP toR6 Path sec-loose
-----------------------------------------------------------------------
LSP Name    : toR6                           Path LSP ID : 55396
From        : 10.10.10.1                     To          : 10.10.10.6
Adm State   : Up                             Oper State  : Up
Path Name   : sec-loose                      Path Type   : Secondary
Path Admin  : Up                             Path Oper   : Down
OutInterface: n/a                            Out Label   : n/a
Path Up Time: 0d 00:00:00                    Path Dn Time: 0d 00:00:04
Retry Limit : 0                              Retry Timer : 30 sec
RetryAttempt: 0                              NextRetryIn : 0 sec
SetupPriori*: 7                              Hold Priori*: 0
Preference  : n/a
Bandwidth   : No Reservation                 Oper Bw     : 0 Mbps
Hop Limit   : 255                            Class Type  : 0
Oper CT     : None
Record Route: Record                         Record Label: Record
Oper MTU    : 0                              Neg MTU     : 0
Adaptive    : Enabled                        Oper Metric : 65535
```

```
Include Grps:                             Exclude Grps:
None                                    None
Path Trans   : 2                          CSPF Queries: 1
Failure Code: noError                     Failure Node: n/a
ExplicitHops:
    No Hops Specified
Actual Hops :
    No Hops Specified
ComputedHops:
    No Hops Specified
Srlg        : Disabled
ResigEligib*: False
LastResignal: n/a                         CSPF Metric : 0
======================================================================
* indicates that the corresponding row element may have been truncated.
*A:R1#
```

Figure 16.4 shows the secondary LSP::Path signaled and active after a link failure on the primary LSP::Path. Listing 16.2 shows how the condition is represented on the 7750 SR.

Figure 16.4 Primary path down, secondary path up.

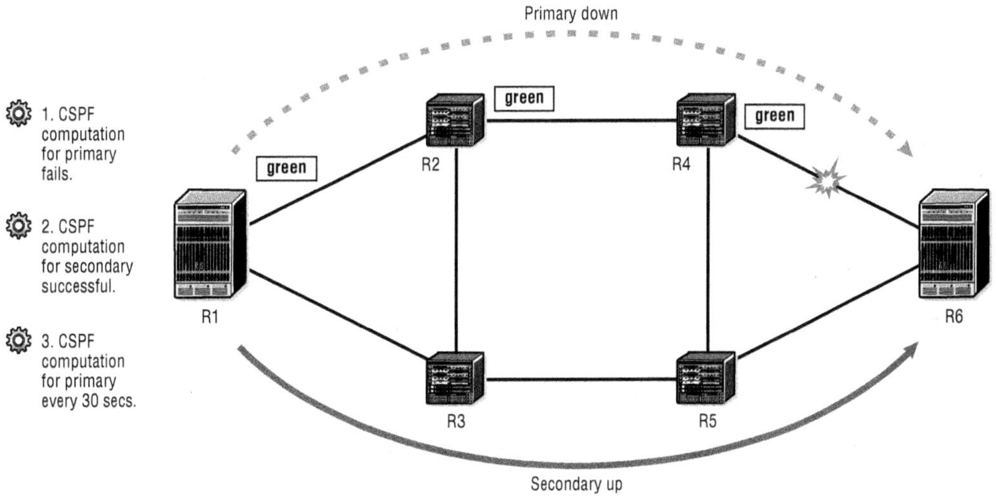

Listing 16.2 Secondary path configuration and secondary up

```
*A:R1# show router mpls lsp "toR6" path detail

===============================================================================
MPLS LSP toR6 Path  (Detail)
===============================================================================
Legend :
    @ - Detour Available              # - Detour In Use
    b - Bandwidth Protected           n - Node Protected
    s - Soft Preemption
===============================================================================
-------------------------------------------------------------------------------
LSP toR6 Path loose
-------------------------------------------------------------------------------
LSP Name    : toR6                         Path LSP ID : 55394
From        : 10.10.10.1                   To          : 10.10.10.6
Adm State   : Up                           Oper State  : Up
Path Name   : loose                        Path Type   : Primary
Path Admin  : Up                           Path Oper   : Down
OutInterface: n/a                          Out Label   : n/a
Path Up Time: 0d 00:00:00                  Path Dn Time: 0d 00:00:06
Retry Limit : 0                            Retry Timer : 30 sec
RetryAttempt: 0                            NextRetryIn : 24 sec
SetupPriori*: 7                            Hold Priori*: 0
Preference  : n/a
Bandwidth   : No Reservation               Oper Bw     : 0 Mbps
Hop Limit   : 255                          Class Type  : 0
Backup CT   : None
MainCT Retry: n/a                          MainCT Retry: 0
    Rem     :                                  Limit   :
Oper CT     : None
Record Route: Record                       Record Label: Record
Oper MTU    : 0                            Neg MTU     : 0
Adaptive    : Enabled                      Oper Metric : 65535
Include Grps:                              Exclude Grps:
green                                    None
Path Trans  : 46                           CSPF Queries: 72
Failure Code: noError                      Failure Node: n/a
ExplicitHops:
```

```
    No Hops Specified
Actual Hops :
    No Hops Specified
ComputedHops:
    No Hops Specified
ResigEligib*: False
LastResignal: n/a                             CSPF Metric : 0
----------------------------------------------------------------------
LSP toR6 Path sec-loose
----------------------------------------------------------------------
LSP Name    : toR6                            Path LSP ID : 55398
From        : 10.10.10.1                      To          : 10.10.10.6
Adm State   : Up                              Oper State  : Up
Path Name   : sec-loose                       Path Type   : Secondary
Path Admin  : Up                              Path Oper   : Up
OutInterface: 1/1/3                           Out Label   : 131070
Path Up Time: 0d 00:00:08                     Path Dn Time: 0d 00:00:00
Retry Limit : 0                               Retry Timer : 30 sec
RetryAttempt: 0                               NextRetryIn : 0 sec
SetupPriori*: 7                               Hold Priori*: 0
Preference  : n/a
Bandwidth   : No Reservation                  Oper Bw     : 0 Mbps
Hop Limit   : 255                             Class Type  : 0
Oper CT     : 0
Record Route: Record                          Record Label: Record
Oper MTU    : 1564                            Neg MTU     : 1564
Adaptive    : Enabled                         Oper Metric : 220
Include Grps:                                 Exclude Grps:
None                                        None
Path Trans  : 3                               CSPF Queries: 2
Failure Code: noError                         Failure Node: n/a
ExplicitHops:
    No Hops Specified
Actual Hops :
    10.1.2.1(10.10.10.1)                      Record Label    : N/A
 -> 10.1.2.2(10.10.10.2)                      Record Label    : 131070
 -> 10.2.4.4(10.10.10.4)                      Record Label    : 131069
 -> 10.4.5.5(10.10.10.5)                      Record Label    : 131071
 -> 10.5.6.6(10.10.10.6)                      Record Label    : 131069
ComputedHops:
```

(continued)

Listing 16.2 *(continued)*

```
    10.1.2.1          -> 10.1.2.2          -> 10.2.4.4          -> 10.4.5.5
  -> 10.5.6.6
Srlg         : Disabled
ResigEligib*: False
LastResignal: n/a                              CSPF Metric : 220
=======================================================================
* indicates that the corresponding row element may have been truncated.
*A:R1#
```

The head end does a CSPF computation to retry the primary LSP::Path at each retry interval. When the link is repaired, the primary LSP::Path becomes operationally up, and the secondary LSP::Path is torn down. Reverting from the secondary to the primary is done in MBB fashion and is *hitless* (no traffic is lost). Listing 16.3 shows the representation on the 7750 SR after the primary LSP::Path is restored.

Listing 16.3 Revert to primary path after link is repaired

```
*A:R1# show router mpls lsp "toR6" path detail

=======================================================================
MPLS LSP toR6 Path  (Detail)
=======================================================================
Legend :
    @ - Detour Available              # - Detour In Use
    b - Bandwidth Protected           n - Node Protected
    s - Soft Preemption
=======================================================================
-----------------------------------------------------------------------
LSP toR6 Path loose
-----------------------------------------------------------------------
LSP Name     : toR6                         Path LSP ID : 55400
From         : 10.10.10.1                   To          : 10.10.10.6
Adm State    : Up                           Oper State  : Up
Path Name    : loose                        Path Type   : Primary
Path Admin   : Up                           Path Oper   : Up
OutInterface: 1/1/3                         Out Label   : 131071
Path Up Time: 0d 00:00:04                   Path Dn Time: 0d 00:00:00
```

```
Retry Limit : 0                              Retry Timer : 30 sec
RetryAttempt: 0                              NextRetryIn : 0 sec
SetupPriori*: 7                              Hold Priori*: 0
Preference  : n/a
Bandwidth   : No Reservation                 Oper Bw     : 0 Mbps
Hop Limit   : 255                            Class Type  : 0
Backup CT   : None
MainCT Retry: n/a                            MainCT Retry: 0
    Rem     :                                    Limit   :
Oper CT     : 0
Record Route: Record                         Record Label: Record
Oper MTU    : 1564                           Neg MTU     : 1564
Adaptive    : Enabled                        Oper Metric : 30
Include Grps:                                Exclude Grps:
green                                      None
Path Trans  : 47                             CSPF Queries: 76
Failure Code: noError                        Failure Node: n/a
ExplicitHops:
    No Hops Specified
Actual Hops :
    10.1.2.1(10.10.10.1)                     Record Label    : N/A
 -> 10.1.2.2(10.10.10.2)                     Record Label    : 131071
 -> 10.2.4.4(10.10.10.4)                     Record Label    : 131070
 -> 10.4.6.6(10.10.10.6)                     Record Label    : 131070
ComputedHops:
    10.1.2.1        -> 10.1.2.2       -> 10.2.4.4       -> 10.4.6.6
ResigEligib*: False
LastResignal: n/a                            CSPF Metric : 30
-----------------------------------------------------------------------
LSP toR6 Path sec-loose
-----------------------------------------------------------------------
LSP Name    : toR6                           Path LSP ID : 55398
From        : 10.10.10.1                     To          : 10.10.10.6
Adm State   : Up                             Oper State  : Up
Path Name   : sec-loose                      Path Type   : Secondary
Path Admin  : Up                             Path Oper   : Down
OutInterface: n/a                            Out Label   : n/a
Path Up Time: 0d 00:00:00                    Path Dn Time: 0d 00:00:02
Retry Limit : 0                              Retry Timer : 30 sec
RetryAttempt: 0                              NextRetryIn : 0 sec
```

(continued)

Listing 16.3 *(continued)*

```
SetupPriori*: 7                             Hold Priori*: 0
Preference  : n/a
Bandwidth   : No Reservation                Oper Bw     : 0 Mbps
Hop Limit   : 255                           Class Type  : 0
Oper CT     : None
Record Route: Record                        Record Label: Record
Oper MTU    : 0                             Neg MTU     : 0
Adaptive    : Enabled                       Oper Metric : 65535
Include Grps:                               Exclude Grps:
None                                      None
Path Trans  : 4                             CSPF Queries: 2
Failure Code: noError                       Failure Node: n/a
ExplicitHops:
    No Hops Specified
Actual Hops :
    No Hops Specified
ComputedHops:
    No Hops Specified
Srlg        : Disabled
ResigEligib*: False
LastResignal: n/a                           CSPF Metric : 0
=======================================================================
* indicates that the corresponding row element may have been truncated.
*A:R1#
```

Standby Secondary LSP::Paths

The secondary LSPs discussed in the previous section provide a solution to ensure that a traffic-engineered primary LSP::Path is protected if there is a failure along its path. However, there is still a traffic outage while the head end signals the secondary LSP::Path.

A solution is the *standby* secondary, which is a secondary LSP::Path that is signaled when the LSP is initially brought up. Because standby secondary LSP paths are pre-signaled, they coexist with the primary LSP::Path. Therefore, standby secondary LSP::Paths must be constrained in a way that ensures they are disjoint from the primary LSP::Path. In this example, admin groups are used to ensure that the secondary LSP::Path is disjoint from the primary LSP::Path (see Figure 16.5). On the 7750 SR, secondary LSP::Paths are pre-signaled when they are configured as `standby` (see Listing 16.4).

Figure 16.5 Primary path up and active, secondary path up and inactive.

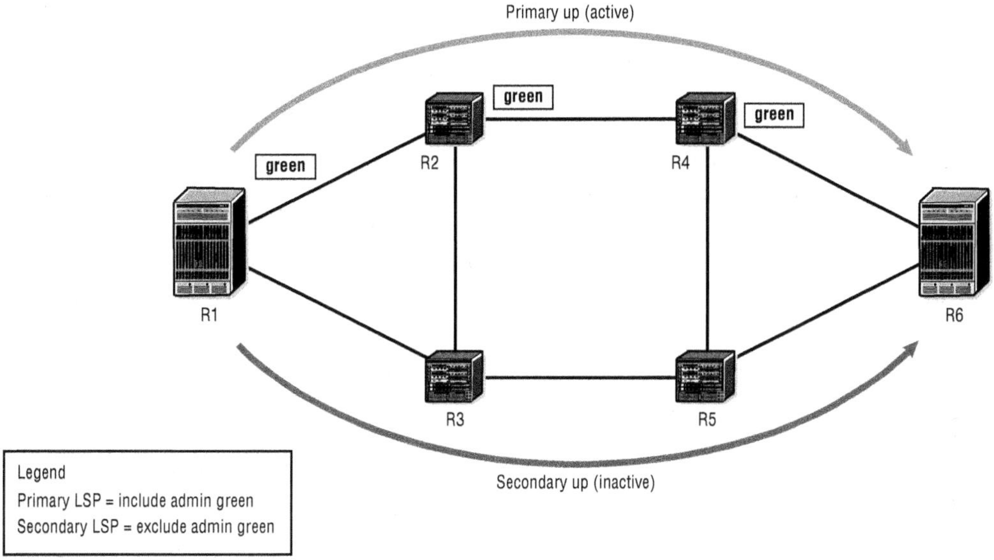

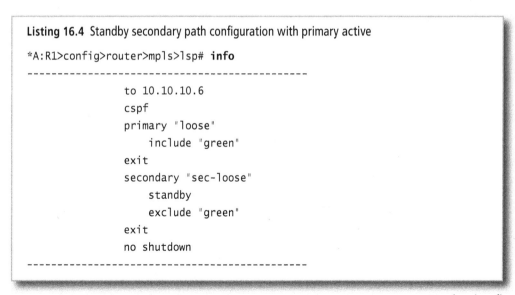

Listing 16.4 Standby secondary path configuration with primary active

```
*A:R1>config>router>mpls>lsp# info
----------------------------------------------
                to 10.10.10.6
                cspf
                primary "loose"
                    include "green"
                exit
                secondary "sec-loose"
                    standby
                    exclude "green"
                exit
                no shutdown
----------------------------------------------
```

(continued)

Listing 16.4 *(continued)*

```
*A:R1>config>router>mpls>lsp#

*A:R1# show router mpls lsp path detail

===============================================================================
MPLS LSP  Path  (Detail)
===============================================================================
Legend :
    @ - Detour Available              # - Detour In Use
    b - Bandwidth Protected           n - Node Protected
    s - Soft Preemption
===============================================================================
-------------------------------------------------------------------------------
LSP toR6 Path loose
-------------------------------------------------------------------------------
LSP Name     : toR6                         Path LSP ID : 55406
From         : 10.10.10.1                   To          : 10.10.10.6
Adm State    : Up                           Oper State  : Up
Path Name    : loose                        Path Type   : Primary
Path Admin   : Up                           Path Oper   : Up
OutInterface: 1/1/3                         Out Label   : 131071
Path Up Time: 0d 00:05:06                   Path Dn Time: 0d 00:00:00
Retry Limit : 0                             Retry Timer : 30 sec
RetryAttempt: 0                             NextRetryIn : 0 sec
SetupPriori*: 7                             Hold Priori*: 0
Preference  : n/a
Bandwidth    : No Reservation               Oper Bw     : 0 Mbps
Hop Limit    : 255                          Class Type  : 0
Backup CT    : None
MainCT Retry: n/a                           MainCT Retry: 0
    Rem      :                                  Limit   :
Oper CT      : 0
Record Route: Record                        Record Label: Record
Oper MTU     : 1564                         Neg MTU     : 1564
Adaptive     : Enabled                      Oper Metric : 30
Include Grps:                               Exclude Grps:
green                                     None
Path Trans   : 49                           CSPF Queries: 86
```

```
Failure Code: noError                         Failure Node: n/a
ExplicitHops:
    No Hops Specified
Actual Hops :
    10.1.2.1(10.10.10.1)                      Record Label    : N/A
 -> 10.1.2.2(10.10.10.2)                      Record Label    : 131071
 -> 10.2.4.4(10.10.10.4)                      Record Label    : 131070
 -> 10.4.6.6(10.10.10.6)                      Record Label    : 131070
ComputedHops:
    10.1.2.1        -> 10.1.2.2        -> 10.2.4.4        -> 10.4.6.6
ResigEligib*: False
LastResignal: n/a                             CSPF Metric : 30
----------------------------------------------------------------------
LSP toR6 Path sec-loose
----------------------------------------------------------------------
LSP Name     : toR6                           Path LSP ID : 55408
From         : 10.10.10.1                     To          : 10.10.10.6
Adm State    : Up                             Oper State  : Up
Path Name    : sec-loose                      Path Type   : Standby
Path Admin   : Up                             Path Oper   : Up
OutInterface: 1/1/2                           Out Label   : 131071
Path Up Time: 0d 00:01:29                     Path Dn Time: 0d 00:00:00
Retry Limit : 0                               Retry Timer : 30 sec
RetryAttempt: 0                               NextRetryIn : 0 sec
SetupPriori*: 7                               Hold Priori*: 0
Preference  : 255
Bandwidth   : No Reservation                  Oper Bw     : 0 Mbps
Hop Limit   : 255                             Class Type  : 0
Oper CT     : 0
Record Route: Record                          Record Label: Record
Oper MTU    : 1564                            Neg MTU     : 1564
Adaptive    : Enabled                         Oper Metric : 300
Include Grps:                                 Exclude Grps:
None                                        green
Path Trans  : 9                               CSPF Queries: 14
Failure Code: noError                         Failure Node: n/a
ExplicitHops:
    No Hops Specified
Actual Hops :
    10.1.3.1(10.10.10.1)                      Record Label    : N/A
```

(continued)

Listing 16.4 *(continued)*

```
 -> 10.1.3.3(10.10.10.3)                      Record Label     : 131071
 -> 10.3.5.5(10.10.10.5)                      Record Label     : 131071
 -> 10.5.6.6(10.10.10.6)                      Record Label     : 131069
ComputedHops:
    10.1.3.1         -> 10.1.3.3         -> 10.3.5.5         -> 10.5.6.6
Srlg        : Disabled
SrlgDisjoint: False
ResigEligib*: False
LastResignal: n/a                             CSPF Metric : 300
===============================================================================
* indicates that the corresponding row element may have been truncated.
*A:R1#
```

Because standby secondary LSP::Paths are pre-signaled, the distinction between an LSP::Path being operationally up and an LSP::Path being active is important. When LSP::Paths are successfully signaled, they are operationally up; however, only the active LSP::Path passes traffic. Listing 16.4 shows that each path of the LSP has a path type that is either `Primary` or `Standby`. In addition, note that both the primary and standby LSP::Paths are operationally up. Because the primary LSP::Path is always used over a secondary LSP::Path, we can deduce from Listing 16.4 that the primary path is the active path passing traffic. Listing 16.5 explicitly shows which LSP::Path is active.

Listing 16.5 Determining the active path

```
*A:R1# show router mpls lsp "toR6" activepath

===============================================================================
MPLS LSP: toR6 (active paths)
===============================================================================
LSP Name      : toR6                            LSP Id        : 55406
Path Name     : loose                           Active Path   : Primary
To            : 10.10.10.6

===============================================================================
*A:R1#
```

The primary and secondary paths of the same LSP have the same Tunnel ID but different LSP IDs (Listing 16.6).

Listing 16.6 Tunnel IDs and LSP IDs of primary and secondary paths

```
*A:R1# show router rsvp session

===============================================================================
RSVP Sessions
===============================================================================
From            To              Tunnel LSP   Name                      State
                                ID     ID
-------------------------------------------------------------------------------
10.10.10.1      10.10.10.6      4      55406 toR6::loose               Up
10.10.10.1      10.10.10.6      4      55408 toR6::sec-loose           Up
-------------------------------------------------------------------------------
Sessions : 2
===============================================================================
*A:R1#
```

Because standby secondary LSP::Paths are pre-signaled, the head end can switch traffic to the secondary as soon as it receives the ResvTear message. The outage time is therefore reduced to the time that it takes the head end router to detect the failure. As shown in Figure 16.6, this is dependent on the number of hops the ResvTear traverses from the failure point to the head end. Listing 16.7 shows the status of the primary and secondary LSP::Paths after the link failure.

Listing 16.7 Standby secondary active and primary down

```
*A:R1# show router mpls lsp "toR6" activepath

===============================================================================
MPLS LSP: toR6 (active paths)
===============================================================================
LSP Name      : toR6                              LSP Id        : 55408
Path Name     : sec-loose                         Active Path   : Standby
To            : 10.10.10.6

===============================================================================
*A:R1#
```

Figure 16.6 Primary LSP::Path down, secondary LSP::Path active.

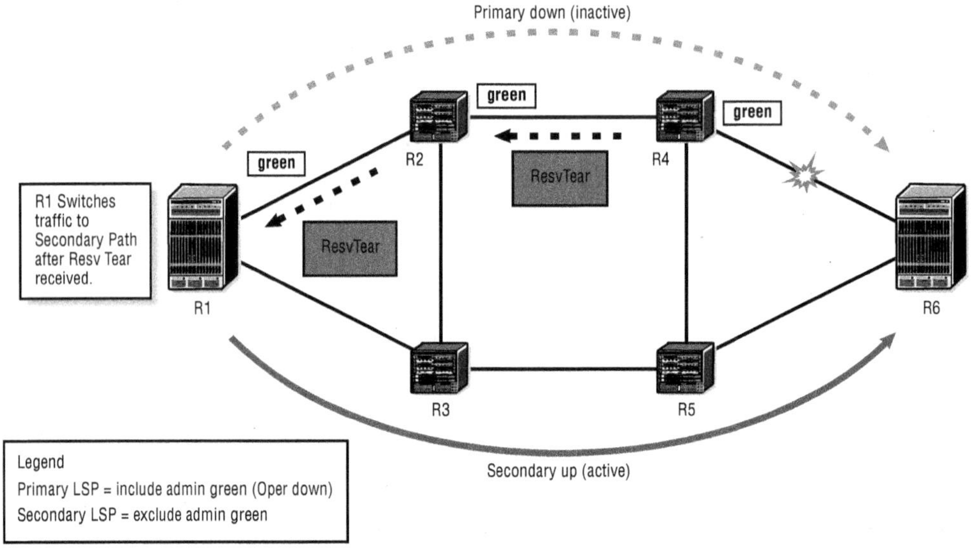

Primary LSP::Paths are always preferred over secondary LSP::Paths, even if the standby secondary LSP::Path is active and passing traffic. Therefore, when the link failure is repaired, the head end reverts to the primary LSP::Path, as shown in Listing 16.8. Another thing to note is that the Tunnel IDs for both the primary and secondary LSP::Paths remain constant. Because the secondary LSP::Path has not changed during the reversion process, its LSP ID stays constant. The LSP ID of the primary LSP::Path has changed because it has been torn down and set up again.

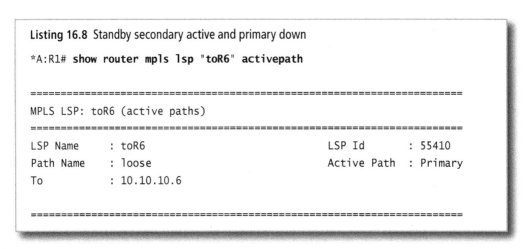

Listing 16.8 Standby secondary active and primary down

```
*A:R1# show router mpls lsp "toR6" activepath

==========================================================================
MPLS LSP: toR6 (active paths)
==========================================================================
LSP Name      : toR6                         LSP Id          : 55410
Path Name     : loose                        Active Path     : Primary
To            : 10.10.10.6

==========================================================================
```

```
*A:R1# show router rsvp session

===============================================================================
RSVP Sessions
===============================================================================
From            To              Tunnel LSP   Name                      State
                                ID     ID
-------------------------------------------------------------------------------
10.10.10.1      10.10.10.6      4      55408 toR6::sec-loose           Up
10.10.10.1      10.10.10.6      4      55410 toR6::loose               Up
-------------------------------------------------------------------------------
Sessions : 2
===============================================================================
*A:R1#
```

Although it may seem preferable to always configure a secondary LSP::Path as `standby`, this is not always the case. A network designer may opt to use a non-standby secondary when another repair mechanism such as fast reroute (FRR) is used to handle the immediate failure. Then the RSVP-TE tunnel can be optimized by signaling the secondary LSP::Path only when it is required. This is described in detail below in the chapter.

Maintaining Path Diversity with Secondary Paths Using Shared Link Risk Groups

As mentioned earlier in the chapter, care must be taken to ensure that the primary and standby secondary LSP::Paths are disjoint. For example, consider the situation shown in Figure 16.7. The primary LSP::Path is constrained by including the admin group `green`, but the secondary LSP::Path is totally loose. If there is a failure anywhere along the primary path, both the primary and secondary LSP::Paths will go down. Because the secondary LSP has a totally loose path, it will be reestablished over the path R1–R3–R5–R6, but not until the 30-second retry timer expires. In this situation there is no benefit to declaring the secondary as standby. In fact, a non-standby secondary is better because it will be signaled as soon as the primary goes down.

For the most effective protection, it is best if the primary and secondary LSP::Paths are totally disjoint. One way to ensure this is through the use of admin groups as shown earlier in this section. Another way to ensure disjoint paths is shared risk link groups

(SRLGs), defined in RFC 4202. Like admin groups, SRLGs are constraints configured on MPLS interfaces. You configure them on links that you do not want shared between primary and secondary LSP::Paths. When the head end node performs the CSPF computation for a standby secondary LSP::Path, it prunes *all* links that belong to any SRLG used in the primary LSP::Path. SRLGs are configured on the egress interface, but because two unidirectional LSPs are required, SRLGs are frequently configured on both ends of a link.

Figure 16.7 Primary path up and active, secondary path follows primary.

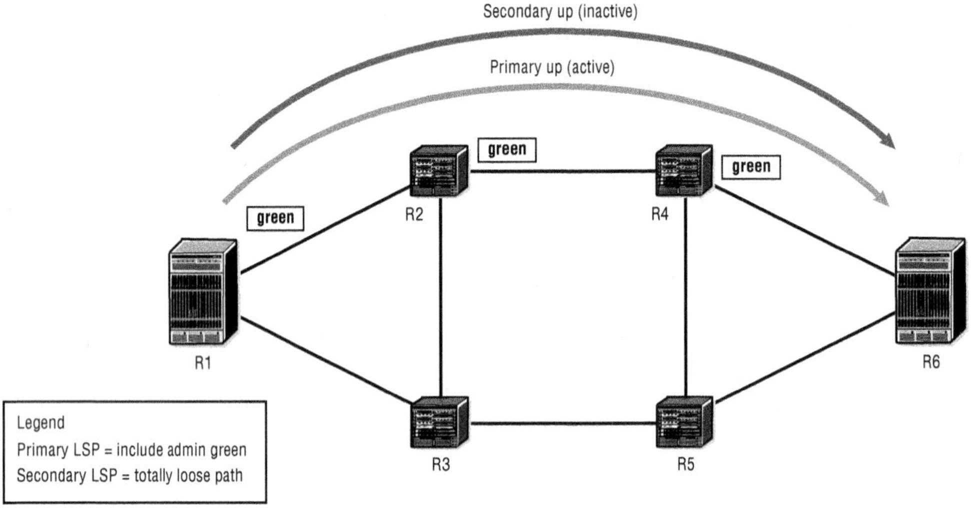

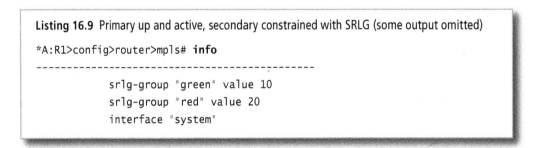

Figure 16.8 and Listing 16.9 show the use of SRLGs to ensure that the secondary LSP::Path is disjoint from the primary LSP::Path. In this case, there are two possible paths for the primary, and each of these is configured with a different SRLG. If the secondary is configured with `srlg`, it will always follow the path other than the primary. The SRLG configuration is only shown on the head end router R1, although a similar interface configuration is required throughout the network.

Listing 16.9 Primary up and active, secondary constrained with SRLG (some output omitted)

```
*A:R1>config>router>mpls# info
----------------------------------------------
            srlg-group "green" value 10
            srlg-group "red" value 20
            interface "system"
```

```
            exit
            interface "toR2"
                srlg-group "green"
            exit
            interface "toR3"
                srlg-group "red"
            exit
            lsp "toR6"
                to 10.10.10.6
                cspf
                primary "loose"
                exit
                secondary "sec-loose"
                    standby
                    srlg
                exit
                no shutdown
            exit
            no shutdown
----------------------------------------------
*A:R1>config>router>mpls#
```

Figure 16.8 Primary up and active, secondary up and constrained with SRLG.

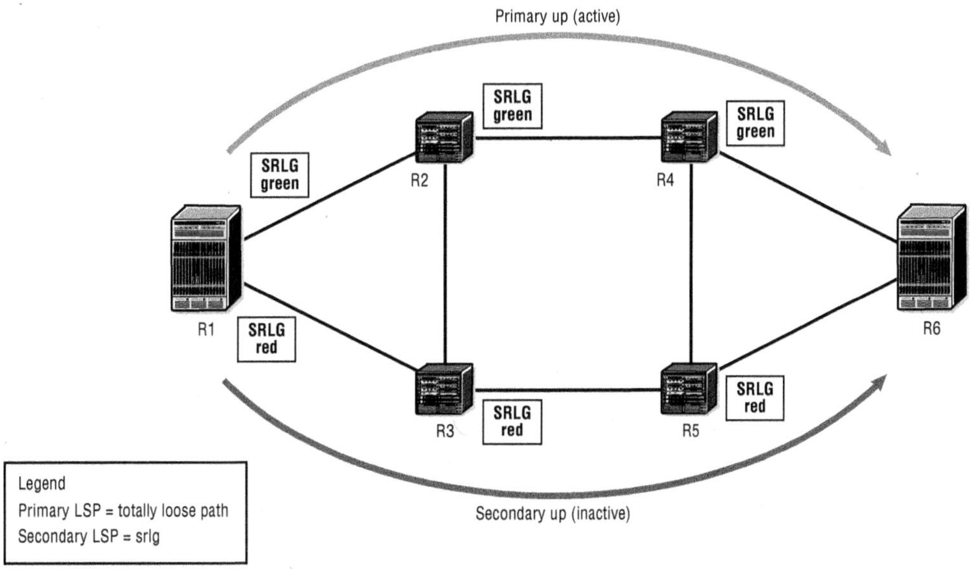

After configuring the SRLG groups, the primary LSP::Path must be resignaled for the SRLG groups to be bound to it. The secondary LSP::Path is then resignaled to avoid the constraint of the SRLG interfaces in the primary LSP::Path.

It is important to remember that when the head end computes the secondary LSP::Path, it removes all interfaces that belong to any SRLG in the primary LSP::Path. Consider the network shown in Figure 16.9. After pruning all SRLG interfaces used by the primary LSP::Path, the secondary LSP::Path cannot be established. The failure code on the 7750 SR is `noCspfRouteToDestination`. To successfully establish the secondary LSP::Path, the SRLG group must be removed from the R1–R2 link and the R4–R6 link. This illustrates a fundamental point: Do not configure SRLG on links that are single points of failure.

Figure 16.9 Primary up and active, secondary down due to excessive SRLG configuration.

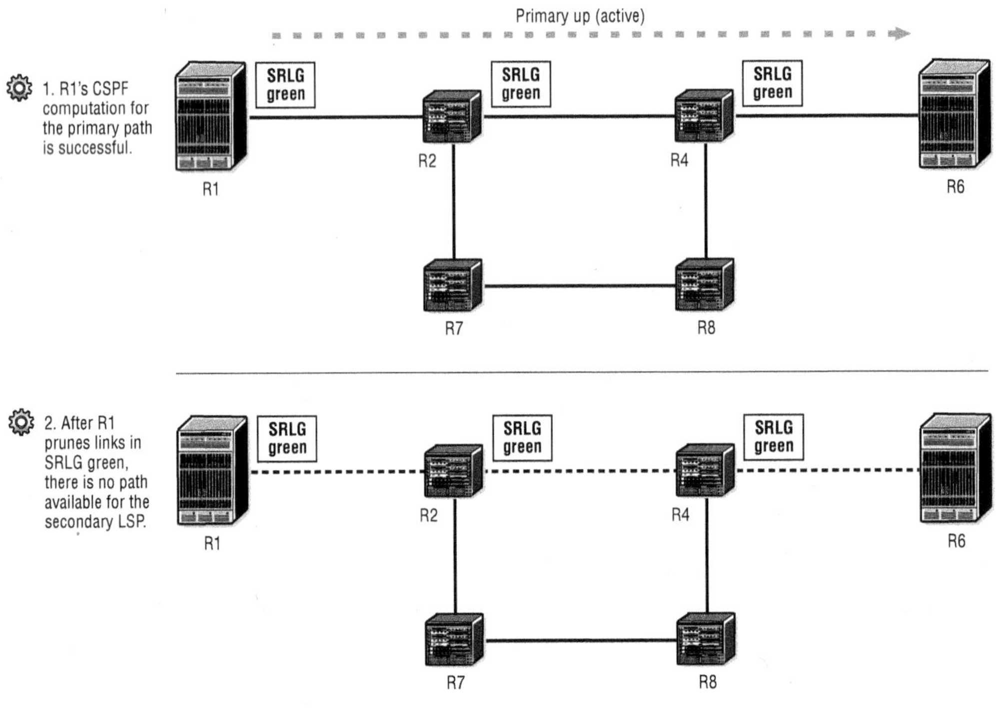

A similar situation can result even if the primary LSP::Path does not use the interface. This is shown in Figure 16.10.

Figure 16.10 Primary up and active, secondary down due to excessive SRLG configuration.

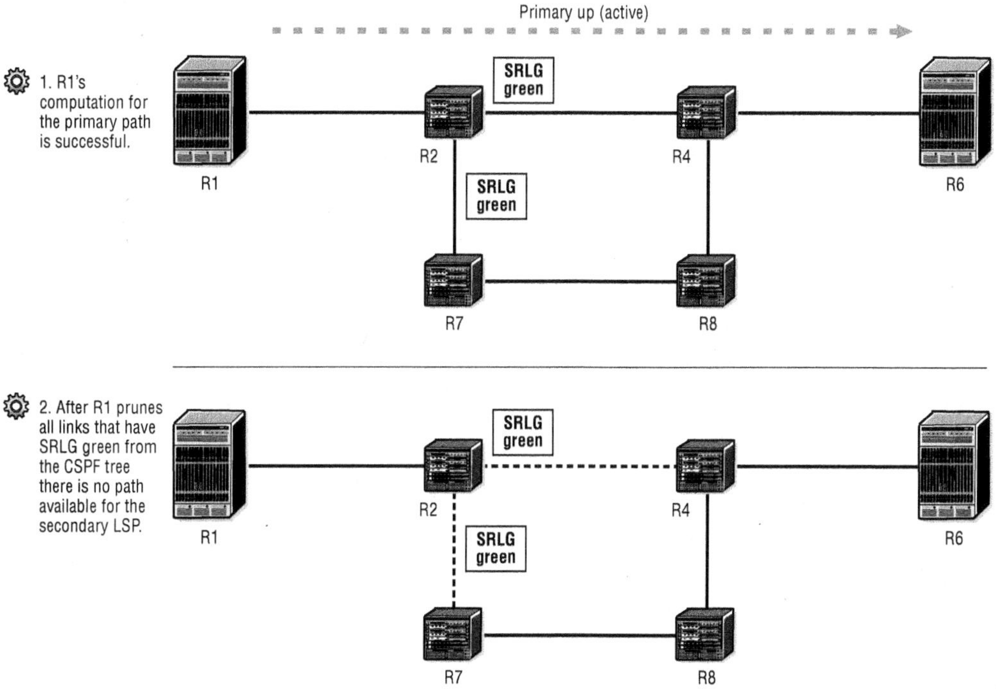

Now that we have described the use of SRLG, we will look at the way SRLGs are advertised throughout the network. SRLGs are advertised much like admin groups in both OSPF (Open Shortest Path First) and IS-IS (Intermediate System to Intermediate System). RFC 4203 describes an optional TLV (type–length–value) subtype to carry the SRLG information in an OSPF Type 10 LSA. RFC 5307 defines a new TLV type for the SRLG information in IS-IS. On the 7750 SR the SRLG TLV is only present when SRLG is configured and bound to an interface.

Unlike admin groups, the SRLG value does not represent a bit pattern, but rather a decimal value. The number of SRLG groups bound to the interface is indicated in the sub-TLV along with the actual SRLG values. Listing 16.10 shows the OSPF Opaque database for R1 used in the example of Figure 16.8. As shown in Listing 16.10, the interface `toR2` (address `10.1.2.1`) has one SRLG group bound to it with a value of 10, which is the configured value for SRLG `green`. The interface `toR3` (address `10.1.3.1`) also has one SRLG group bound to it with a value of 20, which is the configured value for SRLG `red`.

Listing 16.10 SRLG groups in OSPF opaque LSA

```
*A:R1# show router ospf opaque-database adv-router 10.10.10.1 detail

===============================================================================
OSPF Opaque Link State Database (Type : All) (Detailed)
===============================================================================
-------------------------------------------------------------------------------
Opaque LSA
-------------------------------------------------------------------------------
Area Id          : 0.0.0.0              Adv Router Id    : 10.10.10.1
Link State Id    : 1.0.0.1              LSA Type         : Area Opaque
Sequence No      : 0x800000d0           Checksum         : 0x72ce
Age              : 122                  Length           : 28
Options          :  E
Advertisement    :
     ROUTER-ID TLV  (0001) Len   4 : 10.10.10.1
-------------------------------------------------------------------------------
Opaque LSA
-------------------------------------------------------------------------------
Area Id          : 0.0.0.0              Adv Router Id    : 10.10.10.1
Link State Id    : 1.0.0.2              LSA Type         : Area Opaque
Sequence No      : 0x8000000f           Checksum         : 0xb5ac
Age              : 134                  Length           : 132
Options          :  E
Advertisement    :
     LINK INFO TLV  (0002) Len 108 :
       Sub-TLV: 1     Len: 1     LINK_TYPE     : 1
       Sub-TLV: 2     Len: 4     LINK_ID       : 10.10.10.2
       Sub-TLV: 3     Len: 4     LOC_IP_ADDR   : 10.1.2.1
       Sub-TLV: 4     Len: 4     REM_IP_ADDR   : 10.1.2.2
       Sub-TLV: 5     Len: 4     TE_METRIC     : 10
       Sub-TLV: 6     Len: 4     MAX_BDWTH     : 1000000 Kbps
       Sub-TLV: 7     Len: 4     RSRVBL_BDWTH  : 1000000 Kbps
       Sub-TLV: 8     Len: 32    UNRSRVD_CLS0  :
         P0: 1000000 Kbps P1: 1000000 Kbps P2: 1000000 Kbps P3:
         1000000 Kbps
         P4: 1000000 Kbps P5: 1000000 Kbps P6: 1000000 Kbps P7:
         1000000 Kbps
       Sub-TLV: 9     Len: 4     ADMIN_GROUP   : 00000008 (8)
       Sub-TLV: 16    Len: 4     SRLG_LIST     :
```

```
        Num SRLGs: 1
        10

-----------------------------------------------------------------------
Opaque LSA
-----------------------------------------------------------------------
Area Id          : 0.0.0.0             Adv Router Id     : 10.10.10.1
Link State Id    : 1.0.0.3             LSA Type          : Area Opaque
Sequence No      : 0x80000002          Checksum          : 0xa568
Age              : 134                 Length            : 132
Options          :  E
Advertisement    :
     LINK INFO TLV  (0002) Len 108 :
       Sub-TLV: 1     Len: 1     LINK_TYPE     : 1
       Sub-TLV: 2     Len: 4     LINK_ID       : 10.10.10.3
       Sub-TLV: 3     Len: 4     LOC_IP_ADDR   : 10.1.3.1
       Sub-TLV: 4     Len: 4     REM_IP_ADDR   : 10.1.3.3
       Sub-TLV: 5     Len: 4     TE_METRIC     : 100
       Sub-TLV: 6     Len: 4     MAX_BDWTH     : 1000000 Kbps
       Sub-TLV: 7     Len: 4     RSRVBL_BDWTH : 1000000 Kbps
       Sub-TLV: 8     Len: 32    UNRSRVD_CLS0 :
         P0: 1000000 Kbps P1: 1000000 Kbps P2: 1000000 Kbps P3:
         1000000 Kbps
         P4: 1000000 Kbps P5: 1000000 Kbps P6: 1000000 Kbps P7:
         1000000 Kbps
       Sub-TLV: 9     Len: 4     ADMIN_GROUP   : 0 None
       Sub-TLV: 16    Len: 4     SRLG_LIST     :
         Num SRLGs: 1
         20

=======================================================================
*A:R1#
```

SRLG information is advertised in the same way with the IS-IS SRLG TLV.

Multiple Secondary Paths

The network topologies described so far have two equal cost paths between the head and tail end routers, making the choice of a secondary path easy. However, consider the network shown in Figure 16.11. Assuming that all links have equal metrics, there are three equal cost paths between the head and tail end routers in this topology.

Figure 16.11 More than two equal cost paths.

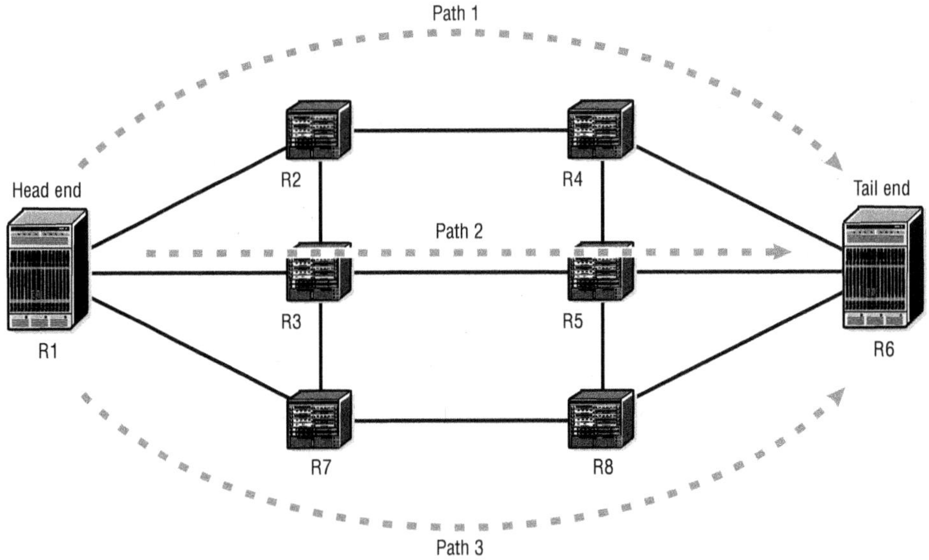

Consider a case in which the network designer wants to ensure that the path R1–R2–R4–R6 is used for the primary LSP. In addition, suppose that the network designer wants to ensure that if the primary path fails, the path R1–R3–R5–R6 is used. The path R1–R7–R8–R6 is used as a last resort.

The 7750 SR supports such network designs by allowing configuration of up to eight LSP::Paths. There can only be one primary LSP::Path and up to seven secondary LSP::Paths configured, or no primary and up to eight secondary paths.

In the case of non-standby secondary LSP::Paths, if multiple secondary LSP::Paths are configured, they are used in the order of configuration. The configuration shown in Figure 16.12 and Listing 16.11 uses non-standby secondary LSP::Paths. In this case, the primary LSP::Path is set to R1–R2–R4–R6 by using an `include` admin group. The first secondary LSP::Path is set to R1–R3–R5–R6 by using another `include` admin group. The other secondary LSP::Path is totally loose. If there is a failure on the first two paths, the totally loose secondary LSP::Path will be R1–R7–R8–R6 because it is the lowest IGP cost. Using a totally loose path provides protection if there are partial failures on all three paths.

Figure 16.12 Non-standby secondary multiple paths.

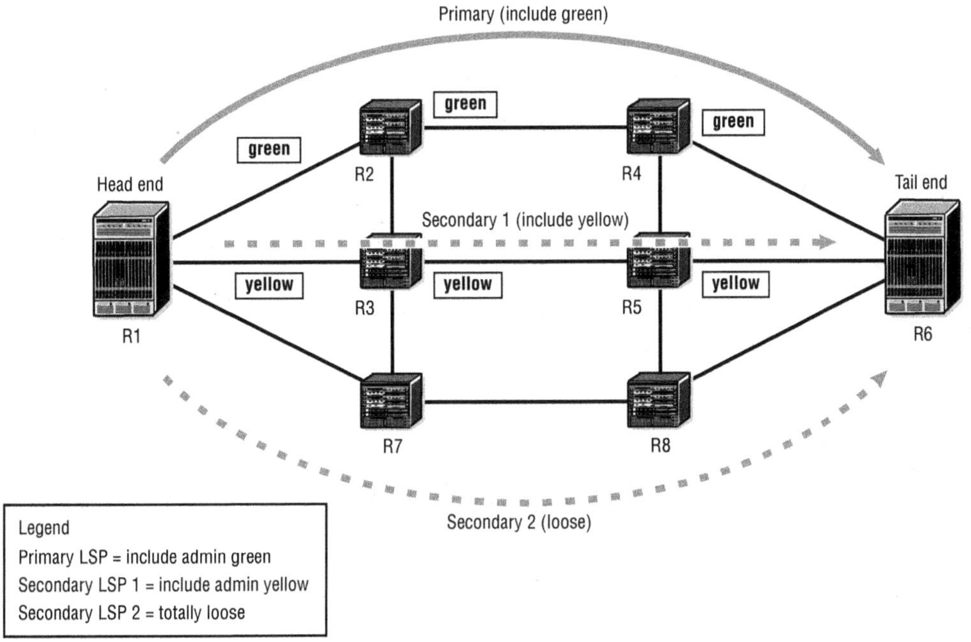

Listing 16.11 Non standby secondary multiple paths

```
*A:R1>config>router>mpls>lsp# info
----------------------------------------------
                to 10.10.10.6
                cspf
                primary "loose"
                    include "green"
                exit
                secondary "sec-loose"
                    include "yellow"
                exit
                secondary "third-loose"
                exit
                no shutdown
----------------------------------------------
*A:R1>config>router>mpls>lsp#
```

In the example shown above, it might be tempting to define admin groups only on the head end router and then use an `exclude` statement to constrain the primary LSP::Path to R1–R2–R4–R6. The problem with this approach is that primary LSP::Paths are always preferred over secondary LSP::Paths. As a result, traffic might be forwarded over a suboptimal primary LSP::Path instead of a more optimal secondary LSP::Path. For example, consider the case in which R1's interface to R7 is configured with admin group `red` and the primary LSP has the constraint `exclude yellow red`. If the link between R4 and R6 fails, as shown in Figure 16.13, the primary LSP will still be active using the suboptimal path of R1–R2–R4–R5–R6.

Figure 16.13 Suboptimal primary path.

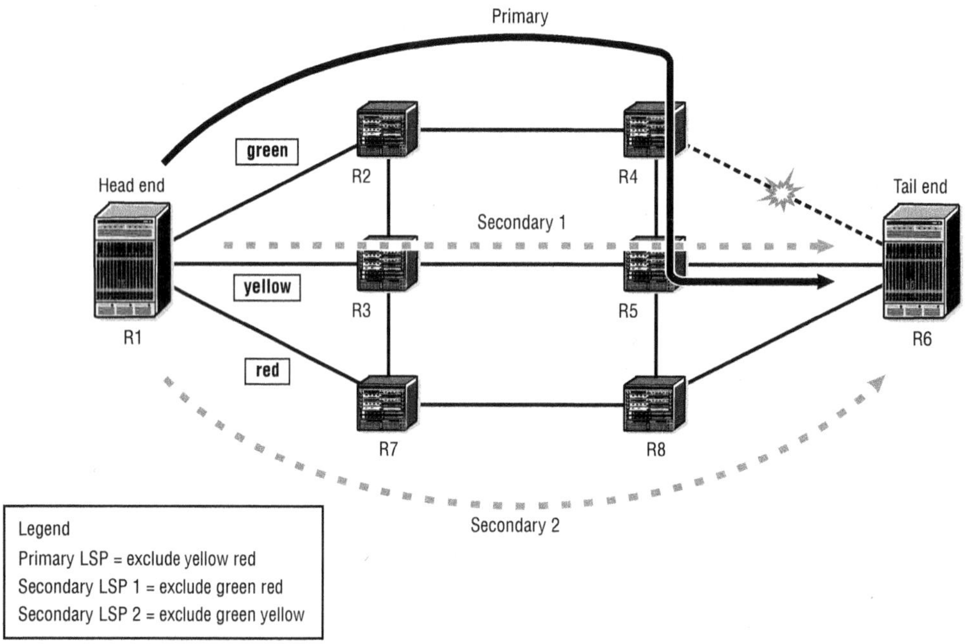

The rules for standby LSP::Paths are a bit different. A path preference can be defined, with the lower value path more preferred. The range is 1–255 with a default value of 255. Secondary path selection is also preemptive. If a standby secondary LSP::Path comes up with a better preference, it becomes the active LSP::Path. In the case that multiple standby LSP::Paths are equal, an SRLG-enabled standby LSP::Path(s) is preferred. Path preference is not applicable to non-standby secondary LSP::Paths.

SRLGs are of limited use when multiple standby secondary LSP::Paths are required. In the topology above, both secondary LSP::Paths can be constrained to not use any SRLG used by the primary path. However, secondary LSP::Paths cannot be constrained to avoid SRLGs used by other secondary LSP::Paths. Additional constraints are required to keep the secondary LSP::Paths disjoint. Admin groups may offer a simpler solution than SRLGs.

Figure 16.13 shows a solution using standby secondary LSP::Paths. It is similar to the non-standby solution, but there are some differences. First, the path preference values must be configured correctly. The second secondary LSP::Path explicitly excludes the `green` and `yellow` admin groups to ensure that it is established over the path R1–R7–R8–R6. To protect against partial link failures on all three paths, a third non-standby secondary is configured with a totally loose path. Standby secondary LSP::Paths are always selected over non-standby secondary LSP::Paths in the secondary LSP selection criteria. The configuration is shown in Figure 16.14 and Listing 16.12.

Figure 16.14 Multiple standby secondary paths.

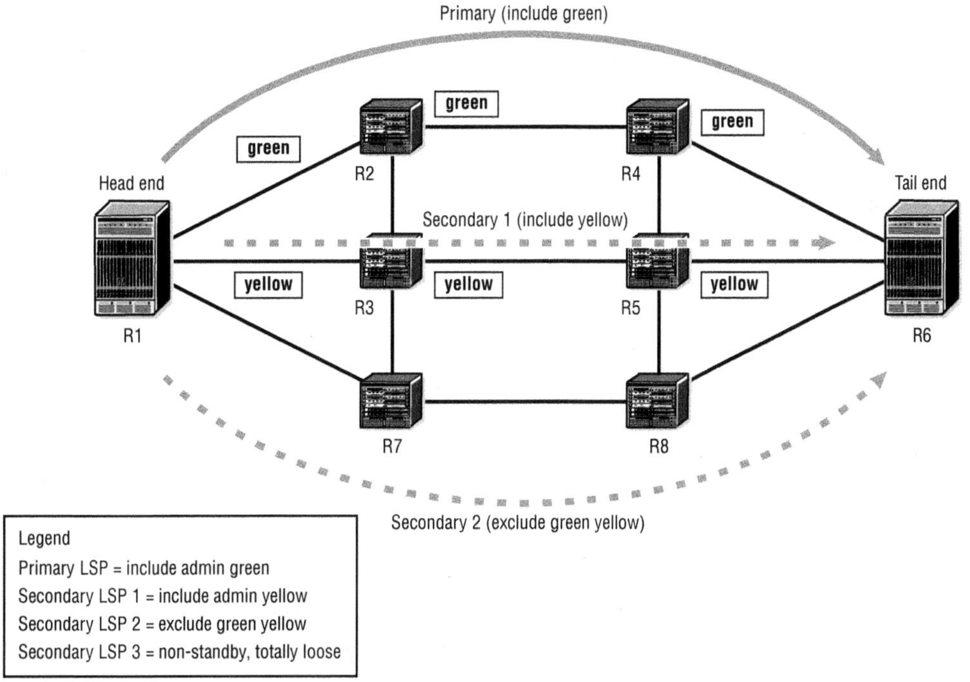

Listing 16.12 Multiple standby secondary paths

```
*A:R1>config>router>mpls>lsp# info
----------------------------------------------
            to 10.10.10.6
            cspf
            primary "loose"
                include "green"
            exit
            secondary "sec-loose"
                standby
                include "yellow"
                path-preference 20
            exit
            secondary "third-loose"
                standby
                exclude "green"
                exclude "yellow"
                path-preference 30
            exit
            secondary "fourth-loose"
            exit
            no shutdown
----------------------------------------------
*A:R1>config>router>mpls>lsp#
```

16.3 Fast Reroute

The previous section described the use of secondary LSP::Paths to protect primary LSP::Paths. The fundamental characteristic of the secondary LSP::Path mechanism is that it uses switching at the head end. Even with standby secondary LSP::Paths, failover time is still dependent on the number of routers the ResvTear messages have to pass through between the point of failure and the head end router.

FRR offers a solution that aims for 50-millisecond failover times and is not dependent on the size of the network or where the failure occurs. RSVP-TE was extended for FRR in RFC 4090. It introduces two new objects, the FAST_REROUTE object and the DETOUR object, as well as extensions to the SESSION_ATTRIBUTE and RECORD_ROUTE objects.

Fast Reroute Overview

The quick failover times of FRR are based on the concept of *local repair.* Instead of waiting for the head end to switch to another LSP, the repair is done at the router immediately upstream from the failure. Only primary LSP::Paths can be protected with FRR secondary LSP::Paths cannot be protected.

There are several terms used in describing FRR:

- **Protected LSP**—The primary LSP::Path that is protected with FRR
- **Protection LSP**—An LSP that protects the protected LSP. The protection LSP is pre-signaled to minimize traffic outages.
- **Point of local repair (PLR)**—The router immediately upstream from the failure that repairs the primary LSP::Path by switching traffic to the protection LSP
- **Merge point (MP)**—The point at which traffic on the protection LSP merges back onto the protected LSP

Figure 16.15 shows a primary LSP::Path protected with FRR. Under normal operation, the path of the protected LSP is R1–R2–R4–R6. After a link failure between R4 and R6, the protected LSP is repaired locally by the PLR (R4) by switching traffic to the protection LSP (R4–R5–R6). In this case, the MP is the tail end router, although examples below in this chapter show that this is not always the case.

The advantage of FRR is that the protection LSPs are signaled when the protected LSP is created. If there is a failure on the primary LSP::Path, the protection LSPs can be used immediately. When the primary LSP:Path is configured for FRR protection, each router along the path that could be a PLR signals a protection LSP. There are two possibilities for the protection LSP:

- **Node protection**—The path of the protection LSP is calculated to bypass the immediate downstream node.
- **Link protection**—The path of the protection LSP is calculated to bypass the immediate downstream link.

Usually node protection is preferred and is the default on the 7750 SR. When the PLR cannot provide node protection, it will signal a protection LSP to provide link protection, if possible. In Figure 16.15, R4 is providing link protection for the protected LSP because there are no nodes between R4 and the tail end router (R6).

Consider Figure 16.16. When R2 is the PLR, it has the ability to offer node protection or link protection. The link protection LSP only protects the link between R2 and R4. The node protection LSP protects against a failure of the entire R4 node.

Figure 16.15 FRR overview.

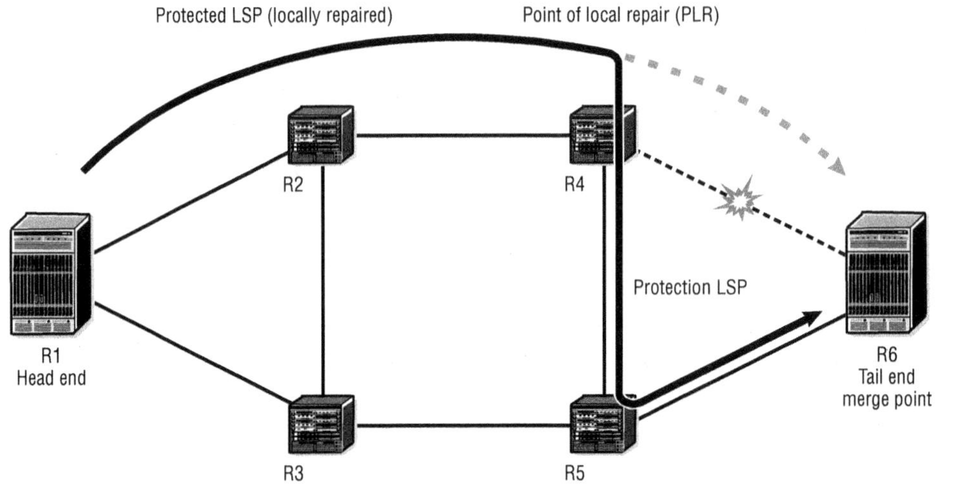

Figure 16.16 Node protection versus link protection.

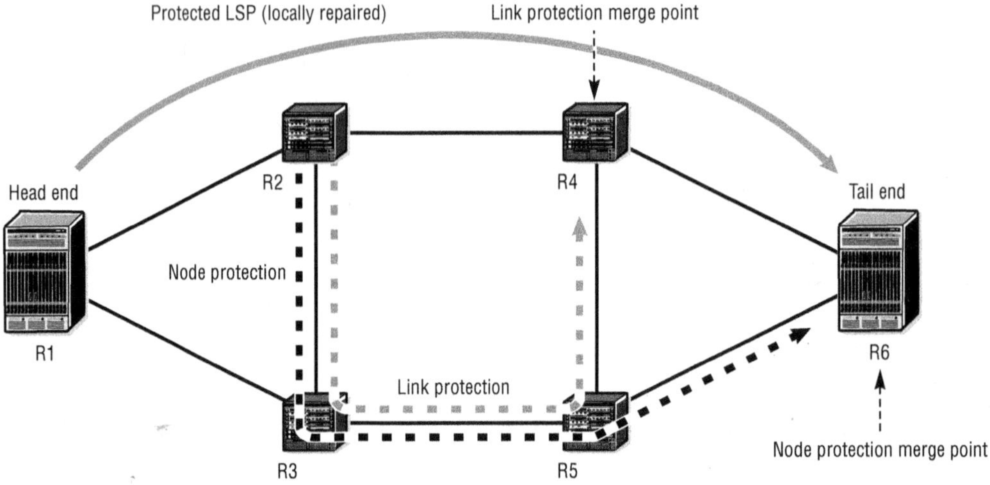

CSPF should always be enabled on the LSP to allow FRR and the associated recovery to work properly. We do not explore the use of FRR without CSPF in this book.

There are two FRR methods—one-to-one backup and facility backup. Each protected LSP can only use one FRR method. The merge points and the path of the protection LSPs are affected by which FRR method is used. The next sections describe the two FRR methods.

One-to-One Backup Method

The first FRR method that we examine is the one-to-one protection method. It's called *one-to-one* because protection tunnels are established for every protected LSP; protection tunnels are never shared between protected LSPs. The protection tunnels used in the one-to-one method are called *detour LSPs*.

The main characteristic of a detour LSP is that it is originated by a PLR with the aim of getting traffic from the PLR to the tail end router using the shortest path possible. This makes sense considering that a detour LSP protects only one LSP and all traffic on the detour LSP has the same destination. This is in contrast to the FRR facility backup method, in which traffic from different protected LSPs is switched over the same bypass tunnel.

FRR is configured for an LSP only on the head end router. The head end router includes the `FAST_REROUTE` object in the Path message and uses the `flags` field to specify the protection method as one-to-one (`0x01`) or facility (`0x02`). Flags are also set in the `SESSION_ATTRIBUTE` object of the Path message for `local-protection-desired` and `node-protection-desired` (if node protection was selected).

Consider the protected LSP shown in Figure 16.17. A primary LSP has been configured on R1 with a totally loose path and CSPF enabled. As shown in Listing 16.13, FRR is only configured on the head end router for the LSP. The default setting of FRR on the 7750 SR is the one-to-one backup method with node protection.

Figure 16.17 FRR one-to-one initial state.

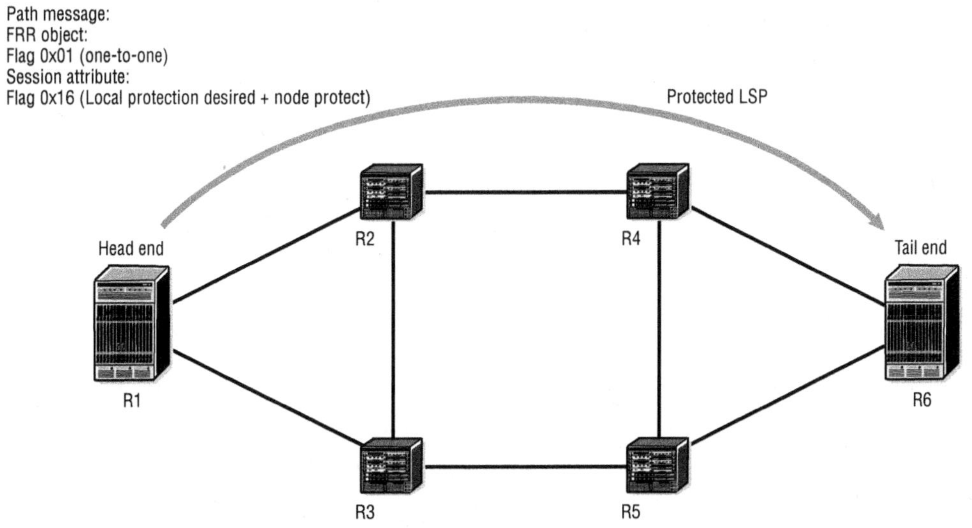

Listing 16.13 Configuration of one-to-one FRR (some output omitted)

```
*A:R1>config>router>mpls# info
----------------------------------------------
            lsp "toR6"
                to 10.10.10.6
                cspf
                fast-reroute one-to-one
                exit
                primary "loose"
                exit
                no shutdown
            exit
            no shutdown
----------------------------------------------
*A:R1>config>router>mpls#
*A:R1>config>router>mpls>lsp>frr# info detail
----------------------------------------------
                    no hop-limit
                    node-protect
----------------------------------------------
*A:R1>config>router>mpls>lsp>frr#
```

Although the FRR flags are set in the initial Path message, the routers wait for the second Resv message (the first refresh message) before calculating and signaling the detours. Every router along the primary LSP::Path that could be a PLR (typically all routers except the tail end) calculates a protection tunnel that originates on itself to provide the protection type requested (see Figure 16.18). Each PLR uses its own CSPF process to calculate the detour, and therefore it is mandatory that traffic engineering be configured network-wide in the IGP.

The LSP in Figure 16.18 is being protected using a one-to-one backup with node protection. These two criteria are significant to the CSPF calculation. The PLR calculates a path for the detour LSP that takes the shortest CSPF route to the tail end router and avoids the next node on the primary path.

To understand the detour LSP calculation, we will consider each potential PLR router separately starting with R1. R1 must signal a detour LSP that avoids node R2 and has the lowest cost to the tail end, R6. If we assume that all router links in the topology have the same cost, the path of the detour LSP is as shown in Figure 16.19. To signal the detour, the PLR sends a separate RSVP-TE Path message on the path of the detour using the same Tunnel ID and LSP ID as the primary LSP::Path. The 7750 SR uses the following format for the LSP name of the detour: `LSP::Path_detour`.

Figure 16.18 FRR one-to-one detour calculation.

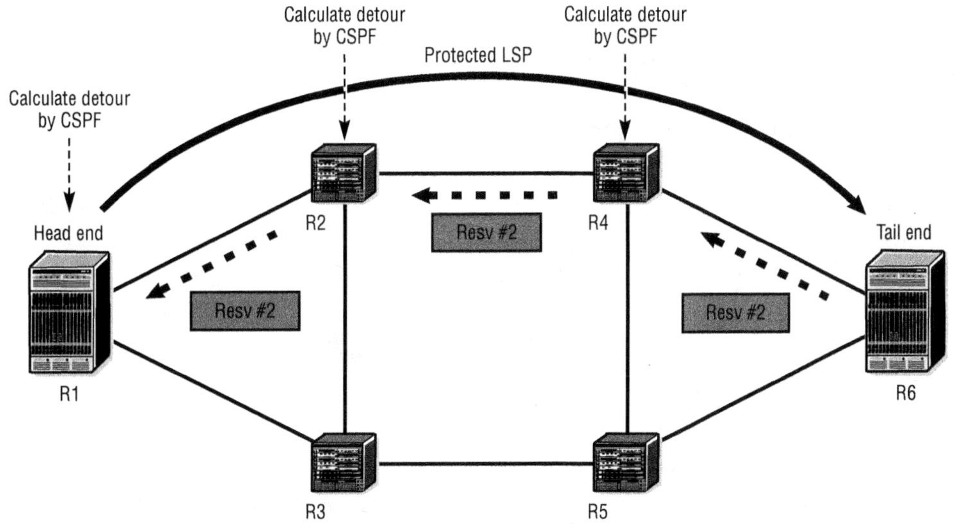

Figure 16.19 FRR one-to-one detour calculation on R1.

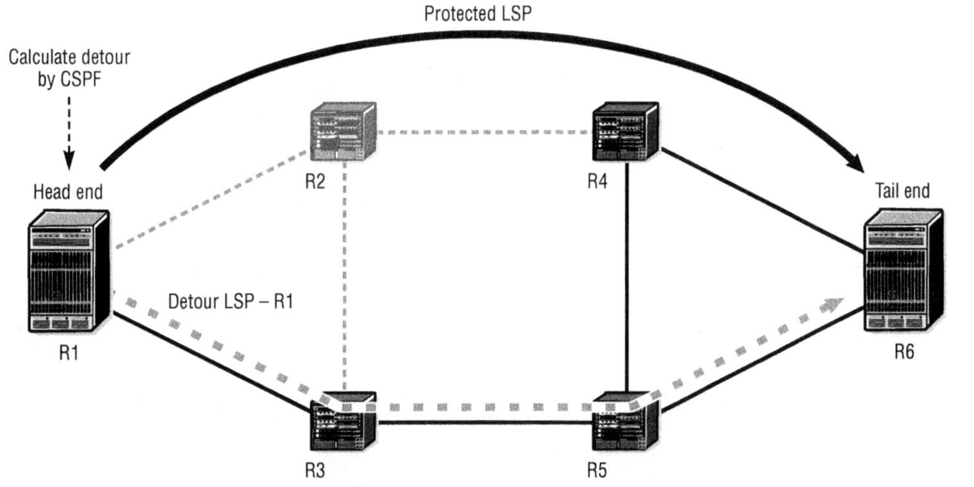

Now consider the actions on R2. Like R1, R2 must signal a detour LSP that follows the shortest path from R2 to the tail end, while avoiding router R4 (see Figure 16.20).

Figure 16.20 FRR one-to-one detour calculation on R2.

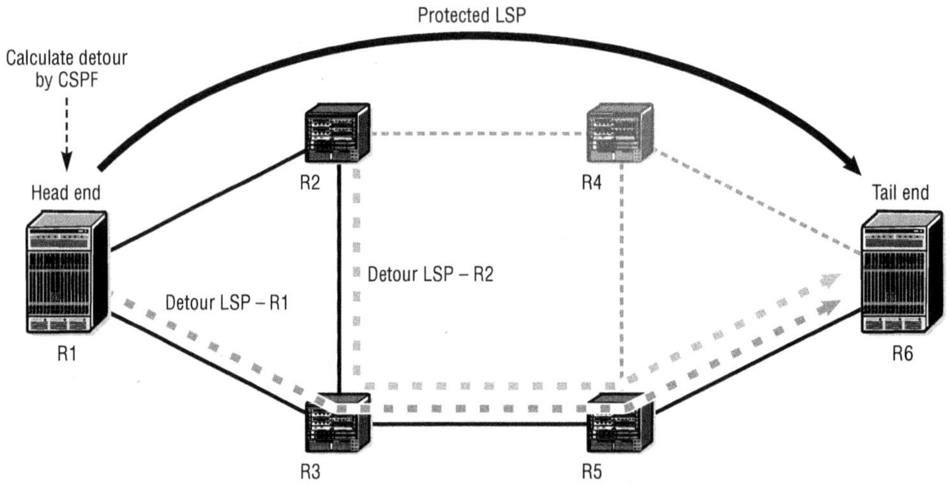

Although R1 is requesting node protection, it is not possible from R4 because the next downstream node is the tail end. Therefore, R4 creates a detour LSP to provide link protection (see Figure 16.21). The PLR immediately upstream from the tail end will always provide link protection if possible.

Figure 16.21 FRR one-to-one detour calculation on R4.

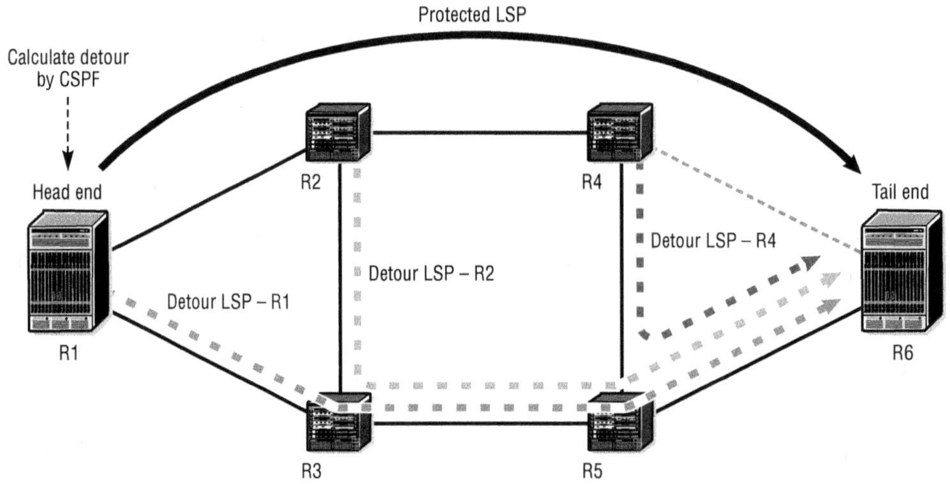

The number of detour LSPs adds up fast because each PLR originates a detour LSP. To help reduce the number of LSPs that need to be maintained at each router, LSPs can be merged at a detour merge point (DMP). Consider the situation on R3. If the detours were not merged, R3 would transit two detour LSPs that follow the same path to the same tail end and are forwarding traffic from the same protected LSP. In practice, R3 acts as a DMP and merges the detour LSPs originated by R1 and R2, as shown in Figure 16.22. A similar process occurs at R5 to merge the detour LSP from R4.

Figure 16.22 FRR one-to-one detour LSP merging.

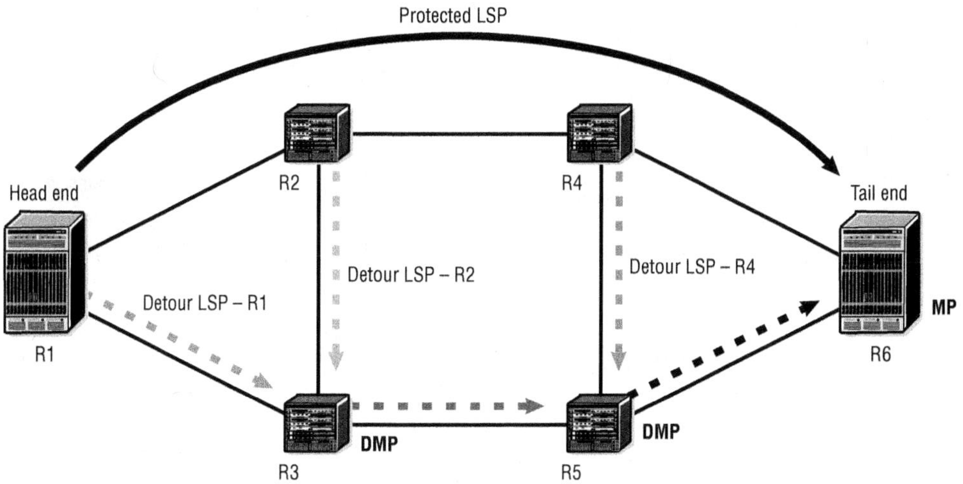

To recap the terminology used above:

- R1 is the head end for the LSP.
- R1, R2, and R4 are PLRs.
- R3 and R5 are DMPs.
- R6 is the MP and tail end.

RFC 4090 also defines a `DETOUR` object that is used to help identify and merge the detours. The `DETOUR` object is included in the Path message originated by the PLR for a detour LSP. Among other fields, the `DETOUR` object contains a `PLR_ID` (system IP address of the PLR) and an `Avoid_Node` field. If the PLR is providing node protection, the `Avoid_Node` field contains the system IP address of the router to be avoided. If the PLR is providing link protection, the field contains the interface IP address of the link to be avoided. When a router receives multiple Path messages for detours with the same `SESSION`, `SENDER_TEMPLATE`, outgoing interface, and next-hop router, it will act as a DMP for the detours (R3 and R5 in Figure 16.22). The `PLR_ID` and `Avoid_Node` pairs are copied into the `DETOUR` object sent downstream, as shown in Figure 16.23.

Figure 16.23 FRR one-to-one detour LSP merging and DETOUR object.

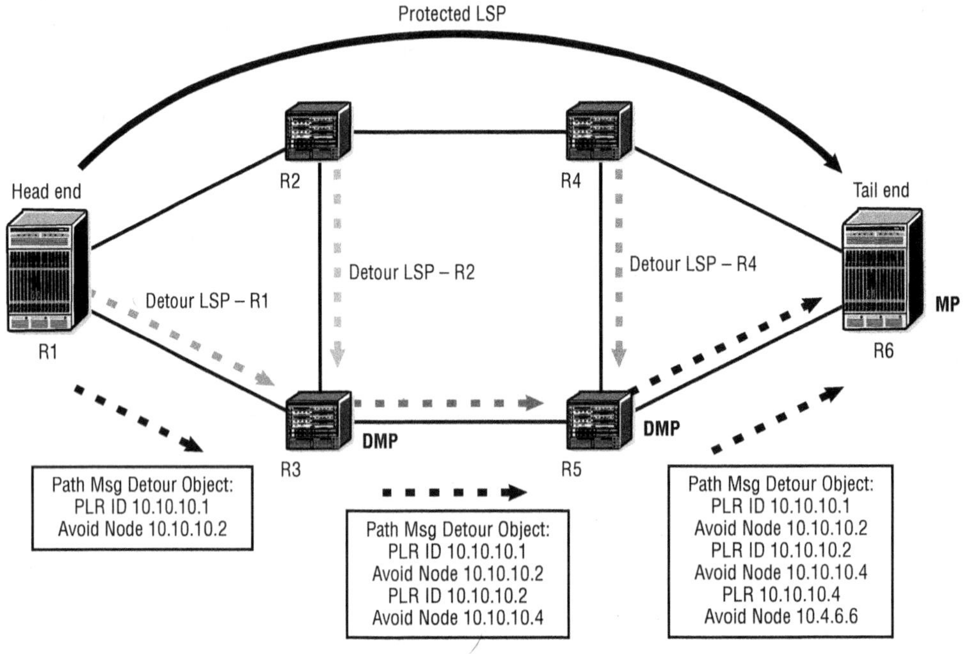

Listing 16.14 shows the output from the head end node. The `Actual Hops` field from the `show router mpls lsp path detail` command shows the expected result. The first three routers in the protected LSP path show `@` to indicate that a detour LSP is available. The first two routers in the protected LSP path also show an `n` to indicate that the protection method is node protection. R4 cannot offer node protection because it is directly connected to the tail end router. The information for these two flags comes from the `RRO` in the Resv message. The status is set by each potential PLR and relayed upstream in the `RRO`. Also notice from the `show router rsvp session` command that the Tunnel ID and LSP ID of the protected LSP and the detour LSP are the same.

Listing 16.14 Viewing the detour LSPs

```
*A:R1# show router mpls lsp "toR6" path detail

===============================================================================
MPLS LSP toR6 Path  (Detail)
===============================================================================
Legend :
    @ - Detour Available              # - Detour In Use
    b - Bandwidth Protected           n - Node Protected
    s - Soft Preemption
===============================================================================
-------------------------------------------------------------------------------
LSP toR6 Path loose
-------------------------------------------------------------------------------
LSP Name     : toR6                          Path LSP ID : 55308
From         : 10.10.10.1                    To          : 10.10.10.6
Adm State    : Up                            Oper State  : Up
Path Name    : loose                         Path Type   : Primary
Path Admin   : Up                            Path Oper   : Up
OutInterface: 1/1/3                          Out Label   : 131069
Path Up Time: 0d 00:01:18                    Path Dn Time: 0d 00:00:00
Retry Limit : 0                              Retry Timer : 30 sec
RetryAttempt: 0                              NextRetryIn : 0 sec
SetupPriori*: 7                              Hold Priori*: 0
Preference  : n/a
Bandwidth   : No Reservation                 Oper Bw     : 0 Mbps
Hop Limit   : 255                            Class Type  : 0
Backup CT   : None
MainCT Retry: n/a                            MainCT Retry: 0
    Rem     :                                    Limit   :
Oper CT     : 0
Record Route: Record                         Record Label: Record
Oper MTU    : 1564                           Neg MTU     : 1564
Adaptive    : Enabled                        Oper Metric : 300
Include Grps:                                Exclude Grps:
None                                       None
Path Trans  : 11                             CSPF Queries: 7
Failure Code: noError                        Failure Node: n/a
ExplicitHops:
```

(continued)

Listing 16.14 *(continued)*

```
    No Hops Specified
Actual Hops :
    10.1.2.1(10.10.10.1) @ n                Record Label    : N/A
 -> 10.1.2.2(10.10.10.2) @ n                Record Label    : 131069
 -> 10.2.4.4(10.10.10.4) @                  Record Label    : 131069
 -> 10.4.6.6(10.10.10.6)                    Record Label    : 131071
ComputedHops:
    10.1.2.1       -> 10.1.2.2       -> 10.2.4.4       -> 10.4.6.6
ResigEligib*: False
LastResignal: n/a                           CSPF Metric : 300

DetourStatus: Standby                       DetourType  : Originate
DetourAvoid*: 10.10.10.2                    DetourOrigin: 10.10.10.1
SetupPriori*: 7                             Hold Priori*: 0
Class Type  : 0
DetourActiv*: n/a                           DetourUpTime: 0d 00:00:55
InInterface : n/a                           InLabel     : n/a
OutInterface: 1/1/2                         OutLabel    : 131071
NextHop     : 10.1.3.3
ExplicitHops:
    10.1.3.1       -> 10.1.3.3       -> 10.3.5.5       -> 10.5.6.6
===============================================================================
* indicates that the corresponding row element may have been truncated.
*A:R1#
*A:R1# show router rsvp session

===============================================================================
RSVP Sessions
===============================================================================
From           To             Tunnel LSP   Name                        State
                              ID     ID
-------------------------------------------------------------------------------
10.10.10.1     10.10.10.6     4      55308 toR6::loose                 Up
10.10.10.1     10.10.10.6     4      55308 toR6::loose_detour          Up
-------------------------------------------------------------------------------
Sessions : 2
===============================================================================
*A:R1#
```

Listing 16.15 illustrates that R3 and R5 are DMPs. R3 takes the detour LSP originated by R1 and merges it with the detour LSP from R2. The output shows that the two LSPs have different ingress interfaces and labels, but the same egress interface and label. The LSP from R1 is the transit LSP, whereas the one from R2 is terminated. R5 takes the merged detour LSP from R3 and merges it with the detour LSP from R4.

Listing 16.15 Viewing the RSVP-TE sessions at the detour merge points

```
A:R3# show router rsvp session detail

===============================================================================
RSVP Sessions (Detailed)
===============================================================================
-------------------------------------------------------------------------------
LSP : toR6::loose_detour
-------------------------------------------------------------------------------
From             : 10.10.10.1           To              : 10.10.10.6
Tunnel ID        : 4                    LSP ID          : 55308
Style            : SE                   State           : Up
Session Type     : Transit (Detour)
In Interface     : 1/1/4                Out Interface   : 1/1/2
In Label         : 131071               Out Label       : 131070
Previous Hop     : 10.1.3.1             Next Hop        : 10.3.5.5
SetupPriority    : 7                    Hold Priority   : 0
Class Type       : 0
SubGrpOrig ID    : 0                    SubGrpOrig Addr: 0.0.0.0
P2MP ID          : 0

Path Recd        : 46                   Path Sent       : 45
Resv Recd        : 43                   Resv Sent       : 89

Summary messages:
SPath Recd       : 0                    SPath Sent      : 0
SResv Recd       : 0                    SResv Sent      : 0
-------------------------------------------------------------------------------
LSP : toR6::loose_detour
-------------------------------------------------------------------------------
From             : 10.10.10.1           To              : 10.10.10.6
Tunnel ID        : 4                    LSP ID          : 55308
```

(continued)

Listing 16.15 *(continued)*

```
Style           : SE                    State           : Up
Session Type    : Terminate (Detour)
In Interface    : 1/1/3                 Out Interface   : 1/1/2
In Label        : 131070                Out Label       : 131070
Previous Hop    : 10.2.3.2              Next Hop        : 10.3.5.5
SetupPriority   : 7                     Hold Priority   : 0
Class Type      : 0
SubGrpOrig ID   : 0                     SubGrpOrig Addr: 0.0.0.0
P2MP ID         : 0

Path Recd       : 44                    Path Sent       : 1
Resv Recd       : 43                    Resv Sent       : 89

Summary messages:
SPath Recd      : 0                     SPath Sent      : 0
SResv Recd      : 0                     SResv Sent      : 0
=======================================================================
A:R3#

A:R5# show router rsvp session detail

=======================================================================
RSVP Sessions (Detailed)
=======================================================================
-----------------------------------------------------------------------
LSP : toR6::loose_detour
-----------------------------------------------------------------------
From            : 10.10.10.1            To              : 10.10.10.6
Tunnel ID       : 4                     LSP ID          : 55308
Style           : SE                    State           : Up
Session Type    : Transit (Detour)
In Interface    : 1/1/3                 Out Interface   : 1/1/4
In Label        : 131071                Out Label       : 131070
Previous Hop    : 10.4.5.4              Next Hop        : 10.5.6.6
SetupPriority   : 7                     Hold Priority   : 0
Class Type      : 0
SubGrpOrig ID   : 0                     SubGrpOrig Addr: 0.0.0.0
P2MP ID         : 0
```

```
Path Recd       : 48                    Path Sent       : 49
Resv Recd       : 49                    Resv Sent       : 90

Summary messages:
SPath Recd      : 0                     SPath Sent      : 0
SResv Recd      : 0                     SResv Sent      : 0
-----------------------------------------------------------------------
LSP : toR6::loose_detour
-----------------------------------------------------------------------
From            : 10.10.10.1            To              : 10.10.10.6
Tunnel ID       : 4                     LSP ID          : 55308
Style           : SE                    State           : Up
Session Type    : Terminate (Detour)
In Interface    : 1/1/2                 Out Interface   : 1/1/4
In Label        : 131070                Out Label       : 131070
Previous Hop    : 10.3.5.3              Next Hop        : 10.5.6.6
SetupPriority   : 7                     Hold Priority   : 0
Class Type      : 0
SubGrpOrig ID   : 0                     SubGrpOrig Addr: 0.0.0.0
P2MP ID         : 0

Path Recd       : 49                    Path Sent       : 1
Resv Recd       : 49                    Resv Sent       : 90

Summary messages:
SPath Recd      : 0                     SPath Sent      : 0
SResv Recd      : 0                     SResv Sent      : 0
=======================================================================
A:R5#
```

Now that we have seen how the control plane signals the detour LSPs, we'll look at the data plane. From the command outputs already shown, we can determine the exact LSP labels that will be used at each hop of the network. Figure 16.24 shows the labels that have been signaled for the protected and protection LSPs. Remember that MPLS labels are locally significant between two routers, thus labels along a path can be the same or different. If there is a failure at any point along the LSP, the PLR uses standard label swapping to switch traffic to the detour LSP. Instead of sending the traffic out the interface for the protected LSP, the PLR sends the traffic out the interface for the detour LSP with the appropriate label for the detour.

Figure 16.24 FRR one-to-one data path.

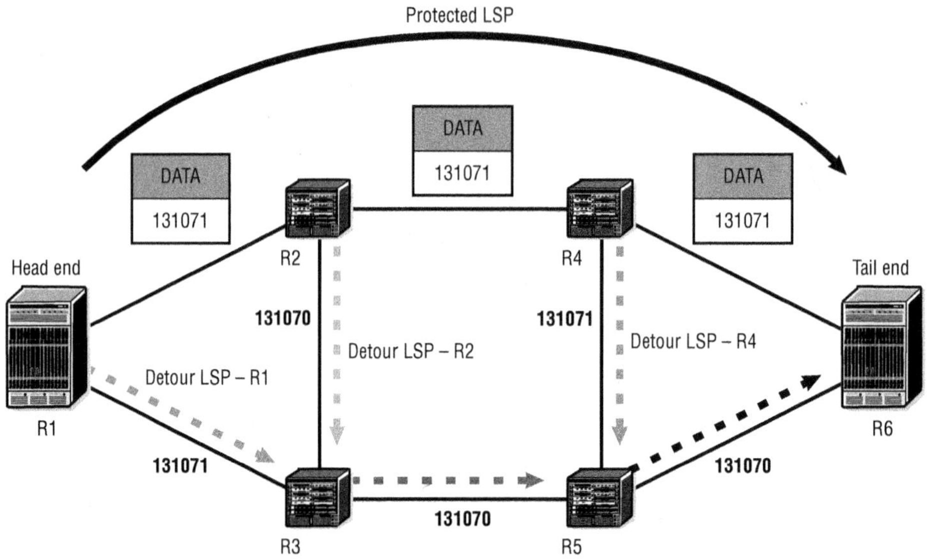

In Chapter 17 we'll see that there is also a service label when the MPLS network is used for VPN services. This label is placed between the MPLS transport label and the data and is omitted from these diagrams for simplicity.

Consider the case in which the link fails between R2 and R4. R2 is the PLR and diverts all traffic to the detour LSP, as shown in Figure 16.25. The PLR is also responsible for notifying the head end that local protection is in use. This is done in two ways. First, the PLR sends a Path Error message to the head end with error code 25 `RSVP Notify Error` and an error value of 3 `Tunnel Locally Repaired`. Second, the `Local Protection in Use` flag is set in the `RRO` of the continuous Resv refresh messages. As shown in Listing 16.16, `Detour In Use` is indicated in the output of the `show router mpls lsp` command on the 7750 SR with a `#` next to the PLR's hop in the *Actual Hops* field.

Figure 16.25 FRR one-to-one failure between R2 and R4.

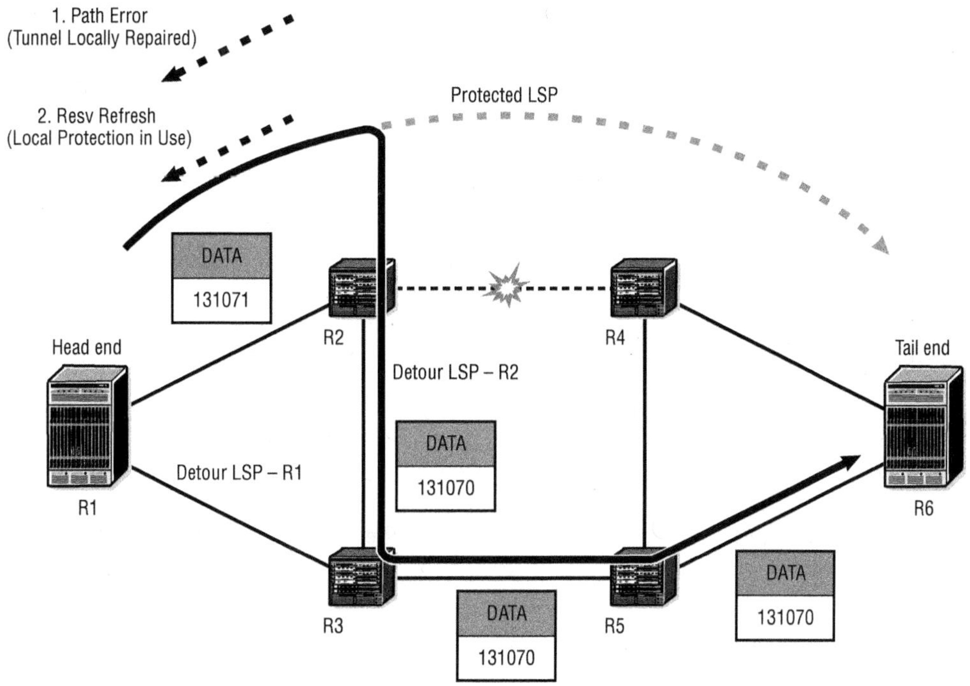

Listing 16.16 FRR one-to-one failure between R2 and R4

```
*A:R1# show router mpls lsp "toR6" path detail

===============================================================================
MPLS LSP toR6 Path  (Detail)
===============================================================================
Legend :
    @ - Detour Available                 # - Detour In Use
    b - Bandwidth Protected              n - Node Protected
    s - Soft Preemption
===============================================================================
-------------------------------------------------------------------------------
LSP toR6 Path loose
-------------------------------------------------------------------------------
LSP Name     : toR6                          Path LSP ID : 55310
From         : 10.10.10.1                    To          : 10.10.10.6
Adm State    : Up                            Oper State  : Up
```

(continued)

Listing 16.16 *(continued)*

```
Path Name    : loose                     Path Type    : Primary
Path Admin   : Up                        Path Oper    : Up
OutInterface: 1/1/3                      Out Label    : 131071
Path Up Time: 0d 20:00:07                Path Dn Time: 0d 00:00:00
Retry Limit : 0                          Retry Timer : 30 sec
RetryAttempt: 0                          NextRetryIn : 0 sec
SetupPriori*: 7                          Hold Priori*: 0
Preference  : n/a
Bandwidth   : No Reservation             Oper Bw     : 0 Mbps
Hop Limit   : 255                        Class Type  : 0
Backup CT   : None
MainCT Retry: n/a                        MainCT Retry: 0
    Rem     :                                Limit   :
Oper CT     : 0
Record Route: Record                     Record Label: Record
Oper MTU    : 1564                       Neg MTU     : 1564
Adaptive    : Enabled                    Oper Metric : 300
Include Grps:                            Exclude Grps:
None                                   None
Path Trans  : 13                         CSPF Queries: 8
Failure Code: tunnelLocallyRepaired      Failure Node: 10.10.10.2
ExplicitHops:
    No Hops Specified
Actual Hops :
    10.1.2.1(10.10.10.1) @ n             Record Label    : N/A
 -> 10.1.2.2(10.10.10.2) @ # n           Record Label    : 131071
 -> 10.2.3.3(10.10.10.3)                 Record Label    : 131071
 -> 10.3.5.5(10.10.10.5)                 Record Label    : 131071
 -> 10.5.6.6(10.10.10.6)                 Record Label    : 131070
ComputedHops:
    No Hops Specified
ResigEligib*: False
LastResignal: n/a                        CSPF Metric : 300
In Prog MBB :
 MBB Type    : GlobalRevert              NextRetryIn : 1 sec
 Started At : 03/20/2011 17:35:56        RetryAttempt: 0
 FailureCode: noError                    Failure Node: n/a
===============================================================================
* indicates that the corresponding row element may have been truncated.
*A:R1#
```

On the 7750 SR, protected LSPs have a *global revertive* behavior. When the head end node is notified that local protection is in use, it performs a CSPF calculation and resignals the primary LSP::Path if there is a route that avoids the failed node and satisfies path constraints. In this case, the primary LSP is totally loose, and the primary LSP::Path is resignaled on the path R1–R3–R5–R6 (see Figure 16.26). Because the link between R2 and R4 is down, protection cannot be established on all links along the new primary path. Only link protection is available, for the first and last hops (see Listing 16.17).

Figure 16.26 FRR one-to-one recovery from failure between R2 and R4.

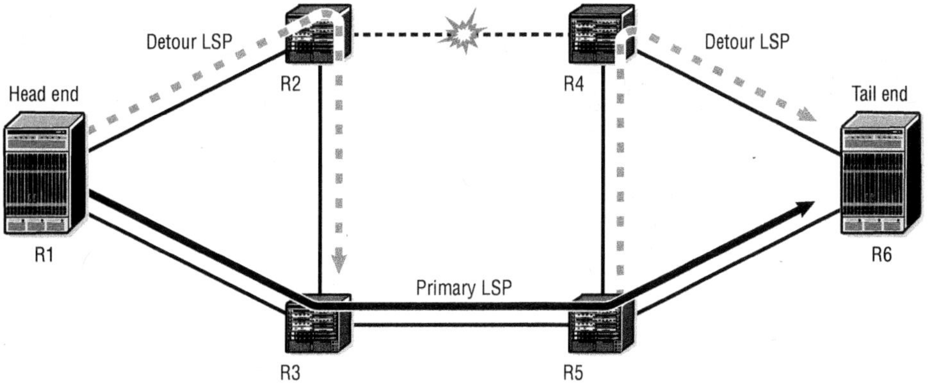

Fast Reroute with Secondary LSPs

If it is desirable to have the primary path be only R1–R2–R4–R6, it can be constrained with admin groups or strict hops. If the link fails between R2 and R4 and there is no other path that meets the constraints, the head end will attempt to reestablish the primary LSP::Path every 30 seconds until the link between R2 and R4 is fixed. In the meantime, traffic will keep flowing on the suboptimal path of the detour LSP. The goal of FRR is fast failover time, not optimal traffic paths.

This situation can be improved by using a secondary LSP::Path in conjunction with fast reroute. When the head end router is notified that local protection is in use, it will use secondary LSP::Paths until the primary LSP::Path is reestablished. Adding a non-standby secondary LSP::Path allows traffic to flow on the most optimal path at the time of failure. Meanwhile, the head end router continually tries to signal the primary LSP::Path (see Figure 16.27). As soon as it is successful, the head end router reverts to the primary LSP::Path. Listing 16.17 shows the LSP before the failure with fast reroute and a secondary

LSP. The detours have been signaled, but the secondary LSP path is down because it is non-standby.

Figure 16.27 FRR one-to-one in conjunction with secondary paths.

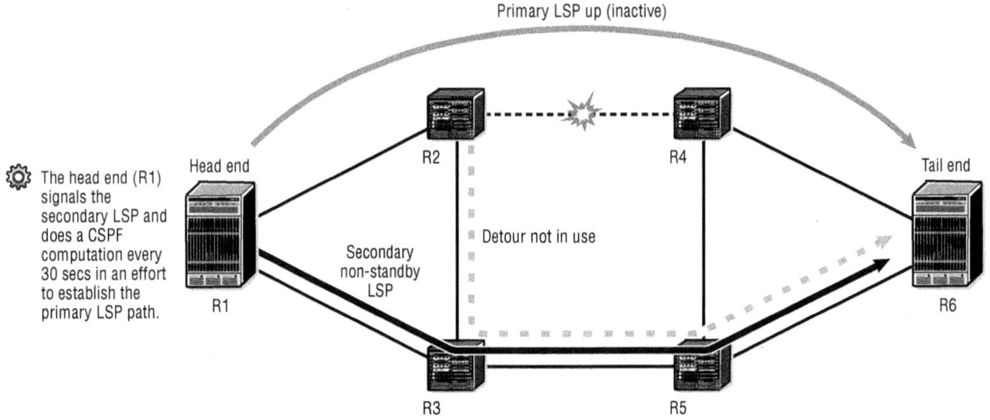

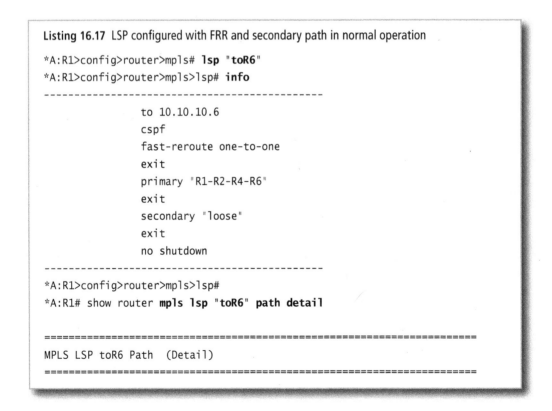

Listing 16.17 LSP configured with FRR and secondary path in normal operation

```
*A:R1>config>router>mpls# lsp "toR6"
*A:R1>config>router>mpls>lsp# info
----------------------------------------------
                to 10.10.10.6
                cspf
                fast-reroute one-to-one
                exit
                primary "R1-R2-R4-R6"
                exit
                secondary "loose"
                exit
                no shutdown
----------------------------------------------
*A:R1>config>router>mpls>lsp#
*A:R1# show router mpls lsp "toR6" path detail

===============================================================================
MPLS LSP toR6 Path  (Detail)
===============================================================================
```

```
Legend :
    @ - Detour Available              # - Detour In Use
    b - Bandwidth Protected           n - Node Protected
    s - Soft Preemption
========================================================================
------------------------------------------------------------------------
LSP toR6 Path loose
------------------------------------------------------------------------
LSP Name     : toR6                       Path LSP ID : 55318
From         : 10.10.10.1                 To          : 10.10.10.6
Adm State    : Up                         Oper State  : Up
Path Name    : loose                      Path Type   : Secondary
Path Admin   : Up                         Path Oper   : Down
OutInterface: n/a                         Out Label   : n/a
Path Up Time: 0d 00:00:00                 Path Dn Time: 0d 00:01:13
Retry Limit : 0                           Retry Timer : 30 sec
RetryAttempt: 0                           NextRetryIn : 0 sec
SetupPriori*: 7                           Hold Priori*: 0
Preference  : n/a
Bandwidth   : No Reservation              Oper Bw     : 0 Mbps
Hop Limit   : 255                         Class Type  : 0
Oper CT     : None
Record Route: Record                      Record Label: Record
Oper MTU    : 0                           Neg MTU     : 0
Adaptive    : Enabled                     Oper Metric : 65535
Include Grps:                             Exclude Grps:
None                                    None
Path Trans  : 2                           CSPF Queries: 1
Failure Code: noError                     Failure Node: n/a
ExplicitHops:
    No Hops Specified
Actual Hops :
    No Hops Specified
ComputedHops:
    No Hops Specified
Srlg        : Disabled
ResigEligib*: False
LastResignal: n/a                         CSPF Metric : 0
```

(continued)

Listing 16.17 *(continued)*

```
-----------------------------------------------------------------------
LSP toR6 Path R1-R2-R4-R6
-----------------------------------------------------------------------
LSP Name     : toR6                          Path LSP ID : 55316
From         : 10.10.10.1                    To          : 10.10.10.6
Adm State    : Up                            Oper State  : Up
Path Name    : R1-R2-R4-R6                   Path Type   : Primary
Path Admin   : Up                            Path Oper   : Up
OutInterface: 1/1/3                          Out Label   : 131070
Path Up Time: 0d 00:01:16                    Path Dn Time: 0d 00:00:00
Retry Limit : 0                              Retry Timer : 30 sec
RetryAttempt: 0                              NextRetryIn : 0 sec
SetupPriori*: 7                              Hold Priori*: 0
Preference  : n/a
Bandwidth    : No Reservation                Oper Bw     : 0 Mbps
Hop Limit    : 255                           Class Type  : 0
Backup CT    : None
MainCT Retry: n/a                            MainCT Retry: 0
    Rem     :                                    Limit   :
Oper CT      : 0
Record Route: Record                         Record Label: Record
Oper MTU     : 1564                          Neg MTU     : 1564
Adaptive     : Enabled                       Oper Metric : 300
Include Grps:                                Exclude Grps:
None                                       None
Path Trans  : 1                              CSPF Queries: 39
Failure Code: noError                        Failure Node: n/a
ExplicitHops:
    10.1.2.2        -> 10.2.4.4       -> 10.4.6.6
Actual Hops :
    10.1.2.1(10.10.10.1) @ n                 Record Label    : N/A
 -> 10.1.2.2(10.10.10.2) @ n                 Record Label    : 131070
 -> 10.2.4.4(10.10.10.4) @                   Record Label    : 131070
 -> 10.4.6.6(10.10.10.6)                     Record Label    : 131070
ComputedHops:
    10.1.2.1        -> 10.1.2.2       -> 10.2.4.4       -> 10.4.6.6
ResigEligib*: False
LastResignal: n/a                            CSPF Metric : 300
```

```
DetourStatus: Standby                          DetourType   : Originate
DetourAvoid*: 10.10.10.2                       DetourOrigin: 10.10.10.1
SetupPriori*: 7                                Hold Priori*: 0
Class Type  : 0
DetourActiv*: n/a                              DetourUpTime: 0d 00:01:03
InInterface : n/a                              InLabel      : n/a
OutInterface: 1/1/2                            OutLabel     : 131070
NextHop     : 10.1.3.3
ExplicitHops:
    10.1.3.1       -> 10.1.3.3       -> 10.3.5.5       -> 10.5.6.6
===============================================================================
* indicates that the corresponding row element may have been truncated.
*A:R1#
```

When the R2–R4 link fails, traffic is immediately switched to the detour. After the head end receives the PathErr message, it signals the secondary LSP::Path. Traffic is switched to the secondary when it comes up because a secondary is preferred over the primary with an active detour. The primary LSP::Path is still up because it is protected; however, the command `show router mpls lsp activepath` shows that the secondary is currently the active forwarding path (see Listing 16.18).

Listing 16.18 LSP configured with FRR and secondary path after failure

```
*A:R1# show router mpls lsp "toR6" path detail

===============================================================================
MPLS LSP toR6 Path  (Detail)
===============================================================================
Legend :
    @ - Detour Available              # - Detour In Use
    b - Bandwidth Protected           n - Node Protected
    s - Soft Preemption
===============================================================================
-------------------------------------------------------------------------------
LSP toR6 Path loose
-------------------------------------------------------------------------------
LSP Name     : toR6                            Path LSP ID : 55320
```

(continued)

Listing 16.18 *(continued)*

```
From         : 10.10.10.1                To           : 10.10.10.6
Adm State    : Up                        Oper State   : Up
Path Name    : loose                     Path Type    : Secondary
Path Admin   : Up                        Path Oper    : Up
OutInterface: 1/1/2                      Out Label    : 131069
Path Up Time: 0d 00:02:02                Path Dn Time: 0d 00:00:00
Retry Limit : 0                          Retry Timer : 30 sec
RetryAttempt: 0                          NextRetryIn : 0 sec
SetupPriori*: 7                          Hold Priori*: 0
Preference   : n/a
Bandwidth    : No Reservation            Oper Bw      : 0 Mbps
Hop Limit    : 255                       Class Type   : 0
Oper CT      : 0
Record Route: Record                     Record Label: Record
Oper MTU     : 1564                      Neg MTU      : 1564
Adaptive     : Enabled                   Oper Metric : 300
Include Grps:                            Exclude Grps:
None                                    None
Path Trans   : 3                         CSPF Queries: 2
Failure Code: noError                    Failure Node: n/a
ExplicitHops:
    No Hops Specified
Actual Hops :
    10.1.3.1(10.10.10.1)                 Record Label     : N/A
 -> 10.1.3.3(10.10.10.3)                 Record Label     : 131069
 -> 10.3.5.5(10.10.10.5)                 Record Label     : 131069
 -> 10.5.6.6(10.10.10.6)                 Record Label     : 131071
ComputedHops:
    10.1.3.1       -> 10.1.3.3       -> 10.3.5.5       -> 10.5.6.6
Srlg         : Disabled
ResigEligib*: False
LastResignal: n/a                        CSPF Metric : 300
-------------------------------------------------------------------------
LSP toR6 Path R1-R2-R4-R6
-------------------------------------------------------------------------
LSP Name     : toR6                      Path LSP ID : 55316
From         : 10.10.10.1                To           : 10.10.10.6
Adm State    : Up                        Oper State   : Up
```

```
Path Name    : R1-R2-R4-R6                        Path Type    : Primary
Path Admin   : Up                                 Path Oper    : Up
OutInterface: 1/1/3                               Out Label    : 131070
Path Up Time: 0d 00:06:25                         Path Dn Time: 0d 00:00:00
Retry Limit : 0                                   Retry Timer : 30 sec
RetryAttempt: 0                                   NextRetryIn : 0 sec
SetupPriori*: 7                                   Hold Priori*: 0
Preference   : n/a
Bandwidth    : No Reservation                     Oper Bw      : 0 Mbps
Hop Limit    : 255                                Class Type   : 0
Backup CT    : None
MainCT Retry: n/a                                 MainCT Retry: 0
    Rem      :                                        Limit    :
Oper CT      : 0
Record Route: Record                              Record Label: Record
Oper MTU     : 1564                               Neg MTU      : 1564
Adaptive     : Enabled                            Oper Metric : 300
Include Grps:                                     Exclude Grps:
None                                            None
Path Trans   : 1                                  CSPF Queries: 43
Failure Code: tunnelLocallyRepaired               Failure Node: 10.10.10.2
ExplicitHops:
    10.1.2.2        -> 10.2.4.4       -> 10.4.6.6
Actual Hops :
    10.1.2.1(10.10.10.1) @ n                      Record Label     : N/A
 -> 10.1.2.2(10.10.10.2) @ # n                    Record Label     : 131070
 -> 10.2.3.3(10.10.10.3)                          Record Label     : 131071
 -> 10.3.5.5(10.10.10.5)                          Record Label     : 131071
 -> 10.5.6.6(10.10.10.6)                          Record Label     : 131069
ComputedHops:
    10.1.2.1        -> 10.1.2.2       -> 10.2.4.4       -> 10.4.6.6
ResigEligib*: False
LastResignal: n/a                                 CSPF Metric : 300
In Prog MBB :
 MBB Type    : GlobalRevert                       NextRetryIn : 24 sec
 Started At : 03/20/2011 18:38:30                 RetryAttempt: 4
 FailureCode: noCspfRouteToDestination            Failure Node: 10.10.10.1

DetourStatus: Standby                             DetourType  : Originate
```

(continued)

Listing 16.18 *(continued)*

```
DetourAvoid*: 10.10.10.2                    DetourOrigin: 10.10.10.1
SetupPriori*: 7                             Hold Priori*: 0
Class Type  : 0
DetourActiv*: n/a                           DetourUpTime: 0d 00:06:11
InInterface : n/a                           InLabel     : n/a
OutInterface: 1/1/2                         OutLabel    : 131070
NextHop     : 10.1.3.3
ExplicitHops:
    10.1.3.1        -> 10.1.3.3        -> 10.3.5.5        -> 10.5.6.6
===============================================================================
* indicates that the corresponding row element may have been truncated.
*A:R1# show router mpls lsp "toR6" activepath

===============================================================================
MPLS LSP: toR6 (active paths)
===============================================================================
LSP Name     : toR6                         LSP Id        : 55320
Path Name    : loose                        Active Path   : Secondary
To           : 10.10.10.6

===============================================================================
*A:R1#
```

Fast Reroute Facility Backup

The primary drawback of the one-to-one backup method is scalability. In a network with hundreds of protected LSPs, LSRs must signal and maintain several times as many detour LSPs. The facility backup method is more scalable because protection LSPs can be used to protect more than one LSP. In facility backup these protection LSPs are called *bypass tunnels* instead of detours. The two significant differences between facility backup and one-to-one backup are:

- **Bypass tunnels rejoin the primary LSP::Path as soon as possible.** For node protect, the bypass tunnel is calculated and signaled to the node immediately downstream from the node being avoided (also known as the *next-next-hop* node). For link protect, the bypass tunnel is calculated and signaled to the node immediately downstream from the PLR.

- **Traffic in the bypass tunnel is encapsulated with an additional label.** Because the bypass tunnel may carry traffic from multiple LSPs, it is not possible to simply label switch traffic onto a new path as in one-to-one backup. Instead, data is encapsulated by pushing on another label that represents the bypass tunnel. This label is popped at the MP.

With facility backup, the default on the 7750 SR is to calculate node-protect bypass tunnels and to use link protect when node protect is not possible (the same as one-to-one backup). Because the bypass tunnel rejoins the primary immediately, the path for a facility backup may be less optimal than for one-to-one backup. Figure 16.28 shows the calculation of bypass tunnels for an LSP protected with facility backup. Notice that the bypass tunnel calculated by R1 results in a path one hop longer (R1–R3–R5–R4–R6) than the one-to-one detour (R1–R3–R5–R6). The network designer must balance the reduced number of RSVP-TE sessions required for facility backup against the more optimal forwarding paths of one-to-one detours when designing a network using fast reroute.

Figure 16.28 Bypass tunnels calculated for facility backup.

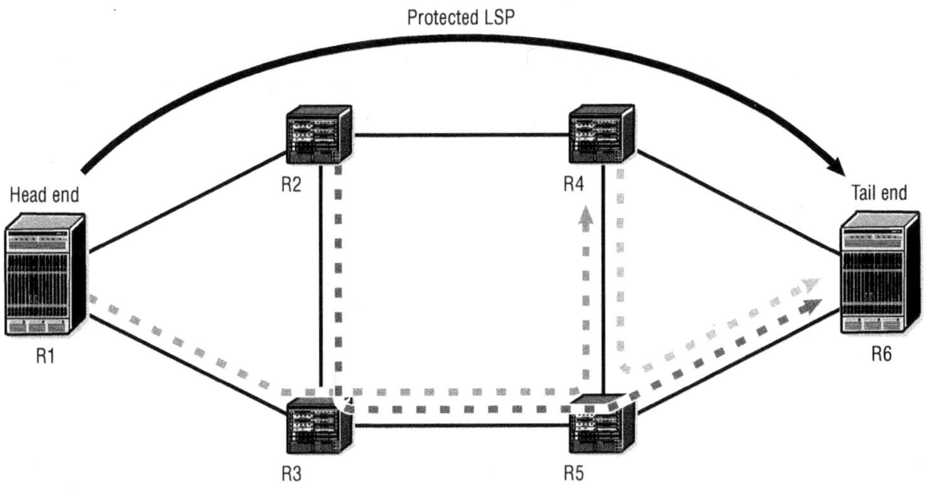

A bypass tunnel is expected to provide protection for multiple LSPs that could easily have different end points. If all traffic entering the bypass tunnel was simply label switched onto the bypass tunnel as with one-to-one backup, there would be no way to sort out the data onto the individual LSPs at the MP. Therefore, the bypass tunnel pushes on an additional label to encapsulate traffic on the bypass.

For the MP to identify the primary LSP::Path to which the packet belongs, the encapsulated packet must contain the label that was originally signaled for the primary

LSP::Path. For link protection, this is the label signaled by the downstream node. For node protection, this is the label signaled to the next-hop router by the next-next-hop router. The PLR extracts the label signaled by the next-next-hop from the `RRO` in the Resv message. The PLR swaps the ingress label for the label expected by the MP before the tunnel label is pushed on the stack.

In Figure 16.29, the primary LSP::Path has been signaled with labels 37, 36, 35 from head end to tail end. A bypass tunnel has also been signaled with labels 103, 102, 101 from the PLR (R1) to the MP (R4) to provide node protection for R2. When the bypass tunnel is in use, the PLR pushes the label signaled by the next-next-hop router (R4) onto the packet. (This would be a swap of the ingress label except that the PLR is the head end router in this example.) Then it pushes the label 103 for the bypass tunnel onto the packet. The MPLS packet is label switched along the bypass until it reaches the MP. R4 pops the bypass label and then label switches using the ingress label (36) based on the contents of the LFIB (label forwarding information base). Because per-platform label space is in use, label 36 indicates the same FEC (Forwarding Equivalent Class) no matter which interface it is received on. The packet is now back on the original primary LSP::Path.

Figure 16.29 Label operations on the bypass tunnel.

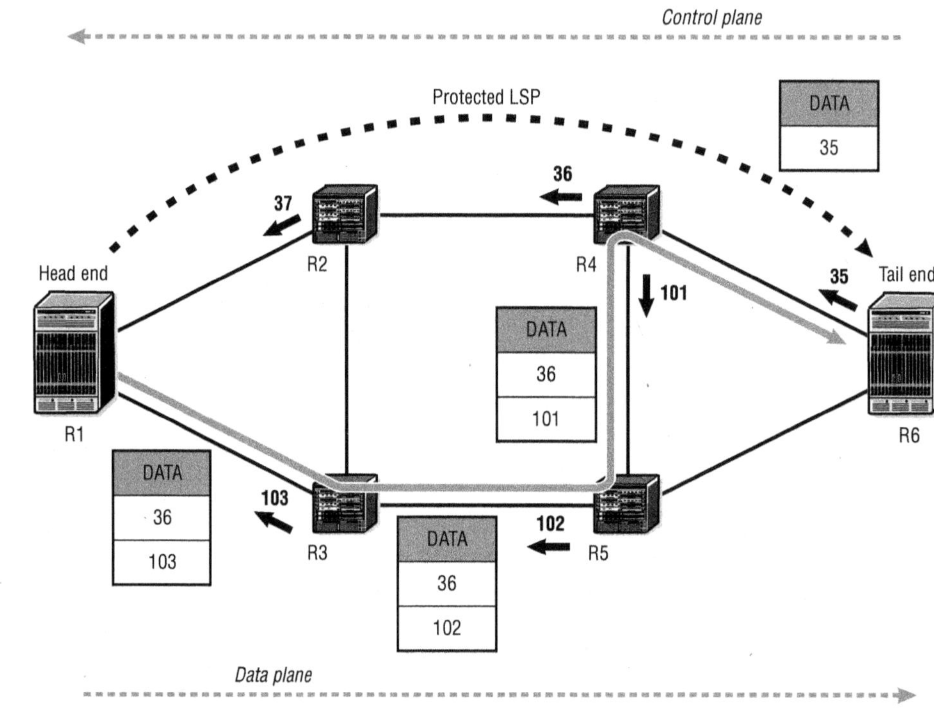

Configuration of the LSP for facility backup is similar to the one-to-one method; it is only required on the head end router (see Listing 16.19). Signaling is also similar. The "local-protection-desired" and "node-protection-desired" flags are set in the SESSION_ATTRIBUTE object, and the facility protection method is specified in the FAST_REROUTE object of the Path message (see Figure 16.30). When configuring facility backup, it is important to consider that an additional 4 bytes is required for the bypass label. This can have an impact on the MTU calculations described in Chapter 18.

Figure 16.30 Initial signaling for facility backup.

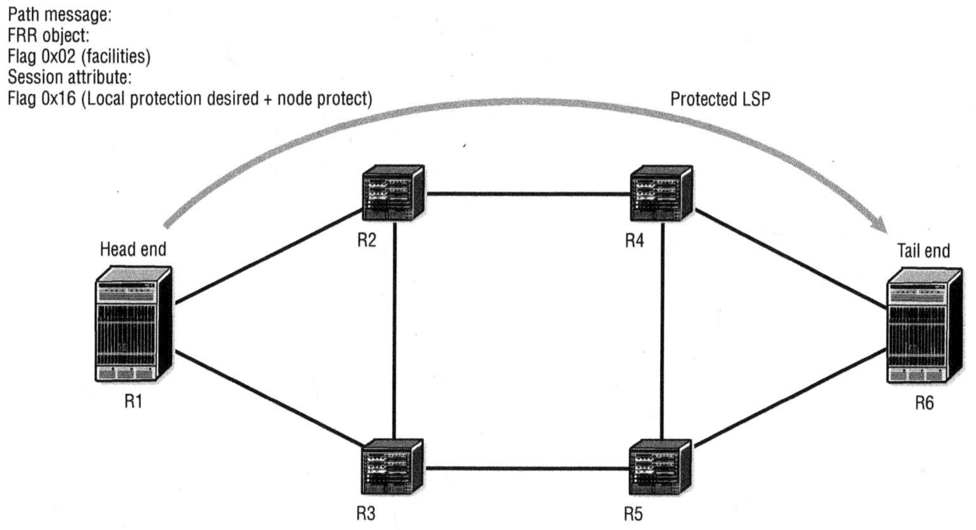

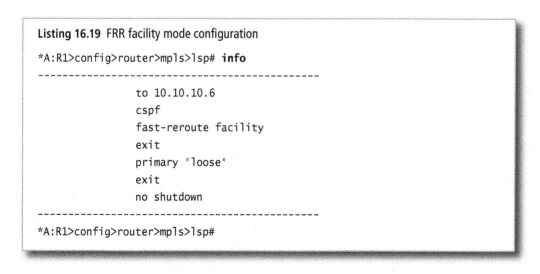

Listing 16.19 FRR facility mode configuration

```
*A:R1>config>router>mpls>lsp# info
----------------------------------------------
                to 10.10.10.6
                cspf
                fast-reroute facility
                exit
                primary "loose"
                exit
                no shutdown
----------------------------------------------
*A:R1>config>router>mpls>lsp#
```

Figure 16.31 shows that the second Resv message is used to trigger the FRR calculations on each potential PLR, as in the one-to-one method. The Path message used for signaling bypass tunnels does not use the `DETOUR` object. Because bypass tunnels can be shared among multiple protected LSPs, the PLR first does a check to see if there is already a bypass tunnel that meets the requirements.

Figure 16.31 Calculation of bypass tunnels for facility backup.

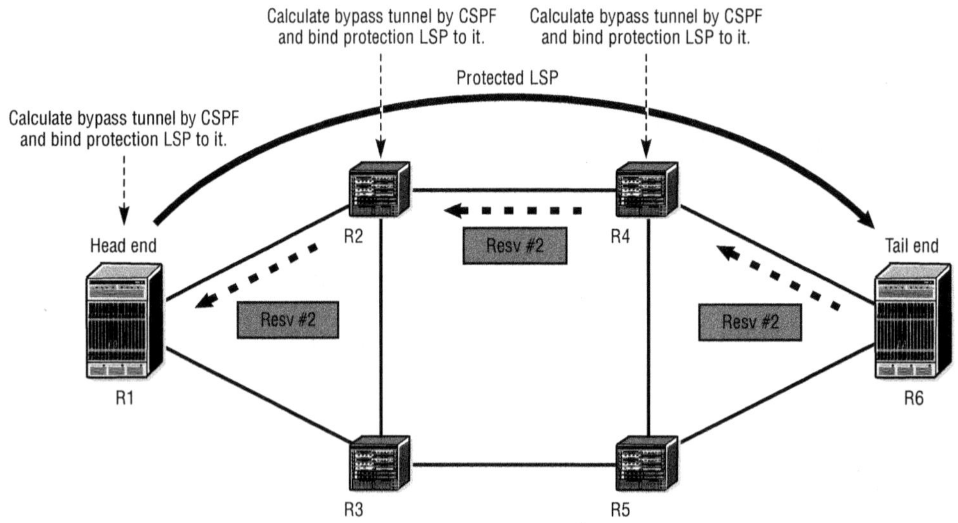

Figure 16.32 shows the bypass tunnel computation done by R1. The router first checks to see if a suitable bypass tunnel exists. There is no bypass tunnel, thus R1 does a CSPF computation to avoid the next-hop node and signals the bypass tunnel. Next R1 binds the protected LSP to the bypass tunnel. In building the association it must also calculate the label value that should be swapped for the protected LSP ingress label. It does this by consulting the MPLS label values found in the `RRO`.

The bypass tunnels that are calculated by all potential PLRs in this network are shown in Figure 16.33. As in the one-to-one method, R4 can only establish a link-protect bypass tunnel because it is directly connected to the tail end router. Listing 16.20 shows the bypass tunnels signaled by R1. The name given to the bypass tunnel follows the format `bypass-node`*<node>*, where *<node>* is the system IP address of the node to avoid. From the `show router rsvp session` command, we see that the Tunnel ID and LSP ID of the bypass tunnel created by R1 have no relation to the Tunnel ID and LSP ID of the protected tunnel. The `show router mpls bypass-tunnel` command shows that the protected LSP count is currently 1.

Figure 16.32 FRR facility bypass tunnel calculation on R1.

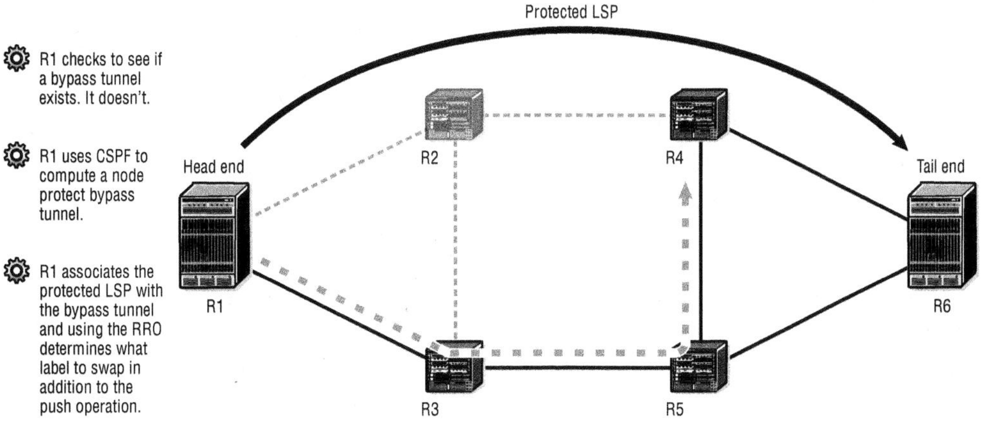

Protected LSP
R1 checks to see if a bypass tunnel exists. It doesn't.
R1 uses CSPF to compute a node protect bypass tunnel.
R1 associates the protected LSP with the bypass tunnel and using the RRO determines what label to swap in addition to the push operation.
Head end
R1
R2
R3
R4
R5
Tail end
R6

Figure 16.33 FRR facility—bypass tunnels.

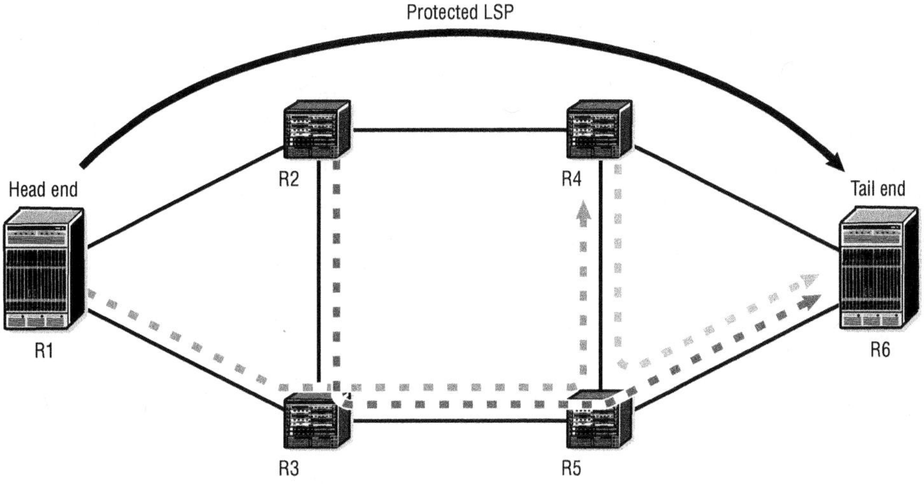

Protected LSP
Head end
R1
R2
R3
R4
R5
Tail end
R6

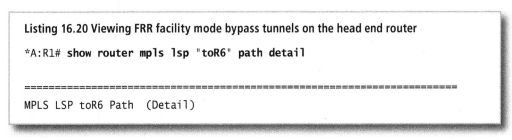

Listing 16.20 Viewing FRR facility mode bypass tunnels on the head end router

```
*A:R1# show router mpls lsp "toR6" path detail

===============================================================================
MPLS LSP toR6 Path  (Detail)
```

(continued)

Listing 16.20 *(continued)*

```
===============================================================================
Legend :
    @ - Detour Available              # - Detour In Use
    b - Bandwidth Protected           n - Node Protected
    s - Soft Preemption
===============================================================================
-------------------------------------------------------------------------------
LSP toR6 Path loose
-------------------------------------------------------------------------------
LSP Name    : toR6                          Path LSP ID : 55348
From        : 10.10.10.1                    To          : 10.10.10.6
Adm State   : Up                            Oper State  : Up
Path Name   : loose                         Path Type   : Primary
Path Admin  : Up                            Path Oper   : Up
OutInterface: 1/1/3                         Out Label   : 131070
Path Up Time: 0d 10:52:21                   Path Dn Time: 0d 00:00:00
Retry Limit : 0                             Retry Timer : 30 sec
RetryAttempt: 0                             NextRetryIn : 0 sec
SetupPriori*: 7                             Hold Priori*: 0
Preference  : n/a
Bandwidth   : No Reservation                Oper Bw     : 0 Mbps
Hop Limit   : 255                           Class Type  : 0
Backup CT   : None
MainCT Retry: n/a                           MainCT Retry: 0
    Rem     :                                   Limit   :
Oper CT     : 0
Record Route: Record                        Record Label: Record
Oper MTU    : 1560                          Neg MTU     : 1560
Adaptive    : Enabled                       Oper Metric : 300
Include Grps:                               Exclude Grps:
None                                      None
Path Trans  : 16                            CSPF Queries: 9
Failure Code: noError                       Failure Node: n/a
ExplicitHops:
    No Hops Specified
Actual Hops :
    10.1.2.1(10.10.10.1) @ n                Record Label    : N/A
 -> 10.1.2.2(10.10.10.2) @ n                Record Label    : 131070
```

```
 -> 10.2.4.4(10.10.10.4) @                      Record Label     : 131070
 -> 10.4.6.6(10.10.10.6)                        Record Label     : 131070
ComputedHops:
    10.1.2.1          -> 10.1.2.2          -> 10.2.4.4          -> 10.4.6.6
ResigEligib*: False
LastResignal: n/a                               CSPF Metric : 300
Last MBB     :
 MBB Type    : ConfigChange                     MBB State    : Success
 Ended At    : 03/20/2011 21:19:23              Old Metric   : 300
===============================================================================
* indicates that the corresponding row element may have been truncated.
*A:R1#
*A:R1# show router rsvp session

===============================================================================
RSVP Sessions
===============================================================================
From            To              Tunnel LSP   Name                        State
                                ID     ID
-------------------------------------------------------------------------------
10.10.10.1      10.10.10.6      4      55348 toR6::loose                 Up
10.10.10.1      10.4.5.4        63555  6     bypass-node10.10.10.2       Up
-------------------------------------------------------------------------------
Sessions : 2
===============================================================================
*A:R1#
*A:R1# show router rsvp session detail

===============================================================================
RSVP Sessions (Detailed)
===============================================================================
-------------------------------------------------------------------------------
LSP : toR6::loose
-------------------------------------------------------------------------------
From            : 10.10.10.1            To              : 10.10.10.6
Tunnel ID       : 4                     LSP ID          : 55348
Style           : SE                    State           : Up
Session Type    : Originate
In Interface    : n/a                   Out Interface   : 1/1/3
```

(continued)

Listing 16.20 *(continued)*

```
In Label        : n/a                     Out Label       : 131070
Previous Hop    : n/a                     Next Hop        : 10.1.2.2
Hops            :
    No Hops Specified
SetupPriority   : 7                       Hold Priority   : 0
Class Type      : 0
SubGrpOrig ID   : 0                       SubGrpOrig Addr: 0.0.0.0
P2MP ID         : 0

Path Recd       : 0                       Path Sent       : 1436
Resv Recd       : 1453                    Resv Sent       : 0

Summary messages:
SPath Recd      : 0                       SPath Sent      : 0
SResv Recd      : 0                       SResv Sent      : 0
-----------------------------------------------------------------------
LSP : bypass-node10.10.10.2
-----------------------------------------------------------------------
From            : 10.10.10.1              To              : 10.4.5.4
Tunnel ID       : 63555                   LSP ID          : 6
Style           : FF                      State           : Up
Session Type    : Bypass Tunnel
In Interface    : n/a                     Out Interface   : 1/1/2
In Label        : n/a                     Out Label       : 131070
Previous Hop    : n/a                     Next Hop        : 10.1.3.3
SetupPriority   : 7                       Hold Priority   : 0
Class Type      : 0
SubGrpOrig ID   : 0                       SubGrpOrig Addr: 0.0.0.0
P2MP ID         : 0

Path Recd       : 0                       Path Sent       : 1428
Resv Recd       : 1424                    Resv Sent       : 0

Summary messages:
SPath Recd      : 0                       SPath Sent      : 0
SResv Recd      : 0                       SResv Sent      : 0
=======================================================================
*A:R1#
```

```
*A:R1# show router mpls bypass-tunnel
===============================================================================
MPLS Bypass Tunnels
===============================================================================
Legend :   m - Manual       d - Dynamic       p - P2mp
===============================================================================
To             State  Out I/F      Out Label     Reserved   Protected  Type
                                                 BW (Kbps)  LSP Count
-------------------------------------------------------------------------------
10.4.5.4       Up     1/1/2        131070        0          1          d
-------------------------------------------------------------------------------
Bypass Tunnels : 1
===============================================================================
*A:R1#
```

Listing 16.21 shows the bypass tunnels on nodes R3, and Listing 16.22 shows the tunnels on R5. Unlike the one-to-one method, the facility method does not use detour merge points.

Listing 16.21 Facility bypass tunnels on router R3

```
*A:R3# show router rsvp session detail

===============================================================================
RSVP Sessions (Detailed)
===============================================================================
-------------------------------------------------------------------------------
LSP : bypass-node10.10.10.4
-------------------------------------------------------------------------------
From            : 10.10.10.2            To              : 10.5.6.6
Tunnel ID       : 63519                 LSP ID          : 8
Style           : FF                    State           : Up
Session Type    : Transit
In Interface    : 1/1/3                 Out Interface   : 1/1/2
In Label        : 131071                Out Label       : 131070
Previous Hop    : 10.2.3.2              Next Hop        : 10.3.5.5
SetupPriority   : 7                     Hold Priority   : 0
Class Type      : 0
```

(continued)

Listing 16.21 *(continued)*

```
SubGrpOrig ID  : 0                SubGrpOrig Addr: 0.0.0.0
P2MP ID        : 0

Path Recd      : 1672             Path Sent      : 1637
Resv Recd      : 1645             Resv Sent      : 1657

Summary messages:
SPath Recd     : 0                SPath Sent     : 0
SResv Recd     : 0                SResv Sent     : 0
-----------------------------------------------------------------------
LSP : bypass-node10.10.10.2
-----------------------------------------------------------------------
From           : 10.10.10.1       To             : 10.4.5.4
Tunnel ID      : 63555            LSP ID         : 6
Style          : FF               State          : Up
Session Type   : Transit
In Interface   : 1/1/4            Out Interface  : 1/1/2
In Label       : 131070           Out Label      : 131069
Previous Hop   : 10.1.3.1         Next Hop       : 10.3.5.5
SetupPriority  : 7                Hold Priority  : 0
Class Type     : 0
SubGrpOrig ID  : 0                SubGrpOrig Addr: 0.0.0.0
P2MP ID        : 0

Path Recd      : 1637             Path Sent      : 1609
Resv Recd      : 1640             Resv Sent      : 1648

Summary messages:
SPath Recd     : 0                SPath Sent     : 0
SResv Recd     : 0                SResv Sent     : 0
=======================================================================
*A:R3#
```

Listing 16.22 Facility bypass tunnels on router R5

```
*A:R5# show router rsvp session detail

=======================================================================
RSVP Sessions (Detailed)
```

```
===============================================================================
-------------------------------------------------------------------------------
LSP : bypass-link10.10.10.6
-------------------------------------------------------------------------------
From            : 10.10.10.4            To             : 10.5.6.6
Tunnel ID       : 63552                 LSP ID         : 4
Style           : FF                    State          : Up
Session Type    : Transit
In Interface    : 1/1/3                 Out Interface  : 1/1/4
In Label        : 131071                Out Label      : 131069
Previous Hop    : 10.4.5.4              Next Hop       : 10.5.6.6
SetupPriority   : 7                     Hold Priority  : 0
Class Type      : 0
SubGrpOrig ID   : 0                     SubGrpOrig Addr: 0.0.0.0
P2MP ID         : 0

Path Recd       : 1597                  Path Sent      : 1640
Resv Recd       : 1580                  Resv Sent      : 1648

Summary messages:
SPath Recd      : 0                     SPath Sent     : 0
SResv Recd      : 0                     SResv Sent     : 0
-------------------------------------------------------------------------------
LSP : bypass-node10.10.10.4
-------------------------------------------------------------------------------
From            : 10.10.10.2            To             : 10.5.6.6
Tunnel ID       : 63519                 LSP ID         : 8
Style           : FF                    State          : Up
Session Type    : Transit
In Interface    : 1/1/2                 Out Interface  : 1/1/4
In Label        : 131070                Out Label      : 131068
Previous Hop    : 10.3.5.3              Next Hop       : 10.5.6.6
SetupPriority   : 7                     Hold Priority  : 0
Class Type      : 0
SubGrpOrig ID   : 0                     SubGrpOrig Addr: 0.0.0.0
P2MP ID         : 0

Path Recd       : 1638                  Path Sent      : 1652
```

(continued)

Listing 16.22 *(continued)*

```
Resv Recd       : 1659                 Resv Sent       : 1647

Summary messages:
SPath Recd      : 0                    SPath Sent      : 0
SResv Recd      : 0                    SResv Sent      : 0
-----------------------------------------------------------------------
LSP : bypass-node10.10.10.2
-----------------------------------------------------------------------
From            : 10.10.10.1           To              : 10.4.5.4
Tunnel ID       : 63555                LSP ID          : 6
Style           : FF                   State           : Up
Session Type    : Transit
In Interface    : 1/1/2                Out Interface   : 1/1/3
In Label        : 131069               Out Label       : 131069
Previous Hop    : 10.3.5.3             Next Hop        : 10.4.5.4
SetupPriority   : 7                    Hold Priority   : 0
Class Type      : 0
SubGrpOrig ID   : 0                    SubGrpOrig Addr: 0.0.0.0
P2MP ID         : 0

Path Recd       : 1610                 Path Sent       : 1631
Resv Recd       : 1692                 Resv Sent       : 1642

Summary messages:
SPath Recd      : 0                    SPath Sent      : 0
SResv Recd      : 0                    SResv Sent      : 0
=======================================================================
*A:R5#
```

We can use the information from the listings above to show the data flow when there is a link failure between R2 and R4 (see Figure 16.34). Although it is not obvious, the ingress label of 131070 was swapped at the PLR for the value expected by R6. It happens that this is also 131070. The outer label used for switching on the bypass tunnel is 131071. The primary LSP::Path is shown in Listing 16.23.

Figure 16.34 FRR facility failure between R2 and R4.

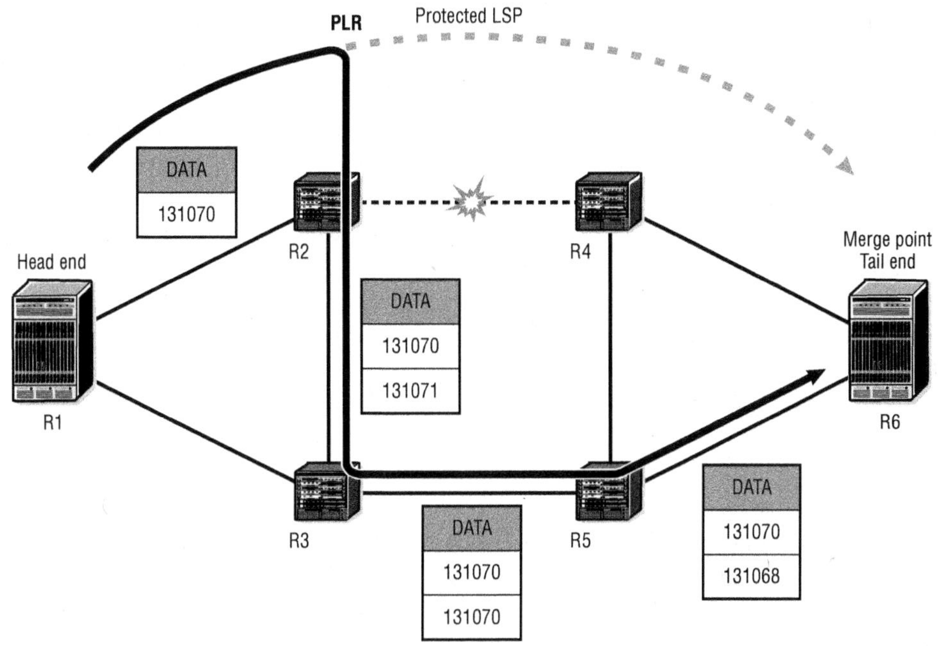

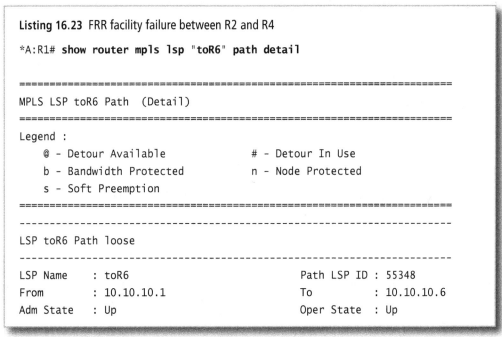

Listing 16.23 FRR facility failure between R2 and R4

```
*A:R1# show router mpls lsp "toR6" path detail

===============================================================================
MPLS LSP toR6 Path  (Detail)
===============================================================================
Legend :
    @ - Detour Available              # - Detour In Use
    b - Bandwidth Protected           n - Node Protected
    s - Soft Preemption
===============================================================================
-------------------------------------------------------------------------------
LSP toR6 Path loose
-------------------------------------------------------------------------------
LSP Name     : toR6                              Path LSP ID : 55348
From         : 10.10.10.1                        To          : 10.10.10.6
Adm State    : Up                                Oper State  : Up
```

(continued)

Listing 16.23 *(continued)*

```
Path Name    : loose                          Path Type    : Primary
Path Admin   : Up                             Path Oper    : Up
OutInterface: 1/1/3                           Out Label    : 131070
Path Up Time: 0d 15:44:11                     Path Dn Time: 0d 00:00:00
Retry Limit : 0                               Retry Timer : 30 sec
RetryAttempt: 0                               NextRetryIn : 0 sec
SetupPriori*: 7                               Hold Priori*: 0
Preference  : n/a
Bandwidth   : No Reservation                  Oper Bw      : 0 Mbps
Hop Limit   : 255                             Class Type   : 0
Backup CT   : None
MainCT Retry: n/a                             MainCT Retry: 0
    Rem     :                                     Limit    :
Oper CT     : 0
Record Route: Record                          Record Label: Record
Oper MTU    : 1560                            Neg MTU      : 1560
Adaptive    : Enabled                         Oper Metric : 300
Include Grps:                                 Exclude Grps:
None                                        None
Path Trans  : 16                              CSPF Queries: 10
Failure Code: tunnelLocallyRepaired           Failure Node: 10.10.10.2
ExplicitHops:
    No Hops Specified
Actual Hops :
    10.1.2.1(10.10.10.1) @ n                  Record Label     : N/A
 -> 10.1.2.2(10.10.10.2) @ # n                Record Label     : 131070
 -> 10.2.4.4(10.10.10.4)                      Record Label     : 131070
 -> 10.4.6.6(10.10.10.6)                      Record Label     : 131070
ComputedHops:
    10.1.2.1        -> 10.1.2.2        -> 10.2.4.4        -> 10.4.6.6
ResigEligib*: False
LastResignal: n/a                             CSPF Metric : 300
Last MBB    :
 MBB Type   : ConfigChange                    MBB State    : Success
 Ended At   : 03/20/2011 21:19:23             Old Metric   : 300
In Prog MBB :
 MBB Type   : GlobalRevert                    NextRetryIn : 0 sec
 Started At : 03/21/2011 13:02:13             RetryAttempt: 1
```

```
  FailureCode: noError                              Failure Node: n/a
===================================================================
* indicates that the corresponding row element may have been truncated.
*A:R1#
```

Now consider what happens in the network when a new LSP is provisioned with a path R1–R2–R4 (see Figure 16.35). If this LSP had the exact same path as the first LSP, the existing bypass tunnels could be used for both protected LSPs and there would be no requirement to signal additional bypass tunnels. R1 is a potential PLR and checks to see what bypass tunnels are available. It does have a node-protect bypass tunnel to R4 and associates the protected LSP with the bypass tunnel. R2 is also a potential PLR, but because it is directly connected to the tail end router, it can only provide link protection. R2 searches to see if it already has a bypass tunnel to R4 that provides link protection. It does not; therefore, R2 signals a bypass tunnel toward R4.

Figure 16.35 FRR facility—protecting more than one primary LSP.

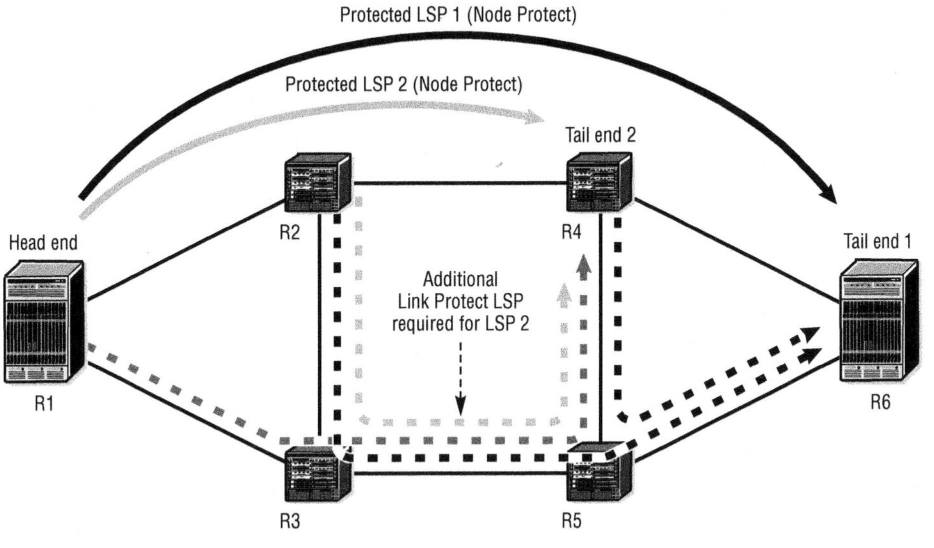

Listing 16.24 shows the configuration of the additional LSP on the head end. It also shows the expected node protection at the first hop and link protection at the last hop. Note that when the `show router mpls bypass-tunnel` command is used on R1, it now shows that the bypass tunnel originated by R1 has a protected LSP count of 2.

Listing 16.24 FRR facility protection of multiple LSPs

```
*A:R1>config>router>mpls>lsp# info
---------------------------------------------
               to 10.10.10.4
               cspf
               fast-reroute facility
               exit
               primary "loose"
               exit
               no shutdown
---------------------------------------------
*A:R1>config>router>mpls>lsp#
*A:R1# show router mpls lsp "toR4" path detail

=======================================================================
MPLS LSP toR4 Path  (Detail)
=======================================================================
Legend :
    @ - Detour Available             # - Detour In Use
    b - Bandwidth Protected          n - Node Protected
    s - Soft Preemption
=======================================================================
-----------------------------------------------------------------------
LSP toR4 Path loose
-----------------------------------------------------------------------
LSP Name     : toR4                          Path LSP ID : 24576
From         : 10.10.10.1                    To          : 10.10.10.4
Adm State    : Up                            Oper State  : Up
Path Name    : loose                         Path Type   : Primary
Path Admin   : Up                            Path Oper   : Up
OutInterface: 1/1/3                          Out Label   : 131071
Path Up Time: 0d 00:00:43                    Path Dn Time: 0d 00:00:00
Retry Limit : 0                              Retry Timer : 30 sec
RetryAttempt: 0                              NextRetryIn : 0 sec
SetupPriori*: 7                              Hold Priori*: 0
Preference  : n/a
Bandwidth    : No Reservation                Oper Bw     : 0 Mbps
Hop Limit    : 255                           Class Type  : 0
```

```
Backup CT    : None
MainCT Retry: n/a                              MainCT Retry: 0
    Rem     :                                      Limit    :
Oper CT     : 0
Record Route: Record                           Record Label: Record
Oper MTU    : 1560                             Neg MTU      : 1560
Adaptive    : Enabled                          Oper Metric : 200
Include Grps:                                  Exclude Grps:
None                                         None
Path Trans  : 1                                CSPF Queries: 1
Failure Code: noError                          Failure Node: n/a
ExplicitHops:
    No Hops Specified
Actual Hops :
    10.1.2.1(10.10.10.1) @ n                   Record Label     : N/A
 -> 10.1.2.2(10.10.10.2) @                     Record Label     : 131071
 -> 10.2.4.4(10.10.10.4)                       Record Label     : 131069
ComputedHops:
    10.1.2.1        -> 10.1.2.2         -> 10.2.4.4
ResigEligib*: False
LastResignal: n/a                              CSPF Metric : 200
=======================================================================
* indicates that the corresponding row element may have been truncated.
*A:R1#
*A:R1# show router mpls bypass-tunnel
=======================================================================
MPLS Bypass Tunnels
=======================================================================
Legend :  m - Manual      d - Dynamic      p - P2mp
=======================================================================
To            State  Out I/F       Out Label   Reserved   Protected  Type
                                               BW (Kbps)  LSP Count
-----------------------------------------------------------------------
10.4.5.4      Up     1/1/2         131069      0          2          d
-----------------------------------------------------------------------
Bypass Tunnels : 1
=======================================================================
*A:R1#
```

Listing 16.25 shows that R2 now originates two bypass tunnels. It still has the node-protect tunnel for the LSP to R6, but now it also originates a link-protect bypass tunnel for the LSP to R4.

Listing 16.25 FRR facility bypass tunnels on R2

```
*A:R2# show router mpls bypass-tunnel
=========================================================================
MPLS Bypass Tunnels
=========================================================================
Legend :  m - Manual      d - Dynamic      p - P2mp
=========================================================================
To            State  Out I/F      Out Label   Reserved   Protected  Type
                                              BW (Kbps)  LSP Count
-------------------------------------------------------------------------
10.5.6.6      Up     1/1/3        131070      0          1          d

10.4.5.4      Up     1/1/3        131071      0          1          d
-------------------------------------------------------------------------
Bypass Tunnels : 2
=========================================================================
*A:R2#
```

Listing 16.26 shows the RSVP-TE sessions on R3. Listing 16.27 shows the RSVP-TE sessions on R5. From these we can tell what labels will be used for the data path on both LSPs.

Listing 16.26 FRR facility RSVP-TE sessions on R3

```
*A:R3# show router rsvp session lsp-name bypass-node10.10.10.2 detail

=========================================================================
RSVP Sessions (Detailed)
=========================================================================
-------------------------------------------------------------------------
LSP : bypass-node10.10.10.2
-------------------------------------------------------------------------
From            : 10.10.10.1             To              : 10.4.5.4
```

```
Tunnel ID       : 63678                    LSP ID          : 16
Style           : FF                       State           : Up
Session Type    : Transit
In Interface    : 1/1/4                    Out Interface   : 1/1/2
In Label        : 131069                   Out Label       : 131071
Previous Hop    : 10.1.3.1                 Next Hop        : 10.3.5.5
SetupPriority   : 7                        Hold Priority   : 0
Class Type      : 0
SubGrpOrig ID   : 0                        SubGrpOrig Addr: 0.0.0.0
P2MP ID         : 0

Path Recd       : 643                      Path Sent       : 659
Resv Recd       : 635                      Resv Sent       : 635

Summary messages:
SPath Recd      : 0                        SPath Sent      : 0
SResv Recd      : 0                        SResv Sent      : 0
=======================================================================
*A:R3#
```

Listing 16.27 FRR facility RSVP-TE sessions on R5

```
*A:R5# show router rsvp session lsp-name bypass-node10.10.10.2 detail

=======================================================================
RSVP Sessions (Detailed)
=======================================================================
-----------------------------------------------------------------------
LSP : bypass-node10.10.10.2
-----------------------------------------------------------------------
From            : 10.10.10.1               To              : 10.4.5.4
Tunnel ID       : 63678                    LSP ID          : 16
Style           : FF                       State           : Up
Session Type    : Transit
In Interface    : 1/1/2                    Out Interface   : 1/1/3
In Label        : 131071                   Out Label       : 131070
Previous Hop    : 10.3.5.3                 Next Hop        : 10.4.5.4
SetupPriority   : 7                        Hold Priority   : 0
Class Type      : 0
```

(continued)

Listing 16.27 *(continued)*

```
SubGrpOrig ID   : 0                    SubGrpOrig Addr: 0.0.0.0
P2MP ID         : 0

Path Recd       : 661                  Path Sent       : 629
Resv Recd       : 677                  Resv Sent       : 637

Summary messages:
SPath Recd      : 0                    SPath Sent      : 0
SResv Recd      : 0                    SResv Sent      : 0
===============================================================================
*A:R5#
```

Figure 16.36 shows the data path when there is a failure on the link between R1 and R2. The labels expected along the primary path are shown for both LSPs. These can be seen in the output in Listing 16.28. The head end node (R1) is also the PLR, and traffic from both LSPs is sent to R4 on the same bypass tunnel. The outer (bottom) label for data from both LSP1 and LSP2 is the same as it all travels on the same bypass tunnel. Before R1 sends traffic on the bypass tunnel, it determines from the `RRO` the label value that R4 expects to receive for each LSP. These are the inner labels and remain constant as traffic is switched over the bypass tunnel. When traffic gets to the MP (R4), it pops the outer labels as it is the termination point for the bypass tunnel. The router then looks at the inner label. For the label `131069` (LSP 2 data), it pops the label as it is the termination point for LSP 2. For label value `131071` (LSP 1 data), it swaps the label for `131070` and forwards the data toward LSP 1's tail end (R6). Because of the use of per-platform label space, R4 treats data received with label `131071` from R5 the same way as it would treat it if received from R2.

Listing 16.28 Facility backup protecting multiple failed LSPs

```
*A:R1# show router mpls lsp path detail

===============================================================================
MPLS LSP  Path  (Detail)
===============================================================================
Legend :
```

```
    @ - Detour Available              # - Detour In Use
    b - Bandwidth Protected           n - Node Protected
    s - Soft Preemption
===============================================================================
-------------------------------------------------------------------------------
LSP toR6 Path loose
-------------------------------------------------------------------------------
LSP Name    : toR6                         Path LSP ID : 55356
From        : 10.10.10.1                   To          : 10.10.10.6
Adm State   : Up                           Oper State  : Up
Path Name   : loose                        Path Type   : Primary
Path Admin  : Up                           Path Oper   : Up
OutInterface: 1/1/3                        Out Label   : 131069
Path Up Time: 0d 06:05:32                  Path Dn Time: 0d 00:00:00
Retry Limit : 0                            Retry Timer : 30 sec
RetryAttempt: 0                            NextRetryIn : 0 sec
SetupPriori*: 7                            Hold Priori*: 0
Preference  : n/a
Bandwidth   : No Reservation               Oper Bw     : 0 Mbps
Hop Limit   : 255                          Class Type  : 0
Backup CT   : None
MainCT Retry: n/a                          MainCT Retry: 0
    Rem     :                                  Limit   :
Oper CT     : 0
Record Route: Record                       Record Label: Record
Oper MTU    : 1560                         Neg MTU     : 1560
Adaptive    : Enabled                      Oper Metric : 300
Include Grps:                              Exclude Grps:
None                                     None
Path Trans  : 21                           CSPF Queries: 13
Failure Code: tunnelLocallyRepaired        Failure Node: 10.10.10.2
ExplicitHops:
    No Hops Specified
Actual Hops :
    10.1.2.1(10.10.10.1) @ n               Record Label    : N/A
 -> 10.1.2.2(10.10.10.2) @ # n             Record Label    : 131069
 -> 10.2.4.4(10.10.10.4) @                 Record Label    : 131071
 -> 10.4.6.6(10.10.10.6)                   Record Label    : 131070
ComputedHops:
    10.1.2.1        -> 10.1.2.2       -> 10.2.4.4        -> 10.4.6.6
```

(continued)

Listing 16.28 *(continued)*

```
ResigEligib*: False
LastResignal: n/a                              CSPF Metric : 300
Last MBB    :
 MBB Type   : GlobalRevert                     MBB State   : Success
 Ended At   : 03/21/2011 15:33:12              Old Metric  : 300
In Prog MBB :
 MBB Type   : GlobalRevert                     NextRetryIn : 8 sec
 Started At : 03/21/2011 21:37:34              RetryAttempt: 0
 FailureCode: noError                          Failure Node: n/a
----------------------------------------------------------------------
LSP toR4 Path loose
----------------------------------------------------------------------
LSP Name    : toR4                             Path LSP ID : 24576
From        : 10.10.10.1                       To          : 10.10.10.4
Adm State   : Up                               Oper State  : Up
Path Name   : loose                            Path Type   : Primary
Path Admin  : Up                               Path Oper   : Up
OutInterface: 1/1/3                            Out Label   : 131071
Path Up Time: 0d 01:12:07                      Path Dn Time: 0d 00:00:00
Retry Limit : 0                                Retry Timer : 30 sec
RetryAttempt: 0                                NextRetryIn : 0 sec
SetupPriori*: 7                                Hold Priori*: 0
Preference  : n/a
Bandwidth   : No Reservation                   Oper Bw     : 0 Mbps
Hop Limit   : 255                              Class Type  : 0
Backup CT   : None
MainCT Retry: n/a                              MainCT Retry: 0
    Rem     :                                      Limit   :
Oper CT     : 0
Record Route: Record                           Record Label: Record
Oper MTU    : 1560                             Neg MTU     : 1560
Adaptive    : Enabled                          Oper Metric : 200
Include Grps:                                  Exclude Grps:
None                                         None
Path Trans  : 1                                CSPF Queries: 1
Failure Code: tunnelLocallyRepaired            Failure Node: 10.10.10.2
ExplicitHops:
    No Hops Specified
Actual Hops :
```

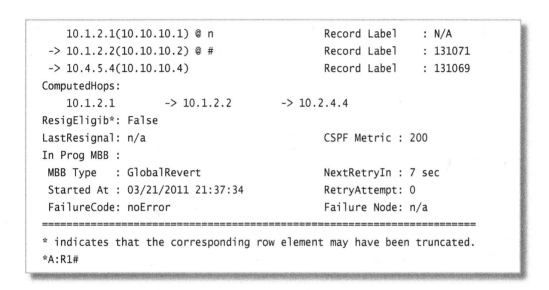

```
    10.1.2.1(10.10.10.1) @ n                    Record Label     : N/A
  -> 10.1.2.2(10.10.10.2) @ #                   Record Label     : 131071
  -> 10.4.5.4(10.10.10.4)                       Record Label     : 131069
ComputedHops:
    10.1.2.1         -> 10.1.2.2         -> 10.2.4.4
ResigEligib*: False
LastResignal: n/a                               CSPF Metric : 200
In Prog MBB :
 MBB Type    : GlobalRevert                     NextRetryIn : 7 sec
 Started At : 03/21/2011 21:37:34               RetryAttempt: 0
 FailureCode: noError                           Failure Node: n/a
===============================================================================
* indicates that the corresponding row element may have been truncated.
*A:R1#
```

Figure 16.36 Data path for facility backup protecting multiple LSPs.

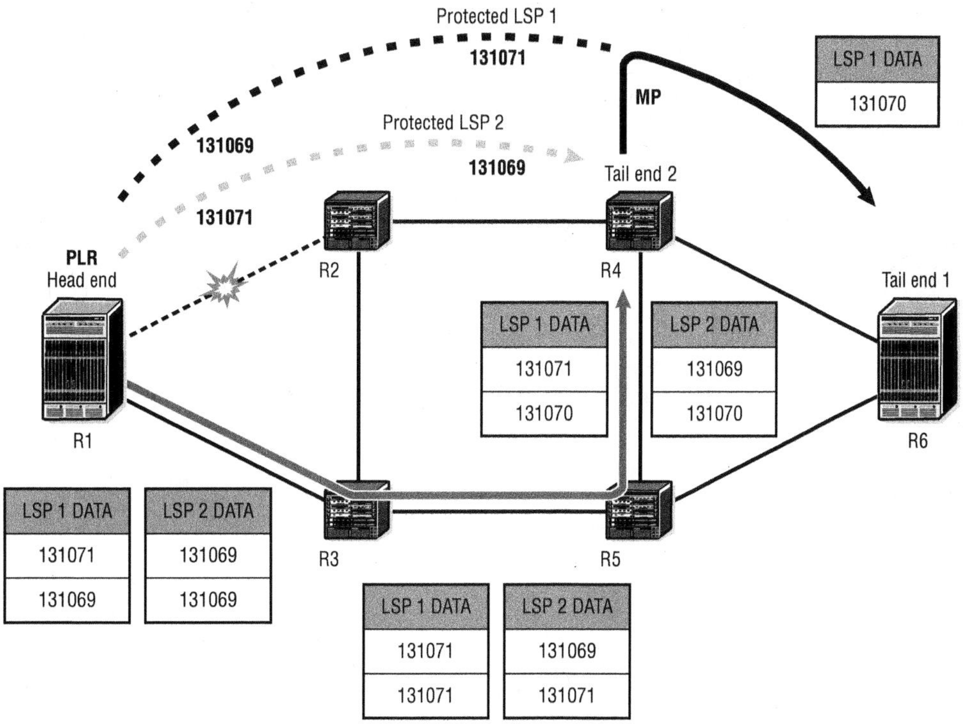

Using SRLG with FRR

Earlier in the chapter, SRLGs were discussed in the context of secondary LSP::Paths. Their purpose is to ensure that secondary LSP::Paths are disjoint from the primary paths they are protecting. As long as an SRLG is used by a primary LSP::Path, any interface that has the SRLG bound to it cannot be used by the secondary LSP::Path, regardless of whether or not it is used in the primary path. Although FRR is not color-aware (it cannot use admin group constraints for protection LSPs), it can take SRLG into account.

System-wide configuration is required for SRLG with the command `configure router mpls srlg-frr [strict]`. With the strict option, CSPF will not establish an FRR protection tunnel if there is no path that meets the SRLG constraint. Without the strict option (default), if CSPF cannot find a path for the protection tunnel with the SRLG constraint, the PLR disregards the constraint and tries to establish a tunnel over links not compliant to SRLG. As with secondary LSP::Paths, after shared risk link groups are added, the primary LSP::Path must be resignaled so that the SRLG constraint is taken into account.

We now look at an example of SRLG used with FRR facility backup. Consider an LSP from R1 to R6 but with a slightly different topology and metrics, as shown in Figure 16.37.

Figure 16.37 FRR facility—SRLG topology metrics.

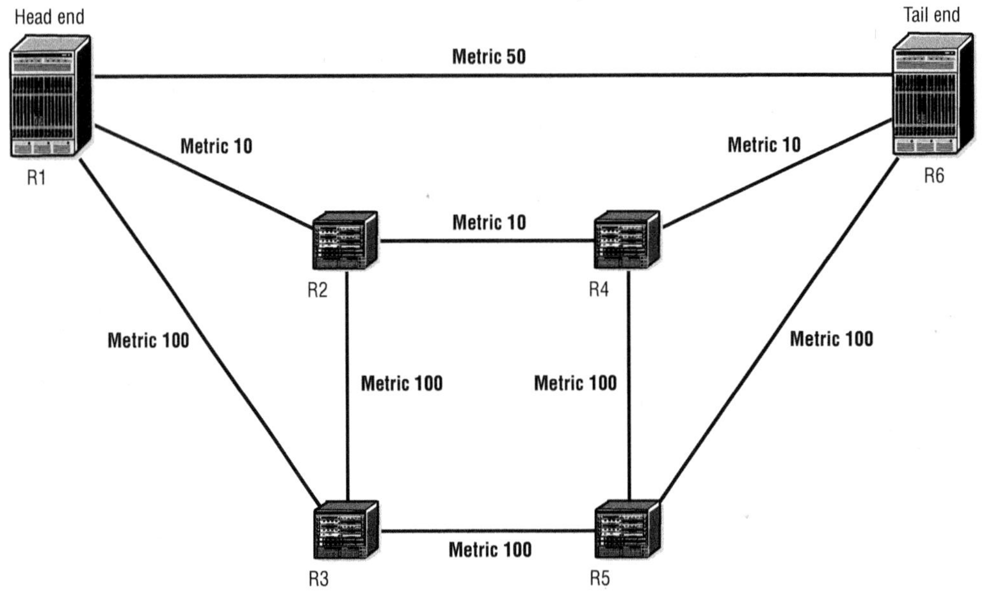

Figure 16.38 shows a primary LSP::Path and its associated bypass tunnels. Listing 16.29 shows the bypass tunnel on R1. Listings 16.30 and 16.31 show the bypass tunnels on R2 and R4.

Figure 16.38 FRR facility bypass tunnels without SRLG.

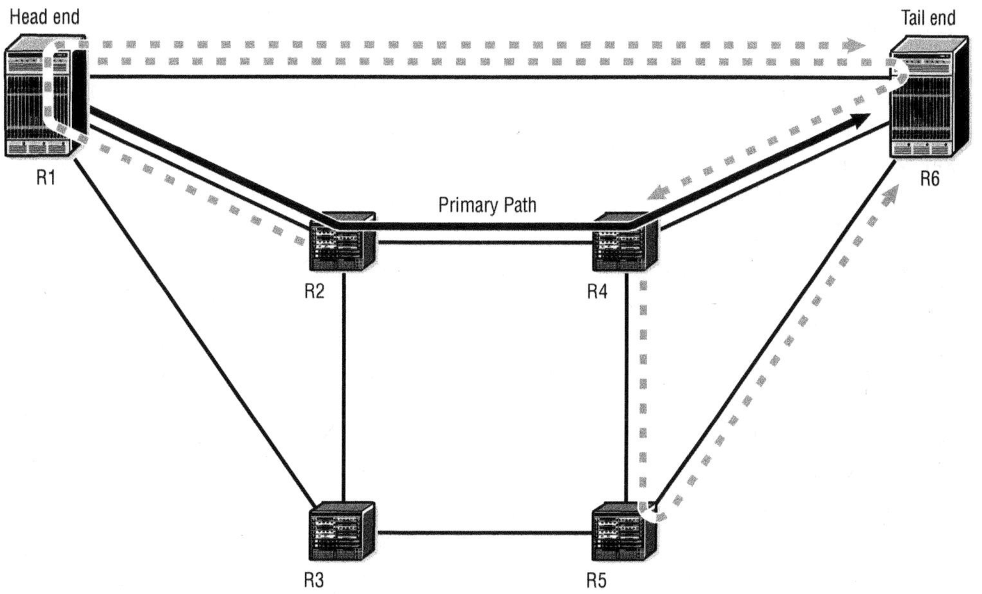

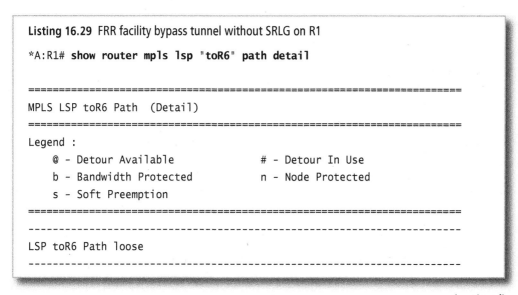

Listing 16.29 FRR facility bypass tunnel without SRLG on R1

```
*A:R1# show router mpls lsp "toR6" path detail

===============================================================================
MPLS LSP toR6 Path  (Detail)
===============================================================================
Legend :
    @ - Detour Available              # - Detour In Use
    b - Bandwidth Protected           n - Node Protected
    s - Soft Preemption
===============================================================================
-------------------------------------------------------------------------------
LSP toR6 Path loose
-------------------------------------------------------------------------------
```

(continued)

Listing 16.29 *(continued)*

```
LSP Name     : toR6                       Path LSP ID : 55368
From         : 10.10.10.1                 To          : 10.10.10.6
Adm State    : Up                         Oper State  : Up
Path Name    : loose                      Path Type   : Primary
Path Admin   : Up                         Path Oper   : Up
OutInterface: 1/1/3                       Out Label   : 131071
Path Up Time: 0d 21:19:28                 Path Dn Time: 0d 00:00:00
Retry Limit : 0                           Retry Timer : 30 sec
RetryAttempt: 0                           NextRetryIn : 0 sec
SetupPriori*: 7                           Hold Priori*: 0
Preference  : n/a
Bandwidth    : No Reservation             Oper Bw     : 0 Mbps
Hop Limit    : 255                        Class Type  : 0
Backup CT    : None
MainCT Retry: n/a                         MainCT Retry: 0
    Rem      :                                Limit   :
Oper CT      : 0
Record Route: Record                      Record Label: Record
Oper MTU     : 1560                       Neg MTU     : 1560
Adaptive     : Enabled                    Oper Metric : 30
Include Grps:                             Exclude Grps:
None                                    None
Path Trans   : 27                         CSPF Queries: 19
Failure Code: noError                     Failure Node: n/a
ExplicitHops:
    No Hops Specified
Actual Hops :
    10.1.2.1(10.10.10.1) @ n              Record Label    : N/A
 -> 10.1.2.2(10.10.10.2) @ n              Record Label    : 131071
 -> 10.2.4.4(10.10.10.4) @                Record Label    : 131071
 -> 10.4.6.6(10.10.10.6)                  Record Label    : 131071
ComputedHops:
    10.1.2.1        -> 10.1.2.2        -> 10.2.4.4        -> 10.4.6.6
ResigEligib*: False
LastResignal: n/a                         CSPF Metric : 30
Last MBB     :
 MBB Type    : ManualResignal             MBB State   : Success
 Ended At    : 03/22/2011 12:51:09        Old Metric  : 100
```

```
===============================================================================
* indicates that the corresponding row element may have been truncated.
*A:R1# show router mpls  bypass-tunnel
===============================================================================
MPLS Bypass Tunnels
===============================================================================
Legend :  m - Manual      d - Dynamic      p - P2mp
===============================================================================
To           State  Out I/F      Out Label      Reserved   Protected  Type
                                                BW (Kbps)  LSP Count
-------------------------------------------------------------------------------
10.4.6.4     Up     1/1/1        131067         0          1          d
-------------------------------------------------------------------------------
Bypass Tunnels : 1
===============================================================================
*A:R1#
```

Listing 16.30 Facility bypass tunnel without SRLG on R2

```
*A:R2# show router mpls bypass-tunnel detail

===============================================================================
MPLS Bypass Tunnels (Detail)
===============================================================================
-------------------------------------------------------------------------------
bypass-node10.10.10.4
-------------------------------------------------------------------------------
To                : 10.1.6.6            State                : Up
Out I/F           : 1/1/4               Out Label            : 131069
Up Time           : 0d 00:19:54         Active Time          : n/a
Reserved BW       : 0 Kbps              Protected LSP Count : 1
Type              : Dynamic
SetupPriority     : 7                   Hold Priority        : 0
Class Type        : 0
Actual Hops       :
    10.1.2.2         -> 10.1.2.1         -> 10.1.6.6

===============================================================================
*A:R2#
```

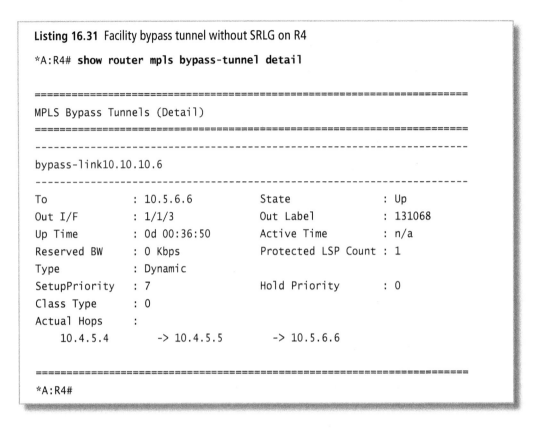

Listing 16.31 Facility bypass tunnel without SRLG on R4

```
*A:R4# show router mpls bypass-tunnel detail

===============================================================================
MPLS Bypass Tunnels (Detail)
===============================================================================
-------------------------------------------------------------------------------
bypass-link10.10.10.6
-------------------------------------------------------------------------------
To               : 10.5.6.6           State               : Up
Out I/F          : 1/1/3              Out Label           : 131068
Up Time          : 0d 00:36:50        Active Time         : n/a
Reserved BW      : 0 Kbps             Protected LSP Count : 1
Type             : Dynamic
SetupPriority    : 7                  Hold Priority       : 0
Class Type       : 0
Actual Hops      :
    10.4.5.4          -> 10.4.5.5          -> 10.5.6.6

===============================================================================
*A:R4#
```

Now suppose that the network designer wishes to have all bypass tunnels totally disjoint from the primary, as shown in Figure 16.39. The steps required to accomplish this with SRLG are:

1. Create an SRLG on all interfaces of the primary path.
2. Apply the global system setting `srlg-frr` on all routers.
3. Resignal the primary LSP.

Listing 16.32 shows the configuration and resulting bypass tunnel on R1. Configuration of SRLG on the interfaces is only shown for the head end router. Listing 16.33 shows the resulting bypass tunnel on R1, and Listing 16.34 shows the tunnel on R2. The link-protect bypass tunnel originated by R4 is unchanged and therefore not shown.

Figure 16.39 FRR facility—resulting topology with SRLG on the primary path.

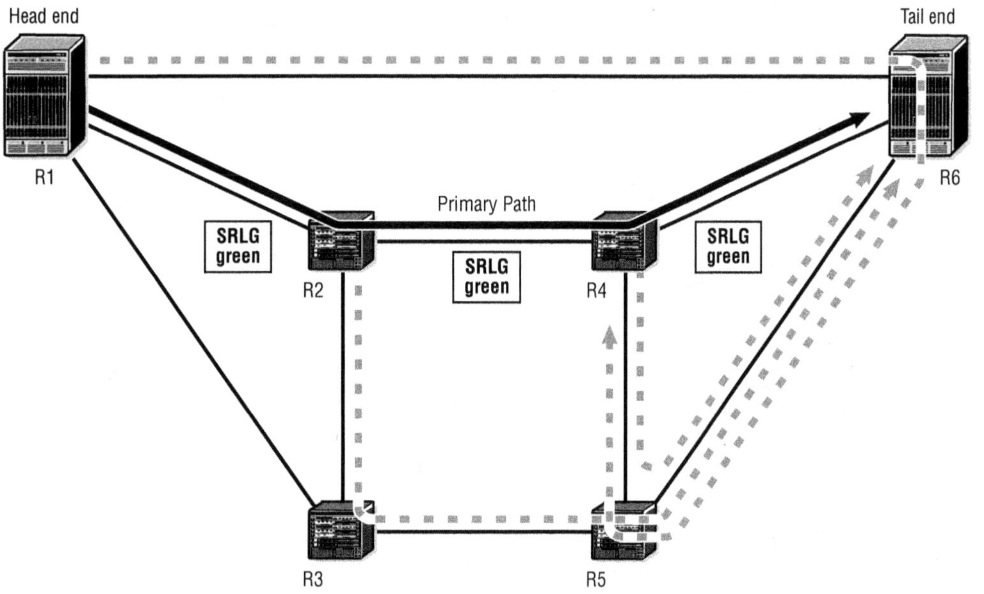

Listing 16.32 FRR facility SRLG configuration (some output omitted)

```
*A:R1# configure router mpls
*A:R1>config>router>mpls# info
----------------------------------------------
            srlg-frr
            srlg-group "green" value 10
            interface "system"
            exit
            interface "toR2"
                srlg-group "green"
            exit
            interface "toR3"
            exit
            interface "toR6"
            exit
            lsp "toR6"
                to 10.10.10.6
                cspf
```

(continued)

Listing 16.32 *(continued)*

```
                fast-reroute facility
                exit
                primary "loose"
                exit
                no shutdown
            exit
----------------------------------------------
*A:R1>config>router>mpls#
```

Listing 16.33 Bypass tunnel on R1 with SRLG on the primary path

```
*A:R1# show router mpls bypass-tunnel detail

=======================================================================
MPLS Bypass Tunnels (Detail)
=======================================================================
-----------------------------------------------------------------------
bypass-node10.10.10.2
-----------------------------------------------------------------------
To                : 10.4.5.4          State              : Up
Out I/F           : 1/1/1             Out Label          : 131068
Up Time           : 0d 00:36:05       Active Time        : n/a
Reserved BW       : 0 Kbps            Protected LSP Count : 1
Type              : Dynamic
SetupPriority     : 7                 Hold Priority      : 0
Class Type        : 0
Actual Hops       :
    10.1.6.1        -> 10.1.6.6       -> 10.5.6.5        -> 10.4.5.4

=======================================================================
*A:R1#
```

Listing 16.34 Bypass tunnel on R2 with SRLG on the primary path

```
*A:R2# show router mpls bypass-tunnel detail
```

```
===============================================================================
MPLS Bypass Tunnels (Detail)
===============================================================================
-------------------------------------------------------------------------------
bypass-node10.10.10.4
-------------------------------------------------------------------------------
To                  : 10.5.6.6          State                 : Up
Out I/F             : 1/1/3             Out Label             : 131071
Up Time             : 0d 00:57:41       Active Time           : n/a
Reserved BW         : 0 Kbps            Protected LSP Count : 1
Type                : Dynamic
SetupPriority       : 7                 Hold Priority         : 0
Class Type          : 0
Actual Hops         :
    10.2.3.2          -> 10.2.3.3         -> 10.3.5.5         -> 10.5.6.6

===============================================================================
*A:R2#
```

Suppose that the network designer also wants the bypass tunnels to avoid the newly attached link between R1 and R6. One way to achieve this is to set the same SRLG group on the interface between R1 and R6. The resulting bypass tunnels are shown in Figure 16.40 and Listing 16.35. The bypass tunnels originated by R2 and R4 are unchanged. Again, the primary LSP::Path must be resignaled for the changes to take effect, as this will also resignal the bypass tunnels.

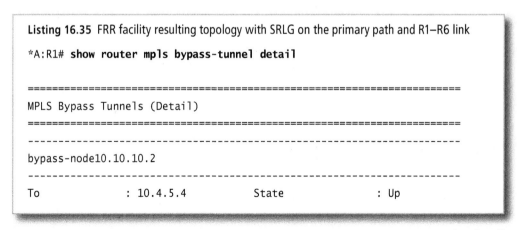

Listing 16.35 FRR facility resulting topology with SRLG on the primary path and R1–R6 link

```
*A:R1# show router mpls bypass-tunnel detail

===============================================================================
MPLS Bypass Tunnels (Detail)
===============================================================================
-------------------------------------------------------------------------------
bypass-node10.10.10.2
-------------------------------------------------------------------------------
To                  : 10.4.5.4          State                 : Up
```

(continued)

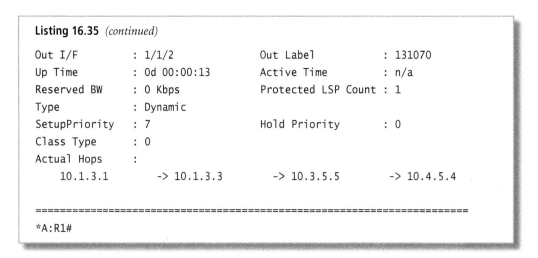

Listing 16.35 *(continued)*

```
Out I/F          : 1/1/2                Out Label           : 131070
Up Time          : 0d 00:00:13          Active Time         : n/a
Reserved BW      : 0 Kbps               Protected LSP Count : 1
Type             : Dynamic
SetupPriority    : 7                    Hold Priority       : 0
Class Type       : 0
Actual Hops      :
    10.1.3.1         -> 10.1.3.3          -> 10.3.5.5          -> 10.4.5.4

===============================================================================
*A:R1#
```

Figure 16.40 FRR facility—resulting topology with SRLG also on R1–R6 interface.

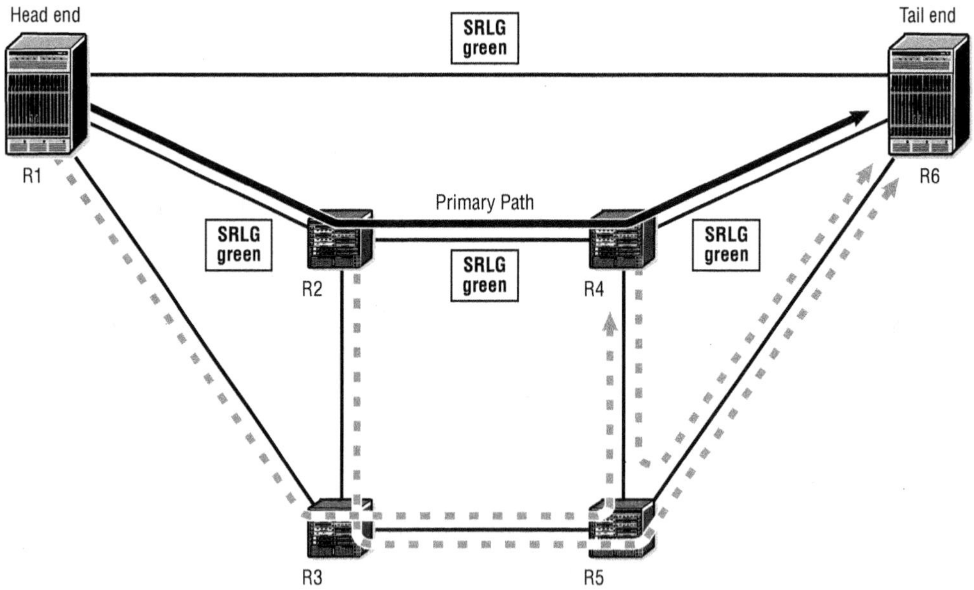

Practice Lab: MPLS Resiliency

The following lab is designed to reinforce your knowledge of the content in this chapter. Please review the instructions carefully, and perform the steps in the order in which they are presented. The practice labs require that you have access to six or more Alcatel-Lucent 7750 SRs or Alcatel-Lucent 7450 ESSs in a non-production environment.

These labs are designed to be used in a controlled lab environment. Please *do not* attempt to perform these labs in a production environment.

Lab Section 16.1: Secondary LSP::Paths

RSVP-TE supports the use of secondary LSP::Paths. This section investigates the use of secondary LSP::Paths on the Alcatel-Lucent 7750 SR that are not declared with the `standby` parameter.

Objective In this exercise, you will configure a topology of six Alcatel-Lucent 7750 SRs with primary and secondary LSP::Paths (see Figure 16.41).

Figure 16.41 Lab topology for RSVP-TE resiliency lab.

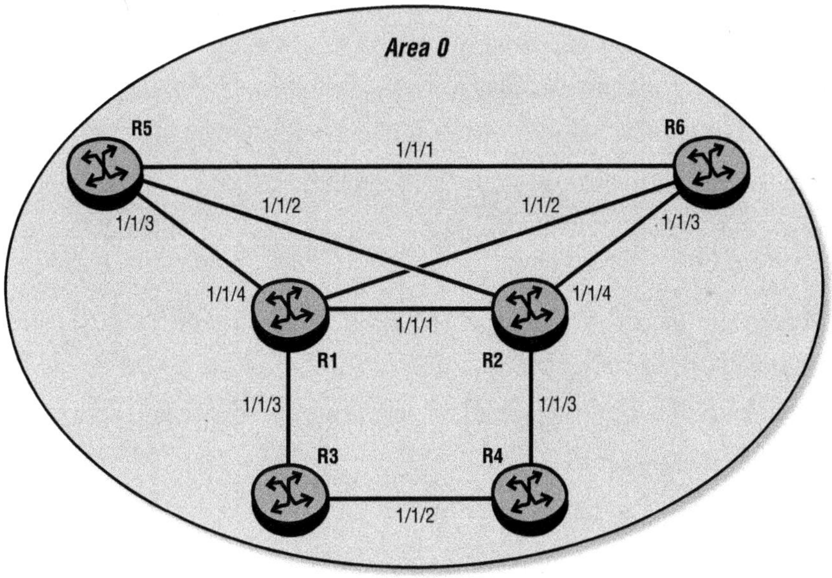

Validation You will know you have succeeded if the secondary LSP::Paths are established to protect the primary LSP::Path at the correct times.

1. Make sure that your IGP is configured as shown in Figure 16.41. All system and link interfaces should be advertised into the IGP, and traffic engineering should be enabled. This lab uses OSPF for the IGP, but you can use IS-IS if you prefer. Also make sure that all RSVP-TE interfaces are functional.

2. Configure a CSPF-enabled LSP from R5 to R6 named `toR6`. Use a totally loose primary path and a totally loose secondary path.
   a. What path does the primary LSP take?
   b. What path does the secondary LSP take? Explain.
   c. What are the Tunnel ID and LSP ID of the primary and secondary LSP::Paths?
   d. Shut down R6's port to R5.
   e. What paths do the primary LSP and secondary LSP take immediately after the port is shut down? Which path is active? Explain.
   f. What paths do the primary LSP and secondary LSP take 1 minute after the port is shut down? Which path is active? Explain.
   g. How can the failover time be characterized for the switchover from the primary LSP::Path to the secondary LSP::Path? What about from the secondary LSP::Path to the primary LSP::Path?
   h. Enable the port on R6 and wait for IGP convergence.
   i. What is the path of the primary LSP? Explain.
3. Constrain the primary LSP::Path with an `include` admin group on R5's interface to R6.
   a. Verify that the path of the primary LSP is directly from R5 to R6 before proceeding.
   b. What path does the secondary LSP take? Which LSP::Path is active? Explain.
   c. Shut down R6's port to R5.
   d. What paths do the primary LSP and secondary LSP take immediately after the port is shut down? Which LSP::Path is active? Explain.
   e. What paths do the primary LSP and secondary LSP take 1 minute after the port is shut down? Which LSP::Path is active? Explain.
   f. What are the Tunnel ID and LSP ID of the primary and secondary LSP::Paths?
   g. Enable R5's port to R6 and wait for IGP convergence.
   h. What paths do the primary LSP and secondary LSP take? Which LSP::Path is active? Explain.

Lab Section 16.2: Standby Secondary LSP::Paths

This section investigates standby secondary LSP::Paths on the 7750 SR.

Objective To observe the behavior of secondary LSP::Paths declared with the `standby` parameter.

Validation You will know you have succeeded if the standby LSP::Paths behave as expected.

1. Declare the secondary LSP::Path used in the previous section as `standby`. Don't modify the primary LSP::Path.
   - **a.** What path does the secondary LSP take? Which LSP::Path is active? Explain.
   - **b.** What are the Tunnel ID and LSP ID of the primary and secondary LSP::Paths? Explain.
   - **c.** Shut down R6's port to R5.
   - **d.** What paths do the primary and secondary LSPs take immediately after the port is shut down?
   - **e.** Wait for at least 1 minute, and then determine which paths the primary and secondary LSPs take. Which LSP::Path is active? Explain.
   - **f.** Is the secondary LSP::Path design in this example practical? If not, explain how it can be improved.
   - **g.** Enable R6's port to R5 before continuing.
2. Configure an SRLG called `green` with a value of 10, and bind it to R5's interface to R6.
   - **a.** How does the IGP propagate the SRLG information to the other routers?
   - **b.** Configure both sides of the R2–R5 link with an IGP cost of 110.
   - **c.** Configure the secondary LSP::Path to take SRLGs into consideration.
   - **d.** What path does the secondary LSP take? Explain.
   - **e.** Resignal the primary LSP::Path. What path does the secondary LSP take? Explain.
   - **f.** Resignal the secondary LSP::Path. What path does the secondary LSP use now? Explain.
   - **g.** Does the same `green` SRLG need to be bound to R6's interface to R5?

h. Configure the same `green` SRLG on R5's port to R1. Do you have to resignal the primary and secondary LSP::Paths? Explain. What path does the secondary LSP take? Explain.

i. What path does the secondary LSP take? Explain.

3. Configure another standby secondary LSP with a strict path of R5–R1–R6 with a preference of 50.

   a. How do the CSPF metric and path preference of the two secondary LSP::Paths compare to each other?

   b. Configure a totally loose non-standby secondary LSP::Path.

   c. What are the Tunnel IDs and LSP IDs of all the LSP::Paths?

   d. Shut down R6's port to R5. Which LSP::Path is active? Explain.

   e. Shut down R6's port to R1. Which LSP::Path is active? Explain.

   f. Shut down R6's port to R2. Which LSP::Path is active? Explain.

   g. Enable R6's port to R2. Which path is active?

   h. Enable R6's port to R1. Which path is active?

   i. Enable R6's port to R5, and make sure that the primary LSP::Path is established. In addition, remove all the secondary LSP::Paths before proceeding.

Lab Section 16.3: One-to-One Fast Reroute

The previous lab sections investigated using the head end switching mechanism of secondary LSP::Paths. This section investigates the local repair mechanism used in the one-to-one fast reroute mode.

Objective In this lab you will configure one-to-one FRR.

Validation You will know you have succeeded if you see the correct protection types at each hop of a protected LSP.

1. Change the primary path of the LSP `toR6` to use a strict path of R5–R1–R2–R6.

   a. Verify that the primary LSP::Path is operationally up before proceeding.

   b. Enable one-to-one FRR on the LSP.

   c. Which PLRs offer node protection? Which PLRs offer link protection?

d. How many detour LSPs are established? Describe the path of each detour LSP. Which routers are detour merge points?

e. How do the Tunnel ID and LSP ID of the detour LSPs relate to the protected LSP?

f. Change the metric of R5's interface to R6 to 2000. Does this have an effect on the detour LSPs? Does the LSP have to be resignaled?

g. Change the metric of R5's interface back to the default value, and resignal the LSP to get the detour LSPs back to their previous state.

h. Configure the LSP so that PLRs take SRLG into account when computing the detour LSPs. Resignal the LSP for the changes to take effect.

i. How has the change influenced the detour LSPs? Explain.

j. Remove the FRR SRLG configuration on all the routers, and resignal the LSP before proceeding.

2. Configure another one-to-one FRR protected LSP named `toR6-2` with a primary path of R5–R2–R6 using strict hops.

   a. Describe the detour LSPs used to protect this LSP. Are any detour LSPs shared between the two protected LSPs `toR6` and `toR6-2`? Explain.

   b. Shut down R1's port to R2.

   c. Describe the path that traffic carried on the LSP `toR6` will take. Which router is the PLR?

   d. Is the head end aware that local protection is in use?

   e. Enable R1's port to R2, and wait for IGP convergence.

   f. Is FRR protection still in use?

Lab Section 16.4: Facility Fast Reroute

This section investigates the use of the facility fast reroute method and compares it to the one-to-one FRR method. It also investigates the use of secondary LSP::Paths in conjunction with FRR to optimize traffic paths.

Objective In this lab you will configure facility backup FRR with secondary LSP::Paths.

Validation You will know you have succeeded if bypass tunnels are created in the expected way and if the secondary LSP::Paths are activated at the correct times.

1. Shut down LSP `toR6-2`, and change the FRR protection mode on the LSP `toR6` to facility backup.
   a. Which routers offer node protection? Which offer link protection?
   b. Describe the bypass tunnels created to protect this LSP. How are the bypass tunnels different from the detour LSPs used for the one-to-one method?
   c. What are the Tunnel IDs and LSP IDs of the bypass tunnels? How do they relate to the protection LSP?
2. Change the FRR protection mode to facility, and enable the LSP `toR6-2`.
   a. Describe the bypass tunnels used to protect this LSP. Are any of them shared with the other protected LSP? Explain.
3. Shut down R6's port to R2.
   a. Describe the path that traffic carried on the LSP `toR6` will take. Which router is the PLR?
   b. Describe the path that traffic carried on the LSP `toR6-2` will take. Which router is the PLR?
   c. What is the problem with this traffic pattern if the failure condition persists for a significant duration?
   d. Enable R6's port to R2, and wait for IGP convergence before proceeding.
4. Configure the LSP `toR6` with a non-standby totally loose path secondary LSP.
   a. Shut down R6's port to R2.
   b. Describe the path that traffic carried on the LSP `toR6` will take.
   c. Describe the path that traffic carried on the LSP `toR6-2` will take. Which router is the PLR?
   d. Why wasn't the secondary LSP::Path declared `standby`?
   e. Bring up R6's port to R2, and describe the paths of both LSPs.

Chapter Review

Now that you have completed this chapter, you should be able to:

- Explain the use of secondary LSP::Paths and the advantages and disadvantages to declaring them as standby.
- Describe the role of admin groups and SRLG in maintaining path diversity between secondary LSP::Paths and primary LSP::Paths.
- Describe the secondary LSP::Path selection criteria.
- Explain why fast reroute offers very fast failover times that are not bound by network size.
- Contrast the one-to-one backup method with the facility backup method.
- Configure FRR for one-to-one backup and verify the detour tunnels.
- Configure FRR for facility backup and verify the bypass tunnels.
- Describe global revertive mode as it pertains to fast reroute.
- Describe the use of SRLG in conjunction with fast reroute.
- Describe the use of secondary LSP::Paths in conjunction with fast reroute.

Post-Assessment

1. An operator configures an Alcatel-Lucent 7750 SR with a primary LSP::Path and a non-standby secondary LSP::Path. The operator mistakenly configures a strict hop in the secondary LSP::Path that does not exist. If the primary LSP::Path is operationally up and FRR is not configured, which statement below is false?

   A. The primary LSP::Path will be active.

   B. The secondary LSP::Path will be operationally down.

   C. The secondary LSP::Path will have a failure code of `noCspfRouteToDestination`.

   D. The secondary LSP::Path will not have any computed hops.

   E. All of the above statements are true.

2. An LSP is configured with a totally loose primary LSP::Path and a totally loose standby secondary LSP::Path. If there are at least two unequal cost totally disjoint paths between the head and tail end routers, which statement below is incorrect?

   A. The LSP::Paths should be made disjoint by the use of strict hops, admin groups, or SRLGs.

   B. The secondary LSP::Path is operationally up.

   C. The secondary LSP::Path will take the second least cost path between the head and tail end routers.

   D. If there is a link failure on the primary LSP::Path, there will be a traffic outage at least as long as the LSP retry interval.

   E. All of the above statements are correct.

3. A 7750 SR is configured with three totally loose secondary LSP::Paths in the following order. The first secondary LSP::Path is non-standby, has no constraints, and has no configured path preference. The second secondary LSP::Path is declared standby, has admin group constraints to achieve path diversity, and has a path preference of 50. The third secondary LSP::Path is declared standby, uses SRLG to achieve path diversity, has no configured path preference, and has a lower CSPF metric than the second secondary LSP::Path. Which secondary LSP::Path will become active if the primary LSP::Path fails? Assume that the failure does not affect the standby LSP::Paths.

   A. The first secondary LSP::Path will become active.

   B. The second secondary LSP::Path will become active.

   C. The third secondary LSP::Path will become active.

   D. None of the secondary LSP::Paths will become active.

4. Consider a router that could be a PLR for two established protected LSPs that have the same tail end router. Which statement best describes the detour LSPs originated by the PLR?

   A. The PLR originates one detour LSP that follows the shortest CSPF path to the destination.

   B. If both protected LSPs have identical paths, the PLR originates one detour LSP; otherwise, two detour LSPs are originated.

   C. If both protected LSPs have the same head end router, the PLR originates one detour LSP; otherwise, two detour LSPs are originated.

   D. The PLR originates two detour LSPs that follow the shortest CSPF path to the destination.

   E. None of the above statements are correct.

5. Consider an LSP protected with facility backup and a primary LSP::Path constrained with strict hops. The LSP also has a totally loose non-standby secondary. Assuming that the primary LSP::Path is operationally up and fully protected, which of the following statements is incorrect?

   A. After a link failure on the primary LSP::Path, the PLR will switch traffic to the bypass tunnel.

   B. After the head end node learns that local protection is in use, it signals the secondary LSP::Path and makes it active.

   C. FRR protection is attempted by every router on the secondary LSP::Path after it becomes active.

   D. The bypass tunnel remains up even if the secondary LSP::Path is active.

   E. All of the above statements are true.

6. An LSP is provisioned with a totally loose primary LSP::Path and a non-standby totally loose secondary LSP::Path. Assuming that there are multiple disjoint paths between the head and tail end routers, which statement is true?

   A. Admin groups should be used to ensure path diversity.

   B. Shared risk link groups should be used to ensure path diversity.

   C. The primary LSP::Path and secondary LSP::Paths will use the same hops.

   D. The primary LSP::Path will use the path with the shortest CSPF cost, and the secondary LSP::Path will use the path with the next shortest CSPF cost.

   E. All of the above statements are incorrect because the secondary is not signaled.

7. A CSPF LSP is configured with a totally loose primary LSP::Path and a non-standby totally loose secondary LSP::Path. The primary LSP::Path is operationally up. There are at least two unequal cost and disjoint paths in the network between the head and tail end routers. If there is a failure on the link of the tail end router that is on the primary LSP::Path, which statement below is false?

   A. After the head end detects the failure, it will immediately signal the secondary LSP::Path over the least cost path available.

   B. After the retry interval expires, the primary LSP::Path will be signaled over the least cost path available, and the secondary LSP::Path will be torn down.

   C. After the link is repaired, the primary LSP::Path will not be resignaled to use the least cost path available.

   D. There will be a traffic outage that is at least as long as the retry interval when the link goes down.

   E. None of the above statements are false.

8. A 7750 SR is configured with an LSP that has a primary LSP::Path constrained with strict hops and a totally loose standby secondary LSP::Path with the `srlg` parameter. The operator mistakenly configures *all* interfaces on the tail end router with the same SRLG instead of just the interface used for the primary LSP::Path. Assuming that there are at least two disjoint paths in the network between the head and tail end routers and the LSP::Paths are configured after SRLG groups have been bound to the interfaces, which statement below is correct?

   A. The primary LSP::Path and the secondary LSP::Path will be operationally up with identical actual hops.

   B. The secondary LSP::Path will be down with the failure code `noCspfRouteToDestination`.

   C. The secondary LSP::Path will be operationally up with no links shared with the primary LSP::Path.

   D. The secondary LSP::Path will be down with the failure code `srlgError`.

   E. None of the above statements are correct.

9. An Alcatel-Lucent 7750 SR is configured with the command `configure router mpls srlg-group blue value 3`. Assuming that traffic engineering is enabled on the IGP, how is this SRLG group information advertised through the network immediately after the command is executed?

   A. The SRLG group name `blue` is transmitted in the TE LSA originated by the router.

   B. The decimal value of 3 is transmitted in the TE LSA originated by the router to represent the SRLG.

   C. The decimal value of 4 is transmitted in the TE LSA originated by the router to represent the SRLG.

   D. The decimal value of 8 is transmitted in the TE LSA originated by the router to represent the SRLG.

   E. The SRLG group is not propagated through the network.

10. An LSP is configured for fast reroute with default settings in a network of 7750 SRs with enough redundant paths to fully protect the LSP. Which of the following best describes the expected behavior?

   A. All hops will show link protection.

   B. All hops will show node protection.

   C. The last hop will show link protection, and all other hops will show node protection.

   D. None of the hops will be protected.

11. Consider an Alcatel-Lucent 7750 SR network that is provisioned with the MPLS one-to-one FRR method with default FRR settings. Which statement below is incorrect regarding the signaling of protection LSPs?

   A. The Path messages of the protected LSP will include the `FAST_REROUTE` object with the `flags` field set to `0x01`.

   B. The router that is directly connected to the tail end will attempt to signal a link protection LSP.

   C. A constraint of every protection LSP is to merge back to the primary LSP::Path as soon as possible.

   D. All protection LSPs will have a `DETOUR` object in their Path messages.

   E. All of the above statements are correct.

12. Consider a network of 7750 SRs in which all primary LSP::Paths are provisioned to use one-to-one FRR. A router transiting a detour LSP receives a Path message to establish a new detour LSP with the same destination and out interface. The Tunnel ID and LSP ID of the second detour LSP are not the same as those of the first. What action does the router take?

A. The router transits two separate detour LSPs that have the same out interface but different out labels.

B. The router merges the detour LSP if detour merge capability is configured on the head end router.

C. The router checks the avoid node statements in the DETOUR object of the path messages. If they match, the LSPs are merged and the router transits one detour LSP.

D. The router merges the two detour LSPs and transits one detour LSP.

E. None of the above statements are correct.

13. Consider a router that can be a PLR for three LSPs protected with facility backup. All three protected LSPs traverse the same egress port on the PLR. The tail end router of one of the protected LSPs is directly connected to the PLR. The other two protected LSPs have identical paths to the same tail end router, which is not directly connected to the PLR. Assuming that default facility mode configurations are used and there are enough paths in the network to provide the requested FRR protection, which statement is correct regarding the bypass tunnels originated by the PLR?

A. The PLR originates three link protection bypass tunnels.

B. The PLR originates three node protection bypass tunnels.

C. The PLR originates one link-protect bypass tunnel and one node-protect bypass tunnel.

D. The PLR originates one link-protect bypass tunnel and two node-protect bypass tunnels.

E. There is not enough information to answer the question.

14. Which statement regarding SRLG for FRR is correct on a 7750 SR?

A. If SRLGs are configured with default settings, a 7750 SR may establish protection LSPs that share links with the primary LSP::Path.

B. SRLGs can be used to influence bypass tunnels but not detour LSPs.

C. SRLG can be enabled on specific LSPs.

D. For the purposes of FRR, SRLG is only enabled on the head end router.

E. None of the above statements are true.

15. Which of the following mechanisms cannot be used to ensure LSP::Path diversity?

A. Strict hops

B. SRLGs

C. Admin groups

D. Any of the above mechanisms can be used to ensure LSP::Path diversity.

III

VPN Services

17 Introduction and Overview of VPN Services

The Alcatel-Lucent NRS II exam topics covered in this chapter include the following:

- Rationale for VPN Services
- Comparison of service router to traditional IP router
- Service types—VPWS, VPLS, VPRN, IES
- GRE tunnels
- Transport and service label encapsulation
- T-LDP and service label signaling
- Service configuration model on the Alcatel-Lucent 7750 SR
- Subscribers, customers, and service identifiers
- Service Access Point (SAP)
- Configuring a local service
- Infrastructure for distributed services
- Service Distribution Point (SDP)
- Configuring a distributed service

This chapter introduces the IP/MPLS service architecture for the Alcatel-Lucent 7750 SR. It introduces the different service types available and the components required to support these services. The encapsulation of service data with a service label and transport label is described. The concept and use of a Service Access Point (SAP) are explained, as well as the concept and use of the Service Distribution Point (SDP). The configuration and verification of an epipe service are shown as an example.

Pre-Assessment

The following assessment questions will help you understand what areas of the chapter you should review in more detail to prepare for the NRS II exam. You can also use the CD that accompanies this book to take all the assessment tests and review the answers.

1. An epipe service is to be deployed in a network. Which routers may need to be configured with the epipe service?

   A. PE routers

   B. CE routers

   C. P routers

   D. Core routers

   E. PE routers and P routers

2. Which statement best characterizes a Virtual Private LAN Service (VPLS) from a customer's point of view?

   A. The service provider network appears as a leased line between customer locations.

   B. The service provider network appears as a single MPLS switch between customer locations.

   C. The service provider network appears as a single IP router between customer locations.

   D. The service provider network appears as a Layer 2 switch between customer locations.

   E. None of the above statements are correct.

3. Consider a network of Alcatel-Lucent 7750 SRs that contains four PE routers, six CE routers, and eight P routers. Assuming that the network is only used to provide VPRN services, which routers need to be configured with SAPs?

A. All CE routers

B. All PE routers

C. All P routers

D. All P and CE routers

E. All PE, CE, and P routers

4. Which of the following best describes the encapsulation of the service payload on an IP/MPLS service network with Ethernet links?

A. The service payload is encapsulated in an Ethernet frame.

B. The service payload is encapsulated in an Ethernet frame with a service label.

C. The service payload is encapsulated in an Ethernet frame with a transport label and a service label.

D. The service payload is encapsulated in an Ethernet frame with an IP header and a service label.

5. Which of the following best describes the signaling of service labels for an epipe?

A. Service labels are signaled when the SDP is created at both ends.

B. Service labels are signaled when the service is created and made administratively up at one end.

C. Service labels are signaled when the service is created and made administratively up at both ends.

D. Service labels are signaled when the SDP binding is created in the service at both ends.

E. Service labels are signaled when the SAP and the SDP binding are created in the service at both ends.

17.1 Introduction to Services

Different technologies have been developed over the years to support the variety of telecommunication services. There are time-division multiplexing (TDM) technologies for real-time voice, Frame Relay and ATM (Asynchronous Transfer Mode) for private network services with specific service levels, and IP for best-effort data services. Historically, telecommunication service providers have deployed completely separate networks to provide these distinct types of services.

Many factors are driving service providers to evolve to a single network infrastructure that supports the delivery of a wide variety of telecommunication services. These include:

- High costs of maintaining and operating discrete, legacy networks
- Service provider desire to continue to support high-revenue legacy services such as Frame Relay and TDM
- Consumer demand for new services such as wireless data and streaming video
- Competitive market creating consumer expectations of higher-bandwidth service at decreasing prices

One approach to building a common infrastructure for deploying a wide range of telecommunication services uses a core IP/MPLS network that supports a range of Virtual Private Network (VPN) services. The Alcatel-Lucent 7750 SR product family was specifically designed for this purpose.

A VPN to the customer is a *private* network. Only their equipment is attached to the network, and their data is not visible or accessible to any other customer. Furthermore, the configuration of their equipment [IP address plan, VLAN (Virtual Local Area Network) assignment, etc.] is not constrained by any other customer's configuration. To the customer, the service provider network appears as its own private network.

A VPN to the service provider is a *virtual* network. They are able to support many instances of private networks for many different customers on one physical infrastructure. The VPN technology supports the provisioning and management of these distinct, private networks and ensures that they are kept separate.

Rationale for VPN Services

The goal for a VPN service network is to deploy a core network that can support a wide variety of telecommunication services in a cost-effective manner. IP/MPLS is ideal for this purpose for several reasons:

- A single core network can be deployed to provide a wide range of services. Capital expenditures and maintenance costs are reduced by having only one network to build and maintain.
- IP has become a universal technology with mature routing and management capabilities.
- Ethernet, IP, and MPLS are non-proprietary, simple, and inexpensive technologies that are widely available and widely deployed.
- MPLS provides a tunneling capability over IP that can support a wide variety of VPN services.
- A single core network with well-defined service access points enables advanced accounting, billing, and service management features.

This chapter provides an introduction to the VPN services that can be offered over an IP/MPLS network built on the 7750 SR.

Comparison of the Service Router to the Traditional IP Router

A *service router* is a scalable IP router that not only offers best-effort IP routing, but also supports many other data services using a service-oriented architecture. Besides supporting a wide variety of network interfaces, a service router such as the 7750 SR must support additional functionality:

- **Quality of service (QoS)**—The ability to provide distinct levels of service depending on the customer, application, or service-level agreement
- **Accounting**—The ability to measure the traffic and service delivered based on a specific customer or service and perform logging and billing accordingly
- **Filtering**—The ability to restrict or monitor specific traffic, based on customer or service
- **Troubleshooting**—The ability to analyze and troubleshoot problems from the perspective of a specific service

These capabilities are supported to varying degrees in traditional IP routers, but generally they are oriented around the router's interfaces or physical ports. It can be difficult to apply these functions to a specific service instance because many services may use the same port.

In a full-function service router, this functionality is provided based on the services supported by the router. These functions are provided at the level of the individual service components, which often do not correspond directly to interfaces or ports.

There are many components involved in a service network, but the key component is the provider edge (PE) router, which provides the interface between the customer network and the core service provider network. All of the service-specific functions are found in the PE router. The service provider network is transparent to the customer devices, and the routers in the service provider core need only label-switch encapsulated traffic.

Figure 17.1 shows the position of the service router that functions as the PE router in a service network. Typical components found in a service network include:

Figure 17.1 Typical components of an IP/MPLS service network.

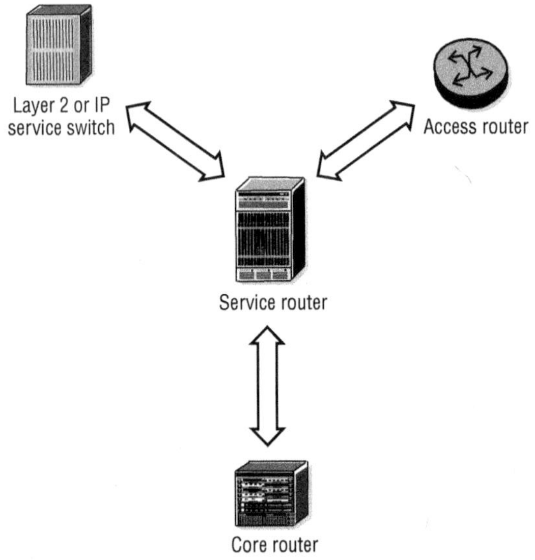

- **Access router**—This provides a simple and specific service such as best-effort IP routing. It may be used to aggregate several lower-speed connections.

- **Layer 2 or IP service switch**—This is a low-cost device with some basic service capabilities, including quality of service and possibly some method of separating different customers.
- **Service router**—This is a scalable, full-function IP/MPLS router that supports the full range of service types, many customers, and the additional service management capabilities described above.
- **Core router**—This is a router with high-speed interfaces capable of forwarding large quantities of data, but with very limited or no service-level knowledge. Quality of service may be applied to data on an aggregated basis.

17.2 Service Types

A variety of different service types are supported in a service network of 7750 SRs, based on a common core of IP/MPLS technology. The different possible VPN services are:

- **Virtual Private Wire Service (VPWS)**—Provides a point-to-point service similar to a leased line.
- **Virtual Private LAN Service (VPLS)**—Provides a multipoint Ethernet service similar to an Ethernet switch.
- **Virtual Private Routed Network service (VPRN)**—Provides a multipoint IP routed service.

Besides the VPN-based services, the 7750 SR supports the Internet Enhanced Service (IES). The IES is a routed IP interface service that includes the service, administration, and management capabilities described above.

Virtual Private Wire Service

The Virtual Private Wire Service (VPWS) is a Layer 2 point-to-point service, also known as a Virtual Leased Line (VLL) service. A VPWS is suitable for the customer who is looking for a simple point-to-point connection supporting Ethernet, Frame Relay, ATM (Asynchronous Transfer Mode), or TDM (time-division multiplexing) circuit emulation.

The VPWS encapsulates customer data and transports it across the service provider's network in a GRE (generic routing encapsulation) or MPLS tunnel. A VPWS is sometimes considered a Layer 1 VPN because it emulates a simple physical connection and there is no MAC (Media Access Control) learning involved.

In Figure 17.2, a service provider network provides an epipe (point-to-point Ethernet) service and an apipe (point-to-point ATM) service. Many different services can be deployed over a common core network.

Figure 17.2 Service provider network with epipe and apipe services.

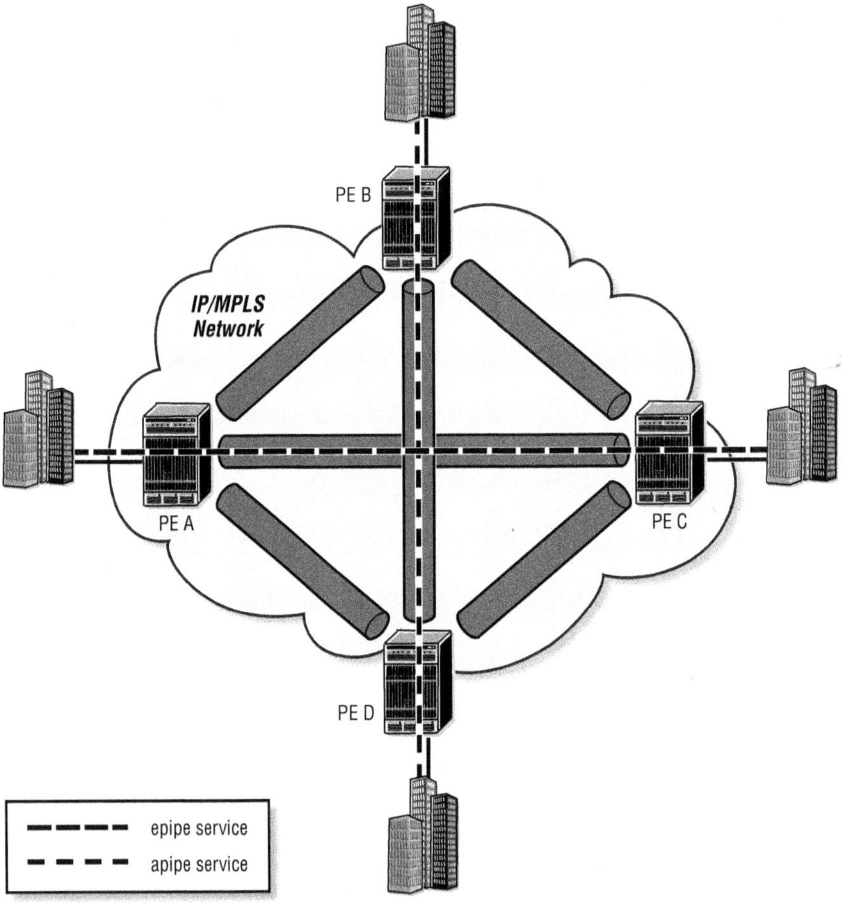

The advantages of a VPWS from the customer's perspective are as follows:

- The VPWS can support ATM, Frame Relay, TDM, or Ethernet.
- The service provider network appears as a leased line between the two customer locations.

- The VPWS is transparent to the customer's data or higher-layer protocols.

The advantages of a VPWS from the service provider's perspective are as follows:

- **Simple configuration**—Only the PE devices require configuration for the VPWS service.
- **Scalability**—The provider can support thousands of customers per node.
- **Flexibility**—Many different services for many different customers can be provided over a single core IP/MPLS network.
- **Service features**—The service provider can apply QoS, billing, ingress/egress traffic shaping, and policing on a per-service basis.

Virtual Private LAN Service

The Virtual Private LAN Service (VPLS) is an Ethernet service that connects multiple sites in a single switched domain over the provider-managed IP/MPLS network. A VPLS is suitable for the customer who is looking for a simple Ethernet service to connect more than two locations.

In Figure 17.3, the service provider has deployed two distinct VPLS services, VPLS 11 and VPLS 22, over the same infrastructure. VPWS services might also be deployed on this infrastructure.

The advantages of a VPLS from the customer's perspective are the following:

- To the customer, it appears as if all sites are connected to a single switched Ethernet network.
- The VPLS is transparent to the customer's data and higher-layer protocols.
- The VPLS can operate over a single, local site or at multiple, geographically dispersed sites.
- The VPLS performs MAC learning so that frames are forwarded only across the required links in the network.

The advantages to the service provider are the same advantages as for a VPWS service. The IP/MPLS infrastructure provides the ability to deploy and manage a wide variety of services in a cost-effective manner.

Figure 17.3 Two VPLS services provided on the same service provider infrastructure.

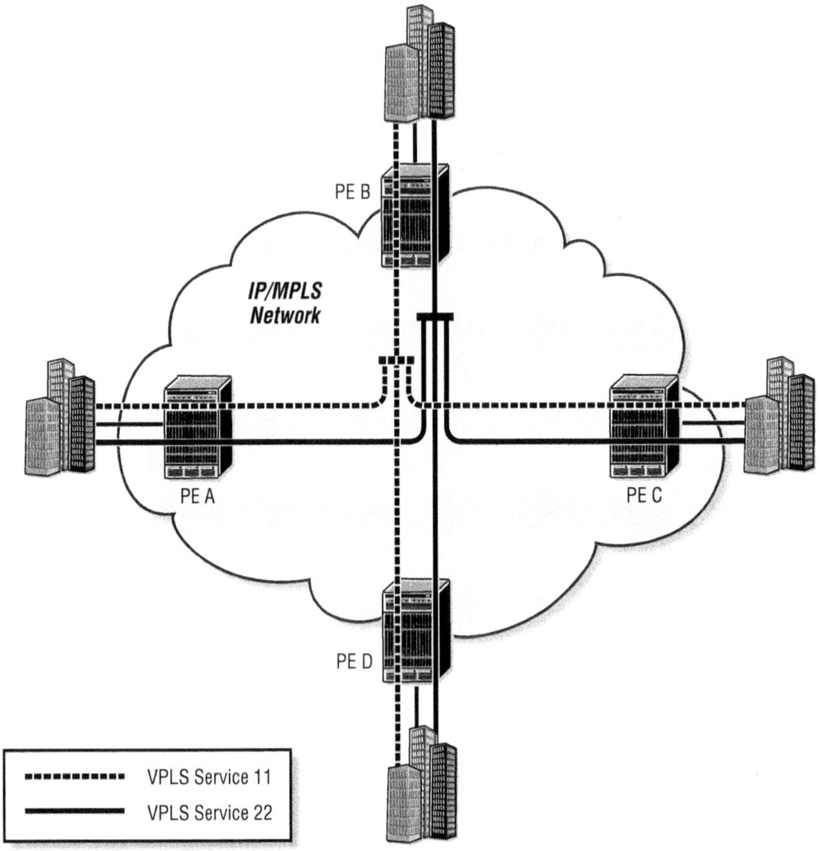

Virtual Private Routed Network

The Virtual Private Routed Network (VPRN) service is an IP (Layer 3) service that connects multiple sites in a single routed domain over the provider-managed IP/MPLS network. A VPRN is suitable for the customer who is looking for a routed IP service to connect multiple locations.

In Figure 17.4, the service provider has deployed two VPRN services, VPRN 1 and VPRN 2. VPWS and VPLS services might also be deployed on this infrastructure.

Figure 17.4 Two VPRN services deployed on the same service provider infrastructure.

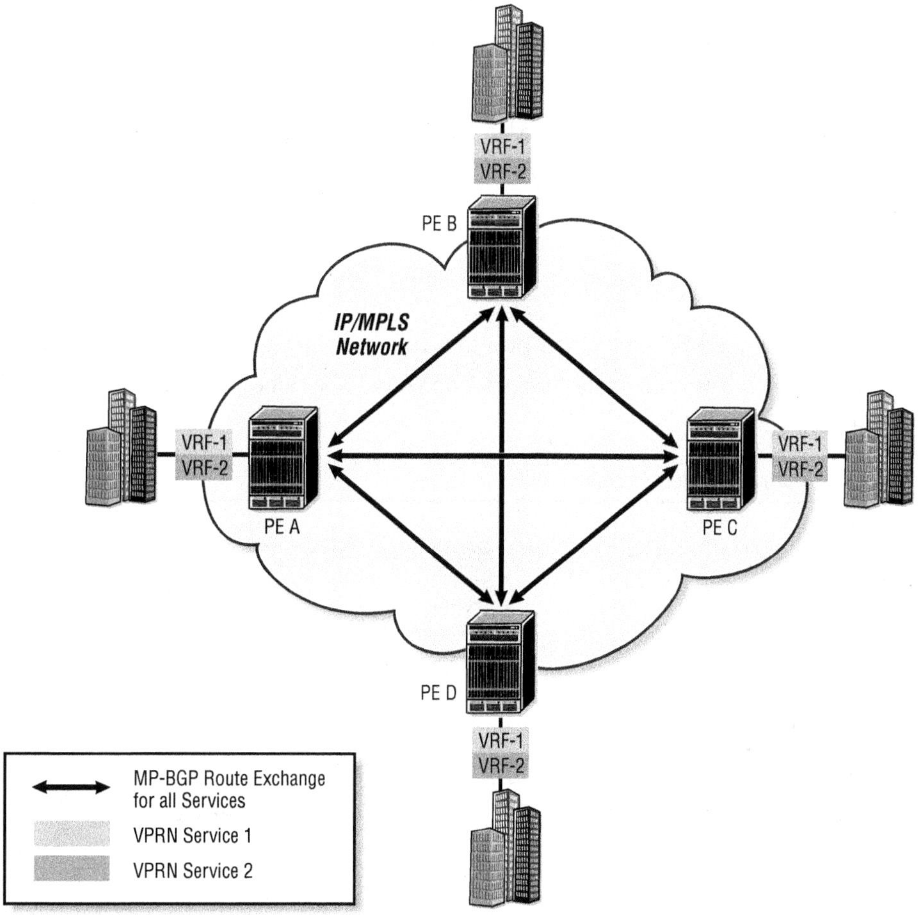

The advantages of a VPRN service from the customer's perspective are the following:

- To the customer, it appears as if all sites are connected to a private, routed IP network. The PE router maintains a separate, virtual router and route table for each VPRN.
- Because the VPRN service operates as a private network, the IP address plan used by the customer is completely separate and independent of any address plan used by the provider or any of its other customers.

- The VPRN service distributes the customer's routes across the service provider's network as if it were an IP router exchanging routes with the customer's routers.
- The VPRN can operate over a single, local site or at multiple, geographically dispersed sites.

The advantages to the service provider are the same as the advantages for a VPWS or VPLS service. The service provider uses MP-BGP (Multiprotocol Border Gateway Protocol) to distribute the routes for the different customer networks.

IES

An Internet Enhanced Service (IES) provides the customer with a Layer 3 IP interface to send and receive Internet traffic. Figure 17.5 shows a service provider network with multiple IES instances.

Figure 17.5 IES provides Internet connectivity.

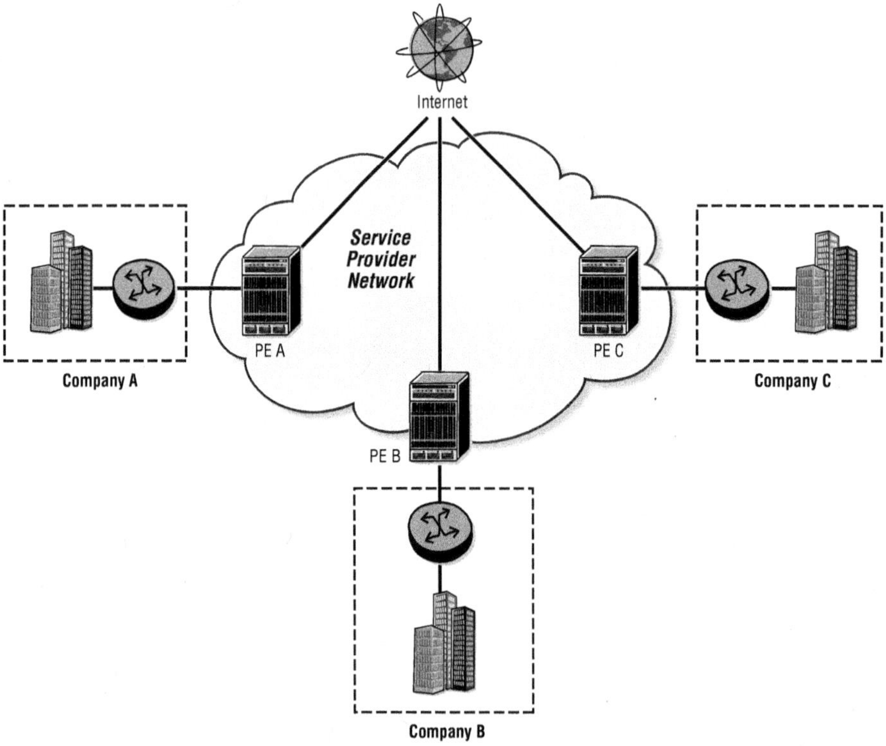

IES provides direct Internet access to a customer. The routing protocols supported by the 7750 SR, including BGP, can be used by the customer on the IES interface. The difference between the IES and a basic network interface is that the service provider can apply all QoS, billing, ingress/egress shaping, and policing available within a service to the IES interface.

17.3 MPLS Transport and Service Label Signaling

All of the IP/MPLS VPN services described above use MPLS or GRE tunnels to transmit customer data across the service provider network. When MPLS is used, customer data is encapsulated with two MPLS labels—an outer transport label and an inner service label. Another way to view this is as a service tunnel carried within a transport tunnel (see Figure 17.6). Multiple service tunnels can be carried within a transport tunnel, and multiple transport tunnels can be configured on a single network port.

Figure 17.6 The inner service label defines the service tunnel; the outer transport label defines the transport tunnel.

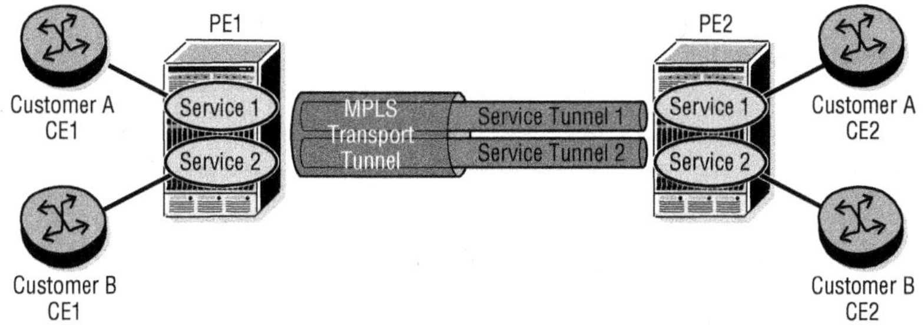

Typically the transport tunnel is a RSVP-TE (Resource Reservation Protocol–Traffic Engineering or LDP (Label Distribution Protocol) signaled LSP, although it may also be a GRE tunnel as described in the next section. Labels for the transport tunnel are signaled using RSVP-TE or LDP, as described in the previous chapters on MPLS.

Because the customer data is MPLS-encapsulated, forwarding across the network is not based at all on the customer data. The encapsulated data is simply forwarded to the tunnel egress, which is the egress PE for the service.

GRE Tunnels

Generic routing encapsulation (GRE) is a method other than MPLS for encapsulating data for the transport tunnel. Instead of an MPLS label signaled by RSVP-TE or LDP

LSP, the data is encapsulated with an IP header. The source IP address is the ingress PE router, and the destination address is the egress PE router. This header is used to route the packet across the network—the customer's data has no influence on forwarding while the packet is in the GRE tunnel. GRE is typically used when there are routers in the transport network that do not support MPLS label switching. Our focus in this book is on the use of MPLS for transport tunnels.

Transport and Service Label Encapsulation

In an IP/MPLS service network, data is encapsulated with at least two labels—the transport label and the service label. (There are some special situations in which additional labels may be used.) Figure 17.7 shows the encapsulation of data for a VPN service.

Figure 17.7 MPLS and GRE encapsulation of VPN service traffic.

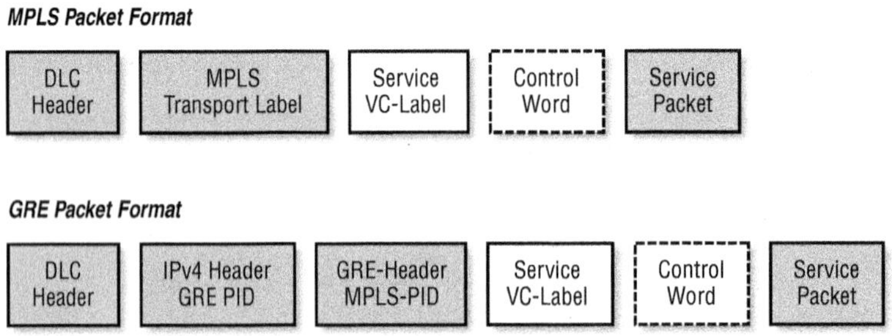

The fields in the MPLS packet are the following:

- **DLC header**—This is the Layer 2 header used to transport the MPLS packet. The 7750 SR supports Ethernet and Packet over SONET/SDH (POS) on its network interfaces, thus the DLC header will be one of these two.
- **MPLS transport label**—This is the label signaled by the next-hop PE that represents the RSVP-TE or LDP transport tunnel.
- **Service VC label**—The service, or virtual circuit (VC), label identifies the service to which the packet belongs. The egress PE uses this label to de-multiplex the packet to the appropriate service.
- **Control word**—The control word is optional and is primarily used for ATM or Frame Relay services. It is usually not present.
- **Service packet**—This is the customer data being transported by the service. For a VPWS or VPLS service, this is a Layer 2 frame. For a VPRN service, this is an IP datagram.

If GRE is used for the transport encapsulation, the fields are similar to MPLS. A service label is still required to de-multiplex the packet to the appropriate service. However, an additional IP header and the GRE header are used instead of the MPLS transport label. The service provider routers use the GRE IPv4 header to route the packet across the network.

T-LDP and Service Label Signaling

In the previous chapters on MPLS, we have seen how the transport labels are signaled using either RSVP-TE or LDP. These labels define the transport tunnel from ingress PE to egress PE that is used to transport customer data. However, one transport tunnel can be used to carry data for many different services. A second label, the service label, is used to identify to which service a specific packet belongs.

RFC 4447, "Pseudowire Setup and Maintenance Using the Label Distribution Protocol (LDP)," describes how service labels are signaled using Targeted LDP (T-LDP). T-LDP is the same protocol as Link LDP, used for signaling transport labels which we studied in Chapter 12, with a few additional capabilities added. VPWS and VPLS (Layer 2 services) both use T-LDP to signal the service labels.

In a VPRN service (Layer 3), MP-BGP is used to exchange customer routes across the VPRN. The BGP updates also include a label for these routes. We examine this in more detail in Chapter 20.

Figure 17.8 shows the signaling of transport and service labels. Although MPLS tunnels are used to carry the data, the IGP is still required to help establish the transport LSPs and to allow the T-LDP peers to communicate with each other.

Figure 17.8 Signaling of transport and service labels using IGP.

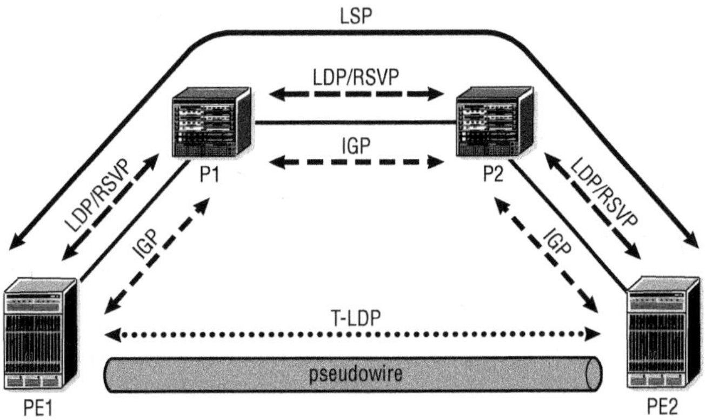

Once we have signaled service labels with T-LDP and created a transport tunnel between the two PE endpoints, we have created a *pseudowire* as defined in RFC 4447. A pseudowire is an emulated, Layer 2 circuit built across an MPLS network that can transport Layer 2 PDUs (protocol data units) as if they were transmitted on their native media. Epipes (Ethernet), apipes (ATM), fpipes (Frame Relay), ipipes (IP Interworking), and cpipes (TDM circuit emulation) are all examples of pseudowire technologies and are described in more detail in Chapter 18.

The difference between link LDP and T-LDP is that T-LDP is used for exchanging service label information and the T-LDP peers do not need to be directly connected. Because they may not be directly connected, a router must know the IP address of its T-LDP peer. It then sends its Hello messages to its peer's unicast address instead of the multicast address. Otherwise, the process for establishing adjacencies and the messages exchanged are the same as for Link LDP (see Figure 17.9).

Figure 17.9 Message exchange between two T-LDP peers.

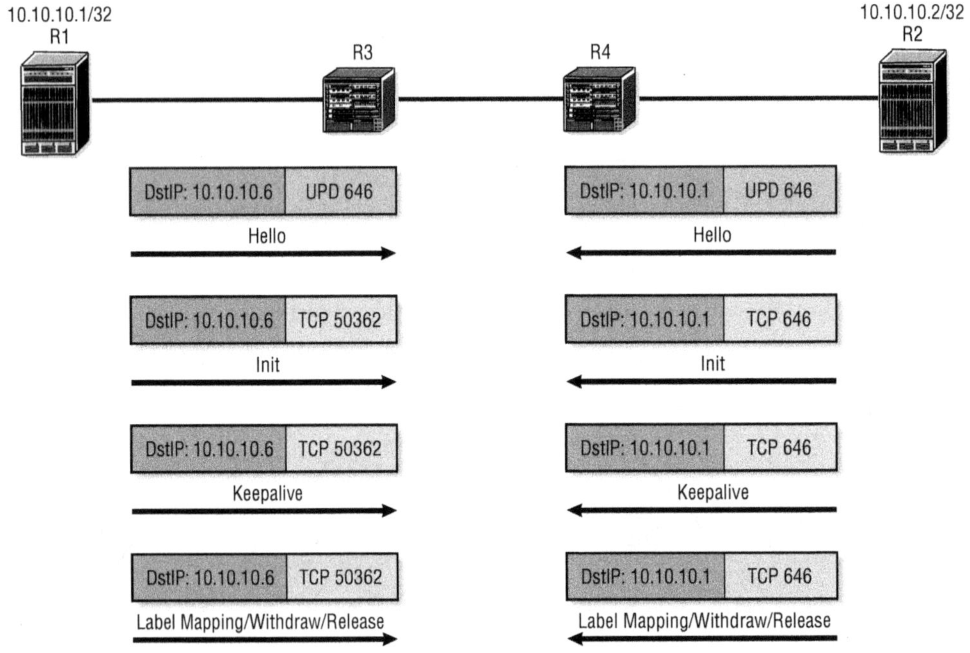

LDP must be enabled to configure VPWS or VPLS services so that T-LDP can signal the service labels, even if RSVP-TE is used for signaling the transport labels. On the 7750 SR, LDP is enabled simply by going to the `configure router ldp` context (see Listing 17.1).

Listing 17.1 Enabling LDP on the 7750 SR

```
*A:R1# show router ldp status
MINOR: CLI LDP is not configured.
*A:R1# configure router ldp
*A:R1>config>router>ldp$ show router ldp status

===============================================================================
LDP Status for LSR ID 10.10.10.1
===============================================================================
Admin State         : Up                    Oper State          : Up
Created at          : 03/19/2011 13:45:49  Up Time             :
 0d 00:00:06
Oper Down Reason    : n/a                   Oper Down Events    : 0
Last Change         : 03/19/2011 13:45:49  Tunn Down Damp Time  : 3 sec
Label Withdraw Del*: 0 sec                 Implicit Null Label :
 Disabled
Short. TTL Prop Lo*: Enabled               Short. TTL Prop Tran*:
 Enabled
Import Policies     : None                  Export Policies     : None
Aggregate Prefix    : False
Agg Prefix Policies: None
Active Adjacencies : 0                     Active Sessions     : 0
Active Interfaces   : 0                     Inactive Interfaces : 0
Active Peers        : 0                     Inactive Peers      : 0
Addr FECs Sent      : 0                     Addr FECs Recv      : 0
Serv FECs Sent      : 0                     Serv FECs Recv      : 0
Attempted Sessions : 0
No Hello Err        : 0                     Param Adv Err       : 0
Max PDU Err         : 0                     Label Range Err     : 0
Bad LDP Id Err      : 0                     Bad PDU Len Err     : 0
Bad Mesg Len Err    : 0                     Bad TLV Len Err     : 0
Unknown TLV Err     : 0
Malformed TLV Err   : 0                     Keepalive Expired Err: 0
Shutdown Notif Sent: 0                     Shutdown Notif Recv : 0
===============================================================================
* indicates that the corresponding row element may have been truncated.
*A:R1>config>router>ldp$ info
----------------------------------------------
            interface-parameters
```

(continued)

Listing 17.1 *(continued)*

```
            exit
            targeted-session
            exit
----------------------------------------------
*A:R1>config>router>ldp$
```

Notice that `targeted-session` is enabled automatically; this enables T-LDP. Interface parameters are required only if Link LDP is to be used for signaling transport labels. T-LDP can be disabled if desired.

T-LDP peers must be explicitly specified because they are not automatically discovered. On the 7750 SR the T-LDP peer is normally specified in the configuration of the far-end router in the SDP (Service Distribution Point). Configuration of the SDP is described below in this chapter. It is also possible to specify the T-LDP peer manually as shown in Listing 17.2. Notice that the Hello timer value and Hello time-out have been modified from the default in this example. An authentication parameter can also be specified for T-LDP sessions. When authentication is specified, LDP authenticates all TCP segments using the MD5 signature option originally defined for BGP in RFC 2385.

Listing 17.2 Manual creation of a T-LDP peer

```
*A:R1>config>router>ldp$ targeted-session
*A:R1>config>router>ldp>targ-session$ peer 10.10.10.2
*A:R1>config>router>ldp>targ-session>peer$ hello 60 5
*A:R1>config>router>ldp>targ-session>peer$ exit
*A:R1>config>router>ldp>targ-session# exit
*A:R1>config>router>ldp# info
----------------------------------------------
            interface-parameters
            exit
            targeted-session
                peer 10.10.10.2
                    hello 60 5
                exit
            exit
----------------------------------------------
```

```
*A:R1>config>router>ldp# show router ldp peer detail

===============================================================================
LDP Peers (Detail)
===============================================================================
-------------------------------------------------------------------------------
Peer 10.10.10.2
-------------------------------------------------------------------------------
Admin State       : Up           Oper State       : Up
Hold Time         : 60           Hello Factor     : 5
Keepalive Timeout : 40           Keepalive Factor : 4
Passive Mode      : Disabled     Last Modified    : 03/19/2011 13:54:41
Active Adjacencies: 0            Auto Created     : No
Tunneling         : Disabled
Lsp Name          : None
Local LSR         : None
BFD Status        : Disabled

===============================================================================
*A:R1>config>router>ldp# show router ldp bindings

===============================================================================
LDP LSR ID: 10.10.10.1
===============================================================================
Legend: U - Label In Use, N - Label Not In Use, W - Label Withdrawn
        S - Status Signaled Up,  D - Status Signaled Down
        E - Epipe Service, V - VPLS Service, M - Mirror Service
        A - Apipe Service, F - Fpipe Service, I - IES Service,
 R - VPRN service
        P - Ipipe Service, WP - Label Withdraw Pending,
 C - Cpipe Service
        TLV - (Type, Length: Value)
===============================================================================
LDP Prefix Bindings
===============================================================================
Prefix            Peer          IngLbl    EgrLbl EgrIntf/    EgrNextHop
                                                 LspId
-------------------------------------------------------------------------------
No Matching Entries Found

===============================================================================
```

(continued)

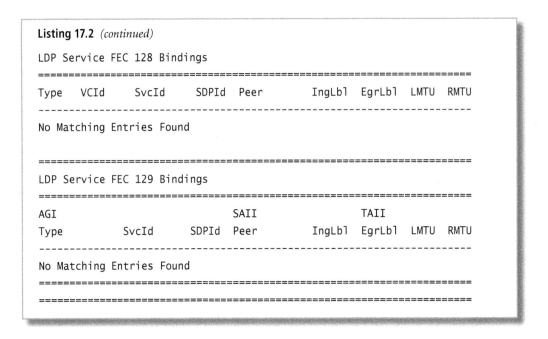

Listing 17.2 *(continued)*

```
LDP Service FEC 128 Bindings
===============================================================================
Type   VCId      SvcId     SDPId  Peer          IngLbl  EgrLbl  LMTU  RMTU
-------------------------------------------------------------------------------
No Matching Entries Found


===============================================================================
LDP Service FEC 129 Bindings
===============================================================================
AGI                               SAII                  TAII
Type            SvcId      SDPId  Peer          IngLbl  EgrLbl  LMTU  RMTU
-------------------------------------------------------------------------------
No Matching Entries Found
===============================================================================
===============================================================================
```

Although a T-LDP session is established with its peer, no service labels have been exchanged. The exchange of service labels occurs when the pseudowire is created. A VC ID (virtual circuit identifier) identifies the pseudowire, and each PE device uses T-LDP to signal the other the service label that it should use for the VC ID. The VC ID must be the same at each end. In Figure 17.10, PE-2 signals PE-1 to use label `11350`, and PE-1 signals PE-2 to use label `21350` for VC ID 50. After the successful exchange of service labels, a pseudowire has been created between the two PE routers.

Figure 17.10 Each PE signals a service label to the other.

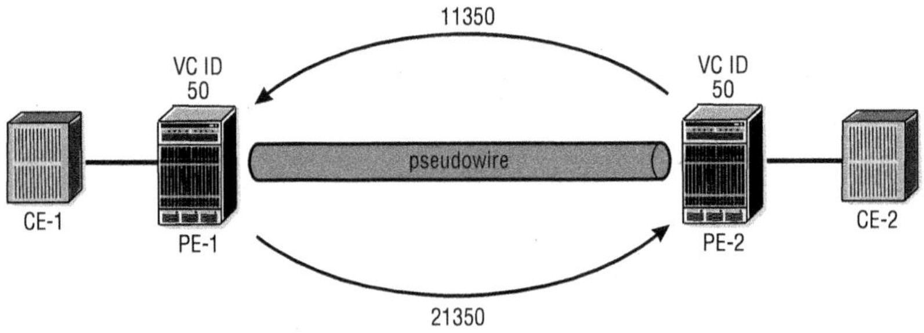

On the 7750 SR, a service is identified on a router by its service ID. Best practice is to use the service ID value for the pseudowire VC ID whenever possible. The pseudowire is created when the service is bound to an SDP at both ends. This process is described in more detail below in this chapter.

Figure 17.11 shows the steps required to enable a Layer 2 service. They are as follows:

Figure 17.11 **Signaling of transport and service labels for a Layer 2 service.**

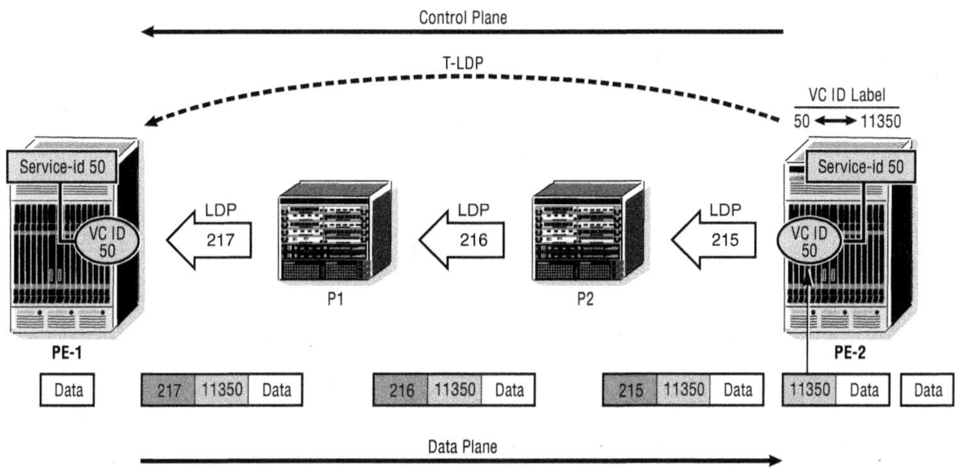

1. A transport tunnel is created. In this case, Link LDP is used to signal the labels `217`, `216`, and `215`, which define an MPLS tunnel from PE-1 to PE-2 (the two endpoints of the service).
2. A service label of `11350` is signaled by PE-2 to PE-1 using a T-LDP Label Mapping message. This label is associated with the service with a VC ID of 50.
3. Transport labels and a service label are signaled in the reverse direction, from PE-1 to PE-2.

The signaling of transport and service labels is a control plane operation.

The service is established when transport and service labels have been signaled in both directions. As seen in Figure 17.11, when router PE-1 receives customer data for transmission over the service, it encapsulates the data using the service label of `11350` and the transport label of `217`. The data is label-switched over the network to the egress, router PE-2. The transport label is popped, and the service label tells PE-2 that the data belongs to the service with VC ID 50. The service label is popped, and the data is transmitted on the correct interface for the service with service ID 50.

Note that the VC ID is associated with the service ID on the router, but the VC ID value is completely different from the value of the service label.

17.4 Service Configuration Model on the 7750

We have seen the basic mechanism of signaling transport and service labels used in the IP/MPLS service model and how data is encapsulated for transport across the service provider network. The 7750 SR uses some very specific terminology to describe and configure services. The major components are shown in Figure 17.12.

Figure 17.12 Service components on the 7750 SR.

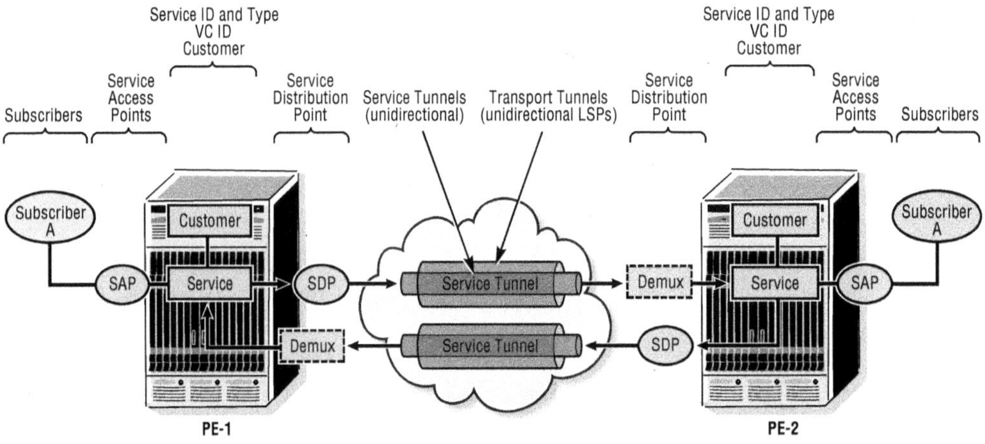

Service Components

The components from Figure 17.12 are the following:

- **Subscriber**—This describes the user of the service.
- **Service Access Point (SAP)**—This is the subscriber's point of interface to the service network.

- **Customer ID**—This is a value associated with the service that can be used to group together several services for reporting purposes.
- **Service ID**—This is the numeric value used on the 7750 SR to identify the service.
- **Service type**—There are several different service types that can be configured on the 7750 SR:
    - A VPWS service can be one of the following service types: `epipe`, `apipe`, `fpipe`, `ipipe`, or `cpipe`.
    - A `vpls` service
    - A `vprn` service
- **VC ID**—The VC ID identifies the service when signaling the service labels. This value must match at both ends of the service. The VC ID is usually the same as the service ID.
- **Service Distribution Point (SDP)**—This is a logical representation of the transport tunnel that will be used to deliver the service data to the egress PE.
- **Transport tunnel**—This is the LSP used to transport the service data, typically signaled with RSVP-TE or LDP. An SDP is associated with the transport tunnel.
- **Service tunnel**—This is the tunnel represented by the service labels signaled end-to-end by the two PEs that are the service endpoints.
- **De-multiplex**—This represents the operation of delivering the data arriving at the egress router to the appropriate service based on the service label.

These components are described in more detail in the following sections.

Subscribers, Customers, and Service Identifiers

We use the term *subscriber* to describe the user of the service. Often the term *customer* is used interchangeably, but on the 7750 SR, customer has a more specific meaning. When a service is created, it must be associated with an existing customer ID (see Figure 17.13). Multiple services can be associated with one customer. The 5620 Service Access Manager (SAM) uses the customer identifier network-wide for provisioning and reporting on services. When using the command-line interface (CLI) to configure services, it is not uncommon to use the default customer ID of 1 to configure all services.

Figure 17.13 Subscriber and customer association with a service.

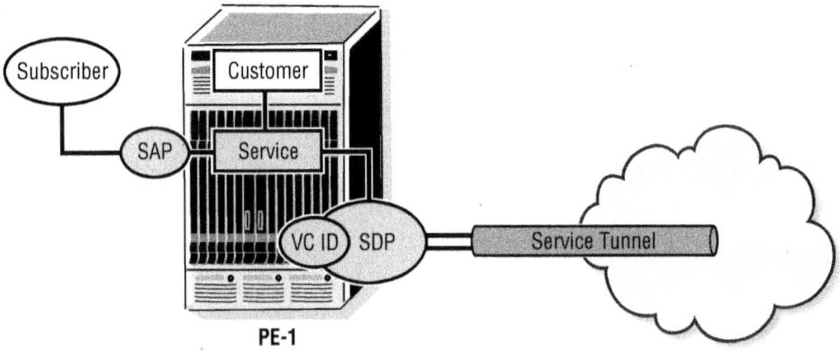

The customer must be created before the service is created (see Listing 17.3). The customer ID for the service cannot be changed once the service is created. Although it is recommended that a globally consistent value be used for the customer ID, it is never signaled to other PEs and has no effect on the service.

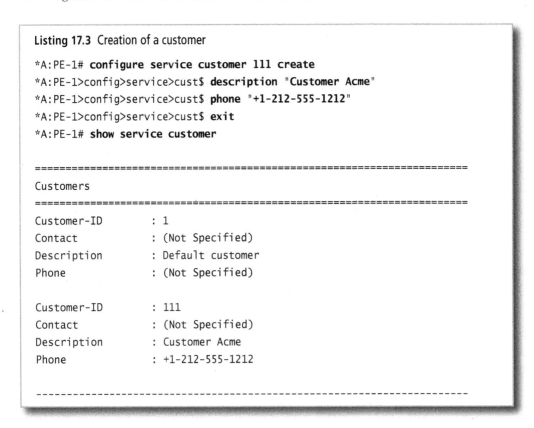

Listing 17.3 Creation of a customer

```
*A:PE-1# configure service customer 111 create
*A:PE-1>config>service>cust$ description "Customer Acme"
*A:PE-1>config>service>cust$ phone "+1-212-555-1212"
*A:PE-1>config>service>cust$ exit
*A:PE-1# show service customer

=========================================================================
Customers
=========================================================================
Customer-ID         : 1
Contact             : (Not Specified)
Description         : Default customer
Phone               : (Not Specified)

Customer-ID         : 111
Contact             : (Not Specified)
Description         : Customer Acme
Phone               : +1-212-555-1212

-------------------------------------------------------------------------
```

```
Total Customers : 2
-------------------------------------------------------------------------
=========================================================================
```

A service must be created using a unique service ID. Once a value is used for one service, it cannot be used for another on that router. For example, if a VPLS service is created using service ID 11, it is not possible to create an epipe with service ID 11 (see Figure 17.14).

Figure 17.14 The service ID identifies the service on the local router.

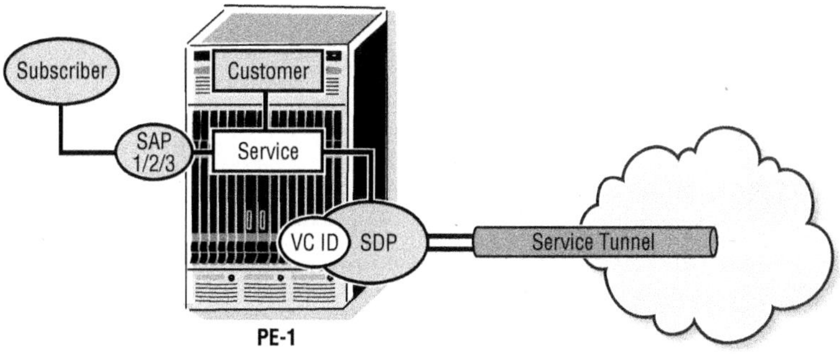

Listing 17.4 shows the creation of an epipe service. The service is operationally down because it is not completely configured.

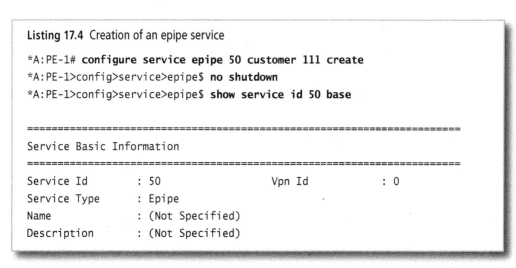

Listing 17.4 Creation of an epipe service

```
*A:PE-1# configure service epipe 50 customer 111 create
*A:PE-1>config>service>epipe$ no shutdown
*A:PE-1>config>service>epipe$ show service id 50 base

=========================================================================
Service Basic Information
=========================================================================
Service Id          : 50                    Vpn Id            : 0
Service Type        : Epipe
Name                : (Not Specified)
Description         : (Not Specified)
```

(continued)

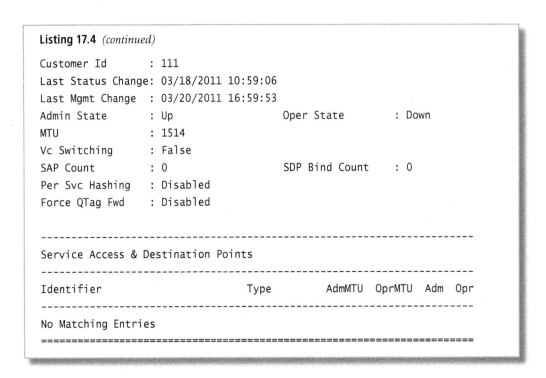

Listing 17.4 *(continued)*

```
Customer Id        : 111
Last Status Change: 03/18/2011 10:59:06
Last Mgmt Change   : 03/20/2011 16:59:53
Admin State        : Up                  Oper State         : Down
MTU                : 1514
Vc Switching       : False
SAP Count          : 0                   SDP Bind Count     : 0
Per Svc Hashing    : Disabled
Force QTag Fwd     : Disabled

-----------------------------------------------------------------------
Service Access & Destination Points
-----------------------------------------------------------------------
Identifier                        Type         AdmMTU  OprMTU  Adm  Opr
-----------------------------------------------------------------------
No Matching Entries
=======================================================================
```

Service Access Point (SAP)

The Service Access Point (SAP) is the subscriber's point of interface with the service (see Figure 17.15). A SAP is specified as a physical port and an encapsulation identifier. The encapsulation identifier may be null, in which case, the SAP is simply the port.

Figure 17.15 Service Access Point.

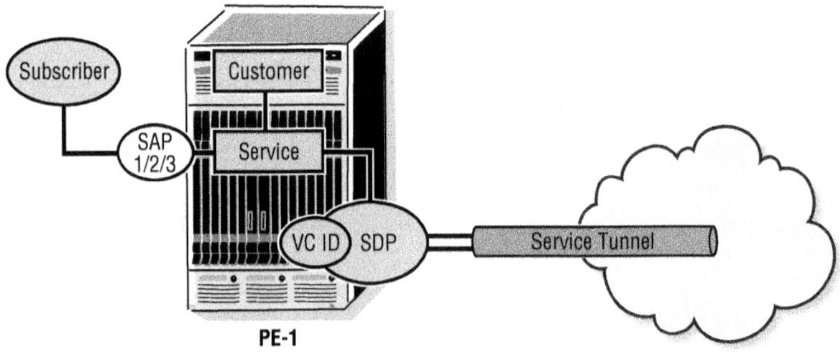

The encapsulation identifier depends on the type of port used as the SAP. For example, if the SAP is an Ethernet port, the encapsulation identifier can be a VLAN tag or a Q-in-Q tag.

Because the 7750 SR is a service router, it defines its physical ports as either access or network ports. An *access port* provides a customer-facing interface; a *network port* provides an interface toward the core network. An access port may support thousands of different services, each with different and extensive QoS queuing, accounting, and filtering capabilities. On the network side, service traffic is aggregated, and the QoS, accounting, and other functions required are much different. Thus, access ports are provided with a distinct set of capabilities from a network port. To be used as a SAP, a port must be configured as an access port. Ports are configured as network ports by default (see Listing 17.5).

Listing 17.5 Ports must be configured as access ports for use as a SAP.

```
*A:PE-1# show port 1

===============================================================================
Ports on Slot 1
===============================================================================
Port          Admin Link Port    Cfg  Oper LAG/ Port Port Port   SFP/XFP/
Id            State      State   MTU  MTU  Bndl Mode Encp Type   MDIMDX
-------------------------------------------------------------------------------
1/1/1         Up    Yes  Up      9212 9212    - netw null gige
1/1/2         Up    Yes  Up      9212 9212    - netw null gige
1/1/3         Up    Yes  Up      9212 9212    - netw null gige
1/1/4         Up    Yes  Up      9212 9212    - netw null gige
1/1/5         Down  No   Down    9212 9212    - netw null gige
1/1/6         Down  No   Down    9212 9212    - netw null gige
1/1/7         Down  No   Down    9212 9212    - netw null gige
1/1/8         Down  No   Down    9212 9212    - netw null gige
1/1/9         Down  No   Down    9212 9212    - netw null gige
1/1/10        Down  No   Down    9212 9212    - netw null gige
===============================================================================
*A:PE-1# configure port 1/1/1
*A:PE-1>config>port# shutdown
*A:PE-1>config>port# ethernet
*A:PE-1>config>port>ethernet# mode access
```

(continued)

Listing 17.5 *(continued)*

```
*A:PE-1>config>port>ethernet# encap-type dot1q
*A:PE-1>config>port>ethernet# exit
*A:PE-1>config>port# no shutdown
*A:PE-1>config>port# exit
*A:PE-1# configure port 1/1/2
*A:PE-1>config>port# shutdown
*A:PE-1>config>port# ethernet mode access
*A:PE-1>config>port# ethernet encap-type dot1q
*A:PE-1>config>port# no shutdown
*A:PE-1>config>port# exit
*A:PE-1# show port 1

===============================================================================
Ports on Slot 1
===============================================================================
Port        Admin Link Port    Cfg  Oper LAG/ Port Port Port   SFP/XFP/
Id          State      State   MTU  MTU  Bndl Mode Encp Type   MDIMDX
-------------------------------------------------------------------------------
1/1/1       Up    Yes  Up      1518 1518    - accs dotq gige
1/1/2       Up    Yes  Up      1518 1518    - accs dotq gige
1/1/3       Up    Yes  Up      9212 9212    - netw null gige
1/1/4       Up    Yes  Up      9212 9212    - netw null gige
1/1/5       Down  No   Down    9212 9212    - netw null gige
1/1/6       Down  No   Down    9212 9212    - netw null gige
1/1/7       Down  No   Down    9212 9212    - netw null gige
1/1/8       Down  No   Down    9212 9212    - netw null gige
1/1/9       Down  No   Down    9212 9212    - netw null gige
1/1/10      Down  No   Down    9212 9212    - netw null gige
===============================================================================
```

Notice that when the ports are configured as Ethernet access ports with `dot1q` encapsulation, they are automatically changed to an MTU (maximum transmission unit) of 1518. This defines the maximum size of frame that will be accepted for a service using this port as a SAP. By default, the 7750 SR configures an Ethernet access port to accept a standard-sized Ethernet frame. Because this port is configured for `dot1q` encapsulation, the MTU is 1518.

Because the 7750 SR does not count the FCS (frame check sequence) field in the frame size, the MTU for a standard Ethernet frame is 1514. A frame with a VLAN tag has an MTU of 1518.

Many other encapsulation types are possible. These depend on the MDA type of the port and the type of service being provisioned. SAP encapsulations are described in more detail in Chapter 18.

Configuring a Local Service

Services can be local or distributed. A *local service* is one in which all of the components of the service are on a single router. A *distributed service* has components on multiple routers and uses the IP/MPLS network to connect the service and deliver data. In this section, we demonstrate the configuration of an epipe service on a single router, as shown in Figure 17.16. The PE router configured as a local epipe effectively acts as a two-port Ethernet repeater. The CE devices have IP addresses configured on the same subnet and are able to ping each other through the epipe once it is configured. The CE devices shown in this picture are routers with IP interfaces, but could in fact be any two devices with Ethernet ports.

Figure 17.16 Local epipe service connecting to CE routers.

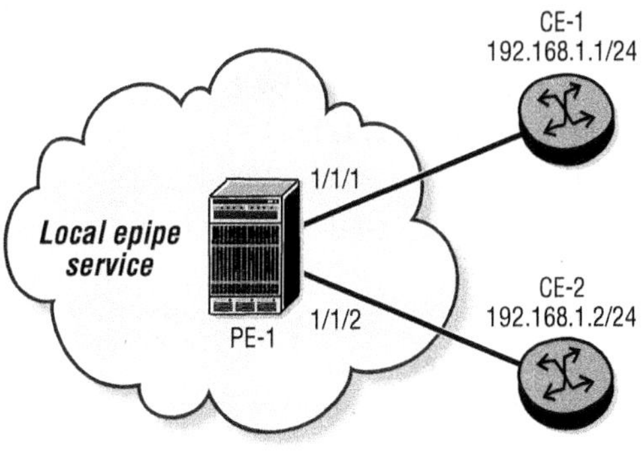

An epipe service was previously created in Listing 17.4, but no SAPs were configured for the service; thus the service is down (see Listing 17.6). The CE devices are configured with IP interfaces that use VLAN tag 11. Listing 17.7 shows that there is no connectivity between the CE devices as expected.

Listing 17.6 Epipe service exists without SAPs

```
*A:PE-1# configure service epipe 50
*A:PE-1>config>service>epipe# info
----------------------------------------------
            no shutdown
----------------------------------------------
*A:PE-1>config>service>epipe# show service service-using epipe

===============================================================================
Services [epipe]
===============================================================================
ServiceId  Type      Adm  Opr  CustomerId Service Name
-------------------------------------------------------------------------------
50         Epipe     Up   Down 111
-------------------------------------------------------------------------------
Matching Services : 1
-------------------------------------------------------------------------------
===============================================================================
```

Listing 17.7 No connectivity between CE devices

```
*A:CE-1# configure port 1/1/1 shutdown
*A:CE-1# configure port 1/1/1 ethernet encap-type dot1q
*A:CE-1# configure port 1/1/1 no shutdown
*A:CE-1# configure router interface "to_CE-2"
*A:CE-1>config>router>if# port 1/1/1:11
*A:CE-1>config>router>if# address 192.168.1.1/24
*A:CE-1>config>router>if# show router interface

===============================================================================
Interface Table (Router: Base)
===============================================================================
Interface-Name                Adm         Opr(v4/v6)  Mode     Port/SapId
   IP-Address                                                  PfxState
-------------------------------------------------------------------------------
system                        Down        Down/--     Network  system
   -                                                           -
to_CE-2                       Up          Up/--       Network  1/1/1:11
```

```
   192.168.1.1/24                                          n/a
-------------------------------------------------------------------------------
Interfaces : 2
===============================================================================
*A:CE-1>config>router>if# ping 192.168.1.2 count 1
PING 192.168.1.2 56 data bytes
Request timed out. icmp_seq=1.

---- 192.168.1.2 PING Statistics ----
1 packet transmitted, 0 packets received, 100% packet loss
```

Once the correct SAPs are added to the epipe service, the service is up (see Listing 17.8), and it is now possible for the two CE devices to reach each other over the Ethernet connection (see Listing 17.9). Notice that after the ping, CE-1 has the MAC address of CE-2's interface in its ARP cache.

Listing 17.8 Local epipe service enabled with two SAPs

```
*A:PE-1# configure service epipe 50
*A:PE-1>config>service>epipe# sap 1/1/1:11 create
*A:PE-1>config>service>epipe>sap$ exit
*A:PE-1>config>service>epipe# sap 1/1/2:11 create
*A:PE-1>config>service>epipe>sap$ exit
*A:PE-1>config>service>epipe# show service id 50 base

===============================================================================
Service Basic Information
===============================================================================
Service Id        : 50                    Vpn Id            : 0
Service Type      : Epipe
Name              : (Not Specified)
Description       : (Not Specified)
Customer Id       : 111
Last Status Change: 03/20/2011 19:24:24
Last Mgmt Change  : 03/20/2011 16:59:53
Admin State       : Up                    Oper State        : Up
MTU               : 1514
```

(continued)

Listing 17.8 *(continued)*

```
Vc Switching       : False
SAP Count          : 2                      SDP Bind Count     : 0
Per Svc Hashing    : Disabled
Force QTag Fwd     : Disabled

-------------------------------------------------------------------------------
Service Access & Destination Points
-------------------------------------------------------------------------------
Identifier                              Type        AdmMTU  OprMTU  Adm   Opr
-------------------------------------------------------------------------------
sap:1/1/1:11                            q-tag       1518    1518    Up    Up
sap:1/1/2:11                            q-tag       1518    1518    Up    Up
===============================================================================
```

Listing 17.9 Two CE devices can communicate through the local epipe service.

```
*A:CE-1>config>router>if# ping 192.168.1.2 count 1
PING 192.168.1.2 56 data bytes
64 bytes from 192.168.1.2: icmp_seq=1 ttl=64 time=4.45ms.

---- 192.168.1.2 PING Statistics ----
1 packet transmitted, 1 packet received, 0.00% packet loss
round-trip min = 4.45ms, avg = 4.45ms, max = 4.45ms, stddev = 0.000ms
*A:CE-1>config>router>if# show router arp

===============================================================================
ARP Table (Router: Base)
===============================================================================
IP Address      MAC Address       Expiry    Type   Interface
-------------------------------------------------------------------------------
192.168.1.1     00:03:fa:0e:93:31 00h00m00s Oth[I] to_CE-2
192.168.1.2     00:03:fa:ac:b8:27 03h58m00s Dyn[I] to_CE-2
-------------------------------------------------------------------------------
No. of ARP Entries: 2
===============================================================================
```

Although the PE router is now behaving like a simple Ethernet connection, a look at the detailed output for one of the SAPs in Listing 17.10 gives a hint at the capabilities available for defining QoS, filtering, and accounting policies on the SAP.

Listing 17.10 Detailed output of configuration and stats for SAP 1/1/1:11

```
*A:PE-1# show service id 50 sap 1/1/1:11 detail

===============================================================================
Service Access Points(SAP)
===============================================================================
Service Id         : 50
SAP                : 1/1/1:11                 Encap             : q-tag
Description        : (Not Specified)
Admin State        : Up                       Oper State        : Up
Flags              : None
Multi Svc Site     : None
Last Status Change : 03/18/2011 10:59:06
Last Mgmt Change   : 03/20/2011 19:24:14
Sub Type           : regular
Dot1Q Ethertype    : 0x8100                   QinQ Ethertype    : 0x8100
Split Horizon Group: (Not Specified)

Admin MTU          : 1518                     Oper MTU          : 1518
Ingr IP Fltr-Id    : n/a                      Egr IP Fltr-Id    : n/a
Ingr Mac Fltr-Id   : n/a                      Egr Mac Fltr-Id   : n/a
Ingr IPv6 Fltr-Id  : n/a                      Egr IPv6 Fltr-Id  : n/a
tod-suite          : None                     qinq-pbit-marking : both
Ing Agg Rate Limit : max                      Egr Agg Rate Limit: max
Endpoint           : N/A
Q Frame-Based Acct : Disabled
Vlan-translation   : None

Acct. Pol          : None                     Collect Stats     : Disabled
Application Profile: None


-------------------------------------------------------------------------------
QOS
-------------------------------------------------------------------------------
```

(continued)

Listing 17.10 *(continued)*

```
Ingress qos-policy : 1                  Egress qos-policy : 1
Shared Q plcy      : n/a                Multipoint shared : Disabled
I. Sched Pol       : (Not Specified)
E. Sched Pol       : (Not Specified)
I. Policer Ctl Pol : (Not Specified)
E. Policer Ctl Pol : (Not Specified)
-----------------------------------------------------------------------
Sap Statistics
-----------------------------------------------------------------------
Last Cleared Time     : N/A

                        Packets                Octets
Forwarding Engine Stats
Dropped                : 0                     0
Off. HiPrio            : 0                     0
Off. LowPrio           : 2                     174
Off. Uncolor           : 0                     0

Queueing Stats(Ingress QoS Policy 1)
Dro. HiPrio            : 0                     0
Dro. LowPrio           : 0                     0
For. InProf            : 0                     0
For. OutProf           : 2                     174

Queueing Stats(Egress QoS Policy 1)
Dro. InProf            : 0                     0
Dro. OutProf           : 0                     0
For. InProf            : 0                     0
For. OutProf           : 2                     174
-----------------------------------------------------------------------
Sap per Queue stats
-----------------------------------------------------------------------
                        Packets                Octets

Ingress Queue 1 (Unicast) (Priority)
Off. HiPrio            : 0                     0
Off. LoPrio            : 2                     174
Dro. HiPrio            : 0                     0
```

```
Dro. LoPrio              : 0                        0
For. InProf              : 0                        0
For. OutProf             : 2                        174

Egress Queue 1
For. InProf              : 0                        0
For. OutProf             : 2                        174
Dro. InProf              : 0                        0
Dro. OutProf             : 0                        0
===============================================================================
```

Infrastructure for Distributed Services

The example above shows the provisioning of a local service. Of course, in most cases, you will be interested in a distributed service. The components described so far are still required, but the network component based on the pseudowire is also required.

To deliver a distributed service, a transport network is required. The first component is the IGP, which is required for routing through the network. Although the IGP is not used directly for routing data, it is important to the operation of the control plane. IP routing is used to establish the transport LSPs and to support the signaling of the T-LDP sessions. Figure 17.17 shows the service provider network that we use to demonstrate a distributed service. Listing 17.11 shows that PE-1 has routes to all the other routers in the core network.

Listing 17.11 PE-1 has routes to all other MPLS routers.

```
*A:PE-1# show router route-table

===============================================================================
Route Table (Router: Base)
===============================================================================
Dest Prefix                                 Type    Proto    Age         Pref
      Next Hop[Interface Name]                                   Metric
-------------------------------------------------------------------------------
10.1.3.0/27                                 Local   Local    02d09h51m   0
      toR3                                                       0
```

(continued)

Listing 17.11 *(continued)*

```
10.2.4.0/27                                  Remote  OSPF      01d07h25m    10
       10.1.3.3                                                     300
10.3.4.0/27                                  Remote  OSPF      01d07h25m    10
       10.1.3.3                                                     200
10.10.10.1/32                                Local   Local     02d10h03m    0
       system                                                     0
10.10.10.2/32                                Remote  OSPF      00h00m51s    10
       10.1.3.3                                                     300
10.10.10.3/32                                Remote  OSPF      01d07h26m    10
       10.1.3.3                                                     100
10.10.10.4/32                                Remote  OSPF      01d07h25m    10
       10.1.3.3                                                     200
-------------------------------------------------------------------------
No. of Routes: 7
=========================================================================
```

Figure 17.17 Infrastructure for a distributed service over an IP/MPLS core.

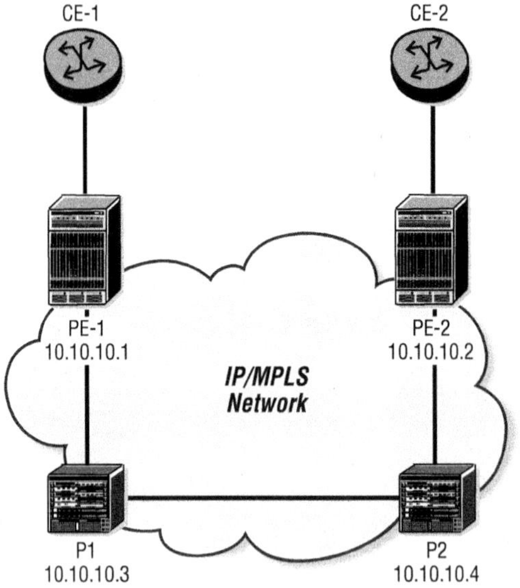

Once the IGP has been configured, a transport LSP is required to support the service. We can use either RSVP-TE or LDP, although RSVP-TE is required if we are interested in traffic engineering or fast reroute (FRR). We will use an RSVP-TE LSP in this example (see Listing 17.12).

Listing 17.12 RSVP-TE LSP configured to support epipe service

```
*A:PE-1# configure router mpls
*A:PE-1>config>router>mpls# no shutdown
*A:PE-1>config>router>mpls# interface "to_P1"
*A:PE-1>config>router>mpls>if$ exit
*A:PE-1>config>router>mpls# path loose
*A:PE-1>config>router>mpls>path$ no shutdown
*A:PE-1>config>router>mpls>path$ exit
*A:PE-1>config>router>mpls# lsp to_PE-2
*A:PE-1>config>router>mpls>lsp$ to 10.10.10.2
*A:PE-1>config>router>mpls>lsp$ cspf
*A:PE-1>config>router>mpls>lsp$ primary "loose"
*A:PE-1>config>router>mpls>lsp>primary$ exit
*A:PE-1>config>router>mpls>lsp# no shutdown
*A:PE-1>config>router>mpls>lsp# exit all
*A:PE-1# configure router rsvp no shutdown
*A:PE-1# show router mpls lsp

===============================================================================
MPLS LSPs (Originating)
===============================================================================
LSP Name                         To                  Fastfail       Adm    Opr
                                                     Config
-------------------------------------------------------------------------------
to_PE-2                          10.10.10.2          No             Up     Up
-------------------------------------------------------------------------------
LSPs : 1
===============================================================================
```

The other routers in the network have all been configured to support RSVP-TE, thus the LSP is up. Because services are bidirectional, an LSP is also required from PE-2 to PE-1.

The final step in preparing the service infrastructure is to ensure that T-LDP is enabled. As was shown in Listing 17.1, we only need to go into the `configure router ldp` context to enable T-LDP.

Service Distribution Point (SDP)

The transport tunnel for the service is represented by the SDP (see Figure 17.18). A distributed service is bound to an SDP when the service is configured. Key characteristics of the SDP include the following:

Figure 17.18 The SDP represents the transport tunnel for multiple services.

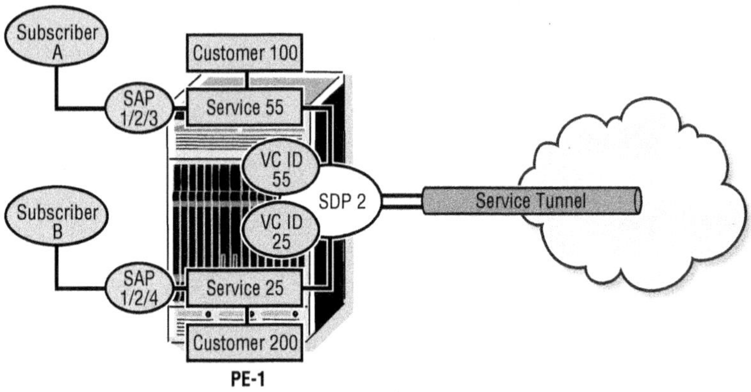

- Multiple services of different service types can use the same SDP for transport. All services that are bound to an SDP share the characteristics of that SDP.
- The SDP defines the encapsulation type to be used for the transport of the service data, either MPLS or GRE.
- An SDP uses the system IP address to identify the far-end PE router. A T-LDP session is established with the far end for Layer 2 services.
- There is a path MTU associated with the SDP. The service MTU of any service bound to the SDP cannot be larger than the path MTU of the SDP.
- The SDP ID is locally unique to the router. Other routers can use the same SDP ID.

The SDP is configured in the `configure service` context (see Listing 17.13). The following information must be included to define the service:

- **Encapsulation type**—Encapsulation is either MPLS or GRE.
- **Far end**—IP address of egress PE for all services bound to the SDP
- **Transport tunnel**—For an MPLS-encapsulated SDP, this specifies either the RSVP-TE LSP or `ldp` to indicate that LDP labels are to be used.

Listing 17.13 Configuration of an SDP

```
*A:PE-1# configure service sdp 2 mpls create
*A:PE-1>config>service>sdp$ far-end 10.10.10.2
*A:PE-1>config>service>sdp$ lsp "to_PE-2
*A:PE-1>config>service>sdp$ no shutdown
*A:PE-1>config>service>sdp$ exit
*A:PE-1# show service sdp detail

===============================================================================
Services: Service Destination Points Details
===============================================================================
-------------------------------------------------------------------------------
 Sdp Id 2  -(10.10.10.2)
-------------------------------------------------------------------------------
Description         : (Not Specified)
SDP Id              : 2                     SDP Source        : manual
Admin Path MTU      : 0                     Oper Path MTU     : 9190
Far End             : 10.10.10.2            Delivery          : MPLS
Admin State         : Up                    Oper State        : Down
Signaling           : TLDP                  Metric            : 0
Acct. Pol           : None                  Collect Stats     : Disabled
Last Status Change  : 03/18/2011 10:59:06   Adv. MTU Over.    : No
Last Mgmt Change    : 03/20/2011 23:08:20   VLAN VC Etype     : 0x8100
Bw BookingFactor    : 100                   PBB Etype         : 0x88e7
Oper Max BW(Kbps)   : 0                     Avail BW(Kbps)    : 0
Net-Domain          : default               Egr Interfaces    : Consistent
Mixed LSP Mode      : Disabled
Flags               : TldpSessDown

KeepAlive Information :
Admin State         : Disabled              Oper State        : Disabled
Hello Time          : 10                    Hello Msg Len     : 0
Hello Timeout       : 5                     Unmatched Replies : 0
Max Drop Count      : 3                     Hold Down Time    : 10
Tx Hello Msgs       : 0                     Rx Hello Msgs     : 0

-------------------------------------------------------------------------------
RSVP/Static LSPs
-------------------------------------------------------------------------------
```

(continued)

Listing 17.13 *(continued)*

```
Associated LSP LIST :
Lsp Name              : to_PE-2
Admin State           : Up                  Oper State          : Up
Time Since Last Tran*: 01h41m55s

-------------------------------------------------------------------------
Class-based forwarding :
-------------------------------------------------------------------------
Class forwarding      : Disabled           EnforceDSTELspFc    : Disabled
Default LSP           : Uknwn              Multicast LSP       : None

=========================================================================
FC Mapping Table
=========================================================================
FC Name             LSP Name
-------------------------------------------------------------------------
No FC Mappings

-------------------------------------------------------------------------
Number of SDPs : 1
-------------------------------------------------------------------------
=========================================================================
* indicates that the corresponding row element may have been truncated.
```

The SDP in Listing 17.13 is operationally down because there is no SDP configured in the reverse direction. Once the SDP from PE-2 to PE-1 is configured, the SDP from PE-1 comes up, as seen in Listing 17.14. Although the T-LDP session is up in both directions, no service labels have been exchanged yet because there is no service bound to the SDP.

Listing 17.14 SDP comes up after an SDP is configured in each direction

```
*A:PE-1# show service sdp

=========================================================================
```

```
Services: Service Destination Points
===============================================================================
SdpId    Adm MTU  Opr MTU  IP address     Adm  Opr      Deliver  Signal
-------------------------------------------------------------------------------
2        0        9190     10.10.10.2     Up   Up       MPLS     TLDP
-------------------------------------------------------------------------------
Number of SDPs : 1
-------------------------------------------------------------------------------
===============================================================================
*A:PE-1# show router ldp bindings fec-type services

===============================================================================
LDP LSR ID: 10.10.10.1
===============================================================================
Legend: U - Label In Use, N - Label Not In Use, W - Label Withdrawn
        S - Status Signaled Up,  D - Status Signaled Down
        E - Epipe Service, V - VPLS Service, M - Mirror Service
        A - Apipe Service, F - Fpipe Service, I - IES Service,
 R - VPRN service
        P - Ipipe Service, WP - Label Withdraw Pending,
 C - Cpipe Service
        TLV - (Type, Length: Value)
===============================================================================
LDP Service FEC 128 Bindings
===============================================================================
Type   VCId     SvcId     SDPId  Peer         IngLbl  EgrLbl  LMTU  RMTU
-------------------------------------------------------------------------------
No Matching Entries Found

===============================================================================
LDP Service FEC 129 Bindings
===============================================================================
AGI                                SAII                 TAII
Type            SvcId     SDPId  Peer         IngLbl  EgrLbl  LMTU  RMTU
-------------------------------------------------------------------------------
No Matching Entries Found
===============================================================================
===============================================================================
```

Listing 17.15 shows the SDP after the transport LSP used by the SDP is shut down. Notice that the flag indicates `TranspTunnDown`. Although the SDP is down, the T-LDP session is still established and the SDP in the reverse direction is still up.

Listing 17.15 SDP down after LSP is shut down

```
*A:PE-1# show service sdp 2 detail

===============================================================================
Service Destination Point (Sdp Id : 2) Details
===============================================================================
-------------------------------------------------------------------------------
 Sdp Id 2  -(10.10.10.2)
-------------------------------------------------------------------------------
Description          : (Not Specified)
SDP Id              : 2                      SDP Source         : manual
Admin Path MTU      : 0                      Oper Path MTU      : 0
Far End             : 10.10.10.2             Delivery           : MPLS
Admin State         : Up                     Oper State         : Down
Signaling           : TLDP                   Metric             : 0
Acct. Pol           : None                   Collect Stats      : Disabled
Last Status Change  : 03/21/2011 09:58:53    Adv. MTU Over.     : No
Last Mgmt Change    : 03/20/2011 23:08:20    VLAN VC Etype      : 0x8100
Bw BookingFactor    : 100                    PBB Etype          : 0x88e7
Oper Max BW(Kbps)   : 0                      Avail BW(Kbps)     : 0
Net-Domain          : default                Egr Interfaces     : n/a
Mixed LSP Mode      : Disabled
Flags               : TranspTunnDown

KeepAlive Information :
Admin State         : Disabled               Oper State         : Disabled
Hello Time          : 10                     Hello Msg Len      : 0
Hello Timeout       : 5                      Unmatched Replies : 0
Max Drop Count      : 3                      Hold Down Time     : 10
Tx Hello Msgs       : 0                      Rx Hello Msgs      : 0

-------------------------------------------------------------------------------
RSVP/Static LSPs
-------------------------------------------------------------------------------
```

```
Associated LSP LIST :
Lsp Name              : to_PE-2
Admin State           : Down                   Oper State          : Down
Time Since Last Tran*: 00h00m24s

-----------------------------------------------------------------------
Class-based forwarding :
-----------------------------------------------------------------------
Class forwarding      : Disabled            EnforceDSTELspFc    : Disabled
Default LSP           : Uknwn               Multicast LSP       : None

=======================================================================
FC Mapping Table
=======================================================================
FC Name              LSP Name
-----------------------------------------------------------------------
No FC Mappings

=======================================================================
* indicates that the corresponding row element may have been truncated.
*A:PE-1# show router ldp peer

=======================================================================
LDP Peers
=======================================================================
Peer         Adm  Opr  Hello   Hold   KA      KA       Passive  Auto
                       Factor  Time   Factor  Timeout  Mode     Created
-----------------------------------------------------------------------
10.10.10.2   Up   Up   3       45     4       40       Disabled Yes
-----------------------------------------------------------------------
No. of Peers: 1
=======================================================================
```

In Listing 17.16, the SDP is changed to use LDP instead of RSVP-TE. However, there is no active label for the far-end router, thus the SDP is still down with the same error flag.

Listing 17.16 LDP-signaled SDP down because there is no active label

```
*A:PE-1# configure service sdp 2
*A:PE-1>config>service>sdp# no lsp "to_PE-2
*A:PE-1>config>service>sdp# ldp
*A:PE-1>config>service>sdp# info
----------------------------------------------
            far-end 10.10.10.2
            ldp
            keep-alive
                shutdown
            exit
            no shutdown
----------------------------------------------
*A:PE-1>config>service>sdp# exit
*A:PE-1# show router ldp bindings active

===============================================================================
Legend:  (S) - Static
===============================================================================
LDP Prefix Bindings (Active)
===============================================================================
Prefix              Op   IngLbl    EgrLbl    EgrIntf/LspId  EgrNextHop
-------------------------------------------------------------------------------
No Matching Entries Found
*A:PE-1# show service sdp 2 detail

===============================================================================
Service Destination Point (Sdp Id : 2) Details
===============================================================================
-------------------------------------------------------------------------------
 Sdp Id 2  -(10.10.10.2)
-------------------------------------------------------------------------------
Description           : (Not Specified)
SDP Id               : 2                   SDP Source        : manual
Admin Path MTU       : 0                   Oper Path MTU     : 0
Far End              : 10.10.10.2          Delivery          : LDP
Admin State          : Up                  Oper State        : Down
Signaling            : TLDP                Metric            : 0
Acct. Pol            : None                Collect Stats     : Disabled
```

```
Last Status Change   : 03/21/2011 09:58:53   Adv. MTU Over.    : No
Last Mgmt Change     : 03/21/2011 10:07:07   VLAN VC Etype     : 0x8100
Bw BookingFactor     : 100                   PBB Etype         : 0x88e7
Oper Max BW(Kbps)    : 0                     Avail BW(Kbps)    : 0
Net-Domain           : default               Egr Interfaces    : n/a
Mixed LSP Mode       : Disabled
Flags                : TranspTunnDown

KeepAlive Information :
Admin State         : Disabled             Oper State         : Disabled
Hello Time          : 10                   Hello Msg Len      : 0
Hello Timeout       : 5                    Unmatched Replies  : 0
Max Drop Count      : 3                    Hold Down Time     : 10
Tx Hello Msgs       : 0                    Rx Hello Msgs      : 0

-----------------------------------------------------------------------
LDP Information :
-----------------------------------------------------------------------
LDP LSP Id           : 0                     LDP Active         : No

-----------------------------------------------------------------------
RSVP/Static LSPs
-----------------------------------------------------------------------
Associated LSP LIST :
No LSPs Associated

-----------------------------------------------------------------------
Class-based forwarding :
-----------------------------------------------------------------------
Class forwarding     : Disabled             EnforceDSTELspFc   : Disabled
Default LSP          : Uknwn                Multicast LSP      : None

=======================================================================
FC Mapping Table
=======================================================================
FC Name              LSP Name
-----------------------------------------------------------------------
No FC Mappings

=======================================================================
```

Configuring a Distributed Service

Once the service infrastructure has been configured, the distributed service can be provisioned. As an example, we show the configuration of an epipe in the topology of Figure 17.19.

Figure 17.19 Service provider network with epipe configured.

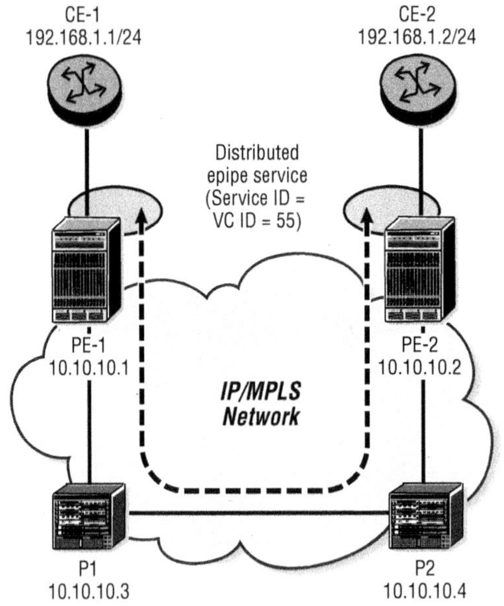

Configuration of a distributed service is very similar to the local service configured in Listing 17.8. The difference is that an SDP binding is required to signal the service labels and define the transport to the remote node. On the 7750 SR the SDP binding is defined as a spoke or mesh binding. Mesh bindings are only used for VPLS services. The difference between the two is described in Chapter 19. Listing 17.17 shows the configuration of a distributed epipe service on PE-1. The SDP binding specifies both the SDP ID and the VC ID in the format `spoke-sdp` *`sdp-id:vc-id`*. This identifies the transport tunnel and service tunnel for the pseudowire that is signaled by T-LDP.

Listing 17.17 Configuration of the distributed epipe

```
*A:PE-1# configure service epipe 55 customer 111 create
*A:PE-1>config>service>epipe$ sap 1/1/2 create
```

```
*A:PE-1>config>service>epipe>sap$ exit
*A:PE-1>config>service>epipe# spoke-sdp 2:55 create
*A:PE-1>config>service>epipe>spoke-sdp$ exit
*A:PE-1>config>service>epipe# no shutdown
*A:PE-1>config>service>epipe# info
----------------------------------------------
            sap 1/1/2 create
            exit
            spoke-sdp 2:55 create
            exit
            no shutdown
----------------------------------------------
*A:PE-1>config>service>epipe# show service id 55 base

===============================================================================
Service Basic Information
===============================================================================
Service Id        : 55                  Vpn Id            : 0
Service Type      : Epipe
Name              : (Not Specified)
Description       : (Not Specified)
Customer Id       : 111
Last Status Change: 03/18/2011 10:59:06
Last Mgmt Change  : 03/21/2011 13:36:16
Admin State       : Up                  Oper State        : Down
MTU               : 1514
Vc Switching      : False
SAP Count         : 1                   SDP Bind Count    : 1
Per Svc Hashing   : Disabled
Force QTag Fwd    : Disabled

-------------------------------------------------------------------------------
Service Access & Destination Points
-------------------------------------------------------------------------------
Identifier                          Type     AdmMTU  OprMTU  Adm  Opr
-------------------------------------------------------------------------------
sap:1/1/2                           null     1514    1514    Up   Up
sdp:2:55 S(10.10.10.2)              Spok     0       0       Up   Down
===============================================================================
```

The service is configured with a null encapsulated SAP and a spoke SDP binding. However, the service is down because the spoke SDP is down. Listing 17.18 shows that the SDP itself is up, but the SDP binding to the service is down. The flag shows `NoEgrVCLabel` because the service has not been configured on the remote PE router (PE-2). The `show router ldp bindings fec-type services` command shows that the local router has created a label for the service but has not received one from the remote router. A pseudowire is bidirectional and is not operational until both ends are successfully signaled.

Listing 17.18 SDP is up, but SDP binding to service is down.

```
*A:PE-1# show service sdp

===============================================================================
Services: Service Destination Points
===============================================================================
SdpId   Adm MTU  Opr MTU  IP address      Adm  Opr       Deliver  Signal
-------------------------------------------------------------------------------
2       0        9190     10.10.10.2      Up   Up        MPLS     TLDP
-------------------------------------------------------------------------------
Number of SDPs : 1
-------------------------------------------------------------------------------
===============================================================================
*A:PE-1# show service id 55 sdp 2:55 detail

===============================================================================
Service Destination Point (Sdp Id : 2:55) Details
===============================================================================
-------------------------------------------------------------------------------
 Sdp Id 2:55  -(10.10.10.2)
-------------------------------------------------------------------------------
Description      : (Not Specified)
SDP Id              : 2:55                 Type                 : Spoke
Spoke Descr      : (Not Specified)
VC Type             : Ether                VC Tag               : n/a
Admin Path MTU      : 0                    Oper Path MTU        : 9190
Far End             : 10.10.10.2           Delivery             : MPLS
Hash Label          : Disabled

Admin State         : Up                   Oper State           : Down
```

```
Acct. Pol            : None                    Collect Stats     : Disabled
Ingress Label        : 131069                  Egress Label      : 0
Ingr Mac Fltr-Id     : n/a                     Egr Mac Fltr-Id   : n/a
Ingr IP Fltr-Id      : n/a                     Egr IP Fltr-Id    : n/a
Ingr IPv6 Fltr-Id    : n/a                     Egr IPv6 Fltr-Id  : n/a
Admin ControlWord    : Not Preferred           Oper ControlWord  : False
Admin BW(Kbps)       : 0                       Oper BW(Kbps)     : 0
Last Status Change   : 03/18/2011 10:59:06     Signaling         : TLDP
Last Mgmt Change     : 03/21/2011 13:36:01     Force Vlan-Vc     : Disabled
Endpoint             : N/A                     Precedence        : 4
Class Fwding State   : Down
Flags                : NoEgrVCLabel
Peer Pw Bits         : None
Peer Fault Ip        : None
Peer Vccv CV Bits    : None
Peer Vccv CC Bits    : None
Application Profile: None

KeepAlive Information :
Admin State          : Disabled                Oper State        : Disabled
Hello Time           : 10                      Hello Msg Len     : 0
Max Drop Count       : 3                       Hold Down Time    : 10

Statistics             :
I. Fwd. Pkts.        : 0                       I. Dro. Pkts.     : 0
E. Fwd. Pkts.        : 0                       E. Fwd. Octets    : 0

-----------------------------------------------------------------------
RSVP/Static LSPs
-----------------------------------------------------------------------
Associated LSP LIST :
Lsp Name             : to_PE-1
Admin State          : Up                      Oper State        : Up
Time Since Last Tr*: 00h01m16s

-----------------------------------------------------------------------
Class-based forwarding :
-----------------------------------------------------------------------
Class forwarding     : Disabled                EnforceDSTELspFc : Disabled
```

(continued)

Listing 17.18 *(continued)*

```
Default LSP        : Uknwn                  Multicast LSP     : None

========================================================================
FC Mapping Table
========================================================================
FC Name             LSP Name
------------------------------------------------------------------------
No FC Mappings

------------------------------------------------------------------------
Number of SDPs : 1
------------------------------------------------------------------------
========================================================================
* indicates that the corresponding row element may have been truncated.
*A:PE-1># show router ldp bindings fec-type services

========================================================================
LDP LSR ID: 10.10.10.1
========================================================================
Legend: U - Label In Use, N - Label Not In Use, W - Label Withdrawn
        S - Status Signaled Up,  D - Status Signaled Down
        E - Epipe Service, V - VPLS Service, M - Mirror Service
        A - Apipe Service, F - Fpipe Service, I - IES Service,
 R - VPRN service
        P - Ipipe Service, WP - Label Withdraw Pending,
 C - Cpipe Service
        TLV - (Type, Length: Value)
========================================================================
LDP Service FEC 128 Bindings
========================================================================
Type   VCId    SvcId     SDPId  Peer          IngLbl  EgrLbl  LMTU  RMTU
------------------------------------------------------------------------
E-Eth  55      55        2      10.10.10.2    131069U   --    1500  0
------------------------------------------------------------------------
No. of VC Labels: 1

========================================================================
LDP Service FEC 129 Bindings
```

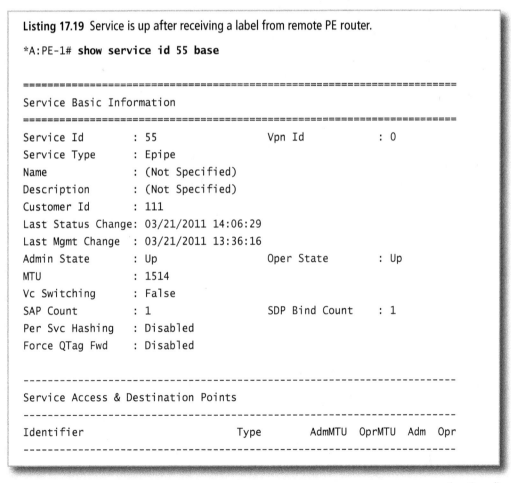

```
===============================================================================
AGI                                    SAII                TAII
Type            SvcId         SDPId    Peer        IngLbl  EgrLbl  LMTU  RMTU
-------------------------------------------------------------------------------
No Matching Entries Found
===============================================================================
===============================================================================
```

Once the service is configured on the remote node with a matching VC ID, a service label is signaled and the service is up, as seen in Listing 17.19.

Listing 17.19 Service is up after receiving a label from remote PE router.

```
*A:PE-1# show service id 55 base

===============================================================================
Service Basic Information
===============================================================================
Service Id        : 55                  Vpn Id            : 0
Service Type      : Epipe
Name              : (Not Specified)
Description       : (Not Specified)
Customer Id       : 111
Last Status Change: 03/21/2011 14:06:29
Last Mgmt Change  : 03/21/2011 13:36:16
Admin State       : Up                  Oper State        : Up
MTU               : 1514
Vc Switching      : False
SAP Count         : 1                   SDP Bind Count    : 1
Per Svc Hashing   : Disabled
Force QTag Fwd    : Disabled

-------------------------------------------------------------------------------
Service Access & Destination Points
-------------------------------------------------------------------------------
Identifier                         Type         AdmMTU  OprMTU  Adm  Opr
-------------------------------------------------------------------------------
```

(continued)

Listing 17.19 *(continued)*

```
sap:1/1/2                        null       1514     1514     Up   Up
sdp:2:55 S(10.10.10.2)           Spok       0        9190     Up   Up
===============================================================================
*A:PE-1# show router ldp bindings fec-type services

===============================================================================
LDP LSR ID: 10.10.10.1
===============================================================================
Legend: U - Label In Use, N - Label Not In Use, W - Label Withdrawn
        S - Status Signaled Up,  D - Status Signaled Down
        E - Epipe Service, V - VPLS Service, M - Mirror Service
        A - Apipe Service, F - Fpipe Service, I - IES Service,
 R - VPRN service
        P - Ipipe Service, WP - Label Withdraw Pending,
 C - Cpipe Service
        TLV - (Type, Length: Value)
===============================================================================
LDP Service FEC 128 Bindings
===============================================================================
Type   VCId     SvcId    SDPId  Peer          IngLbl  EgrLbl  LMTU  RMTU
-------------------------------------------------------------------------------
E-Eth  55       55       2      10.10.10.2    131069U 131069S 1500  1500
-------------------------------------------------------------------------------
No. of VC Labels: 1

===============================================================================
LDP Service FEC 129 Bindings
===============================================================================
AGI                             SAII                  TAII
Type            SvcId    SDPId  Peer          IngLbl  EgrLbl  LMTU  RMTU
-------------------------------------------------------------------------------
No Matching Entries Found
===============================================================================
===============================================================================
```

An IP interface is configured on CE1-1 and CE-2 to verify that the two routers can reach each other through the epipe (see Listing 17.20).

Listing 17.20 CE devices can ping through the epipe.

```
*A:CE-1# configure port 1/1/2
*A:CE-1>config>port# shutdown
*A:CE-1>config>port# ethernet encap-type null
*A:CE-1>config>port# no shutdown
*A:CE-1>config>port# exit
*A:CE-1# configure router interface to_CE-2
*A:CE-1>config>router>if$ port 1/1/2
*A:CE-1>config>router>if$ address 192.168.1.1/24
*A:CE-1>config>router>if$ exit
*A:CE-1# show router interface

===============================================================================
Interface Table (Router: Base)
===============================================================================
Interface-Name                   Adm         Opr(v4/v6)  Mode    Port/SapId
   IP-Address                                                    PfxState
-------------------------------------------------------------------------------
system                           Down        Down/--     Network system
   -                                                             -
to_CE-2                          Up          Up/--       Network 1/1/2
   192.168.1.1/24                                                n/a
-------------------------------------------------------------------------------
Interfaces : 2
===============================================================================
*A:CE-1# ping 192.168.1.2
PING 192.168.1.2 56 data bytes
64 bytes from 192.168.1.2: icmp_seq=1 ttl=64 time=8.17ms.
64 bytes from 192.168.1.2: icmp_seq=2 ttl=64 time=3.52ms.
64 bytes from 192.168.1.2: icmp_seq=3 ttl=64 time=3.56ms.
64 bytes from 192.168.1.2: icmp_seq=4 ttl=64 time=3.54ms.
64 bytes from 192.168.1.2: icmp_seq=5 ttl=64 time=3.55ms.

---- 192.168.1.2 PING Statistics ----
5 packets transmitted, 5 packets received, 0.00% packet loss
round-trip min = 3.52ms, avg = 4.47ms, max = 8.17ms, stddev = 1.85ms
```

Although there are no QoS, filter, or accounting policies configured, the statistics displayed for the SAP give a sense of the administrative policies that can be applied to a SAP (see Listing 17.21).

Listing 17.21 Detailed statistics for the SAP 1/1/2 in the epipe service

```
*A:PE-1# show service id 55 sap 1/1/2 detail

===============================================================================
Service Access Points(SAP)
===============================================================================
Service Id         : 55
SAP                : 1/1/2                    Encap             : null
Description        : (Not Specified)
Admin State        : Up                       Oper State        : Up
Flags              : None
Multi Svc Site     : None
Last Status Change : 03/21/2011 13:36:16
Last Mgmt Change   : 03/21/2011 13:35:35
Sub Type           : regular
Dot1Q Ethertype    : 0x8100                   QinQ Ethertype    : 0x8100
Split Horizon Group: (Not Specified)

LLF Admin State    : Down                     LLF Oper State    : Clear
Admin MTU          : 1514                     Oper MTU          : 1514
Ingr IP Fltr-Id    : n/a                      Egr IP Fltr-Id    : n/a
Ingr Mac Fltr-Id   : n/a                      Egr Mac Fltr-Id   : n/a
Ingr IPv6 Fltr-Id  : n/a                      Egr IPv6 Fltr-Id  : n/a
tod-suite          : None                     qinq-pbit-marking : both
Ing Agg Rate Limit : max                      Egr Agg Rate Limit: max
Endpoint           : N/A
Q Frame-Based Acct : Disabled
Vlan-translation   : None

Acct. Pol          : None                     Collect Stats     : Disabled
Application Profile: None


-------------------------------------------------------------------------------
QOS
```

```
-------------------------------------------------------------------------------
Ingress qos-policy : 1                    Egress qos-policy : 1
Shared Q plcy      : n/a                  Multipoint shared : Disabled
I. Sched Pol       : (Not Specified)
E. Sched Pol       : (Not Specified)
I. Policer Ctl Pol : (Not Specified)
E. Policer Ctl Pol : (Not Specified)
-------------------------------------------------------------------------------
Sap Statistics
-------------------------------------------------------------------------------
Last Cleared Time     : 03/21/2011 14:16:01

                        Packets                 Octets
Forwarding Engine Stats
Dropped               : 0                       0
Off. HiPrio           : 0                       0
Off. LowPrio          : 5                       510
Off. Uncolor          : 0                       0

Queueing Stats(Ingress QoS Policy 1)
Dro. HiPrio           : 0                       0
Dro. LowPrio          : 0                       0
For. InProf           : 0                       0
For. OutProf          : 5                       510

Queueing Stats(Egress QoS Policy 1)
Dro. InProf           : 0                       0
Dro. OutProf          : 0                       0
For. InProf           : 0                       0
For. OutProf          : 5                       510
-------------------------------------------------------------------------------
Sap per Queue stats
-------------------------------------------------------------------------------
                        Packets                 Octets

Ingress Queue 1 (Unicast) (Priority)
Off. HiPrio           : 0                       0
Off. LoPrio           : 5                       510
Dro. HiPrio           : 0                       0
Dro. LoPrio           : 0                       0
```

(continued)

Listing 17.21 *(continued)*

```
For. InProf          : 0                     0
For. OutProf         : 5                     510

Egress Queue 1
For. InProf          : 0                     0
For. OutProf         : 5                     510
Dro. InProf          : 0                     0
Dro. OutProf         : 0                     0
===============================================================================
```

Figure 17.20 summarizes the main components of a service and whether they have local or global significance. The components are as follows:

Figure 17.20 Local or global significance for service components.

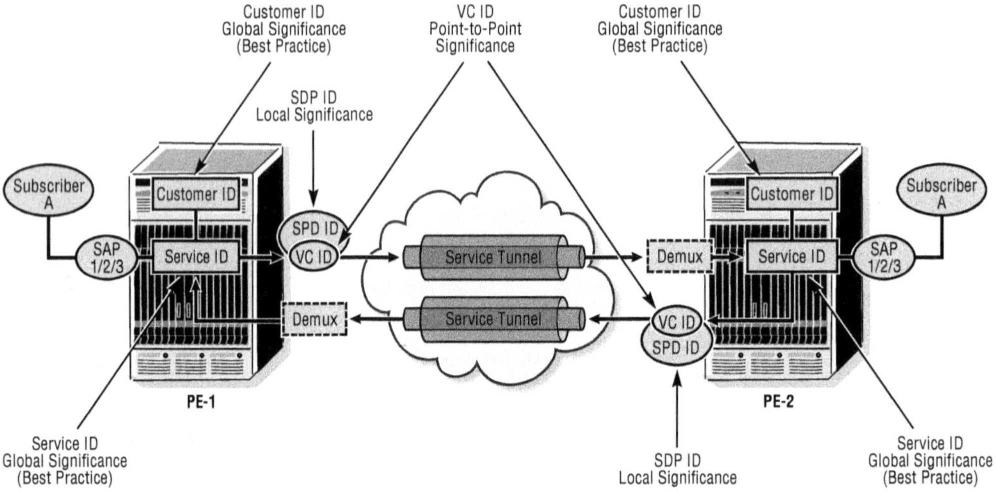

- **Customer ID**—Best practice is to maintain global significance. 5620 SAM requires that the customer ID is treated with global significance.
- **Service ID**—Best practice is to maintain global significance when possible. In some situations, it is necessary to have different service IDs on distributed nodes.

- **VC ID**—Point-to-point significance. The VC ID must match for the distributed components of the service. Best practice is to use the service ID as the VC ID when possible.
- **SDP ID**—Local significance. An SDP ID can be reused on other routers. In this book we use the last octet of the system address of the far-end node as the SDP ID to make the SDPs easier to identify.

Practice Lab: Configuring the Service Infrastructure

The following lab is designed to reinforce your knowledge of the content in this chapter. Please review the instructions carefully, and perform the steps in the order in which they are presented. The practice labs require that you have access to six or more Alcatel-Lucent 7750 SRs or Alcatel-Lucent 7450 ESSs in a non-production environment.

These labs are designed to be used in a controlled lab environment. Please *do not* attempt to perform these labs in a production environment.

Lab Section 17.1: Configuring SDPs

One of the first steps to configuring services on the Alcatel-Lucent 7750 SR is to configure the Service Distribution Points (SDPs) and their underlying infrastructure.

Objective In this exercise you will configure SDPs that will be used for a service provisioned in later sections of this lab exercise (see Figure 17.21).

Validation You will know you have succeeded if the SDPs are operationally up.

1. Make sure that your IGP is configured as shown in Figure 17.21. Note that an IGP should not be configured on R5 or R6 because these nodes will simulate CE routers in this lab. R1 and R2 will simulate PE routers, and R3 and R4 are P routers. This lab uses OSPF for the IGP, but you can use IS-IS if you prefer. Configure your IGP with traffic engineering and make sure that all RSVP-TE interfaces are functional. If you have just completed the previous labs, much of this configuration will already be completed.

Figure 17.21 Lab topology for bandwidth-constrained LSPs.

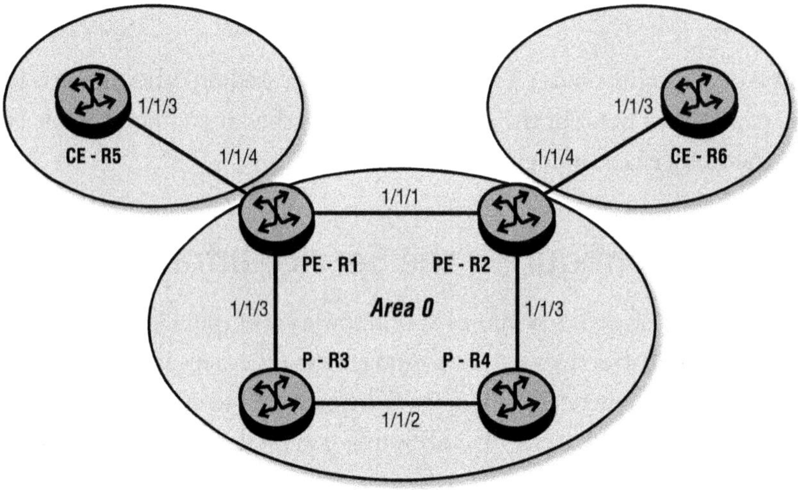

2. Configure an SDP on R1 toward R2. Configure the SDP to use RSVP-TE-signaled LSPs, but don't bind the LSPs to the SDP yet.
   a. Is the SDP operationally up? If not, what are the flags?
   b. Create a loose path LSP from R1 to R2, and bind it to the SDP.
   c. Is the SDP operationally up? If not, what are the flags?
   d. Create an SDP from R2 to R1, and ensure that an RSVP-TE LSP is bound to it.
   e. Are the SDPs operationally up? If not, what are the flags?
   f. Ensure that both SDPs are up before continuing to the next lab section.

Lab Section 17.2: Configuring an Epipe Service

In the previous section an infrastructure was created to support services. This section uses the infrastructure to create an epipe service.

Objective This lab will investigate the creation of an epipe service.

Validation You will know you have succeeded if the epipe service is operationally up and the CE devices can ping each other through the service.

1. Configure R5's port to R1 and R6's port to R2 to have `dot1Q` encapsulations. Delete the existing network interfaces on R5 and R6.
2. Configure a network interface on R5 toward R1 called `toR1-vlan20`. Use an IP address of `192.168.20.5/24` and an Ethernet `dot1Q` encapsulation of 20.
3. Configure a network interface on R6 toward R2 called `toR2-vlan20`. Use an IP address of `192.168.20.6/24` and an Ethernet encapsulation of 20.
   a. From R5, ping the IP address `192.168.20.6`. Is the ping successful? Explain.
4. Configure an epipe service on R1 that uses a customer ID of 2040. Don't create any of the other service components yet.
   a. Is the service operationally up? Explain.
   b. Bind the SDP toward R2 to the epipe service on R1.
   c. Is the SDP binding up? If not, what are the flags? Compare this to the operational status of the SDP itself. Explain.
   d. Configure an epipe service on R2, and bind the SDP toward R1 to the service.
   e. Is the SDP binding on R2 toward R1 operationally up? Explain.
   f. From R5, ping the IP address `192.168.20.6`. Is the ping successful?
   g. Are the epipe services on R1 and R2 operationally up? Explain.
5. Configure the SAPs required for the services.
   a. Where do the SAPs need to be configured?
   b. How do the physical ports have to be configured to support the SAPs?
   c. From R5, ping the IP address `192.168.20.6`. Is the ping successful? Explain.
   d. Describe the MPLS labels applied to traffic sent from R5 to R6.
   e. If the network designer wanted to make sure that traffic for the service is sent through the P routers (R3 and R4), what change is required to the service components?

Lab Section 17.3: Configuring Multiple Services

The previous lab sections provisioned an operational epipe service that could be used for communication between the CE routers. This lab investigates using the same service infrastructure to provision additional services.

Objective In this lab you will configure an additional epipe service that can be used for communications between the CE routers.

Validation You will know you have succeeded if both epipe services are operational and they pass traffic for the correct data sent between the CE routers.

1. Configure a network interface on R5 toward R1 called `toR1-vlan40`. Use an IP address of `192.168.40.5/24` and an Ethernet `dot1Q` encapsulation of 40.
2. Configure a network interface on R6 toward R2 called `toR2-vlan40`. Use an IP address of `192.168.40.6/24` and an Ethernet `dot1Q` encapsulation of 40.
   a. From R5 ping the IP address `192.168.20.6`. Is the ping successful? Explain.
   b. From R5 ping the IP address `192.168.40.6`. Is the ping successful? Explain.
3. Configure an epipe service between R1 and R4 with a service ID of 40.
   a. Configure SDP bindings for the services on both routers. Are new SDPs required? Explain.
   b. Create the required SAPs on both routers. What value should be used for the Ethernet encapsulation of the SAPs?
   c. Verify that the epipe service is operationally up by pinging `192.168.40.6` from R5.
   d. Describe the MPLS labels applied to traffic sent from R5 to R6 that uses epipe 40. How does this compare to traffic sent on epipe 20?
   e. How many entries are in the MAC FDB for each service?

Chapter Review

Now that you have completed this chapter, you should be able to:

- List the reasons for deploying an IP/MPLS services network.
- Describe the differences between an IP/MPLS service router and a traditional IP router.
- Describe the types of routers and switches found in a service network.
- Describe the different service types possible with an IP/MPLS network.
- Explain how GRE can be used as the transport tunnel for a service.
- Describe the service encapsulation and the purpose of the transport and service labels.
- Compare T-LDP and Link LDP.
- Explain how T-LDP is used to exchange service labels.
- Configure and verify T-LDP peers.
- List the service components on the 7750 SR.
- Describe the use of the customer ID, the service ID, and the VC ID.
- Describe the purpose and characteristics of the SAP.
- Configure a local epipe service with two SAPs.
- List the routing infrastructure required to configure a distributed service.
- Describe the purpose and characteristics of the SDP.
- Configure and verify an SDP.
- Configure and verify a distributed epipe service.

Post-Assessment

The following questions will test your knowledge and prepare you for the Alcatel-Lucent NRS II Certification Exam. Compare your responses with the answers listed in Appendix A. You can also use the CD that accompanies this book to take all the assessment tests and review the answers.

1. An epipe service is to be deployed in a network. Which routers may need to be configured with the epipe service?
   - **A.** PE routers
   - **B.** CE routers
   - **C.** P routers
   - **D.** Core routers
   - **E.** PE routers and P routers.
2. Which statement best characterizes a VPLS from a customer's point of view?
   - **A.** The service provider network appears as a leased line between customer locations.
   - **B.** The service provider network appears as a single MPLS switch between customer locations.
   - **C.** The service provider network appears as a single IP router between customer locations.
   - **D.** The service provider network appears as a Layer 2 switch between customer locations.
   - **E.** None of the above statements are correct.
3. Consider a network of 7750 SRs that contains four PE routers, six CE routers, and eight P routers. Assuming that the network is only used to provide VPRN services, which routers need to be configured with SAPs?
   - **A.** All CE routers
   - **B.** All PE routers
   - **C.** All P routers
   - **D.** All P and CE routers
   - **E.** All PE, CE, and P routers

4. Which of the following best describes the encapsulation of the service payload on an IP/MPLS service network with Ethernet links?

   A. The service payload is encapsulated in an Ethernet frame.

   B. The service payload is encapsulated in an Ethernet frame with a service label.

   C. The service payload is encapsulated in an Ethernet frame with a transport label and a service label.

   D. The service payload is encapsulated in an Ethernet frame with an IP header and a service label.

5. Which of the following best describes the signaling of service labels for an epipe?

   A. Service labels are signaled when the SDP is created at both ends.

   B. Service labels are signaled when the service is created and made administratively up at one end.

   C. Service labels are signaled when the service is created and made administratively up at both ends.

   D. Service labels are signaled when the SDP binding is created in the service at both ends.

   E. Service labels are signaled when the SAP and the SDP binding are created in the service at both ends.

6. Which statement best characterizes an epipe service from a customer's point of view?

   A. The service provider network appears as a leased line between two customer locations.

   B. The service provider network appears as a single MPLS switch between two customer locations.

   C. The service provider network appears as a single IP router between customer locations.

   D. The service provider network appears as a Layer 2 switch between customer locations.

   E. None of the above statements are correct.

7. Which of the following is *not* a primary feature of a service router such as an Alcatel-Lucent 7750 SR?

   A. The ability to perform accounting operations based on a specific customer or service

   B. The ability to provide quality of service based on a specific customer or service

   C. The ability to restrict or monitor specific traffic based on customer or service

   D. The ability to analyze and troubleshoot problems from the perspective of a service

   E. All of the above are primary features of a service router.

8. A PE router is provisioned with two epipe services, one apipe service, and four VPLS services. Assuming that all services are operationally up and passing subscriber traffic, how many T-LDP sessions are established on the PE router?

   A. 1

   B. 2

   C. 3

   D. 4

   E. 7

   F. There is not enough information to answer this question.

9. Which of the following is a true statement about an IP/MPLS service network?

   A. GRE can only be used for a Layer 3 service such as VPRN.

   B. The CE routers connected to the service network must support MPLS.

   C. The service provider must provision multiple service instances in order to provide redundancy for a customer.

   D. Layer 2 and Layer 3 services such as VPLS and VPRN can both be provisioned on the same IP/MPLS network.

   E. A new transport tunnel must be configured for each service.

   F. All of the above statements are false.

10. Which of the statements below is incorrect?

- **A.** Link LDP peers do not have to be directly connected.
- **B.** T-LDP peers do not have to be directly connected.
- **C.** Link LDP is used to signal transport labels.
- **D.** T-LDP is used to signal service labels.
- **E.** All of the above statements are correct.

11. Which of the following statements about the number of routers required for an epipe service is true?

- **A.** An epipe service is configured on only one PE router.
- **B.** An epipe service must be configured on two PE routers.
- **C.** An epipe service must be configured on either one or two PE routers.
- **D.** An epipe service may be configured on any number of PE routers.
- **E.** An epipe service is not configured on the PE router, only on the CE routers.

12. Which of the following statements about T-LDP is true?

- **A.** A T-LDP router uses the IGP to discover its peers.
- **B.** After the T-LDP session is established, the peers signal service labels.
- **C.** If RSVP-TE is used for a VPWS, T-LDP is not required.
- **D.** Because LDP is only used in a service provider network, authentication is not required and is not supported.
- **E.** All of the above statements are false.
- **F.** Statements A–D are true.

13. Which of the following statements about an epipe is true?

- **A.** The customer IDs at both ends of an epipe must match.
- **B.** The service IDs at both ends of an epipe must match.
- **C.** The VC IDs at both ends of an epipe must match.
- **D.** The service labels at both ends of an epipe must match.
- **E.** None of the above statements are true.
- **F.** Statements A–D are true.

14. Which of the following statements about the use of physical ports for services on the Alcatel-Lucent 7750 SR is false?

- **A.** One physical port can be used for multiple SAPs in different services.
- **B.** An access port has the same QoS and accounting capabilities as a network port.
- **C.** A port to be used for a SAP must be configured as an access port.
- **D.** A port to be configured for a normal IP interface must be configured as a network port.
- **E.** Ports are network ports by default.
- **F.** All of the above statements are true.

15. Which of the following is a true statement about the configuration of services on the 7750 SR?

- **A.** A new SDP must be configured for any new service that is configured.
- **B.** One SDP can support multiple services, but they must all be the same type of service.
- **C.** One SDP can support multiple different service types.
- **D.** An SDP can use GRE encapsulation for some services and MPLS for others.
- **E.** None of the above statements are true.

18 VPWS Services

The Alcatel-Lucent NRS II exam topics covered in this chapter include the following:

- Epipe encapsulation types
- Special SAP values
- Specifying Ethertype values
- SAP and service MTU considerations
- SDP path MTU
- SDP and VC type
- Fpipes
- Apipes
- Cpipes
- Interworking overview
- Ipipes

Chapter 17 introduced the Alcatel-Lucent 7750 SR service infrastructure and described the signaling and operation of an IP/MPLS pseudowire as described by RFC 4447. As an example, we showed the configuration of one possible Virtual Private Wire Service (VPWS), an epipe.

In this chapter, we examine the details of an epipe configuration and verification. We look in detail at some of the trickier aspects of MTU (maximum transmission unit) configuration for a VPWS. We also introduce the other VPWS types: the apipe, fpipe, cpipe, and ipipe. The chapter concludes with a look at some of the interworking capabilities of the different VPWSs.

Pre-Assessment

The following assessment questions will help you understand what areas of the chapter you should review in more detail to prepare for the NRS II exam. You can also use the CD that accompanies this book to take all the assessment tests and review the answers.

1. Consider an epipe service on an Alcatel-Lucent 7750 SR that has a SAP configured with the CLI syntax `sap 1/1/4:20.10`. Assuming that the epipe service is operationally up, which statement best describes CE traffic that will ingress the service?
   - **A.** CE traffic with an outer VLAN tag of 10 and any non-zero inner VLAN tag will be sent over the service.
   - **B.** CE traffic with an outer VLAN tag of 20 and any non-zero inner VLAN tag will be sent over the service.
   - **C.** CE traffic with an outer VLAN tag of 20 and an inner VLAN tag of 10 will be sent over the service.
   - **D.** CE traffic with an outer VLAN tag of 10 and an inner VLAN tag of 20 will be sent over the service.
   - **E.** None of the above statements describe CE traffic that will ingress the service.

2. Which of the following statements is *false* regarding the MTUs used for an epipe service?

   A. SAP MTUs must be greater than or equal to the service MTU.

   B. The service MTU must be less than or equal to the path MTU.

   C. The path MTU must be greater than the MTU of every network port in the transport path.

   D. Epipe services configured on the same PE can have different service MTUs.

   E. None of the above statements are false.

3. An operator needs to provision an epipe service to accept IP packets as large as 9,000 bytes. What value should be used for the service MTU if the SAP encapsulation on both PE routers has a CLI syntax of `1/1/4:100.*`?

   A. 8,982 bytes

   B. 8,986 bytes

   C. 9,000 bytes

   D. 9,014 bytes

   E. 9,018 bytes

4. An epipe on a PE router receives a frame carrying an IP packet from a CE (customer edge) router that is too large for the service. What action will the PE router take?

   A. It will silently discard the frame.

   B. It will discard the frame and send a notification to the CE router.

   C. It will fragment the frame as long as the do-not-fragment bit is not set.

   D. It will always fragment the frame.

   E. None of the above answers are correct.

5. Which of the following best describes the behavior of the default SAP?

   A. The default SAP receives all frames.

   B. The default SAP receives all untagged frames.

   C. The default SAP receives all tagged frames.

   D. The default SAP receives all untagged frames and all tagged frames not received by another SAP.

   E. The default SAP receives all untagged frames and all frames with a VLAN tag of 0.

18.1 Overview of VPWS

VPWS defines a virtual point-to-point service that emulates a private leased line connection. For this reason, a VPWS is sometimes known as a Virtual Leased Line (VLL) service. The types of VPWS service supported on the Alcatel-Lucent 7750 SR include:

- **Epipe**—Emulates a point-to-point Ethernet service. VLAN (Virtual Local Area Network) tagged Ethernet frames are supported. Interworking with other Layer 2 technologies is also supported.
- **Apipe**—Emulates a point-to-point ATM (Asynchronous Transfer Mode) service. Several subtypes are provided to support different ATM service types.
- **Fpipe**—Emulates a point-to-point Frame Relay circuit. Some features for interworking with ATM are also supported.
- **Cpipe**—Emulates a point-to-point time division multiplexing (TDM) circuit.
- **Ipipe**—Provides IP interworking capabilities between different Layer 2 technologies.

The initial challenge of implementing a VPWS is the encapsulation of the various frame types for transmission over the IP/MPLS network. In addition to encapsulation, there are other complications that arise in supporting the individual characteristics and service capabilities of the Layer 2 technologies. These include issues such as the timing and service level capabilities found in technologies like ATM and TDM. In this book the focus is on the Ethernet epipe service. Many of these additional issues for the other VPWS services are beyond the scope of this book.

18.2 Epipe SAP Encapsulations

In Chapter 17, we introduced the components required for deploying a service and also provided an example of a simple, basic service, the epipe. The 7750 SR implementation of an epipe is based on RFC 4448 ("Encapsulation Methods for Transport of Ethernet over MPLS Networks"). In this chapter, we look into some of the more subtle aspects of Layer 2 service configuration. These can be roughly summarized as two subjects:

- SAP (Service Access Point) encapsulation
- MTU considerations

Epipe Encapsulation Types

There are three types of Ethernet SAP encapsulation supported for an Ethernet service, as shown in Table 18.1.

Table 18.1 Ethernet SAP Encapsulation Types

Encapsulation	VLAN Tags	Access Port MTU (bytes)	SAP Syntax
Null	0	1,514	port
dot1q	1	1,518	port:tag
qinq	2	1,522	port:outer-tag.inner-tag

When a VLAN tag is specified as part of the encapsulation, it is considered to be *service-delimiting*. This means that the VLAN tag is used to determine to which service the frame belongs. For example, if a SAP is created in a service as `1/1/2:11`, all frames arriving at port 1/1/2 with VLAN tag 11 belong to the service. All other frames do not.

Using service-delimiting VLAN tags, multiple SAPs can be defined on a single port for different services. In the service network shown in Figure 18.1, two epipe services have been defined—epipe 11 and epipe 22. Listing 18.1 shows the configuration of the two services on PE-1.

Figure 18.1 Service network with two epipe services.

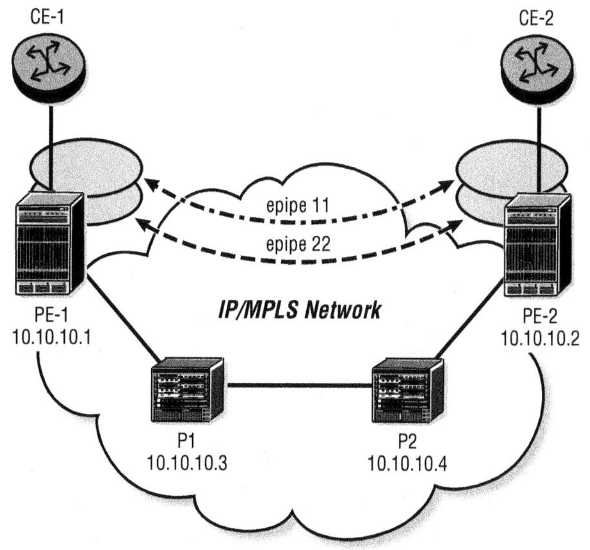

Listing 18.1 Configuring two different epipe services with dot1q SAPs

```
*A:PE-1# configure port 1/1/2
*A:PE-1>config>port# shutdown
*A:PE-1>config>port# ethernet mode access
*A:PE-1>config>port# ethernet encap-type dot1q
*A:PE-1>config>port# no shutdown
*A:PE-1>config>port# exit
*A:PE-1# configure service epipe 11 create customer 111
*A:PE-1>config>service>epipe$ sap 1/1/2:11 create
*A:PE-1>config>service>epipe>sap$ exit
*A:PE-1>config>service>epipe# spoke-sdp 2:11 create
*A:PE-1>config>service>epipe>spoke-sdp$ exit
*A:PE-1>config>service>epipe# no shutdown
*A:PE-1>config>service>epipe# exit
*A:PE-1# configure service epipe 22 customer 111 create
*A:PE-1>config>service>epipe$ sap 1/1/2:22 create
*A:PE-1>config>service>epipe>sap$ exit
*A:PE-1>config>service>epipe# spoke-sdp 2:22 create
*A:PE-1>config>service>epipe>spoke-sdp$ exit
*A:PE-1>config>service>epipe# no shutdown
*A:PE-1>config>service>epipe# show service service-using epipe

========================================================================
Services
========================================================================
ServiceId  Type      Adm  Opr  CustomerId Service Name
------------------------------------------------------------------------
11         Epipe     Up   Up   111
22         Epipe     Up   Up   111
------------------------------------------------------------------------
Matching Services : 2
------------------------------------------------------------------------
========================================================================
```

We simulate two different customer devices on the CE-1 router by configuring two interfaces with different VLAN tags. Listing 18.2 shows the configuration of the interfaces and a ping of the CE-2 router from both interfaces. The second ping uses a larger packet size.

Listing 18.2 Pinging from CE to CE through the two epipes

```
*A:CE-1# configure port 1/1/2
*A:CE-1>config>port# shutdown
*A:CE-1>config>port# ethernet encap-type dotlq
*A:CE-1>config>port# no shutdown
*A:CE-1>config>port# exit
*A:CE-1# configure router
*A:CE-1>config>router# interface to_CE11_2
*A:CE-1>config>router>if$ port 1/1/2:11
*A:CE-1>config>router>if$ address 192.168.11.1/24
*A:CE-1>config>router>if$ exit
*A:CE-1>config>router# interface to_CE22_2
*A:CE-1>config>router>if$ port 1/1/2:22
*A:CE-1>config>router>if$ address 192.168.22.1/24
*A:CE-1>config>router>if$ exit
*A:CE-1>config>router# show router interface

===============================================================================
Interface Table (Router: Base)
===============================================================================
Interface-Name                   Adm          Opr(v4/v6)  Mode    Port/SapId
   IP-Address                                                     PfxState
-------------------------------------------------------------------------------
system                           Down         Down/--     Network system
   -                                                              -
to_CE11_2                        Up           Up/--       Network 1/1/2:11
   192.168.11.1/24                                                n/a
to_CE22_2                        Up           Up/--       Network 1/1/2:22
   192.168.22.1/24                                                n/a
-------------------------------------------------------------------------------
Interfaces : 3
===============================================================================
*A:CE-1>config>router# ping 192.168.11.2
PING 192.168.11.2 56 data bytes
64 bytes from 192.168.11.2: icmp_seq=1 ttl=64 time=11.3ms.
64 bytes from 192.168.11.2: icmp_seq=2 ttl=64 time=3.50ms.
64 bytes from 192.168.11.2: icmp_seq=3 ttl=64 time=3.45ms.
64 bytes from 192.168.11.2: icmp_seq=4 ttl=64 time=3.54ms.
```

(continued)

Listing 18.2 *(continued)*

```
64 bytes from 192.168.11.2: icmp_seq=5 ttl=64 time=3.47ms.

---- 192.168.11.2 PING Statistics ----
5 packets transmitted, 5 packets received, 0.00% packet loss
round-trip min = 3.45ms, avg = 5.04ms, max = 11.3ms, stddev = 3.11ms
*A:CE-1>config>router# ping 192.168.22.2 size 1400
PING 192.168.22.2 1400 data bytes
1408 bytes from 192.168.22.2: icmp_seq=1 ttl=64 time=9.47ms.
1408 bytes from 192.168.22.2: icmp_seq=2 ttl=64 time=4.70ms.
1408 bytes from 192.168.22.2: icmp_seq=3 ttl=64 time=4.70ms.
1408 bytes from 192.168.22.2: icmp_seq=4 ttl=64 time=4.71ms.
1408 bytes from 192.168.22.2: icmp_seq=5 ttl=64 time=4.70ms.

---- 192.168.22.2 PING Statistics ----
5 packets transmitted, 5 packets received, 0.00% packet loss
round-trip min = 4.70ms, avg = 5.65ms, max = 9.47ms, stddev = 1.91ms
```

When we look at the statistics for the two SAPs, we can see the ping packets and can tell that the larger packets were sent through epipe 22 as expected. In Listing 18.3, we first clear the statistics for the SAPs and then ping the two interfaces (not shown). The show commands are performed after the ping to display the SAP statistics.

Listing 18.3 SAP statistics tell us that the larger pings are transmitted through epipe 22

```
*A:PE-1# clear service statistics sap 1/1/2:11 all
*A:PE-1# clear service statistics sap 1/1/2:22 all
*A:PE-1# show service id 11 sap 1/1/2:11 stats

===============================================================================
Service Access Points(SAP)
===============================================================================
Service Id         : 11
SAP                : 1/1/2:11                 Encap             : q-tag
Description        : (Not Specified)
Admin State        : Up                       Oper State        : Up
Flags              : None
```

```
Multi Svc Site     : None
Last Status Change : 03/24/2011 18:42:57
Last Mgmt Change   : 03/24/2011 18:42:42
-------------------------------------------------------------------------------
Sap per Queue stats
-------------------------------------------------------------------------------
                        Packets                 Octets

Ingress Queue 1 (Unicast) (Priority)
Off. HiPrio           : 0                       0
Off. LoPrio           : 6                       598
Dro. HiPrio           : 0                       0
Dro. LoPrio           : 0                       0
For. InProf           : 0                       0
For. OutProf          : 6                       598

Egress Queue 1
For. InProf           : 0                       0
For. OutProf          : 6                       598
Dro. InProf           : 0                       0
Dro. OutProf          : 0                       0
===============================================================================
*A:PE-1# show service id 22 sap 1/1/2:22 stats

===============================================================================
Service Access Points(SAP)
===============================================================================
Service Id         : 22
SAP                : 1/1/2:22                Encap             : q-tag
Description        : (Not Specified)
Admin State        : Up                      Oper State        : Up
Flags              : None
Multi Svc Site     : None
Last Status Change : 03/24/2011 18:43:48
Last Mgmt Change   : 03/24/2011 18:43:34
-------------------------------------------------------------------------------
Sap per Queue stats
-------------------------------------------------------------------------------
```

(continued)

Listing 18.3 *(continued)*

```
                        Packets                 Octets

Ingress Queue 1 (Unicast) (Priority)
Off. HiPrio          : 0                        0
Off. LoPrio          : 6                        7318
Dro. HiPrio          : 0                        0
Dro. LoPrio          : 0                        0
For. InProf          : 0                        0
For. OutProf         : 6                        7318

Egress Queue 1
For. InProf          : 0                        0
For. OutProf         : 6                        7318
Dro. InProf          : 0                        0
Dro. OutProf         : 0                        0
===============================================================================
```

When service-delimiting VLAN tags are used on the 7750 SR, they are stripped at the SAP ingress by default. The FCS (frame check sequence) for the frame is also removed. All other fields of the customer's frame are maintained. Figure 18.2 shows the encapsulation of data on the customer network and its encapsulation as it is transmitted across the epipe service. On the left, an Ethernet frame arrives at PE-1. It has a VLAN tag with a value of 11. The VLAN tag identifies the service that is intended to handle the frame and is stripped from the frame by router PE-1 along with the FCS field. The rest of the frame (header and data) is encapsulated with two MPLS labels. This frame is then encapsulated in a Layer 2 frame (either Ethernet or POS) for transmission to the next-hop. The FCS in this case is for the entire frame carrying the MPLS-encapsulated data.

When the frame reaches the egress PE router (PE-2, in this case), the MPLS labels are popped and the untagged frame is transmitted on the SAP interface. A VLAN tag is added to the frame, depending on the encapsulation ID on the SAP. In this example, the SAP on PE-2 is `1/1/2:111`, thus the VLAN tag added to the customer frame is 111 (see Listing 18.4).

Figure 18.2 Encapsulation of an Ethernet frame in an epipe service.

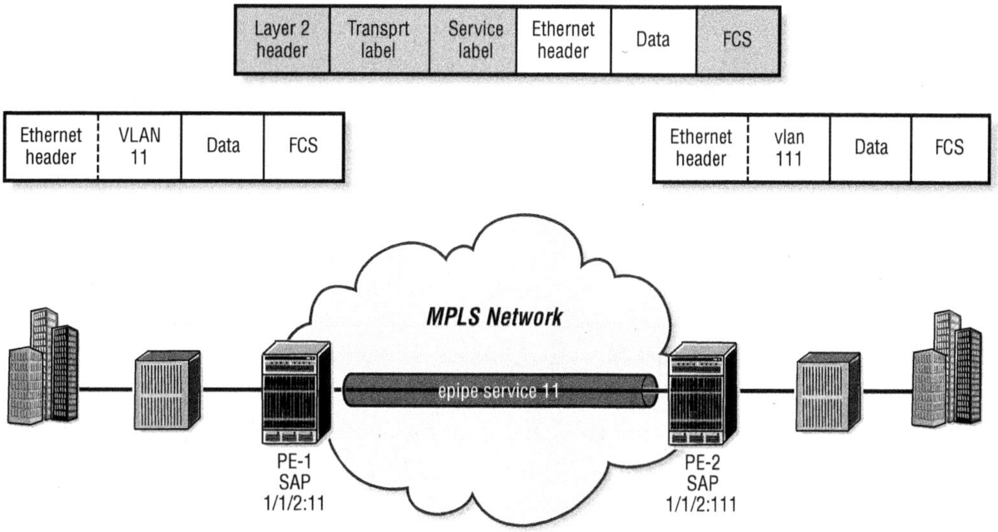

Listing 18.4 The SAP on PE-2 is defined with an encapsulation ID of 111

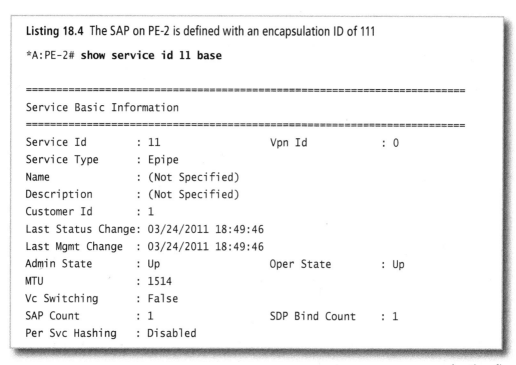

```
*A:PE-2# show service id 11 base

===============================================================================
Service Basic Information
===============================================================================
Service Id        : 11                    Vpn Id            : 0
Service Type      : Epipe
Name              : (Not Specified)
Description       : (Not Specified)
Customer Id       : 1
Last Status Change: 03/24/2011 18:49:46
Last Mgmt Change  : 03/24/2011 18:49:46
Admin State       : Up                    Oper State        : Up
MTU               : 1514
Vc Switching      : False
SAP Count         : 1                     SDP Bind Count    : 1
Per Svc Hashing   : Disabled
```

(continued)

Listing 18.4 *(continued)*

```
Force QTag Fwd     : Disabled

-------------------------------------------------------------------------------
Service Access & Destination Points
-------------------------------------------------------------------------------
Identifier                          Type         AdmMTU  OprMTU  Adm  Opr
-------------------------------------------------------------------------------
sap:1/1/2:111                       q-tag        1518    1518    Up   Up
sdp:1:11 S(10.10.10.1)              Spok         0       9190    Up   Up
===============================================================================
```

We can see in Listing 18.5 that the CE-2 router is expecting a VLAN tag of 111 for epipe service 11 and a VLAN tag of 222 for epipe 22.

Listing 18.5 IP interfaces defined on CE-2 for VLANs 111 and 222

```
*A:CE-2# show router interface

===============================================================================
Interface Table (Router: Base)
===============================================================================
Interface-Name                  Adm         Opr(v4/v6)  Mode    Port/SapId
   IP-Address                                                   PfxState
-------------------------------------------------------------------------------
system                          Down        Down/--     Network system
   -                                                            -
to_CE11_1                       Up          Up/--       Network 1/1/2:111
   192.168.11.2/24                                              n/a
to_CE22_1                       Up          Up/--       Network 1/1/2:222
   192.168.22.2/24                                              n/a
-------------------------------------------------------------------------------
Interfaces : 3
===============================================================================
```

Q-in-Q encapsulation works in a very similar manner to dot1Q encapsulation, except that two VLAN tag values are specified in the SAP as `port:outer.inner`, where `outer` is the outer (sometimes known as provider) VLAN tag and `inner` is the inner (sometimes known as customer) VLAN tag. Listing 18.6 shows the configuration of a port for Q-in-Q encapsulation and the creation of a service with a Q-in-Q SAP.

Listing 18.6 Q-in-Q SAP encapsulation

```
*A:PE-1# configure port 1/1/1
*A:PE-1>config>port# shutdown
*A:PE-1>config>port# ethernet mode access
*A:PE-1>config>port# ethernet encap-type qinq
*A:PE-1>config>port# no shutdown
*A:PE-1>config>port# exit
*A:PE-1# configure service epipe 111 customer 111 create
*A:PE-1>config>service>epipe$ sap 1/1/1:10.111 create
*A:PE-1>config>service>epipe>sap$ exit
*A:PE-1>config>service>epipe# sap 1/1/1:20.222 create
*A:PE-1>config>service>epipe>sap$ exit
*A:PE-1>config>service>epipe# no shutdown
*A:PE-1>config>service>epipe# show service id 111 base

===============================================================================
Service Basic Information
===============================================================================
Service Id        : 111                  Vpn Id            : 0
Service Type      : Epipe
Name              : (Not Specified)
Description       : (Not Specified)
Customer Id       : 111
Last Status Change: 03/26/2011 17:07:38
Last Mgmt Change  : 03/26/2011 17:07:38
Admin State       : Up                   Oper State        : Up
MTU               : 1514
Vc Switching      : False
SAP Count         : 2                    SDP Bind Count    : 0
Per Svc Hashing   : Disabled
Force QTag Fwd    : Disabled

-------------------------------------------------------------------------------
Service Access & Destination Points
-------------------------------------------------------------------------------
```

(continued)

Listing 18.6 *(continued)*

```
Identifier                          Type        AdmMTU  OprMTU  Adm  Opr
------------------------------------------------------------------------
sap:1/1/1:10.111                    qinq        1522    1522    Up   Up
sap:1/1/1:20.222                    qinq        1522    1522    Up   Up
========================================================================
```

Although epipe service 111 shown above is a little nonsensical, it is up and functioning. A frame with VLAN tags 10.111 received on port 1/1/1 will be retransmitted on the same port with VLAN tags 20.222.

Special SAP Values

The examples above illustrate the use of service-delimiting VLAN tags. However, VLAN tags do not have to be service-delimiting and can be passed transparently. If null encapsulation is specified for an access port and SAP, the SAP will accept all frames received on the port whether they are untagged, dot1Q tagged, or Q-in-Q tagged. They will be treated like any Ethernet frame and transmitted with the VLAN tag transparently preserved across the service. There are MTU issues to consider in this situation that are discussed in the next section.

We see similar behavior in a case in which a SAP is defined as a dot1Q service-delimiting SAP and a Q-in-Q frame is received at the port. If the outer tag matches the value in the SAP, it will be stripped and the frame transmitted over the service with the inner tag transparently maintained. If the outer tag does not match the SAP value, the frame is ignored by the service.

In a situation in which there are some frames that are untagged and some with service-delimiting VLAN tags, it is possible to define SAPs to capture the frames without service-delimiting tags. For dot1Q there are two special SAPs:

- **Default SAP** (`port:*`)—This SAP receives all untagged frames and any frames with tag values that are not used as a service-delimiting value on another SAP. VLAN tags are not stripped and are passed transparently.
- **Null SAP** (`port:0`)—This SAP receives all untagged frames and all frames with a VLAN tag of 0.

The default SAP can be used in a situation in which it is desired to pass all customer VLAN-tagged frames transparently, but capture some specific traffic for another purpose.

For example, one SAP can be created to capture management traffic with a specific tag value and a default SAP to capture all remaining traffic.

The null SAP is used when it is desirable to capture untagged traffic in another service. Use of the null SAP and default SAP are mutually exclusive on a port—if one is defined in a service, the other cannot be used.

For Q-in-Q-encapsulated SAPs, there is no default SAP. An encapsulation of `port:*.*` is not valid on the 7750 SR, and thus there is no way to capture all combinations of Q-in-Q-tagged frames, except to configure the port for null or dot1Q encapsulation and use the dot1Q default SAP. However, there are some special SAPs that govern the handling of the inner tag:

- **Wildcard SAP** (`port:x.*`)—This SAP receives all frames with outer tag value `x` regardless of the inner tag. The outer tag is stripped and the inner tag is passed transparently.
- **Null SAP** (`port:0.*`)—This SAP receives all untagged frames and any frames with a VLAN tag of 0.

Specifying Ethertype Values

IEEE 802.1Q specifies a hex value of `0x8100` to be used in the Ethertype field to identify the frame as a tagged frame. This value is also used for the Ethertype value in the inner VLAN tag for Q-in-Q encapsulation. However, some switches use other Ethertype values to identify the outer VLAN tag for Q-in-Q, usually `0x88a8` or `0x9100`. If the 7750 SR, in its default configuration receives a tagged frame with an Ethertype value other than `0x8100`, it is simply treated as an untagged frame.

On the 7750 SR, the port can be configured to use a different Ethertype value to support interoperation with these switches. A different value can be specified for either an outer tag (dot1Q Ethertype) or the inner tag (Q-in-Q Ethertype) or both. Listing 18.7 shows the configuration for changing the dot1Q Ethertype on a port. When the Ethertype value is changed for the port, any frame with an Ethertype that does not match the configured value is treated as an untagged frame.

Listing 18.7 Changing the Ethertype value for dot1Q encapsulation

```
*A:PE-1# configure port 1/1/1
*A:PE-1>config>port# ethernet dot1q-etype ?
```

(continued)

Listing 18.7 *(continued)*

```
  - dot1q-etype <0x0600..0xffff>
  - no dot1q-etype

 <0x0600..0xffff>     : [1536..65535] - accepts in decimal or hex


*A:PE-1>config>port# ethernet dot1q-etype 0x88a8
*A:PE-1>config>port# show service id 111 sap 1/1/1:10.111 base

===============================================================================
Service Access Points(SAP)
===============================================================================
Service Id         : 111
SAP                : 1/1/1:10.111             Encap             : qinq
QinQ Dot1p         : Default
Description        : (Not Specified)
Admin State        : Up                       Oper State        : Up
Flags              : None
Multi Svc Site     : None
Last Status Change : 03/26/2011 17:16:32
Last Mgmt Change   : 03/26/2011 17:07:23
Sub Type           : regular
Dot1Q Ethertype    : 0x88a8                   QinQ Ethertype    : 0x8100
Split Horizon Group: (Not Specified)

Admin MTU          : 1522                     Oper MTU          : 1522
Ingr IP Fltr-Id    : n/a                      Egr IP Fltr-Id    : n/a
Ingr Mac Fltr-Id   : n/a                      Egr Mac Fltr-Id   : n/a
Ingr IPv6 Fltr-Id  : n/a                      Egr IPv6 Fltr-Id  : n/a
tod-suite          : None                     qinq-pbit-marking : both
Ing Agg Rate Limit : max                      Egr Agg Rate Limit: max
Endpoint           : N/A
Q Frame-Based Acct : Disabled
Vlan-translation   : None

Acct. Pol          : None                     Collect Stats     : Disabled
Application Profile: None

===============================================================================
```

18.3 MTU Relationships

A pseudowire implements a service over an IP/MPLS network that can emulate a variety of Layer 2 technologies such as Ethernet and ATM. A fundamental characteristic of any Layer 2 technology is its MTU. When the pseudowire is established with T-LDP (Targeted LDP) signaling, there is an MTU negotiated that must match at each end of the service. However, the MTU subject is complicated in an IP/MPLS network by the fact that frames received at the PE are processed and encapsulated for transmission across the network and then assembled again at the other end. In designing an IP/MPLS network there are several entities for which MTU must be considered:

- Access port, or SAP MTU
- Service and virtual circuit (VC) MTU
- SDP(Service Distribution Point) path MTU
- Network port MTU

MTU is an important consideration in a Layer 2 service because oversized frames arriving at a Layer 2 interface are not fragmented, but simply discarded. Even though a Layer 3 service such as a VPRN will fragment oversized packets for transmission, this is an expensive operation and generally undesirable. Thus, MTU is an important issue in both Layer 2 and Layer 3 services.

SAP and Service MTU Considerations

The service MTU defines the maximum customer payload that can be carried in a VPN service. An Ethernet VPN service such as an epipe or VPLS service has a default service MTU of 1,514 bytes. This is the size required to carry a standard Ethernet frame—a 1,500-byte payload and a 14-byte header with no FCS. In a Layer 2 service, MTU is particularly important because Layer 2 technologies do not support fragmentation. If an oversized frame is received at an Ethernet interface, it is discarded. The configuration of the epipe from Figure 18.1 is shown in Listing 18.8. *MTU* has the default value of 1,514 bytes.

Listing 18.8 SAP and service MTU for an epipe with default parameters

```
*A:PE-1# show service id 11 base
```

(continued)

Listing 18.8 *(continued)*

```
===============================================================================
Service Basic Information
===============================================================================
Service Id        : 11                    Vpn Id          : 0
Service Type      : Epipe
Name              : (Not Specified)
Description       : (Not Specified)
Customer Id       : 111
Last Status Change: 03/24/2011 19:06:01
Last Mgmt Change  : 03/24/2011 18:42:57
Admin State       : Up                    Oper State      : Up
MTU               : 1514
Vc Switching      : False
SAP Count         : 1                     SDP Bind Count  : 1
Per Svc Hashing   : Disabled
Force QTag Fwd    : Disabled

-------------------------------------------------------------------------------
Service Access & Destination Points
-------------------------------------------------------------------------------
Identifier                          Type         AdmMTU  OprMTU  Adm  Opr
-------------------------------------------------------------------------------
sap:1/1/2:11                        q-tag        1518    1518    Up   Up
sdp:2:11 S(10.10.10.2)              Spok         0       9190    Up   Up
===============================================================================
```

Notice that the SAP in Listing 18.8 has an MTU of 1,518 bytes. The customer frame arriving at the SAP is expected to have a VLAN tag (4 bytes long) that is stripped before the frame is transmitted through the epipe. A Q-in-Q-encapsulated SAP such as the one configured in Listing 18.6 has a default MTU of 1,522 bytes, and both VLAN tags are removed before transmitting (see Figure 18.3). Both of these situations require a service MTU of 1,514 bytes because this is the size of the frame once the VLAN tag or tags are removed.

When using default values, the service MTU and SAP MTU are set to the appropriate values for a full-size Ethernet frame. We demonstrate this using two ping commands with specific packet sizes as shown in Listing 18.9. The size value specifies the size of the ping packet but does not include the 20 bytes of the IP header or the 8 bytes of the ICMP (Internet Control Message Protocol) header. Thus, a 1,500-byte IP packet is created with a ping value of 1,500 – 20 – 8 = 1,472 bytes. You can see that the ping of size 1,473 bytes (frame size of 1,515 bytes) is not transmitted through the service.

Figure 18.3 Both VLAN tags are removed at a service-delimiting Q-in-Q SAP.

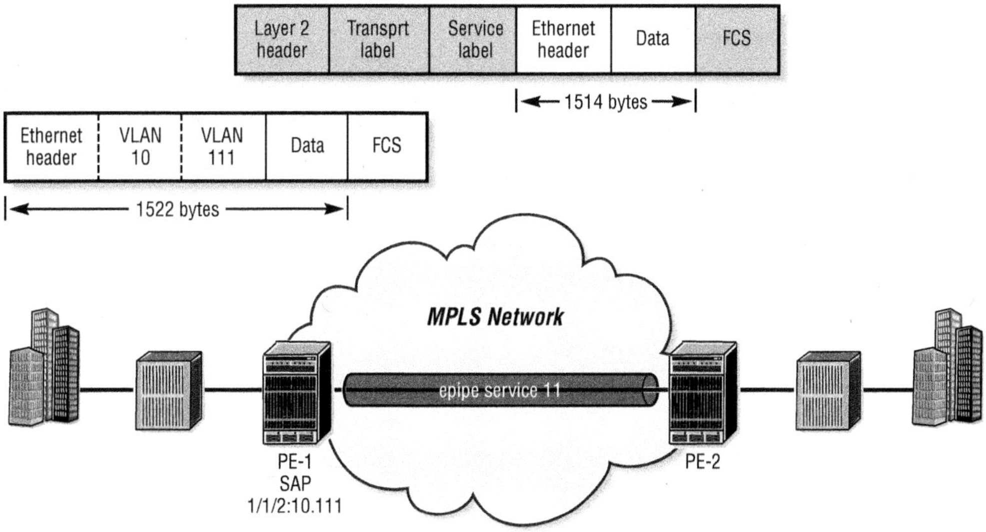

Listing 18.9 Ping through an epipe with maximum size packet

```
*A:CE-1# ping 192.168.11.2 size 1472 do-not-fragment count 2
PING 192.168.11.2 1472 data bytes
1480 bytes from 192.168.11.2: icmp_seq=1 ttl=64 time=4.96ms.
1480 bytes from 192.168.11.2: icmp_seq=2 ttl=64 time=4.88ms.

---- 192.168.11.2 PING Statistics ----
2 packets transmitted, 2 packets received, 0.00% packet loss
round-trip min = 4.88ms, avg = 4.92ms, max = 4.96ms, stddev = 0.038ms
*A:CE-1# ping 192.168.11.2 size 1473 do-not-fragment count 2
PING 192.168.11.2 1473 data bytes
Request timed out. icmp_seq=1.
Request timed out. icmp_seq=2.

---- 192.168.11.2 PING Statistics ----
2 packets transmitted, 0 packets received, 100% packet loss
```

MTU problems arise when we have a configuration different from the regular default configuration. For example, if we configure a default dot1Q SAP in our epipe service, VLAN tags are not stripped at the SAP because they are not service-delimiting (see Listing 18.10).

Listing 18.10 VLAN tags are not removed on the default SAP

```
*A:PE-1# configure service epipe 11
*A:PE-1>config>service>epipe# sap 1/1/2:11 shutdown
*A:PE-1>config>service>epipe# no sap 1/1/2:11
*A:PE-1>config>service>epipe# sap 1/1/2:* create
*A:PE-1>config>service>epipe>sap$ exit
*A:PE-1>config>service>epipe# info
----------------------------------------------
            sap 1/1/2:* create
            exit
            spoke-sdp 2:11 create
            exit
            no shutdown
----------------------------------------------
*A:PE-1# show service id 11 base

===============================================================================
Service Basic Information
===============================================================================
Service Id        : 11                  Vpn Id            : 0
Service Type      : Epipe
Name              : (Not Specified)
Description       : (Not Specified)
Customer Id       : 111
Last Status Change: 03/26/2011 20:40:16
Last Mgmt Change  : 03/24/2011 18:42:57
Admin State       : Up                  Oper State        : Up
MTU               : 1514
Vc Switching      : False
SAP Count         : 1                   SDP Bind Count    : 1
Per Svc Hashing   : Disabled
```

```
Force QTag Fwd      : Disabled

-------------------------------------------------------------------------------
Service Access & Destination Points
-------------------------------------------------------------------------------
Identifier                          Type          AdmMTU  OprMTU  Adm  Opr
-------------------------------------------------------------------------------
sap:1/1/2:*                         q-tag         1518    1518    Up   Up
sdp:2:11 S(10.10.10.2)              Spok          0       9190    Up   Up
===============================================================================
```

The default SAP will accept a full-size frame of 1,518 bytes (1,500-byte payload), but because the VLAN tag is not stripped from the customer frame, the service payload is 1,518 bytes. A frame of this size exceeds the service MTU of 1,514 bytes, and the frame is dropped. Listing 18.11 shows ping commands demonstrating that the maximum frame transmitted by this epipe service is 1,514 bytes. Because the frame includes the VLAN tag, the frame header is 18 bytes, and the Ethernet payload is only 1,496 bytes (see Figure 18.4).

Figure 18.4 Because the VLAN tag is carried in the epipe, the frame header occupies 18 bytes.

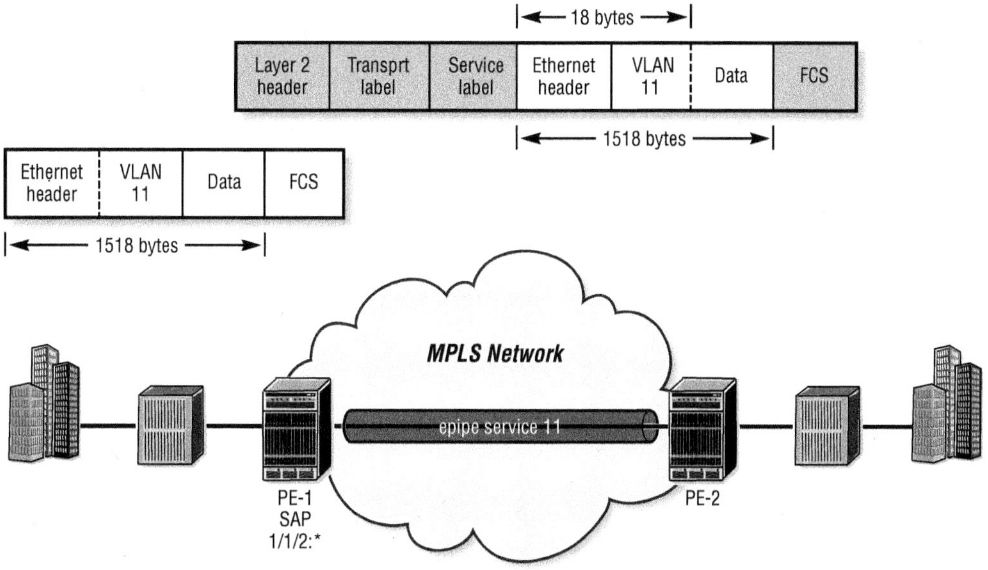

Listing 18.11 Maximum frame transmitted in the epipe is 1,514 bytes

```
*A:CE-1# ping 192.168.11.2 size 1472 do-not-fragment count 2
PING 192.168.11.2 1472 data bytes
Request timed out. icmp_seq=1.
Request timed out. icmp_seq=2.

---- 192.168.11.2 PING Statistics ----
2 packets transmitted, 0 packets received, 100% packet loss
*A:CE-1# ping 192.168.11.2 size 1469 do-not-fragment count 2
PING 192.168.11.2 1469 data bytes
Request timed out. icmp_seq=1.
Request timed out. icmp_seq=2.

---- 192.168.11.2 PING Statistics ----
2 packets transmitted, 0 packets received, 100% packet loss
*A:CE-1# ping 192.168.11.2 size 1468 do-not-fragment count 2
PING 192.168.11.2 1468 data bytes
1476 bytes from 192.168.11.2: icmp_seq=1 ttl=64 time=5.10ms.
1476 bytes from 192.168.11.2: icmp_seq=2 ttl=64 time=4.75ms.

---- 192.168.11.2 PING Statistics ----
2 packets transmitted, 2 packets received, 0.00% packet loss
round-trip min = 4.75ms, avg = 4.93ms, max = 5.10ms, stddev = 0.176ms
```

In Listing 18.12, we clear the statistics on the SAP before attempting the three ping commands in Listing 18.11. Afterward we can see that the four ping frames that were too large for the service were dropped at the SAP.

Listing 18.12 Frames that are too large for the service are dropped at the SAP

```
*A:PE-1# clear service statistics sap 1/1/2:* all
*A:PE-1# show service id 11 sap 1/1/2:* sap-stats

===============================================================================
Service Access Points(SAP)
===============================================================================
```

```
Service Id         : 11
SAP                : 1/1/2:*                  Encap             : q-tag
Description        : (Not Specified)
Admin State        : Up                       Oper State        : Up
Flags              : None
Multi Svc Site     : None
Last Status Change : 03/27/2011 12:17:08
Last Mgmt Change   : 03/26/2011 20:40:16
------------------------------------------------------------------------
Sap Statistics
------------------------------------------------------------------------
Last Cleared Time     : 03/27/2011 14:19:36

                        Packets                 Octets
Forwarding Engine Stats
Dropped               : 4                       6082
Off. HiPrio           : 0                       0
Off. LowPrio          : 2                       3036
Off. Uncolor          : 0                       0

Queueing Stats(Ingress QoS Policy 1)
Dro. HiPrio           : 0                       0
Dro. LowPrio          : 0                       0
For. InProf           : 0                       0
For. OutProf          : 2                       3036

Queueing Stats(Egress QoS Policy 1)
Dro. InProf           : 0                       0
Dro. OutProf          : 0                       0
For. InProf           : 0                       0
For. OutProf          : 2                       3036
========================================================================
```

We can see that in order to carry a full-size Ethernet frame for the default dot1Q SAP, we need a service MTU of 1,518 bytes. Listing 18.13 shows the configuration of the service for this larger MTU. When increasing the service MTU, we must also consider the SDP path MTU, which is discussed in the next section.

Listing 18.13 Configuring a larger service MTU

```
*A:PE-1# configure service epipe 11
*A:PE-1>config>service>epipe# service-mtu 1518
*A:PE-1>config>service>epipe# info
----------------------------------------------
            service-mtu 1518
            sap 1/1/2:* create
            exit
            spoke-sdp 2:11 create
            exit
            no shutdown
----------------------------------------------
*A:PE-1>config>service>epipe# show service id 11 base

===============================================================================
Service Basic Information
===============================================================================
Service Id        : 11                  Vpn Id            : 0
Service Type      : Epipe
Name              : (Not Specified)
Description       : (Not Specified)
Customer Id       : 111
Last Status Change: 03/27/2011 11:40:56
Last Mgmt Change  : 03/27/2011 11:40:56
Admin State       : Up                  Oper State        : Down
MTU               : 1518
Vc Switching      : False
SAP Count         : 1                   SDP Bind Count    : 1
Per Svc Hashing   : Disabled
Force QTag Fwd    : Disabled

-------------------------------------------------------------------------------
Service Access & Destination Points
-------------------------------------------------------------------------------
Identifier                          Type         AdmMTU  OprMTU  Adm  Opr
-------------------------------------------------------------------------------
sap:1/1/2:*                         q-tag        1518    1518    Up   Up
sdp:2:11 S(10.10.10.2)              Spok         0       9190    Up   Down
```

```
===============================================================================
*A:PE-1>config>service>epipe# show service id 11 sdp 2:11 detail

===============================================================================
Service Destination Point (Sdp Id : 2:11) Details
===============================================================================
-------------------------------------------------------------------------------
 Sdp Id 2:11  -(10.10.10.2)
-------------------------------------------------------------------------------
Description      : (Not Specified)
SDP Id              : 2:11                       Type                : Spoke
Spoke Descr      : (Not Specified)
VC Type             : Ether                      VC Tag              : n/a
Admin Path MTU      : 0                          Oper Path MTU       : 9190
Far End             : 10.10.10.2                 Delivery            : MPLS
Hash Label          : Disabled

Admin State         : Up                         Oper State          : Down
Acct. Pol           : None                       Collect Stats       : Disabled
Ingress Label       : 131069                     Egress Label        : 131069
Ingr Mac Fltr-Id    : n/a                        Egr Mac Fltr-Id     : n/a
Ingr IP Fltr-Id     : n/a                        Egr IP Fltr-Id      : n/a
Ingr IPv6 Fltr-Id   : n/a                        Egr IPv6 Fltr-Id    : n/a
Admin ControlWord   : Not Preferred              Oper ControlWord    : False
Admin BW(Kbps)      : 0                          Oper BW(Kbps)       : 0
Last Status Change  : 03/27/2011 11:40:56        Signaling           : TLDP
Last Mgmt Change    : 03/27/2011 11:40:56        Force Vlan-Vc       : Disabled
Endpoint            : N/A                        Precedence          : 4
Class Fwding State  : Down
Flags               : ServiceMTUMismatch
Peer Pw Bits        : pwNotForwarding
Peer Fault Ip       : None
Peer Vccv CV Bits   : lspPing
Peer Vccv CC Bits   : mplsRouterAlertLabel
Application Profile: None

... output omitted ...
```

After the MTU is increased on PE-1, the service is down because the SDP binding is down. The *Flags* field shows an error of `ServiceMTUMismatch`. This MTU is used in the T-LDP signaling of the pseudowire and must match at both ends of the service. Listing 18.14 shows the MTU values signaled by T-LDP for epipe service 11 (LMTU and RMTU). Notice that the value signaled is the service MTU minus 14 (for the Ethernet header). It can be seen that the local MTU is 1,504 bytes and the remote MTU is 1,500 bytes; thus, the service is not up.

Listing 18.14 MTU values signaled by T-LDP between service endpoints

```
*A:PE-1# show router ldp bindings fec-type services

===============================================================================
LDP LSR ID: 10.10.10.1
===============================================================================
Legend: U - Label In Use, N - Label Not In Use, W - Label Withdrawn
        S - Status Signaled Up,  D - Status Signaled Down
        E - Epipe Service, V - VPLS Service, M - Mirror Service
        A - Apipe Service, F - Fpipe Service, I - IES Service,
R - VPRN service
        P - Ipipe Service, WP - Label Withdraw Pending, C - Cpipe Service
        TLV - (Type, Length: Value)
===============================================================================
LDP Service FEC 128 Bindings
===============================================================================
Type   VCId     SvcId     SDPId  Peer           IngLbl  EgrLbl  LMTU  RMTU
-------------------------------------------------------------------------------
E-Eth  11       11        2      10.10.10.2     131069U 131069D 1504  1500
E-Eth  22       22        2      10.10.10.2     131068U 131068S 1500  1500
-------------------------------------------------------------------------------
No. of VC Labels: 2


===============================================================================
LDP Service FEC 129 Bindings
===============================================================================
AGI                                    SAII             TAII
Type                SvcId      SDPId  Peer      IngLbl  EgrLbl  LMTU  RMTU
-------------------------------------------------------------------------------
No Matching Entries Found
===============================================================================
===============================================================================
```

After the service MTU is adjusted on the far side, the service is up. Listing 18.15 shows that the service MTU values signaled are now both 1,504 bytes. Listing 18.16 shows that a full-size frame [1,472 bytes (ping) + 28 bytes (ICMP/IP header) + 18 bytes (Ethernet header including VLAN tag) = 1,518 bytes] can be accommodated by the service.

Listing 18.15 Service is up when service MTUs match

```
*A:PE-1# show service id 11 base

===============================================================================
Service Basic Information
===============================================================================
Service Id         : 11                     Vpn Id           : 0
Service Type       : Epipe
Name               : (Not Specified)
Description        : (Not Specified)
Customer Id        : 111
Last Status Change: 03/27/2011 12:17:08
Last Mgmt Change   : 03/27/2011 11:40:56
Admin State        : Up                     Oper State       : Up
MTU                : 1518
Vc Switching       : False
SAP Count          : 1                      SDP Bind Count   : 1
Per Svc Hashing    : Disabled
Force QTag Fwd     : Disabled

-------------------------------------------------------------------------------
Service Access & Destination Points
-------------------------------------------------------------------------------
Identifier                         Type         AdmMTU  OprMTU  Adm  Opr
-------------------------------------------------------------------------------
sap:1/1/2:*                        q-tag        1518    1518    Up   Up
sdp:2:11 S(10.10.10.2)             Spok         0       9190    Up   Up
===============================================================================
*A:PE-1# show router ldp bindings fec-type services

===============================================================================
LDP LSR ID: 10.10.10.1
===============================================================================
```

(continued)

Listing 18.15 *(continued)*

```
Legend: U - Label In Use, N - Label Not In Use, W - Label Withdrawn
        S - Status Signaled Up,  D - Status Signaled Down
        E - Epipe Service, V - VPLS Service, M - Mirror Service
        A - Apipe Service, F - Fpipe Service, I - IES Service,
 R - VPRN service
        P - Ipipe Service, WP - Label Withdraw Pending, C - Cpipe Service
        TLV - (Type, Length: Value)
========================================================================
LDP Service FEC 128 Bindings
========================================================================
Type   VCId   SvcId      SDPId  Peer          IngLbl  EgrLbl  LMTU  RMTU
------------------------------------------------------------------------
E-Eth  11     11         2      10.10.10.2    131069U 131069S 1504  1504
E-Eth  22     22         2      10.10.10.2    131068U 131068S 1500  1500
------------------------------------------------------------------------
No. of VC Labels: 2


========================================================================
LDP Service FEC 129 Bindings
========================================================================
AGI                           SAII                    TAII
Type         SvcId      SDPId Peer            IngLbl  EgrLbl  LMTU  RMTU
------------------------------------------------------------------------
No Matching Entries Found
========================================================================
========================================================================
```

Listing 18.16 Full-size, VLAN-tagged frames transmitted through epipe with 1,518-byte service MTU

```
*A:CE-1# ping 192.168.11.2 size 1472 do-not-fragment count 2
PING 192.168.11.2 1472 data bytes
1480 bytes from 192.168.11.2: icmp_seq=1 ttl=64 time=4.86ms.
1480 bytes from 192.168.11.2: icmp_seq=2 ttl=64 time=5.22ms.

---- 192.168.11.2 PING Statistics ----
2 packets transmitted, 2 packets received, 0.00% packet loss
```

```
round-trip min = 4.86ms, avg = 5.04ms, max = 5.22ms, stddev = 0.177ms
*A:CE-1# ping 192.168.11.2 size 1473 do-not-fragment count 2
PING 192.168.11.2 1473 data bytes
Request timed out. icmp_seq=1.
Request timed out. icmp_seq=2.

---- 192.168.11.2 PING Statistics ----
2 packets transmitted, 0 packets received, 100% packet loss
```

A null-encapsulated SAP behaves in the same manner as a dot1Q default SAP and has the same issue if it receives VLAN-tagged frames. In Listing 18.17, the far end of the epipe service (PE-2) is configured with a null-encapsulated SAP and a service MTU of 1,518 bytes.

Listing 18.17 Null-encapsulated SAP on a service with tagged frames

```
*A:PE-2# configure service epipe 11
*A:PE-2>config>service>epipe# sap 1/1/2:* shutdown
*A:PE-2>config>service>epipe# no sap 1/1/2:*
*A:PE-2>config>service>epipe# exit
*A:PE-2# configure port 1/1/2
*A:PE-2>config>port# shutdown
*A:PE-2>config>port# ethernet encap-type null
*A:PE-2>config>port# no shutdown
*A:PE-2>config>port# exit
*A:PE-2# configure service epipe 11
*A:PE-2>config>service>epipe# sap 1/1/2 create
*A:PE-2>config>service>epipe>sap$ exit
*A:PE-2>config>service>epipe# info
----------------------------------------------
            service-mtu 1518
            sap 1/1/2 create
            exit
            spoke-sdp 1:11 create
            exit
            no shutdown
----------------------------------------------
```

(continued)

Listing 18.17 *(continued)*

```
*A:PE-2>config>service>epipe# show service id 11 base

===============================================================================
Service Basic Information
===============================================================================
Service Id        : 11                  Vpn Id           : 0
Service Type      : Epipe
Name              : (Not Specified)
Description       : (Not Specified)
Customer Id       : 1
Last Status Change: 03/27/2011 12:57:06
Last Mgmt Change  : 03/27/2011 11:53:33
Admin State       : Up                  Oper State       : Down
MTU               : 1518
Vc Switching      : False
SAP Count         : 1                   SDP Bind Count   : 1
Per Svc Hashing   : Disabled
Force QTag Fwd    : Disabled

-------------------------------------------------------------------------------
Service Access & Destination Points
-------------------------------------------------------------------------------
Identifier                        Type        AdmMTU  OprMTU  Adm  Opr
-------------------------------------------------------------------------------
sap:1/1/2                         null        1514    1514    Up   Down
sdp:1:11 S(10.10.10.1)            Spok        0       9190    Up   Up
===============================================================================
*A:PE-2>config>service>epipe# show service id 11 sap 1/1/2 detail

===============================================================================
Service Access Points(SAP)
===============================================================================
Service Id         : 11
SAP                : 1/1/2                   Encap             : null
Description        : (Not Specified)
Admin State        : Up                      Oper State        : Down
Flags              : PortMTUTooSmall
Multi Svc Site     : None
```

```
Last Status Change : 03/18/2011 10:42:00
Last Mgmt Change   : 03/27/2011 12:58:30
Sub Type           : regular
Dot1Q Ethertype    : 0x8100                    QinQ Ethertype     : 0x8100
Split Horizon Group: (Not Specified)

... output omitted ...
```

The service is down because the SAP MTU is less than the service MTU. In this situation, the service on PE-2 could receive a frame that was too large for the SAP. In a Layer 2 service, the SAP MTU must always be equal to or larger than the service MTU. Of course, if the SAP MTU is larger than the service MTU, there is the risk that a frame will be dropped at ingress to the service. The SAP MTU is changed by changing the port MTU (see Listing 18.18).

Listing 18.18 Increasing the SAP MTU to match the service MTU

```
*A:PE-2# configure port 1/1/2 ethernet mtu 1518
*A:PE-2# show service id 11 base

===============================================================================
Service Basic Information
===============================================================================
Service Id        : 11                    Vpn Id            : 0
Service Type      : Epipe
Name              : (Not Specified)
Description       : (Not Specified)
Customer Id       : 1
Last Status Change: 03/27/2011 13:19:48
Last Mgmt Change  : 03/27/2011 11:53:33
Admin State       : Up                    Oper State        : Up
MTU               : 1518
Vc Switching      : False
SAP Count         : 1                     SDP Bind Count    : 1
Per Svc Hashing   : Disabled
Force QTag Fwd    : Disabled

-------------------------------------------------------------------------------
```

(continued)

Listing 18.18 *(continued)*

```
Service Access & Destination Points
-------------------------------------------------------------------------
Identifier                          Type         AdmMTU  OprMTU  Adm  Opr
-------------------------------------------------------------------------
sap:1/1/2                           null         1518    1518    Up   Up
sdp:1:11 S(10.10.10.1)              Spok         0       9190    Up   Up
=========================================================================
```

These examples demonstrate the need to carefully consider the setting of the service and the SAP MTU. The same principles apply when a service is being deployed to carry jumbo frames with a size of 5,000 bytes or 9,000 bytes. There are additional considerations on the service provider network for supporting larger service MTUs, which are discussed in the next section.

SDP Path MTU

In the previous section, we examined the relationship between frames and MTU in the access network and the service MTU. In this section, we examine the relationship between the service MTU and the SDP path MTU.

The SDP path MTU defines the maximum payload size that can be carried in the SDP transport tunnel. On the 7750 SR, the default value for the SDP path MTU is calculated on the ingress PE router by subtracting the encapsulation overhead of the transport tunnel from the egress network port MTU.

Remember, many different services may be bound to the same SDP. These services may have different service MTUs, but they can never exceed the SDP path MTU.

Figure 18.5 illustrates the relationship between the network port, SDP path MTU, service MTU, and the access port MTU. The MTU rules can be summarized as follows:

- Network port MTU > SDP path MTU + transport tunnel encapsulation overhead
- SDP path MTU > service MTU
- Service MTU < access port MTU (packet drops may occur when the access port MTU is greater than the service MTU)

Figure 18.5 Relationship between network port, path, service, and access port MTU.

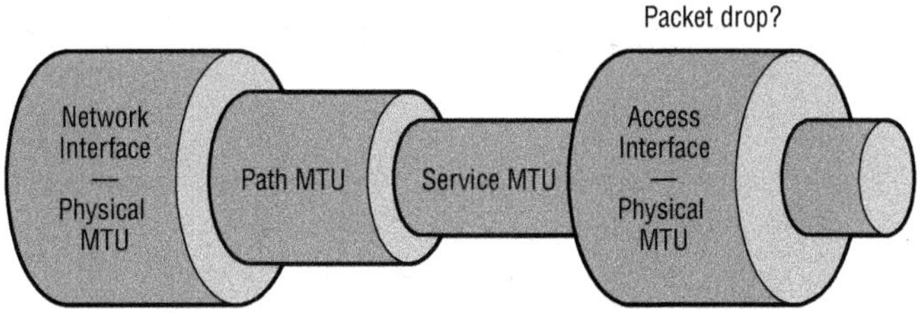

As an example, assume that the SDP network port is a gigabit Ethernet port with an MTU of 9,212 bytes (default on the 7750 SR) and the SDP uses MPLS encapsulation. The encapsulation overhead of the transport tunnel is 14 bytes for the Ethernet header plus 8 bytes for the two MPLS labels. Therefore, the default path MTU for the SDP is 9,212 – 22 = 9,190 bytes. In Listing 18.19, `sdp 2` has an *Oper Path MTU* of `9190` and uses LSP `to_PE-2` as its transport LSP. `to_PE-2` egresses Router PE-1 on interface `1/1/3`, which has an MTU of 9,212 bytes.

Listing 18.19 Derivation of the SDP path MTU from the network port MTU

```
*A:PE-1# show service sdp 2 detail

=======================================================================
Service Destination Point (Sdp Id : 2) Details
=======================================================================
-----------------------------------------------------------------------
 Sdp Id 2  -(10.10.10.2)
-----------------------------------------------------------------------
Description          : (Not Specified)
SDP Id               : 2                    SDP Source         : manual
Admin Path MTU       : 0                    Oper Path MTU      : 9190
Far End              : 10.10.10.2           Delivery           : MPLS
Admin State          : Up                   Oper State         : Up
Signaling            : TLDP                 Metric             : 0
Acct. Pol            : None                 Collect Stats      : Disabled
Last Status Change   : 03/27/2011 17:37:42  Adv. MTU Over.     : No
Last Mgmt Change     : 03/27/2011 17:37:42  VLAN VC Etype      : 0x8100
Bw BookingFactor     : 100                  PBB Etype          : 0x88e7
Oper Max BW(Kbps)    : 0                    Avail BW(Kbps)     : 0
```

(continued)

Listing 18.19 *(continued)*

```
Net-Domain          : default             Egr Interfaces    : Consistent
Mixed LSP Mode       : Disabled
Flags                : None

KeepAlive Information :
Admin State         : Disabled            Oper State         : Disabled
Hello Time          : 10                  Hello Msg Len      : 0
Hello Timeout       : 5                   Unmatched Replies : 0
Max Drop Count      : 3                   Hold Down Time     : 10
Tx Hello Msgs       : 0                   Rx Hello Msgs      : 0

-------------------------------------------------------------------------
RSVP/Static LSPs
-------------------------------------------------------------------------
Associated LSP LIST :
Lsp Name             : to_PE-2
Admin State          : Up                   Oper State         : Up
Time Since Last Tran*: 00h00m51s

-------------------------------------------------------------------------
Class-based forwarding :
-------------------------------------------------------------------------
Class forwarding     : Disabled             EnforceDSTELspFc   : Disabled
Default LSP          : Uknwn                Multicast LSP      : None

=========================================================================
FC Mapping Table
=========================================================================
FC Name             LSP Name
-------------------------------------------------------------------------
No FC Mappings

=========================================================================
* indicates that the corresponding row element may have been truncated.
*A:PE-1# show router mpls lsp "to_PE-2" path

=========================================================================
```

```
MPLS LSP to_PE-2 Path
========================================================================
------------------------------------------------------------------------
LSP Name     : to_PE-2                          To           : 10.10.10.2
Adm State    : Up                               Oper State   : Up
------------------------------------------------------------------------
Path Name                   Next Hop        Type       Out I/F   Adm  Opr
------------------------------------------------------------------------
loose                       10.1.3.3        Primary    1/1/3     Up   Up
========================================================================
*A:PE-1# show port 1/1

========================================================================
Ports on Slot 1
========================================================================
Port         Admin Link Port    Cfg  Oper LAG/ Port Port Port   SFP/XFP/
Id           State      State   MTU  MTU  Bndl Mode Encp Type   MDIMDX
------------------------------------------------------------------------
1/1/1        Up    Yes  Up      1522 1522    - accs qinq gige
1/1/2        Up    Yes  Up      1518 1518    - accs dotq gige
1/1/3        Up    Yes  Up      9212 9212    - netw null gige
1/1/4        Up    Yes  Up      9212 9212    - netw null gige
1/1/5        Down  No   Down    9212 9212    - netw null gige
1/1/6        Down  No   Down    9212 9212    - netw null gige
1/1/7        Down  No   Down    9212 9212    - netw null gige
1/1/8        Down  No   Down    9212 9212    - netw null gige
1/1/9        Down  No   Down    9212 9212    - netw null gige
1/1/10       Down  No   Down    9212 9212    - netw null gige
========================================================================
```

If an SDP is defined with GRE (generic routing encapsulation) for the transport tunnel, it uses a GRE header (4 bytes) and an IP header (20 bytes) instead of the 4-byte MPLS transport label. The encapsulation overhead for a GRE tunnel on the same Ethernet interface is 14 bytes for the Ethernet header plus 20 bytes for the IP header plus 4 bytes for the GRE header plus 4 bytes for the service label = 42 bytes. Thus the default SDP path MTU for a GRE-encapsulated SDP is 9,212 – 42 = 9,170 bytes (see Listing 18.20).

Listing 18.20 The SDP path MTU using a GRE transport tunnel

```
*A:PE-1# configure service sdp 22 gre create
*A:PE-1>config>service>sdp$ far-end 10.10.10.2
*A:PE-1>config>service>sdp$ no shutdown
*A:PE-1>config>service>sdp$ show service sdp 22 detail

===============================================================================
Service Destination Point (Sdp Id : 22) Details
===============================================================================
-------------------------------------------------------------------------------
 Sdp Id 22  -(10.10.10.2)
-------------------------------------------------------------------------------
Description           : (Not Specified)
SDP Id               : 22                     SDP Source        : manual
Admin Path MTU       : 0                      Oper Path MTU     : 9170
Far End              : 10.10.10.2             Delivery          : GRE
Admin State          : Up                     Oper State        : Up
Signaling            : TLDP                   Metric            : 0
Acct. Pol            : None                   Collect Stats     : Disabled
Last Status Change   : 03/27/2011 17:47:48    Adv. MTU Over.    : No
Last Mgmt Change     : 03/27/2011 17:47:48    VLAN VC Etype     : 0x8100
Bw BookingFactor     : 100
Oper Max BW(Kbps)    : 0                      Avail BW(Kbps)    : 0
Net-Domain           : default                Egr Interfaces    : Consistent
Mixed LSP Mode       : n/a
Flags                : None

KeepAlive Information :
Admin State          : Disabled               Oper State        : Disabled
Hello Time           : 10                     Hello Msg Len     : 0
Hello Timeout        : 5                      Unmatched Replies : 0
Max Drop Count       : 3                      Hold Down Time    : 10
Tx Hello Msgs        : 0                      Rx Hello Msgs     : 0

-------------------------------------------------------------------------------
RSVP/Static LSPs
-------------------------------------------------------------------------------
Associated LSP LIST :
SDP Delivery Mechanism is not MPLS

===============================================================================
```

When calculating the required network port MTU, you must also consider any other factors that increase the encapsulation overhead. For example, facility backup or LDP over RSVP-TE (Label Distribution Protocol over Resource Reservation Protocol–Traffic Engineering) each requires an additional MPLS label. If both are used together on the same LSP, this is an additional 8 bytes of encapsulation overhead.

The calculation of SDP path MTU from the egress network port assumes that all ports on the SDP path have an equal or greater MTU. When this is not the case, it may cause problems with services bound to the SDP. In Figure 18.6, the MTU on network ports of Routers PE-1 and PE-2 is 9,212 bytes. However, the network MTU between P1 and P2 is set to 1,514 bytes.

Figure 18.6 Service with lower MTU in the path.

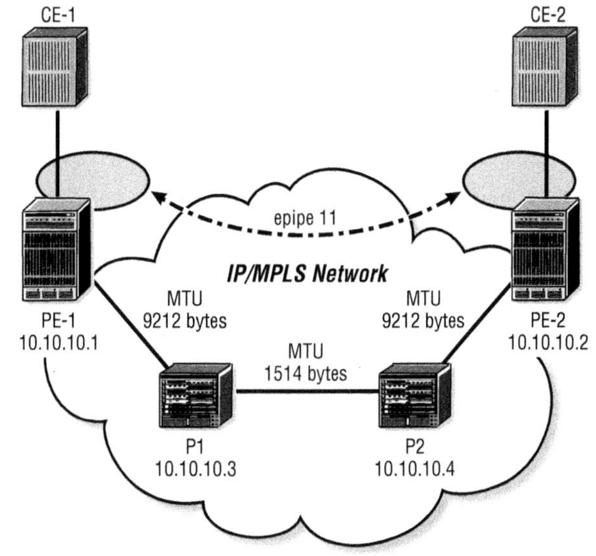

We have configured epipe 11 with a service MTU of 5,000 bytes. This is considerably smaller than the SDP path MTU of 9,190 bytes; thus the service is up (Listing 18.21).

Listing 18.21 Epipe with a service MTU of 5,000 and an SDP path MTU of 9,190

```
*A:PE-1# show service id 11 base

===============================================================================
```

(continued)

Listing 18.21 *(continued)*

```
Service Basic Information
===============================================================================
Service Id        : 11                    Vpn Id            : 0
Service Type      : Epipe
Name              : (Not Specified)
Description       : (Not Specified)
Customer Id       : 111
Last Status Change: 03/27/2011 19:11:51
Last Mgmt Change  : 03/27/2011 18:33:41
Admin State       : Up                    Oper State        : Up
MTU               : 5000
Vc Switching      : False
SAP Count         : 1                     SDP Bind Count    : 1
Per Svc Hashing   : Disabled
Force QTag Fwd    : Disabled

-------------------------------------------------------------------------------
Service Access & Destination Points
-------------------------------------------------------------------------------
Identifier                         Type         AdmMTU  OprMTU  Adm  Opr
-------------------------------------------------------------------------------
sap:1/1/2:11                       q-tag        5004    5004    Up   Up
sdp:2:11 S(10.10.10.2)             Spok         0       9190    Up   Up
===============================================================================
*A:PE-1# show service sdp 2

===============================================================================
Service Destination Point (Sdp Id : 2)
===============================================================================
SdpId    Adm MTU  Opr MTU  IP address    Adm  Opr        Deliver   Signal
-------------------------------------------------------------------------------
2        0        9190     10.10.10.2    Up   Up         MPLS      TLDP
===============================================================================
```

Although we can ping across the epipe, we find that it does not support anywhere near the size frame expected with a service MTU of 5,000 bytes. As seen in Listing 18.22, we find the maximum size ping to be 1,450 bytes. The size of the frame transmitted on the network port for this ping can be calculated as 1,450 + 28 bytes (IP/ICMP header) + 14 bytes (payload Ethernet header) + 22 bytes (transport encapsulation overhead) = 1,514 bytes. This is exactly as expected because the link MTU between P1 and P2 is 1,514.

Listing 18.22 The maximum ping through the epipe is 1,450 bytes although the service MTU is 5,000 bytes

```
*A:CE-1# ping 192.168.11.2 size 1450 do-not-fragment count 2
PING 192.168.11.2 1450 data bytes
1458 bytes from 192.168.11.2: icmp_seq=1 ttl=64 time=5.61ms.
1458 bytes from 192.168.11.2: icmp_seq=2 ttl=64 time=5.66ms.

---- 192.168.11.2 PING Statistics ----
2 packets transmitted, 2 packets received, 0.00% packet loss
round-trip min = 5.61ms, avg = 5.63ms, max = 5.66ms, stddev = 0.060ms
*A:CE-1# ping 192.168.11.2 size 1451 do-not-fragment count 2
PING 192.168.11.2 1451 data bytes
Request timed out. icmp_seq=1.
Request timed out. icmp_seq=2.

---- 192.168.11.2 PING Statistics ----
2 packets transmitted, 0 packets received, 100% packet loss
```

A tool that is useful in determining the effective path MTU of an SDP is the command `oam sdp-mtu`, which transmits increasingly large packets on the SDP. The OAM (operations, administration, and maintenance) commands are described in more detail in Chapter 21. Listing 18.23 shows the use of this tool to determine the effective path MTU for SDP 2 of 1,492 bytes. If we add the transport encapsulation overhead of 22 bytes to this, we get a network port MTU of 1,514 bytes.

Listing 18.23 Use of the oam sdp-mtu command to determine the effective path MTU

```
*A:PE-1# oam sdp-mtu 2 size-inc 1450 1550 step 10
Size     Sent     Response
----------------------------
1450     ..        Success
1460     .         Success
```

(continued)

Listing 18.23 *(continued)*

```
1470     .        Success
1480     .        Success
1490     .        Success
1500     ...      Request Timeout

Maximum Response Size: 1490
*A:PE-1# oam sdp-mtu 2 size-inc 1490 1499 step 1
Size    Sent    Response
----------------------------
1490     .        Success
1491     .        Success
1492     .        Success
1493     ...      Request Timeout

Maximum Response Size: 1492
```

RSVP-TE defines the ADSPEC object that can be used in the Path message to collect information about the path at each router, including MTU information. Negotiated MTU for the LSP (label switched path) is set to the smallest MTU value found on the path. If adspec is configured on the LSP used as the transport for the SDP, the SDP path MTU is derived from the path MTU negotiated by RSVP-TE using the ADSPEC object (see Listing 18.24). Notice that the LSP MTU is 1,500 bytes. The SDP path MTU is 8 bytes less to accommodate the two MPLS labels. If the negotiated MTU of the LSP changes, the SDP path MTU changes accordingly.

Listing 18.24 Use of the ADSPEC object by RSVP-TE to signal the path MTU

```
*A:PE-1# configure router mpls lsp "to_PE-2"
*A:PE-1>config>router>mpls>lsp# adspec
*A:PE-1>config>router>mpls>lsp# info
----------------------------------------------
                to 10.10.10.2
                adspec
                primary "loose"
                exit
                no shutdown
----------------------------------------------
```

```
*A:PE-1>config>router>mpls>lsp# exit
*A:PE-1# show router mpls lsp "to_PE-2" path detail

===============================================================================
MPLS LSP to_PE-2 Path  (Detail)
===============================================================================
Legend :
    @ - Detour Available              # - Detour In Use
    b - Bandwidth Protected           n - Node Protected
    s - Soft Preemption
===============================================================================
-------------------------------------------------------------------------------
LSP to_PE-2 Path loose
-------------------------------------------------------------------------------
LSP Name     : to_PE-2                          Path LSP ID : 44548
From         : 10.10.10.1                       To          : 10.10.10.2
Adm State    : Up                               Oper State  : Up
Path Name    : loose                            Path Type   : Primary
Path Admin   : Up                               Path Oper   : Up
OutInterface: 1/1/3                             Out Label   : 131069
Path Up Time: 0d 00:00:24                       Path Dn Time: 0d 00:00:00
Retry Limit : 0                                 Retry Timer : 30 sec
RetryAttempt: 0                                 NextRetryIn : 0 sec
SetupPriori*: 7                                 Hold Priori*: 0
Preference   : n/a
Bandwidth    : No Reservation                   Oper Bw     : 0 Mbps
Hop Limit    : 255                              Class Type  : 0
Backup CT    : None
MainCT Retry: n/a                               MainCT Retry: 0
    Rem      :                                      Limit   :
Oper CT      : 0
Record Route: Record                            Record Label: Record
Oper MTU     : 1500                             Neg MTU     : 1500
Adaptive     : Enabled                          Oper Metric : 300
Include Grps:                                   Exclude Grps:
None                                          None
Path Trans   : 5                                CSPF Queries: 0
Failure Code: noError                           Failure Node: n/a
ExplicitHops:
    No Hops Specified
```

(continued)

Listing 18.24 *(continued)*

```
Actual Hops :
    10.1.3.1(10.10.10.1)                          Record Label    : N/A
 -> 10.1.3.3(10.10.10.3)                          Record Label    : 131069
 -> 10.3.4.4(10.10.10.4)                          Record Label    : 131069
 -> 10.2.4.2(10.10.10.2)                          Record Label    : 131067
ResigEligib*: False
LastResignal: n/a                                 CSPF Metric : 0
===============================================================================
* indicates that the corresponding row element may have been truncated.
*A:PE-1# show service sdp 2

===============================================================================
Service Destination Point (Sdp Id : 2)
===============================================================================
SdpId     Adm MTU  Opr MTU  IP address     Adm  Opr      Deliver   Signal
-------------------------------------------------------------------------------
2         0        1492     10.10.10.2     Up   Up       MPLS      TLDP
===============================================================================
```

When we examine the service, we see that it is down because the SDP path MTU is now less than the service MTU of 5,000 bytes (see Listing 18.25). The *Flags* field is set to `PathMTUTooSmall`.

Listing 18.25 Service down because the path MTU is smaller than the service MTU

```
*A:PE-1# show service id 11 base

===============================================================================
Service Basic Information
===============================================================================
Service Id        : 11                  Vpn Id            : 0
Service Type      : Epipe
Name              : (Not Specified)
Description       : (Not Specified)
Customer Id       : 111
Last Status Change: 03/27/2011 19:41:09
Last Mgmt Change  : 03/27/2011 18:33:41
```

```
Admin State        : Up                Oper State        : Down
MTU                : 5000
Vc Switching       : False
SAP Count          : 1                 SDP Bind Count    : 1
Per Svc Hashing    : Disabled
Force QTag Fwd     : Disabled

-----------------------------------------------------------------------
Service Access & Destination Points
-----------------------------------------------------------------------
Identifier                        Type        AdmMTU  OprMTU  Adm  Opr
-----------------------------------------------------------------------
sap:1/1/2:11                      q-tag       5004    5004    Up   Up
sdp:2:11 S(10.10.10.2)            Spok        0       1492    Up   Down
=======================================================================
*A:PE-1# show service id 11 sdp 2:11 detail

=======================================================================
Service Destination Point (Sdp Id : 2:11) Details
=======================================================================
-----------------------------------------------------------------------
 Sdp Id 2:11  -(10.10.10.2)
-----------------------------------------------------------------------
Description      : (Not Specified)
SDP Id             : 2:11                   Type               : Spoke
Spoke Descr      : (Not Specified)
VC Type            : Ether                  VC Tag             : n/a
Admin Path MTU     : 0                      Oper Path MTU      : 1492
Far End            : 10.10.10.2             Delivery           : MPLS
Hash Label         : Disabled

Admin State        : Up                     Oper State         : Down
Acct. Pol          : None                   Collect Stats      : Disabled
Ingress Label      : 131071                 Egress Label       : 131070
Ingr Mac Fltr-Id   : n/a                    Egr Mac Fltr-Id    : n/a
Ingr IP Fltr-Id    : n/a                    Egr IP Fltr-Id     : n/a
Ingr IPv6 Fltr-Id  : n/a                    Egr IPv6 Fltr-Id   : n/a
Admin ControlWord  : Not Preferred          Oper ControlWord   : False
Admin BW(Kbps)     : 0                      Oper BW(Kbps)      : 0
```

(continued)

Listing 18.25 *(continued)*

```
Last Status Change : 03/27/2011 19:41:09      Signaling          : TLDP
Last Mgmt Change   : 03/27/2011 18:33:41      Force Vlan-Vc      : Disabled
Endpoint           : N/A                      Precedence         : 4
Class Fwding State : Down
Flags              : PathMTUTooSmall
Peer Pw Bits       : None
Peer Fault Ip      : None
Peer Vccv CV Bits  : lspPing
Peer Vccv CC Bits  : mplsRouterAlertLabel
Application Profile: None
... output omitted ...
```

The service could be made operationally up by setting the service MTU to 1,492 bytes. Once we change the MTU on the link from P1 to P2 back to 9,212, the path can support an MTU of 9,190 bytes. The SDP uses this MTU, and the service is up with a service MTU of 5,000 bytes (see Listing 18.26).

Listing 18.26 Service is up when the path supports 9,190 MTU from end to end

```
*A:PE-1# show router mpls lsp "to_PE-2" path detail

===============================================================================
MPLS LSP to_PE-2 Path  (Detail)
===============================================================================
Legend :
    @ - Detour Available              # - Detour In Use
    b - Bandwidth Protected           n - Node Protected
    s - Soft Preemption
===============================================================================
-------------------------------------------------------------------------------
LSP to_PE-2 Path loose
-------------------------------------------------------------------------------
LSP Name     : to_PE-2                          Path LSP ID : 44550
From         : 10.10.10.1                       To          : 10.10.10.2
Adm State    : Up                               Oper State  : Up
Path Name    : loose                            Path Type   : Primary
Path Admin   : Up                               Path Oper   : Up
```

```
OutInterface: 1/1/3                             Out Label    : 131071
Path Up Time: 0d 00:01:46                       Path Dn Time: 0d 00:00:00
Retry Limit : 0                                 Retry Timer : 30 sec
RetryAttempt: 0                                 NextRetryIn : 0 sec
SetupPriori*: 7                                 Hold Priori*: 0
Preference  : n/a
Bandwidth   : No Reservation                    Oper Bw     : 0 Mbps
Hop Limit   : 255                               Class Type  : 0
Backup CT   : None
MainCT Retry: n/a                               MainCT Retry: 0
    Rem     :                                       Limit   :
Oper CT     : 0
Record Route: Record                            Record Label: Record
Oper MTU    : 9198                              Neg MTU     : 9198
Adaptive    : Enabled                           Oper Metric : 300
Include Grps:                                   Exclude Grps:
None                                          None
Path Trans  : 7                                 CSPF Queries: 0
Failure Code: noError                           Failure Node: n/a
ExplicitHops:
    No Hops Specified
Actual Hops :
    10.1.3.1(10.10.10.1)                        Record Label    : N/A
 -> 10.1.3.3(10.10.10.3)                        Record Label    : 131071
 -> 10.3.4.4(10.10.10.4)                        Record Label    : 131071
 -> 10.2.4.2(10.10.10.2)                        Record Label    : 131068
ResigEligib*: False
LastResignal: n/a                               CSPF Metric : 0
=========================================================================
* indicates that the corresponding row element may have been truncated.
*A:PE-1# show service sdp 2

=========================================================================
Service Destination Point (Sdp Id : 2)
=========================================================================
SdpId    Adm MTU  Opr MTU  IP address    Adm  Opr     Deliver  Signal
-------------------------------------------------------------------------
2        0        9190     10.10.10.2    Up   Up      MPLS     TLDP
=========================================================================
```

(continued)

Listing 18.26 *(continued)*

```
*A:PE-1# show service id 11 base

===============================================================================
Service Basic Information
===============================================================================
Service Id        : 11                  Vpn Id           : 0
Service Type      : Epipe
Name              : (Not Specified)
Description       : (Not Specified)
Customer Id       : 111
Last Status Change: 03/27/2011 19:52:28
Last Mgmt Change  : 03/27/2011 18:33:41
Admin State       : Up                  Oper State       : Up
MTU               : 5000
Vc Switching      : False
SAP Count         : 1                   SDP Bind Count   : 1
Per Svc Hashing   : Disabled
Force QTag Fwd    : Disabled

-------------------------------------------------------------------------------
Service Access & Destination Points
-------------------------------------------------------------------------------
Identifier                           Type         AdmMTU  OprMTU  Adm  Opr
-------------------------------------------------------------------------------
sap:1/1/2:11                         q-tag        5004    5004    Up   Up
sdp:2:11 S(10.10.10.2)               Spok         0       9190    Up   Up
===============================================================================
```

SDP and VC Type

RFC 4448 defines the transport of Ethernet frames over an MPLS network and defines two VC (virtual circuit) types for the Ethernet pseudowire: *tagged mode* and *raw mode*. The 7750 SR supports both, with raw mode the default. The VC type is specified when the SDP is bound to the service and is signaled by T-LDP:

- `ether`—Specifies raw mode (default).
- `vlan`—Specifies tagged mode.

In *raw mode*, the service-delimiting VLAN tag or tags are stripped at the ingress and are not carried across the epipe. In *tagged mode*, a VLAN tag is carried in the frame. Tagged mode is supported on the 7750 SR mainly for interoperability with systems that only support tagged mode. If you do use tagged mode, remember to add an additional 4 bytes when calculating the required service MTU.

When type `vlan` is specified and the SAP is defined with a service-delimiting tag, this value is used for the tag on the pseudowire. If there is no service-delimiting tag, a tag with value of 0 is used. The value for the tag can be configured to use a specific value. Listing 18.27 shows the configuration of an epipe of type `vlan` with a tag value of 166. In this example, the other end of the epipe is type `ether`. T-LDP will not make a pseudowire operational unless the VC ID (virtual circuit identifier) and VC type match. The *Flags* field contains `NoEgrVCLabel`, which is an indication that there is no service at the other end. The `show router ldp bindings` command shows two different services with a VC ID of 66 but different VC types.

Listing 18.27 Epipe configured to operate in tagged mode

```
*A:PE-1# configure service epipe 66 customer 111 create
*A:PE-1>config>service>epipe$ sap 1/1/2:66 create
*A:PE-1>config>service>epipe>sap$ exit
*A:PE-1>config>service>epipe# spoke-sdp 2:66 vc-type vlan create
*A:PE-1>config>service>epipe>spoke-sdp$ vlan-vc-tag 166
*A:PE-1>config>service>epipe>spoke-sdp$ exit
*A:PE-1>config>service>epipe# no shutdown
*A:PE-1>config>service>epipe# info
----------------------------------------------
            sap 1/1/2:66 create
            exit
            spoke-sdp 2:66 vc-type vlan create
                vlan-vc-tag 166
            exit
            no shutdown
----------------------------------------------
*A:PE-1>config>service>epipe# show service id 66 sdp 2:66 detail

===============================================================================
Service Destination Point (Sdp Id : 2:66) Details
===============================================================================
```

(continued)

Listing 18.27 *(continued)*

```
-------------------------------------------------------------------------------
 Sdp Id 2:66  -(10.10.10.2)
-------------------------------------------------------------------------------
Description      : (Not Specified)
SDP Id              : 2:66                      Type              : Spoke
Spoke Descr      : (Not Specified)
VC Type             : VLAN                      VC Tag            : 166
Admin Path MTU      : 0                         Oper Path MTU     : 9190
Far End             : 10.10.10.2                Delivery          : MPLS
Hash Label          : Disabled

Admin State         : Up                        Oper State        : Down
Acct. Pol           : None                      Collect Stats     : Disabled
Ingress Label       : 131067                    Egress Label      : 0
Ingr Mac Fltr-Id    : n/a                       Egr Mac Fltr-Id   : n/a
Ingr IP Fltr-Id     : n/a                       Egr IP Fltr-Id    : n/a
Ingr IPv6 Fltr-Id   : n/a                       Egr IPv6 Fltr-Id  : n/a
Admin ControlWord   : Not Preferred             Oper ControlWord  : False
Admin BW(Kbps)      : 0                         Oper BW(Kbps)     : 0
Last Status Change  : 03/18/2011 10:59:06       Signaling         : TLDP
Last Mgmt Change    : 03/27/2011 20:43:52       Force Vlan-Vc     : Disabled
Endpoint            : N/A                       Precedence        : 4
Class Fwding State  : Down
Flags               : NoEgrVCLabel
Peer Pw Bits        : None
Peer Fault Ip       : None
Peer Vccv CV Bits   : None
Peer Vccv CC Bits   : None
Application Profile: None

... output omitted ...

*A:PE-1# show router ldp bindings fec-type services

===============================================================================
LDP LSR ID: 10.10.10.1
===============================================================================
Legend: U - Label In Use, N - Label Not In Use, W - Label Withdrawn
```

```
        S - Status Signaled Up,  D - Status Signaled Down
        E - Epipe Service, V - VPLS Service, M - Mirror Service
        A - Apipe Service, F - Fpipe Service, I - IES Service,
 R - VPRN service
        P - Ipipe Service, WP - Label Withdraw Pending, C - Cpipe Service
        TLV - (Type, Length: Value)
=========================================================================
LDP Service FEC 128 Bindings
=========================================================================
Type   VCId        SvcId    SDPId  Peer         IngLbl  EgrLbl  LMTU  RMTU
-------------------------------------------------------------------------
E-Vlan 66          66       2      10.10.10.2  131067U   --     1500  0
?-Eth  66          Ukwn     R. Src 10.10.10.2    --     131067S 0     1500
-------------------------------------------------------------------------
No. of VC Labels: 2

=========================================================================
LDP Service FEC 129 Bindings
=========================================================================
AGI                                SAII               TAII
Type              SvcId      SDPId Peer          gLbl  EgrLbl  LMTU  RMTU
-------------------------------------------------------------------------
No Matching Entries Found
=========================================================================
=========================================================================
```

After the remote node (PE-2) is configured as type vlan, the service is operational (see Listing 18.28).

Listing 18.28 Both ends of the epipe configured as type vlan

```
*A:PE-1# show service service-using epipe

=========================================================================
Services [epipe]
=========================================================================
ServiceId  Type      Adm  Opr  CustomerId Service Name
-------------------------------------------------------------------------
```

(continued)

Listing 18.28 *(continued)*

```
11         Epipe     Up   Down 111
22         Epipe     Up   Down 111
66         Epipe     Up   Up   111
111        Epipe     Up   Up   111
-------------------------------------------------------------------------
Matching Services : 4
-------------------------------------------------------------------------
=========================================================================
*A:PE-1# show router ldp bindings fec-type services

=========================================================================
LDP LSR ID: 10.10.10.1
=========================================================================
Legend: U - Label In Use, N - Label Not In Use, W - Label Withdrawn
        S - Status Signaled Up,  D - Status Signaled Down
        E - Epipe Service, V - VPLS Service, M - Mirror Service
        A - Apipe Service, F - Fpipe Service, I - IES Service,
 R - VPRN service
        P - Ipipe Service, WP - Label Withdraw Pending, C - Cpipe Service
        TLV - (Type, Length: Value)
=========================================================================
LDP Service FEC 128 Bindings
=========================================================================
Type   VCId       SvcId    SDPId  Peer         IngLbl  EgrLbl  LMTU  RMTU
-------------------------------------------------------------------------
E-Vlan 66         66       2      10.10.10.2   131067U 131070S 1500  1500
-------------------------------------------------------------------------
No. of VC Labels: 1

=========================================================================
LDP Service FEC 129 Bindings
=========================================================================
AGI                               SAII                 TAII
Type                 SvcId    SDPId  Peer         IngLbl  EgrLbl  LMTU  RMTU
-------------------------------------------------------------------------
No Matching Entries Found
=========================================================================
=========================================================================
```

Encapsulation and VC Type Summary

In the sections above, we have seen that there are many options for SAP encapsulations as well as two options for the VC type on an Ethernet pseudowire. The situation is complicated by the fact that an epipe can be configured with any combination of SAP encapsulation at each end; a null SAP on one side and a Q-in-Q-encapsulated SAP on the other side, for example. Overall, the rules can be summarized as follows:

- **Null SAP or default dot1Q SAP**—All VLAN tags received at ingress are transmitted in the pseudowire. No VLAN tags are added to egressing packets.
- **Dot1Q SAP or wildcard Q-in-Q SAP**—The outer VLAN tag is removed at ingress, and any remaining tags are transmitted in the pseudowire. The specified VLAN tag is added to egressing packets.
- **Q-in-Q SAP**—Two outer VLAN tags are removed at ingress. The two specified VLAN tags are added to egressing packets.

Figure 18.7 shows the different combinations of frame transmission possible for a null-encapsulated SAP with different egress encapsulations. The behavior of the default dot1Q SAP is the same.

Figure 18.7 VLAN tag behavior with a null SAP.

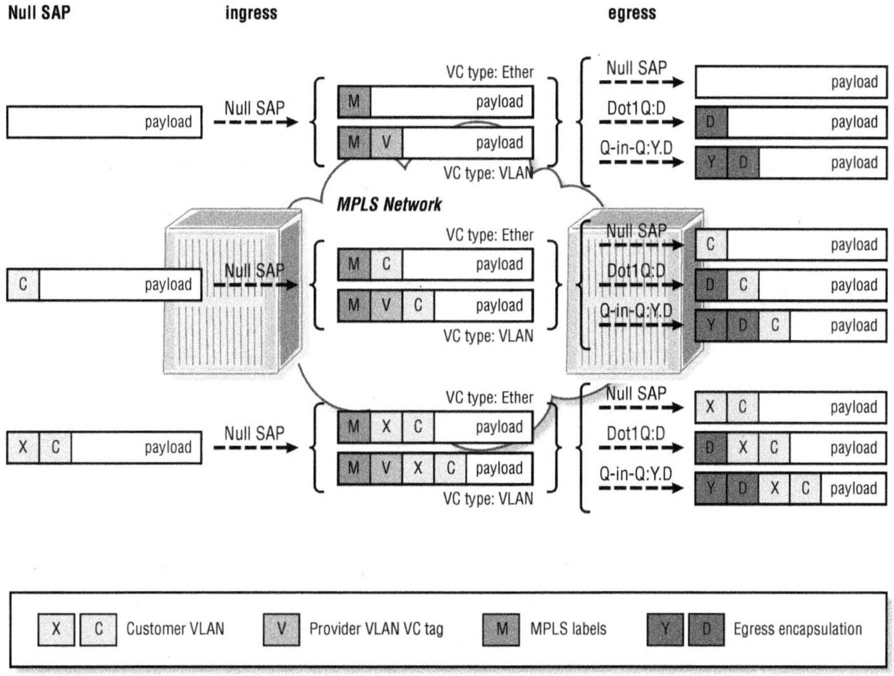

Figure 18.8 shows the different combinations of frame transmission possible for a dot1Q-encapsulated SAP with different egress encapsulations.

Figure 18.8 VLAN tag behavior with a dot1Q SAP.

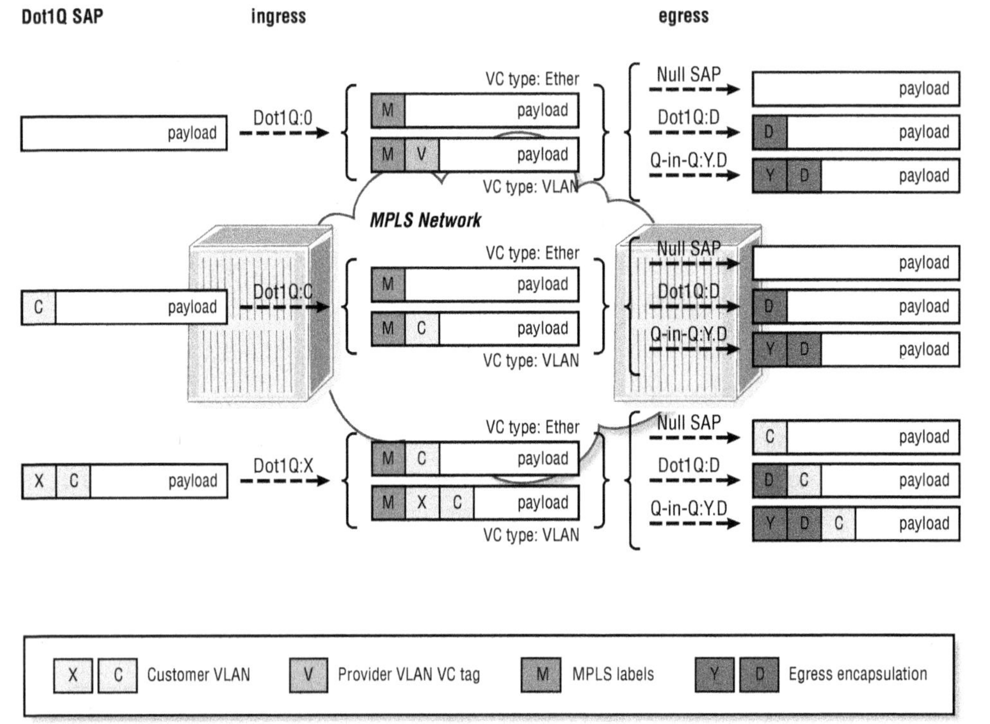

Figure 18.9 shows the different combinations of frame transmission possible for a Q-in-Q-encapsulated SAP with different egress encapsulations.

18.4 Other VPWS Services

In this book most of the attention to Layer 2 services is given to Ethernet. This should not diminish the importance of other Layer 2 pseudowire services supported by the 7750 SR. Although the trend in current network deployments is increasingly to Ethernet for reasons of cost and performance, there is still a very significant demand for other technologies that represent very significant revenues to service providers. These services can be deployed on an IP/MPLS infrastructure that simultaneously provides a base for modern Ethernet and IP services. Layer 2 services available besides Ethernet (epipe) are as follows:

- **Fpipe**—Pseudowire emulating a point-to-point Frame Relay service
- **Apipe**—Pseudowire emulating a point-to-point ATM service
- **Cpipe**—Pseudowire emulating a point-to-point TDM circuit
- **Ipipe**—Pseudowire providing an IP-based interworking service

Figure 18.9 VLAN tag behavior with a Q-in-Q SAP.

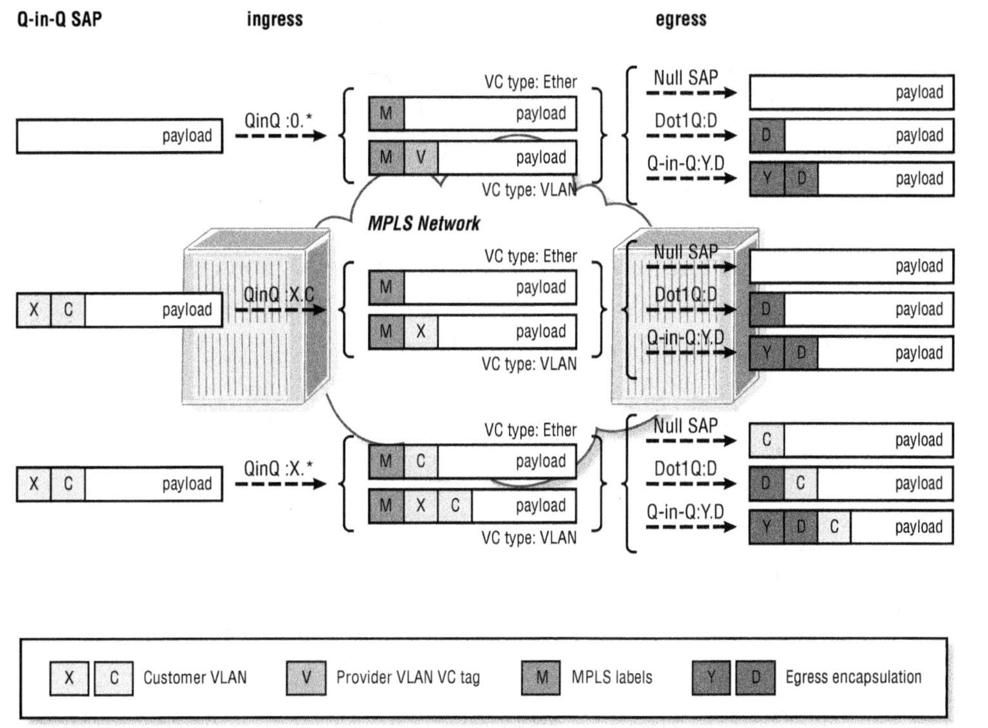

These services are all based on RFC 4447 ["Pseudowire Setup and Maintenance Using the Label Distribution Protocol (LDP)"], and most of the characteristics, configuration, and maintenance that we describe for epipes apply to these services as well. In this section, we introduce each of these services, paying particular attention to any characteristics that distinguish them from an epipe service.

There are also additional interworking services provided for Frame Relay, ATM, and Ethernet. These are described after the VPWS services.

Fpipes

Frame Relay pseudowires are described in RFC 4619 ("Encapsulation Methods for Transport of Frame Relay over Multiprotocol Label Switching (MPLS) Networks"). The 7750 SR supports one-to-one mode for the mapping of a Frame Relay DLCI [data link connection identifier] to a pseudowire. This means that a single Frame Relay circuit is mapped to an fpipe service.

From the customer perspective, the PE router should appear as much as possible like a native Frame Relay UNI (user network interface). The SAP for the fpipe on the 7750 is configured on a SONET/SDH port and specifies Frame Relay encapsulation. The syntax for the SAP is `port:DLCI`.

When a frame arrives at the fpipe SAP, the Frame Relay header and any padding are removed. The frame is encapsulated with a service label and transport label as for any pseudowire service. The fpipe also uses the MPLS control word, which is a 4-byte field directly following the service label (see Figure 18.10). Specific values from the Frame Relay header are copied into the control word.

Figure 18.10 The fpipe appears as a native Frame Relay interface.

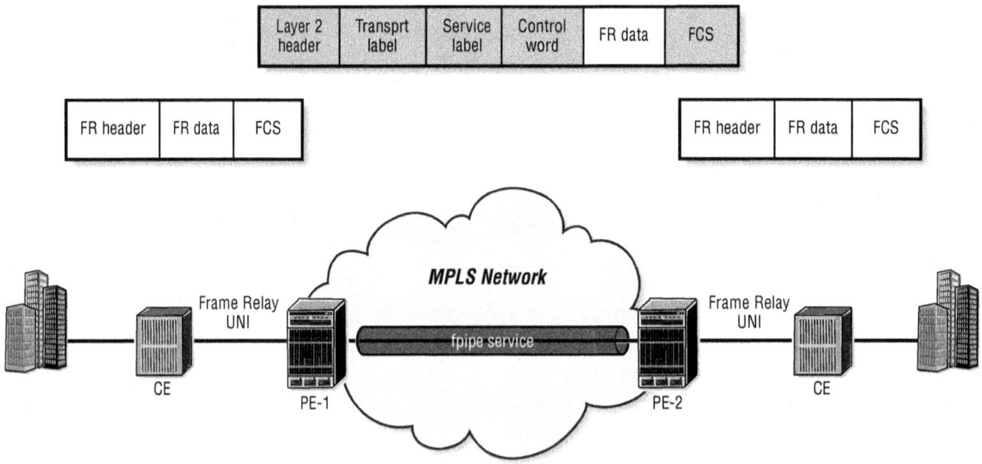

The MPLS control word is an optional field in the RFC 4447 pseudowire encapsulation. It is not generally used in an epipe but is always present in the fpipe encapsulation. The fields of the 4-byte control word (see Figure 18.11) are as follows:

- **Zeroes**—The first 4 bits of the control word must be zero.
- **F**—The Frame Relay FECN (forward explicit congestion notification) bit.
- **B**—The Frame Relay BECN (backward explicit congestion notification) bit.
- **D**—The Frame Relay DE (discard eligibility) bit.
- **C**—The Frame Relay frame C/R (command/response) bit.
- **FRG**—2 bits for optional pseudowire fragmentation (defined in RFC 4623).
- **Length**—Frame Relay payload length if less than 64 bits, zero otherwise.
- **Sequence Number** (Optional)—May be used to ensure packet ordering.

Figure 18.11 Fpipe use of the MPLS control word.

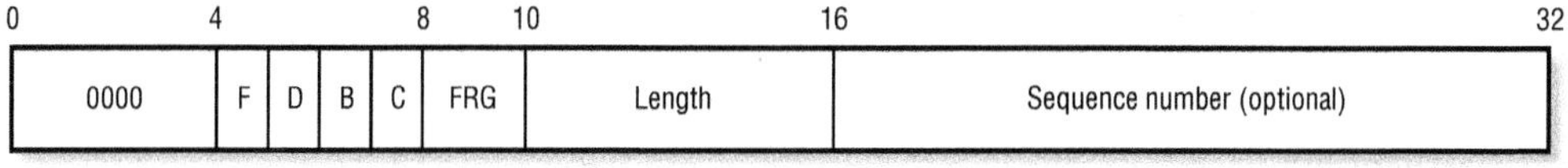

The control word is required for an fpipe because the Frame Relay header is not carried with the encapsulated frame. When the frame is received at the ingress SAP, the F, B, D, and C bits are copied to the control word. When the Frame Relay frame is reconstructed at the egress SAP, these bits are copied to the appropriate bit in the header.

Apipes

ATM pseudowires are described in RFC 4717 ["Encapsulation Methods for Transport of Asynchronous Transfer Mode (ATM) over MPLS Networks"]. An ATM PVC (permanent virtual circuit) is configured on the PE, and the apipe appears as an ATM circuit to the customer (see Figure 18.12). Two different modes of operation are supported on the 7750 SR for ATM apipes:

- **N:1 cell mode**—Individual cells or groups of cells are encapsulated for transmission on the apipe.
- **AAL5 frame mode**—An AAL5 SDU (Service Delivery Unit) frame is encapsulated for transmission on the apipe.

Figure 18.12 ATM cells encapsulated for transmission on an MPLS network.

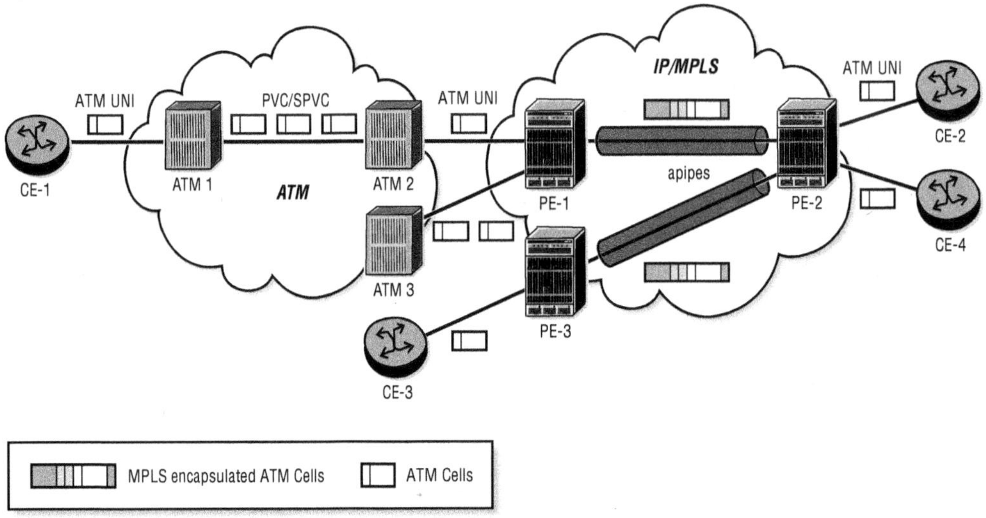

N:1 Cell Mode

In N:1 cell mode, one or more cells are transparently encapsulated in an apipe frame, including the first 4 bytes of the cell header. The HEC field is not carried. N:1 cell mode provides a service that supports the transport of control, signaling, and routing information because cells arriving at the SAP are transparently carried over the apipe (see Figure 18.13).

Figure 18.13 Groups of ATM cells encapsulated in N:1 cell mode.

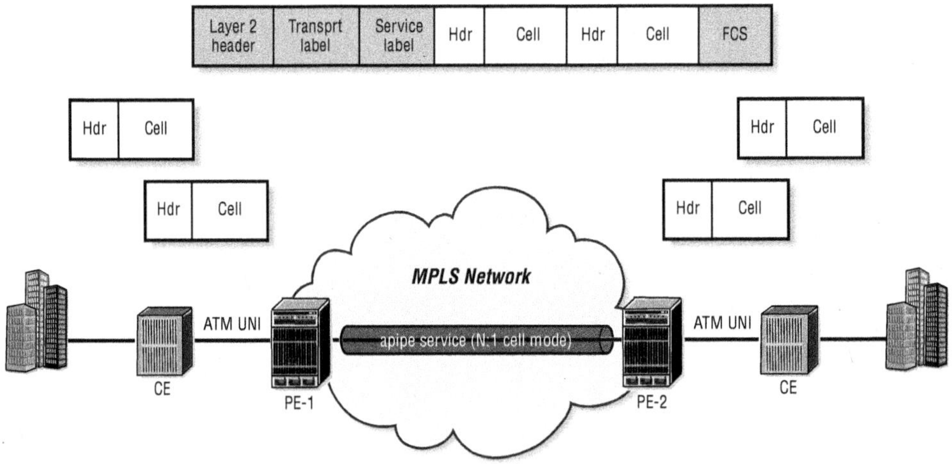

There are a number of different VC types supported by the 7750 SR that use ATM N:1 cell mode. These are the following:

- `atm-vcc`, SAP syntax `port:vpi/vci`—A single ATM VCC (virtual channel connection) is mapped to the apipe. The VPI/VCI (Virtual Path Identifier/Virtual Channel Identifier) that identifies the VCC can be different in the SAPs at either end of the apipe. In the same way that the VLAN tag can be rewritten at egress to the epipe service, the VPI/VCI value can be rewritten for the ATM cells.
- `atm-vpc`, SAP syntax `port:vpi`—An entire ATM VPC (Virtual Path Connection) is mapped to the apipe. The VPI (Virtual Path Identifier) that identifies the VPC can be different in the SAPs at either end of the apipe. In this case, the VPI value is rewritten in the ATM cells.
- `atm-cell`, SAP syntax `port:vpi-1.vpi-2`—ATM trunk mode in which a range of VPI values is specified. All the VPCs from `vpi-1` through `vpi-2` are mapped to the apipe.
- `atm-cell`, SAP syntax `port`—ATM port mode is an ATM trunk in which all of the ATM traffic received on the port is transported in the apipe.

An important characteristic of N:1 concatenation is that multiple cells can be encapsulated in a single MPLS packet. The advantage of concatenation is more efficient bandwidth use because the encapsulated ATM cells are only 52 bytes each. The disadvantage is that the time required to complete an MPLS packet increases the delay for the ATM connection.

The `cell-concatenation` command is used in the `spoke-sdp` context to specify the concatenation parameters for the pseudowire. The default is no cell concatenation. These parameters can be used simultaneously. If multiple parameters are specified, the packet is transmitted as soon as one of the conditions is met. The conditions that can be used to complete cell concatenation and transmit the MPLS packet are as follows:

- `aal5-frame-aware`—Cell concatenation is completed when the AAL5 end-of-frame indication is detected.
- `clp-change`—Cell concatenation is completed when a change is detected in the CLP (cell loss priority) bit.
- `max-cells`—Cell concatenation is completed when this number (1–128) of cells is reached. The default is 1, indicating no cell concatenation.
- `max-delay`—Cell concatenation is completed when this amount of time has elapsed since the first cell was received. The value (1–400) specifies hundreds of microseconds and provides an upper bound on the delay incurred by cell concatenation.

AAL5 Frame Mode

A large percentage of existing ATM circuits carry IP traffic. AAL5 (ATM Adaptation Layer 5) was defined for a best effort, connectionless packet service such as IP. The AAL5 SDU is the payload that the service is intended to carry—in this case, the IP packet. The SDU is encapsulated in an AAL5 PDU that has no header but an 8-byte trailer and is padded so that the SDU, plus trailer, plus padding is an exact multiple of 48 bytes long. The AAL5 PDU is then split into the necessary number of cells for transmission. This operation is known as segmentation and reassembly (SAR).

When the apipe is defined as VC type `atm-sdu`, the PEs perform the SAR operation, and only the AAL5 SDU is carried in the MPLS-encapsulated packet. This provides more efficient use of the bandwidth because the AAL5 overhead (padding and trailer) and the ATM cell headers are discarded. Figure 18.14 shows the operation of an apipe in `atm-sdu` mode. The SAP defines a single PVC in the format `port:pvi/pci`.

Figure 18.14 Apipe operating in atm-sdu mode.

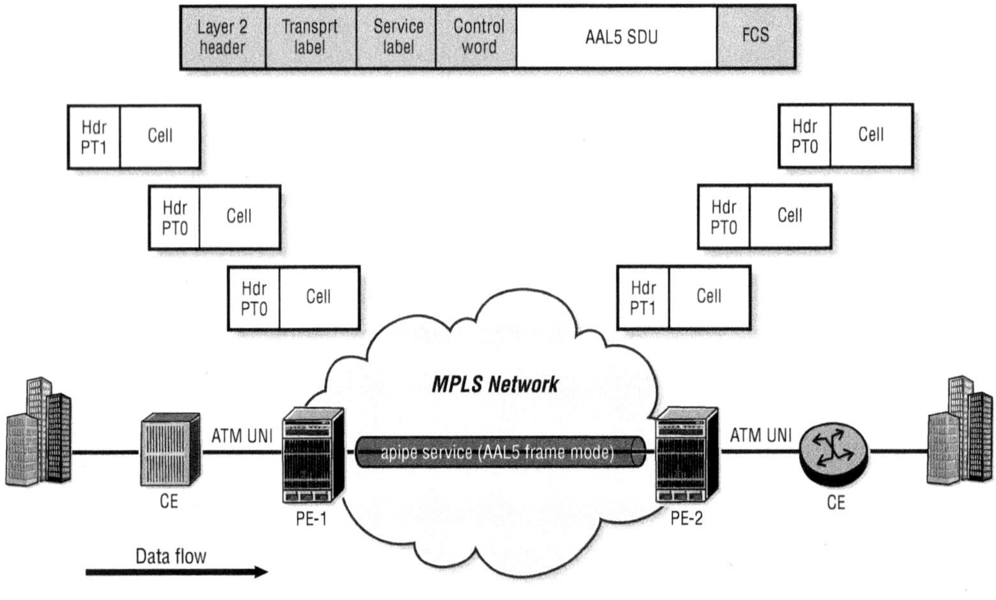

As in the fpipe, the control word is also required for an apipe in AAL5 frame mode. The purpose is to carry the information lost when the cell headers are stripped in the SAR process. The format of the control word is shown in Figure 18.15. The key fields of the control word are as follows:

Figure 18.15 Control word for AAL5 frame mode.

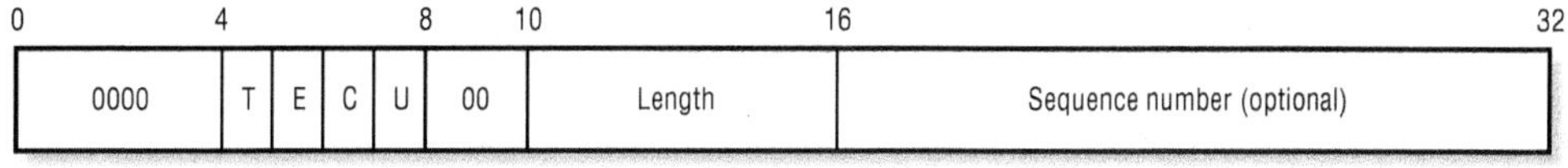

- **T bit (transport type)**—ATM OAM cells may also be transported using N:1 cell encapsulation on the AAL5 frame pseudowire in order to provide transparency of OAM functions. If the T bit is set, the MPLS packet contains an admin cell encapsulated in N:1 cell format. Otherwise, the packet contains an AAL5 SDU.
- **E bit (EFCI)**—This bit is set to match the setting of the EFCI (explicit forward congestion indication) bit in the last cell carrying the AAL5 PDU. (The EFCI is the second bit in the PT field of the cell header.)
- **C bit (CLP)**—This bit is set if the CLP bit is set in the header of any of the cells carrying the AAL5 PDU and is zero otherwise.
- **U bit (Command/Response field)**—This bit relates only to Frame Relay traffic carried for FRF8.1 interworking. A bit in the AAL5 PDU trailer may contain the Frame Relay C/R bit. This value is copied to the U bit.

At the egress PE, the SAR process reconstructs the ATM cells, and the values in the E, C, and U bits are copied to the corresponding bit in the cell header or PDU trailer.

Cpipes

Cpipes are an implementation of TDM pseudowires to transport T1 or E1 circuits. SAPs are configured on a SONET/SDH port. There are two categories of cpipes:

- **Structure agnostic**—SAToP (Structure Agnostic TDM over Packet) pseudowires are defined in RFC 4553 and transport unstructured T1 or E1 circuits.
- **Structure aware**—CESoPSN (Circuit Emulation Service over Packet Switched Network) pseudowires are defined in RFC 5086 and transport multiple DS0 channels from a T1 or E1 circuit.

The encapsulation for all cpipes includes the control word and an optional RTP header (see Figure 18.16). On the 7750 SR, the RTP header is typically only used to interoperate with other equipment.

Figure 18.16 MPLS encapsulation for CESoPSN cpipe.

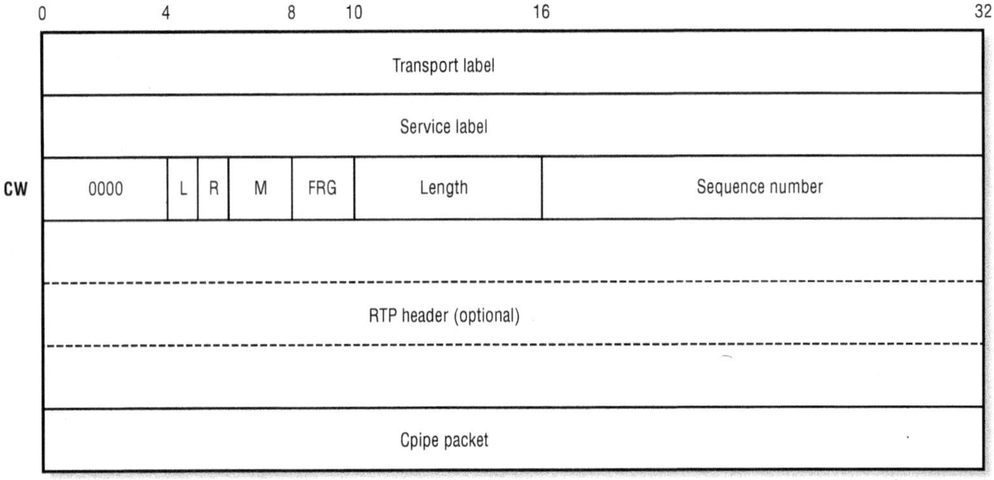

The encapsulation of SAToP packets is the same as the one shown in Figure 18.16 for CESoPSN except that the 2-bit M field in the control word is reserved and always set to zero. For both types of service, the meaning of the key fields is as follows:

- **L (Local)**—An AIS (alarm indication signal) or other error condition is detected by the PE that indicates the frame data being received from the CE is invalid. When the L bit is set, the frame data does not need to be transmitted. However, the PE at the remote end must generate data for the TDM circuit (typically all ones).
- **R (Remote)**—This is a signal to the remote end (ingress PE) from the egress PE receiving the packets from the pseudowire that it is in a *packet loss* state. The packet loss state occurs when the egress PE has not received a preconfigured number of valid packets. Once it is receiving valid packets again, the R bit is cleared.
- **Length**—If the size of the packet is less than 64 bytes, the length of the packet is carried in this field. Otherwise, the field is zero.
- **Sequence number**—The sequence number is used to maintain packet ordering and detect missing packets. It is initially set to a random number and incremented with every packet.

Two important parameters for the cpipe service are the jitter buffer and the payload size. The jitter buffer is required because a cpipe runs over a packet switched network

(PSN) that may have variable delay. However, the receiving TDM circuit is synchronous and must receive data at a constant rate. Packets received from the PSN are queued depending on the size of the jitter buffer and then played out at a regular rate to the TDM circuit.

A larger jitter buffer and larger payload size provide the most efficient transfer and the least chance of losing data. However, larger values increase delay. For delay-sensitive services, the jitter buffer and payload size must be kept small to minimize delay.

The SAToP pseudowire is an unstructured service—essentially a transparent transport of the T1 or E1 frame. The contents of the frames are packetized as they arrive at the ingress SAP. Packet sizes must be a multiple of 32 bytes and must match at each end of the service. Maximum packet size is dependent on the service MTU. Default packet sizes depend on the VC type (Table 18.2).

Table 18.2 Default Payload Sizes for SAToP cpipe

TDM Circuit	VC Type	Default Payload	Default Jitter Buffer
T1	`satop-t1`	192 bytes	5 milliseconds
E1	`satop-e1`	256 bytes	5 milliseconds

The CESoPSN pseudowire is structured because it is aware of, and dependent on, the time slots configured on the TDM circuit. Time slots are specified when the port is configured. Unused time slots are not transported on the pseudowire. The TDM frame is reconstructed on the far-side from the active timeslots. Channel Associated Signaling (CAS) is also supported. Use of the control word is similar to an SAToP cpipe, with additional signaling capabilities supported by the 2-bit M field.

Because the number of DS0 circuits, or time slots, being transported can vary, the default values for the payload size and jitter buffer vary depending on the number of time slots. Payload size must be an integer multiple of the number of time slots and a multiple of 2 if there is only one time slot.

Interworking Overview

Several interworking capabilities are provided with VPWS services. These support the interconnection of different types of services—for example, ATM and Ethernet. The interworking capabilities of the 7750 SR are summarized in Table 18.3.

Table 18.3 VPWS Interworking Matrix

	ATM	Frame Relay	Ethernet
ATM	Apipe	Apipe (FRF.5 interworking)	Epipe (bridged) Ipipe (routed)
Frame Relay	Apipe (FRF.5 interworking)	Fpipe	Epipe (bridged) Ipipe (routed)
Ethernet	Epipe (bridged) Ipipe (routed)	Epipe (bridged) Ipipe (routed)	Epipe

FRF.5 (Frame Relay Forum) defines a standard method for encapsulating and transporting Frame Relay frames over an ATM network (see Figure 18.17). It is configured on the 7750 SR by creating an apipe service that specifies `interworking frf-5` and a Frame Relay SAP with a DLCI encapsulation ID. The port is configured for Frame Relay encapsulation. The other end of the apipe has a regular ATM SAP with VPI/VCI encapsulation ID. The VC type of the apipe must be `atm-sdu`.

Figure 18.17 FRF.5 interworking over an apipe.

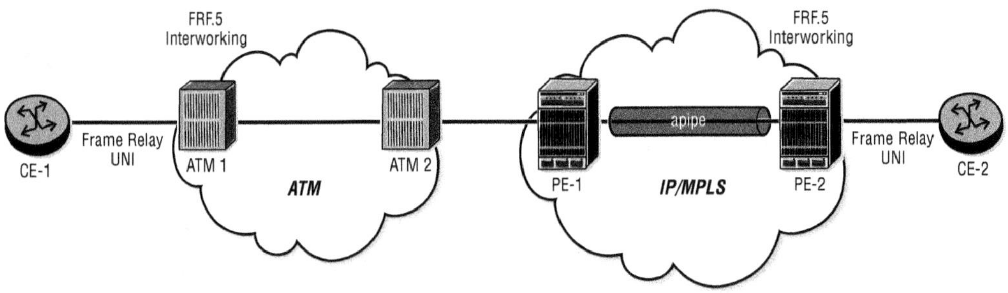

Interworking between either Frame Relay or ATM and Ethernet is also supported on an epipe. The Frame Relay network must be sending and receiving Ethernet-encapsulated frames as defined by RFC 2427 ("Multiprotocol Interconnect over Frame Relay"). The ATM network must be sending and receiving Ethernet-encapsulated frames as defined by RFC 2684 ("Multiprotocol Encapsulation over ATM Adaptation Layer 5"). One side of the epipe has either a Frame Relay or ATM SAP, the other an Ethernet SAP (see Figure 18.18). Any VLAN tags in the encapsulated frames are passed transparently as they would be for a null SAP.

Ipipes

Ipipes provide a routed interworking service. We say *routed* because the encapsulated data are Layer 3 (IP) packets instead of the Layer 2 frames we discussed above. They are not truly routed, because the ipipe is a point-to-point service. An ipipe is an interworking service because it supports interconnection between the following:

- **Frame Relay**—Using RFC 2427 routed encapsulation
- **ATM**—Using RFC 2684 routed encapsulation
- **PPP**—Using IPCP encapsulation as defined in RFC 1332
- **Cisco HDLC**—Routed encapsulation
- **Ethernet**—Using null, dot1Q, or Q-in-Q encapsulation

Figure 18.18 Frame Relay or ATM/Ethernet interworking over an epipe.

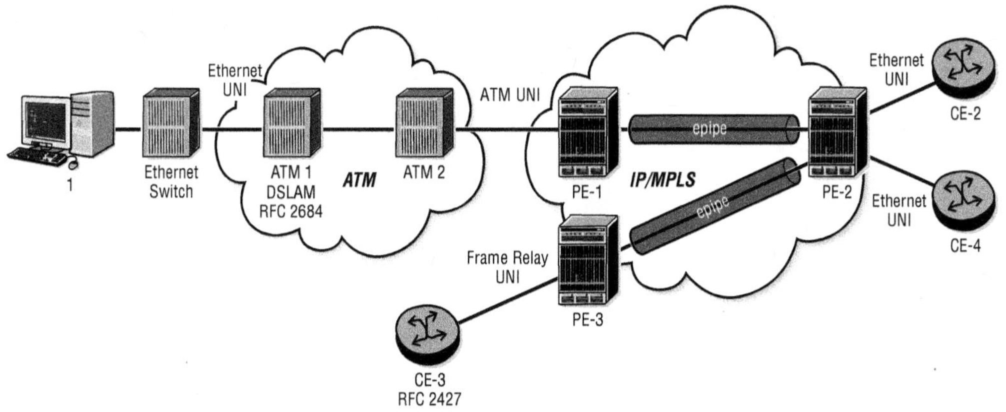

An ipipe is useful when migrating from technologies such as ATM and Frame Relay to an Ethernet infrastructure and a routed encapsulation is being used (see Figure 18.19).

The ipipe in Figure 18.19 is configured with a Frame Relay SAP on PE-1 and a dot1Q-encapsulated SAP configured on PE-2. Both PE devices must also know the IP address of the local and remote CE devices. On PE-1, for example, the SAP is configured with the address of the local CE device and the spoke SDP is configured with the address of the remote CE. PE-2 is configured in a similar manner. When the service is brought up, PE-2 broadcasts an ARP request on the local LAN for the MAC address of the CE device. The two PE routers are now able to exchange encapsulated IP packets over the ipipe between the two CE devices.

Figure 18.19 IP packet transport through an ipipe.

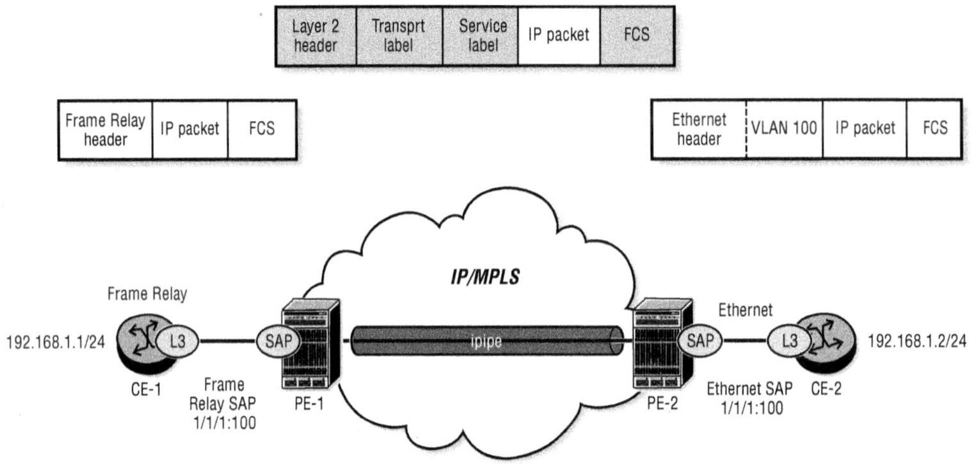

Practice Lab: Configuring a VPWS Service

The following lab is designed to reinforce your knowledge of the content in this chapter. Please review the instructions carefully, and perform the steps in the order in which they are presented. The practice labs require that you have access to six or more Alcatel-Lucent 7750 SRs or Alcatel-Lucent 7450 ESSs in a non-production environment.

These labs are designed to be used in a controlled lab environment. Please *do not* attempt to perform these labs in a production environment.

Lab Section 18.1: Service MTU, SAP MTU, and SDP MTU

The previous chapter's lab focused on configuring an epipe service that was operationally up and passing traffic. This lab section investigates the MTU configurations required to support different frame sizes.

Objective In this exercise, you will configure the service MTU, SAP MTU, and SDP MTU of a service to support different customer frame sizes using the network topology shown in Figure 18.20.

Figure 18.20 Lab topology for VPWS services.

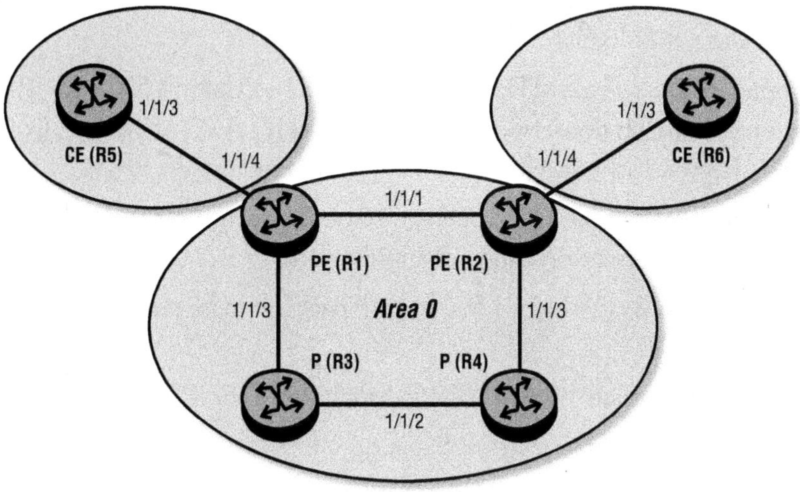

Validation You will know you have succeeded if frames from the CE routers that are larger than the maximum frame size of the service are discarded and frames conforming to the MTU limitations are passed through the service.

1. For the purpose of this lab exercise, configure all network ports on the PE and P routers (R1, R2, R3, and R4) to use an Ethernet MTU of 1,550 bytes (don't change the MTU of the access ports on R1 and R2).
2. Verify that epipe service 20 and epipe service 40 from the Chapter 17 lab are operationally up.
   - **a.** What is the default service MTU on the epipe services? What are the default SAP and Path MTUs?
   - **b.** What is the largest size packet that you expect the epipe services to pass?
   - **c.** Use a ping on R5 to verify the largest size ping that can be sent by pinging the far-end CE addresses `192.168.20.6` and `192.168.40.6`.

You can use the `ping` command on the SR with a size parameter, for example, `ping 192.168.20.6 size 1200`. This sends a packet of 1,228 bytes—20 bytes added for the IP header and 8 for the ICMP header.

3. Configure epipe service 20 to use a default dot1Q SAP encapsulation.
   a. Repeat the ping from the previous step using the same `size` parameter. Is the ping successful? Explain.
   b. Configure the service MTU of epipe 20 on R1 so that a 1,500-byte IP packet will pass through the service when default dot1Q SAPs are in use. Don't configure R2 yet. Is the service operationally up? Explain.
   c. Configure the service MTU of epipe 20 on R2 to match the value configured on R1. Is the service operationally up? Explain.
   d. Use a ping to verify that a 1,500-byte IP packet can be sent between R5 and R6 on epipe 20.
4. Configure epipe service 40 to also use a default dot1Q SAP encapsulation.
   a. Is the configuration successful? Explain.
   b. Ensure that epipe service 40 has SAPs that use a dot1Q SAP encapsulation of 40 before continuing.
5. Configure epipe service 20 to support exactly 1,536-byte IP packets using the existing default dot1Q SAPs. Assume that the service will only use the path directly between the PE routers.
   a. Explain the Ethernet MTU values configured for the access ports on R1 and R2?
   b. What service MTU should be used for epipe service 20?
   c. What Ethernet MTU values should be configured for the network ports between R1 and R2? What path MTU does this correspond to?
   d. Ensure that the service is operationally up with the expected MTU values and that you can ping between R5 and R6 on epipe service 20 with 1,536-byte IP packets.
   e. How is the MTU of epipe service 40 affected by these changes? Explain.

Lab Section 18.2: Using ADSPEC

The previous section investigated the MTU settings on the PE routers for the epipe service. This section investigates how ADSPEC can be used to avoid MTU problems on P routers that transit traffic for the service.

Objective This lab will investigate the use of ADSPEC on transport tunnels for the previously created epipe service.

Validation You will know you have succeeded if the epipe service is operationally down when P routers don't support the required path MTU.

1. Change the transport tunnels used for epipe service 20 and epipe service 40 to use a path through R3 and R4.

You can use admin groups or a strict path to constrain the LSP.

   a. Are both services operationally up?

   b. Change the network ports between R1 and R3 and between R2 and R4 to accommodate the required path MTU. (Do not change the configuration on the ports between R3 and R4.) Is epipe 20 operationally up? Explain.

   c. Use a ping to verify that epipe service 20 can transmit a large IP packet. (Use the same value as the previous section.) Is the ping successful? Explain.

   d. Use the `oam sdp-mtu` command on R1 to verify the effective path MTU of the SDP from R1 to R2. Explain the result.

2. Enable ADSPEC on the transport LSPs used for the service.

   a. Is epipe service 40 operationally up? If not, what error codes are given? Explain.

   b. Is epipe service 20 operationally up? Explain.

   c. Change any MTU values required in the network to bring both epipe services operationally up.

Lab Section 18.3: Ethernet Encapsulations

This lab section investigates the effects of different SAP encapsulations on the CE and PE routers.

Objective In this lab you will configure different combinations of Ethernet encapsulation types on the PE and CE routers.

Validation You will know you have succeeded if you can explain the ping results between CE routers when different encapsulations are used.

1. This lab section uses epipe service 20 exclusively. You can remove the interfaces on the CE routers that were used for epipe service 40.

2. For the purposes of this lab section, decrease the service MTU of epipe 20 to 1,518 bytes and verify that the service is operationally up.

3. Configure CE R5 to use a null-encapsulated network port while R6 still uses a dot1Q encapsulation of 20.

   a. Are pings between R5 and R6 successful? Explain.

   b. Modify the SAP for epipe service 20 on R2 so that the ping is successful using a dot1Q encapsulation type.

   c. Modify the SAP for epipe service 20 on R2 so that the ping is successful using a Q-in-Q encapsulation type.

   You can remove the SAP on epipe service 40.

   d. Configure epipe service 20 on R2 to use a SAP with Q-in-Q encapsulation that has an outer tag of 20 and an inner tag of 10. Is a ping between R5 and R6 successful?

   e. Change epipe service 20 on R2 back to its previous state so that a ping between R5 and R6 is successful using Q-in-Q encapsulation.

Chapter Review

Now that you have completed this chapter, you should be able to:

- Describe the different types of Ethernet SAP encapsulations and their behavior.
- Explain how service-delimiting VLAN tags are used in a service.
- Describe the use and operation of the default SAP, the null SAP, and the Q-in-Q wildcard SAP.
- Explain why it may be necessary to change Ethertype values and how to do it.
- Explain the relationship between the access port MTU and the service MTU.
- Adjust the service and access port MTUs to accommodate transparently passed VLAN tags.
- Describe the relationship between the service MTU and the path MTU.
- Describe the relationship between the network MTU and the path MTU.
- Explain how the path MTU is set on an SDP.
- Explain how `ADSPEC` is used by RSVP-TE to determine the path MTU.
- Describe the difference between the two Ethernet VC types.
- Describe the purpose and operation of an fpipe.
- List the fields of the control word used in an fpipe.
- Describe the purpose and operation of an apipe.
- Describe the operation of N:1 cell mode in an apipe and how cells are concatenated.
- List the different VC types that operate in N:1 cell mode.
- Describe the operation of an `atm-sdu` apipe.
- List the fields of the control word used in an `atm-sdu` apipe.
- Explain the purpose and operation of a cpipe.
- Describe the use of the control word in a cpipe.
- Describe the operation of an SAToP cpipe.
- Describe the operation of a CESoPSN cpipe.
- Describe the bridged interworking services supported by the Alcatel-Lucent 7750 SR.
- Explain the purpose and operation of an ipipe.
- List the interworking capabilities of an ipipe.

Post-Assessment

The following questions will test your knowledge and prepare you for the Alcatel-Lucent NRS II Certification Exam. Compare your responses with the answers listed in Appendix A. You can also use the CD that accompanies this book to take all the assessment tests and review the answers.

1. Consider an epipe service on an Alcatel-Lucent 7750 SR that has a SAP configured with the CLI syntax `sap 1/1/4:20.10`. Assuming that the epipe service is operationally up, which statement best describes CE traffic that ingresses the service?
   - **A.** CE traffic with an outer VLAN tag of 10 and any non-zero inner VLAN tag will be sent over the service.
   - **B.** CE traffic with an outer VLAN tag of 20 and any non-zero inner VLAN tag will be sent over the service.
   - **C.** CE traffic with an outer VLAN tag of 20 and an inner VLAN tag of 10 will be sent over the service.
   - **D.** CE traffic with an outer VLAN tag of 10 and an inner VLAN tag of 20 will be sent over the service.
   - **E.** None of the above statements describe CE traffic that ingresses the service.
2. Which of the following statements is *false* regarding the MTUs used for an epipe service?
   - **A.** SAP MTUs must be greater than or equal to the service MTU.
   - **B.** The service MTU must be less than or equal to the path MTU.
   - **C.** The path MTU must be greater than the MTU of every network port in the transport path.
   - **D.** Epipe services configured on the same PE can have different service MTUs.
   - **E.** None of the above statements are false.

3. An operator needs to provision an epipe service to accept IP packets as large as 9,000 bytes. What value should be used for the service MTU if the SAP encapsulation on both PE routers has a CLI syntax of `1/1/4:100.*`?

   A. 8,982 bytes

   B. 8,986 bytes

   C. 9,000 bytes

   D. 9,014 bytes

   E. 9,018 bytes

4. An epipe on a PE router receives a frame carrying an IP packet from a CE router that is too large for the service. What action will the PE router take?

   A. It will silently discard the frame.

   B. It will discard the frame and send a notification to the CE router.

   C. It will fragment the frame as long as the do-not-fragment bit is not set.

   D. It will always fragment the frame.

   E. None of the above answers are correct.

5. Which of the following best describes the behavior of the default SAP?

   A. The default SAP receives all frames.

   B. The default SAP receives all untagged frames.

   C. The default SAP receives all tagged frames.

   D. The default SAP receives all untagged frames and all tagged frames not received by another SAP.

   E. The default SAP receives all untagged frames and all frames with a VLAN tag of 0.

6. Which of the following statements best describe the function of an ipipe service?

   A. It emulates a point-to-point Ethernet service.

   B. It emulates a point-to-point ATM service.

   C. It emulates a point-to-point Frame Relay service.

   D. It emulates a point-to-point TDM circuit.

   E. None of the above statements describe the function of an ipipe service.

7. Consider a network of four routers that are used to provide an epipe service. The transport tunnels used for the service traverse all four routers. Which of the following statements is correct regarding service configuration?

   A. The epipe service has to be configured on all four routers.

   B. The epipe service has to be configured on one router.

   C. The epipe service has to be configured on the P routers.

   D. The epipe service has to be configured on the CE routers.

   E. The epipe service has to be configured on two routers.

8. A SAP on an epipe service receives an Ethernet frame from a CE router. Which statement below describes the action taken on the FCS?

   A. The FCS is removed.

   B. The FCS is untouched.

   C. The FCS is recomputed.

   D. The action taken depends on how the epipe is configured.

9. Consider an epipe service that is operationally up on a network of 7750 SRs. All network ports have an MTU of 9,212 bytes. The epipe service and access ports use default MTU settings. The SAPs on both ends of the epipe service are configured with the CLI syntax `sap 1/1/4:20`. An operator changes the CLI syntax on both ends of the epipe service to `sap 1/1/4:*`. What additional configuration does the operator need to make for the service to function correctly?

   A. The MTU of the network ports needs to be increased.

   B. The service MTU of the epipe service needs to be increased.

   C. The SAP MTU of the service needs to be increased.

   D. The MTU of the access port used by the SAP needs to be increased.

   E. No other configuration is required.

10. An epipe SAP is configured for dot1Q encapsulation with default values. Which of the following describes the behavior of the SAP when a tagged frame arrives with an Ethertype value of `0x9100`?

A. The frame is discarded.

B. The frame is treated as an untagged frame.

C. An error message is sent to the sender of the frame.

D. It is not possible to have a tagged frame with an Ethertype value of `0x9100`; the Ethertype must be `0x8100`.

E. None of the above answers are correct.

11. Which of the following best describes the `atm-vcc` VC type for an apipe?

A. A single ATM VPI/VCI value is mapped to the apipe.

B. An entire ATM VPC is mapped to the apipe.

C. A range of ATM VPCs is mapped to the apipe.

D. An entire ATM port is mapped to the apipe.

E. `atm-vcc` is not a valid VC type for an apipe.

12. Which of the following statements about cpipes is *false*?

A. The SAToP pseudowire transports unstructured T1 or E1 data.

B. The CESoPSN pseudowire transports data from individual circuits in a T1 or E1.

C. The control word is used in the encapsulation of all packets in a cpipe service.

D. A larger jitter buffer is always preferred because it reduces the chance that data will be lost.

E. All of the above statements are true.

13. Which of the following forms of interworking is *not* supported on the Alcatel-Lucent 7750 SR?

A. Apipe to epipe interworking

B. Apipe to fpipe interworking

C. Apipe to cpipe interworking

D. Fpipe to epipe interworking

E. Epipe to ipipe interworking

14. An Ethernet frame with a single VLAN tag ingresses an epipe service with a Q-in-Q-encapsulated SAP `1/1/2:20.*`. The frame egresses the epipe service on a SAP `1/1/3:20.10`. What are the VLAN tag or tag values after the frame egresses the service?

A. There will be three tags from outer to inner: 20, 10, and the original tag.

B. There will be an outer tag of 20 and an inner tag of 10.

C. There will be a single tag of 20.

D. There will be a single tag of 10.

E. The frame will not be accepted at the ingress SAP because it has only a single tag.

15. A service provider network is made up of redundant 1 Gb/s Ethernet links with all SDPs using RSVP-TE LSPs configured with fast reroute facility backup. An fpipe is configured with a service MTU of 5,000 bytes. What is the minimum MTU for the network ports to be able to support this service?

A. 5,000 bytes

B. 5,014 bytes

C. 5,022 bytes

D. 5,026 bytes

E. 5,030 bytes

F. `ADSPEC` must be configured on the LSP because the specific value cannot be determined

19 VPLS

The Alcatel-Lucent NRS II exam topics covered in this chapter include the following:

- Virtual switch behavior
- VPLS flooding behavior
- MAC learning
- Configuring the infrastructure
- Configuring a Full-Mesh VPLS
- Verifying the VPLS and the FDB
- Hub-and-Spoke Topology
- Hierarchical VPLS
- Spoke-SDP Termination on VPLS

In this chapter, we extend the concept of an epipe into a multipoint configuration: the Virtual Private LAN Service (VPLS). We see how a VPLS emulates a virtual Ethernet switch, in particular its MAC (Media Access Control) learning and flooding behavior. We look at the configuration and verification of a VPLS and some of the different topologies used. These include the full-mesh VPLS, hub-and-spoke VPLS, hierarchical VPLS, and spoke termination in a VPLS.

Pre-Assessment

The following assessment questions will help you understand what areas of the chapter you should review in more detail to prepare for the NRS II exam. You can also use the CD that accompanies this book to take all the assessment tests and review the answers.

1. Which of the following describes a difference in the behavior of an Ethernet switch and a VPLS?
   - **A.** Unknown unicast traffic is flooded to all destinations in a VPLS but is discarded in an Ethernet switch.
   - **B.** Traffic to known multicast and broadcast addresses is flooded to all destinations in a VPLS but only to specific ports in an Ethernet switch.
   - **C.** SAPs with different VLAN values in a VPLS are treated as separate broadcast domains. On an Ethernet switch, different VLAN values are treated as being in the same broadcast domain.
   - **D.** SAPs with different VLAN values in a VPLS are treated as being in the same broadcast domain. On an Ethernet switch, different VLAN values are treated as separate broadcast domains.
   - **E.** None of the above statements describe a difference between a VPLS and an Ethernet switch.
2. Which of the following best describes how a VPLS populates the MAC FDB?
   - **A.** The network administrator programs the FDB with the MAC address of the attached devices.
   - **B.** The PE router uses ARP to discover the MAC addresses of attached devices.
   - **C.** The PE router examines the source MAC address of received frames.
   - **D.** The PE router examines the destination MAC address of received frames.
   - **E.** There is no MAC learning; unicast traffic is flooded to all destinations in the VPLS.

3. Which statement best describes the flooding behavior of a VPLS for unknown unicast traffic received on a mesh SDP?
   - **A.** The traffic is flooded to all SDPs and SAPs configured on the router.
   - **B.** The traffic is flooded to all mesh SDPs in the same service.
   - **C.** The traffic is flooded to all mesh SDPs, SAPs, and spoke SDPs in the same service.
   - **D.** The traffic is flooded to all SAPs and spoke SDPs in the same service.
   - **E.** The traffic is flooded to all mesh SDPs that are not in the same service, and all SAPs and spoke SDPs that are in the same service.
   - **F.** None of the above statements are correct.
4. Consider a metro VPLS network that has four PE routers. Two VPLS instances are created on each PE router. If only mesh SDPs are used in the network, what is the total number of mesh SDPs that have to be configured in the network?
   - **A.** Three mesh SDPs are required.
   - **B.** Four mesh SDPs are required.
   - **C.** Six mesh SDPs are required.
   - **D.** Eight mesh SDPs are required.
   - **E.** Twelve mesh SDPs are required.
   - **F.** Twenty-four mesh SDPs are required.
5. Which of the following statements about mesh and spoke SDPs is true?
   - **A.** Using spoke SDPs in a VPLS removes the requirement for a full mesh of SDP bindings.
   - **B.** Using spoke SDPs in a VPLS eliminates the possibility of looping in the VPLS.
   - **C.** MAC learning is not performed on spoke SDPs in a VPLS.
   - **D.** Spoke and mesh SDPs cannot be used in the same VPLS.
   - **E.** None of the above statements are true.

19.1 VPLS Overview

The VPLS is an Ethernet service that connects multiple sites in a single switched domain over the provider-managed IP/MPLS network. The characteristics of a VPLS service are described in RFC 4665 ("Service Requirements for Layer 2 Provider-Provisioned Virtual Private Networks") and RFC 4762 ("Virtual Private LAN Service [VPLS] Using Label Distribution Protocol [LDP] Signaling). VPLS is essentially an enhancement to a multipoint service of the Ethernet pseudowire service, or Virtual Private Wire Services (VPWS), described in Chapter 18.

The similarities between an epipe and a VPLS are the following:

- They both use the same encapsulation and transport mechanism of an MPLS (Multiprotocol Label Switching) or GRE (generic routing encapsulation) encapsulated packet with an inner service label.
- The signaling of transport and service labels is the same: LDP or RSVP-TE (Resource Reservation Protocol–Traffic Engineering) for transport labels and T-LDP (Targeted LDP) for service labels.
- The SAP (Service Access Point) encapsulation types of null, dot1Q, and Q-in-Q are the same for a VPLS as for an epipe. The treatment of customer data at the SAP is the same in a VPLS as in an epipe.

The differences between an epipe and a VPLS service are the following:

- A VPLS is a multipoint service instead of the point-to-point service of an epipe.
- The VPLS appears as a single switched LAN (Local Area Network) to the customer, whereas the epipe appears as a direct Ethernet connection.
- A VPLS performs MAC (Media Access Control) learning to build a forwarding database (FDB) containing the addresses of customer-attached devices. The VPLS uses the FDB for intelligent forwarding of customer traffic over the IP/MPLS core network.

The advantages of a VPLS from the customer's perspective are as follows:

- To the customer it appears as if all sites are connected to a single switched Ethernet network.
- The VPLS is transparent to the customer's data and higher-layer protocols.
- The VPLS can operate over a single, local site or at multiple, geographically dispersed sites.
- The VPLS performs MAC learning so that frames are forwarded only across the required links in the network.

The advantages to the service provider are the advantages of using an IP/MPLS network for any VPN service:

- Only the PE (provider edge) devices require configuration for the VPLS service.
- There is a clear demarcation of functionality between the service provider and customer networks.
- **Scalability**—The provider can support thousands of customers per node.
- **Flexibility**—Many different services for many different customers can be provided over a single core IP/MPLS network.
- The service provider can apply QoS, billing, ingress/egress traffic shaping, and policing on a per-service basis

The IP/MPLS infrastructure provides the ability to deploy and manage a wide variety of services in a cost-effective manner. Figure 19.1 shows a service provider supporting two different customer VPLS services on a common IP/MPLS core.

Figure 19.1 Multiple VPLS services can be deployed using the same IP/MPLS core.

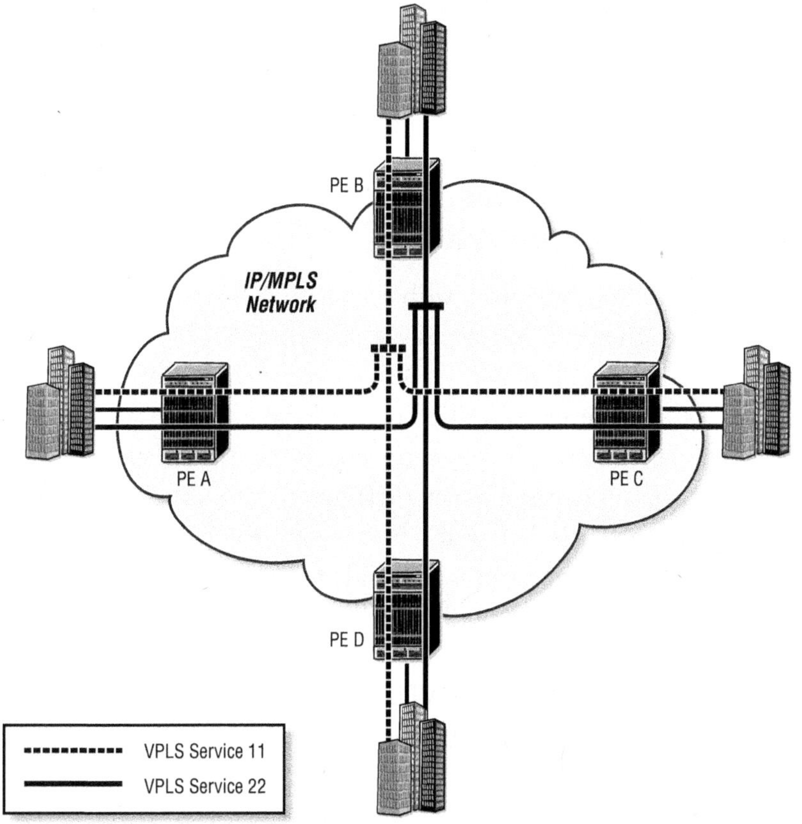

For the transport of customer data, the VPLS acts as if it were a full mesh of epipes between all the PEs in the service. Figure 19.2 shows that each PE has a T-LDP peering session with every other PE and signals a label to use for the service. The VC ID (virtual circuit identifier) configured for the service must match on all PEs in the service. Customer frames are encapsulated with a service label and the outer MPLS transport label. The VPLS instance on each PE router is often referred to as a *virtual switch* (VS) because it emulates the behavior of an Ethernet switch.

Figure 19.2 All PE routers in the VPLS are T-LDP peers and exchange labels for the service.

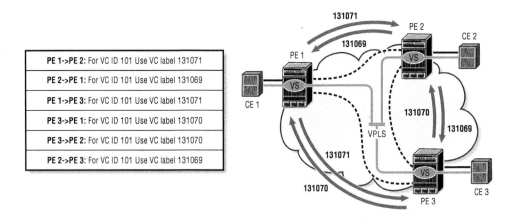

PE 1->PE 2: For VC ID 101 Use VC label 131071
PE 2->PE 1: For VC ID 101 Use VC label 131069
PE 1->PE 3: For VC ID 101 Use VC label 131071
PE 3->PE 1: For VC ID 101 Use VC label 131070
PE 3->PE 2: For VC ID 101 Use VC label 131070
PE 2->PE 3: For VC ID 101 Use VC label 131069

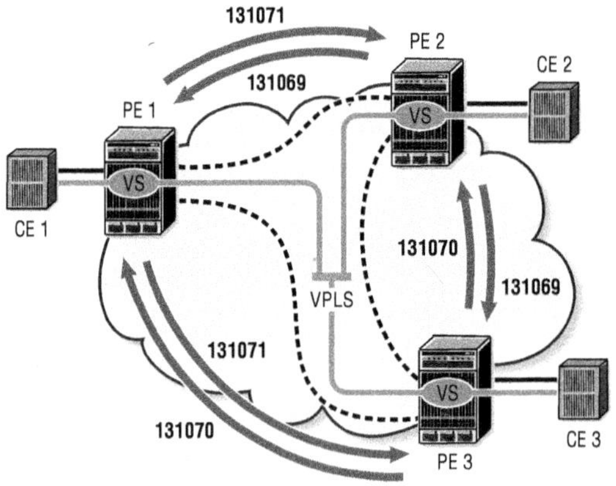

19.2 Virtual Switch Behavior

Figure 19.3 shows an IP/MPLS network with a single VPLS service supporting six different customer sites. There is a full mesh of SDPs (Service Distribution Points) configured between the four PE routers such that every PE has an SDP to every other PE. Like other pseudowire services, a VPLS can be local (multiple sites connected to a single PE) or distributed (multiple sites connected to multiple PEs).

In this chapter, we examine the characteristics of the VPLS that enable it to appear to the customer as though each SAP were a port on an Ethernet switch. The VPLS performs MAC learning so that it can intelligently forward frames across the network and can be configured to participate in the customer's spanning tree protocol (STP) like an Ethernet switch.

One significant difference between the VPLS and an Ethernet switch is that the VPLS joins any VLANs used for service-delimiting tags. On an Ethernet switch, VLAN tags create separate broadcast domains. However, in a VPLS, all the SAPs belong to the same broadcast domain, regardless of the VLAN tags. In Figure 19.3, six different tag values are used at the six different sites. Because service-delimiting tags are stripped at ingress, they are effectively invisible to the VPLS, and the VLANs are joined. If it is desirable to maintain VLAN tags, the SAPs can be defined using a null encapsulation.

Figure 19.3 VPLS connects a customer's multiple locations like a virtual Ethernet switch.

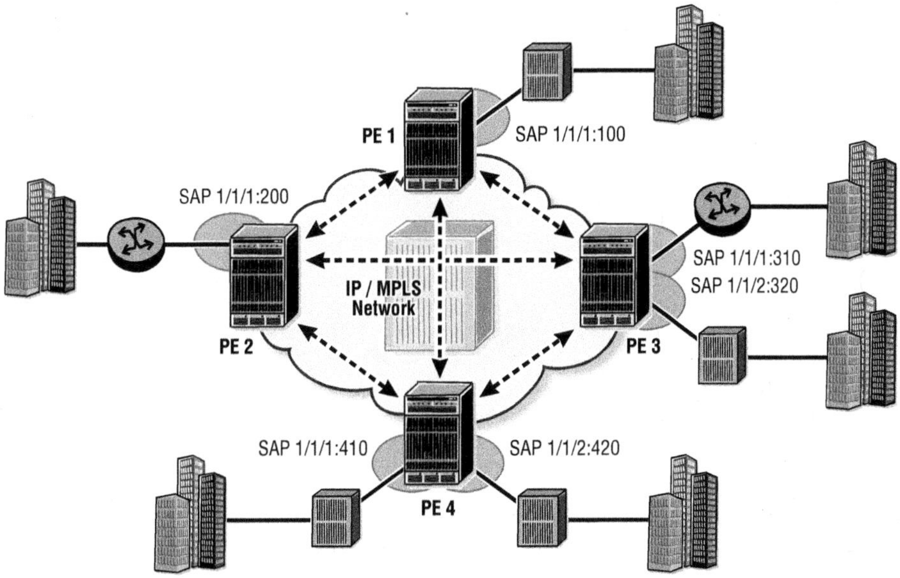

VPLS Flooding Behavior

Because a VPLS provides a multipoint connectivity, traffic entering the service must be appropriately replicated to the other locations. As in an Ethernet switch, known unicast traffic is replicated only to the destination. Figure 19.4 shows an Ethernet frame arriving at PE 4. The FDB on PE 4 contains the destination MAC address of the frame and thus can forward the encapsulated frame to PE 3. The FDB on PE 3 also contains the destination MAC, thus PE 3 forwards the frame out of the appropriate SAP.

On an Ethernet switch, traffic to a multicast, broadcast, or unknown unicast address is flooded to all ports. A VPLS also floods such traffic to all SAPs in the service (see Figure 19.5).

Figure 19.4 Forwarding of an Ethernet frame with a known unicast address over the VPLS.

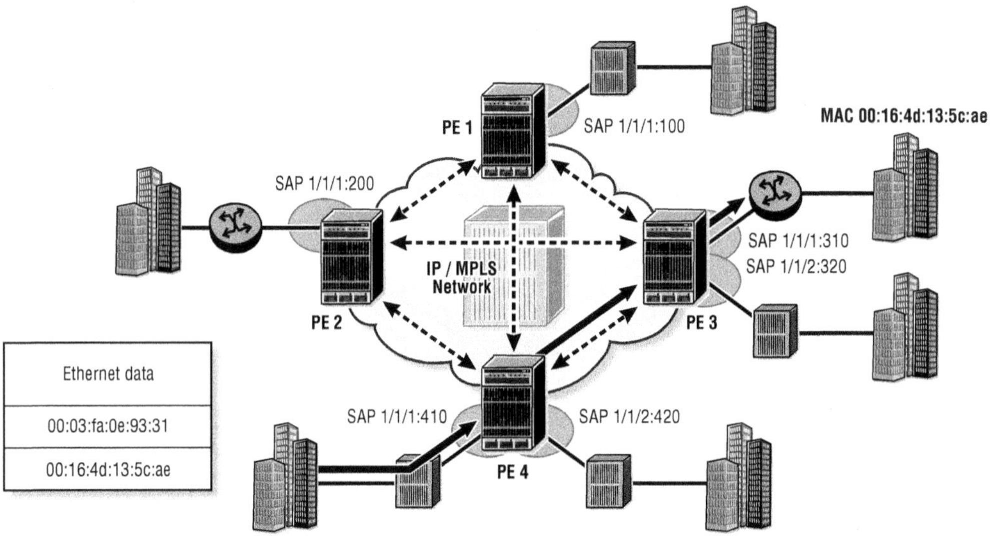

Figure 19.5 Traffic flooded to all SAPs in the VPLS.

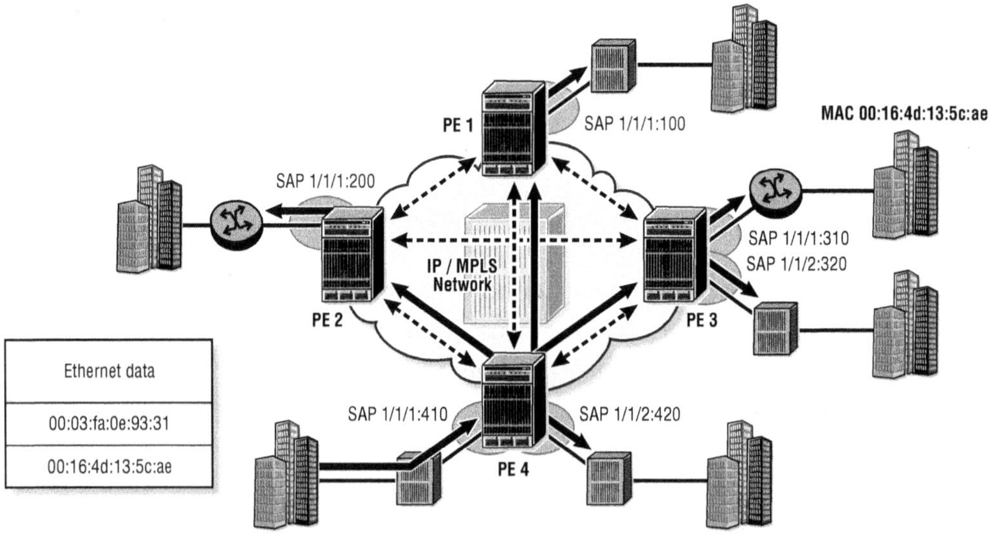

Figure 19.5 illustrates one of the key requirements of a VPLS—the proper flooding of traffic. Notice that PE 3 forwards the frame it receives only to the SAPs and not on the SDP to PE 1 or PE 2. In a basic VPLS such as this one, the SDP is bound to the

service as a *mesh SDP*. In a VPWS, the SDP is bound as a *spoke SDP*. The only difference between the two is their flooding behavior, which can be summarized as follows:

- **Mesh SDP**—Floods frames received from a SAP or from a spoke SDP but does not flood frames received from another mesh SDP.
- **Spoke SDP**—Floods frames received from a SAP, spoke SDP, or mesh SDP.

Figure 19.6 shows a VPLS service on one PE. It has two SAPs on the local PE and four SDPs that lead to other PE devices. A frame received on one SAP and destined to a broadcast, multicast, or unknown address must be flooded through the VPLS. It is transmitted on the other SAP, the two mesh SDPs, and the two spoke SDPs.

Figure 19.6 Replication of a frame received on a SAP.

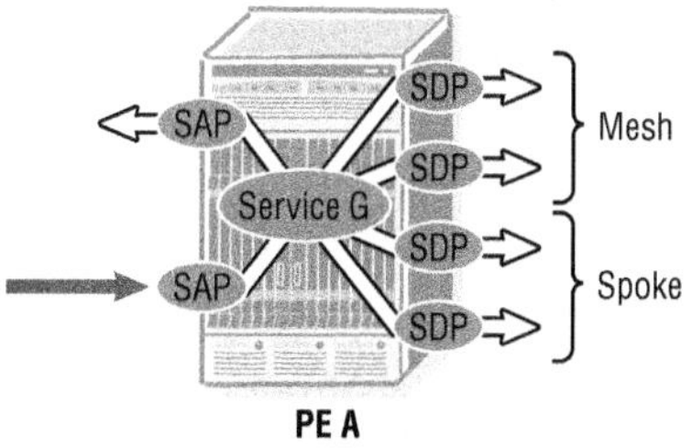

A frame received on a spoke SDP to be flooded through the VPLS is transmitted on both SAPs, the other spoke SDP, and both mesh SDPs (see Figure 19.7).

Figure 19.7 Replication of a frame received on a spoke SDP.

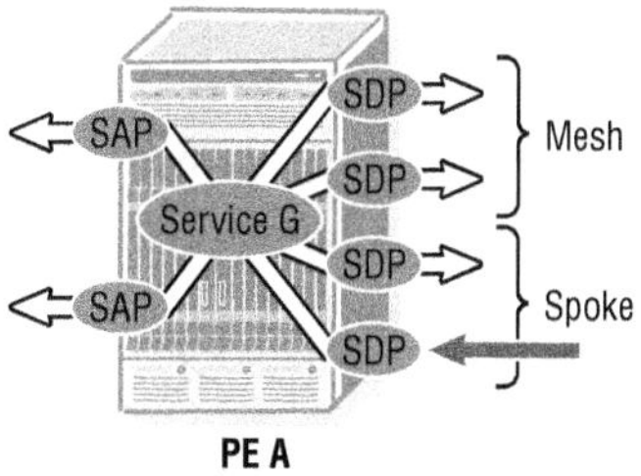

A frame received on a mesh SDP to be flooded through the VPLS is transmitted on both SAPs, both spoke SDPs, but not the other mesh SDP (see Figure 19.8).

A basic VPLS is configured with a full mesh of mesh SDPs between all the PE nodes in the service. You can see from Figure 19.5 that if the service was configured with spoke SDPs between the routers, a frame arriving at PE 3 from PE 1 would be sent on the spoke SDPs to PE 2 and PE 4, resulting in unwanted and uncontrolled flooding of frames in the VPLS. Mesh SDPs ensure that all PE devices receive the frame without looping or duplication of frames. Below in this chapter we describe some specific situations in which spoke SDPs are used in a VPLS.

Figure 19.8 Replication of a frame received on a mesh SDP.

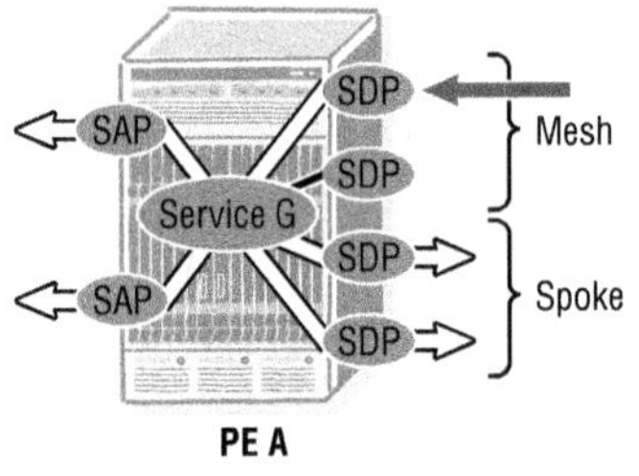

MAC Learning

We saw in Figure 19.4 that data to a known destination is only transmitted on the SDP leading to the destination node and then sent out of only the SAP leading to the destination. The VPLS learns the MAC addresses of the customer's attached devices in the same manner as an Ethernet switch. The learned addresses are stored in a *forwarding database* (FDB) kept on each PE device. Similar to the way an Ethernet switch maintains a separate FDB for each configured VLAN, the PE maintains a separate FDB for every VPLS service configured on the router. Figure 19.9 shows the two FDBs maintained on PE-1 for two different VPLS services.

In Figure 19.10, we examine the transmission of a customer frame across VPLS 101 to see how the PE routers learn MAC addresses. When PE-2 receives a frame from M2 destined to M1, it is flooded because M1 is an unknown address. Afterward, all PE routers in the VPLS have learned M2's address.

The step-by-step process is as follows:

1. M2 transmits a unicast Ethernet frame destined to M1 that is received at the SAP on PE-2.
2. PE-2 learns the location of M2 on the SAP from the source address in the received frame and updates its FDB with M2's MAC address.

3. Because M1's address (the destination address) is unknown, M2 floods the frame to both SDPs in the service.
4. M1 and M3 both receive the frame and learn the location of M2 as being on the SDP to PE-2 and update their FDBs with M2's MAC address.
5. Because the destination address is unknown to M1 and M3, they both flood the frame out of their local SAPs. The frame arrives at the customer device, M1.

Figure 19.9 Two distinct FDBs are maintained on each PE router for each VPLS.

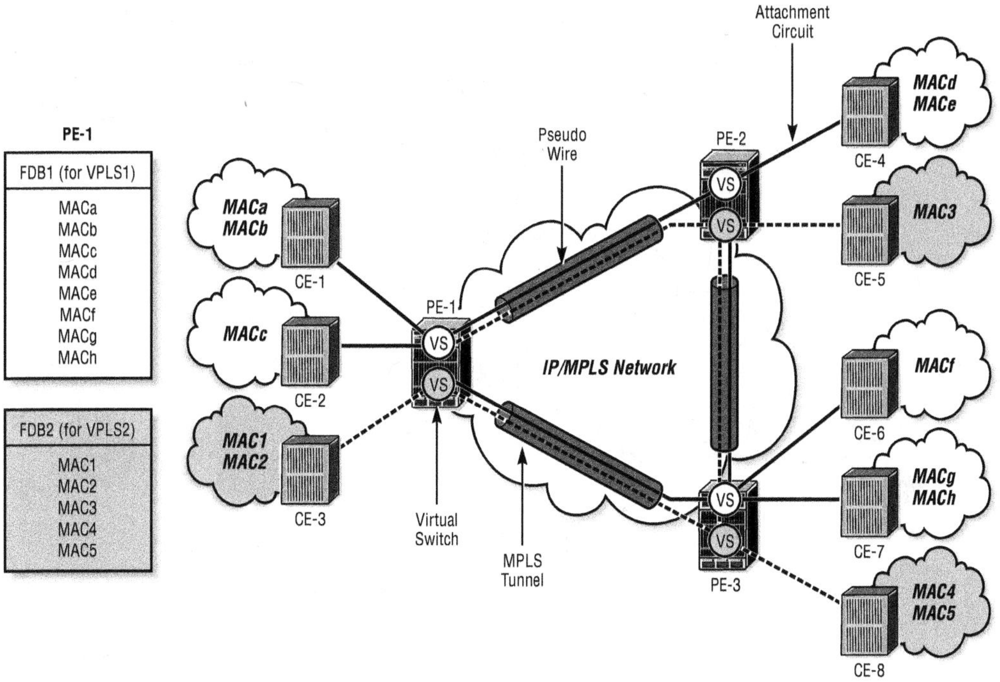

Figure 19.11 shows what occurs when M1 responds to M2. Because M2 is now known in the FDB, the frame does not have to be flooded and can be sent directly to PE-2. Once the frame arrives at M2, both PE-1 and PE-2 have learned M1's MAC address and have it in their FDBs.

The step-by-step process is as follows:

1. M1 transmits a frame with M2 as the destination. The frame arrives at the SAP on PE-1.

2. PE-1 has the MAC address for M2 in its FDB and knows to transmit the frame on the SDP to PE-2. PE-1 learns the location of M1 from the source address in the frame and updates its FDB.
3. PE-2 has the MAC address for M2 in its FDB and knows to transmit the frame out of the SAP. PE-2 learns the location of M1 from the source address in the frame and updates its FDB. The frame arrives at the destination, M2.

Figure 19.10 MAC learning in a VPLS.

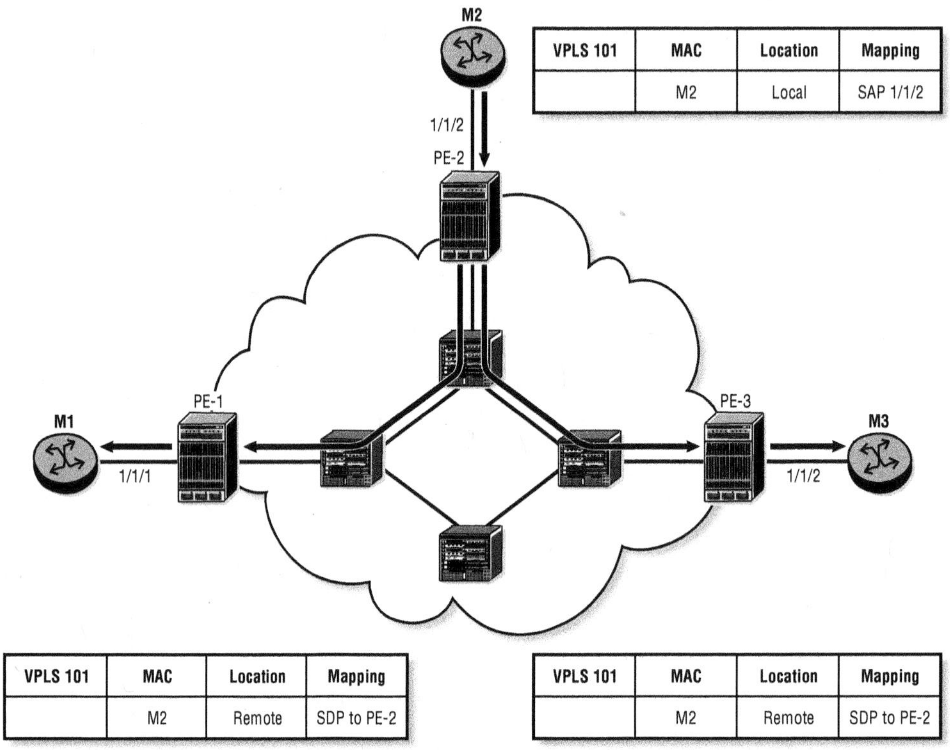

After the transmission from M1 to M2, both PE-1 and PE-2 have an entry for M1 in their FDB. Because the frame from M1 was not flooded in the VPLS, PE-3 does not have M1 in its FDB. If it receives a frame destined for M1, it will be flooded in the VPLS by PE-3.

Figure 19.11 MAC learning in a VPLS with another frame.

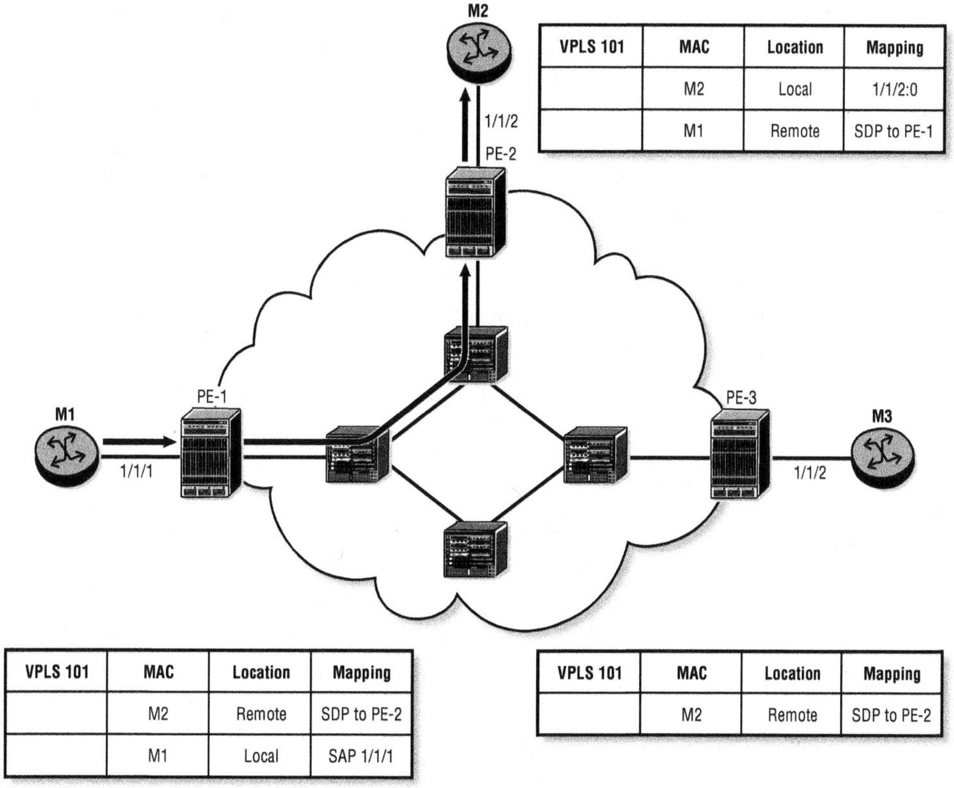

VPLS 101	MAC	Location	Mapping
	M2	Local	1/1/2:0
	M1	Remote	SDP to PE-1

VPLS 101	MAC	Location	Mapping
	M2	Remote	SDP to PE-2
	M1	Local	SAP 1/1/1

VPLS 101	MAC	Location	Mapping
	M2	Remote	SDP to PE-2

19.3 VPLS Configuration and Verification

The configuration and verification of a VPLS are very similar to the configuration of a VPWS, although with potentially more PE locations. The steps for provisioning the service are as follows:

1. Configure the IP/MPLS service infrastructure.
2. Create the VPLS service on each of the PE routers.
3. Verify connectivity through the service.

Configuring Infrastructure

As for any other VPN service, we first require the IP/MPLS infrastructure to support the service. Figure 19.12 shows a network of three PE routers and two P routers on which we will provision a VPLS. The steps for preparing the infrastructure are as follows:

1. Configure IP interfaces and an IGP (interior gateway protocol) for basic routing in the core network.
2. Configure MPLS interfaces and LSPs (label switch paths). Either LDP or a full mesh of RSVP-TE LSPs between all PE routers is required.
3. Configure a full mesh of SDPs between all PE routers.

Figure 19.12 IP/MPLS core infrastructure for deploying a VPLS.

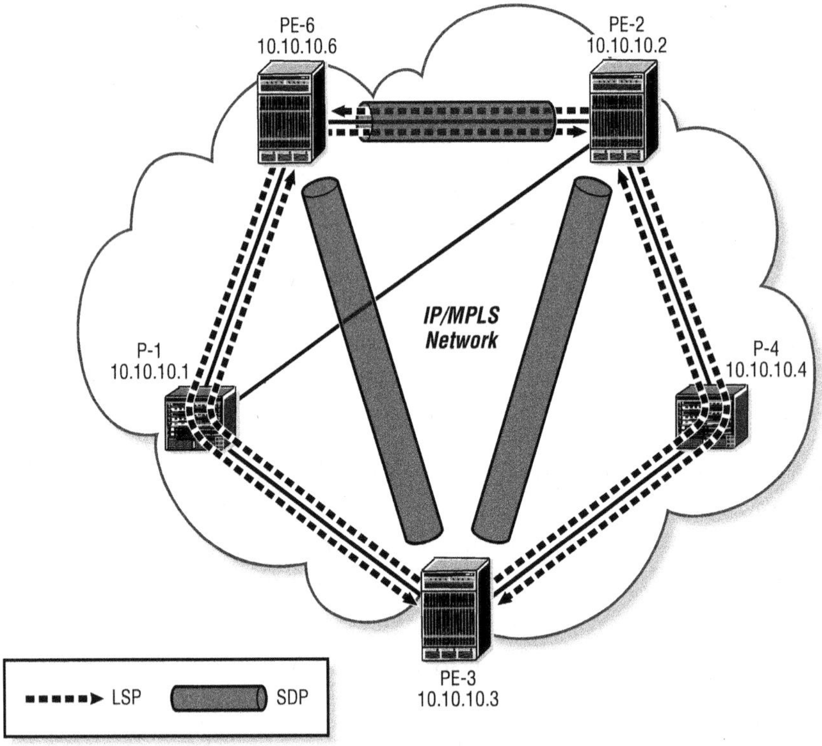

Listing 19.1 shows the configuration on PE-2. The configuration on PE-3 and PE-6 is similar. The following protocols are deployed in the network:

- Single-area OSPF (Open Shortest Path First) with traffic engineering enabled

- A full mesh of RSVP-TE LSPs with fast reroute enabled
- A full mesh of MPLS-encapsulated SDPs

Listing 19.1 Configuration of the PE router for a VPN service infrastructure

```
*A:PE-2# show router route-table

===============================================================================
Route Table (Router: Base)
===============================================================================
Dest Prefix                                 Type    Proto    Age         Pref
       Next Hop[Interface Name]                                Metric
-------------------------------------------------------------------------------
10.1.2.0/27                                 Local   Local    01h29m49s   0
       toP1                                                    0
10.1.3.0/27                                 Remote  OSPF     01h29m43s   10
       10.1.2.1                                                200
10.1.6.0/27                                 Remote  OSPF     01h29m43s   10
       10.1.2.1                                                200
10.2.4.0/27                                 Local   Local    02h42m25s   0
       toP4                                                    0
10.2.6.0/27                                 Local   Local    02h41m52s   0
       toPE-6                                                  0
10.3.4.0/27                                 Remote  OSPF     01h48m28s   10
       10.2.4.4                                                200
10.10.10.1/32                               Remote  OSPF     01h29m43s   10
       10.1.2.1                                                100
10.10.10.2/32                               Local   Local    02h41m38s   0
       system                                                  0
10.10.10.3/32                               Remote  OSPF     01h29m43s   10
       10.1.2.1                                                200
10.10.10.4/32                               Remote  OSPF     01h48m29s   10
       10.2.4.4                                                100
10.10.10.6/32                               Remote  OSPF     01h48m37s   10
       10.2.6.6                                                100
-------------------------------------------------------------------------------
No. of Routes: 11
===============================================================================
```

(continued)

Listing 19.1 *(continued)*

```
*A:PE-2# show router ospf opaque-database

==========================================================================
OSPF Opaque Link State Database (Type : All)
==========================================================================
Type  Id          Link State Id    Adv Rtr Id      Age  Sequence    Cksum
--------------------------------------------------------------------------
Area  0.0.0.0     1.0.0.1          10.10.10.1      1892 0x80000005 0xa03
Area  0.0.0.0     1.0.0.2          10.10.10.1      1474 0x80000009 0xef50
Area  0.0.0.0     1.0.0.3          10.10.10.1      1105 0x80000009 0x61d1
Area  0.0.0.0     1.0.0.4          10.10.10.1      1572 0x8000000a 0x5be5
Area  0.0.0.0     1.0.0.1          10.10.10.2      493  0x80000005 0xefc
Area  0.0.0.0     1.0.0.2          10.10.10.2      831  0x8000000b 0x49f8
Area  0.0.0.0     1.0.0.3          10.10.10.2      831  0x8000000b 0xb87c
Area  0.0.0.0     1.0.0.4          10.10.10.2      68   0x8000000b 0xab80
Area  0.0.0.0     1.0.0.1          10.10.10.3      139  0x80000005 0x12f6
Area  0.0.0.0     1.0.0.2          10.10.10.3      1239 0x8000000c 0xa19b
Area  0.0.0.0     1.0.0.3          10.10.10.3      303  0x8000000a 0x131f
Area  0.0.0.0     1.0.0.1          10.10.10.4      1166 0x80000233 0xb323
Area  0.0.0.0     1.0.0.2          10.10.10.4      206  0x800004c7 0xf480
Area  0.0.0.0     1.0.0.3          10.10.10.4      972  0x8000000f 0xe448
Area  0.0.0.0     1.0.0.1          10.10.10.6      910  0x80000005 0x1ee4
Area  0.0.0.0     1.0.0.2          10.10.10.6      624  0x80000011 0xa685
Area  0.0.0.0     1.0.0.3          10.10.10.6      337  0x80000012 0x170f
--------------------------------------------------------------------------
No. of Opaque LSAs: 17
==========================================================================
*A:PE-2# show router mpls lsp

==========================================================================
MPLS LSPs (Originating)
==========================================================================
LSP Name                    To                   Fastfail     Adm   Opr
                                                 Config
--------------------------------------------------------------------------
to-PE-3                     10.10.10.3           Yes          Up    Up
to-PE-6                     10.10.10.6           Yes          Up    Up
--------------------------------------------------------------------------
```

```
LSPs : 2
===============================================================================
*A:PE-2# show service sdp

===============================================================================
Services: Service Destination Points
===============================================================================
SdpId     Adm MTU  Opr MTU  IP address      Adm  Opr        Deliver   Signal
-------------------------------------------------------------------------------
3         0        9190     10.10.10.3      Up   Up         MPLS      TLDP
6         0        9190     10.10.10.6      Up   Up         MPLS      TLDP
-------------------------------------------------------------------------------
Number of SDPs : 2
-------------------------------------------------------------------------------
===============================================================================
```

The two P routers, P-1 and P-4, must be configured to support IP/MPLS but do not require any service infrastructure. Listing 19.2 shows that P-4 has the IP routing information and is transiting LSPs but does not require any additional configuration.

Listing 19.2 Configuration of the P router for a VPN service infrastructure

```
*A:P4# show router route-table

===============================================================================
Route Table (Router: Base)
===============================================================================
Dest Prefix                                 Type     Proto     Age          Pref
       Next Hop[Interface Name]                                  Metric
-------------------------------------------------------------------------------
10.1.2.0/27                                 Remote   OSPF      01h46m18s    10
       10.2.4.2                                                   200
10.1.3.0/27                                 Remote   OSPF      02h47m31s    10
       10.3.4.3                                                   200
10.1.6.0/27                                 Remote   OSPF      01h46m18s    10
       10.2.4.2                                                   300
10.2.4.0/27                                 Local    Local     11d16h38m    0
       toPE-2                                                    0
```

(continued)

Listing 19.2 *(continued)*

```
10.2.6.0/27                              Remote  OSPF      02h05m06s   10
       10.2.4.2                                                 200
10.3.4.0/27                              Local   Local     02h47m54s   0
       toPE-3                                                   0
10.10.10.1/32                            Remote  OSPF      01h46m18s   10
       10.2.4.2                                                 200
10.10.10.2/32                            Remote  OSPF      02h05m07s   10
       10.2.4.2                                                 100
10.10.10.3/32                            Remote  OSPF      02h47m32s   10
       10.3.4.3                                                 100
10.10.10.4/32                            Local   Local     11d16h38m   0
       system                                                   0
10.10.10.6/32                            Remote  OSPF      02h05m07s   10
       10.2.4.2                                                 200
-------------------------------------------------------------------------
No. of Routes: 11
=========================================================================
*A:P4# show router mpls lsp

=========================================================================
MPLS LSPs (Originating)
=========================================================================
LSP Name                        To               Fastfail     Adm   Opr
                                                 Config
-------------------------------------------------------------------------
No Matching Entries Found
=========================================================================
*A:P4# show router rsvp session

=========================================================================
RSVP Sessions
=========================================================================
From         To              Tunnel LSP   Name                         State
                                ID     ID
-------------------------------------------------------------------------
10.10.10.2   10.10.10.3      2      7680  to-PE-3::loose               Up
10.10.10.2   10.10.10.3      2      7680  to-PE-3::loose_detour        Up
10.10.10.2   10.10.10.6      4      57856 to-PE-6::loose_detour        Up
```

```
10.10.10.3    10.10.10.6       4       35840 to-PE-6::loose_detour      Up
10.10.10.3    10.10.10.2       2       51712 to-PE-2::loose             Up
10.10.10.3    10.10.10.2       2       51712 to-PE-2::loose_detour      Up
10.10.10.6    10.10.10.3       4       45568 to-PE-3::loose_detour      Up
-------------------------------------------------------------------------------
Sessions : 7
===============================================================================
*A:P4# show service sdp

===============================================================================
Services: Service Destination Points
===============================================================================
SdpId     Adm MTU   Opr MTU   IP address     Adm   Opr        Deliver   Signal
-------------------------------------------------------------------------------
No Matching Entries
===============================================================================
```

Configuring the VPLS

The steps we will follow to configure the VPLS in Figure 19.13 are as follows:

1. Configure the customer-facing ports as access ports. Ports are network ports by default.
2. Create the VPLS service on each of the PE routers.
3. Add a full mesh of SDP bindings between the PEs.
4. Add the appropriate customer-facing SAPs.
5. Verify that the service is operationally up on all PEs.
6. Verify connectivity through the service by pinging between the customer devices.

Listing 19.3 shows the configuration of the access ports in preparation for their use as the SAP. We are using null encapsulation, but any encapsulation supported for an epipe is possible in a VPLS. Notice that the port MTU changes to 1,514 bytes when it is configured as an access port.

Figure 19.13 VPLS configured between three PE routers.

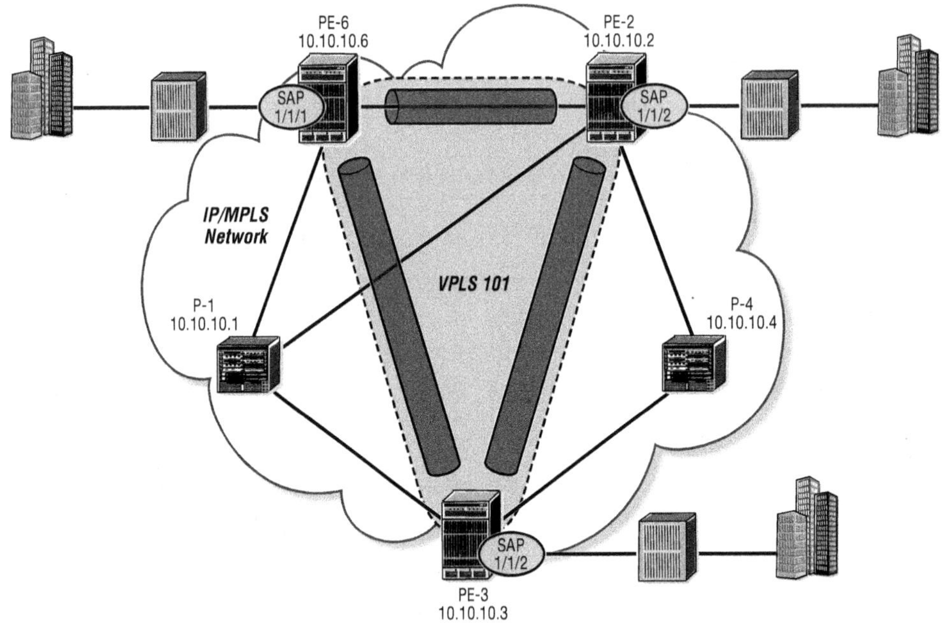

Listing 19.3 Customer-facing ports configured as access ports for use in a SAP

```
*A:PE-2# configure port 1/1/2
*A:PE-2>config>port# shutdown
*A:PE-2>config>port# ethernet mode access
*A:PE-2>config>port# no shutdown
*A:PE-2>config>port# exit
*A:PE-2# show port 1/1

===============================================================================
Ports on Slot 1
===============================================================================
Port        Admin Link Port    Cfg  Oper LAG/ Port Port Port   SFP/XFP/
Id          State      State   MTU  MTU  Bndl Mode Encp Type   MDIMDX
-------------------------------------------------------------------------------
1/1/1       Up    Yes  Up      9212 9212    - netw null gige
1/1/2       Up    Yes  Up      1514 1514    - accs null gige
1/1/3       Up    Yes  Up      9212 9212    - netw null gige
```

```
1/1/4        Up    Yes  Up      9212 9212    - netw null gige
1/1/5        Down  No   Down    9212 9212    - netw null gige
1/1/6        Down  No   Down    9212 9212    - netw null gige
1/1/7        Down  No   Down    9212 9212    - netw null gige
1/1/8        Down  No   Down    9212 9212    - netw null gige
1/1/9        Down  No   Down    9212 9212    - netw null gige
1/1/10       Down  No   Down    9212 9212    - netw null gige
===============================================================================
```

Listing 19.4 shows the creation of the VPLS and the binding of the SDPs to the service. We use mesh SDPs to create a loop-free core for the VPLS. A VC ID is not specified for the mesh SDP; it uses the service number as the VC ID. The service has only been configured on one PE device and thus is not operationally up. The error flag for the SDP shows `NoEgrVCLabel` because there has been no label signaled by the other end.

Listing 19.4 Create the VPLS and bind mesh SDPs to the service

```
*A:PE-2# configure service vpls 101 customer 1 create
*A:PE-2>config>service>vpls$ mesh-sdp 3 create
*A:PE-2>config>service>vpls>mesh-sdp$ exit
*A:PE-2>config>service>vpls# mesh-sdp 6 create
*A:PE-2>config>service>vpls>mesh-sdp$ exit
*A:PE-2>config>service>vpls# show service id 101 base

===============================================================================
Service Basic Information
===============================================================================
Service Id         : 101                  Vpn Id            : 0
Service Type       : VPLS
Name               : (Not Specified)
Description        : (Not Specified)
Customer Id        : 1
Last Status Change: 04/14/2011 11:29:22
Last Mgmt Change   : 04/16/2011 15:10:08
Admin State        : Up                   Oper State        : Down
MTU                : 1514                 Def. Mesh VC Id   : 101
SAP Count          : 0                    SDP Bind Count    : 2
Snd Flush on Fail : Disabled              Host Conn Verify  : Disabled
```

(continued)

Listing 19.4 *(continued)*

```
Propagate MacFlush: Disabled           Per Svc Hashing    : Disabled
Def. Gateway IP    : None
Def. Gateway MAC   : None

-------------------------------------------------------------------------
Service Access & Destination Points
-------------------------------------------------------------------------
Identifier                         Type         AdmMTU  OprMTU  Adm  Opr
-------------------------------------------------------------------------
sdp:3:101 M(10.10.10.3)            Mesh         0       9190    Up   Down
sdp:6:101 M(10.10.10.6)            Mesh         0       9190    Up   Down
=========================================================================
*A:PE-2>config>service>vpls# show service id 101 sdp 3:101 detail

=========================================================================
Service Destination Point (Sdp Id : 3:101) Details
=========================================================================
-------------------------------------------------------------------------
 Sdp Id 3:101  -(10.10.10.3)
-------------------------------------------------------------------------
Description     : (Not Specified)
SDP Id             : 3:101                Type               : Mesh
Mesh Descr      : (Not Specified)
Split Horiz Grp    : (Not Specified)
VC Type            : Ether                VC Tag             : n/a
Admin Path MTU     : 0                    Oper Path MTU      : 9190
Far End            : 10.10.10.3           Delivery           : MPLS
Hash Label         : Disabled

Admin State        : Up                   Oper State         : Down
Acct. Pol          : None                 Collect Stats      : Disabled
Ingress Label      : 131071               Egress Label       : 0
Ingr Mac Fltr-Id   : n/a                  Egr Mac Fltr-Id    : n/a
Ingr IP Fltr-Id    : n/a                  Egr IP Fltr-Id     : n/a
Ingr IPv6 Fltr-Id  : n/a                  Egr IPv6 Fltr-Id   : n/a
Admin ControlWord  : Not Preferred        Oper ControlWord   : False
Last Status Change : 04/14/2011 11:29:22  Signaling          : TLDP
Last Mgmt Change   : 04/16/2011 15:09:58  Force Vlan-Vc      : Disabled
```

```
Endpoint            : N/A                       Precedence          : 4
Class Fwding State : Down
Flags               : NoEgrVCLabel
Peer Pw Bits        : None
Peer Fault Ip       : None
Application Profile: None
MAC Pinning         : Disabled

KeepAlive Information :
Admin State         : Disabled                  Oper State          : Disabled
Hello Time          : 10                        Hello Msg Len       : 0
Max Drop Count      : 3                         Hold Down Time      : 10

Statistics            :
I. Fwd. Pkts.       : 0                         I. Dro. Pkts.       : 0
I. Fwd. Octs.       : 0                         I. Dro. Octs.       : 0
E. Fwd. Pkts.       : 0                         E. Fwd. Octets      : 0
MCAC Policy Name    :
MCAC Max Unconst BW: no limit                   MCAC Max Mand BW    : no limit
MCAC In use Mand BW: 0                          MCAC Avail Mand BW: unlimited
MCAC In use Opnl BW: 0                          MCAC Avail Opnl BW: unlimited

-------------------------------------------------------------------------
RSVP/Static LSPs
-------------------------------------------------------------------------
Associated LSP LIST :
Lsp Name            : to-PE-3
Admin State         : Up                         Oper State          : Up
Time Since Last Tr*: 02h31m37s

-------------------------------------------------------------------------
Class-based forwarding :
-------------------------------------------------------------------------
Class forwarding    : Disabled                  EnforceDSTELspFc    : Disabled
Default LSP         : Uknwn                     Multicast LSP       : None

=========================================================================
FC Mapping Table
=========================================================================
```

(continued)

Listing 19.4 *(continued)*

```
FC Name                 LSP Name
-------------------------------------------------------------------------------
No FC Mappings


-------------------------------------------------------------------------------
Number of SDPs : 1
-------------------------------------------------------------------------------
===============================================================================
* indicates that the corresponding row element may have been truncated.
```

Once the service is configured on the other PE devices and the SAP configured on PE-2, the VPLS on PE-2 is up (see Listing 19.5).

Listing 19.5 VPLS operationally up on router PE-2

```
*A:PE-2# configure service vpls 101
*A:PE-2>config>service>vpls# sap 1/1/2 create
*A:PE-2>config>service>vpls>sap$ exit
*A:PE-2>config>service>vpls# info
----------------------------------------------
            stp
                shutdown
            exit
            sap 1/1/2 create
            exit
            mesh-sdp 3:101 create
            exit
            mesh-sdp 6:101 create
            exit
            no shutdown
----------------------------------------------
*A:PE-2>config>service>vpls# show service id 101 base


===============================================================================
Service Basic Information
===============================================================================
Service Id          : 101                    Vpn Id              : 0
Service Type        : VPLS
Name                : (Not Specified)
```

```
Description        : (Not Specified)
Customer Id        : 1
Last Status Change: 04/16/2011 15:18:30
Last Mgmt Change   : 04/16/2011 15:10:08
Admin State        : Up                    Oper State          : Up
MTU                : 1514                  Def. Mesh VC Id     : 101
SAP Count          : 1                     SDP Bind Count      : 2
Snd Flush on Fail : Disabled               Host Conn Verify   : Disabled
Propagate MacFlush: Disabled               Per Svc Hashing     : Disabled
Def. Gateway IP    : None
Def. Gateway MAC   : None

-------------------------------------------------------------------------
Service Access & Destination Points
-------------------------------------------------------------------------
Identifier                        Type          AdmMTU  OprMTU  Adm  Opr
-------------------------------------------------------------------------
sap:1/1/2                         null          1514    1514    Up   Up
sdp:3:101 M(10.10.10.3)           Mesh          0       9190    Up   Up
sdp:6:101 M(10.10.10.6)           Mesh          0       9190    Up   Up
=========================================================================
*A:PE-2>config>service>vpls#
```

Verifying the VPLS and the FDB

Once the VPLS is up, we should be able to ping through the service from devices in the CE (customer edge) network. Figure 19.14 shows the VPLS with attached customer devices. Listing 19.6 shows a ping from a router on CE-2 to a router on CE-3 and CE-2's ARP (Address Resolution Protocol) table afterward.

Listing 19.6 Ping and ARP table on a customer router

```
*A:CE-2# ping 192.168.1.3
PING 192.168.1.3 56 data bytes
64 bytes from 192.168.1.3: icmp_seq=1 ttl=64 time=4.40ms.
64 bytes from 192.168.1.3: icmp_seq=2 ttl=64 time=2.96ms.
64 bytes from 192.168.1.3: icmp_seq=3 ttl=64 time=3.74ms.
64 bytes from 192.168.1.3: icmp_seq=4 ttl=64 time=3.01ms.
```

(continued)

Listing 19.6 *(continued)*

```
64 bytes from 192.168.1.3: icmp_seq=5 ttl=64 time=3.06ms.

---- 192.168.1.3 PING Statistics ----
5 packets transmitted, 5 packets received, 0.00% packet loss
round-trip min = 2.96ms, avg = 3.43ms, max = 4.40ms, stddev = 0.561ms
*A:CE-2# show router arp

==========================================================================
ARP Table (Service: Base)
==========================================================================
IP Address      MAC Address       Expiry    Type   Interface
--------------------------------------------------------------------------
192.168.1.2     00:03:fa:ac:99:af 00h00m00s Oth[I] toPE-2
192.168.1.3     00:16:4d:13:63:c1 03h54m22s Dyn[I] toPE-2
--------------------------------------------------------------------------
No. of ARP Entries: 2
==========================================================================
```

Figure 19.14 CE routers can ping through VPLS 101.

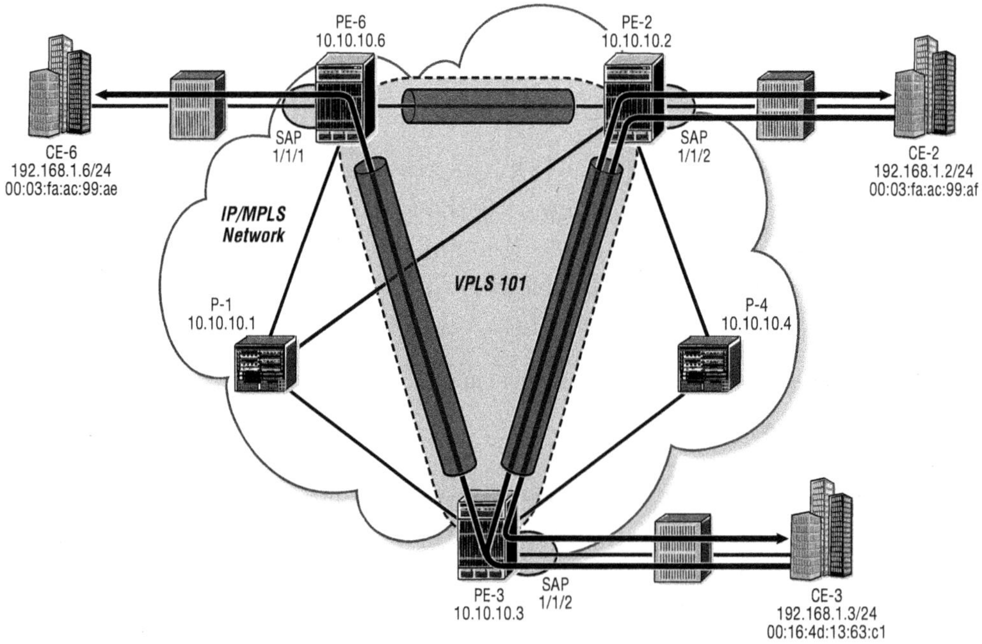

Immediately after the ping, we see that PE-2 has learned the MAC addresses for CE-2 and CE-3 and stored them in its FDB (see Listing 19.7). PE-2 knows that it reaches one device through SAP `1/1/2` and the other through SDP 3.

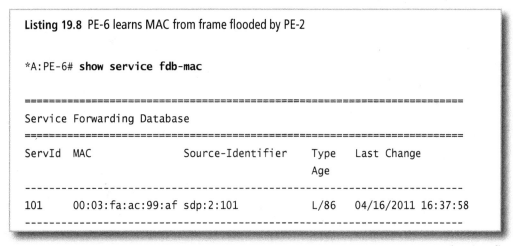

Listing 19.7 FDB contents on PE-2 after the ping

```
*A:PE-2# show service fdb-mac

===============================================================================
Service Forwarding Database
===============================================================================
ServId  MAC               Source-Identifier     Type   Last Change
                                                Age
-------------------------------------------------------------------------------
101     00:03:fa:ac:99:af sap:1/1/2             L/45   04/16/2011 16:25:27
101     00:16:4d:13:63:c1 sdp:3:101             L/45   04/16/2011 16:25:27
-------------------------------------------------------------------------------
No. of Entries: 2
-------------------------------------------------------------------------------
Legend: L=Learned; P=MAC is protected
===============================================================================
```

Listing 19.8 shows that PE-6 has learned the MAC address for CE-2 but not for CE-3, as expected.

Listing 19.8 PE-6 learns MAC from frame flooded by PE-2

```
*A:PE-6# show service fdb-mac

===============================================================================
Service Forwarding Database
===============================================================================
ServId  MAC               Source-Identifier     Type   Last Change
                                                Age
-------------------------------------------------------------------------------
101     00:03:fa:ac:99:af sdp:2:101             L/86   04/16/2011 16:37:58
-------------------------------------------------------------------------------
```

(continued)

Listing 19.8 *(continued)*

```
No. of Entries: 1
-------------------------------------------------------------------------
Legend: L=Learned; P=MAC is protected
=========================================================================
```

19.4 VPLS Topologies

The VPLS above uses a fully meshed topology. The use of mesh SDPs provides a loop-free topology that ensures flooded traffic reaches every SAP. This is a simple and reliable approach to provisioning a VPLS. However, there are circumstances in which other more complex topologies are preferred. Besides fully meshed topologies, we examine several other approaches in this book:

- Hub-and-spoke topology
- Hierarchical VPLS
- Spoke termination on a VPLS

The use of spoke SDPs in a VPLS can lead to loops in the VPLS because frames arriving on a spoke SDP are replicated to all SAPs, mesh SDPs, and spoke SDPs in the service. There are several techniques that can be used to provide redundancy in a VPLS including the spanning tree protocol (STP). Coverage of these are beyond the scope of this book.

Hub-and-Spoke Topology

A hub-and-spoke topology can be deployed when it is necessary to have traffic flowing through a central location (hub). This might be to implement security policies or packet filtering, deep packet inspection, or some other constraint of the physical topology. Figure 19.15 shows the same topology as above but configured with spoke SDPs. Listing 19.9 shows the configuration of the VPLS on PE-3. Notice that there is no spoke SDP between PE-2 and PE-6. A spoke SDP between these two nodes causes a loop in the VPLS.

Figure 19.15 Traffic in hub-and-spoke travels through the central node.

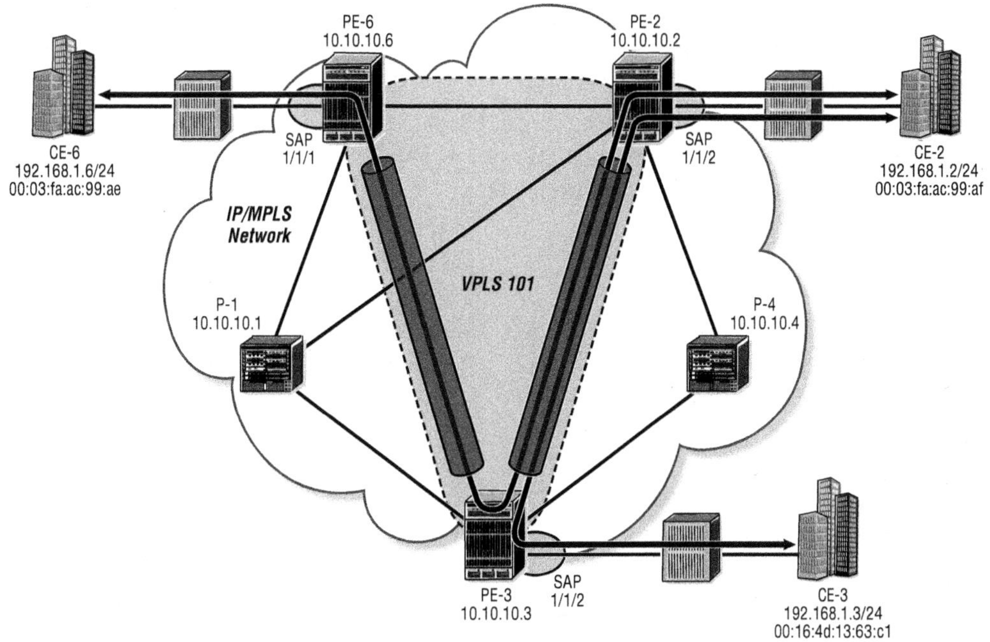

Listing 19.9 Hub-and-spoke VPLS

```
*A:PE-3# configure service vpls 101
*A:PE-3>config>service>vpls# mesh-sdp 2:101 shutdown
*A:PE-3>config>service>vpls# no mesh-sdp 2:101
*A:PE-3>config>service>vpls# mesh-sdp 6:101 shutdown
*A:PE-3>config>service>vpls# no mesh-sdp 6:101
*A:PE-3>config>service>vpls# spoke-sdp 2:101 create
*A:PE-3>config>service>vpls>spoke-sdp$ exit
*A:PE-3>config>service>vpls# spoke-sdp 6:101 create
*A:PE-3>config>service>vpls>spoke-sdp$ exit
*A:PE-3>config>service>vpls# show service id 101 base

===============================================================================
Service Basic Information
===============================================================================
Service Id        : 101                    Vpn Id            : 0
```

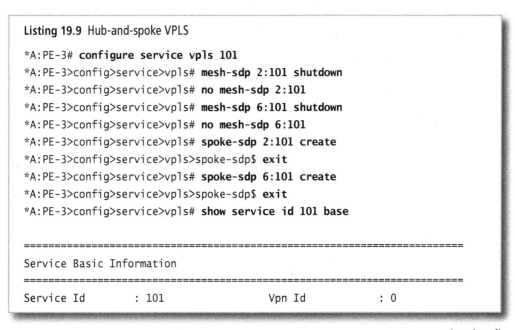

(continued)

Listing 19.9 *(continued)*

```
Service Type      : VPLS
Name              : (Not Specified)
Description       : (Not Specified)
Customer Id       : 1
Last Status Change: 04/16/2011 15:12:43
Last Mgmt Change  : 04/16/2011 18:11:48
Admin State       : Up                   Oper State        : Up
MTU               : 1514                 Def. Mesh VC Id   : 101
SAP Count         : 1                    SDP Bind Count    : 2
Snd Flush on Fail : Disabled             Host Conn Verify  : Disabled
Propagate MacFlush: Disabled             Per Svc Hashing   : Disabled
Def. Gateway IP   : None
Def. Gateway MAC  : None

-------------------------------------------------------------------------------
Service Access & Destination Points
-------------------------------------------------------------------------------
Identifier                          Type         AdmMTU  OprMTU  Adm  Opr
-------------------------------------------------------------------------------
sap:1/1/2                           null         1514    1514    Up   Up
sdp:2:101 S(10.10.10.2)             Spok         0       9190    Up   Up
sdp:6:101 S(10.10.10.6)             Spok         0       9190    Up   Up
===============================================================================
*A:PE-3>config>service>vpls# show service id 101 labels

===============================================================================
Martini Service Labels
===============================================================================
Svc Id     Sdp Binding          Type  I.Lbl                   E.Lbl
-------------------------------------------------------------------------------
101        2:101                Spok  131071                  131071
101        6:101                Spok  131070                  131068
-------------------------------------------------------------------------------
Number of Bound SDPs : 2
-------------------------------------------------------------------------------
===============================================================================
```

Note that a ping from CE-2 to CE-6 must pass through PE-3. In Listing 19.9, we see that there is a service label signaled for each spoke SDP. When traffic from PE-2 arrives at PE-3, the transport label is popped and the service label is swapped for the service label signaled by PE-6.

The FDB on PE-2 shows that all remote destinations in the customer network are reached through the spoke SDP to PE-3 (see Listing 19.10).

Listing 19.10 All destinations in VPLS are reached through the spoke SDP to PE-3

```
*A:PE-2# show service id 101 fdb detail

===============================================================================
Forwarding Database, Service 101
===============================================================================
ServId  MAC               Source-Identifier      Type   Last Change
                                                  Age
-------------------------------------------------------------------------------
101     00:03:fa:ac:99:ae sdp:3:101              L/0    04/16/2011 18:25:43
101     00:03:fa:ac:99:af sap:1/1/2              L/0    04/16/2011 18:25:37
101     00:16:4d:13:63:c1 sdp:3:101              L/0    04/16/2011 18:25:37
-------------------------------------------------------------------------------
No. of MAC Entries: 3
-------------------------------------------------------------------------------
Legend: L=Learned; P=MAC is protected
===============================================================================
```

Hierarchical VPLS

As the size of a VPLS grows, scalability issues may arise. The number of SDPs required for a fully meshed VPLS is $n \times (n - 1)$ because an SDP is required in each direction. Furthermore, the addition of a new node means that an SDP must be configured on every node in the network to the new node.

Consider two metropolitan areas that each contains a VPLS of 10 PE routers. If you want to join the two VPLS services, it will require $20 \times 19 = 380$ SDPs to make a new fully meshed VPLS of 20 nodes. An alternative is to join the two metro VPLS networks with a spoke SDP. Figure 19.16 shows two metro networks of four fully meshed nodes joined by a spoke SDP. Instead of 8 × 7 = 56 SDPs for a fully meshed VPLS, this requires 2 × 3 × 4 = 24 SDPs for the two metro networks plus another two spoke SDPs to join the two.

Figure 19.16 Joining two meshed VPLSs with a spoke SDP.

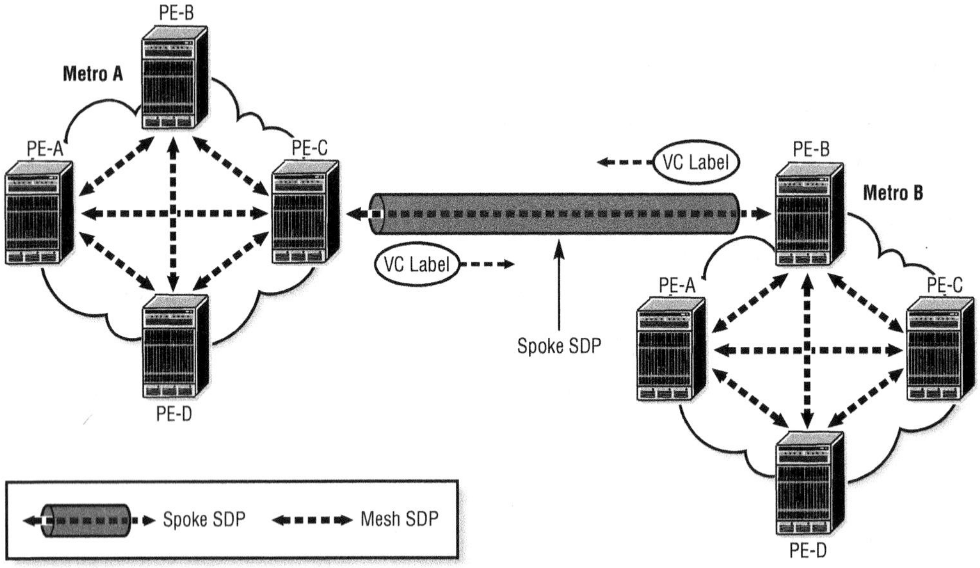

Figure 19.16 shows that PE-C in Metro A and PE-B in Metro B signal VC labels between themselves to create the spoke SDP. A customer frame transported from PE-A in Metro A to PE-A in Metro B will have three different service labels in its passage: one for the mesh SDP in Metro A, another for the spoke SDP, and a third for the mesh SDP in Metro B.

In Figure 19.17, we show two fully meshed VPLSs that are to be joined with a spoke SDP between PE-1 and PE-2. Listing 19.11 shows the full-mesh VPLS on PE-2. Although the spoke SDP between the two may appear to be a single point of failure, remember that it can be transported on a protected LSP. A failure on this link results in the spoke SDP being rerouted through PE-4. If we were to add a spoke SDP between PE-2 and PE-4, this would result in a loop.

Figure 19.17 Spoke SDP used to join two fully meshed VPLSs.

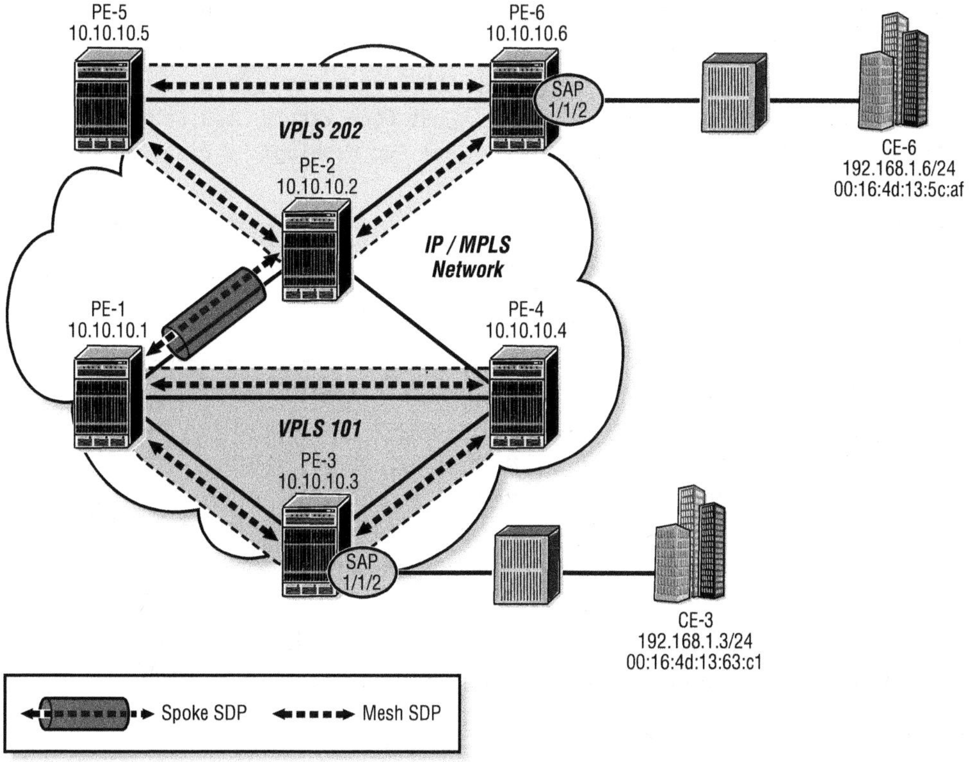

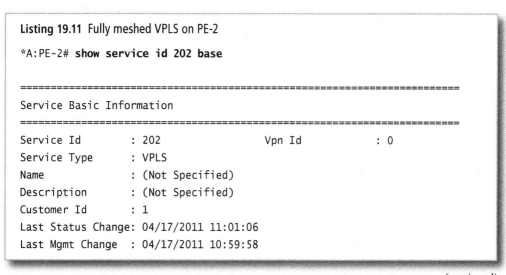

Listing 19.11 Fully meshed VPLS on PE-2

```
*A:PE-2# show service id 202 base

===============================================================================
Service Basic Information
===============================================================================
Service Id        : 202                    Vpn Id            : 0
Service Type      : VPLS
Name              : (Not Specified)
Description       : (Not Specified)
Customer Id       : 1
Last Status Change: 04/17/2011 11:01:06
Last Mgmt Change  : 04/17/2011 10:59:58
```

(continued)

Listing 19.11 *(continued)*

```
Admin State        : Up                  Oper State         : Up
MTU                : 1514                Def. Mesh VC Id    : 202
SAP Count          : 0                   SDP Bind Count     : 2
Snd Flush on Fail : Disabled             Host Conn Verify   : Disabled
Propagate MacFlush: Disabled             Per Svc Hashing    : Disabled
Def. Gateway IP    : None
Def. Gateway MAC   : None

-------------------------------------------------------------------------------
Service Access & Destination Points
-------------------------------------------------------------------------------
Identifier                          Type         AdmMTU  OprMTU  Adm  Opr
-------------------------------------------------------------------------------
sdp:5:202 M(10.10.10.5)             Mesh         0       9190    Up   Up
sdp:6:202 M(10.10.10.6)             Mesh         0       9190    Up   Up
===============================================================================
```

A spoke SDP is configured on PE-2 and on PE-1 to join the two VPLSs. Listing 19.12 shows the configuration and the state of the service on PE-1.

Listing 19.12 Spoke SDP to join VPLS 101 with VPLS 102

```
*A:PE-1# configure service vpls 101
*A:PE-1>config>service>vpls# spoke-sdp 2:101 create
*A:PE-1>config>service>vpls>spoke-sdp$ exit
*A:PE-1>config>service>vpls# show service id 101 base


===============================================================================
Service Basic Information
===============================================================================
Service Id         : 101                 Vpn Id             : 0
Service Type       : VPLS
Name               : (Not Specified)
Description        : (Not Specified)
Customer Id        : 1
Last Status Change: 04/17/2011 11:06:49
Last Mgmt Change   : 04/17/2011 14:06:05
Admin State        : Up                  Oper State         : Up
```

```
MTU                 : 1514              Def. Mesh VC Id    : 101
SAP Count           : 0                 SDP Bind Count     : 3
Snd Flush on Fail : Disabled            Host Conn Verify   : Disabled
Propagate MacFlush: Disabled            Per Svc Hashing    : Disabled
Def. Gateway IP     : None
Def. Gateway MAC    : None

-------------------------------------------------------------------------
Service Access & Destination Points
-------------------------------------------------------------------------
Identifier                      Type         AdmMTU  OprMTU  Adm  Opr
-------------------------------------------------------------------------
sdp:2:101 S(10.10.10.2)         Spok         0       9190    Up   Down
sdp:3:101 M(10.10.10.3)         Mesh         0       9190    Up   Up
sdp:4:101 M(10.10.10.4)         Mesh         0       9190    Up   Up
=========================================================================
*A:PE-1>config>service>vpls# show service id 101 sdp 2:101 detail

=========================================================================
Service Destination Point (Sdp Id : 2:101) Details
=========================================================================
-------------------------------------------------------------------------
 Sdp Id 2:101  -(10.10.10.2)
-------------------------------------------------------------------------
Description       : (Not Specified)
SDP Id              : 2:101                 Type               : Spoke
Spoke Descr       : (Not Specified)
Split Horiz Grp     : (Not Specified)
VC Type             : Ether                 VC Tag             : n/a
Admin Path MTU      : 0                     Oper Path MTU      : 9190
Far End             : 10.10.10.2            Delivery           : MPLS
Hash Label          : Disabled

Admin State         : Up                    Oper State         : Down
Acct. Pol           : None                  Collect Stats      : Disabled
Ingress Label       : 131068                Egress Label       : 0
Ingr Mac Fltr-Id    : n/a                   Egr Mac Fltr-Id    : n/a
Ingr IP Fltr-Id     : n/a                   Egr IP Fltr-Id     : n/a
Ingr IPv6 Fltr-Id   : n/a                   Egr IPv6 Fltr-Id   : n/a
Admin ControlWord   : Not Preferred         Oper ControlWord   : False
```

(continued)

Listing 19.12 *(continued)*

```
Last Status Change : 04/04/2011 22:21:41      Signaling          : TLDP
Last Mgmt Change   : 04/17/2011 14:06:05      Force Vlan-Vc      : Disabled
Endpoint           : N/A                      Precedence         : 4
Class Fwding State : Down
Flags              : NoEgrVCLabel
... output omitted ...

*A:PE-1>config>service>vpls# show router ldp bindings fec-type services

========================================================================
LDP LSR ID: 10.10.10.1
========================================================================
Legend: U - Label In Use, N - Label Not In Use, W - Label Withdrawn
        S - Status Signaled Up,  D - Status Signaled Down
        E - Epipe Service, V - VPLS Service, M - Mirror Service
        A - Apipe Service, F - Fpipe Service, I - IES Service,
 R - VPRN service
        P - Ipipe Service, WP - Label Withdraw Pending, C - Cpipe Service
        TLV - (Type, Length: Value)
========================================================================
LDP Service FEC 128 Bindings
========================================================================
Type   VCId     SvcId    SDPId  Peer          IngLbl  EgrLbl  LMTU  RMTU
------------------------------------------------------------------------
V-Eth  101      101      2      10.10.10.2    131068U   --    1500  0
V-Eth  101      101      3      10.10.10.3    131070U 131071  1500  1500
V-Eth  101      101      4      10.10.10.4    131069U 131071  1500  1500
?-Eth  202      Ukwn     R. Src 10.10.10.2      --    131069S 0     1500
------------------------------------------------------------------------
No. of VC Labels: 4


========================================================================
LDP Service FEC 129 Bindings
========================================================================
AGI                             SAII                  TAII
Type            SvcId    SDPId  Peer          IngLbl  EgrLbl  LMTU  RMTU
------------------------------------------------------------------------
No Matching Entries Found
========================================================================
========================================================================
```

After configuring the spoke SDP on both ends, it is not up with an error flag of `NoEgrVCLabel`. The output of the `show router ldp bindings` command from the listing above shows that the VC ID does not match. This makes sense because each VPLS uses a different VC ID. To join the two, the VC ID on one end of the spoke must be set to match the other. The change is made in Listing 19.13.

Listing 19.13 Spoke SDP configured to use VC ID of the other VPLS

```
*A:PE-1# configure service vpls 101
*A:PE-1>config>service>vpls# spoke-sdp 2:101 shutdown
*A:PE-1>config>service>vpls# no spoke-sdp 2:101
*A:PE-1>config>service>vpls# spoke-sdp 2:202 create
*A:PE-1>config>service>vpls>spoke-sdp$ exit
*A:PE-1>config>service>vpls# show service id 101 base

===============================================================================
Service Basic Information
===============================================================================
Service Id        : 101                     Vpn Id            : 0
Service Type      : VPLS
Name              : (Not Specified)
Description       : (Not Specified)
Customer Id       : 1
Last Status Change: 04/17/2011 11:06:49
Last Mgmt Change  : 04/17/2011 14:15:27
Admin State       : Up                      Oper State        : Up
MTU               : 1514                    Def. Mesh VC Id   : 101
SAP Count         : 0                       SDP Bind Count    : 3
Snd Flush on Fail : Disabled                Host Conn Verify  : Disabled
Propagate MacFlush: Disabled                Per Svc Hashing   : Disabled
Def. Gateway IP   : None
Def. Gateway MAC  : None

-------------------------------------------------------------------------------
Service Access & Destination Points
-------------------------------------------------------------------------------
Identifier                          Type         AdmMTU  OprMTU  Adm  Opr
-------------------------------------------------------------------------------
sdp:2:202 S(10.10.10.2)             Spok         0       9190    Up   Up
```

(continued)

Listing 19.13 *(continued)*

```
sdp:3:101 M(10.10.10.3)          Mesh        0       9190    Up   Up
sdp:4:101 M(10.10.10.4)          Mesh        0       9190    Up   Up
===============================================================================
*A:PE-1>config>service>vpls# show router ldp bindings fec-type services

===============================================================================
LDP LSR ID: 10.10.10.1
===============================================================================
Legend: U - Label In Use, N - Label Not In Use, W - Label Withdrawn
        S - Status Signaled Up,  D - Status Signaled Down
        E - Epipe Service, V - VPLS Service, M - Mirror Service
        A - Apipe Service, F - Fpipe Service, I - IES Service,
 R - VPRN service
        P - Ipipe Service, WP - Label Withdraw Pending, C - Cpipe Service
        TLV - (Type, Length: Value)
===============================================================================
LDP Service FEC 128 Bindings
===============================================================================
Type   VCId    SvcId     SDPId  Peer            IngLbl  EgrLbl  LMTU  RMTU
-------------------------------------------------------------------------------
V-Eth  101     101       3      10.10.10.3      131070U 131071  1500  1500
V-Eth  101     101       4      10.10.10.4      131069U 131071  1500  1500
V-Eth  202     101       2      10.10.10.2      131067U 131069S 1500  1500
-------------------------------------------------------------------------------
No. of VC Labels: 3
===============================================================================
LDP Service FEC 129 Bindings
===============================================================================
AGI                             SAII                   TAII
Type           SvcId     SDPId  Peer            IngLbl  EgrLbl  LMTU  RMTU
-------------------------------------------------------------------------------
No Matching Entries Found
===============================================================================
===============================================================================
```

Once the merged, hierarchical VPLS is up, it is possible to ping from CE-3 to CE-6. If we examine the FDB on router PE-1, we see that it is service-aware and contains the MAC addresses of the CE devices (see Listing 19.14).

Listing 19.14 FDB on Router PE-1

```
*A:PE-1# show service id 101 fdb detail

===============================================================================
Forwarding Database, Service 101
===============================================================================
ServId  MAC               Source-Identifier      Type    Last Change
                                                 Age
-------------------------------------------------------------------------------
101     00:16:4d:13:5c:af sdp:2:202              L/0     04/17/2011 14:24:11
101     00:16:4d:13:63:c1 sdp:3:101              L/0     04/17/2011 14:24:29
-------------------------------------------------------------------------------
No. of MAC Entries: 2
-------------------------------------------------------------------------------
Legend: L=Learned; P=MAC is protected
===============================================================================
```

Spoke-SDP Termination on VPLS

The section above shows how the scalability of a VPLS can be improved by joining together smaller meshed VPLSs with spoke SDPs. Another example of an application of a hierarchical VPLS is a metropolitan VPLS comprised of a mesh or ring of larger, more capable PE routers that each has a large number of smaller, less expensive devices attached (see Figure 19.18). These smaller devices are sometimes known as multi-dwelling units (MDUs) and may be capable of providing an MPLS pseudowire service, but with a more limited capacity.

Imagine a fully meshed VPLS with six core PE routers each attached to 20 MDUs. This requires $120 \times 119 = 14{,}280$ SDPs! Adding an additional MDU to this network means configuring a new mesh SDP on 120 routers. Using a spoke SDP from the PE router to the MDU dramatically reduces the number of SDPs required and simplifies the addition of new nodes.

The MDUs can be included in the hierarchical VPLS by configuring a spoke SDP from the MDU to the PE router. Or, the MDUs can be connected using an epipe. This is sometimes known as a spoke termination to a VPLS. The difference is that an epipe is a simpler service, and the MDU does not perform any MAC learning. The other end of the epipe is a spoke SDP in the VPLS. MAC learning is performed in the VPLS.

Figure 19.19 shows a meshed VPLS with two spoke terminations on PE-2 from MDU-5 and MDU-6. The configuration of MDU-6 is provided in Listing 19.15. The epipe service ID does not need to match that of the VPLS, but the VC ID must be matching.

Figure 19.18 Hierarchical VPLS with meshed core and attached MDUs.

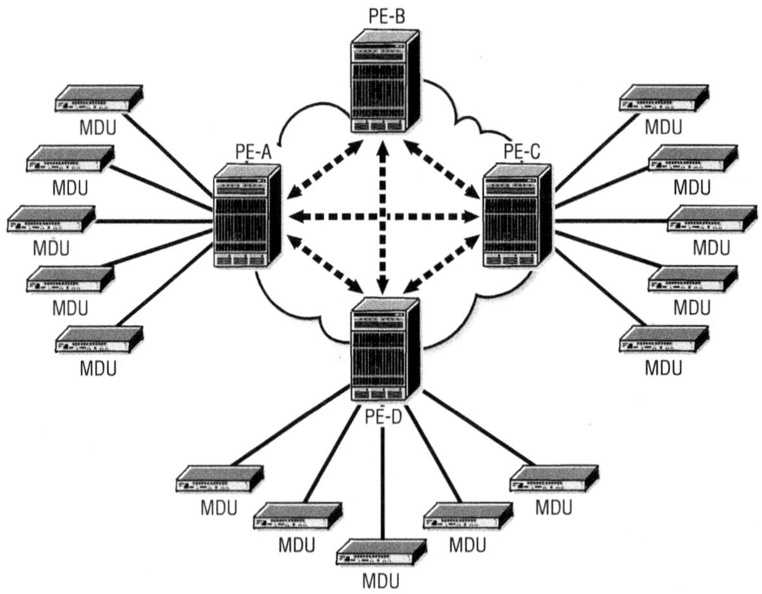

Listing 19.15 Epipe configured on MDU-6

```
*A:PE-6# configure service epipe 101 customer 1 create
*A:PE-6>config>service>epipe$ sap 1/1/2 create
*A:PE-6>config>service>epipe>sap$ exit
*A:PE-6>config>service>epipe# spoke-sdp 2:101 create
*A:PE-6>config>service>epipe>spoke-sdp$ exit
*A:PE-6>config>service>epipe# no shutdown
*A:PE-6>config>service>epipe# show service id 101 base

===============================================================================
Service Basic Information
===============================================================================
Service Id        : 101                    Vpn Id            : 0
Service Type      : Epipe
Name              : (Not Specified)
```

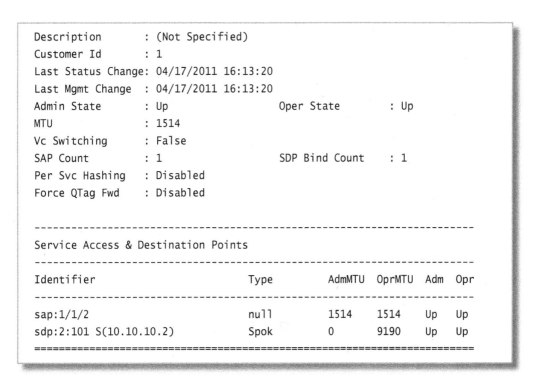

```
Description         : (Not Specified)
Customer Id         : 1
Last Status Change: 04/17/2011 16:13:20
Last Mgmt Change    : 04/17/2011 16:13:20
Admin State         : Up                    Oper State        : Up
MTU                 : 1514
Vc Switching        : False
SAP Count           : 1                     SDP Bind Count    : 1
Per Svc Hashing     : Disabled
Force QTag Fwd      : Disabled

-------------------------------------------------------------------------
Service Access & Destination Points
-------------------------------------------------------------------------
Identifier                          Type         AdmMTU  OprMTU  Adm  Opr
-------------------------------------------------------------------------
sap:1/1/2                           null         1514    1514    Up   Up
sdp:2:101 S(10.10.10.2)             Spok         0       9190    Up   Up
=========================================================================
```

Figure 19.19 Spoke termination in a VPLS.

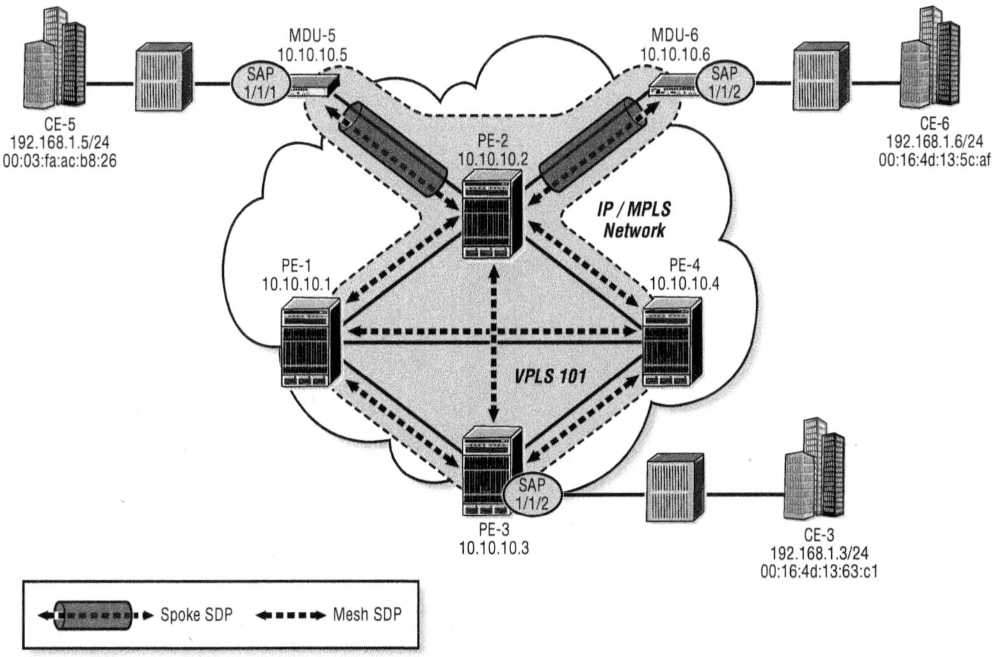

In the VPLS, the epipes are terminated as spoke SDPs (see Listing 19.16).

Listing 19.16 Spoke-SDP termination in a VPLS

```
*A:PE-2>config>service# vpls 101
*A:PE-2>config>service>vpls# info
----------------------------------------------
            stp
                shutdown
            exit
            mesh-sdp 1:101 create
            exit
            mesh-sdp 3:101 create
            exit
            mesh-sdp 4:101 create
            exit
            spoke-sdp 5:101 create
            exit
            spoke-sdp 6:101 create
            exit
            no shutdown
----------------------------------------------
*A:PE-2>config>service# show service id 101 base

===============================================================================
Service Basic Information
===============================================================================
Service Id         : 101                    Vpn Id            : 0
Service Type       : VPLS
Name               : (Not Specified)
Description        : (Not Specified)
Customer Id        : 1
Last Status Change: 04/17/2011 15:57:48
Last Mgmt Change   : 04/17/2011 16:00:15
Admin State        : Up                     Oper State        : Up
MTU                : 1514                   Def. Mesh VC Id   : 101
SAP Count          : 0                      SDP Bind Count    : 5
Snd Flush on Fail : Disabled                Host Conn Verify  : Disabled
Propagate MacFlush: Disabled                Per Svc Hashing   : Disabled
Def. Gateway IP    : None
```

```
Def. Gateway MAC  : None

-------------------------------------------------------------------------
Service Access & Destination Points
-------------------------------------------------------------------------
Identifier                          Type         AdmMTU  OprMTU  Adm  Opr
-------------------------------------------------------------------------
sdp:1:101 M(10.10.10.1)             Mesh         0       9190    Up   Up
sdp:3:101 M(10.10.10.3)             Mesh         0       9190    Up   Up
sdp:4:101 M(10.10.10.4)             Mesh         0       9190    Up   Up
sdp:5:101 S(10.10.10.5)             Spok         0       9190    Up   Up
sdp:6:101 S(10.10.10.6)             Spok         0       9190    Up   Up
=========================================================================
*A:PE-2>config>service# show router ldp bindings fec-type services

=========================================================================
LDP LSR ID: 10.10.10.2
=========================================================================
Legend: U - Label In Use, N - Label Not In Use, W - Label Withdrawn
        S - Status Signaled Up,  D - Status Signaled Down
        E - Epipe Service, V - VPLS Service, M - Mirror Service
        A - Apipe Service, F - Fpipe Service, I - IES Service,
 R - VPRN service
        P - Ipipe Service, WP - Label Withdraw Pending, C - Cpipe Service
        TLV - (Type, Length: Value)
=========================================================================
LDP Service FEC 128 Bindings
=========================================================================
Type   VCId     SvcId      SDPId  Peer           IngLbl  EgrLbl  LMTU  RMTU
-------------------------------------------------------------------------
V-Eth  101      101        1      10.10.10.1     131056U 131054  1500  1500
V-Eth  101      101        3      10.10.10.3     131055U 131067  1500  1500
V-Eth  101      101        4      10.10.10.4     131054U 131055  1500  1500
V-Eth  101      101        5      10.10.10.5     131053U 131065S 1500  1500
V-Eth  101      101        6      10.10.10.6     131052U 131068S 1500  1500
-------------------------------------------------------------------------
No. of VC Labels: 5

=========================================================================
```

(continued)

Listing 19.16 *(continued)*

```
LDP Service FEC 129 Bindings
========================================================================
AGI                                  SAII                  TAII
Type              SvcId       SDPId  Peer          IngLbl  EgrLbl  LMTU  RMTU
------------------------------------------------------------------------
No Matching Entries Found
========================================================================
========================================================================
```

Once traffic flows through the VPLS, the FDB on PE-2 has the MAC addresses of the CE devices (see Listing 19.17).

Listing 19.17 Service FDB on Router PE-2

```
*A:PE-2# show service fdb-mac

========================================================================
Service Forwarding Database
========================================================================
ServId  MAC               Source-Identifier     Type   Last Change
                                                Age
------------------------------------------------------------------------
101     00:03:fa:ac:b8:26 sdp:5:101             L/0    04/17/2011 16:04:54
101     00:16:4d:13:5c:af sdp:6:101             L/0    04/17/2011 16:12:48
101     00:16:4d:13:63:c1 sdp:3:101             L/0    04/17/2011 16:12:43
------------------------------------------------------------------------
No. of Entries: 3
------------------------------------------------------------------------
Legend: L=Learned; P=MAC is protected
========================================================================
```

Notice that there is no FDB on MDU-6 because it is an epipe service (see Listing 19.18).

Listing 19.18 No FDB required on the MDU

```
*A:PE-6# show service fdb-mac

===============================================================================
Service Forwarding Database
===============================================================================
ServId    MAC               Source-Identifier        Type    Last Change
                                                     Age
-------------------------------------------------------------------------------
No Matching Entries
-------------------------------------------------------------------------------
No. of Entries: 0
-------------------------------------------------------------------------------
Legend: L=Learned; P=MAC is protected
===============================================================================
*A:PE-6# show service service-using

===============================================================================
Services
===============================================================================
ServiceId  Type      Adm  Opr  CustomerId Service Name
-------------------------------------------------------------------------------
101        Epipe     Up   Up   1
2147483648 IES       Up   Down 1          _tmnx_InternalIesService
-------------------------------------------------------------------------------
Matching Services : 2
-------------------------------------------------------------------------------
===============================================================================
```

Practice Lab: VPLS Services

The following lab is designed to reinforce your knowledge of the content in this chapter. Please review the instructions carefully, and perform the steps in the order in which they are presented. The practice labs require that you have access to six or more Alcatel-Lucent 7750 SRs or Alcatel-Lucent 7450 ESSs in a non-production environment.

These labs are designed to be used in a controlled lab environment. Please *do not* attempt to perform these labs in a production environment.

Lab Section 19.1: Fully Meshed VPLS

Chapter 18's lab focuses on configuring epipe services. This chapter focuses on configuring Virtual Private LAN Services.

Objective In this exercise, you will configure a fully meshed VPLS, as shown in Figure 19.20.

Figure 19.20 Lab topology for VPLS.

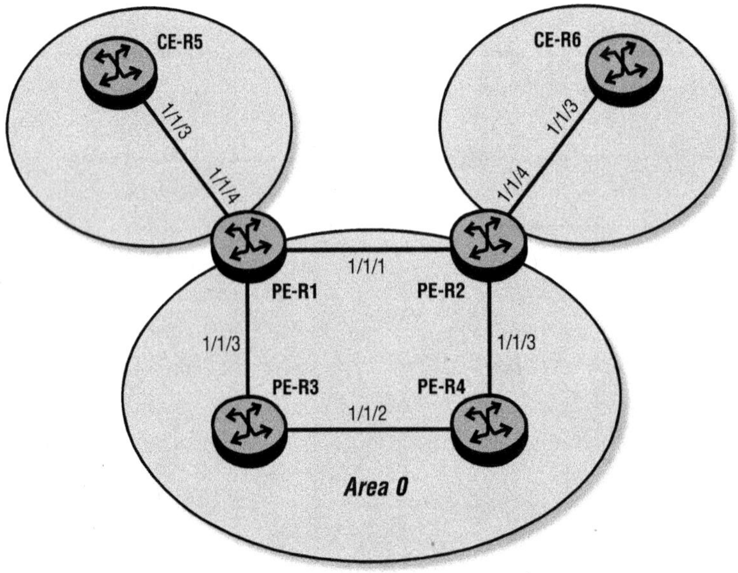

Validation You will know you have succeeded if the CE routers can ping each other over the correct VPLS.

1. Configure CE router R5 with two network interfaces. One interface should use a dot1Q Ethernet encapsulation of 20 with an IP address of `192.168.20.5/24`. The other interface should use a dot1Q Ethernet encapsulation of 40 with an IP address of `192.168.40.5/24`.

If you have just completed previous labs, this configuration may already be done.

2. Set up CE router R6 with two network interfaces. One interface should use a dot1Q Ethernet encapsulation of 40 with an IP address of `192.168.20.6/24`. The other interface should use a dot1Q Ethernet encapsulation of 40 with an IP address of `192.168.40.6/24`.

If you have just completed previous labs, this configuration may already be done.

3. Configure a full mesh of RSVP-TE LSPs that have totally loose paths between R1, R2, R3, and R4. To observe best practice, enable the LSPs with one-to-one FRR and ADSPEC.

You may already have some LSPs created from previous labs that you can simply enable with FRR and ADSPEC.

   a. Verify that all LSPs are operationally up and FRR-protected before proceeding.
   b. Configure a full mesh of SDPs between R1, R2, R3, and R4 that use the LSPs.

You may already have some SDPs created, but make sure that they are bound to an FRR-protected LSP.

   c. Does LDP need to be enabled on every router?
   d. Verify that all SDPs are operationally up before proceeding.

4. Configure a VPLS service on R1, R2, R3, and R4 with a service ID of 40. Use a customer ID of 100. Don't configure any SDP bindings or SAPs yet.
   a. Can an epipe service and a VPLS service on a PE router use the same service ID?
   b. Create a mesh SDP for the VPLS between R1 and R4 with a VC ID of 99. Is the operation successful? Explain.

c. Create mesh SDPs for every VPLS instance to all PE nodes. How many mesh SDPs are required?

d. Is the VPLS on each node operationally up?

e. On R1 and R2, create a SAP with a dot1Q Ethernet encapsulation of 40 toward the CE routers.

f. What is the default service MTU for a VPLS? How does this compare with an epipe?

g. If the requirement is to support an IP packet of exactly 1,500 bytes, does the service MTU need to be changed with the current SAP encapsulations? Explain.

h. From R5, verify that a ping to `192.168.40.6` is successful.

i. Describe which SDPs and LSPs are used for the ping process in the step above. Are the SDPs on R3 and R4 used? Explain.

j. View the MAC FDB on R1 and R2 for VPLS 40, and explain the results.

k. View the MAC FDB on R3 and R4, and explain the results.

l. From R6, ping R5's interface address of `192.168.40.5`. How do the MAC FDB tables on the routers change?

m. View the dynamically learned entries in the ARP table on the CE routers, and explain the results.

5. Shut down the link between R1 and R2, and view the LSPs and SDPs for VPLS service 40 on R1. Which SDPs and LSPs are used for the service now?

   a. Ping `192.168.40.6` on R5. Is the ping successful?

   b. View the MAC FDB on R1 and R2 for VPLS 40. How does it compare with the FDB before the link between R1 and R2 was shut down?

   c. View the dynamically learned ARP entries on the CE routers. How does this compare with the ARP cache before the link between R1 and R2 was shut down?

   d. Shut down the VPLS service instances on R3 and R4.

   e. Repeat the ping of `192.168.40.6` on R5. Is it successful? Explain.

   f. Enable the link between R1 and R2 before proceeding.

Lab Section 19.2: Mesh- and Spoke-SDP Flooding Behavior

This section investigates the differences in flooding behavior between mesh- and spoke-SDP bindings.

Objective In this lab, you will use mesh and spoke SDPs and observe the differences in flooding behavior.

Validation You will know you have succeeded if you can explain the flooding behavior when mesh and spoke SDPs are used.

1. Configure a VPLS instance on R1, R2, R3, and R4 with a service ID of 20 and a customer ID of 200.

> If you have just completed previous labs, you may have to delete the existing epipe services that use the same service ID.

- **a.** Create an Ethernet dot1Q SAP with an encapsulation of 20 toward the CE routers on R1 and R2.
- **b.** Create a mesh SDP between VPLS instance 20 on R1 and R3. Do you need to create a new SDP? Explain.
- **c.** Create a mesh SDP between VPLS instance 20 on R3 and R4. Verify that the binding is operationally up before proceeding.
- **d.** Create a mesh SDP between VPLS instance 20 on R2 and R4. Verify that the binding is operationally up before proceeding.
- **e.** From R5, ping `192.168.20.6`. Is the ping successful? Explain.

2. Change the mesh SDPs between R1 and R3 and between R2 and R4 to spoke SDPs. Do you need to create a new SDP to use for the binding? Explain.

- **a.** From R5, ping `192.168.20.6`. Is the ping successful? Explain.
- **b.** When would a VPLS use spoke SDPs instead of mesh SDPs?
- **c.** If the mesh SDP between R3 and R4 was changed to a spoke SDP, would a Layer 2 loop exist in VPLS 20?
- **d.** View the MAC FDB on R3 for VPLS 20, and explain the entries. How does this compare with the MAC FDB on VPLS 40 in the previous exercise?

Lab Section 19.3: Epipe to VPLS Spoke Termination

This lab section investigates the use of Layer 2–spoke terminations with different service types.

Objective In this lab, you will configure an epipe to VPLS spoke termination.

Validation You will know you have succeeded if CE devices can successfully communicate with each other when an epipe to VPLS spoke termination is used.

1. Delete the VPLS 20 instance on R1, R3, and R4.
2. Replace the VPLS 20 instance on R1 with an epipe service that has a spoke termination to R2. Use a service ID of 99 on the epipe service and a VC ID of 55 for the spoke-SDP binding.
    a. Verify that the epipe service and the VPLS are operationally up.
    b. Ping `192.168.20.6` from R5. Is the ping successful?
    c. View the MAC FDB on R2 of VPLS 20. Explain the results.
    d. View the MAC FDB on R1 of epipe 99. Explain the results.

Chapter Review

Now that you have completed this chapter, you should be able to:

- Compare a VPLS to an Ethernet switch.
- Explain how a VPLS floods unknown traffic.
- Describe the MAC learning process used in a VPLS.
- Describe the VPLS FDB.
- Configure and verify a full-mesh VPLS.
- Configure and verify a hub and spoke VPLS.
- Configure and verify a hierarchical VPLS.
- Configure and verify spoke termination in a VPLS.
- List the reasons for having different VPLS topologies.

Post-Assessment

The following questions will test your knowledge and prepare you for the Alcatel-Lucent NRS II Certification Exam. Compare your responses with the answers listed in Appendix A. You can also use the CD that accompanies this book to take all the assessment tests and review the answers.

1. Which of the following describes a difference in the behavior of an Ethernet switch and a VPLS?
   A. Unknown unicast traffic is flooded to all destinations in a VPLS, but is discarded in an Ethernet switch.
   B. Traffic to known multicast and broadcast addresses is flooded to all destinations in a VPLS, but only to specific ports in an Ethernet switch.
   C. SAPs with different VLAN values in a VPLS are treated as separate broadcast domains. On an Ethernet switch, different VLAN values are treated as being in the same broadcast domain.
   D. SAPs with different VLAN values in a VPLS are treated as being in the same broadcast domain. On an Ethernet switch, different VLAN values are treated as separate broadcast domains.
   E. None of the above statements describe a difference between a VPLS and an Ethernet switch.

2. Which of the following best describes how a VPLS populates the MAC FDB?
   A. The network administrator programs the FDB with the MAC address of the attached devices.
   B. The PE router uses ARP to discover the MAC addresses of attached devices.
   C. The PE router examines the source MAC address of received frames.
   D. The PE router examines the destination MAC address of received frames.
   E. There is no MAC learning; unicast traffic is flooded to all destinations in the VPLS.

3. Which statement best describes the flooding behavior of a VPLS for unknown unicast traffic received on a mesh SDP?
   - **A.** The traffic is flooded to all SDP bindings and SAPs configured on the router.
   - **B.** The traffic is flooded to all mesh SDPs in the same service.
   - **C.** The traffic is flooded to all mesh SDPs, SAPs, and spoke SDPs in the same service.
   - **D.** The traffic is flooded to all SAPs and spoke SDPs in the same service.
   - **E.** The traffic is flooded to all mesh SDPs that are not in the same service, and all SAPs and spoke SDPs that are in the same service.
   - **F.** None of the above statements are correct.
4. Consider a metro VPLS network that has four PE routers. Two VPLS instances are created on each PE router. If only mesh SDPs are used in the network, what is the total number of mesh SDPs that have to be configured in the network?
   - **A.** Three mesh SDPs are required.
   - **B.** Four mesh SDPs are required.
   - **C.** Six mesh SDPs are required.
   - **D.** Eight mesh SDPs are required.
   - **E.** Twelve mesh SDPs are required.
   - **F.** Twenty-four mesh SDPs are required.
5. Which of the following statements about mesh and spoke SDPs is true?
   - **A.** Using spoke SDPs in a VPLS removes the requirement for a full mesh of SDP bindings.
   - **B.** Using spoke SDPs in a VPLS eliminates the possibility of looping in the VPLS.
   - **C.** MAC learning is not performed on spoke SDPs in a VPLS.
   - **D.** Spoke and mesh SDPs cannot be used in the same VPLS.
   - **E.** None of the above statements above are true.

6. Which of the following protocols can be used to signal service labels for a VPLS service?

   A. LDP

   B. RSVP-TE

   C. GRE

   D. OSPF

   E. None of the above protocols can be used to signal service labels for a VPLS service

7. What is the default service MTU for a VPLS service on an Alcatel-Lucent 7750 SR if all SAPs have a dot1Q encapsulation?

   A. 1,500 bytes

   B. 1,504 bytes

   C. 1,514 bytes

   D. 1,518 bytes

   E. 1,522 bytes

8. Which of the following statements concerning VPLS services is false?

   A. A VPLS can be used to provide point-to-point services.

   B. CE routers use a spoke SDP to connect to PE routers offering a VPLS service.

   C. A VPLS does not need a configured SDP binding to be operationally up.

   D. A PE router can offer multiple VPLS services to a single CE router using the same physical port.

   E. Only PE routers need to be configured with a VPLS service.

9. Consider a VPLS metro network that has four PE routers. Two VPLS instances are created on every PE router. If only mesh SDPs are used in the network, what is the total number of T-LDP sessions required?

   A. Three T-LDP sessions are required.

   B. Four T-LDP sessions are required.

   C. Six T-LDP sessions are required.

   D. Eight T-LDP sessions are required.

   E. Twelve T-LDP sessions are required.

   F. Twenty-four T-LDP sessions are required.

10. Consider an Alcatel-Lucent 7750 SR that is a PE router for two VPLS and one epipe service. Additionally, the 7750 SR acts as a P router transiting traffic for three other VPLS instances. How many MAC FDBs are held on the 7750 SR?

A. One

B. Two

C. Three

D. Five

E. Six

F. There is not enough information provided to answer the question

11. Which statement best describes the forwarding behavior of known unicast traffic that is received on a spoke SDP on a 7750 SR?

A. The traffic is flooded to all SDP bindings and SAPs configured on the router.

B. The traffic is flooded to all spoke SDPs in the same service.

C. The traffic is flooded to all spoke SDPs and SAPs in the same service.

D. The traffic is flooded to all mesh SDPs and SAPs in the same service.

E. The traffic is flooded to all spoke SDPs that are not in the same service, and all SAPs and mesh SDPs in the same service.

F. None of the above statements are correct.

12. Which statement is correct regarding the VC ID that needs to be configured on spoke and mesh SDPs in a VPLS on a 7750 SR?

A. Spoke SDPs must have a VC ID that is equal to the VPLS service ID.

B. Mesh SDPs must have a VC ID that is equal to the VPLS service ID.

C. The VC ID used on both ends of a spoke SDP must match.

D. Mesh SDPs don't use a VC ID.

E. Two spoke SDPs on the same PE cannot use the same VC ID.

F. None of the above statements are correct.

13. Which statement best describes the flooding behavior of a VPLS for unknown unicast traffic received on a SAP?

A. The traffic is flooded to all SAPs configured on the router.

B. The traffic is flooded to all SAPs in the same service.

C. The traffic is flooded to all SDP bindings in the same service.

D. The traffic is flooded to all SAPs and spoke SDPs in the same service.

E. The traffic is flooded to all SAPs and SDP bindings in the same service.

F. None of the above statements are correct.

14. A VPLS is configured with two mesh SDPs and one spoke SDP. The VPLS is operationally down, and the output of `show router ldp bindings fec-type services` shows the following information:

```
LDP Service FEC 128 Bindings
==============================================================================
Type    VCId        SvcId       SDPId  Peer             IngLbl  EgrLbl  LMTU  RMTU
------------------------------------------------------------------------------
V-Eth   101         101         2      10.10.10.2       131068U   --    1500  0
V-Eth   101         101         3      10.10.10.3       131070U 131071  1500  1500
V-Eth   101         101         4      10.10.10.4       131069U 131071  1500  1500
?-Eth   202         Ukwn        R. Src 10.10.10.2         --    131069S 0     1500
------------------------------------------------------------------------------
```

What is the likely reason that the service is down?

A. T-LDP is not configured on the PE router at the other end of the spoke SDP.

B. The service MTU values are not matching at both ends of the spoke SDP.

C. The VC ID values are not matching at both ends of the spoke SDP.

D. The service ID values are not matching at both ends of the spoke SDP.

E. The service ID is not configured at the far end of the spoke SDP.

F. It is not possible to configure a VPLS with both spoke and mesh SDPs.

15. Router PE-1 is connected as the hub to routers PE-2 and PE-3 in a hub-and-spoke VPLS using spoke SDPs. Which of the following is a true statement about the behavior of this VPLS?

A. A VPLS cannot use spoke SDPs; it must use only mesh SDPs.

B. PE-2 does not perform MAC learning because all traffic is sent to PE-1 as the hub of the VPLS.

C. To prevent looping in the VPLS, traffic received on a spoke SDP at PE-1 is never flooded to the other spoke SDPs in the service.

D. Each of the three PE routers signals a service label for the VPLS to the other two routers.

E. PE-2 and PE-3 signal a service label to PE-1, and PE-1 signals a service label to PE-2 and PE-3 for the VPLS.

20

Layer 3 Services

The Alcatel-Lucent NRS II exam topics covered in this chapter include the following:

- IES overview
- Spoke termination on an IES
- Components of a VPRN
- CE-to-PE routing
- Route Distinguisher
- MP-BGP
- Route Target
- PE-to-PE routing
- PE-to-CE routing
- VPRN for IPv6 (6VPE)
- Operation of 6VPE

In this chapter, we look at two different Layer 3 services:

- Internet Enhanced Service (IES)
- Virtual Private Routed Network (VPRN)

We see how an IES interface provides a customer-facing Layer 3 interface and how it can be used to provide Internet connectivity. We also look at the configuration and operation of the VPRN service and how it appears as a single IP router to the customer. Finally, we examine 6VPE, which is the use of a VPRN service to interconnect IPv6 networks.

Pre-Assessment

The following assessment questions will help you understand what areas of the chapter you should review in more detail to prepare for the NRS II exam. You can also use the CD that accompanies this book to take all the assessment tests and review the answers.

1. An IES spoke termination is used to connect a CE router to an IES interface through an epipe service. Which statement is correct regarding the IP address configuration?

   A. The IP address of the CE router interface should be the same as the IP address of the IES interface.

   B. The IP address of the CE router interface should be on the same subnet as the IP address of the IES interface.

   C. The IP address of the CE router interface should be on a different subnet from the IP address of the IES interface.

   D. The IP address configuration depends on whether the IES has been configured in switched or routed mode.

   E. None of the above statements are correct.

2. Which statement is *false* regarding the traffic sent between two PE routers of a VPRN in a service provider network that uses RSVP-TE?

   A. The traffic has an MPLS transport label.

   B. The traffic has an MPLS service label.

   C. The traffic has the Layer 2 header sent by the CE router.

   D. The traffic has the IP header sent by the CE router.

   E. None of the above statements are false.

3. Which statement concerning route distinguishers on the Alcatel-Lucent 7750 SR is true?

   A. Route distinguishers are used to determine which routes a VPRN should import.

   B. Different route distinguishers can be used for the same VPRN on different PE routers.

   C. CE routers must be configured with the correct route distinguishers for the VPRN with which they are associated.

   D. P routers only need to be aware of route distinguishers that belong to VPRNs for which they transit traffic.

   E. A route distinguisher is 96 bits in length.

   F. None of the above statements are correct.

4. Which of the following best describes the purpose of MP-BGP in a VPRN?

   A. MP-BGP is an enhanced version of BGP that can carry both IPv4 and IPv6 prefixes.

   B. MP-BGP is an enhanced version of BGP that can carry a service label and customer route prefixes.

   C. MP-BGP is an enhanced version of BGP that can carry a transport label and customer route prefixes.

   D. MP-BGP is an enhanced version of BGP that allows BGP routers to peer with other protocols such as OSPF and RIP for CE-to-PE route exchange.

   E. None of the above statements describes the use of MP-BGP in a VPRN.

5. Which of the following statements regarding 6VPE is *false*?

   A. Both PE and P routers must support both IPv4 and IPv6 addresses; customer routers can use either one.

   B. A single MP-BGP session can be used to carry both VPN-IPv4 and VPN-IPv6 routes.

   C. A single customer's VPRN might contain both IPv4 and IPv6 routes.

   D. Any of the transport methods used for an IPv4 VPRN can be used for 6VPE.

   E. Statements A–D are true.

   F. Statements A–D are false.

20.1 IES Overview

The Internet Enhanced Service is essentially a way of providing a Layer 3 interface to a customer. It is similar to a normal Layer 3 interface, but treated as a service, with the port configured as a SAP (Service Access Point). This provides more flexibility and also the ability to use all of the service-oriented capabilities of an access port such as QoS (quality of service), accounting, and filtering. Like any IP interface, the customer can use the IES interface as a neighbor for a routing protocol such as OSPF (Open Shortest Path First), IS-IS (Intermediate System to Intermediate System), or BGP (Border Gateway Protocol). The IES provides access to the service provider's core routing instance (see Figure 20.1).

Figure 20.1 IES provides a customer with access to the service provider's core routing.

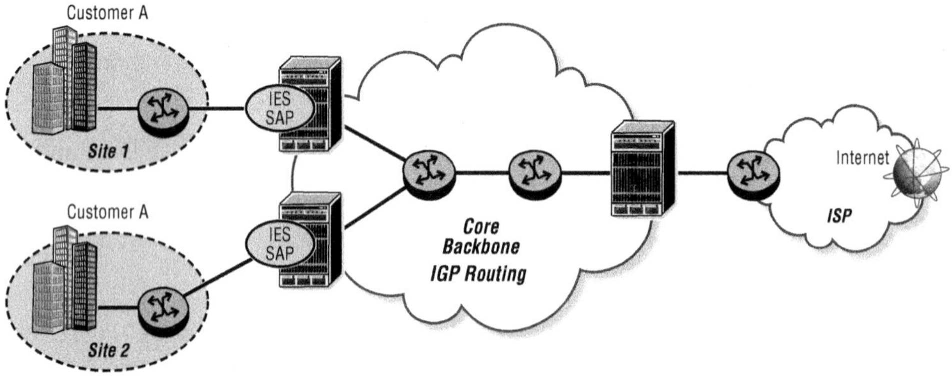

When we look at VPRNs below in this chapter, we see that the PE (provider edge) router has a virtual router for each VPRN. These virtual routers keep a completely separate route table from the core route table. On the Alcatel-Lucent 7750 SR, we refer to the core routing instance as the *base router instance.*

Listing 20.1 shows the configuration of the IES and the Layer 3 interface on the service provider PE router. Multiple interfaces can be configured in a single IES. Notice that the IES interface appears as a regular Layer 3 interface in the base router instance and in this case is added to OSPF.

Listing 20.1 The Layer 3 interface is configured within the IES.

```
*A:PE-1# configure port 1/1/2
*A:PE-1>config>port# shutdown
*A:PE-1>config>port# ethernet mode access
*A:PE-1>config>port# no shutdown
*A:PE-1>config>port# exit
*A:PE-1# configure service ies 1 customer 1 create
*A:PE-1>config>service>ies$ interface toCE create
*A:PE-1>config>service>ies>if$ sap 1/1/2 create
*A:PE-1>config>service>ies>if>sap$ exit
*A:PE-1>config>service>ies>if$ address 192.168.254.1/24
*A:PE-1>config>service>ies>if$ exit
*A:PE-1>config>service>ies# no shutdown
*A:PE-1>config>service>ies# show service id 1 base

===============================================================================
Service Basic Information
===============================================================================
Service Id        : 1                   Vpn Id           : 0
Service Type      : IES
Name              : (Not Specified)
Description       : (Not Specified)
Customer Id       : 1
Last Status Change: 05/03/2011 12:28:27
Last Mgmt Change  : 05/03/2011 12:28:27
Admin State       : Up                  Oper State       : Up
SAP Count         : 1

-------------------------------------------------------------------------------
Service Access & Destination Points
-------------------------------------------------------------------------------
Identifier                          Type         AdmMTU  OprMTU  Adm  Opr
-------------------------------------------------------------------------------
sap:1/1/2                           null         1514    1514    Up   Up
===============================================================================
*A:PE-1>config>service>ies# exit
*A:PE-1# show router interface

===============================================================================
```

(continued)

Listing 20.1 *(continued)*

```
Interface Table (Router: Base)
===============================================================================
Interface-Name                   Adm         Opr(v4/v6)  Mode    Port/SapId
   IP-Address                                                    PfxState
-------------------------------------------------------------------------------
system                           Up          Up/Down     Network system
   10.10.10.1/32                                                 n/a
toCE                             Up          Up/Down     IES     1/1/2
   192.168.254.1/24                                              n/a
toPE-2                           Up          Up/Down     Network 1/1/1
   10.1.2.1/27                                                   n/a
toPE-4                           Up          Up/Down     Network 1/1/4
   10.1.4.1/27                                                   n/a
-------------------------------------------------------------------------------
Interfaces : 4
===============================================================================
*A:PE-1# configure router ospf area 0
*A:PE-1>config>router>ospf>area# interface "toCE" interface-type
point-to-point
*A:PE-1>config>router>ospf>area# exit
```

In Listing 20.2, the customer forms an OSPF adjacency with the provider's router and receives the routes from the provider core. The MTU (maximum transmission unit) is set in the OSPF context because the port MTU on the CE (customer edge) router does not match the SAP MTU of the IES.

Listing 20.2 Customer receiving routes from the service provider core

```
*A:CE# show router interface

===============================================================================
Interface Table (Router: Base)
===============================================================================
Interface-Name                   Adm         Opr(v4/v6)  Mode    Port/SapId
   IP-Address                                                    PfxState
-------------------------------------------------------------------------------
system                           Up          Up/Down     Network system
```

```
   10.10.10.6/32                                                    n/a
toPE-1                          Up           Up/Down      Network 1/1/2
   192.168.254.2/24                                                 n/a
-------------------------------------------------------------------------------
Interfaces : 2
===============================================================================
*A:CE# configure router ospf area 0
*A:CE>config>router>ospf>area# interface "toPE-1"
*A:CE>config>router>ospf>area>if$ interface-type point-to-point
*A:CE>config>router>ospf>area>if$ show router ospf neighbor

===============================================================================
OSPF Neighbors
===============================================================================
Interface-Name                 Rtr Id           State      Pri  RetxQ   TTL
-------------------------------------------------------------------------------
toPE-1                         10.10.10.1       ExchStart  1    0       33
-------------------------------------------------------------------------------
No. of Neighbors: 1
===============================================================================

*A:CE>config>router>ospf>area>if$ mtu 1500
*A:CE>config>router>ospf>area>if$ show router ospf neighbor

===============================================================================
OSPF Neighbors
===============================================================================
Interface-Name                 Rtr Id           State      Pri  RetxQ   TTL
-------------------------------------------------------------------------------
toPE-1                         10.10.10.1       Full       1    1       36
-------------------------------------------------------------------------------
No. of Neighbors: 1
===============================================================================
*A:CE>config>router>ospf>area>if$ show router route-table

===============================================================================
Route Table (Router: Base)
===============================================================================
Dest Prefix                              Type    Proto    Age          Pref
```

(continued)

Listing 20.2 *(continued)*

```
       Next Hop[Interface Name]                                Metric
---------------------------------------------------------------------------
10.1.2.0/27                               Remote  OSPF      00h00m07s   10
       192.168.254.1                                           200
10.1.4.0/27                               Remote  OSPF      00h00m07s   10
       192.168.254.1                                           200
10.2.4.0/27                               Remote  OSPF      00h00m07s   10
       192.168.254.1                                           300
10.10.10.1/32                             Remote  OSPF      00h00m07s   10
       192.168.254.1                                           100
10.10.10.2/32                             Remote  OSPF      00h00m07s   10
       192.168.254.1                                           200
10.10.10.4/32                             Remote  OSPF      00h00m07s   10
       192.168.254.1                                           200
10.10.10.6/32                             Local   Local     01d00h56m   0
       system                                                 0
192.168.254.0/24                          Local   Local     00h03m20s   0
       toPE-1                                                 0
---------------------------------------------------------------------------
No. of Routes: 8
===========================================================================
```

Although the IES interface is similar to a standard IP interface, the SAP provides the QoS, accounting, and billing capabilities of a service interface (see Listing 20.3).

Listing 20.3 QoS and accounting capabilities of the IES SAP

```
*A:PE-1# show service id 1 sap 1/1/2 detail


===========================================================================
Service Access Points(SAP)
===========================================================================
Service Id          : 1
SAP                 : 1/1/2                      Encap              : null
Description         : (Not Specified)
Admin State         : Up                         Oper State         : Up
```

```
Flags               : None
Multi Svc Site      : None
Last Status Change : 05/03/2011 12:56:59
Last Mgmt Change    : 05/03/2011 12:28:03
Sub Type            : regular
Dot1Q Ethertype     : 0x8100                 QinQ Ethertype    : 0x8100
Split Horizon Group: (Not Specified)

Admin MTU           : 1514                   Oper MTU          : 1514
Ingr IP Fltr-Id     : n/a                    Egr IP Fltr-Id    : n/a
Ingr Mac Fltr-Id    : n/a                    Egr Mac Fltr-Id   : n/a
Ingr IPv6 Fltr-Id   : n/a                    Egr IPv6 Fltr-Id  : n/a
tod-suite           : None                   qinq-pbit-marking : both
Ing Agg Rate Limit : max                     Egr Agg Rate Limit: max
Q Frame-Based Acct : Disabled

Acct. Pol           : None                   Collect Stats     : Disabled

Anti Spoofing       : None                   Avl Static Hosts  : 0
                                             Tot Static Hosts  : 0
Calling-Station-Id : n/a
Application Profile: None


--------------------------------------------------------------------------
QOS
--------------------------------------------------------------------------
Ingress qos-policy : 1                       Egress qos-policy : 1
Shared Q plcy       : n/a                    Multipoint shared : Disabled
I. Sched Pol        : (Not Specified)
E. Sched Pol        : (Not Specified)
I. Policer Ctl Pol : (Not Specified)
E. Policer Ctl Pol : (Not Specified)
--------------------------------------------------------------------------
Sap Statistics
--------------------------------------------------------------------------
Last Cleared Time      : N/A

                        Packets                  Octets
```

(continued)

Listing 20.3 *(continued)*

```
Forwarding Engine Stats
Dropped                : 60                    4680
Off. HiPrio            : 0                     0
Off. LowPrio           : 0                     0
Off. Uncolor           : 0                     0

Queueing Stats(Ingress QoS Policy 1)
Dro. HiPrio            : 0                     0
Dro. LowPrio           : 0                     0
For. InProf            : 0                     0
For. OutProf           : 0                     0

Queueing Stats(Egress QoS Policy 1)
Dro. InProf            : 0                     0
Dro. OutProf           : 0                     0
For. InProf            : 243                   21636
For. OutProf           : 2                     204
-------------------------------------------------------------------------------
Sap per Queue stats
-------------------------------------------------------------------------------
                         Packets                 Octets

Ingress Queue 1 (Unicast) (Priority)
Off. HiPrio            : 0                     0
Off. LoPrio            : 0                     0
Dro. HiPrio            : 0                     0
Dro. LoPrio            : 0                     0
For. InProf            : 0                     0
For. OutProf           : 0                     0

Egress Queue 1
For. InProf            : 243                   21636
For. OutProf           : 2                     204
Dro. InProf            : 0                     0
Dro. OutProf           : 0                     0
===============================================================================
```

Spoke Termination on an IES

Sometimes it is desirable to use a Layer 2 service such as an epipe or a VPLS (Virtual Private LAN Service) to connect the customer to the IES interface. This is known as a spoke termination on an IES. In Figure 20.2, the service provider is providing an epipe to its customer that terminates on an IES. This supplies a Layer 3 interface to the customer. Listing 20.4 shows the IES configuration. Notice that the spoke SDP (Service Distribution Point) connected to the service is included in the IES instead of a SAP.

Figure 20.2 Spoke termination on an IES.

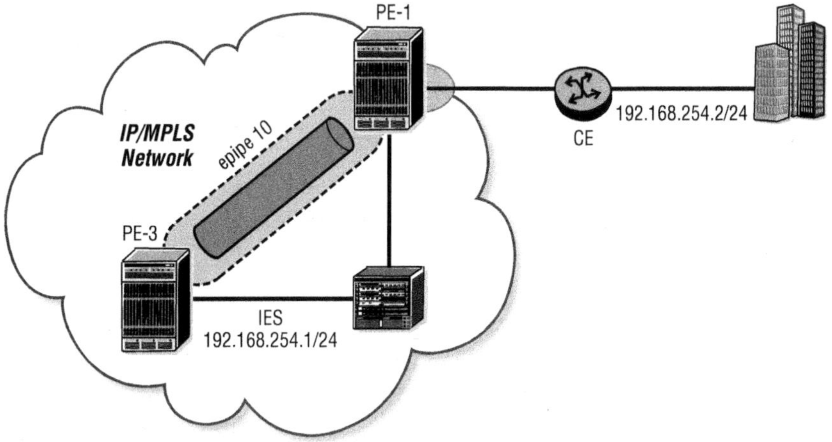

Listing 20.4 Spoke termination on an IES

```
*A:PE-3# configure service
*A:PE-3>config>service# sdp 1 mpls create
*A:PE-3>config>service>sdp$ far-end 10.10.10.1
*A:PE-3>config>service>sdp$ ldp
*A:PE-3>config>service>sdp$ no shutdown
*A:PE-3>config>service>sdp$ exit
*A:PE-3>config>service# ies 2 customer 1 create
*A:PE-3>config>service>ies$ no shutdown
*A:PE-3>config>service>ies$ interface spoke-ies create
*A:PE-3>config>service>ies>if$ address 192.168.254.1/24
*A:PE-3>config>service>ies>if$ spoke-sdp 1:10 create
```

(continued)

Listing 20.4 *(continued)*

```
*A:PE-3>config>service>ies>if>spoke-sdp$ exit
*A:PE-3>config>service>ies>if# no shutdown
*A:PE-3>config>service>ies>if# exit all
*A:PE-3# show service id 2 base

===============================================================================
Service Basic Information
===============================================================================
Service Id         : 2                    Vpn Id            : 0
Service Type       : IES
Name               : (Not Specified)
Description        : (Not Specified)
Customer Id        : 1
Last Status Change: 05/09/2011 11:45:10
Last Mgmt Change   : 05/10/2011 17:18:32
Admin State        : Up                   Oper State        : Down
SAP Count          : 0

-------------------------------------------------------------------------------
Service Access & Destination Points
-------------------------------------------------------------------------------
Identifier                        ype          AdmMTU  OprMTU  Adm  Opr
-------------------------------------------------------------------------------
sdp:1:10 S(10.10.10.1)            pok          0       9190    Up   Down
===============================================================================
*A:PE-3# show service id 2 sdp 1:10 detail

===============================================================================
Service Destination Point (Sdp Id : 1:10) Details
===============================================================================
-------------------------------------------------------------------------------
 Sdp Id 1:10  -(10.10.10.1)
-------------------------------------------------------------------------------
Description      : (Not Specified)
SDP Id             : 1:10                   Type              : Spoke
Spoke Descr      : (Not Specified)
VC Type            : Ether                  VC Tag            : n/a
```

```
Admin Path MTU      : 0                      Oper Path MTU       : 9190
Far End             : 10.10.10.1             Delivery            : LDP

Admin State         : Up                     Oper State          : Down
Acct. Pol           : None                   Collect Stats       : Disabled
Ingress Label       : 131064                 Egress Label        : 131063
Ingr Mac Fltr-Id    : n/a                    Egr Mac Fltr-Id     : n/a
Ingr IP Fltr-Id     : n/a                    Egr IP Fltr-Id      : n/a
Ingr IPv6 Fltr-Id   : n/a                    Egr IPv6 Fltr-Id    : n/a
Admin ControlWord   : Not Preferred          Oper ControlWord    : False
Last Status Change  : 05/09/2011 11:45:10    Signaling           : TLDP
Last Mgmt Change    : 05/10/2011 17:06:41
Class Fwding State  : Down
Flags               : PWPeerFaultStatusBits ServiceMTUMismatch
Peer Pw Bits        : pwNotForwarding
Peer Fault Ip       : None
Peer Vccv CV Bits   : None
Peer Vccv CC Bits   : None
Application Profile: None

... output omitted ...
```

We see in the listing above that the spoke SDP is not operational with a *Flags* value of `ServiceMTUMismatch`. This is because the MTU signaled from the IES side is based on the network port MTU (the network port MTU is 9,212 bytes by default), and the MTU signaled from the epipe is based on the service MTU of the epipe, which is 1,514 bytes by default. The pseudowire will not become operational when the MTUs are not the same.

In Listing 20.5, we see the different MTU values signaled by the two ends of the pseudowire. The MTU values could be made to match by adjusting the network port MTU or the SDP path MTU. The preferred method is to change the service MTU of the IES using the `ip-mtu` command.

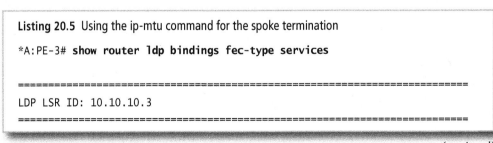

Listing 20.5 Using the ip-mtu command for the spoke termination

```
*A:PE-3# show router ldp bindings fec-type services


===============================================================================
LDP LSR ID: 10.10.10.3
===============================================================================
```

(continued)

Listing 20.5 *(continued)*

```
Legend: U - Label In Use, N - Label Not In Use, W - Label Withdrawn
        S - Status Signaled Up,  D - Status Signaled Down
        E - Epipe Service, V - VPLS Service, M - Mirror Service
        A - Apipe Service, F - Fpipe Service, I - IES Service,
 R - VPRN service
        P - Ipipe Service, WP - Label Withdraw Pending, C - Cpipe Service
        TLV - (Type, Length: Value)
===============================================================================
LDP Service FEC 128 Bindings
===============================================================================
Type   VCId     SvcId    SDPId  Peer             IngLbl  EgrLbl  LMTU  RMTU
-------------------------------------------------------------------------------
I-Eth  10       2        1      10.10.10.1       131064U 131063D 9176  1500
-------------------------------------------------------------------------------
No. of VC Labels: 1

... output omitted ...

*A:PE-3# configure service ies 2 interface "spoke-ies"
*A:PE-3>config>service>ies>if# ip-mtu 1500
*A:PE-3>config>service>ies>if# info
----------------------------------------------
                address 192.168.254.1/24
                ip-mtu 1500
                spoke-sdp 1:10 create
                exit
----------------------------------------------
*A:PE-3>config>service>ies# show service id 2 base

===============================================================================
Service Basic Information
===============================================================================
Service Id        : 2                    Vpn Id           : 0
Service Type      : IES
Name              : (Not Specified)
Description       : (Not Specified)
Customer Id       : 1
Last Status Change: 05/10/2011 17:26:27
Last Mgmt Change  : 05/10/2011 17:18:32
```

```
Admin State          : Up                     Oper State         : Up
SAP Count            : 0


-------------------------------------------------------------------------------
Service Access & Destination Points
-------------------------------------------------------------------------------
Identifier                          Type          AdmMTU  OprMTU  Adm  Opr
-------------------------------------------------------------------------------
sdp:1:10 S(10.10.10.1)              Spok          0       9190    Up   Up
===============================================================================
```

Once the service is up, we can ping the IES interface from the CE router. The CE router ARP (Address Resolution Protocol) cache has the MAC (Media Access Control) address of the PE router with the IES interface (see Listing 20.6).

Listing 20.6 The IES interface is the next-hop address for the CE router.

```
*A:CE# ping 192.168.254.1 count 2
PING 192.168.254.1 56 data bytes
64 bytes from 192.168.254.1: icmp_seq=1 ttl=64 time=2.24ms.
64 bytes from 192.168.254.1: icmp_seq=2 ttl=64 time=2.31ms.

---- 192.168.254.1 PING Statistics ----
2 packets transmitted, 2 packets received, 0.00% packet loss
round-trip min = 2.24ms, avg = 2.28ms, max = 2.31ms, stddev = 0.038ms
*A:CE# show router arp

===============================================================================
ARP Table (Router: Base)
===============================================================================
IP Address      MAC Address       Expiry    Type   Interface
-------------------------------------------------------------------------------
192.168.254.1   00:16:4d:61:0e:8c 03h54m31s Dyn[I] toPE-1
192.168.254.2   00:03:fa:ac:b8:27 00h00m00s Oth[I] toPE-1
-------------------------------------------------------------------------------
No. of ARP Entries: 2
===============================================================================
```

Listing 20.7 shows the configuration of the spoke SDP in the epipe. There is no difference from a normal epipe configuration.

Listing 20.7 Spoke to the IES configured in the epipe

```
*A:PE-1# configure service epipe 10
*A:PE-1>config>service>epipe# info
----------------------------------------------
            sap 1/1/2 create
            exit
            spoke-sdp 3:10 create
            exit
            no shutdown
----------------------------------------------
*A:PE-1>config>service>epipe# show service id 10 base

===============================================================================
Service Basic Information
===============================================================================
Service Id        : 10                  Vpn Id            : 0
Service Type      : Epipe
Name              : (Not Specified)
Description       : (Not Specified)
Customer Id       : 1
Last Status Change: 05/10/2011 15:17:14
Last Mgmt Change  : 05/10/2011 15:17:14
Admin State       : Up                  Oper State        : Up
MTU               : 1514
Vc Switching      : False
SAP Count         : 1                   SDP Bind Count    : 1
Per Svc Hashing   : Disabled
Force QTag Fwd    : Disabled

-------------------------------------------------------------------------------
Service Access & Destination Points
-------------------------------------------------------------------------------
Identifier                          Type         AdmMTU  OprMTU  Adm  Opr
-------------------------------------------------------------------------------
sap:1/1/2                           null         1514    1514    Up   Up
sdp:3:10 S(10.10.10.3)              Spok         0       9190    Up   Up
===============================================================================
```

20.2 VPRN Overview

The VPRN service defined in RFC 4364 provides a multipoint, routed service to the customer over an IP/MPLS core. Figure 20.3 shows an IP/MPLS service provider network supporting three distinct VPRN services.

Figure 20.3 Three VPRN services provisioned on an IP/MPLS core.

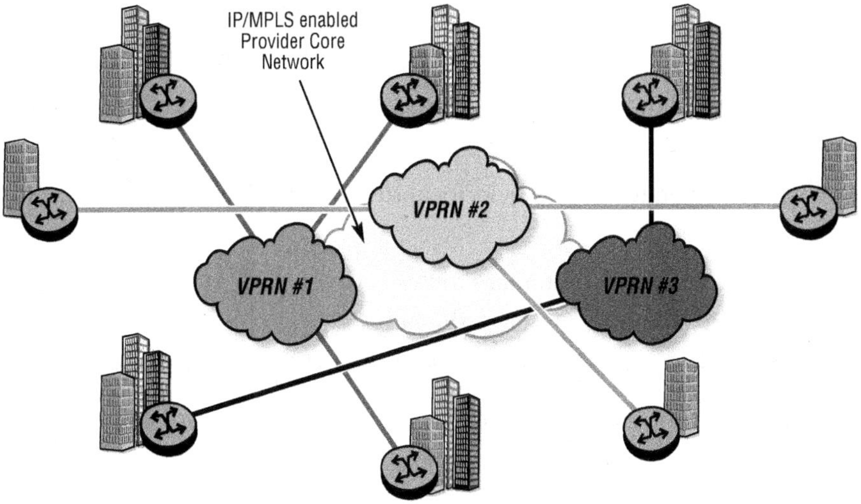

A VPRN is similar in many ways to the Layer 2 VPN services:

- Customer data is transported across the provider network encapsulated with two MPLS labels—the inner one a service label and the outer one a transport label.
- The service provider network is invisible to the customer. The VPRN appears as a virtual IP router to the customer.
- The service provider can use the same IP/MPLS infrastructure to support many different VPRN services as well as Layer 2 services such as VPWS (Virtual Private Wire Services) and VPLS.

There are also some significant differences between the Layer 2 VPN services and a VPRN. These differences include the following:

- CE routers peer with the PE routers using a routing protocol such as RIP (Routing Information Protocol), OSPF, or BGP. The PE router maintains a virtual, private router for each VPRN service.

- Multiprotocol BGP (MP-BGP) is used to carry customer route information across the provider network.
- MP-BGP is used to signal the service labels between the egress and ingress PE routers instead of T-LDP (Targeted LDP).
- Because the VPRN acts as a router, Layer 2 information is removed from the customer data before it is forwarded across the VPRN.

From the customer's perspective, the advantages of a VPRN service are the following:

- The service appears to the customer as if all its sites are connected to an IP router.
- A variety of Layer 2 protocols and IP routing protocols can be used to connect to the VPRN.
- The VPRN can operate over a single, local site or at multiple, geographically dispersed sites.
- The VPRN distributes the customer's routes between customer locations so that data is forwarded appropriately across the network.
- The customer benefits from redundancy built into the service provider network.

The advantages to the service provider are the same advantages of using an IP/MPLS network for any VPN service:

- Only the PE devices require configuration for the VPRN service.
- There is a clear demarcation of functionality between the service provider and customer networks.
- Customer networks are separate, and overlapping address space between customers can be accommodated.
- The service provider can apply QoS, billing, ingress/egress traffic shaping, and policing on a per-service basis.

Components of a VPRN

The operation of the data plane in a VPRN is very much the same as for the Layer 2 services we have looked at in previous chapters. Customer data arriving at the PE router is encapsulated with two MPLS labels—the inner service label and an outer transport label, as shown in Figure 20.4. The difference from a Layer 2 service is that the VPRN appears as an IP router to the customer network. This means that data arriving at the VPRN has the Layer 2 encapsulation removed, and a forwarding decision is made by the PE. It is the IP packet that is encapsulated for transmission across the VPRN.

Figure 20.4 Data plane for a VPRN service.

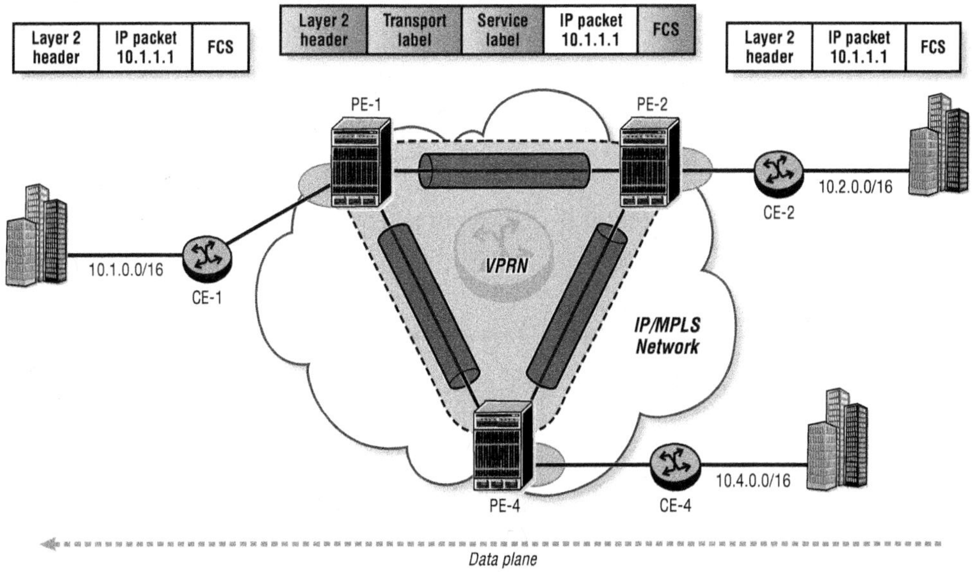

A VPRN differs from a Layer 2 VPN service in that customer routing information must be propagated across the VPRN. The VPRN distributes customer routes between customer locations, and the PE routers make forwarding decisions based on the customer route information (see Figure 20.5).

Figure 20.5 Customer routing information is propagated across the VPRN.

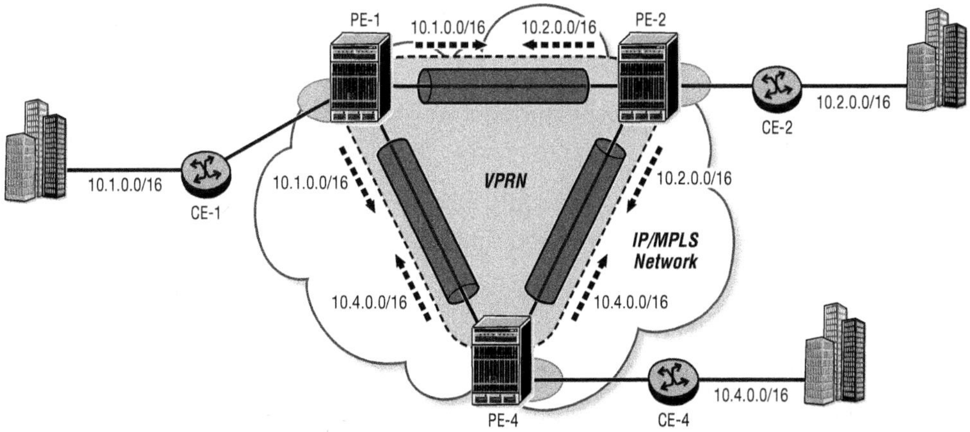

There are several aspects to the distribution of routing information, as shown in Figure 20.6. These are described below:

1. **CE-to-PE routing**—The CE router peers with and distributes routes to the local PE router. The PE router may use these to route IP packets to local networks.
2. **PE-to-PE routing**—The customer's routes are distributed to the other PE routers using MP-BGP.
3. **PE-to-CE routing**—The routes learned from the other PE routers are distributed to the local customer network.

Figure 20.6 Routing interactions in a VPRN.

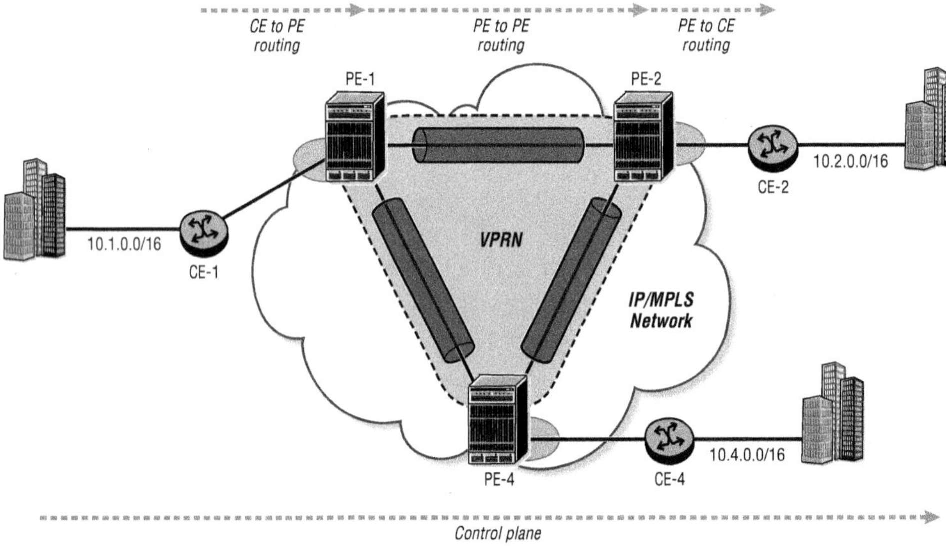

There are several new components introduced with VPRNs. The key new concepts are the following:

- **VRF**—The VPN routing and forwarding table (VRF) is the virtual router on the PE router that contains the customer's routes for the VPRN. Each PE has a VRF for each VPRN service provisioned on the router.
- **Route distinguisher (RD)**—The RD is an additional string added to a customer's routes so that they can be distinguished from other customers' routes in the service provider network.

- **Route target (RT)**—The RT is an extended community string attached to VPN routes. The route target is used to identify which routes are to be exported from MP-BGP into the VRF for the VPRN at a local PE.
- **MP-BGP**—MP-BGP is a version of BGP enhanced to support additional address families. In this case, the address family is the IP VPN routes that are created with the RD. One MP-BGP instance is used in the provider core to carry the IP VPN routes for all of the VPRN services provisioned in the network.

In the sections below, we look at routing across the VPRN and describe the use of these components in more detail. In our example, we look at the distribution of routing information from CE-1 to PE-1, from PE-1 to PE-2, and then from PE-2 to CE-2. Of course, routing information is also distributed in the opposite direction using the same mechanisms.

CE-to-PE Routing

The PE router peers with the CE router to exchange customer route information. On the PE router, this information is kept in the VRF for the VPRN, thus the CE router is effectively peering with the VRF on the PE router. The CE router can use EBGP (External Border Gateway Protocol), OSPF, or RIP to exchange routes with the VRF. Or, in the simplest case, the CE can simply use static routes to route traffic to the VPRN. Figure 20.7 shows a network with a local VPRN configured on router PE-1 and an EBGP peering session with router CE-1.

Figure 20.7 CE-to-PE routing in a VPRN.

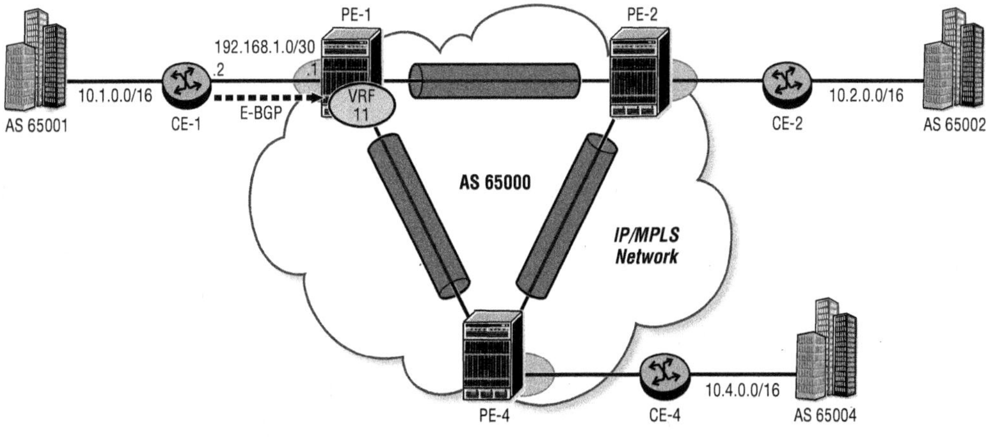

Listing 20.8 shows the configuration of the local VPRN 11. The parameters that need to be configured are the following:

- The PE-to-CE interface, which includes the SAP and the IP address of the interface.
- The CE-to-PE routing protocol, which is BGP in this example.
- A route distinguisher (RD), which is described in the next section. The VPRN does not come up until an RD is configured.

Listing 20.8 VPRN and VRF on Router PE-1

```
*A:PE-1# configure service vprn 11 customer 1 create
*A:PE-1>config>service>vprn$ autonomous-system 65000
*A:PE-1>config>service>vprn$ route-distinguisher 65000:11
*A:PE-1>config>service>vprn$ interface toCE-1 create
*A:PE-1>config>service>vprn>if$ sap 1/1/2 create
*A:PE-1>config>service>vprn>if>sap$ exit
*A:PE-1>config>service>vprn>if$ address 192.168.1.1/30
*A:PE-1>config>service>vprn>if$ exit
*A:PE-1>config>service>vprn# bgp group "customer-11"
*A:PE-1>config>service>vprn>bgp>group$ peer-as 65001
*A:PE-1>config>service>vprn>bgp>group$ neighbor 192.168.1.2
*A:PE-1>config>service>vprn>bgp>group>neighbor$ exit
*A:PE-1>config>service>vprn>bgp>group# exit
*A:PE-1>config>service>vprn# no shutdown
*A:PE-1>config>service>vprn# show service id 11 base

===============================================================================
Service Basic Information
===============================================================================
Service Id        : 11                    Vpn Id           : 0
Service Type      : VPRN
Name              : (Not Specified)
Description       : (Not Specified)
Customer Id       : 1
Last Status Change: 05/01/2011 05:49:32
Last Mgmt Change  : 05/01/2011 05:49:32
Admin State       : Up                    Oper State       : Up

Route Dist.       : 65000:11              VPRN Type        : regular
```

```
AS Number           : 65000                Router Id          : 10.10.10.1
ECMP                : Enabled              ECMP Max Routes    : 1
Max IPv4 Routes     : No Limit             Auto Bind          : None
Max IPv6 Routes     : No Limit
Ignore NH Metric    : Disabled
Hash Label          : Disabled
Vrf Target          : None
Vrf Import          : None
Vrf Export          : None
MVPN Vrf Target     : None
MVPN Vrf Import     : None
MVPN Vrf Export     : None

SAP Count           : 1                    SDP Bind Count     : 0

-------------------------------------------------------------------------------
Service Access & Destination Points
-------------------------------------------------------------------------------
Identifier                          Type         AdmMTU  OprMTU  Adm   Opr
-------------------------------------------------------------------------------
sap:1/1/2                           null         1514    1514    Up    Up
===============================================================================
```

Listing 20.9 shows the BGP configuration and peering session on CE-1. From the customer perspective, PE-1 is a normal IPv4 BGP peer. CE-1 is configured with an export policy to export the `10.1.0.0/16` prefix to the VPRN.

Listing 20.9 Configuration of BGP session on CE-1

```
*A:CE-1# configure router bgp
*A:CE-1>config>router>bgp# info
----------------------------------------------
            group "PE-1_peer"
                export "net_10"
                neighbor 192.168.1.1
                    peer-as 65000
                exit
            exit
----------------------------------------------
```

(continued)

Listing 20.9 *(continued)*

```
*A:CE-1>config>router>bgp# show router policy "net_10"
    entry 10
        from
            prefix-list "10_net"
        exit
        action accept
        exit
    exit
*A:CE-1>config>router>bgp# show router policy prefix-list "10_net"
prefix 10.1.0.0/16 longer
*A:CE-1>config>router>bgp# show router bgp summary
===============================================================================
 BGP Router ID:10.10.10.3       AS:65001       Local AS:65001
===============================================================================
BGP Admin State         : Up          BGP Oper State             : Up
Total Peer Groups       : 1           Total Peers                : 1
Total BGP Paths         : 2           Total Path Memory          : 240
Total IPv4 Remote Rts   : 0           Total IPv4 Rem. Active Rts : 0
Total IPv6 Remote Rts   : 0           Total IPv6 Rem. Active Rts : 0
Total Supressed Rts     : 0           Total Hist. Rts            : 0
Total Decay Rts         : 0

Total VPN Peer Groups   : 0           Total VPN Peers            : 0
Total VPN Local Rts     : 0
Total VPN-IPv4 Rem. Rts : 0           Total VPN-IPv4 Rem. Act. Rts: 0
Total VPN-IPv6 Rem. Rts : 0           Total VPN-IPv6 Rem. Act. Rts: 0
Total L2-VPN Rem. Rts   : 0           Total L2VPN Rem. Act. Rts  : 0
Total VPN Supp. Rts     : 0           Total VPN Hist. Rts        : 0
Total VPN Decay Rts     : 0
Total MVPN-IPv4 Rem Rts : 0           Total MVPN-IPv4 Rem Act Rts : 0
Total MDT-SAFI Rem Rts  : 0           Total MDT-SAFI Rem Act Rts  : 0

===============================================================================
BGP Summary
===============================================================================
Neighbor
                AS PktRcvd InQ  Up/Down   State|Rcv/Act/Sent (Addr Family)
                   PktSent OutQ
```

```
-------------------------------------------------------------------------------
192.168.1.1
                65000        23      0 00h09m41s 0/0/1 (IPv4)
                             26      0
===============================================================================
```

Use the command `show router service-id` to display the router information for the VRF. Once the BGP session is configured on the CE router, the routes from the customer network can be seen in the VRF with the `show router service-id route-table` command (see Listing 20.10).

Listing 20.10 Contents of the VRF for VPRN 11

```
*A:PE-1# show router 11 interface

===============================================================================
Interface Table (Service: 11)
===============================================================================
Interface-Name                   Adm         Opr(v4/v6)  Mode    Port/SapId
   IP-Address                                                    PfxState
-------------------------------------------------------------------------------
toCE-1                           Up          Up/Down     VPRN    1/1/2
   192.168.1.1/30                                                n/a
-------------------------------------------------------------------------------
Interfaces : 1
===============================================================================
*A:PE-1# show router 11 bgp summary
===============================================================================
 BGP Router ID:10.10.10.1        AS:65000        Local AS:65000
===============================================================================
BGP Admin State         : Up          BGP Oper State              : Up
Total Peer Groups       : 1           Total Peers                 : 1
Total BGP Paths         : 2           Total Path Memory           : 248
Total IPv4 Remote Rts   : 1           Total IPv4 Rem. Active Rts  : 1
Total IPv6 Remote Rts   : 0           Total IPv6 Rem. Active Rts  : 0
Total Supressed Rts     : 0           Total Hist. Rts             : 0
Total Decay Rts         : 0

===============================================================================
```

(continued)

Listing 20.10 *(continued)*

```
BGP Summary
===============================================================================
Neighbor
                AS PktRcvd InQ  Up/Down   State|Rcv/Act/Sent (Addr Family)
                   PktSent OutQ
-------------------------------------------------------------------------------
192.168.1.2
                65001     123     0 01h00m08s 1/1/0 (IPv4)
                          123     0
===============================================================================
*A:PE-1# show router 11 route-table

===============================================================================
Route Table (Service: 11)
===============================================================================
Dest Prefix                               Type     Proto    Age         Pref
       Next Hop[Interface Name]                                  Metric
-------------------------------------------------------------------------------
10.1.0.0/16                               Remote   BGP      00h59m46s   170
       192.168.1.2                                               0
192.168.1.0/30                            Local    Local    01h00m44s   0
       toCE-1                                                    0
-------------------------------------------------------------------------------
No. of Routes: 2
===============================================================================
```

Multiple services, including multiple VPRNs, can be configured on a single PE router. In Figure 20.8, VPRN 22 is also configured as a local VPRN on PE-1. PE-1 maintains separate VRFs and separate E-BGP peering sessions for the two different VPRNs. Listing 20.11 shows the VRF for VPRN 22 as well as the route table for the base router instance. You can see that the route tables are completely separate.

Listing 20.11 VRF for VPRN 22 and base route table

```
*A:PE-1# show router 22 route-table

===============================================================================
Route Table (Service: 22)
```

```
===============================================================================
Dest Prefix                                 Type    Proto    Age          Pref
       Next Hop[Interface Name]                                 Metric
-------------------------------------------------------------------------------
10.101.0.0/16                               Remote  BGP      00h01m41s    170
       192.168.101.2                                            0
192.168.101.0/30                            Local   Local    00h06m55s    0
       toPE-1                                                   0
-------------------------------------------------------------------------------
No. of Routes: 2
===============================================================================
*A:PE-1# show router route-table

===============================================================================
Route Table (Router: Base)
===============================================================================
Dest Prefix                                 Type    Proto    Age          Pref
       Next Hop[Interface Name]                                 Metric
-------------------------------------------------------------------------------
10.1.2.0/27                                 Local   Local    01d00h34m    0
       toPE-2                                                   0
10.1.4.0/27                                 Local   Local    01d00h34m    0
       toPE-4                                                   0
10.2.4.0/27                                 Remote  OSPF     01d00h27m    10
       10.1.2.2                                                 200
10.10.10.1/32                               Local   Local    01d00h38m    0
       system                                                   0
10.10.10.2/32                               Remote  OSPF     01d00h27m    10
       10.1.2.2                                                 100
10.10.10.4/32                               Remote  OSPF     01d00h23m    10
       10.1.4.4                                                 100
-------------------------------------------------------------------------------
No. of Routes: 6
===============================================================================
```

From the output above, you can see that PE-1 has the routing information it needs to forward packets it receives from the VPRN to the local customer networks. In the next section, we examine how these routes are distributed across the VPRN, so that the other PE routers also have these prefixes in their VRFs.

Figure 20.8 PE-1 maintains a separate VRF for the new VPRN 22.

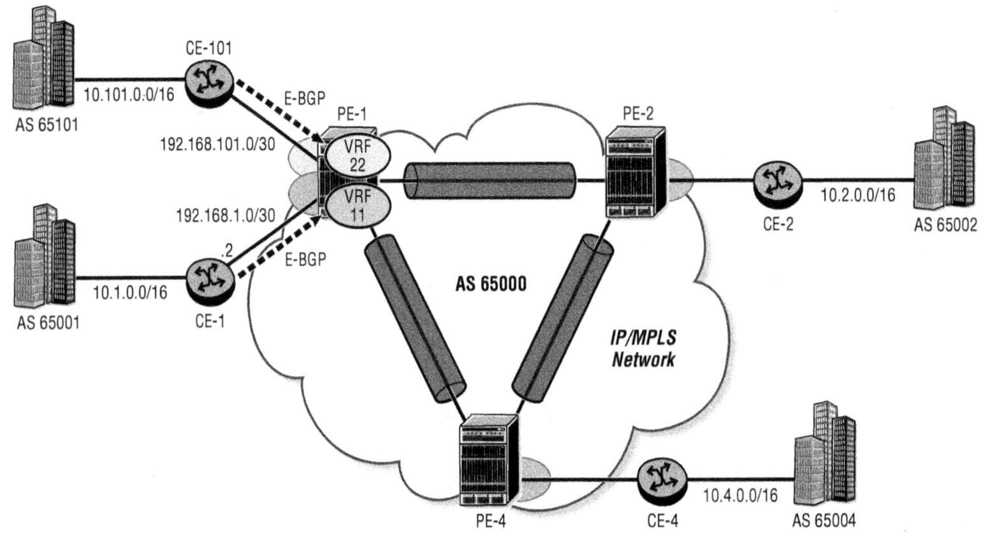

Route Distinguisher

We refer to the distribution of customer routes across the VPRN as *PE-to-PE routing*. In a VPRN this is handled by MP-BGP. A single instance of MP-BGP in the provider's core handles the exchange of updates for all VPRNs in the network; thus a method is required to distinguish between the routes of the different VPRNs. This is the role of the *route distinguisher* (RD). The RD is an 8-byte value that is added to the IPv4 prefix to create a VPN prefix known as the *VPN-IPv4 address*, as shown in Figure 20.9.

Figure 20.9 The VPN-IPv4 address is created by adding the RD to the IPv4 prefix.

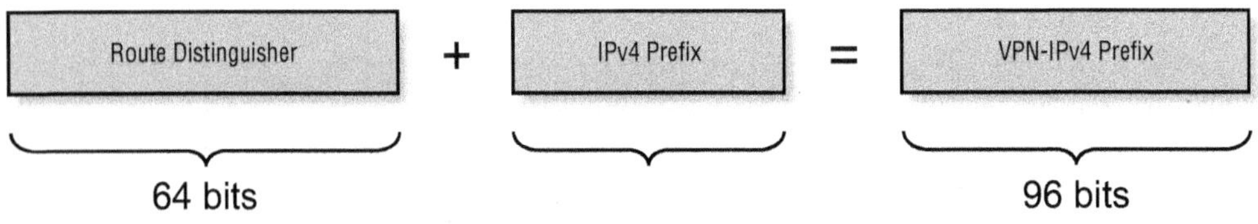

There are currently two different formats supported for the RD:

- **Type 0**—Uses a 2-byte AS number and an assigned number.
- **Type 1**—Uses a 4-byte IPv4 address and an assigned number.

Both RD types are supported by the Alcatel-Lucent 7750 SR and use 8 bytes, as shown in Figure 20.10.

Figure 20.10 Two RD types.

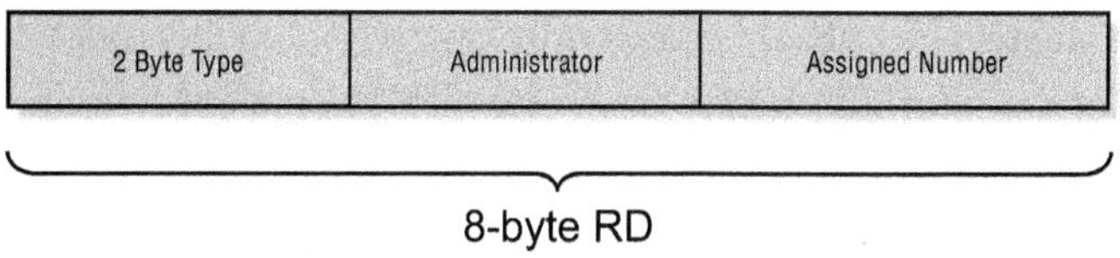

Type	Administrator	Assigned Number	Total Length of RD	VPN-IPv4 Address
2 Bytes (Type 0)	2 Bytes (ASN)	4 Bytes	8 Bytes	65321:100:10.1.1.0/24
2 Bytes (Type 1)	4 Bytes (IP Address)	2 Bytes	8 Bytes	10.10.10.10:100:10.1.1.0/24

The VPN-IPv4 address appears only in the PE control plane—it is added when the prefix is exported from the VRF to the VPRN. The CE router never sees the VPN-IPv4 address, and it never appears in any IP packet anywhere on the network.

The RD is also used with an IPv6 prefix to create a VPN-IPv6 address. This is described later in the chapter.

MP-BGP

BGP was designed as an extensible protocol, and this allows it to be adapted for advertising VPRN routes, as shown in Figure 20.11.

Figure 20.11 BGP update containing VPN-IPv4 prefix, MPLS label, and route targets.

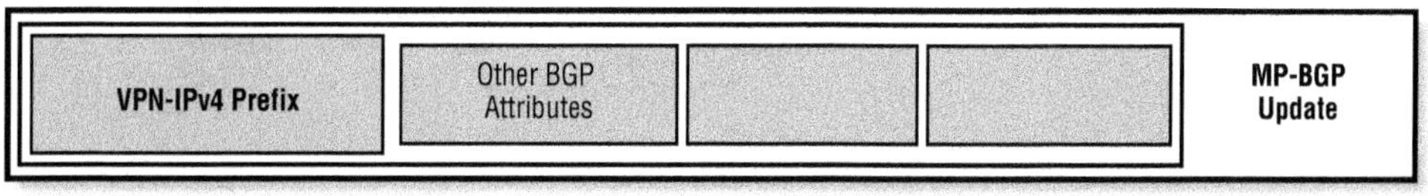

There are really three additional capabilities added to BGP that enable its use for VPRN routing:

- MP-BGP supports the VPN-IPv4 address family. It is able to carry updates with these 12-byte addresses in addition to the regular 4-byte IP addresses.
- The MP-BGP update carries an MPLS label to be used as the service label for this VPRN.

- The MP-BGP update carries one or more extended community strings that determine which routes are extracted to which VRFs. Extended community strings are not new to BGP but are used in VPRNs as the route target (described in the next section).

The Alcatel-Lucent 7750 SR advertises only one VPN label (service label) per VRF. Thus, the BGP updates for all prefixes from one VPRN on a specific PE, will have the same label.

Figure 20.12 shows two distributed VPRNs between three PE routers. The first step in configuring a distributed VPRN is to configure the MP-BGP sessions between the PE routers. If we're not using BGP to carry regular IPv4 routes, we can configure the PEs to use only the VPN-IPv4 address family. Listing 20.12 shows the configuration on PE-1.

Figure 20.12 MP-BGP carries VPN-IPv4 address family updates across the VPRN.

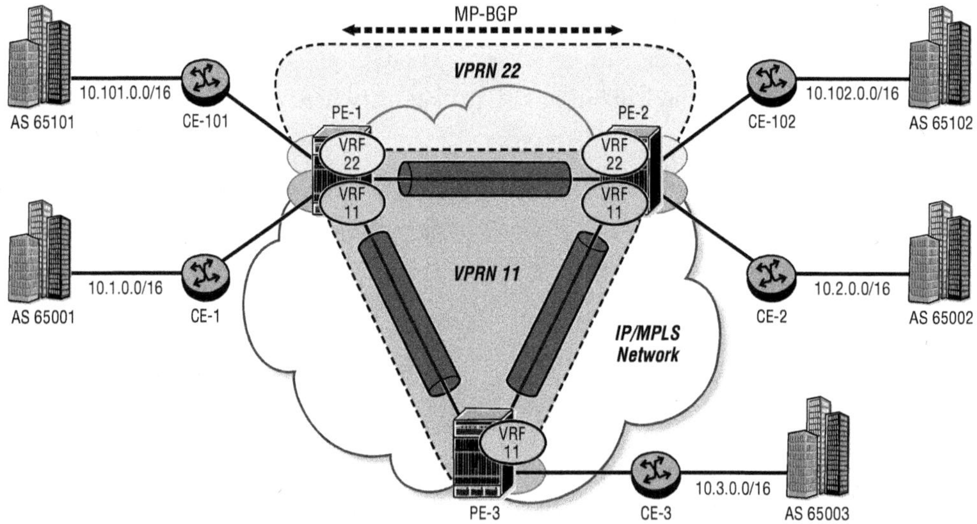

Listing 20.12 MP-BGP configuration on PE-1

```
*A:PE-1# configure router
*A:PE-1>config>router# autonomous-system 65000
*A:PE-1>config>router# bgp group "vprn"
*A:PE-1>config>router>bgp>group# family vpn-ipv4
*A:PE-1>config>router>bgp>group# peer-as 65000
```

```
*A:PE-1>config>router>bgp>group# neighbor 10.10.10.2
*A:PE-1>config>router>bgp>group>neighbor# exit
*A:PE-1>config>router>bgp>group# neighbor 10.10.10.4
*A:PE-1>config>router>bgp>group>neighbor# exit
*A:PE-1>config>router>bgp# show router bgp summary
===============================================================================
 BGP Router ID:10.10.10.1       AS:65000       Local AS:65000
===============================================================================
BGP Admin State         : Up          BGP Oper State              : Up
Total Peer Groups       : 1           Total Peers                 : 2
Total BGP Paths         : 6           Total Path Memory           : 720
Total IPv4 Remote Rts   : 0           Total IPv4 Rem. Active Rts  : 0
Total IPv6 Remote Rts   : 0           Total IPv6 Rem. Active Rts  : 0
Total Supressed Rts     : 0           Total Hist. Rts             : 0
Total Decay Rts         : 0

Total VPN Peer Groups   : 2           Total VPN Peers             : 2
Total VPN Local Rts     : 0
Total VPN-IPv4 Rem. Rts : 0           Total VPN-IPv4 Rem. Act. Rts: 0
Total VPN-IPv6 Rem. Rts : 0           Total VPN-IPv6 Rem. Act. Rts: 0
Total L2-VPN Rem. Rts   : 0           Total L2VPN Rem. Act. Rts   : 0
Total VPN Supp. Rts     : 0           Total VPN Hist. Rts         : 0
Total VPN Decay Rts     : 0
Total MVPN-IPv4 Rem Rts : 0           Total MVPN-IPv4 Rem Act Rts : 0
Total MDT-SAFI Rem Rts  : 0           Total MDT-SAFI Rem Act Rts  : 0

===============================================================================
BGP Summary
===============================================================================
Neighbor
                AS PktRcvd InQ  Up/Down   State|Rcv/Act/Sent (Addr Family)
                   PktSent OutQ
-------------------------------------------------------------------------------
10.10.10.2
                65000    2929    0 01d00h19m 0/0/0 (VpnIPv4)
                         2918    0
10.10.10.4
                65000       3    0 00h00m41s 0/0/0 (VpnIPv4)
                            5    0
===============================================================================
```

Route Target

Although the RD ensures that different VPN routes are all unique, it is not used by the PE to identify to which VPRN (or VRF) the route belongs. This is the purpose of the route target (RT). The *route target* is an extended community string that is added by the PE when the prefix is brought into MP-BGP. The other PEs effectively use a policy on the RT to select the routes they bring into the VRF.

Although an export policy can be used to add the RT and select routes based on the RT, there are simpler ways of doing this on the 7750 SR. The simplest way is to use the `vrf-target` command. For example, the command `vrf-target target:65000:11` will do two things:

1. Add the community string `target:65000:11` to all routes taken from the VRF into MP-BGP.
2. Select all MP-BGP routes with this community string and put them in the VRF.

PE-to-PE Routing

Once MP-BGP and the RT are configured in the VPRN, the routes from the VRF are advertised through MP-BGP to all other PE routers (see Figure 20.13). Listing 20.13 shows the configuration and the routes advertised to its neighbor, PE-2. Notice that the routes are VPN-IPv4 routes with the RD added, and the same label is advertised for both routes. You can also see that the RT is added in the detailed route command.

Listing 20.13 Configuration of distributed VPRN on PE-1

```
*A:PE-1# configure service vprn 11
*A:PE-1>config>service>vprn# info
----------------------------------------------
            autonomous-system 65000
            route-distinguisher 65000:11
            vrf-target target:65000:11
            interface "toCE-1" create
                address 192.168.1.1/30
                sap 1/1/2 create
                exit
            exit
            bgp
```

```
            group "customer-11"
                peer-as 65001
                neighbor 192.168.1.2
                exit
            exit
        exit
        no shutdown
----------------------------------------------
*A:PE-1>config>service>vprn# show router bgp neighbor 10.10.10.2
advertised-routes vpn-ipv4
===========================================================================
 BGP Router ID:10.10.10.1       AS:65000       Local AS:65000
===========================================================================
 Legend -
 Status codes  : u - used, s - suppressed, h - history, d - decayed,
 * - valid
 Origin codes  : i - IGP, e - EGP, ? - incomplete, > - best

===========================================================================
BGP VPN-IPv4 Routes
===========================================================================
Flag  Network                                        LocalPref   MED
      Nexthop                                                    VPNLabel
      As-Path
---------------------------------------------------------------------------
?     65000:11:10.1.0.0/16                           100         None
      10.10.10.1                                                 131071
      65001
i     65000:11:192.168.1.0/30                        100         None
      10.10.10.1                                                 131071
      No As-Path
---------------------------------------------------------------------------
Routes : 2
===========================================================================
*A:PE-1>config>service>vprn# show router bgp routes
65000:11:10.1.0.0/16 hunt
===========================================================================
 BGP Router ID:10.10.10.1       AS:65000       Local AS:65000
===========================================================================
```

(continued)

Listing 20.13 *(continued)*

```
 Legend -
 Status codes  : u - used, s - suppressed, h - history, d - decayed,
 * - valid
 Origin codes  : i - IGP, e - EGP, ? - incomplete, > - best

===============================================================================
BGP VPN-IPv4 Routes
===============================================================================
-------------------------------------------------------------------------------
RIB In Entries
-------------------------------------------------------------------------------


-------------------------------------------------------------------------------
RIB Out Entries
-------------------------------------------------------------------------------
Network         : 10.1.0.0/16
Nexthop         : 10.10.10.1
Route Dist.     : 65000:11                VPN Label      : 131071
To              : 10.10.10.2
Res. Nexthop    : n/a
Local Pref.     : 100                     Interface Name : NotAvailable
Aggregator AS   : None                    Aggregator     : None
Atomic Aggr.    : Not Atomic              MED            : None
Community       : target:65000:11
Cluster         : No Cluster Members
Originator Id   : None                    Peer Router Id : 10.10.10.2
Origin          : Incomplete
AS-Path         : 65001

Network         : 10.1.0.0/16
Nexthop         : 10.10.10.1
Route Dist.     : 65000:11                VPN Label      : 131071
To              : 10.10.10.4
Res. Nexthop    : n/a
Local Pref.     : 100                     Interface Name : NotAvailable
Aggregator AS   : None                    Aggregator     : None
Atomic Aggr.    : Not Atomic              MED            : None
Community       : target:65000:11
```

```
Cluster          : No Cluster Members
Originator Id    : None                      Peer Router Id : 10.10.10.4
Origin           : Incomplete
AS-Path          : 65001

-------------------------------------------------------------------------------
Routes : 2
===============================================================================
```

Figure 20.13 VPN-IPv4 routes are advertised to all PE routers.

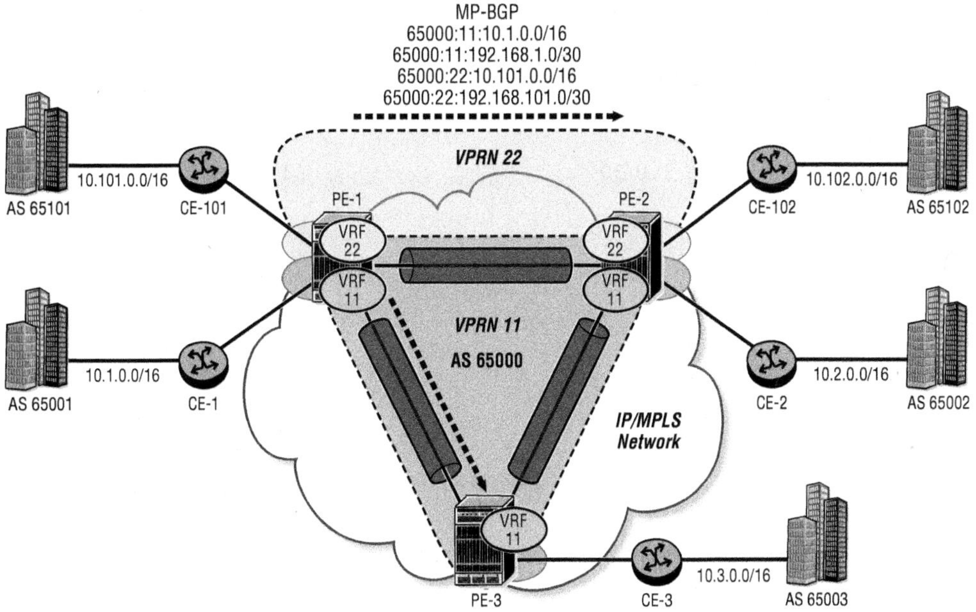

When VPRN 22 is configured on PE-1, we see its routes advertised by MP-BGP as well (see Listing 20.14).

Listing 20.14 Routes from all VPRNs are advertised in a single instance of BGP.

```
*A:PE-1# show router bgp neighbor 10.10.10.2 advertised-routes vpn-ipv4
===============================================================================
 BGP Router ID:10.10.10.1       AS:65000        Local AS:65000
===============================================================================
```

(continued)

Listing 20.14 *(continued)*

```
 Legend -
 Status codes  : u - used, s - suppressed, h - history, d - decayed,
 * - valid
 Origin codes  : i - IGP, e - EGP, ? - incomplete, > - best

===============================================================================
BGP VPN-IPv4 Routes
===============================================================================
Flag  Network                                           LocalPref   MED
      Nexthop                                                       VPNLabel
      As-Path
-------------------------------------------------------------------------------
?     65000:11:10.1.0.0/16                              100         None
      10.10.10.1                                                    131071
      65001
i     65000:11:192.168.1.0/30                           100         None
      10.10.10.1                                                    131071
      No As-Path
?     65000:22:10.101.0.0/16                           100         None
      10.10.10.1                                                    131067
      65101
i     65000:22:192.168.101.0/30                        100         None
      10.10.10.1                                                    131067
      No As-Path
-------------------------------------------------------------------------------
Routes : 4
===============================================================================
```

PE-2 receives the routes for all the VPRNs from all the other PE routers (see Listing 20.15). However, any routes that are not matched by a route target on this PE are not kept.

Listing 20.15 All VPRN routes are received at PE-2, and routes for the VRF are identified by the route target.

```
*A:PE-2# show router bgp routes vpn-ipv4
===============================================================================
 BGP Router ID:10.10.10.2       AS:65000       Local AS:65000
===============================================================================
```

```
 Legend -
 Status codes  : u - used, s - suppressed, h - history, d - decayed,
 * - valid
 Origin codes  : i - IGP, e - EGP, ? - incomplete, > - best

===============================================================================
BGP VPN-IPv4 Routes
===============================================================================
Flag  Network                                            LocalPref   MED
      Nexthop                                                        VPNLabel
      As-Path
-------------------------------------------------------------------------------
?     65000:11:10.1.0.0/16                               100         None
      10.10.10.1                                                     131071
      65001
?     65000:11:10.4.0.0/16                               100         None
      10.10.10.4                                                     131068
      65004
i     65000:11:192.168.1.0/30                            100         None
      10.10.10.1                                                     131071
      No As-Path
i     65000:11:192.168.4.0/30                            100         None
      10.10.10.4                                                     131068
      No As-Path
?     65000:22:10.101.0.0/16                            100         None
      10.10.10.1                                                     131067
      65101
?     65000:22:10.104.0.0/16                            100         None
      10.10.10.4                                                     131067
      65104
i     65000:22:192.168.101.0/30                         100         None
      10.10.10.1                                                     131067
      No As-Path
i     65000:22:192.168.104.0/30                         100         None
      10.10.10.4                                                     131067
      No As-Path
-------------------------------------------------------------------------------
Routes : 8
===============================================================================
```

Routes with community strings that match the route target value should be brought into the VRF. However, we can see in Listing 20.16 that the routes for VPRN 11 are not in the VRF.

Listing 20.16 VPRN routes are not in the VRF.

```
*A:PE-2# show router 11 route-table

===============================================================================
Route Table (Service: 11)
===============================================================================
Dest Prefix                                 Type    Proto     Age        Pref
       Next Hop[Interface Name]                                    Metric
-------------------------------------------------------------------------------
10.2.0.0/16                                 Remote  BGP       03h45m07s  170
       192.168.2.2                                                 0
192.168.2.0/30                              Local   Local     01d04h18m  0
       toCE-2                                                      0
-------------------------------------------------------------------------------
No. of Routes: 2
===============================================================================
*A:PE-2# show router bgp routes vpn-ipv4 65000:11:10.1.0.0/16 hunt
===============================================================================
 BGP Router ID:10.10.10.2       AS:65000       Local AS:65000
===============================================================================
 Legend -
 Status codes  : u - used, s - suppressed, h - history, d - decayed,
 * - valid
 Origin codes  : i - IGP, e - EGP, ? - incomplete, > - best

===============================================================================
BGP VPN-IPv4 Routes
===============================================================================
-------------------------------------------------------------------------------
RIB In Entries
-------------------------------------------------------------------------------
Network         : 10.1.0.0/16
Nexthop         : 10.10.10.1
Route Dist.     : 65000:11                VPN Label       : 131071
From            : 10.10.10.1
```

```
Res. Nexthop     : n/a
Local Pref.      : 100                    Interface Name : toPE-1
Aggregator AS    : None                   Aggregator     : None
Atomic Aggr.     : Not Atomic             MED            : None
Community        : target:65000:11
Cluster          : No Cluster Members
Originator Id    : None                   Peer Router Id : 10.10.10.1
Flags            : Invalid  Incomplete
AS-Path          : 65001
VPRN Imported    : None

---------------------------------------------------------------------------
RIB Out Entries
---------------------------------------------------------------------------
---------------------------------------------------------------------------
Routes : 1
===========================================================================
```

The route is shown as `Invalid` because BGP must have a valid next-hop for the route before it is installed in the route table. In this case, we plan to reach the next-hop through an MPLS tunnel, but we have not configured the MPLS transport in the VPRN. A spoke SDP can be used if you plan to use an RSVP-TE LSP (e.g., for traffic engineering or fast reroute). Or, you can use the `auto-bind` command to automatically use GRE (generic routing encapsulation), RSVP-TE (Resource Reservation Protocol–Traffic Engineering), or LDP (Label Distribution Protocol) for transport. Listing 20.17 shows the use of `auto-bind ldp`. As long as there is an active label for the next-hop PE, BGP can use the route.

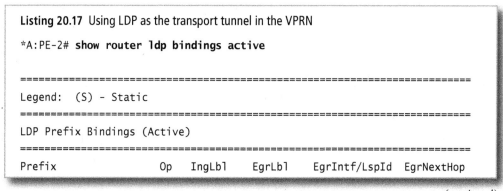

Listing 20.17 Using LDP as the transport tunnel in the VPRN

```
*A:PE-2# show router ldp bindings active

===========================================================================
Legend:  (S) - Static
===========================================================================
LDP Prefix Bindings (Active)
===========================================================================
Prefix                  Op   IngLbl    EgrLbl    EgrIntf/LspId  EgrNextHop
```

(continued)

Listing 20.17 *(continued)*

```
-------------------------------------------------------------------------------
10.10.10.1/32           Push    --      131070    1/1/1          10.1.2.1
10.10.10.1/32           Swap 131070     131070    1/1/1          10.1.2.1
10.10.10.2/32           Pop  131071       --        --              --
10.10.10.4/32           Push    --      131071    1/1/3          10.2.4.4
10.10.10.4/32           Swap 131069     131071    1/1/3          10.2.4.4
-------------------------------------------------------------------------------
No. of Prefix Bindings: 5
*A:PE-2# configure service vprn 11 auto-bind ldp
*A:PE-2# show router 11 route-table

===============================================================================
Route Table (Service: 11)
===============================================================================
Dest Prefix                               Type     Proto     Age         Pref
       Next Hop[Interface Name]                                Metric
-------------------------------------------------------------------------------
10.1.0.0/16                               Remote   BGP VPN   00h06m36s   170
       10.10.10.1 (tunneled)                                     0
10.2.0.0/16                               Remote   BGP       05h21m32s   170
       192.168.2.2                                               0
10.4.0.0/16                               Remote   BGP VPN   00h06m36s   170
       10.10.10.4 (tunneled)                                     0
192.168.1.0/30                            Remote   BGP VPN   00h06m36s   170
       10.10.10.1 (tunneled)                                     0
192.168.2.0/30                            Local    Local     01d05h55m   0
       toCE-2                                                    0
192.168.4.0/30                            Remote   BGP VPN   00h06m36s   170
       10.10.10.4 (tunneled)                                     0
-------------------------------------------------------------------------------
No. of Routes: 6
===============================================================================
```

PE-to-CE Routing

Routes in the VRF are not automatically advertised into the customer's network. In the example above, EBGP was used for CE-to-PE routing. The same EBGP session is used as the PE-to-CE routing protocol. To advertise the routes from the VRF into the local

EBGP session with the CE router, we need an export policy. Listing 20.18 shows the routes in the VRF learned from the VPRN (BGP VPN). The routes are not advertised to the CE router until an export policy is configured in the BGP instance in VPRN 11.

Listing 20.18 Export policy to export the routes into the customer network

```
*A:PE-2# show router 11 route-table

===============================================================================
Route Table (Service: 11)
===============================================================================
Dest Prefix                                 Type    Proto     Age         Pref
       Next Hop[Interface Name]                                     Metric
-------------------------------------------------------------------------------
10.1.0.0/16                                 Remote  BGP VPN   08h08m10s   170
       10.10.10.1 (tunneled)                                        0
10.2.0.0/16                                 Remote  BGP       13h23m05s   170
       192.168.2.2                                                  0
10.4.0.0/16                                 Remote  BGP VPN   08h08m10s   170
       10.10.10.4 (tunneled)                                        0
192.168.1.0/30                              Remote  BGP VPN   08h08m10s   170
       10.10.10.1 (tunneled)                                        0
192.168.2.0/30                              Local   Local     01d13h56m   0
       toCE-2                                                       0
192.168.4.0/30                              Remote  BGP VPN   08h08m10s   170
       10.10.10.4 (tunneled)                                        0
-------------------------------------------------------------------------------
No. of Routes: 6
===============================================================================
*A:PE-2# show router 11 bgp neighbor 192.168.2.2 advertised-routes
===============================================================================
 BGP Router ID:10.10.10.2       AS:65000       Local AS:65000
===============================================================================
 Legend -
 Status codes  : u - used, s - suppressed, h - history, d - decayed,
 * - valid
 Origin codes  : i - IGP, e - EGP, ? - incomplete, > - best

===============================================================================
```

(continued)

Listing 20.18 *(continued)*

```
BGP IPv4 Routes
===============================================================================
Flag  Network                                            LocalPref   MED
      Nexthop                                                        VPNLabel
      As-Path
-------------------------------------------------------------------------------
No Matching Entries Found
===============================================================================
*A:PE-2# configure router policy-options
*A:PE-2>config>router>policy-options# begin
*A:PE-2>config>router>policy-options# policy-statement export-vprn
*A:PE-2>config>router>policy-options>policy-statement$ entry 10
*A:PE-2>config>router>policy-options>policy-statement>entry$ from protocol
bgp-vpn
*A:PE-2>config>router>policy-options>policy-statement>entry# action accept
*A:PE-2>config>router>policy-options>policy-statement>entry>action# exit
*A:PE-2>config>router>policy-options>policy-statement>entry# exit
*A:PE-2>config>router>policy-options>policy-statement# info
----------------------------------------------
                entry 10
                    from
                        protocol bgp-vpn
                    exit
                    action accept
                    exit
                exit
----------------------------------------------
*A:PE-2>config>router>policy-options>policy-statement# exit
*A:PE-2>config>router>policy-options# commit
*A:PE-2>config>router>policy-options# exit
*A:PE-2# configure service vprn 11 bgp group "customer-11" export
"export-vprn"
*A:PE-2# show router 11 bgp neighbor 192.168.2.2 advertised-routes
===============================================================================
 BGP Router ID:10.10.10.2       AS:65000       Local AS:65000
===============================================================================
 Legend -
 Status codes  : u - used, s - suppressed, h - history, d - decayed,
```

```
 * - valid
 Origin codes  : i - IGP, e - EGP, ? - incomplete, > - best

===============================================================================
BGP IPv4 Routes
===============================================================================
Flag  Network                                            LocalPref   MED
      Nexthop                                                        VPNLabel
      As-Path
-------------------------------------------------------------------------------
?     10.1.0.0/16                                        n/a         None
      192.168.2.1                                                    -
      65000 65001
?     10.4.0.0/16                                        n/a         None
      192.168.2.1                                                    -
      65000 65004
i     192.168.1.0/30                                     n/a         None
      192.168.2.1                                                    -
      65000
i     192.168.4.0/30                                     n/a         None
      192.168.2.1                                                    -
      65000
-------------------------------------------------------------------------------
Routes : 4
===============================================================================
```

If the same AS (autonomous system) number is used at both customer sites for VPRN 11, BGP on CE-2 will not accept the routes from CE-1 because they contain CE-2's AS number in the AS-Path. This is the loop-prevention mechanism of BGP. It is possible to modify the BGP updates in the VPRN so that they will be accepted by the CE router. Although it's not complicated, it is beyond the scope of this book. To avoid this situation, we use different AS numbers at each customer site in our example.

Once the PE-to-CE routing is configured on both sides of the VPRN (see Figure 20.14), it is possible to ping between CE-1 and CE-2 (see Listing 20.19). Of course, there is no way to reach a destination in VPRN 22 (such as `10.102.0.1`) from VPRN 11 because the routes from VPRN 22 do not appear in the VRF or CE routers of VPRN 11.

Figure 20.14 PE-to-CE routing is used to distribute routes from the VRF to the customer network.

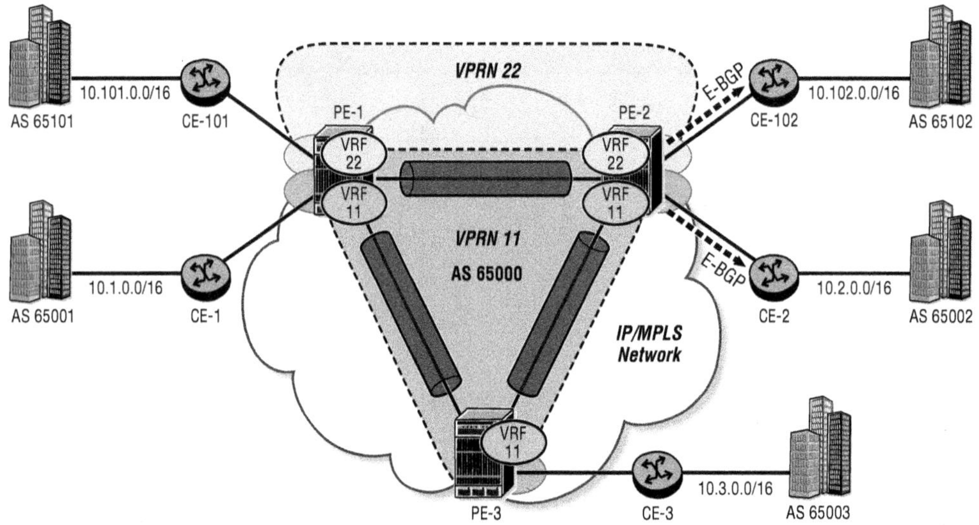

Listing 20.19 Traceroute from CE-1 to CE-2 through the VPRN

```
*A:CE-1# show router route-table

===============================================================================
Route Table (Router: Base)
===============================================================================
Dest Prefix                               Type    Proto    Age         Pref
      Next Hop[Interface Name]                                Metric
-------------------------------------------------------------------------------
10.1.0.0/16                               Local   Local    01d15h29m   0
      loop1                                                    0
10.2.0.0/16                               Remote  BGP      00h00m32s   170
      192.168.1.1                                              0
10.4.0.0/16                               Remote  BGP      00h00m32s   170
      192.168.1.1                                              0
192.168.1.0/30                            Local   Local    01d15h29m   0
      toPE-1                                                   0
192.168.2.0/30                            Remote  BGP      00h00m32s   170
      192.168.1.1                                              0
192.168.4.0/30                            Remote  BGP      00h00m32s   170
```

```
      192.168.1.1                                              0
-------------------------------------------------------------------------------
No. of Routes: 6
*A:CE-1# traceroute 10.2.0.1 source 10.1.0.1
traceroute to 10.2.0.1 from 10.1.0.1, 30 hops max, 40 byte packets
  1  192.168.1.1 (192.168.1.1)    2.27 ms  1.39 ms  1.67 ms
  2  0.0.0.0  *
  2  192.168.2.1 (192.168.2.1)    2.71 ms  2.10 ms
  3  10.2.0.1 (10.2.0.1)    2.95 ms  2.94 ms  2.98 ms
*A:CE-1#
```

20.3 VPRN for IPv6 (6VPE)

6VPE (IPv6 on VPN Provider Edge Router) is an extension to the VPRN standard (defined in RFC 4659) that adds support for the interconnection of IPv6 networks over an IPv4-based core. 6VPE provides a similar service for bridging IPv6 networks as the 6PE technology described in Chapter 13. The difference is that 6VPE uses the VPRN infrastructure to connect customer IPv6 networks.

6VPE is very similar in concept and operation to an IPv4 VPRN. The similarities between the two are the following:

- An RD is used to create prefixes that are unique across multiple VPRNs.
- A single instance of MP-BGP is used to distribute customer IPv6 routes across the VPRN.
- An RT is used to select routes for a specific VPRN.
- PE routers maintain a VRF for each VPRN on that router.
- In the data plane, the ingress PE makes a forwarding decision based on the contents of the VRF. IPv6 data packets are encapsulated with a service and transport label for transmission across the core.

The main differences between 6VPE and a standard (IPv4) VPRN are the following:

- A new address family, VPN-IPv6, is defined. Similar to a VPN-IPv4 address, the VPN-IPv6 address is created by adding the 8-byte RD to a 16-byte IPv6 address.

- The PE routers run a dual stack of IPv4 and IPv6. Only IPv4 is required in the core network.
- IPv6 routes must be resolved to an IPv6 next-hop. IPv4 addresses in the core are mapped to IPv6 addresses to accomplish this.

In this book, we only consider the interconnection of pure IPv6 networks. We do not discuss any of the techniques for interconnecting IPv4 and IPv6 networks or translation between them.

Operation of 6VPE

In Figure 20.15, the customer using VPRN 22 from the previous example has migrated its network to a native IPv6 network. We demonstrate how the VPRN can be used to connect the customer's IPv6 locations, while still supporting a traditional IPv4 VPRN service.

Figure 20.15 IPv6 and IPv4 VPRN services supported on the same core infrastructure.

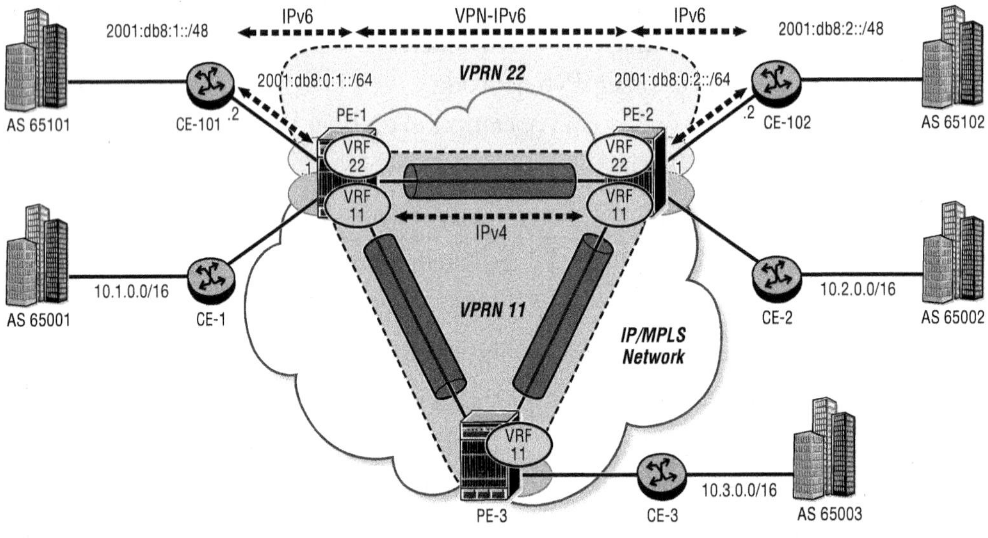

The only real change required in the service provider core is to update MP-BGP on any involved PE routers to support the VPN-IPv6 address family (see Listing 20.20). Of course, no changes are required on the P routers because they do not participate in the MP-BGP peering.

Listing 20.20 PE routers updated to support VPN-IPv6 address family

```
A:PE-1# configure system chassis-mode c force
A:PE-1# configure router bgp group "vprn" family vpn-ipv4 vpn-ipv6
*A:PE-1# show router bgp summary
===============================================================================
 BGP Router ID:10.10.10.1       AS:65000       Local AS:65000
===============================================================================
BGP Admin State         : Up          BGP Oper State              : Up
Total Peer Groups       : 1           Total Peers                 : 2
Total BGP Paths         : 10          Total Path Memory           : 1248
Total IPv4 Remote Rts   : 0           Total IPv4 Rem. Active Rts  : 0
Total IPv6 Remote Rts   : 0           Total IPv6 Rem. Active Rts  : 0
Total Supressed Rts     : 0           Total Hist. Rts             : 0
Total Decay Rts         : 0

Total VPN Peer Groups   : 2           Total VPN Peers             : 2
Total VPN Local Rts     : 4
Total VPN-IPv4 Rem. Rts : 0           Total VPN-IPv4 Rem. Act. Rts: 0
Total VPN-IPv6 Rem. Rts : 0           Total VPN-IPv6 Rem. Act. Rts: 0
Total L2-VPN Rem. Rts   : 0           Total L2VPN Rem. Act. Rts   : 0
Total VPN Supp. Rts     : 0           Total VPN Hist. Rts         : 0
Total VPN Decay Rts     : 0
Total MVPN-IPv4 Rem Rts : 0           Total MVPN-IPv4 Rem Act Rts : 0
Total MDT-SAFI Rem Rts  : 0           Total MDT-SAFI Rem Act Rts  : 0

===============================================================================
BGP Summary
===============================================================================
Neighbor
                AS PktRcvd InQ  Up/Down   State|Rcv/Act/Sent (Addr Family)
                   PktSent OutQ
-------------------------------------------------------------------------------
10.10.10.2
                65000    6302    0 00h00m08s 0/0/0 (VpnIPv4)
                         6267    0           0/0/0 (VpnIPv6)
10.10.10.4
                65000    3386    0 00h00m08s 0/0/0 (VpnIPv4)
                         3403    0           0/0/0 (VpnIPv6)
===============================================================================
```

The next step is to configure the VPRN service on the PE routers to support IPv6 interfaces and route exchange with the CE routers. We use the same RD and RT as for the previous VPRN 22 service (see Listing 20.21).

Listing 20.21 Configuring the VPRN service on the PE for supporting an IPv6 network

```
*A:PE-1# configure service vprn 22
*A:PE-1>config>service>vprn# info
----------------------------------------------
            autonomous-system 65000
            route-distinguisher 65000:22
            vrf-target target:65000:22
            interface "toCE-1" create
                ipv6
                    address 2001:DB8::1:0:0:0:1/64
                exit
                sap 1/1/3 create
                exit
            exit
            bgp
                group "customer_22"
                    family ipv6
                    peer-as 65101
                    neighbor 2001:DB8::1:0:0:0:2
                    exit
                exit
            exit
            no shutdown
----------------------------------------------
*A:PE-1>config>service>vprn# show router 22 interface

===========================================================================
Interface Table (Service: 22)
===========================================================================
Interface-Name                   Adm         Opr(v4/v6)  Mode    Port/SapId
   IP-Address                                                    PfxState
---------------------------------------------------------------------------
toCE-1                           Up          Down/Up     VPRN    1/1/3
   2001:DB8::1:0:0:0:1/64                                        PREFERRED
   FE80::2C:434D:6955:59D5/64                                    PREFERRED
---------------------------------------------------------------------------
```

```
Interfaces : 1
===============================================================================
*A:PE-1>config>service>vprn# show router 22 bgp summary
===============================================================================
 BGP Router ID:10.10.10.1       AS:65000       Local AS:65000
===============================================================================
BGP Admin State         : Up          BGP Oper State              : Up
Total Peer Groups       : 1           Total Peers                 : 1
Total BGP Paths         : 1           Total Path Memory           : 120
Total IPv4 Remote Rts   : 0           Total IPv4 Rem. Active Rts  : 0
Total IPv6 Remote Rts   : 0           Total IPv6 Rem. Active Rts  : 0
Total Supressed Rts     : 0           Total Hist. Rts             : 0
Total Decay Rts         : 0

===============================================================================
BGP Summary
===============================================================================
Neighbor
                AS PktRcvd InQ  Up/Down   State|Rcv/Act/Sent (Addr Family)
                   PktSent OutQ
-------------------------------------------------------------------------------
2001:DB8::1:0:0:0:2
                65101      31     0 00h00m28s 0/0/0 (IPv6)
                           33     0
===============================================================================
*A:PE-1>config>service>vprn# show router 22 route-table ipv6

===============================================================================
IPv6 Route Table (Service: 22)
===============================================================================
Dest Prefix                                 Type     Proto     Age          Pref
       Next Hop[Interface Name]                                     Metric
-------------------------------------------------------------------------------
2001:DB8::1:0:0:0:0/64                      Local    Local     00h00m39s    0
       toCE-1                                                       0
2001:DB8:1::/48                             Remote   BGP       00h00m05s    170
       2001:DB8::1:0:0:0:2                                          0
-------------------------------------------------------------------------------
No. of Routes: 2
===============================================================================
```

We see from Listing 20.22 that the network advertised by the CE router is now in the VRF on PE-1. We are also receiving the routes advertised by CE-2 from MP-BGP (see Listing 20.22), but even though we have a valid route target on PE-1, the routes are not in the VRF. The next-hop for the routes is not valid because we have not defined a transport for the VPRN, and thus they do not get installed in the VRF. Notice that the next-hop address for the IPv6 routes is an IPv4-mapped address. The listing shows that we are also still receiving the routes for the IPv4 VPRN.

Listing 20.22 VPRN routes received at PE-1

```
*A:PE-1>config>service>vprn# show router bgp routes vpn-ipv6
===============================================================================
 BGP Router ID:10.10.10.1       AS:65000       Local AS:65000
===============================================================================
 Legend -
 Status codes  : u - used, s - suppressed, h - history, d - decayed,
 * - valid
 Origin codes  : i - IGP, e - EGP, ? - incomplete, > - best

===============================================================================
BGP VPN-IPv6 Routes
===============================================================================
Flag  Network                                            LocalPref   MED
      Nexthop                                                        VPNLabel
      As-Path
-------------------------------------------------------------------------------
i     65000:22:2001:DB8::2:0:0:0:0/64                    100         None
      ::FFFF:A0A:A02                                                  131067
      No As-Path
?     65000:22:2001:DB8:2::/48                           100         None
      ::FFFF:A0A:A02                                                  131067
      65102
-------------------------------------------------------------------------------
Routes : 2
===============================================================================
*A:PE-1>config>service>vprn# show router bgp routes vpn-ipv4
===============================================================================
 BGP Router ID:10.10.10.1       AS:65000       Local AS:65000
===============================================================================
```

```
  Legend -
  Status codes  : u - used, s - suppressed, h - history, d - decayed,
  * - valid
  Origin codes  : i - IGP, e - EGP, ? - incomplete, > - best

===============================================================================
BGP VPN-IPv4 Routes
===============================================================================
Flag  Network                                          LocalPref   MED
      Nexthop                                                      VPNLabel
      As-Path
-------------------------------------------------------------------------------
u*>?  65000:11:10.2.0.0/16                             100         None
      10.10.10.2                                                   131068
      65002
u*>?  65000:11:10.4.0.0/16                             100         None
      10.10.10.4                                                   131068
      65004
u*>i  65000:11:192.168.2.0/30                          100         None
      10.10.10.2                                                   131068
      No As-Path
u*>i  65000:11:192.168.4.0/30                          100         None
      10.10.10.4                                                   131068
      No As-Path
-------------------------------------------------------------------------------
Routes : 4
===============================================================================
```

In this example, we will use an RSVP-TE LSP as the transport tunnel to illustrate a different transport type from LDP. Listing 20.23 shows the configuration of an LSP with fast reroute and then the SDP to be used for the transport. After the service is bound to the spoke SDP, the routes received from PE-2 are seen in the VRF on PE-1.

Listing 20.23 Configuration of RSVP-TE for the VPRN transport

```
*A:PE-1# configure router mpls
*A:PE-1>config>router>mpls# path loose
*A:PE-1>config>router>mpls>path$ no shutdown
```

(continued)

Listing 20.23 *(continued)*

```
*A:PE-1>config>router>mpls>path$ exit
*A:PE-1>config>router>mpls# lsp toPE-2
*A:PE-1>config>router>mpls>lsp$ to 10.10.10.2
*A:PE-1>config>router>mpls>lsp$ cspf
*A:PE-1>config>router>mpls>lsp$ fast-reroute facility
*A:PE-1>config>router>mpls>lsp>frr$ exit
*A:PE-1>config>router>mpls>lsp# no shutdown
*A:PE-1>config>router>mpls>lsp# primary "loose"
*A:PE-1>config>router>mpls>lsp>primary$ exit
*A:PE-1>config>router>mpls>lsp# info
----------------------------------------------
                to 10.10.10.2
                cspf
                fast-reroute facility
                exit
                primary "loose"
                exit
                no shutdown
----------------------------------------------
*A:PE-1>config>router>mpls>lsp# show router mpls lsp

===============================================================================
MPLS LSPs (Originating)
===============================================================================
LSP Name                        To                  Fastfail     Adm   Opr
                                                    Config
-------------------------------------------------------------------------------
toPE-2                          10.10.10.2          Yes          Up    Up
-------------------------------------------------------------------------------
LSPs : 1
===============================================================================
*A:PE-1>config>router>mpls>lsp# exit all
*A:PE-1# configure service sdp 2 mpls create
*A:PE-1>config>service>sdp$ far-end 10.10.10.2
*A:PE-1>config>service>sdp$ lsp "toPE-2"
*A:PE-1>config>service>sdp$ no shutdown
*A:PE-1>config>service>sdp$ exit all
A:PE-1# configure service vprn 22
```

```
*A:PE-1>config>service>vprn# spoke-sdp 2 create
*A:PE-1>config>service>vprn>sdp$ exit
*A:PE-1>config>service>vprn# show service id 22 base

===============================================================================
Service Basic Information
===============================================================================
Service Id          : 22                    Vpn Id            : 0
Service Type        : VPRN
Name                : (Not Specified)
Description         : (Not Specified)
Customer Id         : 1
Last Status Change: 05/01/2011 07:08:53
Last Mgmt Change    : 05/02/2011 20:43:21
Admin State         : Up                     Oper State        : Up

Route Dist.         : 65000:22              VPRN Type         : regular
AS Number           : 65000                  Router Id         : 10.10.10.1
ECMP                : Enabled                ECMP Max Routes   : 1
Max IPv4 Routes     : No Limit               Auto Bind         : None
Max IPv6 Routes     : No Limit
Ignore NH Metric    : Disabled
Hash Label          : Disabled
Vrf Target          : target:65000:22
Vrf Import          : None
Vrf Export          : None
MVPN Vrf Target     : None
MVPN Vrf Import     : None
MVPN Vrf Export     : None

SAP Count           : 1                      SDP Bind Count    : 1

-------------------------------------------------------------------------------
Service Access & Destination Points
-------------------------------------------------------------------------------
Identifier                              Type         AdmMTU  OprMTU  Adm  Opr
-------------------------------------------------------------------------------
sap:1/1/3                               null         1514    1514    Up   Up
sdp:2:22 S(10.10.10.2)                 Spok         0       9186    Up   Up
```

(continued)

Listing 20.23 *(continued)*

```
===============================================================================
*A:PE-1>config>service>vprn# show router 22 route-table ipv6

===============================================================================
IPv6 Route Table (Service: 22)
===============================================================================
Dest Prefix                             Type    Proto    Age         Pref
       Next Hop[Interface Name]                                Metric
-------------------------------------------------------------------------------
2001:DB8::1:0:0:0:0/64                  Local   Local    07h59m47s   0
       toCE-1                                                  0
2001:DB8::2:0:0:0:0/64                  Remote  BGP VPN  00h01m03s   170
       10.10.10.2 (tunneled)                                   0
2001:DB8:1::/48                         Remote  BGP      07h59m12s   170
       2001:DB8::1:0:0:0:2                                     0
2001:DB8:2::/48                         Remote  BGP VPN  00h01m03s   170
       10.10.10.2 (tunneled)                                   0
-------------------------------------------------------------------------------
No. of Routes: 4
===============================================================================
```

Once the routes are distributed to the CE routers, it's possible to ping across the network, as shown in Listing 20.24.

Listing 20.24 Traceroute between CE routers

```
*A:CE-101# traceroute 2001:db8:2::1 source 2001:db8:1::1
traceroute to 2001:DB8:2::1 from 2001:DB8:1::1, 30 hops max, 60 byte
 packets
  1  2001:DB8::1:0:0:0:1 (2001:DB8::1:0:0:0:1)    1.79 ms  1.15 ms  1.33 ms
  2  2001:DB8::2:0:0:0:1 (2001:DB8::2:0:0:0:1)    2.66 ms  1.84 ms  2.22 ms
  3  2001:DB8:2::1 (2001:DB8:2::1)    3.21 ms  3.01 ms  2.76 ms
*A:CE-101#
```

Practice Lab: Configuring Layer 3 Services

The following lab is designed to reinforce your knowledge of the content in this chapter. Please review the instructions carefully, and perform the steps in the order in which they are presented. The practice labs require that you have access to six or more Alcatel-Lucent 7750 SRs or Alcatel-Lucent 7450 ESSs in a non-production environment.

These labs are designed to be used in a controlled lab environment. Please *do not* attempt to perform these labs in a production environment.

Lab Section 20.1: Internet Enhanced Services

Chapter 19's lab focused on Layer 2 services. This lab section investigates the Internet Enhanced Service (IES), which is a Layer 3 service available on an Alcatel-Lucent 7750 SR.

Objective In this exercise, you will configure an IES toward a CE router and validate connectivity using the network topology shown in Figure 20.16.

Figure 20.16 Lab topology for IES.

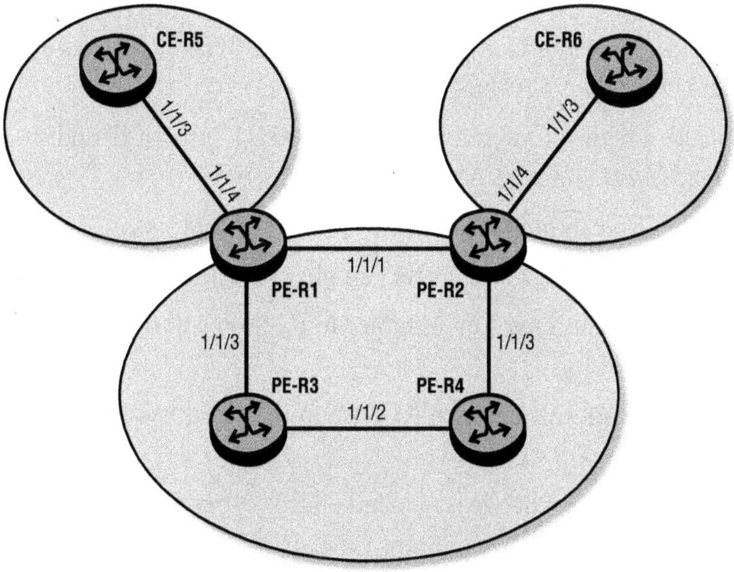

Validation You will know you have succeeded if the CE routers can ping each other.

1. Make sure that an IGP is running, and create a full mesh of SDPs between R1, R2, R3, and R4 using RSVP-TE LSPs.

   If you have just completed a previous lab, this step may already be done. Remove any existing services.

2. Configure a network interface on R2 toward R6 with an IP address of `192.168.6.2/24` and a VLAN tag of 6.
   a. Configure a network interface on R6 toward R2 with an IP address of `192.168.6.6/24` and a VLAN tag of 6.
   b. Can R6 ping R2's directly connected network interface?
   c. Can R4 ping R6's interface to R2? Explain.
   d. Without running an IGP on R6, configure the network so that R4 can ping R6's interface to R2.

   Use a passive interface on R2 and a static default route on R6.

3. Configure a network interface on R1 toward R5 with an IP address of `192.168.5.1/24` and a VLAN tag of 5.
   a. Configure a network interface on R5 toward R1 with an IP address of `192.168.5.5/24` and a VLAN tag of 5.
   b. Verify that R5 can ping R1's directly connected interface.
   c. Configure the network so that R4 can ping R5's interface to R1.
   d. Verify that R5 can ping R6's interface to R2. You will need to specify a source address for the ping.
4. Replace the network interface on R1 with an IES that uses a customer ID of 100 and a service ID of 5.
   a. What configuration change is required on R5 to accommodate the IES? Explain.
   b. Verify that the IES is operationally up before proceeding.

c. Verify that R5 can ping R1's directly connected interface.

d. Can R5 still ping R6's interface to R2?

e. Complete any network configuration required to ensure that the ping is successful before proceeding.

f. Explain the entries in the MAC FDB of the IES.

g. Explain the entries in the ARP table of the IES.

h. What is the difference between the command `show router arp` and the command `show service id <service-id> arp`?

i. Explain the dynamically learned entries in the ARP table of R5.

5. What is the default MTU setting of the SAP bound to the IES interface?

a. Set the interface MTU of router R5 to 1,550 bytes.

b. From R5, generate a ping to R6's interface that will have a frame size of 1,518 bytes (use a ping with a size parameter of 1,472). Is the ping successful? Explain.

c. From R5, generate a ping to R6's interface that will have a frame size of 1,519 bytes (use a ping with a size of 1,473).

d. Repeat the ping form the previous step with the `do-not-fragment` option. Is the ping successful? Explain.

e. Describe which SDPs and LSPs are used to transmit traffic between R5 and R6.

6. Can a Layer 2 service be used for connectivity between the CE routers without changing their interface IP addresses? Explain.

Lab Section 20.2: IES Spoke-SDP Termination

The previous section investigated local IES services that do not have a spoke SDP. This lab uses an IES interface that can provide Layer 3 IP connectivity to a host that is connected through a Layer 2 service using a spoke-SDP termination.

Objective This lab will investigate the use of IES spoke termination to provide Layer 3 connectivity to the CE routers through a Layer 2 service.

Validation You will know you have succeeded if the CE routers can ping each other.

1. Replace the IES service on R1 with an epipe service that has a service ID of 99, a customer ID of 100, and a default service MTU.

The spoke SDP is configured in a later step.

a. Configure an IES service on R4 with a service ID of 400 and a customer ID of 100.

b. Create an interface within the IES service with a spoke termination to the epipe service on R1. What interface IP address should be used? What MTU value should be used?

c. Verify that the IES interface is operationally up before proceeding.

d. Can R5 ping the IES interface? Explain.

e. Configure the network so that R5 can ping R6's interface to R2. Use the source parameter in R5's ping.

f. Describe the dynamically learned entries in the ARP table on R5.

g. Describe the contents of the MAC FDB and ARP tables for the epipe service on R1.

h. Describe how traffic is forwarded from R5 to R6.

2. Replace the network interface on R2 with a VPLS that has a service ID of 199, a customer ID of 100, and a default service MTU.

   a. Within IES 400, configure another interface that can be used for a spoke termination to the VPLS on R6. Ensure that the CE configuration does not need to change.

   b. Verify that the IES interface is operationally up before proceeding.

   c. Verify that R6 can ping the correct IES interface before proceeding.

   d. Verify that R5 can ping R6.

   e. Describe how traffic is forwarded from R5 to R6.

   f. Do the IES interfaces still need to be distributed into the IGP in order for the CE routers to ping each other? Explain.

   g. How do the dynamic entries in the ARP cache of R5 and R6 compare with each other?

   h. Describe the contents of the MAC FDB of the VPLS.

   i. Describe the contents of the ARP cache on the IES of R4.

   j. In this example, is there an advantage to using a VPLS rather than an epipe service?

Lab Section 20.3: VPRN Services Using PE–CE Static Routing

This lab section investigates how a VPRN can be used to provide connectivity between the CE routers used in the previous lab sections without altering configuration on the CE routers.

Objective In this lab, you will configure a VPRN service to provide connectivity between CE routers using static routes for the PE–CE routing protocol (see Figure 20.17).

Figure 20.17 Lab topology for VPRN.

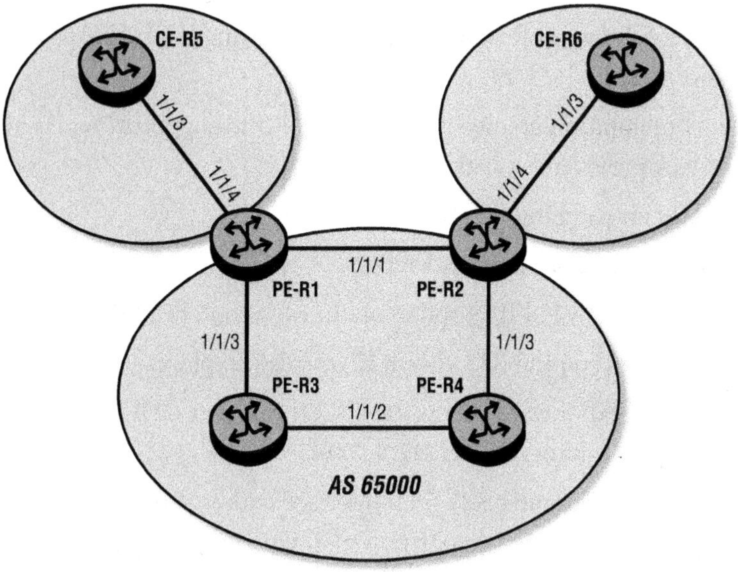

Validation You will know you have succeeded if the CE routers can ping each other.

1. Remove the IES, VPLS, and epipe services from the previous lab section.
2. Configure a full mesh of MP-BGP sessions between R1, R2, R3, and R4 that is capable of supporting the VPN-IPv4 address family. Use an autonomous system of 65000. You can assume that the sessions will not be used to carry regular IPv4 routes.
   a. Verify that all MP-BGP sessions are operationally up before proceeding.
3. Configure a VPRN instance with a service ID of 10 and a customer ID of 100 on R1, R2, R3, and R4.
   a. Use a route distinguisher of 65000:1 on R1, 65000:2 on R2, 65000:3 on R3, and 65000:4 on R4.

b. Configure the VPRN instance on R1 to use an import and export route target of 65000:10.

c. Configure the route target of the other VPRN instances so that all sites of VPRN 10 share routing information.

d. Use the existing SDPs to configure a full mesh of SDP bindings between the PE nodes. What VC ID should be used? Explain.

e. Verify that all spoke SDPs are operationally up on each VPRN before continuing.

f. Check the VRF on several of the PE routers. How many routes are in each VRF?

4. Configure a SAP toward R5 on the R1's VPRN using a VLAN tag of 5 and an IP address of `192.168.5.1/24`.

   a. What configuration change is required on R5 to support the new VPRN in the service provider network?

   b. From R5, can you ping R1's SAP interface?

   c. How many routes are in each VRF?

   d. How many BGP VPN-IPv4 routes are in each router's BGP table?

   e. From R5, can you ping R1's system IP address? Explain.

   f. Configure a SAP toward R6 on the VPRN instance of R2 using a VLAN tag of 6 and an IP address of `192.168.6.2/24`.

   g. Verify that you can ping R2's SAP interface address from R6 before proceeding.

   h. How many routes are in the VRF of each VPRN instance? Explain.

   i. From R5, ping R6's interface to R2. Use the source parameter in the ping

   j. Is the ping successful? Explain.

   k. Configure static routes in the VPRN so that the CE routers can ping each other's system interface.

   l. How many routes are in the VRF of R1 and R2?

5. Shut down the VPRN instances on R3 and R4.

   a. Can the CE routers still ping each other's system interface address? Explain.

   b. Describe the MPLS labels used on the data path between R1 and R2 when traffic is sent between R5 and R6.

Lab Section 20.4 VPRN Services Using PE–CE BGP

The previous lab section used static routes as the PE–CE routing protocol. This lab section changes one of the PE–CE links to use BGP for the PE–CE routing protocol.

Objective In this lab, you will configure one of the PE–CE links to use BGP for the PE–CE routing protocol (see Figure 20.18).

Figure 20.18 VPRN with BGP for PE–CE routing.

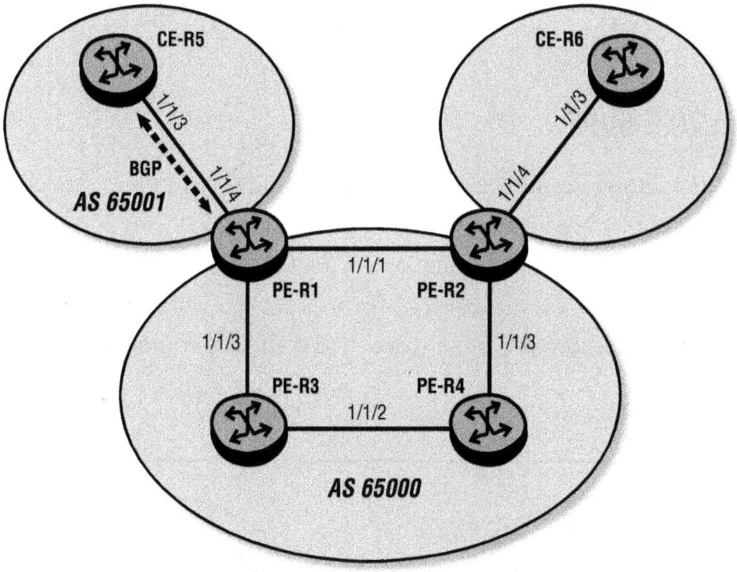

Validation You will know you have succeeded if the CE routers can ping each other.

1. Remove the static default route configuration on R5.
   a. Remove the static route configuration on R1's VPRN interface to R5.
   b. Does the VRF on R2 still have a route for R5's system address?
2. Change the link between R1 and R5 to use BGP for the PE–CE routing protocol. Use an autonomous system of 65001 on R5.
   a. Verify that the BGP session is operationally up before proceeding.
   b. What address families are required on the PE–CE BGP session? Explain.
   c. Advertise R5's system interface into BGP.

d. Is a route policy required on R1 to advertise R5's system interface to R2? Explain.

e. Does the link between R2 and R6 need to be changed to use BGP for communication between the CE routers?

f. Can R1 ping R6's system address from the base router context?

g. Can R1 ping R6's system address from the VPRN router context?

h. From R5, ping R6's system address. Is the ping successful? Explain.

i. Configure an export policy on R1 so that R5 will be able to ping R6's system interface address.

Lab Section 20.5 6VPE

This lab section investigates how a VPRN can be used to provide connectivity between the CE routers used in the previous lab sections.

Objective In this lab, you will configure a VPRN service to provide connectivity between CE routers.

Validation You will know you have succeeded if the CE routers can ping each other (see Figure 20.19).

Figure 20.19 6VPE.

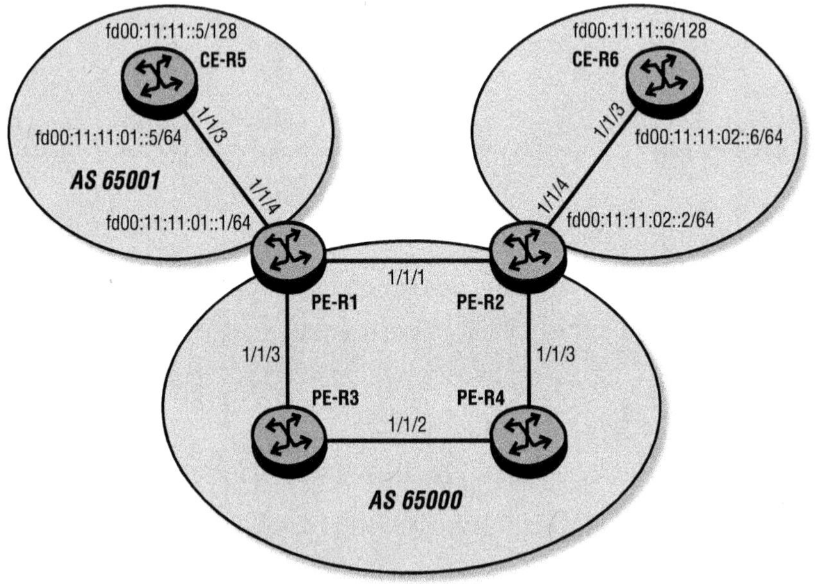

1. Configure the CE routers with the IPv6 system and interface addresses shown in Figure 20.19.
   a. Add the IPv6 interface addresses from Figure 20.19 to the VPRN of each PE router.
   b. Verify that the CE routers can ping their directly connected PE router interfaces.
   c. Configure an IPv6 static default route on R6.
   d. In the VPRN instance of R2, configure an IPv6 static route to R6's system address.
   e. Can R2 ping R6's system interface from inside the VPRN? Explain.
   f. Can R1 ping R6's system address from inside the VPRN? Explain.
   g. Enable the `vpn-ipv6` address family on the MP-BGP sessions between R1 and R2. Assume that the service provider still needs to use the infrastructure to carry `vpn-ipv4` routes.
   h. Can R1 ping R6's system interface from the VPRN router context? Explain.
2. Replace the BGP session between R1 and R5 with one that can exchange IPv6 routes between R1 and R5.
   a. What address family is required?
   b. Verify that the BGP session is operationally up before proceeding.
   c. Configure R5 to distribute its IPv6 system address into BGP.
   d. Can R5 ping R6's system address? Explain.
   e. Configure any required policies to ensure that R5 can ping R6's system interface address.
   f. Can R5 still ping R6's IPv4 system address? Explain.

Chapter Review

Now that you have completed this chapter, you should be able to:

- Describe the purpose of an IES.
- Configure and verify an IES.
- Configure and verify spoke termination on an IES.
- Describe the components of a VPRN.
- Explain the purpose of the VRF.
- Describe CE-to-PE and PE-to-CE routing.
- Explain the purpose of the RD.
- Explain the purpose and operation of the RT.
- Describe how MP-BGP is used for PE-to-PE routing.
- Configure and verify a basic VPRN service.
- Explain the purpose and operation of 6VPE.
- Configure an IPv4 VPRN to interconnect IPv6 networks.

Post-Assessment

The following questions will test your knowledge and prepare you for the Alcatel-Lucent NRS II Certification Exam. Compare your responses with the answers listed in Appendix A. You can also use the CD that accompanies this book to take all the assessment tests and review the answers.

1. An IES spoke termination is used to connect a CE router to an IES interface through an epipe service. Which statement is correct regarding the IP address configuration?

A. The IP address of the CE router interface should be the same as the IP address of the IES interface.

B. The IP address of the CE router interface should be on the same subnet as the IP address of the IES interface.

C. The IP address of the CE router interface should be on a different subnet from the IP address of the IES interface.

D. The IP address configuration depends on whether the IES has been configured in switched or routed mode.

E. None of the above statements are correct.

2. Which statement is *false* regarding the traffic sent between two PE routers of a VPRN in a service provider network that uses RSVP-TE?

A. The traffic has an MPLS transport label.

B. The traffic has an MPLS service label.

C. The traffic has the Layer 2 header sent by the CE router.

D. The traffic has the IP header sent by the CE router.

E. None of the above statements are false.

3. Which statement concerning route distinguishers on the 7750 SR is true?

   A. Route distinguishers are used to determine which routes a VPRN should import.

   B. Different route distinguishers can be used for the same VPRN on different PE routers.

   C. CE routers must be configured with the correct route distinguishers for the VPRN with which they are associated.

   D. P routers only need to be aware of route distinguishers that belong to VPRNs for which they transit traffic.

   E. A route distinguisher is 96 bits in length.

   F. None of the above statements are correct.

4. Which of the following best describes the purpose of MP-BGP in a VPRN?

   A. MP-BGP is an enhanced version of BGP that can carry both IPv4 and IPv6 prefixes.

   B. MP-BGP is an enhanced version of BGP that can carry a service label and customer route prefixes.

   C. MP-BGP is an enhanced version of BGP that can carry a transport label and customer route prefixes.

   D. MP-BGP is an enhanced version of BGP that allows BGP routers to peer with other protocols such as OSPF and RIP for CE-to-PE route exchange.

   E. None of the above statements describes the use of MP-BGP in a VPRN.

5. Which of the following statements regarding 6VPE is *false*?

   A. Both PE and P routers must support both IPv4 and IPv6 addresses; customer routers can use either one.

   B. A single MP-BGP session can be used to carry both VPN-IPv4 and VPN-IPv6 routes.

   C. A single customer's VPRN might contain both IPv4 and IPv6 routes.

   D. Any of the transport methods used for an IPv4 VPRN can be used for 6VPE.

   E. Statements A–D are true.

   F. Statements A–D are false.

6. Which of the following statements concerning Internet Enhanced Services on an Alcatel-Lucent 7750 SR is *false*?

A. An IES can use a mesh SDP.

B. An IES can have a spoke termination to an epipe.

C. An IES can have a spoke termination to a VPLS.

D. An IES can use a SAP.

E. An IES can be advertised into an IGP.

F. An IES can be configured with multiple interfaces.

7. Consider an IES service that has a spoke termination to an epipe service with a service MTU of 9,000 bytes. How should the IES interface MTU be configured?

A. The IES MTU should be configured to exactly 9,000 bytes.

B. The IES MTU should be configured to exactly 9,022 bytes.

C. The IES MTU should be configured to exactly 8,986 bytes.

D. The IES MTU should be configured to exactly 9,014 bytes.

E. The IES MTU should be configured to any value less than 9,000 bytes.

F. The IES MTU should be configured to any value greater than 9,000 bytes.

8. Which of the following statements is *false* regarding an IES spoke termination to an epipe service?

A. Targeted LDP is used to signal service labels for the IES spoke termination.

B. A SAP must be configured on the IES interface.

C. The service ID of the IES and epipe service can be different.

D. The VC ID between the IES interface and epipe must match.

E. The ARP cache of a CE router connected through the spoke termination has the chassis MAC of the PE router with the IES interface.

9. Consider a network of 7750 SRs used to provide VPRN services. There are four PE routers and five P routers in the network. Each PE router has two VPRN services configured. How many T-LDP sessions are required in the network?
   - **A.** No T-LDP sessions are required.
   - **B.** Four T-LDP sessions are required.
   - **C.** Six T-LDP sessions are required.
   - **D.** Eight T-LDP sessions are required.
   - **E.** Twelve T-LDP sessions are required.
   - **F.** Thirty-six T-LDP sessions are required.

10. Consider a network of three 7750 SRs: R1, R2, and R3. A VPRN is configured on all three routers. R1 learns two prefixes from its locally connected CE router. Which statement below is correct about the service labels R1 sends to the other routers for these prefixes?
   - **A.** R1 sends the same service label for both prefixes to R2 and R3.
   - **B.** A single service label is sent to R2 for both prefixes. A different service label is sent to R3 for both prefixes.
   - **C.** A single service label is sent to R2 and R3 for the first prefix. A different service label is sent to R2 and R3 for the second prefix.
   - **D.** A different service label is sent to each router for each prefix.
   - **E.** None of the above statements are correct.

11. Consider a VPRN that is configured on two 7750 SR PE routers, R1 and R2. R1 and its CE router use the PE–CE protocol BGP to exchange routing information. R2 and its CE router use static routes to forward traffic to and from the VPRN. Both sites of the VPRN share all available routing information with each other. Which of the statements below is *false*?

A. The BGP session between R1 and its CE router must be enabled with the IPv4 or IPv6 address family.

B. An export policy must be configured on R1 to advertise routes to the directly connected CE router.

C. An export policy is not required on R2 to advertise routes to the directly connected CE router.

D. An export policy must be configured to advertise routes between the PE routers.

E. None of the above statements are false.

12. An operator needs to provision 6VPE on a 7750 SR that is also used to provide existing IPv4 VPRN services. The IPv6 VPRN customers use BGP as the PE-CE protocol. Which statement below is true regarding the configuration steps required?

A. New LSPs need to be provisioned in the service provider network to support IPv6.

B. New MP-BGP sessions need to be configured in the service provider network to advertise IPv6 routes.

C. The PE-to-CE BGP sessions need to be configured to support the IPv6 and VPN-IPv6 address families.

D. The PE-to-PE BGP sessions need to be configured to support the IPv6 and VPN-IPv6 address families.

E. The route targets on existing IPv4 VPRN services need to be modified.

F. None of the above statements are correct.

13. Which of the following best describes the purpose of the route target?

   A. The route target is added to the IPv4 or IPv6 prefix to create a unique VPN-IPv4 or VPN-IPv6 prefix.

   B. The route target is used by the CE router to identify routes to be taken from its route table and given to the PE router for the VPRN.

   C. The route target is used by the PE router to indentify routes to be taken from MP-BGP and installed in the VRF.

   D. The route target is used by the PE router to identify routes to be taken from the VRF to be sent to the CE router.

   E. None of the above statements describes the purpose of the route target.

14. Which of the following best describes the term *VRF*?

   A. A virtual routing instance that allows a single router to act as multiple virtual routers maintaining multiple route tables

   B. A virtual routing instance that contains a single customer's VPRN routes and peers with the customer's routers

   C. A virtual MP-BGP instance that peers with other MP-BGP instances to exchange routes for a single customer's VPRN across the service provider network

   D. A virtual MP-BGP instance that peers with a single customer's BGP router to exchange the customer's VPRN routes

   E. The Alcatel-Lucent 7750 SR does not support the VRF construct.

15. VPRN routes advertised by PE router R1 (`10.10.10.1`) are not appearing in the VRF on the 7750 SR PE router R2 (`10.10.10.2`). The output from the `show router bgp routes vpn-ipv4` command is shown below:

```
===============================================================================
 BGP Router ID:10.10.10.2       AS:65000       Local AS:65000
===============================================================================
 Legend -
 Status codes  : u - used, s - suppressed, h - history, d - decayed,
 * - valid
 Origin codes  : i - IGP, e - EGP, ? - incomplete, > - best

===============================================================================
BGP VPN-IPv4 Routes
===============================================================================
Flag  Network                                             LocalPref   MED
      Nexthop                                                         VPNLabel
      As-Path
-------------------------------------------------------------------------------
?     65000:11:10.1.0.0/16                                100         None
      10.10.10.1                                                      131071
      65001
i     65000:11:192.168.1.0/30                             100         None
      10.10.10.1                                                      131071
      No As-Path
-------------------------------------------------------------------------------
Routes : 2
===============================================================================
```

Which of the following is the most likely reason these routes do not appear in the VRF?

A. The MP-BGP peering session between R1 and R2 is not operational.

B. The route distinguisher configured for the VPRN on R2 does not match the value configured on R1.

C. The route target configured for the VPRN on R2 does not match the value configured on R1.

D. The transport tunnel between R1 and R2 is not operational.

E. The route distinguisher has not been configured in the VPRN on R2.

21

Operations, Administration, and Maintenance

The Alcatel-Lucent NRS II exam topics covered in this chapter include the following:

- `lsp-ping` and `lsp-trace`
- `sdp-ping` and `sdp-mtu`
- `svc-ping`
- Local service mirroring
- Remote service mirroring
- Mirror slice size

In this chapter, we look at some of the tools available for managing and troubleshooting IP/MPLS service networks. Tools such as `lsp-ping`, `sdp-ping`, and `svc-ping` are available to help diagnose different levels of the service infrastructure.

Another important capability of the Alcatel-Lucent 7750 SR is the ability to perform local and remote service mirroring. This is similar to port mirroring but performed at the level of an individual service. Service mirroring is described in the second section of this chapter.

Pre-Assessment

The following assessment questions will help you understand what areas of the chapter you should review in more detail to prepare for the NRS II exam. You can also use the CD that accompanies this book to take all the assessment tests and review the answers.

1. Which of the following 7750 SR OAM commands can be used to diagnose a far-end epipe service instance that is administratively shut down?

A. `lsp-ping`

B. `lsp-trace`

C. `sdp-ping`

D. `sdp-mtu`

E. `svc-ping`

F. None of the commands can be used to diagnose an epipe service instance that is administratively shut down.

2. An operator issues the command `oam sdp-ping 5` on a 7750 SR. Which of the following statements is true?

A. The `sdp-ping` is sent out-of-band.

B. The `sdp-ping` reply is sent out-of-band.

C. An RSVP-TE LSP must be used for the SDP to use the `sdp-ping` command.

D. An LDP LSP must be used for the SDP to use the `sdp-ping` command.

E. None of the above statements are true.

3. Which of the following statements concerning the `oam lsp-ping` and `oam lsp-trace` commands on the 7750 SR is *false*?

A. Both commands can be used on LDP LSPs.

B. When the `oam lsp-trace` command is used on an RSVP-TE LSP, the hops followed are the same that would be seen with the `traceroute` command to the egress LER.

C. The `lsp-ping` command can be used for measuring round-trip time for a specific forwarding class.

D. For both commands, a UDP packet is encapsulated and sent along the path of the LSP.

E. All of the above statements are true.

4. Which OAM command on the 7750 SR can be used to find the effective MTU of an SDP?

A. `oam lsp-ping`

B. `oam svc-ping`

C. `oam sdp-ping`

D. `oam lsp-trace`

E. None of the above

5. Consider two 7750 SR PE routers that have two epipes between them. One of the epipes is operationally down, and the other is operationally up. Which statement is correct?

A. An `lsp-ping` between the routers will fail.

B. An `sdp-ping` between the routers will fail.

C. An `svc-ping` will be successful for the operationally up epipe and will fail for the operationally down epipe.

D. There is not enough information to answer the question.

21.1 OAM Overview

Operations, administration, and maintenance (OAM) tools are provided in modern routers to help manage and troubleshoot the network. The tools that we examine in this chapter include the following:

- `lsp-ping` and `lsp-trace`—These allow the network operator to diagnose and discover the condition of MPLS paths in the network.
- `sdp-ping` and `sdp-mtu`—These allow the network operator to diagnose and discover details about a configured SDP (Service Distribution Point), including the path MTU (maximum transmission unit).
- `svc-ping`—This tool allows the network operator to diagnose a configured service and the SDP bindings for the service at both the local and remote ends.

`lsp-ping` and `lsp-trace` are based on industry standards defined in RFC 4379 and can interoperate with other vendor's equipment. `sdp-ping` and `svc-ping` are tools proprietary to the Alcatel-Lucent 7750 SR.

These are some of the core OAM tools available on the 7750 SR. There are many other management tools available on the 7750 SR that are outside the scope of this book.

lsp-ping and lsp-trace

`lsp-ping` and `lsp-trace` can be used on either LDP (Label Distribution Protocol) or RSVP-TE (Resource Reservation Protocol–Traffic Engineering) LSPs (label switched paths) to verify the data path for the LSP. A UDP (User Datagram Protocol) packet is MPLS (Multiprotocol Label Switching)–encapsulated and transmitted along the LSP. In the case of an `lsp-trace`, the packet is given to the control plane of each transit LSR (label switch router) for verification. Figure 21.1 shows the network topology used to demonstrate the use of `lsp-ping` and `lsp-trace`. The default metric in this network is 100, and two links have been set with a metric of 1,000 to force traffic on a specific LSP. The default port MTU is 9,212 bytes, but this has been set to 1,514 bytes on the link between R3 and R5. Listing 21.1 shows the use of `lsp-ping` and `lsp-trace` for LDP from R1 to R6.

Figure 21.1 Topology for demonstrating lsp-ping.

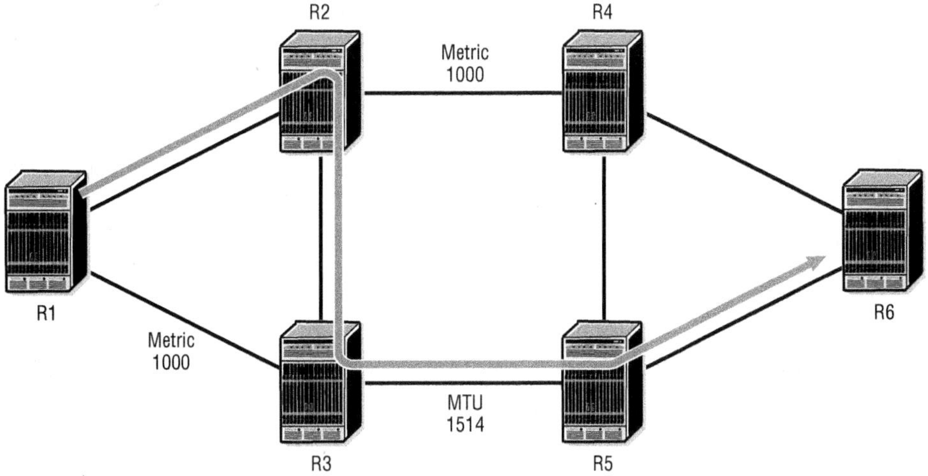

Listing 21.1 lsp-ping and lsp-trace for LDP

```
*A:R1# oam lsp-ping prefix 10.10.10.6/32
LSP-PING 10.10.10.6/32: 80 bytes MPLS payload
Seq=1, send from intf toR2, reply from 10.10.10.6
       udp-data-len=32 ttl=255 rtt=3.36ms rc=3 (EgressRtr)

---- LSP 10.10.10.6/32 PING Statistics ----
1 packets sent, 1 packets received, 0.00% packet loss
round-trip min = 3.36ms, avg = 3.36ms, max = 3.36ms, stddev = 0.000ms

*A:R1# oam lsp-trace prefix 10.10.10.6/32 detail
lsp-trace to 10.10.10.6/32: 0 hops min, 0 hops max, 104 byte packets
1  10.10.10.2  rtt=1.14ms rc=8(DSRtrMatchLabel)
     DS 1: IfAddr 10.2.3.3 MRU=9198 label=131067 proto=3(LDP)
2  10.10.10.3  rtt=1.45ms rc=8(DSRtrMatchLabel)
     DS 1: IfAddr 10.3.5.5 MRU=1500 label=131066 proto=3(LDP)
3  10.10.10.5  rtt=1.69ms rc=8(DSRtrMatchLabel)
     DS 1: IfAddr 10.5.6.6 MRU=9198 label=131071 proto=3(LDP)
```

(continued)

Listing 21.1 *(continued)*

```
4  10.10.10.6  rtt=3.05ms rc=3(EgressRtr)

*A:R1# traceroute 10.10.10.6
traceroute to 10.10.10.6, 30 hops max, 40 byte packets
  1  10.1.2.2 (10.1.2.2)    1.99 ms  1.70 ms  1.70 ms
  2  10.2.3.3 (10.2.3.3)    2.05 ms  2.05 ms  2.06 ms
  3  10.3.5.5 (10.3.5.5)    2.28 ms  2.22 ms  2.23 ms
  4  10.10.10.6 (10.10.10.6)    3.46 ms  9.90 ms  3.12 ms
```

The use of `lsp-ping` and `lsp-trace` is similar for RSVP-TE, although the LSP is specified by name. Listing 21.2 shows the results with an RSVP-TE LSP.

Listing 21.2 Use of lsp-ping and lsp-trace on an RSVP-TE LSP

```
*A:R1# show router mpls lsp

===========================================================================
MPLS LSPs (Originating)
===========================================================================
LSP Name                        To              Fastfail      Adm   Opr
                                                Config
---------------------------------------------------------------------------
toR6                            10.10.10.6      No            Up    Up
---------------------------------------------------------------------------
LSPs : 1
===========================================================================
*A:R1# oam lsp-ping "toR6"
LSP-PING toR6: 92 bytes MPLS payload
Seq=1, send from intf toR2, reply from 10.10.10.6
       udp-data-len=32 ttl=255 rtt=3.52ms rc=3 (EgressRtr)

---- LSP toR6 PING Statistics ----
1 packets sent, 1 packets received, 0.00% packet loss
round-trip min = 3.52ms, avg = 3.52ms, max = 3.52ms, stddev = 0.000ms
*A:R1# oam lsp-trace "toR6" detail
lsp-trace to toR6: 0 hops min, 0 hops max, 116 byte packets
1  10.10.10.2  rtt=1.34ms rc=8(DSRtrMatchLabel)
```

```
      DS 1: IfAddr 10.2.3.3 MRU=9198 label=131065 proto=4(RSVP-TE)
2  10.10.10.3  rtt=1.44ms rc=8(DSRtrMatchLabel)
      DS 1: IfAddr 10.3.5.5 MRU=1500 label=131065 proto=4(RSVP-TE)
3  10.10.10.5  rtt=2.21ms rc=8(DSRtrMatchLabel)
      DS 1: IfAddr 10.5.6.6 MRU=9198 label=131065 proto=4(RSVP-TE)
4  10.10.10.6  rtt=2.86ms rc=3(EgressRtr)
```

`lsp-ping` can be used for additional functions, such as measuring the round-trip time for a specific forwarding class, or testing the path MTU. The size of the MPLS payload can be specified as a parameter and used to determine the effective MTU of the path. Because the R3-to-R5 link has a port MTU of 1,514, the maximum MPLS payload that can be accommodated is 1,514 bytes – 14 bytes (Ethernet header) – 4 bytes (MPLS label) = 1,496 bytes. Verification of this is shown in Listing 21.3.

Listing 21.3 Using lsp-ping to verify LDP path MTU

```
*A:R1# oam lsp-trace prefix 10.10.10.6/32 size 1496 detail
lsp-trace to 10.10.10.6/32: 0 hops min, 0 hops max, 1496 byte packets
1  10.10.10.2  rtt=1.27ms rc=8(DSRtrMatchLabel)
      DS 1: IfAddr 10.2.3.3 MRU=9198 label=131067 proto=3(LDP)
2  10.10.10.3  rtt=1.64ms rc=8(DSRtrMatchLabel)
      DS 1: IfAddr 10.3.5.5 MRU=1500 label=131066 proto=3(LDP)
3  10.10.10.5  rtt=2.40ms rc=8(DSRtrMatchLabel)
      DS 1: IfAddr 10.5.6.6 MRU=9198 label=131071 proto=3(LDP)
4  10.10.10.6  rtt=3.51ms rc=3(EgressRtr)
*A:R1# oam lsp-trace prefix 10.10.10.6/32 size 1497 detail
lsp-trace to 10.10.10.6/32: 0 hops min, 0 hops max, 1497 byte packets
1  10.10.10.2  rtt=1.30ms rc=8(DSRtrMatchLabel)
      DS 1: IfAddr 10.2.3.3 MRU=9198 label=131067 proto=3(LDP)
2  10.10.10.3  rtt=1.76ms rc=8(DSRtrMatchLabel)
      DS 1: IfAddr 10.3.5.5 MRU=1500 label=131066 proto=3(LDP)
3  0.0.0.0  *
4  0.0.0.0  *
5  0.0.0.0  *
6  0.0.0.0  *
7  0.0.0.0  *
*A:R1# oam lsp-ping prefix 10.10.10.6/32 size 1497
LSP-PING 10.10.10.6/32: 1497 bytes MPLS payload
```

(continued)

Listing 21.3 *(continued)*

```
Request timed out.

---- LSP 10.10.10.6/32 PING Statistics ----
1 packets sent, 0 packets received, 100.00% packet loss
```

sdp-ping and sdp-mtu

`sdp-ping` is used to test the encapsulation of an SDP. The ping can be either unidirectional or bidirectional. If the remote SDP is not specified, the ping is unidirectional, and the reply is sent out-of-band as a routed IP packet.

Figure 21.2 shows a network topology with an SDP configured between R1 and R6. The SDP ID at R1 is 6, and the SDP ID on R6 is 1. Listing 21.4 shows a unidirectional ping, a bidirectional ping, and a ping with a count greater than one. A single ping provides a more detailed output.

Figure 21.2 Topology to demonstrate sdp-ping.

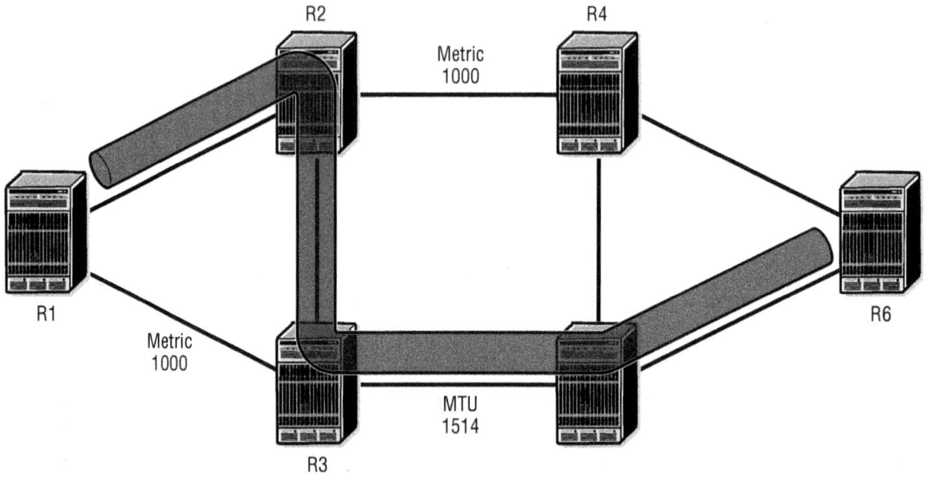

Listing 21.4 Different options for an sdp-ping

```
*A:R1# show service sdp 6

===============================================================================
```

```
Service Destination Point (Sdp Id : 6)
==========================================================================
SdpId    Adm MTU  Opr MTU  IP address     Adm  Opr       Deliver   Signal
--------------------------------------------------------------------------
6        0        9190     10.10.10.6     Up   Up        LDP       TLDP
==========================================================================
*A:R1# oam sdp-ping 6
Err SDP-ID Info              Local           Remote
--------------------------------------------------
    SDP-ID:                  6               N/A
    Administrative State:    Up              N/A
    Operative State:         Up              N/A
    Path MTU:                9190            N/A
    Response SDP Used:                       No

    IP Interface State:      Up
    Actual IP Address:       10.10.10.1      10.10.10.6
    Expected Peer IP:        10.10.10.6      10.10.10.1

    Forwarding Class         be              be
    Profile                  Out             Out

Request Result: Sent - Reply Received
RTT: 2.72(ms)

*A:R1# oam sdp-ping 6 resp-sdp 1
Err SDP-ID Info              Local           Remote
--------------------------------------------------
    SDP-ID:                  6               1
    Administrative State:    Up              Up
    Operative State:         Up              Up
    Path MTU:                9190            N/A
    Response SDP Used:                       Yes

    IP Interface State:      Up
    Actual IP Address:       10.10.10.1      10.10.10.6
    Expected Peer IP:        10.10.10.6      10.10.10.1

    Forwarding Class         be              be
```

(continued)

Listing 21.4 *(continued)*

```
    Profile                      Out                 Out

Request Result: Sent - Reply Received
RTT: 2.89(ms)

*A:R1# oam sdp-ping 6 resp-sdp 1 count 5
Request      Response     RTT
----------------------------------------------------
1            Success      3.72ms
2            Success      2.85ms
3            Success      2.80ms
4            Success      3.14ms
5            Success      3.06ms

Sent: 5     Received: 5
Min: 2.80ms    Max: 3.72ms    Avg: 3.11ms
```

From Figure 21.2, you can see that the link between R3 and R5 on the SDP to R6 has an MTU of 1,514 bytes. However, the SDP has a path MTU of 9,190 bytes, as seen in listing 21.4. As described in Chapter 18, the path MTU is set based on the network port MTU unless `adspec` is configured on the RSVP-TE LSP. The path MTU is calculated as the port MTU of 9,212 bytes – 8 bytes (MPLS overhead) – 14 bytes (Layer 2 header) = 9,190 bytes. The `sdp-mtu` command can be used to find the actual path MTU of the SDP, as shown in Listing 21.5. The value of 1,492 bytes is as expected for a port MTU of 1,514 bytes (1,514 – 8 – 14 = 1,492).

Listing 21.5 Using sdp-mtu to find the effective path MTU for an SDP

```
*A:R1# show service sdp 6

============================================================================
Service Destination Point (Sdp Id : 6)
============================================================================
SdpId     Adm MTU   Opr MTU   IP address      Adm   Opr       Deliver   Signal
----------------------------------------------------------------------------
```

```
6         0         9190      10.10.10.6       Up    Up          LDP         TLDP
=================================================================================
*A:R1# oam sdp-mtu 6 size-inc 1450 1550 step 10
Size     Sent     Response
----------------------------
1450     .         Success
1460     .         Success
1470     .         Success
1480     .         Success
1490     .         Success
1500     ...       Request Timeout

Maximum Response Size: 1490
*A:R1# oam sdp-mtu 6 size-inc 1490 1500 step 1
Size     Sent     Response
----------------------------
1490     .         Success
1491     .         Success
1492     .         Success
1493     ...       Request Timeout

Maximum Response Size: 1492
```

Note that the path MTU is 4 bytes less than the MTU discovered using `lsp-ping` in Listing 21.3. This is because `lsp-ping` uses only a single MPLS label, whereas `sdp-mtu` uses both the service and transport label.

svc-ping

`svc-ping` verifies the correct configuration of a service and can help to verify any misconfiguration. The parameter `local-sdp` specifies that the ping should be sent to the far-end in-band using the SDP, and the parameter `remote-sdp` specifies that the return ping should be sent in-band. If these are not specified, the ping is sent out-of-band. Listing 21.6 shows two examples of `svc-ping` for the epipe configured in Figure 21.3. The first specifies `local-sdp`, and the output shows that the SDP was not used by the remote end.

Figure 21.3 Network for demonstrating svc-ping.

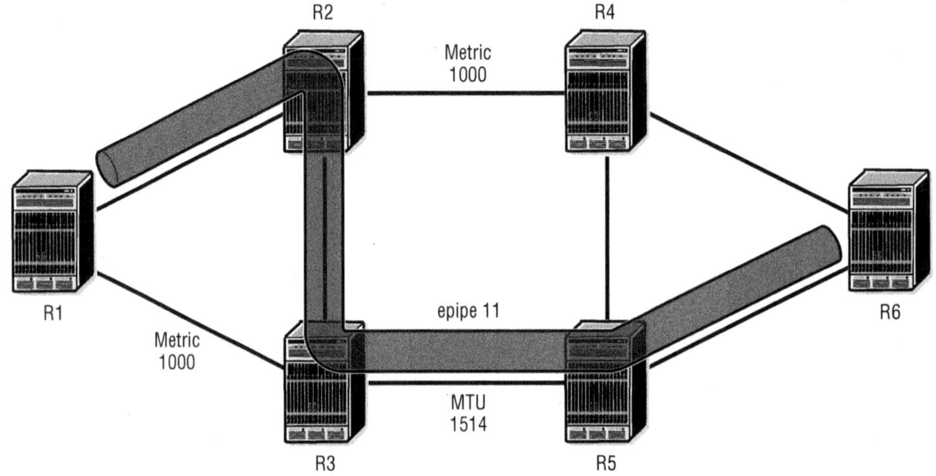

Listing 21.6 Output from svc-ping

```
*A:R1# oam svc-ping 10.10.10.6 service 11 local-sdp
Service-ID: 11

Err Info                 Local           Remote
-----------------------------------------------------
    Type:                EPIPE           EPIPE
    Admin State:         Up              Up
    Oper State:          Up              Up
    Service-MTU:         1514            1514
    Customer ID:         1               1

    IP Interface State: Up
    Actual IP Addr:      10.10.10.1      10.10.10.6
    Expected Peer IP:    10.10.10.6      10.10.10.1

    SDP Path Used:       Yes             No
    SDP-ID:              6               1
    Admin State:         Up              Up
    Operative State:     Up              Up
    Binding Admin State:Up               Up
    Binding Oper State: Up               Up
```

```
    Binding VC ID:       11               11
    Binding Type:        Spoke            Spoke
    Binding Vc-type:     Ether            Ether
    Binding Vlan-vc-tag:N/A               N/A

    Egress Label:        131061           131065
    Ingress Label:       131065           131061
    Egress Label Type:   Signaled         Signaled
    Ingress Label Type: Signaled          Signaled

Request Result: Sent - Reply Received
*A:R1# oam svc-ping 10.10.10.6 service 11 local-sdp remote-sdp
Service-ID: 11

Err Info                 Local            Remote
-----------------------------------------------------
    Type:                EPIPE            EPIPE
    Admin State:         Up               Up
    Oper State:          Up               Up
    Service-MTU:         1514             1514
    Customer ID:         1                1

    IP Interface State: Up
    Actual IP Addr:      10.10.10.1       10.10.10.6
    Expected Peer IP:    10.10.10.6       10.10.10.1

    SDP Path Used:       Yes              Yes
    SDP-ID:              6                1
    Admin State:         Up               Up
    Operative State:     Up               Up
    Binding Admin State:Up                Up
    Binding Oper State: Up                Up
    Binding VC ID:       11               11
    Binding Type:        Spoke            Spoke
    Binding Vc-type:     Ether            Ether
    Binding Vlan-vc-tag:N/A               N/A

    Egress Label:        131061           131065
    Ingress Label:       131065           131061
```

(continued)

Listing 21.6 *(continued)*

```
    Egress Label Type:  Signaled        Signaled
    Ingress Label Type: Signaled        Signaled

Request Result: Sent - Reply Received
```

Notice that the output shows the service MTU as the configured value for the epipe. There is no verification by `svc-ping` that the service is actually able to transport a payload of this size. The `sdp-mtu` command in Listing 21.5 shows that the effective path MTU for this service is actually 1,492 bytes.

21.2 Service Mirroring

Many traditional routers and switches provide the capability of mirroring ports. This capability allows the operator to replicate traffic received or sent on one port to be replicated on another. The 7750 SR provides a similar feature with some much more powerful capabilities. The significant differences are the following:

- The mirror source cannot only be a port, but other service entities such as a SAP (Service Access Point), MPLS label, IP filter, or MAC (Media Access Control) filter.
- The replicated traffic cannot only be sent to a destination on the local switch, but also through an SDP to a remote location.

In the sections below, we look first at traffic mirrored to a local switch and then remote mirroring, in which the traffic is sent to a remote switch.

The replication of packets is handled by the hardware on the Input/Output Module (IOM) and thus has minimal impact on router performance. However, it is important to remember that mirroring involves the duplication of traffic and thus increases the bandwidth required. If ingress and egress traffic on a 1 Gb/s port is mirrored, this could represent as much as an additional 2 Gb/s of traffic to the mirror destination.

Local Service Mirror

A *local service mirror* replicates traffic from a mirror source to a mirror destination on the same device. When defining the local mirror, the mirror destination is created first, as a mirror service. The mirror service includes a SAP that identifies where the traffic is replicated. If a dot1Q encapsulation is used, the same physical port can be used for multiple distinct service destinations.

Once the service destination is created, the mirror source is defined using the `debug mirror-source` command. The mirror source can be one of the following:

- Port
- SAP
- IP filter
- MAC filter
- Ingress label
- Subscriber (the subscriber feature is beyond the scope of this book)

Figure 21.4 shows a service provider network providing an epipe between two customer routers.

Figure 21.4 Local mirror topology.

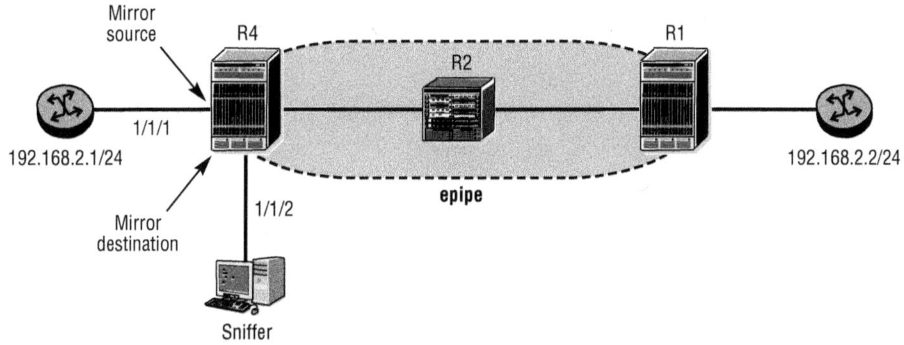

Listing 21.7 shows the configuration of the mirror destination and the mirror source on the PE router for the epipe service. The mirror source is configured on SAP 1/1/1 of the epipe to mirror both ingress and egress traffic.

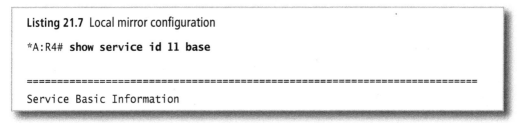

Listing 21.7 Local mirror configuration

```
*A:R4# show service id 11 base

===============================================================================
Service Basic Information
```

(continued)

Listing 21.7 *(continued)*

```
===============================================================================
Service Id        : 11                    Vpn Id            : 0
Service Type      : Epipe
Name              : (Not Specified)
Description       : (Not Specified)
Customer Id       : 1
Last Status Change: 05/23/2011 12:47:59
Last Mgmt Change  : 05/23/2011 12:36:14
Admin State       : Up                    Oper State        : Up
MTU               : 1514
Vc Switching      : False
SAP Count         : 1                     SDP Bind Count    : 1
Per Svc Hashing   : Disabled
Force QTag Fwd    : Disabled

-------------------------------------------------------------------------------
Service Access & Destination Points
-------------------------------------------------------------------------------
Identifier                          Type         AdmMTU  OprMTU  Adm  Opr
-------------------------------------------------------------------------------
sap:1/1/1                           null         1514    1514    Up   Up
sdp:1:11 S(10.10.10.1)              Spok         0       9190    Up   Up
===============================================================================
*A:R4# configure mirror mirror-dest 101
*A:R4>config>mirror>mirror-dest# info
---------------------------------------------
            sap 1/1/2 create
            exit
            no shutdown
---------------------------------------------
*A:R4>config>mirror>mirror-dest# exit
*A:R4# show service service-using mirror

===============================================================================
Services [mirror]
===============================================================================
ServiceId  Type      Adm  Opr  CustomerId Service Name
-------------------------------------------------------------------------------
```

```
101         Mirror     Up    Up    1
-------------------------------------------------------------------------------
Matching Services : 1
-------------------------------------------------------------------------------
===============================================================================
*A:R4# debug mirror-source 101
*A:R4>debug>mirror-source# sap 1/1/1 ingress egress
*A:R4>debug>mirror-source# no shutdown
*A:R4>debug>mirror-source# exit
*A:R4# show debug
debug
    mirror-source 101
        sap 1/1/1 egress ingress
        no shutdown
    exit
exit
```

Figure 21.4 shows a packet sniffer attached to port 1/1/2 of router R4. The mirrored traffic is transmitted on this port and received by the sniffer. For this example, we have configured a router with an IP filter on an epipe SAP to emulate the sniffer. The filter captures traffic sent to the IP address of the far-end router, and its configuration is shown in Listing 21.8.

Listing 21.8 Configuration of an IP filter on the "sniffer" router

```
*A:Sniffer# configure filter
*A:Sniffer>config>filter# info
----------------------------------------------
        log 111 create
            destination memory 100
        exit
        ip-filter 11 create
            entry 10 create
                match
                    dst-ip 192.168.2.0/24
                exit
                log 111
```

(continued)

Listing 21.8 *(continued)*

```
                action drop
            exit
        exit
----------------------------------------------
*A:Sniffer>config>filter# exit
*A:Sniffer# configure service epipe 111
*A:Sniffer>config>service>epipe# info
----------------------------------------------
            sap 1/1/2 create
                ingress
                    filter ip 11
                exit
            exit
            sap 1/1/3 create
            exit
            no shutdown
----------------------------------------------
```

If we ping the far-end CE (customer edge) router with a count of two, the packets are replicated and sent to the mirror destination. This can be seen by viewing the filter log as shown in Listing 21.9. Because the packets are replicated, the original packets are still forwarded through the epipe and a reply received. Both ingress traffic and egress traffic are mirrored, thus we see both the echo request and the echo reply.

Listing 21.9 Mirrored traffic of two ping packets is seen on the "sniffer" router

```
*A:Sniffer# show filter log 111

===========================================================================
Filter Log
===========================================================================
Admin state : Enabled
Description : (Not Specified)
Destination : Memory
Wrap        : Enabled
---------------------------------------------------------------------------
Maximum entries configured : 100
```

```
Number of entries logged    : 4
2011/05/23 19:41:48  Ip Filter: 11:10  Desc:
SAP: 1/1/2  Direction: Ingress  Action: Drop
Src MAC: 00-03-fa-ac-b8-26  Dst MAC: 00-03-fa-c6-f0-9c  EtherType: 0800
Src IP: 192.168.2.1  Dst IP: 192.168.2.2  Flags: 0  TOS: 00  TTL: 64
Protocol: ICMP  Type: Echo Request  Code: 0

2011/05/23 19:41:48  Ip Filter: 11:10  Desc:
SAP: 1/1/2  Direction: Ingress  Action: Drop
Src MAC: 00-03-fa-c6-f0-9c  Dst MAC: 00-03-fa-ac-b8-26  EtherType: 0800
Src IP: 192.168.2.2  Dst IP: 192.168.2.1  Flags: 0  TOS: 00  TTL: 64
Protocol: ICMP  Type: Echo Reply  Code: 0

2011/05/23 19:41:49  Ip Filter: 11:10  Desc:
SAP: 1/1/2  Direction: Ingress  Action: Drop
Src MAC: 00-03-fa-ac-b8-26  Dst MAC: 00-03-fa-c6-f0-9c  EtherType: 0800
Src IP: 192.168.2.1  Dst IP: 192.168.2.2  Flags: 0  TOS: 00  TTL: 64
Protocol: ICMP  Type: Echo Request  Code: 0

2011/05/23 19:41:49  Ip Filter: 11:10  Desc:
SAP: 1/1/2  Direction: Ingress  Action: Drop
Src MAC: 00-03-fa-c6-f0-9c  Dst MAC: 00-03-fa-ac-b8-26  EtherType: 0800
Src IP: 192.168.2.2  Dst IP: 192.168.2.1  Flags: 0  TOS: 00  TTL: 64
Protocol: ICMP  Type: Echo Reply  Code: 0

==========================================================================
```

Remote Service Mirror

In a *remote service mirror*, the router with the mirror source has an SDP as the mirror destination. The mirrored traffic is encapsulated as defined by the SDP (either MPLS labels or GRE [generic routing encapsulation]) and sent to the far-end router. On the far-end router there is a local mirror destination defined that accepts the packets from the remote source. Figure 21.5 shows the same epipe service as above; however, the mirror source in this case is configured on the other PE (provider Edge) router, R1.

Figure 21.5 Remote mirror topology.

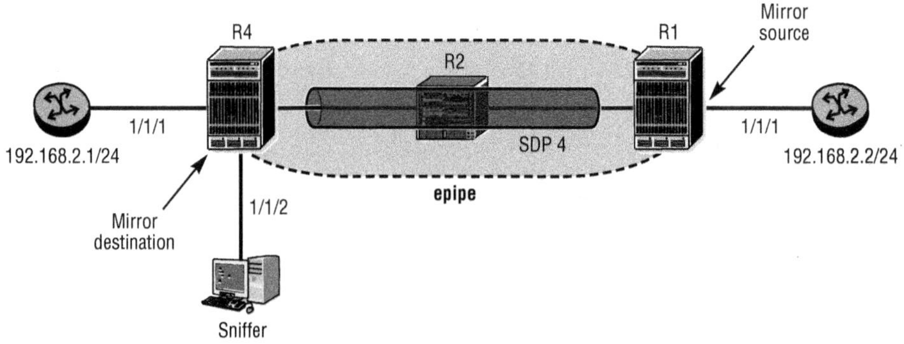

Listing 21.10 shows the mirror source configured as an IP filter on R1. The same result could be achieved by specifying the SAP as in the example above, but we use a filter to demonstrate a different technique. Notice that the destination specified on R1 is SDP 4.

Listing 21.10 Configuration of the mirror source on R1

```
*A:R1# configure mirror mirror-dest 101 create
*A:R1>config>mirror>mirror-dest# spoke-sdp 4:101 create
*A:R1>config>mirror>mirror-dest>spoke-sdp$ exit
*A:R1>config>mirror>mirror-dest# no shutdown
*A:R1>config>mirror>mirror-dest# exit
*A:R1# show service sdp-using

===============================================================================
SDP Using
===============================================================================
SvcId        SdpId              Type    Far End           Opr S* I.Label  E.Label
-------------------------------------------------------------------------------
11           4:11               Spok    10.10.10.4        Up     131064   131069
101          4:101              Spok    10.10.10.4        Down   n/a      0
-------------------------------------------------------------------------------
Number of SDPs : 2
-------------------------------------------------------------------------------
===============================================================================
* indicates that the corresponding row element may have been truncated.
*A:R1# configure filter ip-filter 11 create
*A:R1>config>filter>ip-filter$ entry 10 create
```

```
*A:R1>config>filter>ip-filter>entry$ match dst-ip 192.168.2.2/32
*A:R1>config>filter>ip-filter>entry$ action forward
*A:R1>config>filter>ip-filter>entry$ exit
*A:R1>config>filter>ip-filter# default-action forward
*A:R1>config>filter>ip-filter# info
----------------------------------------------
            default-action forward
            entry 10 create
                match
                    dst-ip 192.168.2.2/32
                exit
                action forward
            exit
----------------------------------------------
*A:R1>config>filter>ip-filter# exit all
*A:R1# configure service epipe 11
*A:R1>config>service>epipe# sap 1/1/1
*A:R1>config>service>epipe>sap# egress filter ip 11
*A:R1>config>service>epipe>sap# exit
*A:R1>config>service>epipe# info
----------------------------------------------
            sap 1/1/1 create
                egress
                    filter ip 11
                exit
            exit
            spoke-sdp 4:11 create
            exit
            no shutdown
----------------------------------------------
*A:R1>config>service>epipe# exit
*A:R1# debug mirror-source 101
*A:R1>debug>mirror-source# ip-filter 11 entry 10
*A:R1>debug>mirror-source# exit
*A:R1# show debug
debug
    mirror-source 101
        ip-filter 11 entry 10
        no shutdown
    exit
exit
```

The spoke binding used for the mirror service is still down, because the far end has not been configured and thus there is no egress label. The next step is to configure the mirror destination at the far end of the tunnel—on R4 in this example. Listing 21.11 shows the configuration of the remote mirror destination. The first step is to remove the local mirror source from the previous example. Only the remote source needs to be specified in the mirror destination service that already exists.

Listing 21.11 Remote mirror destination on R4

```
*A:R4# show debug
debug
    mirror-source 101
        sap 1/1/1 egress ingress
        no shutdown
    exit
exit
*A:R4# debug no mirror-source 101
*A:R4# configure mirror mirror-dest 101
*A:R4>config>mirror>mirror-dest# remote-source
*A:R4>config>mirror>mirror-dest>remote-source# far-end 10.10.10.1
*A:R4>config>mirror>mirror-dest>remote-source# exit
*A:R4>config>mirror>mirror-dest# info
----------------------------------------------
            remote-source
                far-end 10.10.10.1
            exit
            sap 1/1/2 create
            exit
            no shutdown
----------------------------------------------
```

Once the remote mirror destination is configured on R4, an egress label is signaled to R1 using T-LDP (Targeted LDP), and the mirror service is up (see Listing 21.12). There is no egress label signaled by R1 because a mirror service really only requires a one-way pseudowire. The label can also be statically configured.

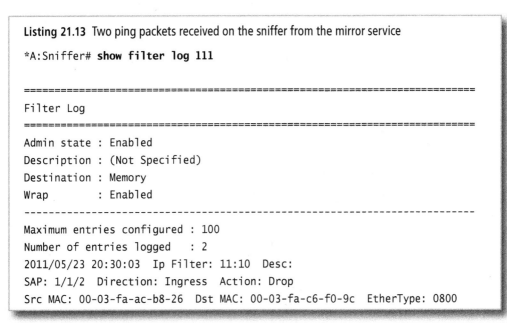

Listing 21.12 Status of the SDP bindings on R1

```
*A:R1# show service sdp-using

===============================================================================
SDP Using
===============================================================================
SvcId        SdpId            Type     Far End          Opr S* I.Label  E.Label
-------------------------------------------------------------------------------
11           4:11             Spok     10.10.10.4       Up     131064   131069
101          4:101            Spok     10.10.10.4       Up     n/a      131066
-------------------------------------------------------------------------------
Number of SDPs : 2
-------------------------------------------------------------------------------
===============================================================================
* indicates that the corresponding row element may have been truncated.
```

After the remote mirror is configured, the filter log is cleared, and two ping packets are sent to the far-end CE router, we see two packets on the "sniffer" router (see Listing 21.13). There are only two in this case because the IP filter for the mirror source specified only the destination IP address of the ping.

Listing 21.13 Two ping packets received on the sniffer from the mirror service

```
*A:Sniffer# show filter log 111

===============================================================================
Filter Log
===============================================================================
Admin state : Enabled
Description : (Not Specified)
Destination : Memory
Wrap        : Enabled
-------------------------------------------------------------------------------
Maximum entries configured : 100
Number of entries logged   : 2
2011/05/23 20:30:03  Ip Filter: 11:10  Desc:
SAP: 1/1/2  Direction: Ingress  Action: Drop
Src MAC: 00-03-fa-ac-b8-26  Dst MAC: 00-03-fa-c6-f0-9c  EtherType: 0800
```

(continued)

Listing 21.13 *(continued)*

```
Src IP: 192.168.2.1  Dst IP: 192.168.2.2  Flags: 0  TOS: 00  TTL: 64
Protocol: ICMP  Type: Echo Request  Code: 0

2011/05/23 20:30:04  Ip Filter: 11:10  Desc:
SAP: 1/1/2  Direction: Ingress  Action: Drop
Src MAC: 00-03-fa-ac-b8-26  Dst MAC: 00-03-fa-c6-f0-9c  EtherType: 0800
Src IP: 192.168.2.1  Dst IP: 192.168.2.2  Flags: 0  TOS: 00  TTL: 64
Protocol: ICMP  Type: Echo Request  Code: 0

===========================================================================
```

Mirror Slice Size

When defining the mirror source, a *slice size* can be defined to reduce mirroring overhead. When a slice size is configured, all mirrored packets are truncated after the specified number of bytes have been replicated. In Listing 21.14, a mirror destination is defined for the remote mirror service with a slice size of 128. The transmitted packet will be slightly larger because of encapsulation overhead, but no more than 128 bytes of the original packet will be transmitted. The original packets are not affected by mirror slicing.

Listing 21.14 Configuring slice size for a remote mirror service

```
A:R1# configure mirror mirror-dest 101
A:R1>config>mirror>mirror-dest# slice-size 128
*A:R1>config>mirror>mirror-dest# info
----------------------------------------------
            spoke-sdp 4:101 create
            exit
            slice-size 128
            no shutdown
----------------------------------------------
*A:R1>config>mirror>mirror-dest#
```

Practice Lab: Operations, Administration, and Maintenance

The following lab is designed to reinforce your knowledge of the content in this chapter. Please review the instructions carefully, and perform the steps in the order in which they are presented. The practice labs require that you have access to six or more Alcatel-Lucent 7750 SRs or Alcatel-Lucent 7450 ESSs in a non-production environment.

> These labs are designed to be used in a controlled lab environment. Please *do not* attempt to perform these labs in a production environment.

Lab Section 21.1: OAM Tools

This lab section investigates the use of the `lsp-ping`, `lsp-trace`, `sdp-ping`, and `svc-ping` OAM tools on a services infrastructure.

Objective In this exercise, you will use OAM tools to diagnose LSPs, SDPs, and service instances (see Figure 21.6).

Figure 21.6 Lab topology for OAM Lab.

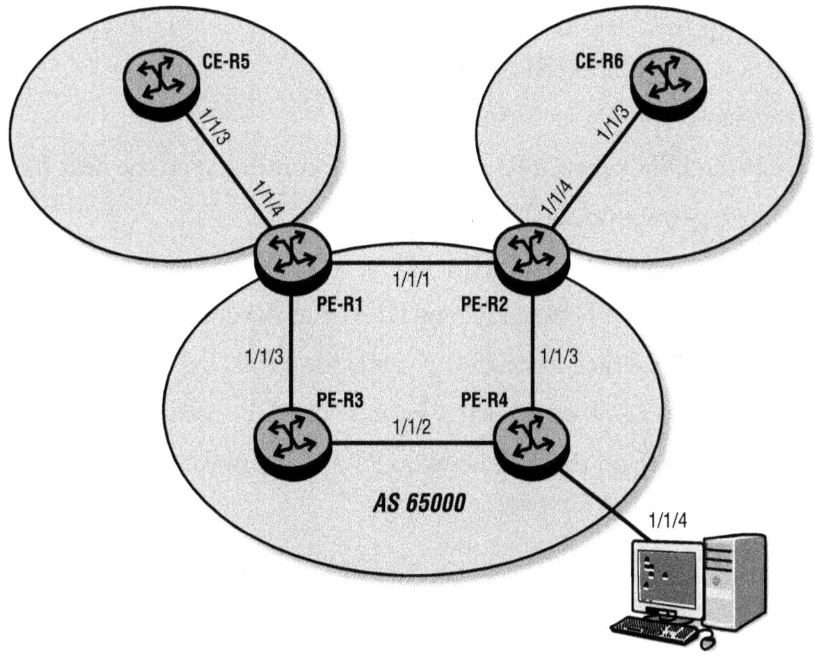

Validation You will know you have succeeded if you can explain the result of the various OAM tools used.

1. Configure an epipe service between R1 and R2 using null-encapsulated SAPs to the CE routers R5 and R6. Use RSVP-TE-signaled LSPs enabled with one-to-one fast reroute (FRR). For the LSP on R5, use a strict path directly to R2. For the LSP on R6, use a loose path.

   If you have completed previous labs, part of this configuration may already be done.

   a. Configure the IP address `192.168.99.5/24` on R5's interface to R1.
   b. Configure the IP address `192.168.99.6/24` on R6's interface to R2.
   c. Verify that you can ping between CE routers before moving to the next step.
2. Perform an `lsp-ping` on the LSP between R1 and R2.
   a. Is the `lsp-ping` successful?
   b. Administratively shut down the LSP on R2 toward R1.
   c. Is the same `lsp-ping` successful? Explain.
   d. Enable the LSP on R2 toward R1.
   e. Shut down the LSP on R1 toward R2.
   f. Is the same `lsp-ping` successful? Explain.
   g. Enable the LSPs between R1 and R2 before continuing to the next step.
3. Perform an `lsp-trace` on the LSP between R1 and R2.
   a. What is the result of the `lsp-trace`?
   b. Shut down the port between R1 and R2 so that the detour LSP becomes active.
   c. Is the same `lsp-trace` successful? What is the result? Explain.
   d. Keep the detour LSP on R1 active because it will be used in the next step.
4. Perform an `sdp-ping` on the SDP between R1 and R2; make sure the response is received in-band. Is the sdp-ping successful?
   a. Shut down the LSP on R2.
   b. Is the same `sdp-ping` successful? Explain.
   c. Is an `sdp-ping` from R1 successful if a remote SDP is not specified? Explain.

d. Enable the LSP on R2.

e. Shut down the epipe service on R2.

f. Is the same `sdp-ping` successful? Explain.

g. Leave the epipe service on R2 shut down and proceed to the next step.

5. Perform an `svc-ping` from R1 to R2 that uses in-band communication.

a. Is the `svc-ping` successful? Explain.

b. Enable the epipe service on R2.

c. Is the same `svc-ping` successful? Explain.

Lab Section 21.2: Local Mirror Service

The Alcatel-Lucent 7750 SR provides the capability of mirroring service traffic to external sources such as a packet sniffer. In this section, you will configure a mirror service to replicate traffic to a directly connected packet sniffer.

Objective This lab will configure a local mirror service to replicate traffic to a directly connected sniffer.

Validation You will know you have succeeded if traffic is replicated from the service provider network and seen on the packet sniffer.

1. For this lab, you will require a PC or equivalent packet sniffer connected to R4. Verify that you can use your sniffer to capture traffic before continuing.

2. Configure a local mirror service on R4 that sends replicated traffic to the packet sniffer.

a. Does the packet sniffer need to be connected to the mirror service with an access port or network port? Explain.

b. Verify that the mirror service is operationally up.

c. Set the mirror to replicate traffic that ingresses port 1/1/2 to the packet sniffer.

d. Verify that you see control traffic (IGP, RSVP, LDP, etc.).

e. Set the mirror to only replicate user traffic that travels on the RSVP-TE LSP from R1 to R2. You will need to find the label for the active detour LSP.

f. Send pings between the CE routers to verify your configuration.

Lab Section 21.3: Configuring a Remote Mirror Service

The previous lab section used a local mirror service to replicate traffic to a directly connected sniffer. A remote mirror service can be used when a packet sniffer is not directly connected, but exists at a different point in the network.

Objective In this lab, you will configure a remote mirror service to replicate traffic to a sniffer in the network that is not directly connected.

Validation You will know you have succeeded if the correct traffic is seen on the packet sniffer.

1. Configure a GRE-encapsulated SDP between R4 and R2 that can be used for the mirror service.
   a. For this section, use T-LDP to signal service labels for the GRE SDP.
   b. Verify that the SDP is operationally up before proceeding to the next step.
2. Configure a remote mirror service so that the sniffer connected to R4 can be used to mirror traffic on the SAP of the epipe service on R2.
   a. Which routers need to be configured with a mirror destination? Which routers need to be configured with a mirror source?
   b. Send a ping between the CE routers, and ensure that you see ICMP traffic on the sniffer.
   c. Is the ICMP traffic captured encapsulated with an MPLS label? Explain.
3. In this step, you will simulate a packet sniffer that has network reachability but is not directly connected to a 7750 SR.
   a. Remove the mirror destination on R4.
   b. Configure R4's port to the sniffer as a network port with a corresponding network interface with an IP address of `10.55.55.1/24` or any other IP address on the same subnet as your packet sniffer.
   c. Distribute the network interface into the IGP on R4.
   d. Verify that R2 has a route to the network where the sniffer is located.
4. Modify the GRE SDP on R2 to have a far-end IP address of the sniffer.
   a. Is the GRE SDP on R2 operationally up? Explain.
   b. Disable signaling on the GRE SDP.

c. Verify that the GRE SDP is operationally up before continuing.

d. Modify the SDP binding on the mirror destination on R2 to use a static vc-label. What value should be used for the label? Explain.

e. Send a ping between CE routers, and verify that you see the ICMP (Internet Control Message Protocol) traffic on the sniffer.

f. Does the ICMP traffic captured on the sniffer have any MPLS labels? Explain.

Chapter Review

Now that you have completed this chapter, you should be able to:

- Use `lsp-ping` and `lsp-trace` to verify MPLS LSPs.
- Use `sdp-ping` and `sdp-mtu` to verify correct configuration of SDPs.
- Use `svc-ping` to verify correct configuration of a VPN service.
- Configure a local mirror service.
- Configure a remote mirror service.
- Set the mirror slice size.

Post-Assessment

The following questions will test your knowledge and prepare you for the Alcatel-Lucent NRS II Certification Exam. Compare your responses with the answers listed in Appendix A. You can also use the CD that accompanies this book to take all the assessment tests and review the answers.

1. Which of the following 7750 SR OAM commands can be used to diagnose a far-end epipe service instance that is administratively shut down?

   A. `lsp-ping`

   B. `lsp-trace`

   C. `sdp-ping`

   D. `sdp-mtu`

   E. `svc-ping`

   F. None of the above commands can be used to diagnose an epipe service instance that is administratively shut down.

2. An operator issues the command `oam sdp-ping 5` on a 7750 SR. Which of the following statements is true?

   A. The `sdp-ping` is sent out-of-band.

   B. The `sdp-ping` reply is sent out-of-band.

   C. An RSVP-TE LSP must be used for the SDP to use the `sdp-ping` command.

   D. An LDP LSP must be used for the SDP to use the `sdp-ping` command.

   E. None of the above statements are true.

3. Which of the following statements concerning the `oam lsp-ping` and `oam lsp-trace` commands on the 7750 SR is *false*?

   A. Both commands can be used on LDP LSPs.

   B. When the `oam lsp-trace` command is used on an RSVP-TE LSP, the hops followed are the same that would be seen with the `traceroute` command to the egress LER.

   C. The `lsp-ping` command can be used for measuring round-trip time for a specific forwarding class.

   D. For both commands, a UDP packet is encapsulated and sent along the path of the LSP.

   E. All of the above statements are true.

4. Which OAM command on the 7750 SR can be used to find the effective MTU of an SDP?

   A. `oam lsp-ping`

   B. `oam svc-ping`

   C. `oam sdp-ping`

   D. `oam lsp-trace`

   E. None of the above

5. Consider two 7750 SR PE routers that have two epipes between them. One of the epipes is operationally down, and the other is operationally up. Which statement is correct?

   A. An `lsp-ping` between the routers will fail.

   B. An `sdp-ping` between the routers will fail.

   C. An `svc-ping` will be successful for the operationally up epipe and will fail for the operationally down epipe.

   D. There is not enough information to answer the question.

6. Consider four routers connected as R1–R2–R3–R4 using Ethernet. The MTU on the R1–R2 and R3–R4 link is 9,212 bytes. The MTU on the link between R2 and R3 is 2,000 bytes. An RSVP-TE LSP is bound to the SDP from R1–R4. If an `oam sdp-mtu` command is used on R1 to find the effective path MTU of the SDP, what is the result?

A. 1,976 bytes

B. 1,978 bytes

C. 1,980 bytes

D. 9,190 bytes

E. 9,212 bytes

F. There is not enough information provided to answer the question.

7. Which of the following entities cannot be used as the source for a mirror service on the 7750 SR?

A. Physical port

B. SAP

C. Ingress MPLS label

D. IP filter

E. MAC filter

F. All of the above entities can be used.

8. Which of the following statements is true regarding the configuration of a remote mirror on the 7750 SR?

A. T-LDP must be used to signal service labels between the PE routers.

B. RSVP-TE or LDP must be used for the SDP encapsulation between the routers.

C. A mirror destination is configured on both PE routers.

D. A mirror source is configured on both PE routers.

E. A SAP to the sniffer is only configured on the mirror source.

F. None of the above statements are true.

9. An operator has been using a remote mirror service on a 7750 SR for a period of time without any problems. The operator performs a reboot for a software upgrade; however, when the router comes back up, the mirror is not working. What is the most probable cause?

A. The mirror source needs to be reconfigured.

B. The mirror destination needs to be reconfigured.

C. The sniffer needs to be reconfigured.

D. There is a problem with the physical topology.

E. The operator must wait longer for control plane convergence.

F. None of the above statements are correct.

10. An operator wants to use remote service mirroring on the 7750 SR but is concerned about the potential increase in bandwidth consumption on network links involved in the mirror. Which of the following can be used to reduce the bandwidth consumption?

A. IP filters

B. MAC filters

C. A filter on the MPLS ingress label

D. Slice size

E. Features A–D can be used to restrict the amount of traffic replicated across the mirror service.

F. None of Features A–D can be used to restrict the amount of traffic replicated across the mirror service.

A

Chapter Assessment Questions and Answers

Assessment Questions

Chapter 2

1. Which of the following is a circuit switched protocol?
   - **A.** POS
   - **B.** ATM
   - **C.** IP
   - **D.** Ethernet
2. What does a switch do when it receives a frame with an unknown destination MAC address?
   - **A.** It sends an ICMP destination unreachable to the source.
   - **B.** It sends an ICMP redirect to the source.
   - **C.** It silently discards the frame.
   - **D.** It floods the frame to all ports except the one the frame was received on.
   - **E.** It holds the packet for the configured time-out value and discards it if the source is still not known.
3. How is communication accomplished between two users on separate VLANs?
   - **A.** The users must be relocated to the same VLAN.
   - **B.** A third VLAN must be created, and both users must be given membership.
   - **C.** A router must be used to route the packets at the IP layer.
   - **D.** The users on separate VLANs must use an IP address on the same subnet to trigger a direct VLAN transfer on the switch.
   - **E.** No special mechanism is required.
4. For what reason was TDM initially developed?
   - **A.** To support high-bandwidth video applications
   - **B.** As a technology to offer improvements over ATM with respect to QoS
   - **C.** To meet the demands of the emerging Internet
   - **D.** For the PSTN
   - **E.** To support the cellular network

5. Which ATM adaptation layer is used for connectionless non-real-time data such as IP?
   A. AAL1
   B. AAL2
   C. AAL3
   D. AAL4
   E. AAL5
6. Which of the following is not an OSI Layer?
   A. Application
   B. Presentation
   C. Establishment
   D. Transport
   E. Physical
7. How is a corrupted frame typically detected in Ethernet? .
   A. Using the framing information in the Layer 2 header
   B. Using the FCS field in the Layer 2 header
   C. By doing a reverse path forwarding check
   D. Frame corruption is not typically detected at Layer 2 as it is handled by the higher-layer protocols.
8. Which of the following pieces of information is stored in the FDB when a frame arrives at an Ethernet switch?
   A. The destination IP address
   B. The source IP address
   C. The source MAC address
   D. The destination MAC address

9. What is the purpose of VLANs?

A. To allow more efficient use of the IPv4 address space

B. To separate broadcast domains

C. To allow direct routing between subnets

D. To separate collision domains

E. To provide full duplex functionality to a regular switch

10. What can be done when VLANs need to span more than one switch?

A. No special mechanism is required.

B. Signaling is used between switches for each destination MAC address in the FDB to build the correct VLAN to MAC associations.

C. Signaling is used between switches for each source MAC address in the FDB to build the correct VLAN to MAC associations.

D. A VLAN tag is attached to the Ethernet frame to indicate VLAN membership.

E. It's not possible for VLANs to span more than one switch.

11. Which statement is correct regarding the use of Ethernet Q-in-Q?

A. The outer tag is commonly used by the service provider, and the inner tag is commonly used by the customer.

B. The inner tag is commonly used by the service provider, and the outer tag is commonly used by the customer.

C. The service provider VLAN tag is identified with the SP field set to 1.

D. The customer VLAN tag is identified with the CE field set to 1.

E. Service provider VLAN tags are identified with Ethertype 8100, and customer VLAN tags are identified with Ethertype 8200.

12. Which statement is correct regarding POS?

A. IP is encapsulated in an Ethernet frame and transported over SONET.

B. IP is encapsulated in PPP and transported over SONET.

C. IP is encapsulated in ATM and transported over SONET.

D. All the above variations are possible.

13. Which of the following is a reason for ATM's fixed 53-byte cell size?
   A. To avoid data fragmentation
   B. To minimize delay and jitter for voice services
   C. To reduce the cell tax
   D. To enable backward compatibility with TDM and Frame Relay

14. How many service classes are defined by ATM?
   A. One
   B. Three
   C. Five
   D. Seven
   E. Eight

15. Which statement is correct regarding the required order for configuration of Alcatel-Lucent 7750 SR ports?
   A. MDAs are configured first, followed by ports, followed by IOMs.
   B. MDAs are configured first, followed by IOMs, followed by ports.
   C. Ports are configured first, followed by MDAs, followed by IOMs.
   D. Ports are configured first, followed by IOMs, followed by MDAs.
   E. IOMs are configured first, followed by ports, followed by MDAs.
   F. IOMs are configured first followed by MDAs, followed by ports.

Chapter 3

1. Which statement is correct concerning the IP network 192.0.2.160 with a subnet mask of 255.255.255.224?
   A. The host address range is 192.0.2.160–192.0.2.190.
   B. The host address range is 192.0.2.161–192.0.2.190.
   C. The host address range is 192.0.2.161–192.0.2.191.
   D. The host address range is 192.0.2.160–192.0.2.191.

2. Which statement best describes the path of data traffic switched between two IOMs in an Alcatel-Lucent 7750 SR?

   A. Data traffic will pass through the SF module.

   B. Data traffic will pass through the SF module and then the CPM module.

   C. Data traffic will pass through the CPM module and then the SF module.

   D. Data traffic does not pass through either the SF or the CPM module.

3. If static routes are used for connectivity between a branch office and corporate headquarters, what is the most likely configuration?

   A. Static route on the corporate router and a default route on the branch router

   B. Default route on the corporate router and a static route on the branch router

   C. Static route on the corporate and branch routers

   D. Default route on the corporate and branch routers

4. An Alcatel-Lucent 7750 SR is configured with a default route and a static route for prefix 198.51.100.160/27. It has an OSPF route for 198.51.100.160/28. All routes are visible in the route table and use default preference values. Which route will be used to forward an IP packet with the source address of 198.51.100.177?

   A. Default route.

   B. Static route.

   C. OSPF route.

   D. There is not enough information to determine.

5. A router-interface on an Alcatel-Lucent 7750 SR is bound to a port and enabled with IPv6. An explicit IPv6 address is assigned to the interface. The port MAC address is 00:03:fa:ac:99:af, and the chassis MAC address is 00:03:fa:bf:b9:f8. Which statement below best describes the link-local address that will be assigned to the router interface?

   A. The link-local interface address is FE80::203:FAFF:FEAC:99AF/64.

   B. The link-local interface address is FC::3:FAFF:FEAC:99AF/64.

   C. The link-local interface address is FC::203:FAFF:FEBF:B9F8/64.

   D. The link-local interface address is FE80::3:FAFF:FEBF:B9F8/64.

   E. A link-local address is not configured for the interface.

6. Which of the following is a capability provided by IP?
   - **A.** Connection-oriented, unreliable datagram delivery service
   - **B.** Connectionless, unreliable datagram delivery service
   - **C.** Connection-oriented, reliable datagram delivery service
   - **D.** Connectionless, reliable datagram delivery service

7. Which of the following is *not* contained in the route table maintained by the Alcatel-Lucent 7750 SR CPM?
   - **A.** Preference
   - **B.** Metric
   - **C.** Layer 2 information of the next-hop
   - **D.** Protocol used to learn the routes

8. Which command can be used on the CLI to view the FIB stored on the IOM in Slot 1 of an Alcatel-Lucent 7750 SR?
   - **A.** `show router route-table`
   - **B.** `show router 1 route-table`
   - **C.** `show router iom 0`
   - **D.** `show router iom 1`
   - **E.** `show router fib 0`
   - **F.** `show router fib 1`

9. Which of the following fields in the IPv4 header identifies that the IP packet is carrying ICMP data?
   - **A.** Version
   - **B.** IHL
   - **C.** IP source address
   - **D.** IP destination address
   - **E.** Protocol

10. Which of the following is *not* part of the Alcatel-Lucent 7750 SR IP interface configuration?

   A. IP address

   B. Subnet mask

   C. Layer 2 media type

   D. Port number

11. Which statement is correct regarding the system interface on the Alcatel-Lucent 7750 SR?

   A. It always has an operational state of up.

   B. It needs to be explicitly configured as a loopback.

   C. It assumes an IP address of the last four octets of the chassis MAC address if one is not configured.

   D. It always has an admin state of up.

   E. It cannot be removed.

12. What is the correct syntax to configure a default route on an Alcatel-Lucent 7750 SR assuming that the local router interface to be used has an IP address of 10.1.1.1/30?

   A. `configure router default-route 0.0.0.0/0 next-hop 10.1.1.1`

   B. `configure router default-route 0.0.0.0/0 next-hop 10.1.1.2`

   C. `configure router static-route 0.0.0.0/0 next-hop 10.1.1.1`

   D. `configure router static-route 0.0.0.0/0 next-hop 10.1.1.2`

   E. `configure router static-route * next-hop 10.1.1.1`

   F. `configure router static-route * next-hop 10.1.1.2`

13. Which statement is true concerning floating static routes?

   A. The floating static route is configured with the keyword `floating`.

   B. The floating static route is used if the active route becomes too congested.

   C. The route with the higher preference is active.

   D. Floating static routes are only beneficial when the physical topology offers more than one next-hop to a prefix.

   E. BFD must be used on the active static route to detect failures.

14. An Alcatel-Lucent 7750 SR is configured with the following routes:

```
configure router static-route 0.0.0.0/0 next-hop 10.1.1.1
configure router static-route 172.16.14.64/27 next-hop 10.1.2.2
  preference 200
configure router static-route 172.16.14.64/28 next-hop 10.1.3.3
```

The router also learns the route 172.16.14.0/24 from OSPF with a next-hop of 10.1.4.4. What is the next-hop for the packet with destination address 172.16.14.82?

A. 10.1.1.1

B. 10.1.2.2

C. 10.1.3.3

D. 10.1.4.4

E. The packet is discarded.

15. Two Alcatel-Lucent 7750 SRs named R1 and R2 are directly connected. The MAC address of the port on R1 is 00:16:4d:13:63:cf, and the MAC address of the port on R2 is 00:16:4d:13:63:c1. The system IP address of R2 is fd00:33:33::1/128, and all interface names follow the convention `toRx`, where *x* is the router number. Which of the following commands can be used on R1 to create a static route to R2's system interface address?

A. `configure router static-route fd00:33:33::1/128 next-hop FE80::216:4DFF:FE13:63C1`

B. `configure router static-route fd00:33:33::1/128 next-hop FE80::216:4DFF:FE13:63C1-toR2`

C. `configure router static-route fd00:33:33::1/128 next-hop FE80::216:4DFF:FE13:63CF-toR1`

D. `configure router static-route fd00:33:33::1/128 next-hop FE80::216:4DFF:FE13:63CF`

E. Static routes cannot be created until a global IPv6 address is assigned to the router interfaces.

Chapter 4

1. Which of the following is the primary goal of an IGP?

   A. To facilitate load balancing

   B. To provide the lowest-cost route to networks within an autonomous system

   C. To provide the best route to Internet destinations considering policy rules and cost

   D. To distribute aggregate routes

2. Which statement is true about link-state protocols?

   A. Sequence numbers are incremented as the updates are passed from router to router.

   B. Updates and Hello messages are sent to a broadcast address so they can be seen by all routers running the protocol.

   C. When an interface changes state, a routing update is flooded to all routers in the domain.

   D. Routing tables are periodically sent between neighbors.

3. What action is taken when a router receives a new LSP from a neighbor?

   A. Run SPF on the LSDB and flood a SYNC message to all routers to start a query and reply process.

   B. Run SPF on the LSDB and send the results of the SPF calculation to its neighbors.

   C. Run an SPF calculation to update the route table and send incremental updates to the routers in its adjacency database.

   D. Flood the LSP to all its neighbors and then run an SPF calculation to update the route table.

4. Which statement is correct regarding the age and sequence number of an LSP as it is flooded throughout a network?

   A. The sequence number and age are increased.

   B. The sequence number and age are not changed.

   C. The sequence number is not changed, but the age is changed.

   D. The sequence number is increased, but the age is held constant.

5. Which statement is true regarding BGP?

   A. BGP discovers its neighbors through the use of Hello messages.

   B. BGP is a path-vector protocol that selects the route that is the least number of hops between autonomous systems.

   C. A BGP policy may cause BGP to choose a route that is not the shortest path to the destination.

   D. BGP routers are always directly connected to their neighbors.

   E. The primary objective of BGP is to offer the lowest-cost route to destination networks.

6. Which of the following is an exterior gateway routing protocol?

   A. OSPF

   B. BGP

   C. IS-IS

   D. RIP

7. Which of the following is a link-state routing protocol?

   A. LDP

   B. BGP

   C. IS-IS

   D. RSVP-TE

   E. RIP

8. What does the `Type` field indicate in the Alcatel-Lucent 7750 SR route table?

   A. The protocol used to learn the route

   B. Whether the prefix is internal or external

   C. Whether the route represents a locally attached network or a remote network

   D. Relative weight of a route that can be used as a tie breaker

   E. Whether the route is active or not

9. Which field is *not* present in the Alcatel-Lucent 7750 SR route table?

- **A.** Protocol
- **B.** Source address
- **C.** Age
- **D.** Preference
- **E.** Next-hop

10. Which statement is true about distance-vector protocols?

- **A.** Each router is aware of the entire network topology.
- **B.** Updates received by a router must be used to update its routing table before an update can be sent to other neighbors.
- **C.** Routing updates are flooded throughout the network.
- **D.** Traffic engineering is an option.
- **E.** Routing updates are flooded throughout an area.

11. Which of the following is *not* a database required by a link-state protocol?

- **A.** Adjacency database
- **B.** Link-state database
- **C.** Metric database
- **D.** Forwarding database

12. What action is taken when a router receives an LSP with a lower sequence number than an LSP already in the LSDB?

- **A.** An ACK is sent to the sending router, and the LSP is discarded.
- **B.** The received LSP is discarded, and an updated LSP is transmitted to the sending router.
- **C.** The received LSP is discarded, and a SYNC message is sent to all neighbors.
- **D.** The received LSP is silently discarded.

13. What action is taken when an LSP is received with the same sequence number as one already in the database?

   A. An ACK is sent to the sending router, and the LSP is discarded.

   B. The received LSP is discarded, and the LSP in the database is sent to the sender.

   C. The received LSP is discarded, and a SYNC message is sent to all neighbors.

   D. The received LSP is silently discarded.

14. An Alcatel-Lucent 7750 SR with default settings has the following routes in its route table:

```
Dest Prefix         Proto    Pref         Next Hop[Interface Name]
192.168.0.0/16      OSPF     10           toR2
192.168.0.0/20ISIS18          toR3
192.168.100.0/24    BGP      170          toR4
0.0.0.0/0           Static   5            toR5
```

   A packet with destination address 192.168.10.111 is forwarded by the router. Which router is the next hop for this packet?

   A. Next hop is R2.

   B. Next hop is R3.

   C. Next hop is R4.

   D. Next hop is R5.

   E. The packet is discarded.

15. A router (R1) with default configuration is running OSPF and IS-IS and learns a network prefix through both protocols. OSPF has two paths to the destination, through R2 with a metric of 200 and through R3 with a metric of 1,000. IS-IS has one path to the destination, through R4 with a metric of 100. What will be the next-hop chosen for this destination, and what will become the next-hop if this path fails?

   A. R2 will be the next-hop, and R3 will become the next-hop if R2 fails.

   B. R2 will be the next-hop, and R4 will become the next-hop if R2 fails.

   C. R4 will be the next-hop, and R2 will become the next-hop if R4 fails.

   D. R3 will be the next-hop, and R4 will become the next-hop if R3 fails.

   E. R3 will be the next-hop, and R2 will become the next-hop if R3 fails.

Chapter 5

1. What is the cost value of an OSPF interface on the Alcatel-Lucent 7750 SR?
   - **A.** It is based on the configuration of the global OSPF cost variable, which has a default value of 10.
   - **B.** It is based on the configuration of the global OSPF cost variable, which has a default value of 100.
   - **C.** It is based on a reference bandwidth, which has a default value of 10 Gbps.
   - **D.** It is based on a reference bandwidth, which has a default value of 100 Gbps.
2. A router has an OSPF broadcast interface declared as passive. How will this be represented in the Router LSA originated by the router?
   - **A.** The Router LSA will contain a stub network link type to describe the interface.
   - **B.** The Router LSA will contain a transit link type to describe the interface.
   - **C.** The Router LSA will contain a point-to-point link type to describe the interface.
   - **D.** The Router LSA will contain a point-to-point link type and a stub network link type to describe the interface.
   - **E.** The Router LSA will not describe the interface.
3. Which statement is *not* correct regarding an OSPF Type 1 LSA?
   - **A.** An OSPF Type 1 LSA is originated by every OSPF router.
   - **B.** An OSPF Type 1 LSA is called a Router LSA.
   - **C.** The OSPF Type 1 LSA is flooded throughout the autonomous system.
   - **D.** The OSPF Type 1 LSA describes the router's directly connected links.
   - **E.** The OSPF Type 1 LSA contains an age field.

4. A 7750 SR has an OSPF adjacency with its neighbor using a router ID derived from the last four octets of the chassis MAC address. The system interface IP address, router ID, and OSPF router ID are then configured. Assuming these are the only commands executed, what router ID will be seen by the OSPF neighbor?

   A. The router ID seen by the neighbor will be derived from the last four octets of the chassis MAC address.

   B. The router ID seen by the neighbor will be derived from the system interface address.

   C. The router ID seen by the neighbor will be derived from the configured router ID.

   D. The router ID seen by the neighbor will be derived from the configured OSPF router ID.

5. Which of the following is not a field in an OSPF Hello packet that must match for a successful state transition to the 2-Way state?

   A. Dead Interval

   B. Authentication Type

   C. MTU

   D. Area ID

   E. Stub Flag

6. When does an OSPF router transition to the 2-Way state?

   A. After a Link State Request is received from a neighbor

   B. After the first link-state update is received from a neighbor

   C. After a Hello packet that contains its own router ID is received from a neighbor

   D. After the first link-state acknowledgment is received from a neighbor

   E. After a Database Description packet is received from a neighbor

7. Two routers R1 and R2 have a point-to-point OSPF adjacency. R1 has a priority of 15 and an OSPF router ID of `10.10.10.10`. R2 has a priority of 25 and an OSPF router ID of `5.5.5.5`. Which router will be the designated router?

   A. R1 will be the Designated Router.

   B. R2 will be the Designated Router.

   C. The first router to initialize will be the designated router.

   D. There will be no designated router.

8. When two routers are in the OSPF ExStart state, how is the initial Database Description sequence number determined?

   A. Both routers send a DBD packet with an initial sequence number, and the highest is used.

   B. The sequence number of the router with the highest priority is used.

   C. The sequence number of the router that sends the first Database Description packet is used.

   D. The sequence number of the router with the highest router ID is used.

9. R1 and R2 are directly connected to each other and running OSPF on the link. The OSPF interface MTU of both routers is different, but the port MTU of each router is the same. What state will the adjacency be in?

   A. The adjacency will be in the Init state.

   B. The adjacency will be in the 2-Way state.

   C. The adjacency will be in the ExStart state.

   D. The adjacency will be in the Full state.

   E. It cannot be determined without details of the DR/BDR election.

10. What is the main purpose of the DBD packet?

   A. The DBD packet is used to carry LSAs between routers.

   B. The DBD packet is used in the OSPF neighbor discovery mechanism.

   C. The DBD packet is used to provide summary LSA information to each router so that specific LSAs can be requested.

   D. The DBD packet is used to withdraw LSA information when there is a topology change.

11. Which statement is correct regarding OSPF LSA exchange between routers?

   A. A router requests one LSA at a time using an LSR.

   B. A router can request multiple LSAs using a single LSR. The size of the LSR is dependent on the MTU settings.

   C. A router can request multiple LSAs using a single LSR. The size of the LSR is dependent on the value of the maximum LSA size parameter.

   D. A router never requests LSAs; they are always flooded.

12. Which statement best describes what happens when an OSPF receives an LSA with a higher sequence number than the LSA in its database?

A. The router acknowledges the LSA but does not add it to its link-state database and does not flood it to its neighbors.

B. The router does not acknowledge the LSA but sends a copy of the LSA from its database to the neighbor from which it received the LSA.

C. The router acknowledges the LSA and floods it to its neighbors but does not add it to its link-state database.

D. The router acknowledges the LSA, adds it to its own database, and floods it to its neighbors.

13. A router has four interfaces that are added to OSPF. Two point-to-point interfaces are in Area 1. There is one point-to-point interface in Area 2 and one broadcast interface in Area 3. How many Network LSAs will be originated by the router?

A. The router will not originate any Network LSAs.

B. The router will originate one Network LSA.

C. The router will originate two Network LSAs.

D. The router will originate four Network LSAs.

E. It is not possible to determine with the given information.

14. Which of the following best describes the election of the DR on a broadcast interface in OSPF when all routers have the same priority value?

A. The router with the lowest router ID is always the DR.

B. The router with the highest router ID is always the DR.

C. The router with the highest IP address on the broadcast interface is always the DR.

D. The router with the lowest IP address on the broadcast interface is always the DR.

E. The router that has been up the longest is usually the DR, since DR election is non-preemptive.

15. A router has been elected the DR on a broadcast OSPF interface on a subnet with three other routers. How will the link-state topology be described by routers on the subnet? Choose the best statement.

   A. The DR originates a Router LSA that includes the broadcast interface. The other routers on the subnet do not originate any LSAs that include the broadcast interface.

   B. The DR originates only a Network LSA that describes the broadcast network.

   C. The DR originates a Router LSA that includes the broadcast interface and a Network LSA that includes the broadcast interface. The other routers on the subnet do not originate any LSAs that include the broadcast interface.

   D. All routers on the subnet originate a Router LSA that includes the broadcast interface and a Network LSA that describes the broadcast network.

   E. All routers on the subnet originate a Router LSA that includes the broadcast interface. Only the DR originates a Network LSA that describes the broadcast network.

Chapter 6

1. Which of the following is the definition of an ASBR?

   A. An OSPF router that routes in the backbone network

   B. An OSPF router that routes in a stub network

   C. An OSPF router that connects two or more different OSPF areas

   D. An OSPF router that connects to an external routing domain

   E. An OSPF router that connects to a BGP network

2. A router has four interfaces configured in OSPF. Two point-to-point interfaces are in Area 0, one point-to-point interface is in Area 1, and one broadcast interface is in Area 2. How many Router LSAs will be originated by the router?

   A. The router will originate one Router LSA.

   B. The router will originate two Router LSAs.

   C. The router will originate three Router LSAs.

   D. The router will originate four Router LSAs.

   E. It is not possible to determine with the given information.

3. What is the default behavior of multi-area OSPF with respect to originating Type 3 Summary LSAs?

   A. Every backbone router originates a Summary LSA for each prefix in its Router LSA.

   B. Every ABR originates a Summary LSA for each Router LSA in its database.

   C. Every backbone router originates a Summary LSA for every prefix listed in the LSDB.

   D. Every ABR originates a Summary LSA for every prefix listed in the LSDB.

   E. Summary LSAs are only originated by backbone routers when manual summarization is configured.

4. R1 is an ABR with an interface connected to R2 that is an Area 1 intra-area router. The network operator wants to summarize the backbone area networks `192.168.1.0/24` and `192.168.2.0/24` routes with the summary route `192.168.0.0/16`. Which statement below is correct regarding the Summary LSA flooded throughout Area 1?

   A. It will have its metric set to the highest cost of the component networks, and the Adv router ID set to R1's router ID.

   B. It will have its metric set to the highest cost of the component networks, and the Adv router ID set to R2's router ID.

   C. It will have its metric set to the lowest cost of the component networks, and the Adv router ID set to R1's router ID.

   D. It will have its metric set to the lowest cost of the component networks, and the Adv router ID set to R2's router ID.

5. Consider an OSPF network topology with Area 0, Area 1, and Area 2. An ASBR in Area 1 is configured to redistribute external routes into OSPF using a policy. Which statement below correctly describes how external routes are advertised to Area 0 and Area 2?

   A. The ASBR originates Router LSAs with the ASBR flag set that are flooded throughout Area 1. The external routes are not learned in Area 0 or Area 2 without additional policy on the ABRs.

   B. The ASBR originates Router LSAs that are flooded throughout Area 1. Area 1 ABRs originate Summary LSAs that are flooded throughout Area 0. The ABRs between Area 0 and Area 2 originate Summary LSAs that are flooded throughout Area 2.

   C. The ASBR originates Router LSAs with the ASBR flag set that are flooded throughout the autonomous system.

   D. The ASBR originates ASBR Summary LSAs that are flooded throughout the autonomous system.

   E. The ASBR originates AS External LSAs that are flooded throughout the autonomous system.

6. Select the *incorrect* statement about multi-area OSPF networks.

   A. Suboptimal routing may occur in a multi-area network.

   B. Traffic engineering calculations cannot be made across a multi-area network.

   C. Troubleshooting of routing issues in a multi-area network is usually more difficult than in a single area network.

   D. The large number of Summary LSAs makes the SPF calculation more complex in a multi-area network.

7. Which of the following is NOT an OSPF area type?

   A. Backbone Area

   B. Virtual Area

   C. Stub Area

   D. Not So Stubby Area

   E. Totally Stubby Area

8. Consider an OSPF network with Area 0, Area 1, and Area 2. R1 is an ABR for Area 1, and R2 is an ABR for Area 2. If default OSPF configurations are used, which statement below is correct?

   A. Area 1 routes are advertised to Area 2 using Router LSAs originated by R1.

   B. Area 1 routes are advertised to Area 2 using Router LSAs originated by R2.

   C. Area 1 routes are advertised to Area 2 using Summary LSAs originated by R1.

   D. Area 1 routes are advertised to Area 2 using Summary LSAs originated by R2.

9. Router R1 is an ABR connected to R2 that is an Area 1 intra-area router. The network operator wants to configure OSPF summarization to reduce routing table sizes of Area 1 routers. Which statement below is correct about the required configuration?

   A. R1 needs to be configured with the `area-range` command in the `configure router OSPF area 0` context.

   B. R1 needs to be configured with the `area-range` command in the `configure router OSPF area 1` context.

   C. R1 needs to be configured with the `aggregate` command in the `configure router` context.

   D. R2 needs to be configured with the `area-range` command in the `configure router OSPF area 1` context.

   E. R2 needs to be configured with the `aggregate` command in the `configure router` context.

10. R1 is an ABR with an interface connected to R2 that is an Area 1 intra-area router. The network operator uses the OSPF `area-range` command to summarize the backbone area networks `192.168.1.0/24` and `192.168.2.0/24` with the summary prefix `192.168.0.0/16`. Which statement below is correct?

   A. R1 will contain entries in its route table for both the /24 networks and for the summarized /16 network.

   B. R2 will contain entries in its route table for both the /24 networks and for the summarized /16 network

   C. R2 will contain entries in its route table for only the /24 networks.

   D. Both answers A and B are correct.

11. Consider an OSPF network topology with Area 0, Area 1, and Area 2, all configured as normal areas. R1 is the only ABR between Area 0 and Area 1. R2 is the only ABR between Area 0 and Area 2. R3 is in Area 1 and is the only router in the entire network configured as an ASBR. Which statement below is correct?

A. Only Area 1 routers have an ASBR Summary LSA with *Adv Rtr-id* of R3.

B. Only Area 0 routers have an ASBR Summary LSA with *Adv Rtr-id* of R1.

C. Area 0 and Area 2 routers have an ASBR Summary LSA with *Adv Rtr-id* of R1.

D. Area 0 routers have an ASBR Summary LSA with *Adv Rtr-id* of R1. Area 2 routers have an ASBR Summary LSA with *Adv Rtr-id* of R2.

E. All routers in the autonomous system have an ASBR Summary LSA with *Adv Rtr-id* of R3.

F. Area 1 routers have an ASBR Summary LSA with *Adv Rtr-id* of R3. Area 0 routers have an ASBR Summary LSA with *Adv Rtr-id* of R1. Area 2 routers have an ASBR Summary LSA with *Adv Rtr-id* of R2.

12. Consider an OSPF network topology with Area 0, Area 1, and Area 2. Area 2 is a simple stub area. Area 1 contains an ASBR that redistributes external routes into OSPF. Which LSA types listed below will *not* be contained in the LSDB of the Area 2 routers?

A. A Summary LSA describing the default route

B. AS External LSAs originated by the ASBR in Area 1

C. Summary LSAs describing Area 0 internal networks

D. Summary LSAs describing Area 1 internal networks

E. Router LSAs originated by Area 2 routers

13. An OSPF network consists of Area 0, Area 1, and Area 2. Area 1 contains an ASBR that originates AS External LSAs. Area 2 is initially declared as a simple stub area. An operator changes the Area 2 intra-area router to be a totally stubby area. How does the configuration change the LSDB of the Area 2 routers?

A. AS External LSAs will be blocked.

B. Summary LSAs will be blocked.

C. Router LSAs originated by Area 2 will not be flooded throughout Area 2.

D. There will not be a Summary LSA to describe a default route.

E. There will be no change.

14. An OSPF network is designed to include Area 0, Area 1, and Area 2. Area 2 is not required to learn any specific routes from the other areas but should use a default route to its ABR instead. Area 2 contains an ASBR that redistributes external routes into the network. Which of the configurations below would be the most likely choice for the Area 2 ABR if it is an Alcatel-Lucent 7750 SR?

A. It should be configured as a `stub` area with the parameter `originate-default-route`.

B. It should be configured as a `stub` area with the parameters `no summaries` and `originate-default-route`.

C. It should be configured as an `nssa` area with the parameter `no summaries`.

D. It should be configured as an `nssa` area with the parameter `originate-default-route`.

E. It should be configured as an `nssa` area with the parameters `no summaries` and `originate-default-route`.

15. Consider an OSPF network topology with Area 0, Area 1, and Area 2. Area 2 is configured as an NSSA area and contains router R10, which is an ASBR redistributing external routes into the OSPF network, but not an ABR. Which statement below is *not* correct?

A. The LSDB of routers in Area 2 contains an NSSA LSA with an advertising router ID of R10.

B. The LSDB of routers in Area 0 contains AS External LSAs with an advertising router ID of R10.

C. The LSDB of routers in Area 1 contains an ASBR Summary LSA with an advertising router ID of the ABR between Area 0 and Area 1.

D. The LSDB of routers in Area 1 contains an AS External LSA with an advertising router ID of the ABR between Area 0 and Area 2.

E. The LSDB of routers in Area 1 does not contain NSSA LSAs from Area 2.

Chapter 7

1. When only IPv6 is configured, how is the OSPFv3 router ID derived on an Alcatel-Lucent 7750 SR?
   - **A.** The router ID is derived from the system interface address if it is assigned; otherwise, it defaults to the last four octets of the chassis MAC address.
   - **B.** The router ID is derived from the system interface address if it is assigned; otherwise, it defaults to `0.0.0.0`.
   - **C.** The router ID is derived from an explicitly configured router ID if there is one assigned; otherwise, it defaults to the system interface address.
   - **D.** The router ID is derived from an explicitly configured router ID if there is one assigned; otherwise, it defaults to the last four octets of the chassis MAC address.
   - **E.** The router ID is derived from an explicitly configured router ID. OSPFv3 does not become active until the router ID is configured.

2. Two routers, R1 and R2, have an OSPFv3 adjacency between them. Both routers are configured with a system interface address, and their directly connected links are configured with a global IPv6 address. When R2 learns routes from R1, which next-hop will be used in R2's routing table? Assume that the OSPFv3 routes from R1 are the best routes received by R2.
   - **A.** The link-local interface address of R2 will be used for the next-hop.
   - **B.** The link-local interface address of R1 will be used for the next-hop.
   - **C.** The global interface address of R2 will be used for the next-hop.
   - **D.** The global interface address of R1 will be used for the next-hop.
   - **E.** The system interface address of R1 will be used for the next-hop.

3. An OSPFv3 router has a system interface, a loopback interface, and a router interface in Area 0. Global IPv6 addresses are assigned only to the system interface and the router interface. Which of the prefixes will appear in the IAP LSA originated by the router?

A. The loopback and router link-local prefixes will appear in the IAP LSA along with the two global prefixes.

B. The system interface and loopback prefixes will appear in the IAP LSA.

C. The loopback prefixes and both router interface prefixes will appear in the IAP LSA.

D. The system interface prefix and the global router interface prefix will appear in the IAP LSA.

E. The loopback prefix and the link-local router interface prefix will appear in the IAP LSA.

4. What is the flooding scope of an OSPFv3 Inter-Area Prefix LSA?

A. Link-local scope

B. External scope

C. Area scope

D. Autonomous System scope

E. None of the above

5. Which of the following statements about OSPFv3 is *not* correct?

A. OSPFv3 supports the equivalent of OSPFv2 stub areas.

B. OSPFv3 does not require global IPv6 addresses for router interfaces.

C. OSPFv3 uses the same authentication mechanisms as OSPFv2.

D. OSPFv3 Router LSAs do not carry IPv6 prefix information.

E. An OSPFv3 router ID is 32 bits long.

6. Consider an OSPFv3 network topology with three normal areas; Area 0, Area 1, and Area 2. An ASBR in Area 1 is configured to redistribute external routes into OSPFv3. Which statement below correctly describes how external routes are advertised to Area 2?

   A. The ASBR in Area 1 originates AS External LSAs that are flooded throughout the AS to describe external routes. The Area 2 ABR originates an Inter-Area Router LSA to describe the ASBR.

   B. The ASBR in Area 1 originates AS External LSAs that are flooded throughout the AS to describe the external routes. The Area 1 ABR originates an Inter-Area Router LSA that is flooded throughout the AS to describe the ASBR.

   C. The ASBR in Area 1 originates AS External LSAs that are flooded throughout the AS to describe the external routes. The Area 2 ABR originates an Intra-Area Router LSA that is flooded throughout the AS to describe the ASBR.

   D. The ASBR in Area 1 originates Inter-Area Router LSAs that are flooded throughout the AS to describe the external routes. The ABR for Area 2 originates an Intra-Area Router LSA to describe the ASBR.

   E. The ASBR in Area 1 originates Inter-Area Router LSAs that are flooded throughout the AS to describe the external routes. The ABR for Area 1 originates an AS External LSA that is flooded throughout the AS to describe the ASBR.

7. Two routers, R1 and R2, have an OSPFv3 broadcast adjacency between them. R1 has a system interface address of `FD00:11:11::1`. R2 has a system interface address of `FD00:11:11::2`. Which of the following LSA types is *not* originated by R1?

   A. Router LSA.

   B. Network LSA.

   C. Intra-Area Prefix LSA.

   D. There is not enough information to determine.

8. Which of the following commands can be used on an Alcatel-Lucent 7750 SR to view Link LSAs?

A. `show router ospf3 database`

B. `show router ospf3 database detail`

C. `show router ospf3 database type link-local detail`

D. `show router ospf3 interface <interface> database detail`

E. None of the above

9. Two routers, R1 and R2, are directly connected and actively exchanging routes over an OSPFv3 broadcast adjacency. How does R1 learn about R2's link-local interface address?

A. From the Router LSA.

B. From the Network LSA.

C. From the IAP LSA.

D. From the Link LSAs.

E. R2 is not aware of R1's link-local interface address.

10. What value is used for the link-state ID of an OSPFv3 Network LSA?

A. The router ID of the DR on the broadcast network.

B. The router ID of the first OSPFv3 router to initialize on the link.

C. The interface ID of the DR's interface to the broadcast network.

D. It is set to match the link-state ID of the Router LSA it refers to.

E. It is derived from the DR's current sequence number and router ID.

11. Each of the following statements compares an OSPv3 LSA with a corresponding OSPFv2 LSA. Which statement is *incorrect*?

A. An IAP LSA is comparable to a Type 1 LSA in OSPFv2.

B. An IEP LSA is comparable to a Type 3 LSA in OSPFv2.

C. An IER LSA is comparable to a Type 4 LSA in OSPFv2.

D. An AS External LSA is comparable to a Type 5 LSA in OSPFv2.

E. An NSSA LSA is comparable to a Type 7 LSA in OSPFv2.

12. Which command can be used on an Alcatel-Lucent 7750 to display the link-local addresses associated with its router interfaces?

   A. `show router ospf3 interface`

   B. `show router ospf interface detail`

   C. `show router route-table`

   D. `show router route-table ipv6`

   E. `show router interface`

13. Which OSPFv3 LSA has a similar function to the OSPFv2 Type 3 Summary LSA?

   A. Inter-Area Router LSA

   B. Inter-Area Prefix LSA

   C. Intra-Area Prefix LSA

   D. AS External LSA

   E. None of the above

14. Consider an OSPFv3 network topology with Area 0, Area 1, and Area 2. Area 1 contains an intra-area router that advertises a prefix in OSPFv3. There is a single Area 1 ABR that advertises a prefix in Area 0. There are two ABRs for Area 2. Assuming that manual summarization is not configured, how are the prefix in Area 0 and the prefix in Area 1 represented in the LSDB of Area 2 intra-area routers?

   A. There are two IEP LSAs. The Area 1 prefix is described by an IEP LSA originated by the Area 1 ABR. The Area 2 prefix is described by an IEP LSA originated by the Area 2 ABR with the least cost to each router.

   B. There are three IEP LSAs. The Area 1 prefix is described by an IEP LSA originated by the Area 1 ABR. Each Area 2 ABR originates an IEP LSA for the Area 0 prefix.

   C. There is one IEP LSA to describe both prefixes. The IEP LSA is originated by the Area 2 ABR with the least cost to each router.

   D. There are two IEP LSAs. Each Area 2 ABR originates an IEP LSA for each prefix; however, only the LSAs to the least-cost ABR are stored in each router's LSDB.

   E. There are four IEP LSAs. Each Area 2 ABR originates one IEP LSA for each prefix.

15. Consider an OSPF network topology with Area 0 and Area 1. Area 1 is configured as a totally stubby area. Which LSA type is used to propagate a default route into Area 1?

A. Intra-Area Router LSA

B. Inter-Area Router LSA

C. AS External LSA

D. Intra-Area Prefix LSA

E. Inter-Area Prefix LSA

Chapter 8

1. Which of the following statements comparing IS-IS and OSPF on the Alcatel-Lucent 7750 SR is false?

A. OSPF and IS-IS are both link-state routing protocols.

B. OSPF uses a reference bandwidth and the bandwidth of an interface to calculate the metric for the link. IS-IS always uses the value of 10 as a metric.

C. Both protocols support hierarchy. In OSPF, an ABR joins different areas; in IS-IS, L2 routers join the different areas.

D. OSPF uses IP to send its messages, whereas IS-IS uses the Layer 2 protocol.

E. OSPF was developed specifically for routing IP, whereas IS-IS was originally developed as an OSI protocol.

F. All of the above statements are true.

2. Which of the following statements best describes the election of the DIS on a broadcast network where all routers have the same priority?

A. The DIS is the router with the highest interface MAC address.

B. The DIS is the router with the highest system IP address.

C. If there is no DIS, the router with the highest interface MAC address is selected; otherwise, the existing DIS continues as DIS.

D. If there is no DIS, the router with the highest system IP address is selected; otherwise, the existing DIS continues as DIS.

E. The first router active on the broadcast network becomes the DIS.

3. Which of the following statements best describes how IS-IS routers ensure that their LSDB is always up-to-date?

   A. Routers periodically exchange Hello PDUs to ensure that the LSDB is up-to-date.

   B. Routers periodically exchange CSNPs that list the LSPs in their LSDB.

   C. Routers acknowledge any new LSPs received. If an LSP is not acknowledged, the router retransmits the LSP.

   D. When the age of an LSP in the LSDB reaches zero, the originating router floods a new LSP to ensure that all of the LSDBs are kept up-to-date.

   E. No special mechanism is required because new LSPs are flooded anytime there is a topology change.

4. Which of the following statements about the flooding of IS-IS LSPs is false?

   A. An L1/L2-capable router floods both an L1 and an L2 LSP.

   B. A router only floods an LSP when there is a topology change or when it receives an updated LSP from a neighbor.

   C. The sequence number of the LSP is set by the originating router and used by other routers to tell if the LSP is an update to their LSDB.

   D. On point-to-point links LSPs are acknowledged with a PSNP.

   E. All of the above statements are true.

5. Which of the following statements about the IS-IS metric is false?

   A. The interface metric can be set to different values for Level 1 and Level 2.

   B. On the 7750 SR the default metric for an IS-IS interface is 10.

   C. IS-IS can be configured on the 7750 SR with a reference bandwidth and wide metrics so that it calculates the link metric the same way that OSPF does.

   D. If an IS-IS router does not use wide metrics, the maximum metric is 63.

   E. All of the above statements are true.

6. Which of the following is not a valid IS-IS PDU type?
   - **A.** Hello
   - **B.** LSP
   - **C.** ACK
   - **D.** PSNP
   - **E.** CSNP
   - **F.** All of the above are valid IS-IS PDUs.

7. Which of the following statements about the NSAP address is false?
   - **A.** The AFI indicates the authority through which the address was assigned.
   - **B.** On the 7750 SR, the IDP and high-order DSP are assigned as the Area ID.
   - **C.** The system ID is always 4 bytes long.
   - **D.** The NSAP selector is always zero for a router.
   - **E.** All of the above statements are true.

8. Which of the following best describes the CSNP?
   - **A.** The CSNP is used to discover neighbors and establish adjacencies.
   - **B.** The CSNP is an index that lists all of the LSPs in the LSDB.
   - **C.** The CSNP is an index that lists some of the LSPs in the LSDB.
   - **D.** The CSNP is the PDU that carries the router's link-state information.
   - **E.** The CNSP is not a valid IS-IS PDU.

9. Which of the following statements about IS-IS adjacencies is incorrect?
   - **A.** There are three types of Hello messages used to form an adjacency: the Level 1 LAN Hello, the Level 2 LAN Hello, and the point-to-point Hello.
   - **B.** An IS-IS router may form both L1 and L2 adjacencies.
   - **C.** L1 adjacencies are only formed if both routers have the same Area ID.
   - **D.** In IS-IS, an adjacency is considered to be established after the successful exchange of Hello PDUs.
   - **E.** All of the above statements are correct.

10. Which of the following best describes how the IS-IS system ID is created on the 7750 SR?

A. The four numbers of the router ID are each represented using three digits to create a 6-byte system ID.

B. The 4-byte router ID is directly copied to the system ID, and the two NSAP selector bytes are added to create a 6-byte system ID.

C. The hexadecimal value of the router ID is converted to a decimal number to create the 6-byte system ID.

D. The chassis MAC address is used to create a 6-byte system ID.

E. None of the above statements describe the creation of the IS-IS system ID.

11. An extract from an IS-IS LSP on the 7750 SR is shown below. Which of the TLVs contains the information used to create the entry in the route table for the subnet corresponding to the interface with IP address `10.1.5.1/27`.

```
*A:R1>config>router>isis# show router isis database R1.00-00 detail
  Router ID   :
    Router ID   : 10.10.10.1
  I/F Addresses :
    I/F Address   : 10.10.10.1
    I/F Address   : 10.1.5.1
  TE IS Nbrs    :
    Nbr   : R1.03
    Default Metric  : 10
    Sub TLV Len     : 6
    IF Addr   : 10.1.5.1
  TE IP Reach   :
    Default Metric  : 0
    Control Info:     , prefLen 32
    Prefix   : 10.10.10.1
    Default Metric  : 10
    Control Info:     , prefLen 27
    Prefix   : 10.1.5.0
```

A. Router ID TLV

B. I/F Addresses TLV

C. TE IS Nbrs TLV

D. TE IP Reach TLV

E. None of the above. The output shown is from a traffic engineering LSP. The prefix information is actually carried in another PDU.

12. The neighbors listed in an LSP are all shown as having a metric of 0. Which of the following is a true statement?

A. All neighbors are connected on point-to-point links.

B. All neighbors are connected on broadcast links.

C. The LSP is the pseudonode LSP.

D. The LSP is from a router that has only the system interface defined in IS-IS.

E. The LSP described is not a valid IS-IS LSP.

13. Given the output from `show router isis database` on router R1 shown below, which of the following is not necessarily a true statement? Assume that all routers in the network have formed adjacencies with all their neighbors.

```
*A:R1# show router isis database

===============================================================================
ISIS Database
===============================================================================
LSP ID                            Sequence Checksum Lifetime Attributes
-------------------------------------------------------------------------------

Displaying Level 1 database
-------------------------------------------------------------------------------
Level (1) LSP Count : 0

Displaying Level 2 database
-------------------------------------------------------------------------------
R1.00-00                          0x67d    0xc95b   905      L1L2
R1.03-00                          0x1      0x9eda   904      L1L2
R2.00-00                          0x84     0x1356   882      L1L2
R5.00-00                          0xab     0x7227   904      L1L2
R3.00-00                          0x1c     0x2699   897      L1L2
Level (2) LSP Count : 5
===============================================================================
```

A. There are four routers in the network that are L2-capable.

B. At least one of the interfaces in the network is a broadcast network.

C. R1 does not have any L1 adjacencies.

D. All routers in the network have the same Area ID.

E. All of the above statements must be true.

14. Which of the following statements about a passive interface in IS-IS is false?

  A. The passive interface is listed in the I/F Addresses TLV.

  B. The passive interface is listed in the TE IS Nbrs TLV.

  C. The passive interface is listed in the TE IP Reach TLV.

  D. All of the above statements are true.

15. An interface is configured for BFD using a transmit and receive interval of 100 milliseconds and a multiplier of 5. The interface is BFD-enabled in IS-IS. What is the maximum length of time it will take after loss of forwarding on the interface to notify IS-IS of the failure?

  A. 5 milliseconds

  B. 10 milliseconds

  C. 100 milliseconds

  D. 500 milliseconds

  E. 5 seconds

  F. 10 seconds

Chapter 9

1. Which of the following best describes the implementation of hierarchy in IS-IS?

  A. L1 routers perform the SPF calculation over their local area. L2 routers connect to L1 routers in different areas and exchange routes between the different areas.

  B. L1 routers perform the SPF calculation over their local area. L2 routers perform the SPF calculation over the L2 topology and route between the different areas.

  C. L1 routers exchange routes only with other L1 routers. L2 routers exchange routes only with other L2 routers.

  D. L1 routers route only in their own area. L2 routers create tunnels between different areas.

2. What is the most likely cause of asymmetric routing in a multi-area IS-IS network?

   A. Asymmetric routing can occur because L1 routers can only forward traffic to other L1 routers and L2 routers can only forward traffic to other L2 routers.

   B. In an IS-IS multi-area network, all traffic between areas must pass through the backbone area.

   C. A prefix learned from an L1 LSP is preferred over one learned from an L2 LSP even if it is not the most direct route.

   D. A prefix learned from an L2 LSP is preferred over one learned from an L1 LSP even if it is not the most direct route.

   E. L1 routers only have a default route to an L1/L2 router, which may not be the most direct route to the destination.

3. Which of the following best describes the advantage of using summarization?

   A. Summarization provides more accurate routing information to routers outside the area.

   B. Summarization simplifies the configuration required on the L2 routers.

   C. Summarization eliminates the possibility of asymmetric routing and suboptimal routing.

   D. Summarization reduces the size of the LSP and of the route table of routers outside the area.

   E. Summarization is not supported in IS-IS because it was not designed as an IP routing protocol.

4. Which of the following statements best describes route leaking in IS-IS?

   A. Route leaking allows prefixes from outside an L1 area to be known inside the area.

   B. Route leaking reduces the number of routes in the route table by replacing a group of prefixes with one less specific prefix.

   C. Route leaking allows prefixes from outside the IS-IS routing domain to be known in the IS-IS domain.

   D. Route leaking allows prefixes from the IS-IS routing domain to be advertised in another routing protocol such as BGP.

5. What is the likely result if there is a break in the L2 backbone?
   A. Some destinations in the network will be unreachable.
   B. Some routes will have an asymmetric path.
   C. Some routes will not take the most optimal path.
   D. The network will take longer to converge after a topology change.
   E. All of the above conditions are likely to occur.
6. Which of the following best describes the purpose of hierarchy in an IS-IS network?
   A. Hierarchy improves the efficiency of packet forwarding through the network.
   B. Hierarchy eliminates the possibility of asymmetric routing in the network.
   C. Hierarchy simplifies the configuration and troubleshooting of routers.
   D. Hierarchy is required in order to implement traffic engineering.
   E. None of the above statements describe the purpose of hierarchy in IS-IS.
7. Which of the following statements is false?
   A. The L1 LSDB is the same for all L1 and L1/L2 routers in the same area.
   B. The L2 LSDB is the same for all L1/L2 and L2 routers in the network.
   C. An L1/L2 router has one LSDB with both L1 and L2 LSPs.
   D. An L1/L2 router has both an L1 and an L2 LSDB.
   E. Both A and B are false.
8. The command `summary-address 192.0.2.0/24 level-2` is used on an L1/L2 router to summarize several `/28` prefixes in the area. Which of the following statements is false?
   A. The L2 LSP originated by the router will contain only the summarized prefix.
   B. The L1 LSP originated by the router will contain a black-hole prefix for the summarized prefix.
   C. The individual prefixes will be seen in the L1 LSDB for the area.
   D. The router will have a black-hole entry in its route table for the summary prefix.
   E. All of the above statements are true.

9. IS-IS routes are being leaked into an L1 area, and the network operator does not want to have the default route used in the area. Where does the operator configure `suppress-default` to accomplish this?

A. The command is configured on any L1/L2 router that is leaking routes into the area.

B. The command is configured on all L1/L2 or L2 routers in the area.

C. The command is configured on all L1/L2 or L2 routers in the IS-IS routing domain.

D. The command is configured on all L1 routers in the area.

E. The command is configured on all routers in the area.

10. Which of the following statements about IS-IS export policies is false?

A. By default, an IS-IS router only advertises interfaces that are defined in IS-IS.

B. An export policy must be applied in IS-IS to advertise routes from another routing domain.

C. By default, routes exported to IS-IS from another routing protocol are always advertised in the L2 LSP only.

D. The metric for the route can be set in the export policy.

E. All of the above statements are true.

11. Which of the following statements about route tags is incorrect?

A. A route tag can be assigned on an IS-IS interface.

B. A route tag can be assigned on an IS-IS summary address.

C. A route tag can be assigned in a route leaking policy.

D. A route tag can be used in a policy to control route leaking.

E. All of the above statements are correct.

12. Router R1 learns a route to `10.10.0.0/20` with next-hop R2 from OSPF, a route to `10.10.10.0/24` with next-hop R3 from an L1 LSP, and a route to `10.10.10.0/24` with next-hop R4 from an L2 LSP, and has a static route to `10.10.0.0/16` with next-hop R5. What will be the next-hop for a packet destined to `10.10.10.10`?

    A. The next-hop is R2.

    B. The next-hop is R3.

    C. The next-hop is R4.

    D. The next-hop is R5.

    E. The packet is discarded.

13. Which of the following statements is false?

    A. Routing in an IS-IS L1 area is similar to routing in an OSPF stub area with no summaries.

    B. Routing in a normal OSPF area is similar to routing in an IS-IS L1 area with all of the L2 routes leaked by the L1/L2 routers in the area.

    C. The IS-IS routing protocol is more likely to create asymmetric routes than OSPF.

    D. IS-IS can be configured to calculate the interface bandwidth the same way as OSPF.

    E. All of the above statements are true.

14. Which of the following statements is false?

    A. An L1 router forms adjacencies with all neighbors in the same area.

    B. An L2 router forms adjacencies with all neighbors regardless of area.

    C. An L1/L2 router forms adjacencies only with other L1 and L1/L2 neighbors in the same area.

    D. Answers A–C are true.

    E. Answers A–C are false.

15. Which of the following best describes the use of the ATT bit in IS-IS?

    A. The ATT bit indicates that the router is in the overload state.

    B. The ATT bit is set by a router to indicate that it is configured for route leaking.

    C. The ATT bit is set by a router that is exporting external routes to IS-IS.

    D. The ATT bit is set by an L1/L2 router to indicate that it can be used for a default route by L1 routers in the area.

Chapter 10

1. Which of the following statements about the operation of IS-IS for IPv6 is false?

   A. Two separate instances of IS-IS must operate on the router in order to support both IPv4 and IPv6 routing.

   B. Operating with IPv4 and IPv6 in a single routing topology could lead to holes in either IPv4 or IPv6 routing.

   C. IS-IS can be configured to exchange IPv6 routes with OSPFv3.

   D. IS-IS can operate on the 7750 SR with a mix of IPv4 and IPv6 interfaces.

   E. All of the above statements are true.

2. The complete output of the `show router isis database detail level 2` is shown below. Which of the following statements about router R1 is true?

```
Displaying Level 2 database
-----------------------------------------------------------------------
LSP ID     : R1.00-00                                   Level      : L2
Sequence   : 0xae7                 Checksum   : 0x4a18  Lifetime   : 1014
Version    : 1                     Pkt Type   : 20      Pkt Ver    : 1
Attributes: L1L2                   Max Area   : 3
SysID Len : 6                      Used Len   : 81      Alloc Len : 1492

TLVs :
  Area Addresses:
    Area Address : (1) 49
  Supp Protocols:
    Protocols       : IPv4
    Protocols       : IPv6
  MT Topology:
    MT ID           : 0                         No Flags
    MT ID           : 2                         No Flags
  IS-Hostname    : R1
  Router ID    :
    Router ID    : 10.10.10.1
  I/F Addresses :
    I/F Address    : 10.10.10.1
    I/F Address    : 10.1.2.1
  TE IP Reach    :
```

```
    Default Metric  : 0
    Control Info:    , prefLen 32
    Prefix   : 10.10.10.1
    Default Metric  : 10
    Control Info:    , prefLen 27
    Prefix   : 10.1.2.0

Level (2) LSP Count : 1
======================================================================
```

A. The router is configured for IPv4 operation only.

B. The router is configured for IPv6 operation only.

C. The router is configured for single-topology IPv4 and IPv6.

D. The router is configured for multi-topology IPv4 and IPv6.

E. There is not enough information to select from the above statements.

3. Given the following extract from the `show router isis database` command, what is the most likely IPv6 system address for Router R1?

```
Displaying Level 2 database
----------------------------------------------------------------------
LSP ID    : R1.00-00                                Level     : L2

TLVs :
  Supp Protocols:
    Protocols      : IPv4
    Protocols      : IPv6
  I/F Addresses :
    I/F Address    : 10.10.10.1
    I/F Address    : 10.1.2.1
    I/F Address    : 10.1.3.1
  I/F Addresses IPv6 :
    IPv6 Address     : 2001:DB8::1
    IPv6 Address     : 2001:DB8::12:0:0:0:1
  TE IP Reach    :
    Default Metric  : 0
    Control Info:    , prefLen 32
    Prefix   : 10.10.10.1
    Default Metric  : 100
    Control Info:    , prefLen 27
```

```
    Prefix    : 10.1.2.0
    Default Metric  : 100
    Control Info:    , prefLen 27
    Prefix    : 10.1.3.0
  IPv6 Reach:
    Metric: ( I ) 0
    Prefix    : 2001:DB8::1/128
    Metric: ( I ) 100
    Prefix    : 2001:DB8::12:0:0:0:0/64
```

- **A.** `2001:DB8::1`
- **B.** `2001:DB8::12:0:0:0:1`
- **C.** An IPv6 address is not assigned to the system interface.
- **D.** It is not possible to tell which is the system address.
- **E.** IPv6 is not enabled on the router.

4. Which of the following best describes how multi-topology capabilities are implemented in IS-IS?

- **A.** No changes are required to the protocol. The IS-IS process on the router is enhanced to support multi-topologies.
- **B.** The existing TLVs are used with an additional sub-TLV added to indicate the topology to which it applies.
- **C.** New TLVs are defined that contain a field identifying the topology to which it applies.
- **D.** Multiple IS-IS instances are implemented on each router to support each of the topologies.
- **E.** The Alcatel-Lucent 7750 SR does not support MT IS-IS for IPv6.

5. Which of the following statements about IPv6 for IS-IS on the 7750 SR is false?

A. Routers can be configured to leak IPv6 prefixes in a similar manner to route leaking for IPv4.

B. An L1 router creates an IPv6 default route to the nearest L1/L2 router in the IPv6 topology.

C. Export policies can be configured on routers to bring IPv6 prefixes from other IPv6 routing protocols into IS-IS.

D. IPv6 global addresses do not necessarily need to be configured on interfaces because routers use the link local addresses to form their adjacency.

E. Statements A–D are true.

F. Statements A–D are false.

6. Which of the following is the TLV that carries the information about IPv6 destinations in the network?

A. Extended IS Reachability TLV (Type 22)

B. Extended IP Reachability TLV (Type 135)

C. IPv6 Interface Address TLV (Type 232)

D. IPv6 Reachability TLV (Type 236)

E. None of the above

7. What is meant by *multi-topology* IS-IS?

A. Multi-topology means that there are multiple address families supported in the same topology.

B. Multi-topology means that the router maintains different LSDBs and route tables for distinct topologies such as IPv4 and IPv6.

C. Multi-topology means that the routing domain is split into multiple areas to provide better scalability in a large network.

D. Multi-topology means that the router is learning routes from multiple different routing protocols.

E. None of the above statements describe a multi-topology network.

8. An extract from the show `routerisis database detail` command is shown below. How many interfaces are enabled for IPv4 and IPv6 in IS-IS? Assume that an adjacency is formed on all enabled interfaces.

```
Displaying Level 2 database
-----------------------------------------------------------------------
LSP ID    : R1.00-00                                    Level     : L2

TLVs :
  TE IS Nbrs    :
    Nbr    : R2.00
    Default Metric   : 100
    Sub TLV Len      : 12
    IF Addr    : 10.1.2.1
    Nbr IP     : 10.1.2.2
  MT IS Nbrs      :
    MT ID            : 2
    Nbr    : R2.00
    Default Metric   : 100
    Sub TLV Len      : 0
  TE IS Nbrs    :
    Nbr    : R3.00
    Default Metric   : 100
    Sub TLV Len      : 12
    IF Addr    : 10.1.3.1
    Nbr IP     : 10.1.3.3
```

A. There are no interfaces in either IPv4 or IPv6.

B. There is one IPv4 interface and two IPv6 interfaces.

C. There are two IPv4 interfaces and one IPv6 interface.

D. There are three IPv4 interfaces and three IPv6 interfaces.

E. It is not possible to tell from this output.

9. Given the output below from the `show router route-table ipv6` command, which of the following statements is most likely true?

```
IPv6 Route Table (Router: Base)
===============================================================================
Dest Prefix                                       Type     Proto    Age        Pref
      Next Hop[Interface Name]                                         Metric
-------------------------------------------------------------------------------
2001:DB8::1/128                                   Remote   ISIS     12h23m44s   18
      FE80::216:4DFF:FE13:5CB0-"toR5"                                   300
2001:DB8::5/128                                   Remote   ISIS     12h27m20s   18
      FE80::216:4DFF:FE13:5CB0-"toR5"                                   100
2001:DB8::6/128                                   Local    Local    01d14h18m   0
      system                                                           0
2001:DB8::12:0:0:0:0/64                           Remote   ISIS     12h27m17s   18
      FE80::216:4DFF:FE13:5CB0-"toR5"                                   400
2001:DB8::6666:0:0:0:0/64                         Remote   ISIS     00h09m40s   255
      Black Hole                                                       1
2001:DB8::6666:0:0:0:1/128                        Local    Local    12h12m36s   0
      loop1                                                            0
2001:DB8::6666:0:0:0:2/128                        Local    Local    12h12m27s   0
      loop2                                                            0
2001:DB8::6666:0:0:0:3/128                        Local    Local    12h12m19s   0
      loop3                                                            0
-------------------------------------------------------------------------------
No. of Routes: 8
```

A. The router does not have any interfaces configured for IPv4.

B. The system address of the router is `2001:DB8::5/128`.

C. The router is a Level 1 router.

D. The router is summarizing its local loopback interfaces as `2001:DB8::6666:0:0:0:0/64`.

E. None of the above statements is likely to be true.

10. Which of the following is *not* one of the MT topologies defined in RFC 5120?
    - **A.** IPv4 in-band management.
    - **B.** IPv6 routing.
    - **C.** IPv4 multicast routing.
    - **D.** IPv6 multicast routing.
    - **E.** Answers C and D are not valid MT topologies.
    - **F.** Answers A, B, C, and D are all valid MT topologies.

Chapter 11

1. Which protocol cannot be transported in MPLS?
    - **A.** IP
    - **B.** Ethernet
    - **C.** ATM
    - **D.** Frame Relay
    - **E.** All of the above protocols can be transported in MPLS.
2. What is the primary purpose of using MPLS for IGP shortcuts?
    - **A.** To provide the shortest path possible for forwarding data across the network
    - **B.** To reduce the number of EBGP sessions required
    - **C.** To reduce the number of IBGP sessions required
    - **D.** To eliminate the use of an IGP in the carrier network
    - **E.** None of the above
3. Which statement is correct regarding the definition of a P router?
    - **A.** P routers are service-aware.
    - **B.** P routers are typically LERs.
    - **C.** P routers perform label PUSH and POP operations.
    - **D.** P routers have all their interfaces inside the service provider domain.
    - **E.** None of the above.

4. When is a packet assigned to an FEC in an MPLS network?
   A. The FEC is assigned at each LSR in the MPLS network.
   B. The FEC is assigned at the ingress LER.
   C. The FEC is assigned at the ingress LER and at each LSR in the MPLS network.
   D. The FEC is assigned at the ingress LER and the egress LER.
   E. There is not enough information provided.
5. Which of the following MPLS signaling protocols are used to signal transport labels?
   A. Multiprotocol BGP
   B. Targeted LDP
   C. GRE
   D. RSVP-TE
   E. All of the above
6. Which of the following is *not* a current application of MPLS today?
   A. Virtual Private Networks
   B. Traffic Engineering
   C. Enabling line rate forwarding
   D. High availability and redundancy
   E. All of the above
7. Which of the following statements about label distribution protocols is correct?
   A. Label bindings are distributed in the downstream direction.
   B. A router using ordered control mode will not generate a label until it receives one from its upstream neighbor.
   C. A router using liberal label retention will have the same contents in its LIB and LFIB.
   D. Answers A and B are correct.
   E. None of the above answers are correct.

8. Consider a network that is used to provide MPLS VPN services. Which statement best describes the packets that egress a CE router that is directly connected to a PE?

   A. The packets are unlabeled.

   B. The packets have one outer transport label and one inner service label.

   C. The packets have one inner transport label and one outer service label.

   D. There is not enough information to answer the question.

9. Which MPLS construct is used to store the active MPLS labels used for switching packets?

   A. RIB

   B. Route table

   C. LIB

   D. FIB

   E. LFIB

10. Consider a network topology with three Alcatel-Lucent 7750 SR routers, R1, R2, and R3. R1 and R3 are PE routers, and R2 is a P router. An operator wants to configure a static LSP for a particular FEC to have a path of R1–R2–R3. Which statement below is correct?

    A. The FEC needs to be configured on all three routers.

    B. R2 needs to have its interface to R1 and its interface to R3 configured with label swap operations.

    C. The same MPLS label must be used for the LSP on all three routers.

    D. None of the above answers are correct.

11. Consider a network with an ingress PE, five P routers, and an egress PE that are all Alcatel-Lucent 7750 SRs used to provide a VPN service. When an unlabeled packet enters the ingress PE, it has an IP TTL of 10. What will the IP TTL be when the packet leaves the egress PE?

    A. 255

    B. 10

    C. 9

    D. 8

    E. 3

    F. There is not enough information to determine.

12. Consider a network topology that contains three Alcatel-Lucent 7750 SRs: R1, R2, and R3. R3 is connected to R1 with port `1/1/1` and to R2 with port `1/1/2`. R3 advertises label 32,800 for a particular FEC to R1. What label will be advertised to R2 for the same FEC assuming that R3 is not advertising any other FECs?

A. 32,800

B. 32,799

C. 32,801

D. There is not enough information to determine.

13. An MPLS router is signaled a label of 3 from its downstream router. What will the router do when it receives a data packet for this LSP from an upstream router?

A. It will perform label swapping and transmit the packet with an MPLS label of 3.

B. It will push the label of 3 and transmit the packet.

C. It will silently discard the packet.

D. It will extract the packet to the CPM for OAM options.

E. It will pop the outer label, and forward the packet to the next-hop.

14. Which statement is correct regarding an Alcatel-Lucent 7750 SR VPN services network?

A. An IGP such as OSPF or IS-IS is required inside the carrier network.

B. All user data traffic that traverses the carrier network contains an MPLS transport label that is held constant through the carrier network.

C. All user data traffic that traverses the carrier network contains an MPLS service label that is swapped at each P router.

D. None of the above statements are correct.

15. Which statement is correct concerning label distribution modes on the Alcatel-Lucent 7750 SR?

A. RSVP-TE uses downstream unsolicited mode.

B. LDP uses downstream-on-demand mode.

C. RSVP-TE and LDP use conservative label retention.

D. RSVP-TE and LDP use ordered control.

E. None of the above statements are correct.

Chapter 12

1. Which of the following statements about LDP is correct?
   - **A.** Link LDP is used to exchange service labels.
   - **B.** Targeted LDP is used to exchange transport labels.
   - **C.** Link LDP peers are always directly connected.
   - **D.** Targeted LDP is required to provide L3 VPN services.
   - **E.** None of the above statements are correct.

2. What is the purpose of an LDP Notification message?
   - **A.** To create, change, and delete label mappings for FECs
   - **B.** To signal errors and other notable events
   - **C.** To establish LDP sessions between neighbors
   - **D.** To announce and maintain the presence of an LSR in a network
   - **E.** None of the above

3. Which statement below best describes the default behavior of LDP label advertisement on the Alcatel-Lucent 7750 SR?
   - **A.** Advertise a label for the system address.
   - **B.** Advertise labels for reachable FECs for which a label has been received.
   - **C.** Advertise a label for the system address and for reachable FECs for which a label has been received.
   - **D.** Do not advertise any labels unless an LDP export policy is configured.
   - **E.** Do not advertise any labels unless an LDP import policy is configured.

4. When an operator uses the `show router ldp bindings active` command on an Alcatel-Lucent 7750 SR, which construct is viewed?
   - **A.** RIB
   - **B.** FIB
   - **C.** LIB
   - **D.** LFIB
   - **E.** RTM

5. Consider a network topology that includes four Alcatel-Lucent 7750 SRs. An IGP is running in the network, and each router advertises its system interface into the IGP. Assuming that export policies are not configured and LDP is converged, how many label prefix bindings are seen on each router when the `show router ldp bindings` command is used?

   A. 4

   B. 8

   C. 12

   D. 16

   E. There is not enough information to determine the answer.

6. Which of the following is *not* a function of LDP?

   A. Discovery

   B. Flow control

   C. Session establishment

   D. Label exchange

   E. All of the above are functions of LDP.

7. Which LDP message type does *not* use TCP as a transport protocol?

   A. Notification

   B. Label Mapping

   C. KeepAlive

   D. Hello

   E. All of the above messages use TCP as a transport protocol.

8. Which of the statements below is correct regarding Link LDP adjacencies on an Alcatel-Lucent 7750 SR?

A. A non-zero label space is indicated in each Hello message.

B. The source IP address in each Hello message is the system interface address of the originating router.

C. The destination IP address in each Hello message is the interface address of the destination router.

D. The Hello time-out value must match between routers for the LDP adjacency to come up.

E. By default, the egress interface address of the originating router is used for the transport address in Hello messages.

F. None of the above statements are correct.

9. Consider a network that contains three Alcatel-Lucent 7750 SRs—R1, R2, and R3. The network is used to provide MPLS VPN services. R1 has two links to R2 and a single link to R3. R2 and R3 do not have a link between them. If Link LDP is used to distribute labels between all three routers, how many LDP sessions will R2 have?

A. 1

B. 2

C. 3

D. 4

E. There is not enough information to determine the answer.

10. Two Alcatel-Lucent 7750 SRs are configured to use Link LDP. R1 has a system interface address of `10.0.0.5`, and R2 has a system interface address of `10.0.0.12`. Which of the following statements is correct regarding LDP session establishment between the routers?

A. R1 is considered the active router for session establishment.

B. R1 does not send any LDP Initialization messages for session establishment.

C. R2 initiates the opening of the LDP session by sending an LDP Notification message.

D. Both routers will attempt to open a TCP connection.

E. LDP Address and Label Mapping messages cannot be exchanged until the active router reaches the operational state.

11. Consider two routers, R1 and R2, running a Link LDP session between them. R2 has a label binding for an FEC that it received from R1; however, a network topology change occurs that causes R1 to no longer recognize the FEC. Which statement best characterizes the LDP message sequence used to indicate the change on R1?

A. R1 sends a Label Withdraw message to R2.

B. R1 sends a Label Release message to R2.

C. R1 sends a Label Withdraw message to R2, and R2 sends a Label Release message to R1.

D. R1 sends a Label Release message to R2, and R2 sends a Label Release message to R1.

12. Consider a network topology that contains three Alcatel-Lucent 7750 SRs—R1, R2, and R3—running Link LDP. R1 is connected to both R2 and R3. Assuming that an export policy is not configured on R1, which statement best describes R1's actions as soon as the LDP adjacencies are established with both routers?

A. R1 originates a Label Mapping message for its system address to R1 and R2. Both Label Mapping messages contain the same label value.

B. R1 originates a Label Mapping message for its system address to R1 and R2. The Label Mapping messages contain different label values.

C. R1 originates a Notification message for its system address to R1 and R2. Both Notification messages contain the same label value.

D. R1 originates a Notification message for its system address to R1 and R2. The Notification messages contain different values.

E. There is not enough information to determine R1's actions.

13. Consider a network topology of three Alcatel-Lucent 7750 SRs in which each router has a single connection to the other two routers. An IGP is running in the network, and each router advertises its system interface into the IGP. All router links in the network are equal cost, and ECMP is configured throughout the network. How many prefix bindings are seen on each router when the `show router ldp bindings active` command is used?

   A. 3

   B. 5

   C. 6

   D. 9

   E. There is not enough information to determine the answer.

14. Consider a network of Alcatel-Lucent 7750 SRs with two OSPF Area 1 ABRs. Both Area 1 ABRs receive the prefixes `192.168.3.0/24` and `192.168.4.0/24` from Area 1 and summarize them as `192.168.0.0/16` toward Area 0. What configuration is required in the network to ensure that Area 0 routers have active LDP bindings for the FECs `192.168.3.0/24` and `192.168.4.0/24`?

   A. The `aggregate-prefix-match` command has to be used on one of the ABRs.

   B. The `aggregate-prefix-match` command has to be used on both of the ABRs.

   C. The `aggregate-prefix-match` command has to be used on Area 0 routers that are directly connected to either of the Area 1 ABRs.

   D. The `aggregate-prefix-match` command has to be used on all Area 0 routers.

   E. No specific configuration is required.

15. Consider a network topology of three Alcatel-Lucent 7750 SRs. Each router has a connection to the other two routers. An IGP is running in the network, and each router advertises its system interface into the IGP. An operator intends to configure the router interfaces between all three routers into LDP but forgets an interface on one of the routers. How many active LDP prefix bindings are on the router that the operator mistakenly configured with only one LDP interface? Assume that all the router links have the same cost.

    A. 0

    B. 1

    C. 2

    D. 3

    E. 5

    F. 6

Chapter 13

1. Which statement is correct regarding the RSVP-TE messages used for setting up an LSP?

    A. The destination IP address of a Path message is always the next-hop neighbor.

    B. Resv messages must contain an RRO so that they can be forwarded appropriately.

    C. Label binding information is carried in Path messages.

    D. The head end signals LSP label values to be used by all other routers in a Path trigger message.

    E. None of the above statements are correct.

2. Consider an operationally up LSP that has a strict path of R1 ➪ R2 ➪ R3 ➪ R4. A link failure occurs between R2 and R3. Which statement best describes the RSVP-TE message sequence that follows?

   A. R1 detects the IGP topology change and sends a PathTear message downstream.

   B. R1 detects the IGP topology change and sends a ResvTear message downstream.

   C. R2 sends a PathErr message upstream, and R3 sends a ResvErr message downstream.

   D. R2 sends a PathTear message upstream, and R3 sends a ResvTear message downstream.

   E. R2 sends a ResvTear message upstream, and R3 sends a PathTear message downstream.

3. Consider an established LSP with a path traversing four routers. There are six routers in the IGP domain, and all routers have operational RSVP-TE interfaces. Which routers will have an RSVP-TE session for this LSP?

   A. Only the head end router will have an RSVP-TE session for the LSP.

   B. The head end router and the tail end router will have an RSVP-TE session for the LSP.

   C. All routers in the LSP::Path will have an RSVP-TE session for the LSP.

   D. All routers in the IGP domain will have an RSVP-TE session for the LSP.

   E. There is not enough information to answer the question.

4. Which statement is correct concerning RSVP Error messages?

   A. PathErr messages travel upstream and are addressed to the head end router.

   B. ResvErr messages travel downstream and are addressed to the tail end router.

   C. ResvErr messages modify the RSB on RSVP routers.

   D. PathErr messages do not modify the PSB on RSVP routers.

   E. None of the above answers are correct.

5. Consider a network that has four routers with EBGP peers and five core routers that only have IBGP peers. A service provider wants to start using MPLS shortcuts for BGP. Which routers need to be provisioned with MPLS shortcuts?

   A. MPLS shortcuts need to be provisioned on the routers that only have IBGP peers.

   B. MPLS shortcuts need to be provisioned on the routers that have EBGP peers.

   C. MPLS shortcuts need to be provisioned on all routers in the autonomous system.

   D. MPLS shortcuts need to be provisioned on all routers that have EBGP connections and their peers in other autonomous systems.

   E. There is not enough information to answer the question.

6. Consider an RSVP-TE LSP that is operationally up. An operator administratively shuts down the LSP at the head end. Which statement best describes the sequence of messages that follows?

   A. A PathTear message is sent from the head end router to the tail end, intercepted by each router along the path of the LSP.

   B. A PathTear message is tunneled from the head end router to the tail end. Upon reception of the PathTear, the tail end originates a ResvTear message that travels back to the head end, intercepted at each hop.

   C. A ResvTear message is sent from the head end router toward the tail end, intercepted by each router in the path.

   D. A PathErr message is tunneled from the head end router to the tail end. The tail end then originates a ResvTear message that travels back to the head end, intercepted at each hop.

   E. A ResvErr message is sent from the head end router toward the tail end, intercepted by each router in the path.

7. A router is the ingress LER for three RSVP-TE–signaled LSPs, the egress LER for two RSVP-TE–signaled LSPs, and the transit LSR for four RSVP-TE–signaled LSPs. The router has 10 Layer 2 VPN service instances configured. How many RSVP-TE sessions exist on the node?

   A. Two

   B. Three

   C. Four

   D. Five

   E. Nine

   F. 19

8. An operator mistakenly does an admin shutdown on an operationally up LSP and later brings it back up. How do the Tunnel ID and LSP ID compare before and after the LSP was shut down?

   A. The Tunnel ID and LSP ID remain unchanged.

   B. The Tunnel ID changes, but the LSP ID stays constant.

   C. The Tunnel ID stays constant, but the LSP ID changes.

   D. The Tunnel ID and the LSP ID change.

   E. There is not enough information to determine the answer.

9. An operationally up LSP in an Alcatel-Lucent 7750 SR network has a totally loose path. CSPF is not configured on the LSP, and the resignal timer has not been changed from default settings. A link failure in the network causes a topology change that affects the path of the LSP. The link is later repaired. Which statement best describes the LSP ID before and after the link failure?

   A. The LSP ID stays constant through the network changes.

   B. The LSP ID changes when the link goes down. It does not change again until the resignal timer expires or the LSP is manually resignaled.

   C. The LSP ID changes when the link goes down and changes again when the link is restored.

   D. There is not enough information to determine the answer.

10. Consider two routers, R1 and R2. There are two LSPs that originate on R1 and terminate on R2. There are two LSPs that originate on R2 and terminate on R1. R1 is a transit LSR for seven LSPs, and three of these also transit R2. Assuming that these are the only LSPs in the network, how many Hello messages will R1 send to R2 at every Hello interval?

   A. Two

   B. Four

   C. Seven

   D. 11

   E. None of the above answers are correct.

11. Which statement is correct regarding RSVP-TE refresh reduction?

   A. A summary refresh message is sent to indicate that a router can support refresh reduction.

   B. A summary refresh message lists the tunnel IDs that the router is refreshing.

   C. A summary refresh message lists the LSP IDs that the router is refreshing.

   D. If a router receives an unknown Message ID, it sends a PathTear message downstream and a ResvTear message upstream.

   E. If a router receives an unknown Message ID, it sends a PathTear message upstream and a ResvTear message downstream.

   F. Message ID values are included in Path and Resv messages when RSVP-TE refresh is enabled on an interface.

12. Consider a totally loose LSP that is established over a network of Alcatel-Lucent 7750 SRs. The LSP is not enabled with CSPF. Routers are added to the network in such a way that the original path of the LSP is not affected but a more optimal path becomes available. The resignal timer is set to 30 minutes, and the retry timer has default settings. How long after IGP convergence does it take for the LSP to take the more optimal path?

   A. It takes 30 seconds to start establishing a new path.

   B. It takes 30 minutes to start establishing a new path.

   C. A new path starts to be established at the next resignal timer interval, which could be as long as 30 minutes.

   D. The LSP will not be optimized until it is manually resignaled.

   E. There is not enough information to determine the answer.

13. Consider a totally loose LSP that traverses four routers in the order R1, R2, R3, and R4. CSPF is not configured on the LSP. Which statement below describes the ERO in the Path message sent by R1?

   A. There will not be an ERO in the Path message.

   B. The ERO only contains the system address of R4.

   C. The ERO contains the system address of R1 and the system address of R4.

   D. The ERO contains the router interface addresses of each router along the path followed by the system interface of R4.

   E. There is not enough information to answer the question.

14. An Alcatel-Lucent 7750 SR is provisioned with MPLS shortcuts for BGP. The command `configure router bgp igp-shortcut mpls` is used on the router. If a prefix has both an LDP label binding and an RSVP-TE LSP to the next-hop, which will be used?

   A. The RSVP-TE LSP will be used.

   B. The LDP label binding will be used.

   C. The tunnel that gives the shortest path through the network will be used.

   D. Native IP forwarding will be used.

   E. The tunnel that became available first will be used.

15. Which statement is correct regarding 6PE networks running over Alcatel-Lucent 7750 SRs?

   A. The outer label is an MPLS transport label, and the inner label is an IPv6 implicit null label.

   B. The outer label is an MPLS transport label, and the inner label is an IPv4 explicit null label.

   C. 6PE is used by a service provider that wants to tunnel IPv6 traffic over an IPv4 core.

   D. 6PE is used by a service provider that wants to tunnel IPv4 traffic over an IPv6 core.

Chapter 14

1. Which statement is correct regarding constraint-based routing?
   - **A.** TE-LSPs always follow the best IGP route.
   - **B.** LDP is commonly used for constraint-based routing applications.
   - **C.** Constraint-based routing can be used to provide QoS functions in the data plane.
   - **D.** The route for a TE-LSP is calculated at the head end router.
   - **E.** None of the above statements are correct.

2. An operationally up LSP in a network of Alcatel-Lucent 7750 SRs has a totally loose path and is following the shortest route from the IGP. CSPF is configured on the LSP, and the resignal timer has not been changed from default settings. A link failure in the network causes a topology change that affects the path of the LSP. The link is later repaired. Which statement best describes the LSP ID before and after the link failure?
   - **A.** The LSP ID stays constant.
   - **B.** The LSP ID changes when the link goes down. It will not change again until the resignal timer expires or the LSP is manually resignaled.
   - **C.** The LSP ID changes when the link goes down and changes again when the link is restored.
   - **D.** There is not enough information to determine the answer.

3. Which statement is *not* correct regarding the processing of ERO and RRO messages on a CSPF-enabled router?
   - **A.** Each transit LSR removes the first hop from the ERO in the Path message and builds a new Path message for the next-hop LSR.
   - **B.** The head end router fills the ERO according to the CSPF calculation results.
   - **C.** Each LSR in the LSP path helps to build the RRO by adding the IP address of the interface on which it transmits the Path message.
   - **D.** When CSPF is enabled, the ERO can contain strict or loose hops.
   - **E.** All of the above statements are correct.

4. Consider an Alcatel-Lucent 7750 SR that has three MPLS interfaces. One interface is configured with the admin group `gold`, one with the admin group `silver`, and one with the admin group `bronze`. These are the only interfaces in the entire network configured with admin groups. An established LSP is configured to exclude the admin group `gold`; however, an operator decides to change the LSP to include the admin group `bronze`. No other routers are changed. Assuming that the ingress LER and egress LER of the LSP are not directly connected, which statement best describes the resulting behavior?

   A. The LSP becomes operationally down until the retry timer expires and then becomes established.

   B. The LSP becomes operationally down and stays in this state until a configuration change is made.

   C. The LSP path does not change until it is manually resignaled or the resignal timer expires.

   D. The LSP path changes to use the interface with admin group `bronze`.

   E. None of the above statements are correct.

5. Which statement is not correct regarding the use of LDP-over-RSVP on a network of 7750 SRs?

   A. CSPF is not required on RSVP-TE LSPs used for LDP-over-RSVP.

   B. For the purposes of LDP-over-RSVP, T-LDP is only required on the ABRs.

   C. Data travels across an area with an outer MPLS label signaled with RSVP-TE, an inner MPLS label signaled with LDP, and possibly a VPN service label.

   D. The IGP must be configured to support LDP-over-RSVP.

   E. All of the above statements are correct.

6. Which statement is incorrect regarding CSPF calculations?

   A. The router doing the CSPF calculation puts itself as the root of the SPF tree.

   B. CSPF calculations are performed on the TED.

   C. Traffic engineering metrics are stored in the LSDB.

   D. Hop count can be used as a constraint for a TE-LSP.

   E. All of the above statements are correct.

7. Which of the following attributes is not carried in link-state packets for Traffic Engineering?

   A. Maximum bandwidth

   B. IGP metric

   C. Administrative groups

   D. Unreserved bandwidth

   E. Maximum reservable bandwidth

   F. All of the above parameters are carried in link-state packets.

8. What type of LSA does OSPF use for flooding traffic engineering information?

   A. Type 7 LSA

   B. Type 8 LSA

   C. Type 9 LSA

   D. Type 10 LSA

   E. None of the above

9. If a non-TE–capable OSPF router in an area receives a traffic engineering LSA, what actions will it take?

   A. It will flood the LSA.

   B. It will silently discard the LSA.

   C. It will discard the LSA and send an error to the originating router.

   D. It will discard the LSA and send an error to the router from which it received the LSA.

   E. It will not take any of the above actions.

10. Which of the following statements about the OSPF-TE Type 10 LSA is incorrect?

   A. The Type 10 LSA has two subtypes.

   B. The subtype 1 of the Type 10 LSA contains the router's IP address.

   C. The subtype 2 of the Type 10 LSA contains TE information for all links on the router.

   D. Each Type 10 LSA only contains one subtype.

   E. All of the statements are correct.

11. An operator configures an LSP with CSPF on an Alcatel-Lucent 7750 SR and specifies a strict hop to an adjacent node followed by a loose hop to the destination node. The command `no record` is used to disable building of the RRO. The operator observes the output of the `show router mpls lsp <lsp-name> path detail` command. Assuming that the LSP is operationally up, which of the following statements is incorrect?

A. The *Explicit Hops* field will list the IP address of the strict hop followed by the IP address of the loose hop.

B. The *Actual Hops* field will list the hops along the entire LSP path.

C. The *Computed Hops* field will list the hops along the entire LSP path.

D. All of the above statements are correct.

12. Consider a network topology that contains four 7750 SRs. R1 is directly connected to R2. Another path from R1 to R2 exists through R3 and R4. The link from R1 to R2 has an IGP cost of 1,000, and all other links in the network have an IGP cost of 100. An LSP is configured from R1 to R2 with a hop limit of 3 and enabled with CSPF. Which path will be taken by the LSP?

A. The path of the LSP will be directly from R1 to R2.

B. The path of the LSP will be through R3 and R4.

C. The LSP will be operationally down because a path that meets the constraint does not exist.

D. There is not enough information to determine the answer.

13. An operator is trying to use traffic engineering to influence the path of a totally loose LSP on a network of 7750 SRs by changing the TE metrics of MPLS interfaces. The path of the LSP does not change. Which statements below could be a possible reason why the LSP path has not changed?

A. A manual resignal is required to create an immediate change in the LSP's path.

B. The operator may not have enabled CSPF on the LSP.

C. The operator may not have explicitly configured the LSP to use TE metrics for its CSPF calculation.

D. A, B, and C could all explain why the LSP path has not changed.

E. None of the answers explain why the LSP path has not changed.

14. Which of the following statements is *not* correct regarding MPLS admin groups on the 7750 SR?

   A. The use of admin groups is also known as link coloring.

   B. The `admin group` attribute is carried as a 32-bit mask in OSPF LSAs.

   C. IS-IS supports admin groups.

   D. Only one admin group at a time can be bound to an MPLS interface.

   E. All of the above statements are correct.

15. An admin group is configured with the command `admin-group "green" 2` and bound to an interface on a 7750 SR. If OSPF is the IGP in the network, which statement best describes how the admin group is advertised?

   A. The Opaque LSA for the interface advertises a value of 0 for the admin group.

   B. The Opaque LSA for the interface advertises a value of 1 for the admin group.

   C. The Opaque LSA for the interface advertises a value of 2 for the admin group.

   D. The Opaque LSA for the interface advertises a value of 3 for the admin group.

   E. The Opaque LSA for the interface advertises a value of 4 for the admin group.

   F. None of the above answers are correct.

Chapter 15

1. A router has just finished a CSPF computation to find a route for a bandwidth-constrained LSP. Which statement best describes the next step for the head end router assuming a path is found for the LSP?

   A. The head end router sends a CAC message to the next-hop router so that it can perform bandwidth reservation.

   B. The head end router floods a TE LSA to all routers in the LSP path so that they can perform bandwidth reservation.

   C. The head end router sends a Path message to the tail end router. The next-hop router intercepts the Path message and performs bandwidth reservation.

   D. The head end router sends a Resv message to the tail end router. The next-hop router intercepts the Resv message and performs bandwidth reservation.

   E. None of the above statements are correct.

2. Consider a network of Alcatel-Lucent 7750 SRs. An operator wants to provision a bandwidth-constrained LSP with a fully loose path. There are two paths between the head and tail end routers. One path has a lower IGP cost but has RSVP-TE interfaces that cannot meet the bandwidth requirement. The RSVP-TE interfaces of all routers along the path with the higher IGP metric can meet the bandwidth requirement. The operator forgets to enable the LSP with CSPF. Which statement below is correct?

   A. The LSP is established and operationally up along the path with the lower IGP cost.

   B. The LSP is established and operationally up along the path with the higher IGP cost.

   C. The LSP is operationally down with the failure code `admissionControlError`.

   D. The LSP is operationally down with the failure code `noCspfRouteToDestination`.

   E. None of the above statements are correct.

3. Consider a network of 7750 SRs. All ports in the network are 1 Gb/s, and default subscription values are used. An operator provisions an LSP with a primary and hot standby secondary path between two nodes. Both paths have a bandwidth constraint of 800 Mb/s and are totally loose. Assume that there are no other RSVP-TE sessions in the network. Which statement below is correct?

   A. If Shared Explicit mode is used, the primary and secondary paths will be established over different paths in the network.

   B. The secondary LSP will not be signaled unless the primary path goes down.

   C. If Fixed Filter mode is used and CSPF is enabled on the LSP, the primary and secondary LSPs will take separate paths through the network.

   D. If Shared Explicit mode is used and CSPF is not enabled on the LSP, the secondary LSP will have a failure code of `admissionControlError`.

   E. All of the above statements are incorrect.

4. Consider a network of 7750 SRs with three CSPF LSPs configured between the same head and tail end router. All ports in the network are 1 Gb/s. Two equal cost paths exist to the tail end router, but ECMP is not enabled on the IGP. The three CSPF LSPs are configured in the following order: a 300 Mb/s LSP, a 400 Mb/s LSP, and a 200 Mb/s LSP. The first and third LSPs have the least-fill option enabled, but the second LSP does not. Assuming that there are no other LSPs in the network, which statement below is correct?

   A. The first and second LSPs will have the same path.

   B. The first and third LSPs will have the same path.

   C. The first and third LSPs will have different paths, but it is not possible to determine which path the second LSP will use.

   D. There is not enough information to determine the path of the LSPs.

5. Which statement below is correct regarding DiffServ-aware traffic engineering on an Alcatel-Lucent 7750 SR?

   A. An Alcatel-Lucent 7750 SR can be configured to use MAM for some LSPs and RDM for other LSPs.

   B. RDM allows lower CTs to allocate the unused bandwidth from higher CTs.

   C. RDM allocates bandwidth discretely to different CTs, and bandwidth cannot be shared between CTs.

   D. If an incorrect class type and priority pair is configured on an LSP, the LSP stays operationally down with a failure code of `admissionControlError`.

   E. None of the above statements are correct.

6. A router receives a Resv message but does not have the required bandwidth resources for the LSP. What action will the router take?

   A. It will flood an LSA to indicate that it cannot service the LSP.

   B. It will send a PathErr message upstream.

   C. It will send a ResvErr message downstream.

   D. It will send a PathTear message downstream and a ResvTear message upstream.

   E. None of the above statements are correct.

7. What is the maximum rate at which an interface can be oversubscribed to actual bandwidth on an Alcatel-Lucent 7750 SR?

   A. 50%

   B. 100%

   C. 1,000%

   D. 10,000%

   E. There is no oversubscription limit.

8. Consider an Alcatel-Lucent 7750 SR that is the head end for a bandwidth-constrained LSP of 600 Mb/s that is operationally up. All of the ports on the router have a speed of 1 Gb/s. The operator changes all RSVP-TE interfaces to have a subscription rate of 50%. Assume there is only one RSVP-TE session on the router. Which statement below is correct?

   A. There is no change to the LSP until the resignal timer expires or the LSP is manually resignaled.

   B. The LSA sent by the head end router for the interface the LSP uses has a maximum bandwidth of 500 Mb/s.

   C. The LSA sent by the head end router for the port the LSP uses has an unreserved bandwidth of 500 Mb/s.

   D. The LSA sent by the head end router for the port the LSP uses has a reservable bandwidth of 0 Mb/s.

   E. There is not enough information to answer the question.

9. A bandwidth-constrained CSPF-enabled LSP is successfully established and passes through two LSRs between the head and tail end routers. Threshold-triggered IGP TE updates are not configured. How many TE LSAs are expected to be flooded in the network because of this LSP establishment?

   A. 0

   B. 1

   C. 3

   D. 4

   E. 6

   F. 8

10. Consider a network of 7750 SRs in which all ports have a speed of 1 Gb/s. The RSVP-TE `te-down` thresholds are configured with a single value of 0% on every router. A physical link failure between two directly connected nodes in the network causes a CSPF-enabled LSP with a totally strict path and a bandwidth reservation of 500 Mb/s to go down. The LSP passes through a total of four routers (including head and tail end). Assuming that there are no other LSPs in the network, how many TE LSAs are generated in the network because of the link failure?

A. 1

B. 2

C. 3

D. 4

E. 6

F. 8

11. Consider a 7750 SR that is a transit LSR for three RSVP-TE tunnels, each configured with a primary and a standby secondary path. All LSPs (primary and secondary) egress the same interface. One of the tunnels has an FF reservation style with a primary and secondary bandwidth constraint of 100 Mb/s. The second LSP uses an SE reservation style with a primary and secondary bandwidth constraint of 200 Mb/s. The third LSP uses an SE reservation style with a primary bandwidth constraint of 300 Mb/s and a secondary bandwidth constraint of 400 Mb/s. Assuming that these are the only RSVP-TE sessions on the router, what should an operator expect to see for the egress interface when they use the `show router rsvp interface` command?

A. The total *Resv BW* is 400 Mb/s.

B. The total *Resv BW* is 600 Mb/s.

C. The total *Resv BW* is 700 Mb/s.

D. The total *Resv BW* is 800 Mb/s.

E. None of the above answers are correct.

12. Consider a network of 7750 SRs. All ports in the network are 1 Gb/s, and all RSVP-TE interfaces have default subscription values. An LSP that is operationally up is configured with a bandwidth constraint of 600 Mb/s and has a Fixed Filter reservation style. There are two distinct paths through the network for the LSP. The LSP is manually resignaled. Assuming that there is no other bandwidth-constrained LSP in the network, which statement below is correct?

  A. The LSP will be operationally down after it is resignaled.

  B. The LSP will be operationally up and will take the same path as before it was resignaled.

  C. The LSP will have the same LSP ID but a different Tunnel ID after it is resignaled.

  D. The LSP will be operationally up but will take a different path through the network after it is resignaled.

  E. None of the above answers are correct.

13. A CSPF LSP with a bandwidth constraint of 600 Mb/s is established with a setup priority of 4 and a hold priority of 3 on a 7750 SR. There are no other LSPs that use the same RSVP-TE interface on the head end router, all ports in the network have a speed of 1 Gb/s, and all RSVP-TE interfaces are configured with default subscription rates. Which statement below is correct regarding the TE LSA that is sent by the head end router as a result of the LSP becoming established?

  A. The unreserved bandwidth for P0–P2 is 1 Gb/s, and the unreserved bandwidth for P3–P7 is 400 Mb/s.

  B. The unreserved bandwidth for P3–P7 is 1 Gb/s, and the unreserved bandwidth for P0–P2 is 400 Mb/s.

  C. The unreserved bandwidth for P3 and P4 is 400 Mb/s, and the rest of the priorities are 1 Gb/s.

  D. The unreserved bandwidth for P3 is 400 Mb/s, and the rest of the priorities are 1 Gb/s.

  E. The unreserved bandwidth for P4 is 400 Mb/s, and the rest of the priorities are 1 Gb/s.

  F. None of the above statements are correct.

14. Consider a network of 7750 SRs. All ports in the network are 1 Gb/s, and all RSVP-TE interfaces have default subscription rates. There are exactly two unequal cost paths in the network between the head and tail end routers. An operator configures three CSPF-enabled totally loose LSPs between the two routers in the following order: an 800 Mb/s LSP with setup and hold priority of 3, a 400 Mb/s LSP with setup and hold priority of 1, and a 700 Mb/s LSP with a setup and hold priority of 2. The operator views the output of the `show router mpls lsp path detail` command immediately after the last LSP is configured. Which statement below is *not* correct?

A. The 400 Mb/s LSP is operationally up along the lowest-cost path.

B. The 700 Mb/s LSP is operationally up along the lowest-cost path.

C. The 800 Mb/s LSP is operationally up along the higher-cost path.

D. All of the above statements are correct.

15. Consider a 7750 SR in which all ports are 1 Gb/s and all RSVP-TE interfaces have a subscription rate of 200. The router is configured for DiffServ-TE using the Russian Dolls Model. Class type 0 is assigned 20% of the reservable bandwidth, class type 1 is assigned 0% of the reservable bandwidth, and class type 2 is assigned 30% of the reservable bandwidth. Assuming that no LSPs are configured, what bandwidth constraints are expected to be in the Traffic Engineering LSAs originated by the router?

A. The BC0 value is 500 Mb/s, the BC1 value is 300 Mb/s, and the BC2 value is 300 Mb/s.

B. The BC0 value is 1 Gb/s, the BC1 value is 600 Mb/s, and and the BC2 value is 600 Mb/s.

C. The BC0 value is 300 Mb/s, the BC1 value is 500 Mb/s, and the BC2 value is 500 Mb/s.

D. The BC0 value is 600 Mb/s, the BC1 value is 1 Gb/s, and the BC2 value is 1 Gb/s.

E. None of the above answers are correct.

Chapter 16

1. An operator configures an Alcatel-Lucent 7750 SR with a primary LSP::Path and a non-standby secondary LSP::Path. The operator mistakenly configures a strict hop in the secondary LSP::Path that does not exist. If the primary LSP::Path is operationally up and FRR is not configured, which statement below is false?

   A. The primary LSP::Path will be active.

   B. The secondary LSP::Path will be operationally down.

   C. The secondary LSP::Path will have a failure code of `noCspfRouteToDestination`.

   D. The secondary LSP::Path will not have any computed hops.

   E. All of the above statements are true.

2. An LSP is configured with a totally loose primary LSP::Path and a totally loose standby secondary LSP::Path. If there are at least two unequal cost totally disjoint paths between the head and tail end router, which statement below is incorrect?

   A. The LSP::Paths should be made disjoint by the use of strict hops, admin groups, or SRLGs.

   B. The secondary LSP::Path is operationally up.

   C. The secondary LSP::Path will take the second least cost path between the head and tail end routers.

   D. If there is a link failure on the primary LSP::Path, there will be a traffic outage at least as long as the LSP retry interval.

   E. All of the above statements are correct.

3. A 7750 SR is configured with three totally loose secondary LSP::Paths in the following order. The first secondary LSP::Path is non-standby, has no constraints, and has no configured path preference. The second secondary LSP::Path is declared standby, has admin group constraints to achieve path diversity, and has a path preference of 50. The third secondary LSP::Path is declared standby, uses SRLG to achieve path diversity, has no configured path preference, and has a lower CSPF metric than the second secondary LSP::Path. Which secondary LSP::Path will become active if the primary LSP::Path fails? Assume that the failure does not affect the standby LSP::Paths.

A. The first secondary LSP::Path will become active.

B. The second secondary LSP::Path will become active.

C. The third secondary LSP::Path will become active.

D. None of the secondary LSP::Paths will become active.

4. Consider a router that could be a PLR for two established protected LSPs that have the same tail end router. Which statement best describes the detour LSPs originated by the PLR?

A. The PLR originates one detour LSP that follows the shortest CSPF path to the destination.

B. If both protected LSPs have identical paths, the PLR originates one detour LSP; otherwise, two detour LSPs are originated.

C. If both protected LSPs have the same head end router, the PLR originates one detour LSP; otherwise, two detour LSPs are originated.

D. The PLR originates two detour LSPs that follow the shortest CSPF path to the destination.

E. None of the above statements are correct.

5. Consider an LSP protected with facility backup and a primary LSP::Path constrained with strict hops. The LSP also has a totally loose non-standby secondary. Assuming that the primary LSP::Path is operationally up and fully protected, which of the following statement is incorrect?

   A. After a link failure on the primary LSP::Path, the PLR will switch traffic to the bypass tunnel.

   B. After the head end node learns that local protection is in use, it signals the secondary LSP::Path and makes it active.

   C. FRR protection is attempted by every router on the secondary LSP::Path after it becomes active.

   D. The bypass tunnel remains up even if the secondary LSP::Path is active.

   E. All of the above statements are true.

6. An LSP is provisioned with a totally loose primary LSP::Path and a non-standby totally loose secondary LSP::Path. Assuming that there are multiple disjoint paths between the head and tail end router, which statement is true?

   A. Admin groups should be used to ensure path diversity.

   B. Shared risk link groups should be used to ensure path diversity.

   C. The primary LSP::Path and secondary LSP::Paths will use the same hops.

   D. The primary LSP::Path will use the path with the shortest CSPF cost, and the secondary LSP::Path will use the path with the next shortest CSPF cost.

   E. All of the above statements are incorrect because the secondary is not signaled.

7. A CSPF LSP is configured with a totally loose primary LSP::Path and a non-standby totally loose secondary LSP::Path. The primary LSP::Path is operationally up. There are at least two unequal cost and disjoint paths in the network between the head and tail end routers. If there is a failure on the link of the tail end router that is on the primary LSP::Path, which statement below is false?

   A. After the head end detects the failure, it will immediately signal the secondary LSP::Path over the least cost path available.

   B. After the retry interval expires, the primary LSP::Path will be signaled over the least cost path available, and the secondary LSP::Path will be torn down.

   C. After the link is repaired, the primary LSP::Path will not be resignaled to use the least cost path available.

   D. There will be a traffic outage that is at least as long as the retry interval when the link goes down.

   E. None of the above statements are false.

8. A 7750 SR is configured with an LSP that has a primary LSP::Path constrained with strict hops and a totally loose standby secondary LSP::Path with the `srlg` parameter. The operator mistakenly configures *all* interfaces on the tail end router with the same SRLG instead of just the interface used for the primary LSP::Path. Assuming that there are at least two disjoint paths in the network between the head and tail end routers and the LSP::Paths are configured after SRLG groups have been bound to the interfaces, which statement below is correct?

   A. The primary LSP::Path and the secondary LSP::Path will be operationally up with identical actual hops.

   B. The secondary LSP::Path will be down with the failure code `noCspfRouteToDestination`.

   C. The secondary LSP::Path will be operationally up with no links shared with the primary LSP::Path.

   D. The secondary LSP::Path will be down with the failure code `srlgError`.

   E. None of the above statements are correct.

9. An Alcatel-Lucent 7750 SR is configured with the command `configure router mpls srlg-group blue value 3`. Assuming that traffic engineering is enabled on the IGP, how is this SRLG group information advertised through the network immediately after the command is executed?

   A. The SRLG group name `blue` is transmitted in the TE LSA originated by the router.

   B. The decimal value of 3 is transmitted in the TE LSA originated by the router to represent the SRLG.

   C. The decimal value of 4 is transmitted in the TE LSA originated by the router to represent the SRLG.

   D. The decimal value of 8 is transmitted in the TE LSA originated by the router to represent the SRLG.

   E. The SRLG group is not propagated through the network.

10. An LSP is configured for fast reroute with default settings in a network of 7750 SRs with enough redundant paths to fully protect the LSP. Which of the following best describes the expected behavior?

   A. All hops will show link protection.

   B. All hops will show node protection.

   C. The last hop will show link protection, and all other hops will show node protection.

   D. None of the hops will be protected.

11. Consider an Alcatel-Lucent 7750 SR network that is provisioned with the MPLS one-to-one FRR method with default FRR settings. Which statement below is incorrect regarding the signaling of protection LSPs?

   A. The Path messages of the protected LSP will include the `FAST_REROUTE` object with the `flags` field set to `0x01`.

   B. The router that is directly connected to the tail end will attempt to signal a link protection LSP.

   C. A constraint of every protection LSP is to merge back to the primary LSP::Path as soon as possible.

   D. All protection LSPs will have a `DETOUR` object in their Path messages.

   E. All of the above statements are correct.

12. Consider a network of 7750 SRs in which all primary LSP::Paths are provisioned to use one-to-one FRR. A router transiting a detour LSP receives a Path message to establish a new detour LSP with the same destination and out interface. The Tunnel ID and LSP ID of the second detour LSP are not the same as of the first. What action does the router take?

A. The router transits two separate detour LSPs that have the same out interface but different out labels.

B. The router merges the detour LSP if detour merge capability is configured on the head end router.

C. The router checks the avoid node statements in the DETOUR object of the Path messages. If they match, the LSPs are merged and the router transits one detour LSP.

D. The router merges the two detour LSPs and transits one detour LSP.

E. None of the above statements are correct.

13. Consider a router that can be a PLR for three LSPs protected with facility backup. All three protected LSPs traverse the same egress port on the PLR. The tail end router of one of the protected LSPs is directly connected to the PLR. The other two protected LSPs have identical paths to the same tail end router, which is not directly connected to the PLR. Assuming that default facility mode configurations are used and there are enough paths in the network to provide the requested FRR protection, which statement is correct regarding the bypass tunnels originated by the PLR?

A. The PLR originates three link protection bypass tunnels.

B. The PLR originates three node protection bypass tunnels.

C. The PLR originates one link-protect bypass tunnel and one node-protect bypass tunnel.

D. The PLR originates one link-protect bypass tunnel and two node-protect bypass tunnels.

E. There is not enough information to answer the question.

14. Which statement regarding SRLG for FRR is correct on a 7750 SR?

A. If SRLGs are configured with default settings, a 7750 SR may establish protection LSPs that share links with the primary LSP::Path.

B. SRLGs can be used to influence bypass tunnels but not detour LSPs.

C. SRLG can be enabled on specific LSPs.

D. For the purposes of FRR, SRLG is only enabled on the head end router.

E. None of the above statements are true.

15. Which of the following mechanisms cannot be used to ensure LSP::Path diversity?

A. Strict hops

B. SRLGs

C. Admin groups

D. Any of the above mechanisms can be used to ensure LSP::Path diversity.

Chapter 17

1. An epipe service is to be deployed in a network. Which routers may need to be configured with the epipe service?

A. PE routers

B. CE routers

C. P routers

D. Core routers

E. PE routers and P routers

2. Which statement best characterizes a VPLS from a customer's point of view?

A. The service provider network appears as a leased line between customer locations.

B. The service provider network appears as a single MPLS switch between customer locations.

C. The service provider network appears as a single IP router between customer locations.

D. The service provider network appears as a Layer 2 switch between customer locations.

E. None of the above statements are correct.

3. Consider a network of 7750 SRs that contains four PE routers, six CE routers, and eight P routers. Assuming that the network is only used to provide VPRN services, which routers need to be configured with SAPs?

   A. All CE routers

   B. All PE routers

   C. All P routers

   D. All P and CE routers

   E. All PE, CE, and P routers

4. Which of the following best describes the encapsulation of the service payload on an IP/MPLS service network with Ethernet links?

   A. The service payload is encapsulated in an Ethernet frame.

   B. The service payload is encapsulated in an Ethernet frame with a service label.

   C. The service payload is encapsulated in an Ethernet frame with a transport label and a service label.

   D. The service payload is encapsulated in an Ethernet frame with an IP header and a service label.

5. Which of the following best describes the signaling of service labels for an epipe?

   A. Service labels are signaled when the SDP is created at both ends.

   B. Service labels are signaled when the service is created and made administratively up at one end.

   C. Service labels are signaled when the service is created and made administratively up at both ends.

   D. Service labels are signaled when the SDP binding is created in the service at both ends.

   E. Service labels are signaled when the SAP and the SDP binding are created in the service at both ends.

6. Which statement best characterizes an epipe service from a customer's point of view?

   A. The service provider network appears as a leased line between two customer locations.

   B. The service provider network appears as a single MPLS switch between two customer locations.

   C. The service provider network appears as a single IP router between customer locations.

   D. The service provider network appears as a Layer 2 switch between customer locations.

   E. None of the above statements are correct.

7. Which of the following is *not* a primary feature of a service router such as an Alcatel-Lucent 7750 SR?

   A. The ability to perform accounting operations based on a specific customer or service.

   B. The ability to provide quality of service based on a specific customer or service.

   C. The ability to restrict or monitor specific traffic based on customer or service.

   D. The ability to analyze and troubleshoot problems from the perspective of a service.

   E. All of the above are primary features of a service router.

8. A PE router is provisioned with two epipe services, one apipe service, and four VPLS services. Assuming that all services are operationally up and passing subscriber traffic, how many T-LDP sessions are established on the PE router?

   A. 1

   B. 2

   C. 3

   D. 4

   E. 7

   F. There is not enough information to answer this question.

9. Which of the following is a true statement about an IP/MPLS service network?
   - **A.** GRE can only be used for a Layer 3 service such as VPRN.
   - **B.** The CE routers connected to the service network must support MPLS.
   - **C.** The service provider must provision multiple service instances in order to provide redundancy for a customer.
   - **D.** Layer 2 and Layer 3 services such as VPLS and VPRN can both be provisioned on the same IP/MPLS network.
   - **E.** A new transport tunnel must be configured for each service.
   - **F.** All of the above statements are false.

10. Which of the statements below is incorrect?
    - **A.** Link LDP peers do not have to be directly connected.
    - **B.** T-LDP peers do not have to be directly connected.
    - **C.** Link LDP is used to signal transport labels.
    - **D.** T-LDP is used to signal service labels.
    - **E.** All of the above statements are correct.

11. Which of the following statements about the number of routers required for an epipe service is true?
    - **A.** An epipe service is configured on only one PE router.
    - **B.** An epipe service must be configured on two PE routers.
    - **C.** An epipe service must be configured on either one or two PE routers.
    - **D.** An epipe service may be configured on any number of PE routers.
    - **E.** An epipe service is not configured on the PE router, only on the CE routers.

12. Which of the following statements about T-LDP is true?
    - **A.** A T-LDP router uses the IGP to discover its peers.
    - **B.** After the T-LDP session is established, the peers signal service labels.
    - **C.** If RSVP-TE is used for a VPWS, T-LDP is not required.
    - **D.** Because LDP is only used in a service provider network, authentication is not required and is not supported.
    - **E.** All of the above statements are false.
    - **F.** Statements A–D are true.

13. Which of the following statements about an epipe is true?

    A. The customer IDs at both ends of an epipe must match.

    B. The service IDs at both ends of an epipe must match.

    C. The VC IDs at both ends of an epipe must match.

    D. The service labels at both ends of an epipe must match.

    E. None of the above statements are true.

    F. Statements A–D are true.

14. Which of the following statements about the use of physical ports for services on the Alcatel-Lucent 7750 SR is false?

    A. One physical port can be used for multiple SAPs in different services.

    B. An access port has the same QoS and accounting capabilities as a network port.

    C. A port to be used for a SAP must be configured as an access port.

    D. A port to be configured for a normal IP interface must be configured as a network port.

    E. Ports are network ports by default.

    F. All of the above statements are true.

15. Which of the following is a true statement about the configuration of services on the 7750 SR?

    A. A new SDP must be configured for any new service that is configured.

    B. One SDP can support multiple services, but they must all be the same type of service.

    C. One SDP can support multiple different service types.

    D. An SDP can use GRE encapsulation for some services and MPLS for others.

    E. None of the above statements are true.

Chapter 18

1. Consider an epipe service on an Alcatel-Lucent 7750 SR that has a SAP configured with the CLI syntax `sap 1/1/4:20.10`. Assuming that the epipe service is operationally up, which statement best describes CE traffic that ingresses the service?

   A. CE traffic with an outer VLAN tag of 10 and any non-zero inner VLAN tag will be sent over the service.

   B. CE traffic with an outer VLAN tag of 20 and any non-zero inner VLAN tag will be sent over the service.

   C. CE traffic with an outer VLAN tag of 20 and an inner VLAN tag of 10 will be sent over the service.

   D. CE traffic with an outer VLAN tag of 10 and an inner VLAN tag of 20 will be sent over the service.

   E. None of the above statements describe CE traffic that ingresses the service.

2. Which of the following statements is *false* regarding the MTUs used for an epipe service?

   A. SAP MTUs must be greater than or equal to the service MTU.

   B. The service MTU must be less than or equal to the path MTU.

   C. The path MTU must be greater than the MTU of every network port in the transport path.

   D. Epipe services configured on the same PE can have different service MTUs.

   E. None of the above statements are false.

3. An operator needs to provision an epipe service to accept IP packets as large as 9,000 bytes. What value should be used for the service MTU if the SAP encapsulation on both PE routers has a CLI syntax of `1/1/4:100.*`?

   A. 8,982 bytes

   B. 8,986 bytes

   C. 9,000 bytes

   D. 9,014 bytes

   E. 9,018 bytes

4. An epipe on a PE router receives a frame carrying an IP packet from a CE router that is too large for the service. What action will the PE router take?
   - **A.** It will silently discard the frame.
   - **B.** It will discard the frame and send a notification to the CE router.
   - **C.** It will fragment the frame as long as the do-not-fragment bit is not set.
   - **D.** It will always fragment the frame.
   - **E.** None of the above answers are correct.
5. Which of the following best describes the behavior of the default SAP?
   - **A.** The default SAP receives all frames.
   - **B.** The default SAP receives all untagged frames.
   - **C.** The default SAP receives all tagged frames.
   - **D.** The default SAP receives all untagged frames and all tagged frames not received by another SAP.
   - **E.** The default SAP receives all untagged frames and all frames with a VLAN tag of 0.
6. Which of the following statements best describes the function of an ipipe service?
   - **A.** It emulates a point-to-point Ethernet service.
   - **B.** It emulates a point-to-point ATM service.
   - **C.** It emulates a point-to-point Frame Relay service.
   - **D.** It emulates a point-to-point TDM circuit.
   - **E.** None of the above statements describe the function of an ipipe service.
7. Consider a network of four routers that are used to provide an epipe service. The transport tunnels used for the service traverse all four routers. Which of the following statements is correct regarding service configuration?
   - **A.** The epipe service has to be configured on all four routers.
   - **B.** The epipe service has to be configured on one router.
   - **C.** The epipe service has to be configured on the P routers.
   - **D.** The epipe service has to be configured on the CE routers.
   - **E.** The epipe service has to be configured on two routers.

8. A SAP on an epipe service receives an Ethernet frame from a CE router. Which statement below describes the action taken on the FCS?

   A. The FCS is removed.

   B. The FCS is untouched.

   C. The FCS is recomputed.

   D. The action taken depends on how the epipe is configured.

9. Consider an epipe service that is operationally up on a network of 7750 SRs. All network ports have an MTU of 9,212 bytes. The epipe service and access ports use default MTU settings. The SAPs on both ends of the epipe service are configured with the CLI syntax `sap 1/1/4:20`. An operator changes the CLI syntax on both ends of the epipe service to `sap 1/1/4:*`. What additional configuration does the operator need to make for the service to function correctly?

   A. The MTU of the network ports needs to be increased.

   B. The service MTU of the epipe service needs to be increased.

   C. The SAP MTU of the service needs to be increased.

   D. The MTU of the access port used by the SAP needs to be increased.

   E. No other configuration is required.

10. An epipe SAP is configured for dot1Q encapsulation with default values. Which of the following describes the behavior of the SAP when a tagged frame arrives with an Ethertype value of `0x9100`?

   A. The frame is discarded.

   B. The frame is treated as an untagged frame.

   C. An error message is sent to the sender of the frame.

   D. It is not possible to have a tagged frame with an Ethertype value of `0x9100`; the Ethertype must be `0x8100`.

   E. None of the above answers are correct.

11. Which of the following best describes the `atm-vcc` VC type for an apipe?

A. A single ATM VPI/VCI value is mapped to the apipe.

B. An entire ATM VPC is mapped to the apipe.

C. A range of ATM VPCs is mapped to the apipe.

D. An entire ATM port is mapped to the apipe.

E. `atm-vcc` is not a valid VC type for an apipe.

12. Which of the following statements about cpipes is *false*?

A. The SAToP pseudowire transports unstructured T1 or E1 data.

B. The CESoPSN pseudowire transports data from individual circuits in a T1 or E1.

C. The control word is used in the encapsulation of all packets in a cpipe service.

D. A larger jitter buffer is always preferred because it reduces the chance that data will be lost.

E. All of the above statements are true.

13. Which of the following forms of interworking is *not* supported on the Alcatel-Lucent 7750 SR?

A. Apipe to epipe interworking

B. Apipe to fpipe interworking

C. Apipe to cpipe interworking

D. Fpipe to epipe interworking

E. Epipe to ipipe interworking

14. An Ethernet frame with a single VLAN tag ingresses an epipe service with a Q-in-Q-encapsulated SAP `1/1/2:20.*`. The frame egresses the epipe service on a SAP `1/1/3:20.10`. What are the VLAN tag or tag values after the frame egresses the service?

A. There will be three tags from outer to inner: 20, 10, and the original tag.

B. There will be an outer tag of 20 and an inner tag of 10.

C. There will be a single tag of 20.

D. There will be a single tag of 10.

E. The frame will not be accepted at the ingress SAP because it has only a single tag.

15. A service provider network is made up of redundant 1 Gb/s Ethernet links with all SDPs using RSVP-TE LSPs configured with fast reroute facility backup. An fpipe is configured with a service MTU of 5,000 bytes. What is the minimum MTU for the network ports to be able to support this service?

   A. 5,000 bytes

   B. 5,014 bytes

   C. 5,022 bytes

   D. 5,026 bytes

   E. 5,030 bytes

   F. ADSPEC must be configured on the LSP because the specific value cannot be determined.

Chapter 19

1. Which of the following describes a difference in the behavior of an Ethernet switch and a VPLS?

   A. Unknown unicast traffic is flooded to all destinations in a VPLS but is discarded in an Ethernet switch.

   B. Traffic to known multicast and broadcast addresses is flooded to all destinations in a VPLS but only to specific ports in an Ethernet switch.

   C. SAPs with different VLAN values in a VPLS are treated as separate broadcast domains. On an Ethernet switch, different VLAN values are treated as being in the same broadcast domain.

   D. SAPs with different VLAN values in a VPLS are treated as being in the same broadcast domain. On an Ethernet switch, different VLAN values are treated as separate broadcast domains.

   E. None of the above statements describe a difference between a VPLS and an Ethernet switch.

2. Which of the following best describes how a VPLS populates the MAC FDB?

   A. The network administrator programs the FDB with the MAC address of the attached devices.

   B. The PE router uses ARP to discover the MAC addresses of attached devices.

   C. The PE router examines the source MAC address of received frames.

   D. The PE router examines the destination MAC address of received frames.

   E. There is no MAC learning; unicast traffic is flooded to all destinations in the VPLS.

3. Which statement best describes the flooding behavior of a VPLS for unknown unicast traffic received on a mesh SDP?

   A. The traffic is flooded to all SDP bindings and SAPs configured on the router.

   B. The traffic is flooded to all mesh SDPs in the same service.

   C. The traffic is flooded to all mesh SDPs, SAPs, and spoke SDPs in the same service.

   D. The traffic is flooded to all SAPs and spoke SDPs in the same service.

   E. The traffic is flooded to all mesh SDPs that are not in the same service, and all SAPs and spoke SDPs that are in the same service.

   F. None of the above statements are correct.

4. Consider a metro VPLS network that has four PE routers. Two VPLS instances are created on each PE router. If only mesh SDPs are used in the network, what is the total number of mesh SDPs that are required in the network?

   A. Three mesh SDPs are required.

   B. Four mesh SDPs are required.

   C. Six mesh SDPs are required.

   D. Eight mesh SDPs are required.

   E. Twelve mesh SDPs are required.

   F. Twenty-four mesh SDPs are required.

5. Which of the following statements about mesh and spoke SDPs is true?
   A. Using spoke SDPs in a VPLS removes the requirement for a full mesh of SDP bindings.
   B. Using spoke SDPs in a VPLS eliminates the possibility of looping in the VPLS.
   C. MAC learning is not performed on spoke SDPs in a VPLS.
   D. Spoke and mesh SDPs cannot be used in the same VPLS.
   E. None of the above statements above are true.

6. Which of the following protocols can be used to signal service labels for a VPLS service?
   A. LDP
   B. RSVP-TE
   C. GRE
   D. OSPF
   E. None of the above protocols can be used to signal service labels for a VPLS service.

7. What is the default service MTU for a VPLS on an Alcatel-Lucent 7750 SR if all SAPs have a dot1Q encapsulation?
   A. 1,500 bytes
   B. 1,504 bytes
   C. 1,514 bytes
   D. 1,518 bytes
   E. 1,522 bytes

8. Which of the following statements concerning VPLS services is false?
   A. A VPLS can be used to provide point-to-point services.
   B. CE routers use a spoke SDP to connect to PE routers offering a VPLS service.
   C. A VPLS does not need a configured SDP binding to be operationally up.
   D. A PE router can offer multiple VPLS services to a single CE router using the same physical port.
   E. Only PE routers need to be configured with a VPLS service.

9. Consider a VPLS metro network that has four PE routers. Two VPLS instances are created on every PE router. If only mesh SDPs are used in the network, what is the total number of T-LDP sessions required?

A. Three T-LDP sessions are required.

B. Four T-LDP sessions are required.

C. Six T-LDP sessions are required.

D. Eight T-LDP sessions are required.

E. Twelve T-LDP sessions are required.

F. Twenty-four T-LDP sessions are required.

10. Consider an Alcatel-Lucent 7750 SR that is a PE router for two VPLS and one epipe service. Additionally, the 7750 SR acts as a P router transiting traffic for three other VPLS instances. How many MAC FDBs are held on the 7750 SR?

A. One

B. Two

C. Three

D. Five

E. Six

F. There is not enough information provided to answer the question.

11. Which statement best describes the forwarding behavior of known unicast traffic that is received on a spoke SDP on a 7750 SR?

A. The traffic is flooded to all SDP bindings and SAPs configured on the router.

B. The traffic is flooded to all spoke SDPs in the same service.

C. The traffic is flooded to all spoke SDPs and SAPs in the same service.

D. The traffic is flooded to all mesh SDPs and SAPs in the same service.

E. The traffic is flooded to all spoke SDPs that are not in the same service, and all SAPs and mesh SDPs in the same service.

F. None of the above statements are correct.

12. Which statement is correct regarding the VC ID that needs to be configured on spoke and mesh SDPs in a VPLS on a 7750 SR?

   A. Spoke SDPs must have a VC ID that is equal to the VPLS service ID.

   B. Mesh SDPs must have a VC ID that is equal to the VPLS service ID.

   C. The VC ID used on both ends of a spoke SDP must match.

   D. Mesh SDPs don't use a VC ID.

   E. Two spoke SDPs on the same PE cannot use the same VC ID.

   F. None of the above statements are correct.

13. Which statement best describes the flooding behavior of a VPLS for unknown unicast traffic received on a SAP?

   A. The traffic is flooded to all SAPs configured on the router.

   B. The traffic is flooded to all SAPs in the same service.

   C. The traffic is flooded to all SDP bindings in the same service.

   D. The traffic is flooded to all SAPs and spoke SDPs in the same service.

   E. The traffic is flooded to all SAPs and SDP bindings in the same service.

   F. None of the above statements are correct.

14. A VPLS is configured with two mesh SDPs and one spoke SDP. The VPLS is operationally down, and the output of `show router ldp bindings fec-type services` shows the following information:

```
LDP Service FEC 128 Bindings
===============================================================================
Type   VCId       SvcId      SDPId  Peer          IngLbl  EgrLbl  LMTU  RMTU
-------------------------------------------------------------------------------
V-Eth  101        101        2      10.10.10.2    131068U   --    1500  0
V-Eth  101        101        3      10.10.10.3    131070U 131071  1500  1500
V-Eth  101        101        4      10.10.10.4    131069U 131071  1500  1500
?-Eth  202        Ukwn       R. Src 10.10.10.2      --    131069S 0     1500
-------------------------------------------------------------------------------
```

What is the likely reason that the service is down?

A. T-LDP is not configured on the PE router at the other end of the spoke SDP.

B. The service MTU values are not matching at both ends of the spoke SDP.

C. The VC ID values are not matching at both ends of the spoke SDP.

D. The service ID values are not matching at both ends of the spoke SDP.

E. The service ID is not configured at the far end of the spoke SDP.

F. It is not possible to configure a VPLS with both spoke and mesh SDPs.

15. Router PE-1 is connected as the hub to routers PE-2 and PE-3 in a hub-and-spoke VPLS using spoke SDPs. Which of the following is a true statement about the behavior of this VPLS?

A. A VPLS cannot use spoke SDPs; it must use only mesh SDPs.

B. PE-2 does not perform MAC learning because all traffic is sent to PE-1 as the hub of the VPLS.

C. To prevent looping in the VPLS, traffic received on a spoke SDP at PE-1 is never flooded to the other spoke SDPs in the service.

D. Each of the three PE routers signals a service label for the VPLS to the other two routers.

E. PE-2 and PE-3 signal a service label to PE-1, and PE-1 signals a service label to PE-2 and PE-3 for the VPLS.

Chapter 20

1. An IES spoke termination is used to connect a CE router to an IES interface through an epipe service. Which statement is correct regarding the IP address configuration?

A. The IP address of the CE router interface should be the same as the IP address of the IES interface.

B. The IP address of the CE router interface should be on the same subnet as the IP address of the IES interface.

C. The IP address of the CE router interface should be on a different subnet from the IP address of the IES interface.

D. The IP address configuration depends on whether the IES has been configured in switched or routed mode.

E. None of the above statements are correct.

2. Which statement is *false* regarding the traffic sent between two PE routers of a VPRN in a service provider network that uses RSVP-TE?

   A. The traffic has an MPLS transport label.

   B. The traffic has an MPLS service label.

   C. The traffic has the Layer 2 header sent by the CE router.

   D. The traffic has the IP header sent by the CE router.

   E. None of the above statements are false.

3. Which statement concerning route distinguishers on the 7750 SR is true?

   A. Route distinguishers are used to determine which routes a VPRN should import.

   B. Different route distinguishers can be used for the same VPRN on different PE routers.

   C. CE routers must be configured with the correct route distinguishers for the VPRN with which they are associated.

   D. P routers only need to be aware of route distinguishers that belong to VPRNs for which they transit traffic.

   E. A route distinguisher is 96 bits in length.

   F. None of the above statements are correct.

4. Which of the following best describes the purpose of MP-BGP in a VPRN?

   A. MP-BGP is an enhanced version of BGP that can carry both IPv4 and IPv6 prefixes.

   B. MP-BGP is an enhanced version of BGP that can carry a service label and customer route prefixes.

   C. MP-BGP is an enhanced version of BGP that can carry a transport label and customer route prefixes.

   D. MP-BGP is an enhanced version of BGP that allows BGP routers to peer with other protocols such as OSPF and RIP for CE-to-PE route exchange.

   E. None of the above statements describe the use of MP-BGP in a VPRN.

5. Which of the following statements regarding 6VPE is *false*?

   A. Both PE and P routers must support both IPv4 and IPv6 addresses; customer routers can use either one.

   B. A single MP-BGP session can be used to carry both VPN-IPv4 and VPN-IPv6 routes.

   C. A single customer's VPRN might contain both IPv4 and IPv6 routes.

   D. Any of the transport methods used for an IPv4 VPRN can be used for 6VPE.

   E. Statements A–D are true.

   F. Statements A–D are false.

6. Which of the following statements concerning Internet Enhanced Services on an Alcatel-Lucent 7750 SR is *false*?

   A. An IES can use a mesh SDP.

   B. An IES can have a spoke termination to an epipe.

   C. An IES can have a spoke termination to a VPLS.

   D. An IES can use a SAP.

   E. An IES can be advertised into an IGP.

   F. An IES can be configured with multiple interfaces.

7. Consider an IES service that has a spoke termination to an epipe service with a service MTU of 9,000 bytes. How should the IES interface MTU be configured?

   A. The IES MTU should be configured to exactly 9,000 bytes.

   B. The IES MTU should be configured to exactly 9,022 bytes.

   C. The IES MTU should be configured to exactly 8,986 bytes.

   D. The IES MTU should be configured to exactly 9,014 bytes.

   E. The IES MTU should be configured to any value less than 9,000 bytes.

   F. The IES MTU should be configured to any value greater than 9,000 bytes.

8. Which of the following statements is *false* regarding an IES spoke termination to an epipe service?

   A. Targeted LDP is used to signal service labels for the IES spoke termination.

   B. A SAP must be configured on the IES interface.

   C. The service ID of the IES and epipe service can be different.

   D. The VC ID between the IES interface and epipe must match.

   E. The ARP cache of a CE router connected through the spoke termination has the chassis MAC of the PE router with the IES interface.

9. Consider a network of 7750 SRs used to provide VPRN services. There are four PE routers and five P routers in the network. Each PE router has two VPRN services configured. How many T-LDP sessions are required in the network?

   A. No T-LDP sessions are required.

   B. Four T-LDP sessions are required.

   C. Six T-LDP sessions are required.

   D. Eight T-LDP sessions are required.

   E. Twelve T-LDP sessions are required.

   F. Thirty-six T-LDP sessions are required.

10. Consider a network of three 7750 SRs: R1, R2, and R3. A VPRN is configured on all three routers. R1 learns two prefixes from its locally connected CE router. Which statement below is correct about the service labels R1 sends to the other routers for these prefixes?

   A. R1 sends the same service label for both prefixes to R2 and R3.

   B. A single service label is sent to R2 for both prefixes. A different service label is sent to R3 for both prefixes.

   C. A single service label is sent to R2 and R3 for the first prefix. A different service label is sent to R2 and R3 for the second prefix.

   D. A different service label is sent to each router for each prefix.

   E. None of the above statements are correct.

11. Consider a VPRN that is configured on two 7750 SR PE routers, R1 and R2. R1 and its CE router use the PE–CE protocol BGP to exchange routing information. R2 and its CE router use static routes to forward traffic to and from the VPRN. Both sites of the VPRN share all available routing information with each other. Which of the statements below is *false*?

A. The BGP session between R1 and its CE router must be enabled with the IPv4 or IPv6 address family.

B. An export policy must be configured on R1 to advertise routes to the directly connected CE router.

C. An export policy is not required on R2 to advertise routes to the directly connected CE router.

D. An export policy must be configured to advertise routes between the PE routers.

E. None of the above statements are false.

12. An operator needs to provision 6VPE on a 7750 SR that is also used to provide existing IPv4 VPRN services. The IPv6 VPRN customers use BGP as the PE–CE protocol. Which statement below is true regarding the configuration steps required?

A. New LSPs must be provisioned in the service provider network to support IPv6.

B. New MP-BGP sessions must be configured in the service provider network to advertise IPv6 routes.

C. The PE-to-CE BGP sessions must be configured to support the IPv6 and VPN-IPv6 address families.

D. The PE-to-PE BGP sessions must be configured to support the IPv6 and VPN-IPv6 address families.

E. The route targets on existing IPv4 VPRN services must be modified.

F. None of the above statements are correct.

13. Which of the following best describes the purpose of the route target?

    A. The route target is added to the IPv4 or IPv6 prefix to create a unique VPN-IPv4 or VPN-IPv6 prefix.

    B. The route target is used by the CE router to identify routes to be taken from its route table and given to the PE router for the VPRN.

    C. The route target is used by the PE router to indentify routes to be taken from MP-BGP and installed in the VRF.

    D. The route target is used by the PE router to identify routes to be taken from the VRF to be sent to the CE router.

    E. None of the above statements describe the purpose of the route target.

14. Which of the following best describes the term *VRF*?

    A. A virtual routing instance that allows a single router to act as multiple virtual routers maintaining multiple route tables.

    B. A virtual routing instance that contains a single customer's VPRN routes and peers with the customer's routers.

    C. A virtual MP-BGP instance that peers with other MP-BGP instances to exchange routes for a single customer's VPRN across the service provider network.

    D. A virtual MP-BGP instance that peers with a single customer's BGP router to exchange the customer's VPRN routes.

    E. The Alcatel-Lucent 7750 SR does not support the VRF construct.

15. VPRN routes advertised by PE router R1 (`10.10.10.1`) are not appearing in the VRF on the 7750 SR PE router R2 (`10.10.10.2`). The output from the `show router bgp routes vpn-ipv4` command is shown below:

```
===============================================================================
 BGP Router ID:10.10.10.2       AS:65000       Local AS:65000
===============================================================================
 Legend -
 Status codes  : u - used, s - suppressed, h - history, d - decayed,
 * - valid
 Origin codes  : i - IGP, e - EGP, ? - incomplete, > - best

===============================================================================
BGP VPN-IPv4 Routes
===============================================================================
Flag  Network                                              LocalPref   MED
      Nexthop                                                          VPNLabel
      As-Path
-------------------------------------------------------------------------------
?     65000:11:10.1.0.0/16                                 100         None
      10.10.10.1                                                       131071
      65001
i     65000:11:192.168.1.0/30                              100         None
      10.10.10.1                                                       131071
      No As-Path
-------------------------------------------------------------------------------
Routes : 2
===============================================================================
```

Which of the following is the most likely reason these routes do not appear in the VRF?

A. The MP-BGP peering session between R1 and R2 is not operational.

B. The route distinguisher configured for the VPRN on R2 does not match the value configured on R1.

C. The route target configured for the VPRN on R2 does not match the value configured on R1.

D. The transport tunnel between R1 and R2 is not operational.

E. The route distinguisher has not been configured in the VPRN on R2.

Chapter 21

1. Which of the following 7750 SR OAM commands can be used to diagnose a far-end epipe service instance that is administratively shut down?

   A. `lsp-ping`

   B. `lsp-trace`

   C. `sdp-ping`

   D. `sdp-mtu`

   E. `svc-ping`

   F. None of the above commands can be used to diagnose an epipe service instance that is administratively shut down.

2. An operator issues the command `oam sdp-ping 5` on a 7750 SR. Which of the following statements is true?

   A. The `SDP-ping` is sent out-of-band.

   B. The `SDP-ping` reply is sent out-of-band.

   C. An RSVP-TE LSP must be used for the SDP to use the `sdp-ping` command.

   D. An LDP LSP must be used for the SDP to use the `sdp-ping` command.

   E. None of the above statements are true.

3. Which of the following statements concerning the `oam lsp-ping` and `oam lsp-trace` commands on the 7750 SR is *false*?

   A. Both commands can be used on LDP LSPs.

   B. When the `oam lsp-trace` command is used on an RSVP-TE LSP, the hops followed are the same that would be seen with the `traceroute` command to the egress LER.

   C. The `lsp-ping` command can be used for measuring round-trip time for a specific forwarding class.

   D. For both commands, a UDP packet is encapsulated and sent along the path of the LSP.

   E. All of the above statements are true.

4. Which OAM command on the 7750 SR can be used to find the effective MTU of an SDP?

   A. `oam lsp-ping`

   B. `oam svc-ping`

   C. `oam sdp-ping`

   D. `oam lsp-trace`

   E. None of the above

5. Consider two 7750 SR PE routers that have two epipes between them. One of the epipes is operationally down, and the other is operationally up. Which statement is correct?

   A. An `lsp-ping` between the routers will fail.

   B. An `sdp-ping` between the routers will fail.

   C. An `svc-ping` will be successful for the operationally up epipe and will fail for the operationally down epipe.

   D. There is not enough information to answer the question.

6. Consider four routers connected as R1–R2–R3–R4 using Ethernet. The MTU on the R1–R2 and R3–R4 link is 9,212 bytes. The MTU on the link between R2 and R3 is 2,000 bytes. An RSVP-TE LSP is bound to the SDP from R1–R4. If an `oam sdp-mtu` command is used on R1 to find the effective path MTU of the SDP, what is the result?

   A. 1,976 bytes

   B. 1,978 bytes

   C. 1,980 bytes

   D. 9,190 bytes

   E. 9,212 bytes

   F. There is not enough information provided to answer the question.

7. Which of the following entities cannot be used as the source for a mirror service on the 7750 SR?
   - **A.** Physical port
   - **B.** SAP
   - **C.** Ingress MPLS label
   - **D.** IP filter
   - **E.** MAC filter
   - **F.** All of the above entities can be used.

8. Which of the following statements is true regarding the configuration of a remote mirror on the 7750 SR?
   - **A.** T-LDP must be used to signal service labels between the PE routers.
   - **B.** RSVP-TE or LDP must be used for the SDP encapsulation between the routers.
   - **C.** A mirror destination is configured on both PE routers.
   - **D.** A mirror source is configured on both PE routers.
   - **E.** A SAP to the sniffer is only configured on the mirror source.
   - **F.** None of the above statements are true.

9. An operator has been using a remote mirror service on a 7750 SR for a period of time without any problems. The operator performs a reboot for a software upgrade; however, when the router comes back up, the mirror is not working. What is the most probable cause?
   - **A.** The mirror source needs to be reconfigured.
   - **B.** The mirror destination needs to be reconfigured.
   - **C.** The sniffer needs to be reconfigured.
   - **D.** There is a problem with the physical topology.
   - **E.** The operator must wait longer for control plane convergence.
   - **F.** None of the above statements are correct.

10. An operator wants to use remote service mirroring on the 7750 SR but is concerned about the potential increase in bandwidth consumption on network links involved in the mirror. Which of the following can be used to reduce the bandwidth consumption?

A. IP filters

B. MAC filters

C. A filter on the MPLS ingress label

D. Slice size

E. Features A–D can be used to restrict the amount of traffic replicated across the mirror service.

F. None of features A–D can be used to restrict the amount of traffic replicated across the mirror service.

Answers to Assessment Questions

Chapter 2

1. B. The correct answer is ATM. POS is a point-to-point technology, IP is packet switched, and Ethernet is a broadcast technology.
2. D. When a switch receives a frame with an unknown destination MAC address it floods the frame to all ports except the one the frame was received on. ICMP messages are used by routers rather than switches.
3. C. A router must be used to route the packets at the IP layer in order to facilitate communication between two users on separate VLANs.
4. D. TDM was initially developed for the PSTN.
5. E. The majority of ATM traffic today is AAL5, which is a simple, connectionless, non-real-time service.
6. C. Establishment is not an OSI Layer (the others are all valid OSI Layers).
7. B. A corrupted frame is typically detected in Ethernet by using the FCS field in the Layer 2 header.
8. C. The source MAC address is stored in the FDB along with the port the frame arrive on when a frame arrives at a port on an Ethernet switch.
9. B. The purpose of VLANs is to separate broadcast domains.
10. D. When VLANs need to span more than one switch, a VLAN tag is attached to the Ethernet frame to indicate VLAN membership. B and C are incorrect since there is no per MAC address signaling done between switches.
11. A. The outer tag is commonly used by the service provider, and the inner tag is commonly used by the customer. C and D are incorrect as these fields do not exist in the VLAN tags. E is incorrect as Ethertype 8200 is not used for VLAN tagging.
12. B. IP is encapsulated in PPP and transported over SONET.
13. B. One of the reasons for ATM's fixed 53-byte cell size was to have a relatively small size to minimize delay and jitter for voice services. Another reason was to simplify high-speed switching requirements for optical networks.
14. C. Five service classes are defined by ATM. The different service classes are AAL1 (CBR), AAL2 (VBR-rt), AAL2 (VBR-nrt), AAL3/4 (ABR) and AAL5 (UBR).
15. F. IOMs are configured first, followed by MDAs, followed by ports.

Chapter 3

1. B. 192.0.2.160 and 192.0.2.191 are not used as host addresses on the subnet because they are reserved as the subnet and broadcast addresses for the subnet.
2. A. Data traffic passes through the switch fabric module. Data traffic does not pass through the CPM.
3. A. The branch router is the stub network, and its only route out is the corporate network. A default route is appropriate to save the burden of manually configuring every possible route toward the corporate network. On the corporate router, however, a static route with a specific prefix needs to be used because it is not a stub and may be connected to many other networks.
4. D. There is not enough information to determine the answer. The question states that 198.51.100.177 is the source IP address. The source IP address has no effect on unicast traffic forwarding. If the question said that 198.51.100.177 is the destination, the correct answer would be B because the static route would be used. Although the OSPF route is more specific than the static route, it is not a match for 198.51.100.177.
5. A. The link-local address is obtained by combining the prefix fe80::/10 with the modified EUI-64 MAC address for the physical port bound to the interface. The modified EUI-64 MAC address is obtained by flipping the seventh most significant bit in the original 6-byte MAC address and adding the hex pattern fffe after the third byte. Note that a link local address is assigned to all IPv6 interfaces regardless of whether a global IPv6 address is also assigned to the interface.
6. B.
7. C. Layer 2 information of the next-hop is information not contained in the route-table maintained by the Alcatel-Lucent 7750 SR CPM. Preference, metric, and the protocol used to learn the routes are all in the route table.
8. F.
9. E. The protocol field identifies the upper-layer protocol carried in the IP datagram. The others are fields in the IP header, but are incorrect.
10. C. Layer 2 media type is not part of the Alcatel-Lucent 7750 SR IP interface configuration (all the other information must be provided to configure an IP interface).

11. E. The system interface cannot be removed. Although it is admin up by default, it can be admin shutdown. Its operational state is down in a default configuration, but it becomes up as soon as there is an IP address. The system interface is essentially a loopback but does not need to be explicitly configured as a loopback.

12. D. The correct syntax to configure a default route on Alcatel-Lucent 7750 SR is configure router static-route 0.0.0.0/0 next-hop 10.1.1.2. Make sure to use the next-hop of the neighbor router. Since you are told that the local address is 10.1.1.1/30, the correct next-hop must be 10.1.1.2.

13. D. Floating static routes are only beneficial when the physical topology offers more than one next-hop to a prefix. If there is no other path to the destination, there is no value in having a second static route. Answer B is incorrect because there is no mechanism in basic IP to respond to congestion on a route. Answer C is incorrect because it is the route with the lowest preference that becomes active. BFD is an option that may be used to detect when a physical link is down, but it does not have to be used. If the port goes operationally down, the static route that uses it will become inactive.

14. B. The next-hop for the packet with destination address 172.16.14.82 is 10.1.2.2. Since all the routes have a different prefix length, the longest matching prefix is the one that is used. The preference of the route is irrelevant in this case. 172.16.14.64/28 is the longest prefix but only matches the range 172.16.14.64 through 172.16.14.79. 172.16.14.64/27 matches the range 172.16.14.64 through 172.16.14.95 and is therefore the entry chosen. The OSPF and default route both match but are a shorter prefix match.

15. B. Just as in IPv4, the correct IPv6 next-hop to use is that of the far end router, in this case, R2. From the given MAC address of R2's port, we can determine that the link-local interface of R2's port is FE80::216:4DFF:FE13:63C1. When using local-link addresses, the local interface name must always be supplied in the syntax so the router can determine which interface to use. In this case, the local interface name on R1 toward R2 is "toR2." A is incorrect because it does not specify the local interface name. C is incorrect because it uses the next-hop of its own interface rather then R2 and it specifies the wrong interface name. D is incorrect because it uses the next-hop of its own interface rather then R2's.

Chapter 4

1. B. The primary goal of an IGP is to provide the lowest cost route to networks within an autonomous system. The other answers are incorrect.
2. C. When an interface changes state, a routing update is flooded to all routers in the domain.
3. D. The action taken when a router receives a new LSP from a neighbor is to flood the LSP to all its neighbors and then run an SPF calculation to update the route table.
4. C. The sequence number is not changed as it represents the version of the LSP and needs to be kept constant as the LSP traverses the network. The age is increased for OSPF and decreased for IS-IS as the LSP is flooded and in the LSDB.
5. C. A BGP policy may cause BGP to choose a route that is not the shortest path to the destination. BGP is not a discovery protocol so Hello messages are not used. Although BGP is a path-vector protocol, route selection is influenced by policies and is not always the least number of hops to the destination. Routers do not need to be directly connected; this is often the case with IBGP sessions.
6. B. BGP is an exterior gateway routing protocol, while the others are IGP protocols.
7. C. IS-IS is a link-state protocol as is OSPF. RIP is a distance-vector routing protocol and BGP a path-vector routing protocol. LDP and RSVP-TE are label signaling protocols and not routing protocols.
8. C. The "Type" field in the Alcatel-Lucent SR route-table indicates whether the route represents a locally attached network or a remote network.
9. B. The source address field is not present in the Alcatel-Lucent 7750 SR route-table.
10. B. Updates received by a router are used to update its routing table before an update is sent to other neighbors.
11. C. Metric database is not a database required by a link-state protocol. The other three are the databases used by a link-state protocol.
12. B. The received LSP is discarded and an updated LSP is transmitted to the sending router. The sending router has out-of-date information and therefore needs to be updated.
13. A. An ACK is sent to the sending router and the LSP is discarded. The LSP is not sent to its neighbors because it does not contain any new information.

14. B. The route chosen for forwarding is the one that has the longest prefix match, which is 192.168.0.0/20 in this case. Although 0.0.0.0/0 and 192.168.0.0/16 have lower preference values, they do not have as many bits matching the destination network as 192.168.0.0/20. Preference value is significant when the router receives the same prefix from two different protocols. For example, if the router received 192.168.0.0/16 from OSPF with a preference of 15 and 192.168.0.0/16 from IS-IS with a preference of 18, the RTM will install the route from OSPF in the route table.

15. A. R2 will be the next-hop, and R3 will become the next-hop if R2 fails. The first criteria for choosing a route is the longest prefix match, but because it is the same prefix, the length is the same for all. Preference is employed by the RTM to determine which protocol to use since protocol metrics cannot be compared directly. Because OSPF has a lower default preference than IS-IS, the OSPF routes will be used first. When comparing routes of a single protocol, the route with the lowest metric is used. Therefore, the OSPF route from R2 will be used first, followed by the OSPF route from R3.

Chapter 5

1. D. The cost value in OSPF is dependent on the default OSPF reference bandwidth, which is 100Gbs.

2. A. All passive interfaces, loopback interfaces, system interfaces, and interfaces that have not yet formed an adjacency are represented in the Router LSA as stub networks.

3. C. The OSPF Router LSA (Type 1 LSA) is not flooded throughout the autonomous system; it is only flooded within the area in which it was originated.

4. A. The router ID value does not change until the OSPF process is restarted. If OSPF is shut down and restarted, the router ID will be configured with the OSPF router ID value.

5. C. The MTU must match, but the MTU value is not in the Hello packet; it is in the Database Description packet. If there is an MTU mismatch on the link, the routers will move past the OSPF 2-Way state. The other four parameters are all contained in the Hello packet and must match for the adjacency to continue.

6. C. An OSPF router transitions to the 2-Way state after a Hello packet that contains its own router ID is received from a neighbor.

7. D. OSPF routers on a point-to-point link do not elect a designated router, only routers on a broadcast link.

8. D. Both OSPF routers send an initial Database Description packet. The router with the highest router ID becomes the master, and the sequence number in its Database Description packet is used.

9. C. By default, the OSPF MTU is derived from the port MTU. However, in this case, the OSPF MTU is explicitly set on the OSPF interface; thus there is definitely an MTU mismatch. Because the MTU is carried in the Database Description packet and the values do not match, the routers will stay in the ExStart state.

10. C. The DBD packet is used to provide summary LSA information to each router so that specific LSAs can be requested.

11. B. A router can request multiple LSAs using a single LSR. The size of the LSR is limited by the OSPF interface MTU setting.

12. D. A higher sequence number indicates that the received LSA has newer information than what the router currently has in its database. Therefore, the router will acknowledge the LSA, flood it to its neighbors, and add the LSA to its own database. Answer A describes the action when the sequence number is the same and B describes the action when the sequence number is lower (the LSA is out of date).

13. E. Network LSAs are originated by the elected DR for an OSPF broadcast network, and we do not know if the router is the DR or not. If the router is the DR for the broadcast network in area 3, the router originates one Network LSA. If the router is not the DR for the broadcast network in area 3, it does not originate any Network LSAs. Network LSAs are not originated for any of the point-to-point networks.

14. E. If the priority of the routers is the same and there is no DR already elected, the router with the highest router ID on the network is elected DR. However, DR election is non-preemptive. If a router is already DR, it remains DR even when a router with a higher priority joins the network. Thus, the DR is often the router on the network that has been up the longest.

15. E. Every OSPF router originates a Router LSA that describes all their interfaces regardless of the interface types. Therefore, answers A, B, and C are incorrect. Only the DR and BDR for a broadcast interface originate the Network LSA and, therefore, D is incorrect.

Chapter 6

1. D. An OSPF router needs to be declared as an ASBR (autonomous system border router) when it has to exchange routes between OSPF and another routing protocol. Answer C is an area border router (ABR). Although an ASBR will often connect to a BGP network, answer E is incorrect because an ASBR may also connect to other external routing domains.
2. C. An ABR originates one Router LSA for each area that it connects to. Each Router LSA includes the interfaces and prefixes declared in that area.
3. D. Only OSPF ABRs originate Summary LSAs. (Backbone routers do not, unless they are ABRs.) By default, the ABR creates a Summary LSA for every prefix in the LSDB resulting in routes advertised to all areas. Summarization can be configured manually using the area-range command to reduce route advertisements between areas.
4. A. Summary LSAs are originated by an ABR with the metric set to the highest cost of the component networks and link-state id set to the summary route.
5. E. The ASBR originates AS External LSAs that are flooded throughout the autonomous system. AS External LSAs are not modified by any ABRs.
6. D. Although there may be a large number of Summary LSAs, they do not affect the SPF calculation because they are not part of the local area's topology. A, B, and C are true statements because individual areas in a multi-area network do not have complete topology information.
7. B. OSPF supports virtual links, but the areas they connect to are not called Virtual Areas. The others are all valid OSPF areas.
8. D. Area 1 routes are advertised to Area 0 using Summary LSAs originated by R1. These Summary LSAs are flooded throughout Area 0. The ABR of Area 2 originates another Summary LSA to flood throughout Area 2. Router LSAs are never used to advertise prefix information into another area. Summary LSAs are also originated and flooded into an area by the ABR for that area.
9. A. The OSPF area-range command is used on an ABR in the context of the area being summarized. In this case, the requirement is to reduce the routing table size of Area 1 routers. Therefore, Area 0 routes are summarized before advertisement to Area 1, and the command is used in the Area 0 context.

10. A. Because R1 is an ABR, its route-table will contain the Area 0 /24 routes. R1's route-table will also contain a black-hole route for the /16 route it advertises to Area 1. Answers B and C are incorrect because R2 will have only the summary (/16) prefix in its route-table.

11. D. An OSPF ASBR Summary LSA is used to advertise the location of an ASBR to areas the ASBR does not reside in. R3 sets the ASBR flag in its Router LSA. An ABR that receives this Router LSA originates an ASBR Summary LSA that is flooded throughout the other areas it is attached to. In this case, R1 receives the Router LSA with ASBR flag set and originates an ASBR Summary LSA that is flooded into Area 0. Because R2 is also an ABR, it has the ASBR Summary LSA originated by R1 in its LSDB. Because R1 is not known in Area 2, R2 originates an ASBR Summary LSA to be flooded into Area 2. Answer F is not correct because an ASBR Summary LSA is not required in the area where the ASBR resides.

12. B. A simple stub area only blocks Type 5 AS External LSAs. If the area was configured as a totally stubby area by configuring an additional no summaries parameter, Type 3 Summary LSAs would also be blocked. Unlike NSSAs, stub areas always contain a default route.

13. E. The no summaries parameter was added to a router that is not the ABR. This has no effect because it is the ABR that originates Summary LSAs into an area. If the no summaries parameter is configured on the ABR, the correct answer would be B because Type 3 Summary LSAs would be blocked in addition to the AS External LSAs.

14. E. Because there is an ASBR in the area, answers A and B can be eliminated. Unlike a stub area, an NSSA does not originate a default route by default; therefore, answer C can be eliminated. Like a stub area, an NSSA needs to be explicitly configured with no summaries to block Summary LSAs. Therefore, the correct answer is E.

15. B. Type 7 NSSA LSAs are advertised by an ASBR in an NSSA and are only flooded throughout the area; therefore, answers A and E are true statements. An ABR that receives an NSSA LSA originates AS External LSAs that are flooded throughout the autonomous system to describe the routes. Answer B is correct because it falsely indicates R10 as the advertising router rather than the ABR for Area 2. An ABR originates an ASBR Summary LSA when it floods an AS External LSA from one area to another. Therefore, answer C is a true statement because Area 1 routers will

indeed have an ASBR Summary LSA with an advertising router ID of the ABR for Area 1. Note that there is no ASBR Summary LSA in Area 0 because the AS External LSA is originated by the ABR for Area 2.

Chapter 7

1. D. An OSPF router needs to be declared as an ASBR (autonomous system border router) when it has to exchange routes between OSPF and another routing protocol. Answer C is an area border router (ABR). Although an ASBR will often connect to a BGP network, answer E is incorrect because an ASBR may also connect to other external routing domains.
2. C. An ABR originates one Router LSA for each area that it connects to. Each Router LSA includes the interfaces and prefixes declared in that area.
3. D. Only OSPF ABRs originate Summary LSAs. (Backbone routers do not, unless they are ABRs.) By default, the ABR creates a Summary LSA for every prefix in the LSDB resulting in routes advertised to all areas. Summarization can be configured manually using the area-range command to reduce route advertisements between areas.
4. A. Summary LSAs are originated by an ABR with the metric set to the highest cost of the component networks and link-state id set to the summary route.
5. E. The ASBR originates AS External LSAs that are flooded throughout the autonomous system. AS External LSAs are not modified by any ABRs.
6. D. Although there may be a large number of Summary LSAs, they do not affect the SPF calculation because they are not part of the local area's topology. A, B, and C are true statements because individual areas in a multi-area network do not have complete topology information.
7. B. OSPF supports virtual links, but the areas they connect to are not called Virtual Areas. The others are all valid OSPF areas.
8. D. Area 1 routes are advertised to Area 0 using Summary LSAs originated by R1. These Summary LSAs are flooded throughout Area 0. The ABR of Area 2 originates another Summary LSA to flood throughout Area 2. Router LSAs are never used to advertise prefix information into another area. Summary LSAs are also originated and flooded into an area by the ABR for that area.

9. A. The OSPF area-range command is used on an ABR in the context of the area being summarized. In this case, the requirement is to reduce the routing table size of Area 1 routers. Therefore, Area 0 routes are summarized before advertisement to Area 1, and the command is used in the Area 0 context.

10. A. Because R1 is an ABR, its route-table will contain the Area 0 /24 routes. R1's route-table will also contain a black-hole route for the /16 route it advertises to Area 1. Answers B and C are incorrect because R2 will have only the summary (/16) prefix in its route-table.

11. D. An OSPF ASBR Summary LSA is used to advertise the location of an ASBR to areas the ASBR does not reside in. R3 sets the ASBR flag in its Router LSA. An ABR that receives this Router LSA originates an ASBR Summary LSA that is flooded throughout the other areas it is attached to. In this case, R1 receives the Router LSA with ASBR flag set and originates an ASBR Summary LSA that is flooded into Area 0. Because R2 is also an ABR, it has the ASBR Summary LSA originated by R1 in its LSDB. Because R1 is not known in Area 2, R2 originates an ASBR Summary LSA to be flooded into Area 2. Answer F is not correct because an ASBR Summary LSA is not required in the area where the ASBR resides.

12. B. A simple stub area only blocks Type 5 AS External LSAs. If the area was configured as a totally stubby area by configuring an additional no summaries parameter, Type 3 Summary LSAs would also be blocked. Unlike NSSAs, stub areas always contain a default route.

13. E. The no summaries parameter was added to a router that is not the ABR. This has no effect because it is the ABR that originates Summary LSAs into an area. If the no summaries parameter is configured on the ABR, the correct answer would be B because Type 3 Summary LSAs would be blocked in addition to the AS External LSAs.

14. E. Because there is an ASBR in the area, answers A and B can be eliminated. Unlike a stub area, an NSSA does not originate a default route by default; therefore, answer C can be eliminated. Like a stub area, an NSSA needs to be explicitly configured with no summaries to block Summary LSAs. Therefore, the correct answer is E.

15. B. Type 7 NSSA LSAs are advertised by an ASBR in an NSSA and are only flooded throughout the area; therefore, answers A and E are true statements. An ABR that

receives an NSSA LSA originates AS External LSAs that are flooded throughout the autonomous system to describe the routes. Answer B is correct because it falsely indicates R10 as the advertising router rather than the ABR for Area 2. An ABR originates an ASBR Summary LSA when it floods an AS External LSA from one area to another. Therefore, answer C is a true statement because Area 1 routers will indeed have an ASBR Summary LSA with an advertising router ID of the ABR for Area 1. Note that there is no ASBR Summary LSA in Area 0 because the AS External LSA is originated by the ABR for Area 2.

Chapter 8

1. B. IS-IS uses 10 as the link metric by default. However, it can be configured to calculate the link metric the same way as OSPF using the reference bandwidth and the link bandwidth.
2. A. IS-IS is not specifically designed for IP and uses the Layer 2 protocol for communication, so it is logical that it would use the highest interface MAC address as a tiebreaker. DIS election is preemptive, so if a new router with a higher priority or higher interface MAC address is added to the network, it becomes the DIS.
3. B. CSNPs are transmitted periodically on broadcast or point-to-point links. Based on this information, a router can request an updated LSP or transmit an updated LSP to its neighbor. Hello messages do not carry any information about the LSDB. Routers on a point-to-point network do acknowledge received LSPs, but also transmit CSNPs. Answer D describes the aging of LSPs, but this is not the mechanism to maintain synchronization of databases.
4. B. An IS-IS router also periodically re-floods its own LSPs with an incremented sequence number to refresh the LSDB of the other routers.
5. E. All the statements are true.
6. C. There is no ACK PDU in IS-IS. On a point-to-point link, LSPs are acknowledged with a PSNP.
7. C. In the IS-IS NSAP address, the system ID is always six bytes long. For example, the router ID of 10.10.10.1 is transformed into a 6 byte value of 0100.1001.0001. The transformation is done by using each of the four parts of the router ID as 3 digits (think of it as 010.010.010.001 divided in three instead of four parts).

8. B. A CSNP is best described as an index that lists all the LSPs in the LSDB. Answer A describes the Hello PDU, answer C describes the CSNP, and answer D describes the LSP.

9. E. All of the statements about the formation of an adjacency in IS-IS are correct. In OSPF an adjacency is not established until both LSDBs are up to date. In IS-IS the adjacency is considered established after the successful exchange of Hello PDUs.

10. A. As an example, the router ID of 10.10.10.1 is transformed into a 6 byte value of 0100.1001.0001. The transformation is done by using each of the four parts of the router ID as 3 digits (think of it as 010.010.010.001 divided in three instead of four parts). Answer B is incorrect because the NSAP selector is added to the six byte system ID. Answer D is incorrect because the last four bytes may be used to create the router ID, but this is then converted to a six byte system ID using the process described by answer A.

11. D. Prefix information is carried in the *TE IP Reach* TLV, (or Extended IP Reachability TLV). Notice the *prefLen* field which indicates the length of the prefix. *Router ID* is the unique router ID and is not necessarily a routeable IP address. *I/F Addresses* lists the IP addresses for interfaces included in IS-IS, but this is not the prefix information. *TE IS Nbrs* identifies the interfaces where the router has formed an adjacency with another IS-IS router, but this is not the prefix information for that link. A number of the fields are described as TE because these TLVs are defined in RFC 5305 which describes the TE extensions to IS-IS.

12. C. The pseudonode LSP lists all the routers attached on a broadcast network as neighbors with a metric of zero.

13. D. The LSP IDs show four different system IDs, so there are four different routers in the network with L2 or L1/L2 capability. Because they are L2 they could be in different areas, so D is not necessarily true. R1 originates two LSPs. R1.03-00 is a pseudonode LSP as indicated by the "03" so there is at least one broadcast network. There could be L1 routers in the network, but R1 does not have an adjacency with any of them because there are no L1 LSPs in its database.

14. B. A passive interface is never listed in the TE IS Nbrs TLV because an IS-IS adjacency is never formed on a passive interface.

15. D. The router transmits and expects to receive a BFD packet every 100 milliseconds. After it has missed 5 consecutive packets (the multiplier) the interface is considered down by IS-IS.

Chapter 9

1. B. An SPF calculation is performed over the topology defined by all the L2 capable routers and used to route between areas. L1 routers only perform the SPF calculation for their local area.
2. E. L1 routers use a default route to the nearest L1/L2 router to forward traffic out of the area, which may not be the most direct route to the destination. Because the L2 routers have more complete routing information, the return traffic may take a more direct route. A route learned through an L1 LSP is preferred over one learned through L2 and can lead to sub-optimal routing. However, this is less likely to result in an asymmetric route since traffic will usually follow the same route in both directions.
3. D. When routes are summarized it reduces the number of entries required in the LSP carrying the routing information and thus reduces the size of the route table in other routers. It does not provide more accurate routing information or eliminate asymmetric and sub-optimal routing; in fact it is more likely to have the opposite effect.
4. A. Normally L1 routers do not have routing information from outside the area, unless L1/L2 routers in the area are configured for route leaking.
5. A. A break in the L2 backbone is likely to result in unreachable destinations since L2 LSPs cannot be distributed throughout the entire network.
6. E. Hierarchy improves the scalability of IS-IS by allowing the SPF calculation to be performed over several smaller areas rather than one large area. It has no effect on the efficiency of packet forwarding. Hierarchy can result in asymmetric routing; configuration and troubleshooting are more difficult in a hierarchical network; traffic engineering calculations cannot be performed over a hierarchical (multi-area) network.
7. C. L1 and L2 LSPs are kept in separate LSDBs. The SPF calculation is performed separately on each database.
8. B. A black hole prefix cannot be advertised in an LSP. The summarizing router adds a black hole entry to its route table so that it will silently discard any packets destined to the summary route that do not match any of the individual prefixes.
9. D. L1 routers create a default route to the nearest L1/L2 router with the ATT bit set unless they are configured to suppress the default route. The route is not

distributed in the LSP from the L1/L2 router in the way that an OSPF ABR distributes the default route in a stub network. Routers with L2 capability do not create a default route entry since they have all the prefix information for the network.

10. C. By default, routes exported to IS-IS on an L1/L2 router are advertised in both the L1 and L2 LSP.
11. E. All of the statements are correct.
12. B. The two IS-IS routes are a longer match than the OSPF and static routes, so the preference of these is not relevant. A route learned from L1 is preferred over an L2 route.
13. C. Asymmetric routing is most likely to occur when an area does not have complete route information. An IS-IS area with route leaking configured has effectively the same routing information as an OSPF normal area, so the protocol itself is not any more likely to create asymmetric routes.
14. E. A is false because an L1 router does not form an adjacency with an L2 router in the same area. B is false because an L2 router does not form an adjacency with an L1 router. C is false because an L1/L2 router also forms adjacencies with L1/L2 and L2 routers in other areas.
15. D. An L1/L2 router sets the ATT bit when it has routes to another area. The L1 routers in the area create a default route to the nearest router with the ATT bit set.

Chapter 10

1. A. Only a single instance of IS-IS is required. Typically this would be configured for multi-topology operation.
2. D. The MT Topology TLV shows that both IPv4 (0) and IPv6 (2) are enabled. This TLV does not appear when the router is configured for single topology operation. However, there are no IPv6 addresses assigned to any interfaces.
3. A. 2001:DB8::1 is shown in the IP6 Reachability TLV with a metric of 0. This is likely the system address, unless there is no system interface defined and there is a loopback with this address.
4. C. New TLVs were defined for MT IS-IS that identify the topology to which the TLV applies.
5. E. All the statements are true.

6. D. IPv6 Reachability TLV carries the information about IPv6 prefixes in the network. The Extended IP Reachability TLV carries the IPv4 prefixes and the Extended IS Reachability TLV carries information about neighbors. The IPv6 Interface Address TLV carries the IPv6 interface addresses.
7. B. Multi-topology IS-IS means that the router maintains different route tables for distinct topologies such as IPv4 and IPv6.
8. C. The output shows two Extended IS Reachability TLVs (used for IPv4) and one MT IS TLV (used for IPv6). Note the MT ID value of 2 for this TLV.
9. D. The black hole entry in the route table is an indication that the router is summarizing the loopback interfaces. It is not possible to deduce anything about the IPv4 status since the command only shows IPv6 routes. The router could be L1/L2 but is not likely to be Level 1 only because the learned routes all have a preference of 18, which is the default value for L2 routes.
10. F. A, B, C, and D are all valid MT topologies.

Chapter 11

1. E. MPLS is a tunneling technology. The format of the tunneled data is not important, since the forwarding of data across a tunneled network is controlled by the tunneling protocol. In fact, MPLS is known as multiprotocol because it can be used to transport any type of packet payload across any Layer 2 network protocol using a simple label switching approach.
2. C. Using MPLS IGP shortcuts eliminates the need to run a full mesh of IBGP sessions in a service provider's core. This is because core routers only need to perform label switching using MPLS labels rather then forwarding IP transit traffic from the Internet. Therefore IBGP sessions are not required on the core routers since they do not need to know the external routes.
3. D. The main function of a P router is label switching of MPLS packets based on their MPLS transport labels. Answer A is incorrect since P routers are not service aware. Answer B is incorrect since P routers are LSRs rather then LERs. Answer C is incorrect since the MPLS label operation associated with an LSR is label swapping rather then label pushing or label popping.
4. B. A FEC defines a group of packets to be forwarded over the same path with the same forwarding treatment. Therefore packets need to be assigned to a FEC at the ingress LER only.

5. D. Answer C is incorrect because GRE is not an MPLS signaling protocol. Answer A is incorrect because Multiprotocol BGP can be used to signal Layer 3 service labels but is not used to signal MPLS transport labels. Answer B is incorrect. Although Link LDP is used to signal MPLS transport labels, Targeted LDP is only used to signal Layer 2 service labels. RSVP-TE is not used to signal service labels but is used to signal MPLS transport labels.

6. C. Answer A is not correct since MPLS is used to provide Layer 2 and Layer 3 VPN services. Answer B is not correct since MPLS traffic engineering is done with RSVP-TE to force an LSP to take a particular path through a service provider network. Answer D is incorrect since RSVP-TE does provide high availability and redundancy mechanisms such as MPLS fast reroute. Although MPLS originated to replace the more complex IP forwarding mechanism, once hardware was developed that could perform IP forwarding at line rates MPLS was no longer required for that purpose.

7. E. Answer A is incorrect because label bindings are distributed in the upstream direction. Answer B is incorrect because a router in ordered control mode only generates a label after it receives one from its downstream (not upstream) neighbor. Answer C is incorrect because routers using liberal label retention will have more label bindings in their LIB then their LFIB.

8. A. One of the requirements of an MPLS VPN is to make sure CE routers are not aware of the VPN. Since CE routers are not aware of the VPN, they do not perform MPLS label operations on packets. Therefore answers B and C are incorrect.

9. E. Answers A, B, and D, are incorrect since they are not MPLS constructs. Answer C is incorrect since the LIB is used to store all MPLS labels received from peers regardless of whether or not they are active.

10. D. Answer A is incorrect since the FEC only needs to be configured on the ingress LER (R1). Answer B is incorrect since R2 only needs to have the interface to R1 configured with label swap operations, although both interfaces must be configured for MPLS. Answer C is incorrect since different MPLS label values can be used between the routers as long as they meet the requirement that R2 is aware of what label to expect from R1 and R3 is aware of what label to expect from R2. Note that this question is only concerned with a single static LSP from R1-R2-R3. In a more realistic situation bi-directional traffic flow would be required between the routers and a static LSP would also be configured from R3-R2-R1.

11. F. The first thing to know is that the Alcatel-Lucent 7750 SR uses pipe mode. Therefore the fact that there are five P routers is not relevant to the solution. The next thing to know is that TTL handling depends on whether the VPN service type is Layer 2 or Layer 3. Since the service type information has not been provided, the question cannot be answered. If a Layer 2 VPN service is being offered, the IP TTL is not affected and is therefore 10 at egress. If a Layer 3 VPN service is being offered the IP TTL is decremented at each PE and the TTL value is 8 at egress.

12. A. The Alcatel-Lucent 7750 SR uses a per platform label space. Therefore the same label value for a FEC is advertised to all other peers.

13. E. An MPLS label value of 3 is called an implicit null and is reserved for penultimate hop popping. Therefore when an MPLS router receives a label value of 3 from a downstream router, it pops the outer label before forwarding data packets downstream.

14. A. Answer B is incorrect because the MPLS transport label is not held constant through the service provider network, it is label swapped at each P router. Answer C is incorrect because the MPLS service label is not label swapped at each P router, it is held constant from PE to PE.

15. D. Answer A is incorrect because RSVP-TE uses downstream on demand mode. Answer B is incorrect because LDP uses downstream unsolicited mode. Answer C is incorrect; although RSVP-TE uses conservative label retention, LDP uses liberal label retention. Ordered control mode means that a router does not generate a label for a FEC until it has received a valid label from its downstream neighbor. Since both LDP and RSVP-TE operate in ordered control mode answer D is correct.

Chapter 12

1. C. Answer A is incorrect because Targeted LDP (not Link LDP) is used to exchange service labels. Answer D is incorrect because Targeted LDP is only used to exchange service labels for Layer 2 services, not Layer 3 services. Answer B is incorrect because Targeted LDP is not used to exchange transport labels (only Link LDP or RSVP-TE can be used to exchange transport labels). Unlike Targeted LDP peers, Link LDP peers must be directly connected.

2. B. The purpose of an LDP notification message is to signal errors and other notable events.

3. C. Answer A and B are incorrect because by default the Alcatel-Lucent 7750 SR advertises labels for its system address AND for reachable FECs for which a label has been received. Answers D and E are incorrect; although import and export policies can be used to influence LDP label distribution, they are not required for default behavior.
4. D. Answer A is incorrect because the RIB is the Routing Information Base and contains all IP routes received. Answer B is incorrect because the FIB represents the IP route table which contains the best IP routes from the RIB to use for unlabelled IP packets. The FIB can be viewed with the show router route-table command. Answer C is incorrect because the LIB is the Label Information Base and contains ALL labels received, not just the active ones. The LIB can be viewed with the command show router ldp bindings. The LFIB is the Label Forwarding Information Base and contains the labels from the LIB that are active. The LFIB can be viewed with the show router ldp bindings active command, therefore the correct answer is D. Answer E is incorrect because the RTM is the Route Table Manager which is a process rather than a storage construct.
5. E. To answer this question you need to know how many LDP interfaces are on each router; however, this information is not provided. Each router will receive an LDP prefix binding for each system address in the network from each of its neighbors. Therefore, if each router has 2 LDP interfaces, it will receive 8 LDP bindings from its neighbors. If each router has 3 LDP interfaces, it will receive 12 LDP prefix bindings from its neighbors.
6. B. Flow control is not a function of LDP.
7. D. LDP Hello messages use UDP rather then TCP. This is logical since LDP Hello messages are used in the neighbor discovery stage and are sent to the all routers multicast address (224.0.0.2). Since the neighbors are initially unknown, a TCP session is not possible.
8. F. Answer A is incorrect because the Alcatel-Lucent 7750 SR always indicates a label space of zero since it uses a per-platform label space. Answer B is incorrect because the source IP address in each Hello message is the egress interface of the router. Answer C is incorrect because the destination IP address is the all router multicast address 224.0.0.2. Answer D is incorrect because the smaller value is used when the hello hold time values do not match between the routers. Answer E is incorrect because the system address of the originating router is used for the transport address, not the egress interface address.

9. E. The question asks for the number of LDP sessions. However this could be Link LDP or Targeted LDP sessions, so the question cannot be answered with the information provided. Although you are told the network is used to provide VPN services, you are not told whether they are Layer 2 or Layer 3 services or how many PE routers there are (versus P routers). For example, since R2 and R3 are not directly connected they do not have a Link LDP session between them. However, if R2 and R3 are both PEs for a Layer 2 service, they will have a Targeted LDP session. If the question specifically asked how many Link LDP sessions there were on R2, the answer would be one session.

10. E. Answer A is incorrect because the router with the highest transport address is considered the active router. Answer B is incorrect because both passive and active routers send LDP initialization messages. Answer C is incorrect because the active router initiates the opening of the LDP session by sending an LDP Initialization message, not an LDP Notification message. Answer D is incorrect because only the active router attempts to open a TCP connection.

11. C. The statement which best characterizes the LDP message sequence used to indicate the change on R1 is: R1 sends a Label Withdraw message to R2 and R2 sends a Label Release message to R1.

12. A. The first thing to consider is that Label Mapping messages are used to advertise FEC prefix bindings to neighbors. Notification messages are used to signal error conditions. Therefore answers C and D are incorrect. The next thing to consider is that because the Alcatel-Lucent 7750 SR uses a per platform label space it will advertise the same label value to both peers. Therefore answers B and D are incorrect.

13. B. Although ECMP is enabled, the topology is a triangle so multiple equal cost paths do not exist. Each router will have a swap and push operation for each of the other two routers' system addresses, and a pop operation for its own system address. Therefore there will be 5 active LDP bindings in each router's LFIB.

14. D. The aggregate-prefix-match command is used on routers that only receive summarized routes to ensure that labels for the more specific prefixes are installed into the LFIB. In this case the aggregate-prefix-match command must be used on all Area 0 routers. Answers A, B, and C are incorrect because the aggregate-prefix-match command does not have to be used on either of the ABRs since they have the more specific routes in their route table.

15. C. The routers in this topology essentially form a triangle. If all the interfaces were properly included in LDP there would be 5 active LDP bindings on each router (a pop operation for its own system interface address, and a swap and a push operation for each of the other two system interface addresses). Now consider the router that was only configured with one LDP interface. This router now only has one LDP neighbor from which it will receive all its LDP bindings so it will never be an LSR (only ingress or egress LER). Therefore it will not have any swap operations in its LFIB. Furthermore, the label it receives from its LDP neighbor for the other directly connected router will not be installed in the LFIB because it does not match the routing table entry for the best route. Therefore the router will only have two active prefix bindings in its LFIB, a push operation for its LDP neighbor and a pop operation for itself. There will also be 2 active bindings on the router directly connected to the interface that was not configured correctly. The other router will have the expected 5 prefix bindings in its LFIB.

Chapter 13

1. E. Answer A is incorrect because the destination IP address of a Path message is the egress LER. Answer B is incorrect because the RRO (Route Record Object) is optional and is not used by the Resv message for forwarding. (There are some cases where an RRO is required to support features such as MPLS FRR, which is covered in later chapters). Answer C is incorrect because RSVP-TE labels are distributed in the upstream direction by Resv messages. Answer D is incorrect because the head end router does not signal the LSP label used by all other routers. Every router along the LSP path signals a label for the LSP to their upstream router in a Resv message.
2. E. Answers A and B are incorrect because an IGP topology change does not affect a strict path LSP. Answer B is also incorrect because Resv Tear messages travel upstream rather then downstream. Answer C is incorrect because Path Error and Resv Error messages don't change the state of an LSP. Answer D is incorrect because Path Tear messages travel downstream rather than upstream and Resv Tear messages travel upstream rather than downstream.
3. C. Every router in the path of an LSP must have an RSVP-TE session for the LSP. Answer D is incorrect because the question states that the path of the LSP traverses four routers but there are six routers in the IGP domain. This means that two of the routers in the IGP domain are not in the LSP's path and do not have an RSVP-TE

session for the LSP. Answers A and B are not correct as they state that the RSVP-TE session is only on the head and tail end routers.

4. D. Answer A is incorrect because although Path Error messages do travel upstream they are addressed hop by hop. Answer B is incorrect because although Resv Error messages travel downstream they are also addressed hop by hop. Answer C is incorrect because Resv Error messages do not modify the RSB, RSVP-TE Error messages are for notification only.

5. B. MPLS shortcuts are used to avoid having a full mesh of IBGP sessions and are therefore only required on routers that have EBGP sessions. When using MPLS shortcuts, the only requirement of transit routers is to support MPLS label swapping. They have no special configuration for the use of MPLS shortcuts. Therefore answers A and C are incorrect. Answer D is incorrect because the use of MPLS shortcuts in an AS is not dependent on whether or not MPLS shortcuts are used in a peer AS. MPLS shortcuts are used for intra-AS communication. Inter-AS communication is achieved with IP routing, not with MPLS.

6. A. Path Tear messages always travel downstream with a purpose of tearing down the LSP state at each router along the LSP path. When an operator administratively shuts down an LSP at the head end router, a Path Tear message is sent from the head end to the tail end router and is intercepted by each router along the path of the LSP. Answer B is incorrect because Path Tear messages are not tunneled. Answer C is incorrect because Resv Tear messages travel upstream not downstream. Answer D is incorrect because Path Error messages travel upstream not downstream and are not used to tear down an LSP. Answer E is incorrect because RSVP-TE Error messages do not modify the state of an LSP.

7. E. An RSVP-TE router has an RSVP-TE session for every LSP for which it acts as an ingress LER, transit LSR, or egress LER. Therefore the number of RSVP-TE sessions on the router is 9 (ingress LER for 3 LSPs + egress LER for 2 LSPs + transit LSR for 4 LSPs). The number of Layer 2 VPN service instances configured is irrelevant as RSVP-TE is not used for signaling service labels.

8. C. The Tunnel ID of an LSP always remains constant unless the LSP configuration is deleted and then re-created. Therefore answer B and D are incorrect. The LSP ID changes whenever an LSP is resignaled, therefore answer A and B are incorrect.

9. C. The LSP has a totally loose path and CSPF has not been enabled on the LSP. The LSP goes down when there is a topology change along the path of the LSP. When the retry timer expires the LSP is signaled along the path chosen by the IGP with a new LSP ID. Because CSPF is not enabled, the LSP must always follow the IGP. The consequence is that when the link is repaired, the LSP goes down again. When the retry timer expires, the LSP is signaled along the path chosen by the IGP with a new LSP ID. The LSP is now on its original path and the LSP ID has changed twice in the process. Answer A is incorrect because the LSP ID always changes when the Path of an LSP changes. Answer B is incorrect as a manual resignal or resignal timer expiry is not required for a non-CSPF enabled LSP to change its path.

10. E. RSVP-TE Hello messages are used to detect when an adjacency between two routers is down; the number of LSPs on the router does not affect the number of Hello messages that need to be sent. Only a single Hello message is sent by a router at each Hello interval, regardless of the number of RSVP-TE sessions on the router; therefore the answer is E.

11. F. Answer A is incorrect because a router does not advertise that it supports refresh reduction by sending a summary refresh message. To indicate that a router supports refresh reduction, it adds a MESSAGE_ID to Path and Resv messages sent on that interface and sets the lowest bit of the Flags field in the RSVP-TE header. Answers B and C are incorrect because individual LSPs are uniquely identified in the Summary Refresh message by the sending router's IP address and Message ID values, not by Tunnel ID or LSP ID. If the router does not find a message corresponding to one of the Message ID values, it sends its neighbor a Summary Refresh message with a MESSAGE_ID_NACK object that indicates the unknown Message ID. The neighbor then transmits the regular Path or Resv message corresponding to the unknown Message ID. Therefore answers D and E are incorrect.

12. A. Because the question states that the LSP is totally loose and not enabled with CSPF it will follow the best IGP path at all times. After the topology change, the head end router starts the retry timer (set to 30 secs by default). When the timer expires the head end establishes the LSP over the shortest IGP path.

13. A. There will not be an ERO in the Path message.

14. A. The command configure router bgp igp-shortcut command specifies one of three options, ldp, rsvp-te, or mpls. When the mpls option is used, an RSVP-TE LSP will be used if one exists, otherwise it will use an active LDP label binding.

15. C. 6PE is used by service providers that want to tunnel IPv6 traffic over an IPv4 core, therefore answer D is incorrect. 6PE uses two labels, the outer label is the MPLS transport label and the inner label has the IPv6 explicit null value of 2 to indicate that the payload is a native IPv6 packet.

Chapter 14

1. D. Answer A is incorrect because TE-LSPs will not follow the best IGP route if there are constraints that force the LSP to use a longer route. Answer B is incorrect. As noted in the text, CR LDP was defined in RFC 3212 but was deprecated in 2003. Answer C is incorrect because constraint-based routing only determines the path of an LSP; independent configuration is required to enforce QoS in the data plane. Answer D is correct because whenever CSPF is enabled on an LSP, the head end router calculates the entire path of the LSP and populates the ERO accordingly. This is in contrast to an LSP that was not enabled with CSPF, which will follow the best IGP route when strict hops are not configured in the path.
2. B. The first consideration is that when an LSP path changes, the LSP ID increases. When the link is repaired, the behavior of the LSP depends on whether or not CSPF is enabled. If CSPF is enabled, the head end router does not resignal the LSP until the resignal timer expires or a manual resignal is performed. If CSPF is not enabled on the LSP, the path will always follow the IGP route and the LSP ID is increased whenever the LSP is resignaled.
3. D. When CSPF is enabled on a router, the head end calculates the entire path of the LSP and populates the ERO accordingly. Because the entire path of the LSP is calculated, the ERO is populated with only strict hops. The other statements are correct.
4. B. The question says that the interfaces on the head end router are the only ones in the entire network configured with admin groups. By definition, LSPs constrained to include admin groups must have the admin group defined on every egress interface the LSP traverses. Because the ingress and egress LERs are not directly connected, there is at least one interface in the LSP that is not configured with the admin group bronze, and thus there is no path that satisfies the constraint. The LSP will be down until the configuration is changed.

5. B. Because LDP-over-RSVP is intended for traffic engineering, it is likely that CSPF will be configured on the RSVP-TE LSPs. However, it is not required, and, therefore, statement A is true. Statement B is false because T-LDP is required not only on the ABRs but also the two PE routers that are the ingress and egress of the LSP. Statement C correctly describes the label stack. Statement D is also true. Although strict-hop LSPs can be signaled without an IGP, it is required for the T-LDP sessions because they are typically not directly connected.
6. C. Traffic-engineering metrics are actually stored in the TED. The other answers are true statements about CSPF.
7. B. Link-state packets for traffic engineering contain TE metrics rather then IGP metrics. The TE metric can be set differently than the IGP metric of the same interface.
8. D. The Type 10 LSA is used by OSPF to carry traffic-engineering information.
9. A. If a non-TE-capable OSPF router receives a traffic-engineering LSA, it will still flood the LSA even though it is not a part of the TE topology. One consequence of this is that if traffic engineering is mistakenly not configured on a transit LSR, a CSPF LSP could be operationally up over a suboptimal path. If traffic engineering is not configured on the ingress LER or egress LER, the LSP will be operationally down.
10. C. There are two Type 10 LSA subtypes. Subtype 1 carries an IP address for the router. Subtype 2 carries the TE information for one interface. Statement C is incorrect because there is one LSA for each interface of the router containing the TE information.
11. B. This question specifically asks about the output of the show router mpls lsp path detail command. The *Explicit Hops* field shows the IP address of each hop that is configured on the LSP's path. The *Computed Hops* field shows the result of the CSPF calculation which is the egress interface IP address of every hop the LSP must traverse. The *Actual Hops* field is populated from the RRO (record route object) in the RSVP-TE Resv Message. Because the question states that building the RRO is disabled for this LSP, there is no RRO and therefore nothing in the *Actual Hops* field. Note that none of the three fields shows whether the hop was configured as strict or loose. In the ERO of a CSPF-enabled LSP, all hops are strict. If CSPF is not enabled on the LSP, the ERO may contain a combination of strict and loose hops.

12. A. The hop-limit parameter indicates the number of routers the LSP must traverse, including the ingress and egress LER. Because the hop limit is 3, the only path that meets the constraint is the high cost link between R1 and R2.

13. D. All three statements are valid reasons why the LSP path would not have changed.

14. D. An interface can be assigned to multiple admin groups because each is represented by a single bit in the 32-bit field. The other statements are correct.

15. E. The value configured for an admin group on the 7750 SR corresponds to the bit position in the admin-group field of the LSA. The least significant bit is zero; therefore, a value of 2 for the admin group indicates the third least-significant bit, or binary 100. The LSA will thus carry a value of 4 for this admin group.

Chapter 15

1. E. Answer A is incorrect because there is no CAC message. Answer B is incorrect because although IGP TE LSAs are used to distribute TE information, they have nothing to do with making bandwidth reservations for specific LSPs. RSVP-TE messages are used for this. TE LSAs are flooded after the LSP is established to indicate the change in bandwidth available. Answer C is correct in that a Path message is signaled from the head end to the tail end router. However it is incorrect because bandwidth reservations for the LSP are done with the Resv message. Answer D is incorrect because Resv messages are sent upstream from the tail end router to the head end router and not from the head end.

2. C. When CSPF is enabled, the head end router is responsible for calculating the entire path of the LSP based on the bandwidth constraints and placing strict hops in the ERO of the Path message. If CSPF is not enabled the CSPF calculation is not performed and the Path message is routed according to the lowest IGP cost. The question states that the RSVP-TE interfaces along the lowest IGP cost cannot meet the bandwidth requirement, therefore a Path Error message will be sent back to the head end node with the failure code admissionControlError. Because CSPF is not enabled the head end will continue to send Path messages routed according to the lowest IGP cost. The LSP will never become operationally up and therefore answers A and B are incorrect. Answer D is incorrect because the noCspfRouteToDestination failure code can only occur if CSPF is configured on the LSP.

3. C. Because the primary and secondary LSP::Paths are totally loose they will follow the shortest CSPF path through the network. Because the secondary is configured standby, it will be signaled immediately, so answer B is incorrect. If fixed filter mode is specified, 800 Mb/s is required for each LSP::Path and thus they will follow separate paths. If the shared explicit reservation style is used for the LSP, only 800 Mb/s is required so both LSPs are established along the same path. Therefore answer A and D are incorrect.

4. D. When the least fill option is specified and equal cost paths exist, the head end establishes the LSP over the path with the most bandwidth available. Note that ECMP is not required on the IGP for the least fill option to function. If the least fill option is not enabled and two CSPF paths exist the head end router will randomly select the path to use. In this case least fill is not enabled on the second LSP so its path is randomly chosen. Because the second LSP's path is randomly chosen it is not possible to determine how the third LSP will be established.

5. B. Answer A is incorrect because the use of MAM or RDM is a global setting that applies to all LSPs. Answer C is incorrect because it is MAM rather then RDM that allocates bandwidth that cannot be shared between CTs. Answer D is incorrect because the failure code is invCtAndSetupAndHoldPri when an incorrect class type and priority pair is configured on an LSP.

6. C. If a router can not allocate the resources requested by a Resv message, a Resv Error message is sent downstream to the tail end router. The tail end sends a Resv Tear to the head end router. Answer A is incorrect because LSAs are used to keep track of resources consumed in the network.

7. C. The maximum rate at which an interface can be oversubscribed to actual bandwidth on an Alcatel-Lucent 7750 SR is 1000%.

8. C. When the subscription rates of the router interfaces are changed to 50% there is insufficient bandwidth for the LSP so the LSA shows 500 Mb/s unreserved bandwidth on the port. The LSP remains operationally up in a soft preemption state until the preemption timer (default 5 mins) expires at which point the LSP is brought operationally down. Therefore answer A is incorrect. Answer B is incorrect because the maximum bandwidth field in the LSA is equal to the physical port speed of 1 Gb/s. Answer D is incorrect because after the subscription rate is changed to 50% the reservable bandwidth of all the ports becomes 500 Mb/s.

9. C. An IGP TE LSA is originated for every egress interface the LSP crosses. Because there is an egress interface on every node except the tail end router, three TE LSAs are flooded through the network.

10. D. Because the LSP has a totally strict path a single failure along the path will cause the LSP to go down. An RSVP-TE te-down setting of zero means that a TE LSA is only flooded when the reserved bandwidth reaches zero. Because there is only one LSP in the network, reserved bandwidth on all links becomes zero when the LSP goes down and three TE LSAs are sent as a result of the LSP going down (one for each egress interface). One interface on the link that went down is an egress interface for the LSP and the other an ingress interface. Bandwidth reservation does not change on the ingress interface when it goes down, but the router will generate a TE LSA as the result of the topology change. Thus there are four LSAs generated as a result of the link failure.

11. D. When the Fixed Filter reservation style is used, bandwidth is always allocated individually for primary and secondary LSPs so the first RSVP-TE tunnel consumes 200 Mb/s. When the Shared Explicit reservation style is used, bandwidth is shared by the primary and secondary LSPs when they traverse the same links. In such a case bandwidth is reserved to accommodate the highest bandwidth configured to a path within the tunnel. Therefore 200 Mb/s is allocated for the second RSVP-TE tunnel and 400 Mb/s is allocated for the third RSVP-TE tunnel.

12. D. When an LSP is manually resignaled, a Make Before Break (MBB) operation is done. If the LSP uses a Fixed Filter reservation style, a separate bandwidth allocation is done for the new LSP ID, so during the MBB process the bandwidth allocated for the Tunnel ID is effectively doubled. In this example, 1.2 Gb/s would be required for the tunnel ID during the MBB process; however, only 1 Gb/s is available on each path. Therefore the new LSP will be resignaled over the path with the available bandwidth, which is the path that the original LSP did not use.

13. A. Setup priority is not relevant to TE LSAs, only holding priority needs to be taken into consideration. Higher priority is indicated by a lower value. Therefore when an LSP of priority 3 is established, bandwidth is reserved for priority level 3 and all the lower priority levels of 4, 5, 6, and 7.

14. B. The 800 Mb/s LSP is first established over the lowest cost path. After this the 400 Mb/s LSP is established over the lowest cost path, pre-empting the 800 Mb/s LSP which is resignaled over the higher cost path. When the 700 Mb/s LSP is

configured its priority is not high enough to pre-empt the 400 Mb/s LSP from the lowest cost path, however the priority is high enough to pre-empt the 800 Mb/s LSP from the higher cost path. Because there is no path left that can support the 800 Mb/s LSP, it enters a soft pre-emption state and, assuming no other changes in the network are made, will time out and become operationally down.

15. B. Because the subscription rate is 200%, each port has 2 Gb/s of reservable bandwidth. Because class type 2 is allocated 30%, BC2 is 600 Mb/s. Although class type 1 is 0%, the Russian Doll Model allows lower classes to use the bandwidth of higher classes, so BC1 is also 600 Mb/s. Similarly class type 0 is allocated 20% which is 400 Mb/s; however, because class type 0 can use bandwidth from class type 1 and class type 2, BC0 is 1 Gb/s.

Chapter 16

1. C. The question states that the primary LSP::Path is operationally up. Non-standby LSP::Paths are not signaled unless there is a failure on the primary LSP::Paths. Therefore there will not be a failure code for the secondary LSP::Path. If the secondary LSP::Path was declared standby answer C would be a true statement.

2. C. Because the secondary LSP::Path is declared standby, the primary LSP::Path and secondary LSP::Path may be operational at the same time (although only the primary will be active). Therefore answer B is a true statement. Answer A is a true statement because two totally loose LSP::Paths will follow the same lowest CSPF cost path, which means a path diversity mechanism should be used. This is also why answer C is false. Answer D is a true statement because if there is a link failure on the primary LSP::Path the secondary LSP::Path will also go down because they are using the same path. In this case the head end will not try and establish the LSPs until the retry interval expires.

3. B. Answer A is incorrect because standby LSPs are always preferred over non-standby LSPs. Answer C is incorrect because the third LSP::Path has a lower preference (higher value) than the second LSP::Path. LSP::Paths with SRLGs are only preferred over LSP::Paths without SRLGs when path preferences are equal.

4. D. The question references detour LSPs rather than bypass tunnels, which means the FRR one-to-one protection method is in use. With this method, a protection LSP is never used for more than one protected LSP. Therefore the PLR must originate two detour LSPs. Another characteristic of detour LSPs is that they follow the shortest CSPF path from the PLR to the destination. Answer B is incorrect because the path of the protected LSPs is irrelevant. Answer C is incorrect because whether or not the protected LSPs have the same head end router is also irrelevant.

5. C. An LSP can be enabled with FRR and still use a secondary LSP::Path. If there is a failure along the path of the LSP, the PLR activates the protection LSP and reports that protection is in use to the head end router. Although the protected LSP is still operationally up, the head end router will still signal and activate the standby secondary LSP::Path. Answer C is a false statement because secondary LSP::Paths cannot be protected with FRR.

6. E. The question states that the secondary LSP::Path is not declared standby. Answers A and B are incorrect; a mechanism to ensure path diversity is not required because the primary LSP::Path and secondary LSP::Path are never established at the same time. This is also why answer C is incorrect: the primary LSP::Path and secondary LSP::Path never have the same hops because both paths are never established at the same time. Answer D is incorrect because the secondary LSP::Path is not established when the primary is. If it were configured as standby, it would follow the same path as the primary.

7. D. Answer C is a true statement because CSPF enabled LSPs are not resignaled when there is a topology change. Answer D is a false statement because the non-standby secondary LSP::Path is signaled as soon as the head end detects the failure. The traffic outage is thus equal to the time it takes for the head end to detect the failure plus the time required to signal the secondary LSP::Path.

8. C. SRLG is only relevant on egress interfaces used on the primary LSP::Path. Although a mistake was made on the tail end router it does not affect this LSP because these are ingress interfaces. Answer A is incorrect if SRLG groups have been provisioned correctly on the egress interfaces of the primary LSP::Path. Answer B is incorrect and answer C is correct because there are multiple disjoint paths available in the network and thus it should be possible to signal the secondary on a disjoint path. Answer D is incorrect because the secondary will be up and the failure code srlgError does not exist.

9. E. The SRLG information is propagated in an LSA only after the SRLG has been assigned to an interface, so answer B is incorrect. After it is assigned, the decimal value of 3 is sent in the LSA for the interface. Unlike admin groups, the configured SRLG value does not indicate a bit position; it is a decimal value for the

SRLG which is advertised through the network. Therefore answers A, C, and D are incorrect.

10. C. Answer A is incorrect because the default FRR settings on the 7750 SR use node protection wherever possible and enough redundant paths exist to fully protect the LSP. Answer B is incorrect because the last hop always shows link protection because the tail end node cannot be avoided. Answer D is incorrect because there are redundant paths in the network.

11. C. Answer A is a true statement because a flag of 0x01 in the FAST_REROUTE object indicates one-to-one FRR protection is desired. Answer D is a true statement because unlike facility bypass tunnels, all detour LSPs have a DETOUR object in their Path messages. Answer C is a false statement because one-to-one detour LSPs use the shortest CSPF route from the PLR to the destination. Answer C describes the behavior of facility mode bypass tunnels.

12. A. A detour merge point (DMP) only merges the detour LSPs that are used for a single protected LSP. Because the question states that the tunnel ID and LSP ID of the detour LSPs are different, the detour LSPs are for different protected LSPs and will not be merged. Answer B is incorrect because detour merging does not need to be explicitly configured on the 7750 SR. Answer C is incorrect because avoid node statements are not used to determine if merging should be done, they are used to ensure the merged LSP satisfies the avoid node constraints of the detour LSPs.

13. C. First consider the case of the protected LSP that has a directly connected tail end router. The PLR needs to originate a link protection bypass tunnel for this protected LSP because node protection cannot be achieved. Although facility bypass tunnels can be used for more than one protected LSP, node protection is preferred by default, so this link protect LSP cannot be used for the other two protected LSPs. Because the other two protected LSPs have the same path, the PLR will originate a single node protect bypass tunnel for them.

14. A. The default setting for FRR SRLG on the 7750 SR is to not use the strict parameter. If the strict parameter is used, protection LSPs that share links with the primary LSP::Path will not be established. Answer B is incorrect because SRLGs can be used for both one-to-one FRR and for facility backup FRR. Answer C is incorrect because SRLG is a global setting when used for the purpose of FRR and cannot be enabled on specific LSPs. However, SRLG can be configured on specific secondary

LSP::Paths. Answer D is incorrect because all PLRs in the network must also be configured for FRR SRLG so that protection LSPs can be signaled properly.

15. D. Strict hops, admin groups, and SRLGs can all be used to ensure LSP::Path diversity.

Chapter 17

1. A. Only PE routers need to be configured with the service. The other routers are not aware of the service.
2. D. A VPLS appears as an Ethernet switch to the customer. Answer A describes a VPWS. Answer C describes a VPRN service. Answer B is incorrect because there is no such service; one of the goals of IP/MPLS VPN services is to shield the customer from the details of the service provider's MPLS network.
3. B. The PE routers are configured with SAPs. Answers A, C, D, and E are all incorrect because only PE routers are aware of the VPRN service and have customer facing interfaces. In fact, the same is true for VPWS and VPLS services.
4. C. Because the question states that the IP/MPLS network uses Ethernet links, the service payload is encapsulated in an Ethernet frame. A transport label is required so that data can be label switched through the service provider's IP/MPLS network to the correct PE router. A service label is required so that the PE router knows which service the payload is destined to.
5. D. When an SDP is created, the PE router attempts to establish a T-LDP session to the far end PE. However establishment of a T-LDP session does not involve the exchange of service labels. The SDPs are configured before the epipe service that uses them. Service labels are not exchanged until the SDP binding is created at both ends of the service.
6. A. The service provider network appears as an Ethernet leased line to the customer. Answer C describes a VPRN service. Answer D describes a VPLS. Answer B is incorrect because there is no such service; one of the goals of IP/MPLS VPN services is to shield the customer from the details of the MPLS network.
7. E. All of the statements list a primary feature of a service router. The main point in each statement is that the feature is oriented toward a service rather than a physical attribute of the router such as a physical port.

8. F. Layer 2 services such as VPWS and VPLS require a T-LDP session to exchange service labels. A single T-LDP session between two PE routers can be used to exchange service labels for many services. If the services all have their endpoint on the same PE router, then only one T-LDP session is required. However, in this case the number of PE routers is not specified. The number of endpoints must be known to answer the question.
9. D. An IP/MPLS network can host any number and mixture of VPN services. Answer A is incorrect because GRE can be used as the transport for any SDP regardless of the type of service the SDP is bound to. Answer B is incorrect because CE routers are entirely unaware of the services and details of the service provider's IP/MPLS network. Answer C is incorrect because a service provider can leverage other mechanisms such as MPLS resiliency features to provide redundancy. Answer E is incorrect because multiple services can share the same SDP that is provisioned with a single transport tunnel.
10. A. Link LDP peers must be directly connected. The other statements are true.
11. C. An epipe is a point to point service that can be configured as a local epipe service with two SAPs on the same PE router, or as a distributed epipe service with a SAP and spoke SDP on two PE routers.
12. E. All of the statements are false. Answer A is incorrect because T-LDP is not a neighbor discovery protocol, peers are explicitly configured. Answer B is incorrect because a T-LDP session can exist before a service is configured, for example an SDP configured between 2 PE routers that doesn't have any configured services bound to it. Answer C is incorrect because RSVP-TE is only used for signaling transport tunnels. Answer D is incorrect because LDP supports authentication using the TCP MD5 signature option.
13. C. The VC ID at both ends must match. Answer A is incorrect because although it is a best practice to use the same customer ID for services that belong to the same subscriber it is not required for the service to be operationally up. Note that problems may be encountered when using the 5620 SAM network manager if customer ID is not treated with global significance. Answer B is incorrect because the service ID is a local attribute that does not have to match on both ends of a service. However, it is considered a best practice to match the service IDs when possible. Answer D is incorrect because the service labels at both ends of an epipe do not have to match. What is important is that each PE knows what service label to use to reach the correct service on the far end PE.

14. B. Because access ports are used for customer-facing services, they have many more service-specific capabilities than network ports. Answer A is a true statement because mechanisms such as Ethernet dot1Q and Q-in-Q encapsulations can be used to create multiple SAPs on a single port. The other statements are true.

15. C. An SDP can support multiple different service types. Answers A and B are incorrect because a single SDP can support multiple services of different types. For example, the same SDP can be used for an epipe, VPLS, and VPRN service simultaneously. Answer D is incorrect because the encapsulation type is an SDP characteristic and must be defined as either MPLS or GRE upon creation.

Chapter 18

1. C. The CLI syntax shown for the SAP corresponds to an outer VLAN tag of 20 and an inner VLAN tag of 10. All other traffic will be rejected.

2. C. Answer C is a false statement because the path MTU should always be less than the MTU of all network ports along the transport path. The MTU of all network ports must be large enough to accommodate the path MTU plus the encapsulation overhead. This includes a four byte MPLS transport label (possibly two if facility FRR is enabled, or an IP header if GRE is in use), one four byte MPLS service label, and the Layer 2 header (14 bytes if it is Ethernet).

3. E. The Q-in-Q SAP encapsulation of 100.* means that the outer VLAN tag of 100 is stripped from frames before they are passed to the service, but the inner VLAN tag is left on the frame. Therefore the service MTU should accommodate the IP packet (9000 bytes) a layer 2 header (14 bytes) and an extra four byte VLAN tag (4 bytes).

4. A. Frames greater then the service MTU of a Layer 2 service are silently discarded Notifications are not sent. Answer C and D are incorrect because Layer 2 services never fragment frames.

5. D. The default SAP receives all frames arriving at a port that are not received by another SAP. Answer E describes the null SAP.

6. E. An ipipe service provides IP interworking capabilities between different Layer 2 technologies. Answer A describes an epipe. Answer B describes an apipe. Answer C describes an fpipe. Answer D describes a cpipe.

7. E. The service is configured on the two PE routers. P routers are not service aware and are only used to transport traffic through the service provider's network. CE routers are not service aware either. Because an epipe is a point-to-point service, the maximum number of PE routers that belong to the service is two.

8. A. Statement A best describes the action taken on the FCS.

9. B. The default Ethernet MTU of a Layer 2 service on a 7750 SR is 1514 bytes. Because the default MTU of an Ethernet dot1Q access port is 1518 bytes, the maximum size frame that can enter the SAP is 1518 bytes. When default SAPs are NOT in use, the four byte VLAN tag is always stripped and the maximum size frame that can be sent to the service is 1514 bytes. When default dot1Q SAPs are in use VLAN tags sent from the CE router are NOT stripped before the frame is sent to the service. Therefore the service MTU needs to be increased by four bytes to 1518 bytes to accommodate the default SAP. Although the service is still up, a full-size frame will be dropped at ingress because the service is unable to carry a 1518 byte frame.

10. B. Although 0x8100 is the standard Ethertype value for dot1Q encapsulation, the 7750 SR supports the use of other Ethertype values. The Ethertype value is specified in the configure port ethernet context. 0x8100 is the default. If the Ethertype value does not match the value configured for the port, the frame is treated as untagged.

11. A. Answer B describes atm-vpc type. Answer C describes atm-cell type operating in trunk mode. Answer D describes atm-cell type operating in port mode.

12. D. Although a larger jitter buffer does reduce the chance that data will be lost, it also increases the delay. For delay sensitive services, a smaller jitter buffer is preferred.

13. C. All the other forms of interworking described are supported on the Alcatel-Lucent 7750 SR.

14. B. The single tag on the ingressing frame must be 20, otherwise the frame would not be received by the service. The single tag is stripped on ingress and the two tags 20 and 10 are added at egress.

15. E. The encapsulation required for the customer frame is: four bytes for the control word (required for an fpipe), four bytes for the service label, four bytes for the transport label, four bytes for the facility bypass label, and 14 bytes for the Ethernet header. The MTU required for a 5000 byte frame is 5000 + 4 + 4 + 4 + 4 + 14 = 5030 bytes.

Chapter 19

1. D. The VPLS merges all SAPs into a common broadcast domain regardless of the VLAN tags. An Ethernet switch uses VLAN tags to create separate broadcast domains. Answer A is incorrect because unknown unicast traffic is flooded to all destinations in a VPLS and to all ports in an Ethernet switch. Answer B is incorrect because multicast and broadcast traffic is flooded to all destinations in a VPLS and all ports in a switch.
2. C. The VPLS performs MAC learning by checking the source address of received frames. It associates this address with the SAP or SDP on which the frame arrived.
3. D. Traffic is never flooded outside of a single service so answers A and E are incorrect. Answers B and C are incorrect because traffic is never flooded from one mesh SDP to another.
4. F. Because only mesh SDPs are used in the network, each PE must have one mesh SDP per service to every other PE router. A full mesh is required because traffic is never forwarded between mesh SDPs. With four PE routers, each PE has 3 mesh SDPs for a total of 12 mesh SDPs per service. Since there are two services there is a total of 24 mesh SDPs.
5. A. Spoke SDPs remove the need for a full mesh since traffic is forwarded from spoke SDPs to other spoke and mesh SDPs. However, this behavior can lead to loops in the network. A mixture of spoke and mesh SDPs are often used in a VPLS, and MAC learning is performed on both types.
6. A. LDP, or more specifically T-LDP is used to signal service labels. Link LDP is used to signal transport labels. Answer B is incorrect because RSVP-TE is only used to signal transport labels. Answer C is incorrect because GRE is not an MPLS signaling protocol, although it can be used to encapsulate and transport data through the service provider network. Answer D is incorrect because OSPF is an Interior Routing Protocol and not an MPLS signaling protocol.
7. C. The default service MTU for a VPLS is always 1514 bytes. SAP encapsulation type does not have an effect on the default service MTU. If default SAPs are used, a network designer may explicitly configure a service MTU to take into account extra VLAN tags passed into the service.
8. B. CE routers are unaware of service components and infrastructure. Answer A is a true statement because a VPLS may provide a point-to-point service the same as

an epipe. The only difference is that the VPLS performs MAC learning. Answer C is a true statement because it is possible to configure a local VPLS service with two or more SAPs and no SDPs. Answer D is a true statement because multiple SAPs can be configured on a single physical port by using a dot1Q or Q-in-Q Ethernet encapsulation. These SAPs may be bound to different services. Answer E is a true statement because P routers and CE routers are unaware of the service.

9. C. Because only mesh SDPs are used in the network, each PE must have an SDP to every other PE. This requires one T-LDP session between each pair of PEs. The fact that there are two services on each PE router is irrelevant because a single T-LDP session is used to signal multiple service labels. If each PE needs an SDP to every other PE, the number of T-LDP sessions on each PE is 3. To find the total number of T-LDP sessions in the network, multiply the number of PE routers (4) by the number of sessions on each (3) and then divide by two because LDP sessions are bi-directional. The formula is $n(n-1)/2$, where n is the number of PE routers.

10. B. The PE router maintains one FDB for each VPLS configured on the router. It does not have a MAC FDB for the epipe service because MAC learning is not performed by epipe services. A MAC FDB is not maintained for the other VPLSs that transit the router because P routers are not service aware.

11. F. Unicast traffic with a known destination is not flooded, it is forwarded to a single SAP or SDP that is associated with the destination MAC address. Answer C describes the behavior for unknown unicast traffic.

12. C. VC-ID on both ends of a pseudowire must always match or the pseudowire will not come up. Although the VC-ID of spoke SDPs can be configured to be the same as the VPLS service ID, it is not a requirement, so answer A is incorrect. Although the default behavior of the 7750 SR is to use a VC-ID equal to the VPLS service ID for mesh SDPs, the def-mesh-vc-id command can be used to explicitly configure the VC-ID used by all mesh SDPs of a VPLS, so answer B is incorrect. Note that all mesh SDPs of a single service must use the same VC-ID. Although the VC-ID of a mesh SDP is not explicitly configured, a VC-ID is still used to signal the service labels, so answer D is incorrect. Answer E is incorrect because VC-IDs have a point-to-point significance. Two spoke SDPs on the same PE can use the same VC-ID if they are to different routers.

13. E. Unknown unicast traffic received on a SAP is flooded to all SDPs and SAPs in the same service. The only exception is that traffic is not flooded back to the SAP where the traffic was received.

14. C. The output shows four entries for three different peers. The fact that there are three peers shows that T-LDP is configured on all the routers, so answer A is incorrect. The two entries to peer 10.10.10.2 show an ingress label and no egress label for one, and an egress label and no ingress label for the other. This is indicative of two halves of a pseudowire that could not be signaled properly. The two different VC-ID values is the cause of the SDP binding not coming up. Since mesh SDPs always use the service ID for the VC-ID, it is expected that this is the spoke SDP that did not come up. Although it shows an MTU of 1500 for one end and 0 for the other, this is because the pseudowire did not become operational. The two ends of the connection both use 1500, so answer B is incorrect. Answer D is incorrect because it is not necessary for the service ID to match at both ends as long as the VC-ID is the same. In fact, this question is the example of two VPLSs connected with a spoke SDP. The two VPLSs have different service IDs, so the VC-ID must be changed on one end of the spoke SDP to match the far end. Answer E is incorrect because there cannot be a service without a service ID, so there would be no label signaled by the far end.

15. E. The VPLS described consists of two spoke SDPs to PE-1: one from PE-2 and one from PE-3. PE-1 signals service labels with each of the PE routers at the other end of each spoke SDP. PE-2 and PE-3 do not signal labels with each other. PE-2 does forward all traffic received on its SAPs to PE-1, but it still performs MAC learning because it is a VPLS, so answer B is incorrect. It's possible that PE-2 could have multiple SAPs configured and would intelligently forward known unicast traffic between them. Answer C is incorrect because traffic is forwarded between spoke SDPs regardless of whether it causes a loop or not. There is no loop in this VPLS because the topology is a single connected line of two spoke SDPs.

Chapter 20

1. B. From the CE router's perspective it is connected directly over an Ethernet connection to the IES interface, even though an epipe service is used. Therefore the CE router and IES interface should be on the same subnet.

2. C. Because a VPRN is a Layer 3 service, the Layer 2 header sent between CE routers (or switches) is not preserved between customer sites. The service provider network appears as a single router to the CE sites. Answer D is a true statement because CE sites expect IP headers to be constant as they are routed through the service provider network.

3. B. A VPRN can use the same route distinguisher on all PE routers or different route distinguishers. Answer A is a false statement because the purpose of route distinguishers is to make routes unique as they are exchanged over the service provider network. The route distinguisher does not affect which routes are imported into a VPRN. Answer C is a false statement because CE routers are unaware of the VPRN service. Answer D is a false statement because P routers are not service-aware. Answer E is a false statement because a route distinguisher is 64 bits in length. It is combined with a 32-bit IPv4 prefix to construct a 96-bit VPN-IPv4 prefix or with a 128-bit IPv6 prefix to construct a 192-bit VPN-IPv6 prefix.

4. B. Answer A is a true statement because MP-BGP may also carry IPv6 routes, but it does not describe the use of MP-BGP in a VPRN. Answer C is incorrect because the transport label is signaled by either LDP or RSVP-TE. Answer D is incorrect because MP-BGP only peers with other BGP routers, not OSPF or RIP.

5. A. The PE routers must support both IPv4 and IPv6. However, P routers only need to support IPv4 since they are not service-aware and only forward MPLS-encapsulated traffic. The other statements are true.

6. A. Mesh SDPs are only used in a VPLS. Answers B and C are true statements because an IES can have a spoke termination to an epipe or VPLS. The IES is not aware of the actual service type that terminates the spoke SDP, it is only aware of a pseudowire to the Layer 2 service.

7. C. The VC-MTU signaled for the pseudowire between the epipe service and the IES interface must match on both ends. The service MTU for a Layer 2 service must accommodate the Layer 2 header, but the value signaled for the VC-MTU is actually the service MTU minus 14. The value signaled by the epipe end will thus be 8986. Since the IES interface is a Layer 3 service, it does not include the Layer 2 header. The IES interface MTU must be set to the value that will actually be signaled, which is 8986 bytes. If there is ever any doubt in this situation, the command show router ldp bindings fec-type services shows exactly the MTU being signaled by each end.

8. B. Answer B is a false statement because a spoke SDP is used in place of a SAP for an IES spoke termination. Answer E is a true statement because the spoke SDP is bound to a transport LSP and not to a physical port. Therefore the router responds to an ARP request for the IES interface IP address with its chassis MAC address.

9. A. Unlike a Layer 2 service, a VPRN service does not use T-LDP to signal a service label. A VPRN uses MP-BGP to signal service labels (or VPN labels). If the question was how many MP-BGP sessions are required in the network the answer would be calculated as follows. MP-BGP sessions are only required on the PE routers because P routers are not service-aware. Furthermore only one MP-BGP session is required between each pair of PE routers regardless of the number of VPRN services configured between them. Because there are four routers, each router needs to have three MP-BGP sessions, and because MP-BGP sessions are bi-directional, we divide by two. The number of MP-BGP sessions is thus calculated as $4*(3)/2 = 6$.

10. A. The 7750 SR advertises one service label (VPN label) per VRF. Thus the BGP updates for all prefixes from one VPRN on a specific PE have the same service label.

11. D. Answer A is a true statement because the CE router is not aware of the VPRN; thus, the BGP adjacency between PE and CE routers does not use the VPN-IPv4 or VPN-IPv6 address family. Answer B is a true statement because the default behavior of the 7750 SR is to not advertise routes learned from a VPRN to a CE peer unless it is explicitly configured to do so using an export policy. Answer C is a true statement because routes are not being advertised between the PE and CE routers that use static routes and therefore no export policy is required. Answer D is a false statement because the default behavior of the 7750 SR is to advertise routes between the PE routers without an export policy.

12. F. Answer A is a false statement because the same LSPs can carry both IPv4 and IPv6 traffic. Answer B is a false statement because MP-BGP sessions can carry VPN-IPv4 routes and VPRN-IPv6 routes simultaneously. Answer C is a false statement because CE routers are not aware of the VPRN or VPN-IPv6 addresses. Answer D is a false statement because the MP-BGP sessions between PE routers only exchange VPN-IPv6 routes and not native IPv6 routes. Answer E is a false statement because 6VPE can be configured without impacting IPv4 VPRN services.

13. C. The route target is used by the PE to identify which routes are to be taken from MP-BGP and installed in the VRF. Answer A describes the purpose of the route distinguisher. Answer C is incorrect because the route target is not used by the CE router. Answer D is incorrect because a regular export policy is used to select routes to be advertised to the CE.

14. B. VRF specifically refers to the virtual router and forwarding instance implemented as part of a VPRN that holds the customer routes on the PE router.

15. D. The routes shown do not appear in the VRF because they are not in use (the u status code does not appear in the output). If the route target matches some routes, but there is no transport tunnel to the next hop, the routes are marked as Invalid and not used by BGP. Answer A is incorrect because there would not be any routes from R1 without a MP-BGP session. Answer B is incorrect because having different route distinguishers has no effect on whether the routes are used or not. Answer C is incorrect because the MP-BGP VPN routes are not kept on R2 if they are not matched by a route target configured in a VPRN on R2. Answer E is incorrect because the VPRN is not operationally up without a route distinguisher and thus no routes would be seen.

Chapter 21

1. E. The epipe service is diagnosed with the svc-ping command. lsp-ping and lsp-trace are used to diagnose LSPs. sdp-ping and sdp-mtu are used to diagnose SDPs.

2. B. The command specifies that the sdp ping should be sent in-band on the sdp 5. To have the reply sent in-band, the parameter resp-sdp <*sdp-id*> must be used. Otherwise it is sent out-of-band. The sdp-ping command can be used on an LDP or an RSVP-TE LSP.

3. B. oam lsp-trace follows the path of the RSVP-TE LSP, which could easily be different than the IGP path if strict hops or other constraints are used. traceroute always follows the IGP path.

4. C. oam sdp-ping can be used with the size parameter to find the effective MTU of the SDP. oam sdp-mtu can also be used to find the effective MTU of the SDP. lsp-ping could be used to find the effective MTU of the LSP and used to calculate the SDP MTU.

5. C. oam svc-ping can be used to verify that a service is up. If one of the epipe services is up, it means that both the SDP and LSP are up.

6. B. The oam sdp-mtu command specifies the size of the payload to be carried over the SDP. When you add the encapsulation overhead for the SDP (8 bytes for the MPLS headers and 14 bytes for the Ethernet header) you get the network port MTU.

7. F. Any one of the entities can be used.
8. C. A mirror destination is created on the PE with the mirror source and specifies the SDP to use to connect to the remote destination. On the destination PE the mirror destination specifies the remote source and the local destination. Answer A is false because the label can be statically assigned. Answer B is false because GRE can be used in addition to MPLS. Answer D is false because the mirror source is only configured on the source PE router. Answer E is false because the SAP for the sniffer is configured on the mirror destination on the destination PE router.
9. A. The mirror source needs to be reconfigured after the reboot because it is implemented as a debug command and is not saved in the router's configuration.
10. E. All the features can be used to restrict the amount of traffic replicated across the mirror service.

Glossary

5620 SAM *5620 Service Aware Manager*—The 5620 Service Aware Manager (SAM) is the network management tool for the 7750 SR, 7705 SAR, 7450 ESS, 7250 SAS, and other Alcatel-Lucent equipment.

6over4 6over4 refers to the tunneling of IPv6 packets over an IPv4 network as defined in RFC 2529.

7210 SAS *7210 Service Access Switch*—The 7210 SAS is a family of compact Ethernet and aggregation devices that extends the reach of MPLS-enabled carrier Ethernet aggregation networks into smaller network locations.

The 7210 SAS family is available in a range of platform variants, including two that support extended temperature ranges (ETR).

7450 ESS *7450 Ethernet Service Switch*—The 7450 ESS is a highly scalable family of MPLS-enabled Ethernet service switches designed to support residential service delivery, business VPN services, and mobile backhaul applications at the carrier Ethernet service edge.

7705 SAR *7705 Service Aggregation Router*—The Alcatel-Lucent 7705 SAR family is an IP/MPLS aggregation router that is available in compact, low-power consumption platforms delivering highly available services over resilient and flexible network topologies.

7750 SR *7750 Service Router*—The Alcatel-Lucent 7750 Service Router (SR) family is a suite of multiservice routers that deliver high-performance, high-availability routing with service-aware operations, administration, management, and provisioning.

AAL *ATM Adaption Layers*—The ATM Adaption Layers are the layers above the ATM layer. They adapt non-ATM bit streams into ATM cells and perform functions such as error checking and correction. The ATM Adaptation Layers are AAL1, AAL2, AAL 3/4, and AAL5.

AAL5 *ATM Adaptation Layer 5*—AAL5 is the simplest of the ATM Adaptation Layers and provides a connectionless datagram delivery service most commonly used for transporting IP over an ATM network.

AAL5 SDU *AAL5 Service Delivery Unit*—The AAL5 SDU contains the AAL5 payload (the IP packet) and the AAL5 overhead. It is always an even multiple of 48 bytes long and is segmented for delivery in ATM cells.

ABR *Area border router*—An OSPF router that has interfaces configured in more than one area.

ABR *Available bit rate service*—The service provided by AAL3/4 on ATM networks. It is a connection-oriented data service and is rarely used.

ACK *Acknowledgment*—In general, an ACK is the way a protocol confirms that it has received the transmitted data. In TCP, ACK is a single-bit flag indicating the receipt of a TCP data segment. The acknowledgment number is a 32-bit field in the header and indicates the number of the next consecutive byte expected in the data stream.

Adjacency An adjacency is a relationship between two routers indicating that they have discovered each other and are able to perform routing or label distribution operations.

Adjacency database The adjacency database is built and maintained through the exchange of periodic Hello messages and is used to keep track of all other directly connected routers.

Administrative group A 32-bit mask assigned by the network administrator that can be used to characterize links for traffic engineering. Assigning administrative groups is also known as *link coloring*.

ADSL *Asymmetric Digital Subscriber Line*—A technology used to provide high-speed Internet service over existing copper infrastructure originally used for POTS.

ADSPEC object An RSVP object optionally used in the Path message to carry additional information about the path. In the case of RSVP-TE, it can be used to carry path MTU information.

AIS *Alarm indication signal*—An AIS is a code sent downstream in a digital network to indicate that a traffic-related defect has been detected.

ANSI *American National Standards Institute*—A private non-profit organization that oversees the development of standards in the United States.

Anycast An anycast address is a unicast address used by more than one host. A packet addressed to an anycast address is delivered to the nearest host as determined by the routing protocol.

Apipe A type of VPWS that provides a point-to-point ATM service. Also known as an ATM VLL service.

ARP *Address Resolution Protocol*—A TCP/IP protocol used to map an IP address to an Ethernet MAC address.

ARPANET *Advanced Research Projects Agency network*—Generally considered the first operational packet-switched network. First operational with four nodes in the United States in 1969, it eventually evolved into today's Internet.

AS *Autonomous system*—A network or group of networks and networking equipment under a common administration.

BGP is designed to route between autonomous systems.

ASBR *Autonomous system boundary router*—A router that connects the OSPF routing domain with another routing domain.

ATM *Asynchronous Transfer Mode*—ATM is a standard for cell switching that uses 53-byte cells (5-byte header and 48-byte payload) as a basic unit of transfer. ATM networks can carry traffic for multiple service types (e.g., voice, video, and data).

BA *Behavior aggregate*—A collection of packets with the same DiffServ codepoint crossing a link in a specific direction.

Backbone router An OSPF router that has at least one interface in Area 0 (may be an intra-area router or an ABR).

Bandwidth Bandwidth is transmission capacity measured in hertz (analog) or bits per second (digital). The greater the bandwidth, the more information can be sent over a circuit or transmission medium in a given time.

BC *Bandwidth constraint*—The allocation of bandwidth to class type in MPLS DiffServ-aware TE.

BDR *Backup designated router*—See *designated router.*

BECN *Backward explicit congestion notification*—A bit in the Frame Relay header indicating that traffic flowing in the opposite direction is experiencing congestion. An endpoint receiving frames with BECN set could reduce its transmission rate to avoid packet drops.

Bellman-Ford algorithm The algorithm used by a distance vector protocol such as RIP in which a router passes a copy of its routing table periodically to all its neighbors. The routers do not have a complete topological view of the network; they only know the best next-hop to the destination.

BFD *Bidirectional forwarding detection*—Used to detect failures on the link and can be enabled on static routes and other protocols such as OSPF and IS-IS.

BGPv4 *Border Gateway Protocol version 4*—BGPv4 provides many features to control traffic flows between autonomous systems and is the exterior gateway protocol currently used on the Internet. It is defined in RFC 4271.

Bit A bit is the smallest amount of information that can be transmitted on a digital network. It can have one of two values: zero or one. A combination of bits can indicate an alphabetic character or a numeric digit, or perform signaling, switching, or other functions.

Black-hole route A black-hole route is an IP route without a next-hop address. Any packets matched by the black-hole route are silently discarded.

BNG *Broadband Network Gateway*—The service provider device used as the logical IP gateway for residential subscribers.

Broadcast A broadcast message is sent to all devices or nodes in a network, rather than only to specific devices. It also refers to the address of all devices in a network.

Byte A byte is a group of 8 bits, also called one octet.

CAC *Connection Admission Control*—The set of actions taken by the network during the connection setup phase to determine whether a connection request can be accepted or should be rejected based on the resources available.

CAS *Channel Associated Signaling*—CAS is a form of signaling used in the PSTN whereby signaling information is carried in the data channel.

CBR *Constant bit rate service*—The service provided by AAL1 on an ATM network. It is a connection-oriented service with minimal delay, jitter, and data loss and is intended for the transport of traditional voice circuits.

CCITT *Comité Consultatif International Téléphonique et Télégraphique*—CCITT was renamed ITU-T in 1993.

CE *Customer edge*—CE devices are the switches or routers in a customer's network that connect to the provider edge routers (PEs).

CESoPSN *Circuit Emulation Service over Packet Switched Network*—CESoPSN pseudowires transport multiple DS0 channels from a T1 or E1 circuit and are defined in RFC 5086.

CFI *Canonical format indicator*—A single-bit flag in the Ethernet VLAN tag field that is always set to zero for Ethernet switches. CFI is used for compatibility between Ethernet type and Token Ring networks.

Checksum The checksum is the sum of a specified set of data calculated for the purpose of error detection. A checksum value is usually included with a data packet so that the receiver can compare it with the calculated checksum and confirm that the data was not altered.

CIDR *Classless Interdomain Routing*—CIDR is an enhancement to IP routing protocols that replaces the older addressing system of classful addressing based on classes A, B, and C. Routing protocols that support CIDR include a subnet mask as part of the prefix in routing updates.

Circuit-based network Contains a collection of devices with point-to-point connections, each of which may contain many circuits (data is transmitted on individual circuits and may include a circuit identifier).

Circuit ID *Circuit identifier*—A value carried in the packet header that indicates the circuit to which the packet belongs.

Classless addressing Exclusive use of the subnet mask to indicate the size of an IP network.

CLI *Command-line interface*—A text-based user interface used to configure a router such as the 7750 SR (in contrast to a graphical user interface, or GUI).

CLP bit *Cell loss priority bit*—The CLP bit is used by ATM to indicate a cell of lower priority than one without the CLP bit set. It is more likely to be dropped if congestion is encountered downstream. Similar to the Frame Relay DE bit.

CO *Central office*—A building used by a service provider or telephone company to house telecommunications and networking equipment.

Convergence time The length of time from when there is a change in the network topology to the point when all of the routers in the network have updated their routing table to reflect the new topology.

Core router A router with high-speed interfaces capable of forwarding large quantities of data, but with very limited or no service-level knowledge.

CPAM *Control Plane Assurance Manager*—The Alcatel-Lucent 5650 CPAM is a route analytics device integrated with the 5620 Service Aware Manager (SAM) to deliver real-time visualization, surveillance, and troubleshooting for dynamic IP/MPLS networks and services.

CPE *Customer premise equipment*—Customer-owned telecommunications equipment at customer premises used to terminate or process information from the public network.

Cpipe A type of VPWS that emulates a point-to-point TDM circuit.

CPM *Control Processor Module*— The CPM is the processor that handles the control plane functions of the 7750 SR.

CRC *Cyclic redundancy check*—A CRC is an error-detection scheme for bit-oriented data communications protocols used to check the integrity of a block of data. A CRC checks the integrity of a received frame using a polynomial calculation based on the content of the frame. This value is matched with the value included in a field appended to the frame (FCS field in an Ethernet frame).

CSMA/CD *Carrier Sense Multiple Access with Collision Detection*—The method of accessing a LAN specified in IEEE 802.3. A device listens until no signals are detected (carrier sense), then transits and checks to see if more than one signal is present (collision detection). If a signal is detected, each device backs off and waits briefly before attempting transmission again. CSMA/CD is used in Ethernet LANs.

CSNP *Complete Sequence Number PDU*—A PDU used in IS-IS to ensure database synchronization.

CSPF *Constrained shortest path first*—An algorithm similar to SPF that finds the shortest route to a destination that meets the specified constraints. CSPF is used to calculate the path for traffic-engineered LSPs.

CT *Class type*—Allows the definition of an aggregate bandwidth to be allocated to a group of LSPs when the MPLS DiffServ-aware TE model is in use.

Customer ID A value associated with every service on the 7750 SR that can be used to group together a number of services for reporting purposes.

DA *Destination address*—The address of the system meant to receive a packet or frame.

DBD *Database description*—The OSPF DBD packet advertises a summary of all LSAs that the advertising router has in its link-state database (it is essentially an index of the LSDB).

DE *Discard eligible*—A bit in the Frame Relay header to indicate that this frame has a higher eligibility to be dropped if congestion is encountered. Similar to the ATM CLP bit.

De-multiplex In an IP/MPLS network, this represents the operation of delivering the data arriving at the egress router to the appropriate service based on the service label.

Detour LSP A protection LSP used with the MPLS fast reroute one-to-one model. A detour LSP protects only one LSP.

DiffServ *Differentiated Services*—DiffServ groups traffic flows with similar QoS requirements into a behavior aggregate that receives the same treatment by the network.

Dijkstra algorithm See *SPF (Shortest path first).*

DIS *Designated Intermediate System*—In IS-IS, the DIS is the IS (Intermediate System) or router on a broadcast LAN that is designated to generate link-state PDUs on behalf of the LAN as the pseudonode.

DIX *Digital-Intel-Xerox*—The original version of an Ethernet frame.

DLCI *Data link connection identifier*—The circuit identifier used in a Frame Relay network.

DMP *Detour merge point*—A point at which detour LSPs used in the fast reroute one-to-one model can be merged for optimization purposes.

DR *Designated router*—The OSPF router connected to a broadcast LAN that is responsible for generating the Network LSA for the LAN

DS1 *Digital Signal 1*—A digital circuit with a total bandwidth or transmission speed of 1.544 Mb/s. It is designed to support 24-voice conversations each encoded at 64 kb/s. Also referred to as a T1 circuit.

DSCP *Differentiated Services Code Point*—A 6-bit value encoded in the TOS field of an IP packet header. It identifies the DiffServ class of service that the packet should receive.

E-1 *E-carrier 1*—A digital circuit with a total bandwidth or transmission speed of 2.024 Mb/s. It provides 32 time slots at 64 kb/s each. One time slot is used for framing, and another may be used for signaling, providing a capacity of 30 or 31 voice circuits.

EBGP *External Border Gateway Protocol*—A BGP session established between routers in different ASs.

ECMP *Equal cost multi-path routing*—Allows traffic to be distributed across multiple paths when there is more than one path of equal cost.

ECN *Explicit congestion notification*—Allows the signaling of congestion information in an IP network. ECN uses the two least significant bits of the TOS field.

EFCI *Explicit forward congestion indication*—A bit in the PT field of the ATM cell header used to indicate that congestion was encountered by the cell.

eLER *egress label edge router*—The router at the end of the LSP. It receives labeled packets from the MPLS domain, removes the labels, and forwards the unlabeled packets outside the MPLS domain.

Encapsulation Encapsulation is the process of adding header (and possibly trailer) information to the data to be transported.

End system An end system is device intended to send and receive data on the network. Usually, an end system is a customer device such as a computer.

Epipe A type of VPWS that provides a point-to-point Ethernet service. Also known as an Ethernet VLL service.

ERO *EXPLICIT_ROUTE object*—Object that may be used in a Path message to specify the route to be followed by the LSP. Hops may be specified as strict or loose hops.

Ethernet The Ethernet protocol is a data link layer protocol for interconnecting computer equipment into CSMA/CD LANs, jointly developed by Xerox, Digital Equipment Corporation, and Intel. This standard forms the basis for IEEE 802.3. The Ethernet protocol specifies how data is placed on, and retrieved from, a common transmission medium.

Ethertype A field in the Ethernet frame header that is used to indicate the type of payload of the Ethernet frame. For example, an Ethernet frame carrying an IP packet has an Ethertype value of hex 0x0800.

Explicit null label The explicit null label has a value of 0 for IPv4 and 2 for IPv6 and is signaled only by an egress LER. Because this is the last hop on the MPLS network, this label can be simply POPped by the egress router without any lookup.

Facility backup Two fast reroute modes are possible: one-to-one detour and facility backup. Facility backup uses a bypass tunnel to provide protection for many LSPs. The bypass tunnel is routed to the next-hop router for link protection and to the next-next-hop router for node protection.

FCS *Frame check sequence*—The FCS is a field at the end of a Layer 2 frame used to detect transmission errors. The CRC calculation is performed by the sender, and the result is stored in the FCS field. The receiver performs the same calculation and compares the result with the contents of the FCS. If they are different, the frame is discarded.

FDB *Forwarding database*—The forwarding database is a table maintained by an Ethernet switch or a VPLS to identify which port should be used to reach the destination address for the frame.

FEC *Forwarding Equivalence Class*—An FEC defines a group of packets to be forwarded over the same path with the same forwarding treatment.

FECN *Forward explicit congestion notification*—A bit in the Frame Relay header that indicates that congestion was encountered on a link by this frame.

FF *Fixed Filter*—When FF mode is used, each LSP::Path in the RSVP-TE tunnel receives its own bandwidth allocation.

FIB *Forwarding information base*—The forwarding information base, also known as the route table, is used by an IP router to determine the next-hop to which the IP packet should be forwarded.

Floating static route An additional static route to a destination that can be used as a backup to the original route.

Flooding Flooding is the technique used by a routing protocol to ensure that routing information reaches all routers in the routing domain.

Flow label A field in the IPv6 header that indicates that a packet belongs to a specific data flow of an upper-layer protocol or application.

Fpipe A type of VPWS that provides a point-to-point Frame Relay connection. An fpipe is also known as a Frame Relay VLL service.

FR *Frame Relay*—Frame Relay is a standard data transmission protocol used to provide Wide Area Network connections.

FRR *Fast reroute*—Fast Reroute is a method of link and node resiliency used by MPLS. Its objective is to provide failover in less than 50 milliseconds.

Full duplex A transmission medium is considered to be full duplex if data can be transmitted in both directions at the same time.

GRE *Generic routing encapsulation*—A method for encapsulating data based on encapsulating data with an additional IP header. GRE is typically used in a VPN service network when there are routers in the transport network that do not support MPLS label switching.

Half-duplex A transmission medium is defined as half-duplex if only one system can transmit at a time.

Hertz A measure of frequency indicating the number of cycles per second.

Hex *Hexadecimal*—Base 16 numbering system in which the digits between 10 and 15 are represented by the letters A through F. Hexadecimal numbers provide a more concise representation of binary numbers and are used for entities such as IPv6 addresses, MAC addresses, and protocol identifiers. In this book, the hexadecimal number 8A4 would be written as *0x8A4*.

Hierarchy Hierarchical networking entails splitting a large domain into smaller subdomains. Routing occurs only within subdomains and between domains, resulting in a simpler SPF calculation.

Hitless A network change is said to be hitless if it does not result in the loss of any traffic. For example, MBB (make-before-break) is a hitless operation because the new LSP is signaled successfully before traffic is switched to it.

Holding time The length of time a device should wait for a Hello PDU before considering the adjacency to be down.

Hop The number of hops in a path indicates the number of full or fractional links a path traverses to get from source to destination. Each link is one hop.

HTTP *Hypertext Transfer Protocol*—Hypertext transfer protocol is a protocol for exchanging files (text, graphic images, sound, video, and other multimedia files) that is the basis of the Web.

Hub A hub is a simple connecting device in a network that joins communication lines, in a star configuration. Unlike a bridge, a hub acts as a simple repeater and does not do any intelligent forwarding of data.

Hyperaggregation A condition common in traditional IP routing that results in link congestion for some paths and link underutilization for other paths through the network.

IANA *Internet Assigned Numbers Authority*—The IANA is the body that oversees the assignment of IP addresses, AS numbers, domain names, and other Internet protocol addresses.

IAP LSA *Intra-Area Prefix LSA*—IAP LSAs carry all the IPv6 prefix information for the area. Each router generates an IAP LSA for its reachable destinations, and the DR generates one to carry the prefix information for a broadcast link.

ICANN *Internet Corporation for Assigned Names and Numbers*—Operates IANA.

ICMP *Internet Control Message Protocol*—ICMP provides an echo service (ping) and the reporting of delivery errors in an IPv4 network.

ICMPv6 *Internet Control Message Protocol version 6*—ICMPv6 provides the functions of an echo service and reporting of delivery errors in IPv6 similar to those provided in IPv4 by ICMP.

IEEE *Institute of Electrical and Electronics Engineers*—The IEEE is a worldwide engineering publishing and standards-making body. It is the organization responsible for defining many of the standards used in the computer, electrical, and electronics industries.

IEP LSA *Inter-Area Prefix LSA*—An IEP is used to flood prefix information between areas in an OSPFv3 network. Similar to a Type 3 LSA in an OSPFv2 network.

IER LSA *Inter-Area Router LSA*—An IER is used to provide reachability information for an ASBR in an OSPFv3 network. Similar to a Type 4 LSA in an OSPFv2 network.

IES *Internet Enhanced Service*—In a network of 7750 SRs, an IES provides the customer with a Layer 3 IP interface to send and receive IP traffic.

IETF *Internet Engineering Task Force*—IETF is responsible for defining the Internet protocols. It is an open standards organization with no formal membership requirements. Standards are published as RFCs and are available at no cost.

IGMP *Internet Group Management Protocol* —A protocol used between hosts and multicast routers on a single physical network to establish hosts' membership in specific multicast groups. IGMPv2 is described in RFC 2236.

IGP *Interior gateway protocol—IGP* is a generic term referring to any routing protocol, for example, OSPF or IS-IS, used to exchange routing within an autonomous system.

IHL *IP header length*—A field in the IP header that indicates the number of 32-bit words that form the IP header.

iLER *ingress label edge router*—The MPLS router at the start of an LSP. It receives unlabeled packets from outside the MPLS domain, applies an MPLS label to the packets, and forwards the labeled packets into the MPLS domain.

Implicit null label The implicit null label is used by the egress LER to signal the penultimate, or second last, router that the label should be popped and forwarded unlabeled to the egress. A value of 3 is used to signal implicit null, but this value never appears in a packet as an actual label.

Intra-area router A router that only has neighbors in its area (all of its interfaces are in the same area).

IOM *Input/Output Module*—A hardware module 7750 SR that provides the data plane function. It contains the MDAs and forwards labeled or unlabeled packets as well as performing Layer 3 traffic management.

IP *Internet Protocol*—The network layer protocol underlying the Internet. It provides an unreliable, connectionless, packet delivery service and allows large, geographically diverse networks of computers to communicate with each other quickly and economically over a variety of physical links. Usually referred to as IPv4.

IP forwarding The processing of packets by the router to send them to the next-hop router. (Often used interchangeably with the term *IP routing.*)

Ipipe A VPWS that provides IP interworking capabilities between different Layer 2 technologies.

IPv4 *Internet Protocol version 4*—The version of IP in use since the 1970s. IPv4 addresses are 32 bits.

IPv6 *Internet Protocol version 6*—The successor to IPv4. IPv6 addresses are 128 bits.

IS-IS *Intermediate System to Intermediate System*—An OSI routing protocol that was adapted for use in IP networks.

ISP *Internet service provider*—A business or organization that provides external connectivity to the Internet for consumers or businesses.

ITU-T *International Telecommunication Union–Telecommunication Standardization Sector*—ITU-T coordinates international telecommunications standards. Its members are national countries as well as public and private sector companies.

Jitter Jitter is the variation in delay for packets in a data stream.

L2 *Layer 2*—The data link layer of the OSI model. It includes protocols that define a standardized method for encoding and transmitting data on a physical medium. Examples of Layer 2 protocols include Ethernet, ATM, and Frame Relay.

L3 *Layer 3*—The third layer in the OSI model. Layer 3 protocols are responsible for the end-to-end delivery of data across the network. IP is the Layer 3 protocol used in the Internet.

Labeled packet A packet into which an MPLS label has been encoded.

LAN *Local Area Network*—A system designed to interconnect computing devices over a restricted geographical area (usually a couple of kilometers at the maximum). Ethernet is the most popular LAN protocol.

LDP *Label Distribution Protocol*—LDP is a label distribution protocol for MPLS that works in conjunction with the network IGP. As routers become aware of new destination prefixes through their IGP, they advertise labels for these destinations. LSPs signaled with LDP always follow the path determined by the IGP.

LER *Label edge router*—Routers at the edge of the MPLS network that add or remove labels. LERs have one or more interfaces outside the MPLS domain and are capable of handling labeled and unlabeled packets.

Level 1 LAN Hello Used to form Level 1 adjacencies on an IS-IS broadcast network.

Level 2 LAN Hello Used to form Level 2 adjacencies on an IS-IS broadcast network.

LFIB *Label forwarding information base*—The LDP labels that correspond to the best IGP route are transferred from the LIB to the LFIB and used for switching packets.

LIB *Label information base*—All MPLS labels that are locally generated with LDP and those received from other devices are stored in the LIB.

Link coloring Technique used to identify specific links and then ask for a traffic-engineered LSP that includes only links of a specific color or one that avoids links of a specific color. *Link coloring* is another name for administrative groups.

Link protection For fast reroute, the two protection options are node protection and link protection. Link protection means that the PLR finds a route that bypasses the immediate downstream link.

LIR *Local Internet registries*—After receiving address blocks from the five RIRs, the local Internet registries further distribute the address blocks to service providers or large organizations.

Loopback address A loopback address is assigned to a virtual interface on a router such as the 7750 SR. Because loopback interfaces are not bound to a physical port, they are always reachable and often used for communication protocols between two routers. The system interface exists by default on the 7750 SR and is used by control protocols to communicate with the router.

LSA *Link-state advertisement*—LSAs contain the data used by OSPF to distribute topology information and used for the SPF calculation. Similar to an LSP in IS-IS. The complete collection of LSAs from the routing domain makes up the OSPF link-state database.

LSDB *Link-state database*—Used by link-state routing protocols such as OSPF and IS-IS. The LSDB contains the most recent topology information sent by all link-state routers in the network.

LSP *Label switched path*—The path over which a packet travels by label switching in an MPLS network.

LSP *Link-state packet*—A generic term used in this book to refer to the packets used by OSPF and IS-IS to flood topology information throughout the network. In OSPF these are LSAs or LSUs, and in IS-IS they are LSPs.

LSP *Link-state PDU*—An IS-IS packet that carries the local topology information for a router, similar to an OSPF LSA. The complete collection of LSPs from the routing domain makes up the IS-IS link-state database.

LSP::Path In an RSVP-TE tunnel there may be multiple LSP::Paths that each have a unique LSP ID but share the same Tunnel ID. The LSP::Paths are used to provide redundancy and are also created whenever a new LSP is signaled for the tunnel.

LSR *Label switch router*—An LSR is a router located in the middle of an MPLS network that forwards labeled packets by label swapping.

LSR *Link-state request*—An LSR is the message used by OSPF to request updated copies of specific LSAs.

LSU *Link-state update*—An LSU is the message used by OSPF to transmit LSAs to its neighbors. An LSU may contain multiple LSAs.

LTE *Long Term Evolution*—The next generation of cellular technology, also known as 4G wireless. An LTE network uses IP exclusively for transmission of voice and data.

MAC *Media Access Control*—One of the subprotocols within the IEEE802.3 (Ethernet) protocol. The MAC protocol defines medium sharing, packet formatting, addressing, and error detection. A MAC address is a globally unique, 6-byte address that identifies an Ethernet interface.

MAM *Maximum Allocation Model*—The MPLS DiffServ TE model in which bandwidth is allocated discretely to different CTs and cannot be shared between CTs.

MAN *Metropolitan Area Network*—A network largely restricted to a single metropolitan area, hence somewhere in geographical size between an LAN and a WAN.

MBB *Make-before-break*—An operation in which a new LSP::Path is established and declared active before the previous one is torn down.

MDA *Media Dependant Adapter*—MDAs are 7750 SR modules that are housed in IOMs and in which a physical interface terminates. An MDA determines the Layer 2 technology that will be used on the link.

MDU *Multi dwelling unit*—An MDU is a small switch or router installed by a service provider in an office or apartment building. The MDU supports the connection of several customers to the service provider network with one or two high-speed uplink connections.

Mesh SDP A mesh SDP floods frames received from a SAP or from a spoke SDP but does not flood frames received from another mesh SDP.

Metric The numerical value used by the routing protocol to calculate the best route to a destination. Depending on the routing protocol, the metric is usually a hop count or a cost assigned to the network link.

MLD *Multicast Listener Discovery*—Protocol to determine multicast group listeners used in IPv6. Performs similar functions to IGMP in IPv4.

MP *Merge point*—The point at which traffic on a protection LSP merges back onto the protected LSP.

MP-BGP *Multiprotocol BGP*—A version of BGP enhanced to support additional address families.

MPLS *Multiprotocol Label Switching*—MPLS supports the delivery of highly scalable, differentiated, end-to-end IP and VPN services. Packets arriving at the MPLS network have a label added and are then forwarded across the network by label switching.

MSO *Multiservice operator*—A cable operator that provides multiple services such as high-speed Internet, video, and voice.

MT *Multi-topology*—A routing protocol instance that supports routing over multiple, distinct topologies. For example, when multi-topology IS-IS is used for the exchange of IPv6 routes, the

IPv6 prefixes and topology are treated as distinct.

MTU *Maximum transmission unit*—MTU is the largest unit of data that can be transmitted over a particular interface type in one packet. The MTU can change from one network hop to the next.

Multicast A multicast address provides an address for a group of hosts.

ND *Neighbor Discovery*—An IPv6 protocol that can be used by a host to discover the addresses of its neighbors, similar to ARP in IPv4.

Network layer See *Layer 3*.

Next-next-hop In facility backup FRR, the node protect bypass tunnel is always calculated to the router two hops downstream from the PLR. This is sometimes called the *next-next-hop router*.

Node protection For fast reroute, the two protection options are node protection and link protection. Node protection means that the PLR finds a route that bypasses the immediate downstream node.

NSAP *Network Service Access Point*—An NSAP is an OSI network address.

NSFNET *National Science Foundation network*—The largest component of the Internet backbone during the early 1990s. The NSFNET was the first major step in moving from the single-backbone structure of ARPANET to the distributed structure of the Internet today.

NSSA *Not-so-stubby-area*—An OSPF stub area that contains an ASBR.

OAM *Operations, administration, and maintenance*—A group of network management functions that provide network fault indication, performance information, and data and diagnosis functions.

OC-1 *Optical Carrier 1*—The basic SONET optical transmission rate of 51.84 Mb/s.

One-to-one detour Two fast reroute modes are possible: one-to-one detour and facility backup. A one-to-one detour provides protection for a single LSP. The one-to-one detour is calculated as the best route to the tail-end router that avoids the next downstream link or router.

OSI *Open Systems Interconnection*—The OSI reference model is a seven-layer model for network architecture. The model was developed by ISO and CCIT (now ITU-T). From top to bottom, the seven layers are Application, Presentation, Session, Transport, Network, Data Link, and Physical layers.

OSPF *Open Shortest Path First*—Dynamic, link-state routing protocol that responds quickly to network topology changes. It uses an algorithm that builds and calculates the shortest path to all known destinations.

OUI *Organizationally Unique Identifier*—A 24-bit number that identifies the manufacturer of an Ethernet adapter. The number is purchased from the IEEE, who ensure its global uniqueness. The vendor then adds a unique 24-bit suffix to create a MAC address.

Outer label The MPLS transport label used for label switching across the network.

P router A router in the core of the service provider network, typically an LSR that is not service-aware.

Payload When referring to a network transmission, the *payload* refers to the information actually useful to the receiver, as opposed to overhead data in the header.

PDU *Protocol data unit—PDU* is the term for a unit of data in the OSI model. An IP packet would be known as a network PDU and an Ethernet frame a data link PDU.

PE router A router at the edge of the service provider network (typically an LER), which connects to customer edge routers.

PHP *Penultimate hop popping*—The removal (popping) of the top label on a packet's label stack at the penultimate (second last) router in an LSP, rather than at the egress node.

Ping An ICMP echo message and its reply. Often used in IP networks to test the reachability of a network device.

Pipe mode When an MPLS network operates in pipe mode, the MPLS routers are effectively invisible from the perspective of the end-to-end connection.

PLR *Point of local repair*—For RSVP-TE fast reroute, the router immediately upstream from a failure that repairs the primary LSP::Path by switching traffic to the protection LSP.

Point-to-point A point-to-point connection is defined as a connection in which there is only one neighbor.

POS *Packet over SONET/SDH*—POS is a standard method of transporting native network layer packets such as IP directly on SONET interfaces using HDLC-like framing and simple link protocols like PPP.

PPP *Point-to-Point Protocol*—PPP is an IETF standard protocol that allows a computer to use TCP/IP with a standard telephone line and a high-speed modem to establish a link between two (and only two) terminal installations. PPP is also used for POS.

Preamble Ethernet is an asynchronous communications protocol because the transmission of a frame can occur at any time. The preamble is required to identify the beginning of the Ethernet frame. The preamble is a 56-bit pattern of alternating ones and zeroes.

P-bits *Priority bits*—A 3-bit value in the Ethernet header that specifies a frame's priority or class of service.

Protected LSP The primary LSP::Path that is protected with FRR.

Protection LSP An LSP that protects the protected LSP.

Protocol preference A value associated with each routing protocol on the 7750 SR. The protocol preference determines which protocol to use in the event that two routing protocols present the same route to the Routing Table Manager. The route from the routing protocol with the lower preference is preferred.

PSB *Path State Block*—The PSB contains the RSVP-TE session information as well as the original Path message used to signal the LSP.

Pseudonode An imaginary router on an IS-IS broadcast LAN that is a neighbor of all other routers on the LAN. The DIS originates an LSP for the pseudonode.

Pseudowire A pseudowire emulates a Layer 2 point-to-point connection over an IP/MPLS network as defined in RFC 3985. Also known as VPWS or VLL.

PSN *Packet switched network*—A data-transmission network that uses packet-switching techniques. Unlike circuit switching, packet switching allocates multiplexing and switching resources only when data is present. There are public and private packet-switched networks.

PSNP *Partial Sequence Number PDU*—A PDU sent by an IS-IS router to ensure synchronization of link-state databases throughout the network.

PSTN *Public Switched Telephone Network*—The network of the world's telephone system, including local, long distance, and international phone companies.

PVC *Permanent virtual circuit*—A PVC is a Frame Relay or ATM end-to-end logical connection that extends between two user/network interfaces. A single PVC may pass through several Frame Relay or ATM switching nodes.

Q-in-Q The Q-in-Q encapsulation type adds an additional IEEE 802.1Q tag to tagged packets entering the network producing a double-tagged frame.

QoS *Quality of service*—The ability of a network to recognize different service requirements of different application traffic flowing through it and to comply with

SLAs negotiated for each application service, while attempting to maximize network resource utilization.

Raw mode When a pseudowire is operating in raw mode (configured with `vc-type ethernet`), the service-delimiting VLAN tags are stripped at the ingress and are not carried across the pseudowire.

RD *Route distinguisher*—In a VPRN, the RD is an additional string added to a customer's routes so that they can be distinguished from other customer's routes in the service provider network.

RDM *Russian Dolls Model*—An MPLS DiffServ model in which unused bandwidth assigned to a higher CT can be used by a lower CT.

Resignal timer An MPLS timer that controls the interval at which the router tries to find a more optimum path for established LSPs.

Retry timer Set on individual LSPs and controls the interval at which the router tries to establish an LSP.

Revertive behavior The behavior of network protocols when a failure is resolved.

RFC *Request for Comments*—RFCs are the documents that define the Internet standards. They are freely available.

RIB *Routing Information Base*—The RIB is a database in which the information for a single routing protocol is stored.

RID *Router ID*—A value used by a routing protocol to uniquely identify each router in the routing domain.

RIP *Routing Information Protocol*—An interior gateway protocol defined in RFC 2453 and based on the distance vector algorithm.

RIRs *Regional Internet registries*—After receiving address blocks from IANA, the five RIRs distribute address blocks to the local internet registries (LIRs).

RRO *RECORD_ROUTE object*—Object that may optionally be included in the RSVP-TE Path message to record the hops used for the LSP.

RSB *Resv State Block*—The RSB contains RSVP-TE session information including the original Resv message used to signal the LSP and the label allocated for the LSP.

RSVP *Resource Reservation Protocol*—RSVP was originally developed by routers to allow an application to reserve network resources by sending a request to all nodes along the path of the flows.

RSVP-TE *Resource Reservation Protocol–Traffic Engineering*—An extension of the original RSVP that allows MPLS routers to request bandwidth resources and labels for an LSP.

RT *Route target*—The RT is an extended community string attached to VPN routes that identifies which routes are to be exported from MP-BGP into the VRF at a local PE.

RTM *Route Table Manager*—The RTM is a process on the 7750 SR that selects routes from each routing protocol based on protocol preference to build the FIB.

SA *Source address*—The address of the device transmitting a frame.

SAP *Service Access Point*—Term used by Alcatel-Lucent to describe the subscriber's point of interface to an IP/MPLS service network. The SAP may be a physical port or may specify a port and encapsulation ID such as a VLAN tag value.

SAR *Segmentation and reassembly*—In an ATM network, the process of constructing the AAL SDU from the service data stream and then converting it to ATM cells (segmentation). At the egress of the ATM network, the reassembly process constructs the AAL SDU and re-creates the service data stream.

SAToP *Structure Agnostic TDM over Packet*—SAToP pseudowires transport unstructured T1 or E1 circuits and are defined in RFC 4553.

Scalability In a network, the relative ability of control protocols to operate efficiently as the size of the network increases.

SDH *Synchronous Digital Hierarchy*—SDH is an ITU-T standard for fiber optic transmission of high-speed digital traffic. SDH defines a physical interface, optical line rates, frame format, and an OAM protocol. The base rate is 155.52 Mb/s (STM -1), and higher rates are multiples of the base rate. SDH is an international standard that is technically consistent with SONET, used in North America. The SDH STM-1 is equivalent to the SONET STS-3c.

SDP *Service Distribution Point*—A term used by Alcatel-Lucent to identify a logical representation of the IP/MPLS transport tunnel that will be used to deliver the service data to the egress PE.

SDU *Service Delivery Unit*—In an OSI network, the unit of information from an upper-layer protocol that defines a service request to a lower-layer protocol. The SDU becomes the payload of the lower-layer PDU.

Service label Inner label used between endpoints (the ingress and egress PE routers) to identify the VPN service to which the packet belongs.

Service router A scalable, full-function IP/MPLS router such as the Alcatel-Lucent 7750 SR that supports the full range of service types, many customers, and additional service management capabilities.

Service tunnel The tunnel represented by the service labels signaled end-to-end by the two PEs that are the service endpoints.

SF/CPM *Switch Fabric/Control Processor Module*—The SF/CPM is the card in the 7750 SR that supports the router control plane functions. Routing, label distribution, and network management functions are handled by the CPM. The switch fabric provides line rate switching between the IOM cards.

SFD *Start frame delimiter*—The SFD occurs after the preamble in an Ethernet frame and is always `10101011`. It indicates the beginning of the actual Ethernet frame.

SLA *Service level agreement*—A contractual agreement between a service provider and customer stipulating the minimum standards of service.

SONET *Synchronous Optical Network*—SONET is an ANSI standard for fiber optic transmission of high-speed digital traffic. SONET defines a physical interface, optical line rates known as OC signals, frame format, and an OAM protocol. The base rate is 51.84 Mb/s (OC-1), and higher rates are multiples of the base rate. SONET is a North American standard that is technically consistent with SDH, which is international.

SONET/SDH *Synchronous Optical Network/Synchronous Digital Hierarchy*—The most widely used technology for long-distance optical transmission. SONET/SDH was designed for the transport of traditional voice traffic and provides a foundation for both POS and ATM.

SPF *Shortest path first*—SPF is an algorithm used by IS-IS and OSPF to make routing decisions based on the state of network links (also known as the Dijkstra algorithm).

Spoke SDP A spoke SDP floods frames received from a SAP, a spoke SDP, or a mesh SDP.

SRLG *Shared Risk Link Group*—SRLG information can be used by CSPF to calculate paths for secondary LSPs and fast reroute detours that ensure path diversity from the primary path.

Static route Route information that is administratively configured rather than learned from a dynamic routing protocol such as OSPF or IS-IS.

STM-1 *Synchronous Transport Module, level 1*—STM-1 defines the basic frame in an SDH network. It is 19,440 bytes and is transmitted 8,000 times per second for a transmission rate of 155.52 Mb/s. The STM-1 is essentially equivalent to the STS-3c SONET frame.

STP *Spanning Tree Protocol*—STP is used by Ethernet bridges and switches to detect and logically remove duplicate paths to create a loop-free Layer 2 topology.

STS-1 *Synchronous Transport Signal 1*—STS-1 is the basic frame in a SONET network. It is one-third the STM-1 frame (6,480 bytes) and is transmitted 8,000 times per second for a transmission rate of 51.84 Mb/s.

STS-3c *Synchronous Transport Signal 3 (concatenated)*—The STS-3c frame is exactly three times the size of an STS-1 (the same size as an STM-1 or an STS-3), but unlike STS-3, it does not contain multiplexed STS-1 frames. A concatenated service is used for services such as ATM or POS where multiplexing of lower rates is not required.

Stub area An OSPF area that does not allow external route advertisements. A default route is advertised into the stub area instead.

Subnet mask A 32-bit-long sequence of ones followed by a sequence of zeroes. The ones correspond to the network component of the IP address, and the zeroes correspond to the host component.

Summarization The process of representing a contiguous group of longer IP prefixes with a shorter one. Summarization is usually performed between areas or routing domains.

T1 *T-carrier 1*—A digital circuit with a total bandwidth or transmission speed of 1.5444 Mb/s. It is designed to support 24-voice conversations each encoded at 64 kb/s. Also referred to as a DS1 and used mainly in North America and Japan.

Tagged mode When a pseudowire is operating in tagged mode (configured with `vc-type vlan`), the service-delimiting VLAN tags are carried across the pseudowire.

Targeted LDP See *T-LDP*.

TC *Traffic Class*—A 3-bit field in the MPLS header used to indicate QoS handling. Originally known as the EXP field, it was renamed as TC in RFC 5462.

TCP *Transmission Control Protocol*—TCP enables two hosts to establish a connection and exchange streams of data over an IP network. TCP guarantees delivery of data and also guarantees that packets will be delivered in the same order in which they were sent.

TDM *Time division multiplexing*—TDM is a process of sharing a communication channel among several users by allowing each to use the channel for a given period of time in a defined, repeated sequence. TDM is the technique used to multiplex traditional voice circuits on a higher capacity link such as a T1 or E1.

TE *Traffic engineering*—The process of selecting a path across the network that meets specific bandwidth or administrative constraints, rather than simply relying on the path selected by the IGP.

TE class Defines a specific pairing of a CT with a preemption priority.

TED *Traffic engineering database*—The TED is used by OSPF-TE and IS-IS-TE to store the traffic engineering information for the network.

T-LDP *Targeted LDP*—A version of LDP that is used by two endpoints of a Layer 2 VPN service to exchange labels for that service.

TLV *Type–length–value*—A flexible method of defining the data fields in a protocol message. *Type* identifies the specific data field that the TLV contains; *length* specifies the length in bytes of the TLV and thus permits a variable length value field; and *value* contains the actual data to be carried in the TLV.

Topology Topology is the arrangement, map, or plan of a network, its components, and their interconnection.

TOS *Type of service*—An 8-bit field in the IP packet header that can be interpreted as a 3-bit IP precedence value or 6-bit DSCP value. This value is used to identify the level of service that a packet receives in the network.

Totally stubby area An OSPF area that does not receive any Summary LSAs. The link-state database of routers in a totally stubby area contains only Router and Network LSAs from the area and a Summary LSA for the default route.

Traceroute A utility similar to ping that determines the route taken (each hop) from a source endpoint to a destination endpoint.

Transit network A transit network carries traffic that neither originates in nor is destined to the local network.

Transit LSR Any intermediate router in the MPLS network between the ingress and egress LERs. A transit router swaps the incoming label for an outgoing label and forwards labeled packets to the next router along the LSP.

Transport label The outer label used to label-switch the user packet across an MPLS network.

Transport tunnel The LSP used to transport the service data.

TTL *Time-to-live*—A field in the IP header that is effectively a hop count. TTL is decremented by each router, and if the value reaches zero, the packet is discarded.

Tunnel A method of encapsulating data for transmission across a network without any reference to the header of the original packet. An MPLS LSP acts as a tunnel because data arriving at the ingress is encapsulated with an MPLS label and then switched across the network without any reference to the fields of the original packet.

Tunnel ID An RSVP-TE tunnel is identified by its Tunnel ID. It may comprise several distinct LSP::Paths, each with a distinct LSP ID.

UBR *AAL5 unspecified bit rate service*—The service provided by AAL5 on ATM networks. It is a simple, connectionless data service commonly used for transporting IP traffic.

UDP *User Datagram Protocol*—A connectionless transport layer protocol belonging to the Internet protocol suite. In contrast to TCP, UDP does not guarantee reliability or ordering of the packets.

UNI *User network interface*—UNI defines the interface point between a private ATM network and the public carrier ATM network.

Unicast address A unicast address provides an address for a single host.

Uniform mode When operating in uniform mode, MPLS routers act as if they were routers in the overall end-to-end connection.

VBR *AAL2 variable bit rate service*—The service provided by AAL2 on ATM networks. It is a connection-oriented service with variable bit rates and a bounded delay. VBR is intended for compressed voice or video traffic and may have real-time constraints (vbr-rt) or not (vbr-nrt).

VC *Virtual circuit*—In an MPLS network, a virtual circuit is a communications link that behaves like a dedicated P2P circuit, even though it is not. Data packets are delivered to the user in guaranteed sequential order, as if they were sent over a true P2P circuit.

VC ID *Virtual circuit identifier*—The VC ID is used by T-LDP to identify a pseudowire. The VC ID must be the same at each end of the pseudowire for it to become operational.

VCC *Virtual channel connection*—The VCC represents the end-to-end connection in an ATM network. It is defined by the VPI and VCI values.

VCI *Virtual channel identifier*—The VCI is part of the address of a VCC and is contained in a 16-bit field in the ATM cell header. A VCI value is assigned for one hop only; each switch cross-connects cells from one VC to the next, reassigning the VCI value.

VID *VLAN identifier*—A 12-bit value that identifies the VLAN that the frame belongs to.

VLAN *Virtual LAN*—A logical group of network devices that appear to be on the same Ethernet LAN, regardless of their physical location.

VLAN trunking VLAN trunking allows the transmission of traffic from multiple VLANs on a single port. A VID is assigned to each VLAN, and by using consistent VID values on all switches, the VLAN can be extended across multiple switches.

VLL *Virtual Leased Line*—A Layer 2 point-to-point service also known as a Virtual Private Wire Service (VPWS). A VLL is a pseudowire service used to transport Layer 2 traffic such as Ethernet over an IP/MPLS core as if it were a native Ethernet connection.

VPI *Virtual path indicator*—The VPI is an 8-bit field in the ATM cell header that is part of the VCC. A VPI value is assigned for one hop only; each switch cross-connects cells from one VPI to the next, reassigning the VPI value.

VPLS *Virtual Private LAN Services*—VPLS is a class of VPN that allows the connection of multiple sites in a single bridged Ethernet domain over a provider IP/MPLS network.

VPN *Virtual Private Network*—A way to provide network links between a customer's different locations as if they were connected by dedicated, private links. A VPN is usually provisioned over a service provider's core such as an IP/MPLS network that provides VPN services to other customers.

VPRN *Virtual Private Routed Network*—VPRN is a class of VPN that allows the connection of multiple sites in a routed domain over a provider managed IP/MPLS network.

VPWS *Virtual Private Wired Service*—A VPWS is a point-to-point Layer 2 service implemented on an IP/MPLS network that emulates a leased line. Also known as a *VLL*.

VRF *VPN routing and forwarding table*—The virtual router on the PE router that contains the customer's routes for a VPRN. Each PE has a VRF for each VPRN service provisioned on the router.

VS *Virtual switch*—The VPLS instance on each PE router is often referred to as a virtual switch because it emulates the behavior of an Ethernet switch.

WAN *Wide Area Network*—A geographically dispersed, long-haul telecommunications network that provides a network interconnection between widely separated locations.

Web *World Wide Web*—A logical collection of computer systems connected to the Internet that provide documents and other services using HTTP.

Afterword

Congratulations for your hard work and perseverance if you have read through this entire book and worked through the exercises. We wish you success in your written exams and the NRS II lab exam. Attainment of the NRS II certification is a major accomplishment. It demonstrates your solid understanding of the theoretical knowledge and practical skills in IP/MPLS service networking.

MPLS and IPv6 are relatively new technologies to most of us, but are critical foundational components of our current and future networks. The skills you acquire through the NRS II certification will be of value to you throughout your career and will give you the confidence and credibility to work in complex network environments. You will be well positioned to help your company or customer succeed in this dynamic and exciting world of advanced communications.

Index

Numbers & Symbols

A

B

C

D

E

F

G

H

I

J

K

L

M

N

O

P

Q

R

S

T

U

V

W

Alcatel-Lucent Scalable IP Networks Self-Study Guide
Alcatel·Lucent
Advanced QoS
for Multi-Service
IP/MPLS Networks
Alcatel·Lucent

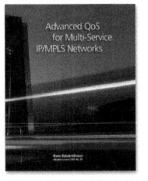